EVIDENCE:
CASES AND MATERIALS

AUSTRALIA
Law Book Co.
Sydney

CANADA and USA
Carswell
Toronto

HONG KONG
Sweet & Maxwell Asia

NEW ZEALAND
Brookers
Wellington

SINGAPORE and MALAYSIA
Sweet & Maxwell Asia
Singapore and Kuala Lumpur

EVIDENCE:
CASES AND MATERIALS
(2nd EDITION)

David H. Sheldon, LL.B (Hons.), Dip. L.P., Advocate
Formerly Lecturer in Law, University of Edinburgh

EDINBURGH
W. GREEN/Sweet & Maxwell
2002

Published in 2002 by W. Green & Son Ltd
21 Alva Street
Edinburgh EH2 4PS

Typeset by J. P. Price, Chilcompton, Somerset
Printed and bound in Great Britain by Athenaeum,
Gateshead, Tyne & Wear

No natural forests were destroyed to make this product;
only farmed timber was used and replanted

A CIP catalogue record for this book is available from
the British Library.

ISBN 0414 01387 5

To my Mother

PREFACE TO SECOND EDITION

Since the first edition of this book was published in 1996, much has happened in the law of evidence. We have indeed been fated to live in interesting times. Perhaps the most important legal development since 1996 has been the advent of devolution and the incorporation of the European Convention on Human Rights into mainstream Scots law. Legal practitioners have begun to test the boundaries of that development and many interesting arguments have been heard on the subject. The Convention impacts on the law of evidence only peripherally, however, since Convention jurisprudence suggests that what is important is not the use of any particular type of evidence but rather the fairness of the proceedings as a whole. I have however, endeavoured to include cases on the Convention rights where they are relevant.

Apart from devolution and the European Convention, there have been many significant examples of evolution in native Scottish species. *Smith v. Lees*, and *Fox v. H.M.A.* in relation to corroboration; *McCutcheon v. H.M.A.* on hearsay; *Thomson v. Crowe* reviving the trial within a trial, and *McLeod, Petitioner* on the recovery of evidence in criminal cases. On the latter subject, it is impossible to ignore the inauguration of the Scottish Criminal Cases Review Commission, a body likely to loom large in the consciousness of every criminal lawyer in the coming years. A section on the SCCRC is included in this book because of its important role in fresh evidence appeals and because of its wide powers to recover material relevant to an appeal—wider powers, it seems, than those available to the defence practitioner at or prior to trial.

A fairly large amount of material has been excised from the first edition, either because it has been superceded or simply because I no longer considered that its relative importance justified its retention in a work which was already quite large enough. Equally, some sections have been retained, which many might rather have seen deleted. I considered, for example, removing that part of the hearsay section relating to *Muldoon v. Herron* and the cases following it. After all, one might say, the battle has been fought and lost, and the views expressed in the articles referred to in that section rejected or forgotten. But law is to some extent like fashion—and sometimes, like flares and kaftans, outmoded arguments come around again. In 1987, I completed an honours dissertation on the subject of the strange demise of the trial within a trial. Although it did not remotely approach the insight and sophistication of later arguments on the subject, it did at least express some disquiet that the procedure authoritatively laid down in *Chalmers v. H.M.A.* had been circumvented without that case having been over-ruled. It did not receive a particularly good mark, not least, one suspects, because those who marked it regarded the subject as (a) unoriginal, (b) boring and (c) of entirely academic interest since the matter was clearly quite settled. And so it was, until along came *Thomson v. Crowe*. The immediate stimulus for that case seems to have been Scotland's accession to the European Convention on Human Rights. In the end, however, the arguments for the appellant were made and accepted purely on the basis of domestic jurisprudence. While I can take no credit whatsoever for the decision, it only goes to show that while in law bad arguments are made every day of the week, an unfashionable argument may eventually succeed, even after 30 years.

Once again, my thanks go to a number of people without whom this book would never have seen the light of day. To Jill Barrington and Lucy Walsh of W. Green goes my gratitude for their gracious nagging, gentle encouragement, and general logistical support. To Laura Irvine of the Scottish Criminal Cases Review Commission for bringing to my attention almost an entire chapter of the law which otherwise might well have escaped my attention; and last but by no means least, to Bill Geake, without whose patience and expertise in computing matters this book might even now be lost in cyberspace hell. Whether you regard his efforts as boon or bane, is a matter for you.

David H Sheldon
Parliament House
May 2002

PREFACE TO THE FIRST EDITION

The purpose of this book is two-fold: first, to set out those materials essential to an understanding of the law of evidence in Scotland, and, secondly, to provide a rough guide to those materials in the form of a commentary or interrogatory. It is not intended to provide a definite statement of the law, but simply to provide a basis for teaching and discussion of the law. It is, therefore, intended primarily for use as a student text, but I hope that practitioners may also find it to be of some use. I have attempted to include at least a reference to the most recent cases in each area, and there is detailed consideration of some of the more important development in the law, such as reform of the hearsay rule in criminal cases, the law of evidence in civil matters, and the treatment of child witnesses.

The structure and content of the book have their origins in the ordinary Evidence course in Edinburgh University. This course and some of the material for lectures I inherited from other, more distinguished teachers—the late Bill Wilson, John Blackie and Robert Black. To each of these scholars I would like to record my gratitude and my enormous respect. Professor Black continues to teach a large part of the course, and his inspiration and assistance have been invaluable. I must also record my thanks to several cohorts of Evidence students whose comments, questions and general air of puzzlement have, I hope, helped to refine and improve both my lectures and this work.

This book would never have been published, however, but for the tolerance, patience and hard work of a number of other people, to whom I owe a large debt of gratitude. In particular, I would like to thank Sally Marr, who quarried much of the material from the law library at Edinburgh University and typed it onto disk, thus making the work of editing the book much less painful. Nick Dyson, the computing support officer at Edinburgh University Law Faculty used the faculty's scanner to "read" some of the material onto disk thus further reducing my workload. Caroline Howell read parts of the manuscript and commented on it. For her help and support I am immensely grateful. Eleanor Swift at the University of California at Berkeley provided the inspiration and some of the material for the Chapter on Relevance, and Professor John McNulty of that University made my visit there possible. I would like to thank my friends, my family and my colleagues at Old College for their support and encouragement over the past year. Their collective boredom threshold has been tested to its limit. Finally, I would like to thank Carole Outterson and all of the staff at W. Green who have, as ever, been most patient and helpful in the face of delay, expense and pedantry.

David H. Sheldon
Old College
August 1996

CONTENTS

		Page
Preface to Second Edition		vii
Preface to First Edition		ix
Table of Cases		xiii
Table of Statutes		xxix
Table of Statutory Instruments		xxxv

1.	Relevance	1
2.	The Burden of Proof	16
3.	Presumptions	43
4.	The Standard of Proof	57
5.	Sufficiency of Evidence	78
6.	The Best Evidence Rule	124
7.	Hearsay	146
8.	Evidence Improperly Obtained	194
9.	Collateral and Character Evidence	268
10.	Opinion Evidence	311
11.	Judicial Knowledge, Agreements, and Admissions	331
12.	Confidentiality, Privilege and the Recovery of Evidence	355
13.	Some Specialties of Civil Evidence	398
14.	Witnesses—Some Specialties	439
15.	Appeals	501

Index		531

TABLE OF CASES

References are to page numbers

1st Indian Cavalry Club v. Commissioners of Customs and Excise [1998] S.T.C. 293; 1998 S.C. 126; 1998 S.L.T. 554, Ex Div 72
A. v. B; *sub nom.* Simpson v. Melvin (1895) 22 R. 402; (1894) 2 S.L.T.515, 1 Div 4, 269, 270, 284, 285
A.B. v. Glasgow and West of Scotland Blood Transfusion Service, 1993 S.L.T. 36 376
AGL v. H.M. Advocate; EDB v. H.M. Advocate 189, 192
Abadom [1983] 1 W.L.R. 126; [1983] 1 All E.R. 364; (1982) 76 Crim.App.R. 48, CA (Crim Div) 317
Abrath v. North Eastern Railway Co. (1886) L.R. 11 App. Cas. 247, HL 19, 28
Adair v. McGarry; Byrne v. H.M. Advocate, 1933 J.C. 72; 1933 S.L.T. 482, HCJ Appeal 206, 207
Adelaide Chemical and Fertilizer Co. Ltd (1940) 64 C.L.R. 514 153
Admiralty v. Aberdeen Steam Trawling and Fishing Co., 1909 1 S.L.T. 5 .... 368, 370, 371, 375
Air Canada v. Secretary of State for Trade (No. 2) [1983] 2 A.C. 394; [1983] 2 W.L.R. 494, HL 371, 391
Aitchison v. Bartlett, 1963 J.C. 27; 1963 S.L.T. 65, HCJ 126
Aitken v. Wood, 1921 J.C. 84; (1921) 2 S.L.T.124, HCJ Appeal 340, 341
Ajodha v. State, The *See* Ajodha v. Trinidad and Tobago
—— v. Trinidad and Tobago; Chandree v. Trinidad and Tobago; Fletcher v. Trinidad and Tobago; Noreiga v. Trinidad and Tobago [1982] A.C. 204; [1981] 3 W.L.R. 1, PC (Trin) 241
Allan v. Ingram, 1995 S.L.T. 1086; 1995 S.C.C.R. 390, HCJ Appeal 328
—— v. Milne, 1974 S.L.T. (Notes) 76, HCJ Appeal 220
Aluwahlia [1992] 4 All E.R. 889 326
Anderson (William) v. Jas B. Fraser & Co. Ltd, 1992 S.L.T. 1129; 1992 S.C.L.R. 417, OH 423, 424, 426
—— v. Buchanan (1848) 11 D. 270 52
—— v. H.M. Advocate, 2001 S.L.T. 1265; 2001 S.C.C.R. 738, HCJ Appeal 91
—— v. Laverock, 1976 J.C. 9; 1976 S.L.T. 62, HCJ Appeal 126, 129, 131
—— v. St Andrews Ambulance Association, 1942 S.C. 555 .... 360, 361
Andrew v. H.M. Advocate, 2000 S.L.T. 402; 1999 G.W.D. 32–1517, HCJ Appeal 305
AP Stephen v. Scottish Boatowners Mutual Insurance Association (The Talisman) [1989] 1 Lloyd's Rep. 535; 1989 S.L.T. 283, HL 315
AR v. Walker, 1999 S.L.T. 1233 482
Ares v. Venner [1970] S.C.R. 608 156
Armit v. O'Donnell, 1999 S.L.T. 1035; 1999 G.W.D. 24–1129, HCJ Appeal 108
Armstrong, 2 Broun 251 .... 468, 469
Arnott v. Burt (1872) 11 M. 62 .... 70, 71
Arthur v. Lindsay 22 R. 417 369
Ashingdane v. United Kingdom (A/93) (1985) 7 E.H.R.R. 528, ECHR; affirming (1982) 4 E.H.R.R. 590, Eur Comm HR 264
Assessor for Dundee v. Elder; *sub nom.* Dundee Assessor v. Elder, 1963 S.L.T. (Notes) 35; (1962) 4 R.I.C.S. 39, LVAC 367
Auld v. McBey (1881) 18 S.L.R. 312 476
Aveson v. Lord Kinnear 1805 6 East 188; 102 All E.R. 1258 151

B. (A Minor) (Rejection of Expert Evidence), Re *See* B (Care: Expert Witnesses), Re
B. (Care: Expert Witnesses), Re; *sub nom.* B (A Minor) (Rejection of Expert Evidence), Re [1996] 1 F.L.R. 667; [1996] 2 F.C.R. 272, CA 316
B. v. Kennedy, 1987 S.C. 247; 1987 S.L.T. 765, 2 Div 69, 71
Baird v. Mitchell (1854) 16 D. 1088 342
Ballard v. North British Railway Co. (1923) 14 Ll. L. Rep. 68; 1923 S.C. 43, HL 54, 55
Balloch v. H.M. Advocate, 1977 S.C. 23; 1977 S.L.T. (Notes) 29, HCJ Appeal ... 230, 232, 238, 239, 240, 241, 242
Barnes v. H.M. Advocate, 2001 S.L.T. 261 298
Barratt Scotland Ltd v. Keith, 1993 S.C. 142; 1994 S.L.T. 1343, 2 Div 74
Bater v. Bater [1951] P. 35; [1950] 2 All E.R. 458, CA 62, 63, 64, 65, 70
Bates v. H.M. Advocate, 1989 S.L.T. 701; 1989 S.C.C.R. 338, HCJ Appeal 470, 472
Baxter v. Scott, 1992 S.L.T. 1125; 1992 S.C.C.R. 342, HCJ Appeal 212
Beattie v. H.M. Advocate, 1995 J.C. 33; 1995 S.L.T. 275, HCJ Appeal 97
Bell v. Lothiansure Ltd, 1990 S.L.T. 58, OH 363, 367
Benendoun, ECHR 382
Beta Computers (Europe) Ltd v. Adobe Systems (Europe) Ltd, 1996 S.L.T. 604; [1996] C.L.C. 821, OH 334

Binnie v. Rederij Theodoro BV, 1993 S.C. 71; 1992 G.W.D. 34–2013, 1 Div 56, 347
Bird v. Bird, 1931 S.C. 731 476
Birkett v. H.M. Advocate, 1993 S.L.T. 395; 1992 S.C.C.R. 850, HCJ 477, 489, 491
Birse v. H.M. Advocate; *sub nom.* Birse v. MacNeill 2000 J.C. 503; 2000 S.L.T. 869; 2000 S.C.C.R. 505, HCJ
     Appeal 219
—— v. MacNeill *See* Birse v. H.M. Advocate
Black v. Annan, 1995 J.C. 58; 1996 S.L.T. 284; 1995 S.C.C.R. 273, HCJ Appeal 251, 254
—— v. Bairds & Dalmellington, 1939 S.C. 472; 1939 S.L.T. 415, 2 Div 359, 360, 361, 362
Blagojevic v. H.M. Advocate, 1995 S.L.T. 1189; 1995 S.C.C.R. 570, HCJ Appeal; affirming 327, 328
Blair v. H.M. Advocate, 1994 S.L.T. 256; 1993 S.C.C.R. 483, HCJ Appeal 110, 493
Blyth v. Blyth (No. 2); *sub nom.* Blyth v. Blyth and Pugh [1966] A.C. 643; [1966] 2 W.L.R. 634, HL 65
Bonczza-Tomaszewski v. H.M. Advocate; *sub nom.* Fraser v. H.M. Advocate 2001 S.L.T. 336; 2000 S.C.C.R.
     657, HCJ Appeal 529
Bonnington Castings Ltd v. Wardlaw; *sub nom.* Wardlaw v. Bonnington Castings Ltd [1956] A.C. 613; [1956]
     2 W.L.R. 707, HL 30
Boyle v. H.M. Advocate, 1976 J.C. 32; 1976 S.L.T. 126, HCJ Appeal 108
——, Petitioner (No. 2), 1993 S.L.T. 1085; 1992 S.C.C.R. 949, HCJ Appeal 171, 275
Brady v. H.M. Advocate, 1986 S.L.T. 686; 1986 S.C.C.R. 191, HCJ Appeal 282, 385
Brannan v. Peek [1948] 1 K.B. 68; [1947] 2 All E.R. 572, DC 197, 202, 203
Bremner v. H.M. Advocate, 1992 S.C.C.R. 476, HCJ Appeal 9, 307
Brennan v. H.M. Advocate, 1954 S.L.T. 255 123
Bricmont v. Belgium (A/158) (1990) 12 E.H.R.R. 217, ECHR 190, 191
Briginshaw v. Briginshaw [1938] 60 C.L.R. 336 64
Brims v. MacDonald, 1994 S.L.T. 922; 1993 S.C.C.R. 1061, HCJ Appeal 339
Britton v. Central Regional Council, 1986 S.L.T. 207, 1 Div 361
Brodie v. H.M. Advocate, 1993 J.C. 92; 1993 S.C.C.R. 371, HCJ Appeal 514, 517, 519
Brotherston v. H.M. Advocate, 1996 S.L.T. 1154; 1995 S.C.C.R. 613, HCJ Appeal 110, 477, 492
Brown v. Brown, 1972 S.C. 123; 1972 S.L.T. 143, OH 63, 71, 74
—— v. Glen, 1998 J.C. 4; 1998 S.L.T. 115, HCJ Appeal 208
—— v. H.M. Advocate, 1964 J.C. 10; 1964 S.L.T. 53, HCJ Appeal 169, 236
—— v. H.M. Advocate, 1966 S.L.T. 105, HCJ Appeal 198, 205, 252, 255, 256, 262
—— v. Macpherson, 1918 J.C. 3; (1917) 2 S.L.T.134, HCJ Appeal 443
—— v. R. (1913) 17 C.L.R. 570 154
—— v. Rolls-Royce [1960] 1 W.L.R. 210; [1960] 1 All E.R. 577; 1960 S.C. (H.L.) 22, HL 30
—— v. Stott; Stott (Procurator Fiscal) v. Brown; Procurator Fiscal, Dunfermline v. Brown; Brown v.
     Procurator Fiscal, Dunfermline [2001] 2 W.L.R. 817; [2001] 2 All E.R. 97; 2001 S.L.T. 59, PC (Sc) 36,
                                            196, 219, 231, 260
Buchanan v. Price, 1982 S.C.C.R. 534, HCJ Appeal 24
Buick v. Jaglar, 1973 S.L.T. (Sh. Ct.) 6, Sh Ct (Tayside) 71
Burke v. Wilson, 1988 J.C. 111; 1988 S.L.T. 749; 1988 S.C.C.R. 361, HCJ Appeal 212
Burnett v. Burnett, 1955 S.C. 183; 1955 S.L.T. 190, 1 Div 223
Burton v. H.M. Advocate, 1979 S.L.T. (Notes) 59, HCJ Appeal 300
Byrne v. Ross, 1992 S.C. 498; 1993 S.L.T. 307, 1 Div 72, 411

C. and L. (Child Abuse: Evidence) [1991] F.C.R. 361 499
C. v. M., 1923 S.C. 1 284
Caffrey v. Lord Inverclyde, 1930 S.L.T. 511, 2 Div 370
Cairns v. Howdle, 2000 S.C.C.R. 742; 2000 G.W.D. 29–1113, HCJ Appeal 114
Cameron v. H.M. Advocate, 1991 J.C. 251; 1988 S.L.T. 169; 1987 S.C.C.R. 608, HCJ Appeal 520, 522, 523
—— v. H.M. Advocate, 1987 S.C.C.R. 608, 1988 S.L.T. 169 47
—— v. Waugh, 1937 S.L.T. 53, HCJ Appeal 278
Campbell v. H.M. Advocate, 1998 S.L.T. 923 .... 508, 509, 510
Campbell (T) v. H.M. Advocate, 1998 S.C.C.R. 214 .... 82, 83, 178
Carberry v. H.M. Advocate, 1975 J.C. 40; 1976 S.L.T. 38, HCJ Appeal 305
Carmichael v. Boyd, 1993 J.C. 219; 1994 S.L.T. 734, HCJ Appeal 231, 258
—— v. Monaghan, 1986 S.C.C.R. 599 305
Carpenter v. Hamilton, 1994 S.C.C.R. 108, HCJ Appeal 117, 119
Carrington v. H.M. Advocate, 1995 S.L.T. 341; 1994 S.C.C.R. 567, HCJ Appeal 38
Carson v. McGlennan, 2000 S.L.T. 810; 2000 S.C.C.R. 631, HCJ Appeal 91, 119
Casey v. H.M. Advocate (No. 1), 1993 S.L.T. 33, HCJ Appeal 449, 458, 475
Cavanagh v. BP Chemicals, 1995 S.L.T. 1287, OH 424
—— v. Ulster Weaving Co. [1960] A.C. 145; [1959] 3 W.L.R. 262, HL 31
Chalmers v. H.M. Advocate, 1954 J.C. 66; 1954 S.L.T. 177, HCJ Appeal ... 199, 225, 230, 231, 234, 236, 237, 238,
                                239, 240, 242, 243, 244, 248, 251, 252, 255, 256, 258, 262
—— v. H.M. Advocate, 1994 S.C.C.R. 651, HCJ Appeal 110, 493
—— v. Speedwell Wire Co. [1944] K.B. 560 22
Chant v. H.M. Advocate, 2001 G.W.D. 14–540, HCJ Appeal 524

Chitambala v. Queen, The [1961] R. & N. at pp.169–170 .... 244, 245, 248
Church v. H.M. Advocate, 1995 S.L.T. 604; 1995 S.C.C.R. 194, HCJ Appeal 327, 508
Church (No. 2) v. H.M. Advocate, 1996 S.L.T. 383, HCJ Appeal 520, 523
Cia Alartiarta v. Royal Exchange Assurance Corp. [1923] K.B. 650 .... 26, 27
——— v. Clark's Trustee; *sub nom.* Clark v. Black, 1948 S.L.T. (Notes) 58, OH 139, 142
——— v. Stuart, 1950 J.C. 8; 1949 S.L.T. 461, HCJ Appeal 131, 248, 249
Clarke v. Edinburgh and District Tramways Co. Ltd, 1919 S.C. (H.L.) 35; (1919) 1 S.L.T.247, HL 502
Cleisham v. British Transport Commission (B.T.C.), 1964 S.C. (H.L.) 8; 1964 S.L.T. 41, HL 92, 399, 401
Coates v. Modern Methods & Materials Ltd [1983] Q.B. 192; [1982] 3 W.L.R. 764; [1982] I.C.R. 763, CA 505
Codona v. H.M. Advocate, 1996 S.L.T. 1100; 1996 S.C.C.R. 300, HCJ Appeal 230, 231, 241, 254, 262
Coffey v. Houston, 1992 J.C. 80; 1992 S.L.T. 520, HCJ Appeal 120
Collins v. H.M. Advocate, 1991 J.C. 204; 1993 S.L.T. 101, HCJ Appeal 171
Comerford v. Strathclyde Regional Council, 1988 S.C.L.R. 67, Sh Pr; reversing 1987 S.C.L.R. 758, Sh Ct
   (Glasgow) 407
Commissioners of Inland Revenue v. Russell, 1955 S.C. 237; 1955 S.L.T. 255, 1 Div 334
Conner v. Lockhart, 1986 J.C. 161; 1987 S.L.T. 392, HCJ Appeal 291, 292, 294, 296
Connolly v. H.M. Advocate, 1958 S.L.T. 79 .... 84, 105, 111, 113
Conway v. Rimmer [1968] A.C. 910; [1968] 2 W.L.R. 998, HL 371, 378
Cook v. Skinner, 1977 J.C. 9; 1977 S.L.T. (Notes) 11, HCJ Appeal 198, 199, 202
Cooper v. Stubbs [1925] 2 K.B. 753 503
——— v. British Railways Board, 1986 S.L.T. 209, OH 426
——— v. H.M. Advocate, 1978 J.C. 64; 1978 S.L.T. 118, HCJ Appeal 305
——— v. H.M. Advocate, 1993 S.L.T. 2; 1991 S.C.C.R. 652, HCJ Appeal 79, 80, 286, 298
Corp. of the City of Glasgow v. Central Land Board, 1956 S.C. (HL) 1 .... 368, 374, 377
Costello, 1922 J.C. 9 229
Cowan v. H.M. Advocate, 2001 G.W.D. 18–692, HCJ Appeal 11, 306
Craig v. H.M. Advocate, unreported, May 18, 2000, High Ct of Justiciary 523
Crombie v. Clark; *sub nom.* Crombie v. Guild, 2001 S.L.T. 635; 2001 S.C.C.R. 231, HCJ Appeal 529
Cryans v. Nixon, 1955 J.C. 1; 1954 S.L.T. 311, HCJ Appeal 123
——— v. Currie, 1950 S.C. 10; 1950 S.L.T. 15, OH 223
——— v. Inland Revenue Commissioners [1921] 2 K.B. 332, CA; reversing [1920] 1 K.B. 801, KBD 506, 507
Custerton v. Westwater, 1987 S.C.C.R. 389, HCJ Appeal 259
Cutts v. Head [1984] Ch. 290; [1984] 2 W.L.R. 349, CA 364, 366

D. (Minors) (Adoption Reports: Confidentiality), Re [1996] A.C. 593; [1995] 3 W.L.R. 483; [1995] 4 All
   E.R. 385, HL 394, 395, 396
D. v. National Society for the Prevention of Cruelty to Children [1978] A.C. 171; [1977] 2 W.L.R. 201, HL ... 378
Daks Simpson Group plc v. Kuiper, 1994 S.L.T. 689; 1994 S.C.C.R. 373, OH 364
Daly v. Vannet, 1999 S.C.C.R. 346; 1999 G.W.D. 16–737, HCJ Appeal 385
Daniels, (unreported) (1960) 358
Davidson v. Brown, 1990 J.C. 324; 1991 S.L.T. 335; 1990 S.C.C.R. 304, HCJ Appeal 208
Davie v. Edinburgh Corp. (No. 2); *sub nom.* Davie v. Edinburgh Magistrates, 1953 S.C. 34; 1953 S.L.T. 54,
   1 Div 311, 315, 316, 317
——— v. Magistrates of Edinburgh *See* Davie v. Edinburgh Corp. (No. 2)
Davies v. McGuire, 1995 S.L.T. 755, OH 420
——— v. Taylor (No. 1) [1974] A.C. 207; [1972] 3 W.L.R. 801, HL 57, 59
——— v. U.S. (1895) 160 U.S. 469 77
Davis v. Davis [1950] P. 125; [1950] 1 All E.R. 40, CA 64
Deacon Brodie 1788 .... 456, 474
Deans' JF v. Deans, 1912 S.C. 448; 1912 S.L.T. 200 435
Deeney v. H.M. Advocate, 1986 S.C.C.R. 393, HCJ Appeal 305
Deighan v. MacLeod, 1959 J.C. 25; 1960 S.L.T. 2; [1961] Crim. L.R. 711, HCJ Appeal 305
Dellow's Will Trusts; *sub nom.* Lloyds Bank v. Institote of Cancer Research [1964] 1 W.L.R. 451; [1964] 1
   All E.R. 771; 108 S.J. 156, Ch D 65
Dempsey v. H.M. Advocate, 1995 J.C. 84; 1996 S.L.T. 289, HCJ Appeal 444
Devine v. Colvilles Ltd; *sub nom.* Colvilles Ltd v. Devine [1969] 1 W.L.R. 475; [1969] 2 All E.R. 53; 1969
   S.C. (H.L.) 67, HL 32, 55
Devlin v. Normand, 1992 S.C.C.R. 875, HCJ 208
Dickie v. H.M. Advocate (1897) 2 Adam 331 .... 7, 9, 285, 307
Dickinson v. Minister of Pensions [1953] 1 Q.B. 228; [1952] 2 All E.R. 1031, QBD 16, 17
Dingley v. Chief Constable of Strathclyde Police (No. 1), 2000 S.C. (H.L.) 77; 2000 S.C.L.R. 309, HL 315
DPP v. A & BC Chewing Gum Ltd [1968] 1 Q.B. 159; [1967] 3 W.L.R. 493, QBD 322
——— v. Boardman; *sub nom.* Boardman v. DPP; R. v. Boardman [1975] A.C. 421; [1974] 3 W.L.R. 673, HL 7,
                                                                                              117, 269
——— v. Kilbourne; *sub nom.* R. v. Kilbourne (John) [1973] A.C. 729; [1973] 2 W.L.R. 254, HL   1, 2, 5, 103, 115,
                                                                                              274
——— v. P; *sub nom.* R. v. P. (A Father) [1991] 2 A.C. 447; [1991] 3 W.L.R. 161, HL 269, 274
——— v. Ping Lin [1976] A.C. 574; [1975] 3 W.L.R. 419, HL 245

Dobson v. Colvilles Ltd, 1958 S.L.T. (Notes) 30, 1 Div 346
Docherty v. H.M. Advocate, 1981 J.C. 6, HCJ 189, 192, 258
—— v. H.M. Advocate, 1987 J.C. 81; 1987 S.L.T. 784, HCJ Appeal 449, 450, 453, 475
—— v. Mcglynn (No. 1), 1983 S.C. 202; 1983 S.L.T. 645, 1 Div 50
Dodds v. H.M. Advocate, 1988 J.C. 21; 1988 S.L.T. 194, HCJ Appeal 286
Donald v. Hart (1844) 6 D. 1255 369
Donnelly v. Carmichael, 1995 J.C. 215; 1996 S.L.T. 153, HCJ Appeal 342
—— v. H.M. Advocate, 1999 S.C.C.R. 508; 1999 G.W.D. 21–993, HCJ Appeal 37
Doorson v. Netherlands (1996) 22 E.H.R.R. 330, ECHR 192, 260
Dosoo v. Dosoo (No. 1), 1999 S.L.T. (Sh. Ct.) 86; 1999 S.C.L.R. 905, Sh Ct (Lothian) 395, 396, 397
Douglas v. Pirie, 1975 J.C. 61; 1975 S.L.T. 206, HCJ Appeal 122, 123
Dow v. MacKnight, 1949 J.C. 38; 1949 S.L.T. 95, HCJ Appeal 450, 451, 452, 453, 454, 457, 458
Dowgray v. Gilmour (1907) 14 S.L.T. 906 .... 140, 370
Downie v. H.M. Advocate, 1952 J.C. 37; 1952 S.L.T. 159, HCJ Appeal 380, 381
Doyle v. Ruxton, 1999 S.L.T. 487; 1998 S.C.C.R. 467, HCJ Appeal 334
Drummond v. H.M. Advocate, 1992 J.C. 88; 1993 S.L.T. 476; 1992 S.C.C.R. 290, HCJ Appeal 211
Dudgeon v. H.M. Advocate, 1988 S.L.T. 476; 1988 S.C.C.R. 147, HCJ Appeal 305
Dudley v. H.M. Advocate, 1995 S.C.C.R. 52, HCJ Appeal 110
Duff v. Duff, 1969 S.L.T. (Notes) 53, OH 285
Duke of Argyll v. Duchess of Argyll (No. 3), 1963 S.L.T. (Notes) 42, OH 223, 224
Dumoulin v. H.M. Advocate, 1974 S.L.T. (Notes) 42, HCJ Appeal 272
Duncan v. Cammell Laird & Co 369, 371, 372
Dunn v. Dunn's Trustees (1930) S.C. 131 .... 501, 502
Dunning v. United Liverpool Hospital Board of Governors [1973] 1 W.L.R. 586; [1973] 2 All E.R. 454, CA   373
Dunstance v. H.M. Advocate, unreported, July 13, 1951 451

Earl v. Vass (1822) 1 Sh. App. 229, HL 369, 370, 371
Earnshaw v. H.M. Advocate, 1982 J.C. 11; 1982 S.L.T. 179, HCJ Appeal 24, 32
Ebrahem v. Ebrahem, 1989 S.L.T. 808; 1989 S.C.L.R. 540, OH 414, 415, 418
Edgley v. Barbour, 1995 S.L.T. 711; 1994 S.C.C.R. 789, HCJ Appeal 217
Edwards v. Bairstow; Edwards v. Harrison [1956] A.C. 14; [1955] 3 W.L.R. 410, HL 503, 504, 505, 506, 507
Elliot v. Joicey, 1935 S.C. (HL) 57 342
Elliott Millar Ark. 355 .... 468, 469
—— v. H.M. Advocate, 1995 S.L.T. 612 .... 508, 509
Eshugbayi Eleko v. Government of Nigeria [1931] A.C. 662, PC (Nig) 64
Eutectic Welding Alloys Co. Ltd v. Whitting, 1969 S.L.T. (Notes) 79, OH 73
Executor of Lady Bath v. Johnston November 12, 1811, F.C 355, 358

F. v. Kennedy (No. 1), 1992 S.C. 28; 1993 S.L.T. 1277, 2 Div 427, 428, 429, 430, 433, 434, 483
—— v. Kennedy (No. 2), 1993 S.L.T. 1284; 1992 S.C.L.R. 750, 2 Div 144, 409, 418, 420, 421, 425, 499
Fagernes, The; sub nom. Coast Lines Ltd v. Societa Nazionale di Navigazione of Genoa (The Fagernes)
    [1927] P. 311; (1927) 28 Ll. L. Rep. 261, CA 332
Fairley v. Fishmongers of London, 1951 J.C. 14; 1951 S.L.T. 54, HCJ Appeal 214
Farmer v. H.M. Advocate, 1991 S.C.C.R. 986, HCJ Appeal 110
Farrell v. Normand, 1993 S.L.T. 793 118
Fayed v. United Kingdom (A/294-B) (1994) 18 E.H.R.R. 393; The Times, October 11, 1994, ECHR 264
Fegan, Shaw 261 .... 468, 469
Ferguson v. H.M. Advocate, 2000 S.C.C.R. 954; 2000 G.W.D. 32–1249, HCJ 110
—— v. S., 1993 S.C.L.R. 712 .... 420, 421
Ferrantelli v. Italy (1997) 23 E.H.R.R. 288, ECHR 190, 191, 192
Fielding v. H.M. Advocate, 1959 J.C. 101; 1960 S.L.T. 105, HCJ Appeal 290, 294
Fisher v. Guild, 1991 S.L.T. 253; 1991 S.C.C.R. 308, HCJ Appeal 121
Fletcher (Margaret Shiells) (1846) Ark 171 .... 281, 282, 283, 288
Forrester v. H.M. Advocate, 1952 J.C. 28; 1952 S.L.T. 188, HCJ Appeal 206, 327, 328
Forsyth v. H.M. Advocate, 1992 S.L.T. 189; 1991 S.C.C.R. 861, HCJ Appeal 281, 306
Foster v. Farrell, 1963 J.C. 46; 1963 S.L.T. 182, HCJ Appeal 255, 260, 261, 266
—— v. H.M. Advocate, 1932 J.C. 75 .... 467, 469
Foulkes v. Chadd (1782) 3 Doug K.B. 157 320
Fox v. H.M. Advocate, 1998 J.C. 94; 1998 S.L.T. 335, HCJ Appeal 83, 92, 93, 103
—— v. Patterson, 1948 J.C. 104; 1948 S.L.T. 547, HCJ Appeal 47, 53, 123
Fraser v. H.M. Advocate, 1989 S.C.C.R. 82, HCJ Appeal 231
Frew v. Jessop, 1990 S.L.T. 396; 1989 S.C.C.R. 530, HCJ Appeal 178, 179, 180
Friel v. Chief Constable of Strathclyde, 1981 S.C. 1; 1981 S.L.T. 113, OH 372
FS (Child Abuse: Evidence), Re; sub nom. FS (Minors) (Care Proceedings), Re [1996] 2 F.L.R. 158; [1996]
    1 F.C.R. 666, CA 315, 437, 478
Funke v. France (A/256-A) [1993] 1 C.M.L.R. 897; (1993) 16 E.H.R.R. 297, ECHR 264
Fyfe v. H.M. Advocate, 1998 S.L.T. 195; 1997 S.C.C.R. 602, HCJ Appeal 315

G's Trustees v. G's Curator Bonis, 1936 S.C. 837; 1936 S.L.T. 631, IH (Ct of 7 judges) 332
Gallacher v. H.M. Advocate, 1951 J.C. 45 .... 510, 511
Gallagher v. H.M. Advocate, 2000 S.C.C.R. 634; 2000 G.W.D. 15–580, HCJ 13, 103
—— v. Paton, 1909 S.C. (J.) 50 .... 272, 277
Gardner v. Gardner 4 R. (HL) 56 .... 48, 49
Gavin v. Normand, 1995 S.L.T. 741; 1995 S.C.C.R. 209, HCJ Appeal 220
George Hopkinson Ltd v. Napier & Son, 1953 S.C. 139; 1953 S.L.T. 99, 1 Div 52
Ghandi Tandoori Restaurant v. Commissioners of Customs and Excise [1989] V.A.T.T.R. 39, VAT Tr 72, 74
Gibson v. British Insulated Callender's Construction Co. Ltd (B.I.C.C.), 1973 S.C. (H.L.) 15; 1973 S.L.T. 2,
    HL 24
—— v. N.C.R., 1925 SC, 500 .... 28, 29
Gillespie v. Macmillan, 1957 J.C. 31; 1957 S.L.T. 283, HCJ Appeal 14, 83, 84, 86, 87
Gilmour v. H.M. Advocate, 1982 S.C.C.R. 590, HCJ Appeal 113
Gladstone v. Stevenson 4F. (J) 66 333
Glaser v. Glaser, 1997 S.L.T. 456; 1997 S.C.L.R. 540, OH 418
Glebe Sugar Refining Co. v. Trustees of the Fort and Harbours of Greenock; *sub nom.* Glebe Sugar
    Refining Co. Ltd and the Westburn Sugar Refineries Ltd v. Greenock Port and Harbour Trustees
    [1921] 2 A.C. 66; (1921) 7 Ll. L. Rep. 147; 1921 S.C. (HL) 76, HL 341
Golder v. United Kingdom (A/18) [1979–80] 1 E.H.R.R. 524, ECHR 261, 263
Gordon v. East Kilbride Development Corp., 1995 S.L.T. 62, OH 367
Gower v. Gower (Divorce: Adultery) [1950] 1 All E.R. 804; 66 T.L.R. (Pt. 1) 717, CA 64
Gracey v. H.M. Advocate, 1987 J.C. 45; 1987 S.L.T. 749, HCJ Appeal 86
Gracie v. Allan, 1987 S.C.C.R. 364, HCJ Appeal 110
Graham v. H.M. Advocate, 1984 S.L.T. 67; 1983 S.C.C.R. 314, HCJ Appeal 303
—— v. Orr, 1995 S.C.C.R. 30, HCJ Appeal 212
Grant v. Grant, 2000 G.W.D. 5–177, Sh Pr 397
Green v. O'Brien, 1988 G.W.D. 10–401 449
Greenshields v. H.M. Advocate, 1989 S.C.C.R. 637, HCJ Appeal 106
Gribben v. Gribben, 1976 S.L.T. 266, 1 Div 72, 73
Griffen v. H.M. Advocate, 1940 J.C. 1; 1940 S.L.T. 175, HCJ Appeal 278, 279, 280

H (Minors) (Sexual Abuse: Standard of Proof), Re; *sub nom.* H (Minors) (Child Abuse: Threshold
    Conditions), Re H and R (Child Sexual Abuse; Standard of Proof), Re [1996] A.C. 563; [1996] 2
    W.L.R. 8, HL 67, 413
H. v. P. (1905) 8 F. (Ct. of Sess.) 232; (1905) 13 S.L.T.615, 1 Div 270, 284, 285
H.M.A. v. Aitken, 1926 J.C. 83 .... 233, 239
—— v. Ashrif, 1988 S.L.T. 567; 1988 S.C.C.R. 197, HCJ Appeal 285, 383, 384, 385
—— v. Aspinall, 2001 G.W.D. 14–546, HCJ Appeal 219
—— v. Bain, 2001 S.C.C.R. 461; 2001 G.W.D. 18–693, HCJ Appeal 193
—— v. Bell, 1985 S.L.T. 349, HCJ Appeal 220
—— v. Campbell, 1964 J.C. 80; 1964 S.L.T. (Notes) 78, HCJ 198, 201, 202, 204, 252, 253, 254
—— v. Carson, 1997 S.L.T. 1119; 1997 S.C.C.R. 273, HCJ Appeal 9, 281
—— v. Cormack, 1995 J.C. 133; 1995 S.C.C.R. 477, HCJ 280
—— v. Cox, 1962 J.C. 27, HCJ 118
—— v. Cumming, 1983 S.C.C.R. 15, Sh Ct (Grampian) 220
—— v. Cunningham, 1939 J.C. 61 .... 229, 234
—— v. Davie (1881) 4 Coup. 450 358
—— v. Forrest, 1998 S.C.C.R. 153; 1998 G.W.D. 8–378, HCJ Appeal 169
—— v. Fox, 1947 J.C. 31; 1947 S.L.T. 52, HCJ 234, 236
—— v. Gilgannon, 1983 S.C.C.R. 10, HCJ 231
—— v. Graham, 1991 S.L.T. 416; 1991 S.C.C.R. 56, HCJ 198, 202, 251, 254
—— v. Grimmond, 2001 S.C.C.R. 708; 2001 G.W.D. 27–1083, HCJ 326, 486
—— v. Grudins, 1976 S.L.T. (Notes) 10, HCJ 294
—— v. Harper, 1989 S.C.C.R. 472, Sh Ct 198, 202, 252
—— v. Hepper, 1958 J.C. 39; 1958 S.L.T. 160, HCJ 211, 214, 215, 216, 263
—— v. Hislop, 1994 S.L.T. 333, HCJ 183, 186
—— v. Joseph, 1929 J.C. 55; 1929 S.L.T. 414, HCJ 117, 269, 273, 277
—— v. Kay, 1970 J.C. 68; 1970 S.L.T. (Notes) 66, HCJ 281
—— v. Kelly, unreported, January 20, 2001, High Ct of Justiciary 208, 358
—— v. Maan; *sub nom.* Maan (Habib), Petitioner 2001 S.L.T. 408; 2001 S.C.C.R. 172, HCJ 284, 382
—— v. McGinlay, 1983 S.L.T. 562, HCJ Appeal 312, 313
—— v. McGuigan, 1936 J.C. 16; 1936 S.L.T. 161, HCJ 216, 217
—— v. McIntosh [2001] UKPC D1; [2001] 3 W.L.R. 107; 2001 S.L.T. 304, PC (UK) 36
—— v. Megrahi (No. 3); Megrahi v. H.M. Advocate (No. 3); H.M. Advocate v. Al Megrahi (No. 3); Al
    Megrahi v. H.M. Advocate (No. 3), 2000 S.L.T. 1401; 2000 G.W.D. 33–1265, HCJ 220
—— v. Mitchell, 1951 J.C. 53; 1951 S.L.T. 200, HCJ 76

H.M.A. v. Monson (1893) 21 R. (J) 5, 1 S.L.T. 405 .... 275, 276, 278, 279, 280
—— v. Mowat *See* H.M. Advocate v. MacMowat, 2001 S.L.T. 738; 2001 S.C.C.R. 242, HCJ 250
—— v. Nulty, 2000 S.L.T. 528; 2000 S.C.C.R. 431, HCJ 192
—— v. O'Donnell, 1975 S.L.T. (Sh. Ct.)22 251
—— v. Parker, 1944 J.C. 49 358
—— v. Peter and Smith 2 Swinton 492 348
—— v. Pritchard (1865) 5 Irv. 88 .... 275, 277, 278, 279
—— v. Pye (1838) 2 Swin. 187 169
—— v. Rigg, 1946 S.L.T. 49; 1946 J.C. 1 .... 228, 233
—— v. Ritchie and Morren (1841) 2 Swin. 581 276
—— v. Shepherd; *sub nom.* H.M. Advocate v. S, 1997 J.C. 131; 1997 S.L.T. 891, HCJ Appeal 206
—— v. Short, unreported, May 30, 1950 228
—— v. Turnbull, 1951 J.C. 96; 1951 S.L.T. 409, HCJ 210, 211, 214, 215
—— v. Von, 1979 S.L.T. (Notes) 62, HCJ 260
—— v. Ward, 1993 S.L.T. 1202; 1993 S.C.C.R. 595, HCJ 378, 381
—— v. Weatherly 4 Adam 353 .... 461, 466
—— v. Whitelaw, 1980 S.L.T. (Notes) 25, HCJ 232, 240, 247 252, 253
—— v. William Dreghorn 1806 .... 461, 464, 465, 466
—— v. Wilson, unreported, June 15, 2000, High Ct of Justiciary 355, 382
Hackston v. Millar 5 Adam 37 .... 446, 448
Halcrow v. Shearer (1892) 20 R. 216 369
Halford v. Brookes [1991] T.L.R. 427 71
Hall v. Edinburgh Corp., 1974 S.L.T. (Notes) 14, OH 426
—— v. H.M. Advocate, 1968 S.L.T. 275, HCJ Appeal 421
Hamill v. H.M. Advocate; *sub nom.* H.M. Advocate v. Hamill, 1999 S.L.T. 963; 1999 S.C.C.R. 384, HCJ
    Appeal 150, 230
Hamilton v. Byrne, 1997 S.L.T. 1210; 1997 S.C.C.R. 547, HCJ Appeal 190
Harley v. H.M. Advocate, 1996 S.L.T. 1075; 1995 S.C.C.R. 595, HCJ Appeal 251
Harris v. DPP; *sub nom.* R. v. Harris [1952] A.C. 694; [1952] 1 All E.R. 1044, HL 1
—— v. F., 1991 S.L.T. 242; 1991 S.C.L.R. 124, 2 Div 69, 71, 411, 419
Hart v. Royal London Mutual Insurance Co. Ltd, 1956 S.L.T. (Notes) 55, OH 271
Hartley v. H.M. Advocate, 1979 S.L.T. 26; [1981] Crim. L.R. 782, HCJ Appeal 106, 108, 110, 230
Hasson v. H.M. Advocate, 1971 J.C. 35; 1971 S.L.T. 199, HCJ 382
Hattie v. Leitch (1889) 16R. 1128 340
Hawkins v. Carmichael, 1992 S.C.C.R. 348, HCJ Appeal 110
Hay 1858 3 Irv. 181 229
—— v. H.M. Advocate, 1968 J.C. 40; 1968 S.L.T. 334, HCJ Appeal 204, 205, 206
—— v. McClory, 1994 S.L.T. 520; 1993 S.C.C.R. 1040, HCJ Appeal 470, 474
—— v. Wither, 1988 J.C. 94; 1988 S.C.C.R. 334, HCJ Appeal 113 118
Hemming v. H.M. Advocate, 1997 J.C. 140; 1998 S.L.T. 213 .... 378, 382
Henderson v. Henderson's Executor, 2000 S.L.T. (Sh. Ct.) 6; 1999 G.W.D. 31–1494, Sh Pr 334
—— v. McGown, 1916 S.C. 821; (1916) 2 S.L.T.65, 1 Div 370, 371, 375
—— v. Robertson (1853) 15 D. 292 .... 369, 375
Hendry v. Clan Line Steamers, 1949 S.C. 320; 1949 S.L.T. 280, 2 Div 58, 63, 73
—— v. H.M. Advocate, 1985 J.C. 105; 1986 S.L.T. 186; 1985 S.C.C.R. 274, HCJ Appeal 164, 165, 166,
                                                                                     167, 168, 169, 170
—— v. H.M. Advocate, 1987 J.C. 63; 1988 S.L.T. 25; 1987 S.C.C.R. 394, HCJ Appeal 312, 313, 317
Hepburn v. Scottish Power plc, 1997 S.C. 80; 1997 S.L.T. 859, Ex Div 358
Herkes v. Dickie, 1958 J.C. 51; 1959 S.L.T. 74, HCJ Appeal 342
Higgins v. Burton, 1968 S.L.T. (Notes) 52, OH 378
—— v. H.M. Advocate, 1990 S.C.C.R. 268, HCJ Appeal 381
—— v. H.M. Advocate; *sub nom.* Higgins, Ferns & Grogan v. H.M. Advocate 1993 S.C.C.R. 542, HCJ
    Appeal 231
Highland Venison Marketing Ltd v. Allwild GmbH, 1992 S.L.T. 1127; 1992 S.C.L.R. 415, OH 421, 424
Hillan v. H.M. Advocate, 1937 S.L.T. 396; 1937 J.C. 53, HCJ Appeal 35
Hoang v. France (A/243) (1993) 16 E.H.R.R. 53, ECHR 36
Hodgson v. Macpherson, 1913 S.C. 68 229
Hoekstra v. H.M. Advocate (No. 6), 2001 J.C. 131; 2001 S.L.T. 632, HCJ Appeal 382
Hogg v. MacNeill, 2001 S.L.T. 873; 2001 S.C.C.R. 134, HCJ Appeal 14
Hopes v. H.M. Advocate; Lavery v. H.M. Advocate 1960 J.C. 104; 1960 S.L.T. 264, HCJ   198, 252, 253, 328, 329
Hornal v. Neuberger Products Ltd [1957] 1 Q.B. 247; [1956] 3 W.L.R. 1034, CA 62, 64, 65, 67
Hotson v. East Berkshire Area Health Board; *sub nom.* Hotson v. Fitzgerald [1987] A.C. 750;
    [1987] 3 W.L.R. 232, HL 58
Houston v. McLeod, 1986 J.C. 96; 1986 S.C.C.R. 219, HCJ Appeal 135
Howden v. H.M. Advocate, 1994 S.C.C.R. 19, HCJ Appeal 119, 121
Howitt v. H.M. Advocate, 2000 S.L.T. 449 467
Hughes v. H.M. Advocate, 2000 S.C.C.R. 250; 2000 G.W.D. 9–327, HCJ Appeal 110

Hughes v. Skeen, 1980 S.L.T. (Notes) 13, HCJ Appeal 132
—— v. Stewart, 1964 S.C. 155, 1 Div 401
—— v. Stewart, 1989 S.C.C.R. 25, HCJ Appeal 92
Hunter v. H.M. Advocate, 1984 J.C. 90 . . . . 358, 470, 473
Hynd v. PF (Kilmarnock), 2000 S.C.C.R. 231 522

Ibrahim v. R. *See* Ibrahim v. King, The [1914] A.C. 599; [1914–15] All E.R. Rep. 874, PC (HK) 228
Imre v. Mitchell, 1958 S.C. 439; 1959 S.L.T. 13, 1 Div 48, 50, 58, 63
Inglis v. National Bank of Scotland (No. 1), 1909 S.C. 1038; (1909) 1 S.L.T. 518, Ex Div 270, 271
Ingram v. Macari, 1983 J.C. 1 . . . . 313, 327
Inland Revenue v. Glasgow Police Athletic Association [1953] A.C. 380; [1953] 2 W.L.R. 625; 1953 S.C.
    (H.L.) 13, HL 342
Inland Revenue Commissioners v. Fraser, 1942 S.C. 493; 1942 S.L.T. 280, 1 Div 504
—— v. Lysaght; *sub nom.* Lysaght v. Inland Revenue Commissioners [1928] A.C. 234; [1928] All E.R. Rep.
    575, HL 503
Iomega Corp. v. Myrica (UK) Ltd (No. 1), 1999 S.L.T. 793; 1997 G.W.D. 39–1980, OH 393
—— v. Myrica (UK) Ltd (No. 2); *sub nom.* Iomega Corp., Petitioners 1998 S.C. 637; 1999 S.L.T. 796,
    1 Div 394
Ireland v. Russell, 1995 J.C. 169; 1995 S.L.T. 1348, HCJ Appeal 196
Irving (1838) 2 Swin 109 . . . . 281, 282, 283
—— v. H.M. Advocate 190, 192
—— v. Jessop; *sub nom.* Irving v. Tudhope, 1988 S.L.T. 53; 1987 S.C.C.R. 505, HCJ Appeal 259
—— v. Minister of Pensions, 1946 S.L.T. 34, 2 Div 59
—— v. Tudhope *See* Irving v. Jessop

J.S. (A Minor), Re [1981] Fam. 22 . . . . 57, 62
Jackson v. Stevenson 2 Adam 255, 24 R. (J) 38 211
Jamieson v. Annan, 1988 J.C. 62; 1988 S.L.T. 631; 1988 S.C.C.R. 278, HCJ Appeal 251, 252, 254
—— v. H.M. Advocate (No. 2), 1995 S.L.T. 666; 1994 S.C.C.R. 610, HCJ Appeal . . . 178, 179, 180, 182, 183, 184,
    187
Japan Leasing (Europe) plc v. Weir's Trustee; *sub nom.* Japan Leasing (Europe) plc v. Hastings 1998 S.L.T.
    224; 1997 S.C.L.R. 519, 1 Div 144
—— v. Weir's Trustee (No. 2), 1998 S.C. 543; 1998 S.L.T. 973, 2 Div 420
John Buchan and Malcolm Maclean (1833) Bells Notes 293 . . . . 437, 478
Johnston v. H.M. Advocate, 1993 J.C. 187; 1994 S.L.T. 300; 1993 S.C.C.R. 693, HCJ Appeal 206, 231, 258
Johnstone v. National Coal Board, 1968 S.C. 128; 1968 S.L.T. 233, 1 Div 360, 361, 362
Jones v. Foxall (1852) 15 Beav. 388 366
—— v. H.M. Advocate, 1992 S.L.T. 115; 1991 S.C.C.R. 290, HCJ Appeal 466
—— v. Leeming; *sub nom.* Leeming v. Jones [1930] A.C. 415, HL; affirming [1930] 1 K.B. 279, CA 503
—— v. Milne, 1975 J.C. 16; 1975 S.L.T. 2, HCJ Appeal 239
—— v. Owen (1870) 34 J.P. 759 194
Joseph Constantine Steamship Line Ltd v. Imperial Smelting Corp. Ltd [1942] A.C. 154; [1941] 2 All E.R.
    165, HL 18

K (Minors) (Alleged Sexual Abuse: Evidence) [1996] 2 F.C.R. 425, Fam Div 315
K. v. Kennedy, 1993 S.L.T. 1281; 1992 S.C.L.R. 386, Ex Div 409, 411, 421, 437
K.P. v. H.M. Advocate, 1991 S.C.C.R. 933 . . . . 326, 478, 483
Kay v. H.M. Advocate 282, 283, 385
Keavney v. H.M. Advocate, 1999 J.C. 240; 1999 S.L.T. 1030, HCJ Appeal 110
Kelly v. Allan, 1984 S.C.C.R. 186, HCJ Appeal 130
—— v. Docherty, 1991 S.L.T. 419; 1991 S.C.C.R. 312, HCJ Appeal 476, 478, 481, 485
—— v. Vannet, 1999 J.C. 109; 2000 S.L.T. 75, HCJ Appeal 358
Kemp v. H.M. Advocate, unreported, September 15, 1950, HCJ Appeal 176
Kennedy v. Smith and Ansvar Insurance Co. Ltd, 1975 S.C. 266; 1976 S.L.T. 110, 1 Div 336
Kenny v. Tudhope, 1984 S.C.C.R. 290, HCJ Appeal 317
Kerr v. H.M. Advocate, 1958 J.C. 14; 1958 S.L.T. 82, HCJ Appeal 424, 425, 426
Khan v. H.M. Advocate, 1992 J.C. 32; 1993 S.L.T. 172, HCJ Appeal 171, 173
Kidd v. H.M. Advocate, 2000 J.C. 509; 2000 S.L.T. 1068, HCJ Appeal 522
King v. Lees, 1993 J.C. 19; 1993 S.L.T. 1184; 1993 S.C.C.R. 28, HCJ Appeal 35, 56, 76
Kinnell v. Peebles, 1890 17 R. 416 501
Kirkwood v. Coalburn District Co-operative Society, 1930 J.C. 38 348
Kirschbaum v. "Our Voices" Publishing Co. (1971) 1 O.R. 737 . . . . 366, 367
Knapp v. State, The 168 Indiana 153, 79 N.E. 1076 (1907) 3, 4, 5, 284
Knowles v. H.M. Advocate, 1975 J.C. 6, HCJ Appeal 171, 443
Knutsen v. Mauritzen (1918) 1 S.L.T. 85 272
Kolbin & Sons v. Kinnear & Co. Ltd; Kolbin & Sons v. United Shipping Co. Ltd (The Eduard Woermann);
    sub nom. Kolbin & Sons v. Kinnear & Co.; Kolbin & Sons v. Kinnear & Co. (SS Altai) (1931) 40 Ll.
    L. Rep. 241; 1931 S.L.T. 464; 1930 S.C. (HL) 57, HL 342

L. v. L., 1998 S.L.T. 672; 1997 S.C.L.R. 866, 1 Div; affirming 1996 S.L.T. 767, OH ... 408, 426, 427, 428, 430, 432, 482
Lamb v. Lord Advocate, 1976 S.C. 110 .... 71, 73
Lambie v. H.M. Advocate, 1973 J.C. 53; 1973 S.L.T. 219, HCJ Appeal 24, 32, 35, 77
Lamont v. Rodger, 1911 S.C. (J.) 24; (1910) 6 Adam 328, HCJ Appeal 76
Langan v. H.M. Advocate, 1989 S.C.C.R. 379, HCJ Appeal 12, 13
Lauderdale Peerage Case (1884–85) L.R. 10 App. Cas. 692, HL 422, 423, 426
Lavallee v. R. [1990] S.C.R. 852 326
Lawrie v. Muir, 1950 J.C. 19; 1950 S.L.T. 37, HCJ Appeal   194, , 196, 204, 206, 207, 218, 221, 222, 223, 224, 258, 263, 266
Leandro v. H.M. Advcoate, 1994 S.C.C.R. 703, HCJ Appeal 13
Leckie v. Miln, 1982 S.L.T. 177; 1981 S.C.C.R. 261, HCJ Appeal 208, 210, 211, 213, 215, 219
Lee v. National Coal Board, 1955 S.C. 151; 1955 S.L.T. 202, 1 Div 343
Lees v. Macdonald 20 R(J) 55, White 468 .... 82, 83
Leggate v. H.M. Advocate, 1988 J.C. 127; 1988 S.L.T. 665; 1988 S.C.C.R. 391, HCJ Appeal 284, 287, 298, 301
Lenaghan v. Ayrshire and Arran Health Board, 1994 S.L.T. 765, Ex Div; reversing 1993 S.L.T. 544, OH 418
Lennie v. H.M. Advocate, 1946 J.C. 79; 1946 S.L.T. 212, HCJ Appeal 33, 34, 35
Lennon v. Co-operative Insurance Society, 1986 S.L.T. 98, OH 68, 69, 70, 71
Lennox v. National Coal Board, 1955 S.C. 438; 1956 S.L.T. 203, OH 347
Lindsay v. H.M. Advocate, 1994 S.L.T. 546, HCJ Appeal 121
Lithgow v. United Kingdom, (A/102) (1986) 8 E.H.R.R. 329; The Times, July 7, 1986, ECHR 264
Little v. H.M. Advocate, 1983 J.C. 16; 1983 S.L.T. 489; 1983 S.C.C.R. 56, HCJ Appeal 12, 79, 103
Livingston v. Murray (1830) 9 S. 161 449
Livingstone v. Strachan, Crerar & Jones, 1923 S.C. 794; 1923 S.L.T. 525 421
Lockhart v. Stainbridge, 1989 S.C.C.R. 220, Sh Ct (Grampian) 327
London and Edinburgh Shipping Co. Ltd v. Admiralty Commissioners (1920) 2 Ll. L. Rep. 342; 1920 S.C. 309, 2 Div 347
Lord Advocate v. Gillespie, 1969 S.L.T. (Sh. Ct.) 10, Sh Ct (Lanark) 346
—— v. Ruffle, 1979 S.C. 371; 1979 S.L.T. 212, OH 72, 74
Lord Advocate's Reference (No. 1 of 1983), Re 1984 J.C. 52; 1984 S.L.T. 337, HCJ Appeal ... 230, 231, 232, 251
Lord Advocate's Reference (No. 1 of 1992), Re 1992 J.C. 179; 1992 S.L.T. 1010; 1992 S.C.C.R. 724, HCJ Appeal 148, 163, 164, 186, 332
Lord Advocate's Reference (No. 1 of 2000), Re 2001 J.C. 143; 2001 S.L.T. 507, HCJ Appeal 342
Louden v. British Merchants Insurance Co. [1961] 1 W.L.R. 798; [1961] 1 All E.R. 705, QBD 336, 337
Loveden v. Loveden [1810] 2 Hagg. Con. 1, 3 63
Low v. H.M. Advocate; sub nom. Low and Reilly v. H.M. Advocate 1994 S.L.T. 277; 1993 S.C.C.R. 493, HCJ Appeal 113, 114
Lowery v. Queen, The; R. v. King; sub nom. R. v. Lowery [1974] A.C. 85; [1973] 3 W.L.R. 235. PC (Aus) ... 318, 319, 320, 321, 323, 324, 325
—— v. R. See Lowery v. Queen, The

M (A Minor) (Application for Care Order), Re [1995] 3 F.C.R. 611, Fam Div 315
M. v. British Railways Board, The Scotsman, September 13, 1995 394
—— v. Ferguson, 1994 S.C.L.R. 487, IH 326, 429, 431
—— v. Kennedy, 1992 S.C.L.R. 69 .... 326, 409, 437, 483
M.(I) v. Kennedy, 1993 S.C. 115; 1993 S.C.L.R. 69, IH 317, 429
McAllister & McLaughlan v. H.M. Advocate (1975) S.C.C.R. Supplement 98 .... 178, 180, 184
—— v. Normand, 1996 S.L.T. 622, HCJ Appeal 3
McAnea v. H.M. Advocate; Dean v. H.M. Advocate; Mcgregor v. H.M. Advocate; McGinnis v. H.M. Advocate 2001 S.L.T. 12; 2000 S.C.C.R. 779; 2000 G.W.D. 26–981, HCJ Appeal 219
McArthur v. Organon Laboratories, 1982 S.L.T. 425, OH 406
McAvoy v. City of Glasgow District Council, 1993 S.L.T. 859; 1993 S.C.L.R. 393, OH 424
—— v. H.M. Advocate, 1982 J.C. 117; 1983 S.L.T. 16; 1982 S.C.C.R. 263, HCJ Appeal 113, 304
—— v. H.M. Advocate, 1991 J.C. 16; 1992 S.L.T. 46; 1991 S.C.C.R. 123, HCJ Appeal 110, 493
—— v. Jessop, 1988 S.L.T. 621; 1988 S.C.C.R. 172, HCJ Appeal 217
McCallum v. British Railways Board, 1991 S.L.T. 5, Ex Div; reversing 1989 S.L.T. 296, OH 406
McCann v. Adair, 1951 J.C. 127; 1951 S.L.T. 326, HCJ Appeal 337
McCarron v. Allen, 1988 S.C.C.R. 9, HCJ Appeal 220
McColl v. Skeen, 1980 S.L.T. (Notes) 53, HCJ Appeal 352
McCormack v. H.M. Advocate, 1993 S.C.C.R. 592, 1993 S.L.T. 1163 509
MacCormick v. Lord Advocate, 1953 S.C. 396; 1953 S.L.T. 255, 1 Div 332
McCourt v. H.M. Advocate, 1977 S.L.T. (Notes) 22 476
McCourtney v. H.M. Advocate, 1977 J.C. 68; 1978 S.L.T. 10, HCJ Appeal 299, 300, 301, 302
McCowan v. Wright (1852) 15 D. 229 .... 355, 357
McCrindle v. MacMillan, 1930 J.C. 56; 1930 S.L.T. 705, HCJ Appeal 81, 82
McCuaig v. H.M. Advocate, 1982 S.L.T. 383; 1982 S.C.C.R. 125, HCJ Appeal 304, 305
McCutcheon v. H.M. Advocate, unreported, December 5, 2001, Ct of 9 Judges 171
Macdonald (J.McF.) v. H.M. Advocate, 1989 S.C.C.R. 559 47

MacDonald (Robert Grant) v. H.M. Advocate, 1999 S.L.T. 533; 1999 S.C.C.R. 146, HCJ Appeal 186, 486
Macdonald v. H.M. Advocate, 1988 S.L.T. 85; 1987 S.C.C.R. 581, HCJ Appeal   113
—— v. H.M. Advocate, 1993 G.W.D. 18–1139   203
McDonald v. H.M. Advocate, 1998 S.L.T. 37   110
MacDonald v. MacDonald, 1985 S.L.T. 244, 2 Div 335, 394
—— v. Skinner, 1979 J.C. 29; 1978 S.L.T. (Notes) 52, HCJ Appeal 198, 200
McDougall v. James Jones & Sons, unreported, November 27, 1970   407
—— v. Macphail, 1991 J.C. 85; 1991 S.L.T. 801; 1991 S.C.C.R. 358, HCJ Appeal   135
Macdougall v. Whitelaw   52
McGaharon v. H.M. Advocate, 1968 S.L.T. (Notes) 99, HCJ Appeal 175, 176, 177, 182
McGhee v. Glasgow Coal Co.   403
McGinley v. H.M. Advocate, 2001 S.L.T. 198; 2001 S.C.C.R. 47, HCJ Appeal   489
—— v. MacLeod, 1963 J.C. 11; 1963 S.L.T. 2, HCJ Appeal 458, 462, 463, 464, 465, 466
McGovern v. H.M. Advocate, 1950 J.C. 33; 1950 S.L.T. 133, HCJ Appeal 206, 207, 208, 210
McGowan v. Belling & Co. Ltd, 1983 S.L.T. 77, OH 135, 145
—— v. Lord Advocate, 1972 S.C. 68; 1972 S.L.T. 188, 1 Div 402, 403, 404, 406, 408
McGrath v. McGrath, 1999 S.L.T. (Sh. Ct.) 90; 1999 S.C.L.R. 1121, Sh Pr 394, 397
McGregor v. D, 1977 S.L.T. 182   70
—— v. Jessop, 1988 J.C. 98; 1988 S.L.T. 719, HCJ Appeal   32
—— v. Stokes [1952] V.L.R. 347   151
—— v. T, 1975 S.L.T. 76   70
McGrory v. H.M. Advocate, 1995 S.L.T. 829; 1995 S.C.C.R. 237, HCJ Appeal   123
McIlveny v. Donald; sub nom. McIlveny v. Donald (Matthew) (t/a M.D.M. Design) 1995 S.C.L.R. 802, Sh Ct
    (North Strathclyde) 143, 420
MacIntosh v. National Coal Board, 1988 S.L.T. 348, 2 Div; reversing in part 1987 S.L.T. 116, OH   502
McIntosh, Petitioner See H.M. Advocate v. McIntosh
Maciver v. Mackenzie, 1942 J.C. 51; 1942 S.L.T. 144, HCJ Appeal 125, 127, 129, 131, 132, 133, 135
Mack v. H.M. Advocate, 1999 S.L.T. 1163; 1999 S.C.C.R. 181, HCJ Appeal   444
McKay v. H.M. Advocate, 1991 J.C. 91; 1992 S.L.T. 138, HCJ Appeal   475
—— v. Yarrow Shipbuilders Ltd, unreported, July 4, 1991, OH   408
McKellar v. Normand, 1992 S.C.C.R. 393, HCJ Appeal   133
McKenna v. H.M. Advocate, 2000 J.C. 291; 2000 S.L.T. 508, HCJ Appeal 9, 189
McKenzie v. H.D. Fraser & Sons, 2001 S.L.T. 116   332
—— v. H.M. Advocate, 1959 J.C. 32 . . . .   62, 73
—— v. H.M. Advocate, unreported, June 26, 1958   452
MacKenzie v. H.M. Advocate, 1995 S.L.T. 743; 1995 S.C.C.R. 141, HCJ Appeal 518, 519
Mackie v. H.M. Advocate, 1994 J.C. 132; 1995 S.L.T. 110, HCJ Appeal   92, 95, 96, 97, 98, 99, 100, 101, 102, 103
McKillen v. Barclay Curie & Co. Ltd, 1967 S.L.T. 41, 1 Div; reversing 1965 S.L.T. (Notes) 19, OH   317
McLaren v. Caldwell's Paper Mills Ltd, 1973 S.L.T. 158, 2 Div 402, 404, 406, 407, 408, 502
—— v. McLeod, 1913 S.C. (J.) 61; (1913) 2 S.L.T.2, HCJ Appeal 162, 163
McLay v. H.M. Advocate, 1994 S.L.T. 873; 1994 S.C.C.R. 397, HCJ Appeal   186
Maclay v. H.M. Advocate (No. 2), 2000 S.L.T. 1076   523
McLean v. Scottish Power plc, 2000 G.W.D. 4–157, OH   28
—— v. Tudhope, 1982 S.C.C.R. 555   304
McLellan V. H.M.A., 1992 S.L.T. 991   89
McLennan v. H.M. Advocate, 1928 J.C. 39 . . . .   81, 82
McLeod v. Fraser, 1986 S.C.C.R. 271   135
—— v. H.M. Advocate, 1995 S.L.T. 145   171
—— v. H.M. Advocate; sub nom. McLeod, Petitioner 1998 J.C. 67; 1998 S.L.T. 233, HCJ Appeal 379, 382,
                                                                                                  383, 384, 392
—— v. Lowe, 1991 J.C. 187; 1993 S.L.T. 471, HCJ Appeal   164
—— v. Woodmuir Miners Welfare Society Social Club, 1961 J.C. 5; 1960 S.L.T. 349, HCJ 127, 129
McLeod, Petitioner See McLeod v. H.M. Advocate
McLory v. McInnes, 1992 S.L.T.. 501   259
McMichael v. United Kingdom (A/308) [1995] 2 F.C.R. 718; (1995) 20 E.H.R.R. 205, ECHR 395, 396
Macmillan v. Murray, 1920 J.C. 13   462
McMillan v. PF (Lanark), unreported, May 29, 2001, High Ct of Justiciary   254
McNeil v. Wilson   122
MacNeill v. McGregor, 1975 J.C. 57; 1975 S.L.T. (Notes) 54, HCJ Appeal   350
McPhee v. H.M. Advocate, 2002 S.L.T. 90; 2001 S.C.C.R. 674, HCJ Appeal   187
McRae v. H.M. Advocate, 1975 S.L.T. 174   121
McVinnie v. McVinnie; sub nom. McVinnie or Doolan v. McVinnie 1995 S.L.T. (Sh. Ct.) 81; 1995 S.C.L.R.
    480, Sh Ct (Lothian) 413, 418, 420, 421
Main v. Andrew Wormald Ltd, 1988 S.L.T. 141, 2 Div   318
—— v. Russell, 1999 G.W.D. 13–592, HCJ Appeal   311
Mair v. Railway Passengers Assurance Co. (1877) 37 L.T. 356   336
Maitland v. Glasgow Corp., 1947 S.L.T. 30, 1 Div   92
—— v. H.M. Advocate, 1983 S.L.T. 645   509

Makin v. Att.-Gen. for New South Wales [1894] A.C. 57, PC (Aus) 268, 278, 319
Malcolm Gillespie and J. Skene Edwards, unreported, 1827 447
Mallett v. McMonagle [1970] A.C. 166; [1969] 2 W.L.R. 767, HL 58
Manuel v. H.M. Advocate, 1958 J.C. 41; 1959 S.L.T. 23, HCJ Appeal 82, 110, 113, 236, 255, 256, 288
Marks and Spencer Ltd v. British Gas Corp., 1983 S.L.T. 196, OH 360, 362
Marsh, 1940 S.C. 202 55
Marsh v. Johnston, 1959 S.L.T. (Notes) 28 .... 197, 199, 200, 202, 203
Martin, 1842 1 Broun 382 229
Martindale v. H.M. Advocate, 1994 S.L.T. 1093; 1992 S.C.C.R. 700, HCJ Appeal 327
Mason v. H.M. Advocate (No. 1), 2000 S.L.T. 1004; 2000 S.C.C.R. 710, HCJ Appeal 458
—— v. S.L.D. Olding Ltd, 1982 S.L.T. 385, OH 406, 407
Matthewson v. Irvine, 1942 J.C. 66 76
Maxwell v. H.M. Advocate, 1990 J.C. 340; 1991 S.L.T. 63, HCJ Appeal 182
Meehan v. H.M. Advocate, 1970 J.C. 11 .... 170, 171
Melon v. Hector Powe Ltd; *sub nom.* Hector Powe Ltd v. Melon [1981] 1 All E.R. 313; 1981 S.C. (H.L.) 1,
    HL; affirming 1980 S.C. 188, 1 Div 504, 505, 507
Meredith v. Lees, 1992 J.C. 127; 1992 S.L.T. 802; 1992 S.C.C.R. 459, HCJ Appeal 106, 110
Micosta SA v. Shetland Islands Council (The Mihalis) [1984] 2 Lloyd's Rep. 525; 1983 S.L.T. 483, 1 Div 356
Middler v. H.M. Advocate, 1994 S.C.C.R. 838, HCJ 231, 259
Milford v. H.M. Advocate, 1973 S.L.T. 12; [1975] Crim. L.R. 110, HCJ 205, 206
Millar v. Mitchell, Cadell & Co. (1860) 22 D. 833 .... 50, 51
—— v. Small (1856) 19D. 142 357
Miller v. H.M. Advocate, 1994 S.L.T. 640; 1994 S.C.C.R. 377, HCJ Appeal 103
—— v. Jackson, 1972 S.L.T. (Notes) 31, OH 425, 426
—— v. Ministry of Pensions [1947] 2 All E.R. 372; 63 T.L.R. 474, KBD 58, 72
—— and Denovan 32
Mills v. H.M. Advocate (No. 1), 1999 J.C. 216; 1999 S.L.T. 680, HCJ Appeal 522
Miln v. Cullen, 1967 J.C. 21; 1967 S.L.T. 35, HCJ Appeal 205, 231, 232, 239, 251, 253, 254, 255, 258, 259, 266
—— v. Fitzgerald, 1978 S.C.C.R. Supp. 205 107
Milne v. H.M. Advocate, 1996 S.L.T. 775; 1995 S.C.C.R. 751, HCJ Appeal 305
—— v. Samson (1843) 6D. 35 140
—— v. Townsend 19 R. 830 .... 54, 55
Mitchell v. Dean, 1979 J.C. 62; 1979 S.L.T. (Notes) 12, HCJ Appeal 305
—— v. H.M. Advocate, 1989 S.C.C.R. 502, HCJ Appeal 509
—— v. H.M. Advocate, 1996 S.C.C.R. 97 114
M'Kie v. Western Scottish Motor Traction Co., 1952 S.C. 206 371
Mongan v. H.M. Advocate, 1989 S.C.C.R. 25, HCJ Appeal 92, 96
Montgomerie & Co. v. Wallace-James (1903) 6 F. (HL) 10 503
Montgomery v. H.M. Advocate 190
Moore v. H.M. Advocate, 1990 J.C. 371; 1991 S.L.T. 278, HCJ Appeal 93, 97
Moorov v. H.M. Advocate; *sub nom.* Moorov v. Lord Advocate 1930 J.C. 69; 1930 S.L.T. 596, HCJ Appeal ... 91,
    114, 115, 116, 117, 118, 119, 120, 121, 192, 269, 274, 350, 351, 483, 484
More v. Brown & Root Wimpey Highland Fabricators Ltd 1983 S.L.T. 669, Ex Div 360, 361, 362
Morrison v. Burrell, 1947 S.L.T. 190; 1947 S.L.T. (Notes) 17, HCJ Appeal 252
—— v. H.M. Advocate, 1990 J.C. 299; 1991 S.L.T. 57; 1990 S.C.C.R. 235, HCJ Appeal ... 146, 164, 171, 172, 173,
    174
—— v. J. Kelly & Sons Ltd, 1970 S.C. 65; 1970 S.L.T. 198, 1 Div 125, 402, 403, 404, 405, 406, 407, 408,
    409, 412, 418, 502, 503
—— v. Mackenzie, 1990 J.C. 185, HCJ 131
—— v. Maclean's Trustees (1862) 24 D. 625 272
—— v. O'Donnell, 2001 S.C.C.R. 272; 2001 G.W.D. 14–541, HCJ Appeal 219
—— v. Somerville (1860) 23D. 232 357
Morrow v. Neil, 1975 S.L.T. (Sh. Ct.) 65, Sh Ct (Glasgow) 72, 73
Morton v. H.M. Advocate, 1938 J.C. 50; 1937 S.N. 108, HCJ Appeal 12, 80, 82, 83, 84, 86, 104, 164
—— v. William Dixon Ltd, 1909 S.C. 807; (1909) 1 S.L.T.346, 1 Div 31
Muirhead 13 R. (J) 52 .... 468, 469
Muldoon v. Herron, 1970 J.C. 30; 1970 S.L.T. 228, HCJ Appeal 151, 174, 178, 179, 181, 182, 183, 184,
    187, 488, 496
Mullan v. Anderson (No. 1), 1993 S.L.T. 835; 1993 S.C.L.R. 506, IH (Ct of 5 judges) 70, 71, 72, 73, 74
Mulligan v. Caird (Dundee) Ltd, 1973 S.L.T. 72, 1 Div 79
Munro v. Fraser (1858) 21D. 103 357
Murdoch v. Taylor [1965] A.C. 574; [1965] 2 W.L.R. 425, HL 300, 302
Murphy v. H.M. Advocate, 1975 S.L.T. (Notes) 17, HCJ Appeal 231, 232, 238, 239
—— v. H.M. Advocate, 1995 J.C. 16; 1995 S.L.T. 725; 1995 S.C.C.R. 55, HCJ Appeal 110
—— v. Waterfront Commission (1964) 378 US 52 247
Murray v. H.M. Advocate, 1996 S.L.T. 648, HCJ Appeal 171
—— v. United Kingdom (1996) 22 E.H.R.R. 29; *The Times,* February 9, 1996, ECHR 249, 261, 264, 265
Myers v. DPP; *sub nom.* R. v. Myers [1965] A.C. 1001; [1964] 3 W.L.R. 145, HL 150, 156, 321

Namyslak v. H.M. Advocate, 1995 S.L.T. 528; 1994 S.C.C.R. 140, HCJ Appeal   206
Neeson v. H.M. Advocate, 1984 S.C.C.R. 72, HCJ Appeal   181
Nelson v. H.M. Advocate, 1989 S.L.T. 215; 1988 S.C.C.R. 536, HCJ Appeal   110
—— v. H.M. Advocate, 1994 J.C. 94; 1994 S.L.T. 389; 1994 S.C.C.R. 192, HCJ Appeal 9, 269, 274, 280, 449
—— v. Nelson, 1988 S.C.L.R. 663, Sh Pr   72
Nethermere (St. Neots) Ltd v. Gardiner [1984] I.C.R. 621   505
Nicol v. Nicol, 1938 S.L.T. 98, OH   285
Nimmo v. Alexander Cowan & Son Ltd [1968] A.C. 107; [1967] 3 W.L.R. 1169; 1967 S.C. (H.L.) 79, HL   20, 24
Nolan v. McLeod, 1987 S.C.C.R. 558, HCJ Appeal 110, 313
Normand v. Walker, 1995 J.C. 5; 1995 S.L.T. 94, HCJ Appeal   24
Norval v. H.M. Advocate, 1978 J.C. 70, HCJ Appeal 12, 13, 14, 15

O'Hara v. Central S.M.T. Co. Ltd, 1941 S.C. 363; 1941 S.L.T. 202, 1 Div 53, 55, 56, 92, 95, 98, 99, 100,
                                                                                                                                149, 150, 153, 170
—— v. H.M. Advocate, 1948 J.C. 90; 1948 S.L.T. 372, HCJ Appeal 289, 290, 291, 292, 293, 294, 295, 296, 297
O'Kelly v. Trusthouse Forte plc [1984] Q.B. 90; [1983] 3 W.L.R. 605; [1983] I.C.R. 728, CA   505
O'Leary v. R. (1946) 73 C.L.R. 566   152
O'Neill v. Wilson, 1983 J.C. 42; 1983 S.L.T. 573, HCJ Appeal 458, 462, 466
Ogg v. H.M. Advocate, 1938 J.C. 152; 1938 S.L.T. 513, HCJ Appeal   116
Oghonogher v. Secretary of State for the Home Department, 1995 S.L.T.733   224
Ogilvie v. H.M. Advocate (No. 2), 1999 S.L.T. 1068; 1999 G.W.D. 14–632, HCJ Appeal   187
Oliver v. Hislop, 1946 S.L.T. 55, HCJ Appeal 332, 334
Omychund v. Barker (1745) Willes 538   124
Ormiston v. H.M. Advocate, 2001 S.L.T. 257   219
Owens v. H.M. Advocate, 1946 J.C. 119; 1946 S.L.T. 227, HCJ Appeal 33, 34, 35, 168, 172
Oyeneyein v. Oyeneyein, 1999 G.W.D. 38–1836   397

P. v. H.M. Advocate, 1991 S.C.C.R. 933 . . . .   118, 482
P. Cannon (Gararges) Ltd v. Lord Advocate, 1983 S.L.T. (Sh. Ct.) 50, Sh Pr   371
Pagan v. Fergusson, 1976 S.L.T. (Notes) 44, HCJ Appeal   31
Paris v. Stepney Borough Council [1951] A.C. 367; [1951] 1 All E.R. 42, HL   31
Parker v. Lanarkshire Health Board, 1996 S.C.L.R. 57, Ex Div   24
Parr v. H.M. Advocate, 1991 J.C. 39; 1991 S.L.T. 208; 1991 S.C.C.R. 180, HCJ Appeal   32
Paterson v. H.M. Advocate, 2000 S.L.T. 833; 1999 S.C.C.R. 750, HCJ Appeal   444
Patterson v. H.M. Advocate, 2000 J.C. 137; 2000 S.L.T. 302, HCJ Appeal 186, 187
Pattison v. Stevenson 5F (J) 43   348
Paxton v. H.M. Advocate, 2000 J.C. 56; 2000 S.L.T. 771, HCJ Appeal   313
Penning v. H.M. Advocate   283
Pennycuick v. Lees, 1992 S.L.T. 763; 1992 S.C.C.R. 160, HCJ Appeal 231, 259
People v. De Simone (1919) 121 NE 761   154
Pepper v. Hart [1993] A.C. 593; [1992] 3 W.L.R. 1032, HL 73, 74
Pervez v. Clark, 2001 S.C.C.R. 138; 2000 G.W.D. 40–1515, HCJ Appeal   14
Phillips v. Queen, The, (1985) 159 C.L.R. 45   297
Pioneer Shipping Ltd v. BTP Tioxide Ltd (The Nema) (No. 2); BTP Tioxide Ltd v. Armada Marine SA; *sub
    nom.* BTP Tioxide Ltd v. Pioneer Shipping Ltd [1982] A.C. 724; [1981] 3 W.L.R. 292, HL   507
Powell v. Streatham Manor Nursing Home [1935] A.C. 243, HL   501
Pragnell O'Neill v. Lady Skiffington, 1984 S.L.T. 282   51
Prentice v. Chalmers, 1985 S.L.T. 168, 2 Div; reversing in part 1984 S.L.T. 63, OH   332
Pullar v. United Kingdom, 1996 S.C.C.R. 755; (1996) 22 E.H.R.R. 391, ECHR   263

Qualcast (Wolverhampton) Ltd v. Haynes [1959] A.C. 743; [1959] 2 W.L.R. 510, HL   31
Queen, The v. Bedingfield (1874) 14 Cox C.C. 341 . . . .   149, 152, 153
—— v. Gibson (1887) L.R. 18 Q.B.D. 537, Crown Cases Reserved   149
Quinn v. Lees, 1994 S.C.C.R. 159, HCJ Appeal 480, 482
—— v. Lowe, 1992 S.L.T. 701; 1991 S.C.C.R. 881, HCJ Appeal   119

R. v. A (Complainant's Sexual History); *sub nom.* R. v. Y; R. v. A (No. 2) [2001] UKHL 25; [2002] 1 A.C.
    45, HL   211
—— v. Abbott [1955] 2 Q.B. 497; [1955] 3 W.L.R. 369; [1955] 2 All E.R. 899, CCA 78, 79
—— v. B. [1987] 1 N.Z.L.R. 362   326
—— v. Baldry (1852) 2 De. C.C. 430 . . . .   237, 238
—— v. Benjafield; R. v. Leal (Manoj); R. v. Milford [2002] UKHL 2; [2002] 2 W.L.R. 235, HL 37, 38
—— v. Bentley [2001] 1 Cr.App.R. 21; [1999] Crim. L.R. 330, CA (Crim Div)   529
—— v. Boardman *See* DPP v. Boardman
—— v. Brophy [1982] A.C. 476; [1981] 3 W.L.R. 103, HL 245, 246, 247, 248, 249, 251, 253
—— v. Camplin; *sub nom.* DPP v. Camplin [1978] A.C. 705; [1978] 2 W.L.R. 679;
    (1978) 67 Cr.App.R. 14, HL   322

R. v. Carr-Briant [1943] K.B. 607, CCA 76
—— v. Ching (1976) 63 Cr.App.R. 7; [1976] Crim. L.R. 687, CA (Crim Div) 60, 62
—— v. Christie [1914] A.C. 545 . . . . 149, 150, 151, 153, 175
—— v. Christou; R. v. Wright [1992] Q.B. 979; [1992] 3 W.L.R. 228, CA (Crim Div) 204
—— v. Clark [1955] 2 Q.B. 469; [1955] 3 W.L.R. 313; [1955] 3 All E.R. 29;
(1955) 39 Cr.App.R. 120, CCA 296, 297
—— v. Cole [1994] Crim. L.R. 820 326
—— v. Cook [1959] 2 Q.B. 340 296
—— v. Curry; R. v. Keeble [1983] Crim. L.R. 737, CA 110
—— v. DPP., ex p. Kebilene; R. v. DPP., ex p. Boukemiche; R. v. DPP., ex p. Souidi; R. v. DPP., ex p.
Rechachi; sub nom. R. v. DPP., ex p. Kebelene [2000] 2 A.C. 326; [1999] 3 W.L.R. 972, HL 36
—— v. Duncan (1981) 73 Cr.App.R. 359; [1981] Crim. L.R. 560, CA 171, 173
—— v. Emery (1993) 14 Cr.App.R.(S.) 394, CA 326
—— v. Everett [1988] Crim. L.R. 826, CA 324, 325
—— v. Exall (1866) 4 F. & F. 922 15
—— v. G.B. [1990] 2 S.C.R. 30 326
—— v. Governor of Brixton Prison, ex p. Ahsan [1969] 2 Q.B. 222; [1969] 2 W.L.R. 618, DC 64
—— v. Gramanatz [1962] Q.W.N.at p.95 297
—— v. Gray (1973) 58 Cr.App.R. 177 61
—— v. Gunewardene [1951] 2 K.B. 600; [1951] 2 All E.R. 290, CCA 323
—— v. Hampshire CC., ex p. Ellerton [1985] 1 W.L.R. 749; [1985] 1 All E.R. 599, CA 66, 67, 69, 70, 71
—— v. Hepworth; R. v. Fearnley [1955] 2 Q.B. 600; [1955] 3 W.L.R. 331; (1955) 39 Cr.App.R. 152 60
—— v. Home [1994] Crim. L.R. 584 326
—— v. Hudson [1912] 2 K.B. 464 296
—— v. Huijser [1988] 1 N.Z.L.R. 577 269
—— v. Inland Revenue Commissioners, ex p. Rossminster; sub nom. Inland Revenue Commissioners v.
Rossminster Ltd; Rossminster and Tucker, Re [1980] A.C. 952; [1980] 2 W.L.R. 1, HL 219
—— v. Jenkins (1945) 31 Cr.App.R. 1 . . . . 296, 297
—— v. Kearley [1992] 2 A.C. 228; [1992] 2 W.L.R. 656; [1992] 2 All E.R. 345, HL   2, 148, 155, 161, 162, 163, 179
—— v. Kilbourne See DPP v. Kilbourne
—— v. King [1967] 2 Q.B. 338; [1967] 2 W.L.R. 612, CA (Crim Div) 6
—— v. King [2000] 2 Cr.App.R. 391; [2000] Crim. L.R. 835, CA (Crim Div) 326
—— v. Kritz [1950] 1 K.B. 82; [1949] 2 All E.R. 406, CCA 59, 60
—— v. Lambert; R. v. Ali; R. v. Jordan [2001] UKHL 37; [2001] 3 W.L.R. 206, HL 36
—— v. Loosely [2001] UKHL 53 203
—— v. Masih [1986] [1986] Crim. L.R. 395, CA 322, 324
—— v. Miller; R. v. Mercado; R. v. Harris [1952] 2 All E.R. 667; (1952) 36 Cr.App.R. 169, Assizes
(Winchester) 318
—— v. Murphy [1965] NILR 248
—— v. Murphy [1980] Q.B. 434; [1980] 2 W.L.R. 743, CA 330
—— v. Murtagh; R. v. Kennedy (1955) 39 Cr.App.R. 72, CCA 58
—— v. Novac; R. v. Raywood; R. v. Andrew-Cohen; R. v. Archer (1977) 65 Cr.App.R. 107, CA (Crim Div) 7
—— v. O'Brien; R. v. Hall; R. v. Sherwood [2000] Crim. L.R. 676; The Times, February 16, 2000, CA (Crim
Div) 326
—— v. Osbourne; R. v. Virtue [1973] Q.B. 678; [1973] 2 W.L.R. 209, CA (Crim Div) 183
—— v. Pendleton [2001] UKHL 66; [2002] 1 W.L.R. 72, HL 523
—— v. Power [1919] 1 K.B. 572, CCA 79
—— v. Preston [1909] 1 K.B. 568 . . . . 290, 296
—— v. Raghip The Times, December 9, 1991 . . . . 324, 325, 326
—— v. Robinson [1994] 3 All E.R. 346; (1994) 98 Cr.App.R. 370, CA (Crim Div) 327
—— v. Sang; R. v. Mangan [1980] A.C. 402; [1979] 3 W.L.R. 263, HL 194, 246
—— v. Secretary of State for the Home Secretary, ex p. Khawaja; R. v. Secretary of State for the Home
Department, ex p. Khera [1984] A.C. 74; [1983] 2 W.L.R. 321, HL 64, 66, 67, 71, 72, 74
—— v. Selvey (No. 1); sub nom. Selvey v. DPP (No. 1) [1970] A.C. 304;
[1968] 2 W.L.R. 1494, HL 292, 293, 295, 296
—— v. Sharp [1988] 1 W.L.R. 7; [1988] 1 All E.R. 65, HL 146, 165, 166, 167, 169, 170, 171, 172
—— v. Shepherd (1988) 85 A.L.R. 387 57
—— v. Shields and Patrick [1977] Crim. L.R. 281, CA 511, 521
—— v. Sims [1946] K.B. 531; [1946] 1 All E.R. 699, CCA 1, 274
—— v. Smith [1987] V.R. 907 327
—— v. Smurthwaite; R. v. Gill [1994] 1 All E.R. 898; (1994) 98 Cr.App.R. 437, CA (Crim Div) 204
—— v. Stafford (No. 1); R. v. Luvaglio (No. 1) [1968] 3 All E.R. 752 (Note); (1969) 53 Cr.App.R. 1, CA
(Crim Div) 61
—— v. Stockwell (1993) 97 Cr.App.R. 260; The Times, March 11, 1993, CA (Crim Div) 327
—— v. Taylor, 1961 (3) S.A. 616 154
—— v. Toohey See Toohey v. Commissioner of Police of the Metropolis
—— v. Turnbull; R. v. Camelo; R. v. Whitby, R. v. Roberts [1977] Q.B. 224; [1976] 3 W.L.R. 445, CA (Crim
Div) 110

R. v. Turner [1944] K.B. 463 296
—— v. Turner [1975] Q.B. 834; [1975] 2 W.L.R. 56; [1975] 1 All E.R. 70,
    CA (Crim Div) 311, 317, 320, 322, 324, 325, 326, 327
—— v. Ward [1993] 1 W.L.R. 619; [1993] 2 All E.R. 577, CA) (Crim Div) 322, 326, 327
—— v. Weightman (1991) 92 Cr.App.R. 291; [1991] Crim. L.R. 204, CA (Cim Div) 322, 326
Ralston v. H.M. Advocate, 1987 S.C.C.R. 467, HCJ Appeal 108
Ratten v. Queen, The; sub nom. Ratten v. R. [1972] A.C. 378; [1971] 3 W.L.R. 930; [1971] 3 All E.R. 801,
    PC (Aus) 150, 151, 155, 158, 162, 186
—— v. R. See Ratten v. Queen, The
Rattray v. Rattray (1895) 25 R. 315; 5 S.L.T. 245 .... 223, 224
Rees v. Lowe, 1989 S.C.C.R. 664 .... 476, 477, 479, 480, 485
Rehmann v. Ahmad, 1993 S.L.T. 741, OH 68, 71
Reilly v. H.M. Advocate, 1981 S.C.C.R. 201, HCJ Appeal 108
Reporter for Strathclyde v. B., 1997 Fam.L.R. 142 394
Rhesa Shipping Co. SA v. Edmunds (The Popi M); Rhesa Shipping Co. SA v. Fenton Insurance Co. Ltd
    [1985] 1 W.L.R. 948; [1985] 2 All E.R. 712, HL 25, 28, 31
Roberts v. British Railways Board, 1998 S.C.L.R. 577; 1998 Rep. L.R. 84, OH 318, 322, 326
Robertson v. Maxwell, 1951 J.C. 11; 1951 S.L.T. 46, HCJ Appeal 123
—— v. Watson; sub nom. Crawford v. Watson 1949 J.C. 73; 1949 S.L.T. 119, HCJ Appeal 76, 279, 280
Robson v. Robson, 1973 S.L.T. (Notes) 4, OH 347
Rodger v. Hislop 6R. (J) 16 333
Rogers v. Orr, 1939 S.L.T. 403; 1939 S.C. 492 .... 370, 374, 377
Runham v. Westwater, 1995 J.C. 70; 1995 S.L.T. 835; 1995 S.C.C.R. 356, HCJ Appeal 242, 248
Russel v. Campbell (1699) 4 Brown's Supp. 468 52
Russell v. Annan, 1993 S.C.C.R. 234, HCJ Appeal 334

S. v. Kennedy, 1987 S.L.T. 667 482
Saidi v. France (A/261-C) (1994) 17 E.H.R.R. 251, ECHR 190, 191, 192
Salabiaku v. France (A/141-A) (1991) 13 E.H.R.R. 379, ECHR 36, 260, 261, 263, 264
Saltire Press Ltd v. AB; sub nom. Saltire Press Ltd, Re; Saltire Press Ltd v. Boyd, 1998 S.C. 718;
    1999 S.L.T. 438, 1 Div 505
—— v. Boyd See Saltire Press Ltd v. AB
Salusbury-Hughes v. H.M. Advocate, 1987 S.C.C.R. 38, HCJ Appeal 509
Sanderson v. McManus; sub nom. S. v. M. (A Minor: Acces Order); Sanderson v. MacManus, 1997 S.C.
    (H.L.) 55; 1997 S.L.T. 629, HL 431, 436, 437
Sands v. George Waterston & Sons, 1989 S.L.T. 174, OH 406
Saunders v. United Kingdom [1997] B.C.C. 872; [1998] 1 B.C.L.C. 362;
    (1997) 23 E.H.R.R. 313, ECHR 249, 264, 265
Science Research Council v. Nasse; Leyland Cars (B.L. Cars Ltd) v. Vyas v. Leyland Cars sub nom. Nasse v.
    Science Research Council [1980] A.C. 1028; [1979] 3 W.L.R. 762, HL 378
Scot v. Elliot 52
Scott v. H.M. Advocate, 1946 J.C. 90 442
—— v. H.M. Advocate, 1987 S.L.T. 389; 1986 S.C.C.R. 346, HCJ Appeal 450
—— v. Howie, 1993 S.C.C.R. 81, HCJ Appeal 259
—— v. Jameson, 1914 S.C. (J.) 187; (1914) 7 Adam 529, HCJ Appeal 14
—— v. The London and St. Katherine Docks Co. 3 H. & C. 596 .... 54, 55
Scott (A.T.) v. H.M. Advocate, 1946 S.C. (J.)187 171
Scott Paper Co. v. Drayton Paper Work Ltd (1927) 44 RFC 151 366
Scottish and Universal Newspapers v. Gherson's Trustees; sub nom. Scottish & Universal Newspapers Ltd v.
    Gherson, 1987 S.C. 27; 1988 S.L.T. 109, 1 Div 129, 135
Scottish Criminal Cases Review Commission v. H.M. Advocate, 2001 J.C. 36; 2001 S.L.T. 905, HCJ ... 386, 527, 529
Scottish Criminal Cases Review Commission, Petitioners, 2001 S.L.T. 1198; 2001 S.C.C.R. 775, HCJ 392
Sereshky v. Sereshky, 1988 S.L.T. 426, OH 68
Shaw v. Lanarkshire Health Board, 1988 S.C.L.R. 13 (Sh. Ct.) 71
Sheridan v. Peel, 1907 S.C. 577 370
Short's Trustee v. Keeper of the Registers of Scotland; sub nom. Laing v. Keeper of the Registers of
    Scotland, 1994 S.L.T. 65; 1994 S.C.L.R. 135, 1 Div 73
Sime v. Union (1897) 24R.(J) 70 340
Simmons v. Heath Laundry Co. [1910] 1 K.B. 543, CA 506, 507
Simpson v. LMS Railway Co., 1931 S.C. (H.L.) 15 63
Sinclair v. Clark, 1962 J.C. 57; 1962 S.L.T. 307, HCJ Appeal 106, 107
Singh v. H.M. Advocate [2001] S.T.C. 790; 2001 J.C. 186;
    2001 S.L.T. 812; 2001 S.C.C.R. 348, HCJ Appeal 196, 219
Singh (Major) v. Secretary of State for the Home Department, 2000 S.C.L.R. 610; 2000 G.W.D. 11–395, OH ... 315
Slack v. H.M. Advocate, 1996 S.L.T. 1084; 1995 S.C.C.R. 809, HCJ Appeal 280
Slater v. H.M. Advocate, 1928 J.C. 94; 1928 S.L.T. 602, HCJ Appeal 380, 382
Slowey v. H.M. Advocate, 1965 S.L.T. 309, HCJ Appeal 449, 451, 458

Smith v. Alexander Baird Ltd, 1993 S.C.L.R. 563, OH 414, 415, 416, 418
—— v. H.M. Advocate, 1952 J.C. 66; 1952 S.L.T. 286, HCJ Appeal 380, 382
—— v. H.M. Advocate, 1986 S.C.C.R. 135, HCJ Appeal 150, 180, 182, 187
—— v. H.M. Advocate, 2001 S.L.T. 438 523
—— v. Innes, 1984 S.C.C.R. 119, HCJ Appeal 220
—— v. Lees, 1997 J.C. 73; 1997 S.L.T. 690, HCJ Appeal 83, 84, 91, 92, 93, 94, 101, 103, 114, 119
Smith's Executors v. Upper Clyde Shipbuilders Ltd (In Liquidation), 1999 G.W.D. 33–1597, OH 28
Sorley v. H.M. Advocate, 1992 J.C. 102; 1992 S.L.T. 867, HCJ Appeal 38
Southern Bowling Club Ltd v. Ross 197, 200, 202
Sporrong and Lönnroth v. Sweden (A/52) (1983) 5 E.H.R.R. 35, ECHR 36, 264
SS Baron Vernon v. SS Metagama (1928) 30 Ll. L. Rep. 132; 1928 S.C. 21, OH 17
SS Bogota v. SS Alconda, 1923 S.C. 526 316
Stark v. H.M. Advocate; Smith v. H.M. Advocate, 1938 J.C. 170; 1938 S.L.T. 516, HCJ Appeal 231
State v. Coetzee [1997] 2 LRC at p.677 (para.220) 36
—— v. Lapage 57 N.H. 288 2
Stevenson v. Stuart 11 Pa. 307 3
Stewart v. H.M. Advocate (No. 1) 1997 S.C.C.R. 330 315
—— v. H.M. Advocate, 1980 J.C. 103; 1980 S.L.T. 245, HCJ Appeal 443, 444
—— v. H.M. Advocate 171
Stewart Abercromby, Hume, ii, 386 12
Stillie v. H.M. Advocate, 1992 S.L.T. 279; 1990 S.C.C.R. 719, HCJ Appeal 62
Stirling Aquatic Technology Ltd v. Farmocean AB (No. 2) 1996 S.L.T. 456, OH 145, 420
Stobo v. H.M. Advocate, 1994 S.L.T. 28; 1993 S.C.C.R. 1105, HCJ Appeal 85, 89, 93, 97
Strathern v. Lambie, 1931 J.C. 137 .... 81, 82
—— v. Sloan, 1937 J.C. 76 .... 347, 350
Styr v. H.M. Advocate, 1993 J.C. 74; 1994 S.L.T. 5; 1993 S.C.C.R. 278, HCJ Appeal 260
Subramaniam v. Public Prosecutor, 1999 S.L.T. 963; 1999 S.C.C.R. 384, HCJ Appeal 151, 155, 158

T. v. T., 2000 S.L.T. 1442 .... 5, 186, 326, 426, 437, 481, 483
Taylor v. Taylor, 2000 S.L.T. 1419; 2001 S.C.L.R. 16, Ex Div 4, 409
Templeton v. H.M. Advocate, 1985 S.C.C.R. 357 287
—— v. McLeod, 1986 S.L.T. 149; 1985 S.C.C.R. 357, HCJ Appeal 287, 289, 291, 292, 294, 297
Teper v. R. [1952] A.C. 480; [1952] 2 All E.R. 447, PC (BG) 149, 151, 153, 170, 175
Texeira de Castro v. Portugal (1998) 28 E.H.R.R. 101, ECHR 204
Thomas v. Queen, The (1874) L.R., 10 Q.B. 44 371
—— v. Thomas; sub nom. Watt v. Thomas [1947] A.C. 484; [1947] 1 All E.R. 582; 1947 S.C. (H.L.) 45, HL ... 28,
        405, 501, 502
Thompson v. Crowe, 1999 S.L.T. 1434 .... 79, 103, 230, 231, 250, 251, 259, 267
—— v. H.M. Advocate, 1968 J.C. 61; 1968 S.L.T. 339 .... 232, 237, 238, 239
—— v. King, The; sub nom. R. v. Thompson [1918] A.C. 221, HL; affirming [1917] 2 K.B. 630, CCA 6
—— v. Trevanion (1693) Skin 402 153
Thomson v. H.M. Advocate, 1989 S.L.T. 170 231
—— v. H.M. Advocate, 2001 S.C.C.R. 162; 2001 G.W.D. 4–153, HCJ Appeal 9, 309
—— v. Jamieson, 1986 S.L.T. 72, OH 426
—— v. Tough Ropes, 1978 S.L.T. (Notes) 5, OH 407
Thorne v. Stott, 2000 J.C. 13; 2000 S.L.T. 113, HCJ Appeal 342
Tobin v. H.M. Advocate, 1934 J.C. 60; 1934 S.L.T. 325, HCJ Appeal 351
Todd v. H.M. Advocate, 1984 J.C. 13 .... 442, 444
Tomlin v. Standard Telephones and Cables Ltd [1969] 1 W.L.R. 1378; [1969] 3 All E.R. 201, CA 364
Tonge v. H.M. Advocate, 1982 S.L.T. 506; 1982 S.C.C.R. 313, HCJ Appeal 200, 231, 232, 251, 258, 259
Toohey v. Commissioner of Police of the Metropolis; sub nom. R. v. Toohey [1965] A.C. 595;
        [1965] 2 W.L.R. 439, HL 318, 322
Torrance v. Thaw, 1970 J.C. 58 106
Townsley v. Lees, 1996 S.L.T. 1182; 1996 S.C.C.R. 620, HCJ Appeal 121
Traynor's Executrix v. Bairds & Scottish Steel Ltd, 1957 S.C. 311; 1957 S.L.T. 71, OH 425, 426
Trivedi v. United Kingdom 190
Trotter v. Trotter, 2001 S.L.T. (Sh. Ct.) 42; 2000 Fam. L.R. 94, Sh Pr 332
Tudhope v. Cullen, 1982 S.C.C.R. 276, Sh Ct (Glasgow) 350
—— v. Dalgleish, 1986 S.C.C.R. 559, HCJ Appeal 107
—— v. Hazleton, 1984 S.C.C.R. 455 .... 117, 119
Tunnicliffe v. H.M. Advocate, 1991 S.C.C.R. 623, HCJ Appeal 231
Turner v. Scott, 1995 J.C. 150; 1996 S.L.T. 200, HCJ Appeal 117

U.S. v. Stevens (1991) 935 F. 2d 1380 (3rd Circuit) 327
Union Carbide 393

Valentine v. Macphail, 1986 S.C.C.R. 321 342

W. (An Infant), Re [1971] A.C. 682; [1971] 2 W.L.R. 1011, HL 505
W. v. Kennedy, 1988 S.C. 82; 1988 S.L.T. 583; 1988 S.C.L.R. 236, 1 Div 409, 412
W.P. v. Tayside Regional Council, 1989 S.C.L.R. 165 .... 355, 378
Waddell v. Kinnaird, 1922 J.C. 40 .... 229, 252
Waddington v. Buchan Poultry Products Ltd 360, 361
Wade v. Robertson, 1948 J.C. 117; 1948 S.L.T. 491, HCJ Appeal 240
Wakelin v. London & South Western Railway Co. (1887) L.R. 12 App. Cas. 41, HL 19
Walker v. Wilsher (1889) L.R. 23 Q.B.D. 335, CA 363, 364
Wallace v. H.M. Advocate, 1952 J.C. 78; 1952 S.L.T. 347, HCJ Appeal 450, 451, 452, 453, 454, 458, 466
Walsh v. H.M. Advocate, 1961 J.C. 51; 1961 S.L.T. 137, HCJ Appeal 350
—— v. Macphail, 1978 S.L.T. (Notes) 29, HCJ Appeal 217
Walters v. Queen, The; *sub nom.* Walters v. R. [1969] 2 A.C. 26; [1969] 2 W.L.R. 60, PC (Jam) 61
Ward v. Chief Constable, Strathclyde Police, 1991 S.L.T. 292 71
Watson Towers Ltd v. Macphail, 1986 S.L.T. 617 .... 365, 366, 367
—— v. Watson, 1934 S.C. 374; 1934 S.L.T. 275, 2 Div 223
Waugh v. British Railways Board, 1998 S.C. 543; 1998 S.L.T. 973, HL 411
Webb v. H.M. Advocate, 1996 J.C. 166; 1997 S.L.T. 170, HCJ Appeal 110
Weir v. Jessop (No. 2), 1991 J.C. 146; 1992 S.L.T. 533; 1991 S.C.C.R. 636, HCJ Appeal 196, 203, 204, 254
Welsh v. H.M. Advocate, 1992 S.L.T. 193; 1992 S.C.C.R. 108, HCJ Appeal 12
Wendo v. Queen, The *See* Wendo v. R.
—— v. R. (1963) 109 C.L.R. 559, HC (Aus) 243
White v. H.M. Advocate, 1986 S.C.C.R. 224, HCJ Appeal 330
—— v. White, 1947 S.L.T. (Notes) 51 476
Whyte v. Whyte (1884) 11R. 712 285
—— v. Whyte (1895) 23R. 320 347
Wilkes v. H.M. Advocate, 2001 S.L.T. 1268; 2001 G.W.D. 26–1024, HCJ Appeal 82
Wilkie v. H.M. Advocate, 1997 G.W.D. 23–1167, HCJ Appeal 122
William Alexander & Sons v. Dundee Corp., 1950 S.C. 123; 1950 S.L.T. 76, 2 Div 2, 270, 271
William Thyne (Plastics) Ltd v. Stenhouse Reed Shaw Scotland Ltd, 1979 S.L.T. (Notes) 93, OH 426
Williamson v. H.M. Advocate, 1978 S.L.T. 38 350
—— v. McClelland, 1913 S.C. 678 332
—— v. Wither, 1981 S.C.C.R. 214, HCJ Appeal 102
Wilson v. Clyde Rigging and Boiler Scaling Co. Ltd [1959] 2 Lloyd's Rep. 345; 1959 S.C. 328;
    1959 S.L.T. (Notes) 59, 2 Div 346
—— v. H.M. Advocate, 1987 J.C. 50; 1987 S.C.C.R. 217, HCJ Appeal 111
—— v. H.M. Advocate, 1988 S.C.C.R. 384, HCJ Appeal 318, 330
—— v. H.M. Advocate, 2001 S.L.T. 1203 .... 91, 119
—— v. Wilson, 1955 S.L.T. (Notes) 81, OH 285
Winter v. Heywood, 1995 J.C. 60; 1995 S.L.T. 586; 1995 S.C.C.R. 276, HCJ Appeal 123
Wong Kam-Ming v. Queen, The [1980] A.C. 247; [1979] 2 W.L.R. 81, PC (HK) 242, 244, 245, 247, 250
Woodhouse v. Hall (1981) 72 Cr.App.R. 39; [1980] Crim. L.R. 645, DC 163
Woodland v. Hamilton, 1990 S.L.T. 565; 1990 S.C.C.R. 166, HCJ Appeal 113
Woods v. W.M. Car Services (Peterborough) Ltd [1982] Com. L.R. 208; [1982] I.C.R. 693, CA 506, 507
Wright v. Doe d. Tatham (1837) 7 Ad. & El. 313; 112 All E.R. 488 .... 156, 157, 159
—— v. H.M. Advocate, 2000 S.L.T. 1026 123
—— v. Wright (1948) 77 C.L.R. 191, HC (Aus) 65

Yates v. H.M. Advocate, 1977 S.L.T. (Notes) 42, HCJ Appeal 90, 102
Young v. H.M. Advocate, 1932 J.C. 63 .... 445, 446, 447, 448
—— v. National Coal Board, 1957 S.C. 99; 1957 S.L.T. 266, 2 Div 360, 361, 363
—— v. National Coal Board, 1960 S.C. 6; 1959 S.L.T. (Notes) 77, OH 425, 426
—— & Woods Ltd v. West [1980] I.R.L.R. 201, CA 507
Yuill v. Yuill, 1973 S.L.T. 158, 2 Div 405, 501, 502

Zenel v. Haddow, 1993 S.C. 612; 1993 S.L.T. 975, 1 Div 502

TABLE OF STATUTES

References are to page numbers

1621 (c.18)........................ 355, 356
1747 (21 Geo. 2, c.34)
    s.20 .... 459, 464, 466
1816 Habeus Corpus Act (56 Geo. 3, c.100).... 64
1828 Circuit Courts (Scotland) Act (9 Geo. 4, c.29)........................ 348
1832 Day Trespass Act...................... 82
1840 Evidence (Scotland) Act
    s.3 410
1853 Evidence (Scotland) Act (16 & 17 Vict., c.20)........................ 476
    s.3 .... 358, 421, 476
1859 Tweed Fisheries Amendment Act (22 & 23 Vict., c.lxx)
    s.2 332
    s.14 332
    s.16 .... 333, 334
1882 Married Women's Property Act (45 & 46 Vict., c.75)
    s.12 469
    s.16 469
1884 Married Women's Property Act (47 & 48 Vict., c.14)
    s.1 469
    Merchant Shipping Act.............. 125
1887 Criminal Procedure (Scotland) Act (50 & 51 Vict., c.35)
    s.36 34
    s.67 295
1898 Criminal Evidence Act (61 & 62 Vict., c.36).................. 301, 443, 448
    s.1 .... 289, 294
        (d) 471
        (f) 289
        (f)(ii) 294
1906 Workmen's Compensation Act (6 Edw. 7, c.58)........................ 506
1907 Sheriff Courts (Scotland) Act (7 Edw. 7, c.51)
    Sched. 1, rule 72A 414
              72A(4)(b) 414
              (5) 414
1908 Summary Jurisdiction (Scotland) Act (8 Edw. 7, c.65)................. 125, 333
    s.41 349
    s.75 .... 125, 132
    Sched. 22
1911 Coal Mines Act (1 & 2 Geo. 5, c.50)..... 343
1912 Protection of Animals (Scotland) Act (2 & 3 Geo. 5, c.14)..................... 219
1915 Finance (No.2) Act (5 & 6 Geo. 5, c.89)
    s.39(c) 506
1918 Income Tax Act (8 & 9 Geo. 5, c.40)
    Sched. D, Case 1 506
1926 Criminal Appeal (Scotland) Act (16 & 17 Geo. 5, c.15)................... 509
    s.2(1) 329, 510
    s.6 .... 509, 511

1928 Food and Drugs (Adulteration) Act (18 & 19 Geo. 5, c.31)
    s.2 279
    s.23 280
1930 Road Traffic Act (20 & 21 Geo. 5, c.43) 81, 347
1936 Finance Act (26 Geo. 5 & 1 Edw. 8, c.34)
    s.21 335
        (1) 334, 335
        (9) 335
        (a) 335
1937 Factories Act (1 Edw. 8 & 1 Geo. 6, c.67)
    s.13 22
    s.26(1) 24
1946 Education (Scotland) Act (9 & 10 Geo. 6, c.72)
    s.35 21
1947 Crown Proceedings Act (10 & 11 Geo. 6, c.44)
    s.47 374
    Town and Country Planning (Scotland) Act (10 & 11 Geo. 6, c.53)......... 368
1949 Criminal Justice (Scotland) Act (12, 13 & 14 Geo. 6, c.94)................... 295
    s.18(2) 351
    s.39(1)(a) 295
        (e) 295
1951 Salmon and Freshwater Fisheries (Protection) (Scotland) Act (14 & 15 Geo. 6, c.26)....................... 127, 128
    s.1 126
    s.2 126
        (1) 126
    s.7 126
        (1) 126
    s.20 127
1952 Income Tax Act (15 & 16 Geo. 6 & 1 Eliz. 2, c.10)
    s.397(1) 335
    s.403 335
1954 Summary Jurisdiction (Scotland) Act (2 & 3 Eliz. 2, c.48)
    s.16(d) 21, 22, 23
    Sched. 2, Pt II 21
1959 Factories Act (7 & 8 Eliz. 2, c.67)
    s.5 24
    Mental Health Act (7 & 8 Eliz. 2, c.72) 321
1960 Road Traffic Act (8 & 9 Eliz. 2, c.16)
    s.1(1) 337
    s.3 255
    s.6(1) 255, 257
    s.232 .... 255, 260
1961 Factories Act (9 & 10 Eliz. 2, c.34)
    s.29 .... 20, 21
        (1) 20, 22, 23, 24
1963 Criminal Justice (Scotland) Act (c.39)
    s.30(1) 295

1966	Police (Scotland) Act (c.52)	
	s.1(1)	526
	s.41(1)(a)	463
1967	Road Safety Act (c.21)	205
1968	Criminal Appeal Act (c.19)	
	s.23	325, 510
	(2)	511
	Firearms Act (c.27)	120
	s.1(1)(a)	287
	s.4(4)	287
	s.17(2)	120
	(5)	120
	Social Work (Scotland) Act (c.49)	74, 395, 414, 428
	s.32	69
	(2)(b)	69
	(d)	69
	(dd)	69
	(g)	70, 143, 410, 419
	s.42	70, 143, 410, 411, 419, 426
	(6)	69, 70
	Law Reform (Miscellaneous Provisions) (Scotland) Act (c.70)	406
	s.9	402, 403, 404, 405, 406, 407, 412, 413
	(2)	402, 403, 404, 405, 406, 407, 408
1969	Family Law Reform Act (c.46)	
	s.26	62
1970	Taxes Management Act (c.9)	
	Pt X	73
	s.99	73
1971	Misuse of Drugs Act (c.38)	36, 196, 201, 208, 379
	s.4(3)	201
	(a)	198
	(b)	274
	s.5(3)	201, 472
	s.23	274
	(2)	196, 220
	s.25	201
	s.28(2)	36
	Sheriff Courts (Scotland) Act (c.58)	
	s.32	416
	(1)(e)	409, 416
	s.38	504
1972	Road Traffic Act (c.20)	178
	s.2	131, 132
	s.3	31
	s.9(3)	24
	s.168	179
	Civil Evidence Act (c.30)	
	s.3	315
	(1)	315
	Administration of Justice (Scotland) Act (c.59)	360, 372
	s.1	372, 373, 375, 376
	(1)	359, 373
	(4)	373, 374
	European Communities Act (c.68)	
	ss.2–3	342
1974	Zetland County Council Act	356
1975	Criminal Procedure (Scotland) Act (c.21)	510
	s.20A	167
	s.20B	167
	s.68(1)	295
	s.82A	445
	s.140A	79, 113, 275
	s.141	287

1975	Criminal Procedure (Scotland) Act—cont.	
	s.141(1)(b)	444
	(f)	287, 289, 292
	(ii)	289, 292, 293, 294
	(2)	446
	s.141A	308
	(1)	308
	(1)(c)	308
	s.141B	308
	(1)(c)	307, 308
	s.143	471, 473, 475
	(2)	471, 475
	s.147	186
	s.151	167
	s.159(1)	295
	s.160	295
	(1)	295, 303, 304, 305
	s.161	295
	(1)	295
	s.166	489
	s.228	471
	(2)	509, 510
	s.252(b)	510
	s.263	528
	s.345A	133, 213, 214, 249
	s.346(1)(b)	444
	(f)	287
	(ii)	291
	s.362	489
	s.452A(1)(d)	341
	s.452B	341
	s.453C(1)	480
	Ministers of the Crown Act (c.26)	
	s.8	526
1976	Licensing (Scotland) Act (c.66)	334
	Sexual Offences (Scotland) Act (c.67)	
	s.3	48
	s.4	48
	s.5	85
1977	Presumption of Death (Scotland) Act (c.27)	
	s.2	46
1978	National Health Service (Scotland) Act (c.29)	376
	Northern Ireland (Emergency Provisions) Act (c.5)	245
	Employment Protection (Consolidation) Act (c.44)	505
	s.133(6)	363
	s.136	504
	(1)	505
	s.153(1)	505
1979	Customs and Excise Management Act (c.2)	
	s.6(3)	353
1980	Education (Scotland) Act (c.44)	
	s.35(1)	24
	Criminal Justice (Scotland) Act (c.62)	448, 453, 509, 510
	s.2	105
	(7)	259
	s.19	242
	s.27	445, 448
	s.28	448
	s.29(1)	471
1981	Forgery and Counterfeiting Act (c.45)	219

1981 Contempt of Court Act (c.49)
    s.8 .... 393, 529
    s.10 358
    Wildlife and Countryside Act (c.69). 219
    s.19 219
1982 Civic Government (Scotland) Act
    (c.45). 212, 213
    s.51(2) 212, 213, 214
1983 Mental Health Act (c.20)
    s.1(2) 487
    s.47 487
    Value Added Tax Act (c.55). 75, 219
    s.39 .... 74, 75
1984 Mental Health (Scotland) Act (c.36)
    s.1(2) 487
    s.71(1) 487
    s.106(1)(a) 307
    s.107 307
    Video Recordings Act (c.39)... 212, 213, 214
    s.1(2) 213
    s.4 213
    s.7 213
    s.8 213
    s.10 .... 212, 213, 216
    s.17(1) 212
    Police and Criminal Evidence Act (c.60) 243
    s.76(2) 242, 324
    (b) 325
    s.78 .... 194, 248
1985 Company Securities (Insider Dealing) Act
    (c.8). 92, 96
    Family Law (Scotland) Act (c.37)
    s.9(1)(b) 414
    Finance Act (c.54). 73, 74
    s.13 .... 72, 74
    (1) 72
    (7) 72
    s.27(1) 72
1986 Law Reform (Parent and Child)
    (Scotland) Act (c.9)
    s.1(1) 50
    s.5 50
    Finance Act (c.41). 73
    s.14 72
1988 Civil Evidence (Scotland) Act (c.32)... 74, 75,
    142, 144, 186, 398, 408, 409, 413, 415, 416,
    419, 420, 421, 423, 424, 426, 431, 432, 434,
    436
    s.1 .... 56, 92, 317, 407, 502
    (1) 408
    s.2   142, 144, 145, 146, 409, 410, 411, 415,
    416, 417, 419, 420, 421, 422, 424,
    433, 434, 436, 438, 488
    (1) 144, 415, 422, 436
    (a) 413, 416, 422, 423, 431, 436
    (b)   144, 409, 415, 416, 417, 419, 422,
    423, 425, 426, 427, 428, 429, 430,
    431, 432, 433, 434, 436, 437, 438
    (2) 434
    (3) 415
    (4) 415
    s.3 .... 410, 419, 420, 421, 424, 438
    s.4 .... 410, 421
    s.6 .... 143, 420
    s.8(3) 409

1988 Civil Evidence (Scotland) Act—cont.
    s.9   70, 74, 143, 144, 410, 419, 421, 424, 425
    s.10(1) 421
    Sched. 421
    Criminal Justice Act (c.33)
    s.25 416
    Court of Session Act (c.36)
    s.5 .... 409, 416
    (e) 415
    Road Traffic Act (c.52). 121, 266
    s.2 339
    s.3 121
    s.5(1)(a) 121
    s.172 .... 260, 265, 266
    (1) 266
    (2) 260, 261, 262
    (a) 266
    (3) 260
    (7) 266
    (9) 266
    (10) 266
1989 Prisons (Scotland) Act (c.45). 208
1990 Law Reform (Miscellaneous Provisions)
    (Scotland) Act (c.40)
    s.56 ...... 490, 492, 494, 495, 496, 497, 498
    (2) 490
    (3) 490, 495
    ss.56–59 ......   s.58 ...... 495, 497, 498
1993 Prisoners and Criminal Proceedings
    (Scotland) Act (c.9)
    ss.33–35 488
1994 Vehicle Excise and Registration Act (c.22)...
    266
    Value Added Tax Act (c.23). 72, 74, 75
    Pt IV 72, 73, 74, 75
    s.59 .... 73, 75
    (7) 75
    (a) 75
    (b) 75
    s.60 .... 72, 73, 74, 75
    (1)(b) 74
    (4)(a) 74
    (5) 75
    (6) 75
    (7) 72
    s.61 .... 72, 73, 75
    (5) 72
    s.62 75
    s.63 75
    ss.65–69 75
    s.70 75
    s.72 .... 72, 73, 75
1995 Civil Evidence (Family Mediation)
    (Scotland) Act (c.6)
    s.1 .... 358, 363
    (1) 429
    s.2 .... 363, 429
    Criminal Justice (Scotland) Act (c.20). ... 186
    Criminal Appeal Act (c.35). 528
    s.4 510
    Children (Scotland) Act (c.36)... 67, 394, 395,
    396, 397, 413
    Pt II, Chap.3 .... 188, 326
    s.6 .... 394, 395
    s.11 395
    (1) 396
    (7) 394, 396

1995 Children (Scotland) Act—*cont.*
   s.65 79
   s.68 74
  Criminal Law (Consolidation) (Scotland)
    Act (c.39)
   ss.1–3 307
   s.5 307
   s.6 307
   s.7(2) 307
    (3) 307
   s.8 307
   s.13(5) 307
  Proceeds of Crime (Scotland) Act (c.43)   36,
                             38
   s.1 37
    (1) 37
    (8) 37
   s.3 .... 36, 37
    (2) 37
   s.9(6) 37
    (8) 37
   s.12 37
  Criminal Procedure (Scotland) Act (c.46)   78,
     184, 188, 285, 287, 306, 307, 352, 353, 354,
               391, 430, 442, 488
   Pt VIII 524
   Pt XA 386, 528
   ss.13–14 217
   ss.13–15 .... 206, 263
   s.14 .... 208, 258
   s.17 .... 186, 187, 390
    (1) 186
    (3) 390
    (4) 390
   s.18 .... 206, 390
    (3) 390
   s.20(4) 188
   s.32 444
   ss.35–38 263
   s.41 48
   s.55(2) 524
   s.57(2) 524
   s.67(5) 185, 286, 353, 441, 442
   s.68 328
   s.76 352
   s.78(4) 185, 286, 353, 441, 442
   s.97 .... 78, 79, 90, 102, 242
   s.101 .... 285, 303, 305
    (1) 304
   s.104(1)(b) 510
   s.106 .... 382, 507, 508, 509
    (3) 509
     (a) 509, 522
     (b) 510
    (3A)   508, 510, 511, 512, 514, 516, 518,
               520, 521, 522
    (3A)–(3D) 509, 510
    (3B) 521
    (3C)   513, 514, 517, 518, 521, 522, 523
    (3C)(a)(i) 513
    (3D) 513, 514, 519, 522
     (a) 519
     (b) 519
     (c) 519, 522
   s.107 507
   s.118(8) 125
   s.123 219

1995 Criminal Procedure (Scotland) Act—*cont.*
   s.124 525
    (3) 509
   s.160 .... 78, 90, 242, 249
   s.175 382
    (3) 504
   s.183(1)(d) 248
   s.185 248
   s.191(3) 248
   s.192(3) 125
   s.194A 524, 528
   s.194A(2) 528
   s.194B 524, 525, 529
    (1) 528
   s.194C 524, 528
    (a) 528
    (b) 528
   s.194D 524
    (1) 529
    (2) 529
     (c) 389
    (3) 529
    (4) 529
    (5) 529
   s.194E 525
   s.194F 525, 529
    (a) 529
    (b) 529
   s.194G 525
   s.194H 525, 529
   s.194I   386, 389, 390, 391, 392, 526, 527, 529
    (1) 391, 392
    (2) 389, 390
    (3) 389, 390
   s.194J 391, 526, 527
   s.194K 526, 527
   s.194L 527
   s.256 352
   s.257 .... 352, 353
   s.258 352
   s.259   184, 186, 188, 189, 190, 191, 192, 240,
              243, 430, 432, 486
    (1) 146, 189, 191, 508
     (b) 430, 431
     (c) 431, 432, 481, 486
    (2) 186, 191, 432
     (a) 189
     (e) 188
      (ii) 186
   s.259(4) 192, 193
    (5) 187, 188, 189
    (6) 188
    (8) 240, 243
   ss.259–261 .... 150, 188
   ss.259–262 124
   s.260 .... 184, 187, 188
   s.261 .... 186, 188
   s.262 188
   s.263 439
    (4) 186, 441
   s.264 .... 439, 469, 473
    (2) 470
     (b) 358
   s.265 440
   s.266 .... 284, 285, 287, 301, 440, 442
    (2) 301
    (3) 244, 301, 449

1995   Criminal Procedure (Scotland) Act—*cont.*
    s.266(4) 286, 301
       (c)   298, 299, 300, 301, 302, 303, 444
      (9) 444
    s.267 441
    s.268 .... 286, 353, 441, 442
    s.269 441
    s.270 .... 284, 285, 286, 287, 442
    s.271 .... 477, 486, 488, 489
      (8)(b) 491
      (12) 488
    s.272(2)–(6) 486
      (8) 486
      (9) 486
    s.274 .... 8, 306, 307
      (1) 307
      (c) 307
    s.275 .... 8, 306, 307, 309
    s.276 .... 129, 135
    s.277 353
    ss.281–286 135
    s.282 353
    Sched. 2 87

1995   Criminal Procedure (Scotland) Act—*cont.*
    Sched. 3 89
       para. 16 24
    Sched. 8, para. 1 352
    Sched. 9A 524
       para. 6(5) 389
1997   Crime and Punishment (Scotland) Act
    (c.48). 510
    s.17 .... 509, 513
      (1) 509
    s.26 508
    s.29 488
    Children Act (Irish)
    s.23 434
1998   Data Protection Act (c.29). 389
    s.35 389
    Human Rights Act (c.42). 35, 189, 396
    s.1 189
    s.2 342
    s.3(1) 35
    s.4 36
    Scotland Act (c.46). 35, 189
    s.57 260
      (2) 189, 249

TABLE OF STATUTORY INSTRUMENTS

References are to page numbers

1901 Sale of Milk Regulations
　　　reg. 1 279
1934 Milk and Dairies (Scotland) Order. 279
1960 Shipbuilding and Ship Repairing Regu-
　　　lations (S.I. 1960 No. 1932). 26
1965 Rules of the Court of Session
　　　r.108A 414, 415, 416
1983 Act of Sederunt (Sheriff Court Ordinary
　　　Cause Rules) (S.I. 1983 No. 747). . . 418
　　　r.72A 413
1985 Video Recordings (Labelling) Regulations
　　　(S.I. 1985 No. 911). 213, 216
　　　reg. 4 213
　　　reg. 7 213
1986 Mental Health (Northern Ireland) Order
　　　(S.I. 1986 No. 595)
　　　art. 3(1) 487
　　　art. 53 487
　　　Road Vehicles (Construction and Use)
　　　Regulations (S.I. 1986 No. 1078). . . . 132
　　　reg. 27(1)(e) 131
　　　　　　　(g) 131

1988 Act of Adjournal (Consolidation) (S.I.
　　　1988 No. 110)
　　　r.61A 490
　　　Electricity Supply Regulations (S.I. 1988
　　　No. 1057)
　　　reg. 34(1)(a) 361
1989 Act of Sederunt (Rules of the Court of
　　　Session Amendment No.1) (Written
　　　Statements) (S.I. 1989 No. 435). 416
1991 Act of Adjournal (Consolidation Amend-
　　　ment No. 2) (Evidence of Children)
　　　(S.I. 1991 No. 1916). 490
1993 Act of Sederunt (Sheriff Court Ordinary
　　　Cause Rules) (S.I. 1993 No. 1956)
　　　r.29.3 . . . . 413, 414
　　　r.29.14 347
1994 Act of Sederunt (Rules of the Court of
　　　Session) (S.I. 1994 No. 1443)
　　　r.36.8 . . . . 414, 418
1997 Act of Sederunt (Child Care and Mainten-
　　　ance Rules) (S.I. 1997 No. 291)
　　　r.3.47(2) 79

Chapter 1

RELEVANCE

When a dispute, whether relating to a civil or criminal matter, reaches court there will always be a number of issues which one party will have to prove in order to persuade the court to find in his or her favour. In a criminal trial, for example, the prosecution will generally have to prove that a criminal act was committed, that it was committed with the appropriate *mens rea*, and that it was committed by the person accused. Failure to prove any of these essential issues (variously referred to as the crucial facts, facts-in-issue, essential facts or *facta probanda*) will lead to the failure of the case. In assessing the evidence that goes towards proof of these issues, a court must ask itself a number of questions, notably whether the evidence is admissible, reliable, and sufficient to establish the facts in issue. But a question usually regarded as being prior to these matters is the question of relevance. In other words, what bearing does the proposed evidence have on the facts-in-issue?

1. R. v. Kilbourne
[1973] A.C. 729

The accused in this case was charged with a number of sexual offences against two groups of boys, all aged between nine and 12. The principal question in the appeal was whether the trial judge had been entitled to direct the jury that uncorroborated evidence from one group of boys could corroborate the evidence of the other group. Lord Simon, however, made the following comments about the question of relevance, another important question being whether evidence of a multiplicity of accusations of sexual assault rendered the facts in issue more probable.

LORD SIMON OF GLAISDALE: "Your Lordships have been concerned with four concepts in the law of evidence: (i) relevance; (ii) admissibility; (iii) corroboration; (iv) weight. The first two terms are frequently, and in many circumstances legitimately, used interchangeably; but I think it makes for clarity if they are kept separate, since some relevant evidence is inadmissible, and some admissible evidence is irrelevant (in the senses that I shall shortly submit). Evidence is relevant if it is logically probative or disprobative of some matter which requires proof. I do not pause to analyse what is involved in 'logical probativeness', except to note that the term does not of itself express the element of experience which is so significant of its operation in law, and possibly elsewhere. It is sufficient to say, even at the risk of etymological tautology, that relevant (*i.e.* logically probative or dis-probative) evidence is evidence which makes the matter which requires proof more or less probable. To link logical probativeness with relevance rather than admissibility . . . not only is, I hope, more appropriate conceptually, but also accords better with the explanation of *Sims* [[1946] K.B. 531] given in *Harris v. Director of Public Prosecutions* [1952] A.C. 694, 710. Evidence is admissible if it may lawfully be adduced at a trial. 'Weight' of evidence is the degree of probability (both intrinsically and inferentially) which is attached to it by the tribunal of fact once it is established to be relevant and admissible in law (though its relevance may exceptionally, as will appear, be dependant on its evaluation by the tribunal of fact).

Exceptionally evidence which is irrelevant to a fact which is in issue is admitted to lay the foundation for other, relevant, evidence (*e.g.* evidence of an unsuccessful search for a missing relevant document, in order to lay the foundation of secondary evidence of the document).

Apart from such exceptional cases no evidence which is irrelevant to a fact in issue is admissible. But some relevant evidence is nevertheless inadmissible."

NOTES

As Lord Simon makes clear, a determination that evidence is relevant is only the first stage in deciding whether the evidence is admissible. There may be other rules which render relevant evidence inadmissible. Many of these are considered in the following chapters. For example, on the admissibility of "collateral" or "similar fact" evidence, a closely related issue, see Chapter 9. On the question of corroboration, see Chapter 5, below.

Lawyers and judges often seem reluctant to attempt a definition of the concept of relevance. As was stated in Field and Raitt, *The Law of Evidence in Scotland* (2nd ed., 1996), paras. 1–12, it is the "ultimate in moving targets". But there must be some rational process by which it is decided whether evidence is relevant. The key appears to lie in "the element of experience" referred to by Lord Simon in *Kilbourne*, above. In *R. v. Kearley* [1992] 2 All E.R. 345, Lord Oliver commented:

"Relevant, cannot, I think, be better defined than in article 1 of Stephen, *Digest of the Law of Evidence* (12th ed., 1936) p.4, that is to say that the word means that any two facts to which it is applied are so related to each other that according to the common course of events one either taken by itself or in connection with other facts proves or renders probable the past, present or future existence or non-existence of the other."

re: Collateral Evidence

2. W. Alexander & Sons v. Dundee Corp.
1950 S.C. 123

This action arose out of an accident sustained by a bus belonging to the pursuers. The pursuers averred that the accident was caused by the polished and greasy condition of the road. That condition was, in turn, caused by the materials used by the defenders in constructing the road which melted in warm conditions and became slippery. The pursuers sought to lead evidence of previous occasions on which their buses had skidded on this stretch of road. That evidence was objected to as irrelevant.

LORD JUSTICE-CLERK (THOMSON): "In my view these incidents are undoubtedly relevant. The real point in the case is the condition of this road. Was it in a reasonably safe condition for traffic, and if not, was that condition known, or ought it to have been known, to the defenders? It seems to me that the behaviour of vehicles on the road may be relevant evidence on these questions. These incidents may either illustrate the condition of the road or they may show that information as to its condition was available for the defenders.

The difficulty arises because the investigation of the behaviour of a vehicle on a road is a complex matter. It is not enough just to show that the vehicle skidded. It is necessary to discover whether the skid was due to the condition of the road or to the failure of the driver or, possibly, to the condition of the vehicle itself. Both the possible condition of the vehicle and the human element introduce complications. It seems to me, however, that although these complications may make the duty of the Judge more difficult in disentangling the evidence as to the condition of the road, nevertheless the evidence, when disentangled, may be relevant to the decision of the case. It was argued to us that the evidence ought to be excluded because this question of the behaviour of the vehicles is a 'collateral issue' in the sense in which that phrase is used in a number of cases which were cited to us. But if it is established that the skidding of these vehicles on these other occasions was truly due to the condition of the road, then it seems to me that that is not a collateral issue at all but something having a direct bearing on the decision of the present case. What we are searching for in a case like this is the cause of the accident. We have to carry out our search for the cause of the accident in a reasonably practical way, and the ultimate test of whether evidence is relevant or not is whether it has a reasonably direct bearing on the subject under investigation. There, no doubt, comes a point at which it is possible to say that the bearing of some fact is too indirect and too remote properly to assist the Court in deciding what the cause of the accident is; but I am quite clear that that point is far from being reached in the averments of other instances in the present case."

NOTES

This case is often referred to in relation to the admissibility of collateral evidence—that is broadly, evidence which is relevant to the facts in issue, but only remotely so. The admissibility of such evidence is considered further in Chapter 9 below. Given the degree to which decisions on relevance turn on the facts of the particular case, and on the practical reasoning of the court, do you consider that decisions on relevance could easily be used as precedents? See the difference of opinion between two of the most distinguished American evidence scholars, Thayer and Wigmore, on this point: Thayer, "Law and Logic" (1900) 14 Harvard Law Review 139; Wigmore, *A Treatise on the Anglo-American System of Evidence* (3rd ed., 1940) p.298 and the American case of *State v. Lapage*, 57 N.H. 288. *McAllister v. Normand*, 1996 S.L.T. 622 provides a rare reported example of a Scottish case that hinged on the relevance of a line of questioning.

3. Knapp v. The State
168 Indiana 153, 79 N.E. 1076 (1907)

The appellant was convicted of murdering a U.S. Marshal. He pled self-defence. To show that he had reason to fear the deceased, the appellant had given evidence that he had heard a story that the deceased had clubbed an old man to death when arresting him. The appellant could not give the names of the people from whom he had heard the story. The prosecution then led evidence in rebuttal that, in fact, the old man in the story had died of senility and alcohol abuse and had no marks or bruises on his body when examined post mortem. The defence argued on appeal that this prosecution evidence was irrelevant and should not have been admitted.

OPINION OF THE COURT: "Counsel for appellant [sic] contend that it was error to admit this testimony; that the question was as to whether he had, in fact, heard the story, and not as to its truth or falsity. While it is laid down in the books that there must be an open and visible connection between the fact under inquiry and the evidence by which it is sought to be established, yet the connection thus required is in the logical processes only, for to require an actual connection between the two facts would be to exclude all presumptive evidence. Within settled rules, the competency of testimony depends largely upon its tendency to persuade the judgement. As said by Wharton: 'Relevancy is that which conduces to the proof of a pertinent hypothesis.' . . . In *Stevenson v. Stuart*, 11 Pa. 307, it was said: 'The competency of a collateral fact to be used as the basis of legitimate argument is not to be determined by the conclusiveness of the inferences it may afford in reference to the litigated fact. It is enough if these may tend in a slight degree to elucidate the inquiry, or to assist, though remotely, to a determination probably founded in truth.'

We are of opinion that the testimony referred to was competent. While appellant's counsel are correct in their assertion that the question was whether appellant had heard a story to the effect that the deceased had offered serious violence to the old man, yet it does not follow that the testimony complained of did not tend to negative the claim of appellant as to what he had heard. One of the first principles of human nature is the impulse to speak the truth. 'This principle', says Dr. Reid, whom Professor Greenleaf quotes at length in his work on Evidence . . . 'has a powerful operation, even in the greatest of liars; for where they lie once they speak truth 100 times'. Truth speaking preponderating, it follows that to show that there was no basis in fact for the statement appellant claims to have heard had a tendency to make it less probable that his testimony on this point was true. Indeed, since this court has not, in cases where self-defence is asserted as a justification for homicide, confined the evidence concerning the deceased to character evidence, we do not perceive how, without the possibility of a gross perversion of right, the state could be denied the opportunity to meet in the manner indicated the evidence of the defendant as to what he had heard, where he, cunningly perhaps, denies that he can remember who gave him the information. The fact proved by the state tended to discredit [the] appellant, since it showed that somewhere between the fact and the testimony there was a person who [was] not a truth speaker, and, [the] appellant being unable to point to his informant, it must at least be said that the testimony complained of had a tendency to render his claim as to what he had heard less probable."

NOTES

Do you agree that the disputed evidence in *Knapp* was relevant? Would it have been admitted in a Scottish court? Compare the views expressed by Lord President Robertson in *A v. B* (1895) 22 R 402, an extract from which is reproduced in Chapter 9. Do you accept the premise that there is a fundamental urge to speak the truth? The latter question is important, and will be considered further later in the book, because it is on that alleged 'principle' that the court in *Knapp* based its judgment. The recent case of *Taylor v. Taylor*, 2000 S.L.T. 1419 provides an interesting Scottish example of legal reasoning about relevance. *Taylor* was a divorce case in which a Christian minister was prevented by the presiding Sheriff from pursuing a line of questioning about the religious principles upon which, he maintained, his marriage was based. His wife gave evidence that she did not believe that God could heal their marriage; nor did she believe that she could tolerate or forgive his behaviour. He sought to cross-examine her on the basis that her failure to forgive was contradictory of her avowed religious beliefs. The Inner House upheld the Sheriff's decision to limit his cross-examination, on the ground that much of it was irrelevant to any issue properly before the court. The court said that:

"What the sheriff refused to allow was inquiry into matters which the court could not resolve, relating to spiritual truth. It can of course be difficult to draw precise boundary lines in an area such as this. But we are satisfied that the causes of breakdown, the reasonable possibility of cohabitation and the likelihood of reconciliation are not matters which can be reduced to issues of logic, or some supposedly inevitable consistency between fundamental religious beliefs and what people can or will do amidst the stresses and tensions of actual behaviour within an actual marriage. We are not persuaded that the sheriff imposed any wrong limitation, or that Mr Taylor was prejudiced by such limitation as was imposed . . ."

These cases demonstrate the essentially practical, almost *ad hoc*, nature of legal reasoning about evidence and proof. The American scholar J.H. Wigmore (1863–1943), author of *A Treatise on the Anglo-American System of Evidence in Trials at Common Law* (1904–5) and *The Principles of Judicial Proof as Founded on Logic, Psychology and General Experience* (1913), was a great advocate of a scientific or systematic approach to matters of evidence. See further: Anderson and Twining, *Analysis of Evidence* (1987); W. Twining, *Rethinking Evidence* (1994). But even Wigmore had to acknowledge the importance of this aspect in fact-finding and reasoning about relevance and weight of evidence.

4. J. H. Wigmore
"Evidence in Trials at Common Law", Vol. 1A, No. 27
Revised Edition by Peter Tiller (Boston, Toronto) 1983

"When a fact is offered as evidence, the very offering of it is an implication that it has some bearing on the proposition at issue—that it tends naturally to produce a conviction about that proposition. The situation is thus in its elements the same as when the persons engaged are not occupied in a legal controversy. One might suppose that the question would be essentially one of the ordinary laws of reasoning, whether it were to be decided, as here, by a judge or a jury, or by the audience of a lecturer, or by a policeman notified of an alleged misdemeanor in his district, or by a class in rhetoric. But the application of the laws of reasoning is here attended with peculiar considerations not existing for any investigation but a judicial one. The first consideration is that so far as the tribunal can attempt expressly to deal at all with logical questions, it can do so only roughly and loosely and in a general way. In the first place, in courts as elsewhere, while the laws of reasoning must underlie inevitably all the operations of reasoning, they are as a rule followed instinctively and not with conscious skill. Little attempt is made deliberately to recognize or to apply them. The process of demonstration and decision in legal tribunals is an employment of the principles of reasoning upon a wider scale than is found in any other activity of life, yet the methods of logic are seldom alluded to in terms by judges or by advocates.

Again, wherever a rule or a principle may be adopted in the effort to employ the recognized tests of reasoning, no attempt can be made to furnish ideal tests. Details, refinements, contingencies, and exact distinctions, which the ideal principle would demand, may be and must often be neglected so that the test may be serviceable. Perhaps it may be necessary to take a mean of convenience and lay down a specific and unshifting rule that will sometimes operate arbitrarily or unequally. Where general principles are declared, they may satisfy themselves with reaching fairness in the main.

Lastly, the logical powers employed must be those of everyday life, not those of the trained logician or scientist. The conclusions and tests of everyday experience must constantly control the standards of legal logic. Moreover, the possibilities of fraud must exclude much that is probative but capable of abuse. Those considerations rest on the circumstances of the situation, patent to all. In the main, they are created by the need of speed in the settlement of litigation, and by the impossibility of expecting aught else in a proceeding where parties, witnesses, advocates, jury and judge represent so many grades of training and accomplishment. The principles of legal proof are in fact affected by these considerations just as we should have expected them to be."

NOTES

Reasoning in relation to the substantive law is generally thought of as being deductive or syllogistic. In deductive reasoning the conclusion follows inevitably from the premises. For example, one may take as a major premise that the crime of murder is committed where a person intentionally or with wicked recklessness causes the death of another. If the minor premise is that a particular accused, X, has intentionally caused the death of another, it necessarily follows (in the absence of any defence such as self-defence or insanity) that the particular accused has committed the crime of murder. It would be self-contradictory and illogical to deny the conclusion while accepting the major and minor premises. See *inter alia* MacCormick, *Legal Reasoning and Legal Theory* (1978).

Reasoning about evidence and proof, on the other hand, is thought to be inductive or empirical. Very rarely, at least without tortuous language, can one cast premises from which a particular conclusion about the evidence is inevitable. Proof in a legal context is based on probabilities, which in turn arise from common sense or experience as to the effect of certain evidence. The following "syllogism" illustrates this: experience shows that people who are seen fleeing the scene of a stabbing with blood-stained clothes, carrying a knife, are often responsible in some degree for the commission of that crime; the accused in this case was seen in just such a situation. The conclusion that the accused was in fact responsible for the crime does not, however, necessarily follow from these premises. It may be regarded as to some extent probable that the accused was responsible; one might properly infer guilt from these premises, but it is not self-contradictory to accept the premises stated and yet to deny the conclusion. The strength of the inferences which can be drawn depends on the probabilities arising from the evidence. This in turn depends to a large extent on the common sense and experience of the tribunal of fact. It is quite conceivable that different tribunals would take different views of the same facts.

It should be noted, however, that while the strength of the inferences to be drawn from evidence is a matter for the tribunal of fact—this is the question of weight, referred to by Lord Simon in the extract from *Kilbourne*, above—the question of *relevance* is a matter of law. It is the judge who must decide whether *any* legitimate inference can be drawn, and further, whether any such inference is outweighed by other considerations, such as disproportionate prejudice or unfairness to the accused. It is the judge who must formulate or approve the initial premise about the probabilities arising from evidence. The difficulty is that an initial premise based on subjective experience or "common sense" is open to abuse through bias or prejudice, unconscious or otherwise, and such prejudice may thus become embedded in the law of evidence. The "principle" adopted in *Knapp*, above—that there is a fundamental urge to speak the truth—is clearly an example of such a "common-sense" premise. No empirical evidence is cited to support it, and the basis for such a generalisation must be seriously open to question. For a Scottish example of a case in which a judicial preconception or "common-sense" premise proved fatal, see *T. v. T.*, 2000 S.L.T. 1442 (see Chapter 13). *T. v. T.* was a case in which, at first instance, a father's contact with his daughter was terminated following an allegation that he had sexually abused her. The sheriff's decision was overturned on appeal because of the basis for the sheriff's reasoning about the allegations of abuse. The appeal court said:

"In his note the sheriff began by setting out the issues which he had to determine. He then said that, in deciding whether there had been some form of sexual abuse, the character of the pursuer was, in his opinion, vital. He set out various sexual activities in which the pursuer had engaged and also noted that, latterly in 1997, the defender's interest in sex had declined. Having completed his survey, the sheriff said: 'This then was the classic background of a male with a high sexual drive and a female who was less keen than she had been in the past for sexual intercourse. It would not be surprising if the pursuer attempted to supply the lack from another available source, namely, his daughter'. "

This was described by the Lord President as an "extraordinary statement", both unjustified and unjustifiable, which was sufficient in itself to render the sheriff's decision unsustainable.

The problem of the legitimacy of generalisations drawn from "common-sense" or experience appears to be particularly acute in relation to sexual offences, although it is by no means confined to such cases. The following case concerned charges of gross indecency, attempted buggery and indecent assault on a number of young boys.

5. R. v. King
[1967] 2 Q.B. 338

LORD PARKER C.J.: "The first point . . . concerns a ruling given by the deputy recorder whereby he permitted the question to be put of the defendant in cross-examination: 'Are you a homosexual?' The deputy recorder ruled that that was a question which he would allow to be asked, and the answer was 'Yes'. Mr Rice before us submits in the first instance that that question ought never to have been allowed, and he refers to the fact that there is no authority which goes so far as to say that such a question in a sexual case of this kind is permissible. He admits that in certain circumstances articles found in the possession of an accused may be spoken to in evidence, as was held in *Thompson v. The King* [1918] A.C. 221. The passage often referred to is a passage in the speech of Lord Sumner. He said:

'No one doubts that it does not tend to prove a man guilty of a particular crime to show that he is the kind of man who would commit a crime, or that he is generally disposed to crime and even to a particular crime; but, sometimes for one reason, sometimes for another, evidence is admissible, notwithstanding that its general character is to show that the accused had in him the makings of a criminal, for example in proving guilty knowledge, or intent, or system, or in rebutting an appearance of innocence which, unexplained, the facts might wear.'

Applying that principle in the case of *Thompson*, certain indecent photographs found on the prisoner were spoken to in evidence as corroborative of the identity of the man who had committed the offences. Mr Rice has sought to argue that to allow that question to be put in the present case is an extension of that principle and ought not to be allowed.

In the judgment of the court it would not be an extension of the principle to allow that question to be put and answered; it comes plainly within the principle. It is no different putting to a man the question 'Are you a homosexual?' from putting to him certain indecent photographs of a homosexual nature found in his possession and saying to him: 'Are these yours?' In the judgement of the court, following *Thompson,* that question was *prima facie* perfectly legitimate.

In passing, it is to be observed that the principle laid down by Lord Sumner is not one of completely general application, but must be limited to certain particular crimes, and the common one to which it has been applied is sexual cases.

The second point under this head taken by Mr Rice is that that question was objectionable in that it implied that this man had committed criminal offences in the past. He says to get the answer 'Yes' to the question 'Are you a homosexual?' is really inviting the jury to accept that he has been guilty of homosexual offences.

The court is quite satisfied that the expression 'I am a homosexual' does not necessarily convey that he has committed homosexual offences; but even if any member of the jury was minded to interpret it in that way there was a full direction by the deputy recorder as to how they should treat the matter. In the summing up he referred to the fact that they must keep out of their minds the prejudice that might arise from this type of case, and referred to the fact that the defendant had admitted in cross-examination that he was a homosexual."

NOTES

The case referred to by Lord Parker C.J., *Thompson v. The King* [1918] A.C. 221 contains the following passage:

"A thief, a cheat, a coiner, or housebreaker is only a particular specimen of the genus rogue and though no doubt each keeps to his own line of business, they all alike possess the by no means extraordinary mental characteristic that they propose somehow to get their living dishonestly. So common a characteristic is not a recognisable mark of the individual. Persons, however, who commit the offences now under consideration seek the habitual gratification of a particular perverted lust, which not only takes them out of the class of ordinary men gone wrong, but stamps them with the hallmark of a specialised and extraordinary class as much as if they carried on their bodies some physical peculiarity."

Thus, where (homo)sexual offences were concerned, it was considered relevant to a charge simply to know that a person was a homosexual. The English courts have now retreated from that rather extreme view—see especially *R. v. Boardman* [1975] A.C. 421, *R. v. Novac* (1976) 65 Cr.App.R. 107 (C.A.)— and it now seems to be accepted that proof of homosexuality or indeed of the commission of previous "homosexual" offences, is not of itself relevant to prove commission of such offences (see also Chapter 9). Compare, however, the recent Scottish case of *H.M.A. v. Beggs (No. 3)*, 2001 S.C.C.R. 891, considered further below, Chapter 9.

6. Dickie v. H.M.A.
(1897) 2 Adam 331

LORD JUSTICE-CLERK (MACDONALD): "Where a woman maintains that she has been indecently attacked, it is competent, upon notice being given, to attack her character for chastity, and to put questions to her involving the accusation of unchastity. And in such cases it has been held competent for the accused to prove that the witness voluntarily yielded to his embraces a short time before the alleged criminal attack. That such proof should be allowed is only consistent with the clearest grounds of justice, for, in considering the question whether an attempt at intercourse be criminal, and to what extent criminal, it is plainly a relevant matter of enquiry on what terms the parties were immediately before the time of the alleged crime. Further, it seems a relevant subject of enquiry whether the woman was at the time a person of reputed bad moral character, as bearing upon her credibility when alleging that she has been subjected to criminal violence by one desiring to have intercourse with her. Such evidence may seriously affect the inferences to be drawn from her conduct at the time. But such evidence is something very different from evidence of individual acts of unchastity with other men at an interval of time. I am not aware that such evidence has ever been allowed, and indeed it could only be allowed upon the footing that a female who yields her person to one man will presumably do so to any man—a proposition which is quite untenable. A woman may not be virtuous, but it would be a most unwarrantable assumption that she could not therefore resist, and resist to the uttermost, an attempt to have connexion with her by any man who might choose to endeavour to obtain possession of her person, and to whom she might have no intention to yield. Every woman is entitled to protection from attack upon her person. Even a prostitute may be held to be ravished if the proof establishes a rape, although she may admit that she is a prostitute. Accordingly, it does not seem to me that the relaxation of the ordinary rules of evidence should be carried any further than it has been in former cases; and that while it is competent to prove a general bad repute at the time of the offence, or to prove that the woman said to have been attacked had yielded her person recently to the same man, it is not competent to prove individual acts of unchastity with other men. Whether proof of such unchastity might be allowed if it occurred just before and practically on the same occasion, I do not say. Such a case might be held as falling within the doctrine of the competency of proof of all matters forming part of the *res gestae*."

NOTES

Another area of controversy has been in relation to the relevance of the sexual "character" of complainers in trials for sexual offences. In *Dickie*, Lord Justice-Clerk Macdonald appeared to take a relatively strict view of the relevance of such evidence. (Do you agree with him that it is relevant in a charge of rape to show that the complainer recently "yielded her person" to the same man?) He did recognise, however, that there might be exceptions to his general rule, and in any event it seems that the rule was honoured more in the breach than in the observance (see "Scottish Law Commission Report" No. 78, para. 3.8). In particular, evidence of "sexual character", which Lord Macdonald was prepared to allow as being relevant only to the complainer's credibility, seems frequently to have been admitted in relation to the quite separate issue of consent. In any event, one might reasonably wonder what relevance a person's sexual history might have to the question of his or her veracity. In 1985, following the Scottish Law Commission's Report on the matter, changes were made to the law to limit the extent to which such complainers may be questioned about their past sexual conduct or character (now contained in the Criminal Procedure (Scotland) Act 1995, ss.274 and 275—see Chapter 10). A recent study cast doubt on the effectiveness of this reform.

7. Brown, Burman and Jamieson
Sex Crimes on Trial (Edinburgh) 1993, p.205

"A key objective of the [1985] legislation was to break the link between sexual immorality and credibility and, hence, to outlaw the notion that because somebody was sexually promiscuous they were also a liar. It has already been noted that this aim can be sabotaged by the introduction of sexual history evidence through other successful appeals to credibility. But a more common form of damage to this intention can be done by the routine use the defence makes of attacks on a complainer's character which are not explicitly sexual yet nonetheless have sexual connotations.

It is in the interests of the defence to suggest simultaneously that the complainer is both a liar and the type of person who would have sex with anybody anywhere. Many were adept at employing cumulative questioning during the course of cross-examination, using non-sexual character evidence as the building bricks in the construction of 'bad sexual character'. 'You are often out late? You drink regularly? You were wearing a low cut dress? Have you ever taken drugs? Are you in the habit of swearing? You are an unmarried mother? Where were your children? Do you often go to this type of pub? How would you describe the discos you go to? You went to a pub on your own? You were happy to get into a car with a strange man?'

Interviews made it clear that there was no consensus among legal practitioners concerning whether such strategies do contravene rules of evidence. Some conceded that they might be dealt with under the exclusion, 'not of good character in sexual matters', other thought not.

The Scottish Law Commission's original draft Bill clearly did cover 'bad character' precisely because of the difficulty of distinguishing sexual character and general character, but it was amended to refer specifically to sexual character. There is no general will among the legal profession to see such attacks stopped despite their prejudicial effect. A number of defence interviewees freely admitted that they would do what they could to suggest that a woman was of 'easy virtue' precisely because they believed that juries were swayed by it.

A generally held view among practitioners was that the defence was inhibited from making character attacks on complainers because they would then face the prospect of the prosecution in turn attacking their client's character. This was not borne out by observation of trials . . .

FEMINIST ISSUES NOT TAKEN ON BOARD

Previous sexual acts with the accused are regarded as being relevant to consent by many (but not all) legal professionals who argue that if a complainer has consented to sex with the accused in the past, then it is more likely she or he will have consented on the occasion in question. The Scottish Law Commission gave tacit support to the view that consent in the past suggests consent in the present. Critics of this reasoning, particularly Rape Crisis Centres, argue that it gives credence to the view that a woman who has had sexual intercourse with a particular man then enters into a permanent contract, rather than recognising that sexual intercourse has to be negotiated on each and every occasion. For example, the judicial statement (case 167), 'There is no reason why a husband should assume his wife is not consenting to intercourse unless she makes it abundantly clear to him she is refusing consent', presents marriage as making a wife available to her husband without any need on his part to check whether or not she wants to have sex. From the perspective of the feminist critique of such views, the legislation has done nothing to challenge the persistence of a view of women which is ultimately inimical to at least some of the aims of the legislation.

In addition to asking about any past relationships, the defence often suggests a recent history of sexually interested or provocative behaviour on the part of the complainer towards the accused. Again, not all legal practitioners accepted that such evidence was relevant but the majority saw it as indicative of consent. Clearly many defence advocates believed that juries could be convinced of consent by presenting such behaviour between the complainer and the accused as dancing together, drinking together, having an intimate conversation, kissing, cuddling, engaging in lewd banter as evidence of an interest in sex, suggesting sexual intercourse is a natural conclusion. In rape and rape related cases, the defence typically suggested consent through this route.

In observed cases this did not result in intervention or counterattack by the prosecution that such behaviour is not always followed by sexual intercourse and need not be intended or interpreted as a desire for intercourse. To treat such behaviour uncritically as indicative of consent is perilously close to condoning the view that if a woman engages in sexual behaviour that is short of sexual intercourse—kissing and flirting—then she is 'leading the man on' and cannot expect to be believed (either at the time or later) when she says 'no'. The legislators and the legislation made no attempt to tackle this view. However, if the defence is correct, such views help considerably in gaining acquittals for their clients and thus work against the aim of reducing wrongful, not proven, or not guilty verdicts."

NOTES

It seems remarkable that attitudes to evidence of previous sexual conduct had developed little since 1897. *Dickie* appears to represent an attitude to such evidence in some respects more enlightened than the views of certain practitioners interviewed by Brown *et al*. There are relatively few reported Scottish cases on the new provisions. However, it is arguable that public awareness and public opinion has now moved decisively in favour of a more progressive approach. In *Bremner v. H.M.A.*, 1992 S.C.C.R. 476, a rape case, the trial judge disallowed questioning about a relationship between the accused and the complainer which ended some eight months prior to the incident. His decision was upheld on appeal. In *Thomson v. H.M.A.*, 2001 S.C.C.R. 162, the High Court again upheld the decision of the judge at first instance to exclude evidence that the complainer had previously made false allegations of rape. It may be significant, however, that in both cases the High Court emphasised the extent of the judge's discretion in relation to such evidence. There is apparently room for different judicial views to be taken. Do you agree that the evidence in *Bremner* and *Thomson* should have been excluded?

It is clear, however, that the relevance of evidence, as opposed to the relevance of a charge, cannot usually be determined in advance of trial. The following case is a very rare example of a case in which the accused objected to a particular line of evidence, very fairly intimated to the defence in the terms of the indictment, prior to trial. This case should be compared with *McKenna v. H.M.A.*, 2000 S.L.T. 508, Chapter 7, which holds that it is only in exceptional cases that a decision can be taken in advance of trial that the admission of certain evidence will lead to an unfair trial, and *Nelson v. H.M.A.*, 1994 S.L.T. 389, Chapter 9.

8. H.M.A. v. Carson
1997 S.L.T. 1119

An accused person was charged on indictment with breach of the peace by clandestinely taking photographs of pupils at a primary school. The libel also included the averments: "and it will be shown that you had in your possession writings of which you were the author relating to the commission of serious sexual offences against children which offences were committed in a context of taking photographs adjacent to a school playground". At a first diet, the sheriff sustained an objection to the relevancy of these averments and deleted them from the libel on the ground that they were solely intended to indicate the accused's intention or motive, which was irrelevant to breach of the peace. The Crown appealed, arguing that the averments were included to give due notice of a line of evidence which the Crown intended to lead, and that any issue of relevancy should be decided at the trial. Before the appeal court the accused's counsel renewed the concession made before the sheriff that no objection would be taken to the evidence on the basis of lack of notice, but contended that the allegations should not be restored to the indictment as they could be prejudicial to the accused.

The following opinion of the court was delivered by Lord Prosser:

OPINION OF THE COURT— "On February 14, 1997, a first diet was held before the sheriff at Arbroath in relation to an indictment against Darren Charles Carson. The indictment contained three charges, of which only the first was and is in point. At the first diet, it was submitted on behalf of the accused that a passage in charge one on the indictment was irrelevant. The sheriff upheld that submission, and ordered deletion of the passage in question. Her Majesty's Advocate now appeals, with leave, to the High Court of Justiciary against that decision, on the ground that the sheriff erred in law in holding that the passage was irrelevant.

The substance of charge one on the indictment was that: 'between August 1 and October 28, 1996, both dates inclusive, at Rosebank Primary School, Rosebank Road, Dundee, you did conduct yourself in a disorderly manner, clandestinely take photographs of pupils at said school . . . and you did commit a breach of the peace'. Those are the whole terms of the charge remaining after deletion of the passage which the sheriff has held to be irrelevant. That passage, as it originally appeared in the indictment, was in the following terms: 'and it will be shown that you had in your possession writings of which you were the author relating to the commission of serious sexual offences against children which offences were committed in a context of taking photographs adjacent to a school playground such as Rosebank Primary School'.

It is to be noted that in this original form, the passage fails to specify the place where the accused was said to have possessed the writings in question. This point of specification was cured by amendment, specifying an address in Glenconnor Drive, Dundee, and another address in Montrose. That change did not however meet the main argument for the accused, which was to the effect that the whole passage was irrelevant.

In view of the positions adopted both by defence counsel and by the advocate depute, before the sheriff and on appeal, it is unnecessary and indeed inappropriate for us to consider any substantive issue of relevancy. Before the sheriff, it was accepted on behalf of the Crown that intention or motive was irrelevant to a charge of breach of the peace, so that the presence of the disputed passage in the charge cannot be justified as a basis for importing evidence of intention or motive. Moreover, in this court it was accepted by the advocate depute that the matters set out in the disputed passage did not constitute a constituent part of the alleged breach of the peace: while the passage had been located between the reference to clandestinely taking photographs of pupils at the school, and the final words 'and you did commit a breach of the peace', the purpose of their inclusion was not to specify a part of the breach of the peace, but merely to give notice on the face of the indictment of a line of evidence which the Crown would intend to lead. As a matter of draftsmanship, and since their only purpose was to give proper notice, the words could well have been located at the end of the charge, after specification of the crime. Moreover, notwithstanding the deletion of the disputed passage from the charge, the Crown indicated, as the sheriff notes at the end of his report, that it intended nevertheless to lead evidence of 'the writings', and counsel for the defence undertook not to object to such evidence on the basis of lack of notice in the libel. That remained the position of both parties at appeal, although both parties emphasised that all issues of relevancy (as opposed to due notice) were regarded as remaining open for objection and argument at the trial, in relation to specific documents or passages in documents, and in the context of the other evidence adduced before the jury.

The advocate depute submitted that the real question was not one about the presence or absence of the words on the face of the charge. Their purpose having been one of giving due notice, and the defence having accepted that no objection as to want of notice would be taken, there was no need for the words to be restored. What did matter was that the sheriff had determined the matter as one of relevancy, saying that he was unable to see the relevance to the charge of the passage complained of, and that as far as he could see, the only purpose of including the averment was to indicate motive. The decision having been taken upon that basis, there was at least a risk that if it were left unchallenged, issues of relevancy might be regarded at trial as having been predetermined, so that the Crown would be disabled from pursuing lines of evidence, covered by the excluded words, which it contended were indeed relevant. The advocate depute submitted that material of the type described in the disputed passage could be relevant in a number of ways. The sheriff's decision on relevancy (as distinct from the technical exclusion of the words from the charge) should stand only if defence counsel contended, and this court were persuaded, that there were no circumstances or ways in which any writing of the type identified in the disputed passage, or any part of any such writing, might be relevant at trial.

Defence counsel did not seek to persuade us of any such all-embracing proposition. He acknowledged that the relevancy of any particular writing, or part of any writing, was a matter which could and should only properly be considered and determined at trial, under reference to the specific matter which the Crown might seek to prove, in the context of all the other evidence adduced. It was, however, contended not only that such matters could properly be decided then in the absence of the jury, but that in view of the possibly prejudicial effect of including such words in the indictment (when nothing might in fact be held relevant) the words should not be restored to the indictment. Sufficient notice could have been given simply by producing the allegedly relevant documents. But in any event, in the events which had happened, ample notice had been given, and the potentially prejudicial words should now be left out.

The advocate depute did not resist this proposed course. We are satisfied that in advance of trial, and without reference to the writings in question, it is impossible to hold that the material identified in the disputed passage is irrelevant. We are satisfied that issues of relevancy should be determined at trial. To that end, the sheriff's decision that the disputed passage is irrelevant is recalled; and to that extent, the appeal succeeds.

We are however satisfied that the restoration of the disputed passage to the indictment would be potentially prejudicial, and is in the circumstances unnecessary. We do not think it appropriate, having regard to the rather special circumstances of this case and the absence of any remaining dispute on this point, to express any general view as to how the need for fair notice and the risk of prejudice might best be reconciled in any particular situations where there is a potential dispute as to the relevancy of material which the Crown include, or consider including, in a charge for the sole purpose of giving notice of this kind.

We should add finally that we have intentionally abstained from any discussion as to how material of the kind covered in the disputed passage might turn out to be relevant. While the advocate depute indicated certain ways in which he contended that the material could be relevant, it was not necessary, in the context of the appeal hearing which took place, for defence counsel either to consider these particular examples or to embark upon a theoretical consideration of lines of evidence which might or might not be relevant to proof of the charge. The whole issue of relevancy must therefore be left at large, for the sheriff at trial."

NOTES

See also *Cowan v. H.M.A.*, High Court of Justiciary, May 3, 2001, unreported. *Cowan* was a case involving a single charge of lewd and libidinous practices in which evidence was led as to the practice of "grooming" children for the purposes of sexual abuse. The evidence was described by the appeal court as "wholly irrelevant".

Difficult cases aside, it will in most cases be obvious that evidence tendered is or is not relevant. Eyewitness evidence of an alleged incident (usually referred to as "direct evidence") will almost always be relevant. Similarly, where the condition or nature of some item or thing is in issue, the production of that object will usually be regarded as relevant. It is in relation to circumstantial evidence that problems may arise. Circumstantial evidence relates to circumstantial or evidential facts; facts which are not themselves in issue, but which have a bearing on the facts in issue. Murphy, *Evidence* (5th ed., 1995), p.5 distinguishes direct and circumstantial evidence in the following way:

"Direct evidence is evidence which requires no mental process on the part of the tribunal of fact in order to draw the conclusion sought by the proponent of the evidence, other than acceptance of the evidence itself. Circumstantial evidence is evidence from which the desired conclusion may be drawn, but which requires the tribunal of fact not only to accept the evidence presented, but also to draw an inference from it. For example, if D is charged with robbery of a bank, and is seen by W running from the bank clutching a wad of banknotes, W's evidence is direct evidence that D was running away from the bank, and circumstantial evidence that D committed the robbery. To arrive at the latter conclusion, the jury must draw certain inferences from the facts perceived by W. This example also shows that circumstantial evidence is not necessarily inferior to direct evidence, if the inference required is obvious and compelling."

9. Langan v. H.M.A.
1989 S.C.C.R. 379

The accused in *Langan* was charged with the murder of an old man who was bludgeoned to death with a blunt instrument. The only evidence against him was that of a fingerprint—his fingerprint—found in a bloodstain by the kitchen sink in the victim's house.

LORD JUSTICE-CLERK (ROSS): "There is no doubt that in appropriate cases fingerprint evidence on its own may be sufficient to entitle a jury to draw an inference that the person whose print it is may be implicated in the commission of the offence. Plainly in this case the jury were entitled to draw the inference that the appellant had been present in the house at a time when the blood of the deceased was still in a liquid state. The question is whether they were entitled to draw any inferences beyond that and to draw the inference that he had been in the house at the time when the crime had been committed and indeed that it was he who had perpetrated the crime. In our view much would in this connection turn upon whether any explanation was put forward by the appellant for the presence of his fingerprint. In this case not only was there an absence of any explanation from the appellant as to how his fingerprint got onto the tap, but he really put forward the position that there was no explanation because he maintained that he had never been in the house. That was his reply to the police. Accordingly he negatived any question of an explanation being put forward for his print being there. In these circumstances we have come to the conclusion that the jury in this case were entitled to draw the inference from the fingerprint not merely that he had been present in the house when the blood was in a liquid state but that it was he who had committed the offence and, as the Crown put it, that the blood had got to the sink when he was cleaning himself up after committing the murder. We accept that the evidence was, as the trial judge put it, minimal, but for the foregoing reasons we are satisfied that the jury were entitled to draw the inference which they obviously did draw and that the trial judge had been well founded in holding that there was sufficient evidence in this case."

NOTES

A comparable case, that of *Stewart Abercromby*, is recorded by Hume (Hume, ii, 386)—"The circumstance which chiefly served to convict him of the murder, was that of his having left his hat in the tavern where he and the deceased had been together, just before the mortal rencounter." Compare *Welsh v. H.M.A.*, 1992 S.C.C.R. 108, in which the crucial evidence was DNA evidence showing that blood found at the scene of a killing involving the use of a knife was that of the accused. However, in *Welsh* there was also evidence that the accused had sustained a fairly serious cut to his arm at around the time the offence took place. There was no such additional evidence in *Langan*. How does *Langan* square with the presumption of innocence, and the correlative idea that the burden of proof always rests on the Crown in a criminal case? See Chapter 2.

It should be noted that each individual item of evidence in a case need not be incriminating. Where a case relies on circumstantial evidence "the question is not whether each of the several circumstances 'points' by itself towards [the facts in issue] but whether the several circumstances taken together are capable of supporting the inference." (*Little v. H.M.A.*, 1983 S.C.C.R. 56 at 61; see also *Morton v. H.M.A.*, 1938 J.C. 50 per Lord Justice-Clerk Aitchison at 52, quoting Hume—"the aptitude and coherence of the several circumstances often as fully confirm the truth of the story, as if all the witnesses were deponing to the same facts".)

10. Norval v. H.M.A.
1978 J.C. 70

The charge in *Norval* was one of armed robbery from Ruchil Hospital in Glasgow. The evidence against the accused was wholly circumstantial.

LORD JUSTICE-GENERAL (EMSLIE): "Before turning to Mr Kerrigan's principal argument, we think it right to indicate what the evidence was on which the Crown case depended. It was a chain of circumstantial evidence and the chain consisted of the following links. The first link was that the getaway car used by the raiders at the hospital was identified by eye-witnesses as a blue car with black roof, the latter part of its number being 541M. The second link in the chain is that Mr Norval, the applicant, owned a blue car with a black roof at the relevant time and the number of that car was NYS 541M. The third link in the chain is that on top of the wall of the hospital over which, according to the evidence, the raiders came in making their escape, there was red anti-climb paint. The fourth link consisted of the finding of a spot of identical paint on the front passenger seat trim of the applicant's car NYS 541M. The fifth link consists of the evidence of a witness Philip Henry. His evidence falls into two parts. The first part of his evidence consisted of an account of a visit from the applicant when the applicant left with him a bag containing certain things. Mr Henry looked in the bag and saw that the things inside the bag might be regarded as of an incriminating character because what Mr Henry claimed to have seen were guns, masks and gloves. The bag did not remain with Mr Henry for long, however, because in the second chapter of his evidence Mr Henry spoke of another visit by Mr Norval who claimed that the police were after him and that he had better take the bag away and dispose of it. The bag was accordingly removed from Mr Henry's control by the applicant, according to the evidence of Mr Henry. Later when he met the applicant the applicant said to Mr Henry, according to Mr Henry, 'I had to dump the stuff in a lay-by at Inchinnan.'

The next link consists of the finding by Ronald Barney, who was out for a walk with his dog, of a bag containing guns, masks and gloves at a lay-by at Inchinnan. The final link is this. Among the gloves in the bag was a white pair, on each of which there were traces of red paint established by forensic evidence to be similar in colour, general and microscopic appearance, texture and chemical composition, to the anti-climb paint on the hospital wall and to the red paint found on the trim of the front passenger seat of the applicant's car.

For the applicant the principal submission was that the chain of circumstantial evidence was defective in two respects. The first was that there was no evidence from any witness, speaking to the events inside the hospital at the time of the robbery or to the escape of the raiders over the wall, that any raider was wearing gloves. The second was that according to Mr Henry he did not see white gloves in the bag when he looked inside it while it was in his possession. Because of these defects or breaks in the chain there was not, said Mr Kerrigan, sufficient evidence in law to entitle the jury to hold that the applicant was one of the gang which had carried out the robbery at the hospital.

This submission in our judgment is without substance. The eyewitness evidence as to whether the raiders wore or did not wear gloves was quite neutral. The question was not raised with any of them. The point of importance is that the forensic evidence provided a clear link between the white gloves found in the bag at Inchinnan and the top of the hospital wall over which the escaping raiders climbed, and the jury were well entitled to conclude upon that evidence that the gloves were worn by a raider in the escape over the wall—an escape which resulted incidentally in the deposit of identical paint upon the inside of the applicant's car. As to Henry's evidence about the gloves he saw in the bag before the applicant took it away, this does not weaken the chain at all. It was not essential to the strength of the chain that Henry should have seen white gloves in the bag. What matters is (i) that the applicant, according to Henry's evidence, took the bag away to dispose of it and reported that he had dumped 'the stuff' in a lay-by at Inchinnan and (ii) that when the bag was found in that lay-by there was evidence for the jury's consideration that it then contained the white gloves with the incriminating paint marks upon them. In our judgment the evidence before the jury was quite sufficient to entitle the jury to hold that the applicant participated in the robbery."

NOTES

Norval is an example of a case in which the facts in issue were proved by circumstantial evidence alone, as was *Langan v. H.M.A.,* above. See also *Leandro v. H.M.A.,* 1994 S.C.C.R. 703; and *Gallagher v. H.M.A.,* 2000 S.C.C.R. 634. In *Gallagher* the accused was charged with assault. He was known to have been with the complainer and a co-accused in the house shortly before the assault took place. He was seen running away from the house shortly after the offence took place. He was found to have blood on his trainers about a week after the incident. In the absence of evidence that he was wearing the trainers at the time of the assault, or whose blood it was, it was held that the evidence was not strong enough to support an inference of guilt. In *Norval* the various adminicles of evidence against the accused were said to form a chain leading to the conclusion averred by the Crown. The "chain analogy" is commonly used in the Scottish case law. It is inaccurate, however, and may be misleading to describe circumstantial evidence in this way.

11.   Gillespie v. Macmillan
1957 J.C. 31

This was a case brought under the Road Traffic Acts and involved a charge of speeding. Controversy centred on proof of the speed at which the accused was travelling. Police officers had measured a set distance on a stretch of road. One officer stood at each end of this measured piece of road, and each had a stopwatch. When the accused passed the first officer, the latter started his stopwatch. When the accused passed the second officer, the second watch was also started. The officers then simultaneously stopped the watches in the presence of the accused, and the difference in the times recorded was taken to be the time in which the measured distance was covered by the accused.

LORD JUSTICE-GENERAL (CLYDE): "It should be observed that in a case of circumstantial evidence it is not a matter of one witness corroborating another, for each may be speaking to a quite separate and independent fact. It is the mutual interlacing and coincidence of these separate facts which can establish the case against the accused.

In the present appeal the Court is dealing with just such a case of circumstantial evidence. The appellant is not accused of passing the entrance to or exit from the measured distance at over 30 miles per hour. The offence consists in what he did between the points of entrance to and exit from that measured distance. The time at which he entered into it and the time at which he left it are separate links in a chain which alone can establish whether the offence was committed. These separate links are part of a single consecutive chain, and are clearly interlaced with one another by the steps taken by the three policemen in their arrangements for ascertaining the speed and identity of vehicles passing over the measured distance. In these circumstances there is no need for separate corroboration for each link in the chain, and a conviction can stand although only one policeman speaks to the time of entry onto the measured distance and one to the time of exit therefrom. Any other conclusion would require to be based upon the view that each separate fact in a case must be proved by two witnesses, a proposition which has been negatived over and over again. It would follow in law from this that the decision in *Scott v. Jameson*, 1914 S.C. (J) 187 is sound in law and should be followed. The material facts in that case are the same as those in the present one, and the method adopted by the police to ascertain the speed of the vehicles over the measured distance in each case was substantially the same. As Lord Guthrie put it:

'If, in order to establish a charge, evidence is only tendered regarding one fact, that fact must be proved by two witnesses. But if several facts require to be proved and these form a consecutive chain, leading to one conclusion, then it appears to me that each may be proved by one witness. If they do not form a consecutive chain leading to one conclusion, then it may be that each of these facts will require to be proved by two witnesses'."

NOTES

Compare *Pervez v. Clark*, 2001 S.C.C.R. 138, and *Hogg v. MacNeill*, 2001 S.L.T. 873. It will be observed that in *Gillespie*, other things being equal, proof of the facts alleged by the police would result necessarily in the conviction of the accused. There was no room for inference or conjecture. Distance divided by time equals speed. Conversely, failure to prove either of the stopwatch times would necessarily have resulted in an acquittal since there would be no basis for the calculation of speed. The court was thus treating as circumstantial evidence, matters which were logically crucial to the case. The stopwatch times should have been proved by corroborated evidence, but in this case the evidence of a single officer as to each time was accepted (see Chapter 5 on Sufficiency of Evidence, and see Wilson, "The Logic of Corroboration" (1960) S.L.R. 101; "Corroboration of Evidence in Scottish Criminal

Law" (Contributed) 1958 S.L.T. (News) 137). The court's reference to a chain of circumstantial evidence appears to have led it into error. The chain analogy is still commonly referred to in Scots cases—as the extract from *Norval* clearly demonstrates. But the chain analogy is an unhappy one, since a case will fail if one link in a chain of evidence should fail. This is not the effect circumstantial evidence is generally thought to have. In *R. v. Exall* (1866) 4 F. & F. 922, Pollock C.B. likened circumstantial evidence to a cord or rope:

> "One strand of the cord might be insufficient to sustain the weight, but three stranded together may be quite of sufficient strength. Thus it may be in circumstantial evidence—there may be a combination of circumstances, no one of which would raise a reasonable conviction, or more than a mere suspicion; but on the whole, taken together, may create a strong conclusion of guilt, that is, with as much certainty as human affairs can require or admit."

The difference between facts in issue and evidential facts is thus related to the difference between deductive and inductive reasoning. Proof of the facts in issue is equivalent to proof of the premises of a syllogism, which proof leads logically to acceptance of the conclusion. Acceptance of evidential facts, on the other hand, does not lead inevitably to acceptance of the facts in issue, but instead requires an assessment, based on common sense or experience, to be made of the probabilities arising from those facts.

Chapter 2

THE BURDEN OF PROOF

---

1. Dickinson v. Minister of Pensions
[1953] 1 Q.B. 228

This case was one of a series arising out of claims for pensions by war widows. Royal Warrant, 1949 Article 4 specified that where a claim was made, it was for the Ministry of Pensions to prove that the claimant was not entitled to a pension. In this case, however, the claim was in respect of a person who died more than seven years after the termination of his war service. This situation was covered by Article 5 of the Royal Warrant, which made no reference to the incidence of the burden of proof. The question, therefore, was whether it was for the Minister of Pensions to prove that the claim was invalid, or for the claimant to prove that the death was "due to or substantially hastened by an injury which was attributable to service". It was held that, in this situation, the onus of proof was on the claimant.

ORMEROD J.: "It is, I think, axiomatic in the administration of our law that, if a person thinks he has a claim against another person, or against a Ministry, the duty is on him to establish that claim. The mere fact that an Act of Parliament does not state that that duty is on him, if it establishes a right, must, I think, automatically establish that the duty is on him to prove what he thinks is his right before he can succeed in his claim. That is, I think, recognised by those who framed this warrant because Article 4 of the warrant, having set out the conditions under which a man may be entitled to a pension, provides specifically that the onus of proof shall in no case be on the claimant; in other words the onus of proof shall be on the Ministry or on the respondents to the claim. That has been done for the specific purpose of providing an exception to what is clearly an accepted rule.

This has not been done in Article 5. In Article 5 no exception is made, and there is no provision that there shall be no onus of proof on the claimant. Therefore, on the face of it, it must, I think, follow that the claimant, in order to succeed, must satisfy the court or the tribunal (whichever body has to decide the matter) that the conditions which entitle him to an award have been satisfied. But Article 5 goes much further than that because it provides in paragraph (2):

'A disablement or death shall be certified . . . if it is shown that the conditions set out in this article and applicable hereto are fulfilled.'

[Counsel for the claimant] argues that there is nothing there to say who shall show that the conditions of the articles are fulfilled; that duty might be on the claimant, or it might be on the Ministry, or it might be on other unspecified persons. That, I think, again is an argument which cannot be accepted. It appears to me clear that, where it is provided that a pension shall be awarded if it is shown that the conditions set out in the article are fulfilled, it must mean that if it is shown by the person making the claim that the conditions applicable thereto are fulfilled."

NOTES

The incidence of the onus or burden of proof is not strictly part of the law of evidence at all, but is rather a product of the substantive law. As noted in the previous chapter, there are a number of elements in every court action which must be proved in order that the case should succeed. These are the facts in issue. A pursuer in an action of reparation for personal injury, for example, must show in the particular circumstances of the case that the defender owed him a duty of care, that that duty was breached, and that the breach caused the injury and loss of which he is complaining. By raising the action, the pursuer puts those facts in issue, and accordingly, as the extract from *Dickinson v. Minister of Pensions* makes clear, must accept the onus of proving those facts to the required standard. The person who asserts a particular state of facts must, in general, prove it. Failure to discharge the onus in relation to any of the facts in issue will lead to failure in the case. It is not, however, only the pursuer who may be required to prove certain issues. By raising specific defences, such as *volenti non fit injuria*, contributory negligence, or frustration, a defender puts those matters in issue and must prove them, if the defences are to succeed.

2.   SS Baron Vernon v. SS Metagama
1928 S.C. (H.L.) 21

The *SS Metagama* collided with the *SS Baron Vernon* in the River Clyde. The latter ship was badly damaged and was beached to prevent her sinking. However, the ship slipped off into the channel again and eventually sank. In an action of damages brought by the owners of the *Baron Vernon* against the owners of the *Metagama* the latter admitted sole responsibility for the collision, but maintained that much of the damage to the *Baron Vernon* was caused not by the collision, but by incompetent handling of the ship after the collision.

VISCOUNT HALDANE: "I have had the advantage of reading the judgment of my noble and learned friend Viscount Dunedin. With his statement of the facts in the appeal, down to that of the result of the reclaiming note to the Second Division, I am in full agreement, and with his statement of the law which follows, so far as the principle is concerned. The question is whether, after the original fault which started matters, there has been a *novus actus interveniens* which was the direct cause of the final damage. Here also I am in agreement with him. I think further that the question whether there was failure to use the engines of the *Baron Vernon* when she was on the north bank, in the first position, is purely one of fact.

But I do not agree that it has been proved that there was such a *novus actus* assuming the form of negligence on the part of those in charge of the *Baron Vernon* in not using the engines. Negligence was not established in the other particulars alleged against those in charge. Apart from the question of not using the engines, there were three other allegations of negligence made against those in charge of the *Baron Vernon*, when in the first position on the north bank. It was alleged at the trial that they should have obtained the assistance of tugs; next, that the steamer should have had her moorings out; and, thirdly, that she should have filled her aft ballast-tanks. If, contended the appellants, these precautions had been taken, the steamer would have remained [beached], and could have been easily and inexpensively salved. But, on these three allegations, the Lord Ordinary, after hearing the evidence, exonerated them, and found the facts in favour of the respondents. It is only in the averment of negligence in not using the engines that he decided against the respondents, and the learned counsel for the appellants are stated in the judgment of the Lord Justice-Clerk to have abstained from challenging the judgment against them on the other grounds referred to.

I therefore turn at once to the crucial question in the case—was there fault in those responsible for the ship in reference to the use of her engines when she was on the north bank? Now, this is a question of evidence, and, in weighing the evidence in order to draw the proper inferences, there are certain principles which have to be kept steadily in view. When a collision takes place by the fault of the defending ship, the damage is recoverable, in an action for damages, if it is the natural and reasonable result of the negligent act, and it will assume this character if it can be shown to be such a consequence as in the ordinary course of things would flow from the situation which the offending ship had created. Further, what those in charge of the injured ship do to save it may be mistaken, but, if they do whatever they do reasonably, although unsuccessfully, their mistaken judgment may be a natural consequence for which the offending ship is responsible, just as much as is any physical occurrence. Reasonable human conduct is part of the ordinary course of things which extends to the reasonable conduct of those who have sustained the damage and who are seeking to save further loss . . . It follows that the burden lies on the negligent ship to show by clear evidence that the subsequent damage arose from negligence or great want of skill on the part of those on board the vessel damaged. It is their duty to do all they can to minimise that damage, but they do not fail in this duty if they only commit an error of judgment in deciding on the best course in difficult circumstances . . .

The burden of showing that the chain of causation started by the initial injury has been broken lies on the defenders. In order to discharge this burden they must prove that the breach in the chain was due to unwarrantable action, and not merely to action on an erroneous opinion by people who have bona fide made a mistake while trying to do their best, which is all that is shown to have happened in the present case. This seems to me to be the standard in the light of which we must examine the evidence of what occurred in the position on the north bank."

3. Joseph Constantine Steamship Line Ltd v. Imperial Smelting Corporation Ltd
[1942] A.C. 154

The appellants chartered a steamship to transport a cargo from South Australia to Europe. Before the ship could begin loading the cargo, it was destroyed by an explosion of "unprecedented character", probably originating in the ship's auxiliary boiler. The explosion was of such violence that the boiler travelled 164 feet, broke through two watertight bulkheads and pierced the shell-plating at the bow. No plausible explanation for the explosion could be found. It proved impossible to load the cargo and the respondents claimed damages from the appellants alleging breach of contract in failing to perform the charter-party. The appellant ship-owners claimed that the contract had been frustrated by the explosion. The arbiter in the dispute could not reach any conclusion on the evidence as to whether the explosion was caused by the negligence of the ship-owners or their employees and the question arose as to the onus of proof where frustration is alleged. The trial judge found that while it was up to the appellants to prove the frustrating event, it was not up to them to prove further that they had not been negligent. That was a matter for the respondents to aver and prove. The Court of Appeal reversed this decision and the matter came before the House of Lords.

VISCOUNT SIMON L.C.: "The question raised by the arbitrator's award is not whether the defence of frustration fails if the frustration is proved to be 'self-induced' (Lord Sumner), or 'due to the act or election of the party' (Lord Wright), or, to use Scott L.J.'s phrase 'brought into operation by his default'. The question here is where the onus of proof lies; *i.e.* whether, when a supervening event has been proved which would, apart from the defendant's 'default' put an end to the contract, and when at the end of the case no inference of 'default' exists and the evidence is equally consistent with either view, the defence fails because the defendant has not established affirmatively that the supervening event was not due to his default.

I may observe, in the first place, that, if this were correct, there must be many cases in which, although in truth frustration is complete and unavoidable, the defendant will be held liable because of his inability to prove a negative—in some cases, indeed, a whole series of negatives. Suppose that a vessel while on the high seas disappears completely during a storm. Can it be that the defence of frustration of the adventure depends on the owner's ability to prove that all his servants on board were navigating the ship with adequate skill and that there was no 'default' which brought about the catastrophe? Suppose that a vessel in convoy is torpedoed by the enemy and sinks immediately with all hands. Does the application of the doctrine require that the owners should affirmatively prove that those on board were keeping a good look-out, were obscuring lights, were steering as directed, and so forth? There is no reported case which requires us so to hold. The doctrine on which the defence of frustration depends is nowhere so stated as to place this onus of proof on the party relying on it . . .

The doctrine of discharge from liability by frustration has been explained in various ways—sometimes by speaking of the disappearance of a foundation which the parties assumed to be at the basis of their contract, sometimes as deduced from a rule arising from impossibility of performance, and sometimes as flowing from the inference of an implied term. Whichever way it is put, the legal consequence is the same. The most satisfactory basis, I think, on which the doctrine can be put is that it depends on an implied term in the contract of the parties . . .

If the matter is regarded in this way, the question is as to the construction of a contract taking into consideration its express and implied terms. The implied term in the present case may well be—'This contract is to cease to be binding if the vessel is disabled by an overpowering disaster, provided that disaster is not brought about by the default of either party.' This is very similar to an express exception of 'perils of the seas', as to which it is ancient law that by an implied term of the contract the ship-owner cannot rely on the exception if its operation was brought about either (a) by negligence of his servants, or (b) by his breach of the implied warranty of seaworthiness. If a ship sails and is never heard of again the ship-owner can claim protection for loss of the cargo under the express exception of perils of the seas. To establish that, must he go on to prove (a) that the perils were not caused by negligence of his servants, and (b) were not caused by any unseaworthiness? I think clearly not. He proves a prima facie case of loss by sea perils, and that he is within the exception. If the cargo owner wants to defeat that plea it is for him by rejoinder to allege and prove either negligence or unseaworthiness."

VISCOUNT MAUGHAM: "For the reasons above stated I have come to the conclusion, with all respect to the Court of Appeal, that their view is incorrect and ought not to prevail. Agreeing with the learned trial judge, I think the burden of proof in any particular case depends on the circumstances under which the claim arises. In general the rule which applies is '*Ei qui affirmat non ei qui negat incumbit probatio*'. It is an ancient rule founded on considerations of good sense and it should not be departed from without strong reasons. The position as to proof of non-responsibility for the event in such a case as the present is not very different from the position of a plaintiff in an action for negligence where contributory negligence on his part is alleged. In such a case the plaintiff must prove that there was some negligent act or omission on the part of the defendant which caused or materially contributed to the injury, but it is for the defendant to prove affirmatively, if he so contends, that there was contributory negligence on the part of the person injured, though here again the onus may easily be shifted: *Wakelin v. London & South Western Ry. Co.*; *Abrath v. North Eastern Ry. Co.* The mere circumstances of the occurrence which led to the event may be sufficient to supply prima facie evidence that the plaintiff is himself responsible for it, but if that is not so it is for the defendant to prove that which he alleges. My Lords, on this view of the law in relation to the onus of proof in a case where frustration is prima facie established, since the voyage admittedly became impossible, we still have to determine whether the facts found in the special case, in the absence of further evidence as to the cause of the explosion, are sufficient to lead to the conclusion that the appellants were to blame for the disaster. The respondents plainly were in no way to blame. The explosion of the auxiliary boiler took place on the appellants' ship, and no doubt it might have been due to a default on the part of the master or the crew . . .

Your Lordships have, of course, no knowledge of the course pursued as regards calling evidence in the arbitration. All that is known is that evidence was called, and that, as the result of it, the arbitrator was not satisfied that any of the servants of the appellants were guilty of any of the negligence alleged, nor did he find that there was any latent defect in the boiler not discoverable by due diligence, or that, if there were such a defect, it caused or contributed to the explosion of the boiler. It is true that he also stated that he was not satisfied that negligence on the part of the servants of the appellants did not cause or contribute to the disaster. That, in my view, amounts to a finding that, notwithstanding the evidence, there was a possibility that there had been negligence or default on the part of the servants of the appellants. If, however, I am right in the opinion above expressed that the onus of establishing absence of default did not rest on the appellants, the mere possibility of default on their part is not sufficient to disentitle them to rely on the principle of frustration. For these reasons I am of opinion that the appeal should be allowed and that the order of Atkinson J. should be restored with costs here and below."

NOTES

As Viscount Simon indicates in this case, it is thought that no party should be required to prove a negative proposition, given the practical and logical difficulties of doing so. This is also one aspect of the maxim *ei qui affirmat non ei qui negat incumbit probatio*, cited by Viscount Maugham. However, in *Cross on Evidence* (7th ed., 1990) p.123, Colin Tapper points out that:

> " . . . this must not be taken to mean that the onus of proof cannot lie upon a party who makes a negative allegation. If this were so, the application of the rule could be made to depend upon the language in which a case happened to be pleaded. For instance, a claim for damages for breach of covenant to keep a house in repair may be stated by saying, either that the defendant did not repair the house, or else that he allowed it to become dilapidated, but the legal burden is borne by the plaintiff, however the claim is expressed."

In some circumstances, however, the law has imposed upon parties the burden of proving a negative, usually because of some overriding practical interest or consideration of policy. It should be noted that in the following extract, the correct view of the law is to be found not in the powerful speech given by Lord Reid, but in that of Lord Guest which follows it.

4.   Nimmo v. Alexander Cowan and Son Ltd
1967 S.C. (H.L.) 79

The pursuer in this case sustained serious injury when a bale of pulp which he was unloading from a railway wagon tipped over. He brought a case against his employers under section 29 of the Factories Act 1961, which required that every place of work must, so far as reasonably practicable, be made and kept safe for those working there. The pursuer's advisers pleaded the case on simple averments that the working place in question was not made and kept safe. The defenders challenged this approach, arguing that in addition, it was for the pursuer to show that it would have been reasonably practicable to make and keep the workplace safer than it was. The majority held that it was for the defender to show that all reasonable steps had been taken to make and keep the workplace safe.

LORD REID (DISSENTING): "A considerable number of statutes prescribe, or enable Regulations to prescribe, what steps an employer or occupier must take to promote the safety of persons working in factories, mines and other premises where work is carried on. Sometimes the duty imposed is absolute. Certain things must be done and it is no defence that it was impossible to prevent an accident because it was caused by a latent defect which could not have been discovered. Still less is it a defence to prove that it was impracticable to carry out the statutory requirement. But in many cases the statutory duty is qualified in one way or another, so that no offence is committed if it is impracticable or not reasonably practicable to comply with the duty. Unfortunately there is great variety in the drafting of such provisions. Sometimes the duty is expressed in absolute terms in one section and in another section it is provided that it shall be a defence to prove that it was impracticable or not reasonably practicable to comply with the duty. Sometimes the form adopted is that the occupier shall so far as reasonably practicable do certain things. Sometimes it is that the occupier shall take all practicable steps to achieve or prevent a certain result. And there are other provisions which do not exactly fit into any of these classes. Often it is difficult to find any reason for these differences.

There has been much doubt about where the onus rests in these cases. About the first class it may well be that it is sufficient for the prosecutor or pursuer to aver and prove a breach of the duty set out in the one section, leaving it to the accused or defender to avail himself of the statutory defence if he can. But in the other cases there is much room for doubt. In the present case the pleadings have been deliberately drawn in such a way as to require a decision at least with regard to the section on which the pursuer relies.

The pursuer, the present appellant, avers that on May 18, 1964 he had, within a factory, to unload railway wagons filled with bales of pulp. In doing this he had to stand on some of the bales, and while he was standing on one of the bales, it tipped up and caused him to fall and fracture his skull and three ribs. He founds on section 29(1) of the Factories Act, 1961, which is in these terms: 'There shall, so far as is reasonably practicable, be provided and maintained safe means of access to every place at which any person has at any time to work, and every such place shall, so far as is reasonably practicable, be made and kept safe for any person working there.'

He avers that the bales were insecurely placed in the wagons, so that the place at which he had to work was not made and kept safe for his working there. He deliberately avoids averring that it was reasonably practicable for the respondents, his employers, to make that place safe. He says that he has averred a relevant case, because under this section it is for the defender to aver and prove, if he can, that it was not reasonably practicable to make the place safe. The respondents, of course, had no control over the loading of the bales in the wagon. That no doubt was done by the seller who sold the pulp to them. They make averments to show that it was not reasonably practicable for them to make the place safe, and they also plead that, the pursuer's averments being irrelevant, the action should be dismissed. This plea to the relevancy was sustained by the Lord Ordinary, and the First Division adhered to his interlocutor. This matter is not a mere technicality. It has important practical consequences. If the respondents are right, the pursuer must not only aver in general terms that it was reasonably practicable to make the place safe. Such an averment without more would be lacking in specification—he must also make sufficient positive averments to give notice to the defender of the method of making the place safe which he proposes to support by evidence. But if the appellant is right, he can simply wait for the evidence which the respondents would have to lead to discharge the onus on them to show that it was not reasonably practicable to make the place safe, and then cross-examine the respondents' witnesses in any relevant way he chooses. He would only have to make positive averments if he intended to lead evidence that some particular method of making the place safe could have been adopted by the defenders. In my opinion this question should be approached by considering first what a prosecutor would have to allege and prove in order to obtain a conviction. For civil liability only arises if there has been a breach of the statutory duty, and I cannot see how a pursuer could succeed in a civil action without averring and proving all the facts essential to establish the commission of an offence. It is true that the standard of proof is lower in a civil case, so that the pursuer only has to show that it is probable that an offence was committed. But that cannot mean that the onus of proof is different with regard to any of the essential elements of the offence.

The appellant's argument is that, although the statute says that every working place 'shall, so far as is reasonably practicable, be made and kept safe', a prosecutor need only allege and prove that the place was not made and kept safe, leaving it to the accused to show that this was not reasonably practicable. He founds on section 16(d) of the Summary Jurisdiction (Scotland) Act, 1954, which provides: 'The charge in a complaint under this Act shall be stated in the form, as nearly as may be, of the appropriate form contained in Part II of the Second Schedule to this Act. No further specification shall be required than a specification similar to that given in that form and . . . (d) any exception, exemption, proviso, excuse, or qualification, whether it does or does not accompany in the same section the description of the offence in the statute or order creating the offence, may be proved by the accused, but need not be specified or negatived in the complaint, and no proof in relation to such exception, exemption, proviso, excuse, or qualification shall be required on behalf of the prosecution . . .'

A large number of forms of complaint are set out in the Schedule. I can find only one which relates to a statutory offence against a section drafted in the same way as section 29 of the Factories Act. That one is in these terms: 'You, being the parent of A.B., a child of school age, aged [blank], who has attended school, and the said child having failed, between [blank] and [blank], without reasonable excuse, to attend regularly at the said school, you are thereby guilty of an offence against section 35 of the Education (Scotland) Act, 1946.' That section provides: '(1) Where a child of school age who has attended a public school on one or more occasions fails without reasonable excuse to attend regularly at the said school, then the parent shall be guilty of an offence.'

Excuse is expressly mentioned in section 16(d), but nevertheless the Schedule makes it quite clear that section 16(d) does not apply to 'without reasonable excuse' in section 35 of the Education Act. And the reason is, I think, plain enough. This section makes it clear that the offence is not failure to attend school regularly: it is failure without reasonable excuse to attend regularly. So the prosecutor must allege and prove absence of reasonable excuse: a complaint which did not contain 'without reasonable excuse' would be immediately dismissed.

The Summary Jurisdiction (Scotland) Act 1908, contains similar provisions, and I have looked through the specimen complaints in the Schedule to that Act. None appears to be so clearly in point, but I find instances where it is necessary to aver in the complaint 'being an unauthorised place' and 'without the required permission'.

The appellant relied on *Chalmers v. Speedwell Wire Co.* [1944] K.B. 560. That complaint arose under section 13 of the Factories Act 1937: 'Every part of the transmission machinery shall be securely fenced unless it is in such a position' as to be as safe as it would be if securely fenced. This exception beginning with the word 'unless' was held to come within the scope of the section of the old Act corresponding to section 16(d) of the 1954 Act. I think that was right. As Lord Justice-Clerk Cooper pointed out (at p.48), the first branch of the section beginning 'every part' sets out the genus of the duty, while the second part beginning 'unless', sets out a species within that genus which is withdrawn from the generality of the opening requirement. But I do not think that that applies to the present case. There is no positive requirement that every working place shall be kept safe followed by an exception that that does not apply to those working places which it is not reasonably practicable to make safe. No doubt all working places can be regarded as a genus, but I do not think that a legal taxonomist would regard as a satisfactory species within that genus such working places as it is not reasonably practicable to make safe.

The Lord President, having analysed the section with which we are concerned, said: 'The words "so far as is reasonably practicable" consequently become, in my view, an integral part of the duty imposed and define the ambit of what is made obligatory.' Lord Guthrie said: 'No breach of the section is committed, and no failure on part of the defenders can take place, unless it is reasonably practicable to take steps to make and keep the working place safe.' And Lord Migdale said that the section 'is not a command to make the place safe, but to make it safe so far as is reasonably practicable.' I agree with these views.

It would be very convenient if one could avoid examination of the method of drafting and have a general rule either that in all these cases the onus is on the pursuer or that it is on the defender. But I do not think that is possible. On the one hand, where the provision is that it 'shall be a defence to prove' something, it would not be reasonable to require the pursuer to disprove that defence. But, on the other hand, take for example section 31 of this Act, which requires that 'all practicable steps shall be taken to prevent an explosion, to restrict its spread and to remove fumes', etc. I cannot see how a prosecutor or pursuer could frame a relevant complaint or condescendence by merely alleging that an explosion occurred, or that it spread, or that fumes were not removed, leaving it to the accused or the defender to show that no practicable steps could have been taken to avoid that. The offence here must be failure to take practicable steps and the prosecutor or pursuer must allege and prove such failure.

I get no assistance in this case from any general presumption that a person is not required to prove a negative or that a person is required to prove facts peculiarly within his own knowledge. I do not lay any stress on the fact that, if the appellant is right, the defenders would have to prove a negative—that it was not reasonably practicable to make the place safe. And I do not think that the question whether this was reasonably practicable is a matter peculiarly within the knowledge of the defenders—an expert witness for the pursuer should be just as able to deal with this as the defenders.

I would dismiss this appeal."

LORD GUEST: "In this action of damages by the appellant against the respondents, which is based on a breach by the respondents of section 29(1) of the Factories Act 1961, the respondents tabled a plea to the relevancy of the appellant's averments. The Lord Ordinary sustained the plea and dismissed the action. The First Division of the Court of Session adhered to the Lord Ordinary's interlocutor.

Section 29(1) of the Factories Act 1961 is in the following terms: [His Lordship quoted section 29(1) and continued]

The appellant avers that he had to unload two railway wagons filled with bales of pulp within the respondents' factory. He had to stand upon and make his way over the bales and, as the wagons were loosely tilled, they formed an insecure foothold. Owing to the bale on which he was standing tipping up, he fell to the floor and was injured. After quoting the terms of section 29(1) of the 1961 Act he avers: 'The place at which the pursuer had to work was not made and kept safe for him working there.' His ground of fault is that the respondents failed to comply with the statutory provision referred to and that this failure was the cause of the accident. Section 29(1) imposes the duty on the occupiers 'so far as is reasonably practicable' and the issue between the parties is whether, in the absence of an averment by the appellant that it was reasonably practicable for the respondents to make and keep his working place safe for him working, he has stated a relevant case. The respondents contend that, as the requirement 'so far as is reasonably practicable' is an ingredient of the offence, its absence renders the appellant's pleadings irrelevant. The appellant contends that it is unnecessary for him to make such an averment and that the question of reasonable practicability is a matter of defence which, if it is to be raised, must be averred by the respondents. The record has been deliberately framed as a test case in order to raise the question in its stark form. The point as raised is one of pleading in Scotland, but the decision has wider implications, as it will inevitably affect the question of onus at the trial.

Although there have been a number of cases in which expressions of opinion on this question have been made, the question is open . . .

The trend of authority in England at any rate is in favour of the appellant's contention. The question is one of the proper construction of section 29(1) and I have not found the question an easy one. The matter may be tested by asking the question as: 'What is the criminal offence which is created by this section?' If there is no criminal offence, there can be no civil liability. The two must go hand in hand. The respondents say that the offence created is failing to make the working place safe so far as is reasonably practicable. In this event the complaint would require to contain this qualification, and in order to establish the commission of the offence the prosecution would require to prove in what way it was reasonably practicable to comply with the terms of the section . . . I am not sure, however, that this necessarily helps to the proper construction of the section. Section 16(d) of the Summary Jurisdiction (Scotland) Act 1954, provides: 'any exception, exemption, proviso, excuse, or qualification, whether it does or does not accompany in the same section the description of the offence in the statute or order cresting the offence, may be proved by the accused, but need not be specified or negatived in the complaint, and no proof in relation to such exception, exemption, proviso, excuse, or qualification shall be required on behalf of the prosecution . . .' If the expression 'so far as is reasonably practicable' can be treated as a 'qualification', in terms of section 16(d), then no difficulty arises, and the complaint need not libel the question of reasonable practicability and it would be for the accused, if so advised, to raise the matter in defence . . .

I therefore return to the construction of section 29(1). Powerful reasons have been given by the Lord Ordinary and the judges of the First Division in favour of the respondents' construction. It is said that the words 'so far as is reasonably practicable' are an integral part of the offence, that they qualify the verbs 'made safe' and 'kept safe' or are, as Lord Migdale graphically puts it, 'woven into the verb'. But these considerations seem to me to pay little or no regard to the purpose of the section. The object of the section was to provide for a safe working place by imposing criminal and civil liability on the occupier in the event of breach. There is doubt as to the construction of this section. The question appears to me to depend upon which construction will best achieve the result to be attained, namely, to make and keep the working place safe. On the one hand, is this result likely to be achieved by requiring the pursuer to condescend on and specify the practicable measures whereby the place could be made and kept safe or by requiring the defenders to specify and establish that it was not reasonably practicable to do this? . . . In this connection . . . I attach some importance to the consideration that the means of achieving the end were more likely to be within the knowledge of the defenders than the pursuer. In some cases it might be comparatively simple for the pursuer to make the necessary averments, but there will be many cases where, particularly in the case of a death of a workman, it would be unreasonable to expect a widow to have to specify what steps which the defenders should have taken to make the working place safe, were reasonably practicable. I may instance the case of a claim by a widow under Regulation 6 of the Shipbuilding and Ship Repairing Regulations 1960, for breach of the duty to provide and maintain a safe means of access, where the form of access provided is inherently unsafe and cannot be made safe, but what was required is a different form of access altogether. In such a case the widow might be faced some time after the accident with the difficult, if not impossible, task of averring what was a reasonably practicable form of access when the ship had been constructed and all the real evidence had disappeared. On the other hand, the employer would be put on inquiry immediately after the accident and would be in a position to investigate the matter timeously. To treat the onus as being on the pursuer seems to equiparate the duty under the statute to the duty under common law, namely, to take such steps as are reasonably practicable to keep the working place safe. I cannot think that the section was intended to place such a limited obligation on employers. It is said by the respondents that to impose the onus on them would mean that they would have to prove a negative. This is not so, in my view. In most cases, the question would be whether the provision of safety measures was reasonable, having regard to the expense involved. This would involve balancing the expense of the precautions suggested against the risks involved. That would be peculiarly within the employer's province.

I attach some importance to the stage at which the latter provision of section 29(1) found its way into the statute book. The particular part of section 29(1) relied on was first enacted by section 5 of the Factories Act 1959, and formed an addition to section 26(1) of the Factories Act 1937. This provision was enacted by Parliament in the knowledge that the current judicial opinion was in favour of the view that section 26(1) placed the onus of proving that the provisions were not reasonably practicable on the employers. Notwithstanding this state of the law the phraseology of section 26(1) was repeated. This is some indication that Parliament was content to leave the onus resting on the employers.

On the whole matter I would allow the appeal, recall the interlocutors of the Court of Session, repel the first plea in law for the defenders and remit to the Court of Session."

NOTES

According to the Scottish rules of pleading, a party may not lead evidence on a matter about which he/ she has not made averments on record—*Parker v. Lanarkshire Health Board*, 1996 S.C.L.R. 57 provides a classic example of the evidential difficulties created by a failure to make precise averments on a crucial issue. In cases such as *Nimmo*, a pursuer is not bound to make averments about the reasonable practicability of precautions to make a workplace safe. Moreover, he/she may be permitted to cross-examine the other party's witnesses on that issue. But if satisfactory admissions from the opposition's witnesses cannot be obtained, the case may be in difficulties. The pursuer may therefore opt to make specific averments about such precautions, in order to be able to lead evidence about them from his/ her own witnesses. If he/she does so, he/she accepts the onus of proving them. Failure by the pursuer to prove such specific averments, however, does not excuse the defender from the general onus of proving that it was not reasonably practicable to take any precautions beyond those which were actually taken—see *Gibson v. B.I.C.C.*, 1973 S.C. (H.L.) 15.

There is an extensive, and somewhat contradictory, jurisprudence on the issue discussed by Lord Reid as to whether the wording of a particular statutory duty or offence requires a pursuer or prosecutor to prove all of the elements referred to in the statute, or whether the statute provides a defence—an "exception, exemption, proviso, excuse or qualification"—which "need not be specified or negatived in the indictment or complaint", but must be established by the accused or the defender (see the Criminal Procedure (Scotland) Act 1995, Schedule 3, para. 16). For example, in *Earnshaw v. H.M.A.*, 1982 S.L.T. 179, it was held that where the Road Traffic Act 1972, s.9(3) created the offence of "failure without reasonable excuse" to provide a laboratory specimen of blood, breath or urine, the onus of proving all the elements of this offence rests throughout on the Crown. This may be thought of as a case where the question of "reasonable excuse" is "woven into the verb" in Lord Migdale's colourful phrase; in *Buchanan v. Price*, 1982 S.C.C.R. 534, on the other hand, it was held that where a parent is charged with an offence under the Education (Scotland) Act 1980, s.35(1), his or her child having failed "without reasonable excuse to attend regularly" at school, the burden of proving that there was a "reasonable excuse" for the failure rests on the parent. Again, what is at issue here is not strictly part of the law of evidence at all, but rather an application of the principles relating to statutory interpretation. As Lord Reid puts it in *Nimmo*: "It would be very convenient if one could avoid examination of the method of drafting and have a general rule either that in all these cases the onus is on the pursuer or that it is on the defender. But I do not think that is possible."

In *Normand v. Walker*, 1995 S.L.T. 94 the High Court expressed the view that the whole issue, at least in relation to criminal charges, may in future have to be re-considered by a Full Bench. Any such consideration may have to include an examination of authorities on the requirements of the European Convention on Human Rights, as to which see the commentary to *Lambie v. H.M.A.*, below. It should be noted that while the defender may bear the onus of proof on certain issues, failure by the defender to discharge the burden does not *necessarily* mean that the pursuer will succeed. The pursuer must still prove the facts in issue to the required standard (in civil cases, the balance of probabilities), and if the court is left unconvinced or is undecided, the onus of proof lying upon the pursuer means that his action will not succeed.

5. Rhesa Shipping Co. SA v. Edmunds ("The Popi M")
[1985] 2 All E.R. 712

A ship belonging to the plaintiffs sank in clear skies and calm seas off the coast of Algeria. The immediate cause of the sinking was a large hole in the ship's hull. In order to claim the insurance money for the vessel, the owners had to establish that it had been lost by "the perils of the sea", which was the main risk against which the ship was insured. The underwriters disputed this and claimed in turn that the ship was lost not because of the ordinary perils of the sea, but merely because it was unseaworthy.

LORD BRANDON OF OAKBROOK: "In approaching this question it is important that two matters should be borne constantly in mind. The first matter is that the burden of proving, on a balance of probabilities, that the ship was lost by the perils of the sea is and remains throughout on the ship-owners. Although it is open to the underwriters to suggest and seek to prove some other cause of loss, against which the ship was not insured, there is no obligation on them to do so. Moreover if they chose to do so, there is no obligation on them to prove, even on a balance of probabilities, the truth of their alternative case.

The second matter is that it is always open to a court, even after the kind of prolonged inquiry with a mass of expert evidence which took place in this case, to conclude, at the end of the day, that the proximate cause of the ship's loss, even on a balance of probabilities, remains in doubt, with the consequence that the ship-owners have failed to discharge the burden of proof which lay on them . . .

The ship-owners relied in their pleadings, and sought to rely at the trial, on the principle that, if a seaworthy ship sinks in unexplained circumstances in good weather and calm seas, there is a rebuttable presumption that she was lost by perils of the seas. This would in the normal case be a classic example of a presumption being used to surmount a burden of proof, and indeed of a situation where it would then be up to the other party to show that the presumption should not apply. But the facts which give rise to the presumption could not be established in this case, and so it could not be applied [see Chapter 3 on Presumptions]. The ship-owners were, however, unable to rely on this principle for two reasons. The first was that Bingham J. [the trial judge] felt unable to make a finding one way or the other on the question whether the ship was seaworthy. The result is that all possible explanations of the ship's loss have to be approached on the basis that it is as likely that she was unseaworthy as that she was seaworthy. The second reason was that, as I have already indicated, the loss did not occur in unexplained circumstances: on the contrary, the reasons why she sank, apart from the cause of the fatal aperture itself, were as clear as they could possibly have been.

The ship-owners felt bound to concede that two causes of the aperture, which they canvassed at the time, could be eliminated as impossible. The first of these was collision with a submerged rock; this could be eliminated because the ship was navigating in a much used sea-lane, and the relevant charts showed deep water all round without any rocks. The second cause was collision with a floating object; this could be eliminated because such an object would have been washed clear of the ship's side in way [sic] of the engine-room by the bow-wave which the ship, proceeding at her full speed of about 11½ knots, would have been creating.

The elimination of these two possibilities left the ship-owners with only one remaining possibility, namely a collision with a submerged object of some kind. In this connection an unarmed torpedo was mentioned, but very sensibly not treated as a serious possibility. That left, as the only remaining possibility for consideration, a collision with a submerged submarine, travelling in the same direction as the ship and at about the same speed, and that was the event which Bingham J, by processes of reasoning which I shall examine shortly, ultimately found to have been the proximate cause of the loss.

My Lords, counsel for the ship-owners contended before your Lordships that his case had never been tied irrevocably to a loss by any specified peril of the seas; in particular, it had never been tied to loss by collision with a submarine. It seems to me, however, that, once it was shown that the water which sank the ship had entered through an aperture in her shell-plating, the burden of proof was on the ship-owners to show that peril of the seas, if any, could be shown, on a balance of probabilities, to have created that aperture. The ship-owners could not, in my view, rely on a ritual incantation of the generic expression 'perils of the seas', but were bound, if they were to discharge successfully the burden of proof to which I have referred, to condescend to particularity in the matter.

I come back now to the processes of reasoning by which Bingham J found that collision with a submarine was, on a balance of probabilities, the proximate cause of the ship's loss. In order to make these processes clear it is necessary to have in mind a matter which I mentioned earlier that, although underwriters sued by ship-owners for the total loss of a ship by perils of the seas are not under any obligation to plead in their defence, or to seek to prove at the trial, some alternative cause of loss against which the ship was not insured, they are perfectly entitled to do so if they wish. In the present case the underwriters did exercise their right to plead and try to prove an alternative cause of loss, the cause so relied on being prolonged wear and tear of the ship's hull over many years, resulting in her shell-plating opening up under the ordinary action of wind and wave and without collision with any external object.

My Lords, the result of the underwriters putting forward this alternative cause of the ship's loss was to lead Bingham J into approaching the decision which he had to make as being a simple choice between the cause of loss relied on by the ship-owners and the alternative cause of loss put forward by the underwriters. Although he had in an earlier part of his judgment referred expressly to the observations with regard to burden of proof made by Scrutton L.J. in *Cia Alartiarta v. Royal Exchange Assurance Corp* [1923] K.B. 650 at 657, which I quoted earlier, he does not seem, when he came later in his judgment to the point of actual decision, to have given any consideration at all to the third possible solution to the case contemplated in those observations. That third possible solution would have been to say that he was left in doubt as to the proximate cause of the ship's loss, and that, in those circumstances, the ship-owners' actions should be dismissed on the simple ground that they had not discharged the burden of proof which lay on them.

Bingham J. had before him a mass of expert evidence relating to the possibilities that the proximate cause of the ship's loss was a collision with a submerged submarine on the one hand or wear and tear of the shell-plating on the other. Dealing with the submarine theory first, he stated seven cogent considerations which militated strongly against that theory. I do not propose to set out, or even try to summarise, those seven considerations. I think it helpful, however, to state the first consideration, which I regard as having a certain convincing simplicity about it, namely that no submarine was seen before or after the casualty.

Having set out the seven cogent considerations which militated strongly against the submarine theory to which I have just referred, Bingham J expressed his conclusion about the theory in this way ([1983] 2 Lloyd's Rep 235 at 246):

> 'I think it would be going too far to describe a collision between the vessel and a submarine, rupturing the shell-plating of the vessel, as impossible. But it seems to me to be so improbable that, if I am to accept the ship-owners' invitation to treat it as the likely cause of the casualty, I (like the ship-owners' experts) must be satisfied that any other explanation of the casualty can be effectively ruled out.'

Bingham J. then went on to examine the alternative wear and tear theory put forward by the underwriters. He went through the essential features of the complex expert evidence which had been adduced before him, and, having done so, expressed his conclusion as follows ([1983] 2 Lloyd's Rep 235 at 248):

> 'They [the underwriters] are not, of course obliged to prove that explanation, even on a balance of probabilities, but unless I am satisfied that some degree of probability attaches to it, I am left with no explanation but the owners.'

Then, after a further reference to the expert evidence, he continued:

'In the result, I find myself drawn to conclude that the [underwriters'] wear and tear explanation must on the evidence be effectively ruled out. That leaves me with the choice between the owners' submarine hypothesis and the possibility that the casualty occurred as a result of wear and tear but by a mechanism which remains in doubt.'

The passages which I have quoted from Bingham J.'s judgment amply support the observations about his approach to the case which I made earlier. These observations were to the effect that he regarded himself as compelled to make a choice between the ship-owners' submarine theory on the one hand and underwriters' wear and tear theory on the other, and he failed to keep in mind that a third alternative, that the ship-owners' had failed to discharge the burden of proof which lay on them, was open to him.

As regards the ship-owners' submarine theory, Bingham J stated in terms that he regarded it as extremely improbable, a view with which I think it unlikely that any of your Lordships will quarrel. As regards the underwriters' wear and tear theory, it was contended by counsel for the ship-owners that Bingham J had ruled it out as impossible. The language used by him in different places is, however, ambivalent, and I think that it would be more accurate to say that he regarded the wear and tear theory not as impossible, but as one in respect of which any mechanism by which it could have operated was in doubt.

My Lords, the late Sir Arthur Conan Doyle in his book *The Sign of Four* describes his hero, Mr Sherlock Holmes, as saying to the latter's friend, Dr Watson: 'How often have I said to you that, when you have eliminated the impossible, whatever remains, however improbable, must be the truth?' It is, no doubt, on the basis of this well-known but unjudicial dictum that Bingham J decided to accept the ship-owners' submarine theory, even though he regarded it, for seven cogent reasons, as extremely improbable. In my view there are three reasons why it is inappropriate to apply the dictum of Mr Sherlock Holmes to which I have just referred to the process of fact-finding which a judge of first instance has to perform at the conclusion of a case of the kind here concerned.

The first reason is one which I have already sought to emphasise as being of great importance, namely that the judge is not bound always to make a finding one way or the other with regard to the facts averred by the parties. He has open to him the third alternative of saying that the party on whom the burden of proof lies in relation to any averment made by him has failed to discharge that burden. No judge likes to decide cases on burden of proof if he can legitimately avoid having to do so. There are cases, however, in which, owing to the unsatisfactory state of the evidence or otherwise, deciding on the burden of proof is the only just course for him to take. The second reason is that the dictum can only apply when all relevant facts are known, so that all possible explanations, except a single extremely improbable one, can properly be eliminated. That state of affairs does not exist in the present case: to take but one example the ship sank in such deep water that a diver's examination of the nature of the aperture, which might well have thrown light on its cause, could not be carried out.

The third reason is that the legal concept of proof of a case on a balance of probabilities must be applied with common sense. It requires a judge of first instance, before he finds that a particular event occurred, to be satisfied on the evidence that it is more likely to have occurred than not. If such a judge concludes, on a whole series of cogent grounds, that the occurrence of an event is extremely improbable, a finding by him that it is nevertheless more likely to have occurred than not, does not accord with common sense. This is especially so when it is open to the judge to say simply that the evidence leaves him in doubt whether the event occurred or not, and that the party on whom the burden of proving that the event occurred lies has therefore failed to discharge such burden.

In my opinion Bingham J. adopted an erroneous approach to this case by regarding himself as compelled to choose between two theories, both of which he regarded as extremely improbable, or one of which he regarded as extremely improbable and the other of which he regarded as virtually impossible. He should have borne in mind, and considered carefully in his judgment, the third alternative which was open to him, namely that the evidence left him in doubt as to the cause of the aperture in the ship's hull, and that, in these circumstances, the ship-owners had failed to discharge the burden of proof which was on them.

If ever a case asked to be treated as coming within the dictum with regard to burden of proof of Scrutton L.J. in *Cia Alartiarta v. Royal Exchange Assurance Corp* [1923] K.B. 650 at 657, this was it. The ship-owners failed to establish that the ship was seaworthy, and they only put forward an extremely improbable cause of her loss. In these circumstances the judge should have found that the true cause of the loss was in doubt, and that the ship-owners had failed to discharge the burden of proof which was on them."

NOTES

The Popi M was distinguished by Lord Cameron of Lochbroom in *McLean v. Scottish Power plc*, 2000 G.W.D. 4–157, January 12. 2000. See also *Thomas v. Thomas*, 1947 S.C. (H.L.) 45, and *Abrath v. North Eastern Railway Company* (1883) L.R. 11 Q.B.D. 440 per Bowen L.J. at 456:

"The test therefore as to the burden of proof or onus of proof, whichever term is used, is simply this—to ask one's self which party will be successful if no evidence is given . . . "

It has been suggested that in a case where the balance of probabilities cannot be determined, but one party's cause has been materially prejudiced by the other party's conduct of the case, the party suffering the prejudice is entitled to succeed—see comments by Lord Bonomy in *Smith's Executors v. Upper Clyde Shipbuilders Ltd (In Liquidation)*, 1999 G.W.D. 33–1597.

Certain comments in the following case, however, suggest that the burden of proof shifts between the parties during the course of a trial or proof. Such suggestions should be treated with caution.

6.   Gibson v. N.C.R. *The shifting burden*
1925 S.C. 500

LORD JUSTICE-CLERK (ALNESS): "The pursuer in this case is a butcher, who carries on business at two shops in Montrose. The defenders manufacture and sell cash registers. In June 1918 the defenders sold to the pursuer, through their agent, Mr Nathan, a cash register at a price of £113, and in August of that year they sold him, through Mr Nathan, another cash register at a price of £115. The sole question in the case is whether it was made plain to the pursuer by Mr Nathan that the cash registers which he sold were not new but secondhand, as in point of fact they were. The pursuer expressly charges the defenders with fraud, and it is, I think, equally clear that the defenders, if their case is well founded, charge the pursuer, though not expressly, yet by necessary implication, with fraud also. The controversy between the parties is accordingly of a disagreeable nature. The pursuer has elected to retain the cash registers which he purchased. He does not seek to rescind the contract, but he contends that, as he was induced to enter into it by the fraud of Mr Nathan, he has suffered loss thereby, and that he is therefore entitled to an award of damages. Alternatively, the pursuer says that he is entitled to damages, as for breach of contract, under the Sale of Goods Act.

The area of discussion was materially narrowed by an admission made by Mr Mackay for the pursuer in the course of the argument, to the effect that he did not attribute fraud to the defenders personally, but only vicarious fraud through their agent Mr Nathan. A careful survey of the pursuer's averments on record leads me to the conclusion that the case with which the pursuer came into Court was not so limited. If it was intended in the pursuer's pleadings so to limit his claim, all I can say is that his averments are most unfortunately expressed. I am of opinion that they attribute fraud to the defenders personally, and I am further of opinion that there is not and never was any justification for that charge. However, as I have said, the ambit of inquiry is now abridged by Mr Mackay's admission, and I shall consider the case on the footing that the defenders personally are freed from an unjustifiable and odious charge.

It appears to me that the question of onus of proof is a vital, if not indeed a conclusive, factor in the decision of the case. Now, it is of course elementary and indisputable that a pursuer who comes into Court averring fraud against his opponent must prove fraud, if he is to succeed in his action. But onus is not an inflexible thing. It may shift as the case progresses. Indeed it may shift more than once in the course of the proceedings. I rather think that the learned Sheriff-substitute, looking to the terms of his note, has not adverted sufficiently to this rudimentary rule. The pursuer's contention is that, while the onus of proving that Mr Nathan did not disclose that the registers which he sold were secondhand originally rested upon the pursuer, there are facts and circumstances in this case, either admitted or proved, which shift the onus, and which impose upon the defenders the necessity of making it plain that their agent disclosed to the pursuer that the registers which he sold were in point of fact secondhand.

The facts and circumstances on which the pursuer relies in support of his contention are: (1) that it is proved, nay, that it is not disputed, that what the pursuer desired to buy were new cash registers; (2) that the defenders hold themselves out to be makers and vendors of such registers; and (3) that what the pursuer obtained from the defenders were secondhand cash registers, which, however, by reason of reconditioning, appeared to be new. The pursuer maintains that in these circumstances it was for the defenders to establish that the pursuer was duly informed by Mr Nathan of the secondhand quality of the goods which he supplied. In this contention I think that the pursuer is well founded.

Much is said on record and in evidence regarding certain letters, 'S.' and 'S.H.', which appear on the registers sold, and which indicate that they were secondhand. Much is also said regarding certain documents or lists alleged to have been exhibited by Mr Nathan to the pursuer before he bought the registers, and which, it is said, yield the same result. But I did not understand the defenders ultimately to maintain that these things, separately or in combination, were sufficient to affect the pursuer with knowledge that the registers sold were secondhand, apart from an explanation to that effect tendered to the pursuer by Mr Nathan. The defenders relied on proving, as indeed on record they offer to prove, that Mr Nathan made it plain to the pursuer that the registers sold to him were in point of fact secondhand. In other words, the defenders did not seriously maintain that the pursuer should have spelt out [sic] of the symbols on the machines and the documents relating to them the secondhand character of the registers. They relied not on what the pursuer saw, but on what Mr Nathan said, as establishing their case.

The issue then appears to be this—Have the defenders discharged the onus, which I hold to rest upon them, of proving that Mr Nathan informed the pursuer that the registers which he was purchasing were secondhand?"

LORD ORMIDALE: "[His Lordship narrated the facts giving rise to the action.] The first question that arises is whether the onus is on the pursuer to prove that what he required and sought to buy were new machines, or on the defenders to prove that they made it plain to him that what they purported to sell were secondhand registers. I agree that it was for the defenders to disclose to the pursuer that what they had on sale were secondhand registers. They hold themselves out as makers of registers. In fact they are sellers of registers made in America by an allied company. As Mr Beeching [a witness for the defenders] puts it, they make the machines in America. Down to the second or third year of the war their trade was the sale of new machines so made. In 1916 the importation of registers was prohibited, and the defenders then commenced to buy up registers that had been sold by them and used. These they overhauled and reconditioned and then resold, and there can be little doubt that by 1918 their trade was almost exclusively in these reconditioned and secondhand registers. In their lists new serial numbers were given to the registers, and the letters 'S' or 'S.H.' were as a rule added to the numbers to denote that they were secondhand. But this complete change in the character of their goods was not advertised and was not generally known, and the pursuer was certainly not aware of it. In these circumstances it was their duty to disclose to an intending customer like the pursuer that a register being sold to him was not new but secondhand, and it is for them to prove that they discharged it.

As the Sheriff-substitute points out, however, the case made by the pursuer on record is that the fact that the registers for which he was in treaty were secondhand was not only not disclosed to him but was, to put it shortly, fraudulently concealed from him. In these circumstances, it appears to me that what I may term the minor onus which I have held to lie on the defenders becomes in some degree subordinated to the greater onus with which every pursuer charges himself when he alleges fraudulent dealing on the part of a defender. For it must be kept in view that there might well be innocent failure to disclose the quality of the goods supplied, *e.g.,* the seller might think that the buyer was aware without express notice that the article for sale was not new but secondhand. That, however, is not the position taken up by the defenders in the present case, for they directly challenge the pursuer's averments and maintain that he was, in fact, fully certiorated that the registers in question were secondhand and not new. In a sense they accept the minor onus incumbent on them. On the other hand it does not appear to me to be possible, standing the averments of fraud, to dispose of this action as if it raised simply a question of breach of contract. The pursuer has elected to retain the registers and to claim damages in respect of the fraudulent representations and concealment of the defenders. The burden of proving the alleged fraud must remain therefore on the pursuer, although the proof of it may be much facilitated if the defenders fail to establish that their agent, Mr Nathan in fact disclosed that the registers were secondhand."

NOTES

From time to time, judges and commentators refer to a shifting of the burden of proof. In the original edition of Walker and Walker, at para. 77 the learned authors said:

"The party upon whom the initial burden of proof rests may discharge that burden by leading evidence which either proves conclusively the fact necessary for his success or gives rise to a presumption that it exists. In the latter case, if the presumption is rebuttable, the burden of proof shifts to the other party, who must either lead evidence to rebut the presumption against him or fail in the action or issue of fact in question."

In the extract from *Gibson v. N.C.R.*, above, Lord Justice-Clerk Alness also talks of the onus of proof shifting in the course of a proof. Such comments and *dicta* accurately reflect the fact that the balance of probabilities arising from the evidence may shift between the parties during the course of a proof, but they are potentially confusing, since they fail to distinguish between the different types of burden which may arise. A clue to this distinction may be found in Lord Ormidale's reference in *Gibson* to the "minor onus" which came to rest on the defenders to show that the secondhand nature of the cash registers had, in fact, been disclosed to the pursuer.

Tactical rendable burden   **7.   Brown v. Rolls-Royce**
                                       1960 S.C. (H.L.) 22

The pursuer in Brown was a machine oiler and his hands were therefore constantly in contact with oil and grease. As a result of such contact he contracted industrial dermatitis. He contended that his condition was caused by the defenders' failure to provide protective cream to their employees. The provision of such cream was proved to be a precaution commonly adopted in industry against the risk of dermatitis. The defenders argued, however, that the use of barrier cream was ineffective, and that their own provision of adequate washing facilities was sufficient to discharge their duty of care toward the pursuer. By a majority, the Inner House of the Court of Session found for the defenders.

LORD DENNING: "The difference between the Judges of the Court of Session turned on the onus of proof. The majority of them (the Lord President, Lord Russell and Lord Sorn) thought that the burden was on the pursuer to prove that the defenders were negligent, and that, looking at the case at the end of the day, the pursuer had not discharged that burden. The minority (Lord Carmont) thought that, once the pursuer proved that the defenders had not followed the common practice of the trade in supplying barrier cream, the burden shifted to the defenders, so that they would not escape liability, unless they proved (not as a mere probability but as matter of reasonable certainty) that, even if they had adopted the common practice and supplied barrier cream, it would have done no good.
    This difference of opinion shows how important it is to distinguish between a legal burden, properly so called, which is imposed by the law itself and a provisional burden which is raised by the state of the evidence. The legal burden in this case was imposed by law on the pursuer. In order to succeed, he had to prove that the defenders were negligent, and that their negligence caused the disease—see *Bonnington Castings Limited v. Wardlaw*, [1956] 1 A.C. 613 at p.620 by Lord Reid and at p.624 by Lord Tucker. In order to discharge the burden of proving negligence, the pursuer proved that 'barrier cream commonly supplied by employers to men doing such work as the pursuer was doing.' This was a cogent piece of evidence and raised no doubt a 'presumption' or a 'prima facie' case, in this sense, that, if nothing more appeared,

the Court might well infer that the defenders were negligent, and in that sense it put a burden on the defenders to answer it. But this was only a provisional burden which was raised by the state of the evidence as it then stood. The defenders might answer it by argument, as indeed they did, by pointing out that there is no evidence as to what, if any, other precautions these employers take or the defenders might answer it by calling evidence themselves as indeed they did, by proving that they 'relied on their medical officer, Dr Collier, who exercised proper care and skill' and that they carried out the precautions advised by him. In this way, a provisional burden may shift from one party to the other as the case proceeds or may remain suspended between them. But it has no compelling force. At the end of the day, the Court has to ask itself not whether the provisional burden is discharged, but whether the legal burden has been discharged, that is to say: Has the pursuer proved that the defenders were negligent?

If the view of Lord Carmont were right it would mean that, once the pursuer proved that the defenders had not followed a precaution usually observed in the trade, there was a compelling presumption that they were negligent, and there was a legal burden on the defender to rebut it. This would introduce a new proposition of law, for which I find no warrant in the judgment of Lord Dunedin in *Morton v. William Dixon Limited*, 1909 S.C. 807. As my noble and learned friend Lord Keith of Avonholm said in *Cavanagh v. Ulster Weaving Co.* [1960] A.C. 145 at p.165 Lord Dunedin was laying down . . . 'no principle of law but stating the factual framework within which the law would fall to be applied.' Nor do I find any warrant for it in the speech of Lord Normand in *Paris v. Stepney Borough Council*, [1951] A.C. 367 at p.382. Lord Normand there said that 'if there is proof that a precaution is usually observed by other persons, a reasonable and prudent man will follow the usual practice in the like circumstances.' That is not a proposition of law at all, but only a proposition of good sense. It is on a par with the propositions about protective clothing discussed by your Lordship, in *Qualcast (Wolverhampton) Limited v. Haynes* [1959] A.C. 743. If the defenders do not follow the usual precautions, it raises a prima facie case against them in this sense, that it is evidence from which negligence is to be inferred, but not in the sense that it must be inferred, unless the contrary is proved. At the end of the day, the Court has to ask itself whether the defenders were negligent or not. It is sufficient if there is a greater probability on one side or the other: but, if, at the end of the case, the evidence is so evenly balanced that the Court cannot reach a determinate conclusion, the legal burden comes into play and requires the Court to reject the case of negligence alleged against them. The majority of the Court of Session here held that the defenders were not at fault in not supplying barrier cream; and I can see no error of law in their findings. I would therefore dismiss the appeal."

NOTES

What Lord Denning refers to as the legal burden and provisional burden may also be called the persuasive and tactical burdens of proof respectively. A provisional or tactical burden arises from the state of the evidence, whereas a persuasive or legal burden arises, as noted above, by operation of the substantive law. Once certain facts are proved by the pursuer, the court may be prepared to presume that the facts in issue have been made out. The defender must then lead sufficient evidence to rebut the provisional presumption arising from the pursuer's evidence, or run the risk of losing the case. But he/she need not *disprove* the pursuer's case. The persuasive burden remains on the pursuer at all times (compare *The Popi M*, above). There is a strong link here with the law relating to presumptions, which is the subject of the next chapter. Certain presumptions arise not from the evidence but from the law, and these presumptions *do* cause a shifting of the legal or persuasive burden.

The idea of the tactical burden applies in criminal as well as civil matters. In *Pagan v. Fergusson*, 1976 S.L.T. (Notes) 44, for example, a motorist was charged with a contravention of section 3 of the Road Traffic Act 1972 (careless driving). It was admitted or proved that he was driving along a perfectly straight road, when the car left the road on its nearside, travelled about 120 feet along the verge and ultimately collided with a rock-face at the side of the road. The road was wet at the time. No evidence was led for the defence but the Sheriff acquitted on the grounds that no inference could be drawn that the respondent was driving at an excessive speed and the prosecution had failed to prove its case. On appeal by the prosecutor the case was remitted by the High Court back to the Sheriff for conviction. Lord Justice-Clerk Wheatley said:

"In my view, looking to the stark facts that this car, for no reason that has been explained, left the road on a perfectly straight stretch, travelled 120 feet along the verge and then collided with a rock-face, is in itself sufficient to raise a prima facie case of negligence that has not been rebutted in any way, since no evidence was led for the defence."

A parallel may be drawn here with the civil "doctrine" of *res ipsa loquitur*, about which more will be said in the section on Presumptions—see, *e.g. Devine v. Colvilles Ltd*, 1969 S.C. (H.L.) 67, below.

There is a third type of burden, sometimes described as the evidential burden. This is the burden of adducing enough evidence on a particular issue to allow a court to consider the matter. In *McGregor v. Jessop*, 1988 S.L.T. 719, the court affirmed that in cases such as *Earnshaw*, above, it was for the court to negative any question of reasonable excuse for failure to provide a blood sample, but only "once the issue of reasonable excuse has been raised by facts and circumstances which are capable of constituting reasonable excuse". While it is difficult to say precisely when sufficient evidence has been led to discharge the persuasive burden, it is relatively simple to show that there is "threshold" evidence of an issue which is capable of evaluation. In *Parr v. H.M.A.*, 1991 S.C.C.R. 180, a man accused of murdering his mother pleaded provocation. The trial judge withdrew that plea from the consideration of the jury and his decision to do so was upheld on appeal. Lord Justice-General Hope quoted with approval the words of one of his predecessors, Lord Clyde, in the unreported case of *Miller and Denovan* where he said that:

"[I]t is no part of the function of a judge at a trial to avoid his responsibility by leaving the issue in all cases to the jury to work out for themselves . . . The judge has a duty to consider the evidence and has a duty to make up his mind whether any of it is relevant to infer that culpable homicide [as opposed to murder] has been committed. If he arrives at the conclusion that there is no evidence in the case from which such a verdict could possibly be reached, it is his plain duty to direct the jury that it is not open to them to consider culpable homicide."

Lord Hope then continued:

"There is no doubt that there are limits as to what a judge may properly do, since questions as to the weight or quality of the evidence are not for him. But if there is no basis at all for the point in the evidence then there is no ground in law for the jury to consider it, and it is the duty of the trial judge to intervene by giving a direction to that effect."

8. Lambie v. H.M.A.
1973 J.C. 53

LORD JUSTICE-GENERAL (EMSLIE): "John Lambie was charged on indictment with theft. To this charge he pled not guilty and lodged a special defence of incrimination, naming certain persons as the perpetrators of the crime. In due course he was tried before a Sheriff and jury. By a majority the jury found him guilty as libelled, and he was sentenced to two years detention in a Young Offenders' Institution. [Having referred to a matter with which this report is not concerned, his Lordship continued—]

After conviction Lambie presented an application for leave to appeal against conviction. The application in its final form was based upon two alleged misdirections in the Sheriff's charge to the jury. [The Lord Justice-General narrated the first ground of appeal with which this report is not concerned.] The second ground of attack was that the Sheriff, it was said, misdirected the jury upon the special defence of incrimination. At the hearing of the application the Court of three judges granted leave to appeal upon the first of these grounds, and, since the point taken in the second ground involved a consideration of what appears to have become a practice in charging juries upon special defences generally, remitted the appeal and the application for hearing by a larger Court.

What we have already said is sufficient for the disposal of the appeal, but since the case was specially remitted to this Court for consideration of the second of the alleged misdirections, and since the full argument which we heard upon it disclosed a need for guidance from us on a matter of general importance, we propose to examine the second alleged misdirection in a little detail now. [Having quoted the passage from the Sheriff's charge which is set out earlier in this report, his Lordship continued—]

As will be seen from the quoted passage the direction plainly asserts: (i) that there is an onus on the accused to prove his special defence; (ii) that the onus can only be discharged by corroborated evidence; and (iii) that there is no corroboration of the accused's evidence incriminating any of the persons named in the special defence. For the applicant it was conceded that the third of these propositions was accurate. It was conceded further, for the purposes of the argument, that in presenting the first two of these propositions to the jury the Sheriff was merely following a widespread practice among trial judges which appears to have developed since the cases of *Lennie v. H.M.A.*, 1946 J.C. 79 and *Owens v. H.M.A.*, 1946 J.C. 119. Against the background of these concessions the submission was that a proper charge required the Sheriff to proceed to tell the jury that although they could not hold the special defence to have been affirmatively proved, they must still consider the appellant's uncorroborated evidence of incrimination and if they believed him or if, while not wholly believing him, found that his evidence created a reasonable doubt as to his guilt of the crime charged, they must acquit him. In this case, however, the Sheriff followed up his first three directions by saying 'Therefore you will not consider that special defence'. Now it was not disputed by the Crown that had the charge stopped there there would have been a plain and grave misdirection by the Sheriff, and the question at the end of the day came to be whether the sufficiency of the charge was saved by reading the quoted sentence in the context of the whole passage dealing with the special defence and, in particular, in conjunction with the sentences which immediately follow it. Upon this question we have come to be of opinion, albeit with some hesitation, that, standing the practice to which we have referred, the charge on the special defence read as a whole would sufficiently inform an intelligent lay jury, in spite of the quoted sentence which might otherwise have misled them, that they were to consider the applicant's evidence of incrimination and to acquit if it produced in their minds a reasonable doubt of his guilt. In these circumstances we would not have been disposed to sustain the appeal on the second ground.

The matter cannot, however, be allowed to rest there since in course of the argument the soundness of the practice to which we have referred, and the soundness of the observations in *Lennie* and *Owens* on which it was based, were seriously questioned. Suffice it to say that the criticisms made were such that it is desirable to look afresh at the whole matter of the proper charge which should be given where there has been lodged by an accused person a special defence of alibi, self-defence or incrimination.

It must be accepted that it has been the practice of many judges since the cases of *Lennie* and *Owens* to direct juries, where any of these special defences is in issue; (i) that there is an onus upon the accused to prove it by evidence sufficient in law on a balance of the probabilities but (ii) that even if the special defence is not established, the jury must nevertheless consider even the evidence of a single witness speaking to alibi, self-defence or incrimination, and if they believe that witness, or find that his evidence creates in their minds a reasonable doubt of the guilt of the accused, they must acquit him, since the burden of proof of guilt is on the Crown throughout. The critical question is whether it is at all appropriate to introduce into a criminal trial, where such a special defence has been lodged, any suggestion that there is at any time any onus on an accused person.

In searching for the answer to this question we begin by noticing what was said in *Lennie* and *Owens*. In *Lennie*, which was a case involving alibi, the Lord Justice-General (Normand) in delivering the opinion of the Court said this—'As regards the question of onus there is no doubt that the onus is throughout on the Crown to prove its case. But it is also true that the onus of proving the alibi was on the appellant. That that has been from the earliest times our law is made clear by the passages in Hume on Crimes upon the proving of alibi in olden days. I refer particularly to vol. II, pages 298 *et seq.* and pages 410 *et seq.*, and these passages also show that it was not uncommon in olden times to take the proof of alibi separately and before remitting the libel to assize. To lay on the Crown the onus of disproving the alibi of which the defence has given notice would be a complete inversion of the rules for the conduct of proofs or trials of which one of the most fundamental and most rational is *semper praesumitur pro negante*. If the jury deal first with the defence of alibi and decide not to sustain it, so that they must then address themselves to the Crown evidence, they must not treat the onus as transferred or affected by the failure of the defence of alibi. The question whether the jury are entitled to reconsider the evidence for the alibi in connexion with the evidence for the Crown and in rebuttal of it does not admit of a simple answer yea or nay.'

In *Owens* where self-defence was in issue the same Lord Justice-General in giving the opinion of the Court said this—'When we speak of the onus being on the panel to set up self-defence we merely mean that the accused must take the sting out of his own admission that he delivered the fatal blow. If he does this by proving that he was attacked and put in danger of his life (or had reasonable apprehension of danger to his life), he has set up his defence so that he must be acquitted. But, although he may choose to undertake complete legal proof as the best line of defence in the circumstances of his case, he is not bound to lead such evidence as would amount to a discharge of proof. He can rely on his own sworn statement that he was acting in self-defence and rely on his own credibility to outweigh any colourable case the Crown has laid before the jury; and the jury, if satisfied on a review of the whole evidence in the case of his credibility, is entitled to accept the panel's single sworn explanation and to reject evidence which would probably, without the explanation, have been sufficient for a conviction . . . It may therefore be necessary for the presiding Judge, not only to ask the jury to consider whether the special defence has been made out, but to ask them also to consider whether it has not had the effect of so shaking reliance on the Crown evidence as to warrant an acquittal from the charge.'

In our opinion there can be no doubt that in *Lennie* and less explicitly in *Owens* the Court did subscribe to the proposition that the onus of proving not only alibi but self-defence affirmatively rests on the accused although the judgments at the same time emphasise that the onus of proof of guilt remains on the Crown throughout and that even if proof of the special defence fails for want of corroboration the jury must still consider in the context of the evidence as a whole, the evidence of even a single witness speaking to alibi or self-defence; and if the evidence of that witness creates in their minds a reasonable doubt of guilt, must acquit. We must accordingly consider whether there was, in law, any warrant for these references to an onus upon the defence, since it is from these references that the charging practice to which we have referred has been derived. What, then, was the state of the law with regard to special defences before 1946? In posing this question we ignore the special defence of insanity at the time since it is quite clear that there is in such a case an onus upon the defence to establish it since proof of insanity is required before the presumption of sanity can be displaced.

Special defences in our law derive from the requirements of the law in earlier centuries for written defences in answer to a criminal libel when accused persons were limited in their defence to evidence in support of these defences, the relevancy of which had to be affirmed by a Court before the matter was remitted to an assize. The 'special defence' of today is the vestigial survivor in modern criminal practice of the written defences of our earlier criminal procedures.

An examination of the earlier authorities discloses no trace of a rule that couples putting forward of a 'special defence' with the necessary acceptance by an accused of an onus of proof of that defence by sufficient, *i.e.* corroborated, evidence, far less of any statement that should he fail to discharge that onus the defence as such must fail. It is not to be found in Hume in the passages dealing with 'special defences' (see Hume, vol. ii, pp.283 and 301) nor in Burnett's *Criminal Law* (1811), p.596, Alison, vol. li, pp.369 and 624 or Macdonald's *Criminal Law* in any editions, nor is it to be found in Andersen's, *Criminal Law of Scotland*, p.274. It is to be observed also that in summary proceedings no notice of such special defences as self-defence or incrimination is required of an accused. In the most recent editions of Renton and Brown's Criminal Procedure the matter is put thus—'The burden of proof that the accused committed the crime libelled against him rests upon the prosecutor throughout the trial. The standard required is proof beyond reasonable doubt. This onus is not transferred or affected by any common law defence pleas other than insanity or diminished responsibility.' The only current statutory requirement relative to the presentation of a special defence in solemn procedure is contained in section 36 of the Criminal Procedure Act 1887.

By the time Hume was writing, the function of a special defence was limited to giving fair notice to the prosecutor of the line which an accused's defence might take and the requirement of the law was that due notice should be given to the prosecution of such an intention. As put by Hume, vol. ii, p.301, it was (and is) because 'to let him maintain silence in that respect till the proof in support of the libel is closed would be downright injustice to the prosecutor who might thus lose the fair means of meeting the defences and strengthening his own case with evidence in the relative and proper parts.'

It is of course true as is pointed out in the judgment of the Court in *Lennie* that in earlier times for reasons which are set out in the passages from Hume cited in that judgment, when in his written defences an accused pleaded alibi, a preliminary proof on the separate issue of alibi was frequently held and if the plea succeeded the libel fell and was not proceeded with. This practice, however, had at least by the time Hume was writing, fallen into desuetude.

In the case of *Hillan v. H.M.A.*, 1937 J.C. 53 one of the grounds of appeal was that the presiding Sheriff in a charge of assault had misdirected the jury in respect that he directed the jury on a plea of self-defence to this effect 'that defence (self-defence) is entirely shouldered and must be discharged by the panel . . . He must have corroborative evidence before you can accept it as established that he did this in self-defence.' The appeal on this point succeeded and Lord Justice-Clerk Aitchison said this: 'I think that direction was unsound. Many cases occur in which from their very circumstances a plea of self-defence must depend upon the evidence of the panel himself . . . It is no doubt true that a plea of self-defence cannot be affirmatively established upon the evidence of the panel himself, but great injustice might arise if the jury were left with a direction that the plea must fail from want of corroboration. Whenever a plea of self-defence is put forward and supported by evidence, the jury should be explicitly directed that the special defence should be weighed by them in light of the whole proved facts in the case.'

This opinion was before the Court in the subsequent cases of *Lennie* and *Owens* and no doubt was cast upon the accuracy of Lord Justice-Clerk Aitchison's statement of the law or of the decision at which the Court arrived.

In light of this review of the law and practice before 1946 we have come to be of opinion that the references in *Lennie* and *Owens* to there being an onus upon the defence were unsound. It follows that the passage in Walkers' Law of Evidence, section 83(b) to the effect that 'When a special defence is stated by the accused the onus of proving it is on him' can now be regarded as an accurate statement of the law only in the case of the plea of insanity at the time. Apart from the unsoundness of its source the practice of referring at all to an onus being upon the defence inevitably complicated the directions of the presiding judge to such an extent as to be calculated to confuse most juries.

The only purpose of the special defence is to give fair notice to the Crown and once such notice has been given the only issue for a jury is to decide, upon the whole evidence before them, whether the Crown has established the accused's guilt beyond reasonable doubt. When a special defence is pleaded, whether it be of alibi, self-defence or of incrimination, the jury should be so charged in the appropriate language, and all that requires to be said of the special defence, where any evidence in support of it has been given, either in course of the Crown case or by the accused himself or by any witness led for the defence, is that if that evidence, whether from one or more witnesses, is believed, or creates in the minds of the jury reasonable doubt as to the guilt of the accused in the matters libelled, the Crown case must fail and that they must acquit. Thus, for example, evidence given of acting in self-defence, as this is defined by law, is in no different position from any other evidence consistent with the innocence of the accused and ought to be considered by the jury in precisely the same way."

NOTES

Following *Lambie* it is clear that, at common law, the accused in a criminal case bears a persuasive burden of proof only in respect of the defence of insanity and the plea of diminished responsibility. Statutes, however, frequently appear to place the persuasive burden of establishing a particular defence on an accused. The case of *King v. Lees*, 1993 S.C.C.R. 28 holds that in discharging such a burden, the accused need not lead corroborated evidence, and requires him only to give some credible evidence of the defence. It has been argued that this is contrary to authority, and in particular to the whole tone of the opinion delivered in *Lambie* which appears to imply that where the persuasive burden does rest on the accused, he must discharge it by corroborated evidence. (See further Sheldon, "Hip Flasks and Burdens" 1993 S.L.T. (News) 33). However, the imposition of a burden of proof on the accused must now be considered in the light of the European Convention on Human Rights, incorporated into Scots law by means of the Human Rights Act 1998 and the Scotland Act 1998. Section 3(1) of the Human Rights Act 1998 provides that:

"So far as it is possible to do so, primary legislation and subordinate legislation must be read and given effect in a way which is compatible with the Convention rights."

Thus, where it is possible to do so, the courts will "read down" legislation which appears to conflict with the Convention. If the legislation in question contains provisions which expressly contradict the meaning which the enactment would have to be given to make it compatible with the Convention, then "reading down" will not be possible, and the only recourse will be to seek a declaration of incompatibility under section 4 of the Act. Before deciding whether a particular provision can be read compatibly with the Convention, however, the courts must first decide whether the provision is potentially in conflict with Convention rights.

9. R. v. Lambert
[2001] 3 W.L.R. 206

Section 28(2) of the Misuse of Drugs Act 1971 provides that where an accused is found to have been in possession of controlled drugs, it shall be defence for him to prove that, "knowing or suspecting" the substance to be a controlled drug, he nevertheless took possession of it for certain specified purposes. In this case, it was argued that that sub-section conflicted with the defendant's rights under Article 6 of the European Convention on Human Rights.

LORD HOPE OF CRAIGHEAD:

"The second issue: the burden on the accused

(a) introduction

73. Article 6(2) of the Convention provides that everyone charged with a criminal offence shall be presumed innocent until proved guilty according to law. There is an important question as to whether a statutory provision which transfers the burden of proof to the accused can ever be compatible with that presumption. But for the purposes of this case it is necessary only to answer the particular questions which have been raised. They are (a) whether the provisions of sections 28(2) and 28(3)(b)(i) of the 1971 Act, which according to the ordinary meaning of the words used require the accused to prove the defences mentioned there on the balance of probabilities, are incompatible with the Convention right; and (b), if so, whether they can be read and given effect to under section 3 of the 1998 Act in a way which is compatible with it.

74. Mr Owen made it clear that the arguments which he presented on these questions were not directed to the defences which are mentioned in section 5(4) of the 1971 Act. This was because section 5(4) relates to things which the accused must establish if he wishes to avoid conviction but are not an essential element of the offence: see *R. v. Edwards* [1975] QB 27, 39–40. In that case the Court of Appeal said that, where an enactment prohibits the doing of an act save in specified circumstances or by persons of specified classes or with specified qualifications, it is for the defendant to prove that he was entitled to do the prohibited act. In *R. v. Hunt* [1987] A.C. 352, 375 Lord Griffiths said that he had little doubt that the occasions upon which a statute would be construed as imposing a burden of proof on a defendant which did not fall within that formulation would be exceedingly rare. It was to cases falling outside that formulation that Mr Owen directed his argument.

75. The section 5(4) defence has not been raised in this case, but I would not wish to be taken as accepting that exceptions of that kind are always immune from challenge on Convention grounds. As I see it, there are three distinct questions, and all three questions need to be asked and answered.

76. The first question is whether, upon the construction of the enactment, the defence is an exception of the kind described in *R. v. Edwards*. The second is whether the language used by Parliament, according to its ordinary meaning, has modified the golden thread rule as described by Viscount Sankey LC in *Woolmington v. Director of Public Prosecutions* [1935] A.C. 462, 481. This rule requires that, subject to the defence of insanity and to any statutory exception which transfers the burden of proof in the case of a particular offence laid down in an enactment, the prosecution must always prove its entire case beyond reasonable doubt. This question too is a question of construction. In a case of a provision such as that found in section 5(4), where the words used are 'it shall be a defence for him to prove', the answer to it is plain on the face of the enactment. A provision which takes this form is understood to be an express statutory exception to the golden thread rule.

77. But there is a third question, which was the subject of some debate in the light of the *Hunt* case but has now been brought right out into the open by sections 3(1) and 6(1) of the Human Rights Act 1998. It

used to be whether placing the burden on the accused by the particular statute can be justified by broader considerations of policy: see Peter Mirfield, "The Legacy of *Hunt*", [1988] Crim. L.R. 19; D. J. Birch, "Hunting the Snark; the Elusive Statutory Exception", [1988] Crim. L.R. 221; Peter Mirfield, "An Ungrateful Reply", [1988] Crim. L.R. 233. It can now be expressed in the language which is appropriate to an examination of the Convention rights.

(b) making use of section 3(1)

78. Section 3(1) of the 1998 Act provides that, so far as it is possible to do so, primary and secondary legislation must be read and given effect in a way which is compatible with the Convention rights. I should now like to explain how, as I see it, this important and far-reaching new approach to the construction of statutes should be employed consistently with the need (a) to respect the will of the legislature so far as this remains appropriate and (b) to preserve the integrity of our statute law so far this is possible.

79. The first point, as I said in paragraph 108 of my speech in *R. v. A.* [2001] UKHL 25, is that the effect of section 3(1) is that the interpretation which it requires is to be achieved only so far as this is possible. The word 'must', which section 3(1) uses, is qualified by the phrase 'so far as it is possible to do so'. The obligation, powerful though it is, is not to be performed without regard to its limitations. Resort to it will not be possible if the legislation contains provisions, either in the words or phrases which are under scrutiny or elsewhere, which expressly contradict the meaning which the enactment would have to be given to make it compatible. The same consequence will follow if legislation contains provisions which have this effect by necessary implication. Further justification for giving this qualified meaning to section 3(1) is to be found in the words 'read and give effect'. As the side note indicates, the obligation is one which applies to the interpretation of legislation. This function belongs, as it has always done, to the judges. But it is not for them to legislate. Section 3(1) preserves the sovereignty of Parliament. It does not give power to the judges to overrule decisions which the language of the statute shows have been taken on the very point at issue by the legislator.

80. The second point, as I said in paragraph 110 of my speech in *R. v. A.*, is that great care must be taken, in cases where a different meaning has to be given to the legislation from the ordinary meaning of the words used by the legislator, to identify precisely the word or phrase which, if given its ordinary meaning, would otherwise be incompatible. Just as much care must then be taken to say how the word or phrase is to be construed if it is to be made compatible. The justification for this approach to the use of section 3(1) is to be found in the nature of legislation itself. Its primary characteristic, for present purposes, is its ability to achieve certainty by the use of clear and precise language. It provides a set of rules by which, according to the ordinary meaning of the words used, the conduct of affairs may be regulated. So far as possible judges should seek to achieve the same attention to detail in their use of language to express the effect of applying section 3(1) as the parliamentary draftsman would have done if he had been amending the statute. It ought to be possible for any words that need to be substituted to be fitted in to the statute as if they had been inserted there by amendment. If this cannot be done without doing such violence to the statute as to make it unintelligible or unworkable, the use of this technique will not be possible. It will then be necessary to leave it to Parliament to amend the statute and to resort instead to the making of a declaration of incompatibility.

81. As to the techniques that may be used, it is clear that the courts are not bound by previous authority as to what the statute means. It has been suggested that a strained or non-literal construction may be adopted, that words may be read in by way of addition to those used by the legislator and that the words may be 'read down' to give them a narrower construction that their ordinary meaning would bear: Clayton and Tomlinson, *The Law of Human Rights*, (Oxford, 2000), p.168 para. 4.28. It may be enough simply to say what the effect of the provision is without altering the ordinary meaning of the words used: see *Brown v. Stott*, 2000 J.C. 328, 355B–C, per Lord Justice General Rodger. In other cases, as in *Vasquez v. The Queen* [1994] 1 W.L.R. 1304, the words used will require to be expressed in different language in order to explain how they are to be read in a way that its compatible. The exercise in these cases is one of translation into compatible language from language that is incompatible. In other cases, as in *R. v. A.*, it may be necessary for words to be read in to explain the meaning that must be given to the provision if it is to be compatible. But the interpretation of a statute by reading words in to give effect to the presumed intention must always be distinguished carefully from amendment. Amendment is a legislative act. It is an exercise which must be reserved to Parliament.

(c) application of section 3(1) in this case

82. The haphazard way in which reverse burden of proof provisions have been introduced into legislation by Parliament has been identified and persuasively criticised: Andrew Ashworth and Meredith Blake, "The Presumption of Innocence in English Criminal Law", [1996] Crim. L.R. 306. As they say, at p.314, nothing could be clearer than the 11th Report of the Criminal Law Revision Committee, *Evidence*

(General), Cmnd. 4991 (1972), para. 140 where the Committee stated: 'we are strongly of the opinion that, both on principle and for the sake of clarity and convenience in practice, burdens on the defence should be evidential only.' It is generally accepted that *Woolmington* changed the law as to the burden of proof in the case of common law defences such as self-defence and non-insane automatism: Professor J C Smith, "The Presumption of Innocence" (1987) 38 NILQ 223, 226; *Vasquez v. The Queen* [1994] 1 W.L.R. 1304, 1309G–H. The same approach has been taken in Scotland to where the onus lies in the case of all common law pleas and defences other than the plea of diminished responsibility and the defence of insanity: *Lambie v. H.M.A.*, 1973 J.C. 53 (incrimination); *Ross v. H.M.A.*, 1991 J.C. 210 (non-insane automatism).

83. The lack of clarity and the inconvenience of applying a different rule to defences created by statute is obvious in the present case. Section 28(4) of the 1971 Act provides that nothing in that section shall prejudice any defence which it is open to a person when charged with an offence to which that section applies to raise apart from that section. In this case the appellant did raise such a defence. It was his defence of duress. That defence was intimately bound up with his defence under the statute, as it depended entirely upon what the jury made of his evidence. But the trial judge had to direct the jury that the onus as regards the defence of duress rested on the prosecution. The jury were not told why there was a difference as to where the onus lay. There was no need for this information to be given to them. But it would not be surprising if they found it hard to maintain a clear distinction between the two positions as to onus when they examined the evidence.

84. There is no doubt that it is possible, in the light of section 3(1) of the Human Rights Act 1998, to read sections 28(2) and 28(3) of the 1971 Act in such a way as to impose no more than an evidential burden on the accused. As it is a rule of construction, the exercise which section 3(1) prescribes makes it necessary to identify the words used by the legislature which would otherwise be incompatible with the Convention right and then to say how these words are to be construed according to the rule to make them compatible. But in this case there is no difficulty. As Lord Cooke of Thorndon said in *R. v. Director of Public Prosecutions, ex p. Kebilene* [2000] 2 A.C. 326, 373G:

'. . . for evidence that it is a *possible* meaning one could hardly ask for more than the opinion of Professor Glanville Williams, 'The Logic of "Exceptions" ' [1988] C.L.J. 261, 265 that "unless the contrary is proved" can be taken, in relation to a defence, to mean "unless sufficient evidence is given to the contrary;" and the statute may then be satisfied by "evidence that, if believed, and on the most favourable view, could be taken by a reasonable jury to support t44he defence".'

85. In *Vasquez v. The Queen* [1994] 1 W.L.R. 1304 the Privy Council were asked to consider the question whether section 116(a) of the Belize Criminal Code which placed the burden on the defendant to prove extreme provocation as a defence to murder contravened the defendant's right under 6(3)(a) of the Constitution of Belize to be presumed innocent until he was proved guilty. Applying the principles described in *Attorney-General of The Gambia v. Momodou Jobe* [1984] A.C. 689, 700 by Lord Diplock and in *Attorney-General of Hong Kong v. Lee Kwong-kut* [1993] A.C. 951, 962 by Lord Woolf, the Board held that section 116(a) was in conflict with the Constitution and that it had to be modified to conform to it. The words 'if either of the following matters of extenuation be proved on his behalf' were to be construed as though they read 'if there is such evidence as raises a reasonable doubt as to whether': p.1314D–E, per Lord Jauncey of Tullichettle. It was by this means that Belize was brought into line with the other Commonwealth countries of the Caribbean, where the onus of proof of unprovoked killing was placed on the prosecution. It provides a good example of the use of an interpretative obligation of the kind that has now been written into our domestic law by section 3(1) of the 1998 Act.

86. More recently, in *Michael Yearwood v. The Queen* [2001] UKPC (June 2001) the Board held that section 239 of the Grenada Criminal Code, which is in the same terms as section 116 of the Belize Criminal Code, had to be read and given effect to in a way that was compatible with the provisions for the protection of the fundamental rights and freedoms to which every person is entitled under the Constitution of Grenada, and in particular with section 8(2)(a) of the Constitution which entitles a person who is accused of a criminal charge to the presumption of innocence. It held that the words 'are proved on his behalf' in section 239 must be read and given effect to as if for those words there were substituted the words 'are the subject of such evidence as to raise a reasonable doubt.'

87. Of course, the fact that it is possible for a statutory provision to be read in this way does not mean that it must be so read. The first question is whether, leaving aside section 3(1), there would be a breach of the Convention. For the reasons which I sought to explain in *R. v. Director of Public Prosecutions, ex p. Kebilene* [2000] 2 A.C. 326, 383–388, I do not think that a reverse onus provision will inevitably give rise to a finding of incompatibility. In *Salabiaku v. France* (1988) 13 E.H.R.R. 379 at p.388, para. 28 the European Court of Human Rights said:

'Presumptions of fact or of law operate in every legal system. Clearly, the Convention does not prohibit such presumptions in principle. It does, however, require the contracting states to remain within certain limits in this respect as regards criminal law . . . Article 6(2) does not therefore regard presumptions of fact or of law provided for in the criminal law with indifference. It requires states to confine them within reasonable limits which take into account the importance of what is at stake and maintain the rights of the defence.'

88. Mr Owen said that the court was not concerned in the *Salabiaku* case with a provision applicable to a person charged with a serious criminal offence which placed the burden of proof on him with respect to an essential element of it. That is true, but I do not think that this deprives it of value as a statement of principle. What it means is that, as the article 6(2) right is not absolute and unqualified, the test to be applied is whether the modification or limitation of that right pursues a legitimate aim and whether it satisfies the principle of proportionality: *Ashingdane v. United Kingdom* (1985) 7 E.H.R.R. 528; see also *Brown v. Stott* [2001] 2 W.L.R. 817. It is now well settled that the principle which is to be applied requires a balance to be struck between the general interest of the community and the protection of the fundamental rights of the individual. This will not be achieved if the reverse onus provision goes beyond what is necessary to accomplish the objective of the statute.

89. The statutory objective is to penalise the unauthorised possession of dangerous or otherwise harmful drugs. But the statute recognises, among other things, that it would be wrong to penalise those who neither knew nor suspected nor had reason to suspect the existence of some fact alleged by the prosecution which it is necessary for the prosecution to prove if he is to be convicted of the offence charged (section 28(2)) or that the substance or product in question is a controlled drug (section 28(3)(b)(i)). That being so, it is hard to see why a person who is accused of the offence of possessing a controlled drug and who wishes to raise this defence should be deprived of the full benefit of the presumption of innocence. The systems of control and prosecution might well be in jeopardy if there were to be an initial onus on the prosecution to establish that the accused knew these things. The right to silence and the covert and unscrupulous nature of drug-related activities must be taken into account in the assessment as to whether a fair balance had been achieved. But we are not concerned here with the initial onus. As I have said in my answer to the first issue, the prosecution do not need to prove that the accused knew that the thing in his possession was a controlled drug. This is a matter which must be raised by the defence.

90. The choice then is between a persuasive burden, which is what the ordinary meaning of the statutory language lays down, and an evidential burden, which is the meaning which it is possible to give to the statutory language under section 3(1) of the 1998 Act. If the evidential burden were to be so slight as to make no difference—if it were to be enough, for example, for the accused merely to mention the defence without adducing any evidence—important practical considerations would suggest that in the general interest of the community the burden would have to be a persuasive one. But an evidential burden is not to be thought of as a burden which is illusory. What the accused must do is put evidence before the court which, if believed, could be taken by a reasonable jury to support his defence. That is what Professor Glanville Williams envisaged when he was giving this meaning to the words 'unless the contrary is proved': 'The Logic of "Exceptions" ' [1988] C.L.J. 261, 265. It is what the Judicial Committee envisaged in *Vasquez v. The Queen* [1994] 1 W.L.R. 1304, 1314G–H and in *Michael Yearwood v. The Queen* [2001] UKPC . It is what the common law requires of a defendant who wishes to invoke one of the common law defences such as provocation or duress.

91. The practical effect of reading section 28(2) and section 28(3) as imposing an evidential burden only on the accused and not a persuasive burden as they have been understood to impose hitherto is likely in almost every case that can be imagined to be minimal. In *Salmon v. H.M.A.*, 1999 J.C. 67, 75C–D, the Lord Justice General said this as to the effect on the accused of the persuasive burden:

'It is perhaps worth stating explicitly that, even though subsections (2) and (3) speak of the accused proving something, this does not imply that, to establish a defence, the accused must necessarily give evidence. Doubtless, that would often be the simplest method of proof, but the necessary evidence might come, for example, from a 'mixed' statement or from witnesses speaking to what the accused was told was in the container or to the accused's apparent astonishment when the contents of the container were revealed and found to be a controlled drug.'

Those words are equally in point as an explanation of what the evidential burden requires of the accused. The change in the nature of the burden is best understood by looking not at the accused and what he must do, but rather at the state of mind of the judge or jury when they are evaluating the evidence. That is why, in the interests of clarity and convenience as well as on grounds of principle, a fair balance will be struck by reading and giving effect to these subsections as imposing an evidential burden only on the accused.

92. It is worth noting in this connection that Parliament itself has recently recognised the force of the argument that as a general rule statutory provisions which require the accused to prove something as a defence to the offence with which he has been charged should be read and given effect to as if they imposed only an evidential burden on him and not a probative one. The Terrorism Act 2000 contains several provisions which say that it shall be a defence for a person charged with an offence to prove something. For example, section 57(2) provides that it shall be a defence for him to prove that his possession of an article was not for a purpose connected with the commission, preparation or instigation of an act of terrorism. But section 118(2), which applies to a number of provisions in the Act including section 57(2) which say that it is a defence for a person to prove something, provides:

'If the person adduces evidence which is sufficient to raise an issue with respect to the matter the court or jury shall assume that the defence is satisfied unless the prosecution proves beyond reasonable doubt that it is not.'

93. Section 53(3) of the Regulation of Investigatory Powers Act 2000 is to the same effect. It provides a defence to the offence of possession described in section 53(2). It places the onus of proving the contrary beyond a reasonable doubt on the prosecutor if sufficient evidence of that fact is adduced to raise an issue with respect to it. It is not unreasonable to think that, if Parliament were now to have an opportunity of reconsidering the words used in section 28(2) and (3) of the 1971 Act, it would be content to qualify them in precisely the same way.

94. I would therefore read the words 'to prove' in section 28(2) as if the words used in the subsection were 'to give sufficient evidence', and I would give the same meaning to the words 'if he proves' in section 28(3). The effect which is to be given to this meaning is that the burden of proof remains on the prosecution throughout. If sufficient evidence is adduced to raise the issue, it will be for the prosecution to show beyond reasonable doubt that the defence is not made out by the evidence. The question whether these provisions must be read and given effect to in that way in this case depends on the issue of retrospectivity, to which I now turn."

NOTES

See also the Scottish cases of *Brown v. Stott*, 2001 S.L.T. 59; *McIntosh, Petitioner*, 2001 S.L.T. 304, both of which went to the Judicial Committee of the Privy Council for determination of the Human Rights issues. The latter case concerned the compatibility with the European Convention of the statutory assumptions made under section 3 of the Proceeds of Crime (Scotland) Act 1995. Lord Bingham of Cornhill said:

[30] "The European Court has made clear its approach to Art. 6(2) and reversal of the onus of proof in *Salabiaku v. France* and *Hoang v. France*, and the topic has been discussed at some length by the House of Lords in *R. v. DPP, ex p. Kebilene* and by the Judicial Committee of the Privy Council in *Brown v. Stott*. It is unnecessary for present purposes to rehearse those authorities. It is plain that the right is not absolute but equally plain that encroachments on the presumption are not to be uncritically accepted. As the Court put it in *Salabiaku* (in para. 28 of its judgment): 'Article 6(2) does not therefore regard presumptions of fact or of law provided for in the criminal law with indifference. It requires States to confine them within reasonable limits which take into account the importance of what is at stake and maintain the rights of the defence'."

As Lord Hope of Craighead put it in *ex p Kebilene* at [2000] 2 A.C. 326: "As a matter of general principle therefore a fair balance must be struck between the demands of the general interest of the community and the protection of the fundamental rights of the individual: see also *Sporrong and Lönnroth v. Sweden* (1982) 5 E.H.R.R. 35, 52, para. 69."

[31] The general interest of the community in suppressing crime, however important, will not justify a state in riding roughshod over the rights of a criminal defendant, as graphically pointed out by Sachs J in *State v. Coetzee* at [1997] 2 LRC, p.677 (para. 220). But it is not irrelevant. Nor is the position of the defendant. In weighing the balance between the general interest of the community and the rights of the individual, it will be relevant to ask (as Lord Hope suggested in *ex p Kebilene* at p.386) what public threat the provision is directed to address, what the prosecutor must prove to transfer the onus to the defendant and what difficulty the defendant may have in discharging the onus laid upon him. In some cases the acceptability of a reverse onus provision will turn not on consideration of the provision in the abstract but on its application in a particular case. The right to a fair trial, guaranteed by Art. 6(1), will ensure that any reverse onus provision is fairly applied in the given case.

[32] The nature of the public threat to which the Misuse of Drugs Act 1971 and the 1995 Act are directed sufficiently appears from the factors listed [his Lordship cited the reference and continued —]. It is significant that the United Nations Convention already referred to provides, in Art. 5.7: [his Lordship quoted its terms and continued—]. In a 1991 report on The Confiscation of the Proceeds of Crime (LRC 35–1991) the Irish Law Reform Commission recommended the adoption of such a presumption (see p.75 of the report; and, as made clear on p.55, para 32, it regarded the presumption of innocence as inapplicable following conviction).

[33] In seeking to justify the reasonableness and fairness of the assumptions which the court is permitted to make under section 3(2), the Solicitor General drew attention to a number of points:

(1) The starting point of the confiscation order procedure is proof beyond reasonable doubt that the accused has committed a drug trafficking offence: section 1(1) of the 1995 Act.
(2) It is open to the accused to rebut the assumptions on a balance of probabilities.
(3) The facts upon which the accused will rely to rebut the assumptions are peculiarly within his personal knowledge.
(4) The proceedings are fully adversarial and the accused has every opportunity to challenge evidence against him and call witnesses: section 9(6).
(5) It is necessary for the prosecutor to prove the possession of property by and the expenditure of the accused under section 3(2).
(6) The court has a discretion whether to make an order and whether to make the assumptions and will order the accused to pay such sum as it thinks fit: sections 1(1) and 3(2).
(7) The accused has a full right of appeal: section 1(8).
(8) The liability of the accused is limited to the sum which may be realised from him, which if overestimated at first may be later reduced: section 12.
(9) The answers of the accused in the confiscation order proceedings cannot be relied upon against him in any later prosecution: section 9(8).

[34] Counsel for the respondent submitted that the statutory assumptions were impermissible in particular because there was no onus on the prosecutor to raise any ground even for suspecting that the accused had during the relevant period engaged in drug trafficking. He placed strong reliance on *Donnelly v. H.M.A.*, 1999 S.C.C.R. 508 in which Lord Coulsfield, giving the opinion of the court of appeal, said (1999 S.C.C.R. 538):

"there is, in our view, nothing in the legislation to suggest that it is necessary that the court should have some evidence, or ground of suspicion, that the accused has profited from drug-dealing before it can make the order. There is nothing in the wording of section 1 to suggest such a requirement. Section 3(2) similarly provides that the court 'may' make the assumptions there set out, but there is nothing in the wording of section 3 which suggests that the court must have evidence or some ground of suspicion that the accused has profited from drug-dealing before it can make those assumptions, and the structure of the legislation suggests the contrary. The only preconditions for the making of the assumptions which can be found in the statute are that the court must be satisfied that the accused has received payments or incurred expenditure, or both".

At p.539 Lord Coulsfield added:

"In all the circumstances, in our opinion, it is not necessary that there should be either evidence that the accused has benefited from drug dealing or grounds for suspicion that he has so profited before the court can make the assumptions set out in section 3(2), and we therefore reject the main argument in principle advanced on behalf of the appellants."

Lord Prosser (p.1290, para. 31 of his judgment) and Lord Allanbridge (p.1294, para. 5 of his judgment) accepted counsel's submission. The Court of Appeal Criminal Division in *R. v. Benjafield* reached a different conclusion.

[35] On this point also I respectfully differ from the court of appeal. The confiscation order procedure can only be initiated if the accused is convicted of a drug trafficking offence. The court is therefore dealing with a proven drug trafficker. It is then incumbent on the prosecutor to prove, as best he can, the property held by the accused and his expenditure over the chosen period up to six years, including any implicative gifts relied on. In practice the prosecutor's statement lodged under section 9 will always particularise such of the accused's sources of income as are known to the prosecutor, and any source of income known to the prosecutor of any person to whom the accused is said to have made an implicative gift. The schedule served by the prosecutor in this case contained those details (whether accurately or not has not yet been determined) relating to the respondent and Ms Black, and had they

not done so the court would inevitably have exercised its power under section 10 to enable further information to be obtained. It is only if a significant discrepancy is shown between the property and expenditure of the accused on the one hand and his known sources of income on the other that the court will think it right to make the section 3(2) assumptions, and unless the accounting details reveal such a discrepancy the prosecutor will not in practice apply for an order. It would be an obviously futile exercise to seek an order where the assets and expenditure of the accused are fully explained by his known sources of legitimate income. If a significant discrepancy is shown, and in the first instance it is for the prosecutor to show it, I do not for my part think it unreasonable or oppressive to call on the accused to proffer an explanation. He must know the source of his assets and what he has been living on. In the respondent's case (unlike Mr Donnelly's) the sums involved are relatively small, but it cannot be hard for the respondent to explain the source of his and Ms Black's assets and expenditure, matters very much within his knowledge.

[36] The statutory scheme contained in the 1995 Act is one approved by a democratically elected Parliament and should not be at all readily rejected. I would for my part endorse the conclusion of the Court of Appeal Criminal Division in para. 88 of its judgment in *R. v. Benjafield*: "It is very much a matter of personal judgment as to whether a proper balance has been struck between the conflicting interests. Into the balance there must be placed the interests of the defendant as against the interests of the public, that those who have offended should not profit from their offending and should not use their criminal conduct to fund further offending. However, in our judgment, if the discretions which are given to the prosecution and the court are properly exercised, the solution which Parliament has adopted is a reasonable and proportionate response to a substantial public interest, and therefore justifiable."

It should be noted that while in certain types of case the courts have made clear that the burden on the accused is an evidential one only, in practice, that burden can be discharged only by very strong evidence. In criminal cases where the defence of automatism is pleaded, for example, the High Court has made clear that the defence cannot be made out without expert evidence to back up other evidence for the accused—a *de facto* requirement for corroboration, in effect. (See, *e.g. Sorley v. H.M.A.*, 1992 S.L.T. 867; *Carrington v. H.M.A.*, 1995 S.L.T. 341).

Chapter 3

PRESUMPTIONS

A presumption "is an inference as to the existence of one fact, drawn from the existence of another fact". Once certain facts have been established, certain other facts will be presumed by the court. Parties, therefore, can use such presumptions in the discharge of their burdens of proof. Conversely, presumptions may also create burdens for the party against whom the presumption operates. The cases reproduced in Chapter 2 regarding Article 6 of the European Convention on Human Rights arose because of the interaction of the presumption of innocence in criminal cases, which is given particular prominence by Article 6(2) of the Convention, and the statutory incidence of the burden of proof in those cases.

In the same way that there may be provisional burdens, there may also be provisional presumptions—that is, a presumption which may be rebutted by leading contrary evidence. But one must distinguish between presumptions which can be rebutted only by proving the contrary position to some formal standard, and those presumptions which arise merely as a result of the state of the evidence which may be rebutted simply by providing some credible explanation for the evidence proffered. This is the difference between presumptions of law and presumptions of fact. Presumptions of law "represent what are probably the only occasions on which the legal [or persuasive] onus can properly be said to shift from one party to another". (Wilkinson, *The Scottish Law of Evidence*, pp. 194–195.)

1. T. Denning,
"Presumptions and Burdens" (1945) L.Q.R. 379

"Much confusion is often caused by failing to recognise the different senses in which the words 'presumption' and 'burden' are used. Nearly 50 years ago Professor Thayer of Harvard analysed the position, but his work is little known in this country and the confusion has persisted. Recent cases tend more and more to show that the division of presumptions into presumptions of fact and presumptions of law should be discarded. That division is comparatively modern in English law and should be replaced by a division into provisional presumptions, compelling presumptions, and conclusive presumptions. Burdens should not be left in a heterogeneous mass but should be divided into legal burdens, provisional burdens and ultimate burdens. Before I criticise the existing position, I propose to state the meaning of the new distinctions.

1. *Legal Burdens*. When the law puts on a party the burden of proving a certain fact in issue as a condition of giving him judgement, that burden never shifts and must be discharged or he will fail. For instance, when the issue is whether the prisoner is guilty of murder; or of receiving; or whether the defendent was negligent; or whether the ship was unseaworthy; or whether the goods were lost without the default of the bailee; or whether the will was the last will of a free and capable testator; the law places the burden of proof on the person who puts forward the proposition. This is the legal burden of proving the fact in issue. The incidence of it does not depend on whether the averment is positive or negative, for that can be varied by a change of language. It depends on the rules of substantive policy, as Professor Stone has recently pointed out.

2. *Provisional Presumptions and Burdens*. In order to discharge a legal burden, the person on whom it lies will often prove relevant facts or rely on presumptions from which he asks the Court to infer the fact in issue which he has to establish in order to succeed. In the instances I have taken he will prove that the prisoner killed a man; or was found in possession of goods

recently stolen; or that the thing which caused the accident was under the control of the defendant; or that the ship was lost within a short time of sailing; or that the goods were stolen; or he will rely on the presumption that the testator was of testamentary capacity. Those relevant facts or circumstances are often said to raise a 'presumption' or make a 'prima facie' case, and so they do in the sense that from them the fact in issue may be inferred, but not in the sense that it must be inferred unless the contrary is proved. The Court will decline before the end of the case to rule whether the fact in issue should be inferred. It will leave it to the other party to take his own course. He may seek to repel the inference by argument, as by submitting that the facts proved only raise a suspicion as distinct from a legitimate inference; or by contradicting the evidence; or by giving evidence of other facts to explain why the fact in issue should not be inferred; or by raising suspicions which counter-balance the presumptions. As the case proceeds the evidence may first weigh in favour of the inference and then against it, thus producing a shift from one party to the other as the case proceeds or may remain suspended between them. The party on whom it rests must call evidence or take the consequences, which may not necessarily be adverse: for the place where the burden eventually comes to rest does not necessarily decide the issue: because at the end of the case the Court has to decide as a matter of fact whether the inference should be drawn or not. These presumptions and burdens are therefore provisional only. It is a mistake to raise these provisional presumptions into propositions having the force of law. They are recognised by the law but their force depends on ordinary good sense rather than on law. They are only guides to the Court in deciding whether to infer the fact in issue or not. The degree of probability needed to establish an inference varies. When considering the guilt of a person accused of an offence of a criminal nature, the Court requires a high degree of probability. It must be satisfied beyond reasonable doubt. On all other issues, whether in civil or criminal cases, the Court is satisfied with a moderate degree of probability. It is sufficient if there is a greater probability on one side or the other; but if at the end of the case the evidence is so evenly balanced that the Court cannot come to a determinate conclusion, the legal burden comes into play and requires the Court to reject the inference.

3. *Compelling Presumptions*. It often happens that a party proves facts from which the Court must in law draw an inference in his favour unless the other side proves the contrary or proves some other fact which the law recognises as sufficient to rebut the inference. For instance, once money is proved to have been received by a public servant from a person who is seeking a Government contract, it is deemed to have been received corruptly unless the contrary is proved; or, once a child is proved to have been born in wedlock, it is presumed to be legitimate unless the other side prove non-access or incapacity by the husband; or when two people die at about the same time, the younger is presumed to have survived the elder, unless it is proved that the elder survived the younger. These presumptions differ from provisional presumptions in that they have the compelling force of law; and whereas provisional presumptions give rise to provisional burdens within a single issue, a compelling presumption gives rise to a separate issue on which the legal burden is on the other side.

4. *Ultimate Burdens*. Where the ultimate decision of a case depends on the determination of a number of separate issues, the burden on the ultimate issue needs to be distinguished from the burden on the separate issues. For instance, where a holder sues an acceptor of a bill of exchange, the ultimate decision depends on whether he is a holder in due course; or where charterers claim against shipowners for failure to lead, the ultimate decision depends on whether the owners broke their contract. At the outset the plaintiff will often content himself by proving facts, or relying on admitted facts, from which the Court must in law draw an inference which will decide the case in his favour unless the defendant proves some other facts. For instance, the plaintiff will prove that he is the holder of the bill and that the defendant signed it as acceptor or that the ship did not arrive within the contract time. Those facts are often said to raise a 'presumption' or make a 'prima facie' case, and so they do and of a compelling kind, because from them the Court not only may, but must in law decide the case in favour of the plaintiff unless the defendant makes good a defence such as fraud in the negotiation; or that the contract was frustrated by destruction of the ship. That is a separate issue on which the legal burden is on the defendant. If he discharges it, the Court must in law

decide the case in favour of the defendant unless the plaintiff makes good a reply such as value in good faith subsequent to the fraud; or that the destruction of the ship was due to the owner's fault. That again is a separate issue and the legal burden of proving it is on the plaintiff. So on, to and fro the legal burden of proof on each separate issue is on the party who has by law to establish it in order to succeed, and the ultimate decision will depend on which of the parties has in his turn discharged the legal burden resting on him. This shifting to and fro is often described as a shifting of the burden of proof and so it is, but it is a shifting of the ultimate burden: and the compelling presumption and circumstances, which produce the shift, have the force of law. The burden of proof on each of the separate issues is a legal burden which never shifts.

5. *Conclusive Presumptions*. It is a misuse of language to speak of any presumption being conclusive, but the meaning is clear enough. On proof of certain facts the Court must draw a particular inference, whether true or not, and it cannot be rebutted. For instance, once it appears that a deserting husband has been certified as a lunatic for any part, maybe only a week, of the three years preceding the petition, the Court must find him not guilty of desertion for that period, however strong the evidence of desertion may be for the remainder of the period for which he was sane.

Now let me turn to the existing distinctions

1. *Presumptions of Law and Presumptions of Fact*. The distinction is not clearly drawn in the books, but it would appear that presumptions of law are presumptions of general application recognised by the law; whereas presumptions of fact are presumptions from the facts of a particular case. The division is unsatisfactory because the line between them is difficult to draw and it does not connote any difference in the legal effect of the presumptions. On the one hand take the presumption of negligence in cases of *res ipsa loquitur*; and the presumption of unseaworthiness in case of loss shortly after sailing. Both are recognised by the law but they are classed as presumptions of fact and are provisional only. On the other hand, take the presumption that a man intends the probable consequences of his acts; and the presumption of death after seven years' absence. Both are classed as presumptions of law, but they also are provisional only. For instance, when the legal burden is on a party to prove a specific intent, such as an intent to prefer creditors, or an intent to resist arrest, or the intent to injure involved in conspiracy, the presumption that a person intends the probable consequences of his acts may carry little weight; and when a husband has deserted his wife for seven years, and she has made no inquiries as to his whereabouts, the fact that she has no reason to believe him to be living within that time may be insufficient to persuade the Court to presume his death. Then again there are some presumptions of law the effect of which appears to vary according to the issue in which they arise. For instance, the presumption of sanity appears to be a compelling presumption in criminal cases where the legal burden is on the accused who pleads insanity to prove it, whereas it appears to be only a provisional presumption in probate cases where the legal burden is on the person who propounds a will to prove sanity; and the presumption of innocence appears to be a compelling presumption in criminal cases where the legal burden is on the prosecution of proving guilt, whereas it appears to be only a provisional presumption in divorce cases where the legal burden is on the petitioner of negativing collusion. The correct view probably is that these presumptions of sanity and innocence are in all cases provisional only, and that the decisive factor is the legal burden. Once it is seen that there are many presumptions of law which are not provisional only and have therefore the same effect as presumptions of fact (which are always provisional) there is no useful purpose to be served by maintaining the distinction.

2. *Burdens*. Whilst the trouble about presumptions is that they have been grouped into unscientific categories, the trouble about burdens is that the different categories are not commonly distinguished at all. In familiar cases one finds judges reported as saying that the burden of proof may shift during the course of a case, without noticing that it is only provisional or ultimate burdens which may shift. The legal burden never shifts. Many errors

have occurred because judges have not kept the distinction in mind and the position has had to be put right by appellate tribunals. The leading example occurred in an action on a marine policy where the defence was unseaworthiness. The judge directed the jury that the fact that the ship was unable to proceed shortly after sailing, gave rise to a presumption of unseaworthiness which shifted the burden of proof and threw it on the assured. On appeal, this was held to be a misdirection, because the legal burden remained throughout on the underwriters. The presumption of unseaworthiness in such a case is a provisional presumption only. Another notable example occurred in a murder case. The judge directed the jury that, once the accused was proved to have killed the deceased, it was presumed to be murder unless he proved he was not guilty; and the direction was approved by the Court of Criminal Appeal. The House of Lords reversed the decision, pointing out that the legal burden was on the prosecution to prove the guilt of the accused and it never shifted. The presumption from the fact of killing, like the presumption from being found in possession of goods recently stolen, is provisional only and gives rise to a provisional burden. It is not compelling and does not give rise to a legal burden. Another striking example occurred when the Ceylon Legislature enacted that 'when any fact is especially within the knowledge of any person, the burden of proving that fact is on him'. A judge trying a criminal case interpreted that as meaning that the legal burden was on the accused to prove he had not committed the offence. The Privy Council pointed out that that is not the law. The burden referred to in the enactment is provisional only. It cannot supply the want of necessary evidence. A recent example occurred in an *obiter dictum* when a Lord Justice drew a parallel between the burden arising in cases of *res ipsa loquitur* and the burden on a bailee of proving that the goods were lost without his fault. He said they were the same doctrine. In truth, the one is a provisional burden and the other a legal burden, and the difference may often be decisive. It is unnecessary, however, to multiply illustrations. The confusion has often been pointed out. The only way to avoid it, whenever the words 'burden of proof' are used, is to make clear which particular sense is intended.

3. *Conflicting Presumptions.* The only distinction has led to difficulties when presumptions have come into conflict. For instance, when a man has gone through a ceremony of marriage with three women and is charged with bigamy in marrying the third during the life of the second, there may be a presumption of innocence on the occasion of the second marriage so as to presume its validity (classed as a presumption of law) which may conflict with a presumption in favour of the duration of life of the first woman (classed as a presumption of fact). Any nice discussion on conflicting presumptions is foreign to English law. The preferable approach in such a case would be to recognise that the presumptions are provisional presumptions only which can and should be discarded when they conflict, leaving the issue to be determined by the jury on the facts, the legal burden being in the last resort decisive.

The reader will have noticed that the illustrations in this article are all taken from familiar cases, but I have not given the references to many of them. This is because I am concerned here, not with particular branches of law, but with a new set of distinctions running through the whole law, in an attempt to remove the confusion produced by the old."

NOTES

Presumptions do not render evidence wholly unnecessary. They do not exist in a vacuum, and must be "triggered" by proof of certain facts. For example, once it is shown that a person has not been known to be alive for a period of seven years, that person will be presumed to have died (Presumption of Death (Scotland) Act 1977, s.2). Again, if it is proved that a person was found in possession of recently stolen goods, and the circumstances of that possession are shown to be incriminating, then it will be presumed that that person stole the goods. These "trigger facts", and the presumptions which arise from them, may be the result of common law development or statutory intervention. "In many cases they have little more to recommend them than practical convenience, public policy or long usage, and in some cases they fail to reflect modern attitudes and practices." (Field and Raitt, *The Law of Evidence in Scotland* (2nd ed., 1996) para. 3–05). Moreover, in the case of the so-called doctrine of recent possession, for example, it is unclear precisely when the "presumption" is triggered. What precisely are "incriminating" circumstances?

2. Fox v. Patterson
1948 J.C. 104

The accused, who was a scrap metal dealer, was charged with the theft of a quantity of phosphor bronze alloy. He claimed to have bought the metal from a man in Glasgow, who gave him his name and a receipt for the purchase price. This man could not be traced by the police. The metal was then sold for a "fair price" on the open market to one of the accused's regular customers. The prosecution relied on the presumption that a person found in possession of recently stolen goods is the thief. The accused was convicted and appealed to the High Court.

LORD JUSTICE-GENERAL (COOPER): "When applied with due regard to its limitations, the rule of recent possession of stolen goods is salutary and sensible but, if its limitations are not observed, the cardinal presumption of innocence may easily be transformed into a rash assumption of guilt. The rule and its limitations are stated in substantially the same sense by Hume (Commentaries, vol. i, p.111), Alison (Criminal Law, vol. i, pp.320 *et seq*) and Dickson (Evidence [Grierson's ed.] vol. i, sections 73 and 157), and to these classical citations I add a quotation aptly given by Dickson (section 73) from Bentham: 'Nothing can be more persuasive,' he says, 'than the circumstance of possession commonly is, when corroborated by other criminative circumstances; nothing more inconclusive, supposing it to stand alone . . . Possession of the jewel, actual possession, may thus belong to half a dozen different persons at the same time; and as to antecedent possession, the number of possible successive possessors is manifestly beyond all limit.'

If the rule is to have full effect in shifting the onus from the prosecution to the accused and raising a presumption of guilt which the accused must redargue or fail, three conditions must concur: (a) that the stolen goods should be found in the possession of the accused; (b) that the interval between the theft of the goods and their discovery in the accused's possession should be short—how short I need not in this case inquire; and (c) that there should be 'other criminative circumstances' over and above the bare fact of possession. If all these conditions are not present—if, for instance, the interval between the theft and the discovery is prolonged, or if the accused has only had temporary possession of the goods and has parted with them normally and openly—the facts which can be proved may well constitute ingredients (*quantum valeat*) in the case, and may combine with other factors to enable the Crown to establish guilt. But, unless all three conditions concur, the accused cannot be required to accept the full onus of positively excluding every element of guilt. Even when they concur, the weight of the resulting presumption, and the evidence required to elide it, will vary from case to case."

NOTES

This case, and particularly the passage in which Lord Justice-General Cooper refers to "the full onus of positively excluding every element of guilt" suggests that the presumption is one of law, which in turn gives rise to a persuasive burden of rebuttal on the accused. That suggestion was severely criticised by Gordon, "The Burden of Proof on the Accused", 1968 S.L.T. (News) 29 at 37, on the ground that it conflicted with the presumption of innocence—the very difficulty Lord Cooper wished in this case to avoid. Moreover, such a conflict may also give rise to questions about the accused's Convention rights, as we saw in Chapter 2. The High Court appears now to have retreated from the position taken up in *Fox v. Patterson*, although the law is by no means absolutely settled. In *Macdonald (J.McF.) v. H.M.A.*, 1989 S.C.C.R. 559, the Sheriff directed the jury that once facts were present which allowed the doctrine to be invoked, it was for the accused to prove his or her innocence. The accused's conviction was overturned on appeal. Lord Justice-General Emslie said (at p.562):

"We stress that the phrase which we criticise is the phrase 'to prove his or her innocence', which goes further than any formulation of the effect of the shifting of the onus in any of the authorities to which we were referred. In *Fox v. Patterson*, Lord Justice General Cooper referred to the rule as having the effect of shifting the onus from the prosecution to the accused and raising a presumption of guilt which the accused must redargue or fail. In *Cameron v. H.M.A.* Lord Justice-General Clyde referred to Lord Justice-General Cooper's formulation as the standard definition of the doctrine of recent possession, of which he said:

'The doctrine is, of course, an exception to the general rule, that throughout the onus of proof remains upon the Crown. But the nature of the offence is the justification for the exception'.

It is clear therefore, as the learned Advocate-Depute pointed out, that the doctrine cannot be confined within the ordinary rule that the onus of proof remains throughout on the Crown. But it is another matter to assert, without further guidance or explanation, that [it] is for the accused to prove his or her innocence."

If it is the case that the burden imposed by the presumption is a tactical one only, is there any need for a "presumption" at all? Evidence of all sorts may give rise to inferences, which in turn place tactical burdens on an opposing party to find an explanation for the evidence. The status of "presumption" therefore arguably gives more weight to certain circumstances than they might otherwise merit. This, of course, is a criticism of presumptions of fact generally, since like the "doctrine" of recent possession, all depend for their effect on the precise circumstances of the case.

Two other categories of "presumption" may be mentioned. The first is the so-called irrebuttable presumption of law. One example of such a "presumption" is the rule that children under the age of eight are not criminally liable for their actions (Criminal Procedure (Scotland) Act 1995, s.41); another is the similar rule that children under the age of 12 are incapable of consent to sexual intercourse (Sexual Offences (Scotland) Act 1976, ss.3, 4). The more accurate view is that these are not truly presumptions at all, but fixed rules. (See Denning's article, "Presumptions and Burdens", part of which is reproduced above). Evidence in rebuttal of such rules is incompetent. A second category is the presumption which does not require proof of any "trigger facts". Again, these are not strictly presumptions at all, but rules governing the burden of proof—the presumptions of innocence and sanity are examples of these, respectively requiring the prosecution to prove guilt and an accused person to prove insanity in a case where the defence is raised.

3.   Imre v. Mitchell
1958 S.C. 439

The pursuer met the defender, Mitchell, and had sexual intercourse with him in April 1948. In August of that year, she told him that she was pregnant, and he suggested that they get married. The baby was born prematurely in December and they were married in January of the following year, thus legitimising the child. The pursuer subsequently began a relationship with another man and Mitchell divorced her in 1951. To try to circumvent the custody award made in Mitchell's favour, the pursuer then raised an action for declarator that the child was a bastard and to put Mitchell to silence from claiming paternity of the child. The evidence led for the pursuer included evidence of the result of blood tests which purported to show that the defender could not have been the father of the child.

LORD PRESIDENT (CLYDE): "I turn therefore to the main issue in this case, and to the question whether the pursuer has succeeded in establishing that her child is a bastard. The law of Scotland has never approached such a question from the point of view of a mere balancing of probabilities, or even as a question where the ordinary rules of onus of proof alone apply. On the contrary, our law has always regarded the label of illegitimacy as involving a taint which the Courts will be slow to attach to any child unless the circumstances clearly warrant it. For once the label is attached it will almost certainly accompany that child to the grave. It is unnecessary to speculate whether this approach is based on considerations of public policy or of fairness to the child whose fate in this world is being decided at a time when the child is too young to stand up for itself. But the authorities establish two matters of prime importance in this connexion each of which has a direct bearing on the circumstances of the present case.

In the first place it is well settled, in my opinion, that in cases such as the present there is a very strong presumption in favour of legitimacy. In the case of a child conceived and born during marriage this presumption is described in the phrase *pater est quem nuptiae demonstrant*. As Erskine [Inst. (Nicolson's ed.), i, vi, 49.] puts it, 'This legal presumption may doubtless be overruled by a contrary proof; but the favour of marriage is so strong and the securing of the point of legitimacy so important to society that it cannot be defeated but by direct evidence that the mother's husband could not be the father of the child.' But the presumption is not limited to such cases. There may in certain circumstances be a similar presumption even in the case of a child conceived before marriage, and legitimated by a subsequent marriage. As Lord Blackburn said in *Gardner v. Gardner* 4 R. (HL) 56 at p.68: 'I take it that we cannot express what I think is really the leading point here in better words than those which were used by Lord Gifford' (in the court below) 'namely: "Wherever an avowed and open courtship has taken place, and there have been opportunities of access, and thereafter the man marries the woman in an advanced state of pregnancy knowing that she is so, and hurrying on the marriage, as happened here, for that very reason, I do not say that the presumption of paternity is absolutely conclusive, but I do say that it is almost as strong as such a presumption can be." ' 'Such' (said Lord Blackburn) 'are the words of Lord Gifford, and that, I apprehend, is correct. That is my opinion, and I think it is what any man, who knows what would be the ordinary way in which a human being might be expected to act, would say. The inference to be drawn is that a man must, when he married under such circumstances, have believed that he was the parent of the child, and consequently . . . must have known that he had had connexion with the mother at such a time that she who was to his knowledge with child when he married her might have been with child by him. I think my Lords the conclusion from that is excessively strong—almost irresistible.'

In my opinion, this almost irresistible presumption applies to the circumstances of the present case. The Lord Ordinary holds it proved that there was intercourse between the pursuer and Mitchell in April 1948 when the child was conceived. The marriage was arranged because the husband knew that she was pregnant and married her because he believed he was the father. It is true that the child was actually born before the marriage took place, but this is truly irrelevant since the child was born prematurely and it was only because of that prematurity that the wedding has not taken place before the birth. All the circumstances necessary to raise the presumption are therefore present.

It was argued that Gardner's case merely dealt with a presumption that intercourse must have taken place, and not with a presumption of paternity. But the speeches in the House of Lords do not bear this out and I have felt unable to interpret the decision or the principles laid down as confined to so narrow a compass.

But in the second place, and apart from this question of a presumption, there is a further factor in regard to the pursuer's acknowledgement of the child as being Mitchell's which is also of material importance in the present case. This factor was not present in *Gardner v. Gardner*, and it makes it even more difficult than it was in *Gardner's* case, for a parent seeking to persuade the Court to bastardise a child.

Before considering the law on this aspect of the case it will make for clarity if I summarise the salient facts established in the evidence regarding the pursuer's acknowledgement of the child as Mitchell's. They are as follows: The pursuer represented to Mitchell in August 1948 that he was the father of the child she was then carrying: she went to live with Mitchell along with the child, and allowed his relations to regard the child as his: she acquiesced in the child being registered in the Register of Births as fathered by Mitchell, and she represented to the minister when the child was baptised that Mitchell was the father. Finally, she did not oppose Mitchell obtaining from the Court a decree for custody of the child as being his, and she has allowed this decree to remain operative and unreduced since 1951. Had the pursuer established some honest and convincing explanation which would have justified her having falsely acknowledged the child as Mitchell's, the Court might have put some reliance on her evidence. Such an explanation must inevitably be forthcoming only very rarely, and there is nothing of the kind in the present case. In these circumstances, in my opinion, the Court should in this case give no weight to the evidence of a mother who after acknowledging the child as Mitchell's subsequently on oath denies that Mitchell is the father.

The reason is not merely that no Court will look with favour upon a pursuer who on oath gives the lie to all her previous conduct. It is based on a more deeply rooted principle than that. Under the Canon Law declarations by parents made on oath denying the legitimacy of their children were sufficient to bastardise them. But even in the Canon Law it was recognised that if anyone acknowledges someone as their son, and he is so commonly reputed, no belief is to be given to either parent who afterwards swears the contrary (Decretals of Gregory IX, II, xix, 10). The law of Scotland has not placed such conclusive reliance on the sworn declaration by the parent that a child is illegitimate, because of the presumptions to which I have already referred. But the law of Scotland has incorporated from the Canon Law the reluctance to accept evidence by a parent that the child is illegitimate if that child has once been acknowledged as legitimate. Hence Bankton [Inst., I, ii, 3] states: 'If they (the parents) once own the child, they cannot afterwards prejudice its legitimacy, nor will the assertion of one of them avail to that purpose.' The passage in question is dealing with children born in lawful wedlock where the presumption *pater est* of course operates. But I see no reason in principle why the situation should be any different where the child is legitimated *per subsequens matrimonium* in which case an almost irresistible presumption may arise—see Gardner. The matter is put thus by Erskine [Inst. (Nicolson's ed.), I, vi, 49.]: 'It is an agreed point by all writers, that if either of the two (parents) have before making such oath, acknowledged the child as lawful, there is a right acquired to him by that acknowledgement which is not to be taken away by any posterior testimony to the contrary.' In my opinion, this principle applies in the present case and renders the testimony of the pursuer in the present case of no avail for the purpose of establishing her case of illegitimacy.

It was contended that the principle could be carried further and would operate as a complete personal bar against the pursuer's success in this action. But I can find no authority for such a contention, nor any logical justification for it. The principle has never been regarded as excluding other evidence apart from that of the parents themselves which might establish the bastardy of the child.

In the result, therefore, I approach the facts with two considerations in view: firstly that there is in the circumstances of this case an almost irresistible presumption of legitimacy; and secondly that the testimony of the pursuer herself can be of no avail to overcome that presumption.

The evidence for legitimacy consists firstly of the testimony of the pursuer, and secondly of evidence regarding certain blood tests. I disregard the evidence of the pursuer as not availing anything towards contradicting her repeated acknowledgements of Mitchell as the father of the child. The only evidence left therefore upon which the pursuer can succeed is the evidence of the blood tests. I can hardly imagine a case in which a Court of law would hold a child to be illegitimate solely on evidence regarding blood tests. But I am clearly of opinion that in the present case the evidence regarding the tests which were made was not sufficiently conclusive to overcome the strong presumption which the facts disclosed that the child was legitimate. If the question had been an ordinary matter of the onus of proof the evidence might have been enough, but in this case the onus on the pursuer is a particularly heavy one and in my opinion the blood tests are not sufficiently infallible to overcome it."

NOTES

The presumption of law described in *Imre v. Mitchell* was clearly a very strong one—"almost irresistible", as the Lord President puts it. The blood test evidence in this case indicated that the chance of the defender actually being the father was about 100,000 to one against. Nevertheless, that evidence was not considered strong enough to overcome the presumption of legitimacy. It is arguable that the standard imposed in this case rendered the presumption virtually irrebuttable. The *ratio* of this case has since been overruled, partly as a result of changes in the law which abolish the legal disadvantages of the former status of illegitimacy (Law Reform (Parent and Child) (Scotland) Act 1986, s.1(1)). The presumption *pater est* remains, but can be rebutted by leading evidence to the ordinary civil standard—the balance of probabilities (1986 Act, above, section 5. See also *Docherty v. McGlynn*, 1983 S.L.T. 645). Clearly, however, the distinction between a presumption of law and a presumption of fact is an important one, since a presumption of law may place a significantly heavier burden on a defender than a presumption of fact.

4. Millar v. Mitchell, Cadell and Co.
(1860) 22 D. 833

In this case, the defenders acted as agents for a German principal in the sale of a quantity of bones to the pursuers. The German firm committed a breach of contract and the question arose as to whether the defenders were personally liable for the breach. The usual rule is that where agents act for a principal who is disclosed to the third party, only the principal is liable under the contract. In this case, however, it was argued by the pursuers that where the principal was foreign a different rule applied.

OPINION OF THE COURT: "We should have gathered . . . that the Lord Ordinary meant to affirm, as a general proposition, that when an agent in this country contracts for a foreign seller, though *factorio nomine*, and with the name of his principal disclosed, the law presumes that he pledges, and that the buyer relies on his personal credit, and that he is therefore liable to fulfil the seller's part of the contract; or, in other words, that there is a presumption or rule of law to this effect. But in the note appended to the interlocutor, the Lord Ordinary states that he is 'inclined to think that it is merely a presumption or probability in point of fact.' But if it be mere presumption of fact, or, as the institutional writers express it, *praesumptio hominis*, we think it ought not to have been made the subject of a finding, apart from 'the circumstances of the case altogether;' for such presumptions, as Mr Erskine says (iv 2, 37), 'daily emerge from the various circumstances of the special cases, and on which it is the duty of a judge to lay more or less weight, according to the several degrees of evidence which they carry with them.' The ultimate fact to be supported in this case by presumption, is the intention of the parties in making the contract, and if it is to be presumed in all cases, according to our practice, that a home agent selling for a disclosed foreign principal binds himself personally, till the contrary be proved by the agent, then this is a presumption of law, for it is the essential characteristic of a presumption of law, that it is conclusive till it be rebutted by contrary probation. But if it be only a presumption of fact, then as the intention of the parties in making the contract (unless directly expressed by the terms of the contract) is not a physical fact cognisable by the senses, but a fact as purely psychological as the intention of a testator, or the dole of a murderer, no inference, or, in other words, no presumption of fact can be safely made or applied to the case, except as the result of an examination of the whole circumstances in evidence. It depends on what we popularly call circumstantial evidence. And in a case of this description we are of opinion that the proper tribunal to draw the inference from the circumstances, is a jury, under the direction of a judge, and we think it is much to be regretted, that the shape in which the parties brought this case before the Lord Ordinary, prevented the usual course and mode of inquiry from being followed.

But apart from the ground of judgment adopted by the Lord Ordinary, we understand, further, that our opinion is asked whether there is any *praesumptio juris*, or rule of law, that where an agent in this country sells for a foreign house to a merchant in this country, he is personally liable to fulfil the seller's part of the contract, though he contract expressly *factorio nomine*, and disclose his principal at the time of contracting.

We are of the opinion that there is no such presumption or rule in the law of Scotland . . . In the absence of any authoritative recognition of this presumption, it is difficult to understand how it can have any place in our jurisprudence as a proper presumption of law. A *praesumptio juris* may be introduced, either by statute or custom; it may have its origin in some strong natural probability assented to by the general voice of mankind, or in some usage of trade, drawing uniformly the same inference from a certain fact or combination of facts; but before it can have the authority of a proper *praesumptio juris*, it must be recognised, and take its place as a part of the system to which it belongs. Till it has been so recognised it is fact and not law."

NOTES

Miller v. Mitchell, Cadell and Co. suggests that the distinction between these two different types of presumption hinges on whether or not the rule inverts the burden of proof, requiring the other party to establish the contrary to some formal standard (usually the civil one). Furthermore, it seems that a presumption remains one of fact unless and until it is accepted as a presumption of law. This leads to the rather unhelpful and circular view that a presumption of law is one which is accepted as such by the courts. In the taxonomy of presumptions, however, it may be that other factors require consideration.

5. Pragnell O'Neill v. Lady Skiffington
1984 S.L.T. 282

In this case, the pursuer had lived with the defender for some years, during which time they acquired an extensive collection of works of art, ornaments, and furniture. The relationship ended acrimoniously and the pursuer left, taking with him only a few essentials. A dispute arose as to the ownership of various items in the collection which the pursuer claimed belonged to him.

LORD HUNTER: "The second main argument presented by counsel for the respondent in answer to the submission by counsel for the appellant was based on the presumption derived from the possession by the defender at the date of the raising of the present action of the articles listed in findings-in-fact 16 and 17. It was contended on behalf of the respondent, and conceded by counsel for the appellant, that the defender, having been in possession of the said articles at the time when the action was raised, must be presumed to be their owner unless the pursuer has succeeded in displacing the presumption in the manner required by the institutional writers: Stair's Institutions, II I. 42; Erskine's Institute, II. I. 24; see also *Scot v. Elliot*; *Russel v. Campbell*; *Macdougall v. Whitelaw*. It is clear from the authorities that the presumption of ownership arising from proof of possession of moveables is one 'of fact, more or less strong according to the circumstances, but capable of being redargued' (*George Hopkinson Ltd v. Napier & Son*, per Lord President Cooper at p.102). It has also been said that the presumption is one 'liable to be rebutted, and perhaps liable to be rebutted easily' (*Anderson v. Buchanan* per Lord Cockburn at p.284). Whether it may be easy or difficult to rebut the presumption depends on circumstances, which may vary greatly. The method by which the presumption may be rebutted has been expressed as follows: 'In overcoming the presumption by proving the property, it must be shown not only that the moveables once belonged to the person seeking to recover them, but that his possession terminated in such a way that the subsequent possessor could not have acquired a right of property in them' (Dickson on Evidence (3rd ed.), s.150). In my opinion the passage just quoted, which itself is followed by quotation of the concluding passage in the report of the opinion of their Lordships in *Russel v. Campbell* at p.469, embodies a correct statement of the law. It demonstrates, in particular, that the party seeking to rebut the presumption must surmount two obstacles.

The application of the principle, thus derived from the authorities, to the circumstances of the present case in my opinion presents a certain amount of difficulty . . . I am satisfied that the defender starts with a presumption in her favour of ownership of the articles still in dispute, that presumption, which is one of fact, being based on her possession of the said articles as at the date when the present action was raised. I am prepared to assume that in his attempt to rebut the presumption the pursuer has succeeded in surmounting the first of the two obstacles. In the case of the articles listed in finding-in-fact 16 it is found in fact that the articles were 'at one time' in the pursuer's possession. In the case of the articles listed in finding-in-fact 17 it is found in fact that the pursuer 'purchased' the articles. As the word 'purchased' is unqualified, I am prepared to assume that in each case covered by finding-in-fact 17 the pursuer made the purchase on his own behalf, and therefore at different times prior to 21 June 1979 became the owner and possessor of them. However, even if the pursuer has succeeded in surmounting the first obstacle, I have reached the conclusion that he has failed to surmount the second. My reason for reaching this conclusion is that on the findings the pursuer has failed to establish that his possession of the articles listed in findings-in-fact 16 and 17 terminated in such a way that the defender, who was subsequent possessor, could not have acquired a right to property in them. In other words, to adopt the language used by the court in *Russel v. Campbell* in p.469, the pursuer has failed to prove *quomodo desierat possidere*."

LORD DUNPARK: "The last paragraph of his note suggests that [the Sheriff] decided the question of disputed ownership in the respondent's favour because he believed her. If that is so, then I am of the conclusion that he reached the correct conclusion for the wrong reason. However, at an earlier stage of his note he says this: 'At best for the pursuer, on the evidence, as regards of the bulk of the items his claim is no better than that of the defender. If so the defender has possession. I think that in these circumstances the maxim in *pari causa melior est condition possidentis* would apply and the defender would succeed'. If he has not applied the maxim in the respondent's favour, then, in my opinion, he ought to have done so. She has had exclusive natural possession of all the articles in dispute since at least June 21, 1979. As the sheriff says, the appellant's claim to the bulk of the items was no better than the respondent's. I am of opinion that the respondent is presumed to be owner of these articles by virtue of that possession and that the appellant has failed to prove that he was the owner of the articles claimed by him except the Tricity freezer and the cat group aforementioned."

LORD GRIEVE: "Having rejected the respondent's submission to the effect that she had established ownership of the disputed articles prior to June 21, 1979, I was initially attracted to the submissions made on behalf of the appellant but, on reflection, I have come to the conclusion that they are not well founded. It is common ground that the disputed articles were in the possession of the respondent on June 21, 1979. Her ownership of them as at that date must be presumed unless it can be demonstrated that she only acquired possession of them by some unlawful act. If the appellant is to succeed in demonstrating that the closing of the door of Innergellie House was the unlawful act by which the respondent gained possession of the articles in question he must be able to point to a finding, or findings, in fact from which it can be clearly inferred that as at 21 June 1979 he was the rightful owner of the articles. He sought to do so by pointing to the opening words of findings 16 and 17. It is true that these findings simply re-echoed the terms of a joint minute of admissions, but it is significant in my opinion that the sheriff left them just as they had been in that minute, and made no finding that the articles 'at one time' possessed by the appellant, and at some time purchased by him, had remained in his possession until June 21, 1979. In my opinion no more can be taken from finding 16 than that the articles therein listed were at one time in the possession of the appellant, and no more can be taken from finding 17 than that the articles therein listed were at some time purchased, and owned by, the appellant. In the absence of a finding that these articles remained in the appellant's possession until he was deprived of it by being excluded from Innergellie House, the admitted possession of the articles by the respondent cannot be said to have been unlawful. As counsel for the respondent submitted in answer to the appellant's submissions, it was for the appellant to prove ownership of the articles in respect of which he sought delivery from the respondent, and he had failed to do so. The fact that the respondent had failed to prove that she owned the articles prior to June 21, 1979 did not assist the appellant, the onus of proof being on him. Until the appellant's ownership of the disputed articles as at June 21, had been established, these articles admittedly having been in the possession at that date, the presumption that the respondent owned them could not be displaced. I think these submissions are well founded, and that this appeal fails. Put very shortly the absence of a finding that the appellant owned the disputed articles as at 21 June 1979 is in my opinion fatal to his submissions. Authority for this is to be found in the institutional writers, Stair, II. I. 42 and Erskine, II. I. 24, and in Dickson on *Evidence* (3rd ed.), s.150."

NOTES

It is clear that the application and strength of presumptions of fact will depend on the precise circumstances of the case, as we saw in relation to *Fox v. Patterson*, above. Thus, the "trigger facts" for such presumptions may be prone to an almost infinite degree of variation. Conversely, the "trigger facts" for presumptions of law are fixed and unchanging. But although the judges in the preceding case took the view that the presumption of ownership arising from possession is one of fact, it is clear that the pursuer had to prove certain matters on a balance of probabilities before his claim could succeed. This suggests that the presumption cast a persuasive burden on the pursuer which in turn suggests a presumption of law. On the other hand, the burden of proving ownership would normally rest on a pursuer seeking delivery of articles in any event, and so it is difficult to see how the burden of proof is affected or *shifted* by this presumption. Wilkinson describes the presumption arising from the possession of moveables as one of law, while Field and Raitt follow the conventional view that it is one of fact. A still more difficult example relates to the so-called doctrine of *res ipsa loquitur* in the law of delict.

6. O'Hara v. Central S.M.T. Co.
1941 S.C. 363

A bus operated by the defenders, which was coming to a stop to allow passengers to alight, suddenly swerved violently. The pursuer, who was standing on the rear platform of the bus waiting to get off, fell onto the road, sustaining serious injury. It was argued by the pursuer that this occurrence was in itself sufficient evidence of negligent driving to justify a finding against the defenders. The defenders maintained that the driver had been forced to swerve by a pedestrian who ran into the road in front of the bus. The Lord Ordinary assoilzied the defenders, holding that they had made out a satisfactory explanation for the accident which was consistent with the exercise of proper care on the part of their servant, the driver.

LORD PRESIDENT (NORMAND): "The next question is whether the Lord Ordinary has put too heavy an onus on the respondents by requiring that the explanation or justification shall be established by full legal proof. On this point the respondents rely on the dicta of Lord Dunedin in *Ballard v. North British Railway Co.*, (1923 S.C. (H.L.) 43 at p.54). Lord Dunedin discusses the various cases in which it is said *res ipsa loquitur*. He points out that in certain cases the mere fact of the accident is relevant to infer negligence, and says that the Lord Ordinary went too far when he said 'that there is then raised a presumption of negligence which the defender has got to rebut'. He draws a distinction between 'relevant to infer' and 'necessarily infers' and says that, where the accident is relevant to infer negligence, 'if the defenders can show a way in which the accident may have occurred without negligence, the cogency of the fact of the accident by itself disappears,' and he subsequently contrasts the 'explanation' which he desiderates with 'proof. The respondents wish to use these dicta to support the view that it is enough for them to tender on record or in evidence an explanation, not amounting to legal proof, that the swerve in this case was caused by the necessity of avoiding collision with a pedestrian. In my view this is not warranted by what Lord Dunedin said. But before coming to that it is necessary to point out that Lord Dunedin was dissenting. The majority of their Lordships held that the railway company was liable for the accident, which was caused by the breaking of a link between an engine and wagons which it was pushing up a hill and over a crest. They held that the wagons were sent over the crest at too great a speed, and that the driver was in fault in this respect. The consequence was that, when the wagons reached the crest and the engine driver tried to stop them by engine power from going down the other side, the strain put on the link which broke was too great. There was a latent defect in the broken link, and there was no fault in failing to discover the defect. But it was held that the system of working subjected the link to excessive strain. In reaching a decision Lord Finlay expressly relies on the occurrence of the accident (at p.52) as casting upon the railway company the burden of proving that it happened without fault on their part. Lord Shaw refers to the Lord Ordinary's opinion, which, he says, gave to the expression *res ipsa loquitur* its own place and no more. Lord Dunedin's observations cannot, therefore, be treated as if they stood alone, and I desire to say, with respect, that I prefer the clearer discussion of *res ipsa loquitur* which is to be found in Lord Shaw's speech. Nevertheless, I think that what Lord Dunedin had in view was a necessary safeguard in applying the expression *res ipsa loquitur* as if it expressed a legal presumption. Lord Shaw pointed out that it is not a legal principle. It is merely a presumption of fact, and its force depends on the facts in each case. Now there are cases where an accident happens through some object falling or breaking when no one is present and in actual physical control of the object at the time. In the part of Lord Dunedin's speech on which the respondents rely he mentions *Scott v. The London and St Katherine Docks Co.* (3 H.&C. 596) where a bag of flour fell from a warehouse though it was not actually being handled by anyone at the time, and *Milne v. Townsend* (19 R. 830) where a strap of a derrick crane broke, causing the derrick to fall when there was no load on it. In these cases there was no question of the negligence of some person actually working the derrick or handling the bags. And in such cases those who were responsible, as having control of the premises or derrick, in Lord Dunedin's view might escape liability if they could put forward an explanation, short of full legal proof, showing that the accident might have occurred without their negligence. I think that Lord Dunedin did not mean that nothing need be proved, but only that the proof need not establish that the accident was in fact caused in a particular way which excluded negligence. It would be sufficient if it were proved that there were conditions present which might have caused the accident without negligence on their part. To take an illustration; in *Scott v. The London and St Katherine Docks Co.* (3 H.&C. 596) if the defendants had proved that there had been an explosion in neighbouring premises which might have disturbed the sack, that might have discharged the onus on them, though they had not proved that the explosion was in fact the cause of the sack's falling from their building. In *Ballard*, (1923 S.C. (H.L.) 43) Lord Dunedin did not base his judgement on something short of legal proof, although he expressly treated the case as one 'where the circumstances warrant the view that the fact of the accident is relevant to infer negligence.' He held it proved that the speed of the train of wagons was not excessive, which excluded a ground of negligence specifically pleaded against the engine-driver, and he also held it proved that the link which broke did so because of a latent defect not discoverable by any ordinary examination. Then he asks; 'Where then is the negligence?' and he answers; 'There is none except such as may be inferred from the mere fact of the accident'. Finally he held that there was no fault in trusting that the train could be held in check on the gradient by the couplings. I cannot find that Lord Dunedin at any stage of the case relied on an explanation short of full legal proof. The present case is not similar to cases like *Scott* or *Milne* (19 R. 830). If this were a case in which the omnibus swerved and it was discovered that the steering gear had broken through a latent defect, there would have been a similarity to *Ballard*, as Lord Dunedin saw it. In the circumstances figured the swerve of the omnibus would have given rise to no inference of negligence against the driver, for the defect of the steering gear would have been adequate to explain it, though it would still have been open to the pursuer to prove that the driver had so mismanaged things that even sound steering gear would have broken, and that it was his fault rather than defective steering gear which caused the accident. But the defenders would never have shifted the onus back to the pursuer except by legal proof that the steering gear was in fact broken and that it was defective. It would have been quite useless for them to say either through the mouth of counsel or through the mouth of a witness that the accident could be accounted for by latent defect causing a break of the steering gear, unless there had been proof that the necessary conditions were present. In my view, therefore, Lord Dunedin's observations should be limited to these cases where the starting point of the action is some accident not immediately brought about by voluntary human action; and they do not suggest that no proof at all is required, but only that, if the conditions are proved which are adequate to account for the accident, the onus is discharged, though there is no proof that these conditions rather than some antecedent mismanagement of the defenders actually caused it. In the present case it is just and in accordance with the views both of Lord Dunedin and of the other learned and noble Lords who took part in the decision of *Ballard* that a driver whose voluntary action is challenged should explain and justify by legal proof a swerve caused or allowed to take place by him. This proposition also is in accordance with the views expressed by the Court in *Marsh* (1940 S.C. 202)."

NOTES

Lord President Normand refers to a requirement for "full legal proof" of the explanation or justification. This infers a persuasive burden—full legal proof at that time required corroborated evidence of the particular fact in issue, and as we have seen, a party which places a fact in issue must generally accept the persuasive burden of proving it. The presence of a persuasive burden in rebuttal of a presumption then infers that the presumption is one of law.

7. Devine v. Colvilles Ltd
1969 S.C. (H.L.) 67

A violent explosion in a steel-works caused the pursuer to jump from the high platform on which he was working. A crucial issue in the case was whether the explosion was sufficient to raise a *prima facie* inference of negligence under the doctrine of *res ipsa loquitur*.

LORD WHEATLEY: "A very crucial issue in the case is whether the Lord Ordinary was entitled to hold that in the proved circumstances the pursuer was entitled to invoke the presumption of negligence against the defenders flowing from the brocard *res ipsa loquitur*. The pursuer has perilled his case on being able to do so, and, if he has failed in this, that is the end of his case. Although the phrase *res ipsa loquitur* does not appear in the report of the case, the classical explanation of it is attributed to Erie, C.J. in *Scott v. The London and St Katherine Docks Co.*, 3 H.&C. 596, in a passage at p.601, where he said: 'There must be reasonable evidence of negligence. But where the thing is shewn to be under the management of the defendant of his servants, and the accident is such as in the ordinary course of things does not happen if those who have the management use proper care, it affords reasonable evidence, in the absence of explanation by the defendants, that the accident arose from want of care.' This has been accepted as being the law of Scotland in a long series of cases, and I need refer only to *Ballard v. North British Railway Co.*, 1923 S.C.(H.L.) 43 and *O'Hara v. Central S.M.T. Co.*, 1941

S.C. 363, by way of illustrations. There is always the primary responsibility on a pursuer to prove that the accident occurred through the negligence of the defender. In the normal case a pursuer has to condescend on a particular negligence and breach of duty on the part of the defender, by prima facie negligence can be inferred if the pursuer proves (a) that the 'thing' causing the accident was under the management of the defender or his servants, and (b) that the accident was such as in the ordinary course of things would not happen if those who had the management had used proper care. In so far as this is founded not on proof of a specific act of negligence but merely on a presumption of negligence unspecified in detail but arising from a prima facie logical inference, the presumption, which is only a presumption of fact dependent on the facts of the particular case, can be rebutted if the defender tenders an explanation which renders the inference invalid. What this involves for a defender was considered in *O'Hara v. Central S.M.T. Co.*

I pause here to note that both parties were agreed that there was a distinction between a case where the accident was immediately brought about by voluntary human action, as in *O'Hara*, and the case where it was not so brought about. In the former case full legal proof is required of the defender to rebut the prima facie case of negligence which has been established against him, whereas in the latter case it would be sufficient if it were established that there were conditions present which could have caused the accident without negligence on his part. This would appear to be the effect of the opinion of Lord President Normand in *O'Hara*, and pursuer's counsel accepted that in this case the defenders could rebut the presumption of negligence against them (if established) on this lesser standard of proof."

NOTES

See also *Binnie v. Rederij Theodoro B.V.*, 1993 S.C. 71. It appears that the "doctrine" *res ipsa loquitur* may be either a presumption of law or a presumption of fact, depending upon the circumstances in which it is invoked. However, the distinction between these different types of presumption is probably of rather less significance in civil actions now that the requirement for corroboration has been abolished in such cases (Civil Evidence (Scotland) Act 1988, s.1—see Chapter 13 below). Formerly, corroborated evidence was necessary to establish some matter, such as a *praesumptio juris*, which required full legal proof. That is no longer the case and any presumption may be rebutted by leading sufficient credible and reliable evidence to satisfy the court that it should not be applied, whether the presumption is one of law or one of fact. More evidence, or better quality evidence may be required to rebut a presumption of law, but the question becomes largely a matter of the weight which can be attached to any particular evidence. The distinction may be of rather more significance in criminal cases (although note the case of *King v. Lees*, 1993 S.C.C.R. 28, which holds that the accused may discharge a persuasive burden of proof by means of uncorroborated evidence).

Chapter 4

THE STANDARD OF PROOF

We have seen that, thanks to the concept of the burden of proof, a person who seeks some remedy or court order must generally accept the onus of proving the facts or state of affairs which justify the granting of the remedy or the making of the order. But what does it mean to prove something? Is proof in law similar to proof in science or mathematics, and if not, what will a court accept as constituting "proof" of any particular matter?

1.   Davies v. Taylor
[1974] A.C. 207

The plaintiff's husband died in a road accident. She had been committing adultery and in fact deserted her husband some five weeks before the fatal accident. The husband was apparently anxious for a reconciliation, but she refused his offer and he initiated divorce proceedings against her. On his death, she claimed damages as a "dependant", but her claim was dismissed because she had not established that a reconciliation with her husband was more probable than not, and she accordingly did not qualify for an award under the legislation concerned.

LORD SIMON OF GLAISDALE: "Beneath the legal concept of probability lies the mathematical theory of probability. Only occasionally does this break surface—apart from the concept of burden of proof on a balance of probabilities, which can be restated as the burden of showing odds of at least 51 to 49 that such-and-such has taken place or will do so. But courts may sometimes be concerned with actuarial calculations (as to expectation of life in assessing damages for personal injuries, for example). And the weight of circumstantial evidence is sometimes expressed mathematically; for example, a fingerprint expert may give the mathematical probability (remote) of a fingerprint identical with that of an accused person being that of some other person. Perhaps forensic science experts could use the mathematical theory more frequently—for example, in combining items of circumstantial evidence (say similarities of boot-prints, dust and cigarette ash); and the respective odds do not combine simply, simply by addition.

But much proof depends on credibility, as to which probability is (at least, as yet) only one factor to be weighed. And when it comes to prediction, there are so many factors to be considered (not least the extra-ordinary vagaries of human nature) that mathematical theory can have in general only marginal significance. So the law ordinarily proceeds to treat probability according to certain easily understood standards. If a possibility is conceivable but fanciful, the law disregards it entirely, on the maxim *de minimus non curat lex*. Most matters in civil litigation have to be proved on a balance of probabilities—in other words is it more likely than not? Most matters in criminal litigation have to be proved beyond reasonable doubt—in other words, is it shown that, though the alternative is possible, it is not in the least probable?"

NOTES

The nature of "legal probability" is controversial, but it certainly seems to be unlike mathematical or "Pascalian" probability. (See, *inter alia, Re J. S. (a minor)* [1981] Fam. 22 at 29, below; *R. v. Shepherd* (1988) 85 A.L.R. 387 at 392; Cohen, "The Probable and the Provable" (1977); and compare Sir

Richard Egglestone's, "Evidence, Proof and Probability" (1983)). It is rarely possible to demonstrate that an accused person committed an offence with the same degree of certainty by which it is possible to demonstrate, for example the truth of Pythagoras' theorem. Instead, what is required is evidence sufficient to instil in the court the requisite degree of belief or conviction as to the facts in issue. This degree of belief has been described as "subjective probability". Given an infinite variety of fact-situations and the presence of so many subjective variables in the fact-finding process, it is difficult or impossible to express the appropriate standard of subjective probability in anything other than very general, common-sense terms.

Faced with the practical problem that decisions must be made in imperfect conditions, the courts will usually accept evidence which falls short of certainty—although compare *Imre v. Mitchell*, 1958 S.C. 461, Chapter 3, above. The nature and amount of evidence is required to convince the court will inevitably vary from case to case. Once the court is convinced to the appropriate standard, however, the issue is regarded as "proved"—"In determining what did happen in the past a court decides on the balance of probabilities. Anything that is more probable than not it treats as certain". (Lord Diplock in *Mallett v. McMonagle* [1970] A.C. 166 at 176, approved by Lord Mackay in *Hotson v. East Berkshire Area Health Board* [1987] A.C. 750 at 785). What is regarded as the "appropriate standard" however, may differ depending upon the nature of the proceedings.

2. Hendry v. Clan Line Steamers
1949 S.C. 320

A stevedore brought an action for damages against Clan Line Steamers in respect of injuries he sustained while working aboard a ship operated by them. His claim was rejected and he appealed on the basis that the Lord Ordinary had misdirected the jury as to the standard of proof to be applied.

LORD JUSTICE-CLERK (THOMSON): "What the Lord Ordinary did tell the jury was that 'the pursuer had to satisfy the jury beyond reasonable doubt that the defenders were to blame for the accident'. That is the familiar formula of the criminal courts. It is a high and exacting standard of proof for the simple reason that an accused person is presumed to be innocent. Such a situation is entirely different to that in a reparation case. There is no presumption that the defender is blameless. It is recognised by our criminal law that there is a distinction between the onus laid upon the Crown and that laid upon the accused, even in cases where the burden of proof is laid on him by statute."

NOTES

It has occasionally been doubted whether any distinction can realistically be made between different standards of proof—in the course of argument in *R. v. Murtagh and Kennedy* (1955) 39 Cr.App.R. 72, for example, Hilbery J. said that:

"I personally have never seen the difference between the onus of proof in a civil and criminal case. If a thing is proved, it is proved, but I am not entitled to that view."

Nevertheless, the difference between the civil and the criminal standard is firmly established and indeed appears to be regarded as a fundamental one in the law of evidence.

3. Miller v. Minister of Pensions
[1947] 63 T.L.R. 474

This case was one of a series which arose out of claims for pensions by ex-service personnel injured or afflicted with disease during the Second World War, or by the relatives of those killed during war service. To establish a claim for such a pension, it had to be shown that the injury, disease or death was caused by the war service. To facilitate such claims, however, the legislation created a presumption in favour of the claimant which, in certain cases, could be rebutted only by proof beyond reasonable doubt.

MR JUSTICE DENNING: "The first point of law in the present appeal is whether the tribunal properly directed itself as to the burden of proof. The proper direction is covered by decisions of this Court. It is as follows: In cases falling under article 4(2) and article 4(3) of the Royal Warrant of December, 1943 (which are generally cases where the man was passed fit at the beginning of his service, but is later afflicted by a disease which leads to his death or discharge), there is a compelling presumption in the man's favour which must prevail unless the evidence proves beyond reasonable doubt that the disease was not attributable to or aggravated by war service, and for that purpose the evidence must reach the same degree of cogency as is required in a criminal case before an accused is found guilty. That degree is well settled. It need not reach certainty, but must carry a high degree of probability. Proof beyond reasonable doubt does not mean proof beyond the shadow of a doubt. The law would fail to protect the community if it admitted fanciful possibilities to deflect the course of justice. If the evidence is so strong against a man as to leave only a remote possibility in his favour, which can be dismissed with the sentence "of course it is possible, but not in the least probable" the case is proved beyond reasonable doubt, but nothing short of that will suffice . . .

In cases falling under article 4(2) (which are generally cases where the man was fit on his discharge, but incapacitated later by a disease) there is no compelling presumption in his favour and the case must be decided according to the preponderance of probability. If at the end of the case the evidence turns the scale definitely one way or the other, the tribunal must decide accordingly, but if the evidence is so evenly balanced that the tribunal is unable to come to a determinate conclusion one way or the other, then the man must be given the benefit of the doubt. This means that the case must be decided in favour of the man unless the evidence against him reaches the same degree of cogency as is required to discharge a burden in a civil case. That degree is well settled. It must carry a reasonable degree of probability, but not so high as is required in a criminal case. If the evidence is such that the tribunal can say 'we think it more probable than not' the burden is discharged, but if the probabilities are equal, it is not."

NOTES

In relation to the criminal standard of proof, compare Lord Justice-Clerk Cooper in *Irving v. Minister of Pensions*, 1945 S.C. 21 at 29: "the doubt must, of course, be a reasonable doubt, and not a strained or fanciful acceptance of a remote possibility". These *dicta* or definitions reflect the common-sense standards referred to by Lord Simon in the passage from *Davies v. Taylor*, above. And yet, in practice, how helpful are the standard formulations?

4. R. v. Kritz
[1950] 1 K.B. 82

The appellant, Kritz, was convicted of obtaining money by false pretences, and appealed on the ground that the trial judge had misdirected the jury as to the standard of proof. He had told the jury that they must be "reasonably satisfied" of the accused's guilt and did not use the words "satisfied beyond reasonable doubt". In dismissing his appeal Lord Goddard made the following remarks:

LORD GODDARD C.J.: "The only other point which has been seriously argued is that because the Common Sergeant told the jury that they must be reasonably satisfied, and did not use the words 'satisfied beyond reasonable doubt', he was not sufficiently stating the onus of proof. It would be a great misfortune, in criminal cases especially, if the accuracy of a summing-up were made to depend upon whether or not the judge or the chairman had used a particular formula of words. It is not the particular formula that matters: it is the effect of the summing-up. If the jury are made to understand that they have to be satisfied and must not return a verdict against a defendant unless they feel sure, and that the onus is all the time on the prosecution and not on the defence, then whether the judge uses one form of language or another is neither here nor there.

In our opinion, there was a perfectly fair and proper summing-up by the Common Serjeant here. We do not think that any jury could have been left in any doubt what was their duty. Juries are not such fools as they are very often thought to be. They know, when they have been in the jury box a short time, that it is the duty of the prosecution to prove the case and that they have to be fully and thoroughly satisfied; and they very seldom want guidance on that point. It is right that they should have it—that they should be reminded that the onus is on the prosecution all the way through the case. It is right that they should be reminded in a criminal case that they must be fully satisfied of the guilt of the accused person and should not find a verdict against him unless they feel sure. That is the direction which I myself constantly give to juries. When once a judge begins to use the words 'reasonable doubt' and to try to explain what is a reasonable doubt and what is not, he is much more likely to confuse the jury than if he tells them in plain language: 'It is the duty of the prosecution to satisfy you of the prisoner's guilt.' The Common Serjeant did not use that formula of words, and I am not saying that it is to be preferred to all others; but what I do say—and I am sure that I can say it with the full assent of my brethren—is that it is not the actual formula used, but the effect of the summing-up which matters; and that, if the effect of the summing-up is to convey to the jury what is their duty, that is enough."

NOTES

Do you agree with Lord Goddard C.J. that to try to define the concept of reasonable doubt is only likely to confuse juries and that a direction along the lines suggested by him is preferable? Is his opinion in any way self-contradictory? It is doubtful whether a direction by a trial judge in Scotland which omitted the words "beyond reasonable doubt" in relation to the criminal onus, would be regarded as sufficient—see *Mackenzie v. H.M.A.*, 160 S.L.T. 41.

5. R. v. Ching
(1976) 63 Cr.App.R. 7

Ching was convicted of theft and appealed, as in *Kritz*, above, on the ground of misdirection by the trial judge. In attempting—after the jury had retired—to clarify for confused jury members what was meant by "reasonable doubt", the judge had said that a reasonable doubt was one to which you could give a reason, as opposed to a merely fanciful speculation. He also said that the doubt would have to be a matter which would influence a reasonable person on a business matter, such as the mortgage of a house. These directions are described in Lord Justice Lawton's opinion as the "final direction". Counsel for the appellant objected to these formulations.

LORD JUSTICE LAWTON: "It is against that background that we turn now to the judge's summing-up. He dealt with the burden of proof at the beginning of the summing-up. In the judgement of this Court, that is the best place in a summing-up to deal with it. He did so in these terms: 'So far as the law is concerned, the first matter is one which, quite rightly, has already been referred to, namely, that in this, as in every criminal case, it is for the prosecution to prove the charge, or charges, and to prove them so that you are sure that they have been made out—to prove them beyond a reasonable doubt—these being two different ways of saying what is really the same thing. If you are not satisfied to that degree, then your verdict, or verdicts, must necessarily be ones of not guilty.' Nothing could have been clearer, nothing could have been more accurate.

[Counsel for the appellant] accepted that when this Court comes to consider the effect of the final direction which the judge gave to the jury, it must be looked at against the whole background of the case, and in particular against the whole of the summing-up. That has been said time and time again in this Court. If any authority is required for the proposition it is to be found in *Hepworth and Fearnley* (1955) 39 Cr.App.R. 152; [1955] 2 Q.B. 600. There Lord Goddard C.J. said: 'But I desire to repeat what I said in the case of *Kritz* (1949) 33 Cr.App.R. 169; [1950] 1 K.B. 82: "It is not the particular formula of words that matters; it is the effect of summing-up. If the jury are charged whether in one set of words or in another and are made to understand that they have to be satisfied and must not return a verdict against a defendant unless they feel sure, and that the onus is all the time on the prosecution and not on the defence, that is enough. I should be very sorry if it were thought that cases should depend on the use of a particular formula or particular word or words".'

The task therefore for us has been to consider what was the effect of the summing-up as a whole, including the final direction. [Counsel for the appellant] attacked that final direction on three grounds. He said that it was unsatisfactory for a judge to define a 'reasonable doubt' as one for which a reason could be given; he pointed to a criticism of that phrase which was made by Lord Justice Edmund Davies (as he then was) in *Stafford and Luvaglio* (1968) 53 Cr.App.R. 1. Edmund Davies L.J. sitting with Fenton Atkinson L.J. and Waller J. said at p.2: 'We do not, however, ourselves agree with the trial judge when, directing the jury upon the standard of proof, he told them to "Remember that a reasonable doubt is one for which you could give reasons if you were asked," and we dislike such a description of definition.' So do we. It does not help juries. But that is not the problem in this case. The problem is whether its use made this conviction unsafe.

The next ground of complaint was that by using the mortgage of a house analogy, the learned judge was doing something which had been condemned a number of times in this Court. Counsel called our attention to two recent decisions. One was *Gray* (1973) 58 Cr.App.R. 177. In that case the phrase which was disapproved of was 'doubt which might affect you in the conduct of your everyday affairs'. The other, even more recently, is the decision of this Court, on January 13, 1976 in *Knott*. In that case the phrase 'the sort of doubt that can influence you as prudent men and women in the conduct of your everyday affairs'. In the past this Court has criticised trial judges for using that kind of analogy. The use of any analogy is to be avoided whenever possible.

The final criticism was that when giving the direction of which complaint is made, the judge did not emphasise once again that the jury had to be sure. But we have no doubt that by the time the jury retired for the last time, they must have appreciated that they had to be sure before they could return a verdict of guilty.

Nevertheless, in most cases—but not in this one—judges would be well advised not to attempt any gloss upon what is meant by 'sure' or what is meant by 'reasonable doubt'. In the last two decades there have been numerous cases before this Court, some of which have been successful, some of which have not, which have come here because judges have thought it helpful to a jury to comment of what the standard of proof is. Experience in this Court has shown that such comments usually create difficulties. They are more likely to confuse than help. But the exceptional case does sometimes arise. This is the sort of case in which, as I have already pointed out, the jury possibly wanted help as to what was meant by 'doubt'. The judge thought they wanted help and he tried to give them some. He was right to try and that is all he was doing. He seems to have steered clear of the formulas which have been condemned in this Court such as 'such doubt as arises in your everyday affairs or your everyday life'; or using another example which has been before the Court, 'the kind of doubts which you may have when trying to make up your minds what kind of motor car to buy'.

[Counsel for the appellant] said that the judge did not stress that the relevant doubts were those which have to be overcome in important business affairs. What he did was to pick an example, which for sensible people would be an important matter. We can see nothing wrong in his so doing.

In conclusion we invite attention to what was said in *Walters v. The Queen* [1969] 2 A.C. 26, where the Board had to consider the kind of problem which is now before us. In that case the trial judge in Jamaica gave the jury a long explanation as to what was meant by 'reasonable doubt'. That explanation was criticised upon the same lines as the final direction given by the trial judge in this case was criticised by Mr Latham. The Privy Council considered the criticisms. It objected to certain phrases which had been put forward in the course of argument, and the opinion of Lord Diplock at p.30 ended as follows: 'By the time he sums-up the judge at the trial has had an opportunity of observing the jurors. In their Lordships' view it is best left to his discretion to choose the most appropriate set of words in which to make that jury understand that they must not return a verdict against a defendant unless they are sure of his guilt; and if the judge feels that any of them, though unfamiliarity with court procedure, are in danger of thinking that they are engaged in some task more esoteric than applying to the evidence adduced at the trial the common sense with which they approach matters of importance to them in their ordinary lives, then the use of such analogies as that used by Small J. in the present case, whether in the words in which he expressed it or in those used in any of the other cases to which reference has been made, may be helpful and is in their Lordships' view unexceptionable.' That opinion is the opinion of this Court.

There is no reason for saying in this case that the verdict was unsafe. As I said earlier, and I repeat, this is one of a large number of cases which have come before this Court in recent years, raising fine points about the terms in which judges have directed the jury as to the standard of proof. We point out and emphasise that if judges stopped trying to define that which is almost impossible to define there would be fewer appeals. We hope there will not be any more for some considerable time. The appeal is dismissed."

NOTES

Is it satisfactory in relation to such an important matter as a finding of criminal guilt to adopt a standard which is "almost impossible to define"? What alternatives are there? "Experiments in re-formulation" are also discouraged in Scotland: see *McKenzie v. H.M.A.*, 1959 J.C. 32 and *Stillie v. H.M.A.*, 1990 S.C.C.R. 719. In modern Scottish practice, judges commonly direct the jury that a reasonable doubt is one that would make them hesitate or pause before taking an important decision in their own lives, see *Macdonald v. H.M.A.*, 1996 S.L.T. 723; *Buchanan v. H.M.A.*, 1998 S.L.T. 13. How would that direction have been viewed by the court in *Ching*?

6.   Re J. S. (a minor)
[1981] Fam. 23

LORD ORMEROD: "In the instant case, there is the further objection that to make an order declaring that A is the father of B, largely on serological evidence, is to transmute a mathematical probability into a forensic certainty when there is no necessity to do so. When it is necessary to give effect to statistical evidence of this kind in order to determine the rights of the parties, the court does so on the usual basis of deciding where the onus of proof lies and whether the party on whom it lies has sufficiently discharged it. The weight of the evidence may or may not be sufficient, depending on the issue which the court has to decide. But to make a formal declaration 'in the air' so to speak, is another thing altogether. It poses the question of the standard of proof. Mr Swinton Thomas argued strenuously that the judge should have been satisfied on 'the balance of probabilities', that J was the father of the child, but what that much used phrase means in the context of a case like the present is by no means clear.

The concept of 'probability' in the legal sense is certainly different from the mathematical concept; indeed, it is rare to find a situation in which these two usages co-exist although, when they do, the mathematical probability has to be taken into the assessment of probability in the legal sense and given its appropriate weight. Nor is the word 'balance' much clearer. Cases like *Hornal v. Neuberger Products Ltd* [1957] 1 Q.B. 247 and *Bater v. Bater* [1951] P. 35, both of which were referred to by Heilbron J., make it clear that, in deciding the balance of probability, the court must take into account the gravity of the decision and determine 'the degree of probability which is proportionate to the subject matter'. Perhaps we should recognise that our time-honoured phrase is not a happy one to express a concept which, though we all understand it, is very elusive when it comes to definition. In the criminal law the burden of proof is usually expressed in the formula 'the prosecution must satisfy you so that you are sure that the accused is guilty.' The civil burden might be formulated on analogous lines, 'the plaintiff (or the party on whom the burden rests) must satisfy the court that it is reasonably safe in all the circumstances of the case to act on the evidence before the court, bearing in mind the consequences which will follow'.

The judge, rightly in our opinion, adopted this test. In the course of her judgement she said:

'The degree of probability in an issue of paternity should, in my opinion, be commensurate with the transcending importance of that decision to the child.'

We would express the proposition differently. In our judgement, if there is power to make a bare declaration that A is the father of B the court should not exercise its discretion to make such a declaration unless the evidence is conclusive or very nearly so. (We do not think that section 26 of the Family Law Reform Act 1969, which deals with the presumption of legitimacy and provides that it may be rebutted by evidence which shows that it is more probable than not that the person concerned is illegitimate, is in point in the present case where there is no presumption to rebut.)"

NOTES

Compare *Imre v. Mitchell*, 1958 S.C. 439, Chapter 3, above. Note that both civil and criminal standards are based on probability. The criminal standard requires a very high degree of probability but not absolute certainty, which in most cases is likely to be unattainable. In *Simpson v. LMS Railway Co.*, 1931 S.C. (H.L.) 15 at 20, Lord Dunedin said that "there is no such thing as absolute certainty even where there is direct testimony so that if analysed strictly any conclusion is based on the balance of probabilities".

Nevertheless, there is no doubt that the criminal standard is a different and a higher standard, as the quoted passage from *Hendry v. Clan Steamers*, above, demonstrates. Moreover, it seems that the criminal standard is intended to invoke the highest practicable standard of proof. In *Brown v. Brown*, 1972 S.C. 123 the pursuer raised an action of divorce on the grounds of his wife's adultery and sought declarator that the child of the marriage was illegitimate. It was argued for the defender that while the standard of proof in allegations of adultery was the criminal standard, the standard in relation to declarator of bastardy was higher still! (See the passage from *Imre v. Mitchell*, 1958 S.C. 461, in Chapter 3, above.) In relation to this argument, Lord Emslie said that:

"The standard required [to prove illegitimacy] is clearly not that of the balance of probabilities. So far as I am aware, there is only one other standard of proof known to the law of Scotland, proof beyond reasonable doubt, and it is difficult to conceive of a higher standard which could be applied in practice."

In civil cases, furthermore, what must be weighed is not the respective quantities of evidence, but rather the *probabilities* arising from the evidence (see Macphail, *Evidence*, para. 22.30). Difficulties may arise however, since certain events or states of affairs may be regarded as inherently less probable than others.

7. Bater v. Bater
[1951] P. 35

Mrs Bater petitioned for divorce on the grounds, then competent, of her husband's cruelty. The question arose as to the standard of proof applicable to this allegation, and it was held that a direction that it must be proved "beyond reasonable doubt" was not a misdirection. The Court of Appeal regarded the standard invoked by the trial judge as one different from that appropriate in criminal cases, however, and it is perhaps not surprising that this case has given rise to some confusion.

LORD DENNING: "The difference of opinion which has been evoked about the standard of proof in recent cases may well turn out to be more a matter of words than anything else. It is of course true that by our law a higher standard of proof is required in criminal cases than in civil cases. But this is subject to the qualification that there is no absolute standard in either case. In criminal cases the charge must be proved beyond reasonable doubt, but there may be degrees of proof within that standard.

As Best, C.J., and many other great judges have said, 'in proportion as the crime is enormous, so ought the proof to be clear'. So also in civil cases, the case may be proved by a preponderance of probability, but there may be degrees of probability within that standard. The degree depends on the subject-matter. A civil court, when considering a charge of fraud, will naturally require for itself a higher degree of probability than that which it would require when asking if negligence is established. It does not adopt so high a degree as a criminal court, even when it is considering a charge of a criminal nature; but still it does require a degree of probability which is commensurate with the occasion. Likewise, a divorce court should require a degree of probability which is proportionate to the subject-matter.

I do not think that the matter can be better put than it was by Lord Stowell in *Loveden v. Loveden* [1810] 2 Hagg. Con. 1, 3. 'The only general rule that can be laid down upon the subject is, that the circumstances must be such as would lead the guarded discretion of a reasonable and just man to the conclusion.' The degree of probability which a reasonable and just man would require to come to a conclusion—and likewise the degree of doubt which would prevent him coming to it—depends on the conclusion to which he is required to come. It would depend on whether it was a criminal case or a civil case, what the charge was, and what the consequences might be; and if he were left in real and substantial doubt on the particular matter, he would hold the charge not to be established: he would not be satisfied about it. But what is a real and substantial doubt? It is only another way of saying a reasonable doubt; and a reasonable doubt is simply that degree of doubt which would prevent a reasonable and just man from coming to the conclusion. So the phrase 'reasonable doubt' takes the matter no further. It does not say that the degree of probability must be as high as 99 per cent or as low as 51 per cent. The degree required must depend on the mind of the reasonable and just man who is considering the particular subject-matter. In some cases 51 per cent would be enough, but not in others. When this is realised, the phrase 'reasonable doubt' can be used just as aptly in a civil case or a divorce case as in a criminal case; and indeed it was so used by my Lord in *Davis v. Davis* [1950] P. 125 and *Gower v. Gower* 66 T.L.R. [Pt 1] 717 to which we have been referred. The only difference is that, because of our high regard for the liberty of the individual, a doubt may be regarded as reasonable in the criminal courts, which would not be so in the civil courts. I agree therefore with my brothers that the use of the phrase 'reasonable doubt' by the commissioner in this case was not a misdirection any more than it was in *Briginshaw v. Briginshaw* [1938] 60 C.L.R. 336.

If, however, the commissioner had put the case higher and said that the case had to be proved with the same strictness as a crime is proved in a criminal court, then he would, I think, have misdirected himself, because that would be the very error which this court corrected in *Davis v. Davis* [1950] P. 125. It would be adopting too high a standard. The divorce court is a civil court, not a criminal court, and it should not adopt the rules and standards of the criminal court. I agree that the appeal should be dismissed."

NOTES

In spite of the direction that Mrs Bater's allegations of cruelty must be proved "beyond reasonable doubt", it appears that the Court of Appeal regarded the standard invoked by the trial judge as one different from that appropriate in criminal cases. The following cases attempt, with varying degrees of clarity, to explain *Bater v. Bater*.

8. R. v. Home Secretary, *ex parte* Khawaja
[1984] A.C. 74

Khawaja was a Pakistani who obtained leave to enter the United Kingdom on the basis of statements which later proved to be false. The Home Secretary began proceedings to have him deported as an illegal immigrant. It was held that the burden of proving his status as illegal immigrant lay on the Home Secretary.

LORD SCARMAN: "The law is less certain as to the standard of proof. The choice is commonly thought to be between proof beyond reasonable doubt, as in criminal cases, and the civil standard of the balance of probabilities: and there is distinguished authority for the view that in habeas corpus proceedings the standard is beyond reasonable doubt, since liberty is at stake. This appears to have been the view of Lord Atkin (*Eshugbayi Eleko v. Government of Nigeria* [1931] A.C. 662, 670), and certainly was the view of Lord Parker C.J. (*Reg. v. Governor of Brixton Prison, Ex parte Ahsan* [1969] Q.B. 222). But there is a line of authority which casts doubt upon their view. The Court of Appeal has held that the standard of proof of criminal offences in civil proceedings is that of the balance of probabilities: *Hornal v. Neuberger Products Ltd* [1957] Q.B. 247. As judicial review whether under the modern statutory procedure or section 3 of the Habeus Corpus Act 1816 is a civil proceeding, it would appear to be right, if *Hornal's* case was correctly decided, to apply the civil standard of proof. My Lords, I have come to the conclusion that the choice between the two standards is not one of any great moment. It is largely a matter of words. There is no need to import into this branch of the civil law the formula used for the guidance of juries in criminal cases. The civil standard as interpreted and applied by the civil courts will meet the ends of justice.

The issue has been discussed in a number of cases. In *Bater v. Bater* [1951] P.35, the trial judge had said that the petitioner, who alleged cruelty by her husband, must prove her case beyond reasonable doubt. This was held by the Court of Appeal not to be a misdirection. But Denning L.J. observed that, had the judge said the case required to be proved with the same strictness as a crime in a criminal court, that would have been a misdirection. He put it thus, at pp.36–37:

'The difference of opinion which has been evoked about the standard of proof in recent cases may well turn out to be more a matter of words than anything else. It is of course true that by our law a higher standard of proof is required in criminal cases than in civil cases. But this is subject to the qualification that there is no absolute standard in either case.'

And a little later he added, at p.37:

'So also in civil cases, the case may be proved by a preponderance of probability, but there may be degrees of probability within that standard. The degree depends on the subject-matter. A civil court, when considering a charge of fraud, will naturally require for itself a higher degree of probability than that which it would require when asking if negligence is established. It does not adopt so high a degree as a criminal court, even when it is considering a charge of a criminal nature; but still it does require a degree of probability which is commensurate with the occasion.'

It is clear that all three members of the court (Bucknill, Somervell and Denning L.J.) found difficulty in distinguishing between the two standards. If a court has to be satisfied, how can it at the same time entertain a reasonable doubt (Bucknill L.J. at p.36)?

In *Hornal v. Neuberger Products Ltd* [1951] 1 Q.B. 247, the Court of Appeal had to consider the standard of proof where fraud is alleged in civil proceedings. The court held that the standard was the balance of probabilities. But, since the degree of probability required to tip the balance will vary according to the nature and gravity of the issue, 'no real mischief results from an acceptance of the fact that there is some difference of approach in civil actions . . . the very elements of gravity become a part of the whole range of circumstances which have to be weighed in the scale when deciding as to the balance of probabilities:' per Morris L.J., at p.266. A notable application of the principle that civil courts apply the balance of probabilities is to be found in the will case in which Ungoed-Thomas J. had to decide whether the wife had feloniously killed her husband: In *re Dellow's Will Trusts* [1964] 1 W.L.R. 451. He held the crime proved upon the balance of probabilities. Hornal's case was approved by this House in the divorce case, *Blyth v. Blyth* [1966] A.C. 643. Lord Denning picked up what he had said in *Bater v. Bater* [1951] P.35 and *Hornal's* case and concluded, at p.669, that:

'so far as the grounds for divorce are concerned, the case, like any civil case, may be proved by a preponderance of probability, but the degree of probability depends on the subject-matter. In proportion as the offence is grave, so ought the proof to be clear.'

My Lords, I would adopt as appropriate to cases of restraint put by the executive upon the liberty of the individual the civil standard flexibly applied in the way set forth in the cases cited: and I would direct particular attention to the words of Morris L.J. already quoted. It is not necessary to import into the civil proceedings of judicial review the formula devised by judges for the guidance of juries in criminal cases. Liberty is at stake: that is, as the court recognised in *Bater v. Bater* [1951] P. 35 and in *Hornal v. Neuberger Products Ltd* [1957] 1 Q.B. 247, a grave matter. The reviewing court will therefore require to be satisfied that the facts which are required for the justification of the restraint put upon liberty do exist. The flexibility of the civil standard of proof suffices to ensure that the court will require the high degree of probability which is appropriate to what is at stake. ' . . . The nature and gravity of an issue necessarily determines the manner of attaining reasonable satisfaction of the truth of the issue': Dixon J. in *Wright v. Wright* (1948) 77 C.L.R. 191, 210. I would, therefore, adopt the civil standard flexibly applied in the way described in the case law to which I have referred. And I completely agree with the observation made by my noble and learned friend, Lord Bridge of Harwich, that the difficulties of proof in many immigration cases afford no valid ground for lowering the standard of proof required.

Accordingly, it is enough to say that, where the burden lies on the executive to justify the exercise of a power of detention, the facts relied on as justification must be proved to the satisfaction of the court. A preponderance of probability suffices: but the degree of probability must be such that the court is satisfied. The strictness of the criminal formula is unnecessary to enable justice to be done: and its lack of flexibility in a jurisdiction where the technicalities of the law of evidence must not be allowed to become the master of the court could be a positive disadvantage inhibiting the efficacy of the developing safeguard of judicial review in the field of public law.

For these reasons I conclude that in these two appeals, once the applicant had shown, as each did, that he had entered the United Kingdom with the leave of the immigration officer, the burden of proving that he had obtained leave by deception was upon the executive and the standard of proof was the balance of probabilities. In Khera's case, the executive failed to prove that he was guilty of deception. In Khawaja's case the evidence that he deceived the immigration authority was overwhelming. Accordingly, I would allow the appeal of Khera and dismiss that of Khawaja."

NOTES

Certain dicta in these cases appear to imply that the civil standard of proof is itself variable. Indeed, Lord Scarman goes so far as to dismiss the distinction between the standards as a mere "matter of words". What criticisms could be made of these *dicta*? The next case, *Ellerton*, attempts to make clear the distinction between a flexible standard of proof and a variable one. Are you convinced by this distinction, or is this too a mere matter of words?

9.   R. v. Hants CC *ex parte* Ellerton
[1985] W.L.R. 749

A fire officer was found to have engaged in corrupt practices contrary to Fire Services regulations. He appealed on the basis that the fire authority had been in error in applying the civil standard of proof to the allegation. His appeal was dismissed.

LORD JUSTICE SLADE: "The second of the two main points raised, though not stressed, on behalf of the applicant has caused me slightly greater difficulty. The passages from the speech of Lord Scarman in *Reg. v. Secretary of State for the Home Department, Ex parte Khawaja* [1984] A.C. 74, which have already been cited by May, L.J., well illustrate that the civil standard of proof on the balance of probabilities is a 'flexible' one and that the graver the issue involved, the higher is the degree of probability which the court should require. The very fact that all of their Lordships in that case thought it necessary, albeit in rather different forms of words, to stress this point for the guidance of lower courts gives rise to the question whether the disciplinary appeal panel of the fire authority gave itself a sufficient direction in deciding that 'it was appropriate for the case to be decided on the balance of probabilities, as was customary in employment tribunals of this nature'.

The judge grasped this nettle in his judgement. He specifically asked himself, 83 LGR 54, 63, the question whether the five members of the panel 'would automatically have appreciated that a less serious allegation is more easily proved to the required standard that is a more serious one.' He gave his answer to this question as follows:

'I have reminded myself of the nature of the allegations here, allegations of corrupt practice, the particulars of which, I think, can be summarised as "using a fire brigade vehicle to carry a private load and pretending to the man then in charge of the civic amenity tip to which the load was taken that it had come from the fire brigade". I have been influenced too by my belief that, as a matter of ordinary human experience, a person is less easily satisfied that a serious allegation is made out than that a trivial one is made out. Consider a parent anxious to decide whether one of his children stole a sum of money and whether another had the light on in his bedroom after it had been put out and he had been told to go to sleep. Taking all of these factors into account, I am unable to say that the panel applied to the case before it a lower standard of proof than the law required. In any event, to speak more generally, I believe that a tribunal of fact will automatically take the relative seriousness of an allegation into account as one of the factors bearing on the question of whether the civil burden of proof has been discharged.'

A number of the speeches in the *Khawaja* case [1984] A.C. 74 use phrases such as a 'high degree of probability' or corresponding phrases: see, for example, p.97G per Lord Fraser of Tullybelton, p.113H per Lord Scarman, p.124E per Lord Bridge of Harwich and p.128C per Lord Templeman. Lord Scarman referred, at p.113H, to the 'flexibility of the civil standard of proof'. However, my understanding of the concept of the flexible standard of proof reflected in the speeches in the *Khawaja* case is not that it involves proof on (say) a 51 to 49 balance of probabilities in some cases and (say) a 75 to 25 balance in others: any sliding scale of this nature would lead to intolerable uncertainty in application. My understanding of the concept, which I think was that of the judge, is simply that the relative seriousness of the allegation is a relevant factor (on occasions a highly relevant factor) in considering whether or not the civil burden of proof on the balance of probabilities has been discharged in any given case. This, as I understand it, was essentially the point which their Lordships thought it right to spell out in the *Khawaja* case in the particular context of an allegation of illegal entry. However, in other cases, of which I think the present was one, the point may be so obvious that it does not need to be put into words."

NOTES

Thus, in England it now seems reasonably clear that there are only two standards of proof. Equally it is clear that where serious allegations are made in a civil case, more, or more convincing evidence may be required to tip the balance of probability. The point is well put by Morris L.J. in *Hornal v. Neuberger Products Ltd* [1957] Q.B. 247, part of whose opinion is quoted by the court in *Ellerton*, above:

"Though no court and no jury would give less careful attention to issues lacking gravity than to those marked by it, the very elements of gravity become part of the whole range of circumstances which have to be weighed in the scale when deciding as to the balance of probabilities".

Particular problems may arise in cases where allegations are of a highly sensitive or emotive nature. Proceedings brought under the Children (Scotland) Act 1995 provide a good example, particularly where allegations of abuse have been made. In *Re H. (Minors) (Sexual Abuse)* [1996] A.C. 563, Lord Nichols of Birkenhead said:

"The balance of probability standard means that a court is satisfied an event occurred if the court considers that, on the evidence, the occurrence of the event was more likely than not. When assessing the probabilities the court will have in mind as a factor, to whatever extent is appropriate in the particular case, that the more serious the allegation the less likely it is that the event occurred and, hence, the stronger should be the evidence before the court concludes that the allegation is established on the balance of probability. Fraud is usually less likely than negligence. Deliberate physical injury is usually less likely than accidental physical injury. A step-father is usually less likely to have repeatedly raped and had non-consensual oral sex with his under-age stepdaughter than on some occasion to have lost his temper and slapped her. Built into the preponderance of probability standard is a generous degree of flexibility in respect of the seriousness of the allegation.

Although the result is much the same, this does not mean that where a serious allegation is in issue the standard of proof required is higher. It means only that the inherent probability or improbability of an event is itself a matter to be taken into account when weighing the probabilities and deciding whether, on balance, the event occurred. The more improbable the event, the stronger must be the evidence that it did occur before, on the balance of probability, its occurrence will be established."

He concluded that in such cases:

> "I am conscious of the difficulties facing judges when there is conflicting testimony on serious allegations. On some occasions judges are left deeply anxious at the end of a case. There may be an understandable inclination to 'play safe' in the interests of the child . . . [However, parents] are not to be at risk of having their child taken from them and removed into the care of the local authority on the basis only of suspicions, whether of the judge, or of the local authority or anyone else. A conclusion that the child is suffering . . . harm must be based on facts, not just suspicion."

In other words, while in such cases it may be tempting to apply a lower standard of proof, in fact, depending on the nature and seriousness of the allegations involved, stronger evidence may be required.

What is the position in Scotland? There have, from time to time, been suggestions of a third or intermediate standard of proof. What standard is applied when, in a civil case, an allegation of criminal conduct is made?

10.   Lennon v. Co-operative Insurance Society
1986 S.L.T. 98

A boarding-house was damaged beyond economic repair by a fire. The owner of the boarding-house had insured against the risk of fire, and sought indemnity under his insurance policy. At the time he had been in financial difficulties. The insurers contended that the owner had himself deliberately set fire to the house. At the outset of his opinion the Lord Ordinary (Kincraig) said:

> "The sole question for decision in this case, is whether the defenders have proved that the fire in the pursuer's boarding-house was started by the pursuer. I accept the submission by counsel for the pursuer that the standard of proof which the defenders must attain in order to be entitled to judgement is lower than the criminal standard, namely, beyond reasonable doubt but higher than on a balance of probabilities. There is, in my judgement, a higher onus on the defenders where an allegation of wilful fire-raising is made. I am not able to state in words the extent of that onus, but it is enough that I consider that it is higher than on a balance of probabilities, somewhere half-way between that and beyond reasonable doubt."

At the proof it was accepted by the owner that the fire had been started deliberately with the use of petrol. On the evidence his Lordship held that the owner alone had been in the building at about the time when the fire was started, that the fire had been started from within the house and that it was unlikely that an intruder had gained admission. There was further evidence accepted by his Lordship that the pursuer's clothes had been contaminated with petrol, that despite the smell of petrol in the building after the fire the owner had not suggested that the house had been set on fire by an intruder, and that one seat of the fire was at an electrical junction-box and could thus have been designed to make it appear that the fire had been caused by an electrical fault. The explanation that he gave at the time of the fire, which was not accepted by the Lord Ordinary, was consistent with such an electrical fault.

In holding that the owner had started the fire his Lordship concluded:

> "It is not without significance, in my judgement, that the pursuer has not been able to suggest any person as a possible intruder who would break into his house and set fire to it. I am quite satisfied, upon the evidence, that it was the pursuer who set fire to the house. In my judgement the pursuer's defence is based upon the occurrence of a series of possibilities, many of which are speculative; others founded on fact but all individually mere possibilities. They are, in my judgement, all too speculative to displace the inference from the facts that the fire was ignited by the one person in the house at the time, and it is not insignificant in my judgement that no facts, apart from the evidence given by the pursuer, point to the fire having been more probably started by an intruder than by the pursuer himself. I shall accordingly assoilzie the defenders from the conclusion of the summons."

NOTES

See also *Sereshky v. Sereshky*, 1988 S.L.T. 426. In *Lennon*, Lord Kincraig appears to state a standard of proof higher than the ordinary civil standard. But does he in fact apply that higher standard? In

Rehmann v. Ahmad, 1993 S.L.T. 741, Lord Penrose, with reference to cases such as *Lennon*, highlighted the difficulties of "an approach which depends on indefinable qualitative distinctions". He went on to say that in a case involving rectification of documents, where there was a strong presumption in favour of the accuracy of the document, that "careful and precise proof" would be required to overcome the presumption, an approach which in substance seems similar to English cases such as *Ellerton*. In any event, it appears that the questions raised by *Lennon*, and indeed the English case on the question of the variable civil standard have been largely answered by the following cases.

11.   B. v. Kennedy
1987 S.L.T. 765

A child was referred to a Children's Hearing under the Social Work (Scotland) Act 1968, s.32(2)(b) and (d) in respect of allegations of lewd and libidinous practices towards her by her rather. The father disputed the grounds for referral, and at the hearing before the sheriff, contended that the standard of proof applicable in such a case was higher than the normal civil standard.

LORD JUSTICE-CLERK (ROSS): "We can deal shortly with the second of counsel for the appellant's main submissions, which was that: 'the sheriff should have applied a higher standard of proof than the balance of probabilities'. This submission was based upon an article in 1978 S.L.T. (News) 301, p.305, where the author may seem to suggest that there is an intermediate standard of proof between that applicable to the criminal law of beyond reasonable doubt and that applicable to the civil law, the balance of probabilities. We do not agree. There are only the two standards of proof. The words of Lord Denning quoted in this article: 'the more serious the allegation the higher degree of probability that is required' are unfortunately phrased. We construe that statement as meaning that the weight of evidence required to tip the scales may vary with the gravity of the allegation to be proved. For example, the weight of evidence required to prove fraud in a civil case may be greater than that required to prove breach of contract, but the standard of proof is fixed as 'the balance of probabilities'. The converse is also true, namely, that in a case such as this, where the alleged offence is unlikely, to put it no higher, to be committed *coram publico*, the decree of corroboration available is bound to be less than in a case in which there is corroboration by eye witnesses. The purpose of section 32 of the Social Work (Scotland) Act must be kept in mind, namely, that the child may be in need of compulsory measures of care. Section 42(6) of the Act requires proof beyond reasonable doubt only where the ground of referral is that the child has committed an offence. The ordinary civil law standard applies to all other grounds."

NOTES

> The article referred to in the opinion of the court is Grant, "More Bridge Building: Four Decisions on Children's Hearings" 1978 S.L.T. (News) 301.

12.   Harris v. F.
1991 S.L.T. 242

This was another case brought under the Social Work (Scotland) Act 1968, s.32. Again, the grounds of referral were contested and again it was argued that the standard of proof to be applied where a person was, indirectly, being accused of a criminal offence, should be the higher standard. All of the judges held that proceedings under the 1968 Act were in a special position and the standard to be applied was clearly the civil standard. All reserved their opinion as to the standard to be applied in other types of civil case, where allegations of criminal behaviour were made. Lord Macdonald, however, made the following remarks.

LORD MACDONALD: "The present case relates to a ground of referral under section 32(2)(dd) under which it may be necessary to identify such an individual. This raises sharply the question as to the standard of proof to be applied in deciding whether such ground of referral has been established. Is it to be proof beyond reasonable doubt, or proof on a balance of the probabilities? In my opinion the latter is the appropriate standard.

It is now clear that applications to the sheriff under section 42 of the 1968 Act are to be regarded as civil judicial proceedings, albeit of a special kind (*McGregor v. T; McGregor v. D*). Moreover it is now provided by section 9 of the Civil Evidence (Scotland) Act 1988 that, with one significant exception, the relaxed provisions of that Act are to apply to such applications. The exception arises where the ground of referral is under section 32(2)(g) of the 1968 Act which involves a finding that the child has committed an offence. It is specifically provided by section 42(6) of the Act that in that case the standard required is proof beyond reasonable doubt. In my opinion it must follow from this that all other grounds of referral may be established by the only other standard known to the law of Scotland, *viz.* a balance of the probabilities. This applies even where the ground of referral involves, expressly or by implication, the identification of an individual as the perpetrator of an offence.

It is sufficient to satisfy this standard that the scale falls in favour of the fact to be established. I dissociate myself with judicial dicta which suggest that in certain situations a high degree of probability may be required. There can be no intermediate standard between a bare balance of the probabilities on the one hand, and proof beyond reasonable doubt on the other.

We heard a wider argument as to the appropriate standard of proof required where acts of a criminal nature have to be proved in the course of civil actions generally. This was based upon dicta contained in *Arnott v. Burt* and certain subsequent cases. In my opinion it is neither necessary nor expedient in the present case to comment on the general matter. The social work legislation is a code which is *sui generis* and although it contains provisions which are properly described as involving civil judicial proceedings, these proceedings fall to be conducted strictly in accordance with that code."

NOTES

Can Lord Macdonald's remarks be reconciled with cases such as *Bater v. Bater* and *Ellerton*, above?

13. Mullan v. Anderson
1993 S.C.L.R. 506

The pursuers were the widow and children of a man who had been stabbed to death. The defender had been tried for, and acquitted of, murder. The deceased's family raised an action against the defender for damages for the death of their father, averring that he had deliberately or recklessly stabbed the deceased and thereby caused his death.

LORD MORISON: "It was also submitted that the sheriff erred in holding that 'the standard of proof in this case . . . will be balance of probability'. It was submitted that it was not clear on the authorities that this was so in a case in which an allegation of murder had been made and that the uncertainty of the law on the matter raised a question of importance and created a difficulty which the sheriff had ignored. In my opinion, there is no such importance or difficulty, since the sheriff was correct in his determination of the appropriate standard of proof. The Scottish authorities cited to us as indicating the contrary were, first, dicta contained in *Arnott v. Burt*, particularly Lord Cowan at p.71 and Lord Neaves at p.74. This was a case in which an allegation of forgery was made, but the observations founded on were plainly *obiter*, were not supported by any authority and were not made by the Lord Ordinary, whose decision was affirmed, nor by the Lord Justice-Clerk or Lord Benholme, who concurred in it. The appellants also cited a decision of a Lord Ordinary in *Lennon v. Co-operative Insurance Society*, in which he stated in a case involving an allegation of fire raising that the onus was 'higher than on a balance of probabilities, somewhere halfway between that and beyond reasonable doubt'. It is not stated in the report of this decision that any submission was made on that matter and, in spite of what he had said, the Lord Ordinary appears to have determined the case on the basis that 'no facts, apart from the evidence given by the pursuer, point to the fire having been more probably started by an intruder than by the pursuer himself. In my view these authorities are plainly insufficient to displace the well-established principle that in civil cases the standard of proof required of a pursuer is that he prove his case on a balance of probabilities and the suggestion that there exists in Scotland some standard intermediate between a balance of probabilities and beyond reasonable doubt has expressly been rejected in *Brown v. Brown* at p.126; *Lamb v. Lord Advocate* at pp.116 and 119; and *B v. Kennedy* at p.768. My view that any civil case, including this one, must be determined on a balance of probabilities does not ignore the obvious fact that it is more difficult to prove, according to the required standard, an allegation of murder or serious crime, because it is inherently unlikely that a normal person will commit such a crime. Certain English authorities cited, including the similar case of *Halford v. Brookes*, appear to have proceeded on the basis that this difficulty is to be reflected in a variation of the normal standard of proof, but in my view there is no justification in Scotland for that approach and if it were applied it might well lead to uncertainty in any case where an allegation of serious criminal or immoral conduct was made."

LORD PENROSE: "The sheriff proceeded on the view that the standard of proof to be applied in this case was the ordinary civil standard of balance of probabilities. For the appellant it was argued that that involved an error of law. Counsel referred to *Lennon v. Co-operative Insurance Society*; *Arnott v. Burt*; *Halford v. Brookes*; *B v. Kennedy*; *Harris v. F*; *Buick v. Jaglar*; *Rehman v. Ahmad*; and *Shaw v. Lanarkshire Health Board*. Counsel for the respondents referred, in addition, to *Brown v. Brown*; *Lamb v. Lord Advocate*; *R. v. Home Secretary ex parte Khawaja*; *R. v. Hampshire County Council ex parte Ellerton*; and *Ward v. Chief Constable, Strathclyde Police*. In my opinion the English authorities are not helpful in this context. As a matter of general impression I found Slade L.J.'s opinion in *Ellerton* at p.761 attractive. However, the development of the law in the two jurisdictions has been different and it is not possible to be confident that the use of similar expressions reflects common understanding of the issues involved. The Scottish authorities establish, in my opinion, that there are two standards of proof only in Scotland, proof beyond reasonable doubt and proof on balance of probabilities: *Brown*, per Lord Emslie at p.126; *Lamb* per Lord Justice-Clerk Wheatley at p.116 and Lord Kissen at p.119; *B v. Kennedy* at p.768. The two standards differ in character, not in degree. Proof to a standard which excludes reasonable doubt on the whole evidence available to the tribunal of fact involves a process of analysis and reasoning which differs from that involved in reaching a view whether, among the possibilities which emerge on a consideration of the evidence as a whole, one can be identified which probably reflects the truth. In my opinion, it is wholly consistent with such an approach to recognise that certain facts may require evidence of particular weight if they are to be established on either approach. In *Ward* the Lord President adopted precisely that approach, as I understand his comments, at p.294, as did Lord Sutherland at p.297 and Lord Clyde at pp.298–299. In *Rehman* I attempted to follow the same approach, in adopting the test of 'careful and precise' proof of the facts required to overcome the presumption that a written document embodied the agreement of the parties who subscribed it. In some cases one may have an allegation which, of its very nature is, or appears to be, improbable. It would require evidence of more significant weight to persuade one that a fact of that nature was probably true than it would to persuade one to the same standard that a commonplace event had occurred. It is not clear that the observations of Lord Neaves in *Arnott*, at p.74, are inconsistent with this approach. In *Lennon* Lord Kincraig applied the standard of balance of probabilities when he came to decide the case. The opinion of the court in *B. v. Kennedy* is clearly consistent with the same approach."

NOTES

The English case of *Halford v. Brookes* [1991] T.L.R. 427, cited to the court in *Mullan*, was another case in which murder was alleged. In *Halford* it was held that the standard of proof should be the criminal standard, given the seriousness of the allegations involved. As we have seen, the Scottish court did not accept this argument. But there have in the past been suggestions that Scots law should adopt the same approach. Such suggestions appear to originate in the case of *Arnott v. Burt* (1872) 11 M. 62, and in particular in Lord Neaves' view that allegations of criminal conduct in a civil case should be proved by "as good evidence as would be required to support a criminal charge". Following *Mullan v. Anderson* it is clear that in Scotland there are only two standards of proof and that no intermediate or variable standard is recognised. Furthermore, dicta in *Mullan* suggest that the standard of proof in civil cases will always be the civil balance of probabilities standard. There is some authority to suggest, however, that in quasi-criminal proceedings, such as those involving allegations of breach of interdict, decree *ad factum praestandum*, or for imposition of a civil penalty, the standard to be met is the criminal one. This is because of the prospect that the defender may be imprisoned or fined should the averments be proved—see *Lord Advocate v. Ruffle*, 1979 S.C. 371; *Gribben v. Gribben*, 1976 S.L.T. 266; *Nelson v. Nelson*, 1988 S.C.L.R. 663, and on contravention of lawburrows *Morrow v. Neil*, 1975 S.L.T. (Sh. Ct.) 65 at 69, above. (It has been held, however, that the purposes of that Act, proceedings for breach of interdict, are to be regarded as a civil proceeding. Accordingly, corroboration in such cases is not required, even although the standard of proof is the criminal one—see *Byrne v. Ross*, 1993 S.L.T. 307.) In relation to proceedings under statute, much may depend on the construction of the particular provision. In this context, caution must now be exercised in relation to cases such as *Lord Advocate v. Ruffle*, above.

14.   1st Indian Cavalry Club v. Commissioners of Customs and Excise
1998 S.L.T. 554

Section 60 of the Value Added Tax Act 1994 provides that where, for the purpose of evading VAT, a person does any act or omits to take any action, and his conduct involves dishonesty (whether or not it is such as to give rise to criminal liability), he shall be liable to a penalty. In this case the appellants appealed an assessment to a civil penalty under the Act. They argued that, in considering allegations of dishonest conduct, the commissioners should have applied the criminal standard of proof. The Inner House rejected this contention.

LORD MCCLUSKEY: "A body corporate and its managing officer appealed to the VAT and duties tribunal against penalties assessed against them under sections 60 and 61 of the 1994 Act. The tribunal concluded on an application of the civil standard of proof that dishonesty had been established and that a penalty was appropriate. The issue before this court was therefore a simple issue of the standard of proof which the commissioners had to meet in an appeal to which section 60(7) applied. It was not suggested that the provisions of section 61(5) had any bearing on the issue in this appeal or upon the second appellant's right to pursue the appeal.

In support of his ground of appeal, counsel who appeared for the second appellant pointed out that the 1994 Act was a consolidation measure. Section 60 was derived from section 13 of the Finance Act 1985, as amended by later Acts, with the exception of subsection (7) which derived from section 27(1) of the Finance Act 1985. Section 61 re-enacted provisions taken from section 14 of the Finance Act 1986. He drew attention to the wording of sections 60 and 61 and to the other provisions of Pt IV, notably section 72 which deals with offences which can render the taxpayer liable on conviction to certain penalties in respect of conduct specified in that section. Although it was not in dispute that the provisions in sections 60 and 61 followed the publication of a report (Cmnd 8822, 1983) by a Committee on Enforcement Powers of The Revenue Departments chaired by Lord Keith of Kinkel, he submitted that the provisions in Pt IV of the 1994 Act, and notably sections 60 and 61, did not in fact expressly provide that the standard of proof was to be the standard appropriate in civil proceedings. Counsel was not aware of any ruling by a court as to the standard of proof applicable under the provisions enacted in 1985 and 1986. However he drew attention to *Ghandi Tandoori Restaurant v. Commissioners of Customs and Excise* where the tribunal in London held that the standard of proof required establishing an act or omission and conduct involving dishonesty on the part of the taxpayer under section 13 of the Finance Act 1985 was the civil standard of proof "requiring a high degree of probability". He did not suggest that such language would be appropriate to describe the standard of proof in Scottish proceedings. That was a case in which there was no contradictor and the tribunal did not appear to give weight to the most important consideration, the nature of the proceedings. He drew attention to other English cases in which opinions had been expressed as to a burden of proof that appeared to lie somewhere between the balance of probabilities and proof beyond reasonable doubt: in this regard reference was made to *Miller v. Minister of Pensions* and *Khawaja v. Secretary of State for the Home Department*, per Lord Scarman at [1983] 1 All E.R., p.784. In the tribunal decision in Norman Wood & Sons the tribunal had applied the ordinary civil standard of proof to a case under section 13(1) of the Finance Act 1985. In so doing they referred to *Mullan v. Anderson* as authority for the proposition that there did not exist in Scotland any intermediate standard between a balance of probabilities and proof beyond reasonable doubt. In counsel's submission, however, *Mullan v. Anderson* was not a case which decided what standard of proof was appropriate in quasi-criminal proceedings like the present. He submitted that any proceedings in which a public body sought a penalty could properly be described as quasi-criminal proceedings. He drew attention to the comparatively recent clarification of the distinction between the different standards of proof applicable in civil and in criminal proceedings. He referred to Dickson on *Evidence*, Vol. 1, para. 37, to *Hendry v. Clan Line Steamers* and to the opinion of the Lord Justice Clerk in *McKenzie v. H.M.A.*. He founded strongly upon *Inland Revenue v. Ruffle* in which Lord Jauncey held that proceedings under section 99 of the Taxes Management Act 1970 were of a quasi-criminal nature and that the standard of proof was proof beyond reasonable doubt. At 1979 S.C. 377; 1979 S.L.T. 215 Lord Jauncey said of that section 99: 'Section 99 is one of a number of sections to be found in Part X of the Taxes Management Act 1970 headed 'Penalties etc.'. As a penal section it falls to be construed strictly and the proceedings thereunder being of a quasi-criminal nature proof of the facts resulting in liability to a penalty must be beyond reasonable doubt.'

Lord Jauncey had also made reference to *Gribben v. Gribben* in which it had been held that the same high standard of proof applied in proceedings for breach of interdict. Part of the importance of *Inland Revenue v. Ruffle* was that it preceded both the Keith report and the legislation of 1985. If that legislation had been intended to change the law as explained in *Ruffle* it was to be expected that that would be done expressly. The essential key to determining what standards fell to be applied to proof of the facts was to ascertain the nature of the proceedings. These were proceedings to exact a penalty: they were therefore quasi-criminal. Other quasi-criminal proceedings in Scotland attracted the higher standard of proof. That standard was also held to apply to proceedings for breach of interdict in *Eutectic Welding Alloys Co Ltd v. Whitting*. In *Lamb v. Lord Advocate*, Lord Kissen at 1976 S.C. 117; 1976 S.L.T. 155 drew the distinction between, on the one hand, a civil case and, on the other, cases which were criminal or quasi-criminal. The civil standard was applied in the lawburrows case of *Morrow v. Neil*; but proceedings for contravention of lawburrows appeared to attract the criminal standard of proof: see the opinion of Sheriff Macphail at 1975 S.L.T. (Sh.Ct.) 69. There was a consistent line of authority which held that the higher standard of proof applied in quasi-criminal proceedings. In anticipation of the submissions on behalf of the commissioners he argued that the court could not look at the Keith report. In any event the committee's discussion of the matter proceeded upon a failure to take account of the background, including the case of *Ruffle*, which was not referred to in the relevant part of the report, though it was referred to elsewhere. If the law as expressed in *Ruffle* was to be changed then it would have been necessary to make an express change, and that had not been done. Nor was it appropriate to look at proceedings in Parliament because there was no ambiguity of the kind seen to be necessary in the light of *Pepper v. Hart*. The appeal should be allowed and the penalty quashed.

In replying, counsel for the commissioners explained that fines were paid to the Treasury but penalties under Pt IV were paid to the commissioners. That circumstance and others indicated that there were two separate regimes, one for criminal offences and one for civil penalties. Even if it was technically possible for a person to face criminal prosecution as well as being made liable for a civil penalty, the commissioners, although not a prosecuting authority in Scotland, would have the option not to report for prosecution a case in which they had decided to seek a civil penalty. The existence of two separate regimes was plain from the structure of Pt IV of the 1994 Act and the contrasts between sections 59, 60 and 61 on the one hand and section 72 on the other. He submitted that it was appropriate to look at the Keith report and the parliamentary proceedings as background to the 1985 and 1986 Finance Acts. In addition to *Pepper v. Hart*, he drew attention to *Short's Tr v. Keeper of Registers*, per Lord President Hope at 1994 S.C. 138; 1994 S.L.T. 69C. It was submitted that, in the absence of any express provision and having regard to the arguments submitted in the present appeal, there was an ambiguity in the legislation of the kind envisaged in *Short's Tr*. The Keith report (Cmnd 8822), paras 18.4.7–18.4.19, made it plain that that committee was recommending the introduction of civil penalties into VAT proceedings in order to align the arrangements for VAT and direct taxes. The committee specifically said: 'we endorse the generally civil nature of Inland Revenue offence proceedings'. The thinking behind the recommendation to introduce a "civil fraud", with the civil standard of proof, was fully explained in these paragraphs. He drew attention to the proceedings in Standing Committee B on the Finance Bill on May 16, 1995. Clause 12 of that Bill became section 13 of the Finance Act 1985 and the minister dealing with the Bill made it plain that the intention in relation to the provisions now contained in section 60 of the 1994 Act was to move from the standard of proof appropriate to criminal cases to the balance of probabilities: col. 136. The only express statutory reference specifying the standard of proof that he had been able to find was contained in section 68 of the Children (Scotland) Act 1995 which re-enacted provisions contained in the Social Work (Scotland) Act 1968. He also referred to the Civil Evidence (Scotland) Act 1988. This Act made fresh provision in relation to civil proceedings in Scotland. Section 9 provided that 'civil proceedings' included 'any proceedings before a tribunal or inquiry, except in so far as, in relation to the conduct of proceedings before the tribunal or inquiry, specific provision has been made as regards the rules of evidence which are to apply'.

It followed that the rules of evidence applicable in an appeal to the VAT tribunal were those applicable in civil proceedings. This important rule of law was entirely consistent with the submission that the proceedings before the tribunal under Pt IV of the 1994 Act were civil proceedings attracting the civil standard of proof. The 1988 Act innovated upon old rules such as those applied to adultery: see *Brown v. Brown*. The *Khawaja* case did not in fact introduce an intermediate standard of proof, contrary to the misunderstanding of that case in *Ghandi Tandoori Restaurant*. It was not contended that *Mullan v. Anderson* dealt with the precise point at issue in this appeal. What was clear was that the Finance Act 1985 swept away the previous law regarding evasion of value added tax contained in section 39 of the previous consolidation statute: the Value Added Tax Act 1983. That statute dealt with offences and penalties in an entirely criminal context. Lord Jauncey in the *Ruffle* case was not dealing with value added tax. However, it was submitted that he had fallen into error in the passage quoted. It was not clear whether or not the point as to standard of proof had been fully argued before him.

In replying to the submissions inviting this court to look at the Keith report and the proceedings in Parliament, counsel for the second appellant drew a distinction between an ambiguity of the kind which Lord Browne-Wilkinson was dealing with in *Pepper v. Hart* and an uncertainty which might be thought to arise because the statute had failed to deal with the matter at all. It was plain from the passage in Lord Browne-Wilkinson's speech at [1993] A.C. 634–635 that he had in mind ambiguous words or phrases, not just uncertainty. It was not disputed that the Keith committee envisaged that the civil standard of proof would be introduced; nor could it be disputed that, if one could look at parliamentary proceedings, the minister in charge of the Finance Bill 1985 thought and said that the provisions contained in what was to become section 13 of the 1985 Act would achieve the result of introducing the civil standard of proof. However, it was essential to look at the wording of the provision to see whether or not the result envisaged had in fact been achieved. That was the approach adopted to a consideration of memoranda by the Scottish Law Commission in *Barratt Scotland Ltd v. Keith*. The Lord Justice Clerk there considered that it was not appropriate to have regard to the terms of the Scottish Law Commission memoranda for the purpose of construing a subsequent statute unless the language of the statute was ambiguous or there was any doubt about the construction to be placed upon the statutory language. In the present case there was nothing in the 1994 Act in the way of words, phrases or language generally giving rise to any ambiguity. He acknowledged that the court might look at the Keith report to identify the mischief which the subsequent Bill, the Finance Bill 1985, was intended to cure, but nothing in that report could assist if Parliament in fact failed to deal with the matter at all.

In my opinion, the tribunal reached the correct conclusion on the issue before this court. They also appear to me to have decided that issue upon the correct basis; namely a consideration of the language and form of the provisions in Pt IV of the 1994 Act. It is apparent from the terms of section 60 that a clear distinction is drawn between criminal liability and liability to a 'civil penalty'. That distinction is made both by the words in section 60(1)(b), namely 'whether or not it *i.e.* his conduct is such as to give rise to criminal liability', and by the express reference in subsection (4), para. (a) to the assessing by the commissioners of 'an amount due by way of a civil penalty instead of instituting criminal proceedings'. The same distinction runs through subsections (5) and (6). Section 72 expressly deals with *offences* in terms similar to those found in section 39 of the Value Added Tax Act 1983. Accordingly, I see the provisions for civil penalties in section 60 of the 1994 Act as additional (having been added in 1985) to the previous, purely criminal, provisions found in the 1983 Act. It is also to be observed that other sections in Pt IV give rise to a liability to payments of what are truly penalties. Section 59 renders a taxable person 'liable to a surcharge' calculated in accordance with the provisions of the section in respect of a failure to furnish the necessary return within the prescribed time. Section 62 renders a taxable person liable to a penalty in respect of his providing to named parties an incorrect certificate as to zero rating etc. Section 63 prescribes a penalty for misdeclaration or neglect in certain specified respects and the liability to other penalties may be found elsewhere, including sections 65–69. Section 70 permits some of those penalties to be reduced by the commissioners or by a tribunal. In my opinion, the whole scheme of Pt IV is to enact two distinct and separate schemes. In the one, civil proceedings allow the recovery of civil penalties (including surcharges). In the other, persons may be prosecuted for the offence of "fraudulent evasion of VAT". Section 60 falls within the civil regime and thus gives rise to civil proceedings which, in my opinion, attract the civil standard of proof.

In making the submission that proceedings for recovery of a section 60 civil penalty were quasi-criminal proceedings, not civil proceedings, counsel for the second appellant recognised that proceedings for recovery of a default surcharge would also logically have to be characterised as quasi-criminal proceedings: otherwise there would be three categories of proceedings envisaged by Pt IV, namely; civil (s.59), quasi-criminal (s.60) and criminal (s.72). But I do not consider that section 59 envisages quasi-criminal proceedings necessitating proof beyond reasonable doubt. Default under section 59 is established by the mere non-receipt by the commissioners of the VAT return or the VAT due by the appropriate date. The taxable person is then liable for a 'surcharge' and can escape it only if he discharges the onus placed upon him by section 59(7) to satisfy the commissioners, or a tribunal on appeal, of one of the matters specified in paras (a) or (b) of subsection (7). This placing of the onus on the taxable person strongly suggests that the proceedings are not quasi-criminal. The headnote to sections 59–72 is 'Default surcharge and other penalties and criminal offences'. This suggests that the default surcharge is properly also to be regarded as a civil penalty. This headnote also draws the distinction already noted between what are certainly civil penalties and offences which are punishable in the criminal courts. No question of dishonesty or other criminal behaviour arises under section 59 and I can see no reason to read into the provisions in that section a requirement for proof beyond reasonable doubt that the commissioners have not received the return or the VAT by the due date. When the provisions of section 13 of the 1985 Act are compared and contrasted with those in section 39 of the 1983 Act it is clear that in 1985 Parliament was intending to create an entirely new system allowing for the recovery of civil penalties, whether or not the liability was attributable to conduct which had any truly criminal character. In these circumstances, it is entirely appropriate that the Civil Evidence (Scotland) Act 1988 should provide that the rules of evidence applicable in civil proceedings should be the rules applicable in proceedings before *inter alia* VAT tribunals. It is, of course, possible to envisage that the civil rules of evidence might apply in circumstances where the burden of proof was to the higher criminal standard; but I consider it would require clear language to show that the standard of proof was to be the criminal standard, but that the tests of admissibility and sufficiency were to be the less stringent ones applicable in civil proceedings. On my construction of the relevant provisions of the 1994 Act, I consider that the proceedings for the recovery of a civil penalty under sections 60 and 61 are civil proceedings attracting the civil standard of proof. In my opinion, the mischief identified by the Keith committee, and in respect of which they made recommendations for the introduction of a civil fraud, was the mischief of having to resort to criminal proceedings and sanctions in respect of a whole range of failures by the taxable person to perform his obligations to make due returns or appropriate payments etc. The remedy was to provide a civil regime in respect of liabilities arising from defaults which were less serious, while leaving open the possibility of a prosecution where the conduct was sufficiently serious. This consideration also points in favour of the result arrived at by the tribunal."

15.   Robertson v. Watson
1949 J.C. 73

Two farmers were convicted of selling adulterated milk contrary to Food and Drugs legislation. They appealed against conviction and in the course of his opinion, Lord Cooper made the following remarks about the standard of proof applicable where a persuasive burden of proof rests on an accused person.

LORD JUSTICE-GENERAL (COOPER): "Admitting that production of a properly vouched analysis of a properly taken sample showing certain deficiencies in milk shifts the onus of proof to the supplier to show that the milk was 'genuine' (*i.e.* that it was milk as it came from the cow), it is plain that doubts still prevail as to what exactly is involved in that onus and how it may be discharged. There are certain dicta in the cases which have apparently been read as implying that the onus on the supplier is to prove exhaustively a universal negative, and to prove it with the same stringency as is applicable to the prosecution in establishing criminal guilt beyond reasonable doubt. I cannot accept that view, for it would be tantamount in most cases to refusing to the accused any defence whatever. In the words of Lord Justice-Clerk Normand in *Matthewson v. Irvine*, 'the evidence . . . need not be exhaustive of all possible persons who might have somehow come in contact with the milk. It is normally sufficient, for example, to adduce the evidence of the dairyman and his servants.' The example given in that statement is only an example, for the circumstances must vary from case to case. Moreover, as clearly appears from *Lamont v. Rodger* it is not essential that the evidence tendered by the supplier should be independently corroborated, if the evidence is credible and given by the witnesses reasonably available to him. Finally, I adopt as an accurate statement of Scots law of general validity the rule laid down in *Rex v. Carr-Briant* that, when (as in this instance) some matter is presumed against an accused person unless or until the contrary is proved, the burden of proof on the accused is less than that required at the hands of the prosecutor in proving the case beyond reasonable doubt, and that this burden may be discharged by evidence satisfying the jury or the Court of the probability of that which the accused is called upon to establish."

15.   H.M.A. v. Mitchell
1951 J.C. 53

The accused was charged with murder and pleaded not guilty on the grounds of insanity. Lord Justice-Clerk Thomson gave the jury the following directions on standard of proof.

LORD JUSTICE-CLERK (THOMSON): "Now, members of the jury, on this issue the burden of proof is on the defence, because in our law there is a presumption that a man is sane. But you must keep clearly in mind that the burden in the case of an accused person is not so heavy a burden as the burden that is laid on the Crown. I have told you that on the first issue, when the burden is on the Crown, the Crown has to prove its case beyond reasonable doubt, and that is a high standard. It is the standard which our law imposes to prevent, so far as humanly possible, the conviction of innocent people. Where, however, the burden of proof is on the accused, it is enough if he brings evidence that satisfies you of the probability of what he is called upon to establish. You must weigh the evidence which points to sanity alongside the evidence which points to insanity, and if, having done so, you think that on balance it is more probable that he was insane than that he was not insane, you will hold the special defence proved; otherwise you would have to reject it. That is all I have to say to you about the burden of proof. It is a question of the balance of probabilities."

NOTES

These cases hold that on those rare occasions where the persuasive burden of proof does rest on the accused, that burden need be discharged only on a balance of probabilities. In discharging that burden the accused need not lead corroborated evidence—*King v. Lees*, 1993 S.C.C.R. 28. Does Lord Cooper's opinion in *Robertson v. Watson* imply that corroborated evidence is required? There is authority to suggest that where the accused fails to discharge the persuasive burden in such cases, his defence must fail and the Crown must succeed, provided of course that they have themselves led sufficient, satisfactory evidence of the accused's guilt—see *Lambie v. H.M.A.*, 1973 J.C. 53. What difficulties are there with that view? Does it conflict with the obligation on the Crown to prove a case beyond reasonable doubt, or with the accused's Convention rights? See, generally, Macphail, *Evidence*, para. 22.09 and the passage reproduced there from the American case, *Davies v. U.S.* (1895) 160 U.S. 469.

Chapter 5

SUFFICIENCY OF EVIDENCE

In any case, whether civil or criminal, the evidence must be such as to satisfy the court to the appropriate standard of proof. The degree to which the evidence convinces the court about the facts in issue is a question of fact, and, as we have seen, is probably not a matter about which precise rules can be laid down, given the infinite variety of fact-situations which may arise (although Wigmore's so-called "Chart Method" represents a sustained attempt at least to give structure to the fact-finding process—see Wigmore, *The Science of Judicial Proof* (1937); Anderson and Twining, *Analysis of Evidence* (1987) and Twining, *Rethinking Evidence* (1994)).

Behind the question of the weight to be given to the evidence, however, is the question of sufficiency. Sufficiency is a question of law, and prior to the question of weight. If there is insufficient evidence in law, then the case should be withdrawn from the fact-finder before any question as to the quality of the evidence can arise.

1. Criminal Procedure (Scotland) Act 1995

"97.—(1) Immediately after the close of the evidence for the prosecution, the accused may intimate to the court his desire to make a submission that he has no case to answer both—

(a) on an offence charged in the indictment; and

(b) on any other offence of which he could be convicted under the indictment.

(2) If, after hearing both parties, the judge is satisfied that the evidence led by the prosecution is insufficient in law to justify the accused being convicted of the offence charged in respect of which the submission has been made or of such other offence as is mentioned, in relation to that offence, in paragraph (b) of subsection (1) above, he shall acquit him of the offence charged in respect of which the submission has been made and the trial shall proceed only in respect of any other offence charged in the indictment.

(3) If, after hearing both parties, the judge is not satisfied as is mentioned in subsection (2) above, he shall reject the submission and the trial shall proceed, with the accused entitled to give evidence and call witnesses, as if such submission had not been made.

(4) A submission under subsection (1) above shall be heard by the judge in the absence of the jury."

NOTES

Section 160 of this Act is the equivalent provision for summary proceedings. It is important to emphasise that even if the judge rejects a submission under section 97, the accused will not necessarily be convicted. The judge's ruling decides only the legal question of sufficiency and says nothing about the quality or weight of the evidence against the accused. Of course, should the submission be rejected, a tactical problem arises for the defence. If there is sufficient evidence in law to justify conviction, there is clearly a risk that, unless they provide some exculpatory evidence from the accused or some other witness, a conviction will follow—in other words, a tactical burden arises, or may arise, depending on the perceived quality of the evidence. But in some cases, supposedly favourable witnesses only make matters worse by giving evidence which appears to a jury to be untrustworthy, or, worse, is positively incriminating. What if the judge wrongly rejects a submission under section 97, and the defence witnesses then go on to give damning evidence in this way? The matter was considered in relation to the equivalent English provisions in *R. v. Abbott* [1955] 2 All E.R. 899. In that case, the Court of

Appeal decided that any incriminating evidence given after the mistaken rejection should be disregarded and the accused acquitted. *Abbott* was, however, a rather special case, turning on proof of concert between two defendants; it seems that the prosecution led *no* satisfactory evidence on this point. The trial judge allowed the case to continue and one of the two defendants gave evidence hostile to the other. Both were convicted. In distinguishing a previous relevant decision of the Court, *R. v. Power* [1919] 1 K.B. 572, Lord Goddard C.J. said:

> "What the court said in [*Power*] was that if the case did go to the jury, then the evidence given by the prisoners respectively was part of the sum of the evidence in the case, and that this court when asked to quash a conviction might take the whole of the evidence into account. They did not say that the court must, but they said that this court might, take the whole of the evidence into account. They certainly did not say that, if there was no evidence given against one of two or more prisoners, the learned judge could simply leave the case to the jury to see whether when the case for the defence was opened one or other of the prisoners would support the case set up by the prosecution."

Accordingly, if there is *some* evidence, albeit insufficient in law to convict, it seems that incriminating evidence given subsequently to a wrongly rejected "no case" submission might in England be admissible against the defendant. The problem has not arisen acutely in Scotland. However, in *Little v. H.M.A.*, 1983 S.C.C.R. 56, below, Lord Justice-General Emslie made the following comments on the Scottish provisions (then section 140A of the Criminal Procedure (Scotland) Act 1975):

> "In view of the conclusions at which we have arrived we are fortunate that we do not have to resolve this problem in these appeals without a much more comprehensive exploration of the proper interpretation to be placed on section 140A than was presented on behalf of the appellants. That section which is entirely novel to our accustomed and well-tried procedure, would appear to echo rules of law long familiar to other jurisdictions, and the problem to which we have referred has, we apprehend, been examined in the courts of England and in courts of the Commonwealth, including the Supreme Court of Victoria, in relation to their own systems of prosecution and criminal procedure. No relevant decisions in these other jurisdictions were cited to us and when the problem requires to be resolved in a criminal appeal in Scotland we would expect to have a full discussion of relevant foreign decisions to assist us to appreciate clearly the full implications of the new factor which has been introduced by Parliament into the law of Scotland in the shape of [section 97] of the Act of [1995]."

See also *Cordiner v. H.M.A.*, 1991 S.C.C.R. 652—an accused should not be deprived of the right to make a submission of no case to answer by combining what is truly a number of separate charges in one long narrative (or libel) in an indictment. Finally, if any objection has been taken to evidence led by the Crown—for example, evidence of incriminating statements made by an accused person—the trial judge must decide on the admissibility of that evidence before determining the question of sufficiency—see *Thomson v. Crowe*, 1999 S.L.T. 1434, per Lord Justice General Rodger at 1445.

A similar, though less formal, procedure to that under section 97 may be adopted in civil cases—see *e.g. Mulligan v. Caird (Dundee) Ltd*, 1973 S.L.T. 72, and there is provision for such a submission in referrals by the Children's Reporter to the Sheriff under section 65 of the Children (Scotland) Act 1995 (see the Child Care and Maintenance Rules 1997, rule 3.47(2)).

2. Hume
Vol. ii, pp. 382–84

"These things are what have occurred to me as most worthy of observation, respecting the province of the Court, in the matter of proof and admission of witnesses: For to them, and them only it belongs, to judge of the competency of the evidence, of whatsoever sort, that is offered, and the regularity of the form in which it is brought forward. By what rules a jury shall be guided, in forming their opinion of the sufficiency of the evidence; what circumstances shall weigh with them, and how far, and on what occasions; how to decide between contradictory testimonies; how to distinguish between what amounts to evidence, and what to grounds of suspicion only: these are delicate and arduous inquiries, in which I am unwilling to engage; being well aware how difficult it is to deliver any thing about them in a general way, which shall be of real service towards the performance of this important duty in particular cases. Two or three particulars only I will venture to take notice of, as grounded in universal opinion, and confirmed with numerous examples in every period of our practice. One relates to the direct mode of evidence, by the testimony of such persons who have seen the deed done; and it is this, that no-one shall in any case be convicted on the testimony of a single witness. No matter how trivial the offence, and how high soever the credit and character of the witness, still our law is averse to rely on his single word, in any inquiry which may affect the person, liberty or fame of his neighbour; and rather than run the risk of such an error, a risk which does not hold when there is a concurrence of testimonies, it is willing that the guilty should escape . . .

It would not be a reasonable thing, nor is it our law, that the want of a second witness to the fact cannot be supplied by the other circumstances of the case. If one man swear that he saw the pannel stab the deceased, and others confirm his testimony with circumstances, such as the pannel's sudden flight from the spot, the blood on his clothes, the bloody instrument found in his possession, his confession on being taken, or the like; certainly these are as good, nay better even than a second testimony to the act of stabbing.

Neither is it to be understood in cases of circumstantial evidence, either such as the foregoing case, or one where all the evidence is circumstantial, that two witnesses are necessary to establish each particular; because the aptitude and coherence of the several circumstances often as fully confirm the truth of the story, as if all the witnesses were deponing to the same facts."

NOTES

This passage forms the basis for the rule requiring corroboration in Scotland. It is explicitly adopted in the following case, which still reflects much of the present law on corroboration. The basic requirement of corroboration is that the evidence against the accused should come from two separate and independent sources. *Cordiner v. H.M.A.*, 1993 S.L.T. 2, for example, was a rape case in which the complainer testified that the accused had tied her legs together with a blue pullover. A blue pullover was indeed found not far from the scene of the assault, and the Crown relied on this to provide corroboration of the complainer's account. It was held that the finding of the pullover could not *per se* provide corroboration, however, because the only person who spoke to the pullover having been used or possessed by the accused, was the complainer herself. Things might have been different had a third person seen the accused with such a pullover at or around the time of the alleged offence. But what precisely is it that must be corroborated, and what is the nature of corroborative evidence?

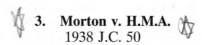

3. Morton v. H.M.A.
1938 J.C. 50

This case concerned a charge of indecent assault in relation to which the complainer identified the accused immediately after the incident and again in court. There was evidence from a woman who observed the assault from her window but was unable to identify the accused as the assailant, and from the complainer's brother who spoke to her distressed condition when relating the incident to him shortly after the event. The accused was convicted and appealed to the High Court.

LORD JUSTICE-CLERK (AITCHISON): "It is a firmly established rule of our criminal law that a person cannot be convicted of a crime, or a statutory offence, on the uncorroborated testimony of one witness however credible, except in the case of certain statutory offences where the Legislature has directed that the evidence of one credible witness shall be sufficient. Subject to these statutory exceptions the rule is inflexible. The law is stated in the clearest terms by Baron Hume in his Commentaries on the Law of Scotland respecting Crimes (Vol. ii. p.383), in the following passage: 'No one shall in any case be convicted on the testimony of a single witness. No matter how trivial the offence, and how high soever the credit and character of the witness, still our law is averse to rely on his single word, in any inquiry which may affect the person, liberty, or fame of his neighbour; and rather than run the risk of such an error, a risk which does not hold when there is a concurrence of testimonies, it is willing that the guilty should escape.' In this passage Hume was dealing with direct evidence, but he goes on to say (at p.384): 'It would not however be a reasonable thing, nor is it our law, that the want of a second witness to the fact cannot be supplied by the other circumstances of the case. If one man swear that he saw the pannel stab the deceased and others confirm his testimony with circumstances, such as the pannel's sudden flight from the spot, the blood on his clothes, the bloody instrument found in his possession, his confession on being taken, and the like: certainly these are as good, nay better even than a second testimony to the act of stabbing. Neither is it to be understood in cases of circumstantial evidence, either such as the foregoing case or one where all the evidence is circumstantial, that two witnesses are necessary to establish each particular; because the aptitude and coherence of the several circumstances often as fully confirm the truth of the story, as if all the witnesses were deponing to the same facts.'

These general propositions as laid down by Hume were hardly disputed by the Crown, but the Solicitor-General thought it right to bring to the notice of the Court the cases of *McCrindle v. MacMillan*, 1930 J.C. 56 and *Strathern v. Lambie*, 1931 J.C. 137, as appearing to support the view that an accused person can be convicted upon the testimony of one witness.

In the case of *McCrindle* an accused person was convicted on a summary complaint which charged an indecent assault upon a girl of 13. At the trial the girl identifie[d] the accused, whom she knew prior to the assault, as her assailant, and there was evidence that he had been near the locus of the assault about the time it was committed. There was also evidence that within a few minutes of the assault the girl stated to her parents and others that the accused had committed it, and she repeated this statement shortly afterwards on being confronted with the accused. It was held that the girl's evidence was sufficiently corroborated by her statements and actions *de recenti*. In my opinion, this judgement proceeded upon a misconception as to the true character of corroboration. A statement made by an injured party *de recenti*, unless it can be brought within the rule of *res gestae*, is ordinarily inadmissible as being hearsay only, but an exception is allowed in the case of sexual assaults upon women and children, including sexual offences against young boys. In cases of that kind the Court will allow the evidence of complaints or statements *de recenti* made by the injured party, for the limited purpose of showing that the conduct of the injured party has been consistent and that the story is not an afterthought, and, in the case of assaults upon women, to negative consent. A complaint *de recenti* increases the probability that the complaint is true and not concocted, and the absence of complaint where sexual offences are alleged is always a material point for the defence. But it must be clearly affirmed that the evidence is admissible as bearing upon credibility only, and the statements of an injured party, although made *de recenti* of the commission of a crime, do not in law amount to corroboration. The essential idea of corroboration is that the testimony of one witness, whether direct to the actual commission of the crime, or indirect to some circumstance implicating the panel in the commission of the crime, is enforced by the testimony, direct or indirect, of some other witness, so that there are concurrent testimonies, either to the same or to different facts, each pointing to the panel as the person by whom the crime was committed. It is this conjunction of separate and independent testimonies, each incriminating, that makes corroboration. A statement of the injured party *de recenti* is nothing but the statement of the injured party. And it is not evidence of the fact complained of.

The case of *McCrindle* purported to follow the case of *McLennan v. H.M.A.*, 1928 J.C. 39. In *McLennan's* case the appellant was convicted upon indictment of lewd and libidinous practices against a boy six years of age. There was evidence of a statement made by the boy to his parents *de recenti*. There were other facts proved which could be relied on as corroboration, but in the opinion of the Court the statements *de recenti* were treated as corroboration of the boy's direct testimony. For the reasons already stated, that view is unsound. The case of *McCrindle* must be overruled, and the observations in *McLennan* can no longer be regarded as authoritative.

In the case of *Strathern v. Lambie* the respondent, who had been charged with the offence of reckless driving under the Road Traffic Act 1930, was acquitted by the Sheriff-substitute upon the ground that he had been insufficiently identified. The identification stood upon the evidence of one witness, a police constable, who deponed that the respondent had given his name and address to him as the driver of the motor car. The only question put in the case was whether the respondent was sufficiently identified as the driver of the motor car, and the question was answered in the affirmative by the appeal Court. The case was not stated so as to raise the question whether the respondent could be legally convicted upon the evidence of one witness. The general principle of the common law that no one can be held guilty of crime upon the uncorroborated testimony of a single witness was undisputed, and was referred to by Lord Hunter as 'a well-established and salutary rule.' But, in indicating a view that there was corroboration by facts and circumstances, two of the learned judges omitted to notice that the facts and circumstances relied on were spoken to by the same witness as had identified the respondent as being at the locus. This is not enough for corroboration. A witness cannot corroborate himself. The correct rule is that formulated by Hume in the passage already quoted, namely, that the corroborative facts and circumstances must be deponed to by some other witness or witnesses. In the same case it was suggested that some corroboration was afforded by the fact that no cross-examination was directed to the evidence of the police constable. But it is surely obvious that the absence of cross-examination upon any point, while it may lead the Crown to think it unnecessary to lead further evidence upon that point, can never absolve the Crown from the duty of proving the guilt of the accused person by the testimony of two witnesses. In view of the decision in the present case the observations in *Lambie* upon these two matters can no longer be regarded as authoritative.

The Solicitor-General also referred to the case of *Lees v. Macdonald* (20 R(J) 55, 3 White 468). That was a prosecution under the Day Trespass Act, 1832, in which the Court held that the title of the prosecutor could be established by the testimony of one witness. In terms of the Act the statutory offence could be proved by the evidence of one credible witness, but apart from this specialty Lord McLaren said (at p.58): 'All that the law demands is that there should be two witnesses to prove a case, and provided that is so, any fact in the case may be proved by the testimony of one credible witness.' This statement of the law does not appear to be open to objection, but it is a very different thing from saying that, if there is only one witness to implicate an accused person, that will be sufficient in law to warrant his conviction. I do not read Lord McLaren as laying down any such proposition.

In order to remove any such doubts to which the cases of *McCrindle*, *McLennan* and *Lambie* may have given rise, it is desirable to reaffirm clearly and explicitly that, by the law of Scotland, no person can be convicted of a crime or a statutory offence, except where the Legislature otherwise directs, unless there is evidence of at least two witnesses implicating the person accused with the commission of the crime or offence with which he is charged. This rule has proved an invaluable safeguard in the practice of our criminal Courts against unjust conviction, and it is a rule from which the Courts ought not to sanction any departure."

NOTES

A number of important points emerge from this case.

(1) In general, a witness cannot corroborate himself or herself. No matter how many times a person makes incriminating statements or complaints, the evidence comes from only one source, and must be independently corroborated. In *Wilkes v. H.M.A*, 2001 S.L.T. 1268, for example, the complainer gave evidence of certain incriminating replies made by the accused when she confronted him in relation to allegations of sexual abuse and rape. Evidence of such incriminating statements is obviously relevant, and subject to certain safeguards, admissible. In this case however, it could not provide corroboration since the evidence of the statements came from the same source as the principal evidence. There must accordingly be at least two witnesses in any case—although that is not necessarily enough to satisfy the requirement for corroboration—see paragraph (3), and the next extract, below. It is a necessary, but not a sufficient condition of corroboration that there should be two witnesses.

It should be noted however, that certain utterances by an accused person are regarded not as statements but as "conduct". Thus, in *Campbell (T.) v. H.M.A.*, 1998 S.C.C.R. 214 (at 232E–F) it was held that where an accused gives an instruction, makes a promise, or as was the case in *Campbell*, expresses his thanks to an accomplice for the commission of the crime, in circumstances directly related to the commission of that crime, this falls to be regarded as incriminating conduct, and not an incriminating statement. As such it is capable of providing corroboration because evidence of the conduct comes from a third party who witnesses it, and not from the maker of the statement himself.

"Special knowledge" confessions form another important exception to the general rule—see cases such as *Manuel v. H.M.A.*, 1958 J.C. 41, reproduced below. In "special knowledge" cases, information about the facts of the case contained in the accused's statement can be taken to corroborate the statement itself, provided the jury are satisfied that the information was obtained because the accused committed the offence in question.

Finally, the distressed state of the complainer, spoken to by an independent witness, may provide corroboration of his or her account and is a further anomaly, not considered in *Morton*. Clearly the distress emanates from the same source as the principal complaint or statement. However, as with the *Campbell* case, above, distress may be regarded as "conduct" which can be independently observed and spoken to in evidence by the person who observed it. The ambit of corroboration by distress has been considerably reduced by the case of *Smith v. Lees*, 1997 S.L.T. 690, below.

(2) Complaints made by the victim soon after an alleged offence (*de recenti* complaints) are admissible as bearing upon the credibility of the witness, but do not provide corroboration.

(3) Lord Justice-Clerk Aitchison describes as unobjectionable a *dictum* in the case of *Lees v. Macdonald* to the effect that: "All that the law demands is that there should be two witnesses to prove a case, and provided that is so, any fact in the case may be proved by the testimony of one credible witness." It appears, however, that Lord Justice-Clerk Aitchison did not appreciate the ambiguity of that *dictum*, and, given his adoption of Hume's views on corroboration, would presumably not have approved the use to which it was put in the subsequent case of *Gillespie v. Macmillan*, 1957 S.L.T. 283, a case widely thought to have been wrongly decided—see W. Wilson, "The Logic of Corroboration" (1960) S.L.R. 101 and the following extract. It is not enough that there be two witnesses in the case. What is required is corroboration of each of the crucial facts, or *facta probanda*—see the cases of *Smith v. Lees*, 1997 S.L.T. 690, and *Fox v. H.M.A.*, 1998 S.L.T. 335 below.

(4) *Morton* requires that in all cases, there must be evidence from "at least two witnesses implicating the person accused with the commission of the crime or offence with which he is charged". But in many cases, there will be only one eyewitness to the events. In some cases, there will be no eyewitness at all. It is clear that circumstantial evidence can provide the necessary corroboration in those circumstances. So how does this dictum from *Morton* fit with Hume's view that in cases involving circumstantial evidence, "the aptitude and coherence of the several circumstances often as fully confirm the truth of the story, as if all the witnesses were deponing to the same facts"? Does this mean that every item of circumstantial evidence requires to be incriminating? Or is sufficient if the evidence as a whole is incriminating? Is there a difference between those cases where there is direct evidence, and those in which the evidence is purely circumstantial? It is with these questions that the following extracts are concerned.

4. "Corroboration of Evidence in Scottish Criminal Law"
(Contributed) 1958 S.L.T. (News) 137

"It is vital to ask why Hume said, when referring to direct evidence—'our law is averse to rely on [a witness's] single word'. There can only be one answer to that question—namely, human fallibility. It may be noted that the risk of fallibility is double—that of the witness, and that of the tribunal which holds the witness to be credible. If that answer is correct, it provides the key to the whole subject of corroboration.

Two consequences emerge from it. In the first place the rule must apply to every witness, whether he is testifying that he saw the deed done, or testifying to something of a collateral nature (*e.g.* that the accused confessed to the crime): to decide otherwise would be to hold, without any reason, that only a witness of the former type was to be assumed fallible. The other consequence is that a simple test must be applied to the testimony of every credible witness at the end of the trial, whether he be speaking to seeing the deed done or to a collateral fact. The test is temporarily to put aside the testimony of each witness in turn, examine what is left and replace that testimony. If while the testimony is thus suspended, there is something beneath or alongside it, *however flimsy*, to point to the accused's guilt, there is sufficient corroboration in law: if not, a conviction cannot follow, and in a jury trial, the jury must be told that [it] may not convict. The words 'however flimsy' have been italicised to emphasise that the point presently under consideration is sufficiency *in law*: it is for the jury to judge *in fact* the strength or weight of the evidence which is competently laid before it for decision.

The first criticism of the decision in *Gillespie* [1957 S.C. 31, the facts of which are set out in Chapter 1, above.] is a general one—namely that, in order to reach a conclusion that the accused was guilty, it was necessary to *rely* on the evidence of a single witness. If the testimony of *either* of the constables was faulty, there was a gap in the only line of proof between the accused and his guilt: there was no other fact in the case from which anything could be deduced or inferred to bridge that gap. The Court, in reaching its decision, departed from the principle laid down by Hume, by *relying* on the testimony of a single witness.

Another way of expressing the general criticism ventured above is that whereas Hume insisted on concurrence of testimonies the Court in *Gillespie's* case relied on testimonies which were only set out *consecutively*. Whereas Hume regarded the testimonies in parallel, the Court in *Gillespie* regarded them in series. Whereas two testimonies in parallel confirm one another, two testimonies in series do not. Whereas two testimonies in parallel reduce the risk of error, two testimonies in series (as in *Gillespie's* case) may increase that risk.

Turning to the *rationes decidendi* set out in the opinions, it would be interesting to consider whether the evidence of the constables was direct or circumstantial, according to Hume (pages 383 to 385; see also Dickson, *Evidence*, 2nd ed., section 244); but it will be assumed that the Court was right in treating it as circumstantial evidence. The principle of corroboration applies to both types of proof.

In applying what Hume laid down regarding circumstantial evidence the Court appears to have proceeded upon a fallacy which vitally affected the decision. Both their Lordships founded on the words of Hume (*supra*) which they quote, regarding the 'aptitude and coherence' of the evidence of the two constables. The only 'aptitude and coherence' of their evidence, so far as 'confirming the truth of the story', lay in the undoubted fact that it agreed with the speed charged in the complaint. That was not true confirmation, since it was on the evidence of the two constables that the prosecutor had libelled the speed of 52 mph in the first place.

The Court would appear to have omitted to notice a feature of considerable importance in Hume's illustration of what he meant by 'circumstances'. In his quotation from Hume (page 284) the Lord Justice-Clerk omitted the whole of Hume's illustration regarding 'circumstances, such as the pannel's sudden flight from the spot, the blood on his clothes . . .' etc. It will be noted that each of Hume's 'circumstances' stood on its own feet: each was independent of the others: each, by itself, pointed towards the accused's guilt: if one was removed, there was another one left pointing towards the accused's guilt. Such 'circumstances' as these, although each could be established by the testimony of a single witness only, 'confirmed the truth of the story'. In *Gillespie* the facts on which the Court proceeded to convict were of a different type. None of the three facts—the evidence of either constable or the measured distance—pointed by itself to the accused's guilt, and each fact was dependent on the others; it was only when they were strung together that they made one 'circumstance' of Hume's type which pointed to the guilt of the accused. There was no other 'circumstance' to confirm it. If one of the facts in *Gillespie's* case was removed, the whole case collapsed. It is submitted that by omitting to quote Hume's explanation of what he meant by 'circumstances' the Lord Justice-Clerk may have overlooked a matter of radical importance.

The Lord Justice-Clerk's reasoning (page 286) emphasises the omission. He said: 'I do not think that the sufficiency of proof of a criminal charge can be any more precisely defined than by saying that there must be facts emanating from at least two sources'. The Lord Justice-Clerk did not define what he meant by 'facts' in that proposition. If he had done so, the difference would have emerged between Hume's 'circumstances' on the one hand and the 'facts' in *Gillespie's* case on the other hand, and that not only the sources but also two at least of the facts themselves had to be independent of each other. Hume's 'circumstances' were mutually consistent, but they did not necessarily depend on each other as did the 'facts' founded on by the Court in *Gillespie*."

NOTES

This article sets out what might be described as the "traditional view" of corroboration, implied by Hume, and repeated in *Morton* and in *Connolly v. H.M.A.*, 1958 S.L.T. 79, that the testimony of the independent witnesses, whether involving direct or indirect evidence, must be separately incriminating—the evidence of each witness "pointing" to the accused as the perpetrator of the crime. Thus, it is not enough, on the traditional view, that the independent evidence should corroborate the witness or the witness's story—what is required is evidence which corroborates guilt. A more sophisticated view—one which the article above skirts around without ever making explicit—is that there must be corroborative evidence "pointing" to at least one of the facts in issue. This is view taken by the modern authorities on corroboration.

5. Smith v. Lees
1997 S.L.T. 690

An accused person was charged on a summary complaint with using lewd, indecent and libidinous practices and behaviour towards a 13-year-old girl by placing his hand on her hand and causing her to handle his naked private member, contrary to section 5 of the Sexual Offences (Scotland) Act 1976. The complainer gave evidence describing the acts libelled in the charge. The Crown relied for corroboration of the complainer's account on evidence of her distressed condition after the event. The sheriff repelled a submission that there was no case to answer. The accused was convicted and appealed, arguing that there was insufficient evidence to corroborate the complainer's account of the commission of the crime.

THE LORD JUSTICE GENERAL (RODGER): "The circumstances giving rise to the appeal can be shortly stated. The appellant and his brother in law, Mr [C], took five children; three girls and two boys, to a campsite to camp out overnight. The children were related to the appellant and his brother-in-law. One of the girls was the complainer who was aged 13. Two tents were pitched. The girls went into one and the boys into the other. Mr [C] decided to stay outside beside the fire. The appellant chose to sleep in the girls' tent. He lay down between the complainer and one of her cousins. In her evidence the complainer spoke to waking up and finding the appellant's penis on her hand, to his putting his other hand on top of her hand and to him moving his penis up and down against her hand. She said that she was upset and deliberately made funny noises of a kind which she had been told that she made when sleeping. She said she did this to pretend she was sleeping. According to the complainer, she then left the tent and was crying and upset, too upset to tell her uncle, Mr [C]. She said that the appellant came out of the tent later. The other witness of importance for the Crown was Mr [C]. He spoke to hearing the funny noises which the complainer said that she had made and that this was the first time that he thought anything might be wrong in the tent. He also spoke to the complainer coming out of the tent quickly and to her having a tear in her eye. According to Mr [C], when the appellant came out of the tent, he said to the complainer 'You can go back in the tent now', and the complainer then looked at Mr [C], who did not know what to do and shrugged his shoulders.

In his note the sheriff tells us that, although Mr [C] did not speak to the complainer actually crying, he did speak to her being distressed and to her showing her distress by means of a tear in the eye, by coming out of the tent and by making a gesture towards the tent. Mr [C] said that he was so concerned that he asked the complainer what was the matter with her. He noticed that, instead of going back into the tent with the other girls, the complainer went into the other tent. He asked one of the boys to speak to the complainer. Mr [C] was very concerned about what might have happened in the tent and the next morning he took the complainer to see his sister-in-law, Mrs [C].

Mrs [C] gave evidence of a *de recenti* statement of the complainer which was consistent with her evidence. The Crown also led evidence from a police constable of a statement given by the appellant in the early hours of August 8, 1995. It appears that, in resisting the motion under section 345A before the sheriff, while the Crown relied for corroboration solely on the evidence of Mr [C], the procurator fiscal depute prayed in aid a number of aspects of his evidence. In particular the procurator fiscal depute relied on his evidence as to the complainer's distress, his evidence of hearing the funny noises which she said that she had made, his evidence of the appellant choosing to go into the girls' tent, and his evidence of the appellant's remark 'You can go back in the tent now'. The sheriff attached significance in particular to the evidence of the funny noises as providing an element of corroboration of the complainer's account. Before this court, however, the Solicitor General relied exclusively on Mr [C]'s evidence of the complainer's distress and did not seek to argue that the other factors could be taken into account as corroboration. To some extent at least, therefore, this court was invited to deal with the matter on a different basis from that which was put forward in the sheriff court.

As the matter was presented to this court, the question for decision was whether the evidence of Mr [C] as to the distress of the complainer when she left the tent was in itself sufficient corroboration of her account that she had woken up to find the appellant's penis on her hand and to his putting his other hand on top of her hand and moving his penis up and down against her hand. We were invited to consider the wider issue of the role of distress as an element in corroboration and in particular whether it could ever be sufficient corroboration of a complainer's account of some sexual activity, as had been held in *Stobo*.

The question in the appeal is important since the doctrine of corroboration has always been seen as an important part of our law. Long ago Burnett, *A Treatise on Various Branches of the*

Criminal Law of Scotland (1811), p.518, said that corroboration guarded effectually against the risk of injustice, while more recently Lord Justice Clerk Thomson described the principles of corroboration as being 'of great importance to our criminal law': *Gillespie v. Macmillan*, 1957 J.C. 41; 1957 S.L.T. 287. The safeguard against wrongful conviction which the requirement of corroboration affords is needed as much today as it ever was. In the present appeal the court was asked in effect to take stock of some recent cases which affect the operation of this important area of our criminal law . . .

The court was faced . . . in the first place with two fairly extreme arguments: the appellant arguing that evidence of distress could never corroborate a complainer's evidence, and the Crown arguing that evidence of distress by itself could provide all the necessary corroboration of a complainer's account of a distressing episode. I begin with the principal argument for the appellant. I have no hesitation in rejecting the argument that evidence of the distress of the complainer could not provide corroboration because it came from the same source as the evidence of the complainer. Fundamentally counsel was arguing that evidence of a complainer's distress should be regarded in the same way as evidence of a *de recenti* statement by the complainer. In other words, just as a complainer might say things shortly after the event, so equally she might display signs shortly after the event. If evidence of what she said could not constitute corroboration (*Morton v. H.M.A.*), neither could evidence of what she did. But in my view that argument takes no account of the kind of evidence which the court has admitted as a possible source of corroboration in distress cases. As the court explained in *Gracey v. H.M.A.*, before they can use evidence of distress as corroboration, the jury have to be satisfied that the complainer was exhibiting genuine distress as a result of the alleged incident, rather than putting it on or feigning it. In other words the jury must be satisfied that the distress was something which arose spontaneously due to the nature of the incident rather than to circumstances outside the incident. Where that is the nature of the distress, then I am satisfied that evidence of such distress can be used as corroboration of certain aspects of the complainer's account.

The principle can be tested by taking a simple example where the only issue in a rape trial is whether the complainer consented to have intercourse with the accused. Suppose a witness were to have seen the accused having intercourse with the complainer and, before either of them was aware of his presence, the witness noticed that the complainer was in tears or showing other signs of distress. In the subsequent trial, it could hardly be suggested that the witness's evidence of seeing the complainer in distress during the intercourse would be irrelevant to the question of whether she had consented to the intercourse, as the accused was contending, or had submitted only due to force, as the complainer was contending. If the jury were satisfied that the signs of distress seen by the witness were genuine, then they would be entitled to find in the witness's evidence corroboration of the complainer's evidence that she had not consented to intercourse, but had simply submitted due to the force used by the accused.

If that is correct, then in principle evidence of distress caused by the incident can provide corroboration of the complainer's evidence that she did not consent to intercourse. No new issue of principle arises if the complainer is observed displaying signs of distress not during, but after, the alleged incident. Always provided the jury continue to be satisfied that the distress was caused by the incident itself, they can use evidence of that distress in the same way to corroborate the complainer's evidence that she did not consent to intercourse.

Counsel made the obvious point that a complainer's distress can be caused by all kinds of factors, such as shame at having too readily agreed to have intercourse or worry about a boyfriend or parents discovering what has happened. These are, of course, precisely the suggestions which are regularly put to complainers and which juries are already asked to take into account when deciding whether the evidence of distress really supports the complainer's evidence that she did not consent to intercourse. Counsel suggested, however, that, if this court confirmed that evidence of distress could be used to provide corroboration, then in future defence lawyers might require to have complainers psychologically examined to check whether the symptoms of distress had been genuine or not. In such a situation the Crown would have to instruct similar reports. A battle of experts would develop. I see no reason to believe that such a development is likely since the issues can be, and in practice are, sharply focused for the jury without such expert evidence. In any event, even if there may be difficulties in establishing the cause of the complainer's distress in certain cases, that is not a reason for excluding evidence of distress in all cases.

For these reasons I reject the extreme argument advanced by counsel. It is convenient to turn next to the Solicitor General's argument that Mr [C]'s evidence of the complainer's distress corroborated her account of the appellant's conduct. This argument raises very basic issues about the role of corroboration in our law. It is all the more important therefore to remember that the Crown can establish many facts in a criminal case by uncorroborated evidence. But there are certain facts which can be established only by corroborated evidence. These facts are variously described as 'fundamental' or 'crucial' or 'essential' facts, or as the *facta probanda*, the facts which require to be proved. They are the elements which need to be established if the accused is to be found guilty of the crime in question—so, in rape, for instance, the Crown requires to prove (1) penetration of the complainer's vagina by (2) the accused's private member, (3) forcibly, and (4) without the complainer's consent. These four fundamental facts require to be established by corroborated evidence. Now in practice, in a rape—or indeed in any other kind of case—the Crown may draft the indictment in such a way as to give notice to the accused that they intend to prove all kinds of incidental facts. But these other facts are not crucial, as can be seen from the very short forms for indictments in Schedule 2 to the Criminal Procedure (Scotland) Act 1995. Since these other facts are not crucial to conviction, the jury may find them proved even though the evidence on them is not corroborated.

The question which was debated before the court therefore arises only in the case of crucial facts, *facta probanda*. In the hearing before us the Solicitor General very properly accepted that the Crown required to corroborate not only the identification of the accused as the person who committed the crime but also the fact that the crime itself had been committed, since that fact is a crucial fact. The crucial facts which the Crown required to prove in the present case include the identity of the appellant as the perpetrator of the offence and the fact that he placed his hand on the complainer's hand and caused her to handle his naked private member.

In view of the concession by the Solicitor General, there is no need to examine the passages which are found in some of the authorities to the effect that it is only the accused's involvement in the crime rather than the actual commission of the crime itself which requires to be corroborated. See, for example, the opinion of the Lord Justice General (Lord Clyde) in *Gillespie v. Macmillan* at p.38 (p.286). It is perhaps sufficient to say two things. First, there is nothing in Hume, Commentaries, ii, 384, or in Alison, Practice, p.552, which supports such a doctrine. Secondly, the concession by the Solicitor General mirrors the approach which is taken every day in courts throughout Scotland.

In this case the Crown does not seek to corroborate the complainer's account by the evidence of another eyewitness to the events in the tent. Rather, it is a case where the Crown seeks to corroborate the direct testimony of the complainer by evidence of facts and circumstances, *viz.* Mr [C]'s evidence of the complainer's distress. The institutional writers recognise that the direct testimony of one witness can be corroborated by evidence of facts and circumstances: Hume, Commentaries, ii, 384; Burnett, Treatise, Chap XX; and Alison, Practice, p.551. Where facts and circumstances are used in this way to corroborate the evidence of an eyewitness, their function is to 'support' or 'confirm' the evidence of the eyewitness: Hume, Commentaries, ii, 384, and Burnett, Treatise, p.518. But the older authorities do not spell out what kinds of circumstances are necessary or sufficient to supply the required support or confirmation of the eyewitness's evidence. This appears to be because the questions of the weight of the evidence and its technical sufficiency are rather run together. As Burnett, Treatise, p.519 puts it: 'What those circumstances are which ought to confirm and render complete the *semiplena probatio* of one witness, it is impossible to determine by any rule, as the result depends upon the nature and quality of each circumstance, and their joint effect when combined; and also on the view taken of them by those who are to judge of the case. This only may be noticed, that the circumstances founded on must be extrinsic of the witness.'

So the only rule which Burnett advances is that the evidence of the corroborating facts and circumstances must be independent of the witness whose evidence is to be corroborated. It is therefore apparent that we do not find in the old authorities any answer to the question which confronts the court in this case. In that situation, while some guidance is said to be found in recent cases, it may be useful first of all to look at the Solicitor General's argument simply on its merits and without reference to authority.

The Crown's position as presented by the Solicitor General is not that the complainer's evidence in this case is simply supported or confirmed in a general way by Mr [C]'s evidence about her distress. Rather, the Crown contend that his evidence of her distress provides all the necessary corroboration of her evidence that the specific crime libelled was committed. That is to say, Mr [C]'s evidence of her distress is said to corroborate her detailed evidence that she found the appellant's penis on her hand and that he put his other hand on top of her hand and moved his penis up and down against her hand.

The Solicitor General's argument that this was indeed the position began from the proposition that certain kinds of behaviour would 'according to ordinary human experience' be likely to cause distress to the victim of that behaviour. Hence, where there was evidence of distress following an alleged incident of potentially distressing conduct, the jury or sheriff should first ask themselves whether the distress had been caused by the accused's conduct. If it had been, then the jury or sheriff were entitled to find in the evidence of that distress the necessary support or confirmation of the complainer's evidence that the conduct had taken place. So, in the present case, the sheriff accepted the complainer as a credible witness who gave careful and convincing evidence which he accepted and which supported the libel. The sheriff then had to ask himself whether Mr [C]'s evidence of the complainer's distress corroborated her evidence. The conduct described by the complainer was of a kind which, according to ordinary human experience, would be likely to provoke distress. Therefore, if the sheriff accepted Mr [C] as a credible and reliable witness, he would require to ask himself whether the distress which Mr [C] observed was actually caused by the accused's conduct and not by something else. If he were satisfied that it was indeed caused by the accused's conduct, then he could find in Mr [C]'s evidence of the complainer's distress on leaving the tent the necessary support or confirmation of her evidence as to the accused's conduct.

I have no difficulty with the Solicitor General's argument insofar as it suggests that evidence of a complainer's distress can corroborate her evidence that she was subjected to conduct which caused her distress. It seems to me to be equally legitimate in an appropriate case to infer from the fact that the conduct caused actual distress that it occurred against the complainer's will and hence that force was used by the offender. Evidence of distress can therefore corroborate a complainer's evidence that she did not consent to the accused's conduct and that he used force to overcome her will. But the Solicitor General seeks to take it further and to use the evidence of distress, not simply to corroborate the complainer's evidence that something distressing occurred, but to corroborate her evidence as to what exactly the appellant did.

In my view that is not a legitimate use of the evidence of distress. The simple fact is that in itself the evidence of distress cannot tell the jury or sheriff more than that something distressing occurred. An example was discussed during the hearing. Suppose that there had been two tents each containing a girl and a man. In one case the girl emerges and says that the man committed the same act as is alleged in the present case. In the other the girl emerges and says that the man in her tent showed her some pornographic photographs. Though no photographs are discovered in the police investigation, it is accepted that photographs of the kind described by her would be likely to provoke distress in the girl. A witness says that each of the girls was distressed. As the Solicitor General accepted, if his argument is correct, then the witness's evidence of the girl's distress provides the necessary corroboration in each case that conduct of the kind spoken to by the girl occurred. In other words exactly the same evidence of distress would be corroborating two quite different accounts. This simply shows that in cases like these the evidence of distress is not really confirming or supporting anything more than the girl's evidence that something distressing occurred. Any further conclusion is based, not on the independent evidence of distress, but on the evidence of the girl herself—in the one case that she was forced to touch the man and in the other that she was shown photographs of a particular kind.

Another weakness in the Crown argument soon emerged. If that argument were correct, then one would expect that evidence of a complainer's distress could corroborate her evidence of any essential element in a distressing criminal act, for instance, her evidence of penetration in a rape case. But the Solicitor General drew back from pressing his argument that far and accepted that more than evidence of distress was required to corroborate a complainer's evidence of penetration. This was said to be because, according to ordinary human experience, penetration is not in itself distressing: it forms an essential part of ordinary sexual intercourse which is generally regarded as pleasurable. So evidence of distress cannot point to penetration—which is not distressing—having taken place. Such an argument is wholly unconvincing. Where intercourse takes place by agreement, penetration will not be distressing; but where intercourse takes place forcibly and without the woman's consent, penetration will undoubtedly be distressing. If therefore the Solicitor General's argument as to the legitimate effect and value of such evidence were correct, it would follow that evidence of distress could corroborate a complainer's evidence of penetration in a rape case. But the Solicitor General accepts that evidence of distress cannot provide that kind of corroboration. This concession in effect confirms that the Crown do not accept the logical implications of their own argument and shows that the argument as a whole is unsound. . .

To be valid, any approach which is applied to evidence of distress must fit into our law of corroboration as a whole. In order to corroborate an eyewitness's evidence on a crucial fact, the corroborating evidence must support or confirm the eyewitness's evidence by showing or tending to show that what the eyewitness said happened did actually happen. So, if a complainer says that she did not consent to intercourse but was forced to submit, then evidence of her distress will tend to confirm her evidence since a jury will be entitled to infer that the complainer was distressed because she was forced to submit to the intercourse and did not agree to it. But in a case like the present, evidence of distress cannot support or confirm the complainer's evidence that a particular form of sexual activity occurred because there is no basis upon which the jury can use the evidence of distress to draw the necessary inference that it did. Since, however, the court in *McLellan* and *Stobo* held that in such cases evidence of distress could by itself provide the necessary corroboration of the complainer's account, it follows that they were wrongly decided and must be overruled.

If the approach which I have outlined is applied in the present case, the evidence of Mr [C] as to the complainer's distress cannot in itself corroborate the complainer's account. There was therefore insufficient evidence for the sheriff to convict the appellant and question two in the stated case must be answered in the negative and the appeal allowed."

LORD MCCLUSKEY: "In Scotland, it is essential to prove the facts which constitute the crime, as well as the accused's responsibility for the commission of those acts. In our form of indictment the facts which must be established (*facta probanda*) have to be averred in the narrative contained in the indictment; but the narrative will commonly contain averment of facts which are not essential facts. I consider that the law and practice in this area are correctly summarised in Walkers, *Evidence*, Chap. XXX, paras 382–384. There the authors discuss crucial facts, '*facta probanda*; the crucial facts include *commission of the crime*'. The commission of the crime is without doubt a crucial fact which requires full legal proof. Thus, for example, in a case in which the accused is charged with theft, he could not be convicted, whatever the other evidence, if there was no evidence, other than from his confession, that the article was stolen. The stealing of the article would require to be corroborated by other evidence: *cf. Sinclair v. Tudhope*. In certain types of case the age of the victim is a crucial fact which requires to be proved by evidence from two sources—unless there is some special statutory provision. Plainly, evidence of the victim's distress would shed no light upon that crucial fact, her age; it would therefore have no corroborative value whatsoever in that regard. It appears to me beyond question that in this type of common law case, having regard to the terms of Schedule 3 to the Criminal Procedure (Scotland) Act 1995 and the very long practice in relation to the bringing and proof of indictments, it is essential to have two separate, independent and reliable pointers in the evidence towards the truth of each of the crucial facts, the *facta probanda*. In the present case the charge was that the accused did 'use lewd, indecent and libidinous practices and behaviour towards' the victim. That, however, is really just a statement of the *nomen iuris*. The *facta probanda* are identified by the words occurring in the complaint 'and did place your hand upon her hand and cause her to handle your naked private member'. It is these facts taken together that constitute the crime which he is said to have committed on the occasion averred. It is obviously true that if such a thing were to happen a very likely consequence would be that the girl would be distressed; and it follows that proof of such distress would be proof of a fact which was entirely consistent with her evidence that it did happen. But if one had nothing but the evidence that she emerged from the encounter in a distressed condition it would be impossible to guess whether the accused had immediately beforehand deliberately placed her hand upon his naked private member against her will, or had physically assaulted her, or that she had had a nightmare or that she had come to regret some consensual conduct some time after it had finished or that some other event had occurred of a nature that might cause distress to a girl of her age. Where a person exhibits anger or joy or fear or distress an observer can infer that something has angered, pleased, frightened or upset the person. But it is hardly possible from observing the display of emotion to identify its precise cause. The first question one asks a stranger whom one encounters in a distressed condition is, 'What happened?' That is because the observed distress tells you that something has happened, but little more. Evidence of nothing more than the existence of the emotion is not evidence as to its cause. In a case like the present, it follows that where the woman gives evidence of the crucial facts and her evidence is to the effect that there was some sexual molesting which caused no injury and left no trace, and the only other evidence is evidence that she was distressed shortly afterwards, there is no other evidence to assist in establishing the crucial fact that she was sexually molested at all, *i.e.* that a crime was committed. All that can be inferred is what the other witness in this case, [C], did infer, namely that something had happened inside the tent to upset the girl. But there is no additional evidence to prove the commission of the crime which has been charged, namely the placing of the girl's hand upon the accused's member. In this type of case it is, in my opinion, always necessary to identify what the *facta probanda* are and to ensure that there is evidence from at least two independent sources pointing to the existence of each of these crucial facts. If that were not to be the rule, then our traditional reliance upon a rule requiring corroboration would be entirely worthless. There is, in my opinion, no legitimate stopping place between the requirement for full legal proof of each of the *facta probanda* and the dispensing altogether with the need for corroboration. A mere formality such as a requirement that there be two or more witnesses adduced by the prosecution would not be a sufficient compliance with our traditional rules about corroboration, unless each were able to give evidence probative of the essentials of the crime.

It is, of course, true that facts may be proved by direct evidence as primary facts or may be established by inference from other facts. In a *Yates* type of case the distress is a primary fact observed and described by an eyewitness. The absence of consent is established and corroborated by putting together: (1) the evidence of the girl that she did not consent; and (2) the inference of no consent yielded by the fact of distress shortly after, and held to be caused by the sexual intercourse. So the direct evidence is corroborated by an 'incriminating' inference shown from evidence separate from and independent of that of the girl.

Obviously, the weight to be attached to any particular piece of evidence is a matter for determination by the jury, as are the inferences to be drawn from proof of several different circumstances. But the judge has to decide as a matter of law whether the evidence as a whole is sufficient, on any tenable view of it, to establish the crime. That duty arises most sharply in modern practice because of the requirement laid upon the judge by sections 97 and 160 of the Criminal Procedure (Scotland) Act 1995 to satisfy him or herself as to whether or not 'the evidence led by the prosecution is insufficient in law to justify the accused being convicted of the offence charged'. Sufficiency of evidence is judged on the basis that the judge or jury will give full weight to the evidence pointing to guilt; the actual weighing of the evidence is not attempted at the 'no case to answer' stage.

In certain of the cases referred to by counsel, the *dicta* are contradictory. It is unnecessary for me to address them all. But it was suggested by the Solicitor General that corroborative evidence may be found in a piece of evidence which is 'consistent' with the account given by the victim which it is necessary to corroborate. I do not understand how mere consistency could ever be enough to provide corroboration. The victim of a sexual assault might say that she was wearing a white blouse, blue jeans and red shoes and that the accused put his tattooed hand on her breast. Evidence from other witnesses that the girl was dressed in the manner described and that the accused's hand was tattooed would be entirely consistent with her evidence, but, if there was nothing else, it would go no way at all to establishing what the accused is alleged to have done. In my opinion, in this type of case, where what is sought as corroboration is evidence which supports the evidence of the girl who is to be corroborated, what must be looked for is evidence which in itself points in some way towards the truth of one or more of the *facta probanda* which are in issue. Evidence which points to the truth of a crucial fact, a *factum probandum*, may in itself appear entirely innocuous and neutral: in that sense it may not appear to be incriminatory; but it may acquire its incriminating character when it is placed in context. So, in that sense, evidence can properly be said to be of a corroborative character even although it does not appear of itself to point to guilt. But it cannot be corroborative in character unless it points positively towards the truth of one of the essential facts which constitute the crime. Evidence which is merely consistent with the victim's story but sheds no light at all upon the criminal event said to have occurred, cannot amount to corroboration. I wish to re-emphasise, for the sake of clarity, that different considerations may apply in those cases where all the evidence relied on is truly circumstantial. In such cases, of course, the various circumstances may, when looked at together, acquire aptitude and coherence as incriminatory circumstances, and different issues as to corroboration arise.

I should only wish to add one other comment. Sheriff Gordon's article discusses the case of Susanna and the Elders (Daniel 13, 1–62) and remarks that the biblical story 'shows what a godsend the two-witness rule is to a cross-examiner; it is only if there are two witnesses that their evidence can be probed for inconsistencies'. I agree entirely, provided that their testimony relates to one or more of the same facts in issue; there must be some overlap of their evidence before consistency or inconsistency can emerge. If the law requires corroboration in the sense in which I believe it does, then the two pieces of evidence relied upon as each pointing towards the guilt of the accused must be capable of being examined separately not just to determine whether they are consistent with each other but to determine whether they are concurrent. Mere consistency, unless both are speaking to the same *factum probandum*, is not decisive. (Inconsistency even as to a *factum non probandum* might be telling as to credibility and reliability, but no more.) In Susanna's case, the evidence of the two alleged eyewitnesses was discredited because they were making statements which contradicted each other as to the species of tree under which Susanna and the young man misbehaved. But the species of tree under which Susanna was alleged to have sinned was not a *factum probandum*; so the case does not really deal with the need for corroboration as a formal requirement of the law of evidence. (Indeed it is far from clear what corroboration there was against the two elders; yet they were put to death.) Corroborative evidence in our law must be evidence which can be used to test the truth or falsity of the accounts of material matters, *i.e.* those which constitute *facta probanda*. In this case, the fact to be corroborated was what the accused did to and with the girl's hand. Her distress is relevant to establish her credibility and to show that something has distressed her; but tells us nothing about whose hand did what or indeed that anybody's hand did anything.

I agree with the disposal of the case proposed by your Lordship in the chair."

NOTES

See also *Anderson v. H.M.A.*, 2001 S.L.T. 1265; *Carson v. McGlennan*, 2000 S.L.T. 810. The latter case should be read along with the case of *Wilson v. H.M.A.*, 2001 S.L.T. 1203, with which it appears on the face of it, to conflict. This point is considered further below in relation to "*Moorov*" doctrine.

Corroboration by means of distress exhibited by the complainer is a partial anomaly in the law of corroboration. It is explicable by emphasising that the independent evidence required by the general rule is provided by a third party who observes the distress. Nevertheless both complaint and distress emanate from the same source. Moreover, distress *per se* may be highly ambiguous, if what a court is looking for is corroboration of the particular facts in issue. The limitations placed on the use of distress in *Smith v. Lees* are accordingly to be welcomed.

Smith v. Lees also gives further guidance on the nature of corroboration. It is clear from the opinions delivered that in modern practice what is required is corroboration of the *evidence*, not corroboration of the *witness*. In particular, it is clear that what must be corroborated is the evidence relating to *the facta probanda*, or crucial facts. Facts other than the facts in issue do not require to be corroborated. Thus, it is enough that one witness speaks to an item of circumstantial evidence, no matter how important that circumstance might prove to be in the case as a whole.

The distinction between the use of circumstantial evidence as a test of credibility on the one hand, and as corroboration on the other, most clearly expressed in Lord McCluskey's opinion, is a useful one, and it re-appears in the next case; *Fox v. H.M.A.* While circumstantial evidence may be used for both purposes, those purposes must be analysed separately. As Lord McCluskey notes, evidence which is merely consistent with a witness's account may bolster that witness's credibility, but it is not corroborative. To corroborate, evidence must support or confirm the witness's evidence in relation to the particular facts in issue. To further illustrate the distinction between corroboration of evidence and "corroboration" of a witness, it is useful to consider the following case, *Fox v. H.M.A.*, 1998 S.L.T. 335.

In *Smith v. Lees*, the appellant put forward a subsidiary argument based on the earlier case of *Mackie v. H.M.A.*, 1995 S.L.T. 110. The Lord Advocate, in turn, asked the court to overrule that case. In the event, the court was not required to consider *Mackie* because of the view it took on the main points. In the next case, the point could not be avoided, and *Mackie* was overruled. The difficulties seem to have arisen largely because of the court's adoption in *Mackie* of the following *dictum* from *O'Hara v. Central S.M.T. Co.*, 1941 S.C 363. The requirement for corroboration in civil cases has now been abolished—see the Civil Evidence (Scotland) Act 1988, s.1, and Chapter 13 below. But Lord President Normand's dictum from *O'Hara* may have led the criminal courts into error. Lord President Normand said that:

"Corroboration may be by facts and circumstances proved by other evidence than that of the single witness who is to be corroborated. There is sufficient corroboration if the facts and circumstances proved are not only consistent with the evidence of the single witness, but more consistent with it than any other competing account of the events spoken to by him. Accordingly, if the facts and circumstances proved by other witnesses fit into his narrative so as to make it the most probable account of the events, the requirements of legal proof are satisfied."

The last sentence from that passage illustrates precisely a test based on evidential support for a witness rather than for his or her evidence. In *Maitland v. Glasgow Corporation*, 1947 S.C. 20 Lord President Normand said that:

"The fact that the story told by the pursuer is probable may render it more easy to accept her evidence as truthful, but it is not corroboration . . ."

Again, in *Cleisham v. B.T.C.*, 1964 S.C. (H.L.) 22 Lord Devlin said:

"It is unnecessary for the pursuer to do more than to establish that, in the light of the surrounding circumstances, her account is more probable than any other account that is given in evidence or can reasonably be suggested, so as not to leave it a case of one man's word against another's."

However, this dictum was criticised by Lord President Clyde in *Hughes v. Stewart*, 1964 S.C. 155. He said:

"As a test for the credibility of a witness, that may well be justifiable, but it has never been regarded as satisfying the needs of corroborative evidence as understood in Scotland. A witness's account, however probable it may be, is not sufficient to constitute legal proof of a ground of action . . . [The pursuer] can secure corroboration only if he leads other evidence than his own of facts more consistent with his own account of [the fact in issue] than any other account of it."

In *Mackie v. H.M.A.*, 1995 S.L.T. 110, Lord President Hope, as he then was, may have been led into error by the dicta from *O'Hara* quoted above. *Mackie* was a case involving charges under the Company Securities (Insider Dealing) Act 1985. Proof of those charges depended on which of two conflicting accounts of what took place at a meeting was to be believed. Corroboration of the incriminating account was essential. The Lord President said that:

"Circumstantial evidence which was equally consistent with the appellant's account of the meeting cannot be said to support Mr Runciman's account of it. At best for the Crown such evidence is neutral and if it is neutral it cannot provide corroboration in such a case. This was the basis for the decision in *Mongan v. H.M.A.*, in which it was held that evidence that the complainer was shaken or upset after the alleged incident was neutral and could not corroborate her evidence that she had been assaulted. If the evidence is of such a kind that it is open to the jury to hold that distress was caused by an alleged incident, but there is nevertheless some other possible explanation for it, the question whether it was caused by the alleged incident must be carefully examined and explained to the jury. It is not sufficient for corroboration if the evidence is merely neutral on this point: *Moore v. H.M.A.*; *Stobo v. H.M.A.* at p.1111D–E."

6. Fox v. H.M.A.
1998 S.L.T. 335

The charge in this case was clandestine injury. The complainer had gone to a party and become very drunk. At one stage she had consensual sexual intercourse with a man in a bathroom although she subsequently had no recollection of it. Her evidence was that she was later put to bed and fell into unconsciousness. She awoke to discover the accused having intercourse with her. When she objected the accused desisted and left her. The complainer was later seen to be distressed. The Crown also led evidence of the accused's statement to the police to the effect that he had intercourse with the complainer when she was in bed and both conscious and consenting, but that she had later objected when she discovered that the accused was not the man with whom she had earlier had intercourse. The trial judge repelled a submission of no case to answer and the accused was convicted. The accused appealed, contending that as the complainer's distress was not more consistent with her account than with his statement, it could not be corroborative of the complainer's evidence.

THE LORD PRESIDENT (RODGER): "This is a case where the Crown led one witness to give direct evidence of the events (the complainer) and relied for corroboration on the appellant's admission of intercourse plus circumstantial evidence, including evidence from the witnesses who said that she was upset later that morning. In the light of *Smith v. Lees* counsel accepted, of course, that, while evidence of distress could not corroborate a complainer's evidence that particular sexual activity had occurred, it could corroborate her evidence that she had not consented to the sexual activity. If therefore the complainer's evidence and the evidence of distress had stood on their own, the evidence of distress would have been capable of corroborating her evidence that the intercourse took place without her consent. Here, however, the appellant gave an alternative account in his interview with the police and the complainer's subsequent distress was consistent with that account also. Counsel's submission was that the appellant's alternative account, as contained in the evidence, changed the situation. Once that alternative account was introduced, the evidence of the complainer's distress could not corroborate her evidence that she had not consented to intercourse. The reason was said to be that the evidence of her distress was not more consistent with the complainer's evidence than with the account given by the appellant. The general proposition underlying this submission was that circumstantial evidence could amount to corroboration of direct evidence only if the circumstantial evidence was more consistent with the direct evidence than with any competing account of the events spoken to by the witness giving direct evidence. Since the submission has profound implications for the law of corroboration, it is appropriate to look at the wider context in which the question arises.

Our law proceeds on the idea that in deciding matters of fact it is unsafe for a court simply to rely on the testimony of a single witness. Burnett, Treatise, p.509 explains the thinking in this way: 'To constitute legal direct evidence, the law of Scotland requires two concurring witnesses; *nam testis unus suspicionem, non fidem facit*. This rule, the principle of which was acknowledged both in the Jewish and Roman laws, seems to have prevailed with us from the earliest times, as well in civil as in criminal matters, and is founded both in reason and in humanity. It is true, the denial of the party, and the presumption of innocence, is not equal to the assertion upon oath of a disinterested witness; yet it is such as to call for some additional circumstance to corroborate his testimony. The law, therefore, has required that something more shall appear than the testimony of a single witness, however unexceptionable he may be in credit, and however high in rank or station (*etiamsi praeclarae curiae honore praefulgeat*, as the Imperial Edict speaks), before another shall be deprived of his civil rights or subjected to punishment.' (The reference is to a constitution of Constantine, August 25, 334, C.Th.11.39.3.)

A similar idea has been found in different contexts in different legal systems at different periods. What is required in addition to the single witness depends on the particular system. In our law it is now said that there must be corroboration of the evidence of the single witness. In itself such a statement may not tell us a great deal. The entries for 'corroborate' and 'corroboration' in the Oxford English Dictionary suggest, however, that the essence of 'corroboration', in ordinary usage at least, is something which strengthens, or confirms, or supports a statement or the testimony of a witness. This is indeed very much the idea which runs through our law. Although we were not referred to their works, it is apparent not only from Burnett, but also from Hume and Alison, that what we would now describe as a requirement for corroboration formed part of the law as known to them.

In the present case we are concerned with the evidence of a direct witness which the Crown argue is corroborated by circumstantial evidence. Hume, Burnett and Alison readily acknowledge that the requirements of legal proof can be satisfied by the direct testimony of one witness plus evidence of facts and circumstances.

Hume, Commentaries, ii, 384 says: 'It would not however be a reasonable thing, nor is it our law, that the want of a second witness to the fact cannot be supplied by the other circumstances of the case. If one man swear that he saw the pannel stab the deceased, and others confirm his testimony with circumstances, such as the pannel's sudden flight from the spot, the blood on his clothes, the bloody instrument found in his possession, his confession on being taken, or the like; certainly these are as good, nay better even than a second testimony to the act of stabbing.'

It is noteworthy that the circumstantial evidence is said to 'confirm' the direct evidence.

The same idea of the role of circumstantial evidence in such cases is found in Burnett, Treatise, pp.518–519 where he says:

'And here it is, that our law guards so effectually against the risk of impunity to offenders on the one hand, and of injustice on the other, by admitting the proof of circumstances to confirm a single witness to the fact, and yet holding his evidence insufficient without such confirmation.

What those circumstances are which ought to confirm and render complete the *semiplena probatio* of one witness, it is impossible to determine by any rule—as the result depends upon the nature and quality of each circumstances, and their joint effect when combined; and also on the view of them by those who are to judge of the case. This only may be noticed, that the circumstances founded on must be extrinsic of the witness. No evidence, which goes merely to support the credibility of the witness in the account he has given of the fact to be proved, as by establishing that he had recently after communicated what he had seen or heard to another person, and had been all along consistent in his story, will be held as sufficient to supply the want of another witness to the fact.'

Burnett envisages that what is required is evidence of facts and circumstances which are extrinsic to the direct evidence and which may 'confirm' that direct evidence. It is noticeable that Burnett emphasises the role of the jury in deciding what the effect of the evidence is.

Alison, Practice, p.551 states as a general proposition that: 'The evidence of a single witness, how clear and conclusive soever, is not sufficient to warrant a conviction; but the evidence of one witness is sufficient, if it is supported by a train of circumstances'.

Lower down the same page he paraphrases the passage of Hume which I have quoted and later (at pp.552–553) explains that 'numerous cases, especially of robbery, have occurred where the pannels have been convicted, with the approbation of the Bench, on no other evidence, as to the *corpus delicti* than a single witness, supported by circumstances tending to bring home the guilt to the prisoner . . . And the want of a second witness to the corpus may be supplied by the same *indicia* which go to fix the crime on the prisoner; as, for example, if the man robbed depone to the fact of his watch having been seized and carried off; and a second, to the same watch being found in the prisoner's custody. But the confirmation must be extrinsic to the witness.'

Alison refers to the direct evidence being 'supported' by a train of circumstances and of independent evidence of those circumstances providing 'confirmation' of the direct evidence.

In essence the picture has not changed since these works were written. Corroborative evidence is still said to be evidence which supports or confirms the direct evidence of a witness.

See *Smith v. Lees,* 1997 J.C. p.90B; 1997 S.L.T., p.703D. The way in which the matter has been formulated in these authorities in itself tells us something about how our law perceives corroboration as operating in such cases. The law might have been, for instance, that a jury could not accept a direct witness as credible unless there were independent evidence supporting that witness. But that is not how the matter is approached in these passages. Rather, the starting point is that the jury have accepted the evidence of the direct witness as credible and reliable. The law requires that, even when they have reached that stage, they must still find confirmation of the direct evidence from other independent direct or circumstantial evidence. Unless they find that confirmation, the jury must acquit the accused even though they may be completely convinced by the direct evidence of the single witness.

This does not mean to say that the jury can look at the circumstantial evidence only at this final stage of their deliberations. How the jury approach their task of assessing credibility and reliability is, of course, very much a matter for them. When examining the direct evidence to see whether they accept it, the jury may well test it by reference to various matters, including the available circumstantial evidence. Nevertheless, once the jury have accepted the direct evidence, the same circumstantial evidence may come into the picture once more when, as the law requires, the jury are looking for evidence which confirms the direct testimony.

While evidence can provide corroboration only if it is independent of the direct evidence which it is to corroborate, the evidence is properly described as being corroborative because of its relation to the direct evidence: it is corroborative because it confirms or supports the direct evidence. The starting point is the direct evidence. So long as the circumstantial evidence is independent and confirms or supports the direct evidence on the crucial facts, it provides corroboration and the requirements of legal proof are met.

According to *Mackie,* however, circumstantial evidence is corroborative only if it is more consistent with the direct evidence than with a competing account given by the accused. This introduces a new element. It amounts to saying that circumstantial evidence cannot confirm or support direct evidence, which the jury have accepted, simply because the facts and circumstances could also be explained on a different hypothesis. I reserve my opinion as to whether there may be cases where the circumstantial evidence is ambiguous, but no reasonable jury could choose the interpretation which would support the direct evidence. With that possible exception it is of the very nature of circumstantial evidence that it may be open to more than one interpretation and that it is precisely the role of the jury to decide which interpretation to adopt. If the jury choose an interpretation which fits with the direct evidence, then in their view—which is the one that matters—the circumstantial evidence confirms or supports the direct evidence so that the requirements of legal proof are met. If on the other hand they choose a different interpretation, which does not fit with the direct evidence, the circumstantial evidence will not confirm or support the direct evidence and the jury will conclude that the Crown have not proved their case to the required standard.

There seems to be no good reason why circumstantial evidence should not be available to the jury as a potential source of corroboration simply because the accused has put forward a possible scenario which could furnish an innocent explanation of the facts and circumstances. The jury may reject the accused's evidence and his scenario. Indeed in any case where the direct evidence of the Crown witness is inconsistent with the accused's account, in accepting the evidence of the Crown witness, the jury will have rejected the accused's account. With the accused's account out of the way as a possible explanation for the circumstantial evidence, the jury can consider any other possible explanations for the facts and circumstances. Having done so, they will be entitled to find that the circumstantial evidence fits with the direct evidence of the Crown witness. If that is their conclusion, then the circumstantial evidence as interpreted by them will confirm or support the direct evidence and complete the legal proof.

Although the matter is not generally spelled out in the cases, some such analysis underlies the approach to corroboration which is adopted every day in our courts by judges who have to charge juries and consider submissions of no case to answer. That analysis is not, however, consistent with *Mackie.* It is therefore necessary to examine both *Mackie* and the case of *O'Hara v. Central SMT* which is the foundation for what the Lord Justice General says in *Mackie.* In one important respect *Mackie* was similar to the present case: just as in the present case, the Crown led one witness to give direct evidence of the crucial fact and for corroboration relied on evidence of certain facts and circumstances. The cases arose out of very different situations, however.

In *Mackie* the charge was one of insider dealing under the Company Securities (Insider Dealing) Act 1985. Putting the matter shortly, the accused, who was an investment analyst, was charged with counselling or procuring salesmen in his firm to deal in securities when he had knowingly obtained price sensitive information about the securities. At about 11 o'clock in the morning of the day in question the accused went to see a Mr Runciman who was the chairman of Shanks & McEwan Group plc ('SME'). It was proved that on the previous day the board of directors of SME had discussed the need to issue a profits warning to the market. Mr Runciman had been strongly of the view that such a warning should be issued, but the board had decided to take further advice from the company's advisers, Hoare Govett. Information about the profits warning was price sensitive information. According to Mr Runciman, at his meeting with the accused, Mr Runciman told him that there was going to be a profits warning which still had to be discussed with Hoare Govett. Later that day, after the accused returned to his office, between about three and four o'clock, he told the salesmen in the firm that investors should now be advised to 'top slice' their holdings in SME. Before the Stock Exchange closed at half past four, one of the salesmen sold shares belonging to a private discretionary client. Instructions to sell were given by salesmen in the firm over the following days. The volume of sales by the firm was so large as to attract attention and, following a complaint from Mr Runciman, the firm's compliance director placed an embargo on further dealings.

It was in these circumstances that the accused was charged with insider dealing. In order to establish the charge it was essential for the Crown to prove by corroborated evidence that at their meeting Mr Runciman had told the accused about the profits warning. The Crown relied on the evidence of Mr Runciman that he had told the accused about the profits warning. For corroboration the Crown relied on the facts and circumstances of the large volume of sales instructed by the accused's firm after he returned from his meeting with Mr Runciman.

It is important to note that the accused emphatically denied that Mr Runciman had told him about the profits warning. He denied it both to Department of Trade and Industry investigators and in evidence at his trial. According to the accused, Mr Runciman had given him certain confidential information which he had not passed on and which did not include any information about a profits warning. The accused said that his advice to the salesmen that investors should top slice their holdings was based on nothing more than his view, derived from what he had been told during his visit to SME, that there would be little or no growth in the earnings per share of the company.

The trial judge rejected a submission of no case to answer and the jury convicted the accused. He appealed. This court allowed his appeal and quashed his conviction. Lord Cowie's opinion is not altogether easy to interpret, but the Lord Justice General, with whom Lord Mayfield agreed, held that the Crown had led insufficient evidence in law. They held that the evidence as to the sales of shares could not constitute corroboration of Mr Runciman's evidence that he had told the accused about the profits warning since the evidence of sales was equally consistent with the account given by the accused that he had not been told about the profits warning but had advised that investors should sell shares in SME because he had formed a certain view about the prospects of the shares. The Lord Justice General observed (at 1994 J.C., p.141D; 1995 S.L.T., p.118H): 'in my opinion the question which then had to be considered was whether the facts and circumstances, when taken together, were more consistent with Mr Runciman's evidence than with the appellant's evidence'.

He went on to say (at p.141E–H (p.118I–L)): 'The advocate-depute submitted that, where the circumstantial evidence might give rise to various inferences, it was enough that one of them was consistent with the account given by Mr Runciman. All that was needed, she said, was independent evidence which was capable of supporting Mr Runciman's testimony. The remaining questions as to the weight to be given to that evidence were for the jury to assess. It seems to me, however, that this overlooks the fact that what was required in this case was independent evidence to support one of two different accounts of what was said. Circumstantial evidence which was equally consistent with the appellant's account of the meeting cannot be said to support Mr Runciman's account of it. At best for the Crown such evidence is neutral and if it is neutral it cannot provide corroboration in such a case. This was the basis for the decision in *Mongan v. H.M.A.*, 1989 S.C.C.R. 25, in which it was held that evidence that the complainer was shaken or upset after the alleged incident was neutral and could not corroborate her evidence that she had been assaulted. If the evidence is of such a kind that it is open to the jury to hold that distress was caused by an alleged incident, but there is nevertheless some other possible explanation for it, the question whether it was caused by the alleged incident must be carefully examined and explained to the jury. It is not sufficient for corroboration if the evidence is merely neutral on this point: *Moore v. H.M.A.*, 1990 J.C. 371; *Stobo v. H.M.A.*, 1994 J.C. 28 at p.35B.'

In this passage the Lord Justice General rejects the advocate depute's submission that it is sufficient if the Crown leads independent circumstantial evidence which is capable of supporting the direct evidence. He holds that there required to be independent evidence to support one of two different accounts of what was said. It is, of course, correct that, before the jury could convict, they required to have independent evidence which supported Mr Runciman's evidence. But the question of whether the circumstantial evidence actually supported his evidence was for the jury to determine. At the stage when the court required to consider whether the Crown had led evidence which would entitle the jury to convict the accused, in my view the appropriate question for the court to ask was indeed whether there was independent evidence which was capable of supporting the direct evidence. To demand anything more than that is to encroach upon the jury's role as the masters of all matters of fact.

There is nothing to suggest that the court intended that the approach which it adopted in *Mackie* should be confined to any particular kind of case. The formulation is quite general and it was mentioned (*albeit obiter*) in connection with a charge of murder in the later case of *Beattie v. H.M.A.*, 1995 J.C. at p.53F–H; 1995 S.L.T. at p.287C–E. Applied across the board, its effects would be far reaching indeed.

We may suppose the following imaginary case. A lady gives evidence that an accused, who was not known to them, gained entry to the house where she lived with her husband. She says that he then stabbed her husband who died as a result. There is ample evidence to corroborate the wife's evidence that her husband was stabbed to death. The issue at the trial is whether the Crown has proved that the accused was the perpetrator. For corroboration of the wife's evidence that the accused committed the murder the Crown rely on two adminicles of evidence. First, there is evidence of a fingerprint of the accused having been lifted from the door of the room where the husband's body was found. There is also evidence of a stain of the husband's blood on the accused's clothes. When interviewed by the police the accused denies killing the husband, but says that he met him earlier that day in a public house and went back to his house. He goes on to say that, as a result of a quarrel, they fought and in the course of the fight he got some of the husband's blood on his clothing. The accused says that the fight was comparatively minor, however, and that, when he left the house, the husband was perfectly fit. Moreover the accused says that, as he was leaving, he touched the door of the room. Evidence of what the accused said at the interview is led by the Crown for the purpose of showing that the accused had been in the company of the husband on the day of his murder. The accused's account is therefore competent evidence for the jury's consideration.

Evidence of an accused's fingerprint at the locus and of the deceased's blood on his clothing is normally apt to provide powerful corroboration of an eyewitness's evidence that the accused stabbed someone to death. This is not because such circumstantial evidence is open to only one interpretation and that interpretation is one which confirms the evidence of the eyewitness. After all the jury will often be invited to consider more than one possible explanation of that kind of circumstantial evidence. Rather, it is up to the jury to decide what inference they draw from the circumstantial evidence. If, having considered the matter, the jury draw the inference that the circumstantial evidence points to the accused's involvement in the crime, then the circumstantial evidence does indeed confirm the evidence of the eyewitness and so provides the corroboration which our law requires. In my view that remains the position, irrespective of whether one of the competing explanations comes from something said by the accused.

Faced with evidence of the kind which I have outlined in the imaginary case, whether at interview or in the witness box, a guilty accused who wishes to try to escape conviction will seek to put forward an account which is consistent with the finding of the blood and the fingerprint. He may well devise a story of the kind which I have put into the imaginary accused's mouth. If he does, the evidence of the blood and the fingerprint will be equally consistent with the wife's evidence that he came into the house and stabbed her husband and with the accused's account that he came to the house earlier and fought with the husband but left him alive. It follows that, if the *Mackie* approach is correct, neither the evidence of the fingerprint nor the evidence of the husband's blood on the accused's clothes—nor indeed both pieces of evidence together—could constitute corroboration of the wife's evidence. The trial judge would therefore require to sustain a defence submission of no case to answer on the basis that the Crown had not led sufficient evidence in law.

Counsel did not demur to the proposition that this would be the kind of result which would follow from applying the reasoning in *Mackie*. In my view that result would indeed be inescapable. Yet I know of no authority—and none was cited to us—for holding that in the imaginary case the evidence of the wife plus the evidence of the fingerprint and blood would be insufficient in law to entitle a jury to conclude that the accused was the person who carried out the murder. Indeed countless convictions must have been secured on just that kind of evidence.

Moreover the approach in *Mackie* would work somewhat capriciously in practice. In the case which I have supposed, just as in the present case, the accused's account was to be found in the evidence of his interview with the police. It would therefore form part of the evidence for the Crown which would be before the trial judge at the time of the submission of no case to answer—hence the need to sustain that submission if *Mackie* is correct. If, however, we suppose that the accused said nothing to the police but gave his account in the witness box, then the evidence about the blood and the fingerprint would constitute competent corroboration of the wife's account at the end of the Crown case, but would cease to be competent corroboration the moment that the accused gave his account in the witness box. Once that evidence had been given, counsel for the accused could close his examination and, assuming that the accused did not depart from his account in cross examination, counsel could make a common law submission that the accused should be acquitted. The notion of the corroborative effect draining out of evidence in this way is curious, to say the least.

What I have said so far suggests that the test as laid down in *Mackie* does not represent the law. It is therefore all the more important to examine *O'Hara v. Central SMT* upon which the Lord Justice General relied. *O'Hara* was a civil case and, so far as counsel's researches could discover, *Mackie* marks its entry into the reported decisions of our criminal courts. The Lord Advocate indeed submitted that *O'Hara* was an unsafe guide in this matter simply because it was a civil rather than a criminal case and in civil cases the standard of proof was proof on the balance of probabilities rather than proof beyond reasonable doubt. These are certainly points of distinction, but I am not persuaded that they would, of themselves, be a proper basis for concluding that *O'Hara* was an unsafe guide in the present context. For these reasons I prefer to look at *O'Hara* in a little more detail.

The facts take us back to the early months of the Second World War. On a dark December evening the pursuer was on a bus in Clydebank. Because of the blackout the street lamps were not lit and the beam from the headlights of the bus illuminated a distance of only about 25 feet in front of the bus. When the bus was approaching the stop where she wanted to get off, the pursuer left her seat and went to the rear platform where she took hold of the rail. At that point the bus took a violent and unexpected swerve which caused the pursuer to be thrown headlong on to the street. She sued the bus company for damages for her injuries and it was held that the occurrence of the swerve gave rise to a prima facie presumption of negligence on the part of the driver. The defenders sought to displace that presumption by showing that the swerve had not been caused by negligence on the part of the driver, but rather by the driver having to swerve to the offside to avoid killing a man who had suddenly run across the road about two or three yards in front of the bus. The court held that, in order to displace the presumption of negligence, the defenders required to lead full legal proof that the driver had swerved because of the man running in front of the bus.

The only person who gave direct evidence about the man running in front of the bus was the driver. According to the defenders, corroboration for his account might be found in a number of different ways, only one of which matters for present purposes. The defenders argued that corroboration was to be found in evidence of various facts and circumstances. It was proved that the conductor signalled to the driver that he was to stop at the bus stop and that he responded by slowing his speed and turning in towards the bus stop. The bus then swerved. When, after the accident, the conductor rang the bell for an emergency stop, the driver immediately stopped the bus. It was also proved that, after helping the pursuer into a shop, the driver spoke to a man standing beside the bus door and challenged him with being the man who had run in front of the bus. This man handed the conductor a piece of paper with his name on it. The court held that the direct evidence of the driver was corroborated by evidence of these facts and circumstances so that the defenders had adduced full legal proof to displace the prima facie presumption of negligence on the part of the driver.

It was in defining what would amount to 'sufficient corroboration' in this context that Lord President Normand expressed the view which was adopted in *Mackie*. Lord Normand said (1941 S.C. at p.379; 1941 S.L.T. at p.211): 'Corroboration may be by facts and circumstances proved by other evidence than that of the single witness who is to be corroborated. There is sufficient corroboration if the facts and circumstances proved are not only consistent with the evidence of the single witness, but more consistent with it than with any competing account of the events spoken to by him. Accordingly, if the facts and circumstances proved by other witnesses fit in to his narrative so as to make it the most probable account of the events, the requirements of legal proof are satisfied.'

He went on (at p.380 (p.211)) to apply the test to the facts and circumstances on which the defenders relied: 'The sequence of events seems to me to afford sufficient corroboration of the driver's story. The movements of the omnibus correspond with his account of his speed and steering. His response to bell signals shows that he was alert and minding his business. The swerve is no longer an isolated incident, it has a setting which points to the probability of the driver's evidence that it was a change of direction, opposite to the direction in which he was deliberately going, forced upon him by an emergency. This is much more probable than that it was a casual, one might say inexplicable, act of negligence. The choice is between a story into which details spoken to by other witnesses fit naturally and convincingly, and an inference arising from one movement isolated from the preceding and subsequent movements of the omnibus, all of which are indicative of careful driving. There is, therefore, in my opinion, evidence from independent sources which in law is corroborative of the driver's testimony, and which is, in the absence of any contradiction by competent evidence, sufficient corroboration.'

In *Mackie* the Lord President's description of sufficient corroboration was applied to the situation where the Crown relied on circumstantial evidence to corroborate the direct evidence of Mr Runciman about what had been said at the meeting with the accused, but the defence argued that the circumstantial evidence was equally consistent with the accused's account of the meeting with Mr Runciman. In other words the court applied Lord Normand's test to a situation where there were two competing accounts given in evidence.

That was not the situation, however, of which Lord Normand was speaking in *O'Hara*. There the pursuer's case was founded simply on the evidence that the bus suddenly swerved and caused her to fall off. That was held to give rise to a prima facie presumption of negligence. The pursuer led no evidence whatever as to the cause of the swerve and in particular she led no evidence to contradict the driver's evidence as to the man running in front of the bus. Her case was therefore based on the inference which she invited the court to draw from the fact that the bus swerved suddenly. So, when Lord Normand speaks of a competing 'account' of the accident, he is not referring to an account to be found in the direct evidence of another witness; he is simply referring to the account of the accident which fell to be derived by inference from the fact that the bus had suddenly swerved.

Just before the crucial passage in his opinion Lord Normand accepted that the driver's evidence about the man running in front of the bus was to be believed. He was then concerned to decide what evidence, when added to the driver's evidence, would constitute full legal proof which would displace the prima facie presumption of negligence on the part of the driver. The Lord President's view was that there would be 'sufficient corroboration' if the facts and circumstances were not only consistent with the driver's evidence, but more consistent with it than with the inference that the swerve had been due to negligence on the part of the driver. When he refers to 'sufficient corroboration' he is really considering what evidence will be required to displace the prima facie presumption that the driver was negligent. It is therefore not clear whether the Lord President was actually concerned with what could constitute bare corroboration of the driver's account. In any event he plainly did not have in mind the very different kind of situation where the circumstantial evidence would have been consistent with the direct evidence of the driver but also with a different account given by some other witness whom the Lord Ordinary would have required to disbelieve in order to accept the driver's evidence. For that reason the relevant passage in the Lord President's opinion is not to be interpreted as meaning that circumstantial evidence can corroborate truthful direct evidence only if the circumstantial evidence is more consistent with the account given in that evidence than with a competing and different account given by an opposing witness. Therefore Lord Normand's opinion does not provide authority for the particular approach to corroboration adopted by the court in *Mackie*.

The description of corroborative evidence in *Mackie* must stand or fall without the aid of *O'Hara*. No other authority from the institutional writers has been quoted in support of it. The Lord Justice General refers to three cases, one of which has since been overruled. The other two deal with distress as a potential source of corroboration, but neither is authority for the particular novel doctrine laid down in *Mackie*. Moreover the approach in *Mackie* does not correspond to the practice in our courts and would require judges to acquit accused persons in many cases where there was a body of evidence against them upon which a jury could readily convict under the law as generally understood. In these circumstances, I have reached the view that the approach in *Mackie* is incorrect and should be disapproved. Where the Crown rely on the direct evidence of a single witness plus circumstantial evidence to establish the crucial facts in a charge, all that needs to be done is to apply the usual approach to corroboration. The jury must not only accept the direct evidence of the single witness, but must also find independent circumstantial evidence which they accept and which confirms or supports the direct evidence on the crucial facts. At the stage when a submission of no case to answer is made, the submission will fall to be rejected if the Crown has led direct evidence and independent circumstantial evidence which is capable of confirming or supporting the direct evidence on the crucial facts.

During the course of the argument before us the Lord Advocate made various submissions about the way in which the court dealt with the particular facts in *Mackie*, but for the purposes of the present appeal I do not require to say more than that the court may have trespassed on matters of fact which were truly for the jury to determine.

It only remains to apply the approach which I have identified to the present case where the appellant contends that the trial judge misdirected the jury as to how they should deal with the evidence of the distress exhibited by the complainer. The evidence of distress was independent of the complainer's evidence. The trial judge directed the jury that they had first to decide whether they accepted the complainer's evidence. If they did not, they would acquit the appellant. Their verdict shows that the jury accepted the complainer as a truthful and reliable witness on the essential matters. Since her evidence was that she had been unconscious during the intercourse, while the appellant's account was that she had been conscious and had encouraged him, in accepting the complainer's account the jury must have rejected the appellant's account. His account was simply one of a number which the jury had to assess. The jury were directed by the judge that they required to consider whether the distress was genuine, when it was observed, how great it was and how long it lasted. Those were entirely appropriate directions to the jury on how they might approach their task of assessing this aspect of the evidence. Having considered the circumstances and the competing explanations, the jury were entitled to conclude that the complainer had been distressed because the appellant had had intercourse with her without her consent. On that basis, as the trial judge directed them, the jury were entitled to find in the evidence of the complainer's distress confirmation of that part of her evidence where she said that she had not consented to the sexual intercourse.

I am satisfied therefore that there was no misdirection by the trial judge and that this second ground of appeal falls to be rejected."

LORD JUSTICE CLERK (CULLEN): "I am in full agreement with the opinion of your Lordship in the chair. I would, however, add some observations of my own in regard to the decision in *Mackie v. H.M.A.*

In that case it was essential for the Crown to establish that the appellant was knowingly in possession of certain price sensitive information, namely a profits warning. A witness, Mr

H.L.I. Runciman, gave evidence that he had told the appellant about the profits warning, whereas the appellant denied receiving that information and stated that Mr Runciman had given him some confidential information which did not include any information about a profits warning. The Crown had sought to find corroboration for the evidence of Mr Runciman in evidence relating to certain facts and circumstances. However, at p.141C–D (p.118H) the Lord Justice General (Hope) said: 'The trial judge said that it was appropriate to look at the whole context and all the evidence, and to that extent I agree with him. But in my opinion the question which then had to be considered was whether the facts and circumstances, when taken together, were more consistent with Mr Runciman's evidence than with the appellant's evidence.'

He went on to say, also on p.141G (p.118J): 'Circumstantial evidence which was equally consistent with the appellant's account of the meeting cannot be said to support Mr Runciman's account of it. At best for the Crown such evidence is neutral and if it is neutral it cannot provide corroboration in such a case.'

In considering the soundness of these observations, which appear to be applicable to corroboration generally and not limited to the particular case, it is, in my view, important to begin by considering the general nature of what is required by way of corroboration.

The general rules are not in doubt. In regard to the proof of a fact which is an essential element in the charge which is before them the jury are not entitled to find that fact established solely on the basis of their acceptance of the evidence of a single witness who gave evidence as to that fact, no matter how cogent that evidence may be. The jury are only entitled to find it established if there is evidence from some independent source—such as circumstantial evidence—which they also accept and which they regard as supporting or confirming the evidence of the first witness as to the *factum probandum*. In the result the requirement for corroboration operates as a rule preventing the jury from holding an essential fact established unless that is based on the coherence of two independent sources of evidence.

Hume, Commentaries, ii, 384 illustrates the corroborative effect of circumstantial evidence in these words:

> 'It would not however be a reasonable thing, nor is it our law, that the want of a second witness to the fact cannot be supplied by the other circumstances of the case. If one man swear that he saw the pannel stab the deceased, and others confirm his testimony with circumstances, such as the pannel's sudden flight from the spot, the blood on his clothes, the bloody instrument found in his possession, his confession on being taken, or the like; certainly these are as good, nay better even than a second testimony to the act of stabbing.
>
> Neither is it to be understood in cases of circumstantial evidence, either such as the foregoing case, or one where all the evidence is circumstantial, that two witnesses are necessary to establish each particular; because the aptitude and coherence of the several circumstances often as fully confirm the truth of the story, as if all the witnesses were deponing to the same facts.'

A number of features of circumstantial evidence should also be borne in mind. It is not direct evidence as to the events which form the subject of the charge or as to the person or persons who were responsible for them. It is indirect evidence, the significance of which depends on inference from the evidence at large, and in particular from its consideration in conjunction with the direct evidence. It is not necessary that circumstantial evidence should of itself incriminate the accused or that it should be unequivocally referable to the essential element of the charge which is to be established. What matters is whether it is capable of providing support or confirmation in regard to the *factum probandum* of which direct evidence has been given.

The Lord Justice General in *Mackie* stated that, if the court regards the circumstantial evidence as equally consistent with the explanation given by the appellant in his own exculpation, the circumstantial evidence cannot provide corroboration. To describe evidence as 'consistent' with something else conveys an unfortunate ambiguity: it may mean on the one hand that the evidence tends to confirm the latter proposition, or on the other hand that it offers no conflict with it. (See Lord McCluskey in *Smith v. Lees*, 1997 S.C.C.R. at p.174A–D; 1997 S.L.T. at pp.714K–715B.) However, when the remarks of the Lord Justice General are considered in their context it is reasonably plain that he was referring to a situation which the circumstantial evidence could equally avail to confirm the explanation given by the appellant as well as the account given by the Crown witness. It follows that in that situation there would be the remarkable result that evidence which otherwise could have provided corroboration of the evidence of the Crown witness cannot do so because of the existence of the alternative explanation given by the appellant.

The question of corroboration plainly cannot arise unless the jury accept the evidence of the witness who gave direct evidence as to the *factum probandum* and hence reject the contradictory evidence of the accused. No doubt in arriving at that view they will have had to make their assessment of the conflicting accounts, and for that purpose may have found it useful to do so against the background of the evidence as a whole. Thus, one factor which may assist them in reaching a view as to the credibility and reliability of these accounts may be the extent to which each is consistent or in conflict with the circumstantial evidence. There will, of course, be other factors of significance, such as their assessment of the demeanour of the witnesses. However, if they reach the view that they accept the account given by the direct witness, and hence reject the contradictory account of the accused, it is illogical to say that evidence which otherwise was capable of providing corroboration is robbed of that quality because it was equally consistent with the account which has been rejected.

In this context it is also important to bear in mind the respective functions of judge and jury. Where the prosecutor relies upon circumstantial evidence as supporting or confirming the evidence given by a direct witness as to the *factum probandum*, it is for the jury to decide whether they accept the circumstantial evidence, and, if so, whether it does in fact provide the corroboration for which the prosecutor contends. How they go about their task and what significance or weight they attach to the evidence are, of course, matters exclusively for them to decide. It is, on the other hand, for the court to decide whether there is evidence which, if accepted, is capable of providing corroboration. This may be illustrated by the decision in *Yates v. H.M.A.* and the series of decisions following that case. It is important that the court should not encroach on the province of the jury by substituting its own assessment of the corroborative effect of the circumstantial evidence.

Thus, when dealing with a submission of no case to answer under s.97 of the Criminal Procedure (Scotland) Act 1995, a judge requires to consider whether the evidence led by the prosecution is insufficient in law to justify the accused being convicted. It is well recognised that for this purpose the judge will require to consider whether there is evidence which, if accepted, could corroborate the evidence of the principal witness, assuming that evidence is also accepted (*Williamson v. Wither*). If circumstantial evidence is regarded as capable of having that effect, why should it make any difference to the sufficiency of evidence that an accused thereafter gives an alternative explanation in his own exculpation, with which the court considers that the circumstantial evidence is equally consistent? In my view it would have no such effect, since at the stage when the trial judge gives his directions to the jury the question for him as to the sufficiency of the evidence is the same as it was at the stage when a submission was made of no case to answer, namely whether the circumstantial evidence is capable of providing corroboration, and he will charge the jury accordingly. I should add that it is common experience that an alternative explanation may readily arise at an earlier stage in the trial during the course of the Crown evidence. It may be contained in evidence as to a statement made by the accused to the police which is admissible as evidence of the truth of what occurred. It may arise from points elicited during the cross examination of Crown witnesses. However and whenever it arises as a contradictory explanation of the circumstantial evidence it does not affect the answer to the question whether there is or is not evidence capable of providing corroboration. There may on the other hand be cases in which circumstantial evidence is inevitably ambiguous in nature, and the court reaches the conclusion that it is incapable of providing the necessary support or confirmation.

In the light of these considerations I am of the opinion that the Lord Justice General in *Mackie* was in error in stating that, for the purpose of corroboration, evidence as to facts and circumstances requires to be more consistent with the evidence of the direct witness than with the evidence of the appellant. In my view this statement should be disapproved."

NOTES

Corroborative facts and circumstances must "point", in the context of the other evidence, to the fact in issue which requires to be corroborated. Circumstances which did not so "point" would in any event be irrelevant—see Macphail, *Evidence*, para. 23–08. It may be this issue that the Lord Justice-General had in mind when he reserved his opinion "as to whether there may be cases where the circumstantial evidence is ambiguous, but no reasonable jury could choose the interpretation which would support the direct evidence". This reservation was considered in the unreported case of *Mackie v. H.M.A.*, High Court of Justiciary, July 26, 2001, which seems to indicate that in most cases it will be a matter for the jury whether or not the particular (ambiguous) evidence relied upon by the Crown is capable of providing corroboration. On one view this might be thought strange in the context of a case like *Thompson v. Crowe*, 1999 S.L.T. 1434, see Chapter below. Sufficiency is a matter of law, and it might be argued that in general, the question whether evidence can be regarded as corroborative should be decided by the judge following no case to answer submission.

Thus, corroborative evidence might be described very simply as independent evidence which is relevant (in the sense described in Chapter 1) to the facts in issue. The English view of corroboration is instructive here, a view which the most recent Scottish cases closely parallel. In *R. v. Kilbourne*, [1973] A.C. 729, at p.758 Lord Simon of Glaisdale said that:

"[Corroboration] is required because experience has shown that there is a real risk that an innocent person may be convicted unless certain evidence against an accused . . . is confirmed by other evidence. Corroboration is therefore nothing other than evidence which 'confirms' or 'strengthens' or 'supports' other evidence . . . It is, in short, evidence which renders other evidence more probable. If so, there is no essential difference between, on the one hand, corroboration and, on the other, 'supporting evidence' or 'evidence which helps to determine the truth of the matter'. Each is evidence which makes other evidence more probable. Once it is accepted that the direct evidence on one count is relevant to another by way of circumstantial evidence, it follows that it is available as corroboration if corroboration is required."

English law, it should be noted, did not at this time require corroboration in all criminal cases, but only in those cases, characteristically sexual offence cases, where the evidence was thought likely to be "suspect". This connection between corroboration and relevance accords with the principle of the Scottish trial system. It reserves to the judge the task of deciding whether the evidence led is *capable* of yielding inferences as to the facts in issue, but leaves to the jury the task of deciding whether, in all the circumstances, that inference should be drawn. See further Sheldon, "Corroboration and Relevance" 1999 S.L.T. (News) 1.

Evidence which merely "offers no conflict with" the principal witness may serve to bolster that witness's credibility but it does not provide corroboration. The courts have repeatedly held or implied that evidence which is merely "neutral" is not sufficient. *Miller v. H.M.A.*, 1994 S.L.T. 640, provides a classic example of a case in which there were two inconsistent versions of events with no way of properly deciding which was preferable. *Gallagher v. H.M.A.*, 2000 S.C.C.R. 634 provides an example of circumstantial evidence which neither confirmed nor supported the facts in issue.

Both *Smith v. Lees*, and *Fox v. H.M.A.* were cases in which corroboration of an eyewitness was required. In other words, there was direct evidence of the facts in issue, which then required corroboration from another source. Difficulties may arise in cases involving purely circumstantial evidence, as it may be difficult to say whether any particular item of evidence is independently incriminating in the sense apparently required by the traditional view. In such cases, different considerations apply, and it seems that there will be corroboration if the circumstantial evidence, taken as a whole, supports the necessary inferences about each of the crucial facts, and where the circumstantial evidence comes from at least two sources.

7. Little v. H.M.A.
1983 S.C.C.R. 56

Two women, Mrs Little and her friend Elaine Haggerty, were charged with the murder of Mrs Little's husband. Mr Little was shot by one MacKenzie, and the case turned on the question of whether the two women had paid him money to carry out the killing and had thus instigated the murder.

LORD JUSTICE-GENERAL (EMSLIE): "There was no direct evidence of the instigation libelled against [Mrs Little]. The evidence upon which the learned advocate-depute relied (and we ignore for the moment MacKenzie's evidence) was circumstantial. According to counsel for Mrs Little each of the several circumstances founded upon by the Crown was quite neutral. None pointed to instigation by itself and, taken together, they supported, at best, merely the inference that Mrs Little was aware before the killing of her husband that MacKenzie contemplated shooting him. We do not agree. The question is not whether each of the several circumstances 'points' by itself towards the instigation libelled but whether the several circumstances taken together are capable of supporting the inference, beyond reasonable doubt, that Mrs Little in fact instigated the killing of her husband by MacKenzie. As was pointed out by the Lord Justice-Clerk (Aitchison) in *Morton v. H.M.A.*, 1938 J.C. 50 at p.52, quoting the words of Baron Hume, 'the aptitude and coherence of the several circumstances often as fully confirm the truth of the story, as if all the witnesses were deponing to the same facts'.

The evidence disclosed that the killer MacKenzie had no personal animosity towards Little and no personal motive to shoot him. It also disclosed a very close association between Mrs Little and Elaine Haggarty in spite of the fact that the latter, a sixteen-year-old girl, was involved in a sexual relationship with the deceased. There was uncontroverted evidence, too, that Mrs Little hated her husband, no doubt with good reason. A letter from Mrs Little to the witness Mrs Ross dated September 11, 1981 (Production 50) recorded Mrs Little's despair and in it she wrote (referring to her husband) that she prayed to God to take it [*sic*] off this earth. In an undated letter (Production 74) Mrs Little told her husband that she would never be happy as long as he was alive, that he was the worst man on this earth, and that she hated him. Further, a barmaid in the Labour Club frequented by Mrs Little and Elaine Haggarty, always together, testified that about six months before the trial Mrs Little had stated that she was going to shoot the bastard (referring to her husband). Mrs Gray (the barmaid) did not, of course, treat this statement seriously.

The remaining evidence can be discussed in two chapters.

The first chapter is concerned with events before the murder which it will be recalled took place shortly after 11 p.m. on Wednesday November 25, 1981. About four or five months before the trial which was in March 1982, Mrs Little, accompanied by Elaine Haggarty, met MacKenzie and the witness Vincent Haggarty outside the Lincluden café. According to Vincent Haggarty, Mrs Little asked MacKenzie if he had a gun. MacKenzie said yes and after the two women had walked on MacKenzie added that Mrs Little 'wasn't getting it'. A bullet hole was found after the murder in the mattress of the bed in a bedroom of Mrs Little's house—a room normally occupied by Elaine Haggarty when from time to time she spent the night in Mrs Little's house. Fragments of the bullet which were recovered bore traces of gold washing. The bullet was, accordingly, similar to those possessed by MacKenzie and there was evidence which permitted the inference that a round had been discharged through the mattress some short time before the murder. On November 24 and 25, 1981 there was a remarkable flurry of activity. On each day about 6 p.m. Elaine Haggarty called to see MacKenzie at the house where he lived. This was unusual for there was no association between them and on the first visit at least, according to Sandra MacKenzie, the excuse made by Miss Haggarty was that she brought a message for MacKenzie from her brother Vincent—an excuse shown to be false. Further, on each day MacKenzie visited Mrs Little's house. This was also most unusual because Mrs Little was not friendly with MacKenzie and, including these visits, claimed to have met MacKenzie only on four or five occasions in all. He came on the evening of Tuesday November 24, 1981. According to Mrs Little he came for a cup of tea which Elaine Haggarty made for him. On November 25, 1981, according to Mrs Little, he called again, this time about 8 p.m., asking, she said, if Elaine was in. All that remains to be said of the events of November 24 and 25, 1981, before the murder had been committed, was that on the afternoon of November 25, 1981 Mrs Little, carrying a passbook in the name of Miss Haggarty, entered the offices of the Nationwide Building Society leaving Miss Haggarty outside. Mrs Little who had, it appeared, opened the account in about September 1981 by depositing about £1,000 of Elaine Haggerty's money, withdrew £100 in banknotes, the largest single withdrawal which had ever been made.

The second chapter deals with the events which happened after the shooting of Little by MacKenzie. According to Mrs Little's own evidence, MacKenzie arrived on her doorstep carrying his rifle, almost immediately after he had used it to kill Little. MacKenzie, an apparently casual acquaintance of Mrs Little, knocked at the door gave his name as 'Wull' and was at once admitted. No reason or explanation was given for this apparently unexpected and untimely call, yet he was at once admitted and, according to Mrs Little, he announced that he had just shot her husband. Thereupon MacKenzie and Miss Haggarty, again according to Mrs Little, set off to dispose of the corpse. Mrs Little refused to go, she said, because she had her child to look after. We should mention that Mrs Little's version of these bizarre events was that MacKenzie had demanded the help of one of the two appellants to 'shift the body' or he would 'rope youse into it'. On Mrs Little's evidence, of course, there was no possible basis for the appellants to be roped in, and no rational explanation for MacKenzie's first act after shooting Little, namely, going at once with the rifle barrel still warm, to inform the victim's wife and, as it turned out, Miss Haggarty, of the deed which he had just accomplished. For the next three days the two appellants maintained a discreet silence, reporting nothing of the murder to the police or to anyone else. The body of Little was discovered in its place of concealment on Saturday November 28, 1981. The police called to report this tragic matter to his widow. She appeared calm but surprised. At this time the police entertained no suspicion that Mrs Little had had anything to do with Little's murder, yet on Sunday November 29, 1981 she informed the witness Miss Beresford, in presence of Miss Haggarty, that 'the police thought they might have had something to do with it'. On the same day when she was seen by Detective Inspector Gilchrist her first question to him was 'How did he die?' All she was told was that he had been shot. On Tuesday December 1, 1981, however, Mrs Little told Miss Beresford that the police had told her that Little had been shot four or five times. We come now to Wednesday December 2, 1981. Mrs Little was detained under section 2 of the Criminal Justice (Scotland) Act 1980 and taken to the police station where she was cautioned. She was asked if she knew MacKenzie. Immediately she became distressed and wept for about ten minutes. Because of this surprising reaction she was cautioned again and at once said this: 'I did not think Wull (MacKenzie) would do it. I got a shock when he said he had done it. I'll tell it all now. God Almighty, I wish I was dead.' To complete the account of the relevant evidence in this chapter we go back in time to Thursday November 26, 1981. On the late afternoon of that day MacKenzie went to a food shop and persuaded a friend, Miss Tracy Muir, to cash for him an Inland Revenue cheque for about £31. Miss Muir, who was called as a witness for Mrs Little, stated that MacKenzie had been paid that day and that his wages were about £23 a week. To Miss Muir, however, MacKenzie bragged about having a bundle of money in his pocket. He produced the bundle to let her see it and it appeared to consist of over £100 in notes. He was, he said, going to bank it the next day. On November 27, 1981 MacKenzie deposited in his bank account £120 in notes. This was the only transaction in the account between November 1, 1981 and December 4, 1981 and the sum deposited was far in excess of MacKenzie's known resources.

Upon a consideration of the whole relevant evidence which we now summarise we have no hesitation in saying that it was quite sufficient in law, if it was accepted, to support the inference beyond reasonable doubt that Mrs Little instigated the killing of her husband by MacKenzie, within the scope of the libel. We have only to add that in our opinion there was sufficient evidence in law against Mrs Little even before she elected to give and lead evidence on her own behalf and that when MacKenzie's evidence, which we do not rehearse, is added to the reckoning, there was left no room for any reasonable doubt upon the crucial issue in the case against her."

NOTES

Although sufficiency of evidence is, as we have seen, a matter of law, it is clearly for the jury to decide whether, at the end of the case, the evidence relied upon as corroborative is strong enough to carry the weight of the inferences required. The next extracts are concerned with the question whether some types of principal evidence are so strong that a jury need not strain to find corroboration in the other evidence led. In *Connelly v. H.M.A.*, 1958 S.L.T. 79, Lord Justice-Clerk Thomson said:

"While it is necessary that there should be evidence from two independent sources, the weight to be attached to each source may vary. If one source is unimpeachable, the standard required of the other may be lower than if the first source carries less weight. It is the conjunction of testimonies which is important."

However, to this one must add *dicta* from the case of *Meredith v. Lees*, 1992 S.C.C.R. 459, below, that what is required in each and every case is evidence which forms a sufficient independent check on the principal evidence. There is no rule, contrary to suggestions by Lord Avonside in *Hartley v. H.M.A.*, 1979 S.L.T. 29, that in cases involving unequivocal confessions of guilt, very little in the way of corroboration is required. In *Hartley* Lord Dunpark said that:

> "The standard of corroboration of an unequivocal confession of guilt is, in my opinion, different from the standard to be applied when seeking corroboration of a Crown eye-witness at a criminal trial or of the evidence of a pursuer of defender in a civil case. The reason for the different standard is that, unlike such other evidence, the confession of guilt by an accused person is prejudicial to his own interests and may, therefore, initially be assumed to be true. Accordingly, one is not then looking for extrinsic evidence which is more consistent with his guilt than with his innocence, but for extrinsic evidence which is consistent with his confession of guilt. If, therefore, a jury is satisfied that a confession of guilt was freely made and unequivocal in its terms, corroboration of that confession may be found in evidence from another source or other sources which point to the truth of the confession."

However, *per* Lord Dunpark, cases involving such confessions are *not* in a different category—the normal rules regarding corroboration continue to apply:

8. Meredith v. Lees
1992 S.C.C.R. 459

The appellant was charged with lewd and libidinous practices towards a four-year-old girl. The main evidence against the accused was a clear confession which was held by the Sheriff to have been freely and voluntarily given. There was also evidence from the complainer who spoke to indecent conduct by the appellant, but her account "did not correspond in every detail with the confession".

LORD JUSTICE-GENERAL (HOPE): "The fundamental rule is that no one who confesses to a crime, unless by a formal plea of guilty, can be convicted solely on his own confession. There must be evidence from some other source which incriminates the accused. The clearest expression of this rule is that given by Lord Justice-Clerk Thomson in *Sinclair v. Clark* at p.62:

> 'There is a rule in our law—a somewhat archaic rule—the merit of which in modern conditions is not always obvious, at all events where the admission is made in circumstances beyond suspicion, that short of a solemn plea of guilt, an admission of guilt by an accused is not conclusive against him, unless it is corroborated by something beyond the actual admission. One reason for this rule is to ensure that there is nothing phoney or quixotic about the confession. What is required in the way of independent evidence in order to elide such a risk must depend on the facts of the case, and, in particular, the nature and character of the confession and the circumstances in which it is made.'

That passage was quoted by Lord Avonside in *Hartley v. H.M.A.* at p.29 and by Lord Grieve at p.31. Lord Dunpark's discussion of the point at p.33 in that case is difficult to follow, due partly to a misprint which is corrected at p.300.

As the Lord Justice-Clerk has pointed out in *Greenshields v. H.M.A.* at p.642, it has often been said that if there is a clear and unequivocal admission of guilt, then very little evidence in corroboration of such an admission is required. In the right context that is a perfectly correct statement of the position, and a comment to the same effect is to be found in Lord Grieve's opinion in Hartley at p.31. In *Torrance v. Thaw* at p.64, for example, where the question was whether there was corroboration of the appellant's admission that he was driving a motor-car at the time of the accident which led to his being required to provide a specimen of breath for a breath test, Lord Justice-Clerk Grant said:

> 'On this crucial matter corroboration is clearly required. The appellant admitted on three separate occasions that he was driving at the time, and he behaved throughout the whole

procedure carried out under the 1967 Act, and after warnings of possible prosecution, on the basis that he was the driver. Little corroboration is accordingly necessary.'

The same point arose in *Miln v. Fitzgerald* where, in the course of delivering the opinion of the court, Lord Cameron said this [at p.206–207]:

'In our opinion the admissions made by the respondent are clear and unequivocal to the effect that at the relevant time he was the driver of the motor-car. In such circumstances, very little circumstantial or other corroboration is required to establish the essential fact that the person accused was, at the relevant time, the driver of the vehicle concerned in the events libelled.'

That passage was quoted by the Lord Justice-Clerk in *Tudhope v. Dalgleish* at p.652, where the appellant's statement that she had been driving the vehicle a short time previously was held not to be a clear and unequivocal statement to the effect that she was the driver at the relevant time, and the conclusion was that the whole evidence was insufficient to establish that this was the fact.

But it is not appropriate that this approach to what is required to corroborate a clear and unequivocal confession should be described as a rule. A confession may be clear and unequivocal in its terms, yet the circumstances in which it was made may leave room for doubt as to whether it is true and can be relied upon. There is a risk that, by describing the requirement in minimal terms by using words such as 'very little' and then elevating it into a rule, there will be a weakening of the principle that there must be a sufficient independent check of the confession to corroborate it. What is required to achieve this must depend on the circumstances of the case, and one ought not to say that very little is required until the circumstances of the case have been analysed and it has become clear precisely what it is about the confession that must be corroborated.

In some cases there may be ample evidence from other sources that the crime libelled has been committed. The remaining question will then be whether the accused committed the crime. A clear and unequivocal confession of guilt on his part may then require little more by way of evidence to corroborate it, if the admission is in terms which leave no room for doubt on this point and there is no reason to suspect that it was not freely made. This is the situation which Lord Justice-Clerk Thomson had in mind in *Sinclair v. Clark* when he referred to an admission made in circumstances which were beyond suspicion. The only question would then be whether there was evidence from another source which confirms the truth of the confession. That evidence may amount only to a little more in quantity, but it must be of sufficient quality to provide an independent check of the guilt of the accused. That raises a question of fact and degree which must vary according to the circumstances of each case.

In the present case the identity of the appellant as the person who committed the offence is not in issue. There was ample evidence that he and the child were together in the same room at the time. Her account about the time, place and circumstances was entirely consistent with the account which he gave to the police. It is her account of what he did to her which requires to be examined, in order to see whether it provided a sufficient independent check of his confession to establish the truth of it and that he was guilty of the crime. The sheriff held it proved that the confession was made freely by the appellant, so there is nothing in the circumstances in which it was made to suggest that it was not true. In quantity the child's evidence was very little, as the sheriff has pointed out. She was unable to say much about what happened, partly because of defects in her understanding and partly because of the passage of time. But it is the quality of her evidence and the weight to be attached to it which matter here, rather than the amount of detail or the accuracy with which the incident was described.

We cannot accept therefore Mr Douglas's submission that the fact that the child did not describe the particular acts of indecency which the appellant had confessed to deprives her evidence of all corroborative effect. There are indications in what she said that the appellant's behaviour towards her was lewd, libidinous and indecent in character. Her statement, while pointing to her stomach, that he touched her on the leg, taken together with her description that this was not nice and she did not like it, was not very explicit. But it was for the sheriff to decide what she meant, taking account of her age and her ability to understand and express herself. He gave very careful attention to the matter, and his conclusion was that her evidence, properly understood, was consistent with the confession. This was a conclusion which he was entitled to reach. The only remaining question for him was whether this evidence was sufficient to corroborate the confession. His answer to this question was that, since he believed that this was a genuine confession, it was sufficient corroboration of it. This answer depended on his assessment of the quality of the evidence and the weight to be attached to it, and we are not persuaded that the conclusion which he reached was one which he was not entitled to reach in all the circumstances.

For these reasons we shall answer the . . . remaining questions in the case in the affirmative and refuse this appeal."

NOTES

On the facts of this case, was the corroborative evidence incriminating rather than merely consistent? In particular, were the ingredients of the offence of lewd and libidinous practices properly corroborated? It should be noted that while this case clearly holds that there is no general rule on the matter, the courts sometimes accept in practice that there is corroboration when the evidence is very thin indeed. In *Armit v. O'Donnell*, 1999 S.L.T. 1035, for example, a case involving a charge of vandalism, the court accepted that there was corroboration of a confession where there was evidence that, when the police arrived, the appellant was standing outside the premises where the window had been broken, and there was no-one else in the vicinity at the time. Would this have been accepted as sufficient corroboration in a murder case?

Finally, it was always doubtful whether a different rule on corroboration of confessions could be justified in the way Lord Dunpark suggests in *Hartley*. False confessions do occur—see for example the case of *Boyle v. H.M.A.*, 1976 S.L.T. 126, and *inter alia* Gudjonsson and Gunn in 141 British Journal of Psychiatry 624; Baldwin and McConville, Royal Commission on Criminal Procedure, Research Study No. 5 (1980).

9.   Ralston v. H.M.A.
1987 S.C.C.R. 467

The appellant was convicted of assaulting a security van guard and attempting to rob him. The evidence against him consisted of a positive identification by the victim, who had struggled with Ralston for a few seconds; evidence from a second guard who identified the accused at an identity parade on the basis of his "resemblance" to the accused and who said in court that at that time he could see no-one resembling the assailant; and from a third guard who said that the accused was "possibly the assailant but not for definite". He was convicted and appealed to the High Court on the ground that the evidence against him was insufficient in "character, quality and strength" under reference to the case of *Reilly v. H.M.A.*, 1981 S.C.C.R. 201.

LORD JUSTICE-GENERAL (EMSLIE): "The appellant is Samuel Paul Ralston who went to trial on an indictment along with James William McLean and a man called Gallagher. At the end of the day the appellant was found guilty of charge (3) in that indictment which was directed against him alone, and that was a charge that on August 14, 1986 near the Trustee Savings Bank in the Easterhouse Township Centre he assaulted two named security guards, brandishing an iron bar at them and menacing them with the bar, ordering Stewart, one of them, to drop a bag containing £25,000 and, the libel goes on, he did strike him on the hand with the said iron bar and all this he did with intent to rob them of the said money bag containing £25,000, and he did attempt to rob them thereof.

In this appeal to challenge conviction the simple proposition presented by Mr Welsh is that there was no sufficient evidence in law to identify the appellant as the perpetrator of the crime. In introducing that submission Mr Welsh reminded us of what the evidence at the trial had been. It will be clear that the crime took place when three security guards were delivering money to the bank. Two of the security guards were outside the van and one was inside the van. One security guard in particular was carrying a bag of money, the very bag mentioned in the charge; his name was Stewart. At an identification parade on September 19, just over a month after the crime, Stewart identified the appellant in a positive and clear way although he had never met him before. He did so in court also, in a way which seemed to the trial judge to be impressive, although the attack upon him had lasted only for a few seconds, and although Mr Stewart was wearing a helmet and glasses. Mr Scott, who was the other guard outside the van, did not have the same opportunity as Stewart had to see the assailant as clearly. What he said was that he glanced at the assailant's face and then looked round in case he had companions with him. He too went to an identification parade on September 19, and when he was asked if he could pick out the assailant positively on the parade he was unable to do that, but he was then asked if he could see anybody on the parade who resembled the assailant. He immediately pointed to No. 2 in the parade, who happened to be the appellant, and he explained that he found resemblance by reason of the shape of the appellant's face and the shape of the [face at] the crime. At the trial, however, he did not identify the appellant from the witness box and at one point said he could see no one in court who resembled the assailant. He added, however, at some time during the course of his evidence, that possibly the appellant was the man he had seen and picked out at the identification parade. The remaining security guard, McKenna, who, of course, was inside the van at the time the assault took place, said that he had seen Stewart with his back against the wall and he had seen the assailant run past the van. He could not say for sure that the appellant was the assailant. He apparently stated that he did not get a very good look at him, and that is not at all surprising, and when the sharp issue of identification was examined further he apparently said this: 'I could not say for definite but it is possibly him, the appellant, there.' In short, said Mr Welsh, there was one clear-cut and positive identification of the appellant by one witness. There was one witness who at the identification parade was able to say only that the appellant resembled the assailant, and one witness who in court was able to say only that the assailant was possibly the appellant.

The submission accordingly came to be that the evidence of Scott and McKenna was insufficient in law and in character and quality to provide what the law requires in the way of corroboration of the clear-cut positive evidence of identification given by Stewart. Mr Welsh's submission was that such evidence as had been given by Scott and McKenna was certainly not enough to provide the necessary corroboration of Stewart and in presenting that submission he drew our attention to the well-known case of *Reilly and Ors*. He appeared to seek to draw comfort from that case but it has to be said at once that that was a very special case because although the question in the case was the same as the question which arises here, namely, whether there was sufficient evidence to corroborate the evidence in that case, Reilly's case, was evidence from a witness who found a resemblance between the accused and the perpetrator at the trial. So far so good, but that was not the end of the matter because the evidence was that the resemblance had a very weak basis indeed and in one case was founded upon a feature which contradicted flatly the evidence of the eyewitness who had made the positive identification.

We accordingly come back to the question—was the evidence of Scott and McKenna capable of affording sufficient corroboration for the impressive evidence given by Mr Stewart? It has been said before in a number of cases that where one starts with an emphatic positive identification by one witness then very little else is required. That little else must of course be evidence which is consistent in all respects with the positive identification evidence which has been given. At the end of the day one must look at the whole evidence to ask whether the supporting evidence consistent with the positive identification evidence, taken together with the positive identification evidence, is sufficient to entitle the jury beyond reasonable doubt to conclude that the particular accused was the perpetrator of the particular crime. In this case we are satisfied that the evidence of Scott and McKenna was sufficient at least for the jury's legitimate purpose, and, in particular, we emphasise the nature of the evidence given by Scott that at the identification parade just over a month after the event he was able to pick out at the parade the appellant as a man resembling the assailant. Having regard to the nature of the crime and the circumstances that, in our judgement, provided that degree of sufficiency in the way of other evidence to satisfy the requirement in law of corroboration. The appeal against conviction by Ralston will accordingly be refused."

NOTES

See also *Murphy v. H.M.A.*, 1995 S.C.C.R. 85. *Ralston* appears to take a view on corroboration of identification evidence similar to that taken by *Hartley* on corroboration of confessions. It would seem logical to assume that the comments made by Lord Justice-General Hope in *Meredith v. Lees*, 1992 S.C.C.R. 459, above, should also be applied to this type of case, and that accordingly there is no rule of law that in cases of an "emphatic positive identification, very little corroboration is required". It might be argued, indeed, that the requirement for corroboration should be strengthened in cases where the identity of the accused is disputed, given the "ghastly risk" of mistaken identification and research which suggests that mistaken identification and unreliable confessions are the two most significant causes of wrongful convictions (see *inter alia* Woocher, "Did your eyes deceive you" 29 Stanford Law Review 969; Shepherd, Ellis and Davies, *Identification Evidence: A psychological evaluation* (1982); Gudjonsson and Gunn, *The competence and reliability of a witness in a criminal court: a case report*, 141 British Journal of Psychiatry 624; Baldwin and McConville, Royal Commission on Criminal Procedure Research Study No. 5 (1980) *Confessions in Crown Court Trials*). In Scotland, however, evidence has been accepted as demonstrating an emphatic positive identification which seems far from satisfactory. In *Gracie v. Allan*, 1987 S.C.C.R. 364 the accused was said to be "very like" the perpetrator; in *Nolan v. Mcleod*, 1987 S.C.C.R. 558, the witnesses were "75 or 80 per cent sure" that the accused was the perpetrator; in *Farmer v. H.M.A.*, 1991 S.C.C.R. 986, it was accepted that there was sufficient identification even though the perpetrators had been masked at the time of the offence. The level of accuracy in such identifications has been described as "chance"—see Sheldon and Macleod, "From Positive to Normative Data: Expert Psychological Evidence Re-examined" [1991] Crim.L.R. 811, note 60; finally in *Nelson v. H.M.A.*, 1988 S.C.C.R. 536 the accused was picked out of an identification parade on the basis of his build. This was said to provide sufficient corroboration of a more positive identification. Evidence of identification on the grounds of a person's build might be thought to be vague enough—indeed an identification parade in which the foils are of markedly different builds from that of the suspect is not a properly constructed parade—but additionally, in this case two other persons were picked out of the same parade by the witness, each of whom was said to resemble the perpetrator. *Hawkins v. Carmichael*, 1992 S.C.C.R. 348 was a contrasting case in which the evidence fell "well short" of what would be required to corroborate a positive ID, and which illustrates the importance of being able to take good notes. In *McDonald v. H.M.A.*, 1998 S.L.T. 37, a conviction was quashed where it was held that there was no positive identification of the accused at all. The identifying witness has said that the accused "didn't look unlike" the perpetrator in terms of build and facial appearance. That was held to be insufficient, the court distinguishing *Ralston*, *Nelson* and *Farmer*. While it is clear that each case will turn on its own facts, this case is useful as it shows that the court will examine questions of identification as a matter of law, and in appropriate cases, over-turn convictions.

In England, the case of *R. v. Turnbull* [1977] 1 Q.B. requires judges to direct juries in detail about the dangers of identification evidence and to provide detailed guidelines for such directions (contrast, however *Curry and Keeble* [1983] Crim.L.R. 737, a case in which the Turnbull guidelines were circumvented). In Scotland, it has been accepted that in appropriate cases, juries should be warned about the dangers of identification evidence, but no particular form of warning is required and the matter is largely one for the discretion of the trial judge. See, *inter alia*, *McAvoy v. H.M.A.*, 1991 S.C.C.R. 123; *Blair v. H.M.A.*, 1993 S.C.C.R. 483; *Chalmers v. H.M.A.*, 1994 S.C.C.R. 651; *Brotherston v. H.M.A.*, 1995 S.C.C.R. 613; *Webb v. H.M.A.*, 1997 170; *Keavney v. H.M.A.*, 1999 S.L.T. 1030; *Ferguson v. H.M.A.*, 2000 S.C.C.R. 954; and *Hughes v. H.M.A.*, 2000 S.C.C.R. 250.

Finally, in spite of the obvious perils of the "dock identification", in which the accused is pointed out by a witness in court, often while sitting in the dock flanked by uniformed police officers, it has been held that such identifications are perfectly acceptable, even when the public have been cleared from the court—see *Dudley v. H.M.A.*, 1995 S.C.C.R. 52.

10. Manuel v. H.M.A.
1958 J.C. 41

The accused was convicted of seven murders. The evidence against him in relation to one of the charges consisted of a statement made by him in which he referred to his disposal of the victim's body and items of her clothing. There was further evidence that he led the police to the place he had mentioned in the statement and that at that place they found the body and the clothing he had referred to. He appealed on the ground that the statement and the evidence of the finding of the body and clothes were insufficient evidence to justify conviction.

LORD JUSTICE-GENERAL (CLYDE): "This brings me to the sixth ground of appeal, which relates to the murder of Isabelle Cooke. The evidence for the Crown here was the appellant's confession, plus the fact that the appellant led the police to the place where they found that the appellant had buried the murdered girl's body and the fact that the appellant showed them where he had hidden one of her shoes just before, or immediately after, he had murdered her. The argument for the appellant was that all the evidence relating to the finding of the body and the shoe was so closely related to, and bound up with, the confession itself, that it could not constitute legal corroboration of the confession, as the presiding Judge directed the jury that it could. It was submitted that, in order to constitute proper legal corroboration, there must be some independent fact incriminating the accused, altogether apart from the statements or confessions which he may have made. If, it was said, the confession was rejected as inadmissible, the facts which came to light in consequence of it must be rejected also; and a passage in Alison on Criminal Law, vol. ii, p.584, was founded on in support of this contention. But if the confession is not rejected, and was properly before the jury and was accepted by them, then by the law of Scotland the confirmation of the contents of the confession by the finding of the murdered girl's body and the shoe in the very field where the appellant has confessed that he buried them, and in the very spots where he had confessed that he had hidden them, can be sufficient corroboration to entitle the jury to convict the appellant. The matter is precisely covered in terms which might have been written for this case in a passage in Alison on Criminal Law, vol. ii., p.580, where the learned author says: 'If a person is apprehended on a charge of theft, and he tells the officer who seized him, that if he will go to such a place, and look under such a bush, he will find the stolen goods; or he is charged with murder or assault, and he says that he threw the bloody weapon into such a pool, in such a river, and it is there searched for and found; without doubt, these are such strong confirmations of the truth of the confession, as renders it of itself sufficient, if the corpus is established aliunde, to convict the prisoner.' We were referred to the case of *Connolly v. H.M.A.*, 1958 S.L.T. 79. But I can see nothing in that case which in any way detracts from the clear and unequivocal statement which I have just quoted from Alison. Indeed in that case the present point did not arise. For in that case there was a series of quite independent facts which, in the view of the Court, constituted all the corroboration of the confession which was needed. As the Lord Justice-Clerk indicated towards the end of his opinion, it was not necessary for the Court in that case to consider whether, and to what extent, the evidence establishing the truth of the confession could serve the additional function of providing legal corroboration of it. In the present case we are satisfied that the direction of the presiding Judge in regard to the finding of the body and the shoe, to the effect that they could constitute corroboration of the confession, was quite proper and correct."

NOTES

The logic and authority of this case is difficult to dispute, at least in the situation where the accused leads the police to other evidence which only the perpetrator of the offence, or someone closely involved in its perpetration, could have known about. In fact, the law is not now based on this idea and focuses instead merely on the knowledge displayed in the confession itself—see cases such as *Wilson v. H.M.A.*, below.

11. Wilson v. H.M.A.
1987 S.C.C.R. 217

The two appellants in this case were charged with the murder of a young girl and with gross indecency, both on the same date. The latter charge was later dropped by the Crown. The evidence against them consisted of detailed confessions made separately by each to the police about a month after the murder took place. By the time the confessions were made, details of the murder were widely known and they appealed against their convictions for murder on the ground that their confessions provided insufficient evidence to convict. The victim was the half-sister of the second appellant, Murray.

LORD JUSTICE-GENERAL (EMSLIE): "The evidence at the trial disclosed that the body of the girl had been found by three children who called three other children, and later some adults, to see what they had discovered. It was lying near the bottom of a steep slope below a footpath and it was observed that the girl, naked apart from her socks, was lying on her back spread-eagled, up the slope, with her arms above her head.

There was something round her neck, her jacket was on her arms, and the ground between the path and where she was found was 'all flattened out'. In fact the girl had been strangled with her brassiere. An intensive police investigation then took place over a period of three and a half weeks. It was thought that more than one person had been involved and that they probably belonged to the local Drumchapel community. Many people were interviewed. House-to-house enquiries were made. The assistance of Radio Clyde was obtained and it was disclosed in a broadcast that the girl had been strangled with her brassiere. It appears, too, that those who had seen the body in the wood told relatives and friends what they had observed and that all the members of the Murray family were told by the police that the girl had been murdered, that she had been sexually assaulted but not raped, and that her body had been almost completely naked. In the course of the police investigations each of the appellants was interviewed. Each stated that they had been out together on the day of the murder but, since there were discrepancies in the two accounts, each was seen again to try to clear them up. There was no particular suspicion of the appellants but on this second interview each revealed that they had been in the vicinity of the wood at a time very close to the time of the crime. Although there were still discrepancies in the accounts given by the two appellants, no further progress was made until Sunday June 15, 1986.

On that day Murray was taken into custody and to Drumchapel Police Station in connection with allegations that he had had sexual relations with a girl who was under sixteen years of age. At about midday, at the request of the police, Wilson went to Clydebank Police Station to discuss his earlier statements further. The remarkable thing is that each, in separate police stations, then made a detailed confession of guilt of the murder which, subject to quite insignificant differences of detail, was identical. The essential details disclosed in each of the accounts given by the appellants tallied precisely with what had been found at the scene of the crime. The circumstances in which these detailed confessions were made—and there is now no suggestion that they were unfairly obtained—and the contents of each confession are described at length by the trial judge in his charge to the jury . . . We refer to that passage of the charge for its terms and do not find it necessary to repeat the sordid story here. Suffice to say that each appellant introduced his confession by explaining that the two of them had been engaged in disgusting homosexual practices in the wood when the half-sister of Murray passed by and observed what they were doing. The appellants were terrified that she would report what she had seen to her parents and they then proceeded to make sure that she would be unable to do that.

The case for the Crown at the trial depended essentially upon these confessions, corrobo-rated by evidence of the accuracy of the detailed knowledge of the crime and the manner of its commission which each confession contained. The Crown position was that the jury should be satisfied that the appellants could not and would not have made the detailed statements which they did if they had not been present at the commission of the crime

In these appeals against conviction, counsel for each appellant very properly accepted that no criticism could legitimately be made against the careful directions given by the trial judge to the jury upon the way in which they should approach their task in this case. The jury were in particular directed that it was for them to decide whether the only reasonable explanation for the knowledge of the details of the crime disclosed in each of the confessions made in different police stations was that the appellants were the perpetrators of the crime. The submission made by counsel for each respondent in different language was that having regard to the widespread knowledge of the details of the murder, the case against the appellants should not have been allowed to go to the jury at all. In other words, it was said that the trial judge should have acquitted each appellant at the end of the Crown case upon the ground that the evidence of the accuracy of the appellants' detailed knowledge of the crime, contained in the statement of each of them, was in the special circumstances of his case incapable of being regarded as providing the corroboration required by law (see section 140A of the Criminal Procedure

(Scotland) Act 1975). In this connection the only reported case to which reference was made was *McAvoy v. H.M.A.*, 1982 S.C.C.R. 263 in which Lord Hunter said this:

'I am satisfied that in the circumstances disclosed to this court the ratio of such cases as *Connolly v. H.M.A.*, 1958 S.L.T. 79 and *Manuel v. H.M.A.*, 1958 J.C. 41 applied. I refer in this connection to the charge of the learned sheriff, which in my opinion dealt very adequately with this aspect of the case. I would only add that it is not, in my opinion, necessarily fatal to the application of the ratio of the cases to which I have referred that persons other than the accused had become aware of the facts and circumstances used as corroboration of a detailed confession before the confession itself had been made. This, however, does not mean to say that passage of time between the date of the crime and the date of a detailed confession is of no moment, since such a delay might in some circumstances make it more likely that an accused person had acquired his knowledge of detail not as a perpetrator of the crime or offence but as a recipient of information from other sources.'

In our opinion the trial judge would not have been entitled in this case to sustain a motion that there was no case to answer. There was, in law, quite sufficient evidence capable of providing corroboration of these remarkable, almost identical, confessions made by each appellant in separate police stations to the appalling murder of the half-sister of Murray. Each provided an identical and powerful motive for the dreadful crime, and was redolent of having been made by someone who had been present when the crime was committed. The evidence of the coincidence between the details of the killing which each confessed disclosed, and what was found after the event, was sufficient in law for corroborative purposes if the jury were prepared to find that the accurate knowledge of the crime revealed in the statements of each appellant was his own knowledge as one of the perpetrators. It was not for the trial judge to evaluate the weight which should be given to the circumstance that by June 15, 1986 many people knew or had heard of many of the details of the crime. That was essentially a matter for the jury to consider under the proper directions which were given and that, indeed, is precisely what Lord Hunter had in mind when he said what he did in *McAvoy*. Well though each appeal was presented, we have no doubt that each must be refused."

NOTES

The direction approved in this case is *not* to the effect that the jury must be satisfied that only the perpetrator could have had the knowledge possessed by the accused, but simply that the jury are satisfied that the accused gained the information by reason of his or her participation in the crime. The development of the "self-corroborating" confession has been widely criticised—see Gordon, *At the Mouth of Two Witnesss: Some Comments on Corroboration in "Justice and Crime"* (Hunter, (ed.) 1993), and McCannell, "Special Knowledge Confessions", 1993 S.L.G. 142. It is one thing to say, as in *Manuel*, that a confession may be confirmed by the discovery of evidence previously unknown to the authorities, and quite another to say, as in *Wilson*, that confessions may be corroborated simply by the presence in the confession of facts or knowledge which already known to the police and which indeed may be public knowledge. If the purpose of seeking corroboration in such cases is to avoid the acceptance of a confession which is "phoney or quixotic" in some way, then it seems unlikely that the present view of the law fulfils that purpose. This is particularly so where "special knowledge" accepted as corroborative is shown to be inaccurate or false—as in *Gilmour v. H.M.A.*, 1982 S.C.C.R. 590. The use of special knowledge confessions reached its nadir in the case of *Macdonald v. H.M.A.*, 1987 S.C.C.R. 581, in which the statement accepted as showing special knowledge was "I told you, I did that one with Kenny and Bruce", where there were two co-accused whose first names were Kenneth and Bruce. There have been suggestions, however, that there are limits to the extent to which self-corroborating confessions will be accepted—see *Woodland v. Hamilton*, 1990 S.C.C.R. 166; and *Low v. H.M.A.*, 1993 S.C.C.R. 493. In *Woodland*, Lord Sutherland said:

"We consider that the test to be applied is whether the matters about which an accused person speaks are things of which he would have no reason to be aware if he was not the perpetrator of the crime. Putting it another way, does he have special knowledge, the only reasonable explanation of which is that he was the perpetrator."

It is not clear, however that the two forms proposed by Lord Sutherland come to the same thing. In *Cairns v. Howdle*, 2000 S.C.C.R. 742, the High Court rested its judgment only on the second part of that test and rejected a defence argument that whenever an accused person, as in *Cairns*, could have obtained his knowledge simply by witnessing the offence, the doctrine of self-corroboration could not apply.

Low holds that where it is proposed to rely upon a special knowledge confession, that confession must be proved by two witnesses. This is in contrast to "ordinary" confessions, which may be spoken to by a single witness, since they are corroborated by other witnesses. In *Mitchell v. H.M.A.*, 1996 S.C.C.R. 97, however, it was held that it is enough if the confession is spoken to by two witnesses; it is not necessary that two witnesses speak to every element in the confession relied upon as demonstrating special knowledge. In *Smith v. Lees*, 1997 S.L.T. 690, Lord McCluskey hinted that the time was ripe was a reconsideration of this area of the law. *Cairns* appears to demonstrate, however, that the High Court may be slow to act upon that hint.

12. Moorov v. H.M.A.
1930 J.C. 68

The accused was charged with a series of assaults and indecent assaults against female employees, all except one of which took place at short intervals over a period of about three years. At his appeal the question arose as to whether evidence in relation to the separate charges could corroborate one another.

LORD JUSTICE-GENERAL (CLYDE): "The question in the present case belongs to the department of circumstantial evidence. This consideration is vital to the whole matter; and I do not think the real question in the case can be understood or appreciated otherwise. In a case of purely circumstantial evidence there may be no direct proof at all of the *factum probandum*; yet each circumstance is held to be sufficiently supported by the evidence of a single credible witness. The explanation is that 'the aptitude and coherence of the several circumstance often as fully confirm the truth of the story, as if all the witnesses were deponing to the same facts'— Hume on Crimes, vol.ii, p.384. The *factum probandum* starts as a simple hypothesis; but it becomes a *factum probatum* as soon as it is seen to coincide with the conclusion to which the several circumstances (when collated) necessarily lead according to human knowledge and experience.

In the present case there is direct evidence in support of the *factum probandum* as regards each charge which the jury found proved. But the evidence is that of a single credible witness only to each charge. Corroboration is sought from the circumstance that the charges thus supported are numerous and of the same kind, and the question is whether the case is one in which resort may legitimately be had to corroboration derived from this circumstance.

It is beyond doubt, in the law of Scotland, that corroboration may be found in this way, provided that the similar charges are sufficiently connected with, or related to, each other— Hume on Crimes, vol. ii, p.384; Alison's Criminal Law, vol. ii, p.552. But what is the test of sufficiency? The test I think is whether the evidence of the single witnesses as a whole— although each of them speaks to a different charge—leads by necessary inference to the establishment of some circumstance or state of fact underlying and connecting the several charges, which, if it had been independently established, would have afforded corroboration of the evidence given by the single witnesses in support of the separate charges. If such a circumstance or state of fact was actually established by independent evidence, it would not occur to anyone to doubt that it might be properly used to corroborate the evidence of each single witness. The case is the same, when such a circumstance is established by an inference necessarily arising on the evidence of the single witnesses, as a whole. The only difference is that the drawing of such an inference is apt to be a much more difficult and delicate affair than the consideration of independent evidence. No merely superficial connection in time, character, and circumstance between the repeated acts—important as these factors are—will satisfy the test I have endeavoured to formulate. Before the evidence of single credible witnesses to separate acts can provide material for mutual corroboration, the connection between the separate acts (indicated by their external relation in time, character, or circumstance) must be such as to exhibit them as subordinates in some particular and ascertained unity of intent, project, campaign, or adventure, which lies beyond or behind—but is related to—the separate acts. The existence of such an underlying unity, comprehending and governing the separate acts, provides the necessary connecting link between them, and becomes a circumstance in which corroboration of the evidence of the single witnesses in support of the separate acts may be found—whether the existence of such underlying unity is established by independent evidence, or by necessary inference from the evidence of the single witnesses themselves, regarded as a whole. It is just here, however, that the pinch comes, in such a case as the present. The Lord Advocate spoke as if it would be enough to show from the evidence of the single witnesses that the facts had occurred in what he called 'a course of criminal conduct'. Risk of confusion lurks behind a phrase of that kind; for it might correctly enough be applied to the everyday class of case in which a criminal recurs from time to time to the commission of the same kind of offence in similar circumstances. It might be justly said, in relation to the evidence in support of any indictment in which a number of such similar crimes committed over a period of (say) three years are charged together, that the accused had been following 'a course of criminal conduct'. If any of the crimes in the series had formed the subject of a former prosecution or prosecutions, and convictions had been obtained, neither the commission of such former crimes nor the previous convictions could afford any material for corroborating the evidence of a single witness in support of the last member of the series. And therefore—especially in view of the growing practice of accumulating charges in one indictment—it is of the utmost importance to the interests of justice that the 'course of criminal conduct' must be shown to be one which not only consists of a series of offences, the same in kind, committed under similar circumstances, or in a common locus—these are after all no more than external resemblances—but which owes its source and development to some underlying circumstance or state of fact such as I have endeavoured, though necessarily in very general terms, to define."

NOTES

The so-called "Moorov Doctrine" appears to have its origins in the cases referred to in Hume ii, p.385:

"The evidence of single witnesses has been held sufficient even to establish separate acts of the same crime. In July 1738, Thomas Souter, and James Hog, minister of the Parish of Caputh, were prosecuted at the instance of Hagart of Cairnmuir, for the crime of attempting to suborn false evidence against him; and of this the libel charged a number of instances, which had happened at different times and places, and with different persons. The jury 'found that the crime of subornation, or endeavouring to suborn people to be witnesses, as libelled, against the pannel, Mr James Hog, proven in sundry facts, each fact *only* by one single witness . . .

In this instance, the several acts, though all of one sort, were truly distinct crimes, being attempts on the conscience of several persons, though relative chiefly to one and same charge, that of fire-raising, and thus far connected one with another. That judgement affords therefore an inference *a fortiori*, with respect to those cases where the accusation is truly of the same crime, such as adultery or incest, committed with the same person on sundry occasions, or during a certain period of time. That is to say, such a charge may be made good, though there be no concurrence of testimony as to any one act of incest or adultery, but only a number of witnesses, each deponing to that act which fell under his own observation . . . But there seems to be little risk of so extensive a combination among witnesses, to swear a falsehood; and indeed persons conspiring to destroy the fame or state of any one, are not likely to lay their project in that way, but rather to support each other in the proof of some single act. Certainly, however, no inference is to be made from such a case as that of *Hog*, to one where the several acts, though of the same crime, have no sort of relation to or connection with each other; as for instance, in the case of successive acts of uttering forged notes to different persons, and at different times and places."

It seems that what Hume had in mind, in allowing the possibility of mutual corroboration, was the situation in which each separate incident of, for example, uttering, is related by some underlying purpose, such as a more general, unified, fraudulent scheme. This is what the court in *Moorov* attempts to emphasise when it speaks of the need to show an "underlying unity of intent, project, campaign or adventure". It seems fairly clear, however, that the law has moved on from this position, so that all that is now required is a course of conduct involving the same or similar crimes.

The House of Lords in England have, incidentally, approved of the *Moorov* principle—see *R. v. Kilbourne*, [1973] A.C. 729, and particularly Lord Simon of Glaisdale's comments on corroboration at p.758 where he says:

"[Corroboration] is required because experience has shown that there is a real risk that an innocent person may be convicted unless certain evidence against an accused . . . is confirmed by other evidence. Corroboration is therefore nothing other than evidence which 'confirms' or 'strengthens' or 'supports' other evidence . . . It is, in short, evidence which renders other evidence more probable. If so, there is no essential difference between, on the one hand, corroboration and, on the other, 'supporting evidence' or 'evidence which helps to determine the truth of the matter'. Each is evidence which makes other evidence more probable. Once it is accepted that the direct evidence on one count is relevant to another by way of circumstantial evidence, it follows that it is available as corroboration if corroboration is required. Whether it operates as such depends on what weight the jury attaches to it, and what inferences the jury draws as to whether the offences demonstrate an underlying unity. For that purpose, the jury will be directed to take into account the proximity in time of the offences, their multiplicity, their similarity in detail and circumstance, whether such similarity has any unusual feature, what, if any, risk there is of collaboration in presenting a false case, and any other matter which tends to suggest or rebut an underlying unity—a system—something which would cause common sense to revolt at a hypothesis of mere co-incidence."

The model directions in relation to mutual corroboration are interesting, and probably rather fuller than the directions typically given to juries in *Moorov* cases in Scotland.

13.   Ogg v. H.M.A.
1938 J.C. 152

The accused was charged with a number of offences involving "gross indecency" with other men. The incidents were said to have taken place on various occasions between January 1, 1930 and June 1, 1937. The precise dates of some of the incidents were unknown and the time intervals between the incidents relatively long, and the alleged offences all took place at different locations.

LORD JUSTICE-CLERK (AITCHISON): "I come now to the main question which the appeal raises, *viz.*, whether, taking the four offences of which the appellant was found guilty, each offence can be taken as corroborating, or as tending to corroborate, each of the others. The evidence of the offences of which the appellant was acquitted must be left out of account. All four offences were sexual in character and were instances of sex perversion. In each case the victim of the offence was a stranger; in each case he was accosted by the appellant. The question is whether these similarities in character and circumstance are sufficient to allow the law of *Moorov* to be applied. *Moorov* is a decision of the highest authority by a Court of seven judges which authoritatively laid down the general proposition in relation to sexual crimes, although not entirely limited to such crimes, that similar sexual crimes each deponed to by a single credible witness may afford mutual corroboration, provided always that they are so inter-related by character, circumstances and time—the presence of all these features is not essential—as to justify an inference that they are instances of a course of criminal conduct systematically pursued by the accused person. That is a most valuable doctrine of our criminal law, and nothing to be said in this case is to be read as in any way whitt[l]ing down that doctrine or impugning the authority of *Moorov's* case, even if it were in the power of [t]his Court to impugn the authority of that case. The only question is—Is there a sufficient basis of fact for the application of the doctrine of *Moorov* in this case?

Whether one offence can be used in proof of another depends in every case upon whether it is relevant to proof of that other. The only test is relevancy. In some cases inter-relation is plain and no difficulty arises. Forgery of a will may be relevant to a charge of murder, or the theft of a motor car to a charge of bank robbery. The difficulty arises where the inter-relation is not direct and obvious, and the question must depend upon the circumstances of the individual case. Where the inter-relation is sought between similar offences as in this case, it must be possible to say that there is not only a series of separate similar offences, but that there is a reasonable and practical certainty, based not on conjecture of suspicion, nor a mere moral certainty, that the similar offences are instances of one course of criminal conduct persistently pursued by the accused person. In deciding such a question the relation of the offences in time is a most material consideration. If the intervals of time between the offences are substantial, an inference of their inter-relation becomes difficult and, as a matter of evidence, may be impossible to draw. In the present case the dates are important. Offences 2 and 3, according to W.K., were committed on a date approximately September 15, 1934; offence 6, according to L.I.J., was committed some time between September and November 1935; and offence 13, according to T.L., was committed in June 1937. The intervals of time therefore were between offences 2 and 3 and offence 6, one year, and between offence 6 and offence 13 approximately 18 months.

As I have said, the doctrine of *Moorov* is a valuable doctrine, but it must be applied with great caution. If it is not applied with caution there is a danger that evidence showing a general disposition to commit some kind of offence might be treated as corroboration. That must always be guarded against, and the doctrine ought not to be applied unless interrelation of the similar offences in some substantial sense can be with certainty affirmed. I have come to the conclusion in the present case that the conviction of the appellant upon charges 2, 3 and 6 cannot be supported upon the evidence through failure of corroboration, in respect that there was not a sufficient basis for the application of the doctrine of *Moorov*, and that the conviction upon these charges must be set aside."

NOTES

Although in this case, the conviction was set aside on the grounds that there was insufficient temporal connection between the offences, the court's reference to the fact that the charges were all instances of "sex perversion", illustrates the danger in *Moorov* cases that the "underlying unity" necessary to the invocation of the doctrine becomes equated merely with propensity to commit a particular sort of crime. Any "course of criminal conduct" may be characterised in this way, as, to some extent, the court in *Moorov* recognised. The charges of simple assault in that case were said to be unfounded since "although all the acts flowed from a certain erotic propensity on the part of the appellant . . . that is saying no more than that they were all of the same kind—like a series of unconnected thefts by a servant who is prone to thieving from his master's wardrobe". The nine charges of indecent assault, on the other hand, were said to be evidence of "a campaign of lustful indulgence at the expense of his female employees". Although the High Court has emphasised—see, *e.g. Tudhope v. Hazleton*, 1984 S.C.C.R. 455—that a mere similarity between incidents is insufficient to invoke *Moorov*, it is arguable that the criterion for allowing mutual corroboration is more akin to a requirement for a "striking similarity" between the incidents—compare, for example, *Hay v. Wither*, 1988 S.C.C.R. 334, the "borderline" case of *Turner v. Scott*, 1996 S.L.T. 200 and English cases such as *DPP v. Boardman* [1975] A.C. 421. See also Lord Justice-Clerk Wheatley in *Tudhope v. Hazleton*, 1984 S.C.C.R. 455 where he says:

"The phrase 'course of conduct' did not commend itself to Lord Justice General Clyde in *Moorov*, but it is a phrase which has been much used by judges in recent years, and as long as the reservations expressed by Lord Clyde are borne in mind, it seems to me to be a phrase which aptly focuses this important factor for the benefit of a judge or a jury".

Finally, how closely is this case (and the *Moorov* doctrine generally) connected to cases such as *H.M.A. v. Joseph*, 1929 J.C. 55, considered in Chapter 9 below?

14. Carpenter v. Hamilton
1994 S.C.C.R. 109

The appellant in this case was charged with (1) breach of the peace and (2) indecent exposure. The relevant facts are set out in the opinion of Lord Justice-General Hope.

LORD JUSTICE-GENERAL (HOPE): "By way of background to what we have to say on the *Moorov* doctrine, we should describe a little more the two incidents as they are narrated in the findings of fact. So far as the first incident is concerned, which occurred at about 6 p.m. on February 9, 1993, the complainer was walking alone in the park and the appellant was walking towards her in the opposite direction. As he passed her he made an audible sound with his mouth which the complainer described in her evidence as a 'Hannibal Lector slither' and which she was able to describe in more detail by reference to a character in a well-known film. She described this sound as disgusting, and the sheriff made a finding to the effect that the sound was suggestive of indecency, intimacy and violence. Once he had passed the complainer the appellant stopped and stared at her directly as she walked away from him. He then left the path and proceeded to follow her over a distance, running parallel to it and dodging in and out of bushes, disappearing and reappearing as he did so. The elements of the conduct which are described in these findings involve the initial approach, the making of a sound which was suggestive, among other things, of indecency, and the continuation of contact after making the sound, all without actually making any physical contact with the complainer.

So far as the second incident is concerned, which occurred at about 6 p.m. on April 16, 1993, the complainer was once again walking through the park in the opposite direction to that being taken by the appellant. As the appellant was walking towards the complainer he had his hands in the pockets of his jeans. As he approached her he moved his hands away from his thighs in such a manner that his penis, which was hanging out of his trousers, was exposed to the complainer. She was taken aback and angered by the conduct of the appellant. So far as this incident is concerned then, there is the initial approach and there is the act of indecency which is described in the charge and was spoken to by the complainer, with whom the appellant did not make any physical contact.

In his submissions today Mr Muir submitted that the offences were not so closely connected in time, place and circumstances as to enable the *Moorov* doctrine to be applied. So far as time, place and circumstances in general were concerned, however, there really was nothing much to be said for that submission. The place was the same, the time was 6 p.m. in the evening on days which were within three months of each other, and the general circumstances as we narrated them were broadly similar. But Mr Muir made the point that if one looked more closely at the nature of the conduct there was insufficient in the character of each activity to provide the necessary link. He accepted that the suggestive noise was suggestive of indecency, but he submitted that there was a material difference in the activity which was spoken to by the two complainers. He suggested also that the second charge, that of shameless indecency, was a more serious charge than the first, and that on that basis also there was no opportunity for the first charge, which was spoken to by the complainer to whom the suggestive noise was made, to corroborate the second.

He supported these submissions by reference to what was said in *Farrell v. Normand*. In that case there was a material difference between two charges of breach of the peace, and the court concluded that although there were similarities the charges were in essence so different that the rule of *Moorov* could not be relied upon. The Lord Justice-Clerk pointed out at p.862 in that case that the principal feature of one charge was the making of an indecent suggestion, whereas in the other there was no such allegation and the terms of the second charge were simply in the standard form of disorderly conduct. The conclusion reached in that case was that there was such a material difference between the essential features of the two charges that it was not one where one could affirm that the rule of *Moorov* would apply.

In her response to these submissions the learned advocate-depute submitted that the *nomen juris* of each crime was not the test. She invited us to look at the nature of the conduct, and to examine the question whether there was an underlying similarity in it which would provide the necessary link. She referred to a number of authorities in that connection. There was *H.M. Advocate v. Cox*, where the trial judge held that a charge of incest and a charge of sodomy did not involve crimes of the same type and accordingly that *Moorov* did not apply. By way of contrast there was *P v. H.M.A.*, where the trial judge took the opposite view in a case involving child abuse of a sexual nature amounting to rape and sodomy. She referred especially to *Hay v. Wither*, where there were two charges of breach of the peace. One of these involved the accosting of a young male person by the appellant together with an embrace, which although not charged as an indecent assault might well have been, and the other was a breach of the peace involving the accosting of another young male person by the appellant. In that case the sheriff's decision that the necessary link was present was upheld on appeal. The Lord Justice-Clerk noted that there had been, in each case, an accosting, and he said that that was enough to provide the required underlying similarity. So far as the facts here were concerned, the advocate-depute's submission was that there was something amounting to an accosting and the activity on each occasion was broadly and sufficiently similar to justify the application of the doctrine.

We recognise that these cases must always be approached with care, and that is particularly so where, as in this instance, only two charges are before the court. There must be an underlying similarity between them to enable the conclusion to be drawn that there is a course of conduct which was being persisted in by the appellant. Questions of fact and degree, however, are raised in a case such as we have here. The sheriff had to assess the question whether one charge was more serious than the other, and he had to consider also whether the nature of the conduct in each case had the required underlying similarity.

The sheriff tells us in his note that he considered that there were aspects in the evidence relating to the first charge which enabled him to think that it was on balance more serious than the second, although by looking simply at the terms of the two charges one might form a different conclusion. We have reached the view that, on that issue, he was entitled to take the view that he did, weighing up all the evidence. So far as the remaining matter is concerned, which is whether the underlying similarity is present, he found that the suggestive noise was suggestive, among other things, of indecency. There was the underlying similarity of character whereby, in very similar circumstances, at the same place and at the same time the appellant approached the complainer and conducted himself in a manner suggestive in both cases of indecency but without making physical contact with the complainer. Treating the question, therefore, as one of nature and degree, given the closeness of the two charges to each other in time, place and general circumstances, we have reached the view that the sheriff was entitled to come to the conclusion which he did, and that he was entitled to convict the appellant on the second charge as well as on the first."

NOTES

Hume spoke of the need to show that the various incidents relied upon for mutual corroboration were examples of the "same crime". That view has gradually been eroded, until the point has been reached where mutual corroboration is possible in cases involving legally distinct crimes which are merely similar in nature. It remains the case, however, that the commission of one crime can be corroborated by evidence relating to another, less serious nature. "The greater includes the lesser, but not vice versa"—see *H.M.A. v. Brown*, 1970 S.L.T. 121; *Hutchison v. H.M.A.*, 1998 S.L.T. 679.

It should be emphasised that there were two separate complainers in this case, and it is clear that this is a bare minimum for the operation of the doctrine. However, it is possible to invoke the doctrine where the charges arise out of, and the complainers were involved in the same incident—see *Quinn v. Lowe*, 1992 S.L.T. 701.

It has been accepted that the doctrine can be applied in cases other than those involving sexual offences—*Tudhope v. Hazleton* and *Carpenter v. Hamilton*, above, are examples of this. In *Wilson v. H.M.A.*, 2001 S.L.T. 1203, however, it was held that the *Moorov* doctrine could be applied to two charges of theft in which the nature of the items stolen was different. It might be argued that this conflicts with the case of *Carson v. McGlennan*, 2000 S.L.T. 810 in which it was held that the identity of the property stolen is one of the crucial facts requiring corroboration. On this point, see also Lord McCluskey's opinion in *Smith v. Lees*, 1997 S.L.T. 690, above. It is submitted that the matter is one which requires clarification, particularly since *Moorov* cases involving charges of theft are likely to be common. Lord Marnoch dissented in *Wilson* and said that:

". . . I am in no doubt that the jury was entitled to hold that in respect of both charges the crime of theft of 'something' had been established. However, with the greatest of respect to your Lordship in the chair, I find it difficult to see how evidence of the loss of a camera can corroborate loss of a bag, purse and £472 or thereby of money, a bus pass and card, or vice versa.

[4] Speaking for myself, I might, I think, have been prepared to consider substituting a verdict of guilty on both charges in respect of 'household goods', or the like but, in the absence of argument, I express no concluded view as to whether such a description would have been appropriate or, indeed, sufficiently precise. I mention the possibility only to make the point that, while I respectfully agree with your Lordship that the *Moorov* doctrine could, in appropriate circumstances, be applied to proof of items stolen, that, in my view, would only be so where the various items are capable of some generic description."

15. Howden v. H.M.A.
1994 S.C.C.R. 19

The appellant was charged with two robberies, one from a building society, and one from a bank. The incidents took place in Edinburgh, within two weeks of each other, and in similar circumstances. There was a positive identification of the appellant in relation to the incident at the building society, but not in relation to the one at the bank.

LORD JUSTICE-GENERAL (HOPE): "The appellant is John Howden who was found guilty in the High Court at Edinburgh of attempting to carry out an armed robbery at premises occupied by the National & Provincial Building Society at 213 Morningside Road, Edinburgh, on August 21, 1992. He was also found guilty of carrying out an armed robbery at premises occupied by the Bank of Scotland at 263 Canongate, Edinburgh, about 2 weeks later on September 3, 1992. The weapon which he was said to have had with him on both occasions was a handgun, and there were additional charges under section 17(2) and (5) of the Firearms Act 1968 in respect of and ancillary to the two principal offences.

The appellant has not sought to challenge his conviction on the first offence and its associated charge under the Firearms Act 1968. He accepts that there was sufficient evidence to identify him as the perpetrator of the attempted robbery at that address. But he has appealed against his conviction so far as it relates to the second incident, together with the associated charge under the Firearms Act, on the ground that there was sufficient evidence to identify him as the perpetrator. He also submits that there was a misdirection by the trial judge as to the approach which they might take to the evidence.

So far as the first incident is concerned, it is clear that there was ample evidence to identify him as the person who entered the [building society] and attempted to commit the robbery. Three employees of the building society identified the appellant in positive terms and they gave other evidence about him which formed the basis for later directions by the trial judge.

So far as the second incident is concerned, however, the three witnesses in the bank premises who gave evidence were unable to say positively that the appellant was the perpetrator. As the trial judge put in his charge to the jury . . . the evidence of these witnesses was somewhat tentative and it was clear from what he then said that the jury could not properly convict the appellant on the charges relating to this incident on the evidence of these eyewitnesses alone.

It was in the light of that feature of the evidence that he then proceeded to direct the jury . . . to the effect that, if they were to conclude that the same person must inevitably have been responsible for both incidents, the question would then become 'Who was that person?' and that they would then be entitled to look at any evidence which they thought helpful to decide what the answer to that question should be. He went on to say that they would be entitled to test their conclusion by looking at the identification given by the witnesses in the building society, in other words to take the positive identification of the appellant in regard to the first charge, and by means of circumstantial evidence to link the appellant with the second incident in the bank and conclude that he was responsible for that incident also.

The submission which has been advanced today by Miss Johnston in support of the ground of appeal proceeded upon the basis that what the trial judge was really doing was seeking to apply the *Moorov* doctrine to this case, although she accepted that it was not precisely the type of case to which that doctrine applied. She took as her starting point the observation in *Coffey v. Houston* at p.207B that the *Moorov* doctrine is available to be applied where one has the evidence of at least two credible witnesses, one speaking to each of the incidents which have been charged against the accused. In the present case there was no dispute that there was a positive identification in regard to the first incident. But so far as the second incident is concerned, it is clear that there was no positive identification at all. That being so, said Miss Johnston, it was not open to the trial judge to direct the jury that they should attempt to link the appellant with the second offence by pointing to the fact that he had been identified as the perpetrator of the first. She said that he had taken the wrong starting point by inviting them to look at the similarity of the two incidents. What he should have done was ask them whether they were able to find a positive identification by at least one witness that he was responsible for the second incident. The implication of her argument was that, unless the jury could conclude that at least one of those in the bank identified the appellant positively as the perpetrator, then there was no basis for the exercise which the trial judge was inviting the jury to carry out, which was to look to the similarities between the two incidents as disclosed by the evidence in order to decide whether it has been proved that he was the perpetrator of both of these.

We should add that there were a number of points of similarity to which the trial judge drew attention in the course of his charge. These have been set out in detail in the trial judge's report and we do not need to set them out in detail for the purposes of this opinion. There were eight points of one kind or another relating to clothing, conduct and things said and other such matters which the jury could look at to enable them to reach the conclusion that it was the same person who was responsible for both incidents. Miss Johnston said there was no necessary identity on all these points and that there were differences. But in the end of the day such differences as there might have been were not crucial to the argument which she wished to support. As we indicated earlier, the crucial point she made was that, without at least one positive identification from a witness in the bank, the exercise of looking to the similarities was misconceived.

In our opinion the present case has nothing to do with the *Moorov* doctrine, and the approach which the trial judge invited the jury to follow was a sound one and there was no misdirection. The jury had available to them evidence from which they could conclude, based on the identifications given by the three employees there, that the appellant was the perpetrator of the incident in the building society. They were warned that the evidence of the employees in the bank was not of that character and that for this reason they could not convict the appellant of the second offence without some other evidence. What the trial judge then invited them to do was to look to the circumstantial evidence to examine the question whether it was proved beyond reasonable doubt that it was the same person who committed both offences. The strength or otherwise of the identifications of the person who committed the offence in the bank was not of any importance in these circumstances, so long as the jury were satisfied beyond reasonable doubt by the circumstantial evidence that it was the same person who was responsible for both of them, and so long as they were satisfied beyond reasonable doubt that the appellant was the perpetrator of at least one of these offences. That approach was the one which the jury were told they could follow, and is to be presumed from their verdict that they followed it.

In all the circumstances we are not persuaded that there was a miscarriage of justice in this case, and we shall refuse the appeal."

NOTES

It was for long thought to be the law that in any case in which *Moorov* was invoked, there had to a positive identification of the accused in respect of each incident relied upon—see *e.g. McRae v. H.M.A.*, 1975 S.L.T. 174. It has been held, however, that the identification need not be by an eye-witness, and may be by way of circumstantial evidence—*Lindsay v. H.M.A.*, 1994 S.L.T. 546. Does *Howden* simply represent a logical extension of this trend? Alternatively, is it correct to claim, as the court does in this case, that *Howden* is not a case about *Moorov* at all, but is purely and simply a case about circumstantial evidence? If the latter alternative is correct, where does this leave the *Moorov* doctrine in general and the requirement for a positive identification in each case in particular? *Townsley v. Lees*, 1996 S.L.T. 1182 confirms the decision in *Howden*, and arguably, extends it, since in *Howden*, there was at least a sufficiency of evidence in relation to one of the charges. That was not the case in *Townsley v. Lees*.

16.   Fisher v. Guild
1991 S.L.T. 253

LORD JUSTICE-GENERAL (HOPE): "The appellant is Julian Paul Fisher who was found guilty at the sheriff court in Kirkcaldy of five offences under the Road Traffic Act 1988. The first of these was driving a motor vehicle with an excess of alcohol in his breath, contrary to section 5(1)(a) of the Road Traffic Act 1988. There was then a charge of careless driving by causing that vehicle to collide with another, the other vehicle being a car which was parked in the street, contrary to section 3 of the Act. There were then charges of failing to stop and of failing to report the accident and, finally, there was a charge of failing to give information as to the identity of the driver of the vehicle.

The appellant has now appealed against this conviction. The only issue which arises in the appeal, and which counsel sought to argue today, was a point which formed the basis for a submission at the trial that there was no case to answer. This is whether there was sufficient evidence of identification to establish that the appellant was the driver of the vehicle involved in these incidents. Before dealing with this matter we should mention that the conviction on charge 5 was not challenged, since that charge alone amongst the five in the complaint did not depend upon the proof of the fact that the appellant was driving the vehicle at the time.

The circumstances as summarised in the stated case are as follows. On the night of 21 and into 22 July 1989 the appellant and another man named Paul Davidson were travelling together in a Chevette motor car. They were the only persons in the vehicle at the time. As it was being driven down the street the driver lost control of it, causing it to strike another vehicle which was parked in the street. Shortly afterwards the two men emerged from the motor car at the house of somebody called Gary Dickson and, when they arrived at his house, they both appeared to be drunk. It is not necessary to go into further details except to say that the police were summoned to investigate the collision with the vehicle which was parked in the street. They entered the house where the appellant and the companion Paul Davidson had gone. When the police saw the appellant they asked him if he owned the Chevette motor car and he admitted that he did. He was then asked to provide the identity of the driver. His reply was: 'I was sleeping. I don't know anything.' He was then asked to undertake a breath test, and when the result proved to be positive he was arrested and taken to the police station.

The sheriff says that he found the witness Paul Davidson to be entirely credible and reliable. He identified the appellant as having been the driver, and the sheriff says that he found corroboration for Paul Davidson's evidence in the fact that the appellant pretended that he did not know who the driver was when he must have known and was bound to provide the name. In his submissions today in support of the appeal counsel contended that the sheriff misdirected himself on this point. He submitted that he was not entitled to use the appellant's false denial as corroboration of the evidence of Paul Davidson about the identity of the driver. The denial was without value, and it should simply have been disregarded since, as was held in *Wilkie v. H.M.A.*, the doctrine has no application in our criminal law. He referred also to *Douglas v. Pirie* in which the appellant had submitted to a breath test and had not done or said anything to suggest that he was not the driver of the car. It was held that the evidence of a single police officer that the appellant was the driver of the car was not corroborated. Lord Justice-Clerk Wheatley said that the appellant's failure to assert or to do or say something to suggest that he was not the driver could not give rise to the inference that he was. Counsel also referred us to *McNeil v. Wilson* which he sought to distinguish, because in that case the evidence of a single witness that the lorry in question was being driven by the appellant was corroborated by a witness who emerged from a house and saw the appellant close to the vehicle immediately after it had shed its load.

Turning to the present case, we should say at once that we accept that the sheriff misdirected himself as to where corroboration for Paul Davidson's evidence was to be found. In our opinion he was not entitled to find this in the fact that the appellant pretended that he did not know who was the driver of the car. No doubt this was a lie, but this is not to say that it was an admission that the appellant was in fact the driver of the car. It was a worthless piece of evidence which the sheriff should have left out of account. On the other hand, there are other facts and circumstances in this case which, taken together, do, we think, provide a sufficiency of evidence. The starting point is the evidence of Paul Davidson, whom the sheriff found to be entirely credible and reliable. He identified the appellant as not only being present in the car, but also as having been the driver. His evidence was that they were the only two people in the vehicle. That evidence was corroborated by the evidence of the householder Gary Dickson who spoke to the two people arriving at his house shortly after hearing a bang in the street. That was sufficient to prove that the appellant was alone in the vehicle with Paul Davidson at the material time. Counsel submitted that Paul Davidson's evidence that the appellant was the driver was nevertheless not corroborated. But when we take account of a further factor in the case we think that corroboration of this fact was available. We find it in the point that the vehicle belonged to the appellant, as the appellant himself admitted was the case. When this circumstance is taken into account along with the fact that he was the only other person in the car, we think that it provides what was necessary to corroborate the credible and reliable evidence of Paul Davidson, by which he had in effect excluded himself from being the driver of the car.

For these reasons which are different from those relied on by the sheriff, we consider that there was a case to answer here and that the sheriff was right to repel the submission which was made to him. We also consider that, having accepted as he did the evidence of Paul Davidson, he was entitled to proceed to a conviction on the various charges as libelled in the complaint. For these reasons we shall answer the first question in the case in the affirmative, the second in the negative and the third in the affirmative and refuse the appeal."

NOTES

Although this case is decisive authority that a false denial affords no corroboration of a criminal charge, the courts nevertheless can and do take such denials into account in assessing the credibility of a witness. (Although compare the bizarre case of *Wright v. H.M.A.*, 2000 S.L.T. 1026 in which the accused was accused of changing his story to preserve an alibi, but who was apparently the only person in court to have got the facts correct). Similarly, the silence of the accused in reply to police questioning or charge does not provide corroboration—see *Robertson v. Maxwell*, 1951 J.C. 11; *Douglas v. Pirie*, 1975 S.L.T. (Notes) 63—except possibly in reset cases where silence or an inadequate explanation of possession of stolen goods may be regarded as a "criminative circumstance" for the purposes of the "doctrine" of recent possession—*Fox v. Patterson*, 1948 J.C. 104; *Brennan v. H.M.A.*, 1954 S.L.T. 255; *Cryans v. Nixon*, 1954 S.L.T. 311. (Compare the position in England—see Nash, "Silence as Evidence" 1996 S.L.T. (News) 69). It seems, however, that corroboration may be afforded in certain circumstances where an accused person provides false information to the police—*Winter v. Heywood*, 1995 S.C.C.R. 276; and in *McGrory v. H.M.A.*, 1995 S.C.C.R. 237, a case which was described as a "very narrow one", the evidence of the complainer in an assault case was corroborated by evidence that the accused had apparently threatened a witness in order to prevent her giving evidence against him. The court emphasised in *McGrory* that they did not intend to suggest that uttering threats to a witness would provide corroboration in every case, but confined their judgment to the particular facts of the case.

Chapter 6

THE BEST EVIDENCE RULE

---

1. Dickson on the Law of Evidence in Scotland, Vol. I,
Title I: Of the rule that requires the best evidence

"195. We have already treated of evidence as divided into direct and indirect; and we have seen that indirect evidence is not necessarily substitutionary in its character. It is rather a method of proving that which otherwise might not be provable at all; and consequently, to adduce indirect evidence is in no degree to infringe upon the one primary rule of the law of evidence,—the rule, namely, that a party must adduce the best attainable evidence of the facts he means to prove . . . This rule is founded on the presumption that one who tenders the less trustworthy of two kinds of proof within his reach, does so in order to produce an impression which the better proof would not create; for, if they would lead to the same result, he would probably not select the less convincing of them. The rule is also designed for preventing trials from being burdened with unnecessary investigations into the authenticity of secondary proofs; by which the time of the judge and jury would be wasted, and their attention might be diverted from the real points in issue. The rule is thus directed to the specific character, not to the strength or amount of the proof. It excludes evidence, the substitutional nature of which implies that more original evidence can be obtained . . .

The rule, however, does not require each fact to be proved by the greatest attainable amount of evidence; for all proof beyond what will satisfy the judge or jury is superfluous and unnecessary; and it must be left to the party to determine what amount of evidence is sufficient for that purpose. The rule is chiefly directed against the admission of copies or parole of the contents of documents and of hearsay evidence; these all inferring the existence of more general proof of the facts which they set forth. The exception by which these secondary proofs are admitted, when the original document has been lost, or the original witness has died, tends to illustrate the general rule; because the circumstances under which they are admitted show that the party did not select inferior evidence to mislead the jury."

NOTES

In *Omychund v. Barker* (1745) Willes 538, Lord Harwicke said that:

"The judges and sages of the law have laid it down that there is but one general rule of the law of evidence, the best that the nature of the case will allow."

The best evidence rule in this form was promulgated to a large extent by Sir Geoffrey Gilbert's work *The Law of Evidence* (1754). However, it seems very doubtful, whether even at the time of writing, Gilbert's views represented an accurate statement of the law—see Twining, *Rethinking Evidence*, (1994), Chapter 3. Today it is arguable that the rule has virtually ceased to exist in criminal cases, and its importance in civil cases has been much reduced. However, recent reforms to the rule against hearsay in criminal cases appear to be based on some version of the rule—see the Criminal Procedure (Scotland) Act 1995, ss.259–262, Chapter 7, below. The treatment in civil cases of the rule abolishing corroboration also appears to owe something to the idea that evidence is forbidden which is "substitutionary" or secondary in character—see *Morrison v. J. Kelly and Sons Ltd*, 1970 S.C. 65, and Chapter 15, below.

2. Maciver v. Mackenzie
1942 J.C. 51

The accused was charged with a taking possession of wreck, consisting of pit props, battens and logs of wood, and not being the owner of the goods, failing to deliver them to the Receiver of Wreck, contrary to the Merchant Shipping Act 1884. The wreck was not produced at his trial, but evidence about its condition was led by the prosecutor without objection. The accused was convicted and appealed on the ground that the wreck should have been produced. He argued that the prosecutor was bound to produce any article referred to in the complaint unless it was beyond his power to do so, and in any event, he was not entitled to lead evidence as to the condition of the wreck, since the wreck itself, if produced, would have been the best evidence.

LORD JUSTICE-GENERAL (NORMAND): "The learned counsel for the appellant asserted that there was an obligation on the prosecutor to produce any article which was referred to in an indictment or complaint, unless it was beyond his power to do so. There is certainly no such rule. It is, no doubt, the proper practice to produce any article referred to in the indictment or complaint where there is no practical difficulty in doing so. There are, however, many cases where it is inconvenient, though not wholly impossible, to make articles productions in the case because of the size of the articles. Livestock cannot conveniently be made productions, and there are other examples. The question in each case is whether the real evidence is essential for proving the case against the accused. In a case of forgery I can conceive it would be very difficult to prove the charge unless the document alleged to be forged was in Court, but even in that case I am not satisfied that the proof would be impossible.

In this case, however, the real question seems to me to be related rather to the competence of questions put to the witnesses than to the alleged duty of the prosecutor to produce the timber referred to in the complaint. When the witness was asked about the marks upon the timber alleged to have been found in the possession of the appellant, the agent for the accused was entitled to object to the question on the ground that it was an attempt to elicit evidence about markings on the wood when the wood itself might have been produced and examined, for the timber itself would have been the best evidence of its condition. What would have happened if that objection had been taken we do not know. There might have been some reasonable explanation which would have shown that it was impracticable to have the timber produced, or the result might have been that the timber would have been instantly produced, or there might have been an adjournment to allow it to be produced. But in the absence of objection we really do not even know why it was that the timber was not produced.

The case therefore falls within the terms of section 75 of the Summary Jurisdiction (Scotland) Act of 1908, which provides that no conviction shall be quashed in respect of any objection to the competency or admission or rejection of evidence at the trial unless such objection shall have been timeously stated at such trial by the law agent for the accused. That applies, of course, when the accused has a law agent representing him at the trial, as was the case here."

The court refused the appeal.

NOTES

The result of this case demonstrates the importance of objecting timeously to evidence which is thought to be inadmissible—the provisions of the Summary Jurisdiction (Scotland) Act 1908 are re-enacted in the Criminal Procedure (Scotland) Act 1995, s.192(3), of which the equivalent in solemn proceedings is s.118(8). The court seems to imply that the conviction might have been quashed in this case had the defence objected timeously and had the prosecution been unable to establish a good reason for the non-production of the wreck.

3. Anderson v. Laverock
1976 J.C. 9

Police officers found salmon in the possession of the accused some time after 11 p.m. on a certain date. The police officers asked him to accompany them to the police station and to bring the fish with him, which he did. At the police station the fish were examined by the police officers and a water bailiff outwith the presence of the accused. The fish were impounded and the following day were destroyed without giving the accused any opportunity to examine the fish. The accused was convicted in the Sheriff Court of an offence against section 7(1) of the Salmon and Freshwater Fisheries (Protection) (Scotland) Act 1951. In the course of the trial, his agent objected to any oral evidence being led about the condition of the fish, on the ground that such evidence was secondary, and therefore inadmissible, the primary evidence being the fish, which were not produced. The defence further argued that the fish should have been kept until they could be examined on behalf of the accused, or in any event that photographs of the salmon should have been produced.

The Sheriff repelled the objection, on the grounds: (i) that there was no obligation on the prosecution to produce the salmon; (ii) that there would only have been an obligation on the prosecution to preserve the fish if the accused had indicated when the fish were impounded that he wanted them inspected; and (iii) that photographs of the salmon would have been of no assistance. The accused appealed to the High Court.

LORD JUSTICE-CLERK (WHEATLEY): "This is a stated case at the instance of the Appellant who was convicted of a charge that he was found in possession of 26 salmon in circumstances which afforded reasonable ground for suspecting that he had obtained the said salmon as a result of committing an offence against the provisions of section 1 or 2 of the Salmon and Freshwater Fisheries (Protection) (Scotland) Act 1951, contrary to section 7(1) of that Act.

The manner in which section 7 of the Act operates was fully set out by Lord Justice-General Clyde in *Aitchison v. Bartlett*, 1963 J.C. 27 at p.32, to which *brevitatis causa* we refer. Counsel for the appellant submitted that certain procedural faults had occurred which vitiated the conviction, but conceded that if these were not established he could not argue that on the facts stated in the case the Sheriff was not entitled to convict. In our view this was a concession that on the facts could scarcely have been withheld, since there was ample evidence to constitute the suspicious circumstances which section 7(1) requires, and the appellant's explanations were so incredible and suspicious that the Sheriff had more than ample justification for rejecting them and treating him as a witness of no credit.

An essential matter in the case presented by the respondent was the appearance of the fish in order to establish that they had not been taken by rod and line in violation of section 2(1) of the Act. The fish were found in the appellant's possession some time after 11 p.m. on December 23 and were destroyed on the following day, the time not being stated. The fish were out of season and were therefore 'unclean.' On arrival at the police station to which they had been taken the fish were examined by one of the two policemen who had discovered them in the appellant's car and by a water bailiff who had been asked by the policemen to assist them. This examination was carried out in the presence of the second policeman. The appellant was in the police station at the time, but was not present at the inspection. According to the evidence of the witnesses who examined the fish, all of them were marked with large holdes (sic) and tears of the type made by cleeks or gaffs. The mouths revealed no signs of hook marks or signs of blood. Such marks are normally seen when fish of the size of these fish (10–16 lbs) are caught by rod and line, even on a small hook, although it is possible that a hook can be swallowed so that the mouth is not marked. The Sheriff accepted this evidence as establishing that important aspect of the case. At the beginning of the trial the appellant's agent submitted that since the fish, which were essential to the charge and were the best evidence, were not produced it was not competent for the prosecution to lead secondary evidence about them. He accordingly invited the Sheriff to dismiss the case there and then on that ground. We pause to point out that this was not the correct procedure. The correct procedure was to object at the appropriate time to the leading of evidence about the physical condition of the fish in their absence as productions. In any event the Sheriff repelled the submission and motion in *hoc statu*, and subsequently at the hearing on evidence repelled further submissions by the appellant's agent on the matter of the non-production of the fish on the ground of prejudice to the appellant.

It will be noted that question one of the questions in law submitted for the opinion of the Court does not reflect what should have been the question had the proper procedure been followed. If it had, the question would have been: 'In the circumstances was I correct in repelling the objection to the leading of secondary evidence about the physical condition of the fish?' Be that as it may, we are of the Opinion that the Sheriff's attitude towards the production or rather the non-production of the fish at the trial was correct. In rejecting the defence submission on the point she properly founded upon what Lord Justice-General Normand said in *Maciver v. Mackenzie*, 1942 J.C. 51 about the exclusion of perishable goods from the best evidence rule and from being necessary productions, and what Lord Justice-General Clyde said in *MacLeod v. Woodmuir Miners Welfare Society Social Club*, 1961 J.C. 5 about the competency of leading secondary evidence where it was not reasonably practicable and convenient to lead primary evidence. Whether goods are perishable or whether it is reasonably practicable and convenient to retain them as primary evidence in the form of a production will depend on the circumstances and evidence in each particular case. In the present case the Sheriff was satisfied that the fish were perishable and that it was not reasonably practicable and convenient to retain them. Moreover, section 20 of the Act of 1951 provides that where under the Act a fish seized is liable to forfeiture the person by whom it is seized may sell it, and the net proceeds of the sale shall be liable to forfeiture in the same manner as the fish sold. This authorises the fish to be sold before it would otherwise be produced in Court, and by necessary inference opens the door to the leading of secondary evidence about the fish. In our view there was no validity in this objection. A subsidiary argument namely that esto the fish could not be produced it was incumbent on the prosecution to produce photographs of them and labels is equally untenable. These in themselves would be secondary evidence, and if secondary evidence is permissible to prove an essential fact it is for the party seeking to prove the fact to decide what form of secondary evidence will be tendered and for the Court to decide whether that evidence establishes it. The production of photographs and labels may strengthen the oral secondary evidence, but is not a prerequisite of that evidence.

This brings us to the last point which was debated before us, namely, whether the fish should have been retained for inspection by an expert witness on behalf of the appellant before being destroyed. It is incorporated in question two. This is the one point in the case which has given us concern. On this point the Sheriff in her note says: 'The submission that the fish should have been preserved for examination by an expert witness on behalf of the appellant would have been relevant only if the appellant had indicated to the police when the fish were impounded that he wanted them to be held for such inspection. No such request was made at the time, nor did the appellant ask that he should be allowed to inspect them himself. Of course, since the fish had been in his possession prior to being seized by the police it is clear that he had ample opportunity to examine them had he wished to do so.' The relevant finding is finding 17. The appellant's argument was this. Esto it was in order to destroy the fish and subsequently lead secondary evidence about their physical condition at the trial, since witnesses for the prosecution had been afforded (and in fact had taken advantage of) the opportunity to examine the physical condition of the fish for relevant evidence equity demanded that the defence should have been given the same opportunity. This entailed that before the fish were destroyed the appellant should have been informed by the police of the intention to destroy them and if he signified a wish to have them examined by himself or by an expert a reasonable time should have been allowed to elapse to enable such a wish to be fulfilled. The Sheriff had taken the view that the question of preserving the fish for examination by an expert on behalf of an accused was only relevant if the accused informed the police when the fish were impounded that he wanted them to be preserved for such a purpose. In the instant case the Sheriff had found in fact that no such request was made by the appellant, and she had accordingly rejected the submission that prejudice had been suffered by the appellant. The Sheriff was wrong in law in ruling that the onus was on the appellant to inform the authorities of his wish and to ask for a postponement of the disposal of the fish until an examination by him or on his behalf was made. On the contrary, the onus was on the authorities who had impounded the fish to inform an accused of the intention to dispose of them and to afford the accused a reasonable time before disposal to allow an examination to be made, if desired. This was a matter which went beyond the instant case and was one of general interest and importance. So ran the argument.

It seems almost unnecessary to propound that in the interests of justice and fair play the defence, whenever possible, should have the same opportunity as the prosecution to examine a material and possibly contentious production. The fact that such opportunity has not been afforded to the defence is not per se a ground for quashing a conviction. There may be a variety of reasons, some good some bad, why the opportunity was not provided. The production may have been lost or destroyed before the opportunity reasonably presented itself. It was said by the Advocate-depute that, even if the opportunity was available but was not presented, the only effect of this was possibly to affect the quality of the evidence of the prosecution witnesses who testified to the appearance of the production. In our opinion it goes further than that. It becomes a question whether prejudice was suffered. The questions then arise: 'Was there prejudice?' and 'If so, was it of such materiality as to cause such an injustice that the ensuing conviction falls to be quashed?' The materiality of the production will always be an important factor. It is impossible to lay down hard and fast rules to cover every possible case. Each case will depend on its own facts. In the present case from the Crown point of view the important feature of the production, namely the fish, was to establish that there were present on the fish or absent from the fish marks which would indicate beyond reasonable doubt that the fish had not been caught by rod and line. The prosecution led evidence, which was eventually fully accepted by the Sheriff, to the effect that there were significant marks present and significant marks absent which led to the conclusion that the fish had not been caught by rod and line. It is clear from the stated case that the police, in whose custody the fish were, offered no opportunity to the appellant to have the fish examined by himself or by an expert on his behalf before they were destroyed on the following day. There is nothing in the stated case to indicate that the appellant was informed by the police that the fish were going to be destroyed.

The Sheriff took the view that the obligation to provide an opportunity to the appellant to inspect the fish or have them inspected on his behalf by an expert would only arise if the appellant asked for it. If she was right, then no prejudice was suffered because the appellant did not ask for it. Provision is made in the Act for forfeiture of any fish seized, and persons seizing the fish are authorised to sell it, the net proceeds of the sale being used in lieu of the fish for forfeiture. The Act specifies the three categories of persons who may seize the fish, but does not say that such persons have to warn the persons from whom the fish has been seized of their intention to sell it, or provide him with an opportunity to inspect it before it leaves their possession for sale. That, however, does not entitle us to ignore the canons of justice and fair play. Where it is reasonably practicable, as it was here, we are of the Opinion that a person who has lawfully seized a fish and intends disposing of it one way or another should inform the person from whom it has been seized that the fish is going to be disposed of and that, before it is, he will have the opportunity of examining it or having it examined. Reasonable practicability will depend on the circumstances, which could include such considerations as the delay that would be occasioned by the request and the effect of such delay on the effective disposal of the fish. Here the appellant was provided with no such information or opportunity. The question of reasonable practicability did not therefore arise, but as the fish were going to be destroyed and not sold for consumption there was no obvious extreme urgency. The suggestion by the Advocate-depute that the information given to the appellant that he could have his solicitor present at the police station (an offer which incidentally was not accepted) was an effective substitute is not a tenable one in the circumstances of this case.

We are accordingly of the opinion that the Sheriff applied the wrong test here, and what we conceive to be the correct procedure was not followed. That in itself, however, is not sufficient. It has to be established that the appellant suffered a material prejudice thereby before the conviction is quashed. The Sheriff has stated in her note, though not as a finding in fact, that as the fish had been in the appellant's possession prior to being seized by the police, he had ample opportunity to examine them if he wished to do so. His own story was disbelieved by the Sheriff, and in our view it was so incredible that it would be unsafe to latch on to any part of it that was not established aliunde or was not disputed. Twenty-six salmon or sea-trout weighing 10–16 lbs were stacked in the back of his car. He was alone in the car. It is a reasonable inference that he stacked them there or was a party to that operation. He is an expert fisherman. For the past three years he has held the British and World Fly-casting Championships. He is an instructor in the art, and has held classes on it in the Borders. In the course of a normal year he expects to catch between three and four hundred salmon and sea-trout. If he had the opportunity properly to examine the fish, he would have known what to look for since he was an expert. But the whole affair took place at night when it was dark, and while one might suspect that he had the opportunity to examine the fish before they were impounded, that cannot be assumed. In any event, because of his personal involvement he may well have wished to have the services of another expert if he had been certiorated of his right to have one before the fish were destroyed. This he was undoubtedly denied. Since the marks or absence of significant marks on the fish were crucial to establishing the Crown case, and we are informed by the Sheriff that the Crown witnesses who made the inspection were cross-examined at length and in detail about the physical appearance of the fish, we cannot say that the deprivation of the opportunity to have them examined before disposal by or on behalf of the appellant did not result in substantial prejudice to him. It may be that even if such an opportunity had been provided and evidence contradictory of the Crown case had been adduced, even from an independent expert, the Sheriff would have reached the same conclusion, but that is a matter of pure speculation and one which this Court is not entitled to take into account. We are accordingly of the opinion that for the reasons stated this conviction cannot stand and must be quashed. We reach this conclusion with regret because in our view the appellant's conduct that night reeked of suspicion. His exculpation derives not from his actions and evidence but from a mistake in procedure."

NOTES

Section 276 of the 1995 Act now provides that:

"(1) Evidence as to the characteristics and composition of any biological material deriving from human beings or animals shall, in any criminal proceedings, be admissible notwithstanding that neither the material nor a sample of it is lodged as a production.

(2) A party wishing to lead such evidence as is referred to in subsection (I) above shall, where neither the material nor a sample of it is lodged as a production, make the material or a sample of it available for inspection by the other party unless the material constitutes a hazard to health or has been destroyed in the process of analysis."

In *Macleod v. Woodmuir Miners Welfare Society Social Club*, 1961 J.C. 5, Lord Justice-General Clyde said that:

"Primary evidence is not always essential, and secondary evidence is not necessarily incompetent. Secondary evidence is competent if it is not reasonably practicable and convenient to produce the primary evidence."

The emphasis in *Anderson v. Laverock*, and in the following cases, is on the need to establish prejudice to the defence through the non-production of the evidence. This seems to come close to a reversal of the burden of proof on this point—the older cases seemed to imply that primary evidence should be produced unless a good reason could be given for its non-production. See on this point *Maciver v. Mackenzie*, above, and the critique of the current rule in Nicol, "Best Evidence in Criminal Cases", 1990 S.L.T. (News) 149. Compare also the attitude of the civil courts in *Scottish and Universal Newspapers v. Gherson's Trustees*, 1988 S.L.T. 109.

Among the requirements of article 6, in broad terms, is the requirement for "equality of arms" between the parties to a case. It is arguable that Scottish rules on recovery of evidence place the defence at a disadvantage in comparison with the Crown. In that context it is submitted that the following *dictum* of the Lord Justice-Clerk in *Anderson v. Laverock* is highly significant:

"It seems almost unnecessary to propound that in the interests of justice and fair play the defence, whenever possible, should have the same opportunity as the prosecution to examine a material and possibly contentious production."

It was clearly the principle of equality of arms, albeit argued without reference to the Convention, that led to the quashing of the conviction in this case. This matter is considered further in Chapter 12 on Confidentiality and Privilege.

4. Kelly v. Allan
1984 S.C.C.R. 186

The appellant was charged with reset of a motorcycle. The cycle was recovered from the appellant but was not produced. The appellant in evidence did not deny that the cycle recovered from him possessed the characteristics in respect of which it was identified by the complainer. The appellant was convicted and appealed on the ground that the cycle had not been produced.

LORD JUSTICE-GENERAL: "The appellant is Scott Kelly who was convicted after trial in the sheriff court under the second alternative form of the charge, namely, that between certain dates at a disused coal bing in Newcraighall Road, Edinburgh, or elsewhere in Edinburgh, he did reset a motorcycle, registered number CTS 432V, the same having been dishonestly appropriated by theft. That was the motorcycle mentioned in the first alternative form of the charge which was, of course, a charge of the theft of the bicycle itself.

At the trial there was evidence given by Ian Prentice and his brother, that they had a motorcycle and that it had been stolen, all as described in the charge. No evidence was apparently given of the registration number of the bicycle and the remainder of the evidence consisted of evidence about the discovery of a motorcycle in the possession of the appellant without a registration plate, and without the frame and engine numbers which had been knocked off. The bicycle had apparently been resprayed and various parts of it had been replaced. It was necessary, of course, for the Crown to lead evidence to indicate that the bicycle found in the appellant's possession in circumstances which clearly showed that he knew that it was a stolen bicycle, was in fact the bicycle described in the libel, that is to say the bicycle belonging to Mr Ian Prentice. And what the Crown did was to lead the evidence of Mr Ian Prentice, that when he saw the bicycle which had been recovered from the appellant by the police, he saw that it possessed certain characteristics which were common to it and the bicycle which he had owned and which had been stolen.

In this appeal the conviction is attacked upon the ground that the Crown ought to have produced the motorcycle in court, in the unusual circumstances of this case, and that the Crown's failure to produce that bicycle caused such material prejudice to the appellant as to lead to the conclusion that his conviction of the charge of reset was a miscarriage of justice. According to Mr Macdonald, for the appellant, he had to satisfy us in order to succeed, first, that production was essential in proof of the Crown case against the appellant. Second, he had to satisfy us that there was no trace in the trial or in the stated case of the Crown having attempted to persuade the sheriff that it was neither practicable nor convenient to produce the motorcycle as a production at the trial, and, of course, the third and cardinal proposition was that the absence of the bicycle caused for the appellant such material prejudice as to lead to the desired conclusion about the conviction.

It appeared in the course of the argument that although objection had been taken to evidence being given about the bicycle which had been examined by the Prentices in the hands of the police, the appellant himself gave evidence and when faced with the evidence of the Prentices that they recognised the bicycle, which had changed its appearance somewhat, as theirs, because of the presence of a long list of characteristics, the appellant did not in evidence deny that the bicycle which he had had in his possession did possess these very same characteristics. We need only accordingly address ourselves to the last of the three propositions which Mr Macdonald relied on, and we ask ourselves simply whether, leaving the other questions aside, the absence of the motorcycle as a production in this case caused for the appellant such material prejudice as to lead to the conclusion that his conviction represented a miscarriage of justice. The short answer is no, for this reason. Mr Macdonald very frankly admitted that all he could say was that if the bicycle had been in court it might have been possible for the appellant's solicitor to find something which might have enabled him to cross-examine the owners of the bicycle. That simply will not do. The reality of this trial was that there was a weight of evidence indicating possession by the appellant of a stolen motorcycle. There was no real quarrel with the owners as to the motorcycle being theirs and in all the circumstances we have no doubt whatever that in this case the absence of the motorcycle cannot be prayed in aid in an attack upon this conviction. We shall accordingly refuse the appeal and we shall do so by answering the only two questions which remain, namely questions one and three, in the affirmative."

NOTES

What distinctions can be drawn between this case and that of *Anderson v. Laverock*, above. Why was there material prejudice to the accused in that case, but not in this?

5.   Morrison v. Mackenzie
1990 J.C. 185

"An accused person was convicted of *inter alia* contraventions of section 2 of the Road Traffic Act 1972 and regulations 27(1)(g) and 27(1)(e) of the Road Vehicles (Construction and Use) Regulations 1986 in respect of driving his motor car with bald tyres. At his trial the tyres were not produced but the sheriff allowed police officers to give oral evidence of the condition of the tyres. The sheriff in his note explained that the non-production of the tyres was excusable on the ground of inconvenience. The accused appealed to the High Court by stated case contending that the sheriff had erred in law in admitting oral evidence as to the condition of the tyres. Before the High Court it was accepted that the accused had suffered no prejudice by the non-production of the tyres . . . The sheriff found the following facts to be admitted or proved: (1) About 11.30 p.m. on Saturday October 22, 1988 the appellant was driving his Ford Capri motor car on the A859 road between the villages of Northton and Tarbert, Isle of Harris; (2) Police Constables Smith and Henderson had previously seen the said car parked outside the Rodel Hotel. Their attention had been drawn to it because of the poor state of the tyres on the car; (3) The constables decided to follow the car. They could not catch the car. The car was being driven at speeds in excess of 80 mph on a road which was mostly single track with blind corners and summits. The distance over which the appellant was pursued between Northton and Tarbert was in the region of 17 miles; (4) During the course of the journey John Morrison and Ann Macleod, both passengers in the appellant's car were alarmed at the manner of the appellant's driving. Morrison thought 'it was a bit crazy, but I felt safe' and Macleod said 'I was scared going round corners'; (5) The condition of three of the four tyres on the appellant's car was dreadful. Both front tyres were devoid of tread and the rear offside tyre was devoid of tread and some canvas and wire was showing. The latter tyre could easily have burst at any time rendering the car difficult to keep on the road, particularly at the speed at which the appellant was driving; (6) The front nearside sidelight was inoperative; (7) The appellant was using the said car without a current test certificate.

In his narrative of events preceding these findings, the sheriff set forth, *inter alia*, that:

'During the course of the evidence of PC George Smith, the appellant's solicitor objected to oral evidence being given as to the condition of the tyres on the appellant's car. The nature of the objection and the arguments for and against the leading of the evidence is set out in the note appended to the case. I repelled the appellant's objection and allowed the evidence to be led subject to its relevancy and competency and so that all evidence could be before the court should an appeal be taken (*Clark v. Stuart*, 1950 J.C. 8 at p.11). At the close of the Crown case the objection was renewed and I was moved to find that there was no case to answer. I rejected the motion. No evidence was led for the appellant. I found the appellant guilty as libelled.'

In his note appended to the findings-in-fact, the sheriff set forth that: 'The single matter raised in this appeal by stated case is whether I erred in law in admitting oral evidence of the condition of the tyres on the appellant's car. The tyres were not productions in the case. I allowed oral evidence of their condition to be given by two police officers who had examined the tyres. The agent for the defence submitted that it was neither impractical nor inconvenient to produce the tyres. In their absence, oral evidence of their condition at the time of the offence offended against the best evidence rule. He referred me to Walker and Walker on Evidence, p.445, para. 420. The respondent referred me to *Maciver v. Mackenzie*, 1942 J.C. 51

at 54 per Lord Justice-General Normand. I allowed the evidence to be led because I wished to hear whether production of the tyres was impractical or inconvenient. Both police officers were of the view that it was inconvenient to remove the three tyres from their wheels. They did not consider it either impracticable or inconvenient to photograph the wheels. There was no question of prejudice raised by the appellant's solicitor. He stated that he would feel in some difficulty were he to advance that argument. The accused was left in possession of the tyres and could himself have produced the tyres had he so wished. I took the view that there would be some inconvenience if one or more tyres were to be removed from all vehicles found contravening these regulations. It is within judicial knowledge that a large number of such prosecutions are taken each year and it might well be necessary for the police to keep not only the tyres but also the wheels and, possibly, the car from which the wheels were taken. This would cause inconvenience to the owners and to the police. I considered that the non-production of the tyres could be excused on the ground of inconvenience. In the case of *Maciver v. Mackenzie* the remarks by the Lord Justice-General (Normand) were strictly *obiter* because the decision turned on the terms of section 75 of the Summary Jurisdiction (Scotland) Act 1908—objection not timeously stated. The Lord Justice-General said (at p.54) that there was no general rule that there was an obligation on the prosecutor to produce any article which was referred to in a complaint unless it was beyond his power to do so. 'The question in each case is whether the real evidence is essential for proving the case against the accused. In a case of forgery I can conceive it would be very difficult to prove the charge unless the document alleged to be forged was in court, but even in that case I am not satisfied that the proof would be impossible.' In any event, I am not at all certain that the evidence of what the police saw themselves is anything other than primary evidence. Different considerations might apply to the assessment of that evidence if the depth of the tread remaining on the tyre was challenged.'

The matters desired to be brought under review were: 'That the learned sheriff erred in law in admitting oral testimony by police officers pertaining to the state of the tyres on the appellant's vehicle when said tyres were not produced in court and when it would have been reasonably practicable and convenient to do so'.

The questions of law posed for the opinion of the High Court of Justiciary were the following terms: '(1) Did I err in law in admitting oral evidence by the police officers as to the condition of the tyres on the appellant's car, the said tyres not having been lodged as productions at the trial? (2) On the facts stated, was I entitled to convict the appellant of charges 1, 3, 4 and 5 as libelled?' "

OPINION OF THE COURT: "The appellant is Gordon Alexander Morrison who went to trial in the sheriff court at Stornoway on a complaint libelling a number of charges. What we are concerned with in the present appeal is the fact that he was convicted of charges 1, 3, 4 and 5 on the complaint. Charge 1 was a contravention of section 2 of the Road Traffic Act 1972 and charges 3, 4 and 5 were charges of contravening the Construction and Use (Regulations) in relation to specific tyres on the vehicle which the appellant was driving at the time. There are two questions put forward for the answer of this court. The first is in these terms: [Their Lordships thereafter quoted the terms of the first question of law and continued] As the sheriff says in his note, that is the single matter raised in this appeal. The tyres were not productions in the case and the sheriff allowed oral evidence of their condition to be given by two police officers who had examined the tyres. Counsel for the appellant has drawn attention to the fact that this was a case where the appellant was not suggesting that there was any prejudice to him from the failure to produce the tyres. No doubt that was because the appellant was left in possession of the tyres and had he wished to do so could have produced them himself.

Counsel referred to the case of *Hughes v. Skeen*, 1980 S.L.T. (Notes) 13. That again was a case where it was agreed that there was no prejudice to the appellant from the non-production of the articles involved in that case. In the course of delivering the opinion of the court in that case, Lord Cameron cited from the well known case of *Maciver v. Mackenzie*, 1942 J.C. 51. In the course of delivering an opinion in that case Lord Carmont said at p.551 'There is no rule such as was being contended for, and it is a mere matter of considering whether the production is practicable and convenient.' In *Hughes v. Skeen* Lord Cameron remarks that the appellant in that case was unable to explain what particular purpose in the interests of his client or in the administration of justice would have been served by the production of the articles concerned. It is not unfair to say that in the present case counsel for the appellant also has really been unable to explain what particular purpose in the interests of the appellant or in the interests of justice would be served by the production of these tyres. The sheriff heard evidence from police officers who had examined the tyres and they spoke to what they had seen. The sheriff in his note explains that he took the view that there would have been some inconvenience if one or more of the tyres were to be removed from all vehicles found contravening these regulations and he therefore reached the conclusion that the non-production of the tyres should be excused on the ground of inconvenience. Counsel maintained that there was no finding-in-fact to that effect, but we read the sheriff in this portion of his note as explaining the reasons which he had for arriving at his conclusion that he should allow oral evidence to be given by the police officers.

We are satisfied in this case that the sheriff was well founded in arriving at that conclusion. He recognised that insisting upon production of tyres in a case of this kind could cause practical difficulties and could be regarded as inconvenient. Accordingly, in accordance with the law laid down in *Maciver v. Mackenzie* he decided that this was a case where it was inconvenient for tyres to be produced and that, accordingly, it was competent to hear the evidence of the police officers. We are satisfied that there was no error of law on the sheriff's part in this respect and, accordingly, we answer the first question in this case in the negative. The second question will be answered in the affirmative and the appeal is refused."

6. McKellar v. Normand
1992 S.C.C.R. 393

"The appellant was charged with the reset of a bed and a blanket which were found in her house. Neither bed, [nor] blanket, nor labels in lieu thereof were produced at the appellant's trial. The Crown relied for proof of guilty knowledge on a statement by the appellant that she had received the articles at her house door on a date which was the day after they had been stolen. She was convicted and appealed to the High Court . . . The Justice made the following findings in fact:

'1. Robert Smith was temporarily residing at the house of his mother at 76 Dunterly Avenue while his wife was in hospital. He returned to his house at 10 Blackcraig Avenue on December 9, 1989, when the police informed him that his house had been broken into. Mr Smith informed the police that a bed, bedding and other articles had been removed from the house. The house was in a state of disorder. Mr Smith stated that the bed was returned by the police to his mother (who was not a witness). Mr Smith had not signed a production label. Mr Smith also said that he had seen the bed later and that it was his own.

2. Acting on an anonymous report that goods from Mr Smith's house could be found there the police visited the house at 4 Kinclaven Avenue on December 10, 1989 and interviewed Maureen McKellar, who was identified in court, and advised her that they were making enquiries about stolen goods. The appellant admitted receiving a bed and a blanket at the door of her house. The appellant was co-operative with the police in allowing a search of the house but refused to say where the items came from or give the value thereof. The police removed the bed and blanket and returned them to 10 Blackcraig Avenue where they were received by Mrs Smith. Detective Sergeant Andrew asked the appellant if she had received the goods at her door. Detective Sergeant Andrew stated that he had used the word "received" to the appellant. The appellant had been cautioned that she need not make any reply to the questions put to her by the police officers. Detective Sergeant Weir stated that the appellant was asked if she bought household goods at the door and she agreed she had done so.'

The questions for the opinion of the High Court were:

'1. On the evidence led, was I entitled to repel the appellant's submission under section 345A of the Criminal Procedure (Scotland) Act 1975?

2. On the facts stated, was I entitled to convict the appellant as libelled?' "

LORD JUSTICE-GENERAL (HOPE): "The appellant is Maureen McKellar who went to trial in the district court at Glasgow charged with the reset of a bed and blanket at a dwellinghouse occupied by her at 4 Kinclaven Avenue, Glasgow. At the end of the Crown case a motion was made that there was no case to answer but the magistrate refused that motion. The appellant did not give evidence and at the end of the trial she was found guilty of the charge and fined the sum of £50.

In the appeal against conviction which Mrs Clarke has presented today two short points were argued. The first is that evidence about the bed and blanket which were the subject of this charge was inadmissible because these items were not produced at the trial nor were there labels relating to these items, and the second is that in the circumstances there was insufficient evidence to establish that the appellant had the necessary guilty knowledge to convict her of reset of these items.

The narrative in the stated case is brief. [His Lordship summarised the findings in fact as set out above, and continued:]

The appellant was co-operative with the police in allowing a search of her house, but she refused to say where the items came from or to give the value of these items.

There is a narrative in the findings about the questions which were put to her by the police officers, but nothing of any real importance turns on their terms because it is not suggested that the use of the word 'received' by one of the police officers was of any particular significance in the circumstances of this case.

So far as the first ground of appeal is concerned, Mrs Clarke submitted that there was no good reason why at least a label relating to these items could not have been produced. An objection to the admissibility of the evidence about these articles was timeously taken, and her short point was that the evidence as to finding and ownership of these items was inadmissible. We accept, however, the response which the learned Solicitor-General made to this argument. It is good practice for items which are the subject of charges of this kind to be produced if it is convenient to do so or, failing production, for labels relating to the items to be produced in their place. But the question must always be, if an objection is taken as to the admissibility of the evidence, whether in the absence of the items or labels relating to them some injustice is likely to result to the accused. For obvious reasons, Mrs Clarke has not contended that the bed itself should have been produced. No doubt considerations of convenience would play a part in a decision on that matter and as to whether in the absence of the bed, the blanket only should be produced. But so far as the absence of labels is concerned, it has not been suggested that any point of significance arose because of the fact that no labels were produced. That provides the complete answer to the question which she has raised, because it would only be if there were some particular significance to be attached to the absence of the labels, liable to result in injustice to the appellant, that there would be any substance in this ground of appeal.

So far as the second point is concerned, the evidence relevant to the question of guilty knowledge was in short compass. The appellant, having been cautioned, admitted to receiving or accepting the bed and blanket at the door of her house. She was not prepared to say anything about where the items came from or give the value thereof, but no point can be taken against her for refusing to answer questions by the police on these matters since she was under caution. Nevertheless what we have here is a transaction which, to say the least, was unusual. She admitted to receiving these two items—a bed and a blanket—at the door of her house just one day after the break-in at the house of Mr Smith. The question is what inferences the justice could properly draw from this combination of circumstances, and we have reached the view that once the appellant admitted, as she did, to accepting these two items at the door of her house, there was sufficient to entitle the Justice to draw the necessary inferences. We stress that it is the nature of the transaction by which she acquired the items, the combination of these two items together in the single transaction and the unusual place at which it took place, which provides the essential basis for these inferences. The appellant did not give evidence, so the matter rested entirely on the evidence led for the Crown.

For these reasons we shall answer the two questions in the case in the affirmative and refuse the appeal."

NOTES

Do these cases demonstrate a drift in the law, from the requirement of practicality of production, which seemed to be the relevant criterion in *Maciver v. Mackenzie*, above, to a test of convenience, which is a rather different and apparently less stringent test? In *McDougall v. Macphail*, 1991 S.C.C.R. 358, it was held that the Crown did not have to produce a particular bodily sample, and that evidence from an analyst was sufficient. This was so, even although in *McDougall*, it would have been quite possible to produce the sample. In the commentary to this case, Sheriff Gordon suggests, under reference to two other cases, *McLeod v. Fraser*, 1986 S.C.C.R. 271 and *Houston v. McLeod*, 1986 S.C.C.R. 219, that the best evidence rule is of little importance in modern criminal law. (The ratio of *McDougall* is now of purely academic interest thanks to section 276 of the Criminal Procedure (Scotland) Act 1995, which explicitly permits parties to lead secondary evidence of biological material. See also sections 281–286 of that Act.)

Compare the following cases, which relate to the best evidence rule in civil cases. Do you consider that the best evidence rule should be applied more or less stringently in civil proceedings?

7. McGowan v. Belling & Co. Ltd
1983 S.L.T. (Notes) 77

Various people were injured in a house fire in a house occupied by the McGowan family. The injured persons raised actions against the manufacturers of an electric room heater in respect of an alleged defect in the design and manufacture of the heater and against the electricity board who had sold the heater in respect of failure to act on alleged complaints by the owner of the heater about overheating of the cable and plug and in respect of an alleged breach of the Sale of Goods Act. After a proof the Lord Ordinary (Cowie) held the cause of the fire not established and assoilzied both defenders. In relation to evidence in support of the alleged design defect his Lordship said:

"As I have already indicated, there was expert evidence given to the effect that because of the design of this particular type of heater, it was probable that the cable had overheated and caused the fire. This theory was put forward by Mr Grant and Dr Davidson and while I have no reason to doubt their sincerity and expertise, it was based, first, on the evidence given about the behaviour of the McGowans' electric heater which they never saw themselves and second, it was based on evidence which as I have already indicated I found unacceptable. Furthermore the evidence of Mr Grant and Dr Davidson was based on the condition of a heater which they examined in 1978, and which, although it may well have been of the same type as the McGowans' with the same type of connectors attached to the fixed wiring this could not be confirmed because the heater was not produced in court. Objection was taken to evidence relating to the condition of this heater, and any inferences to be drawn from that condition, because it had not been produced, and the defenders had had no opportunity of examining it. I allowed the evidence subject to competency and relevancy, and I must now rule on the objection. It became clear in the course of Mr Grant's evidence, that, although he had examined this heater in 1978, it was still available and at the date of the proof was still at Strathclyde University, where he had originally examined it. Dr Davidson had examined the same heater as late as the end of 1980 or early 1981. Accordingly it was quite clear that the heater which formed the foundation of the expert evidence could have been lodged as a production in the case, and there was no suggestion that its condition had materially altered in any way since 1978.

In these circumstances it seems to me that the heater should have been lodged, since that would have been the best evidence of its type and condition, not only at the time of the proof, but to all intents and purposes, at the time of the examination of it by the experts. Accordingly, in my opinion, an oral description of its condition in its absence was inadmissible and any expert evidence based on its alleged condition was also inadmissible. See Walkers on the *Law of Evidence in Scotland*, p.445, para. 420 and the cases referred to therein.

In these circumstances I am not prepared to take any account of the expert evidence as to the condition of the heater which was examined in 1978 by Mr Grant and in 1980 by Dr Davidson, nor as to the cause of the fire based on that examination."

8. Scottish & Universal Newspapers v. Gherson's Trustees
1988 S.L.T. 109

A company purchased the entire shareholding of a private limited company. The selling shareholders warranted as accurate the audited balance sheet, audited profit and loss account and other financial documents. Those records had in part been prepared from a sales day book which contained information about creditors as well as debtors. The purchasing company carried out an examination of the accounts and purportedly discovered three particular errors in the balance sheet comprising an overstatement of debtors, an overstatement of prepaid charges and an understatement of creditors. The purchasing company then resold the shareholding at a loss and sued the previous shareholders. At the proof the pursuers attempted to lead evidence as to the errors in the balance sheet through a witness who had discovered the errors from a consideration of prime financial records such as the sales day book. Those prime financial records were not produced. Objection was taken to the line of evidence on the basis that it was incompetent in the absence of the prime financial records themselves. The pursuers argued that the books had been lost without fault on the pursuers' part. They had been in the pursuers' hands until the share-holding was resold. Some of the prime financial records had then been taken by the new purchasers and none of them could now be found. The pursuers argued that the absence of fault was demonstrated by the reasonable belief of the pursuers that these records would be retained by the subsequent purchasers. The pursuers further argued that before being barred from using the evidence tendered it would be necessary that there was such a gross degree of fault as would in equity bar the leading of the proposed evidence. The Lord Ordinary sustained the objection, holding (1) that there was a high likelihood of prejudice to the defenders in that it would be impossible to test the accuracy of the witness's conclusions to discover the reason for any discrepancy between the original books and the accounts, and (2) that there was no rule requiring gross fault to be established. The pursuers reclaimed.

THE LORD PRESIDENT (EMSLIE): "In terms of a written agreement of February 23, 1979 the defenders, the whole shareholders of a small travel agency known as Cruisair International Travel Ltd., a private company, sold the equity shareholding in Cruisair to the pursuers for £75,000. The sale proceeded on the faith of, *inter alia*, Cruisair's audited balance sheet and their audited profit and loss account as at April 30, 1978, and the defenders warranted that the accounts as defined in the agreement were true, complete, and accurate in all respects, that they correctly set forth all the assets and liabilities of Cruisair at that date, and that they showed a true and fair view of the financial position of that company. These accounts had been prepared by the third parties on the material contained in the prime financial records of the company, which included the particular books described by the Lord Ordinary in his opinion, together with the invoices, statements and the like from which these books had been written up.

In this action the pursuers sue in respect of alleged breach of the warranty upon the ground that, according to their averment, investigations carried out on their behalf, after the sale, disclosed that there were errors in three items stated in the balance sheet of Cruisair as at April 30, 1978. On the assets side, according to the pursuers, the figure for debtors had been understated by £3,941 and the figure for 'prepayments' had been overstated by £3,000; and on the liabilities side, the figure for creditors had been understated by £36,496. A revised balance sheet was then prepared and it is clear that it was prepared upon the basis of the same financial records as had been used in the preparation of the original balance sheet mentioned in the agreement of sale. In other words, the pursuers' case depends upon establishing that the alleged errors were revealed by the contents of the prime financial records of Cruisair themselves.

Now the defenders deny that their balance sheet was inaccurate in the respects averred by the pursuers and go on to say that their financial records were complete and accurate and that if their balance sheet was inaccurate in these respects this was the result of professional negligence on the part of the third parties. The position of the third parties in their pleadings is that they do not admit that there were inaccuracies in the balance sheet which they prepared for the purposes of the sale agreement, and contend that, if there were inaccuracies, these were attributable to inaccurate and inadequate information given by the first and second named defenders as directors of Cruisair. In this state of the pleadings it was evident that the contents of the prime financial records were of critical importance in the search for the truth in this dispute.

In due course the action went to proof before answer and the pursuers led certain evidence in support of their averments, designed to persuade the Lord Ordinary that the prime financial records of Cruisair had been lost, or at least could not be found, and thereafter adduced as a witness a Mr Connell, an accountant employed by them, who had, after their acquisition of Cruisair, examined the prime financial records of the company with the assistance of a Mr

Forbes, an employee of the third parties, and had, on the basis of that examination, prepared the revised balance sheet which purported to correct the alleged errors in the entries of debtors, prepayments and creditors. What the pursuers then attempted to do was to take evidence from Mr Connell about the contents of the missing prime financial records of Cruisair for the relevant period which had revealed to him these alleged errors in the original balance sheet. Counsel for the defenders and the third parties objected to the admissibility of this evidence on the ground that it was incompetent, and, after a lengthy debate, the Lord Ordinary sustained the objection for the reasons which he gives in a full and lucid opinion.

In these circumstances, when the proof resumed, counsel for the pursuers intimated that they would lead no further evidence, and on the unopposed motion of the defenders the Lord Ordinary assoilzed them from the conclusions of the summons and sustained the third plea in law for the third parties. The pursuers have now reclaimed to this court and have sought to persuade us that the Lord Ordinary erred in holding that the evidence which they had proposed to take from Mr Connell was incompetent.

For a complete account of the history of the events which happened after the pursuers' acquisition of Cruisair on February 23, 1979 I refer with gratitude to the opinion of the Lord Ordinary. All that I propose to do therefore in order to provide the setting for the reclaiming motion to which we listened is to mention what appear to me to be the important parts of the story. The pursuers were a subsidiary of a subsidiary company within the Lonrho group of companies. Two of their directors, Mr Bruce and Mr Campbell, both of whom gave evidence for the pursuers, became directors of Cruisair. After the pursuers' acquisition of that company its prime financial records were in the effective control of the pursuers. They were kept at Cruisair's premises in Queensferry Street in Edinburgh. Soon after the acquisition Mr Connell felt that there were 'apparent differences in the accounts' which required investigation. With the assistance of Mr Forbes, Mr Connell then spent about five weeks investigating the prime financial records of Cruisair and reported that he had discovered the alleged errors in the balance sheet on which the pursuers found in this action. In the early summer of 1979 the pursuers' solicitors were instructed to write to the sellers intimating the pursuers' intention to make a claim for alleged breach of the warranty.

Correspondence then followed in which the defenders made it clear that they could not accept Mr Connell's unvouched figures and the revised balance sheet to April 30, 1978. The pursuers then decided to bring this action, the summons in which was signeted on November 9, 1979. Defences were lodged on December 19, 1979. The prime financial records of Cruisair which were obviously of critical importance in the resolution of the dispute between the parties were still in effective control of the pursuers. In the spring of 1980 it was apparently decided that another company in the Lonrho group could more easily carry on the Cruisair business and in June 1980 the pursuers sold the equity of Cruisair to that company, Kendall Globe Ltd., which later changed its name to Kendall Travel Ltd. The prime financial records of Cruisair were passed to its new owners and remained in the Queensferry Street premises. Thereafter certain records, and no one knows which, were taken by a Mr Clark from Edinburgh to the London office of Kendall Globe. The financial records of Cruisair which remained in Edinburgh were the responsibility of successive office managers of that company. In parenthesis I should say that counsel for the pursuers led the evidence of a Mr Bett, the bookkeeping accountant of Cruisair from June 1978 until the sale to Kendall Globe and informed the Lord Ordinary that he did not intend to call Mr Clark or any of the employees of Cruisair who had responsibility for the care of Cruisair 5 records (see the Lord Ordinary's opinion, 1986 S.L.T. at p.411B–D). At all events what is perfectly clear is that when Cruisair passed into the ownership of Kendall Globe in June 1980 the pursuers took no steps whatever then or thereafter to make sure that the prime financial records of Cruisair for the relevant period would be preserved as evidence which would be of critical importance in this action. Although Mr Bruce, the financial director of the pursuers, was well aware that Mr Connell's conclusions depended upon the contents of these records, and that the revised balance sheet could not have been prepared without them, he simply assumed that they would be available whenever they were required. His reasons for making this assumption are set out in the Lord Ordinary's opinion at p.413H–J and I do not repeat them here. All that remains to be said is that the pursuers did nothing at all about the vital Cruisair records until, in October 1984, the defenders sought to recover them by diligence. By that time, alas, Kendall Globe had moved its accounting premises in London twice and Cruisair had moved to a different location in Queensferry Street. The evidence led by the pursuers was to the effect that thorough searches of all possible repositories in London and of the premises of Cruisair in Edinburgh had failed to discover the records. The witnesses who were called by the pursuers were unable to say what, if anything, had happened to them or when.

In sustaining the objection to the admissibility of the evidence which the pursuers hoped to elicit from Mr Connell the Lord Ordinary concluded first that the financial records were primary evidence of their contents and that what the pursuers were attempting to do was to lead secondary evidence of their contents through Mr Connell speaking to his investigation of the records and making use of his working papers. He then appears to have decided that such secondary evidence would only be admissible if it could be shown that the important prime financial records had been lost or destroyed without fault on the part of the pursuers and his conclusion on that matter is summarised in the following passage at the end of his opinion (1986 S.L.T. at pp.414.1–415A):

'I consider that the documents are absolutely essential to the proof of the two important issues which I have identified. I consider that the pursuers are solely responsible for bringing about the situation in which the critically important records were not preserved. Not only did they part with them after raising the action but they took no steps whatsoever to ensure that they were retained and kept separate from other records. The evidence suggested that there were large quantities of records of various kinds kept in warehouses at Heathrow and elsewhere in and around London, furthermore the pursuers were aware that both Kendall Globe and Cruisair had at various times changed their premises and moved their records around and it appears to me to be elementary that standing the present action and the denials therein by the defenders, the pursuers should have taken steps to ensure that the relevant documents were preserved and kept available. It would have been a simple matter to do so, but it was not done.

In the whole circumstances, upon the basis of the authorities referred to in Dickson, I have come to be of the view that the pursuers have not shown any reason why I should not apply the general rule which excludes parole proof of the contents of documents not produced when the documents and their contents are critically important to the proof of matters which lie at the heart of the litigation. I have decided therefore that I must sustain the objection to the line of evidence.'

I have only to add that in course of his opinion the Lord Ordinary devoted considerable attention to the material prejudice which the defenders and the third parties would be likely to suffer in the absence of the records which provide the foundation for the pursuers' case and expressed the view, for all the reasons which he gives, that the prejudice would be likely to be substantial and (indeed possibly critical) for the pursuers. Counsel began by questioning whether the missing records ought properly to be regarded as primary evidence and, indeed, whether the evidence which Mr Connell was able to give ought to be classified as secondary. Be that as it may, however, the submission was that upon a proper understanding of the relevant paragraphs of Dickson on the Law of Evidence in Scotland (3rd ed.) and a number of cases which were cited in the course of the argument, the only principle in the law of evidence is that a party is entitled to lead secondary evidence of the contents of documents if it is the best evidence available to him because the primary evidence thereof has been lost. That rule or principle suffers exception in only two sets of circumstances. The first is where the party tendering the secondary evidence is unable to displace the suspicion that he is doing so because the primary evidence, allegedly not available, would not be to his advantage. The second is that where the primary evidence is shown to have been lost after it has come into the possession of the party seeking to lead secondary evidence it appears that the loss is attributable to blameworthy conduct on his part 'tantamount to destruction' of the primary evidence. The Lord Ordinary proceeded from the wrong starting point. In particular he appeared to think that evidence of the contents of documents, lost in the hands of the party founding on it, will only be admissible if the loss appears to have occurred without fault on his part. In any event he did not trouble to consider what is meant by fault in that context. If he had done so he should have appreciated that it does not mean merely a failure to take reasonable care to preserve the primary evidence. Fault in this context connotes grave culpability. Further and in any event, the Lord Ordinary erred in holding that in the circumstances known to the pursuers, and in particular to Mr Bruce, any duty there may have been to take reasonable care to see that the records would be available for the proof did not require him to take any steps which he failed to take. He had every reason to expect that the records would be accessible whenever they were required. A further major error on the part of the Lord Ordinary is that he introduced prejudice to the pursuers' opponents as a vital consideration in deciding the issue of competency. There is no authority for the view that secondary evidence is not admissible if it can be seen that the opposing party is likely to be prejudiced thereby. Prejudice is a consideration which goes to the weight which ought to be given to secondary evidence and it has no role to play in a decision upon its admissibility which is a pure question of competency. This was not a case in which there was the slightest suspicion that the secondary evidence sought to be led was being tendered improperly. There is no suggestion of fraud or grossly culpable conduct on the part of the pursuers. The evidence objected to should accordingly have been admitted.

I am not persuaded that the submissions for the pursuers should receive effect. There is no doubt that in the circumstances of his case the primary evidence of the contents of the vital records were the records themselves. They represent the fountainhead of the investigation and contain the source material upon which the alleged findings of Mr Connell's five weeks of analysis depend. There is, accordingly, no doubt either that the Lord Ordinary was well founded in saying that what the pursuers were attempting to do, when objection was taken, was to lead secondary evidence of the contents of these records. Now the best evidence rule, stated generally, is that the contents of documents must be proved by the documents themselves and cannot be proved by parole evidence (Dickson, "Law of Evidence in Scotland" (3rd ed.), para. 204). In that paragraph it is stated that the reason is: 'that witnesses are extremely apt, from want of observation or memory, to mistake the terms of writings, the effect of which depends on their precise words; and that, each document being intended to be read as a whole, its meaning would often be misunderstood if a statement of only a part of it were admissible'. Our law of course does permit secondary evidence of the contents of documents in certain circumstances where the documents themselves are not available. The question is: what is the law governing the admissibility of secondary evidence applicable to the particular circumstances of this case? The pursuers' position is that the prime financial records of Cruisair cannot now be found and contend that in such circumstances the rule is that secondary evidence of the contents of the missing documents will be admitted save in the exceptional circumstances defined in the submissions of their counsel. I do not accept that contention which finds no support in authority or principle. The secondary evidence which the pursuers proposed to take from Mr Connell is derived from the contents of the missing primary evidence thereof. It is not the rule that save in exceptional circumstances a party in the position of the pursuers in this case may competently lead such secondary evidence merely by showing that the records themselves cannot be found after thorough search. The true rule may safely be taken from Chap. IV of Dickson, cit. sup., in a number of passages in paras. 236, 237 and 241 which have not been the subject of adverse comment or criticism, judicial or otherwise, since 1887. From these passages I take the true rule applicable to a case such as this to be that secondary evidence of the contents of the missing records will be admitted only if it is shown that they have been destroyed or lost without fault on the part of the pursuers who had effective control of the records which the action began. A party in the position of the pursuers indeed will, according to Dickson, para. 237, probably be required to show a special *casus omissionis* not attributable to any fault on his part. It must be recognised accordingly that the leading of secondary evidence to prove the contents of missing documents—a manifestly unsatisfactory expedient—is a privilege to be earned by a party in the position of the pursuers in this case. The Lord Justice-Clerk (Inglis) indeed, in *Clark v. Clark's Trs.* at p.79 called it an 'extraordinary privilege'. In this case the pursuers have merely shown that the prime financial records of Cruisair could not be found after thorough search of various premises in October 1984. They have certainly not established any special *casus omissionis* and had no intention of leading any evidence from those employees of Cruisair who, after June 1980, might have been in a position to say what became of these records. Be that as it may, however, I have to ask whether it has been shown that the non-availability of these records has arisen without fault on the part of the pursuers in whose effective control they were when the action began and indeed until they surrendered that effective control to an associate company in June 1980. There is no difficulty in interpreting the word 'fault' in this context. It simply means failure in a duty to take all proper steps or to use all due diligence to see that these records were preserved and remained accessible for use in the proof. Many of the decided cases are concerned with the question of the degree of care and diligence required of a party in searching for and recovering documents not in his control, but the meaning of the word fault as it has to be applied in the particular circumstances of any case is clear enough. For example, in *Dowgray v. Gilmour* (1907) 14 S.L.T. 906 the pursuer was not permitted to give oral evidence of the contents of a document in the hands of the Lord Advocate because, as the Lord President (Dunedin) said, he had failed to take the proper and only real steps to recover it. Again, for example, in *Milne v. Samson* (1843) 6D. 35 the Lord Justice-Clerk (Hope) at p.357, in sustaining an objection to secondary evidence of the contents of missing documents containing measurements, declared: 'It was the duty of the pursuer to have preserved the original measurements from which the list was made, if he intended to prove by such measurements that the oak really was of the size specified in the agreement of parties; and that, having destroyed or lost these originals, a copy made, after the dispute began, by a third party could not be received'. It must, I think, depend on the circumstances of each case whether the party tendering the secondary evidence has expended the appropriate amount of care and diligence, and the steps required of such a party will no doubt be affected by the nature and importance of the documents, the contents of which are of vital importance in the proof, to the ascertainment of the truth, and to the interests of all parties. The more important the documents the more necessary will it be for the party who has them to take all proper steps to preserve them. Now it was said by counsel for the pursuers that prejudice to the defenders and the third parties had no role to play in deciding on the competency of secondary evidence. I accept at once, of course, that the leading of secondary evidence of the contents of documents cannot be incompetent merely because the absence of the documents themselves will gravely prejudice the opponents in the litigation. To say, however, that the question of prejudice has no role to play in deciding upon the admissibility of secondary evidence of the contents of documents is to go too far. In my opinion, and this was evidently the view taken by the Lord Ordinary, it is entirely relevant in ascertaining the importance of the documents in the litigation to consider to what extent their absence will obviously prejudice the other parties. The greater the obvious prejudice which would be occasioned by the loss of the documents the more necessary will it be for the party who controls the documents to take whatever steps are required to see that they are not lost.

From what I have said so far it will be seen that I do not accept at all that the Lord Ordinary misdirected himself in his approach to the disposal of the defenders' objection, and I have no doubt that upon the material before him the Lord Ordinary was well entitled to conclude that the vital records were not available at the proof because the pursuers had failed to take proper and elementary steps to see that they were preserved. Upon the evidence they were not entitled, having regard to the critical importance of the records, merely to assume that they would be available when they wanted them.

Mr Bruce, the pursuers' financial director, would not (and indeed could not) suggest that there was any practical difficulty in taking steps to ensure that the records were preserved for the purpose of resolving the issue in this case, and when the pursuers relinquished effective control over them to their associate company in June 1980 it was all the more necessary that some simple special and practicable steps were taken to ensure that these records were kept separate from all other records of Cruisair and retained. No such steps of any kind were taken.

Upon the whole matter I am of opinion that the reclaiming motion should be refused. Before parting with the case I feel bound to say that if the pursuers had successfully resisted the defenders' objection, or if the Lord Ordinary had allowed the secondary evidence to be led under reservation of the issue of competency, their victory would in all probability have been an empty one. The prejudice likely to be suffered by the defenders and the third parties is already obvious and grave. In these circumstances it is not improbable that a reasonable judge would have been reluctant to decide the case in the pursuers' favour upon the secondary evidence of Mr Connell and Mr Forbes, however credible and reliable they appeared to be, because, as seems likely, the defenders and the third parties would have been in no position to test their alleged findings in the absence of the records themselves."

LORD GRIEVE: "The primary rule of the law of evidence in Scotland is that: 'a party must adduce the best attainable evidence of the facts he means to prove (Dickson's Law of Evidence in Scotland (3rd ed., 1887), para. 195). This rule was not challenged by the reclaimers, as indeed it could not have been. The position taken up by the reclaimers however was that, as the best evidence, namely the accounts of Cruisair and the material from which they had been prepared, was no longer available, it having gone amissing, the secondary evidence, namely that of the working papers of Messrs Connell and Forbes, had become the best evidence available. According to the reclaimers the Lord Ordinary should have allowed them to lead the evidence of Mr Connell, not as a privilege, but as an application of the best evidence rule. If secondary evidence is not allowed, once it is accepted that the primary evidence is not available a litigant is debarred from proceeding with a claim. The person relying on the secondary evidence is not required to prove that the loss of the primary evidence was not due to any fault on his part; he just has to prove that it has been lost. Counsel did however accept that in a situation in which the party seeking to rely on the secondary evidence has deliberately destroyed the primary evidence, that party will be debarred from relying on the secondary evidence. Counsel seemed to accept that the same result might follow if the loss was wholly unexplained, but he maintained that a failure by a party to take elementary steps to preserve the primary evidence, would not debar the party from leading the secondary evidence. To debar a party from leading secondary evidence when the primary evidence was not available, it had to be apparent that the non-availability of the primary evidence was due to some blameworthy act of the party seeking to found on the secondary evidence. I am bound to say I found this submission very difficult to follow, and in my opinion it is inconsistent with what is said in paras. 236 and 237 of Dickson, cit. sup. In para. 236 the learned author says: 'Secondary evidence is admitted to prove the contents of documents which are with-held by an opponent, or which have been destroyed or lost without fault in the party founding on them'. In the last paragraph of para. 237, which appears to be particularly relevant to the circumstances of this case, it is stated: 'When the loss of a document has occurred while it was in the hands of the party founding on it, the Court will hesitate to admit secondary proof of its contents; as such cases are usually attended with suspicion. They will probably require the party to show a special *casus omissionis* not attributable to any fault on his part'. These passages have never been criticised in the last 100 years and, in its context, the word 'fault' can only mean a failure to take reasonable care to preserve primary evidence when there is a duty to do so. In my opinion such a duty will always arise where the primary evidence is of critical importance for the resolution of a dispute between the parties to a litigation. As junior counsel for the respondents, in his clear and well presented submission pointed out, such a view is consistent with the later passage in Dickson at para. 241 to this effect: 'it must of course depend on the circumstances of each case, whether the party has expended such an amount of care and diligence in searching for the document, as would entitle him to prove its contents by secondary evidence. He does not require to exhaust every possible chance of recovering it. But he must show that he has in bona fide used every means prudence would suggest as likely to attain that object.'

Counsel for the reclaimers maintained that all possible steps had been taken to recover the primary evidence. Exhaustive searches had been made in Edinburgh, and later in the London area. Nothing more could have been done. The fact however remains that the evidence led did not establish that the primary evidence had been lost; all it established was that no one had been able to find it. While its whereabouts remain unknown the fact remains that at the time this action was raised it was under the control of the reclaimers, who allowed it at some unspecified date to pass out of their control. As set out earlier in this opinion Mr Bruce, who was a director of Cruisair as well as the reclaimers, agreed that there would have been no practical difficulty in taking steps to preserve the evidence. As he admitted, he appreciated that the evidence was not only critical for the reclaimers purposes, but also for the purposes of the respondents and the third parties. As I have already said, the circumstances were such that the reclaimers were under a duty to take all reasonable and practicable steps to preserve the primary evidence for the purposes of the proof. It is clear from the evidence of Mr Bruce that not only could such steps have been taken, but that they were not taken. Accordingly, I conclude that it was due to fault on the reclaimers part that the primary evidence was not available at the proof.

In *Clark v. Clark's Trustees* the Lord Justice-Clerk (Inglis) described the substitution of parole evidence for written evidence as 'an extraordinary privilege'. Senior counsel for the reclaimers did not demur to that, but maintained that in this case the exhaustive inquiries made as to the non-availability of the primary evidence were sufficient to allow the reclaimers to avail themselves of that privilege. For the reasons set out above I do not agree. Had it been established that the primary evidence had been accidentally destroyed, for example by fire, the matter might have been different, but the only relevant evidence as to the disappearance of the primary evidence is that at the date of the raising of this action it was under the control of the defenders, and thereafter it was allowed to pass out of their control, but where to nobody could say. On no view can such evidence justify the 'extraordinary privilege' of leading secondary evidence in substitution for the primary evidence which was no longer available, particularly when it was in the power of the reclaimers to produce it, had they taken steps which they could have taken to see that it was preserved (Dickson, cit. sup., para. 203).

The view which I have expressed above seems to me to coincide with what I consider to be the foundation of the Lord Ordinary's decision in the concluding passage of his opinion at 1986 S.L.T., pp.414J-415A, which starts with the words, 'I consider that the documents are absolutely essential to the proof of the two important issues which I have identified'.

For the reasons which I have tried to set out I agree with your Lordship that the reclaiming motion should be refused and that the interlocutor of the Lord Ordinary should be affirmed.

There is one further matter which figured prominently both in the opinion of the Lord Ordinary and in the debate before us. That was the question of the prejudice which would have been suffered by both the respondents and the third parties if the reclaimers had been allowed to lead the secondary evidence relative to the respondents' accounts. There is no doubt that if the secondary evidence had been admitted it could not properly have been tested by reference to the missing primary evidence on which it bore to be based. That however, in my opinion, does not bear on the competency of the secondary evidence. The secondary evidence is either competent because it is the best evidence available—no fault being attributable to the reclaimers for the absence of the primary evidence or incompetent because it is not. The fact however that the primary evidence is of critical importance for the resolution of the dispute between the parties, and that the truth can probably not be ascertained without it, has a bearing on the duty of the party in whose possession it is when the question of the resolution of a dispute arises, to take all reasonable steps to see that the primary evidence is preserved until the questions in dispute are resolved. Accordingly it was a factor affecting the duty of care which in my opinion the reclaimers were required to exercise at the time their action was raised."

NOTES

The emphasis in this case is very much on the importance of the best evidence rule itself, rather than any prejudice which might arise from non-observance of the rule. (Compare Lord Johnston's approach in the dictum quoted below, see his opinion in *Stirling Aquatic Technology Limited v. Farmocean AB (No. 2))*. Indeed Lord Grieve describes the rule, under reference to Dickson, as "the primary rule of the law of evidence in Scotland". Accordingly, it seems that in these civil cases, the best evidence rule has been applied more stringently than in criminal cases, which, arguably, is rather odd. On the other hand, considerable inroads have been made into the rule by the Civil Evidence (Scotland) Act 1988.

9. Civil Evidence (Scotland) Act 1988

"2.—(1) In any civil proceedings—
    (a) evidence shall not be excluded solely on the ground that it is hearsay;

  (b) a statement made by a person otherwise than in the course of the proof shall be admissible as evidence of any matter contained in the statement of which direct oral evidence by that person would be admissible; and

  (c) the court, or as the case may be the jury, if satisfied that any fact has been established by evidence in those proceedings, shall be entitled to find that fact proved by the evidence notwithstanding that the evidence is hearsay . . .

6.—(1) For the purposes of any civil proceedings a copy of a document, purporting to be authenticated by a person responsible for the making of the copy, shall, unless the court otherwise directs, be

  (a) deemed a true copy; and

  (b) treated for evidential purposes as if it were the document itself.

(2) In subsection (1) above, "copy" includes a transcript or reproduction . . .

9.—In this Act, unless the context otherwise requires—

  "business" includes trade or profession;

  "civil proceedings" includes, in addition to such proceedings in any of the ordinary courts of law—

  (a) any hearing by the sheriff under section 42 of the Social Work (Scotland) Act 1968 of an application for a finding as to whether grounds for the referral of a child's case to a children's hearing are established, except in so far as the application relates to a ground mentioned in section 32(2)(g) of that Act (commission by the child of an offence);

  (b) any arbitration, whether or not under an enactment, except in so far as, in relation to the conduct of the arbitration, specific provision has been made as regards the rules of evidence which are to apply;

  (c) any proceedings before a tribunal or inquiry, except in so far as, in relation to the conduct of proceedings before the tribunal or inquiry, specific provision has been made as regards the rules of evidence which are to apply; and

  (d) any other proceedings conducted wholly or mainly in accordance with rules of procedure agreed between the parties themselves (or as respects which it would have been open to them to agree such rules had they wished to do so) except in so far as any such agreement makes specific provision as regards the rules of evidence which are to apply;

  "court" shall be construed in accordance with the definition of "civil proceedings";

  "document" includes, in addition to a document in writing,—

  (a) any map, plan, graph or drawing;

  (b) any photograph;

  (c) any disc, tape, sound track or other device in which sounds or other data (not being visual images) are recorded so as to be capable (with or without the aid of some other equipment) of being reproduced therefrom; and

  (d) any film, negative, tape or other device in which one or more visual images are recorded so as to be capable (as aforesaid) of being reproduced therefrom;

  "film" includes a microfilm;

  "hearsay" includes hearsay of whatever degree;

  "made" includes "allegedly made";

  "proof" includes trial or other hearing of evidence, proof on commission and any continued proof;

  "records" means records in whatever form;

  "statement" includes any representation (however made or expressed) of fact or opinion but does not include a statement in a precognition; and

  "undertaking" includes any public or statutory undertaking, any local authority and any government department."

NOTES

  Section 6 of the 1988 Act effectively abolishes one branch of the best evidence rule by allowing secondary evidence of documents to be led. But who is "the person responsible for the making of the copy"? Is it simply the person who physically created the copy, for example, by photocopying a document? If so, that person may be certifying as a true copy a document about which he or she knows almost nothing. Or does it refer to the person who is ultimately responsible for making the copy? The latter view would seem preferable, but it is by no means clear that that is what the section implies. There does not appear to be any authority on this question, although in *McIlveny and another v. Donald*, 1995 S.C.L.R. 802, it was held that copy documents which were not authenticated at all, could not be authenticated later during the proof and were held to be inadmissible.

A more difficult point arises from the operation of sections 2 and 9 of the 1988 Act. The definition of "statement" in section 9 includes "any representation (however made or expressed) of fact or opinion". Therefore, a statement made in a document appears to fall within the section 9 definition. By section 2, "a statement made by a person otherwise than in the course of the proof shall be admissible as evidence of any matter contained in the statement of which direct oral evidence by that person would be admissible", and accordingly, it might be argued on that basis that it is permissible to lead oral evidence about the contents of a document, notwithstanding that the original document is not produced. In *F. v. Kennedy (No. 2)*, 1992 S.C.L.R. 750, Lord Justice-Clerk Ross said:

> "It is significant that 'statement' is defined in section 9 of the Act of 1988 as including 'any representation (however made or expressed) of fact or opinion'. There is no suggestion there that 'statement' is limited to a statement by a witness who has not given oral evidence. On the contrary, it is plain from section 9 that the only exception arises where the statement has been made in a precognition. Accordingly, reading section 2 and section 9 together, I am satisfied that the fact that the maker of the statement has given oral evidence does not prevent hearsay evidence being given of what he has said upon another occasion. In this connection the effect of these two sections is that the best evidence rule is overridden."

These comments were made in a very different context to the one under consideration here. However, if they were to be regarded as being of general application, then there would be no room in civil cases for objections to the leading of secondary evidence based upon non-production of either original documents or copies. However, that argument has been foreclosed by the case of *Japan Leasing (Europe) plc v. Weir's Trustee*, 1998 S.L.T. 224. In that case creditors made a claim in a sequestration based upon a hire purchase contract which they said they had entered into with the debtor. To prove the agreement they produced photocopies of the contract and related documents. The Inner House upheld an objection to the use of those copies. Delivering the opinion of the court Lord Justice Clerk Cullen (as he then was) said that:

> "For Japan Leasing counsel submitted that the use of copy documents such as those lodged in process had been rendered admissible as evidence of the contents of the principal documents by reason of the terms of section 2(1)(b) of the Civil Evidence (Scotland) Act 1988. It provided: [his Lordship quoted the terms of section 2(1) set out supra and continued]
>
> This provision had the effect of abolishing the best evidence rule as it applied to written statements. A statement could be a document, and a document could be anything which contained evidential matter. It followed that the evidence of a witness would be admissible as to the contents of an affidavit which was not produced. In the present case each of the copy documents to which the objection related was in itself a 'statement' for the purposes of the statutory provision. A copy document was a form of hearsay, namely hearsay of the original document. It was still open to the court to decide what weight should be attached to hearsay evidence which was rendered admissible. In the present case the sheriff had found that the evidence of Mr Bailey was entirely reliable. He had given evidence that there had been no tampering with the photocopies. Counsel also observed that the terms of section 6 also implied that the best evidence rule no longer applied, since not only was it no longer necessary to produce a principal document, but it was only necessary to have the evidence of the person who was responsible for the copying.
>
> Counsel submitted the further argument that, having regard to the fact that the appeal to the sheriff was by way of summary application, it was open to the sheriff to relax the normal rules of procedure. He pointed out that, unlike the rules relating to litigation in the Court of Session and to ordinary causes in the sheriff court, there were no rules which related specifically to documents rendered admissible by the Civil Evidence Act 1988.
>
> In our view the use which counsel for the respondent sought to make of section 2(1)(b) of the 1988 Act was misconceived. It is clear that this provision is intended to apply to the past statement of a person, whether that statement was given orally or in writing. Evidence given in court as to that statement is made admissible as evidence of any matter contained in it, provided

that direct oral evidence by that person as to that matter would be admissible. However, it does not appear to us that this renders what purports to be a copy of the type of document with which the present case is concerned admissible as evidence of the contents of the principal. First, we do not accept that the copy document is 'a statement made by a person otherwise than in the course of the proof'. Assuming that this description is capable of applying to a contractual document, it applies to the principal document. On this basis it would be a statement by the signatories. Even if the copy document were to be regarded as a statement within the expression to which we have referred, this would not render it admissible as evidence of the contents of the principal document, since direct oral evidence of the signatories would not be admissible (*i.e.* apart from the effect of section 2) as evidence of those contents. That is because the best evidence rule would entail that their oral evidence as to its contents would be inadmissible."

The best evidence rule also continues to apply in civil cases in relation to items of real evidence. There is no question of treating such items as "statements" of any sort, and accordingly, the ratio of *McGowan v. Belling & Co.*, above, still represents good law in relation to the production of such items. In *Stirling Aquatic Technology Limited v. Farmocean AB (No. 2)*, 1996 S.L.T. 456, however, secondary evidence was permitted to be led as to the state of nets used by the pursuers in their fish farm. This was on the basis that the nets were, by the stage of the trial, no longer in a condition in which they could usefully be examined, and the court, although permitting secondary evidence about the nets, said that the burden of proof on the pursuers would be increased owing to the absence of the nets. Lord Johnston said that:

"In my opinion the best evidence rule is essentially tied up with questions of prejudice in the sense that if there is better evidence than that adduced before the court, the party affected by it is prejudiced in his attack upon it and the preferring party thus gains an unfair advantage. I do not see how this rule can apply if it is no longer possible to bring the net to court in any useful state. The question of preservation raises another question. In my view the proper approach to the issue is to view the pursuer's case with more care as to its quality than might otherwise be necessary if the net had been produced, or preserved for production, imposing a heavier burden of proof upon the pursuers than might otherwise have been necessary. On this basis I shall repel the objection but approach the matter as indicated."

Chapter 7

HEARSAY

Hearsay has been statutorily defined in Scotland as "evidence of a statement made by a person otherwise than while giving oral evidence in court"—see section 259(1) of the Criminal Procedure Scotland Act 1995, below. The general rule can be relatively simply stated. In *Morrison v. H.M.A.*, 1991 S.L.T. 57 at p.62 the High court accepted as the law of Scotland the definition of hearsay given in Cross, *Evidence* (6th ed.) p.38 quoted by Lord Havers in *R. v. Sharp*, that is: "an assertion other than one made by a person while giving oral evidence in the proceedings is inadmissible as evidence of any fact asserted". However, the rule forbidding the use of hearsay evidence is one of the most obscure and complex in the law of evidence. It is subject to many quirks and exceptions, and has recently been the subject of radical statutory reform. The rule has been altogether abolished in civil cases—see the Civil Evidence (Scotland) Act 1988, section 2 and Chapter 13 below; in criminal cases, its application has been fairly comprehensively circumscribed both by the courts and by statutory intervention.

1.   "Hearsay: A Scottish Perspective"
A. B. Wilkinson in *Justice and Crime: Essays in Honour of Lord Justice-General Emslie* (1993) ed. R. F. Hunter

"In the *Berkeley Peerage case* Lord Mansfield said:
  'In Scotland and in most continental countries, the judges determine about the facts in dispute as well as on the law; and they think that there is no danger in their listening to evidence of hearsay because when they come to consider of their judgement on the merits of the case they can trust themselves to disregard entirely the hearsay evidence, or give it any little weight which it seems to deserve. But in England, where the jury are the sole judges of the facts, hearsay evidence is properly excluded because no man can tell what effect it might have upon their minds.' (1811 4 Camp 401).
  Yet the Scottish lineage of the rule against hearsay is ancient. Stair put it simply: 'testimonies *ex auditu* prove not', and Balfour, Hume and Burnett were to the same effect (Stair IV, xliii, 15; Balfour, *Practicks*, 381; Hume on *Crimes* (3rd ed.), ii, 406; Burnett, *Criminal Law*, 600). Nor, if there had been no rule against hearsay, would the absence of jury trial have been an adequate explanation. Lord Mansfield spoke before jury trial was introduced, or re-introduced, to Scottish civil practice but the criminal jury was already long-established and had similar historical roots to its English counterpart. Lord Mansfield's views are, however, of interest for two reasons. First, he may from experience of Scottish appeals in the House of Lords have acquired some impression of how, at least in civil cases, hearsay evidence was handled by Scottish courts. Lord Devlin has said that the law of evidence as expounded on the basis of the authorities bears the same relation to the law of evidence as practised in the courts as the King's English bears to pidgin English. Lord Mansfield is, perhaps, an eloquent if unwitting witness to that dichotomy. Closing or reducing the gap between law and practice may be a legitimate object of reform. Secondly, however mistaken Lord Mansfield's comparative researches may have been (Hammelman, 1951 L.Q.R. 67)—and the continental sources give little more support to his thesis than do the Scottish—he is of interest as an early exponent of the view that the rationale for the rule against hearsay is to be found in the jury. That view was taken up by Thayer and controversy has since flourished on whether it is to the jury or to

adversary procedure that the common law legal world should look for the origins of the rule (Thayer, *Preliminary Treatise on Evidence at the Common Law*; Morgan, *Law of Evidence: some proposals for its reform*; and *Introduction to the American Law Institute's Model Code of Evidence*).

The controversy on origins, if pursued on traditional lines, is largely sterile. The material from early sources, such as the explanation of the exclusion of evidence on the ground that the author of the statement had not been on oath or was not available for cross-examination, is now usually thought to support the adversary, rather than the jury, theory, but none of the material is unequivocal. The exigencies both of jury trial and of adversary procedure have doubtless influenced later developments but, at least so far as Scotland is concerned, it is difficult to accept that either was a formative source. Until 1686 civil procedure was essentially inquisitorial and it retained something of that character until the reforms at the beginning of the nineteenth century. Yet the rule against hearsay is at least as old as the early seventeenth century. On the other hand, as juries were unknown to post-mediaeval civil procedure until 1815, distrust of, or lack of confidence in, the jury is unlikely to have played a determinant part. The search for origins can be pursued more profitably elsewhere. The dominant historical influence here, as in much of both the substantive and adjective law, seems to have been civilian. Indeed, nowhere is civilian (or canonist) influence stronger than in pre-nineteenth century adjective law, as can be seen from the forms of procedure and proof. There are traces of a rule against hearsay in the Novels and the Digest (Nov 90, 2; D22, 3, 28; *cf* C4, 21, 13). Conservative and liberal interpretations may be found in the later civilian tradition. In eighteenth century German law *testimonium de audita* was regarded as worthless and so, with an exception for questions of blood relationship in matrimonial disputes, the *testis de audita* was excluded (Hammelman, p.69). Pothier too considered that hearsay testimony could not make proof (*Traits des Obligations* No. 786), and pre-Napoleonic French law admitted hearsay only in exceptional circumstances. Voet, on the other hand, was more liberal. He discusses hearsay only in connection with public rumour and broadcast reports. These, he says, are not properly evidence but 'only provide a kind of token by which in criminal matters the judge may direct his further tracking down of the truth.' They may also strengthen other evidence. But 'for the rest rumour is as much a grasper at what is made up and is evil as it is a messenger of the truth.' His conclusion, while acknowledging that the commentators he cites would narrow the discretion of the judge in various ways, is that 'the extent of belief to be given to rumour must be left to the discretion of a cautious judge.' (Commentary on the Pandects, XXII, 3,4). Scots law, it seems clear, inclined to the conservative side of the civilian debate, although a place was found for proof by reputation in questions of marriage and legitimacy and other cases in which reliance could be put on public report so as to yield at least *prima facie* proof.

If one looks for the rationale on which civilian ideas were assimilated and applied it is to be found, quite simply, in an ancient distrust of oral testimony. That distrust is typical of Roman law and found its way into the civilian tradition (Morrison, *Some Features of the Roman and the English Law of Evidence*, 1959 33 Tulane LR 577, 585; Voet, XXII, 5). It has also influenced the historical course of English law (Cross, *Evidence* (7th ed.) pp.201–206). It was a marked feature of Scots law as reflected in the numerous categories of witnesses who were for long excluded from giving evidence (Stair IV, xliii; Erskine, *Institute* IV, ii; Hume, ii, 339). Some of these excluded categories may in part be explained by a reluctance to burden men's consciences with a conflict between their own interests, or the interests of those to whom they were bound by familial or other allegiance, and the duty of speaking the truth under oath, but the main reason was that oral testimony was thought so unreliable that any feature which might heighten the risk of falsehood or error led to the witness's exclusion. 'Yet great caution,' says Stair, 'hath been always adhibited in admitting of witnesses; because many are apt to mistake, through inadvertancy or precipitancy, and through the secret insinuation of favour or hatred, which even the witnesses themselves do not perceive.' (Stair IV, xliii). The same distrust of oral testimony, if in a more acceptable form, may be seen in the requirement of corroboration and in the rules that writing is necessary for the constitution of certain obligations and that the writ or oath of the party having the interest to deny the obligation is necessary for the proof of others. In the latter connection Erskine's comment is of interest that, when the art of writing are rare [sic], proof by witnesses was admitted in almost every case, but 'after writing became a more general accomplishment, the lubricity and uncertain faith of testimonies made it necessary to bring the doctrine of parole evidence within narrower limits.' (Erskine, IV, ii, 19) Our ancestors were very conscious of the fallibility of testimony and until the nineteenth century was well advanced there was little of the modern confidence, perhaps now waning, in the ability of the trier of fact, whether judge or jury, to separate the true from the false. At the beginning of the modern development More commented:

'According to the old notions entertained in Scotland, all persons were incompetent as witnesses whose testimony was supposed to be liable to bias, or to whose evidence full and implicit credit might not be given. Every person admitted as a witness was not only presumed to tell the truth, and the whole truth, but the capacity of every witness for accuracy of observation, and distinctness of recollection, seemed to be placed on the same footing, so that no room was left for the exercise of that discrimination, perhaps the most essential, as it is undoubtedly the most difficult, duty of those who are called upon to judge of evidence, which consists in giving to the testimony even of the most upright witnesses, only that degree of weight to which their opportunities and accuracy of observation entitle it. But when, instead of exercising this discrimination, every person admitted as a witness was held to stand upon the same level, and the evidence of each was received with the same attention, and held to be entitled to the same weight, it is obvious that much precaution was necessary as to the persons who should be allowed to give evidence.' (More's *Notes on Stair* cccix, note on IV, xliii)

Reluctance to admit oral evidence went then hand-in-hand with reluctance to evaluate it once admitted. More stood at the dawn of the modern era and although he saw some of the hazards he did not shrink from the challenge. His confidence in the trier of fact was well-nigh complete. Grotesque though some of the results were, the distrust of oral testimony was not, however, in itself irrational. Witnesses lie. Memory fails. Sentiments of loyalty or compassion, hatred or repulsion, cloud the mind. Threats or inducements, sometimes subtle, sometimes almost unconscious, play a part. Reflection on what was perceived leads imperceptibly to reconstruction. To close the door on all that, or most of it, by shutting out all but the stoutest testimony was intelligible policy. However much we may reject it, or believe we have progressed beyond it, we cannot deny its claim to reason. For long, thinking of that kind underlay attitudes to evidence. It is as old as Justinian or older. A climate of opinion which severely restricted the scope of direct oral testimony and erected elaborate safeguards around it would also, of necessity, be impatient of the reception of indirect testimony dependent on the narrative of others. The authority of the civil law and native caution combined in support. It is there, rather than in the specialities of jury trial or adversary procedure that the *fons et origo* of the rule against hearsay lie.

The question may be asked why, if the rule had its origins in a distrust of oral testimony, it continued to flourish when that distrust had declined. Here, no doubt, the exigencies of adversary procedure, and perhaps also of the jury, played a part. The new confidence in the capacity of the trier of fact to evaluate oral testimony, went hand-in-hand with, was largely based on, confidence in cross-examination as the key to truth. The new era was the era of the great advocates. They were great pleaders and also great cross-examiners. Evidence which was not susceptible to the test of cross-examination remained suspect."

NOTES

See also Wilkinson, "The Hearsay Rule in Scotland" (1982) J.R. 213. It may be questioned whether hearsay should really be the subject of an exclusionary rule at all. The current trend, both in the civil and criminal courts, seems to be towards regarding the admission of hearsay as a matter of the weight to be accorded to the evidence rather than one of admissibility. In this context, see the notes to *R. v. Kearley* [1992] 2 All E.R. 345, below, and the discussion of the hearsay rule in the Scottish Law Commission's Report, "Hearsay Evidence in Criminal Proceedings" (Scot. Law Com. No. 149, 1995). There is relatively little authority on hearsay in Scotland, which may suggest that the rule has caused the Scottish courts little difficulty in practice. The same does not appear to be true of the English courts and many of the cases reproduced here are English. They must accordingly be read with a certain amount of caution, given the apparent divergence of views about hearsay between the two jurisdictions—see the *Lord Advocate's Reference No. 1 of 1992*, 1992 S.C.C.R. 724, and the discussion below.

2. Teper v. R.
[1952] A.C. 480

This was a case from British Guiana which came before the Privy Council on appeal. The appellant was charged with deliberately setting fire to his own dry goods shop with intent to defraud his insurers. A police officer gave identification evidence at Teper's trial, which was not objected to by defence counsel, that he had heard a woman's voice shouting "your place burning and you going away from the fire". The incident took place at least a furlong from the fire and not less than 26 minutes after the fire was said to have been started. *Teper* was convicted and appealed on the ground that the evidence of the woman's statement was hearsay and inadmissible.

LORD NORMAND: "The rule against the admission of hearsay evidence is fundamental. It is not the best evidence and it is not delivered on oath. The truthfulness and accuracy of the person whose words are spoken to by another witness cannot be tested by cross-examination, and the light which his demeanour would throw on his testimony is lost. Nevertheless, the rule admits of certain carefully safeguarded and limited exceptions, one of which is that words may be proved when they form part of the *res gestae*. The rules controlling this exception are common to the jurisprudence of British Guiana, England and Scotland. It appears to rest ultimately on two propositions, that human utterance is both a fact and a means of communication, and that human action may be so interwoven with words that the significance of the action cannot be understood without the correlative words, and the dissociation of the words from the action would impede the discovery of truth. But the judicial application of these two propositions, which do not always combine harmoniously, have never been precisely formulated in a general principle. Their Lordships will not attempt to arrive at a general formula, nor is it necessary to review all of the considerable number of cases cited in the argument. This, at least, may be said, that it is essential that the words sought to be proved by hearsay should be, if not absolutely contemporaneous with the action or event, at least so clearly associated with it, in time, place and circumstances, that they are part of the thing being done, and so an item or part of real evidence and not merely a reported statement: *The Queen v. Bedingfield* 14 Cox CC 341, *O'Hara v. Central SMT Co.,* 1941 S.C. 363.

How slight a separation of time and place may suffice to make hearsay evidence of the words spoken incompetent is well illustrated by the two cases cited. In *Bedingfield's* case a woman rushed with her throat cut out of a room in which the injury had been inflicted into another room where she said something to persons who saw her enter. Their evidence about what she said was ruled inadmissible by Cockburn C.J. In *O'Hara's* case, a civil action, the event was an injury to a passenger brought about by the sudden swerve of the omnibus in which she was travelling. The driver of the omnibus said in his evidence that he was forced to swerve by a pedestrian who hurried across his path. Hearsay evidence of what was said by a man on the pavement at the scene of the accident as soon as the injured party had been attended to was held to be inadmissible in corroboration of the driver's evidence. But what was said 12 minutes later, and away from the scene, by the same man was held not part of the *res gestae*. In *Christie's* case ([1914] A.C. 545), the principle of the decision in *Bedingfield's* case was approved by Lord Reading, with whom Lord Dunedin concurred, and no criticism of it is to be found in the speeches of the other noble and learned Lords who sat with them. In *The Queen v. Gibson* (18 Q.B.D. 537) the prosecutor gave evidence in a criminal trial that, immediately after he was struck by a stone, a woman going past pointing to the prisoner's door said, 'the person who threw the stone went in there'. This evidence was not objected to at the trial, but it was admitted by counsel for the prosecution in a case reserved that the evidence was incompetent. The conviction was quashed, and from their judgements it is clear that the judges who took part in the decision were far from questioning the correctness of counsel's admission. In *Gibson's* case the words were closely associated in time and place with the event, the assault. But they were not directly connected with that event itself. They were not words spontaneously forced from the woman by the sight of the assault, but were prompted by the sight of a man quitting the scene of the assault and they were spoken for the purpose of helping to bring him to justice.

The special danger of allowing hearsay evidence for the purpose of identification requires that it shall only be allowed if it satisfies the strictest test of close association with the event in time, place and circumstances. 'Identification is an act of the mind, and the primary evidence of what was passing in the mind of a man is his own testimony, where it can be obtained. It would be very dangerous to allow evidence to be given of a man's words and actions, in order to show by this extrinsic evidence that he identified the prisoner, if he was capable of being called as a witness and was not called to prove by direct evidence that he had thus identified him.': *Christie's* case, *per* Lord Moulton.

There is yet another proposition which can be affirmed, that for identification purposes in a criminal trial the event with which the words sought to be proved must be so connected as to form part of the *res gestae*, is the commission of the crime itself, the throwing of the stone, the striking of the blow, the setting fire to the building or whatever the criminal act may be. The respondent's counsel submitted that any relevant event or action may be accompanied by words which may have to be proved in order to bring out its true significance. There is a limited sense in which this is true, but it is not always true, and much depends on the use to be made of the evidence. In *Christie's* case hearsay evidence of certain words uttered by a child, the victim of an indecent assault, in the presence and hearing of the accused were held to be admissible in explanation of the demeanour of the accused in response to them. But the evidence was held inadmissible for the purpose of showing that the child identified the accused as his assailant. In the present case identification is the purpose for which the hearsay was introduced, and its admission goes far beyond anything that has been authorised by any reported case".

The evidence was found to be inadmissible and the conviction was quashed.

NOTES

(i) Lord Normand's rationale for the hearsay rule has often been cited and approved by the courts. Is it true to say, however, that hearsay evidence is not the best evidence? In his commentary to *Smith v. H.M.A.*, 1986 S.C.C.R. 135, below, Sheriff Gordon said that:

"There is much to be said for the view that the likelihood is that what a witness says shortly after an incident is more accurate than his recollection at a trial which may take place a year later, but that is not in general the view taken by the law of evidence."

In *Myers v. D.P.P.* [1965] A.C. 1001, Lord Reid said:

"The whole development of the exceptions to the hearsay rule is based on the determination of certain classes of evidence as admissible or inadmissible and not the apparent credibility of particular evidence tendered. No matter how cogent particular evidence may seem to be, unless it comes within a class which is admissible, it is excluded. Half a dozen witnesses may offer to prove that they heard two men of high character who cannot now be found discuss in detail the fact now i[n] issue and agree on a credible account of it, but that evidence would not be admitted although it might be by far the best evidence available."

Recent reforms of the hearsay rule in Scotland, considered below, are based on the idea that in certain circumstances hearsay is or may become the best evidence available. What are the arguments for and against the acceptance of evidence which, by implication, is second best?

(ii) *Res gestae* means, in this context, "the whole thing that happened". The concept is analysed further in *Ratten v. R.* [1972] A.C. 378; [1971] 3 All E.R. 801, below. Where a statement is admitted under this heading it is admissible as evidence of the facts asserted or implied in it, although it has, on occasion, been argued that it is not hearsay at all, but a species of real evidence—see, for example, Lord Moncrieff in *O'Hara v. Central S.M.T. Co.*, 1941 S.C. 363 at 390. Other common law exceptions to the hearsay rule are listed by Wilkinson in (1982) J.R. 213. See also Macphail, *Evidence*, chap. 19, and the new exceptions created by the Criminal Procedure (Scotland) Act 1995, ss.259–261, set out below.

(iii) For a rare Scottish discussion of the meaning of *res gestae*, see the difficult case of *Hamill v. H.M.A.*, 1999 S.L.T. 963, in which the statement in question incriminated a co-accused. The majority held (Lord Philip dissenting) that in the absence of evidence of concert, the statement could not be admissible, even as part of the *res gestae*, because the co-accused had not been present when it was made. See also chapter 8.

(iv) Note the comments in this case, and in that of *Christie* [1914] A.C. 545, referred to in *Teper*, on the dangers of using hearsay evidence as evidence of identification, and compare them with the cases set out below on evidence of previous identification, such as *Muldoon v. Herron*, 1970 J.C. 30. What distinctions, if any, can be drawn between *Teper* and cases such as *Muldoon*?

3. Ratten v. R
[1971] 3 All E.R. 801

Ratten was an Australian case which came to the Privy Council on appeal. The accused was charged with the murder of his wife. His defence was that his wife's death, which was caused by gunshot wounds, was accidental. The prosecution case depended in part on evidence that a phone-call was made to the local telephone exchange from the accused's house shortly before the fatal incident took place. In the phone-call, a woman, clearly distressed, gave her telephone number and asked the operator to connect her with the police. It was evidence which clearly tended to negative the defence of accident, since it was not said that anyone was in the house other than the accused, his wife and their young children. The question arose as to whether it was nevertheless inadmissible as hearsay. Lord Wilberforce delivered the opinion of the Board.

LORD WILBERFORCE: "The next question related to the further facts sought to be proved concerning the telephone call. The objection taken against this evidence was that it was hearsay and that it did not come within any of the recognised exceptions to the rule against hearsay evidence. In their Lordships' opinion the evidence was not hearsay evidence and was admissible as evidence of fact relevant to an issue.

The mere fact that evidence of a witness includes evidence as to words spoken by another person who is not called is no objection to its admissibility. Words spoken are facts just as much as any other action by a human being. If the speaking of the words is a relevant fact, a witness may give evidence that they were spoken. A question of hearsay only arises when the words spoken are relied on 'testimonially', *i.e.* as establishing some fact narrated by the words. Authority is hardly needed for this proposition but their Lordships will restate what was said in the judgment of the Board in *Subramaniam v. Public Prosecutor* ([1956] 1 W.L.R. 965 at 970):

'Evidence of a statement made to a witness by a person who is not himself called as a witness may or may not be hearsay. It is hearsay and inadmissible when the object of the evidence is to establish the truth of what is contained in the statement. It is not hearsay and is admissible when it is proposed to establish by the evidence, not the truth of the statement but the fact that it was made.'

A fuller statement of the same principle is provided by Dean Wigmore in his work on Evidence. He emphasises, as their Lordships would emphasise, that the test of admissibility, in the case last mentioned, is relevance to an issue.

The evidence relating to the act of telephoning by the deceased was, in their Lordship's view, factual and relevant. It can be analysed into the following elements. (1) At about 1.15 p.m. the number Echuca 1494 rang. I plugged into that number. (2) I opened the speak key and said number please. (3) A female voice answered. (4) That voice was hysterical and sobbed. (5) The voice said 'Get me the police please'.

The factual items numbered (1)–(3) were relevant in order to show that, contrary to the evidence of the appellant, a call was made, only some three to five minutes before the fatal shooting, by a woman. It not being suggested that there was anybody in the house other than the appellant, his wife and small children, this woman, the caller, could only have been the deceased. Items (4) and (5) were relevant as possibly showing (if the jury thought fit to draw the inference) that the deceased woman was at this time in a state of emotion or fear (*cf Aveson v. Lord Kinnear* per Lord Ellenborough C.J.). They were relevant and necessary evidence in order to explain and complete the fact of the call being made. A telephone call is a composite act, made up of manual operations together with the utterance of words (*cf McGregor v. Stokes* and remarks of Salmond J. therein quoted). To confine the evidence to the first would be to deprive the act of most of its significance. The act had content when it was known that the call was made in a state of emotion. The knowledge that the caller desired the police to be called, helped to indicate the nature of the emotion—anxiety or fear at an existing or impending emergency. It was a matter for the jury to decide what light (if any) this evidence, in the absence of any explanation from the appellant, who was in the house, threw on what situation was occurring or developing at the time.

If, then, this evidence had been presented in this way, as evidence purely of relevant facts, its admissibility could hardly have been plausibly challenged. But the appellant submits that in fact this was not so. It is said that the evidence was tendered and admitted as evidence of an assertion by the deceased that she was being attacked by the appellant, and that it was, so far, hearsay evidence, being put forward as evidence of the truth of facts asserted by his statement. It is claimed that the learned Chief Justice so presented the evidence to the jury and that, therefore, its admissibility, as hearsay, may be challenged.

Their Lordships, as already stated, do not consider that there is any hearsay element in the evidence, nor in their opinion was it so presented by the trial judge, but they think it right to deal with the appellant's submission on the assumption that there is, *i.e.* that the words said to have been used involve an assertion of the truth of some facts stated in them and that they may have been so understood by the jury. The Crown defended the admissibility of the words as part of the 'res gestae' a contention which led to the citation of numerous authorities.

The expression 'res gestae', like many Latin phrases, is often used to cover situations insufficiently analysed in clear English terms. In the context of the law of evidence it may be used in at least three different ways:

1. When a situation of fact (*e.g.* a killing) is being considered, the question may arise when does the situation begin and when does it end. It may be arbitrary and artificial to confine the evidence to the firing of the gun or the insertion of the knife without knowing, in a broader sense, what was happening. Thus in *O'Leary v. Reginam* (1946 73 C.L.R. 566) evidence was admitted of assaults, prior to a killing, committed by the accused during what was said to be a continuous orgy. As Dixon J. said (1946 73 C.L.R. at 577):

'Without evidence of what, during that time, was done by those men who took any significant part in the matter and specially evidence of the behaviour of the prisoner, the transaction of which the alleged murder formed an integral part could not be truly understood and, isolated from it, could only be presented as an unreal and not very intelligible event.'

2. The evidence may be concerned with spoken words as such (apart from the truth of what they convey). The words are then themselves the *res gestae* or part of the *res gestae, i.e.* are the relevant facts or part of them.
3. A hearsay statement is made either by the victim of an attack or by a bystander—indicating directly or indirectly the identity of the attacker. The admissibility of the statement is then said to depend on whether it was made as part of the *res gestae*. A classical instance of this is the much debated case of *R. v. Bedingfield* (1874 14 Cox CC 341) and there are other instances of its application in reported cases. These tend to apply different standards, and some of them carry less than conviction. The reason why this is so is that concentration tends to be focused on the opaque or at least imprecise Latin phrase rather than on the basic reason for excluding the type of evidence which this group of cases is concerned with. There is no doubt what this reason is: it is twofold. The first is that there may be uncertainty as to the exact words used because of their transmission through the evidence of another person than the speaker. The second is because of the risk of concoction of false evidence by persons who have been the victim of assault or accident.

The first matter goes to weight. The person testifying to the words used is liable to cross-examination: the accused person (as he could not at the time when earlier reported cases were decided) can given his own account if different. There is no such difference in kind or substance between evidence of what was said and evidence of what was done (for example between evidence of what the victim said as to an attack and evidence that he (or she) was seen in a terrified state or was heard to shriek) as to require a total rejection of one and admission of the other.

The possibility of concoction, or fabrication, where it exists, is on the other hand an entirely valid reason for exclusion, and is probably the real test which judges in fact apply. In their Lordships' opinion this should be recognised and applied directly as the relevant test: the test should not be the uncertain one whether the making of the statement was in some sense part of the event or transaction. This may often be difficult to establish: such external matters as the time which elapses between the events and the speaking of the words (or vice versa), and differences in location being relevant factors but not, taken by themselves, decisive criteria. As regards statements made after the event it must be for the judge, by preliminary ruling, to satisfy himself that the statement was so clearly made in circumstances of spontaneity or involvement in the event that the possibility of concoction can be disregarded. Conversely, if he considers that the statement was made by way of narrative of a detached prior event so that the speaker was so disengaged from it as to be able to construct or adapt his account, he should exclude it. And the same must in principle be true of statements made before the event. The test should be not the uncertain one, whether the making of the statement should be regarded as part of the event or transaction. This may often be difficult to show. But if the drama, leading up to the climax, has commenced and assumed such intensity and pressure that the utterance can safely be regarded as a true reflection of what was unrolling or actually happening, it ought to be received. The expression 'res gestae' may conveniently sum up these criteria, but the reality of them must always be kept in mind: it is this that lies behind the best reasoned of the judges' rulings.

A few illustrations may be given. One of the earliest, and as often happens also the clearest, is that of Holt C.J. at Nisi Prius in *Thompson v. Trevanion* ((1693) Skin 402). He allowed that 'what the wife said immediate upon the hurt received, and before that she had time to devise or contrive anything for her own advantage' might be given in evidence, a statement often quoted and approved. *R. v. Bedingfield* ((1874) 14 Cox CC 341) is more useful as a focus for discussion, than for the decision on the facts. Their Lordships understand later indications of approval (*R. v. Christie* [1914] A.C. 545 and *Teper v. Reginam* [1952] All E.R. 447), to relate to the principle established, for, although in a historical sense the emergence of the victim could be described as a different 'res' from the cutting of the throat, there could hardly be a case where the words uttered carried more clearly the mark of spontaneity and intense involvement.

In a lower key the evidence of the words of the careless pedestrian in *O'Hara v. Central SMT Co* (1941 S.C. 363) was admitted on the principle of spontaneity. The Lord President (Lord Normand) said that there must be close association: the words should be at least *de recenti* and not after an interval which would allow time for reflection and concocting a story. Lord Fleming said:

'Obviously statements made after there has been time for deliberation are not likely to be entirely spontaneous, and may, indeed, be made for the express purpose of concealing the truth',

and Lord Moncrieff refers to the 'share in the event' which is taken by the person reported to have made the statement. He contrasts an exclamation 'forced out of a witness by the emotion generated by an event' with a subsequent narrative. The Lord President reaffirmed the principle stated in this case in an appeal to this Board in *Teper v. Reginam* stressing the necessity for close association in time, place and circumstances between the statement and the crucial events.

In Australia, a leading authority is *Adelaide Chemical and Fertilizer Co. Ltd v. Carlyle* ((1940) 64 C.L.R. 514) in which the High Court considered the admissibility of a statement made soon after the breaking of a sulphuric acid jar over his legs by the injured man. This question was not decisive to the decision, but was discussed by

Starke and Dixon JJ with numerous citations. Both emphasise and illustrate the uncertainty of decided cases and legal writers on the question of admissibility of statements of this type and on the question what they may be admitted to prove. Dixon J. with some caution reaches the conclusion that although English law, in the general view of lawyers, admits statements only as parts or details of a transaction not yet complete, while in America, greater recognition is given to the guarantee of truth provided by spontaneity and the lack of time to devise or contrive, yet English decisions do show some reliance on the greater trustworthiness of statements made at on[c]e without reflection. In an earlier case in the High Court (*Brown v. R.* ((1913) 17 C.L.R. 570]) where evidence was excluded, Isaacs and Powers J.J. in their joint judgment put the exclusion on the ground that it was a mere narration respecting a concluded event, a narration not naturally or spontaneously emanating from or growing out of the main narration but arising as an independent and additional transaction.

In *People v. De Simone* ((1919) 121 NE 761) the Court of Appeals of New York admitted evidence that a passer-by immediately after a shooting had shouted 'He ran over Houston Street'. Collin J. referred to deeds and acts which are—

'forced or brought into utterance or existence by and in the evolution of the transaction itself, and which stand in immediate causal relation to it.'

The evidence was, expressly, not admitted as part of the *res gestae*, because it was not so interwoven or connected with the principal event (*i.e.* the shooting which the person did not see) as to be regarded as part of it.

These authorities show that there is ample support for the principle that hearsay evidence may be admitted if the statement providing it is made in such conditions (always being those of approximate but not exact contemporaneity) of involvement or pressure as to exclude the possibility of concoction or distortion to the advantage of the maker or the disadvantage of the accused.

Before applying it to the facts of the present case, there is one other matter to be considered, namely the nature of the proof required to establish the involvement of the speaker in the pressure of the drama, or the concatenation of events leading up to the crisis. On principle it would not appear right that the necessary association should be shown only by the statement itself, otherwise the statement would be lifting itself into the area of admissibility. There is little authority on this point. In *R. v. Taylor* (1961 (3) S.A. 616) where witnesses said they had heard scuffles and thuds during which the deceased cried out 'John, please don't hit me any more. You will kill me', Fannin AJ said that it would be unrealistic to require examination of the question (of close relationship) without reference to the terms of the statement sought to be proved.

'Often the only evidence as to how near in time the making of the statement was to the act it relates to, and the actual relationship between the two, will be contained in the statement itself.'

Facts differ so greatly that it is impossible to lay down any precise general rule: it is difficult to imagine a case where there is no evidence at all of connection between statement and principal event other than the statement itself, but whether this is sufficiently shown must be a matter for the trial judge. Their Lordships would be disposed to agree that, amongst other things, he may take the statement itself into account.

In the present case, in their Lordships' judgment, there was ample evidence of the close and intimate connection between the statement ascribed to the deceased and the shooting which occurred very shortly afterwards. They were closely associated in place and in time. The way in which the statement came to be made (in a call for the police) and the tone of voice used, showed intrinsically that the statement was being forced from the deceased by an overwhelming pressure of contemporary event. It carried its own stamp of spontaneity and this was endorsed by the proved time sequence and the proved proximity of the deceased to the appellant with his gun. Even on the assumption that there was an element of hearsay in the words used, they were safely admitted. The jury was, additionally, directed with great care as to the use to which they might be put. On all counts, therefore, their Lordships can find no error in law in the admission of the evidence. They should add part of the self-exonerating statement and that accordingly, on the basis of in the exercise of discretion."

NOTES

In *Subramaniam v. Public Prosecutor* [1956] 1 W.L.R. 965 it was said that:

"Evidence of a statement is hearsay and inadmissible when the object of the evidence is to establish the truth of what is contained in the statement. It is not hearsay and is admissible when it is proposed to establish by the evidence, not the truth of the statement, but the fact that it was made."

Evidence about a prior statement is admissible where the making of the statement constitutes original evidence of some relevant fact—see Wilkinson, *The Scottish Law of Evidence*, p.34. This has sometimes been described as a distinction between "secondary" and "primary" hearsay. The court insisted in *Ratten* that evidence of the disputed phone-calls was relevant as evidence merely that a statement was made—that is, primary hearsay, or "original evidence"—and that there was no question of admitting it as evidence of the facts asserted in the call, which would constitute secondary hearsay and therefore be inadmissible. Is this convincing? There seems little doubt that certain facts were implied by the phone call, and in any event, evidence of the call would barely have been relevant without reference to the content of the call. Can *Ratten* realistically be distinguished from the next case, *R. v. Kearley*? The House of Lords in the latter case attempted to do so.

4. R. v. Kearley
[1992] 2 All E.R. 345

The Crown sought to lead evidence of certain telephone calls and visits made to a house during a police search for controlled drugs. The callers had all asked for the appellant, "Chippie", and asked to be supplied with drugs. None of the telephone callers or visitors were called as witnesses, and the Crown sought instead to rely on police evidence of the calls. This was objected to as hearsay, an objection which the House of Lords ultimately sustained, Lords Griffiths and Browne-Wilkinson dissenting.

LORD GRIFFITHS (DISSENTING): "My Lords, I have had the advantage of reading the speech of Lord Browne-Wilkinson. Were it not for the fact that there is a division of opinion among your Lordships I would have been content to say that I entirely agree with it and for the reasons he gives I too would dismiss this appeal. In view however of the opinions expressed by others of your Lordships with which I cannot agree I shall add some observations of my own.

The appellant was suspected by the police of trading as a drug dealer. On October 7, 1988 the police arrested the appellant and searched his flat. Drugs were found in the flat but not in such quantities as to raise the irresistible inference that the appellant was dealer as opposed to having the drugs for his own consumption. However, whilst the police were searching the flat, ten telephone calls were made to the flat in which the caller asked for the appellant and asked for drugs. In addition to this seven people called at the flat asking for the appellant and offering to buy drugs for cash. The prosecution did not call the telephone callers or those who visited the flat as witnesses. I do not know the reason but I suspect they could not identify the telephone callers and in the case of the visitors to the flat it is of course notoriously difficult to persuade a user of drugs to give evidence against his supplier: self-incrimination, fear of violent physical reprisals and loss of the source of supply are all powerful deterrents acting on the mind of such a potential witness.

The prosecution however wished the police to give evidence of the telephone calls and the visits including the words spoken on each occasion. If this evidence was admitted it would point overwhelmingly to the conclusion that the appellant was not only in possession of drugs but was on October 7 actively carrying on his trade as a drug dealer.

The defence objected to the admission of the evidence upon the grounds that the words spoken by the telephone callers and the visitors, who were not called as witnesses, were inadmissible by virtue of the hearsay rule of evidence and that evidence of the telephone calls and the visits without evidence of what was said provided no proof of any activity by the appellant and were therefore irrelevant.

The trial judge overruled the objection and admitted the evidence. It is hardly surprising that the jury convicted the appellant, for as a matter of common sense it is difficult to think of much more convincing evidence of his activity as a drug dealer than customers constantly ringing his flat to buy drugs and a stream of customers beating a path to his door for the same purpose.

The Court of Appeal also held that the evidence was admissible and the appellant now appeals to your Lordships.

Unless compelled to do so by authority I should be most unwilling to hold that such evidence should be withheld from the jury. In my view the criminal law of evidence should be developed along common-sense lines readily comprehensible to the men and women who comprise the jury and bear the responsibility for the major decisions in criminal cases. I believe that most laymen if told that the criminal law of evidence forbade them even to consider such evidence as we are debating in this appeal would reply, 'Then the law is an ass.' If I was driven by authority to hold that the law of evidence had been developed by the judges to the point at which the evidence was inadmissible, then I would think that a powerful case had been made out to re-examine the wisdom of the decision in *Myers v. DPP* [1964] 2 All E.R. 881; [1965] A.C. 1001, in which it was held by a majority of three to two that no further judicial development of the law of hearsay was permissible and that future correction must be left to the legislature. Over a quarter of a century has passed since that decision but no overall legislative review of hearsay evidence in criminal law has been attempted. The hearsay rule was created by our judicial predecessors and if we find that it no longer serves to do justice in certain conditions then the judges of today should accept the responsibility of reviewing and adapting the rules of evidence to serve present society. I find the dissenting speeches of Lord Pearce and Lord Donovan more persuasive that the speech of the majority and I note that it was this dissenting view that found favour with the Supreme Court of Canada in *Ares v. Venner* [1970] S.C.R. 608.

Mr de Navarro QC on behalf of the appellant presented a skilful and beguiling argument founded upon the old case of *Wright v. Doe d Tatham* (1837) 7 Ad. & El. 313, 112 All E.R. 488 and encapsulated in the following submission:

> 'Evidence is only relevant if weight can properly be attached to it as a step towards the proof of an issue in the case. If no such weight can be attached to it, the evidence is irrelevant and therefore inadmissible. In this case, the rule against hearsay precluded the jury from concluding that the beliefs of the caller[s] (that the appellant would supply them with drugs) were in fact true. Without such a conclusion, no weight could properly be attached to the evidence, and it was therefore irrelevant and inadmissible.'

In *Wright v. Doe d Tatham* the question to be decided was whether the testator had testamentary capacity at the time he made his will. Those seeking to uphold the will wished to introduce into evidence three letters written by deceased persons to the testators for the purpose of establishing that the testator was of sound mind.

It was submitted that the contents of the letters were such that the writers must have held the opinion that they were writing to a sane man, and that following precedents in the ecclesiastical courts the letters should be admitted to establish that opinion. The judges refused to follow the ecclesiastical precedents. They held that as an opinion as to the testator's sanity expressed by the letter writers to a third party would not be admissible in evidence because it would offend against the hearsay rule, being neither on oath nor possible to test by cross-examination, so also the statements tendered for the purpose of inviting a jury to draw an inference as to the opinion of the writer were likewise inadmissible.

Alternatively, it was submitted that the letters were admissible because there was evidence of the way in which the testator had dealt with them which pointed towards his sanity. If there was evidence to connect the testator's actions to the letters the judges were agreed that the contents of the letters would be admissible, but upon this issue as to whether or not there was such evidence the judges were evenly divided.

We are not here concerned with this second ground of admissibility, as the appellant being in custody had no opportunity to deal with either the telephone callers or the visitors to his flat. We are, however, concerned with the first ground, for it is said that evidence of what was said by those who telephoned or called at the flat asking to be supplied with drugs was evidence of no more than their belief or opinion that they could obtain drugs from the appellant and on the authority of *Wright v. Doe d Tatham* to be treated as inadmissible hearsay.

I cannot accept this submission. It is of course true that it is almost certain that the customers did believe that they could obtain drugs from the appellant, otherwise they would not have telephoned or visited his premises. But why did all these people believe they could obtain drugs from the appellant? The obvious inference is that the appellant had established a market as a drug dealer by supplying or offering to supply drugs and was thus attracting customers. There are of course other possible explanations, such as a mistaken belief or even a deliberate attempt to frame the appellant, but there are very few factual situations from which different inferences cannot be drawn and it is for the jury to decide which inference they believe they can safely draw.

The evidence is offered not for the purpose of inviting the jury to draw the inference that the customers believed they could obtain drugs but to prove as a fact that the telephone callers and visitors were acting as customers or potential customers, which was a circumstance from which the jury could if so minded draw the inference that the appellant was trading as a drug dealer, or to put it in the language of the indictment that he was in possession of drugs with intent to supply them to others.

The requests for drugs made by the callers were not hearsay as generally understood, namely an out-of-court narrative description of facts which have to be proved in evidence. The callers were neither describing the appellant as a drug dealer nor stating their opinion that he was a drug dealer. They were calling him up or visiting him as customers, a fact revealed by the words they used in requesting drugs from him."

LORD BRIDGE OF HARWICH: "The question certified by the Court of Appeal, Criminal Division as raising a point of law of general public importance in this case is expressed in the following terms:

'Whether evidence may be adduced at a trial of words spoken (namely a request for drugs to be supplied by the Defendant), not spoken in the presence or hearing of the Defendant, by a person not called as a witness, for the purpose not of establishing the truth of any fact narrated by the words, but of inviting the jury to draw an inference from the fact that the words were spoken (namely that the Defendant was a supplier of drugs).'

In my opinion this question not only defines accurately the essential issue which falls to be determined in the appeal; it also provides the only correct starting point for the inquiry on which the House must embark. If the answer to the certified question is affirmative, that will be the end of the matter. If the answer to the certified question is negative, it may be necessary to ask the further question whether a different answer should be given in the case where the evidence proposed to be tendered is to the effect that a multiplicity of persons, not called as witnesses, all made similar requests for drugs to be supplied by the defendant and, if so, in what circumstances. But to start from the proposition that evidence of a multiplicity of such requests made at the same place and within a limited space of time must be admissible because of their manifest probative force and to proceed from this premise to the conclusion that the certified question must *therefore* be answered affirmatively seems to me, with respect, to be a wholly illegitimate approach to the problem and to be rendered doubly suspect by the circumstance that the conclusion has to be qualified by saying that evidence of a single request of the kind referred to in the certified question, though technically admissible, ought properly to be excluded in the exercise of the judge's discretion on the ground that its prejudicial effect must outweigh its probative value.

The first question then is whether the fact of the request for drugs having been made is in itself relevant to the issue whether the defendant was a supplier. The fact that words were spoken may be relevant for various purposes, but most commonly they will be so when they reveal the state of mind of either the speaker or the person to whom the words were spoken when that state of mind is itself in issue or is relevant to the matter in issue. The state of mind of the person making the request for drugs is of no relevance at all to the question whether the defendant is a supplier. The sole possible relevance of the words spoken is that by manifesting the speaker's belief that the defendant is a supplier they impliedly assert that fact. This is most clearly exemplified by two of the requests made to police officers in the instant case by callers requesting drugs from the defendant where the speaker asked for a supply of his 'usual amount'. The speaker was impliedly asserting that he had been supplied by the defendant with drugs in the past. If the speaker had expressly said to the police officer that the defendant had supplied him with drugs in the past, this would clearly have been inadmissible as hearsay. When the only relevance of the words spoken lies in their implied assertion that the defendant is a supplier of drugs, must this equally be excluded as hearsay? This, I believe, is the central question on which this appeal turns. Is a distinction to be drawn for the purposes of the hearsay rule between express and implied assertions? If the words coupled with any associated action of a person not called as a witness are relevant solely as impliedly asserting a relevant fact, may evidence of those words and associated actions be given notwithstanding that an express assertion by that person of the same fact would only have been admissible if he had been called as a witness? Unless we can answer that question in the affirmative, I think we are bound to answer the certified question in the negative . . .

[The judgment in *Ratten v. R*], considered as a whole, seems to me to support, rather than to refute, the proposition that words are spoken involving an implied assertion of a relevant fact, certainly if they are not otherwise relevant, are excluded by the hearsay rule unless they can be brought within some established exception to the rule. In *Ratten v. R* itself the making of the telephone call was unquestionably relevant and the words spoken were admissible both on the ground mat they were part of the 'composite act' of the call itself and as evidence of the wife's emotional state, but not as implying an assertion that she was being attacked by the accused.

In the instant case, even if we enlarge the certified question to take account of the fact that the requests for drugs of which police officers gave evidence were made either by telephone calls or personal calls to the defendant's house, we get no further. I accept the proposition that, if an action is of itself relevant to an issue, the words which accompany and explain the action may be given in evidence, whether or not they would be relevant independently. But the mere fact of the calls being made to the defendant's house was by itself of no relevance whatever, so we are back to the bare issue as to whether the implied assertion involved in the request for drugs should be excluded as hearsay. As English law presently stands, I am clearly of the opinion that it should."

LORD OLIVER: "My Lords, granted that, to use Lord Normand's words, the rule against the admission of hearsay evidence is 'fundamental' (for the reasons which he gave), it is necessary in every case where evidence is tendered of words spoken by a person who is not called as a witness to have clearly in mind the purpose for which such evidence is sought to be adduced. Such evidence does not fall foul of the hearsay rule if its purpose is to prove not the correctness of what was said (or, more accurately, of what is said to have been said) but the fact that it was said. That fact, as was observed in the opinion of the Board of the Privy Council in *Subramaniam v. Public Prosecutor* [1956] 1 W.L.R. 965 at 970, may, apart altogether from the truth of the statement, quite frequently be relevant in considering the mental state and conduct of the witness or of some other person in whose presence the statement was made, not excluding the maker of the statement himself. The distinction between utterance as relevant fact and utterance as evidence of the accuracy of what is uttered is neatly expressed in the opinion of the Board of the Privy Council delivered by Lord Wilberforce in *Ratten v. R* [1971] 3 All E.R. 801 at 805, [1972] A.C. 378 at 387:

'The mere fact that evidence of a witness includes evidence as to words spoken by another person who is not called is no objection to its admissibility. Words spoken are facts just as much as any other action by a human being. If the speaking of the words is a relevant fact, a witness may give evidence that they were spoken. A question of hearsay only arises when the words spoken are relied on "testimonially", *i.e.* as establishing some fact narrated by the words.'

Thus, in that case, a telephone call from the wife of the accused, who had been shot dead by him, as he claimed accidentally, and in which she asked for the police, was held to be rightly admitted as evidence simply of a telephone call made by a lady in a distressed state made at a time when the accused denied that any call was made and in the context of his contention that the shooting was accidental. It is to be noted, however, that, in so far as it was admissible as evidence from which the jury could be invited to infer that the caller was being attacked by her husband, the Boards found it admissible only as part of the *res gestae, i.e.* as an exception to the hearsay rule.

Thus the question which presents itself in the instant appeal can be expressed thus: was the evidence of the police officers being tendered simply as evidence of the fact of the conversation or was it introduced 'testimonially' in order to demonstrate the truth either of something that was said or of something that was implicit in or to be inferred from something that was said?

Miss Goddard Q.C., for the Crown, has submitted that the evidence admitted by the judge of what was said by the callers did not fall foul of the hearsay rule at all. It was not tendered as hearsay evidence but simply as probative of the fact that calls were made on the day in question either at or to the house and that the callers were seeking to purchase drugs from 'Chippie'. There was independent evidence of the presence of drugs at the premises and the fact that there were calls at or to the house by persons seeking drugs was relevant, simply as a fact, as tending to show that the accused had an intent to supply, the contents of the conversations being admissible as material explaining the making of the calls. Mr de Navarro Q.C., for the appellant, contends that this submission simply fails to analyse both the true purpose and the effect of the evidence tendered. The fact that callers asked for drugs in the absence of the appellant, there being no evidence of any reaction by him to the requests, cannot possibly, it is said, go any distance at all towards showing what had to be proved, that is to say that the appellant had an intention to supply drugs. It proved no more than that the callers made the calls in the belief, which the jury were invited to infer from the words spoken, that the appellant had drugs and was willing to supply them. That belief, no grounds being stated or capable of being investigated, was being tendered as evidence that the fact believed was true and in the form in which it was tendered could not have been admitted even if the callers had themselves given evidence. So, it is said, the jury were being invited to draw a double inference, that is to say, first an inference that what the callers were saying was, in effect, 'Chippie has drugs and intends to supply them', and, secondly, an inference that, because the caller believed this to be the case, it was therefore true. Thus this was evidence which, standing alone, and without supplementary information indicating the grounds of the caller's belief, could not have been admitted even if given directly by the caller; and, tendered as it was through the mouth of the police officer who heard the statement, it was in any event hearsay and thus inadmissible.

My Lords, to any ordinary layman asked to consider the matter, one might think that the resort of a large number of persons to 11 Perth Close, all asking for 'Chippie', all carrying sums of cash and all asking to be supplied with drugs, would be as clear an indication as he could reasonably expect to have that 11 Perth Close was a place at which drugs were available; and if he were to be asked whether or not this showed also that 'Chippie' was dealing in drugs, I cannot help feeling that his answer would be, 'Of course it does.' But so simple—perhaps, one might say, so attractively common sense—a layman's approach is not necessarily a reliable guide in a criminal trial. I have in mind Parke B's observation in *Wright v. Doe A Tatham* (1837) 7 Ad. & El. 313 at 386, 112 All E.R. 488 at 516 that, although an inference from a statement that an act would not have been done unless the statement were true, or at least believed to be true, 'no doubt would be raised in the conduct of the ordinary affairs of life, if the statement were made by a man of veracity . . . it cannot be raised in a judicial inquiry . . .' Indeed, even accepting the layman's immediate impression, if one goes on to ask, 'Why do you say, "Of course"?' the matter becomes a little more complex. The answer to that question has to be,

'Because, of course, they would not go and ask for drugs unless they expected to get them.' But then if one asks, 'Well, why did they expect to get them?', even the layman is compelled into an area of speculation. They expected to get them either because they had got them before or because they had been told, rightly or wrongly, or had heard or thought or guessed that there was somebody called 'Chippie' at 11 Perth Close who supplied drugs. So, straight away, even the layman is, on analysis, compelled to accept that his instinctive 'of course' rests upon a process of deductive reasoning which starts from an assumption about the state of mind or belief of a number of previously unknown individuals of whom the only known facts are that they telephoned or called at 11 Perth Close and made offers to purchase drugs.

Now, if we translate that inquiry into the context of a criminal trial in which the accused, by pleading not guilty, is saying to the prosecution, as he is entitled to do; 'I challenge you to prove, by relevant and admissible evidence, that I was in possession of the drugs found at 11 Perth Close with intent to supply them', we have to start with the terms of the charge and ask ourselves whether and to what extent the evidence of police officer that he heard a number of callers to or at the premises asking for drugs goes any way at all towards establishing that the accused, one of the three residents at the premises, was intending to supply drugs.

The first inquiry must be: is it relevant evidence? For nothing that is not relevant is admissible. 'Relevant' cannot, I think, be better defined than in article 1 of Stephen's Digest of the Law of Evidence (12th ed., 1936) p.4, that is to say that the word means that—

> 'any two facts to which it is applied are so related to each other that according to the common course of events one either taken by itself or in connection with other facts proves or renders probable the past, present or future existence or non-existence of the other.'

To put it, perhaps, more succinctly, a fact to be relevant must be probative, and if one asks whether the fact that a large number of persons called at the premises seeking to purchase from 'Chippie' renders probable the existence of a person at the premises called 'Chippie' who is willing to supply drugs, the answer can, I think, only be in the affirmative. But the difficulty here is that it is only the combination of the facts (a) that persons called, (b) that they asked for 'Chippie' and (c) that they requested drugs which renders the evidence relevant. The mere fact that people telephoned or called, in itself, is irrelevant, for it neither proves nor renders probable any other fact. In order to render evidence of the calls relevant and therefore admissible there has to be added the additional element of what the callers said, and it is here that the difficulty arises. What was said—in each case a request for drugs—is, of course, probative of the state of mind of the caller. But the state of mind of the caller is not the fact in issue and is, in itself, irrelevant, for it is not probative of anything other than its own existence. It becomes relevant only if and so far as the existence of other facts can be inferred from it. So far as concerns anything in issue at the trial, what the caller said and the state of mind which that fact evinces become relevant and probative of the fact in issue (namely the intent of the appellant) only if, or because of, (i) what was said amounts to a statement, by necessary implication, that the appellant has in the past supplied drugs to the speaker (as in two cases in which requests were made for the 'usual') or (ii) it imports the belief or opinion of the speaker that the appellant has drugs and is willing to supply them. And here, as it seems to me, we are directly up against the hearsay rule which forms one of the major established exceptions to the admissibility of relevant evidence. Clearly if, at the trial, the prosecution had sought to adduce evidence from a witness to the effect that the appellant had, in the past, supplied him with quantities of drugs, that evidence would have been both relevant and admissible; but equally clearly, if it had been sought to introduce the evidence of a police constable to the effect that a person not called as a witness had told him, in a conversation in a public house, that the appellant had supplied drugs, that would have been inadmissible hearsay evidence and so objectionable. It cannot, it is cogently argued, make any difference that exactly the same evidence is introduced in an indirect way by way of evidence from a witness that he has overheard a request by some other person for 'the usual', from which the jury is to be asked to infer that which cannot be proved by evidence of that other person's direct assertion. Equally if, at the trial, the prosecution had sought to adduce evidence from a witness not that drugs had been supplied but that it was his opinion or belief that drugs had been or would be supplied, that evidence would be inadmissible as amounting to no more than a statement of belief or opinion unsupported by facts upon which the belief is grounded. A fortiori, it is argued, that same inadmissible belief or opinion cannot be introduced by inference from the reported statement of someone who is not even called as a witness. Thus, it is said, in seeking to introduce the evidence of the police officers of what callers said, the Crown faces the difficulty that it has to contend that by combining two inadmissible items of evidence—that is to say the evidence of the calls (which are, standing alone, inadmissible because irrelevant) and the evidence of what was said by the callers (which might be relevant but is inadmissible because hearsay)—it can produce a single item of admissible evidence."

NOTES

(i) A curious feature of *Kearley* was the court's unanimous acceptance of the irrelevance of the callers' states of mind. Even the minority judges appear to have taken the view that the evidence was relevant not because of the callers' states of mind but because it showed the existence of a potential market for drugs to which the appellant could sell. The majority did not even accept that arguably modest proposition. Lord Oliver said:

"The pith of the argument . . . is that the acts of the callers in going or telephoning to the premises, explained by their states of mind as revealed by their contemporaneous words, is some evidence which a jury could properly take into account in deciding whether the accused had an intention to supply because it demonstrates that there was an established potential market, *i.e.* a pool of willing purchasers, which the accused had the opportunity of supplying. It is the relevance of this in relation to the only issue in the case—the intention of the accused to supply that market—that I have not felt able to accept. 'Some evidence which a jury could properly take into account' means no more than that the evidence is probative. But then one asks: of what is it probative? What is it about the existence of a potential customer or of a body of potential customers, whether substantial or not, that tends to render it more or less likely that a given individual intends to supply their requirements? Can one, for instance, legitimately infer an intention to make a gift to charity from evidence of calls made by collectors seeking donations?"

The answer to Lord Oliver's rhetorical question at the end of this passage is clearly intended to be negative. But is his analogy a good one? Can it really be true that the presence of large numbers of people at a particular address, all requesting drugs from the householder, is irrelevant? If it is relevant, is it relevant only in so far as it shows that the callers all believed that they could obtain drugs at that address? And, in turn, is the state of mind of the callers really irrelevant, as the court in *Kearley* holds?

(ii) This, of course, leads on to consideration of the hearsay point. The majority were of the opinion that evidence of the callers' states of mind could be rendered relevant only by reference to the facts impliedly asserted—that "Chippie" was a drug dealer—therein. To do so would infringe the hearsay rule, and so the evidence was inadmissible. But if one accepts the definition of hearsay suggested in *Kearley*—that an assertion other than one made by a person while giving oral evidence in the proceedings is inadmissible as evidence of any fact asserted in or implied by it—and couple that definition with the way the facts impliedly asserted in *Kearley* were formulated, would *any* prior statement be admissible? The House of Lords seem to have conflated the question of what facts are asserted by a statement, with the question of what may be inferred from those facts. Lord Oliver, for example, asked:

"Is the existence of [the accused's intent to supply drugs] rendered more or less probable by the fact that a third person, not even proved to have been known to him, has called at the premises where he and two other persons live and has asked a police officer to supply drugs? I find it very difficult to see how it can be except by treating it as an assertion by the caller to the police officer that the appellant is a supplier of drugs, an assertion clearly inadmissible as hearsay because tendered as evidence of fact."

However, it is only by a very artificial process—a process basically of inference—that such an assertion can be formulated. In reality little or nothing is asserted by the request "give me some drugs please".

One might or might not think it legitimate to draw the inference from this request or from a number of them that the recipient of the request was a supplier of drugs. But what the Judicial Committee forbade in *Ratten* was the use of statements "testimonially—*i.e.* as establishing some fact narrated by the words". Is any fact "narrated" either in *Ratten* or in *Kearley*? Is it the case that as soon as one tries to infer things from the content of statements, one is in the area of inadmissible hearsay?

It is here that the difficulty with *Kearley* really becomes acute. If one accepts that implied assertions—inferences drawn from a statement—fall foul of the hearsay rule, two undesirable possibilities follow. First, virtually any statement, or indeed any conduct, may be said to give rise to an inadmissible inference; or secondly, juries may have to be instructed that they may draw certain inferences from statements, but must not draw certain others. Contrast *Ratten v. R.*, above. In *Kearley*, Lord Bridge, referring to *Ratten*, said that:

> "in [that case] the making of the telephone call was unquestionably relevant and the words spoken were admissible both on the ground that they were part of the 'composite act' of the call itself and as evidence of the wife's emotional state, but not as implying an assertion that she was being attacked by her husband."

Thus, the jury in *Ratten* were invited or allowed to draw the inference that the shooting was no accident. In the circumstances, one obvious, perhaps inevitable, further inference was that the deceased made the call because she was about to be attacked, but this inference was not permitted, a prohibition which seems nothing short of bizarre. In *Kearley*, of course, the calls were held to be inadmissible—because irrelevant—without reference to the assertions implied. That conclusion seems surprising enough, but clearly had they been regarded as relevant, any inference as to the defendant's intention to supply drugs would have been forbidden, just as the jury were forbidden in *Ratten* from making the "ultimate" inference in that case. Both cases therefore appear artificially to circumscribe the jury's ability to draw inferences from the making of statements in certain circumstances.

One justification, stated by Lords Ackner and Oliver, for the exclusion of hearsay is that juries are unable properly to evaluate it. One must ask whether, if that is true, it is sensible to tell them that, as in *Ratten*, they may draw certain inferences from a statement but not others, no matter how logical or natural such further inferences might be. Williams, *The Proof of Guilt* (3rd ed., 1963) p.207 said:

> "Thus juries are credited with the ability to follow the most technical and subtle directions in dismissing evidence from consideration, while at the same time they are of such low-grade intelligence that they cannot, even with the assistance of the judge's observations, attach the proper degree of importance to hearsay."

The Law Commission for England and Wales has recently recommended reform of the hearsay rule, although on rather different lines to those now adopted in Scotland. See Law Commission Consultation Paper No. 138, 1995. The Law Commission proposals include a tentative recommendation that hearsay should be defined as follows:

> "an assertion other than one made by a person while giving oral evidence in the proceedings is inadmissible as evidence of any fact or opinion that the person intended to assert."

This proposed definition would exclude implied assertions from the rule. The Law Commission's proposals are considered in some detail in the January issue of 1996 Criminal Law Review. See especially Zuckerman, "The Futility of Hearsay" (1996) Crim. L.R. 4.

5. McLaren v. McLeod
[1913] S.C. 61

The charge in this case was one of brothel-keeping, and the prosecution sought to lead evidence of certain conversations overheard by police officers in the house concerned, in which female occupants of the house were heard to say that the accused had introduced "short time" to the house. This evidence was objected to as hearsay.

LORD JUSTICE-GENERAL (DUNEDIN): "This conviction is objected to on the ground that evidence was improperly admitted. The evidence which was said to be improperly admitted was that of certain constables; while the constables were listening outside this house they heard certain conversations going on between some of the inmates, and the prosecutor asked them what it was they heard. That was objected to upon the ground that it was not said that the accused—the present complainer—was present, and that it was not proposed to call the persons who took part in those conversations. If the matter depended upon the truth of what was said in the conversations, that, I think, would be a good objection; but I take it that those conversations became relevant not in respect of their truth, but of their character. I think they really came into the same category as any noises or exclamations which were heard, and which might have been testified to by those who were watching. The weight that should have been given to them is another matter, but I cannot think it was wrong to admit them. I hope that it is clear that there is nothing in this judgement to countenance the idea that hearsay conversations may be used as evidence to prove what is contained in them. I look upon this as a mere question of something that showed what I may call the atmosphere of the place, and nothing more. I think, therefore, the conviction should stand."

LORD KINNEAR: "I entirely concur with your Lordship. I think the evidence was admissible. I do not think it could properly be described as hearsay, although that is no doubt an ambiguous term, because the thing to be proved is not that the witness heard other people making statements which it is proposed to adduce as testimony in the cause, but simply that he in fact heard certain things. The thing to be proved was that a certain conversation took place. That that was relevant to the question at issue seems to me not doubtful, because the question is whether a house was of a certain character or not, and it is evidence tending to show the affirmative that certain things are done and conversations heard in that house. But if the fact that the conversation took place is relevant at all, there is no difference between the way of proving that fact and the way of proving any other fact. If oral evidence is admissible it must be the direct evidence of witnesses who speak to what they themselves heard or saw. But the evidence of a man who depones that he heard a certain thing said is just as direct and as little to be confounded with hearsay as the evidence of one who depones that he saw a certain thing happen.

I agree entirely with your Lordship in the chair that the inference to be drawn from the fact so proved is a totally different matter, but with that we have nothing to do."

LORD MACKENZIE: "I am of the same opinion. The question in the case was as to the character of the house, and that of course depended upon the character of the people who were frequenting it. I take it that the evidence here has a direct bearing upon the character of the people who were engaging in this conversation, and in that way reflected upon the character of the complainer. This is the point of the evidence. We have nothing to do with the truth or falsity of what was said against the complainer during the conversation. I am unable to see that the objection taken that the accused was not present was a good objection."

NOTES

Compare the similar English case of *Woodhouse v. Hall* (1980) 72 Cr.App.R. 39. The relevance of the statement in *McLaren* that the accused had introduced "short time" to the house can be explained only by reference to the fact impliedly asserted, that the women in the house were working girls. Whether or not the accused had in fact introduced "short time" to the house was wholly irrelevant to any issue in the case. The Scots law of hearsay therefore seems to differ from the English view to the extent that statements containing implied assertions are not prohibited by the rule. In *Lord Advocate's Reference (No. 1 of 1992)*, 1992 S.C.C.R. 724, Lord Justice-General Hope said that the grounds for the dissenting opinions delivered in *Kearley*:

"would cause no surprise in Scotland [since] the evidence in question was direct evidence of a relevant fact, that is to say the existence of potential customers willing and anxious to purchase drugs at the premises from the defendant."

In its recent Report on Hearsay Evidence in Criminal Proceedings S.L.C. No. 149, 1995, paras 5.11–5.13 the Scottish Law Commission recommended that to the extent that implied assertions do not presently count as inadmissible hearsay, no change in the law was required.

The situations in which Scots law recognises the admissibility of primary hearsay, as expounded in the passage from *Lord Advocate's Reference (No. 1 of 1992)*, above, are numerous. For example, in *McLeod v. Lowe*, 1993 S.L.T. 471, the question was whether the police had reasonable grounds to suspect that the accused was in possession of controlled drugs and were therefore entitled to search him. Their suspicion was said to rest on a statement made to them by members of staff at the hotel where the accused was arrested. On an appeal against his conviction the accused argued that there was no evidence before the court to justify the finding that the police had reasonable grounds to suspect him of the offence. The Court said:

> "What was at issue was the information on which the police acted. Evidence about that could competently have been given by either the hotel staff or the police officers themselves. The evidence of the police officers to this effect would not have proved the truth of what they were told by the hotel staff but it could have proved that the statements were made. In other words what the Crown were endeavouring to lead from the police witnesses was primary hearsay which was admissible as direct evidence that the statement was made irrespective of its truth or falsehood (Walker and Walker, *Law of Evidence in Scotland*, p.394). Subsequently at p.396 it is observed that it is frequently necessary to prove that a statement has been made, and it is stated: 'The party leading the evidence does so merely to establish that the statement was made. He is probably not concerned with its truth, and indeed his case may be that it was untrue'. I accordingly agree with the Advocate Depute that the Sheriff was wrong to have upheld the objection to the evidence which it was sought to take from the police officers as to what was said to them by members of the hotel staff."

Other situations in which primary hearsay statements are admissible include the situation in which the statement forms the subject matter of the charge; where the statement is relevant to demonstrate a state of mind such as knowledge of certain facts, or perhaps insanity; or where they are relevant to show consistency of story and hence bolster credibility—although the *de recenti* complaint appears to be the only example of this—see *Morton v. H.M.A.*, Chapter 5 above. In general, evidence which merely supports the credibility of a witness is not admissible.

6. Morrison v. H.M.A.
1990 S.C.C.R. 235

The appellant was charged with rape. When interviewed by the police he admitted having had intercourse with the complainer but claimed that she had consented to what occurred. Evidence was led by the Crown that the intercourse had been preceded by kissing to which the complainer had consented, and that the complainer's daughter had slept through the incident. The appellant did not give evidence. The trial judge directed the jury in terms of *Hendry v. H.M.A.*, 1985 S.C.C.R. 274; 1985 J.C. 105 and told them that anything said by the appellant which was self-exonerating was not a substitute for evidence. The appellant was convicted and appealed to the High Court on the ground that the trial judge had misdirected the jury as to the evidential value of his self-exonerating statement.

LORD JUSTICE-CLERK: "The appellant went to trial in the High Court at Edinburgh on an indictment libelling two charges of rape. In the course of the trial the first charge was amended so as to become a charge of attempted rape. The jury by a majority found the first charge as amended not proven, and by a majority found the appellant guilty as libelled on charge (2). The appellant appealed against conviction. At the first hearing of the appeal in December 1989 questions arose as to the soundness of the decision of five judges in *Hendry v. H.M.A.*, and the appeal was accordingly remitted to a court of seven judges. The appeal has now proceeded upon the basis of amended grounds of appeal which are in the following terms:

> 'That the learned trial judge misdirected the jury in law when he instructed them that anything said in a statement which is self-exonerating is not a substitute for evidence in the witness box, and by implication directed the jury that in considering Crown Label Production No. 1, *i.e.*, the tape recording of the police interrogation of the appellant, they should ignore any statement made therein which was self-exonerating, and said misdirection amounted to a miscarriage of justice.'

In presenting this appeal, Mr Daiches submitted that the decision in *Hendry v. H.M.A.* would require to be reconsidered. He put forward two principal submissions. (1) He contended that even if the decision in *Hendry v. H.M.A.* was correct, nevertheless the trial judge had erred in directing the jury as he did in respect that he did not exactly follow what was stated in *Hendry v. H.M.A.* (2) In the event that his first submission was unsound, Mr Daiches further submitted that this court should hold that *Hendry v. H.M.A.* had been wrongly decided and that the doctrine laid down in *R. v. Sharp* [1988] 1 W.L.R. 7 should be adopted as the law of Scotland.

What has given rise to these submissions is that evidence was led before the jury of a lengthy police interrogation of the appellant which took place on the day following the attempted rape which was the subject of charge (1) and the rape which was the subject of charge (2). The two charges arose out of one incident which took place over a period of time. The police interrogation had been taped and the tape had been transcribed. The transcription constituted Crown Production No. 1. In the course of answering questions put to him by the police the appellant admitted having sexual intercourse with the complainer but maintained that what took place had been with her consent.

In the course of charging the jury, the trial judge explained that if an accused person makes a statement which is proved to have been accurately recorded and fairly obtained, the statement forms part of the evidence in the case and may be taken into consideration by the jury. He then stated:

> 'Insofar as it is self-incriminating, it is, of course, admissible evidence, because it would be against the interests of the person making it to say anything of an incriminatory nature and in this instance the accused freely conceded, and Mr Henderson [defence counsel] took this as a point in his favour, that from the very outset he never denied knowing the girl, he never denied being with the girl and he never denied having sexual intercourse with the girl twice, in fact, and that is relevant evidence that you can take into account. On the other hand, anything made, said in a statement which is self-exonerating, is not a substitute for evidence in the witness box.'

Subsequently he reminded the jury that there was no obligation upon the appellant to give evidence and that he had not given evidence and that they should not draw any adverse inference from the fact that he had not given evidence. He then added:

> 'The onus of proof, as I have already said, remains on the Crown, but insofar as he has, he is alleged to have said things which were self-exonerating, then you will bear in mind that these statements are not a substitute for the evidence which he might have given, if he had chosen to do so or been advised to do so in the witness box.'

The accused did not give evidence and the defence sought to rely upon the answers which he had given in the police interrogation to the effect that sexual intercourse had taken place with the consent of the complainer. Mr Daiches recognised that at a later portion of his charge the trial judge appeared to be inviting the jury to consider the whole transcript. The trial judge explained that he was not to go into the evidence in any detail and he then added:

> 'Mr Henderson [defence counsel] in particular very fairly canvassed both the evidence of the complainer herself . . . in some detail, and the position of the accused, particularly as set out in the transcript and the tape recording to which I have already referred.'

However, he submitted that, having regard to what the trial judge had said earlier, the clear implication was that the jury were being directed that they should disregard and ignore any statement of the appellant in the transcript which was self-exonerating. At the hearing in December the Crown conceded that the effect of the trial judge's charge to the jury was that the self-serving parts of the appellant's statements were to be ignored. Before this court the advocate-depute reminded us that at the trial, when he came to address the jury, the advocate-depute had said nothing about the admissibility of those parts of the statement which were self-exonerating, whereas counsel for the defence had the self-exonerating parts of the statement as if they were evidence in the case. The trial judge in his charge had gone through the whole of the case for the Crown but had proceeded as if there was no case for the defence to be considered. In his report the trial judge states that in giving the jury the directions which he did he was endeavouring to follow *Hendry v. H.M.A.*

Hendry v. H.M.A. was concerned with what has come to be referred to as a mixed statement. In *R. v. Sharp* a mixed statement is defined as 'a statement that is in part admission and in part exculpatory'. In our opinion, it is more accurate to describe a mixed statement as one which is capable of being both incriminatory and exculpatory, and it is in this sense that we use the expression 'mixed statement'. In *Hendry v. H.M.A.* the accused was charged with attempted murder and lodged a plea of self-defence. He did not give evidence nor call any witnesses. The record of his judicial examination, which contained an account of events supporting the plea of self-defence was read to the jury as part of the Crown case. The trial judge directed the jury under reference to the report of the judicial examination as follows [at p.276]:

> 'If in the course of that examination the accused makes a statement which incriminates him, then of course that would be evidence against him, but by the same token, and you might find this a little difficult to understand but you must take it from me that this is the law, any statement which he makes in his favour, any exculpatory statement, is not evidence in his favour.'

The accused was convicted of assault and appealed. The court of five judges held that where the record of a judicial examination led in evidence by the Crown contains self-serving statements, these statements have no evidential value unless they are supported by other evidence in the case, in which event they may add to the weight and credibility of that evidence. They further held that since there was no such other evidence in the case the trial judge had directed the jury correctly.

In view of the conclusion at which we have arrived in relation to Mr Daiches's second submission, it is not strictly necessary to deal with his first submission. However, on the assumption that the law is as stated in *Hendry v. H.M.A.*, we have to consider whether the self-exonerating portion of the statement either supported or was supported by other evidence in the case. Mr Daiches submitted that there was evidence from the complainer and her daughter which confirmed part of the self-exonerating statement and that accordingly, on the basis of *Hendry v. H.M.A.*, the jury should have been permitted to examine the statement to see whether they were satisfied that this other evidence supported or was supported by what was contained in the statement. In this connection he referred to evidence from the complainer that while she and the appellant were in her house together some familiarities took place between them with her consent. She testified that he put his arm round her and kissed her and that she gave him a kiss. In cross-examination, when she was asked if she thought she had led the appellant on, she replied, 'Yes, if by kissing him, if I led him on, yes, I led him on by kissing him.' This, it was said, supported what the appellant had said during the interrogation, namely, 'So I went over and sat on the couch, on the chair and we started neckin' fae there.' Mr Daiches also submitted that support for what the appellant said could be found in the evidence of the complainer's daughter to the effect that after she left the room where the appellant and the complainer were, she had heard nothing, being in a deep sleep. Mr Daiches maintained that, having regard to the fact that the complainer had maintained in her evidence that at one stage she had shouted on her daughter, the daughter's evidence could be regarded as confirming the statement of the appellant to the effect that everything had taken place with the complainer's consent.

Although it is unnecessary to reach a concluded opinion upon the matter, and although it is not easy to determine how much other evidence is required before the statement of an accused can be admitted for the purpose of confirming the other evidence, we are inclined to think that, unlike *Hendry v. H.M.A.*, this was a case where the other evidence in the case provided some confirmation of what the appellant had said in his statement, and that, accordingly, in the light of what was stated in *Hendry v. H.M.A.*, the jury should have been told that the whole statement was before them and was relevant for their consideration as to whether or not it confirmed the other evidence in the case to which we have referred. Accordingly, on the assumption that *Hendry v. H.M.A.* was correctly decided, we are inclined to think that the trial judge in the present case should have allowed the jury to have regard to the self-exonerating portions of the statement for the limited purpose indicated.

So far as Mr Daiches's second submission was concerned, he relied principally upon the case of *R. v. Sharp* and he invited this court to hold that what was laid down in *R. v. Sharp* is also a correct statement of the law of Scotland. At the forefront of his submissions was the proposition that where there has been a mixed statement, it would be unfair to admit that portion which amounts to an admission without also admitting other portions which excuse or explain the admission or are intended to show that the admission does not bear the inference of guilt which it might otherwise attract.

The advocate-depute accepted that what was raised in this appeal was an important question relating to the evidential status of what are called mixed statements made by an accused prior to his trial. He pointed out that such statements might be made to police officers or other persons after the commission of the alleged crime and before the trial. He submitted in this connection that judicial examinations were the same as extrajudicial statements. He contended that the law was well understood regarding statements led of admissions made by an accused person and as to statements led of denials of guilt by an accused person. The problem arose in relation to mixed statements. These would normally be led by the Crown, but it was conceivable that the defence might also attempt to lead them and if the defence were successful in having them admitted as evidence, the question would arise as to how they should be treated. The advocate-depute agreed with Mr Daiches that *Hendry v. H.M.A.* had been wrongly decided and he submitted that the critical question was what rules were to take the place of *Hendry v. H.M.A.* The advocate-depute maintained that quite apart from the correctness or otherwise of the decision in *Hendry v. H.M.A.*, it was difficult to understand exactly what the decision meant, it was unworkable in practice, and it resulted in unfairness.

It is important to realise that what apparently lay behind the decision in *Hendry v. H.M.A.* was that there was concern at the use which accused persons were endeavouring to make of the record of a judicial examination, which was a procedure introduced in 1980 and to which sections 20A, 20B and 151 of the Criminal Procedure (Scotland) Act 1975 refer. In delivering the opinion of the court in that case, the Lord Justice-Clerk said [at p.278]:

> 'The learned advocate-depute expressed concern about the increasing number of cases where accused persons were introducing into their statements at the judicial examination evidence in support of a defence such as alibi or self-defence, and then not giving evidence at the trial, but having their said statements used by their lawyer when addressing the jury as if they were evidence given at the trial. We can sympathise with the advocate-depute's concern, but, if the evidential nature of such statements has been defined with such limitations in their use as can be prescribed, the trial judge should be able to take control of the situation and direct the jury along the proper lines to avert such improper use of the statement.'

It was no doubt because of that concern that the Lord Justice-Clerk subsequently stated that it was illegitimate to use the content of a self-serving statement in a judicial examination as a substitute for evidence on oath, when the accused has not given evidence.

With all respect to the distinguished judges who constituted the court in *Hendry v. H.M.A.*, we are bound to say that we agree with the advocate-depute that it is not easy to understand exactly what the decision means. Thus, in the penultimate paragraph of his opinion, the Lord Justice-Clerk says that a self-exonerating statement cannot be used by the defence as evidence in the case to that effect, since the law provides that the statement cannot prove its contents. Subsequently he says that such a statement has been placed in evidence and is before the jury and that it is for their consideration 'whether it is acceptable'. It is not clear to us what is meant by 'acceptable' in this context; if the statement cannot prove its contents, in what sense are the jury to regard it as acceptable? Further, the decision of the court in *Hendry v. H.M.A.* is said to be based upon a passage in Alison's Practice of the Criminal Law where it is stated that the declaration of the accused is not evidence of the truth of what it contains, but can be founded upon by an accused as a material circumstance in his favour if it is confirmed by what the witnesses on one side or the other prove at the trial. In delivering the opinion of the court, the Lord Justice-Clerk [at p.280] states the converse to what Alison has stated and says that it is for the jury's consideration whether the statement confirms other evidence in the case from whatever source. We also agree with the advocate-depute that a jury would not find it easy to appreciate the difference when told that a statement of the accused was not evidence of the truth of its contents but was 'a material circumstance in his favour'. Moreover, although Alison is an important authority, it must be borne in mind that he was writing at a time when the accused was not a competent witness and what he stated about declarations, when that was the law, is not necessarily applicable to the situation which has obtained since 1898 when the accused became a competent witness.

We also agree with the learned advocate-depute that the decision is unworkable in practice and may result in unfairness In *Hendry v. H.M.A.* the accused admitted striking the victim but stated that he was acting in self-defence. The effect of the decision was that the admission that he struck the victim was admitted but the explanation that he had been acting in self-defence (which, if true, would justify acquittal) was not admitted. In our opinion that was an obviously unfair result. The present case is a further example of the difficulty of applying the decision in *Hendry v. H.M.A.* The effect of the decision is that the admission that the appellant had sexual intercourse with the complainer was admitted but his explanation that what took place had been with her consent was not. In our opinion, that too was an obviously unfair result.

In our opinion, the reasoning in *Hendry v. H.M.A.* is fatally flawed because the court appears not to have recognised that the statement in question was truly a qualified admission. It is well recognised in the law of Scotland that an admission which is qualified must be taken along with the qualification. When dealing with a declaration as an article of evidence, Hume states:

> 'For though the degree of faith that is due to a confession may be different, according to the occasion on which it is made; yet still, whatever the occasion may have been, the man's serious and deliberate impeachment of himself in a written form, must always weigh less or more in the scale against him. Of course, it cannot weigh at all against any other pannel; and even as against himself, it must be taken, qualified as he has chosen to give it, but liable always to be overcome, in those favourable particulars, by the other evidence or presumptions in the case, which often prevail against it' (Hume on Crimes, ii, 327).

When dealing with admissions in civil causes, Dickson states at paragraph 311:

> 'It would be in the highest degree subversive of justice were it permissible for a party to pick out certain expressions in a conversation, or certain letters in a correspondence, and found upon them as instructing an admission by his antagonist, and not permissible for the latter to prove the whole conversation or correspondence, of which these expressions or letters form selected portions' (Dickson on Evidence).

In paragraph 312 Dickson states:

> 'When an admission is made under a qualification, the party who founds on it must take it as it stands, and he may not adduce the portion which is favourable to him and exclude the remainder.'

Although these passages appear to relate to civil causes, we are of opinion that the same principle applies in a criminal case. This was plainly recognised in *Owens v. H.M.A.* [1946 J.C. 119] at p.124, per the Lord Justice-General:

> 'The onus is, of course, on the Crown throughout. It must prove that the fatal act was the accused's, and that it was deliberate or committed with a reckless disregard of the consequences. The panel relieved the Crown of the first part of the burden by himself admitting the stabbing with a lethal weapon, but attached to this admission the

explanation of its being done in self-defence in the circumstances explained by him. The Crown cannot, we think, take advantage of the admission without displacing the explanation or at all events presenting to the jury a not less strong casse that shows directly or indirectly that the explanation is false.'

Accordingly the jury must consider the whole statement, both the incriminating parts and the exculpatory parts. In our opinion the direction in *Hendry v. H.M.A.* to the effect that anything in the statement which was self-exonerating could not be used by the defence as evidence was plainly incorrect. As we have said, the jury has to consider the whole statement and not only that part upon which the Crown relies as amounting to an admission. Indeed it is for the jury to determine whether the statement as a whole amounts to an admission or not. In *R. v. Sharp* Lord Havers said (p.15D–E):

'It is only if the jury think that the facts set out by way of excuse or explanation might be true that any doubt is cast on tine admission, and it is surely only because the excuse or explanation might be true that it is thought fair that it should be considered by the jury.'

In these circumstances we have reached the conclusion that the case of *Hendry v. H.M.A.* must be overruled. In delivering his opinion in that case the Lord Justice-Clerk indicated that the court had been invited to overrule *Brown v. H.M.A.* (1964 J.C. 10). He stated that far from overruling *Brown v. H.M.A.*, the court approved of it. In *Brown v. H.M.A.* evidence of a statement by the accused was led by the Crown, but the sheriff excluded evidence of an explanation of the accused contained in the statement. The court held that the sheriff had been wrong when he directed the jury to that effect. In their opinions the Lord Justice-Clerk and Lord Strachan made it clear that they were satisfied that when the Crown leads evidence that a statement in certain terms had been made by an accused, he is not entitled to rely on that evidence as tending to show the truth of the contents of the statement. They did, however, hold that since evidence of the statement had been led by the Crown and had become part of the evidence in the case, the accused was not wholly debarred from founding upon it. Founding upon the passage in Alison to which we have already referred, the Lord Justice-Clerk and Lord Strachan held that it was for the jury to decide what weight, if any, they should give to the accused's statement and to decide whether, taken along with other evidence in the case, it cast any reasonable doubt on the accused's guilt.

We are satisfied that the court arrived at the correct decision in *Brown v. H.M.A.*, but insofar as the reasoning of the Lord Justice-Clerk and Lord Strachan is based on the passage in Alison to which we have referred, we are of opinion that the reasoning is unsound. As we have already explained, the passage in Alison is, in our opinion, no longer applicable. Both the Lord Justice-Clerk and Lord Strachan also rely on a passage in Macdonald, *Criminal Law* (5th ed.), p.316. That passage is in the following terms:

'Statements by the accused are not evidence in his favour. Thus an accused cannot prove letters written by herself to prove ignorance of the probable date of the birth of a child which she was accused of murdering. But where what is said is part of the *res gestae*, it may be proved, as shewing that the accused has throughout told a consistent story. But the facts stated are not thereby set up in his favour. It is only upon the making of the statement that he can found.'

In our opinion the first sentence of that passage is stated too widely and is incorrect. Statements by an accused may be evidence in his favour where there is a mixed statement containing material which is capable of being both incriminatory and exculpatory. The third sentence referring to statements which are part of the *res gestae* is also, in our opinion, incorrect. If a statement is part of the *res gestae*, it is evidence of the truth of the facts (Walker and Walker, *Law of Evidence in Scotland,* pp.398–400). The authorities which are relied on to support the proposition contained in the third sentence are in fact cases dealing with the admissibility of a *de recenti* statement by an accused for the purpose of showing that he has told a consistent story (*H.M.A. v. Forrest; H.M.A. v. Pye*). But if words spoken are truly part of the *res gestae* as described in *Teper v. The Queen* and *O'Hara v. Central S.M.T. Co.*, they are available as evidence of the truth of the facts.

Since we are satisfied that *Hendry v. H.M.A.* must be overruled, the question arises as to the rules which ought to replace what was laid down in that case. Before determining this, we should stress two matters. First, we are not concerned in this case with statements of an accused which are solely incriminating. Secondly, it must be emphasised that the present case, unlike *Hendry v. H.M.A.*, is not concerned with statements made in the course of judicial examination. In the present case the statements were made, as we have observed, in the course of an interrogation by police officers before the appellant was charged. Accordingly it is unnecessary for us to make any comment about the particular position of the report of a judicial examination. What we are about to say applies generally to statements made by an accused person after the commission of the alleged offence and prior to his trial, provided, of course, that the statement has been accurately recorded and fairly obtained. The following is intended as a statement of the law which applies to all such statements.

(1) The general rule is that hearsay, that is evidence of what another person has said, is inadmissible as evidence of the facts contained in the statement. We accept as the law of Scotland the definition of hearsay in Cross on Evidence (6th ed.), p.38, quoted by Lord Havers in *R. v. Sharp* [at p.11E]:

'[A]n assertion other than one made by a person while giving oral evidence in the proceedings is inadmissible as evidence of any fact asserted.'

We also approve what was stated in the opinion of the court in *Meehan v. H.M.A.* at p.13:

'But it has never been competent for the defence to avoid the giving of evidence by the accused by leading evidence of the accused having denied his guilt extrajudicially to friends or advisers as proof of his innocence.'

The matter is put by Hume as follows:

'There are obvious reasons why a pannel's denial of his guilt, or his statements, in conversation afterwards, of his defences against the charge, or his narrative of the way in which the thing happened, cannot be admitted as evidence on his behalf' (Hume on Crimes, ii, 401, paragraph 5 of note (a)).

So an accused is not entitled to lead in evidence a prior exculpatory statement as evidence of the truth of its contents. This rule embraces statements which are to any extent exculpatory. An exception to this rule exists where the statement is truly part of the *res gestae*.

(2) Where the Crown lead in evidence, or where evidence is led by the defence without objection from the Crown, of a statement made by an accused person prior to the trial which is capable of being both incriminatory and exculpatory, the whole statement is admissible as evidence of the facts contained in the statement. This is because it would be unfair to admit the admission without also admitting the explanation. The jury should be directed that they must consider the whole statement, both the incriminatory and exculpatory parts, and determine whether the whole or any part of the statement is accepted by them as the truth.

(3) A prior statement of an accused which is not to any extent incriminatory is admissible for the limited purpose of proving that the statement was made and of the attitude or reaction of the accused at the time when it was made, which is part of the general picture which the jury have to consider, but it is not evidence of the facts contained in the statement. Thus a statement may be admitted for the sole purpose of showing that the accused's story has been consistent. An accused may lead evidence of a prior exculpatory statement when he has given evidence and his account has been challenged as a late invention. Evidence of his statement, however, is admitted for the limited purpose of rebutting the challenge to his credibility. This rule also applies to the situation where the Crown lead in evidence a statement by an accused person prior to the trial which is wholly exculpatory, for example, a reply to caution and charge which is a complete denial of guilt. The accused may found on that statement only for the limited purpose of showing that his story has been consistent.

When directing a jury regarding a mixed statement, the trial judge may well feel it desirable to comment on the weight which the jury may wish to place upon different parts of the mixed statement. It will normally be appropriate for him to remind the jury that the statement was not made on oath and was not subject to cross-examination, leaving it to the jury to determine what weight should be attached to the statement in such circumstances. In *R. v. Duncan*, which was approved in *R. v. Sharp*, it was observed that there was no reason why, where appropriate, the judge should not comment in relation to the exculpatory remarks upon the election of the accused not to give evidence. Without seeking to inhibit a judge's right to make such comment, we would merely stress that under our law a comment of this kind should be made with restraint and only where there are special circumstances which require it (*Scott (A.T.) v. H.M.A.; Knowles v. H.M.A.*). The circumstances in which such comments may be proper and permissible have never been defined (*Stewart & Others v. H.M.A.*)."

NOTES

The words underlined in Rule 2, above, have been disapproved by a Bench of Nine judges in the following case, *George McCutcheon v. H.M.A.* The defence may now lead evidence of a statement which is capable of being both incriminating and exculpatory. It remains the case that the defence cannot lead evidence of a statement which is wholly exculpatory, except for the purpose of bolstering the accused's credibility.

In *Collins v. H.M.A.*, 1993 S.L.T. 101, it was held that a mixed statement, which contained some material suggestive of coercion was not admissible as evidence in favour of the accused since the accused had not otherwise raised the issue of coercion in his defence, and accordingly the statement was not capable of exonerating him. See also *Khan v. H.M.A.*, 1993 S.L.T. 172; *Boyle, Petitioner*, 1993 S.L.T. 1085, *McLeod v. H.M.A.*, 1995 S.L.T. 145, and *Murray v. H.M.A.*, 1996 S.L.T. 648 which emphasises that while a mixed statement by an accused may be used for or against him, it is not evidence against his co-accused.

It should be noted that in modern practice, the Crown very often leads evidence of tape-recorded interviews with an accused person. Such interviews may be very lengthy, and may contain material which is neutral, irrelevant or only marginally incriminating, as well as material which is clearly incriminating or clearly exculpatory. It may be difficult in practice to determine which parts of the interview may be regarded as exculpatory and which incriminating. *McCutcheon* modifies the rules laid down in *Morrison*, and indicates that, in considering the contents of statements made by an accused person, a broad approach should be taken to the questions of admissibility, particularly in relation to tape-recorded interviews.

7.   George McCutcheon v. H.M.A.
[2002 S.C.C.R. 101]

In this case a court of nine judges was convened to re-consider the rules laid down in *Morrison*. Although they refused the appeal, the court did recast the second of the rules in that case.

OPINION OF THE COURT: "[6] . . . Mr. Findlay invited the court to re-formulate Rule 2 in *Morrison* so as to remove the reference to lack of objection by the Crown, so that evidence as to the contents of a 'mixed statement' could be led in evidence by the Crown or by the defence.

[7] In approaching these submissions, it is, in our view, important to bear in mind the reasons for the way in which evidence of the statements of accused persons has been treated.

[8] One of the main reasons why hearsay evidence in a criminal case is in general inadmissible as evidence of the truth of what the witness has heard is 'that it is not the best evidence, and is not delivered on oath, for the oath of the narrator cannot attach to the original statement that safeguard against falsehood' (Dickson on *Evidence*, (3rd ed.,) para. 245). Thus, as this applies to evidence of a statement of an accused, 'it has never been competent for the defence to avoid the giving of evidence by the accused by leading evidence of the accused having denied his guilt extrajudicially to friends or advisers as proof of his innocence' (*Meehan v. H.M.A.*, 1970 J.C. 11 at p.13). There was no attempt in the argument before us to suggest that this long-established rule should be modified or that the reasons underlying it were unsound.

[9] An admission by an accused against his interest has been treated as standing in a different position. Lord Havers observed in *R. v. Sharp* at p.11:

'The justification for the adoption of that exception was presumably that, provided the accused had not been subjected to any improper pressure, it was so unlikely that he would confess to a crime he had not committed that it was safe to rely on the truth of what he said.'

As Lord Havers pointed out, the exception extended to include any matter which required to be established if the crime alleged was to be proved against the accused. Thus the prosecutor is entitled to found on evidence of an admission by an accused in proof of his guilt, whereas, by reason of the general rule against hearsay, the defence could not found on evidence of a statement by the accused as to his innocence. This again is not in controversy.

[10] We come then to a 'mixed statement'. Subject to what we say later, this expression has been applied to the whole of what an accused has said on a particular occasion, as distinct from particular words or passages in parts of what he said on that occasion. The courts in England and in Scotland have had to determine the appropriate way to treat the admissibility of what is said by the accused in the course of such a statement when a part of what he has said is capable of incriminating him and another part is capable of exculpating him. We use the words 'capable of' advisedly since whether his words do in fact incriminate or exculpate him is a matter for those who are judges of fact. In this type of case the jury are the judges of fact.

[11] It is plain that it was consideration of fairness to the accused, that is to say fairness where the prosecutor was founding on part of the statement, which led the courts to hold that the defence were entitled to found on another part of his statement which was capable of exculpating him. An obvious example would be where an accused admitted that he had killed the victim but added that at the time he was acting in self-defence. In *Owens v. H.M.A.*, 1946 J.C. 119 Lord Justice General Normand said at p.124:

'The onus is, of course, on the Crown throughout. It must prove that the fatal act was the accused's, and that it was deliberate or committed with a reckless disregard of the consequences. The panel relieved the Crown of the first part of the burden by himself admitting the stabbing with a lethal weapon, but attached to this admission the explanation of its being done in self-defence in the circumstances explained by him. The Crown cannot, we think, take advantage of the admission without displacing the explanation or at all events presenting to the jury a not less strong case that shows directly or indirectly that the explanation is false.'

These remarks referred to evidence given by the accused in his own defence, but have also been applied to the prior statements of an accused (see *Morrison* at p.310).

In a number of cases it has been pointed out that the need for treating evidence relating to a 'mixed statement' in this way may be reinforced by a consideration of the relationship between its different parts. Thus in *R. v. Sharp* Lord Havers at p.15 observed:

'How can a jury fairly evaluate the facts in the admission unless they can evaluate the facts in the excuse or explanation? It is only if the jury think that the facts set out by way of excuse or explanation might be true that any doubt is cast on the admission, and it is surely only because the excuse or explanation might be true that it is thought fair that it should be considered by the jury'.

A number of points may be noted. First, it is plainly desirable that there should be no doubt as to when the prosecutor is founding on a 'mixed statement' so that the defence are entitled to found on part of it in exculpation of the accused. In our view if the Crown leads evidence of such a statement they should be taken as relying on it for the incrimination of the accused. Secondly, what the defence may found upon has in the past been often referred to as a qualification, excuse or explanation of the admission against interest. However, in practice the relationship between the two may not be susceptible of a sophisticated analysis. This is particularly so in the light of the common practice of tape recording police interviews, which are often of considerable length and detail. There was force in the observation of the Lord Advocate that it is difficult to determine the scope of a qualification, excuse or explanation. These considerations indicate that a broad approach should be taken to the question whether a part of the statement is so connected to the admission as to form a qualification, excuse or explanation. Considerations of fairness to the accused are reinforced by the need to provide the jury with comprehensible directions. In *R. v. Duncan* (1981) 73 Cr. App. R. 359 Lord Lane stated on behalf of the court at page 365:

> 'Where a 'mixed' statement is under consideration by the jury in a case where the defendant has not given evidence, it seems to us that the simplest, and, therefore, the method most likely to produce a just result, is for the jury to be told that the whole statement, both the incriminating parts and the excuses or explanations, must be considered by them in deciding where the truth lies. It is, to say the least, not helpful to try to explain to the jury that the exculpatory parts of the statement are something less than evidence of the facts they state.'

[12] What then is the position if the defence seek to elicit evidence of a 'mixed statement' by the accused? This may arise in the course of the cross-examination of a witness in the Crown case or in the course of the defence case. We do not accept the submission that to deny the defence the opportunity to use such evidence in exculpation of the accused is in some way unfair to him or compromises his right to silence. Mr. Findlay's argument on this point was its own undoing, since there is no logical way of stopping short of the result that evidence of all statements made by the accused, whether 'mixed' or wholly exculpatory, would be admissible in his exculpation. Yet this would run counter to the general rule against the admission of hearsay, which Mr. Findlay expressly did not seek to question. Likewise, the submission that there is some unfair inconsistency between evidence of a 'mixed statement' being admissible when it is led by the Crown and being inadmissible when it is led by the defence is misconceived. As we have already said, the justification for making part of the first admissible in exculpation is that this is necessary in order to secure fairness where the Crown have led evidence of other parts which are capable of incriminating the accused. The same justification does not apply when the defence seek to introduce a mixed statement. To secure the admission of the statement, the defence would be in the strange position of trying to show that it was in some way incriminatory. If they succeed in doing so, it would be odd indeed to regard the defence as entitled to counteract what they themselves have introduced. The truth of the matter is that the interests of the defence lie in the exculpatory words: those which tend to incriminate the accused pose a risk which they consider to be worth running.

[13] It is, however, important to distinguish the situation, which does not arise in the present case, where the defence seek to lead evidence of a statement of the accused which has a close connection in time, place, and circumstances to a statement which has been led in evidence by the Crown. In such a situation the two statements may be regarded as so interconnected that they require to be treated as parts of a single statement.

[14] The second rule in *Morrison* plainly envisages that, where the Crown do not object to the leading by the defence of evidence of a 'mixed statement' the parts of it which are exculpatory of the accused should be treated in the same way as if evidence of the statement had been led by the Crown. While it may be that there has been an increasing practice of the Crown in conceding such admissibility—from which the Lord Advocate did not appear to be inclined to depart—we consider that it rests on no secure principle. It cannot be justified either on the basis of a fiction that the evidence is being led at the behest of the Crown or on the basis of an assumption that the Crown will seek to rely upon any part which is capable of incriminating the accused. To leave the question of admissibility for later resolution in the light of the Crown's ultimate approach to it would, we consider, be likely to be productive only of uncertainty and doubt which, as we have clearly indicated, it is desirable to avoid. Nor can what is envisaged in the second rule in *Morrison* be justified on the basis that a waiver by the Crown can confer admissibility on evidence which would not otherwise be admissible. The question of admissibility is a question of law, the answer to which cannot be affected by the inaction of the

Crown. Thus, to this extent, we agree with Mr. Findlay that the lack of objection by the Crown should not affect the position. The result of following what Rule 2 says about the effect of the lack of objection by the Crown is illustrated in *Khan v. H.M.A.*, 1992 J.C. 32. At pages 40–41 the court pointed out that the result of the application of the rule in that case was wholly unsatisfactory. They observed:

> 'The use made of the statement at the trial was all one way, and that was to exculpate the appellant without putting him into the witness box. There was no question of any part of the statement being used against him in any way which was unfair, since no mention of it was made at any stage by the Crown'.

It follows that it should be clearly understood that there is no duty on the Crown to lead evidence of a mixed statement, or to refrain from objecting if the defence seek to do so.

[15] In these circumstances we are of the opinion that, where the defence seek to introduce evidence of a statement by the accused, evidence of its terms, if admissible at all, will be admissible for the limited purpose referred to in Rule 3 of *Morrison*, and that the question of admissibility is unaffected by lack of objection by the Crown. We accordingly disapprove of the words in Rule 2 of *Morrison* 'or where evidence is led by the defence without objection by the Crown'.

[16] Having regard to what we have said above we are of the opinion that rule 2 in *Morrison* is in need of correction insofar as it stated that the admissibility of evidence of a mixed statement was the same where it was led by the defence without objection from the Crown as where it was led by the Crown. It may be convenient for future reference if we restate the main rules and in so doing take account of the opinion which we have expressed. The main rules which apply are as follows:

(i) It is a general rule that hearsay, that is evidence of what another person has said, is not admissible as evidence of the truth of what was said.

(ii) Thus evidence of what an accused has been heard to say is, in general, not admissible in his exculpation, and accordingly the defence are not entitled to rely on it for this purpose. Such evidence can be relied on by the defence only for the purpose of proving that the statement was made, or of showing his attitude or reaction at the time when it was made, as part of the general picture which the jury have to consider.

(iii) There is, however, an exception where the Crown have led evidence of a statement, part of which is capable of incriminating the accused. The defence are entitled to elicit and rely upon any part of that statement as qualifying, explaining or excusing the admission against interest.

[17] What we have said above should, of course, be understood as subject to all considerations as to the weight which should be attached to evidence of what an accused has said in his own exculpation. As the court observed in *Morrison* at p.313, it will normally be appropriate for the trial judge to remind the jury that the statement was not made on oath, and was not subject to cross-examination, leaving it to the jury to determine what weight should be attached to the statement in such circumstances.

[18] We should add that if a situation should arise in which the defence lead evidence of a statement which is wholly or partly exculpatory and the Crown do not object, the trial judge will require to direct the jury that evidence of the statement is admissible solely for the purpose indicated in para. (ii) above.

[19] In the present case the appeal turns on whether or not the trial judge was correct in sustaining the objection by the Advocate depute. In the light of our earlier discussion it is plain that he was correct in doing so. This appeal accordingly is refused."

8. Muldoon v. Herron
1970 J.C. 30

Three youths were charged with a breach of the peace. At their trial the only two eye-witnesses to the offence gave evidence that, soon after the offence was committed, they had pointed out to the police several of those involved. Neither witness identified the accused in court and one said that the accused were not among those she had pointed out as being among those implicated. The Sheriff-substitute disbelieved her. Two police officers deponed that the accused were among those pointed out and these witnesses were believed by the Sheriff-substitute. There was no other evidence against the accused. All were convicted and appealed against conviction to the High Court.

LORD JUSTICE-CLERK (GRANT): "Mr Brand's first and major argument was based on the wide ground that, where a witness depones that he identified the culprit to the police after the crime, but fails, or is unable, to identify the accused at the trial, the gap in his evidence cannot be filled by police evidence that the person so identified was the accused. If that be so, it seems to me (although this was not conceded) that the decision in *McGaharon* (1968 S.L.T. 99) must be wrong. No opinions were delivered in that case, but it is clear that the evidence of identification which was relied upon successfully as justifying the conviction was that of two eye-witnesses who identified the accused to the police shortly after the event, but were unable to identify him at the trial, coupled with police evidence that the accused was the person so identified. Had Mrs Miller's evidence here been similar to that of Mr MacDonald, the situation would have been identical in all material respects with that of *McGaharon*. Her evidence, however, differed from Mr MacDonald's in what is said to be a material respect, and accordingly, even if the appellants fail in demolishing *McGaharon*, that is not the end of the matter.

In my opinion, they do so fail. Direct authority is lacking, but the textbook writers, so far as they go (*cf* in particular Alison, vol. ii, pp.627–8; *Macdonald* (5th ed.) p.325) seem to me, despite the criticisms made of them, to be against the appellants' major contention. I note in passing that the passage in Macdonald just cited stems back to the first edition in 1867, at p.555. Apart from that, however, what happened (and was upheld) in *McGaharon* was in accordance with what is, and has been for years, the normal practice of the Courts. Not infrequently one has, for example, the situation where a witness who identified the driver of a motor car to the police at the time and so depones in the box, is unable, by reason of lapse of time perhaps, to identify the accused in court. This gap in his evidence is completed by police evidence that the accused was the person so identified. A similar situation arises (as it did in a recent trial) where a witness notes the number of the robbers' getaway car, gives it to the police and is unable to remember it at the trial. The passage in the first edition of Macdonald to which I have referred indicates that the practice followed in *McGaharon* was also the recognised practice over a century ago.

Furthermore, it is in my opinion a practice which is based on law and logic, and I think that the criticisms made of it were largely based on fallacy and misapprehension. This was exemplified by the reliance placed on certain authorities which I gladly accept but which seem to me to have no bearing on the real issue here. I refer in particular to *Rex v. Christie* (1914 A.C. 545) and the dicta of Lord Moulton at p.558, which were approved by Lord Normand in *Teper v. The Queen* (1952 A.C. 480). It is perfectly true that evidence of what a witness said (I am not, of course, concerned here with admissions of parties) is not evidence of truth of that statement and that, as Lord Moulton pointed out, an act of identification is an act of the mind and its accuracy cannot be established by the evidence of witnesses who merely heard or saw it being made. If the Crown were seeking here to rely on the police evidence as supporting the accuracy of the eye-witnesses' identification at the locus, then on the principle applied in such cases as *Christie* they would fail. Equally it cannot be said that evidence that a witness picked out a person at an identification parade is evidence of the accuracy of that identification.

The situation here, however, is quite different. As so often happens, no single witness at the trial identified the appellants in the dock as participants and such identification must therefore be sought from a combination of facts and circumstances spoken to in evidence by different witnesses. The combination in the present case, so far as Mr MacDonald is concerned, is his evidence that he identified seven of the culprits to the police at the time, coupled with the police evidence that three of those seven were the appellants. In the light of what I have already said it seems to me to be perfectly clear that the police evidence is direct, competent and relevant evidence, given on oath, which, when taken in conjunction with that of Mr MacDonald, inculpates the appellants as guilty parties. It is evidence, however, which stems back to a single source, Mr MacDonald, and there must, of course, be corroboration from another source before conviction can properly follow. The appellants say there is no such corroboration and that brings me to the subsidiary argument, which raises, to my mind, the crucial question in the case.

That argument, put shortly, is that, *esto* Mr MacDonald is covered by the *McGaharon* umbrella, Mrs Miller is not, and that her evidence, even in conjunction with that of the police, cannot provide the corroboration required. In *McGaharon* the two eye-witnesses were, like Mr MacDonald, 'unable to identify' the accused at the trial. Alison, vol. ii, p.628, refers to the witness who 'cannot say' that the accused is the person previously identified, and Macdonald (5th ed.) p.325, deals with the witness who is 'in difficulty in this matter'. Mrs Miller, however, categorically deponed, not that she had any such inability or doubt, but that the appellants were neither identified by her at the locus nor involved. Accordingly it was argued that, even accepting *McGaharon* the police evidence in that case merely provided a link in the evidence (as in the case of Mr MacDonald) which the eye-witnesses themselves were unable to provide and was thus the best available evidence: whereas in Mrs Miller's case there was no missing link and the police were not entitled to destroy the link she had provided and to replace it with another link provided by their own second-best evidence. (This appears to assume that the evidence of the person making an identification to the police is better evidence, in the legal sense, in regard to who was identified than that of the policemen to whom it was made.) It was also said that, if one founded upon Mrs Miller's evidence that the persons she had identified to the police were participators (and that evidence is, of course, essential to the Crown case), one must take it with her qualification that the appellants were neither identified nor involved. In any event, it was said, the police evidence, *quoad* Mrs Miller's identification, went only to credibility.

I think that some confusion may have arisen here, through the loose use of language. A question such as 'is this the best (or direct or primary) evidence?' has little meaning unless one obtains the answer to the counter-query 'Evidence of what?' It is the answer to the latter which bulks large in the present case. Furthermore, the phrase 'going to credibility only' is not one to be used without due consideration of the particular circumstances, and indeed of the point which I have just made. Evidence may competently be led to establish the fact that a witness made on another occasion a statement different from his evidence in the box. That evidence, having been led, becomes competent evidence in the case and, if accepted, falls to be considered in relation to any issue in the case to which it is relevant, *i.e.* which it tends either directly or indirectly to prove or disprove. In the normal case, evidence that a witness made a different statement on another occasion is relevant solely on the question of credibility: for the fact that the statement was made, while highly relevant on the issue of credibility, is not evidence of the truth of the statement and accordingly does not normally have any relevant bearing or evidential value *quoad* the basic issues in the case. Here, however, the evidence of the police as to Mr MacDonald's identification is highly relevant on the vital issue of whom he identified. Similarly, it seems to me that their evidence as to Mrs Miller's identification, having been competently and properly admitted, is evidence in the case which is relevant not merely on the question of her credibility but also, as in Mr MacDonald's case, on the vital issue—were the appellants among those whom she identified?

The situation, as I see it, is this: If a witness states on oath in the witness-box that he identified the culprit to the police shortly after the event, when his memory was still undimmed, it may be established by the evidence of the police concerned who the person was who was so identified. If that be done, the identification of that person by the witness is complete. The evidence of the police as to who was identified is primary and direct evidence of that matter and no question arises of hearsay evidence in the sense of evidence designed to establish the truth of a statement by proving that the statement was made. The evidence of the police is evidence, not of the accuracy of the identification which was made, but of who was in fact identified. On this matter the evidence of the police is just as direct and primary as that of the person who made the identification. Where there is a conflict between the two, it is for the Court (or jury) to decide which of them is telling the truth. Thus, if a witness says, 'I identified my assailant to the police at the locus,' the first condition for the operation of the rule is satisfied. (Contrast the unreported case of *Kemp*, September 15, 1950, to which we were referred.) If the witness goes on to say, 'The man whom I identified is not the accused,' and two policemen depone that the man identified was the accused, the fulfilment of the second condition depends upon whether the evidence of the identifying witness or that of the police is accepted. If the evidence of the police is accepted, the rule applies and the chain is complete.

In my opinion, that is the situation here and no question of hearsay (in the sense indicated above) arises. The Sheriff-substitute accepted Mrs Miller's evidence that she identified seven participants to the police, but he has rejected her evidence, as he was entitled to do, that she did not so identify the appellants and they were not present. On the crucial question of whom she in fact identified, he has preferred the evidence of the police. The purpose and effect of that evidence, as in *McGaharon* was not to establish the accuracy of the identification (in regard to which it could only be secondary and hearsay) but to establish the vital fact that the appellants were some of those identified. On this matter the police evidence is just as primary and direct as that of Mrs Miller."

LORD WHEATLEY (DISSENTING): "What was the basic issue in this case? It was whether the appellants were parties to the breach of the peace. There were only two eye-witnesses called to give evidence about this, and one of them—Mrs Miller—was adamant in her evidence that they were not. The basic issue was not whether she had made an identification to the police which contradicted her evidence on oath. This was an ancillary issue relevant to her credibility. Unlike the position in MacDonald's case, the police evidence did not otherwise fill in a gap in the eyewitness's evidence. Its effect was to contradict it. It was argued that, once she had admitted identifying the seven participants, the issue became simply 'Whom was it she identified?' And if the Court accepted the police evidence on this, you rubbed out her evidence on the point and substituted the police evidence, so that in the result you had Mrs Miller's evidence identifying the appellants. I cannot accept this argument. The issue of who was involved in the proven breach of the peace was something only those who were present could speak to and according to our rules of evidence it is only what the witnesses (apart from the accused) say on oath in the witness box that can be regarded as the measure of their evidence and not what they may have said differently on another occasion. Such other statements may be put to them in order to challenge their credibility or reliability, but they cannot be treated as a replacement of the evidence given in court if that evidence is disbelieved. You cannot say, 'I disbelieve that part of her evidence in the witness box. That leaves a gap in her evidence, so I can prove *aliunde* what she said or did on another occasion and that can be fitted into her evidence even if it contradicts her evidence on oath.' Yet that in effect is what the Crown is seeking leave to do here. It is not a matter of filling in an admitted lacuna in the witness's evidence by the best available evidence in the circumstances, as could be done in MacDonald's case. It is an endeavour to substitute something which the witness is alleged to have said or done outside of court for the evidence given by the witness in court. If Mrs Miller had identified an accused in court as her brother and had admitted that she had made a statement to the police, in which she had named the participants, but had denied on oath that her brother was a participant and that she had named him in her statement to the police, I do not think that the evidence by police officers that she had named her brother in the statement would be allowed to replace her discredited evidence on oath—*cf* Alison's Criminal Law vol. ii p.522. I cannot see how that differs in principle from the circumstances surrounding the evidence of Mrs Miller. How can one logically differentiate between evidence that she pointed to X and said 'That is the man' and evidence that she told the police that X was the man? In each case the evidence relates to a fact about what the witness did or said on a previous occasion. As I have said, this type of evidence can be and often is used to discredit a witness, but it has never been allowed in my experience to be substituted for the evidence given by the witness on oath in court, and I do not see in principle how it can be. If it can be justified on the ground that it is simply a fact that is being proved, namely, who it was that the witness identified, then it seems to me to be a short step to allowing similar evidence to prove that as a fact the witness had made an identification although she depones on oath that she had not. Moreover, the practice of holding identification parades could take on a new significance. At present these can have a two-fold advantage. They provide an opportunity for a witness to see a suspected person at a much earlier stage and may make identification or non-identification easier. Reference to this at the subsequent trial may have a bearing on the reliability of the witness's evidence in court. And in the MacDonald type of case it may provide the best available evidence to fill a gap in the witness's evidence when it is consistent with and not contradictory of the witness's other evidence. If, however, the Crown's contention here is right, identification can be established from the evidence of police witnesses who depone that a witness picked out the accused at such a parade, provided the witness admits having attended a parade and picked out a person, although he or she attests on oath that the accused was not that person. The position can thus be reached where the only two eye-witnesses depone in court that the accused was not the perpetrator of the crime libelled but identification of the accused can be established from the evidence of other witnesses that on a previous occasion the eye-witnesses had pointed to the accused as the culprit or had said that he was. I do not think that is the law of Scotland as it stands at present."

NOTES

   Two broad views of *Muldoon* have been advanced. The first, taking the case more or less at its face value, is that identification evidence of this sort is admissible as direct, primary evidence of an event, namely the earlier identification of the accused as the perpetrator—see Sheldon, "Remembrance of Things Past", 1992 S.L.T.(News) 9; Sheldon, "The Hearsay Rule Devoured" (1995) J.R. 504, and *McAllister & McLaughlan v. H.M.A.*, below. The second is that, on its facts, the case is authority for a wider exception to the hearsay rule on the basis that what the first view characterises as an "act" of identification, is truly an example of assertive conduct—conduct, in other words, in which an assertion of fact is implied—and if evidence of it is admissible it is admissible as an exception to the hearsay rule—see *inter alia* Wilkinson, *The Scottish Law of Evidence* (1987) pp.54–55, Sheriff Gordon's commentary to *Jamieson v. H.M.A.*, 1994 S.C.C.R. 610, and the case of *Frew v. Jessop*, 1990 S.L.T. 396, below. Compare also the case of *Campbell (T) v. H.M.A.*, 1998 S.C.C.R. 214 discussed in chapter 5 above. Of course, as Lord Wheatley recognised in his dissenting opinion in *Muldoon*, if the second view is accepted, then it becomes difficult—unless one is very careful to circumscribe the extent of the acceptable "acts"—to confine the exception created to "acts" of identification and the case becomes authority for a much wider breach in the hearsay rule. This is the problem raised by the next case, *Frew v. Jessop*.

9.   Frew v. Jessop
1990 S.L.T. 396

A man was accused of a number of road traffic offences after a collision between a motor car and a pick-up truck. Two passers-by who saw the collision observed that the two occupants of the pick-up truck were male and made a mental note of their descriptions. They later gave these descriptions to the police. These two passers-by gave evidence at the trial that they had seen the occupants and given the descriptions to the police, but they were unable to identify the accused or recall the terms of their descriptions. Police witnesses gave evidence of the descriptions and this was held to be sufficient to corroborate evidence of an incriminating statement given by the accused to the police. The accused appealed on the basis that the descriptions were hearsay and therefore inadmissible.

LORD JUSTICE-CLERK (ROSS): "The appellant is Stephen Frew who went to trial in the district court at Glasgow on a complaint libelling a number of charges. He was found guilty of several of these charges on the complaint, being offences under the Road Traffic Act 1972. He has appealed against conviction and there are a number of issues raised in the stated case. Today counsel has maintained that the stipendiary magistrate ought to have upheld a submission of no case to answer and that it is plain from the findings and the stipendiary magistrate's note that he relied upon hearsay evidence. In finding 4 and finding 5, the stipendiary magistrate records what the situation was regarding two witnesses Norwood and Robertson. It appears that these two witnesses were on the pavement at the time of an accident involving a motor car and a motor pickup. These witnesses each observed that the occupants of the motor pickup were two young men and they mentally noted a description of them before the pickup drove off. The police came on the scene shortly afterwards and it is recorded that each of these witnesses related to the police officers the description of the men. In the case of Robertson he also related to them the registered number of the pickup vehicle.
   When these two witnesses came to give evidence before the stipendiary magistrate they apparently indicated that they had seen the driver and the passenger of the pickup and they

also testified that shortly after they gave the descriptions to which we have referred to the police officers. It appears that the registered number given was A661 SGB and the description was that the driver was the taller of the two with longer and lighter coloured hair and that the passenger was smaller with shorter and darker coloured hair. In their evidence before the stipendiary magistrate the two witnesses were unable to recall the description which they had given to the police and they were now of course unable to identify the appellant or his co-accused in court. Evidence was however led from the two police officers as to the description which had been conveyed to them at the time by these two witnesses. The point which counsel has made is that that was hearsay evidence and he submits it ought not to have been admitted. Finding 10 in the case records that the appellant was interviewed by the police and required in terms of section 168 of the Road Traffic Act 1972 to state who was driving the vehicle A661 SGB when it was involved in an accident at the time and that he replied 'OK me'. Accordingly there was a clear admission by the appellant that he was the driver and the question is whether corroboration can be obtained from the evidence to which we have already referred.

The advocate-depute has submitted that what took place in this case was very similar to what took place in the well known case of *Muldoon v. Herron*. That case concerned evidence of identification which two witnesses had made to the police at the time but which the witnesses were unable to recall by the time that evidence was given in court. It is now well recognised that where a witness is unable to identify an accused in court but gives evidence that the person whom he had pointed out to the police at an earlier stage was the perpetrator of the crime, and the police witnesses then state that the accused was the person identified to them by the witness, that that is competent evidence of their identification. The advocate-depute contended that the same principle could and should be properly applied to evidence of this description given by the witnesses in this case.

In our opinion the advocate-depute is well founded in that contention. We do not see why any different principle should be applied to evidence of this kind that is frequently applied to evidence of positive identification which the witness has been able to make shortly after an offence has been committed but which he is unable to recall by the time he gives his evidence in court. It is not at all unusual for a witness to testify that he witnessed an accident and had noted the number of the vehicle and had informed the police of this at the time, but that by the time he gives his evidence he is quite unable to recall the registered number of the vehicle which he had reported to the police. In that situation it is quite competent for evidence to be led from police officers as to the number of the vehicle which he had reported to them at the time. In our opinion the same principle would apply to evidence of this kind where a description of driver and passenger were given by the witnesses at the time to police officers. It is quite understandable that after a considerable lapse of time the witnesses might be unable to recall what that description was and in that situation we are of opinion that it is competent for police officers to give evidence as to what the description was which was conveyed to them by the witnesses at the time. No doubt that evidence is hearsay evidence but it is hearsay evidence which forms an exception to the rule that hearsay evidence is inadmissible.

We are satisfied in this case that the evidence was properly admitted by the stipendiary magistrate and that having regard to that evidence there was sufficient evidence along with the admission to justify the stipendiary magistrate in convicting the appellant in charges 2 to 5. We shall accordingly answer the questions in the case as follows: we shall answer the first question in the negative, the second question in the affirmative, the third question in the negative and the fourth question in the affirmative. It follows that the appeal is refused."

NOTES

It is notable that, apart from *Muldoon v. Herron*, no authority is cited for the "exception" to the hearsay rule which this case approves. Whatever the merits of that case, it is submitted that *Frew v. Jessop* is very clearly distinguishable, since in that case there was no "act" of identification, only a narrative description of the vehicle concerned, which was then used "testimonially" in the manner proscribed in *Kearley*. Is it true to say that *Frew* follows naturally and logically from *Muldoon*, as Wilkinson argues? Might it be possible to distinguish the cases on the basis that *Muldoon* was a case about implied assertions, about which, as we seen, Scots law has never had any difficulty, whereas the evidence in *Frew v. Jessop* was very clearly being used testimonially, as a narrative relating to facts in issue? Have both positions in any event been superceded by *Jamieson v. H.M.A.*, below?

10.   McAllister & McLaughlan v. H.M.A.
(1975) S.C.C.R. Supplement 98

LORD JUSTICE-GENERAL (EMSLIE): "We have before us two applications for leave to appeal against conviction. The first is by Michael McLaughlan; the second is by Alan McAllister. They were charged on indictment together and the charge was that acting along with a man called William Egli Kasper, they broke into certain premises in Kilmarnock (a café) and stole a quantity of cigarettes and tobacco. They were tried in the sheriff court and the jury convicted by a majority. It appears perfectly plainly from the sheriff's charge that the principal evidence against both applicants came from the *socius criminis*, William Egli Kasper, and it may be assumed that his evidence implicated both in the crime to the full. The critical question at the trial was, however, whether there was sufficient corroboration in law of Kasper's evidence. The only source of that corroboration as it turned out, could be in the evidence of a witness called Mrs Wotherspoon. In the witness box she spoke of Kasper's arrival at her house on the evening of the theft, with a sack presumably containing the proceeds of the housebreaking. She said that he was accompanied by two men whom she did not see, because they were downstairs. That was her evidence in the box. The Crown then proceeded to lead the evidence of police officers or a police officer, purporting to speak to a statement said to have been made by Mrs Wotherspoon to them on an earlier occasion during the police investigation of the crime. That statement, which the sheriff allowed to go before the jury, bore to disclose that when Kasper arrived at the witness's house he was accompanied by both of the applicants. Objection was, of course, very properly taken to the admission of this statement in evidence at the trial. The sheriff repelled the objection holding that the evidence was competent and admissible upon the basis of the well-known case of Muldoon. In our view he was wholly wrong in so doing. Muldoon is a case which covers the provision of a missing link in the act of identification of a witness. This statement has nothing to do with identification of that kind. It is no more than an account of what the witness is said to have spoken to a third party. It is hearsay. It is plainly incompetent and in no circumstances should that evidence have been admitted as evidence against the applicants. That is enough for disposal of the applications. The applications will be allowed and the convictions will be quashed. The learned advocate-depute, may we add, very properly indicated that he did not wish to address us in support of the conviction."

NOTES

    See also the brief report of this case in (1976) 40 J.C.L. 116. Can *McAllister and McLaughlan* be distinguished from *Frew v. Jessop*? Can it be reconciled with *Jamieson v. H.M.A.*, below? It does not appear from the opinion of the court whether in her evidence, the witness Mrs Wotherspoon acknowledged making the earlier statement to the police, a matter which, standing *Jamieson*, may be crucial.

11.   Smith v. H.M.A.
1986 S.C.C.R. 135

The appellant was convicted of assault and robbery. The case against him depended on three eye-witnesses. There was one positive identification. The second witness accepted that she had made an unqualified identification at an earlier identity parade, but said that she should have qualified her identification by saying that the accused was similar to the culprit because she had been confused at the parade. In relation to the third witness, the police said that she had made an unqualified identification at the identity parade, but her evidence in court was that she had said at the parade that she had thought that the accused was the culprit and in court she said he was very much like the culprit. The accused was convicted and appealed on the ground that there was no corroboration of the principal witness.

LORD JUSTICE-CLERK (ROSS): "The appellant is Michael Smith who was found guilty on two charges, one of breaking into garage premises and stealing therefrom and the second of assault and attempted robbery at a sub-post office in the Kilsyth Road, Banknock. The sole ground of appeal which has been presented today is to the effect that there was insufficient evidence to corroborate the identification of the appellant as being one of the perpetrators of the crime. It is also pointed out in this ground of appeal that at the conclusion of the Crown case the submission was rejected by the presiding sheriff. The contention is that the sheriff erred in rejecting this submission. It is not disputed that there was one positive identification of the appellant by the witness Heather Vass and the question is whether there was sufficient evidence to corroborate that evidence of identification.

There were two sources from which the corroboration was sought to be taken. One was the evidence of a Mrs Rankine and the other of a Mrs Cooper. In his charge the sheriff pointed out to the jury that Mrs Rankine had identified the accused in the dock as the person whom she had identified earlier at an identification parade, but that she went on to say that the accused was similar to the man whom she had seen holding a white stick, and he reminded the jury that she had said in evidence while pointing at the accused 'he looked like him, he is like the man but I am not certain'. So far as Mrs Cooper is concerned the sheriff reminded the jury that according to his notes when giving her evidence in court she had said, and I quote, 'he looked very much like the one.' The witness Mrs Rankine stated that she had gone to an identification parade and that she had identified the appellant but she went on to say that the appellant was similar to the man. She was asked whether the police had enquired of her if she could identify an individual on the parade and she had said she could. She was asked whether she had told the police that the man in the parade was similar and she said no. When she was asked why she did not tell the police she was only saying that the man was similar as opposed to being the actual man, she said that she did not know but had been confused that day apparently because her child had been involved in an accident. As far as the witness Mrs Cooper is concerned she apparently said that when she went to the identification parade she identified No. 2 on the parade and according to her had said 'I think it's No. 2.' The record of the parade itself, however, shows that what she had said was 'It's No. 2', so that there was in this respect a conflict in the evidence.

It was for the jury to evaluate and determine whether on the evidence before them they were satisfied that positive and unqualified identification had been made by one or other or both of these witnesses at the parade or whether the witnesses had given less than a full and unqualified identification. That matter was left by the sheriff to the jury and in our opinion that was the correct course to take. We were referred to the cases of *Muldoon v. Herron* and *Neeson v. H.M.A.* Mr Hamilton on behalf to the appellant sought to distinguish the case of *Neeson* upon the ground that in *Neeson* there had been a confession and that accordingly all that was required was corroboration of that confession. We do not consider that that is a sound distinction to make between *Neeson* and the present case. In the present case there was positive evidence of identification from Heather Vass and the question was similar to the question in *Neeson*, namely whether there was corroboration for that. It is plain from *Neeson* and from the earlier case of *Muldoon* that a jury is entitled to treat the evidence of what a witness had said at an identification parade as corroboration in circumstances of this kind. The case of *Neeson* in fact is very similar to the present case because it appears from the report in that case that the witness whose evidence was being considered had positively identified the accused at an identification parade but had subsequently indicated that he was not sure whether the person he had identified was the man whom he had seen at the time of the offence. In that connection the Lord Justice-General at p.75 said this and I quote:

> 'In this case all that can be said is that Sharpe [the witness in question], while admitting that he had identified somebody at the parade, added the rider, "but I was not sure if it was the same man". The rider was a matter for the jury to evaluate because the police evidence indicated that without qualification or hesitation or comment, the identification had been short, sharp and certain. That is the effect of the evidence and upon the whole matter, and under reference to the well-known case of *Muldoon v. Herron*, this appeal must be refused.'

In exactly the same way in the present case, it was for the jury to evaluate the evidence of the witness because on the one hand there was evidence that the witness had made a positive identification at the identification parade and on the other hand as regards Mrs Cooper there was an indication that she was no longer sure if that was the same individual. For these reasons it appears to us that the matter was properly put to the jury. There was sufficient evidence in law to corroborate the identification of the appellant if the jury chose to accept that evidence. The matter was fairly put to the jury and it is clear that they must have concluded that the evidence available did satisfy them that there was the necessary corroboration. In these circumstances the appeal is refused."

NOTES

Does this case support the first or the second view of *Muldoon*, set out above? On one view, *Muldoon* was dependent on the original witness at least acknowledging that an accurate identification was made, if not that the person identified was the person now charged with the offence (see Sheriff Gordon's commentary to *Smith*). This case appears to take the view that the police evidence can wholly replace that of the original witness. If police evidence of what took place at the identity parade is truly to be regarded as direct evidence of those events, then that would indeed be a logical view. It is doubtful if *Smith* (and see also *Maxwell v. H.M.A.*, 1991 S.L.T. 63) can be reconciled with the next case, which in turn casts some doubt on the idea that *Muldoon* is a case about hearsay at all!

12.   Jamieson v. H.M.A. (No. 2)
1994 S.C.C.R. 610

The appellant was charged with attempted murder. A Crown witness gave evidence that she could not remember what had happened and could not remember telling the police that the appellant had been kicking the complainer, but she said that if she had said this to the police at the time then it must have been true. Evidence was later led that she had indeed told the police that she had seen the appellant kicking the complainer. The trial judge directed the jury that they could use her earlier statement as evidence since she had incorporated it into her evidence by her evidence in court that what she had told the police was true.

LORD JUSTICE-GENERAL (HOPE): "The issue raised by the first point in Mr Di Rollo's argument is encountered most frequently in identification evidence, but in our opinion the principles which must be applied here are the same. In *Muldoon v. Herron* neither of the two witnesses to the incident could identify the accused in court. But they gave evidence that, very soon after the incident, they had identified to the police seven youths as having participated in the disturbance. The evidence of the two police officers was led without objection and the sheriff-substitute held that the youths who had been identified by the witnesses included the appellants. It was contended in that case that the gap in the evidence of the witnesses who were unable to identify the culprits at the trial could not be filled by the police evidence that the persons they identified at that time were the accused. Lord Justice-Clerk Grant pointed out at p.34, however, that what happened in that case, and in *McGaharon v. H.M.A.* in which no opinions were delivered, was in accordance with what was, and had been for years, the normal practice of the courts.

'Not infrequently one has, for example, the situation where a witness who identified the driver of a motor car to the police at the time and so depones in the box, is unable, by reason of lapse of time perhaps, to identify the accused in court. This gap in his evidence is completed by police evidence that the accused was the person so identified.'

He went on to say that in his opinion it was a practice which was based on law and logic. Evidence of what a witness said was not evidence of the truth of that statement. But when taken in conjunction with the witness's evidence that he identified the culprits to the police at the time, there was there direct, competent and relevant evidence, given on oath, as to the guilt of the accused. Later in his opinion at p.36 the Lord Justice-Clerk said that the situation as he saw it was this.

'If a witness states on oath in the witness-box that he identified the culprit to the police shortly after the event, when his memory was still undimmed, it may be established by the evidence of the police concerned who the person was who was so identified. The evidence of the police as to who was identified is primary and direct evidence of that matter and no question arises of hearsay evidence in the sense of evidence designed to establish the truth of the statement by proving that the statement was made. The evidence of the police is evidence, not of the accuracy of the identification which was made, but of who was in fact identified. On this matter the evidence of the police is just as direct and primary as that of the person who made the identification.'

Lord Cameron at pp.46–47 referred to long-standing practice and to a long tract of authoritative opinion to the effect that the evidence of the witness as to an identification made by him at the time to police officers and that of the police officers linking the persons thus identified with the appellants was properly admitted and was relevant and competent evidence tending towards identification of the accused.

The *Muldoon* case dealt with the position of a missing link in evidence of identification. The opinions in that case, including the dissenting opinion by Lord Wheatley, were all directed to the question of identification evidence and the case does not provide direct authority for the direction which was given by the trial judge in this case. But in our opinion the principle upon which the evidence of identification was held to be admissible in that case is of wider application and is not confined to identification evidence. Where a person identifies the alleged culprit to police officers, he is in effect telling them what he saw. He is making a statement to the police officers which is a statement of fact and ought, if possible, to be spoken to by the witness in the witness box. But if he is unable to recollect what he said to the police when he comes to give evidence, the gap in his recollection can be filled by what the police said he said to them at the time. This evidence, when taken with the witness's own evidence that he made a true statement at the time to the police, is held to be admissible because there are two primary sources of evidence. One is the evidence of the police officers as to who was in fact identified and the other is the witness's own evidence that he identified the culprit to the police. The consistency between these two pieces of evidence provides the link between them and completes the chain. As Lord Cameron said in *Muldoon* at p.46, neither of these facts proves identity, but both are elements in the structure of evidence from which identification may be held proved.

In the present case there were two primary sources of evidence. One was the evidence of D.C. Farman as to what Marianne Robertson said to him in her statement. The other was Marianne Robertson's evidence that she made a statement to he police officer and that what she said to him at the time was true. Her evidence that she had made a statement to the police officer did not go to the length of admitting any of the details of what she may have said to him. She said that she could not remember this, so there was a gap in her evidence. But her evidence that she told the police the truth and that, if she said at the time she saw the appellant hitting Camy it must be true, had the effect, as the trial judge said, of incorporating her statement to the police into her own evidence. Taken separately neither the evidence of the police officer nor what she said in her own evidence implicated the appellant in the assault on the complainer. But taken together, as elements in the whole structure of the evidence, they had that effect.

We do not therefore accept Mr Di Rollo's primary submission."

NOTES

The explicit adoption of *Muldoon* in this case throws into doubt the whole basis for the discussion about *Muldoon*. Is it correct to say that the present problem is simply one of "linking up" the evidence of a number of witnesses, thus implying that this is not a hearsay problem at all? As Lord Wheatley pointed out in *Muldoon*, the fact that a witness who gives evidence is shown to have made a previous statement inconsistent with his or her evidence was thought to be relevant only to the credibility of that witness. It is perhaps worth noting that it has been held (by Sir Gerald Gordon QC, sitting as a Temporary Judge) that a witness who claims to be unable to remember past events is making an inconsistent statement for these purposes—see *H.M.A. v. Hislop*, 1994 S.L.T. 333. Compare also the English case of *R. v. Osborne; R. v. Virtue* [1973] Q.B. 678, a similar case in which the hearsay rule was explicitly invoked. To what extent, if any, does *Jamieson* limit the *Muldoon* "doctrine"? In particular what is involved in the idea that the witness must acknowledge in court that he was telling the truth when he made a "true" statement to the police on the earlier occasion? In *Muldoon* the witness admitted having identified someone, but denied having identified the accused. Would this count as a "true" statement for the purposes of *Jamieson*? Moreover, is it correct to say that section 260 of the Criminal Procedure (Scotland) Act 1995 reflects the principles expounded in Jamieson, as it was apparently intended to do? (See S.L.C. No. 149, 1995, paras. 7.8 and 7.39–7.49). In terms of section 260 the witness must indicate in his or her evidence that "the statement was made by him and that he *adopts* it as his evidence" [emphasis added]. See the notes to section 260 of the 1995 Act, below. Finally, in so far as *Jamieson* is consistent with the views expressed in *McAllister and McLaughlan*, above, that "*Muldoon* is a case which covers the provision of a missing link in the act of identification of a witness", can *Frew v. Jessop* be said to remain good law?

13. Criminal Procedure (Scotland) Act 1995

Exceptions to the rule that hearsay evidence is inadmissible

"259.—(1) Subject to the following provisions of this section, evidence of a statement made by a person otherwise than while giving oral evidence in court in criminal proceedings shall be admissible in those proceedings as evidence of any matter contained in the statement where the judge is satisfied—

    (a) that the person who made the statement will not give evidence in the proceedings of such matter of any of the reasons mentioned in subsection (2) below;

    (b) that evidence of the matter would be admissible in the proceedings if that person gave direct oral evidence of it;

    (c) that the person who made the statement would have been, at the time the statement was made, a competent witness in such proceedings; and

    (d) that there is evidence which would entitle a jury properly directed, or in summary proceedings would entitle the judge, to find that the statement was made and that either—

        (i) it is contained in a document; or

        (ii) a person who gave oral evidence in the proceedings as to the statement has direct personal knowledge of the making of the statement.

(2) The reasons referred to in paragraph (a) of subsection (1) above are that the person who made the statement—

    (a) is dead or is, by reason of his bodily or mental condition, unfit or unable to give evidence in any competent manner;

    (b) is named and otherwise sufficiently identified, but is outwith the United Kingdom and it is not reasonably practicable to secure his attendance at the trial or to obtain his evidence in any other competent manner;

    (c) is named and otherwise sufficiently identified, but cannot be found and all reasonable steps which, in the circumstances, could have been taken to find him have been so taken;

    (d) having been authorised to do so by virtue of a ruling of the court in the proceedings that he is entitled to refuse to give evidence in connection with the subject matter of the statement on the grounds that such evidence might incriminate him, refuses to give such evidence; or

    (e) is called as a witness and either—

        (i) refuses to take the oath or affirmation; or

        (ii) having been sworn as a witness and directed by the judge to give evidence in connection with the subject matter of the statement refuses to do so, and in the application of this paragraph to a child, the reference to a witness refusing to take the oath or affirmation or, as the case may be, to having been sworn shall be construed as a reference to a child who has refused to accept an admonition to tell the truth or, having been so admonished, refuses to give evidence as mentioned above.

(3) Evidence of a statement shall not be admissible by virtue of subsection (1) above where the judge is satisfied that the occurrence of any of the circumstances mentioned in paragraphs (a)

to (e) of subsection (2) above, by virtue of which the statement would otherwise be admissible, is caused by—

    (a) the person in support of whose case the evidence would be given; or

    (b) any other person acting on his behalf,

        for the purpose of securing that the person who made the statement does not give evidence for the purposes of the proceedings either at all or in connection with the subject matter of the statement.

(4) Where in any proceedings evidence of a statement made by any person is admitted by reference to any of the reasons mentioned in paragraphs (a) to (c) and (e)(i) of subsection (2) above—

    (a) any evidence which, if that person had given evidence in connection with the subject matter of the statement, would have been admissible as relevant to his credibility as a witness shall be admissible for that purpose in those proceedings;

    (b) evidence may be given of any matter which, if that person had given evidence in connection with the subject matter of the statement, could have been put to him in cross-examination as relevant to his credibility as a witness but of which evidence could not have been adduced by the cross-examining party; and

    (c) evidence tending to prove that that person, whether before or after making the statement, made in whatever manner some other statement which is inconsistent with it shall be admissible for the purpose of showing that he has contradicted himself.

(5) Subject to subsection (6) below, where a party intends to apply to have evidence of a statement admitted by virtue of subsection (1) above he shall, before the trial diet, give notice in writing of—

    (a) that fact;

    (b) the witnesses and productions to be adduced in connection with such evidence; and

    (c) such other matters as may be prescribed by Act of Adjournal, to every other party to the proceedings and, for the purposes of this subsection, such evidence may be led notwithstanding that a witness or production concerned is not included in any list lodged by the parties and that the notice required by sections 67(5) and 78(4) of this Act has not been given.

(6) A party shall not be required to give notice as mentioned in subsection (5) above where—

    (a) the grounds for seeking to have evidence of a statement admitted are as mentioned in paragraph (d) or (e) of subsection (2) above; or

    (b) he satisfies the judge that there was good reason for not giving such notice.

(7) If no other party to the proceedings objects to the admission of evidence of a statement by virtue of subsection (1) above, the evidence shall be admitted without the judge requiring to be satisfied as mentioned in that subsection.

(8) For the purposes of the determination of any matter upon which the judge is required to be satisfied under subsection (1) above—

    (a) except to the extent that any other party to the proceedings challenges them and insists in such challenge, it shall be presumed that the circumstances are as stated by the party seeking to introduce evidence of the statement; and

    (b) where such a challenge is insisted in, the judge shall determine the matter on the balance of probabilities, and he may draw any reasonable inference—

        (i) from the circumstances in which the statement was made or otherwise came into being; or

        (ii) from any other circumstances, including, where the statement is contained in a document, the form and contents of the document.

(9) Where evidence of a statement has been admitted by virtue of subsection (1) above on the application of one party to the proceedings, without prejudice to anything in any enactment or rule of law, the judge may permit any party to lead additional evidence of such description as the judge may specify, notwithstanding that a witness or production concerned is not included in any list lodged by the parties and that the notice required by sections 67(5) and 78(4) of this Act has not been given.

   (10) Any reference in subsections (5), (6) and (9) above to evidence shall include a reference to evidence led in connection with any determination required to be made for the purposes of subsection (1) above."

NOTES

This section implements the S.L.C.'s recommendations in their Report on Hearsay Evidence in Criminal Proceedings (Scot. Law Com. No. 149, 1995); indeed it follows closely the wording of the draft bill contained in that report. In making its recommendations the S.L.C. took as its guiding principle certain *dicta* of Lord Justice-General Hope in *Lord Advocate's Reference (No. I of 1992)*, 1992 S.C.C.R. 724 at 743–744 in which he suggested that the hearsay rule might be modified or disapplied where first-hand evidence is unavailable and hearsay thus becomes the best evidence available (see paras. 3.5, 3.6). Thus, broadly, section 259 allows the admission of hearsay evidence where the maker of the statement is not reasonably available to give evidence in person. See generally Sheldon, "Evidence in Criminal Trials: The Evidential Provisions of the Criminal Justice (Scotland) Act 1995" (1996) 41 J.L.S.S. 25. In particular, however, the effect of section 259(2) and section 261 is that the case of *McLay v. H.M.A.*, 1994 S.C.C.R. 397 is partially overruled. In *McLay,* the appellant had been convicted of murder. He had gone to trial with a co-accused, who was acquitted. It was held that evidence of an incriminating statement made after the trial by the co-accused was not admissible as additional evidence at McLay's appeal. Under the new law, hearsay evidence can be led of a confession by a third party, provided that party has been called as a witness and either refuses to do so, or simply cannot be found. It can also be led in relation to any confession by a co-accused, should that co-accused refrain from giving evidence.

It is worth emphasising that where these new provisions apply, hearsay is admissible as evidence of the facts asserted by or implied in the statement (section 17(1)). In other words, the statement can be used "testimonially" (see *Ratten v. R.*, above); that is, as if it was made by the witness while giving evidence in the proceedings. It remains the law that a previous inconsistent statement may be used to discredit a witness (1975 Act, s.147, now CPSA, s.263(4)) where he or she gives evidence at the trial which is at variance with that previous statement. In *H.M.A. v. Hislop*, 1994 S.L.T. 333 it was held that a witness who states at the trial that she simply cannot remember a particular incident may be giving a statement different from one she made on an earlier occasion. In such circumstances, a party is permitted to lead evidence under section 263(4) of the witness's previous statement. Under the new provisions, however, it is only where a witness refuses to give evidence about a particular matter—"the subject matter of the statement"—that evidence will be admissible under section 17 as evidence in the case, as opposed to mere evidence of credibility. It is not sufficient to satisfy the terms of section 259(2)(e)(ii) that the witness simply refuses to give evidence or answer questions. He or she must be directed to answer the particular questions put, and it may be that a prior statement should be put to the witness before its terms can be led under section 259—see *MacDonald (Robert Grant) v. H.M.A.*, 1999 S.L.T. 533. The court in *MacDonald* said that "section 259 involves a substantial innovation in the law of evidence in criminal cases and, in our view, the terms of the section require to be strictly observed". The effect of this is that a child witness who becomes distressed and is unwilling or unable to answer particular questions cannot be regarded as refusing to answer until he or she has been positively directed to answer those questions.

Each of the exceptions created by section 17 is subject to a number of further qualifications. Thus, in order to adduce evidence under section 17:

1. It must be shown that evidence of the matter in question would be admissible if the maker of the statement gave direct oral evidence of it—for example, a hearsay statement about the criminal convictions of the accused would not normally be admissible, even if the evidence satisfied the other provisions of section 17. A recent example is the case of *H.M.A. v. Beggs, (No. 3)*, 2001 S.C.C.R. 891.
2. That the person who made the statement would have been, at the time the statement was made, a competent witness in the proceedings—this is a refinement of the civil hearsay provisions, which do not impose a competency test in relation to a witness whose hearsay statement it is sought to adduce—see *T v. T*, 2000 S.L.T. 1442. In *Patterson v. H.M.A.*, 2000 S.L.T. 302 it was held that to be regarded as incompetent for the purposes of section 259, a witness has to be either permanently or temporarily insane or at least in such a condition as to be unable to understand the difference between truth and falsehood. A witness, even if unreliable, cannot be regarded as incompetent just because he or she is an alcoholic. There is a general presumption that humans are sane, possess ordinary powers and faculties and know the difference between truth and falsehood. That presumption requires to be displaced by the person seeking to have the hearsay evidence excluded.
3. The statement should have been made in a document, or should be one about which the person giving evidence in the proceedings has direct personal knowledge. This latter provision is clearly aimed at ensuring the reliability of the evidence so far as possible, and effectively rules out double hearsay (or hearsay of hearsay), which is permitted under the 1988 Act. Finally, it should be noted that hearsay will not be admitted where the unavailability of first-

hand evidence was caused by the person (or any person acting on his behalf) seeking to adduce a hearsay statement on that matter. For example, it will not do for an accused to intimidate a witness into silence and then seek to adduce a favourable hearsay statement by that witness.

In general, notice must be given in writing, albeit at any point before the trial, of a party's intention to lead hearsay under this section. Notice is not required in relation to headings (d) or (e), above, since clearly, the conditions can be satisfied only once the trial has commenced. Nor is notice required if good reason can be established for the lack of such notice. The High Court has indicated that the requirement to give notice under section 259(5) is not to be regarded as a mere formality. In *McPhee v. H.M.A.*, 2001 S.C.C.R. 674, the court held that an unexplained failure to give notice under section 259(5) could not be cured by an adjournment to allow the defence to consider the evidence, and quashed the appellant's conviction.

Unless there is an objection to the admission of the evidence, there is no need to satisfy the court that the conditions for the admission of such evidence have been met, and, subject to any such objection, it will be presumed that the circumstances are as stated by the party seeking to introduce evidence of the statement. Where any of the conditions for the admission of hearsay are disputed, the trial judge must determine the matter on the balance of probabilities. Although the matter is not made explicit, the burden of satisfying the Court as to the existence of any of the section 17 conditions will presumably lie on the person seeking to adduce evidence of the hearsay statement—see *Patterson v. H.M.A.*, above.

A statement which amounts to a precognition will not be admitted under s.259 — see s.262(1) and compare *H.M.A. v. Beggs (No. 3)*, 2001 S.C.C.R. 891.

Admissibility of prior statements of witnesses

"260.—(1) Subject to the following provisions of this section, where a witness gives evidence in criminal proceedings, any prior statement made by the witness shall be admissible as evidence of any matter stated in it of which direct oral evidence by him would be admissible if given in the course of those proceedings.

(2) A prior statement shall not be admissible under this section unless—
    (a) the statement is contained in a document;
    (b) the witness, in the course of giving evidence, indicates that the statement was made by him *and that he adopts it as his evidence* [emphasis added]; and
    (c) at the time the statement was made, the person who made it would have been a competent witness in the proceedings.

(3) For the purposes of this section, any reference to a prior statement is a reference to a prior statement which, but for the provisions of this section, would not be admissible as evidence of any matter stated in it.

(4) Subsections (2) and (3) above do not apply to a prior statement—
    (a) contained in a precognition on oath; or
    (b) made in other proceedings, whether criminal or civil and whether taking place in the United Kingdom or elsewhere, and, for the purposes of this section, any such statement shall not be admissible unless it is sufficiently authenticated."

NOTES

Section 260 provides that where a witness gives evidence in criminal proceedings, any prior statement made by him may be admissible as evidence in the case, provided: (i) that the statement is contained in a document; (ii) that the witness indicates in his evidence that he made the statement and that he adopts it as his evidence and (iii) the witness would have been a competent witness in the proceedings at the time the statement was made. For an example of a case in which the requirements of section 260 were not fulfilled—see *Ogilvie v. H.M.A.*, 1999 S.L.T. 1068. Point (ii) is the operative part of the section and is said to constitute a statutory form of the principle laid down in *Jamieson v. H.M.A. (No. 2)*, 1994 S.C.C.R. 610. (See S.L.C. No. 149 para. 7.8 and 7.43.) It may be doubted whether this is correct.

In *Jamieson*, the Court applied what it took to be the *ratio* of *Muldoon v. Herron*, 1970 S.L.T. 228; 1970 J.C. 30. This was said to be that where a witness cannot recall the terms of an earlier statement, but acknowledges that it was a true statement, the terms of that statement may be proved by other witnesses. It is arguable that this is a different thing from adopting one's previous statement. The whole point about *Muldoon* was that the witness in question insisted that the person accused was not the person she earlier identified. In a sense she did not "adopt" her previous statement at all. To require a witness to "adopt" his previous statement is surely a stricter test than that applied in the cases following *Muldoon*, or indeed in *Jamieson*. Furthermore, *Jamieson* may represent a reining in of the *Muldoon* doctrine. Certainly, by requiring that a witness should "adopt" her previous statement, doubt is cast on cases such as *Smith v. H.M.A.*, 1986 S.C.C.R. 135 in which the witness was unsure that his previous identification of the accused was an accurate one, and police evidence was allowed wholly to replace that of the witness. Whatever they may be, the 1995 Act specifically preserves the common law rules on admissibility of statements made otherwise than in the course of giving oral evidence (section 20(4)).

Statements by accused

"261.—(1) Subject to the following provisions of this section, nothing in sections 259 and 260 of this Act shall apply to a statement made by the accused.

(2) Evidence of a statement made by an accused shall be admissible by virtue of the said section 259 at the instance of another accused in the same proceedings as evidence in relation to that other accused.

(3) For the purposes of subsection (2) above, the first mentioned accused shall be deemed—
  (a) where he does not give evidence in the proceedings, to be a witness refusing to give evidence in connection with the subject matter of the statement as mentioned in paragraph (e) of subsection (2) of the said section 259; and
  (b) to have been, at the time the statement was made, a competent witness in the proceedings.

(4) Evidence of a statement shall not be admissible as mentioned in subsection (2) above unless the accused at whose instance it is sought to be admitted has given notice of his intention to do so as mentioned in subsection (5) of the said section 259; but subsection (6) of that section shall not apply in the case of notice required to be given by virtue of this subsection."

Construction of sections 259 to 261

"262.—(1) For the purposes of sections 259 to 261 of this Act, a 'statement' includes—
  (a) any representation, however made or expressed, of fact or opinion; and
  (b) any part of a statement,
      but does not include a statement in a precognition other than a precognition on oath.

(2) For the purposes of the said sections 259 to 261 a statement is contained in a document where the person who makes it—
  (a) makes the statement in the document personally;
  (b) makes a statement which is, with or without his knowledge, embodied in a document by whatever means or by any person who has direct personal knowledge of the making of the statement; or
  (c) approves a document as embodying the statement.

(3) In the said sections 259 to 261—

"criminal proceedings" include any hearing by the sheriff of an application made under Chapter 3 of Part II of the Children (Scotland) Act 1995 for a finding as to whether grounds for the referral of a child's case to a children's hearing are established, in so far as the application relates to the commission of an offence by the child, or for a review of such a finding;

"document" includes, in addition to a document in writing—
  (a) any map, plan, graph or drawing;
  (b) any photograph;
  (c) any disc, tape, sound track or other device in which sounds or other data (not being visual images) are recorded so as to be capable (with or without the aid of some other equipment) of being reproduced therefrom; and
  (d) any film, negative, tape, disc or other device in which one or more visual images are recorded so as to be capable (as aforesaid) of being reproduced therefrom;

"film" includes a microfilm;

"made" includes allegedly made.

(4) Nothing in the said sections 259 to 261 shall prejudice the admissibility of a statement made by a person other than in the course of giving oral evidence in court which is admissible otherwise than by virtue of those sections."

14.   McKenna v. H.M.A.
2000 S.L.T. 508

In this case the accused took a preliminary objection to the admission of hearsay evidence under section 259, pleading *inter alia* that it would be contrary to the European Convention on Human Rights. That Convention was incorporated into Scots law by the Scotland Act 1998 and the Human Rights Act 1998. Article 6 of the Convention provides that:

"(1) In the determination of his civil rights and obligations or of any criminal charge against him, everyone is entitled to a fair and public hearing within a reasonable time by an independent and impartial tribunal established by law. . .

(3) Everyone charged with a criminal offence has the following minimum rights . . . (d) to examine or have examined witnesses against him and to obtain the attendance and examination of witnesses on his behalf under the same conditions as witnesses against him."

OPINION OF THE COURT: "The appellant, Michael McKenna, is charged on indictment with the murder of Robert Potts Halliday on June 21, 1999 by striking him repeatedly on the head with an axe. The crime is alleged to have been committed in premises at 9 Waddell Court, Kilmarnock. The appellant understands that it will be the Crown's position at his trial that the only persons present in those premises at the material time were the victim, the appellant and Colin Alexander Copeland. Mr Copeland has since died. He is said to have made statements to the police in which he exculpated himself and blamed the appellant for the death of Mr Halliday. The Lord Advocate gave notice, as required by section 259(5) of the Criminal Procedure (Scotland) Act 1995, of his intention to apply to have evidence of those statements admitted at the appellant's trial in terms of subsections (1) and (2)(a) of that section. In response the appellant lodged two minutes of notice. In one minute, the appellant contended that the Lord Advocate's actions in serving the section 259 notices infringed the appellant's right to a fair trial and therefore were actions incompatible with his rights under article 6(1) and 6(3)(d) of the European Convention on Human Rights in terms of section 57(2) of the Scotland Act 1998, and section (1) of the Human Rights Act 1998. In the other minute, the appellant sought a ruling that the proposed leading of evidence relating to the statements of the late Mr Copeland would be oppressive. Lord Caplan refused the applications, and granted leave to appeal.

Before this court it was explained that the parties anticipated that there might be evidence pointing to the appellant's guilt from a number of sources. The Lord Advocate had lodged as productions statements given to investigating officers by three witnesses who might say that the appellant had made self incriminating comments to them. Two of the witnesses might speak to comments containing considerable detail. There was scientific evidence. There was evidence of bloodstaining on the appellant's shoes which had been linked to the victim. There were bloody footprints on the floor of the room where the victim was found which were said to match the soles of the shoes worn by the appellant. There was no relevant bloodstaining on the clothing of the late Mr Copeland. His shoes could not have made the footprints found. There might be evidence of the appellant disposing of clothing at his brother's house after the killing. There might be evidence of scratching on the appellant. The appellant had in general made no comment at interview or on judicial examination. On one occasion he denied killing the victim. There was one defence witness who might say that Mr Copeland admitted responsibility for the killing.

The court was asked to consider the argument on the assumption that there might be an incrimination of Mr Copeland. The situation then would be similar to that considered in *Docherty v. H.M.A.*. That case demonstrated the difficulty a trial judge could have in giving proper directions in such circumstances. *AGL and EDB v. H.M.A.* was a further illustration of the same difficulty. The preponderance of the evidence suggested that the perpetrator in this case had to be one or other of the appellant and Mr Copeland. It was not alleged that the two men had acted in concert though at one stage it had clearly been contemplated that they might become co-accused. In such an extreme case the introduction of an eyewitness account of the appellant committing the murder would of necessity be of such enormity and gravity that it would properly be described as decisive evidence. It would be of such a decisive nature in the circumstances that it was hard to imagine that it would not be taken as the main evidence pointing to the appellant's guilt. The statements by Mr Copeland were extremely detailed. They were more detailed than other possible sources of evidence. In the course of the police interview of Mr Copeland, the possibility of the appellant turning the tables on him and blaming him for the murder had been canvassed.

The evidence which the Crown intended to lead was of a character which the court would have been slow to allow as the law stood before the introduction of section 259. The reasoning in the authorities reflected an approach which was closely parallel to the Convention jurisprudence: Lauderdale Peerage Case; *Irving v. H.M.A.*. The court would not admit hearsay of a deceased witness where that person had had an interest or it was perceived that the person had had an interest in the subject matter of the case. The Convention jurisprudence was found in *Trivedi v. United Kingdom; Saidi v. France; Bricmont v. Belgium* and *Ferrantelli v. Italy.* The appellant would be so materially disadvantaged by the admission of the evidence that there would necessarily be a violation of his Convention rights. He would not be able to challenge the truth and accuracy of Mr Copeland's statements without abandoning his right of silence and giving evidence. There was a basis for adverse criticism of Mr Copeland's character. Exploration of that issue might expose the appellant to prejudice if he were obliged to give evidence and submit to cross examination. The argument in support of the section 72 minute was the same, leading to the conclusion that to introduce the evidence of Mr Copeland's statements would be oppressive.

As was observed by the Lord Justice General in *Montgomery v. H.M.A.*: 'The only right which article 6(1) protects is the right to a fair trial and so, in considering a case founded upon that article, the court is concerned only with whether the appellants will receive a fair trial . . . The appellants' rights under the Human Rights Convention exist . . . to ensure that any trial which the appellants face is fair. In this respect the protection afforded to accused persons under the Convention is similar to the protection afforded by the plea of oppression: *Hamilton v. Byrne*, 1997 S.C.C.R. at p.549 E–F; 1997 S.L.T. at p.1211 I–J'. Intimation of a notice or notices under section 259 of the 1995 Act anticipates a course of events which may happen at the subsequent trial. The prosecutor may apply to the trial judge to have evidence about the statements of the deceased witness admitted. On the other hand, in the proper exercise of his or her discretion, the prosecutor may elect to close the Crown case on the basis of the other evidence available to the court with the result that the contentious material is never tendered in evidence. If that were to happen in the present case, the issue whether the appellant had received a fair trial would be determined wholly without reference to the evidence anticipated in the section 259 notices. One of the present applications falls within section 72(1)(d) on the basis that the oppression issue is a matter which might be resolved with advantage before the trial diet. The devolution issue, on the other hand, has its focus in the proposition that if the prosecutor were to make an application at the trial diet for the contentious evidence to be admitted that would be an act of the Lord Advocate that necessarily, and at that point, infringed the appellant's Convention rights by depriving him of a fair trial. It was accepted that the mere service of the notices could not have that effect, notwithstanding the terms of the minutes, in respect that at that stage the proposition would have to be tested on the assumption that the prosecutor might not seek leave to introduce the evidence as matters developed at the trial. It was recognised that it was in extreme circumstances only that an accused person could contend in advance of trial that the introduction of evidence under section 259 would be so prejudicial to the prospects of a fair trial that the court could determine the issue in advance.

An irregularity in the admission of evidence according to the rules of national law may be of such materiality that it is sufficient in itself to amount to a miscarriage of justice and to undermine a conviction. One can envisage situations in which the court might determine in advance that evidence obtained irregularly should not be admitted at trial. Recoveries under a defective search warrant might come into that category. But, more generally, the question whether there are obstacles to a fair trial can be resolved in the normal course only in the light of the proceedings as a whole, and having regard to the whole evidence led. In *Ferrantelli*, at para. 48, the court said: "[The Court] recalls that the admissibility of evidence is primarily a matter for regulation by national law and, as a rule, it is for the national courts to assess the evidence before them. The Court's task is to ascertain whether the proceedings considered as a whole, including the way in which the evidence was taken, were fair". There is a similar observation in *Saidi* at p.264, para. 40.

In relation to section 259, the trial judge's function is prescribed. Where the judge is satisfied that the requirements of subs (1) are met, and the reason that the relevant evidence will not be given by the originator of the statement falls within subs (2), as it does where that person has since died, evidence of the statement is admissible. The admission of hearsay evidence of statements by persons who have died is justified on grounds of necessity: Scottish Law Commission Report no 149 (1995), "Hearsay Evidence in Criminal Proceedings" para. 4.47. The rules of national law regulate the matter. As a matter of domestic law there is no possible objection to the competency of the course proposed by the Crown. The trial judge must, of course, direct the jury as to the differences between hearsay evidence and other evidence that they have heard in court and on oath. Those directions will typically refer to the absence of oath or affirmation, and to the fact that the statement was not subject to cross examination. In the present case it may be that the evidence will disclose grounds for criticism of Mr Copeland which may bear on his credibility or reliability as a source of evidence. He may be represented to the jury as a person having a material interest in exculpating himself and in incriminating the appellant. The trial judge may have to give explicit directions that the hearsay evidence may be unreliable. These, however, are the commonly available means of ensuring that juries apply their minds to the relevant and material considerations which arise out of the evidence. The court has an obligation to ensure that a trial is fair irrespective of the accused person's Convention rights. In the ordinary course that obligation extends to hearing and ruling on objections to the admission of evidence, and to formulating and giving proper directions on the use which may be made of evidence in arriving at a verdict. The issues which arise in relation to the admission of hearsay evidence of statements of deceased persons are not dissimilar in kind from other issues of admissibility. There is similarly no fundamental objection in Convention jurisprudence to the fairness of proceedings in which use is made of hearsay evidence. *Trivedi*, a decision of the Commission, provides the clearest example of the general approach to this matter. The application was held inadmissible. The hearsay statement of a witness had been relied on at trial. The witness had become incapacitated and could not appear at the trial. It was held that the requirements of Article 6(1) and 6(3)(d) were satisfied by the procedures at trial which tested the evidence of the witness's condition, and which allowed for investigation into the statements and for comment on them by the defence and by the judge in summing up. In general, the procedural requirements of Scottish criminal law provide the same safeguards for the accused's position.

The decision of the court in *Bricmont* is not helpful in the present case. The court found that the Belgian proceedings before the Court of Appeal had relied on the 'accusations' or 'submissions' of the Prince of Belgium, the claimant: p.241, para. 84. The Prince's status as a party disqualified him from the benefit of certain provisions of the Code of Criminal Procedure which were available only to witnesses: p.224, para. 28(b). His 'accusations' or 'submissions', so far as material, were never the subject of confrontation, despite repeated requests that confrontation should be arranged. It is difficult to relate the procedures described to any equivalent in Scottish procedure. But it appears that the material relied on, as evidence, was irregularly obtained. None of the steps which might have given the Prince the status of a witness were taken. The Belgian Court of Appeal nevertheless relied on the material in arriving at its conclusion. So far as one can compare the situations, the treatment of the 'accusations' or 'submissions' as evidence would be an irregularity in Scots criminal procedure which might give rise to a miscarriage of justice whether or not there was corroboration.

The second part of the court's observation in *Ferrantelli* emphasises the need to consider the question of fairness of the trial in the light of the whole circumstances. The requirement for corroboration ensures that, however cogent, the statements of Mr Copeland could never be sufficient for a conviction. The narrative of the other possible sources of evidence against the appellant in the present case suggests that when the Crown case is completed there may be sufficient evidence to support a conviction without reference to the contentious statements, and that, if they are relied on, there may be ample corroboration for the statements if they are viewed as a primary source of criminative evidence against the appellant. In *Saidi* hearsay constituted the whole basis for the conviction: p.270, para. 44. The circumstances were quite different from the present case. The procedures adopted denied the applicant the opportunity of confronting witnesses who were alive and available. But so far as one can compare the cases it is clear that in the present case the hearsay which may be introduced could not have the criminative effect of the evidence admitted in *Saidi*. The trial judge would be bound to acquit the appellant if the only evidence against him derived from Mr Copeland. If at the close of the Crown case there were a case to answer it would inevitably be on the basis that some or all of the other sources of evidence pointing to guilt had come before the jury. The relative weight of the several possible sources is impossible to predict. One could form a view on that matter only in the light of the proceedings as a whole.

The sole issue at this stage is whether this court could make the declaratory finding sought, out of context of the evidence at the trial, to the effect that an application for the admission of the evidence of Mr Copeland's statements would necessarily be a breach of the appellant's Convention rights. There is no basis in authority, either domestic or Convention, on which one could reach that view. The relative weight of different sources of evidence would depend on views which could be formed only after the whole evidence had been led. The interaction of any issue which might arise from directions to meet the requirements of *Docherty* and *AGL* and the weight to be given to a source of evidence such as the statements of Mr Copeland would again depend on the view one formed retrospectively of the proceedings as a whole. It may be that the trial judge would require to give very particular directions on the need to use caution in considering the statements if indeed the preponderance of the evidence pointed to the perpetrator as necessarily being one or other of the appellant and Mr Copeland. But that cannot support the present appeal. Mr Copeland's interest in exculpating himself is similarly a matter which may require particular focus in directions. In that connection it is only to be observed that in *Irving* Lord Cameron did not adopt the argument on the effect of the *Lauderdale* case which was advanced before the court. The oppression argument must fail on the basis that it was simply a reformulation in domestic language of the Convention test.

Nothing in this opinion would preclude the appellant from raising the devolution issue afresh in the light of events at the trial, or otherwise instructing an appeal on grounds which related *inter alia* to the use, if any, made of Mr Copeland's statements at the trial. Each party will require to consider the approach to be adopted to the statements. The appellant may require to consider whether to give evidence and be subjected to cross examination in the light of his approach to Mr Copeland's statements. But his position in that respect will be no different from the position which would have obtained if Mr Copeland had survived and appeared at the trial."

NOTES

In *H.M.A. v. Nulty*, 2000 S.L.T. 528 Lord Abernethy rejected an argument that the Court retained a discretion to refuse to admit hearsay evidence even although all the requirements of section 259 have been met. *Nulty* was a case in which the Crown relied on hearsay evidence in the form of a tape-recording of evidence from the victim, V, who had become mentally unwell prior to the trial. His Lordship also refused a devolution minute lodged on the basis that the admission of hearsay evidence would be contrary to Article 6. He did so on the basis that there would be no unfairness *in the circumstances of the case*. He said:

"In my opinion the submissions of the advocate depute are to be preferred. I accept that the question of fairness in the context of Article 6(1) and 6(3)(d) of the Convention must be approached in an overall way (*Ferrantelli, Doorson*). There is no necessary unfairness to the accused in his not being able to cross examine V (*Ferrantelli*). The question of unfairness must depend on the particular circumstances of the case. I accept, of course, that being the complainer in charge 6, V's evidence is critical to that charge and is of major, even critical, importance also in charges 2 and 9. But in Scotland, however cogent the complainer's evidence is, there has to be corroboration. That is in my opinion one important safeguard against any unfairness in admitting this evidence. The fact that the corroboration here can only come by application of the *Moorov* doctrine is not in my opinion of any weight. The application of the *Moorov* doctrine is no more than the use of circumstantial evidence to provide the necessary corroboration. There is nothing inherently weaker in circumstantial evidence being used for that purpose. A second important safeguard is that the defence will be able to make use of the provisions of section 259(4). I think that the advocate depute was correct to point out that in drafting section 259(4) the draftsman was aware of the potential difficulties presented by admitting hearsay evidence and section 259(4) was an attempt to deal with some of them. Thirdly, I think it is possible to deal with any difficulties created by admitting the evidence by way of suitable directions from myself as trial judge as to how the jury should approach that evidence. In my view these considerations would be sufficient to justify my admitting the evidence, even if it was in the form of a transcript of what was said in the earlier trial. If the evidence is presented in the form of a tape recording in which the present jury can hear V say what she said, that is, as the solicitor advocate fairly recognised, an advantage. I fully recognise, of course, that with the information now available the solicitor advocate's cross examination in the earlier trial would have been different from what it was. In particular, it would not only have been directed in support of the accused's position that the events charged did not occur, but also at trying to show that V had transferred responsibility for what had allegedly happened between herself and her brother, E2, to the accused. To that extent the solicitor advocate has not had the chance to examine or cross examine V and the basis on which the earlier cross examination and the pre-trial precognition took place was on the present information a somewhat false basis. I am not persuaded, however, having regard to all the circumstances that to admit this evidence would amount to a breach of the accused's rights in terms of Article 6(1) and Article 6(3)(d) of the Convention. For these reasons I will refuse the solicitor advocate's motion and allow V's evidence in the earlier trial to be admitted as evidence in this trial."

All the reasons given by Lord Abernethy are general points about the Scottish criminal justice system, and are not peculiar to the particular case. It seems therefore that it will only be in exceptional circumstances, if at all, that hearsay evidence will be excluded before or during trial on the grounds of fairness under the Convention. Further support for that view is to be found in *H.M.A. v. Bain*, High Court of Justiciary (Lord Reed), May 14, 2001, unreported. In *Bain*, objection was taken during the trial to hearsay evidence in relation to which notice had been given by the Crown in advance of trial. It was held that objection during the trial was competent, in spite of the notice. The accused was allowed to raise as a devolution issue an argument based on Article 6 of the Convention. However, the argument was again rejected on the basis that (a) there is no absolute rule that an accused person has a right to question a witness and (b) that sufficient procedural safeguards exist within the Scottish system to avoid prejudice to the defence by the admission of such evidence.

Chapter 8

EVIDENCE IMPROPERLY OBTAINED

The manner in which evidence is obtained may have an important effect on its admissibility. This section looks first at the admissibility of real and documentary evidence where it is alleged to have been improperly obtained, and then at the admissibility of statements made by the accused. There are theoretical questions here as to the propriety of using the law of evidence as a vehicle for controlling the executive or the police. Should relevant evidence be excluded for this reason? In the English case of *Jones v. Owen* (1870) 34 J.P. 759, Mellor J. said that "It would be a dangerous obstacle to the administration of justice if we were to hold, because evidence was obtained by illegal means, it could not be used against a party charged with an offence". That approach was re-affirmed by the House of Lords in the case of *R. v. Sang* [1980] A.C. 402. In general, English law did not therefore regard evidence as inadmissible merely because of some impropriety in the way it was obtained. The Police and Criminal Evidence Act 1984, section 78 modified the English common law approach so that the court could exclude evidence where in all the circumstances of the case to admit the evidence would have an adverse effect on the fairness of the proceedings. Do you approve of this approach? What is the *evidential* relevance of the method by which evidence is obtained? If clear evidence exists that a person has committed a serious offence, is it unfair to the individual to use that evidence? If so, why? Both the English and Scottish systems adopt a somewhat uneasy compromise between questions of fairness to the accused, and fairness to the public interest in the administration of justice and suppression of crime. The Scottish Law Commission's Report, "Hearsay Evidence in Criminal Proceedings" Scot. Law Com. No. 149 (1995) para. 2.8 *et seq.* contains an illuminating discussion of the principles properly applicable.

1. Lawrie v. Muir
1950 J.C. 19

Two inspectors from the Milk Marketing Board searched the accused's premises in order to locate a number of stolen milk bottles, and found the bottles there. They purported to be acting under warrants issued by the Board and on that basis that they had permission from the accused to carry out the search. In fact, they had no authority to search under the warrants since the accused was not a distributor for the Board. Both the inspectors and the accused believed that the search was authorised. It was argued nevertheless that the evidence of the discovery of the stolen bottles was inadmissible because of the innocent misrepresentation of authority to search.

LORD JUSTICE-GENERAL (COOPER): "From the standpoint of principle it seems to me that the law must strive to reconcile two highly important interests which are liable to come into conflict—(a) the interest of the citizen to be protected from illegal or irregular invasions of his liberties by the authorities, and (b) the interest of the State to secure that evidence bearing upon the commission of crime and necessary to enable justice to be done shall not be withheld from Courts of law on any merely formal or technical ground. Neither of these objects can be insisted upon to the uttermost. The protection of the citizen is primarily protection for the innocent citizen against unwarranted, wrongful and perhaps high-handed interference, and the common sanction is an action of damages. The protection is not intended as a protection for the guilty citizen against the efforts of the public prosecutor to vindicate the law. On the other hand, the interest of the State cannot be magnified to the point of causing all the safeguards for the protection of the citizen to vanish, and of offering a positive inducement to the authorities to proceed by irregular methods. It is obvious that excessively rigid rules as to the exclusion of evidence bearing upon the commission of a crime might conceivably operate to the detriment and not the advantage of the accused, and might even lead to the conviction of the innocent; and extreme cases can easily be figured in which the exclusion of a vital piece of evidence from the knowledge of a jury because of some technical flaw in the conduct of the police would be an outrage upon common sense and a defiance of elementary justice. For these reasons, and in view of the expressions of judicial opinion to which I have referred, I find it quite impossible to affirm the appellant's extreme proposition. On the contrary, I adopt as a first approximation to the true rule the statement of Lord Justice-Clerk Aitchison that 'an irregularity in the obtaining of evidence does not necessarily make that evidence inadmissible'.

It remains to consider the implications of the word 'necessarily' which I have italicised. By using this word and by proceeding to the sentence which follows, Lord Aitchison seems to me to have indicated that there was, in his view, no absolute rule and that the question was one of circumstances. I respectfully agree. It would greatly facilitate the task of Judges were it possible to imprison the principle within the framework of a simple and unqualified maxim, but I do not think that it is feasible to do so. I attach weight to the fact that the word used by Lord Chancellor Chelmsford and by Horridge, J., when referring to the disregarding of an irregularity in the obtaining of evidence, was 'excuse'. Irregularities require to be excused, and infringements of the formalities of the law in relation to these matters are not lightly to be condoned. Whether any given irregularity ought to be excused depends upon the nature of the irregularity and the circumstances under which it was committed. In particular, the case may bring into play the discretionary principle of fairness to the accused which has been developed so fully in our law in relation to the admission in evidence of confessions or admissions by a person suspected or charged with crime. That principle would obviously require consideration in any case in which the departure from the strict procedure had been adopted deliberately with a view to securing the admission of evidence obtained by an unfair trick. Again, there are many statutory offences in relation to which Parliament has prescribed in detail in the interests of fairness a special procedure to be followed in obtaining evidence; and in such cases (of which the Sale of Food and Drugs Acts provide one example) it is very easy to see why a departure from the strict rules has often been held to be fatal to the prosecution's case. On the other hand, to take an extreme instance figured in argument, it would usually be wrong to exclude some highly incriminating production in a murder trial merely because it was found by a police officer in the course of a search authorised for a different purpose or before a proper warrant had been obtained.

There the general question must be left. To apply the law to the present relatively trivial case is not easy, for the circumstances combine to make it singularly unsuitable as a test case. Indeed I cannot but think that it is a pity that the Procurator-Fiscal insisted in the prosecution, after the point of difficulty had arisen. I am unable to accept the suggestion that a distinction should be drawn between the statutory offence (the *malum prohibitum*) and the common law crime (the *malum in se*), for the interests of the State are as much involved in offences against penal statutes as in offences against the common law, and the former category has greatly expanded in recent times. In England, the former category is the larger of the two. Next, it was argued that in this case the whole of the evidence on which the conviction was obtained was tainted; but in practically every case in which this type of question is worth raising, the admission or exclusion of some piece of evidence must be vital to the conviction, otherwise the point would not be taken. It is specially to be noted that the two inspectors who, in this instance, exceeded their authority were not police officers enjoying a large residuum of common law discretionary powers, but the employees of a limited company acting in association with the Milk Marketing Board, whose only powers are derived from contracts between the Board and certain milk producers and distributors, of whom the appellant is not one. Though the matter is narrow, I am inclined to regard this last point as sufficient to tilt the balance against the prosecution, upon the view that persons in the special position of these inspectors ought to know the precise limits of their authority and should be held to exceed these limits at their peril. It is found that the inspectors acted in good faith, but it is incontrovertible that they obtained the assent of the appellant to the search of her shop by means of a positive misrepresentation made to her. I would therefore answer question 1 in the negative, upon which view question 2 also falls to be answered in the negative".

The Court answered both questions of law in the negative and quashed the conviction.

NOTES

The solution adopted to the problem of irregularly obtained evidence is one of typically Scottish pragmatism. Irregularities in the obtaining of evidence may be fatal to its admissibility, but then again, they may not. It all depends upon the circumstances, and upon the court's assessment of the question of "fairness". The latter question is one which arises time and again in this area of the law. Indeed it might be argued that the whole of the law can be reduced to this one, rather elliptical, question. If that is the case, then it seems that the Scots approach very closely mirrors the (occasionally Delphic) jurisprudence of the European Court of Human Rights. In *Brown v. Stott*, 2000 S.L.T. 59, below, Lord Hope of Craighead said that:

> "the jurisprudence of the European Court tells us that the questions that should be addressed when issues are raised about an alleged incompatibility with a right under Article 6 of the Convention [in broad terms the right to a fair trial] are the following:
>   (1) is the right which is in question an absolute right, or is it a right which is open to modification or restriction because it is not absolute? (2) if it not absolute, does the modification or restriction which is contended for have a legitimate aim in the public interest? (3) if so, is there a reasonable relationship of proportionality between the means employed and the aim sought to be realised? The answer to the question whether the right is or is not absolute is to be found by examining the terms of the article in the light of the judgments of the Court. The question whether a legitimate aim is being pursued enables account to be taken of the public interest in the rule of law. The principle of proportionality directs attention to the question whether a fair balance has been struck between the general interest of the community in the realisation of that aim and the protection of the fundamental rights of the individual."

What are the merits and demerits of this approach? What does the "public interest in the rule of law" demand? For example, look at the case of *Ireland v. Russell*, 1995 S.L.T. 1348. The Misuse of Drugs Act 1971, s.23(2) gives the police power to search individuals on reasonable suspicion of their possession of controlled drugs. In *Ireland v. Russell*, the police had received information that the accused was in possession of cannabis. It was not until some two months after this information was received that they were able to stop and search him. The accused in fact proved to be in possession of drugs, and the question arose as to whether the police were entitled in the circumstances to conduct the search on the basis of "reasonable suspicion". It was held that they were not, given the lapse of time between the receipt of the information and the search. Do you regard this as a sensible or a fair decision? Was it a predictable result on the basis of the dicta in *Lawrie v. Muir*? What if the drug found had been heroin and not cannabis? And should the latter question make any difference to the outcome? Compare *Ireland* with the case of *Singh v. H.M.A.*, 2001 S.L.T. 812, an extract from which is reproduced in the notes to *McAvoy v. Jessop* below.

2. Weir v. Jessop (No. 2)
1991 S.C.C.R. 636

The accused was charged with possession of cannabis with intent to supply it. The principal evidence against him came from a police officer who, in plain clothes, went to the accused's house and asked to be supplied with the drug, saying, falsely, that the accused's brother Charlie had sent him. The accused duly supplied the drug to the police officer who paid for it with a marked £10 note. The police then returned to the accused's house and searched it under a valid warrant, finding a quantity of cannabis resin large enough to suggest an intention to supply, rather than mere personal use. At his trial evidence of the transaction was objected to on the ground that it had been obtained unfairly because of the police officer's deception as to his identity.

LORD JUSTICE-CLERK (ROSS): "The advocate-depute recognised that this was a very important case because police officers investigating possible contravention of the provisions of the Misuse of Drugs Act 1971 frequently used the method employed by D.C. Dinnen in this case. The advocate-depute submitted that a number of cases under the Licensing Acts supported the view that the police were entitled to use these methods. On the other hand, he also acknowledged that cases relating to the admissibility of statements by accused persons or suspects appear to recognise a different principle. The advocate-depute, however, maintained that it was possible to reconcile the decisions given in these two types of cases and he urged the court to follow the Licensing Act cases and to hold that there was no unfairness in what the police had done in this case.

The starting-point is *Southern Bowling Club Ltd v. Ross*. That was a case in which the pursuers sought declarator and interdict upon the ground that it was illegal for the police to enter club premises in disguise for the purpose of detecting whether illegal trafficking in excisable liquor was being carried on. The Lord Justice-Clerk indicated that decree could not be pronounced because it might prevent the police from doing their duty in many cases in which they would have a proper duty to perform. Lord Young said [at p.415]:

'The only way that occurs to me of detecting offences is for the police to employ detectives, and where a club is suspected of shebeening the only mode of discovering the truth of the matter is for detectives to go to the club and ask to be supplied with spirits. There is no other mode that occurs to me of detecting the offence, and if these detectives (not being members of the club, and there being no reason on the part of those supplying them with liquor to suppose that they are members of the club) are supplied with liquor, then the offence is detected, and the result of stopping it by a prosecution is attained.'

In the reclaiming motion the court adhered to the interlocutor of the Lord Ordinary and the Lord Ordinary is reported as saying [at p.413]:

'There is, so far as I know, no statute on the subject. I am not aware of any judicial dictum as to the limits of the devices to which the detective police force may resort in their pursuit of crime.'

That case was followed in *Marsh v. Johnston*. That case concerned evidence given by two police officers who had gone to licensed premises, had seen two customers being supplied with excisable liquor after closing time and had then ordered excisable liquor for themselves from the licence holder. The licence holder was convicted of selling liquor outside permitted hours. He appealed and his appeal was refused. In the course of delivering his opinion the Lord Justice-General said:

'It may be that in ordering a drink outside permitted hours and in tasting it the police were guilty of a technical offence under the Act, but this was a sheer technicality and was not done to procure the commission of an offence but to detect and confirm that offences were being committed. In the circumstances it does not appear to me that there was anything in the conduct of the police which was in the least improper, still less does it make their evidence incompetent.'

Subsequently in his opinion the Lord Justice-General referred to *Southern Bowling Club Ltd v. Ross* and observed that where it is suspected that a licence holder is selling liquor outside the permitted hours, it would be difficult to prove such offences unless police evidence of this kind was used. If such evidence were to be regarded as incompetent, there would be a wholesale flouting of the provisions of the Licensing Acts. He added:

'It would have been a very different matter if any unfairness to the complainer had been established. If, for instance, the police had pressed him to commit the offence or had tricked him into committing an offence which he would not otherwise have committed the position would have been quite different.'

In the circumstances the Lord Justice-General held that the evidence in question was not in any way unfair. The Lord Justice-General also contrasted that case with the earlier English case of *Brannan v. Peek*, in which the policeman concerned had deliberately misled the accused as to who he was in order to induce the accused to accept a better bet laid by the policeman. The conduct of the policeman in that case was held to be grossly unfair and amounted to a trick upon the accused in order to induce him to commit an offence.

Cook v. Skinner and *MacDonald v. Skinner* were also cases where police officers in civilian dress purchased liquor in licensed premises where the conditions of the hotel certificate did not permit the sale. It was held that the evidence obtained by the police officers had been obtained fairly and that nothing done by them could reasonably be regarded as amounting to a trick upon the appellants or as inciting the appellants to commit an offence. In delivering the opinion of the court the Lord Justice-General said (p.13):

> 'It is clear, however, from the decided cases to which we were referred, that where the Court has held that evidence has been obtained unfairly there has been established, on the part of the police officers concerned, conduct which clearly amounted to a trick upon the accused, and, in particular, a trick which involved positive deception and pressure, encouragement or inducement to commit an offence which, but for that pressure, encouragement or inducement, would never have been committed at all.'

In *Cook v. Skinner* the Lord Justice-General described the part played by the police officers in the whole transaction as purely passive since the appellant had taken the initiative in the matter of supplying liquor to the police constables at the time. That element was not present in *MacDonald v. Skinner* but the court still held that there had been no deception on the part of the police and no improper pressure or inducement to lead the appellant to authorise the commission of the offence.

H.M. Advocate v. Harper was a case dealing with the supply of controlled drugs contrary to section 4(3)(a) of the Misuse of Drugs Act 1971. The sheriff followed the Licensing Act cases to which I have referred and in effect applied them to a case concerning the supply of controlled drugs.

In the course of his submissions Mr Ferguson sought to derive support from *H.M.A. v. Campbell* [1964 J.C. 80]. As already observed, the statement in that case was not made directly to the police officer but was made to a newspaper reporter. Moreover, it was the accused who had made the approach to the reporter, and it is difficult to understand why the court held that the statement was not a voluntary statement. In Renton and Brown, "Criminal Procedure" (5th ed.) [para. 18–28], the learned editor states that it may be that nowadays the statement would have been admitted, having been obtained without any inducement or pressure or the actual making of a false statement to the accused. I agree with him. In my opinion, there is no reason to regard the statement made by the accused in that case as other than a voluntary and spontaneous statement. Moreover, it is difficult to reconcile the decision of the Lord Justice-Clerk in that case with *Hopes and Lavery v. H.M.A.* [1960 J.C. 104]. We were also referred to *H.M.A. v. Graham* [1991 S.L.T. 416]. On the basis of the limited report that is available, it is difficult to reach any firm conclusion on the soundness of that decision, but the decision may well be justified upon the view that the statement made was not a truly voluntary and spontaneous statement, but was one which the accused was induced to make by the person with whom he was conversing at the time.

So far as making a statement or giving evidence is concerned, it is a well-established principle of our law that no man is bound to incriminate himself. Thus a witness is entitled to decline to answer a question if the answer might lead to his conviction of a crime and he has to be warned that he need not answer such a question. As regards statements made to the police by an accused person or a suspect, there is a large body of law dealing with the admissibility of such statements. It is now well recognised that the test is whether what had taken place was fair or not. In *Brown v. H.M.A.* [1966 S.L.T. 105] at p.107 the Lord Justice-General said:

> 'Questioning by the police, therefore, which is tainted with any element of bullying or pressure or third degree methods designed to secure admissions of guilt by suspected persons prevents the replies being proved in evidence before the jury at the ultimate trial. For, according to our standards of fair play, this would be unjust to the person accused. On the other hand the police have a right, and indeed a duty, to make investigations and to question people in order to find out whether and by whom a crime has been

committed, and for the purpose of conducting these investigations to interrogate persons who may be involved. Where exactly the line is to be drawn between legitimate questioning and proceedings which are tainted with undue pressure on or bullying of a person ultimately accused of the crime, may sometimes be a difficult matter. It is not possible to lay down *ab ante* the precise circumstances in which answers given to the police prior to a charge being made are admissible in evidence at the ultimate trial or where they are inadmissible. This is so much a question of the particular circumstances of each case and those circumstances vary infinitely from one another. But the test in all of them is the simple and intelligible test which has worked well in practice—has what has taken place been fair or not?'

In my opinion that principle of fairness also applies when judging the admissibility of evidence of the kind objected to in the present case. It was submitted to us that at the material time the appellant must have been a suspect and that, accordingly, the police would not have been entitled to address questions to him where the answers sought were likely to be incriminating. In my opinion, although the same test of fairness falls to be applied in each of these two situations, statements made to the police in response to questioning may be in a special situation. One reason for that may be that if the police were entitled to interrogate and cross-examine an accused and to adduce evidence of what he had said, the prosecution would in effect be able to make the accused a compellable witness, which he is not (*Chalmers v. H.M.A.* [1954 J.C. 66], per Lord Justice-General at p.79).

Where as here a police officer poses as a drugs buyer in order to establish whether the accused is dealing in controlled drugs, there is no question of the Crown being able in effect to make the accused a compellable witness. There is no question of the evidence of the police being used as a substitute for the evidence of the accused. On the contrary, the evidence given by the police officers was merely evidence of investigations which they carried out in order to ascertain whether there was dealing in controlled drugs at this house.

Admittedly D.C. Dinnen deceived the accused as to his identity. He gave every appearance of being a member of the public and not a police officer. He also deceived the appellant in another respect. In order to establish his bona fides, he professed to have been sent to the house by the appellant's brother. None the less, apart from representing that he would like to obtain cannabis, he applied no pressure, encouragement or inducement to incite the appellant to commit an offence which he would otherwise not have committed. It might be different if the appellant had appeared reluctant to carry out the transaction and the police officer had pleaded with him to do so. Again it might have been different if the appellant had indicated that he was not in the habit of carrying out such transactions or that he had never sold drugs before in this way. But there was no such suggestion in the evidence and the only reasonable inference from the evidence is that the appellant was prepared to supply controlled drugs to callers, always provided that the callers could offer some colourable explanation for having come to his door for that purpose. There is nothing at all in the findings to suggest that supplying drugs was something which the appellant would never have done but for the approach made to him by the police officer. Accordingly, applying the test of fairness as it was described in *Cook v. Skinner*, I am of the opinion that the conduct of D.C. Dinnen did not amount to an unfair trick upon the accused. Moreover, even though there was an element of deception in the two respects already described, I am satisfied on the findings that there was no pressure, encouragement or inducement to commit an offence which the appellant would never otherwise have been committing at all. I regard the present case as one like *Marsh v. Johnston* where what the police were doing was not so much procuring the commission of an offence as seeking to detect and confirm that offences were being committed at this address at the material time. I am accordingly satisfied that the sheriff was well founded in repelling the objection taken to the evidence.

I did not understand Mr Ferguson to repeat the submission made to the sheriff to the effect that the police officers were obliged to execute the search warrant instead of taking steps to ascertain whether anyone was in the house and to establish whether there were illegal drugs there. Having regard to the fact that the police officers concluded that it would be difficult to carry out observations on the house, I am satisfied that they were entitled to take the steps which they did take. For the foregoing reasons I am also satisfied that there was sufficient evidence to justify the conviction of the appellant on charge (1).

So far as charge (2) is concerned, I am satisfied also that there was sufficient evidence to justify conviction. Apart from the evidence of D.S. Thorn to the effect that the amount of the controlled drug and the way in which it was packaged suggested that these items were a supply intended for sale, the evidence of the transaction between the appellant and D.C. Dinnen shows that the appellant was engaged in selling controlled drugs that day.

In these circumstances I would move your Lordships to answer the three questions in the case in the affirmative and to refuse the appeal."

LORD MORISON: "If a policeman suspects that a person is dealing in drugs, I see nothing inherently unfair in his asking that person to supply him with a quantity of that substance in order to confirm his suspicion. As was observed by Lord Young in *Southern Bowling Club v. Ross*, at p.415, the request is a method of discovering the truth and of obtaining the result of stopping commission of an offence by prosecution. The procedure necessarily involves an element of deception in the concealment by the policeman of his true identity. As the Lord Justice-Clerk expressed it in the same case, the persons making the request must be 'disguised so that they might not be known as emissaries of the police'. According to the circumstances of the case, this deception may also necessarily involve that the policeman provides some verbal indication that he is the kind of person that he is pretending to be. Such an indication was given by D.C. Dinnen in the present case when, on being questioned as to who had sent him, he gave a name which apparently satisfied the appellant that he was a bona fide customer. By doing so he was not in my opinion doing anything which went beyond the necessary pretence that he was a person to whom drugs could be supplied without risk of prosecution.

But although deception as to the policeman's true identity was involved, that deception cannot reasonably be regarded as having induced the commission of the crime of supply, if the supply was one which would in any event have taken place as a result of a request by a genuine customer. The criminality of the appellant's act lay in the fact that he supplied drugs to another, not that he did so to someone who turned out to be a policeman. That essential feature of the crime was not one which resulted from any undue pressure or persuasion on the part of the policeman. It was a purely voluntary act on the part of the appellant. The appellant was not tricked into doing something which he would not ordinarily do. I see no reason in principle to exclude evidence of the act merely because the appellant thought that he was dealing with an authentic customer. His criminal behaviour was induced not by the deception, but by the fact that he was a person willing to supply drugs on request to anybody in whom he had confidence.

This view is directly supported by the authority of this court in the case of *MacDonald v. Skinner*, which followed the similar case of *Marsh v. Johnston*. In the case of *MacDonald* policemen posing as ordinary customers asked for and obtained alcoholic drinks after hours, with the permission of the licensee. For the licensee it was submitted that the offence had been committed at the instigation of the police. It was held that there was no substance in the submission that evidence of the sale had been unfairly obtained, there having been no deception on the part of the police and no improper pressure or inducement to lead the licensee to authorise the commission of the offence. I can see no ground for distinguishing that case from the present, or for reconsidering whether it was correctly decided.

On behalf of the appellant it was submitted that the evidence of self-incriminating conduct by the accused in the present case was analogous to evidence of self-incriminating statements made by a person under suspicion, which would be held as unfairly obtained and inadmissible in the absence of a caution given to the accused before he made the statement. Even if the comparison were a valid one, I should prefer to rely on the direct authority to which I have referred rather than on inference from cases dealing with the admissibility of extrajudicial statements, a field in which the law has developed separately from that concerned with the question whether a crime has been induced by unfair conduct.

However, in spite of the advocate-depute's apparent acceptance of the validity of the comparison, I do not regard it as apt to provide assistance in the circumstances of the present case. Cases in which evidence of a self-incriminating statement has been held inadmissible have proceeded on the basis that the statement could not be affirmed as truly a voluntary one: *Tonge v. H.M.A.* This may be either because the circumstances or pressures were such as to induce the making of the statement, or because the accused's decision to make it was taken in the absence of a caution which would have made it clear to him that he had a right to remain silent and that, if he did not do so, evidence of what he said might be used against him. It was the absence of such a caution which was held in the case cited on behalf of the appellant, *H.M.A. v. Campbell*, to render the statement inadmissible as having been improperly obtained. It is unfair to elicit a statement from a suspect if he has not been cautioned that he is not required to make it.

But it is well established that it is not unfair for a policeman to question a suspect if he has observed safeguards which are necessary for securing that the statement is truly voluntary. Although a suspect must be informed of his right to remain silent because he may be in ignorance of that right and the possible consequences of his failure to exercise it, there is no obligation imposed on the questioner to advise the suspect not to incriminate himself, and it would hinder the ascertainment of the truth if such an obligation existed. The considerations which apply to the questioning of a suspect therefore have no application to the circumstances of the present case. For the reasons which I have mentioned, the appellant's self-incriminating conduct was voluntary and not induced by any pressure on the part of the police. Although it is necessary to inform a suspect of his right to remain silent because he may be in ignorance of that right, it is not, in my opinion, necessary to inform him that he is entitled to refrain from committing a criminal offence nor to advise him that if he commits one he may be prosecuted for it. There is no unfairness on the part of the police in their failing to point out the obvious, and cases dealing with the absence of a caution in the terms in which it is usually given are not therefore in point. The analogy proceeds upon a misunderstanding of the nature of the caution which fairness requires should be given before a statement is elicited.

The prevention of crime would clearly be hindered if the police were prohibited from adopting the procedure which they adopted in the present case. Both as a matter of principle and on the basis of authority I consider it clear that they are entitled to adopt it. I would answer the questions as proposed by your Lordship in the chair."

LORD CAPLAN: "On October 19, 1990 the appellant was found guilty at Glasgow Sheriff Court after trial of two offences under the Misuse of Drugs Act 1971. In particular he was found guilty of the first charge in the complaint where the offence was that of supplying cannabis resin to Detective Constable James Dinnen, in contravention of section 4(3) of the said Act, and of charge (2) where the offence was that of possessing cannabis resin with intent to supply it, in contravention of sections 5(3) and 25 of the Act. In terms of the sheriff's findings in fact the police had suspected that controlled drugs were on the premises occupied by the appellant at 52 Smeaton Street, Glasgow, and had obtained a warrant to search these premises. However, for a number of reasons, including in particular the reason that it was difficult to carry out observations on the house without being seen, the police had decided to resort to what can be described as an undercover operation. While a colleague posted himself out of sight but in a position to overhear what happened, Detective Constable Dinnen had gone to the door of the premises and rattled the letter box. When a female answered he had asked, 'Is Charlie in? I was told I would get some hash.' When the female asked who had sent him, he replied that he had been over at Charlie's brother's house and that he had sent him. Then the appellant came to the door and asked Detective Constable Dinnen what he was wanting. The constable replied, 'A half half quarter.' The appellant went back into his house and returned a few seconds later with a piece of resinous substance. The detective constable then gave the appellant a marked £10 note. Fifteen minutes or so later the police returned to the premises and exercised their rights under the search warrant to search the house. They found seven pieces of cannabis resin in the possession of the appellant. In respect of the first charge the conviction depended on the evidence of Detective Constable Dinnen and Detective Sergeant Thorn, who had overheard what took place when the former was supplied by the appellant with cannabis. With regard to the second charge Detective Sergeant Thorn had given evidence that the character and weight of the pieces of cannabis discovered in the house were such as to suggest dealing rather than a supply for personal use. However, the sheriff acknowledged that in finding the appellant guilty of the second charge, she had taken into account the transaction involving Detective Constable Dinnen as being admissible. This evidence, it was contended for the appellant, had been unfairly obtained. Any distinction between the cases which establish that a suspect should not be allowed by police to incriminate himself without a caution being administered and the line of authority which appeared to allow the police to test a supplier's willingness to supply in licensing cases was invalid and could not be justified in principle. *H.M.A. v. Harper* had been wrongly decided. We were referred to *H.M.A. v. Campbell; Southern Bowling Club Ltd v. Ross; Graham v. H.M.A.* If the chapter of evidence involving Detective Constable Dinnen was excluded then not only would the first charge fall but there was insufficient evidence remaining to justify a conviction on the second charge.

In addition to discussing the cases cited by the appellant, the Crown cited *Marsh v. Johnston; Brannan v. Peek* and *Cook v. Skinner*. The learned home-depute went some way toward acknowledging that it may be difficult to reconcile licensing law cases such as Cook with the line of authority governing the taking by the police of voluntary statements from a suspect. Indeed he suggested that a larger court may be required to arrive at a satisfactory resolution of the law.

For my own part, I find no particular difficulty in reconciling the licensing investigation cases with the cases setting out rules for voluntary statements by a suspect to the police. The cases which govern voluntary statements have evolved within the context of a particular historical background. Originally the interrogation of a suspect was carried out by the sheriff and not by the police. When the police began to assume a more positive role in the examination of suspects, concern arose to protect an accused against abuse by the police. In particular, there was concern in case a suspect might be induced to confess by unfair treatment or pressure being applied to him by police interrogators. Thus a body of distinct rules and principles has evolved over the years but these relate and are intended to relate only to the situation where the commission of a crime has been reported or noted and the police collect evidence directly from a suspect, particularly by way of an incriminatory statement. The fundamental objective is always to ensure that no unfair methods are used to induce a suspected person to incriminate himself and one particular rule that is clearly acknowledged is that if a person is specifically suspected by the police of having committed a crime then he should be cautioned that he need not say anything which might incriminate him. The position of the police is, however, quite different where the primary objective is not to seek evidence against a person suspected of a particular crime but rather to carry out an investigative function to ascertain whether crime is in fact being committed. In respect of the investigative function of the police it would be quite unrealistic to suppose that a certain amount of covert investigative work requiring a degree of what could be described as deception is not sometimes necessary. This must be particularly so under modern conditions where the police are often faced with requiring to investigate crimes, such as drug dealing, carried out by organised professional criminals who themselves, without hesitation, resort to more than a fair degree of deception. The public have a considerable interest to secure the detection of crime and if a reasonable and necessary degree of undercover operation is necessary to achieve that end then there is justification for tolerating it, provided that the process is not in any respect unfair to the supposed perpetrator of the crime. That, however, is not to say that deception is a desirable technique for the police to employ except in circumstances where it is necessary. However, deception should not in any event be used indiscriminately and certainly not in any way that might unfairly induce a person to commit a crime which he might not otherwise have been prepared to commit. Thus the circumstances under which police carrying out investigations may employ undercover techniques in order to secure information later to be used in evidence against a perpetrator of the crime are also governed by rules of law and the most important of these is that an accused should not be jeopardised by investigative methods which on a balanced view could be described as unfair. Just what investigative procedures may be regarded as fair or unfair will vary with the circumstances but I will confine myself here to a situation where the police require to investigate whether a particular substance is being supplied illegally. In such a situation cases such as *Marsh* and *Cook* can offer valid guidance. It seems to me that when there is no other effective way of ascertaining whether or not a person is engaged in supplying a substance illegally, the police are justified in testing the situation by representing themselves as interested purchasers. What is critical is that the investigator should not in any way seek to tempt, persuade or otherwise put pressure on a supplier to engage in a transaction that he was not otherwise perfectly prepared to transact. The investigation should be designed to discover whether or not, as a matter of course, the suspected person is engaging in a particular category of illegal transaction and certainly not whether it is possible to induce him so to transact. This may explain the reservations which Lord Justice-General Clyde expressed in *Marsh* about the conduct of the police in *Brannan*. Not only are the observations of the Lord Justice-General obiter but the report in the latter case suggests that the investigating policemen persuaded the suspect to enter into a betting transaction which he was hesitant to engage in. If it was necessary for a policeman seeking to discover by direct action if a substance was being supplied illegally to declare his identity and to administer a caution then such enquiries would be a waste of time.

Looking to the circumstances of the present case there was evidence accepted by the sheriff that it was difficult to carry out surveillance operations on the suspected house without being seen. The police therefore decided that Detective Constable Dinnen should go to the house and pretend to have been sent by the appellant's brother. When a female came to the door Detective Constable Dinnen said, 'Is Charlie in? I was told I would get some hash.' This observation was in no sense an attempt to induce another to supply the drug unless Charlie (the appellant) was perfectly prepared to supply the drug to a stranger on request. When the female asked Detective Constable Dinnen who had sent him he replied that he had been over at Charlie's brother's and that he had sent him. That was certainly an untruth but it was clearly designed only to establish Detective Constable Dinnen's identity as a bona fide purchaser of drugs. It was designed to assist the detective constable in concealing his true identity and that was necessary if the investigation was to have had any hope of success. I do not see how the attempt to vouch identity by reference to Charlie's brother could have induced the appellant to supply an illegal drug if he was not already engaged in the supply of such drugs. Indeed within seconds he was able to produce a suitable package of the drug from his house. Thus what Detective Constable Dinnen did was effectively to establish that the appellant was engaged in the supply of drugs and he did this without any kind of unfair tactic such as might have distorted the situation or cast doubt on the result of his enquiry. If, instead of sending Detective Constable Dinnen to the door of the house, the police had executed their warrant, they would certainly have found drugs in the house but may well not have been able to ascertain whether such drugs were for private use or for supply. Indeed the appellant's counsel makes a point of what he claims is the inadequacy of the results of the search in respect of the supply of drugs. The sheriff in Harper had to deal with a situation similar to the present case and in my opinion the case was properly decided by him. Thus I consider that the first two questions in the stated case fall to be answered in the affirmative. Since this means that the evidence of the supply to Detective Constable Dinnen was also available to support Detective Sergeant Thorn's evidence that the drugs discovered within the house were intended for supply, it is not necessary to consider what would be the position were this not so. Clearly with the evidence of Detective Constable Dinnen there is a sufficiency of evidence to establish the second charge and the third question in the stated case also falls to be answered in the affirmative."

NOTES

See also *Macdonald v. H.M.A.*, 1993 G.W.D. 18–1139. *Weir v. Jessop (No. 2)* is an important case, holding that while there is no substantive defence of entrapment in Scots law, evidence of the commission of a crime may be excluded if it can be shown that pressure was applied or inducements offered to the accused. This approach is very similar to that adopted by the English courts. In the recent case of *R. v. Loosely* [2001] UKHL 53 (October 25, 2001), it was held that the English courts will grant a stay of the proceedings (*i.e.* bring them to an end) where the conduct of the police is such as bring the administration of justice into disrepute. In examining that question, the court should consider the nature of the offence—is it one which tends to be committed secretly, such as drug-dealing; the reason for the police conduct—is it part of a campaign directed at drug-dealers generally, for example, or is it simply a vendetta carried out against a particular person whom the police distrust or dislike; the nature and extent of the police participation in the offence—to what extent is there pressure on the accused to commit the offence; and whether the accused's criminal record has any relevance to the question whether he is likely to be committing further offences now. The court in *Loosely* held that the approach of English law is substantially the same as, and therefore compliant with, that of the European Court of Human Rights in the case of *Texeira de Castro v. Portugal*, (1998) 28 E.H.R.R. 101. It accordingly seems likely that the Scottish approach to the question, if properly applied, would also comply with the Convention. On the question of entrapment generally, see *inter alia* A. Choo, "A Defence of Entrapment" (1990) 53 M.L.R. 453; Harris, "Entrapment" (1994) 18 Crim. L.J. 197; Fisse, "Entrapment as a Defence" (1988) 12 Crim. L.J. 367; Fraser, "Undercover law enforcement in Scots law" 1994 S.L.T. (News) 113. See also the English cases of *R. v. Christou* [1992] 3 W.L.R. 228, and *R. v. Smurthwaite and Gill* [1994] 1 All E.R. 898 considered by Pipe, "Entrapment Evidence" (1994) 138 Solicitors Journal 522.

Weir v. Jessop (No. 2) does make clear, however, in contrast to *Lawrie v. Muir*, above, that a certain degree of deception on the part of investigating officers, even deliberate deception, is acceptable. It is submitted, however, that the scope for such deception is limited. *Weir v. Jessop (No 2)* is not directly analogous to *Lawrie v. Muir*. In the latter case, specific and express false representations were made as to the extent of specific statutory powers of search after the completion of any crime. In the former case, any misrepresentations were largely implied, and simply induced the accused to believe that he was selling drugs to an ordinary member of the public, something which, on any view of the law, he should not have been doing.

Finally, how does the situation in *Weir v. Jessop (No 2)* differ from the cases reproduced below dealing with incriminating statements? The Lord Justice-Clerk in particular seems to have had difficulty in finding any distinction—see his comments on *H.M.A. v. Campbell* in particular. In the light of the cases below, what criticisms might be made of his view of *Campbell*? See the analyses of Lords Morison and Caplan on this point.

3. Hay v. H.M.A.
1968 J.C. 40; 1968 S.L.T. 334

A warrant was sought to take an impression of a murder suspect's teeth, in order to match that impression with a bite mark found on a murder victim's body. The warrant was granted, and the accused was subsequently convicted. He appealed on the ground that the warrant was incompetent and should not have been granted.

LORD JUSTICE-GENERAL (CLYDE): "As regards the first and main issue in the appeal— namely the legality of the warrant—it has been observed in more than one of the cases . . . that two conflicting considerations arise. On the one hand there is the need from the point of view of the public interest for promptitude and facility in the identification of accused persons and the discovery on their persons or on their premises of indicia either of guilt or innocence. On the other hand the liberty of the subject must be protected against any undue or unnecessary invasion of it.

In an endeavour as fairly as possible to hold the balance between these two considerations three general principles have been recognised and established by the court. In the first place, once an accused has been apprehended and therefore deprived of his liberty, the police have the right to search and examine him. In the second place, before the police have reached a stage in their investigations when they feel warranted in apprehending him, they have in general no right by the common law of Scotland to search or examine him or his premises without his consent. There may be circumstances, such as urgency or risk of evidence being lost, which would justify an immediate search or examination, but in the general case they cannot take this step at their own hand. But, in the third place, even before the apprehension of the accused they may be entitled to carry out a search of his premises or an examination of his person without his consent if they apply to a magistrate for a warrant for this purpose. Although the accused is not present nor legally represented at the hearing where the magistrate grants the warrant to examine or to search, the interposition of an independent judicial officer affords the basis for a fair reconciliation of the interests of the public in the suppression of crime and of the individual, who is entitled not to have the liberty of his person or his premises unduly jeopardised. A warrant of this limited kind will, however, only be granted in special circumstances. The hearing before the magistrate is by no means a formality, and he must be satisfied that the circumstances justify the taking of this unusual course, and that the warrant asked for is not too wide or oppressive."

NOTES

This passage sets out the three main situations in which the question of the legality of recovery of evidence may arise. The police may recover evidence in pursuit of a legal right or purported legal right—which may be granted by a specific warrant as in Hay, or by a general statutory power; they may recover it with the consent or supposed consent of the accused or some other individual; or they may recover it without any specific legal right to do so in situations of urgency or emergency. If in any of these situations the evidence is recovered in an illegal or irregular way, that irregularity may be excused by the court if the circumstances justify such an exception.

4.   Milford v. H.M.A.
1973 S.L.T. 12

TEMPORARY SHERIFF MACPHAIL: "This petition has been presented by the procurator-fiscal on the instructions of the Crown Office. It sets forth that a named woman has complained that on July 29, 1972 she was assaulted, ravished, and robbed in a lane in Aberdeen, and on August 1, 1972 identified Eric Milford at an identity parade as the person responsible. Trousers belonging to *Milford* have been taken into the possession of the police, and examination of these shows four small spots of blood on the inside of the fly which belonged to blood group A, the same group as a sample of blood which has been taken from the complainer. The petition goes on that it thus appears to the petitioner that it is necessary in the interest of justice that a sample of blood be taken from *Milford*, who is now in the prison of Aberdeen to ascertain his blood group and compare that with the blood spots found on his trousers. I am therefore asked to grant warrant to a named medical man to proceed to the prison and take from *Milford* such a sample of blood as the medical man considers reasonably necessary for the furtherance of the comparison of the blood groups.

This petition, unlike the petition in *Hay v. H.M.A.*, 1968 J.C. 40; 1968 S.L.T. 334, which was presented before arrest, has been intimated to the accused, and both the procurator-fiscal depute and the accused's solicitor have appeared before me in chambers today and made submissions. When they originally appeared, at 10.30 a.m., the accused's solicitor, who had not had an opportunity to study the petition, indicated that he desired to take counsel's opinion. It then seemed to me, however, that the effect of an adjournment could be to hold up a serious criminal investigation for several days, that counsel were not normally instructed at this stage, and that the application, which might be urgent, could be competently dealt with by the solicitor at short notice having regard to the guidance afforded by *Hay* (supra), to which I referred him. It was agreed that I should hear argument in chambers at 12.30 p.m.

In considering an application of this kind it is my duty to reach a fair reconciliation of the interests of the public in the suppression of crime and the interests of the individual, who is entitled not to have the liberty of his person unduly jeopardised. A warrant of this limited kind will only be granted in special circumstances. The hearing before the sheriff is by no means a formality, and he must be satisfied that the circumstances justify the taking of this unusual course, and that the warrant asked for is not too wide or oppressive: for the sheriff is the safeguard against the grant of too general a warrant (see *Hay* at p.46). This petition is presented at a later stage than the petition in *Hay*, but I think that I should keep these considerations in view. In addition to *Hay*, the procurator-fiscal depute has made reference to Hume on Crimes, vol. ii, p.77; *Miln v. Cullen*, 1967 J.C. 21; 1967 S.L.T. 35; and *Brown v. H.M.A.*, 1966 S.L.T. 105.

I have been given the following agreed information about the factual background of the application. The accused has been in custody since August 1, 1972, the date of the identification parade. He has been committed for trial and it is proposed that he should ultimately appear in the High Court, but no indictment has yet been served. He has been asked to give a blood sample, but has refused to do so.

The procurator-fiscal depute argued that the complainer had been the victim of a grave crime. He stated that he could not say that investigation of the crime was being hampered, but corroborative evidence was required. He accepted that there was not in this case the element of urgency which had been present in Hay, because in this case the evidence sought could not be altered or eliminated. He pointed out that the invasion of the person for the purpose of taking a blood sample had been sanctioned by the Road Safety Act 1967.

The accused's solicitor submitted that the accused was being called upon to give evidence against himself, that the taking of blood samples under the road safety legislation was sanctioned for a limited purpose only, and that the medical process desiderated in this case involved the insertion of an instrument into the body and was not limited to observation and the taking of impressions. He argued that the taking of a blood sample without consent was an unprecedented invasion of personal liberty, and, if warranted, could lead to further such investigations of a more repugnant kind.

It was agreed that in this case there was no question of the accused being conveyed, irrespective of his wishes, from one place to another (*cf. Hay* p.42).

Bearing in mind the agreed facts and the submissions, I return to the line of approach laid down in *Hay* and endeavour to reconcile the two conflicting considerations to which I have referred. It seems to me that I have to consider, on the one hand, that a very grave crime is alleged to have been committed, and that it is in the interests of the public that the perpetrator of such a crime should be brought to justice. On the other hand, the infringement of the liberty of the person which is being considered is the comparatively innocuous process of the taking of a sample of blood. Any humiliation of the person inspected which may be involved in that process seems to me to be outweighed in this case by the public interest in the ascertainment of the truth and the dispensation of justice in relation to an allegedly very serious crime. As to the argument that the accused is being called upon to give evidence against himself, it has to be noted, I think, that much may already be legitimately done by the police without warrant or consent in searching a legally arrested person for evidence as to his connection with the crime and his identity with the criminal (see *Adair v. McGarry*, 1933 J.C. 72; 1933 S.L.T. 483 and *Forrester v. H.M.A.* 1952 J.C. 28; 1952 S.L.T. 188). It seems to me that there is no difference in kind but only a very slight difference, if any, in degree, between taking the finger prints of such a person and taking a sample of blood. The argument that successful further applications for invasions of personal liberty may follow the success of this application seems to me to be an unrealistic plea to extremities, having regard to the duty of the sheriff to safeguard the liberty of the subject when considering each application.

The taking of a blood sample accordingly seems to me, in the exceptionally grave circumstances of this case, to be a reasonable and necessary step in the interests of justice, and I am inclined to the view that the arguments that an invasion of bodily integrity is involved and that the accused is being obliged to supply evidence against himself are not strong enough to succeed in this case, having regard to the gravity of the crime under investigation and the necessity for the ascertainment of the truth. I am satisfied that the circumstances justify me in granting the warrant, which I consider neither too wide nor too oppressive. I shall accordingly grant the warrant."

NOTES

Milford provides a good example of the sort of balancing exercise referred to in *Lawrie v. Muir*, above, and illustrates the sort of special circumstances envisaged in *Hay v. H.M.A.*, above, in which warrants may be granted to confer particular powers on the investigator. In *Hay v. H.M.A.*, above, the warrant was applied for before arrest, presumably because it was thought that there was insufficient evidence to justify arrest. Such a situation is unlikely to arise in modern practice, partly because of the introduction in 1980 of powers of detention (now in the Criminal Procedure (Scotland) Act 1995, ss.13–15), and partly because of the decision in *Johnston v. H.M.A.*, 1993 S.C.C.R. 693, which holds that arrest may be justified even though there is insufficient evidence to charge a suspect. It remains the case, however, that even following arrest or detention, a warrant would be required to conduct the sort of invasive procedure sought to be carried out in *Milford*. The police have "ordinary" power only to take non-invasive, non-intimate body samples, including fingerprints and swabs for the purposes of DNA testing or "fingerprinting"—these powers are now contained in the Criminal Procedure (Scotland) Act 1995, s.18. The power to take finger-prints also existed at common law, but again, only once an accused person had been arrested—see *Adair v. McGarry*, 1933 J.C. 72, and *McGovern v. H.M.A.*, 1950 J.C. 33, below. Thus, arrest or detention is generally a necessary prerequisite of the police's power to take fingerprints and other bodily samples from a suspect. However, in *Namyslak v. H.M.A.*, 1994 S.C.C.R. 140, a failure to arrest the accused before fingerprinting him in relation to a charge of theft was not fatal to the admissibility of the prints since the accused had already been fingerprinted in relation to a charge of attempting to pervert the course of justice. In these circumstances the court excused the irregularity in obtaining the prints and allowed the evidence. See also *H.M.A. v. Shepherd*, 1997 S.L.T. 891, and *H.M.A. v. Kelly*, High Court of Justiciary (Lord Mackay), unreported, February 20, 2001, below.

5. McGovern v. H.M.A.
1950 J.C. 33

LORD JUSTICE-GENERAL (COOPER): "The applicant was convicted and sentenced to eighteen months' imprisonment on an indictment which charged him that on a date in August 1949 he broke into the office at Westrigg Colliery, Westcraigs, Harthill, occupied by the National Coal Board, and did by means of explosives force open a lockfast safe. The charge was that he stole a sum of money from that safe, but the jury confined their verdict to one of forcing the safe with intent to steal. The evidence on which that conviction was obtained consisted of a long chain of circumstantial evidence of which an important and perhaps essential, link was certain evidence to the effect that there were found beneath the finger nails of the applicant nitro-glycerine and ammonium nitrate, indicating that his fingers had been in recent contact with a 'non-permitted' explosive such as had been used for blowing the safe.

The single question argued to us in this appeal was whether the evidence as regards the contents of the finger nails was competently admitted, and, if not, whether the conviction can stand.

As was pointed out by Lord Morrison in the case of *Adair v. McGarry* . . . —the case that dealt with the taking of finger prints from a person already apprehended—it is clear that no police officer has any right to search any person whom he does not apprehend; and for present purposes I find it difficult to draw any distinction between the taking of finger prints and the taking of scrapings from finger nails. Technically, the taking of those scrapings without the consent of the applicant was an assault. Some point was made to the effect that it is nowhere stated in evidence that force was used against the applicant, or that his consent was withheld; but my reading of the evidence is that his consent was never asked—at least in such circumstances as to satisfy the requirements of the law—because no consent would avail in the situation here presented unless it was given after a fair intimation that the consent could be withheld.

It follows that the evidence derivable from the analysis of the contents of the finger nails was improperly obtained, and I think it right to say that no attempt whatever was made by the Crown to maintain the contrary. The only matter to which the Crown's argument was directed was whether, assuming the irregularity and incompetence of the method by which this piece of evidence was obtained, the conviction must nevertheless stand upon the principle dealt with the other day by a Full Bench of this Court, when it was held that an irregularity in the manner of obtaining evidence is not *necessarily* fatal to its admissibility.

As I said at the outset, this conviction was obtained on a chain of circumstantial evidence. It seems to me obvious that the evidence as to the contents of the finger nails must have been most material as a link in that chain, and that its admission must to a substantial extent have prejudiced the appellant in the minds of the jury. Where evidence has been wrongly admitted and is of such a nature as to prejudice a fair trial of the applicant, it cannot easily be said that there has been no miscarriage of justice. To look at the matter from the other standpoint discussed in the Full Bench case of *Lawrie*, irregularities of this kind always require to be 'excused' or condoned, if they can be excused or condoned, whether by the existence of urgency, the relative triviality of the irregularity, or other circumstances. This is not a case where I feel disposed to 'excuse' the conduct of the police. The proper procedure for search of the appellant's house by obtaining a search warrant was duly followed out, and it would have been very simple for the police to have adopted the appropriate procedure in relation to a search of his person. Why they did not do so, we do not yet know. Exactly the same information was available to them when they scraped the appellant's finger nails as when they charged and apprehended him shortly afterwards; and, if the charge and apprehension were justified, these should have preceded and not followed the examination of his person.

In the whole circumstances, although with some regret, for the matter was never properly raised in the Court below, I feel that there is no option but to quash this conviction because, unless the principles under which police investigations are carried out are adhered to with reasonable strictness, the anchor of the entire system for the protection of the public will very soon begin to drag. I move that the appeal be allowed."

NOTES

The consent of the person searched may render legal a search for which there is otherwise no proper warrant. *McGovern* takes a fairly liberal view of the issue of consent, appearing to lay down a rule which approaches a requirement for informed consent in the criminal law. The subsequent cases of *Davidson v. Brown*, 1990 J.C. 324; 1990 S.C.C.R. 304, and *Devlin v. Normand*, 1992 S.C.C.R. 875, however, cast doubt on this approach. In *Devlin*, the accused had hidden a packet of cannabis resin in her mouth. Without cautioning her, or informing her under what authority he was doing so (such as the Misuse of Drugs Act 1971 or the Prisons (Scotland) Act 1989), a prison officer required her to open her mouth and lift her tongue, which she did without objection. Evidence of this incident and of the finding of the drug was objected to on the ground that it constituted an illegal search. This argument was rejected on appeal, the High Court taking the view that the procedure followed did not amount to a search:

> "In our opinion when someone is requested in that way to behave as the appellant was requested to do, that does not constitute a search. We think there is force in the Advocate-depute's submission that the situation is analogous to the situation which would have existed if the individual had been asked to open a handbag or to show what was in his or her pockets. Plainly if such an individual declines to comply with the request and any force is used to ascertain what is in the bag or in the pocket, then one could say that a search had taken place, but if the individual to whom the request has been addressed voluntarily complies with the request and opens the bag and takes out of it what has been in it or removes from his or her pocket what is in the pocket, then there is no question of any search having taken place. In the same way in the present case when the appellant was requested to open her mouth and told to lift her tongue, and did so, and when she was asked to hand over what was in her mouth and she did so, we are not persuaded that any search of her person took place on the part of the prison officer. It follows that the whole basis of Miss Scott's challenge of this conviction is not well founded."

Any possibility of distinguishing *Devlin* from *McGovern* on the basis that the former case involved no search seems to have been extinguished by the case of *Brown v. Glen*, 1998 S.L.T. 115. In that case the High Court followed *Devlin* and *Davidson v. Brown*, distinguishing *McGovern* on the basis that in that case the accused was already a suspect for a specific crime in relation to whom particular care had to be taken:

> "In our view there is no doubt that in *McGovern* the applicant was a suspect for a specific crime and accordingly had already been cautioned and a search warrant obtained for search of his house. It was 'in the situation here presented', to use the words of the Lord Justice General, that it was said that intimation should have been made to the applicant that he could refuse consent to have scrapings taken from his fingernails. If an accused is in a position that requires that he should be cautioned as to his right to decline to say anything in response to questions put to him by the police, then equally it is logical that he should be cautioned as to his right to decline to do anything in response to a request made of him by the police. The *obiter* observations of the Lord Justice General in *McGovern* are entirely consistent with that approach. (It is perhaps unlikely that a similar situation would now arise since the introduction of what is now section 14 of the Criminal Procedure (Scotland) Act 1995, and in particular the right of the police to search a detained suspect without his consent.) Where, however, the police are making general inquiries and the person with whom they are dealing has not reached the stage where he could be described as a suspect, except in the most general and nebulous sense, the police are not obliged to caution the person as to his answers to questions and there appears to us to be no logical reason why they should be obliged to issue any caution to accompany a request for a search to be carried out when it must be perfectly obvious that the answer to that request may be either yes or no."

H.M.A. v. Kelly, High Court of Justiciary (Lord Mackay), unreported, February 20, 2001, provides a less obvious example of evidence obtained by consent. In that case a person gave a sample of blood while in prison on the understanding that the results of the test would be confidential. It was held that the results of the test were admissible in evidence at his trial on charges of recklessly endangering the life of his partner by infecting her with the HIV virus.

6. Leckie v. Miln
1982 S.L.T. 177

An accused person was charged on summary complaint with four charges of theft, but was convicted of two charges only. The evidence disclosed that a search of the accused's home had been carried out and that certain items allegedly stolen were found therein. The defence had objected to the admission of evidence of what was found during the search on the ground that the articles were not referred to in the original petition warrant authorising the search, nor had consent to an unlimited search been given by the householder at the material time. The sheriff repelled the objection and convicted the accused, who appealed by stated case. The principal question for the High Court was whether the police were entitled to carry out the search. On October 20, 1981 the High Court answered this question in the negative and quashed the convictions. The following excerpt from the opinion of the court sets out the facts, arguments and grounds of decision:

OPINION OF THE COURT: "Both these charges tell the story of sneak thefts and in particular charge 1 libelled the theft of a wallet from certain office premises and proceeds to narrate that the wallet contained a number of articles including money and some business cards which turned out to be in the name of a Mr Eisner. So far as charge 2 is concerned that charge libelled the theft of a wallet, containing various items including a library card and a receipt, from a room at Harris Academy Annex in Dundee. Let it be said at once that the Crown case in support of conviction on these charges depended essentially upon evidence given by two police officers of finding, during a search of the appellant's dwelling-house which he occupied with a lady, of certain articles stolen during the thefts described in charges 1 and 2. The articles were in the first place certain business cards in the name of Mr Eisner and in the second place a library card in the name of the owner of the wallet taken from Harris Academy together with the receipt which had been in that wallet. The findings-in-fact which describe the search are findings 8, 9 and 10. According to finding 8 two police officers learned from their inspector that the appellant had been arrested on petition at Perth on a charge of sneak theft. That was all they were told. They were then instructed by the inspector to go to the appellant's house and search it. This they proceeded to do. But finding 8 tells us that the officers in question never saw the petition upon which the appellant had been arrested; that they were completely unaware of the nature of any charge in that petition except to the extent that it was a charge of theft of the sneak theft variety; that they did not know at all what articles had been stolen during that theft and did not, of course, in the circumstances, have the petition in their possession, containing the warrant to search, when they went to the appellant's house. On arrival at the house they met a lady called Miss Dailly (known as Mrs Leckie) and they informed her that they were police officers and that the appellant had been arrested by the police at Perth on a petition warrant. Having said that they informed Miss Dailly that they wished to search the house. No objection to the proposed search was made. Finding 10 them describes the search which took place and the discovery, in the course of that search, of the business cards to which we have referred in the top drawer of a chest of drawers in the only bedroom of the house, a top drawer which contained the clothing of Miss Dailly, and the discovery of the library ticket and the receipt which we have already mentioned inside a jacket hanging in the wardrobe of that bedroom. For the appellant the submission was that the search which was carried out in all the circumstances disclosed in findings 8, 9 and 10 was quite unlawful in respect that it was neither authorised by the warrant to search in the petition on which the appellant had been arrested in Perth nor was it authorised by any implied consent given by Miss Dailly. If that submission is sound, as counsel for the appellant urged us to accept, then it followed, according to counsel, that the evidence given by the police officers about their findings was inadmissible. This was not a case in which officers carrying out an active search within the scope of a lawful warrant came across articles unrelated to the particular crime with which they were concerned. In such a case the finding of other articles indicating guilt of other crimes may be perfectly admissible in evidence. The fundamental proposition here was that neither upon the warrant nor upon any implied consent was the active unlimited search carried out by the officers justified in law. The Crown position was simply this. There existed, no doubt, authority for a search of the appellant's premises and that authority was the warrant granted upon the petition on which the appellant had appeared in Perth. It is the case that the officers admittedly did not carry out an active search within the limitations of that warrant to search for they were wholly ignorant of the contents of the petition and the scope of the warrant to search granted upon its presentation. But given the authority for a lawful search of the premises the search which was carried out was carried out by the officers in the manner in which they carried it out with the full consent given by Miss Dailly by plain implication. The question in the case therefore comes to be whether Miss Dailly did give consent for the unlimited search carried out by the officers, all as described in findings 8, 9 and 10. We are of opinion that by no stretch of the imagination can it be said that the consent given by Miss Dailly was consent of an active unlimited search regardless of the limitations in the warrant which admittedly existed. Finding 9 tells us that before Miss Dailly was informed that the officers wished to search the premises they told Miss Dailly that they were police officers and that the appellant had been arrested by the police at Perth on a petition warrant. It follows from that that any consent given by Miss Dailly must be assumed to have been given upon the footing that the officers intended to carry out a search within the authority contained in the warrant to which they referred, and that authority was, it is perfectly plain, an authority of a limited character. The search was nothing of the kind for, as we have already pointed out, the officers had no knowledge of the contents of the petition and what they did was to carry out a random search of the appellant's house in the hope of finding something which might conceivably have been the proceeds of a sneak theft anywhere. In these circumstances we are satisfied that the evidence of the finding of labels 2 and 4 should not have been admitted and if that is right then it follows that the conviction cannot stand for the evidence *aliunde* was insufficient to warrant the conviction of the appellant. The relevant questions in the case are three. The first question in the case we answer of consent in the affirmative in respect that no submission was made upon it. Question 2 goes to the entitlement of the officers to carry out the search which they did and to that question , which is perhaps not perfectly expressed to focus the argument, we give a negative answer. Having given a negative answer to question 2 it is inevitable that the answer to question 3 must also be in the negative. The conviction will accordingly be quashed."

NOTES

This is, for a number of reasons, a strange case. Wilson Finnie, "Police Powers of Search in the Light of *Leckie v. Miln*", 1982 S.L.T. (News) 289, finds no fewer than six grounds on which the evidence in question could have been admitted. Not the least strange aspect of the decision is the view taken of Miss Dailly's consent, which, it was said, was consent limited to a search within the terms of the warrant. As Finnie points out, this confuses two separate grounds upon which a search may be justified—that there was a lawful warrant for the search, or failing a warrant, that the householder consented to the search. The court did not resort to the idea of "informed consent" invoked in *McGovern*, which would, as Finnie suggests, have been a principled approach to the problem. Instead, the court took the view that the extent of Miss Dailly's consent to the search depended upon the police officers' subjective knowledge of the contents of the warrant. But is it realistic to talk of degrees of consent, particularly where the degree of consent is dependent on a matter likely to be wholly outwith the contemplation of the householder? Surely there is either consent to a search or there is not? Objectively, the search carried out by the police would have been the same regardless of their state of knowledge about the warrant. Nevertheless, Scots law in this area does appear to attach much importance to the motive, knowledge and intention of the searcher. In *H.M.A. v. Turnbull*, 1951 J.C. 96, a warrant was obtained to search an accountant's business premises for evidence of the making of fraudulent tax returns on behalf of a client. Police and Inland Revenue inspectors removed large numbers of documents some of which pertained to the client in question, but many of which related to other clients. Each file was clearly marked with the name of the client to which it pertained. Some months later a warrant was granted which covered the further documents, although this was never used, since all the documents necessary to the case against the accused had already been recovered. The accused was later charged on an indictment which related to four of the other clients as well as the original one. An objection to the admissibility of the additional documents was sustained. Lord Guthrie said that:

> "In the present case there were, firstly, no circumstances of urgency. Secondly, the retention and use over a period of six months of the documents bearing to relate to other matters than that mentioned in the petition show that the actions complained of were deliberate. The police officers did not accidentally stumble upon evidence of a plainly incriminating character in the course of a search for a different purpose. If the documents are incriminating, their incriminating character is only exposed by careful consideration of their contents. Thirdly, if information was in the hands of the criminal authorities implicating the accused in other crimes, these could have been mentioned in the petition containing the warrant under which the search was authorised. If they had no such information, the examination of private papers in the hope of finding incriminating material was interference with the rights of the citizen. Therefore to hold that evidence so obtained was admissible would, as I have said, tend to nullify the protection afforded to a citizen by the requirement of a magistrate's warrant, and would offer a positive inducement to the authorities to proceed by irregular methods. Fourthly, when I consider the matter in the light of the principle of fairness to the accused, it appears to me that the evidence so irregularly and deliberately obtained is intended to be the basis of a comparison between the figures actually submitted to the inspector of taxes and the information in the possession of the accused. If such important evidence upon a number of charges is tainted by the method by which it was deliberately secured, I am of the opinion that a fair trial upon these charges is rendered impossible."

Lord Guthrie's explicit reference to the question whether the admission of the evidence could result in a fair trial is significant in the context of the European Convention on Human Rights, given the view expressed in cases such as *R. v. A.,* [2001] UKHL 25, and *McKenna v. H.M.A.*, 2000 S.L.T. 508 that in general an objection to the admission of evidence based on the Convention rights will be unlikely to succeed in advance of trial, since at that stage it is impossible to say whether the proceedings viewed as a whole have resulted in unfairness to the accused.

7. H.M.A. v. Hepper
1958 J.C. 39

Police acting in connection with another matter searched the accused's house. They did so with his permission. In the course of the search, they found and removed an attaché case which was unconnected with the matter then under investigation. The case was found to contain the name and address of another person and the accused was charged with the theft of the case. Objection was taken to the admission of the evidence since the accused's permission to search did not relate to a theft charge but to the other matters under investigation.

LORD GUTHRIE: "On November 19, 1957 police officers called at the residence of the accused on business not connected with the present charge. The accused was at home and consented to the police searching his house. In the course of his examination in the witness-box, the detective superintendent who called at the accused's house was asked whether he had taken possession of anything, and objection was taken to the line of evidence. Counsel for the panel stated that the consent to a search was restricted to the business upon which the police had called at the accused's residence, and that, if the police in the course of that search discovered and removed an article which it was proposed to prove in evidence as relating to the present charge, such evidence should be excluded on the ground that it had been improperly obtained. Reference was made to *H.M.A. v. Turnbull* (1951 J.C. 96, . . .) and *Jackson v. Stevenson* (2 Adam 255, 24 R. (J) 38). In such cases, as the Lord Justice-Clerk, Lord Thomson, has repeatedly pointed out in recent years, the problem is always to reconcile the interest of society in the detection of crime with the requirement of fairness to an accused person. In the present case I am of opinion that the evidence is admissible. The police, in the course of their duty, when searching the accused's house with his consent in connection with another matter, came upon the article which they removed. In *Turnbull* at p.103, I distinguished that case, in which I excluded evidence as to documents taken possession of by police officers searching the accused's premises under a search warrant which clearly did not cover these documents, from a case in which police officers accidentally stumbled upon evidence of a plainly incriminating character in the course of a search for a different purpose. That distinction was based upon earlier authorities to which I was referred in *Turnbull's* case. It may be that the article which the police officers stumbled upon in their search of the accused's house was not an article of a plainly incriminating character, but it was at least an article of a very suspicious character, since it was an attaché case which contained within it the name and address of another person. In the circumstances, I do not think that the police officers acted in any way improperly in taking away that article in order to make further inquiries about it. If they had not done so, it might have disappeared. It appears to me that in the circumstances it was their duty, being officers charged with the protection of the public, to have acted as they did. But even if it cannot be put so highly, and if it be thought that their action was irregular, I am still of opinion that the evidence, even if irregularly obtained, is admissible in view of the interest of society in the detection of crime. I do not think that this is a case in which the evidence ought to be excluded because of a breach of the principle of fairness to the accused. I therefore hold that the evidence is admissible."

NOTES

The "paradoxical" consequences of cases like *Hepper* and *Leckie v. Miln* are well illustrated by the case of *Drummond v. H.M.A.*, 1992 S.C.C.R. 290. In that case, two police officers conducted a search of the accused's house under a warrant allowing them to search for goods stolen from a furniture store in Edinburgh. In the course of the search they found, hidden in a wardrobe, items of clothing stolen from premises in Penicuik and the accused was subsequently charged with the theft of that clothing.

One of the officers said that he had opened the wardrobe suspecting that it might contain the stolen clothing. His evidence was ruled to be inadmissible since the warrant did not cover those items and he had deliberately set out to look for them. The other officer said that he had been looking for smaller items stolen from the Edinburgh theft, and had stumbled upon the clothing by accident. His evidence was admitted.

The importance of the knowledge and intention of the officers carrying out a search is further emphasised by the contrast between two cases involving the search of motor cars.

In *Baxter v. Scott*, 1992 S.C.C.R. 342, the accused was arrested in connection with a motoring offence and the police took possession of his car. They opened the boot of the car and found a number of stolen items in it. This evidence was admitted on the basis that no search had taken place at all. The police were said to be entitled to check the contents of the car, since they were responsible for both car and contents while it remained in their possession.

In *Graham v. Orr*, 1995 S.C.C.R. 30, on the other hand, the police became suspicious of the accused when he was detained on another motoring charge and an officer conducted a search of his car. Evidence of the controlled drugs which they found in the car was ruled inadmissible because there had been no authority for the search. This case implies that cars may count as premises and that accordingly that there is no automatic right to search them when an accused person is arrested or detained, even in relation to a motoring offence. Any search must be justified either by a warrant or statutory power, or by reference to the sort of "security check" which took place in *Baxter v. Scott*. Do these cases lay down a sensible or practical rule? Would it be an improvement to hold that provided a search is conducted in pursuance of a legal warrant, any plainly incriminating material found in the course of that search should be admitted, whether the evidence relates to the warrant or not, and regardless of the searchers' state of mind? Compare the case of *Burke v. Wilson*, 1988 S.C.C.R. 361, below.

8.   Burke v. Wilson
1988 S.C.C.R. 361

A warrant was obtained by the police under the section 17(1) of the Video Recordings Act 1984 to search certain premises for evidence of the possession of unclassified video recordings, an offence under section 10 of that Act. In the course of their search, the police found a number of videos which did not bear the usual evidence of the issue of a classification certificate and which had an amateurish appearance. They took possession of these videos, which proved to contain obscene material, and the accused was later charged with an offence under section 51(2) of the Civic Government (Scotland) Act 1982. It was argued that the videos had been irregularly obtained since the warrant had related to unclassified videos under the 1984 Act and not to obscene videos under the 1982 Act.

LORD DUNPARK: "The sole issue in this case is whether a number of video tapes, which were by joint minute admitted to contain obscene material, were admissible productions in a trial of the appellants for possessing such tapes with a view to their eventual sale or distribution, contrary to section 51(2) of the Civic Government (Scotland) Act 1982. These tapes were found in a shop owned jointly by the appellants, and both appellants were convicted of the charge.

The policemen who found these obscene tapes in the shop on March 20, 1986 were in possession of a search warrant granted by the sheriff on that date in terms of the crave of a petition by the procurator fiscal in the following terms:

'That from credible information which the petitioner has received, it appears that video works as defined by the Video Recordings Act 1984 and for which no classification certificates in terms of section 7 of the said Act have been issued, are to be found in the premises known as A/B Video/Belville Off-Sales, 74 Belville Street, Greenock, for the purpose of supply, in contravention of section 10 of said Act.

Therefore the petitioner craves the court to take the evidence of the foregoing on oath from Detective Sergeant Arthur Miller of the Strathclyde Police, X Division, Greenock, and to grant warrant to said Detective Sergeant Arthur Miller and other officers of Strathclyde Police to enter and search said premises within one month from the date of issue of the warrant.'

Section 10 of the Video Recordings Act 1984 creates the offence of possessing a video recording containing a video work in respect of which no classification certificate has been issued for the purpose of supply, subject to certain exemptions which need not concern us. Section 1(2) is in the following terms:

'Video work means any series of visual images (with or without sound)—
(a) produced electronically by the use of information contained on any disc or magnetic tape, and
(b) shown as a moving picture.'

Section 4 provides for the determination of 'whether or not video works are suitable for classification certificates to be issued in respect of them, having special regard to the likelihood of video works in respect of which such certificates have been issued being viewed in the home'. Section 7 refers to different types of classification certificates. The Video Recordings (Labelling) Regulations 1985 (S.I. No. 911), which was made in pursuance of section 8 of the Act, states the symbols appropriate for the different types of classification certificates and paragraph 4 of the Regulations requires the appropriate symbol to be shown on the face of every disc, on every magnetic tape which is not kept in a spool, on the face of every spool on which a magnetic tape was kept and on the spine of every case or cover in which a video recording is kept, unless one of the dimensions of the spine is less that two centimetres, and paragraph 7 narrates the manner in which the various symbols are to be shown.

On March 20, 1986 four policemen searched the shop under this warrant. The relevant findings in fact are as follows: [His Lordship narrated findings in fact 7 to 16 as set out above.]

At the trial counsel for the appellants objected timeously to *inter alia* the production of these tapes upon the ground that they were unlawfully taken by the police. The submission was that the warrant covered the recovery only of tapes without classification certificates, contrary to section 10 of the Video Recordings Act. This was repeated in support of a submission of no case to answer under section 345A of the Criminal Procedure (Scotland) Act 1975. The sheriff repelled the objection and found that there was a case to answer.

For the appellants Mr Bell maintained that the objection and submission were sound on the ground that a search warrant granted for the recovery of tapes without classification certificates as required by the Video Recordings Act did not cover the seizure of tapes forming the basis of a charge in terms of section 51(2) of the Civic Government (Scotland) Act 1982. He did not suggest that these tapes carried classification certificates, nor could they, as they admittedly contained obscene material, but Mr Bell contended that, as the terms of the search warrant did not cover the seizure of material contrary to section 51(2), these obscene tapes were not lawfully recovered under the warrant and that evidence about their recovery and production in support of the charge under the 1982 Act were inadmissible.

The only case upon which he founded was *Leckie v. Miln*. In that case the appellant was arrested on petition on a charge of theft of a wallet and a purse from a dentist's surgery, and the sheriff granted the usual warrant to search for articles connected with that charge. The police officers, who were instructed to search the appellant's house, were simply told that the appellant had been arrested on petition on a charge of sneak theft. They were not informed of the articles referred to in the charge. It is not even clear from the report if they took with them the warrant to search the house. In any event, they had no idea what were the articles referred to in the charge. On arrival at the appellant's house police officers informed Miss D, who occupied the house with the appellant, that they had a search warrant. Miss D allowed them to search the house. In the course of their search they found articles which formed the basis of subsequent charges of theft from an office, a school and another place. The sheriff held these other articles to be admissible in evidence in support of charges relating to the theft of them and convicted the appellant of theft of articles from the office and the school. On appeal the court quashed these convictions, holding that the seizure of these articles was not authorised by the petition warrant and that it was not authorised by any implied consent on the part of Miss D, since any consent given by her must be assumed to have been given upon the footing that the officers intended to carry out a search within the authority contained in the warrant to which they referred. As the Lord Justice-General pointed out at p.265, the warrant authorised a search of a limited character, whereas the officers carried out 'a random search of the appellant's house in the hope of finding something which might conceivably have been the proceeds of a sneak theft anywhere'.

In the present case we are not concerned with consent. The only question is whether this warrant authorised recovery of these obscene tapes.

The advocate-depute, in support of the conviction, founded upon *H.M.A. v. Hepper*; but that was a consent case in which the police officers do not appear to have had a search warrant. They were searching for evidence in the course of their investigation of the disappearance of bottles of whisky and, in the course of a search with the consent of the accused, they took possession of an attaché case which contained within it the name and address of another person. The appellant was subsequently tried on charges of theft of 36 bottles of whisky and the attaché case. Lord Guthrie held that the attaché case was an article of a very suspicious nature and that the police had not acted improperly in taking it away 'in order to make further inquiries about it. If they had not done so, it might have disappeared'. At the end of his opinion on p.40 Lord Guthrie added:

'It appears to me that in the circumstances it was their duty, being officers charged with the protection of the public, to have acted as they did. But even if it cannot be put so highly, and if it be thought that their action was irregular, I am still of opinion that the evidence, even if irregularly obtained, is admissible in view of the interest of society in the detection of crime. I do not think that this is a case in which the evidence ought to be excluded because of a breach of the principle of fairness to the accused.'

I agree with Lord Guthrie's ruling in *Hepper*. In *H.M.A. v. Turnbull*, Lord Guthrie held, again in the course of the trial, that a warrant to search an accountant's premises for the purpose of recovering documents tending to show that he had made fraudulent income tax returns on behalf of a named client did not authorise police officers to take away a quantity of business files which related to other clients and which later formed the bases of additional charges. I endorse that decision but, in my opinion, every case concerning the legality or otherwise of the recovery of items under a search warrant must depend upon the facts of the particular case.

Now, in this case, the warrant authorised the search for video works for which no classification certificates had been issued. These obscene tapes could have no classification certificates. The sheriff found that some were unlabelled and others were labelled in an unprofessional manner, and the schedule to the complaint shows that these labels only contained the titles of the tapes. The police 'did not know what these tapes were' but 'considered their appearance to be suspicious and took possession of them to ascertain their real content'. This was not 'a random search', nor did the police deliberately remove articles which they knew were not covered by their warrant. In my opinion, the warrant authorised them to remove all tapes which bore no classification certificates in terms of the Act and Regulations made thereunder. Accordingly, the police were entitled to remove these tapes under the search warrant. Having lawfully removed them, they were fully entitled to ascertain their contents and, on finding them to be obscene, the Crown was entitled to charge the appellants under section 51(2) of the Civic Government (Scotland) Act 1982.

As it is competent to charge persons with crimes or offences upon the basis of articles irregularly obtained (see, *e.g.*, *Fairley v. Fishmongers of London*), there is no question but that these obscene tapes, which the police were authorised to remove under the warrant, albeit for the purposes of the Video Recordings Act, may form the basis of prosecution under section 51(2) of the Civic Government (Scotland) Act 1982.

The questions stated for the opinion of the court are as follows:

1. Having regard to the circumstances of the search and the circumstances in which obscene videos were found, was I entitled to repel the defence submission that the evidence of the search, the seizure of the videos found and referred to in the schedule and the production thereof in evidence were inadmissible against the two appellants?
2. Was I, in the circumstances found proved, entitled to reject the defence submission of no case to answer in terms of section 345A of the Criminal Procedure (Scotland) Act 1975?
3. On the foregoing facts admitted or proved, was I entitled to convict the appellants?

For the reasons given above I would answer each of these questions in the affirmative.

I have now read the opinion of your Lordship in the chair. From what I have said I believe that it can be seen that I agree with the excerpts from the decisions which you have cited, which I would have applied to this case if I had not decided to take the obvious direct route, although it was not argued."

LORD JUSTICE-CLERK (ROSS): "Lord Dunpark has set out the facts in this case and I need not rehearse them again. I agree that the questions in the case should be answered as proposed by Lord Dunpark, and that the appeal should be refused. However, I arrive at this conclusion by a somewhat different route from that followed by Lord Dunpark.

I agree with Lord Dunpark that the case of *Leckie v. Miln*, upon which the appellant founded, was a different type of case; the warrant authorised a search of a limited character, but the officers in fact carried out a random search. In my opinion, however, the cases of *H.M.A. v. Turnbull* and *H.M.A. v. Hepper* provide clear support for the conclusion at which the sheriff arrived in the present case.

In *H.M.A. v. Turnbull* the documents which were held to have been illegally obtained were documents which showed *ex facie* that they had no relation to the charges specified in the petition under which the search warrant was granted, and the documents were not *ex facie* incriminating. In the present case, the situation was different. The videos in question were of suspicious appearance and the police took possession of them in order to ascertain their real content; they turned out to be obscene. Lord Guthrie gave as one of the reasons for holding that the documents had been illegally obtained [at p.103].

'The police officers did not accidentally stumble upon evidence of a plainly incriminating character in the course of a search for a different purpose. If the documents are incriminating, their incriminating character is only exposed by careful consideration of their contents.'

The clear inference is that if the police officers had accidentally stumbled upon evidence of an incriminating character, Lord Guthrie would have arrived at a different conclusion. He repeated this view in *H.M.A. v. Hepper* when he said:

'In *Turnbull* at p.103, I distinguished that case, in which I excluded evidence as to documents taken possession of by police officers searching the accused's premises under a search warrant which clearly did not cover these documents, from a case in which police officers accidentally stumbled upon evidence of a plainly incriminating character in the course of a search for a different purpose. That distinction was based upon earlier authorities to which I was referred in *Turnbull's* case. It may be that the article which the police officers stumbled upon in their search of the accused's house was not an article of a plainly incriminating character, but it was at least an article of a very suspicious character, since it was an attaché case which contained within it the name and address of another person. In the circumstances, I do not think that the police officers acted in any way improperly in taking away that article in order to make further inquiries about it.'

It should be noted that in *Leckie* and *Miln* it was stated [at p.774]:

'This is not a case in which officers carrying out an active search within the scope of a lawful warrant came across articles unrelated to the particular crime with which they were concerned. In such a case the finding of other articles indicating guilt of other crimes may be perfectly admissible in evidence.'

In addition, it is plain from the authorities that in determining whether articles have been illegally obtained, one consideration must be whether there were circumstances of urgency. In *H.M.A. v. Turnbull*, Lord Guthrie observed that there were no circumstances of urgency.

On the other hand, in *H.M.A. v. Hepper*, where the actings of the police officer were approved of, Lord Guthrie observed:

'In the circumstances, I do not think that the police officers acted in any way improperly in taking away that article in order to make further inquiries about it. If they had not done so, it might have disappeared.'

In the present case the sheriff expresses the view that if the police officers had not taken away these videos to make further inquiries, they would not have been there the next time they visited the shop. In my opinion the sheriff was fully justified in expressing that opinion.

In all the circumstances I am satisfied that, as the advocate-depute contended, this was a case like *H.M.A. v. Hepper* where the police officers did not act in any way improperly in taking away the videos in order to make further inquiries about them.

It is for the foregoing reasons that I agree that the questions in the case should be answered in the manner proposed by Lord Dunpark. It is clear from Lord Dunpark's decision that he has based his decision in part upon a consideration of the terms of section 10 of the Video Recordings Act 1984 and the Video Recordings (Labelling) Regulations 1985 (S.I. No. 911). As neither counsel addressed us on these provisions, I express no opinion upon the relevance of these provisions and I prefer to base my opinion upon the three authorities to which we were referred by counsel."

NOTES

Note the difference of approach here between the Lord Justice-Clerk, Lord Ross, and Lord Dunpark. In Lord Dunpark's view, this was not a "stumbling" case at all, but one in which the removal of the obscene video-tapes was fully justified by the terms of the warrant. The Lord Justice-Clerk appears to equivocate between the view that this was just such a *Hepper*-type case and an implication in his concluding paragraphs that this search was justified not by the warrant, as Lord Dunpark thought, but by considerations of urgency—"if the police officers had not taken away these videos to make further inquiries, they would not have been there the next time they visited the shop". What difficulty can be foreseen if this latter view is correct? See the following cases.

9. H.M.A. v. McGuigan
1936 J.C. 16

McGuigan was arrested and charged with rape and murder at eight o'clock one evening. Between nine and ten o'clock the same evening, the police visited and searched a tent where the accused lived with his mother and stepfather and took possession of a number of incriminating articles. Objection was taken to the search since it had not been authorised by a search warrant.

Lord Justice-Clerk (Aitchison): "Mr Burnet has raised a point of some importance which he was quite entitled to raise. He takes objection to evidence proposed to be led by the Crown as to a search made by the police, on the evening of August 28, of the tent in which the accused lived along with his mother and stepfather. The ground of the objection is that this search was carried out, and I take it certain articles seized, without the warrant of a magistrate; and it is said, accordingly, that the search and the seizure of the articles were both illegal. Now, the facts are these: On the evening of August 28, the accused had been identified—or was alleged to have been identified—by Marjory Fenwick, and immediately thereafter he was apprehended and charged. The charges made against him were three in number. First, murder; second, rape; third, theft of a pocket book; the apprehension and charge took place about eight o'clock at night. Thereafter the accused was searched. Both the apprehension and the search of the accused were carried out without warrant. I have no doubt that, in the circumstances, this was quite regular. The police were amply justified in acting at their own hand. Between 9 and 10 o'clock the same night Inspector Davidson went to the accused's tent. He found the tent occupied by the accused's mother and the accused's stepfather. He disclosed who he was, and what his purpose was. No objection was raised, as was natural enough. On the other hand, no consent was asked for, and the search proceeded. Now it must be obvious that, the accused having been arrested on so grave a charge as murder, it might be of the first importance to the ends of public justice that a search of the tent in which the accused had been living should be made forthwith. The police acted at their own hand, just as they acted at their own hand in apprehending and searching the person of the accused. In the circumstances, the matter being in the view of Inspector Davidson one of urgency, the police were entitled, in my view, to act without delay and without having obtained a warrant from a magistrate.

Even if I thought otherwise, and that the police had acted irregularly, it would not in the least follow that the evidence proposed to be led would be inadmissible. An irregularity in the obtaining of evidence does not necessarily make that evidence inadmissible. In the present case thirteen articles to which the objection would apply have already been put in evidence, bearing labels showing where these articles were found, to which no objection of any kind was taken, and it appears to me to be out of the question to exclude them now. Rules as to search and warrant must, no doubt, be strictly observed and never lightly departed from; but, on the other hand, they must always be reasonably interpreted in the light of the circumstances of the particular case. While I think, as I have already said, that Mr Burnet was justified in raising the point, I have no hesitation, after giving it careful consideration, in repelling the objection and allowing the evidence."

Notes

McGuigan probably represents the paradigm of a search justified on the grounds of urgency. The offence was a very serious one and there was clearly an imminent likelihood of destruction of evidence. Putting the matter another way, there seems in this case to be a "reasonable relationship of proportionality between the means employed and the aim sought to be realised". As noted above, however, urgency is a highly elastic concept. In *Walsh v. Macphail*, 1978 S.L.T. (Notes) 29, a search was conducted for cannabis on a military air-base. Sniffer dogs had located the approximate location of the drugs in an accommodation block, the area was sealed off, and the inmates of the block in question told to report to the commanding officer. A search was carried out and drugs were found. There was no valid warrant for the search, but it was held that the search was justified on the grounds of urgency, since it would have been "impractical" to obtain a warrant in the time available. Do you agree that urgency was a sufficient justification in this situation? Compare *Edgley v. Barbour*, 1994 S.C.C.R. 789, in which it was held that urgency justified the search of a car for a radar detection device where the driver had been stopped late at night, since there was no facility easily to obtain a warrant, and where it was doubtful whether there was power to detain the accused (see Criminal Procedure (Scotland) Act 1995, ss.13–14). What limits ought to be placed on "urgency" as a justification for illegal searches? For further comment, see *Finnie* in the article cited above, 1982 S.L.T. (News) 289.

10. McAvoy v. Jessop
1988 S.C.C.R. 172

The police obtained a warrant to search for a stolen video recorder in a house occupied by the appellant's brother at a named address. That house proved to be a flat which was divided up in to a number of separately occupied bedsitting-rooms, one of which was occupied by the appellant and one of which was occupied by her brother. When the police discovered that the appellant's brother was not in his room, they showed the warrant to the appellant who did not object to a search of her room. The stolen video recorder was discovered in the appellant's room and she was charged with resetting it. The magistrate repelled an objection to the admissibility of evidence of the finding of the video recorder on the view that what occurred was analogous to the search of different rooms in a family home. The appellant appealed to the High Court.

LORD JUSTICE-GENERAL (EMSLIE): "After trial in the district court in Glasgow before the stipendiary magistrate, the appellant was convicted of a charge that between September 6, 1985 and February 5, 1986, in the house occupied by her at 31 Melville Street, Glasgow, she did reset a video recorder which had been stolen.

In the stated case, the following facts were found: [His Lordship narrated the findings in fact set out above.]

The search warrant which is referred to in findings 2 and 6 was a warrant to search for certain property stolen from a house occupied by Maureen McLaren in Troon consisting of cash, electrical goods and jewellery. The preamble to the warrant states that there were reasonable grounds for believing that the stolen property 'is in the houses occupied by Thomas McAvoy at 31 Melville Street, Glasgow, and 7 Hamiltonhill Road, Glasgow'. The search authorised by the warrant was of these 'houses occupied by Thomas McAvoy'.

The critical question at the trial related to the admissibility of the evidence of the two police officers who found the video recorder in the appellant's room. The point taken on the appellant's behalf was that the search was unlawful and that there were no circumstances rendering the results of the search admissible in evidence. In repelling the submission on behalf of the appellant upon this matter, the stipendiary magistrate in his note reported as follows:

'I overruled this objection and held that the police officers acted correctly in searching the appellant's room situated off the same hallway at the same address as that occupied by Thomas McAvoy. I was of the opinion that they were in a situation similar to that of carrying out a search in a family home which would involve a search of separate rooms occupied by individual members of one family.'

As we understand this passage the stipendiary magistrate appears to have taken the view that the search of the appellant's room was authorised by the warrant, and that the evidence about the finding of the video recorder was accordingly admissible.

Before us counsel for the appellant renewed the submission which had been rejected by the stipendiary magistrate, and the first question for us is whether on the findings in fact he was entitled to hold that the search was authorised by the warrant. It is not suggested in this case that the search was lawful because of any implied consent on the part of the appellant. The question accordingly falls to be answered upon a consideration of what was authorised by the warrant and of the findings in fact. In our opinion the authority of the warrant permitted only a search of the house occupied by Thomas McAvoy at 31 Melville Street. There is no finding that Thomas McAvoy occupied upon the basis of ownership, tenancy or otherwise the flat at that address in which the appellant was the occupier of a bedsitting-room. The findings merely disclose that Thomas McAvoy occupied a bedsitting-room therein when he was not in prison. The picture painted by findings 3, 4 and 5 is of a flat in which the bedsitting-rooms were in separate occupation, and that only one of these was occupied by Thomas McAvoy. In these circumstances it is our opinion that the warrant authorised only the search of the bedsitting-room which is found to have been occupied by Thomas McAvoy and that the search of the appellant's room was unlawful. The stipendiary magistrate was not entitled on the findings in fact to hold that the police officers were in effect carrying out a search of separate rooms in a flat which could be regarded as the family home of Thomas McAvoy.

The fact that the evidence about the finding of the video recorder was irregularly obtained does not necessarily of course make the evidence inadmissible (*Lawrie v. Muir*). As was pointed out in the opinion of the court in that case [at p.27]:

'Irregularities require to be excused, and infringements of the formalities of the law in relation to these matters are not lightly to be condoned. Whether any given irregularity ought to be excused depends upon the nature of the irregularity and the circumstances under which it was committed. In particular, the case may bring into play the discretionary principle of fairness to the accused which has been developed so fully in our law in relation to the admission in evidence of confessions or admissions by a person suspected or charged with a crime.'

For the Crown the submission was that the irregularity in this case was clearly excusable in that the police officers, acting in good faith, could properly have taken the view that their warrant authorised them to search the appellant's quarters. We do not agree. On the findings in fact, and in particular findings 3, 4 and 5, it was not open to them, reasonably, to take that view, and upon the whole matter, in the particular circumstances disclosed in this stated case, we are of the opinion that the evidence of the police officers should have been held to be inadmissible. We shall answer all three questions in the negative, allow the appeal, and quash the conviction."

NOTES

Does this case imply that even if investigating officers are mistaken in their interpretation of a warrant, and the warrant does not in fact give them power to conduct a particular search, the irregularity will be excused if their error was a reasonable one? How does this approach fit with the rather stricter one taken in *Leckie v. Miln*, above? In relation to statutory powers, it seems that a stricter view is appropriate, and it may be that in such cases, one is approaching the type of "absolute right" referred to by Lord Hope in the *dictum* from *Brown v. Stott*, cited above. In *Morrison v. O'Donnell*, 2001 S.C.C.R. 272 the police suspected the accused of setting traps to catch falcons. They detained the appellant under section 19 of the Wildlife and Countryside Act 1981 and searched his rucksack. In it they found a live pigeon and he was charged with causing unnecessary suffering to the bird, an offence under the Protection of Animals (Scotland) Act 1912. The detention was illegal, however, since the 1981 Act grants a power of arrest only where a person fails to give a satisfactory name and address. The appeal court held that this was an irregularity which could not be excused. Delivering the opinion of the court, Lord Coulsfield said:

"The statute under which the police officers were acting contains only a limited power of arrest. The limitation must have been deliberate, and that indicates that Parliament took the view that, in the ordinary case, a person suspected of an offence under the statute should not be detained. In these circumstances it seems to us that there would have to be something to justify the detention before it could be treated as an excusable irregularity, and we do not think that it could be said that there was anything to justify the detention in this case. The search was carried out in the context of the detention and cannot be divorced from it. The consequence is that the evidence in regard to the finding of the live pigeon in the rucksack is inadmissible."

In *McAnea v. H.M.A.*, 2001 S.L.T. 12, a warrant which bore to have been granted under the (non-existent) Forgery and Counterfeiting Act 1989 instead of the (real) Forgery and Counterfeiting Act 1981, was held to be invalid.

Singh v. H.M.A., 2001 S.C.C.R. 348, was a very technical case in which eight Customs officers searched premises under a warrant granted under the Value Added Tax Act 1983. Unfortunately, the warrant was granted for a search by "not more than four authorised persons". However, the warrant also allowed the persons authorised by the warrant to take with them "such other persons (not being authorised persons) as appear to him or them to be necessary." It was held that the "extra" searchers were not lawfully present at the search since they were neither authorised persons for the purposes of the warrant; nor were they "necessary . . . persons (not being authorised persons)". The court held that the irregularity could not be excused, quoting with approval the following dictum of Lord Wilberforce in *R. v. IRC ex parte Rossminster* [1980] A.C. 952:

"The integrity and privacy of a man's home, and of his place of business, an important human right has, since the second world war, been eroded by a number of statutes passed by Parliament in the belief, presumably, that this right of privacy ought in some cases to be over-ridden by the interest which the public has in preventing evasions of the law . . . The courts have the duty to supervise, I would say critically, even jealously, the legality of any purported exercise of those powers. They are the guardians of the citizens right to privacy."

The court laid some significance (a) on the fact that the accused was not aware of the restrictions in the warrant, and could not therefore object to the search; and (b) on the fact that the presence of the extra officers "not only increased the number of individuals physically within the premises but diverted the appellants' attention from the search itself since the occasion was used to interview the second appellant and to attempt to interview the first appellant". Do you agree that these factors are sufficient to render the irregularity "inexcusable"?

In the dictum quoted above, Lord Wilberforce refers to the integrity and privacy of a person's home as being an important human right, and there can be little doubt that on the face of it, the search of a person's home will normally amount to a breach of Article 8 of the European Convention on Human Rights. However, where the search is carried out under a warrant which is *ex facie* valid, and which has been granted by a Sheriff or justice, that provides a complete answer to any argument that a search (or arrest) constitutes a breach of the complainer's Convention rights under Article 8—see *Birse v. Macneill*, 2000 J.C. 503; (*sub nom Birse v. H.M.A.*, 2000 S.C.C.R. 505); *Ormiston v. H.M.A.*, 2001 S.L.T. 257. A similar difficulty to that which arose in *Singh*, arose in *H.M.A. v. Aspinall*, unreported, November 15, 2001, Linlithgow Sheriff Court, a case involving charges of possession of child pornography. That case has been referred to the High Court by the Lord Advocate under section 123 of the Criminal Procedure (Scotland) Act 1995, and it may be that the High Court will issue further guidance on this difficult area.

Where there are formal defects in a warrant any evidence found as a result of a search under that warrant will generally be excluded, but minor defects will not generally be fatal. In *H.M.A. v. Cumming*, 1983 S.C.C.R. 15, for example, a warrant was granted under section 23(2) of the Misuse of Drugs Act 1971. A discrepancy between the name of the person specified in the deposition of the warrant and the name of the accused was not fatal to the warrant's validity; nor was a failure to date the warrant, since a date had been appended by a Justice of the Peace who had signed the warrant. A failure in the warrant to specify the police officer who had authority under the warrant to conduct the search was described as being a breach of section 23(2) however, as was a failure to specify the premises to be searched. These defects taken together were fatal to the validity of the warrant, and items recovered under the warrant were ruled inadmissible. See also *Smith v. Innes*, 1984 S.C.C.R. 119; *H.M.A. v. Bell*, 1985 S.L.T. 349; and compare *Allan v. Milne*, 1974 S.L.T. (Notes) 76.

A warrant which is *ex facie* defective as a result of amendment may still be regarded as valid if it can be shown that the alterations were made after the warrant was executed—see *H.M.A. v. Beggs (No. 4)*, 2002 S.C.C.R. 62.

Finally in this connection, is a person who comes to the door of a property which is being searched under warrant, "found" on those premises for the purposes of section 23(2) of the Misuse of Drugs Act 1971? See *McCarron v. Allen*, 1988 S.C.C.R. 9, which gives an affirmative answer to this question, and *Gavin v. Normand*, 1995 S.C.C.R. 209, which implies a negative one. The former case does not appear to have been before the court in the latter.

11.　H.M.A. v. Megrahi (No. 3)
2000 S.L.T. 1401

This case arises from the trial of the two men accused of murder by planting a bomb aboard Pan Am flight 103 which exploded over Lockerbie, killing everyone on board as well as a number of people on the ground. The Crown sought to lead evidence of a diary belonging to one of the accused. The diary had been found in the office of a company in Malta of which the accused was one of two directors. Two Scottish police officers, an FBI special agent and a Maltese police officer had interviewed the other director in the office under an agreement with the Maltese authorities by which Maltese criminal law and procedures applied. In the course of the interview the diary was found, apparently during a search. The director did not object to the search, though no warrant had been produced; nor did he object to the removal of the diary, which he identified as belonging to the accused. There was evidence that under Maltese law a search was lawful if carried out in the presence of an inspector of police or under a warrant signed by him, though a warrant was normally required to take possession of property. The accused objected to the introduction of this evidence on the grounds that the manner in which it had been obtained rendered it inadmissible. A trial within a trial was held, and the court issued the following opinion:

LORD COULSFIELD: "[5] In March and April 1991, Detective Chief Inspector Bell (now Detective Chief Superintendent) was making inquiries about the second accused [Megrahi]. By February 1991 he had become aware of evidence which might identify the first accused as a person who had purchased, in Malta, certain articles of clothing, similar to remnants of clothing identified by forensic scientists as having formed part of the contents of the suitcase which contained the explosive device which had destroyed PA103. He was also aware that the second accused had been the Libyan Arab Airlines station manager at Malta until October 1988, that the first accused had travelled from Tripoli to Malta on December 20, 1988, and had stayed at the Holiday Inn in Malta, and that on December 21, 1988, while he was there, a telephone call had been made from his room to a flat at Spring Street of which the second accused was then the tenant. Mr Bell took steps to check the lease of the property to the second accused and accounts for water and electricity supplied to it. The lease had by then expired. Mr Bell also checked immigration records for December 20, 1988 to ascertain that the second accused had entered Malta on that date. On March 18, 1991, Mr Bell with other officers went to the flat at Spring Street. They were admitted to the flat by the landlady. The second accused was not in actual occupation of the flat at the time: he had not been in Malta since about August 1990. The flat was almost empty of furniture. The officers examined the flat, took photographs of the interior and took possession of two items, a brown holdall and a small piece of putty, with a view to forensic examination. Bell also checked the time and distance from Luqa Airport to the second accused's flat.

[6] From their meeting with the proprietor of the flat, the officers ascertained that the second accused had a business partner, Mr Vincent Vassallo. Further inquiries revealed that the second accused and Mr Vassallo were the directors of a limited company, Medtours Services Ltd. On April 18, 1991, Mr Vassallo was interviewed at his place of work at Luqa Airport. At the conclusion of the interview, arrangements were made to meet Mr Vassallo at Medtours' office on April 22, 1991, in order to continue the interview.

[7] At the continued interview, Mr Bell was accompanied by another Scottish officer, Sgt Avent, and by an FBI special agent, Philip Reid, and a Maltese police officer, Sgt Galea. They were admitted to the office by Mr Vassallo who was interviewed there over a period of several hours. The office was on the first floor of the building and consisted of a large room subdivided by partitions. It contained a secretary's desk and two other desks, one of which was Mr Vassallo's own desk: the other was that of the second accused. During the interview, Mr Vassallo gave the officers his own diary for 1988. Later in the interview, the diary which is the subject of this question came into the possession of the police officers. There was some difference of evidence as to how that came about. Mr Bell thought that Mr Vassallo had obtained the diary either from a drawer in the second accused's desk or, less probably, from the top of the desk, and handed it over. Sgt Avent thought that Mr Vassallo had offered to show them round the office and gone to the desk and produced the diary and then, at Avent's request, handed it to him. Reid's recollection was not clear, but he thought that Mr Vassallo had allowed them to look around the office and that either he or Sgt Avent had noticed the diary: he could not recall whether or not it was on the desk, but in any event Mr Vassallo agreed that it could be taken. Sgt Galea said that a Scottish officer had opened a drawer and produced the diary. Mr Vassallo said that the officers had gone round the office looking in drawers and other places and that the diary had been produced in the course of their doing so. He gave evidence that he had repeatedly asked the officers what they were looking for and offered to give them what they required but that he had not been told what it was that they wanted. He did not, however, suggest, in his evidence, that he had required the officers to stop what they were doing, or demanded that they show him some authority for a search. It should, however, be added that his evidence was to the effect that he did not think that he could refuse to allow them to do what they were doing. On any view, however, it is reasonably clear that Mr Vassallo did not attempt to prohibit the officers from carrying out any steps which they did take. There is nothing to indicate that Sgt Galea regarded anything that was done as being done without authority (although, as will be noted later, he seemed to be under the impression that there was a warrant to search the premises). It is also clear from the evidence of all the witnesses that when the diary was produced, Mr Vassallo was asked about it and said that it was the second accused's personal diary, but that he did not state any objection to the officers taking it, as they did. Subsequently, the diary was taken to the Maltese police HQ.

[8] In addition to the witnesses to the actual circumstances in which the diary was recovered, we heard evidence from Mr Grech in regard to police practice in Malta and from Dr Donatella Dimech, a Maltese lawyer, who is now a member of the Attorney General's office, in regard to relevant rules of Maltese law. The general effect of their evidence was that in Maltese law and practice a search is lawful if it is carried out under the authority of an inspector of police, either

by his personal presence or under a warrant granted by him. However, both agreed that a warrant was normally required to take possession of the property of a suspect, subject to certain exceptions in circumstances of urgency.

[9] On behalf of the second accused, it was submitted that under the principles of international law, the Scottish courts must take note of any unlawfulness in the recovery of evidence in a foreign jurisdiction. On the evidence, the police officers had had ample reason to suspect the second accused, and the court should approach the issue on the basis that he was a suspect, even though the officers had denied that they regarded him as a suspect at the time of the interview. What had taken place in the Medtours office was a search, and there was reason to hold that it was not a lawful search according to Maltese law. Sgt Galea had thought that there was a warrant, but no warrant had been produced. There had not been any proper consent to the taking of the diary given by a person with authority to agree to the taking of the personal property of the second accused. On the evidence as to Maltese law and practice, it was not lawful to take the property of a suspect without a warrant. There had been other means of recovering evidence in Malta, for example by the use of letters of request, but the police had chosen not to use them. It was accepted, in accordance with the decision in *Lawrie v. Muir*, that the court could allow evidence unlawfully recovered to be led, if the unlawfulness could be excused. In the circumstances of this case, the recovery of the diary amounted to compulsion on the accused to incriminate himself, and in view of the status of the accused as a suspect and the availability of other methods of recovering evidence, the court should not allow the evidence to be led. The advocate depute submitted that there was no objection under international law to the police officers acting as they had done, that the second accused was not at the material time a suspect and that the taking of the diary was lawful. In any event, he submitted that in the circumstances any irregularity could be excused and that the evidence should be allowed.

[10] In these circumstances, in our opinion, the first question is whether the second accused should be regarded as having been a suspect at the time of the visit to the office. There were evidently circumstances which had directed the officers to making particular inquiries into the possibility that the second accused had been involved in the bombing of PA103. It could not however be said that there was any evidence known to the officers which was directly incriminatory of the second accused. The circumstances which led to the investigation were, rather, that there was information to associate him with the first accused, who could be said to be directly incriminated, and to indicate that his position in Malta might suggest that there was an opportunity for him to have been concerned in the placing of the bomb. Both Mr Bell and Sgt Avent said that they did not regard the second accused as a suspect at the time. On balance, we have come to the conclusion that the second accused was not properly to be regarded as a suspect at the material time, but the question is a narrow one and in the circumstances of this case we think it right to consider what the position would have been if he had properly fallen to be regarded as a suspect.

[11] The second question is whether the taking of the diary should be regarded as lawful according to the law and procedure of Malta. One aspect of this question is whether there was any search undertaken by the officers. The evidence is not altogether clear, but, in our opinion, it does appear that the officers did not merely ask questions of Mr Vassallo but did, to however minor an extent, look round the premises and that it was in the course of their doing so that attention was drawn to the diary. In these circumstances, it appears to us that there was a search of the premises, even if a limited one, and that the diary was recovered in the course of that search. On the evidence of Dr Dimech and Mr Grech, a search of premises is lawful under Maltese law if it is authorised by an inspector of police either by personal presence or by issuing a warrant, or if it is consented to by a person who has the right to consent. No inspector was present. Sgt Galea thought that there was a warrant but there is no other evidence to that effect and no warrant has been produced. However, Mr Vassallo was present and did not seek to prevent the search, such as it was. Mr Vassallo was a director of Medtours and therefore, on the evidence, had the authority to consent to a search of the premises. In these circumstances, it does not appear that anything unlawful by the law of Malta occurred, up to the point when the diary was actually identified, however precisely that came about.

[12] The next question then is whether once the diary was identified as the property of the second accused, the taking of it was lawful according to the law of Malta. There was evidence

from Dr Dimech that the consent of Mr Vassallo did render it lawful, but she was not actually asked whether her opinion on that precise point would be affected if the second accused was a suspect, and, in any event, the questions put to her did not focus very precisely on the position in regard to the taking of personal property of the second accused as opposed to company property. The evidence on this aspect of the case is not completely satisfactory, and we have come to the conclusion that the proper conclusion is that the Crown have not demonstrated that the actual taking of the diary, after it was identified, was lawful by the law of Malta.

[13] In these circumstances it is necessary to consider whether the Crown should nevertheless be permitted to lead evidence of the diary and its contents on the principles of *Lawrie v. Muir*. On this aspect of the case, there is, in our opinion, no real difficulty. On the assumptions we think it right to make, the second accused was being investigated as a suspect, but a suspect by reason of his association with the first accused rather than in virtue of any directly incriminating evidence against him. The interview with Mr Vassallo and the search, such as it was, of the premises were not unlawful, up to the point when the diary was identified as the property of the second accused. The Scottish officers were acting in virtue of an agreement with the Maltese authorities, and there was a Maltese officer present whose specific duty it was to see that the proceedings conformed to the proper law and practice in Malta. There is no question of any device or trick having been employed nor of any deliberate evasion of the requirements of the law or collusion in such evasion. The diary had been left, presumably, by the second accused in the company premises, and he had not been in those premises, or even in Malta, for about seven months. In all these circumstances, it seems to us that what occurred can properly be regarded as excusable. It is significant that this is a murder case and that, as the Lord Justice General pointed out in *Lawrie*, in such a case the public interest in the prosecution of crime has to be given due weight. In all these circumstances, the objection falls to be repelled."

12.   Duke of Argyll v. Duchess of Argyll
1963 S.L.T. (Notes) 42

"In an action of divorce on the ground of adultery at the instance of a husband against his wife certain diaries belonging to the defender were put in evidence by the pursuer. It was established at the proof that the pursuer acquired these diaries by breaking into the house occupied by the defender while the parties were living apart and taking them from her bedroom and that the defender was in the habit, while the parties were living together, of keeping the diaries on her bedside table or in an open drawer to which the pursuer, among others, had access. In these circumstances, the Lord Ordinary held that the diaries could not be excluded from consideration as confidential and that, notwithstanding that they were deliberately stolen, they were admissible in evidence. His Lordship referred to *Rattray v. Rattray* (1895) 25 R. 315; 5 S.L.T. 245; *Watson v. Watson* 1934 S.C. 372; 1934 S.L.T. 275; and *Lawrie v. Muir* 1950 J.C. 19; 1950 S.L.T. 37; and observed: "Insofar as historically adultery was regarded as a quasi-criminal offence, and its historical background is reflected in our present law at least to the extent of making proof of adultery dependent upon the criminal standard of proof beyond reasonable doubt (*cf* Lord Guthrie in *Currie v. Currie*, 1950 S.C. 10; 1950 S.L.T. 15 and Lord President Clyde in *Burnett v. Burnett*, 1955 S.C. 183 at p.186; 1955 S.L.T. 190), it may not be inapposite to consider the question of admissibility in a criminal trial of evidence illegally obtained. This question was canvassed by a Full Bench in the case of *Lawrie v. Muir*. In that case, two inspectors of the Milk Marketing Board made an inspection of the accused's premises and an examination of the milk bottles therein. All contracts between the Board and distributors of milk contained a condition that the inspectors of a company formed for the purpose of restoring milk bottles to their rightful owners, on production of their warrants, were entitled to inspect the distributors' premises and examine bottles. The accused had no contract with the Milk Marketing Board, but she permitted the inspectors, who produced their warrants, to make an inspection. On the evidence which they obtained as a result of the inspection, a prosecution was instituted against her under the appropriate order for using, for the sale of her milk, bottles belonging to other persons and she was convicted. On appeal the court held that the inspectors, although acting in good faith, had illegally obtained entry into the premised by a misrepresentation and that their evidence was inadmissible. In these circumstances the conviction was quashed. The opinion of the court was given by Lord Justice-General Cooper, and on the point at issue his judgement is conveniently summarised in the rubric which reads: 'An irregularity in the method by which evidence has been obtained does not necessarily make that evidence inadmissible in a criminal prosecution. There is no absolute rule governing the matter, the question whether any irregularity ought or ought not to be excused depending in each case upon the nature of the irregularity and the circumstances in which it was committed, and important consideration always being whether the admission of the evidence will be fair to the accused. No distinction can be drawn in this matter between a prosecution for a statutory offence and a prosecution for a common law crime.' It would seem from the judgement that greater latitude may be given to police officers who obtain evidence by irregular methods than to offenders who are not the guardians of public order and safety but are private individuals. It would, accordingly, appear to follow that the narrower rather than the broader approach would be taken in the case of a person who obtains evidence by illegal means to further his own ends in a civil process.

Nevertheless, I am of the opinion that the above statement of the law made by Lord Justice-General Cooper in *Lawrie v. Muir* can properly be applied to a case like the present one. There is no absolute rule, it being a question of the particular circumstances of each case determining whether a particular piece of evidence should be admitted or not. Among the circumstances which may have to be taken into account are the nature of the evidence concerned, the purpose for which it is used in evidence, the manner in which it was obtained, whether its introduction is fair to the party from whom it has been illegally obtained and whether its admission will in fairness throw light on disputed facts and enable justice to be done. It may well be that in a particular case something will turn on whether the proposed evidence relates to an admission of adultery or to collateral matters used in an empirical process of establishing facts, circumstances, and qualifications from which proof of adultery can properly be inferred.

In the present case, I have reached the decision that the diaries in question can properly be admitted in evidence.

Some of the evidence in the case had been taken on commission. With regard to the practice of making evidence taken on commission available to the parties before the proof, Lord Wheatley said: 'Moreover, I understand that in conformity with modern practice there was available to her before the proof the evidence taken on commission, so that she had access in advance, if she desired to use it, to the text of that evidence. Of course, as a party she was entitled to be present when such evidence was being taken, and to be certiorated of it in that manner, but I cannot but feel that the modern practice is wrong, and that evidence taken on commission should lie *in retentis* and not be available before the proof to the parties or their advisors, who should decide on its use from their recollection of its contents, and not have it available before it is formally put in as evidence in the case.'

Decree of divorce was granted."

NOTES

Scots law as to the admissibility of improperly obtained evidence in civil causes is far from settled. In *Rattray v. Rattray* (1897) 25 R. 315, two out of four Inner House judges held that improprieties have no effect on admissibility. Lord Trayner said that "the policy of the law in later years (and I think a good policy) has been to admit almost all evidence which will throw light on disputed facts and enable justice to be done". Lord Moncrieff agreed with him. *Rattray* is a somewhat dubious authority, however (see Macphail, paras 21.08–21.12), and it is submitted (with Macphail, *Evidence*, para. 21.14) that the views of Lord Wheatley in the *Duke of Argyll's* case are preferable. Lord Wheatley's interlocutor in this case was challenged on other grounds and the case ultimately went to the House of Lords. In the Inner House, the only mention of the point of admissibility raised above was in a dissenting opinion by Lord Guthrie in which he said:

"It was argued to us at the hearing on the reclaiming motion that, as the object of the Court is to ascertain the truth, and as the truth may be revealed by the diary, its contents should be available to the Court. But while it is correct that the Court endeavours to arrive at the truth, it seeks to ascertain the truth by fair methods. Therefore, it does not compel an accused person to testify against himself nor allow a person to be questioned about his alleged adultery unless he has previously denied it in evidence. It is for the same reason of fairness that the Court does not allow the use in evidence of a party's personal, private and undisclosed documents against his will. It is because the facts concerning this diary may be such that its use in evidence against the will of the defender would offend against the principle of fairness that I am of opinion that the proposed amendment should not be disallowed. I regard the matter before us as of great importance, and requiring me to utter this dissent."

Oghonoghor v. Secretary of State for the Home Department, 1995 S.L.T. 733 is a more modern case on fairness in obtaining evidence in a civil case. A Nigerian woman had entered the United Kingdom on a visitor's visa. She then embarked on a course of study. She sought permission to remain and study, but permission was refused. She nevertheless stayed beyond the expiry date of her visa. An immigration officer instructed to inquire into the circumstances interviewed the woman under caution in relation to her overstaying. During the interview the officer formed the view that the woman might not be merely an "overstayer" but might in fact be an illegal immigrant, since she had obtained her visitor's visa at a time when she had already formed the intention of studying in the United Kingdom. In spite of this the immigration officer continued to question her without issuing a further caution. Lord Cameron of Lochbroom opined that in the circumstances of the case, information obtained from Ms Oghonghor in these circumstances had been obtained unfairly. He accepted the operation of a general principle that "where the liberty of an individual was at stake, a high level of fairness was required of those who were concerned to establish the facts upon which that liberty might be interfered with." He continued:

"In the present case, not only was [a proper caution] not given, but the material upon which Mr Pearson made his report, namely the questions and answers contained in form ISCP4, was but a synthesis of the earlier conversation between the petitioner and Mr Pearson at which time the petitioner understood that it was the circumstances of her overstaying which were being inquired into. In the particular circumstances of this case, I would hold that the decision taken by Mr Gillespie to the effect that the petitioner was an illegal entrant, taken as it was upon information made available to him by Mr Pearson, was taken upon material which had been unfairly obtained from the petitioner and that that unfairness was not removed by the fact that the petitioner was agreeable to signing what appeared as her answers on form ISCP4."

His Lordship did not explicitly hold that such evidence was inadmissible, but it is submitted that is the necessary implication of his decision, in which he held that the Secretary of State had not discharged the onus of proving that the petitioner had gained entry to the country by deception. This is, of course, a rather special case, and has more in common with the following cases regarding the admissibility of statements made by an accused person in criminal cases.

13.   Chalmers v. H.M.A.
1954 J.C. 66

A youth of 16 was suspected of having committed a murder and was brought to a police station where, without being charged, he was cautioned and questioned regarding information he had previously given. At this stage he had received neither legal advice nor parental support. He was reduced to tears by the questioning and made a lengthy and incriminating statement. In consequence of this statement he was taken by the police to a cornfield where he pointed out to them the whereabouts of a purse which belonged to the deceased. He was later formally charged and made a second statement. Evidence was not tendered by the Crown of the first statement, but was led in relation to the second statement and the actings in the cornfield. Objection was taken to the admissibility of this evidence, on the basis that it had been obtained unfairly by the police.

LORD JUSTICE-GENERAL (COOPER): "The appellant was convicted by a majority verdict, after a trial before Lord Strachan and a jury at Stirling, on a charge of robbery and murder, and, in respect that at the date of the crimes he was 16 years of age, he was ordered to be detained during Her Majesty's pleasure. The grounds of appeal against the conviction are (1) wrongful admission of evidence, and (2) insufficient admissible evidence to support the conviction.

The crimes were committed in foundry premises at Larbert in the late afternoon of July 24, 1953, and there is no doubt that the deceased was then robbed and seriously assaulted by someone. The live issue at the trial was whether the Crown could identify the appellant as the assailant.

In the course of their investigations the police made many inquiries, and on July 26, and again on August 7, questioned the appellant. The statements then given by him were not incriminating. The police later obtained certain information from the witnesses Mrs Oliver and her small son, which tended to cast some doubt upon the truth of the statements made by the appellant, and the police decided to see the appellant again. Their attitude at this point is frankly explained by the detective inspector in charge of the investigation, who says that, from the information received from Mrs Oliver, he was 'inclined to suspect' that the appellant might have some connection with the crime, and that the appellant 'was under suspicion'. In that situation a police car with two officers was sent from Falkirk on August 15 to fetch the appellant from Clackmannan, where he was still in bed; and he was brought to the police station at Falkirk at 11.10 a.m. and there interviewed by a detective inspector in the presence of another officer of the same rank. The appellant (who was never at liberty again) was told that he was to be further questioned, and was cautioned in the usual terms. The inspector then proceeded to interrogate the appellant, telling him the information which had come into the possession of the police and reopening the statement made by him on August 7. The inspector admits he was 'cross-examining' the appellant, and making suggestions to him which were contradictory to his previous statement, saying, *inter alia*, that the police had reason to believe that he 'might have been' at the locus at the time when the crimes were committed. The interrogation lasted for about five minutes, until the appellant was reduced to tears. He was then cautioned a second time, and asked whether he wanted his father or a solicitor to be present 'when he did a certain thing'. The appellant declined. The second inspector was then asked to take a note of the appellant's statement but, before doing so, he gave a third (or fourth) caution to the appellant and repeated the offer that his father or a solicitor should be present. A statement was then taken, which we can only assume was highly incriminating: but this statement was not tendered in evidence by the Crown.

Matters did not end there. Immediately after the statement had been taken the first inspector questioned the appellant about certain matters contained in his statement, and, in consequence of answers thus obtained, the appellant was taken about 11.45 a.m. in a police van by the inspector and two other police officers to a cornfield near the locus, where the purse of the deceased was found at a spot pointed out by the appellant under the surveillance of the police. The appellant was then taken back to the police station about 12.10 p.m.. An interval of about two hours then ensued while the appellant's father was being fetched by the police, and at this stage, though there had been neither charge nor arrest, the appellant is described by the police as being 'detained in connection with the murder', whatever that may mean. The father arrived about 2.15 p.m., and the appellant again broke down. At 2.25 p.m. he was cautioned and formally charged in presence of his father, whereupon the appellant is said to have replied: 'I did it. He struck me.'

A speciality is introduced by the reasons given by the presiding Judge in determining to admit the evidence regarding the cornfield. As I have observed, the 'statement' was not tendered in evidence, presumably because it was regarded as unfair so to do, and the presiding Judge indicated that he would disallow any evidence of statements made by the appellant at the cornfield, but that, in the absence of authority, he would not reject evidence as to the 'actings' of the appellant at the cornfield—*i.e.* the evidence that the appellant, when taken to the cornfield, pointed out the place where the purse was found. The whole of the evidence bearing upon the circumstances of the interrogation at the police station and of the subsequent conducted visit to the cornfield was adduced in the presence and hearing of the jury. This evidence the Judge left to the jury with certain comments upon its weight and value, and with the direction that, if they thought that there was such unfairness in the police proceedings as to force them to disregard this piece of evidence, they were entitled to do so. According to the argument for the appellant this line of approach indicated a fatal inconsistency. On behalf of the Crown it was maintained (a) that the cornfield episode was separable from the proceedings which culminated in the 'statement', and (b) that 'the statement' at the police station, if tendered, would have been admissible. The two contentions are so closely related in argument and in the reasoning of the presiding Judge that we allowed the debate to proceed though the second question is not properly before us, and it is right that I should indicate my views upon both questions.

I take first the 'statement', with regard to which I am of opinion that in the circumstances a decision to reject this evidence would have been right. The charge, if there was to be a charge, was bound to be one of murder. The accused was a juvenile. On August 15, he was under suspicion of being a murderer; and, as I read the police evidence, he was then, in their view, not merely a possible but a likely perpetrator of the crime; and it is very significant of the state of mind of the police that the proceedings began with a caution, and that several further cautions followed within the next five minutes. The process to which the appellant was subjected was one not merely of interrogation but of 'cross-examination' and of being confronted with police information contradictory of the statement which he had already made; and this process was continued until the appellant broke down. It is said that the appellant was not technically in custody, that no warrant for his apprehension had been issued, and that he had not been formally charged. This is true, and I recognise that in several cases distinctions have very properly been drawn between 'routine questioning', during exploratory police investigation of a crime, and the interrogation of prisoners, after arrest or in prison awaiting trial. But when a person is brought by police officers in a police van to a police station, and, while there alone, is faced with police officers of high rank, I cannot think that his need for protection is any less than it would have been if he had been formally apprehended. The ordinary person (least of all a youth of sixteen) is not to know that he could have refused to be taken to the police station or to answer any questions, and, even if he knew that, he would be unlikely to adopt such a course and it would probably avail him little if he did. Taking all the circumstances into account I am unable to regard a confession or other incriminating statement extracted by such methods as presenting those features of a 'voluntary' and 'spontaneous' statement on which strong emphasis has been laid in so many of the cases, and such a confession or statement cannot be laid before a jury. I am unable to draw the line or to describe it in terms universally or generally applicable, but I am satisfied that in this case the line was crossed and the statement would have been inadmissible if it had been offered in evidence.

I take next the episode of the cornfield. This is related to the interrogation in two ways. In point of time the visit to the cornfield followed immediately after the further interrogation which followed the taking of the 'statement'. Moreover it is admitted that during the further interrogation the appellant was asked what happened to the purse, and that it was 'in consequence of' his answer to that question that he was taken to the cornfield 'to facilitate any search'. I therefore regard the visit to the cornfield under the surveillance of the police as part and parcel of the same transaction as the interrogation, and, if the interrogation and the 'statement' which emerged from it are inadmissible as 'unfair', the same criticism must attach to the conducted visit to the cornfield. Next I feel unable to accept the distinction drawn by the presiding Judge between statements and 'actings', and I suspect that a fallacy lurks in the word 'actings'. The actings of an accused, if unattended by such circumstances as are here presented, are normally competent evidence against him. For instance, if the police had kept watch on the accused and had seen him go to the cornfield to retrieve the purse, such evidence would have been perfectly competent. Again 'actings' in the sense of conduct, may be perfectly neutral as a communication of specific information; but 'actings' in the sense of a gesture or a sign, may be indistinguishable from a communication by word of mouth or by writing. The question here was—Where exactly is the purse? And this question might have been answered by an oral description of the place where it was, or by going to the place and silently pointing to that place. It seems to me to make no difference for present purposes which method of answering the question was adopted; from which it follows that, if, in the circumstances of this case, the 'statement' was inadmissible, the episode of the cornfield was equally inadmissible. The significance of the episode is plain, for it showed that the appellant knew where the purse was. If the police had simply produced, and proved the finding of, the purse, that evidence would have carried them little or no distance in this case towards implicating the appellant. It was essential that the appellant should be linked up with the purse, either by oral confession or by its equivalent—tacit admission of knowledge of its whereabouts obtained as a sequel to the interrogation.

That, I am afraid, is an end of the case; for I did not understand it to be maintained, and in any event I do not think that it could successfully be maintained, that the verdict could stand in so narrow a case without the evidence of either the 'statement' or the cornfield episode. All that is left is some exceedingly imperfect evidence of bare opportunity, and the alleged admission made when the appellant was charged. The presiding Judge admitted the evidence of this final admission with express hesitation arising from the fact that considering the youth and condition of the appellant, and considering also the evidence (*ex hypothesi* inadmissible) of his visit to the cornfield, it is not easy to attach full significance and value to the further statement made when he was charged, the charge was made at 2.25 p.m. after the appellant's father had reached the police station, and the presiding Judge found in this interval of time sufficient to separate the charge from the proceedings which had taken place earlier that day. I do not consider that this time interval was sufficient in the circumstances to overcome the difficulty, nor am I satisfied that the appellant's answer to the charge would have been the same if the police questioning had stopped at the line beyond which self-incriminating statements became inadmissible in evidence; but I prefer to rest my judgement upon the wider ground that, even accepting the final statement, there is not enough left in the case and that the verdict is vitiated by the erroneous admission of the evidence regarding the cornfield episode.

I have sympathy with the police in the difficult position in which they are often placed. We have no power to give instructions to the police but we have the power and the duty to exclude from the cognisance of a jury evidence which, according to our practice and decisions, is inadmissible; and the police have an interest to know why such decisions are taken. Were it possible to do so, I should like to be able to lay down comprehensive rules for the guidance of the police in all the situations which may arise in practice, but I am satisfied that this is impossible because in the border-line case so much turns upon the exact circumstances. To such cases it is possible to apply the words of Lord Sumner in *Ibrahim v. Rex* (1914 A.C. 599) in which, after reviewing a large number of cases, his Lordship said (p.614): 'The English law is still unsettled, strange as it may seem since the point is one that constantly occurs in criminal trials. Many Judges in their discretion exclude such evidence for they fear that nothing less than the exclusion of all such statements can prevent improper questioning of prisoners, by removing the inducement to resort to it . . . Others, less tender to the prisoner or more mindful of the balance of decided authority, would admit such statements . . . If, as appears even on the line of authorities which the trial Judge did not follow, the matter is one for the Judge's discretion, depending largely on his view of the impropriety of the questioner's conduct and the general circumstances of the case, their Lordships think, as will hereafter be seen, that in the circumstances of this case his discretion is not shown to have been exercised improperly.' In quoting this passage I am not to be taken as suggesting that English law is the same as Scottish law, for it is not, the English Courts being in use to admit certain evidence which would fall to be rejected in Scotland and the procedure in the two countries being materially different. But the dictum stresses the undoubted fact that it is inherent in the problem that wide generalisation is impossible. This, however, it is possible to say with regard to Scots law. It is not the function of the police when investigating a crime to direct their endeavours to obtaining a confession from the suspect to be used as evidence against him at the trial. In some legal systems the inquisitorial method of investigation is allowed in different degrees and subject to various safeguards; but by our law self-incriminating statements, when tendered in evidence at a criminal trial, are always jealously examined from the standpoint of being assured as to their spontaneity; and if, on a review of all the proved circumstances, that test is not satisfied, evidence of such statements will usually be excluded altogether. The theory of our law is that at the stage of initial investigation the police may question anyone with a view to acquiring information which may lead to the detection of the criminal; but that, when the stage has been reached at which suspicion, or more than suspicion, has in their view centred upon some person as the likely perpetrator of the crime, further interrogation of that person becomes very dangerous, and, if carried too far, *e.g.* to the point of extracting a confession by what amounts to cross-examination, the evidence of that confession will almost certainly be excluded. Once the accused has been apprehended and charged he has the statutory right to a private interview with a solicitor and to be brought before a magistrate with all convenient speed so that he may, if so advised, emit a declaration in presence of his solicitor under conditions which safeguard him against prejudice. The practice of emitting declarations has very largely fallen into disuse since the Evidence Act of 1898, but the underlying principle survives, and it may be applicable to situations which arise before apprehension and charge. Much reference was made to a person 'detained under suspicion', an expression which has been used ambiguously in many of our decisions, but the emphasis is on the suspicion and not on the detention. Putting aside the case of proper apprehension without a warrant of persons caught more or less red-handed, no person can be lawfully detained except after a charge has been made against him, and it is for this reason that I view with some uneasiness the situation disclosed in this case, and illustrated by the recent cases of *Rigg* (1946 J.C. 1) and *Short* (May 30, 1950, unreported), in which a suspect is neither apprehended nor charged but is simply 'asked' to accompany two police officers to a police office to be there questioned. In former times, such questioning, if undertaken, would be conducted by police officers visiting the house or place of business of the suspect and there questioning him, probably in the presence of a relation or friend. However convenient the modern practice may be, it must normally create a situation very unfavourable to the suspect. In the eyes of every ordinary citizen the venue is a sinister one. When he stands alone in such a place confronted by several police officers, usually some of high rank, the dice are loaded against him, especially as he knows that there is no one to corroborate him as to what exactly occurred during the interrogation, how it was conducted and how long it lasted. If under such circumstances cross-examination is pursued with the result, though perhaps not with the deliberate object, of causing him to break down and to condemn himself out of his own mouth, the impropriety of the proceedings cannot be cured by the giving of any number of formal cautions or by the introduction of some officer other than the questioner to record the ultimate statement. In the ordinary case, as many decisions now demonstrate, that statement, if tendered in evidence at the trial, will not be treated as possessing that quality of spontaneity on which our law insists, and its rejection, when tendered in evidence, may, and sometimes does, wreck the prosecution. The practice exemplified by this and other recent cases in substance puts the suspect in much the same position as if he had been arrested, while depriving him of the privileges and safeguards which are extended by the statute and the decisions to an accused person who has been apprehended. The police have, of course, the right and the duty to produce all the incriminating evidence they can lay their hands on, from whatever source they may legitimately derive the clue which leads to its discovery, so long as any admission or confession by the accused is not elicited before the jury as an element in proof of guilt. The matter may be put in another way. The accused cannot be compelled to give evidence at his trial and to submit to cross-examination. If it were competent for the police at their own hand to subject the accused to interrogation and cross-examination and to adduce evidence of what he said, the prosecution would in effect be making the accused a compellable witness, and laying before the jury, at second hand evidence which could not be adduced at first hand, even subject to all the precautions which are available for the protection of the accused at a criminal trial.

In expressing the above views I am only reiterating principles which have been stated and restated in over a score of decisions in the last eighty or ninety years. All these cases turned upon their own facts (as every case of this kind must inevitably do); but there are numerous dicta of high authority, which latterly founded upon the principle of 'fairness' as the ultimate test of the propriety or otherwise of admitting self-incriminating evidence of the type here in question. In Alison on Criminal Law, vol. ii. p.584, there is a singularly apt passage which was founded upon by the appellant as negativing the admissibility of the evidence about the cornfield. So long ago as 1842 Lord Justice-Clerk Hope observed (*Martin* 1842 1 Broun 382) that 'it is not the duty of a criminal officer to act as the examination of prisoners'; and in 1858 Lord Justice-Clerk Inglis said (*Hay* 3 Irv. 181: 'When a person is under suspicion of a crime it is not proper to put questions, and receive answers, except before a magistrate.' In *Hodgson v. Macpherson* (1913 S.C. 68) Lord Kinnear said: 'A criminal officer is not entitled to examine a person suspected of a crime in order to obtain confessions or admissions from the criminal, and so in fact to obtain from him what is to serve the purpose of a declaration without giving him the protection of the magistrate, before whom alone declarations have to be taken.' In *Costello* (1922 J.C. 9) Lord Justice-Clerk Scott Dickson drew a distinction between the truly voluntary or spontaneous statement and statements elicited by cross-questioning by the police; and the same distinction was central to the decision in *Waddell v. Kinnaird* (1922 J.C. 40) where the earlier authorities are reviewed. There are numerous recent illustrations of these principles to which I need not refer.

There is one final matter which merits consideration. In this case, following certain precedents (such as *Cunningham* (1939 J.C. 61)), the presiding Judge excluded the jury during the argument as to the admissibility of the evidence as regards the cornfield, but took the evidence as to the circumstances attending the interrogation in the police station and its sequel in the cornfield in the presence and hearing of the jury. In my view, this course is open to objection and should no longer be followed. In some cases (of which the present is an instance) such a course not only unduly ties the hands of counsel in examining and cross-examining the witnesses, but almost inevitably leads to the disclosure to the jury, directly or by inference, of matters which ought to be withheld from their knowledge. When objection is taken to a line of evidence based upon the alleged unfairness of the methods used in eliciting it, the jury ought to be excluded, and the evidence bearing upon the attendant circumstances should be heard by the Judge in the absence of the jury, including, if so advised, the evidence of the accused himself. If, in the light of such evidence and argument, the Judge sustains the objection, the jury should be told nothing about the matter. If on the other hand the Judge repels the objection, the case will proceed in the presence and hearing of the jury, and, if either prosecution or defence choose to do so, the evidence bearing upon the attendant circumstances can be made the subject of examination and cross-examination a second time. In the end of the day it will be for the judge to direct the jury that, in considering the weight and value of the evidence to which objection has been taken and repelled, it is for the jury to have regard to the attendant circumstances as proved before them, and, in so far as they may consider that the evidence objected to is not to be relied upon by reason of the circumstances in which it arose, to discount it or exclude it from their deliberations. I recognise that this procedure may give rise to difficulty and may not always achieve the desired ideal of avoiding prejudice to the accused. But it will at least minimise the risk of such prejudice to an extent unattainable by our past practice. In a murder trial the jury, being enclosed, will hear nothing of evidence which the presiding Judge has ruled to be inadmissible. In other types of cases the jury may acquire information through the medium of the Press; and all that can be done in such cases is to request the Press not to report the matter pending the conclusion of the trial, and to warn the jury to refrain from discussing the case with others, and from reading newspaper reports, during any overnight adjournment. I have had an opportunity of considering the supplementary opinion of the Lord Justice-Clerk and I concur with it.

As regards the present appeal, I am of the opinion, as already announced, that the conviction must be quashed."

NOTES

1. An accused person is never bound to give evidence at his or her own trial. However, incriminating statements made by an accused person are admissible when led by the Crown, even although they are hearsay of the accused. The rationale for this exception to the hearsay rule is that, in general, statements made against one's own interests are assumed to be reliable. However, a statement which incriminates another accused, and which was made outwith the presence of that other accused, is not admissible against the other accused, even if the statement forms part of the *res gestae*—see *Hamill v. H.M.A.*, 1999 S.L.T. 963, and Chapter 7. The only exception to this is where the Crown have proved that the accused were acting in concert.

2. *Chalmers* is the *locus classicus* in this area of the law. It is a case which has had a tremendous influence on the law relating to confessions, and has recently undergone a startling rehabilitation in at least two important respects, following a period during which the High Court seemed intent on "gutting" it (Finnie, 1982 S.L.T. (News) 289).
   (i) In *Thompson v. Crowe*, 1999 S.L.T. 1434, below, the so-called "trial within a trial" inaugurated by Lord Cooper in *Chalmers* was revived, and the case of *Balloch v. H.M.A.*, 1977 J.C. 23 overruled.
   (ii) In *Hartley v. H.M.A.*, 1979 S.L.T. 26 and *Lord Advocate's Reference No. 1 of 1983*, 1984 S.L.T. 337 it was held that vigorous questioning was allowed in spite of the prohibition in *Chalmers* on "cross-examination". The case of *Codona v. H.M.A.*, 1996 S.C.C.R. 300, appears to modify this view somewhat, and re-emphasises that where "questioning is carried too far, by means of leading or repetitive questioning or by pressure in other ways in an effort to obtain from the suspect what they are seeking to

obtain from him, the statement is likely to be excluded on the ground that it was extracted by unfair means." This is particularly so where, as in *Codona*, "the suspect, due to age or mental impairment or other disability, may be vulnerable under police questioning." The appellant in *Codona* was 14 years old. She was questioned for a prolonged period and finally made certain incriminating statements. Ruling that those statements were inadmissible, the court noted that:

"It is clear from the transcript that the two policewomen engaged in a prolonged cross examination of the appellant, during which both officers were putting questions to her, often one after the other before answers were obtained. Despite numerous denials that she had kicked the deceased—we have counted 19 such denials between pp.51 and 68 of the transcript—she was questioned repeatedly on that issue. She was told repeatedly that her negative response to these questions was contrary to information in the possession of the police officers. We have the clear impression from what is recorded in the transcript that the questioning was designed to persuade the appellant to change her answers and to admit to what was being put to her. In the event it was only at a late stage, more then three hours after the start of the interview when she had been crying and was clearly at her most vulnerable, that the answers were obtained from her upon which the Crown case depends."

3. In relation to other forms of vulnerability see *Gilgannon v. H.M.A.*, 1983 S.C.C.R. 10, in which a statement was excluded because it appeared that the accused's mental state was such that he was unable to give a coherent, complete and accurate account of events. *Gilgannon* was distinguished in the case of *Higgins v. H.M.A.*, 1993 S.C.C.R. 542 in which it was said that a statement made by someone who is mentally ill or disturbed may still be admissible if the accused had an "insight into what was going on". Certain other factors may render statements inadmissible even if voluntary. Age is one factor, as in *Codona* and *H.M.A. v. B.*, 1991 S.C.C.R. 533 (Sh.Ct.). Another may be the influence of drink or drugs. In *Thomson v. H.M.A.*, 1989 S.L.T. 170 it was argued that the accused had been so drunk when he made a voluntary statement to the police that the statement should be disregarded. Lord Justice-Clerk Ross said that in this case there was no evidence that the accused was "out the game with drink" or that at the time the statement was made the accused "did not know what he was saying". Does this imply that the accused was simply not drunk enough?

4. It should be noted, however, that the "fairness test" has itself been modified so as to include considerations of fairness to the public interest as well as to the accused—*Miln v. Cullen*, 1967 J.C. 21. While this may constitute a watering down of the principles expounded in *Chalmers*, it is arguable that the test remains consistent with the jurisprudence of the European Court of Human Rights on this matter—see *Brown v. Stott*, 2001 S.L.T. 59.

5. *Chalmers* sets out a graduated range of protection for an accused person or suspect, depending on the stage the investigative procedure has reached. The final stage mentioned by Lord Cooper in *Chalmers* was that occurring after arrest and charge, at which time, it seemed, all questioning must cease. However, this view has been modified by the High Court. It remains the law that after an accused has been *charged* with an offence—and on the basis of *Tonge v. H.M.A.*, 1982 S.C.C.R. 313, it seems that charge may be formal or informal—no further questioning is permitted in relation to *that* offence, although questioning may be allowed in relation to other separate offences—see *Stark* and *Smith v. H.M.A.*, 1938 S.L.T. 516 and *Carmichael v. Boyd*, 1993 S.C.C.R. 751, below. But arrest and charge are different things and need not occur at the same time—see *Johnston v. H.M.A.*, 1994 S.L.T. 300. In an earlier case, *Murphy v. H.M.A.*, 1975 S.L.T. (Notes) 17, it was held that statements by a suspect were admissible even although he was by that stage a "chargeable suspect"—that is, there was enough evidence to justify charging him with the offences in respect of which he had been arrested. There is some suggestion in *Murphy*, however that the statements were given voluntarily and not as a result of questioning at all, which rather diminishes its value as an authority on the matter considered in *Johnston*. See, generally, and in particular, on *Murphy* in Gordon, "The Admissibility of Answers to Police Questioning in Scotland" in *Reshaping the Criminal Law*, P. Glazebrook, (ed.), 1978. *Murphy* does not appear to have been cited to the court in *Johnston*. Another case not apparently cited to the court in that case was *Fraser and Freer v. H.M.A.*, 1989 S.C.C.R. 82 which implied that, at least in some circumstances, questioning could continue even after a formal charge in relation to that matter had been made. What are the implications of the decision in *Johnston*? Does the decision expand police powers, particularly in relation to their power to detain the accused? For discussion, see Sheriff Gordon's commentary to the case in 1993 S.C.C.R. at p.707. Finally, on tape recording of

interviews, see *Lord Advocate's Reference (No. 1 of 1983)*, 1984 S.L.T. 337, and *Tunnicliffe v. H.M.A.*, 1991 S.C.C.R. 623.

6. It seems that there is no longer any general rule as to cautioning a suspect—*Pennycuick v. Lees*, 1992 S.C.C.R. 160; *Middler v. H.M.A.*, 1994 S.C.C.R. 838, considered further below.

7. It is clear that the question of admissibility is one which must be decided by the judge, and not left to the jury.

14. Thompson v. Crowe
1999 S.L.T. 1434

An accused person was tried on summary complaint on 10 charges of forcing open or entering motor vehicles and stealing articles from them. The Crown sought to lead evidence of answers given by the accused during a police interview. The accused objected to this evidence on the basis that it had been unfairly obtained, and moved the court to hold a trial within a trial as to the circumstances of the interview. The sheriff refused the motion and heard the evidence under reservation. The accused, who declined to give evidence, was convicted on nine charges and sought suspension on the ground that the procedure had been unfair as he had been unable to challenge fully the admissibility of the statement without requiring to answer questions, the answers to which might tend to incriminate him. The appeal was remitted to a full bench to review the law and practice relating to objections to the leading of evidence on extrajudicial admissions generally.

LORD JUSTICE-GENERAL (RODGER):

Judge's role in determining admissibility

"The present law on the admission of evidence about extrajudicial confessions is encapsulated in a passage from the opinion of Lord Justice Clerk Wheatley in *Balloch v. H.M.A.*, 1977 J.C. at p.28; 1977 S.L.T. (Notes) p.30): Suffice to say, a Judge who has heard the evidence regarding the manner in which a challenged statement was made will normally be justified in withholding the evidence from the jury only if he is satisfied on the undisputed relevant evidence that no reasonable jury could hold that the statement had been voluntarily made and had not been extracted by unfair or improper means.

The stages by which the law developed until it reached this formulation can be easily traced in cases such as *Miln v. Cullen, Thompson v. H.M.A.* and *Murphy v. H.M.A.* Once uttered, Lord Wheatley's formula soon swept all before it, being reflected, for instance, in the *extempore* ruling of Lord Cameron in *H.M.A. v. Whitelaw* before being applied in *Tonge v. H.M.A.* and (without specific attribution) in *Lord Advocate's Reference No. 1* of 1983. It is within the personal knowledge of all the members of the court that the *Balloch* test has been used repeatedly in courts throughout the country for many years. Its most notable feature perhaps is that under it the judge's power to withhold evidence from the jury is very circumscribed and the real decision on whether the jury are entitled to take account of the evidence in question is left for the jury themselves.

The success which has attended Lord Wheatley's test is doubtless due in part at least to the fact that it appears at first sight to combine the twin virtues of simplicity and elegance. But on the complainer's behalf counsel set out to show that these virtues are specious, concealing a profound error: in *Balloch* the court had abdicated to the jury what was in truth the historic and peculiar duty of the court to determine issues of the competence and admissibility of evidence, in particular the admissibility of evidence of extrajudicial confessions. In performing that duty the judges had been used to deciding issues of fact and to making judgments which were nowadays, wrongly, left to the jury.

So far as history is concerned, even the most casual reader of the works of Hume and Alison must have paused from time to time to marvel at the array of over subtle and exotic objections—infamy, relationship, enmity and partial counsel, and interest and undue influence—which once could be stated to the admission of witnesses. This whole catalogue was to be swept away in the reforming statutes of the 1850s but, while they flourished, such objections were often pressed by counsel, in the hope of excluding a potentially damaging witness. Questions of fact could and did arise in connection with such objections and appropriate evidence had to be led. For instance, of the conviction of a crime inferring infamy (Alison on Criminal Law, ii, 443–444) and as to whether a witness had attempted to suborn three other witnesses or had been guilty of some officious conduct (Alison on Criminal Law, ii, 487). Similarly, where questions were raised as to the mental infirmity of a proposed witness, Alison on Criminal Law, ii, 436 describes it as being 'the province of the Court alone, to decide upon an objection of this description, as upon every other matter which relates to the admissibility of or legal objection to testimony. When, therefore, the objection of insanity or idiocy is stated, it is their duty to proceed to take the evidence that may be offered, and either to admit the witness, reject him, or admit him *cum nota*, as the justice of the case may seem to require'.

The rule was that objections of these kinds had to be stated before the witness was sworn and there was then an examination *in initialibus*. The passages which I have selected, almost at random, from Alison—which could be matched with passages from Hume—demonstrate that, if the objection was relevant, a proof was held and the court determined the issue in the light of the evidence.

Although almost all traces of these procedures have vanished from our law, I mention them to underscore the point that in the first half of the nineteenth century there was nothing unusual in the presiding judges at a criminal trial hearing evidence on questions of fact in order to determine whether a witness was admissible. [His Lordship then reviewed the nineteenth century cases and continued.]

That the intertwined factual and legal questions relating to admissibility remained the exclusive province of the court 40 years later is apparent from *H.M.A. v. Aitken*, a murder case involving an appellant aged about 17. Objection was taken to the admission of evidence about a statement which the appellant gave to a police officer. The police officer was examined and cross examined on the circumstances. This was done in the presence of the jury: neither in the report nor in the minute book nor in the minute of proceedings is there anything to suggest that the jury were excluded. Once the evidence was out, it appears that only one aspect of the circumstances remained controversial. In deciding to uphold the objection and to exclude the statement, Lord Anderson applied the test as stated by the advocate depute in the case: 'whether it would be fair in the circumstances of the accused person to admit the evidence of the statement as evidence'. There is not the slightest indication that Lord Anderson considered that the jury had any role whatever to play in determining the admissibility of the evidence about the statement. His approach was commended by the distinguished editor of Renton and Brown, "Criminal Procedure" (2nd ed. 1928), p.271, n.9.

In *H.M.A. v. Rigg*, Lord Justice Clerk Cooper, sitting as a trial judge, applied the test formulated by Lord Anderson in *Aitken*, in deciding whether to admit evidence of a statement by the appellant to a police officer. Again the case concerned a young man on trial for murder. When the statement had been taken, he had been in the police station for some hours. The Crown led evidence of the circumstances leading up to the statement and defence counsel then objected to evidence of its terms being received, on the ground that it would not be fair to admit it. Lord Cooper sustained the objection and disallowed the evidence, the critical passage in his decision being in these terms (1946 J.C., p.4; 1946 S.L.T., p.49):

'Now, what happened? As I have observed, one statement had been taken in the afternoon, and a second—a long statement and a detailed statement—by the superintendent about 7 p.m. I have looked at the third statement now objected to with a view to acquainting myself with its general characteristics, and I find that it is in substance a detailed precognition of the accused, extending to upwards of 700 words, and giving a coherent and elaborate account of his movements and of the relevant facts of the preceding day and the day in question, with numerous references to persons, places, and hours. To my mind, it is quite incredible that such a statement could have been taken from any person, least of all from a person of the age and apparent experience and condition of the accused, as a truly spontaneous and voluntary statement in the sense in which that expression has been used in the decisions, or without such interrogation as would in common experience be indispensable to the taking of such a detailed precognition.

The ultimate test to be applied in determining questions of this kind is the test of fairness to the accused. Treating the matter not so much as one of technical competence as of the exercise of a just discretion in the light of the surrounding circumstances, so far as elicited, and of the inherent characteristics of the statement sought to be proved, I feel bound, in conformity to the principles of the decisions to which reference has been made, and particularly the case of *Aitken*, to sustain the objection and to disallow the evidence relating to this matter.'

The report of counsel's argument tends to suggest that they did not focus on the nature of the statement attributed to the appellant. This makes it all the more striking that Lord Cooper did. Plainly, he examined the statement and found, in the characteristics which he noticed, a sufficient basis for holding that it could not have been a truly spontaneous and voluntary statement of the kind which would have been admissible. Lord Cooper saw the decision on admissibility as very much one which he, as the judge, required to take himself, using his own appreciation of the circumstances and applying the law as he understood it. It is equally apparent that it never crossed his mind that, in doing so, he was in any sense guilty of usurping a function of the jury in the law of Scotland.

Other examples of trial judges deciding the issue of the admissibility of evidence of a statement by the accused, while leaving it to the jury to assess the weight to be attached to the statement emitted in the particular circumstances, can readily be found in the books. I mention *H.M.A. v. Lieser*; *H.M.A. v. Cunningham* and *H.M.A. v. Fox*. While the exact procedure adopted seems to have varied, the trial judge performs essentially the same role in each. The cases which I have cited paint a consistent picture, from the early nineteenth century through to the middle of the twentieth century, of trial judges taking legal decisions on the admissibility of evidence and of those judges, where necessary, hearing evidence on which they formed a view of the circumstances against which they required to determine the legal question. They also indicate that, although counsel made their submissions and the judge reached his decision on admissibility in the absence of the jury, the evidence bearing upon the point of admissibility was led in front of the jury who, in the event of the accused's statement being admitted, could take it into account in deciding what weight they attached to the statement.

Thus was the stage set for *Chalmers v. H.M.A.*, yet another murder trial in which the appellant was aged 16 at the time of the offence. [His Lordship then went on to state the facts of *Chalmers* and review the decisions taken on the various points at first instance and on the appeal.]

We are not, of course, concerned in this case with the merits of those decisions. It is noteworthy, however, that, having heard the evidence of the circumstances leading up to the events in the cornfield and the reply to caution and charge, Lord Strachan decided for himself the question of the admissibility of the evidence on those matters. Moreover, he clearly took the view that his decision to admit the evidence was a matter of law since he was comforted (1954 J.C., p.70; 1954 S.L.T., p.180) by the fact that, if he had erred in repelling the objection, his decision could be reviewed by the court of criminal appeal. Equally clearly, this court proceeded on the same footing in dealing with the appeal. Once more I detect no hint in this case that any of the judges considered that any aspect of the matter of admissibility could be one for determination by the jury.

During the course of the first hearing of the appeal in *Chalmers* the court allowed the appellant to add to his stated reasons of appeal a ground to the effect that evidence of the circumstances attending the disputed actings and statement had been heard in the presence of the jury before any ruling as to admissibility was given. The point was argued at the end of the submissions for the appellant at the hearing before the five judges. So it came about that, having disposed of the appeal, the Lord Justice General added a passage (pp.80–81 (p.185)) which was to become one of the most controversial statements in our law:

'There is one final matter which merits consideration. In this case, following certain precedents (such as *H.M.A. v. Cunningham*), the presiding Judge excluded the jury during the argument as to the admissibility of the evidence as regards the cornfield, but took the evidence as to the circumstances attending the interrogation in the police station and its sequel in the cornfield in the presence and hearing of the jury. In my view, this course is open to objection and should no longer be followed. In some cases (of which the present is an instance) such a course not only unduly ties the hands of counsel in examining and cross-examining witnesses, but almost inevitably leads to the disclosure to the jury, directly or by inference, of matters which ought to be withheld from their knowledge. When objection is taken to a line of evidence based upon the alleged unfairness of the methods used in eliciting it, the jury ought to be excluded, and the evidence bearing upon the attendant circumstances should be heard by the Judge in the absence of the jury, including, if so advised, the evidence of the accused himself. If, in the light of such evidence and argument, the Judge sustains the objection, the jury should be told nothing about the matter. If on the other hand the Judge repels the objection, the case will proceed in the presence and hearing of the jury, and, if either prosecution or defence choose to do so, the evidence bearing upon the attendant circumstances can be made the subject of examination and cross-examination a second time. In the end of the day it will be for the Judge to direct the jury that, in considering the weight and value of the evidence to which objection has been taken and repelled, it is for the jury to have regard to the attendant circumstances as proved before them, and, in so far as they may consider that the evidence objected to is not to be relied upon by reason of the circumstances in which it arose, to discount it or exclude it from their deliberations. I recognise that this procedure may give rise to difficulty and may not always achieve the desired ideal of avoiding prejudice to the accused. But it will at least minimise the risk of such prejudice to an extent unattainable by our past practice. In a murder trial the jury, being enclosed, will hear nothing of evidence which the presiding Judge has ruled to be inadmissible. In other types of cases the jury may acquire information through the medium of the Press; and all that can be done in such cases is to request the Press not to report the matter pending the conclusion of the trial, and to warn the jury to refrain from discussing the case with others, and from reading newspaper reports, during any overnight adjournment.'

Lord Cooper was concerned to make a procedural change which was intended to avoid possible prejudice to the defence if the evidence about the circumstances in which a statement had been made were led in front of the jury. In future, he said, that evidence should be led in the absence of the jury; similarly, the submissions on the evidence should be made, and the trial judge's decision should be announced, in the absence of the jury. If the judge upheld the defence objection, evidence of the contents of the statement would not be given. If he repelled the objection, the evidence of the circumstances in which the statement was made would be led again in front of the jury who would also, of course, hear the evidence of the statement itself. In deciding what weight, if any, to attach to the statement, when considering their verdict, the jury would be entitled to have regard to the evidence of the circumstances in which it had been made.

Part of the separate opinion of Lord Justice Clerk Thomson is also important for present purposes. Having dealt with the substantive point, he went on (pp. 82–83 (p.186)) to make some observations on the matter of procedure:

'The question of whether evidence is admissible is primarily for the presiding Judge. In the interests of fair trial the law has laid down certain rules as to the circumstances under which statements made by an accused are admissible, and it is for the Judge to say if these have been transgressed. In order to decide the question he may have to hear evidence of the circumstances under which the accused came to give the evidence to which objection is taken. What the Judge has to decide is whether the legal safeguards were observed, so that it can be said that the evidence was freely and voluntarily given. This evidence ought to be heard outwith the presence of the jury. Experience shows that if the jury is present some prejudice to the accused is likely to occur. If the Judge rejects the evidence, that is an end of the matter. If the Judge admits the evidence, what the accused said becomes an item of evidence to be weighed by the jury in relation to the other elements in the case. But it appears to follow that the defence cannot be prevented from putting before the jury the circumstances under which the statement was made. These circumstances, although, in the opinion of the Judge who admitted the evidence, they may be insufficient to show that the safeguards imposed by the law were disregarded, may nevertheless, in the jury's view of the case as a whole, detract from or modify or destroy the *ex facie* value of the statement. Nevertheless, the effect seems to be to hand the whole thing over to the jury. The Judge says no more than that, on what he has heard in evidence outwith the jury's presence, the accused's position was adequately safeguarded and his statement falls to be accepted as a voluntary one. The jury, on what evidence they hear, which may be less or more than the Judge had before him, have the duty of weighing the truth of the statement in relation to the evidence as a whole, but, once one so puts it, it becomes clear that they are entitled to consider whether it was freely and voluntarily given. The only logical alternative is to refuse to allow the defence to put before the jury the circumstances under which the statement was made. In that situation, the Judge would say to the jury: "In your absence I heard evidence on a legal point. I have now to tell you, and you are bound to take it from me, that the accused made a statement and he made it freely and voluntarily."

This seems to me to be a situation where logic must yield. It is impossible to ask a jury to accept as an item of evidence a statement made by an accused while preventing it from considering the circumstances under which it was made. As the circumstances under which a statement is made must include the relationship between the giver and the receiver, the questions asked and so forth, its value as evidence depends on the extent to which it was voluntarily and freely given. The jury's problem is to find out the truth; in their search for the truth a statement made freely by the accused may be of immense significance, but the degree of that significance must depend for the jury on their view of its spontaneity.'

Although *Chalmers* can be seen as making a distinct break with previous practice, it is vital to notice just how limited was the change which the court envisaged. The only difference in the new approach would be that in future the jury would be absent when the evidence about the circumstances surrounding a statement was led for the purpose of obtaining the trial judge's ruling on admissibility. The nature of the trial judge's role would, on the other hand, remain exactly the same: in other words, the judge was to continue to consider the circumstances revealed in the evidence and to decide whether the evidence about the statement should be admitted. This was indeed what happened, for instance, in the trial of Peter Manuel in 1958 where, as the Lord Justice General records, the *Chalmers* procedure was used and the trial judge, Lord Cameron, then ruled on the admissibility of statements made by him: *Manuel v. H.M.A.*, 1958 J.C., p.49; 1959 S.L.T., p.29). Similarly, the *Chalmers* procedure was used, for instance, in *Brown v. H.M.A.*

In *Chalmers* both Lord Cooper and Lord Thomson took the opportunity to make certain comments on the respective roles of the judge and the jury. Those comments, no doubt, gave expression to points which had occurred to the judges when they were considering the new procedure. But the respective roles of the judge and jury were not in substance changed under the new procedure: it had always been for the judge to determine the admissibility of the evidence of a statement and for the jury to determine the weight which they should give to it. Similarly, the circumstances surrounding the statement had always been relevant both to the matter of admissibility and to the matter of weight. In these respects nothing had changed. So the remarks of the Lord Justice Clerk would have been apposite even if the court had not decided to change the procedure. Nonetheless the aspect of the jury's role which he and Lord Cooper discussed was to prove important for the future development of the law.

The Lord Justice Clerk, whose discussion was the fuller and with whose views the other members of the court agreed, began by declaring that the question of the admissibility of evidence was 'primarily' for the judge and that the law had laid down 'rules' as to the circumstances in which a statement made by an accused was admissible. '[I]t is for the Judge to say if these have been transgressed'. That is the premise from which the Lord Justice Clerk begins. Moreover, when he says that questions of admissibility of evidence are 'primarily' for the trial judge, he is not suggesting that, as a technical matter, questions of the admissibility of evidence ever become a matter for the jury. Rather, as the rest of the passage makes clear, the Lord Justice Clerk was simply recognising that, where the judge allowed the statement to go to the jury because he considered that it had been freely and voluntarily given, the jury would be likely to have to consider the same issue of the free and voluntary nature of the statement when considering what weight, if any, to attach to it. In reality, both the judge and the jury would be considering the same question—the judge in order to decide whether evidence of the statement was admissible, the jury in order to decide what weight to attach to it. The Lord Justice Clerk rejected the idea that the trial judge could impose his view on the jury by giving them a direction to the effect that the statement had been given freely and voluntarily: the jury had to be free to consider that matter for themselves and, in that sense, 'the effect seems to be to hand the whole thing over to the jury'.

In making these observations the Lord Justice Clerk was doing nothing more than reflecting what had been the position in trials long before *Chalmers*. For instance, in *H.M.A. v. Fox*, Lord Moncrieff repelled a defence objection and allowed evidence of a statement to be led. At the time of his ruling he explained to the jury (1947 J.C., p.32; 1947 S.L.T., p.53) that: 'Ladies and gentlemen, this is a case where the decision as to law, which is mine, and the decision as to facts, which is yours, rather interact on one another. Please understand that, in what I have said, I have only decided that the statement has not yet been shown to be other than competent as evidence. It is only available as evidence, though competent, if you decide the question of fairness in favour of the police. If you hold, as a matter of fact, that, although competent to have it before you, it is tainted by such unfairness as results from undue pressure or undue inducement, or from concealment of a right to be advised, then these are questions of fact for you. Please understand that, while the statement is before you, it is for you to give it or to refuse to give it a value; I do not give it a value, I only let it come before you so that you may value it.'

In his charge to the jury Lord Moncrieff, having referred to the failure of the police to tell the accused that he was entitled to be advised by a solicitor, said (p.32 (p.53)): 'I do not think, however, that, having in view the complete intelligence, the adult age of the accused, and the general tenor of the events which preceded his arrest and the events which followed, that circumstance alone is likely to induce you to hold that the statement was unfairly taken. Still you must have the circumstance in view and give it such value as you think right.'

In these passages Lord Moncrieff is at pains to explain to the jury that, while he has reached a view, for the purposes of admissibility, on the issue of whether the statement was unfairly taken, the issue remains at large for the jury when they are considering what value to give to the statement. Doubtless, trial judges had long been in the habit of charging juries along these lines, but, despite this, the fact that the issue of voluntariness or fairness would often come to be considered by the jury was seized upon by the court subsequently, when the new procedure in *Chalmers* proved unpopular and the court was considering how questions of admissibility should be handled.

The test of admissibility

For *Chalmers* did indeed prove unpopular with the judges. Their views surfaced in a considered *obiter* passage in the opinion of the court delivered by Lord Justice General Clyde in *Thompson v. H.M.A.*, 1968 J.C., p.66; 1968 S.L.T., pp.341–342:

'We should add that the trial within a trial procedure laid down in *Chalmers v. Lord Advocate*, which was followed in this case, was an innovation in the law of Scotland in 1954. Experience has shown that it has several undesirable features. Apart from the repetition of evidence (first before the judge alone, and then before the jury) with the consequent addition to the length of time occupied by the trial, it affords an opportunity for the reconstruction of evidence for the second trial after the witnesses have seen how they are cross-examined in the first one. Moreover the jury in the second trial have no opportunity of testing the consistency of the evidence in the two trials, because they are not present at the first one, whereas the judge is, although he cannot properly disclose the inconsistencies to the jury. It seems unfair to both sides that the judge should be put in a stronger position than the jury to decide on a matter where the ultimate responsibility for deciding rests exclusively with the jury.

It appears that the procedure laid down in *Chalmers* case may have to be reconsidered, particularly as these trials within trials are increasing in number. It would be unfortunate if the law of Scotland in regard to confessions were to reach the stage it reached in England, which induced Parke B. in *Reg. v. Baldry* (1852) 2 Den. C.C. 430 to say (at p.445): "I confess that I cannot look at the decisions without some shame when I consider what objections have prevailed to prevent the reception of confessions in evidence . . . justice and common sense have, too frequently, been sacrificed at the shrine of mercy." If the question is whether the confession has been freely and voluntarily given—and that is usually the question—and if, as seems clear, the jury must have an opportunity of determining whether the confession was fairly obtained, in cases where the confession is part of the Crown evidence in the trial, it seems difficult to justify a separate trial on this matter before the judge alone as well. It would seem that there is much to be said for leading the evidence once and for all before the jury. If the judge takes the view that the Crown has not led evidence that the confession was freely and voluntarily given, he can at the end of the day direct the jury to disregard the evidence on the confession, or, if the Crown case is otherwise insufficient, he may direct them to return a verdict of not guilty. But if he considers that the confession was freely and voluntarily given, then he leaves the matter to the jury. Time would be saved and the interests of the accused would be quite adequately safeguarded in this way. Until the decision in *Chalmers* is to be reconsidered, however, the present trial within a trial procedure would appear to have to go on.'

On analysis the passage contains two distinct elements which tend perhaps to be run together but which must be kept distinct.

The first is the view that the practice of holding a trial within a trial does not work well—it involves evidence being led twice, with the result that trials take longer; evidence which is given before the judge and is the subject of cross examination may be altered in the light of that cross examination when subsequently given before the jury and the judge cannot tell the jury this; the judge is therefore put in a better position to assess the evidence than the jury whose responsibility it actually is to do so. These are perceived disadvantages of the system of holding a trial within a trial—the quotation from *Baldry* relates to the substance of decisions and therefore appears out of place. If the desire of the court had merely been to eliminate those disadvantages, then all that would have been required would have been for the court to reconsider *Chalmers* and to indicate that the practice which had existed before *Chalmers* should be followed: in other words, the trial judge should hear any evidence relating to admissibility in the presence of the jury and then, in the absence of the jury, hear submissions and decide the question.

But it is clear that the thinking of the court had gone further. It is this new thinking which constitutes the second element in the passage. The Lord Justice General is hinting at quite a different scheme in which 'the evidence' would be led once and for all before the jury. But, crucially, by 'the evidence' Lord Clyde means the evidence including the terms of the accused's statement. So, under this scheme, all the evidence about the circumstances in which the statement was given and about its terms would be led in front of the jury. At the end of the case, if the judge took the view that the Crown had not led evidence that the statement had been freely and voluntarily given, then, depending on the other available evidence, he could either 'direct the jury to disregard the evidence on the confession' or direct them to acquit the accused. If on the other hand he considered that the confession had been freely and voluntarily given, then he would leave the matter to the jury—presumably to consider what weight should be attached to it. The justification for adopting such an approach is said to lie in the fact that, even under the existing (*Chalmers*) approach, the jury required to consider whether a statement had been freely and voluntarily given. If the jury had to consider that issue and if the question of admissibility depended on it, the court saw little advantage in a trial within a trial and much to be said for simply leading all the evidence before the jury.

The Lord Justice General is in effect contemplating a seismic shift in the law—from a system, whether pre or post *Chalmers*, under which the admissibility of a statement is determined by the judge before the Crown leads it to a system under which the 'admissibility' of a statement is determined by the judge after its terms are given to the jury. Any such change really empties the concept of admissibility of all content since evidence which has been led before the jury has by definition been admitted and cannot be unadmitted. All that the judge can do, if it turns out that the statement was not freely and voluntarily given, is to direct the jury to disregard it.

Although the court thought that no such scheme could be introduced unless *Chalmers* were reconsidered, this proved to be unduly pessimistic. These *obiter* reflections in *Thompson* were in fact the original blueprint for the substantially similar system which in effect came into existence as a result of Lord Wheatley's opinion in *Balloch*. The change did not occur overnight. The trial within a trial procedure continued to be used—for example, in *Murphy v. H.M.A.* and, most notably, in *Balloch* itself. Nevertheless the practice of the court did change: in *Balloch* counsel for the appellant referred to 'the present practice of leaving it to the jury to decide if a confession was fairly elicited' and said that it was 'open to challenge'. That challenge was firmly rejected by the court.

The appellant in *Balloch* had been convicted of murder, part of the Crown case being evidence of a confession which he had made to police officers. The trial judge, without the jury, heard the evidence of the circumstances in which the appellant had made the confession and ruled that it was admissible. As can be seen from the report of the argument and from the account in the Lord Justice Clerk's opinion, the submission that the confession evidence should be excluded depended on the supposed combined effect of a number of elements in the circumstances leading up to the moment when the appellant broke down and made the incriminating statement. Lord Wheatley records (1977 J.C., pp.27–28) that the advocate depute put a different picture of the relevant circumstances and finished by arguing that 'In all these circumstances it could not be said that no reasonable jury could hold that the statement "I did it for Marion's sake" had been fairly and properly obtained, and accordingly the trial Judge had properly left the question of fairness, subject to proper directions thereon, to the jury.'

It was against this background that the court rejected the argument for the appellant. The court's reasoning was explained by the Lord Justice Clerk (at p.28; 1977 S.L.T. (Notes), p.30):

> 'The law on this subject has been canvassed in many cases, some of them very recent, such as *Jones v. Milne*, 1975 S.L.T. 2; *Murphy v. H.M.A.*, 1975 S.L.T. (Notes) 17; and *Miln v. Cullen*, 1967 J.C. 21; and we find it unnecessary to rehearse the trend of these authorities. Suffice to say, a Judge who has heard the evidence regarding the manner in which a challenged statement was made will normally be justified in withholding the evidence from the jury only if he is satisfied on the undisputed evidence that no reasonable jury could hold that the statement had been voluntarily made and had not been extracted by unfair or improper means. Applying the test to the instant case, we are of the opinion that, to say the least, the question was so open that the trial Judge acted perfectly correctly in allowing the issue to go to the jury for their determination. That having been done, it is not suggested that proper directions were not given to the jury by the Judge. In point of fact the Judge's directions to the jury on this point were wholly in consistence with the law that has been laid down.
>
> Counsel for the applicant made the somewhat startling proposition that in any event a Judge should be reluctant to remit such a question to the jury because of the difficulty of a jury understanding what is involved in unfairness. That proposition not only flies in the face of the test which the Judge has to apply in deciding whether the evidence should be admitted to or excluded from the jury, but would appear to desiderate that the Judge should usurp the function of the jury in what *ex hypothesi* has become a question of fact.'

Since this passage really lays down the current law, it deserves careful scrutiny. First, the court still envisages, in theory at least, that a trial judge may actually be called upon to rule on the admissibility of a statement before the jury hear evidence of its terms, since Lord Wheatley describes the limited circumstances in which the judge will be 'justified in withholding the evidence from the jury'. Secondly, whereas under the old law the judge considered 'whether it would be fair in the circumstances of the accused person to admit the statement as evidence'

(*Aitken* at p.86 (p.311)) and withheld the evidence if he considered that it would not be fair to admit it, here the court changes the emphasis so that a trial judge is not justified in withholding evidence except in particular circumstances. Thirdly, whereas under the *Aitken* test the judge decides whether the statement has been given fairly and voluntarily and so can properly be admitted, under the formulation in this passage—which develops the reasoning in *Thompson*—the judge does not decide that issue at all: he merely decides whether any reasonable jury could hold that the statement had been voluntarily made and had not been extracted by unfair or improper means. Finally, whereas under the old procedure the judge had to decide admissibility even if the evidence on the issue was disputed, under the new approach the judge can withhold the statement only if the evidence of the surrounding circumstances is 'undisputed'. Since in the majority of cases the evidence will be disputed, this test means that in practice a trial judge will usually have to allow evidence of the statement to be led. As a well informed commentator on the decision observed, on this approach there was little necessity for the procedure by way of a trial within a trial ("A Question of Fairness", 1977 S.L.T. (News) 141 at p.142). Not surprisingly, that procedure soon fell into virtual desuetude.

The transformation in our law which *Thompson* and *Balloch* effected is remarkable by any standard. Particularly remarkable is the fact that it occurred without *Chalmers* or any of the long line of cases which preceded it ever being overruled. The result has been to create a somewhat strange legal landscape. The general rule is that evidence of a statement by an accused is admissible if a reasonable jury could consider that it had been voluntarily made and had not been extracted by unfair or improper means; but every so often one comes across outcrops of an older, different, approach. So, for instance, if the accused has been arrested on a charge and a police officer subsequently asks him a question relating to the matter, the answer is regarded as inadmissible (*Wade v. Robertson*). In this area the general rule does not apply: the judge cannot simply allow the evidence of the answer to go to the jury and direct them to consider whether it was voluntarily made and not extracted by unfair or improper means—as they might conclude, perhaps, if they heard a tape recording of a quietly conducted interview in which the police officers posed a number of questions and the accused person gave considered answers. In truth, as Lord Justice Clerk Thomson explained in *Chalmers*, cases like *Wade* contain rules of law laid down by the judges as to the circumstances in which evidence of a confession is admissible and it is the duty of the judge to say if those rules have been transgressed. Such legal rules prescribed by judges are manifestations of the pre-*Balloch* approach, which regards the judge rather than the jury as having the primary responsibility for deciding in what circumstances evidence of a confession by the accused can properly be taken into account by the jury.

The success of the new approach in sweeping away the old is at first sight surprising but can perhaps be accounted for. As I observed at the outset, the formula used by the Lord Justice Clerk in *Balloch* is both brief and elegant. It is therefore easily absorbed, easily remembered and easily applied. Equally importantly perhaps, the approach may be attractive to judges, since in most cases it relieves them of the need to decide what can be crucial questions of admissibility and passes those questions to the jury to answer. Moreover, decisions on admissibility do indeed sometimes involve decisions on controversial matters of fact. So it can be argued that it is more in keeping with the spirit of a system of trial by jury for the jury to decide, having looked at the facts, whether they should consider the confession as part of the evidence against the accused. Lord Cameron made exactly this point both extrajudicially ("Scottish Practice in relation to admissions and confessions by persons suspected or accused of crime", 1977 S.L.T. (News) 265 at p.267) and judicially in *H.M.A. v. Whitelaw*, 1980 S.L.T. (Notes) at p.26, in a passage which was incorrectly transcribed and should read: 'Now since the case of *Chalmers* there has been growing a feeling that, as it is both the right and the duty of the jury to hear and pass judgment on all the relevant evidence, evidence as to statements of a possibly incriminating character alleged to have been made by an accused person is prima facie of the highest relevance and the jury's function should not be in fact usurped and, unless it is abundantly clear that the rules of fairness and fair dealing have been flagrantly transgressed, it would be better for a jury seised of the whole evidence in the case and of all the circumstances, under such guidance as they should receive from the presiding judge, themselves to take that decision as to the extent to which, if at all, they will take into account evidence of statements given by a suspect after due caution.'

With this we reach what is really the heart of the matter. In the course of the argument before us the advocate depute came to recognise that there had indeed been a change in the approach of the court in *Balloch*. He maintained, however, that the new approach was preferable, precisely because, in a system of trial by jury, in principle matters of fact should be determined by the jury and not by the judge, who should simply deal with matters of law. He acknowledged that this principle could not be regarded as absolute since in section 259 of the Criminal Procedure (Scotland) Act 1995 ('the 1995 Act') Parliament had specifically provided for certain matters of fact, relating to the admissibility of hearsay evidence, to be decided by the trial judge on the balance of probabilities (s.259(8)). Nonetheless for the first day of his submissions the advocate depute's position was that the court should uphold the principle by affirming the law as laid down in *Balloch*.

Although it would be wrong to deny the apparent attractions of such an argument, it is in fact fundamentally unsound. What the judge is being asked to decide is whether evidence of a statement by the accused is admissible—in other words whether evidence of that statement can be led before the jury. It is a logical impossibility to answer that question by first leading the evidence and then directing the jury as to the basis upon which they should either disregard it or take it into account. It follows that, by definition, the question of admissibility is one for the judge rather than for the jury and, if the judge requires to determine issues of fact in order to answer that question, then the determination of those issues of fact is a matter properly falling within the area of responsibility of the judge.

The problem is in no sense peculiar to Scots law. Precisely the same problem must arise in any system of trial by jury where decisions have to be taken about admitting or excluding evidence. In *Ajodha v. The State*, in an appeal to the Privy Council from Trinidad and Tobago, Lord Bridge observed ([1982] A.C., pp.220–221):

> 'It has to be remembered that the rule requiring the judge to be satisfied that an incriminating statement by the accused was given voluntarily before deciding that it is admissible in evidence is anomalous in that it puts the judge in a position where he must make his own findings of fact and thus creates an inevitable overlap between the fact-finding functions of judge and jury. In a simple case, where the sole issue is whether the statement, admittedly made by the accused, was voluntary or not, it is a commonplace that the judge first decides that issue himself, having heard evidence on the voir dire, normally in the absence of the jury. If he rules in favour of admissibility, the jury will then normally hear exactly the same evidence and decide essentially the same issue albeit not as a test of admissibility but as a criterion of the weight and value, if any, of the statement as evidence of the guilt of the accused.'

Although the criteria of admissibility in Scots law may be different, the statement of Lord Bridge describes, exactly, the respective roles of the judge and jury as they are described in the older Scottish authorities. In my view the overlap in the fact finding function is indeed, as Lord Bridge says, inevitable and must be accepted in any system if, like Scots law, it attaches importance to the principle that only legally admissible evidence should be placed before the jury.

This principle is itself no more than one aspect of the long established wider principle of Scots law and many kindred systems, that an accused person has a right to a fair trial. It follows also that, although they may be minimised, any inherent disadvantages of this necessary procedure for determining admissibility must be accepted—in particular the possible need for the judge to reach a view on the credibility of an accused who gives evidence on the point.

The main defect in the approach enshrined in *Balloch* has already been noted: in effect it robs the concept of the admissibility of evidence of all real content in those cases where evidence of the statement is actually admitted and the jury are told that it is for them to decide whether they can take it into account. But another important consequence of the approach is that the court no longer takes responsibility for decisions on admissibility except in the most extreme case where the only possible reasonable view is that the evidence is inadmissible. In all other cases the jury are left to decide whether they can have regard to the evidence and to do so on the basis of their view as to whether the statement was freely and voluntarily given or extracted by unfair or improper means. The effect—and indeed the intended effect—of this approach is that, even if the trial judge considers on undisputed facts that a statement was obtained by unfair or improper means, the judge must still allow the evidence of that statement to go before the jury if he also considers that a reasonable jury could hold that the means had not been unfair or improper. This approach greatly diminishes the power of the judge to ensure that the accused has a fair trial. Nor can any damage readily be put right by the appeal court since, as is apparent in *Balloch*, the test means that the court cannot and will not intervene unless it can be said that no reasonable jury could have held that the means had not been unfair or improper—in other words that the trial judge had erred in allowing evidence of the statement to be led before the jury. Although an appeal can sometimes succeed even on that exacting standard (for example, *Codona v. H.M.A.*, especially at 1996 S.C.C.R., p.321C; 1996 S.L.T., p.1105F), the appeal court has no more scope than the trial judge for determining the admissibility of the statement in such a case. Therefore, even if all three judges regard it as having been extracted by unfair or improper means and consider that it should not have been admitted, they ought not to quash the conviction unless they can say that no reasonable jury could reach a different view. Not only does such a system make it harder to do justice in an individual case, but it also means that the courts cannot develop meaningful rules for having the issue determined consistently—making it at best difficult for them to fulfil a basic requirement of justice, that like cases should be treated alike.

The test prescribed in *Balloch* suffers from another serious drawback: it distorts the procedure by which the accused has a right to make a submission of no case to answer at the end of the Crown case—under section 97 of the 1995 Act in solemn proceedings and under section 160 in summary proceedings. This procedure was not introduced into our law until the Criminal Justice (Scotland) Act 1980 (s.19), and so the judges in *Balloch* could not have foreseen this particular consequence of their approach. By their terms, section 97 and section 160 require the judge to determine whether 'the evidence led by the prosecution is insufficient in law to justify the accused being convicted'. Although this is not spelled out, the proper basis for determining the sufficiency of evidence in a jury trial must be the evidence which the jury are entitled to take into account—the evidence led by the Crown which is legally admissible. Under the present system, however, evidence is admitted and led on behalf of the Crown and the decision on whether the jury can lawfully take it into account is postponed, not being taken until the jury come to consider their verdict. In determining the defence submission of no case to answer the judge may therefore require to include as part of the evidence for the Crown a statement which he himself would have regarded as extracted by unfair means and as inadmissible but which he had nonetheless been unable to withhold in terms of the *Balloch* test. Moreover, it may be evidence which the jury will in due course require to leave out of account because they too regard it as having been extracted by unfair means. As a result the judge may have to conclude that the Crown has led sufficient evidence in a case where, had he determined the issue of admissibility himself and excluded the accused's statement, the Crown would have been left with insufficient evidence and the judge would have upheld the defence submission. In the words of Lord Justice Clerk Ross in *Runham v. Westwater*, 1995 S.C.C.R. at p.360 (1995 S.L.T., p.837), the accused is thus 'deprived of the right conferred upon him' under section 97. The accused's right under that section can be vindicated only if the decision on the admissibility of evidence in a jury trial is taken, as it should be, when the Crown attempts to lead the evidence in question, with the result that the Crown case comprises only legally admissible evidence and the judge can uphold or reject the defence submission on the basis of that admissible evidence.

For these reasons I am satisfied that the rule in *Balloch* is unsatisfactory and should not be applied. Indeed the advocate depute eventually accepted that it could not stand unamended; he therefore suggested certain refinements which I consider—and reject—below. In my view the correct course is for the court to overrule *Balloch* and to revert to the previous law as it applied in Scotland up to the time of *Chalmers*. In doing so, Scots law will once more accord to the judiciary in full measure the power to exclude statements obtained by improper methods, a power which has been regarded as a necessary hallmark of any civilised system of criminal jurisprudence (*Wong Kam-Ming v. The Queen* [1980] A.C. at p.261 per Lord Hailsham of St Marylebone). Once again, accordingly, it will be for the trial judge to decide questions of the admissibility of the evidence of statements by the accused, just as it is for the trial judge to decide all other questions of admissibility. The decision will depend, of course, on the facts of the particular case and, where there are conflicts in the evidence about the circumstances, it will be for the trial judge to resolve those conflicts and so to settle the factual basis upon which to take the decision. The judge will exclude the statement if it was taken in circumstances which render it inadmissible under any rule laid down by the law. In other cases the judge will admit the statement if the Crown satisfies the court that it would be fair to do so, by proving that the statement was made freely and voluntarily and was not extracted by unfair or improper means.

At the hearing counsel for the appellant conceded that the appropriate standard for the judge to apply in deciding an issue of admissibility would be proof on a balance of probabilities, rather than proof beyond a reasonable doubt. In other words the Crown would have to prove, on a balance of probabilities, that the statement was made freely and voluntarily and that it was not extracted by unfair or improper means. Not surprisingly, the advocate depute did not demur. We therefore heard no argument on the point which in any event does not, strictly speaking, arise for decision.

I incline to the view that the concession was sound. In saying this, I am conscious that in England, under section 76(2) of the Police and Criminal Evidence Act 1984, the Crown has to prove the necessary facts beyond a reasonable doubt. This reflects the position under the pre-existing common law. On the other hand, in *Wendo v. The Queen* (1963) 109 C.L.R. at pp.572–573, Sir Owen Dixon CJ, giving the judgment of the High Court of Australia, held that the appropriate standard of proof of the facts relating to the admissibility of a statement was the balance of probabilities. I have found no discussion of the point in any of the Scottish authorities to which we were referred; there is nothing in the cases, however, to suggest that, where trial judges used to decide whether a statement was admissible, they were conscious of applying a particularly high standard in determining whether the Crown had established the necessary factual basis. More positively, perhaps, Parliament's approach to a not dissimilar point can be gauged from section 259 of the 1995 Act, which deals with the admission of other types of hearsay evidence. Subsection (8) provides that, where the trial judge has to be satisfied of any matter relating to the admissibility of that evidence, the judge is to determine the matter on the balance of probabilities. More generally, there is no requirement in our law that the Crown should prove every fact in a case beyond a reasonable doubt. The requirement is, rather, that, on the admissible evidence as a whole, the Crown should prove the accused's guilt beyond a reasonable doubt. It is not inconsistent with that approach for a judge to determine the factual basis for admissibility on the balance of probabilities.

Trial within a trial

The question which now arises is whether the judge requires to hear the evidence relating to the circumstances of a statement in a trial within the trial. The submission for the complainer is that in the circumstances of the present case the sheriff ought to have adopted that procedure. The procedure is usually discussed in the context of jury trials but counsel for the complainer argued that it should be used in appropriate cases under summary procedure. This was said to be such a case. Although the specific issue in the case therefore concerns summary procedure, I have found it helpful to begin by considering the matter in the context of trial by jury.

As the argument developed, it became apparent that it was necessary to identify precisely what is meant by a trial within a trial. In English law the term which is frequently used to describe the equivalent procedure is "voir dire". When the judges referred to a trial within a trial in *Chalmers*, they were thinking of a procedure in which evidence was led before the judge but in the absence of the jury, the whole purpose of the innovation being to avoid the jury hearing the evidence in question. On the other hand, before the Police and Criminal Evidence Act 1984 came into force, Archbold, *Criminal Pleading, Evidence and Practice* (41st ed. 1982), para. 15–28, could say: 'At the appropriate time, whenever that might be, the judge conducts a trial on the voir dire to decide the question of admissibility. This will normally be done in the absence of the jury, but only at the request or with the consent of the defence' . . .

Similar statements are to be found in the pre-1984 cases and, from them, one can see that evidence can be led on the voir dire in the presence of the jury. This in turn makes it clear that the essential characteristic of the hearing of evidence on the voir dire is not the absence of the jury but the fact that it is discrete from the hearing of the evidence in the substantive trial. In other words all the evidence relating to the issue of admissibility is taken together, so as to constitute a distinct chapter. As is apparent from some of the cases discussed below, the evidence is "ring fenced" and can be used only for the purpose for which it was led.

As I pointed out above, a somewhat similar approach can be detected in *Barbara Simpson* where evidence was led in front of the jury about the circumstances in which the appellant had made a statement, after Lord Kyllachy gave his ruling admitting the statement: '[t]he evidence led by the appellant as to the circumstances under which the statement was made was held evidence in the case'. It appears to have been thought that, if that had not been done, the evidence of the circumstances would have remained outside the body of evidence in the substantive case. There is no sign, however, of a similar procedural step in later cases where it seems to be assumed that the jury can take the evidence into account in determining the weight to be attributed to the statement. Be that as it may, the essential characteristic of a trial within a trial as being something distinct from the rest of the trial is of particular importance in relation to summary procedure. If the only purpose of holding a trial within a trial were that it allowed evidence to be led in the absence of the jury, then there could be no room for a trial within a trial in summary procedure where the judge who deals with admissibility also decides the substantive issue of guilt or innocence. But once it is realised that the trial within a trial can be used to cordon off the evidence led in it, it soon becomes apparent that the procedure can have a place in summary proceedings. I examine that point more fully below.

It seems clear that the practice of holding a trial within a trial without the jury was unknown in Scots law until *Chalmers*. Up until that time the evidence relating to the circumstances in which a statement had been made was led in front of the jury who retired only for the phase during which the submissions were made and the decision was announced. It is worth noting that there appears to be no reported case in which the accused gave evidence on the point. The court in *Chalmers* decided that that procedure was open to objection and should no longer be followed because it tended to tie the hands of counsel in examining and cross examining the witnesses and also tended to lead to the disclosure to the jury of matters which ought to be withheld from their knowledge. They also envisaged that the accused could be a witness. It is not hard to figure cases where, for instance, in resisting the admission of evidence of a statement, the defence would wish to be able to refer to the accused's previous convictions or perhaps to a habit of drug taking in order to elucidate the relevant circumstances but, if possible, would not wish the jury to become aware of those matters. In such a case the trial within a trial allows the relevant circumstances to be explored before the judge who has to rule on admissibility, but at the same time avoids any risk that the jury may become aware of prejudicial matter which has no direct bearing on their decision as to the accused's guilt or innocence of the charges in the indictment. In cases of this kind a court should ordinarily use the procedure if the defence ask for it. On the other hand there may be cases where, because of the nature of the circumstances surrounding the emitting of the statement or for other tactical reasons, the defence prefer to have the evidence about the circumstances led in front of the jury.

The arguments in *Chalmers* in favour of adopting the trial within a trial procedure are essentially practical. The argument advanced by counsel for the complainer in the present case is quite different and raises an issue of importance which was not considered in *Chalmers*, or indeed in any other Scottish authority. The defence position at the trial in this case was that they did not intend that the complainer should give evidence at large after the Crown case was closed. On the other hand, they did wish to lead his evidence to show that he made the statement only because he had been told that, if he did so, he would be released on bail. In other words the defence wished to lead the evidence of the complainer in relation to the single issue of the admissibility of the statement without exposing him to general cross examination on the substance of the charges. This was the reason why the complainer's agent moved the sheriff to hold a trial within the trial so that he could hear the evidence relating to admissibility—including the complainer's evidence—and then rule on the matter before the close of the Crown case. The sheriff refused the motion and the complainer did not give evidence. It was submitted that, by refusing to hold a trial within the trial, the sheriff had failed to ensure a fair trial since he had made it impossible for the complainer to deploy his full case against the admissibility of the statement without requiring to answer questions, the answers to which might tend to incriminate him (section 266(3) of the 1995 Act). In this way the complainer had been put under improper pressure to abandon his right not to incriminate himself; he had resisted that pressure but at the cost of not being able to give the evidence necessary to advance his case against the admissibility of the statement. His right to a fair trial had therefore been breached. Although the argument is novel in Scots law, its origin is not far to seek since it is to be found in outline in Renton and Brown, "Criminal Procedure" (6th ed.), para. 24–61.

Perhaps the clearest statement of the point of principle is to be found in the opinion of Clayden AFCJ in the Federal Supreme Court of Rhodesia and Nyasaland in *Chitambala v. The Queen* [1961] R & N at pp.169–170. The passage, which is quoted with approval by Lord Edmund-Davies in *Wong Kam-ming v. The Queen* at p.257, is in these terms:

'In any criminal trial the accused has the right to elect not to give evidence at the conclusion of the Crown case. To regard evidence given by him on the question of admissibility as evidence in the trial itself would mean either that he must be deprived of that right if he wishes properly to contest the admissibility of a statement, or that, to preserve that right, he must abandon another right in a fair trial, the right to prevent inadmissible statements being led in evidence against him . . . To me it seems clear that deprivation of rights in this manner, and the changing of a trial of admissibility into a full investigation of the merits, cannot be part of a fair trial.'

Clayden AFCJ went on to observe (at p.170) that 'evidence given by an accused must be disregarded on the issue of guilt'. It is noteworthy that in *Chitambala* the Federal Supreme Court were dealing with a case which had been tried before the resident magistrate in Lusaka, sitting without a jury. The underlying philosophy of this general approach is articulated by Lord Hailsham in *Wong Kam-ming* where he says (at p.261):

'I have stated elsewhere (*Director of Public Prosecutions v. Ping Lin* [1976] A.C. 574) that the rule, common to the law of Hong Kong and that of England, relating to the admissibility of extra-judicial confessions is in many ways unsatisfactory, but any civilised system of criminal jurisprudence must accord to the judiciary some means of excluding confessions or admissions obtained by improper methods. This is not only because of the potential unreliability of such statements, but also, and perhaps mainly, because in a civilised society it is vital that persons in custody or charged with offences should not be subjected to ill treatment or improper pressure in order to extract confessions. It is therefore of very great importance that the courts should continue to insist that before extra-judicial statements can be admitted in evidence the prosecution must be made to prove beyond reasonable doubt that the statement was not obtained in a manner which should be reprobated and was therefore in the truest sense voluntary. For this reason it is necessary that the defendant should be able and feel free either by his own testimony or by other means to challenge the voluntary character of the tendered statement. If, as happened in the instant appeal, the prosecution were to be permitted to introduce into the trial the evidence of the defendant given in the course of the voir dire when the statement to which it relates has been excluded whether in order to supplement the evidence otherwise available as part of the prosecution case, or by way of cross-examination of the defendant, the important principles of public policy to which I have referred would certainly become eroded, possibly even to vanishing point.'

The main part of this passage was quoted with approval by Lord Fraser of Tullybelton, with whom the remaining Lords of Appeal concurred, in *R. v. Brophy* [1982] A.C. at p.482.

Subject only to a reservation in respect of the standard of proof, I find the reasoning of Lord Hailsham compelling, in particular his emphasis on it being of very great importance that the courts should insist that before extrajudicial statements can be admitted in evidence the Crown should prove that they have been properly obtained. Because this important matter has to be addressed in the course of the Crown case, it follows that the accused must be able to give any necessary evidence on the point at that stage. This separates and distinguishes the accused's right to give evidence in relation to the admissibility of evidence of a statement from his right to give evidence on other matters, such as alibi or self defence. Because the situations are different, there is no inconsistency in holding that the accused has a right to give evidence during the Crown case only in relation to admissibility, while insisting that on other matters his sole right is to give evidence after the Crown case is closed and subject to cross examination at large. For that reason I reject the advocate depute's argument that the accused's evidence on admissibility should be treated in the same way as his evidence on other matters.

The speech of Lord Fraser of Tullybelton in *R. v. Brophy* is of particular interest. The House of Lords were dealing with an appeal by the Crown from a decision of the Court of Appeal in Northern Ireland in a case where the trial had been conducted before Kelly J, sitting without a jury, under the Northern Ireland (Emergency Powers) Act 1978. In that respect the procedure was similar to the summary proceedings in this case where the sheriff was sitting, of course, without a jury. The respondent was charged on indictment with 49 counts, including 12 of murder, 36 of causing explosions or possessing explosives or firearms and one, count 49, of belonging to an illegal organisation, the IRA. The Crown case was based on a number of statements which the respondent was alleged to have made to the police after his arrest. He challenged the admissibility of the statements on the ground that they had been induced by torture or inhuman or degrading treatment while he was in custody. Kelly J. held a voir dire on the issue of admissibility and the respondent gave evidence, *inter alia* admitting expressly that he had been a member of the IRA. Having considered the evidence led, the judge excluded the evidence of the statements from the substantive trial, with the result that the respondent was acquitted of all but count 49. On count 49 the judge admitted as evidence in the substantive trial the defendant's admission during the voir dire that he had been a member of the IRA. On that basis he convicted the respondent of count 49. The Court of Appeal allowed his appeal against conviction on the ground that that evidence had been inadmissible. The House of Lords refused the Crown appeal without calling upon counsel for the respondent.

In giving judgment in the Court of Appeal Lord Lowry C.J. had observed (*R. v. Brophy* [1981] NILR at p.94E) that 'it is only relevant evidence which is protected' against admission at the substantive trial. In the appeal to the House of Lords the Crown argued that the respondent's confession to having been a member of the IRA had not been relevant to the issue in the voir dire and that the judge had therefore been right to admit it. Lord Fraser first rejected the argument on a ground relating to the particular facts and then continued:

'I would rest my opinion of relevance also on a wider ground. Where, as in this case, evidence is given at the voir dire by an accused person in answer to questions by his counsel, and without objection by counsel for the Crown, his evidence ought in my opinion to be treated as relevant to the issue at the voir dire, unless it is clearly and obviously irrelevant. The accused should be given the benefit of any reasonable doubt. Of course if the accused, whether in answer to questions from his own counsel or not, goes out of his way to boast of having committed the crimes with which he is charged, or if he uses the witness box as a platform for a political speech, his evidence so far as it relates to these matters will almost certainly be irrelevant to the issue at the voir dire, and different considerations will apply to its admissibility at the substantive trial. But on any reasonable view of the respondent's evidence in this case, it cannot be said to be clearly and obviously irrelevant.

Once it has been held that the material part of the respondent's evidence was relevant to the issue at the voir dire, a necessary consequence is, in my opinion, that it is not admissible in the substantive trial. Indeed counsel for the Crown did not argue to the contrary. If such evidence, being relevant, were admissible at the substantive trial, an accused person would not enjoy the complete freedom that he ought to have at the voir dire to contest the admissibility of his previous statements. It is of the first importance for the administration of justice that an accused person should feel completely free to give evidence at the voir dire of any improper methods by which a confession or admission has been extracted from him, for he can almost never make an effective challenge of its admissibility without giving evidence himself. He is thus virtually compelled to give evidence at the voir dire, and if his evidence were admissible at the substantive trial, the result might be a significant impairment of his so-called 'right of silence' at the trial. The right means 'No man is to be compelled to incriminate himself; *nemo tenetur se ipsum prodere*' see *Reg. v. Sang* [1980] A.C. 402, 455, per Lord Scarman. The word 'compelled' in that context must, in my opinion, include being put under pressure. So long as that right exists it ought not to be cut down, as it would be if an accused person, who finds himself obliged to give evidence at the voir dire, in order to contest a confession extracted by improper means, and whose evidence tends to show the truth of his confession, were liable to have his evidence used at the substantive trial. He would not receive a fair trial, as that term is understood in all parts of the United Kingdom.'

Although Lord Fraser's observations are not, of course, binding on this court, the weight to which they would in any event be entitled is only enhanced by the fact that, as the last sentence shows, he considered that the argument of principle applied as much in a Scottish context as in the context of the other legal systems of the United Kingdom.

Again, I find the reasoning which I have quoted compelling. As counsel for the appellant submitted, Lord Fraser identifies a quite fundamental reason for holding a trial within a trial. It may at first sight appear startling, even to a lawyer, that the respondent in *Brophy* could give evidence admitting that he was a member of the IRA and yet the judge was not entitled to use that evidence to convict him of the charge of being a member of that organisation. That line is drawn, however, just exactly because of the importance which the law attaches to two principles. The first is the principle that the court should admit only evidence which is admissible according to the rules of the legal system in question. The other is the principle that no man is to be impelled to incriminate himself—meaning *inter alia* that a person who committed the crime with which he is charged cannot be impelled to contribute to his own conviction by admitting it. There is no doubt that this principle or privilege, though asserted only in respect of 'capitall crymes' in the Claim of Right, 1689 c.13, has long been recognised as applying more generally in Scots law (Hume, Commentaries, ii, 336-337 and Alison, Criminal Law, ii, 586–587). I find it unnecessary for present purposes to identify the precise scope of the privilege or to determine whether the values which underpin it in our law are in all respects the same as those articulated by Justice Goldberg, writing for the United States Supreme Court, in *Murphy v. Waterfront Commission*, 378 US 52 (1964) at p.55. It is enough that any system which recognises these two principles must ensure that its trial procedures respect them. A trial within a trial provides an appropriate procedural solution—permitting the accused to give any evidence necessary to support his objection to the admissibility of a statement but in a manner which means that he does not thereby give evidence against himself in the substantive trial.

Brophy was, of course, an unusual case, but it is not difficult to envisage other cases where essentially the same problem might arise—where, for instance, the accused wished to lead evidence to the effect that he had been caught committing one of the offences libelled but had been pressurised into making a false admission of other offences. In such circumstances the accused would be entitled to give evidence admitting the single offence in a trial within the substantive trial in order to deal with the matter of admissibility. For the reasons given by Lord Fraser, the accused's admission in the trial within the trial could not be used against him in the substantive trial.

A question which has caused difficulty in systems where the voir dire has been used is whether the Crown can ever make any reference in the substantive trial to the evidence of the accused in the trial within the trial. While reserving my opinion until such a case arises for decision, I note that in *Wong Kam-ming* both the majority of the board (at pp.258F–260D) and Lord Hailsham (at pp.261E—262A) agreed on the approach which should be taken. They held that, if the judge ruled that the statement was inadmissible, then no reference whatever could be made to what the accused had said in the voir dire. The position would be different, however, if the judge held that the statement was admissible and the accused subsequently gave evidence—relevant to the jury's determination of the weight to be attached to it—about the circumstances in which the statement had been made. If the accused departed materially from the evidence which he had given on the same matter in the voir dire, then their Lordships could see no reason why the discrepancies should not be elicited and demonstrated in cross examination. Lord Edmund-Davies envisaged indeed that the Crown might lead evidence of what the accused had said in the voir dire in rebuttal.

When these various points are considered, it becomes clear that the hostility to the trial within a trial procedure which has been expressed in many Scottish cases is in certain respects misconceived. The criticism tends to be based on the possible effect which the procedure will have in lengthening trials, on inconvenience to jurors and on the risk that evidence when led for a second time before the jury will be tailored in the light of the cross examination in the trial within a trial. All these are disadvantages which are indeed inherent in the procedure and which will be more or less serious in any particular case. They should not be exaggerated, however: the voir dire has operated without undue difficulty for many years in other parts of the United Kingdom as well as in the Commonwealth and a similar procedure operates in the United States. In any event what the criticisms tend to overlook is that the existence of such disadvantages, even if substantial, cannot be a conclusive argument against the use of the procedure. For the reasons which I have sought to explain, there are situations where the general duty to ensure a fair trial will impose on the judge a particular duty to hold a trial within a trial since, otherwise, the accused will be unable properly to challenge the admissibility of evidence against him. In such circumstances the holding of a trial within a trial is unavoidable and any attendant practical disadvantages of the procedure, though unfortunate, are the price which society must pay in order to achieve the important objective of ensuring that persons charged with crimes receive a fair trial.

Even though a trial within a trial may be the best way of securing a fair trial, it will not, of course, always work perfectly. As Lord Cooper acknowledged in *Chalmers* (at p.80 (p.185)), it may give rise to difficulty and may not always achieve the desired ideal of avoiding prejudice to the accused. In particular, difficulties are likely to arise where the judge hears evidence in the trial within a trial and decides on that basis to admit the statement, but then the evidence of the circumstances is subsequently led before the jury and comes out differently, in a form which would mean that the statement should be excluded. The court has to respond to such difficulties, always bearing in mind its duty to ensure a fair trial. The appropriate response will depend on the exact circumstances. If the terms of the statement have not yet been put to the jury, I can see no reason why the defence should not renew the objection or why the judge should not give a further ruling in the light of the new evidence. It is relevant to notice that, though the judge cannot now reconsider his ruling on an objection in England and Wales because of the terms of section 78 of the Police and Criminal Evidence Act 1984, the judge could do so under the pre-existing law. See Archbold, *Criminal Pleading, Evidence and Practice* (41st ed.), para. 15–28, citing *R. v. Murphy* [1965] NILR at p.150 per Lord MacDermott C.J., and *R. v. Watson*. If the terms of the statement have been given to the jury before the additional evidence emerges, the problem may be more complicated. Where the judge concludes that evidence of the statement should not have been led, then he will, of course, take no notice of that evidence in determining a no case to answer submission. Where there remains a case to answer, it will be possible in many cases for the judge, having regard to the evidence as a whole, simply to direct the jury to disregard the statement. There may, however, be cases where the likely impact of the statement on the jury is such that the judge feels that they could not realistically be expected to put it out of their minds when considering their verdict. If the judge is of that opinion, then, depending on the reason for the change in the evidence, it may be appropriate for him to desert the diet *pro loco et tempore* . . .

. . . I turn now to deal with the position under summary procedure. As *Chitambala* and *Brophy* show, the trial within a trial procedure can play a vital role even where it is a judge who has to decide both the issue of admissibility in the trial within the trial and the issue of guilt or innocence in the substantive trial. The opinion of Lord Lowry C.J. in *Brophy* at [1981] NILR, pp.86G–88A contains a useful survey of three Commonwealth cases, all involving non-jury trials. From what is said in *Brophy*, in particular, it follows that a trial within a trial will in principle be the appropriate procedure to adopt in summary proceedings in our law. The advocate depute submitted, however, that any system under which a judge in summary proceedings held a trial within a trial and then excluded evidence would be inconsistent with the indication given by Lord Justice General Cooper in *Clark v. Stuart*, 1950 J.C. at p.11; 1949

S.L.T., p.463, that in summary proceedings 'it seems to me that only exceptional circumstances . . . justify the exclusion of an important chapter of evidence outright, with the effect of placing matters beyond the control of any appellate tribunal. The normal and proper course would be to allow such evidence under reservations as to competency, so that the question of law could, if necessary, be examined by a higher Court.'

Lord Cooper was speaking in the context of a system in which there could be no retrials and the earlier part of his opinion shows that this was what he had in mind when he spoke of matters being placed beyond the control of any appellate tribunal. That particular argument no longer has force since, under section 183(1)(d) and, if appropriate, section 191(3) of the 1995 Act, the court can set aside the verdict of the lower court and grant authority to the Crown to bring a new prosecution in accordance with section 185. I should accordingly wish to reserve my opinion on the weight to be attached to this particular statement in our current system.

In any event Lord Cooper indicated that the rule which he was laying down was subject to exceptions. More importantly, in *Runham v. Westwater* Lord Justice Clerk Ross specifically recognised that a refusal by a sheriff to rule on an issue of admissibility before the end of the Crown case in a summary case could deprive the accused of his right under the equivalent to section 160 of the 1995 Act. Referring to *Clark v. Stuart*, he said, at 1995 S.C.C.R., p.360; 1995 S.L.T., p.837:

'We have come to the conclusion that the present case is sufficiently unusual and exceptional. What is complained of is an irregularity of procedure in that the sheriff erroneously considered that it was not competent for him to rule upon the admissibility of this reserved evidence at the conclusion of the Crown case. As a result of his holding that he could not rule upon that matter, the complainer has been placed in the position that he was not able to put forward his submission of no case to answer under section 345A of the Criminal Procedure (Scotland) Act 1975 in the knowledge of whether or not the particular evidence, which has been allowed under reservation, was admissible. The submission which was made had to be made upon the basis that the evidence led by the Crown included the evidence which has been allowed under reservation. If the sheriff had appreciated that it was competent for him to rule upon that matter of admissibility at the conclusion of the Crown case, he has told us that he would have done so. If he had done so and had upheld the objection taken to the evidence which had been allowed under reservation, then he would have had to consider whether there was sufficient evidence in law on the basis only of the admissible evidence that had been led before him.

It therefore appears to us that, as a result of the sheriff holding that it was not competent for him to make the ruling at that stage, the complainer has been deprived of the right conferred upon him under section 345A of the Act of 1975. He was forced to put forward his submission of no case to answer without knowing whether the evidence objected to was to be held admissible or not. We are accordingly satisfied that that was prejudicial to the complainer and we are not persuaded that that is something which can necessarily be rectified at a later stage.'

This passage confirms that there is no reason why a judge in a summary case who has held a trial within the trial should not forthwith rule on the admissibility of evidence of a statement of the accused and so be in a position properly to consider any no case to answer submission at the close of the Crown case . . .

Human rights

I should record that counsel for the appellant based part of her argument in support of the appeal on Article 6(1) of the European Convention for the Protection of Human Rights and Fundamental Freedoms and on the privilege against self incrimination, which is not mentioned but is nonetheless said to lie at the heart of the notion of a fair procedure under Article 6 (*Saunders v. United Kingdom* (1997) 23 E.H.R.R. 313 at para. 68; *Murray v. United Kingdom* (1996) 22 EHRR 29 at para. 44). Since none of the European Court of Human Rights cases considered the nature or scope of the privilege in a way which added to what could be derived from the other material which was placed before us, I did not derive any real assistance from them. For that reason I shall not extend this already lengthy opinion by examining them. I should also record that counsel, doubtless anticipating possible procedural complications, specifically eschewed any argument based on section 57 (2) of the Scotland Act 1998 and the Lord Advocate's membership of the Scottish Executive. I have therefore not considered the possible implications, if any, of that section for the complainer's argument.

Summary

Finally, it may be useful if I enumerate in summary form the main practical conclusions which I have reached.

(1) *Balloch* should be overruled. In all cases it is for the trial judge to decide whether any evidence, including evidence of a statement by the accused, is legally competent and can be led.

(2) The judge must decide any issues of fact which are necessary to enable that legal decision to be taken.

(3) Since the trial judge has to determine any issue of fact before ruling on admissibility, if the facts are disputed, the judge must first hear all the relevant evidence, including any evidence which the accused wishes to give on the point.

(4) If the defence ask for the evidence on admissibility to be heard in the absence of the jury, the judge should ordinarily grant that motion.

(5) The Crown cannot use any evidence given by the accused in the trial within a trial as proof of his guilt. There may, however, be circumstances in which the accused can be cross examined about that evidence if he subsequently gives evidence in the substantive trial which is materially different. *Cf Wong Kam-ming.* Other witnesses can, of course, be cross examined on any differences in their evidence.

(6) Where an issue arises on the evidence, it is for the Crown to satisfy the judge that the statement is admissible. The appropriate standard of proof would appear to be the balance of probabilities, as the defence conceded in this case.

(7) The judge will exclude evidence of a statement if it was taken in circumstances which render it inadmissible under any rule laid down by the law. In other cases the judge will admit the statement if the Crown satisfy the judge that it would be fair to do so, by proving that the statement was made freely and voluntarily and was not extracted by unfair or improper means.

(8) Any ruling on the admissibility of the evidence of a statement should be given, in both solemn and summary proceedings, after the evidence of the circumstances had been led and any submissions on the evidence have been heard. In this way, any defence submission that there is no case to answer will fall to be made on the basis of the legally admissible evidence led by the Crown.

(9) Where the judge admits the evidence of a statement, evidence of the circumstances in which it was taken remains relevant to any determination of the weight which should be attached to it.

(10) If the judge admits the evidence of a statement and fresh circumstances emerge in subsequent evidence which cast doubt on that ruling, the defence may renew their objection and invite the judge to reconsider the ruling. On reconsideration the judge may confirm or reverse the original ruling in the light of the new evidence. If the evidence of the statement has not yet been led, the judge may exclude it. If it has been led, the judge may direct the jury to disregard it or, if, because of its likely impact, the judge considers that the jury could not realistically be expected to put the evidence out of their minds, then, depending on the circumstances, the judge may desert the diet *pro loco et tempore.* In the case of a summary trial, the judge will disregard the evidence in reaching a verdict; only rarely would it be appropriate for the judge in a summary trial to desert the diet on the ground that it would be impossible to disregard the evidence in reaching a verdict."

NOTES

The decision in *Thompson v. Crowe* restores a valuable safeguard for an accused person, since the jury will no longer hear incriminating evidence which ought properly to have been excluded by the trial judge. However, it seems that the operation of the trial within a trial may create serious practical difficulties. In *H.M.A. v. Mowat*, 2001 S.L.T. 738, a lengthy trial within a trial was held. Repelling a number of defence objections, Lord Osborne said:

"Before parting with this matter, I feel bound to make certain observations about the appropriateness of the procedure which I have just conducted, in the context of an ongoing trial. The objection which resulted in the trial within the trial was taken on February 22, 2001. After a brief discussion, I concluded that the holding of a trial within a trial was inevitable. That trial within a trial continued from day to day. The evidence in it was concluded on March 1, 2001 and legal submissions were heard on March 2, 2001. Since I considered it necessary to take time to reach and formulate a decision, the matter was adjourned over the weekend until the morning of March 5, 2001, when I issued my decision. Thereafter, unfortunately the evidence in the trial itself could not be resumed on account of the failure of certain witnesses to attend on that date. Accordingly the trial itself was resumed on March 6, 2001. I am driven to conclude that the procedure which I have described must have been highly disruptive so far as the jury were concerned. Since the precise duration of the trial within the trial was uncertain throughout, the jury were instructed to keep in telephone contact with the court authorities, with a view to being told when they should make themselves available for the resumption of the trial itself. Thus, for a period of more than a week, they were kept in a position of uncertainty. Furthermore, their recollection of the evidence which they had heard before the trial within the trial must to some extent have been damaged by the lapse of time.

[45] I should say that the only other experience which I have had of a trial within a trial since the decision in *Thompson v. Crowe* was of a similar character; the trial within the trial there involved lasted for a similar period of time with similar likely consequences. In these circumstances, it appears to me that it would be appropriate for those charged with the responsibility of keeping under review our system of criminal procedure to consider whether arrangements should be made under which issues requiring to be determined at a trial within a trial under solemn procedure should be determined prior to the empanelling of the jury, either when the trial diet is called first, or even before the trial diet at a special diet established for the purpose. If that were to be done, plainly disruption and inconvenience to the jury of the kind experienced in this case would be avoided. It might be thought that there would be difficulty in foreseeing the need for a trial within a trial in advance of the commencement of the trial itself. While that might be so in some cases and any new arrangements would require to take account of that, in many cases the need for a trial within a trial becomes evident as soon as preparations for the trial itself have been made. In any event, I understand that arrangements of the kind mentioned already exist and are satisfactorily operated in England for the determination of such issues, taking the form of the voir dire procedure. It appears to me that the creation of such arrangements in Scotland would almost certainly require legislation. However that might be a small price to pay for the avoidance of the serious disruption of trials which the present procedure involves."

For further examples of cases in which evidence has been excluded as unfairly obtained, see *H.M.A. v. Graham*, 1991 S.L.T. 416, below; and *Harley v. H.M.A.*, 1995 S.C.C.R. 595, in which a conviction was quashed when it emerged that the police had threatened to search the house of a married woman with whom the accused was associating, should he not provide them with certain information. Note that the burden of proving that a statement was fairly obtained rests on the Crown (albeit to the lower standard of proof). The defence does not have to prove that the statement was obtained unfairly, although it will almost certainly have to produce sufficient evidence of this to meet the evidential burden—see Chapter 2, above, and *Black v. Annan*, 1995 S.C.C.R. 273. Some of the dicta in the following cases must be read with some caution, given that, in determining the admissibility of the evidence in question, they refer on occasion to the discredited test laid down in *Balloch*.

15. Graham v. H.M.A.
1991 S.L.T. 416

The accused was tried in the High Court for conspiracy including serious assault. The Crown sought to lead evidence of statements allegedly made by the accused to a certain businessman, R. The police had already interviewed the accused under caution because they suspected him of involvement in the assault but had no evidence against him. They learned that R was to have a business meeting with the accused and arranged for a radio transmitter to be concealed in R's clothing to record their conversation. Counsel for the defence objected to the admission of the recorded statements.

LORD CAMERON: "The submission for the panel shortly put was that the incriminating statements made by the panel, so recorded and transcribed were obtained unfairly. The panel being a suspect, the police were bound by the usual rules regarding admissibility of incriminating statements in evidence, and in particular the giving of a caution, and could not seek to elide them by the use of a third party, and thereby to secure material evidence by means which, if they themselves had employed them would have been objectionable. He reminded me of the principles adopted by the courts in judging of these matters, developed since *Chalmers v. H.M.A.* in case such as *Miln v. Cullen*, and *Lord Advocate's Reference (No. 1 of 1983)*. This was not an accidental overhearing of a spontaneous conversation voluntarily entered into with others who are unconnected with the criminal inquiry. Reference was made to *Jamieson v. Annan* and *H.M.A. v. O'Donnell*.

The general approach adopted by the court in cases such as *H.M.A. v. Whitelaw* and *Tonge v. H.M.A.*, while concerned with interrogation by police officers, supported the view that what was done in this case was to use the meeting with the panel, then a suspect, to elicit incriminating material, while transgressing the rules protecting his right to silence as a suspect. The fact that the incriminating statements were made to a private person and not an official in the circumstances of this case, did not save it. Reference was made to Walkers on Evidence, para. 40, *Morrison v. Burrell*, *Waddell v. Kinnaird* and *H.M.A. v. Campbell*.

Here the inquiry recorded in the transcript was made at least with the connivance of the police, of a suspect who at the time had no means of knowing he was still under suspicion, who received no warning by way of caution, and who was unaware that police officers were listening to the course of the conversation. Looking to the terms of the transcript, which counsel examined in detail, the incriminating statements could not be said to be fairly obtained.

For the Crown, the advocate-depute accepted that the matter had to be judged by the test of fairness. He said that at this stage it could only be said that the statements were inadmissible if the evidence measured up to the standard required in *H.M.A. v. Whitelaw*. There was no police interrogation here. The conversation had been voluntarily entered into by the panel, the statements were spontaneous and not induced by police officers engaged in the inquiry. It could not be said that Rahman was acting as an agent of the police, or acting in support of a police trick or subterfuge. These were statements made to a private person, and the transcript was competent evidence of the statements. Reference was made to Renton and Brown, "Criminal Procedure", paras 18–38 and 18–41, and *Hopes and Lavery v. H.M.A.*. There was no question of entrapment, albeit the police hoped to receive information helpful to their inquiry. Reference was made to *Jamieson v. Annan* and *H.M.A. v. Harper*. The facts in *H.M.A. v. Campbell* were materially different, and the decision there was no guide to the present case. Looking to the whole transcript, it could not be said that Rahman was in the category of a person acting as an arm of the police, albeit the police officers had taken advantage of the opportunity presented to them by Rahman to overhear the conversation between him and the panel at the meeting set up by Rahman. The police officers had not sought out Rahman in order to persuade him to set up the meeting; the statements were not unfairly obtained, and evidence regarding the conversation in the transcript and hence the incriminating statements was admissible.

It is important to note at the outset that in this case the police were inquiring into a crime already committed. Therefore the present case does not fall within that category of cases of which *Hopes and Lavery v. H.M.A.* is an example, where eavesdropping is taking place on the commission of a crime, albeit by arrangement between the intended victim and the police beforehand. In *Hopes and Lavery v. H.M.A.*, 1960 S.L.T. at p.265, the Lord Justice-Clerk Thomson made clear the difference when he said this: 'Now, there can be no doubt at all that in the investigation of certain kinds of crime, especially those involving blackmail or fraud in its various aspects, it is quite a common practice, especially when the intended victim has gone to the police, for the police to suggest an apparent yielding to the criminal demands in circumstances where police officers can observe or can overhear what is going on. The taking of such a course is not an irregularity in the sense in which that word is used in the authorities with whose citation I have been so bountifully favoured. It does not contravene any principle or infringe any right: indeed, it is often the only practical way in which such crimes as I have mentioned can be brought home to the persons who commit them. My view of the matter is, that evidence given by the person who overhears a conversation in those circumstances is competent evidence, and can be properly admitted.'

The test which is applied in our courts in determining such matters as that set out by Lord Justice-General Clyde in *Brown v. H.M.A.*, 1966 S.L.T. at p.107, where he said this: 'The test, which time and again has been applied in Scotland to determine a matter of this nature occurring prior to a suspect being charged with the crime, is whether or not the proceedings which led up to his statement were fair to him or not. As Lord Justice-General Cooper said in *Chalmers v. H.M.A.*, 1954 J.C. 66, 1954 S.L.T. 177 at p.78 (S.L.T. p.184). "It is not the function of the police when investigating a crime to direct their endeavours to obtaining a confession from a suspect to be used as evidence against him at the trial. In some legal systems the inquisitorial method of investigation is allowed in different degrees and subject to various safeguards." But our Scottish standards of fairness have always rendered inadmissible as evidence at the trial answers or admissions or statements obtained by methods of that sort.'

No doubt, as has been said in other cases in looking at the test, fairness will not only comprehend fairness from the point of view of the accused but fairness also from the point of view of the public, who have an interest in the police being able to investigate crimes and bring to justice those who commit them. Furthermore, I bear in mind that it is only in an exceptional case that a judge should withhold evidence of a statement made by an accused from a jury, and that only upon the grounds set out in *Balloch v. H.M.A.* and *H.M.A. v. Whitelaw*.

Upon the agreed facts, the panel had already been interrogated by police officers under full common law caution. He was then a suspect. He continued to be a suspect, and thus one in whose favour the law may intervene to safeguard him when questioned, from possible self-incrimination. Against this background, the police officers, with no evidence available to them against the panel, but proceeding upon wholly unsupported suspicion, then promoted the eavesdropping upon the conversation between the panel and Rahman, who was aware of the purpose for which the equipment was provided. Having read and reread the transcript, it is clear that the most incriminating material in the transcript was obtained after the business between the panel and witness Rahman appears to have been concluded, and after new topics were specifically introduced by the latter. I instance questions on pp.28, 35, 43, 50, 67, 68, 71 and 75 of the transcript, and information offered by him elsewhere relating to incidents libelled and individuals named in charge 6. If such questions had been put at that time by police officers in the course of interrogation of the panel without due caution, statements should be rendered admissible by the fact that they were secured by a third party, not a police officer, where the third party asks them in the knowledge that he is being overheard by police officers concerned in an inquiry into the matters about which he is asking questions, and who has been provided by the police with equipment to enable them to overhear what passes. While it may be that the witness was not directly primed with questions, he was well aware of the subject matter of the inquiry by the police officers, and looking to the form and manner of the conversation in the transcript, it is impossible, in my opinion, to suggest that it was simply the kind of disinterested questioning by a third party, statements made in reply to which are competent; see, *e.g.* Renton and Brown, para. 18–39. Rather, such statements in my view fall into the class of statements which have been extracted. In principle I see no distinction between a case such as the present and one where the third party is provided by the police officers investigating the crime with a list of questions to ask the suspect in the hope of securing admissions of guilt, or the example of the inadmissible evidence cited in Macdonald, *The Criminal Law of Scotland*, p.314, where an official procures a fellow prisoner to inveigle the accused into conversation to be overheard by the official, which last could only be regarded as entrapment.

I am accordingly of the opinion that this is just such a special case where it can be asserted at this stage upon agreed facts, that the rules of fairness and fair dealing were flagrantly transgressed, and that any reasonable jury would have been bound to hold that the statements had been induced by unfair or improper means, and that they had been thereby deprived of any voluntary character. In reaching this conclusion I am fortified by the approach adopted in

H.M.A. v. Campbell, by Lord Justice-Clerk Grant (who was subsequently party to the decision in *Miln v. Cullen*), where as here, the accused was under suspicion at the time when the statement objected to was made. I shall therefore in the circumstances sustain the objection to the evidence."

NOTES

Hopes and Lavery v. H.M.A., 1960 J.C. 104, referred to in this case, involved a charge of blackmail. Evidence was admitted of a conversation between the accused and their intended victim, recorded by means of a transmitter, as in Graham, in which the accused attempted to extort money. Lord Justice-General Clyde said:

> "It was . . . contended that the Inspector's evidence was not the best evidence, and should, therefore, have been disallowed. In my opinion, this contention is unsound. The Inspector's evidence of the conversation was as much primary evidence as the evidence from the replaying of the tape recorder. Each received it at the same time, the one recording it in the human memory, the other upon a piece of tape. Owing to the employment of the wireless machine, the Inspector was put into the position of a person present at and overhearing the conversation as it took place. As it is perfectly competent for the Inspector to speak to a conversation which he hears directly, because he is physically present at it, and hears it with his own unaided ear, it appears to me that it is equally competent for him to give evidence of a conversation which he hears with the help of a hearing aid, or, as in this case, when the conversation is transmitted to him over a distance by wireless. There may be, of course, questions as to the reliability of the transmission, but these are criticisms of the quality and not of the competency of his evidence of what he hears.
>
> It was suggested that there was something improper or underhand in eavesdropping of this kind. But, if this kind of crime is to be stopped methods such as the present one are necessary to detect and prove a particularly despicable type of crime, which is practised in secret and away from observation. It hardly lies in the mouth of a blackmailer to complain that the jury are told the truth about his conversation when he is exerting pressure on his cornered victim. His remedy is not to blackmail. In my opinion, therefore, the Inspector's evidence regarding the conversation was perfectly competent."

Lord Cameron's distinction between that case and *Graham* is consistent with the line taken in *Weir v. Jessop*, above, that there is a distinction between direct evidence of the actual commission of a crime, and evidence of a statement made or evidence found after the crime has been committed. It is not clear, however, whether *Graham* can be reconciled with Lord Ross's obiter dictum in *Weir v. Jessop*, above, implying that *H.M.A. v. Campbell*, 1964 J.C. 80 was wrongly decided. In *Campbell*, a police officer disguised as a reporter was present when the accused made an incriminating statement. This statement was excluded on the ground that, in the circumstances, a caution should have been administered. Is the distinction made in *Weir v. Jessop* a valid one? Clearly a person should not have to be cautioned to refrain from committing an offence; but having committed one, is a person in all cases entitled to be cautioned not to incriminate herself? (See *Miln v. Cullen*, 1967 J.C. 21, below, and the cases following it.) The recent case of *McMillan v. P.F. (Lanark)* High Court of Justiciary, May 29, 2001, unreported, provides a rather bizarre counterpoint to *Graham*. In *McMillan*, the *accused* made a covert tape recording of his interview with the police. The Sheriff ruled that evidence of that recording was inadmissible on the basis that it would have involved a "departure from the basic rules of fairness and fair dealing". During the appeal, which ultimately foundered because of a failure to show that there had been a miscarriage of justice, the High Court noted that:

> "the advocate depute did not seek to dispute that that ruling was misconceived, since, although the recording had been covert, the rules of fairness and fair dealing were generally established to prevent oppression or conduct prejudicial to an accused on the part of the Crown. It could not be said to be prejudicial to the Crown to allow the transcript to be lodged standing the fact that the officer had himself given evidence that the appellant's statement had been noted."

If the police, or indeed anyone else, accidentally overhear an incriminating statement, the statement will very likely be admissible. In *Jamieson v. Annan*, 1988 S.C.C.R. 278, a police officer overheard two accused shouting to one another in the cells after they had been charged with theft. The Sheriff held their statements to be admissible and that decision was upheld by the High Court:

> "In our opinion there was nothing wrong with what [the police officer] did at all. He heard the conversation begin by accident and he then took steps to bring some of his colleagues to join

him in listening to what was being said. It is plain from the findings that what these two men said to one another on the occasion in question was entirely voluntary; it was spontaneous, there had been no question of any inducement, no question of any trap and there was also, in our view, no question in the circumstances of any unfairness. Accordingly, the objection to the admissibility of evidence of this conversation is not well founded."

What do these cases tell us about the factors being taken into consideration by the High Court in determining admissibility? Is fairness the only consideration? In a sense, considerations of fairness to the accused are equal in *Graham* and *Jamieson v. Annan*, since in neither case were the accused cautioned; in neither case were they informed of their right to remain silent. Is the issue here really the acceptability of police methods, rather than a pure question of "fairness"? And is it appropriate for the judiciary to define which methods are appropriate and which are not? Is the reliability of the statement a factor? While the case of *Codona v. H.M.A.*, 1996 S.C.C.R. 300, above, emphasises that self-incriminating statements must be voluntarily made, *Black v. Annan*, 1995 S.C.C.R. 273 suggests that there is no need for the accused to show a causal connection between the impropriety alleged and the statement actually made.

16. Miln v. Cullen
1967 J.C. 21

LORD JUSTICE-CLERK (GRANT): "On the evening of April 14, 1965 the witness George Sievwright was driving a motor lorry when it was involved in a collision with a motor car. Twenty minutes later Constables Blair and Laing came on the scene. Sievwright pointed out the respondent to them as being the driver of the car, indicated that the respondent was responsible for the accident and informed them that he thought the respondent was drunk. The constables went up to the respondent and formed the opinion that he was unfit to drive through drink or drugs—as, in fact he admittedly was. Constable Blair then asked him if he was the driver of the car and the respondent replied that he was. The respondent, having given his name and address and produced his driving licence, was then cautioned and charged with contraventions of sections 3 and 6(1) of the Road Traffic Act 1960. He made no reply.

It is conceded by the Crown that the sole corroboration of Sievwright's evidence in the court below that the respondent was the driver of the car is the respondent's reply to Constable Blair. The question is whether that reply was admissible in evidence. The respondent's contention, which, after legal argument, was upheld by the Sheriff-substitute in the end of the day, is that it was not, on the ground that, when the respondent was asked if he was the driver of the car he was under suspicion of having driven the car while under the influence of drink, that he had not been cautioned and that it would accordingly be unfair to him to admit the reply. I should add that it is also conceded by the Crown that Constable Blair had not been authorised by the Chief Constable under section 232 of the Road Traffic Act 1960, to request the giving of information which he sought from the respondent.

In sustaining the respondent's objection the Sheriff-substitute proceeded in the light of the concessions made by the Crown and the decision in *Foster v. Farrell* (1963 J.C. 46). All that was decided in Foster, however, was the question whether a particular statement was admissible under section 232 of the 1960 Act. It was on the provisions of that section that the Crown wanted a ruling in *Foster*, and, whether or not their concession that the statement was not admissible at common law was over-generous, it ensured that a ruling on the statutory provisions was in fact obtained. Accordingly Foster does not help us in the present case, where it is admissibility at common law and not under section 232 that is the sole question in issue. The test to be applied in answering that question has been frequently and authoritatively laid down. In the most recent case to which we were referred, *Brown v. H.M.A.*, (1966 S.L.T. 105) Lord Justice-General Clyde described it (at p.107) as 'the simple and intelligible test which has worked well in practice—has what has taken place been fair or not?'

In applying this test it is well to keep in mind that 'incrimination' and 'unfairness' are far from being synonymous terms. While, according to our common law, no man is bound to incriminate himself, there is, in general, nothing to prevent a man making a voluntary and incriminating statement to the police if he so chooses, and evidence being led of that statement at his subsequent trial on the charge to which his statement relates. (See *e.g. Manuel v. H.M.A.* (1958 J.C. 41) at p.48). It is said, however, that in the present case there are three factors which, when taken cumulatively amount to unfairness—Constable Blair's 'suspicion', the absence of a caution and the fact that the respondent's admission was in reply to a question. One must, however, look at the realities of the situation. The two constables and Sievwright had apparently all formed the opinion that the respondent was unfit to drive through drink: but Constable Blair had only the uncorroborated statement of Sievwright that the respondent was the driver of the car. In that situation it seems to me that Constable Blair, in asking the simple question which he did, was not merely acting reasonably, properly and fairly, but was acting in accordance with the duties incumbent upon him.

In saying this I have fully in mind the well-known passage in Lord Justice-General Cooper's opinion in *Chalmers v. H.M.A.* (1954 J.C. 66), where he points out (at p.78): 'The theory of our law is that at the stage of initial investigation the police may question anyone with a view to acquiring information which may lead to the detection of the criminal; but that, when the stage has been reached at which suspicion, or more than suspicion, has in their view centred upon some person as the likely perpetrator of the crime, further interrogation of that person becomes very dangerous, and, if carried too far, *e.g.* to the point of extracting a confession by what amounts to cross-examination, the evidence of that confession will almost certainly be excluded.'

Where exactly the danger line is to be drawn will vary according to the particular circumstances (*cf Brown*). But I am satisfied that we are well short of it in the present case. I would be prepared to hold that this case had never got beyond the investigation stage. In any event, however, there was no interrogation in the proper sense of that word, no extraction of a confession by cross-examination, no taint of undue pressure, cajoling or trapping, no bullying and nothing in the nature of third degree and it is not suggested that the respondent, by reason of low intelligence, immaturity or drink, was incapable of appreciating what was going on. Had Constable Blair gone on to interrogate the respondent about how the accident had happened, where he had been and what he had had to drink, a different situation might have been created. As it was, he merely asked what was, in my opinion, a fair and proper question and received a reply which can fairly and properly be admitted in evidence. It is well to keep in mind that, in applying the test of fairness, one must not look solely and in isolation at the situation of the suspect or accused: one must also have regard to the public interest in the ascertainment of the truth and in the detection and suppression of crime.

I would allow the appeal and answer the question in the affirmative."

LORD WHEATLEY: "The legal principles in this field of evidence were exhaustively canvassed in *Chalmers v. H.M.A.*, and it would appear from the arguments addressed to us by counsel for the respondent and other expressions of opinion voiced elsewhere that certain misconceptions have arisen from the decision and opinions in that case. If that be so, then the sooner these misconceptions are cleared, the better it is for all concerned. For instance, counsel for the respondent submitted that once a person came under suspicion, no questions by a police officer and a fortiori no answers by the suspect were admissible in evidence. In *Chalmers* the Lord Justice-General, supported by a Full Bench, reviewed the legal position at three different and progressive stages, namely (1) where routine investigations are being carried out and the person ultimately accused has not fallen under suspicion, (2) where that person has fallen under suspicion but has not been cautioned and charged, and (3) where that person has been cautioned and charged. I need not rehearse all that was said by Lord Cooper in that context, but I deem it important to stress that in the variety of circumstances which might attend cases in each of these categories the basic and ultimate test is fairness. While the law of Scotland has always very properly regarded fairness to an accused person as being an integral part of the administration of justice, fairness is not a unilateral consideration. Fairness to the public is also a legitimate consideration, and in so far as police officers in the exercise of their duties are prosecuting and protecting the public interest, it is the function of the Court to seek to provide a proper balance to secure that the rights of the individuals are properly preserved, while not hamstringing the police in their investigation of crime with a series of academic vetoes which ignore the realities and practicalities of the situation and discount completely the public interest. Even at the stage of routine investigations, where much greater latitude is allowed, fairness is still the test, and that is always a question of circumstances. It is conceivable that even at that stage a question might be asked or some action might be perpetrated which produced an admission of guilt from the person being interviewed, and yet the evidence might be disallowed because the circumstances disclosed an unfairness to that person. At the other end of the scale, it is wrong to assume that, after a person has been cautioned and charged, questioning of that person is no longer admissible. All that was said in *Chalmers* and in the subsequent cases of *Manuel v. H.M.A.* (1958 J.C. 41) and *Brown v. H.M.A.* (1966 S.L.T. 105) was that at that stage questions, or indeed actions, which induced by some means or other self-incriminating statements by an accused which were not voluntary or spontaneous were liable to be ruled out as inadmissible. But once again the test is one of fairness. A question asked merely to clear up an ambiguity and not calculated to produce an incriminating answer might result in a self-induced incriminating answer by an accused person. Whether such evidence should be admitted or not will always be a question for the Court, having regard to all the circumstances and the basic touchstone of fairness. Statements voluntarily made after caution, or spontaneous statements, are properly admitted in evidence and any suggestion that such statements should not be admitted, or should be admitted only if they are the product of a judicial declaration before a Sheriff or a magistrate, cannot command my approval or support. While this latter procedure is available, and has the attraction that it minimises and possibly removes any question of challenge as to the validity of the evidence, it is manifestly impracticable in the multitude of cases which the police have to handle, and not least of these are Road Traffic Act offences.

When one comes to consider the position of a 'suspect', the situation becomes even more complicated. The point at which a person becomes a 'suspect' in the eyes of a police officer may be difficult to define with exactitude. The test is basically a subjective one, but the police officer may have to justify his attitude by reference to the facts in his possession or the knowledge which he had at the given point of time. The degree of suspicion may vary from a very slight suspicion to a clearly formed one. What happens after that has again to be judged by the test of fairness. If the 'suspect' is cautioned (but not charged), he is being warned that he is going to be asked questions but that he is not under any obligation to answer them. On the basis that such a caution is properly given and properly understood, it is unrealistic to proceed on the basis that questions which might elicit answers which might tend to incriminate him should automatically be disallowed. To adopt such a rule would be so to circumscribe police investigation that the public interest, the protection of the public and the administration of justice might be completely ignored. In each case the issue is—was the question in the circumstances a fair one?

I now turn to consider the position in the present case, where the respondent was a 'suspect' and was asked whether he was the driver of the car without being cautioned. Once again I return to the test of fairness. The police officers were only suspicious of him because Sievwright had stated to them that he, the respondent, (1) was the driver of the car, (2) was the person responsible for the accident and (3) was drunk. The question asked by Blair was merely to discover whether the respondent was the driver of the car, not whether he had caused the accident or was drunk. If a question had been asked without a caution being administered, and the question had been directed to elicit an admission of culpability for the accident or an admission that he was drunk in charge of his car, then the question might have been properly objected to. But when the question was solely directed to ascertaining whether he was the driver of the car, which was not *per se* a criminal offence either at common law or under statute, then it seems to me that *quoad* that point the police officers were still at the point of initial investigations, albeit, once that point had been established, they might have to proceed on the basis that they were suspicious that the driver of the car might have been responsible for the accident and might have been unfit to drive his car through drink at the time. That, as I understand the position, is the proper effect of the concession by the Crown that the respondent was 'under suspicion'. In any event, the degree of suspicion was rather tenuous, resting as it did on the then unsupported statement of Sievwright, who was an interested party. Sievwright's story had to be investigated and checked, and in that process his complaint about the respondent might have been proved to be unfounded. The police officers had to try and elicit the facts. Manifestly their first duty was to ascertain the identity of the driver of the car involved in the collision. They were at the locus within twenty minutes of the occurrence and there was a crowd of people gathered round, one of whom had been identified as the driver of the car. To suggest that in that situation the police officers required to administer a caution before asking the respondent whether he was the driver of the car is to place too great a restriction and confinement on police officers in the discharge of their duties in the public interest.

It was argued by counsel for the respondent that the question was 'loaded', because, once an affirmative answer was obtained, an admission of guilt of at least a section 6(1) offence naturally followed. That is looking at the matter in retrospect. At that stage the police officers, once they had ascertained the identity of the driver of the car, had still to prosecute inquiries in order to ascertain whether that driver had been guilty of an offence, and an admission that he was the driver of the car did not at that point involve an admission of any offence. If all that Sievwright had said to the police officers had been that the driver of the car was in his opinion drunk, but that he could not identify him, then according to the argument of the respondent's counsel every person thereafter interviewed by the police officers in their endeavours to ascertain the identity of the driver of the car would have had to be cautioned before any questions on identity were asked. Such a proposition cannot stand the scrutiny of any test of bilateral fairness, and for this Court to endorse such a restrictive practice as a general rule to be followed in all cases would be to make a nonsense of the investigation of crime and the administration of justice.

This is not to say that in other circumstances, where the police had already in their possession information which clearly pointed to an offence having been committed and the only further point of inquiry left for them was to establish the identity of the perpetrator of the offence, a question without caution designed to extract an admission of identity would be equally unobjectionable. As I have repeatedly noted, each case must be determined on its own circumstances. In the present case I am satisfied that for the reasons I have stated the Sheriff-substitute erred in rejecting the evidence in question. I accordingly agree with your Lordship in the chair that the question of law should be answered in the affirmative and that the case should be disposed of in the manner proposed."

NOTES

Lord Wheatley's view that questioning of a suspect may continue after caution and charge must itself be read with some caution—see *Carmichael v. Boyd*, 1993 S.C.C.R. 751, and compare *Johnston v. H.M.A.*, 1993 S.C.C.R. 693. It is this case, and Lord Wheatley's opinion in particular, which really began the revision of *Chalmers* in earnest. On one view, however, Lord Wheatley's bilateral fairness test simply brings the law of admissions and confessions into line with the balancing test set out in *Lawrie v. Muir*, above, and indeed with the jurisprudence of the European Court of Human Rights. What are the proper limits of the extent to which the public interest should be taken into account in determining admissibility? Indeed, what is the public interest, what does it demand, and to what extent should the judiciary (a) interpret it, and (b) take it into account?

One topic which has proved to be of some difficulty is that of the caution administered to a suspect before he or she is questioned. Most common law jurisdictions insist that some form of warning is given to a suspect that anything he says may be noted, and/or tape-recorded and used in evidence at a subsequent trial. Some of the older cases suggested that a caution had to be administered to every suspect—see, for example, *Docherty v. H.M.A.*, 1981 J.C. 6, in which Lord Cowie said that: "It is a basic right of every accused person to be allowed to remain silent when he comes under suspicion of a crime".

But in relation to modern practice that *dictum* is now too widely expressed. The idea emerges in *Miln v. Cullen* that a caution is not required in every case in which a suspect is questioned. It is an idea which resurfaces in the more recent cases. But before dealing with those cases, mention must be made of the case of *Tonge v. H.M.A.*, 1982 J.C. 130. In *Tonge* a statement was excluded because no proper caution had been given when the accused were informally accused of having committed rape. The short form of caution given on detention (now provided for in section 14 of the Criminal Procedure (Scotland) Act 1995) was held to be insufficient to guarantee fairness to the accused. The court said:

"A wholly new chapter began when Detective Sergeant McMorran and Constable Jenkins approached these two appellants in detention. They had little or no evidence that the alleged crime had been committed or that either Gray or Tonge had been among its perpetrators. They hoped to get such evidence from Gray himself and it is an inescapable inference from the evidence that they hoped for the same response from Tonge. What they did was to accuse Gray and Tonge of participation in the alleged crime without first cautioning either. This was clearly calculated to provoke a response and the opening words of the response which the accusation elicited from each demonstrated that each was about to make a statement, possibly self-incriminating. Even then they did not caution either man and they did not caution either thereafter when it clearly began to appear that he was, in fact, about to incriminate himself. In these circumstances the unfairness of the police officers was manifest and it is clear from their own evidence that proper practice, prior to 1980, demanded the giving of a caution at least once to persons in the position of Gray and Tonge."

If *Tonge* appeared to take a fairly strict line with respect to the need for a caution, that case has since been distinguished on a number of occasions, and the courts have emphasised that the lack of caution is not necessarily fatal to the admissibility of a statement:

(i) It is clear that while the short form of caution now contained in section 14 of the 1995 Act is insufficient in the absence of a full common law caution, the reverse is not true. In *Scott v. Howie*, 1993 S.C.C.R. 81, the accused was detained on suspicion of housebreaking. He was not given the [short form] warning under section 2(7) of the 1980 Act at that time. He was then taken to the police station where he was given the standard common law caution and the statutory warning. Under questioning he made certain statements which the Sheriff ruled inadmissible because of the failure to give the section 2(7) warning. Allowing an appeal by the Crown, the Lord Justice-General (Hope) said that:

" . . . the section 2(7) warning is no substitute for a full caution at common law. The situation in the present case differs from that in *Tonge* [1982 S.C.C.R. 313], in that while in that case the appellant was accused of a crime without a caution having been administered the respondent here was merely being questioned in the police station. But the effect of the caution which he was given was that he was made fully aware of his right to silence and of the use which might be made of any response to the questioning. The limited information prescribed by subsection (7) had nothing to add to the caution at common law on these points . . . "

(iii) In *Pennycuick v. Lees*, 1992 S.C.C.R. 160 the court explicitly affirmed the approach taken in *Miln v. Cullen*. The appellant was convicted of fraudulently claiming social security benefit. He appealed to the High Court, arguing that certain statements made to social security investigators should not have been admitted, since they were made without any caution having been given. He had been interviewed on two occasions. On the first occasion, he signed a form giving details of his name and address and of the fact that he was employed for more than the statutory number of hours below which he would be entitled to benefit. On the second occasion, he admitted signing forms claiming benefit during the period concerned. On neither of these occasions was he cautioned. His appeal was refused, the absence of a caution being treated as only one of a number of factors. Lord Justice General Hope said:

"In all these cases where enquiries are being conducted into activities which may be criminal the question is whether, looking at all the circumstances of the case, there has been unfairness to the accused in what took place. This was the test which was applied in *Miln v. Cullen* [1967 J.C. 21, above] in which it was conceded by the Crown that, when the accused was asked by the police officers whether he was the driver of the car, he was a suspected person. As Lord Strachan put it at p.27: 'The whole circumstances must be taken into account, and the test in every case is whether in the particular circumstances there has been unfairness on the part of the police.'

There is, therefore, no rule of law which requires that a suspect must always be cautioned before any question can be put to him by the police or by anyone else by whom the enquiries are being conducted. The question in each case is whether what was done was unfair to the accused."

(iv) Pennycuick v. Lees was followed by Lord Marnoch in *Middler v. H.M.A.*, 1994 S.C.C.R. 838. However, one aspect of his opinion must be viewed with caution in the light of the decision in *Thompson v. Crowe*, above. He said with respect to *Tonge* that: "It is to be observed that the Lord Justice-General's *dictum* [at p.348] anent a full caution being a requirement of the substantive law is specifically restricted to the situation where a charge or equivalent accusation is about to be made", and after continued:

"In my opinion, the recent authority of *Pennycuick*, following on those of *Tonge* and *Miln v. Cullen*, makes clear that the question of whether and, if so, at what stage a caution should be given falls to be determined as part of the more general test of fairness to the accused which, unless in exceptional circumstances, is a matter for the jury in the light of the whole evidence and appropriate directions in law given in the charge. Despite Mr Hamilton's forceful submissions to the contrary, I am of the opinion that that is the course which should be followed in the present case. In reaching this view, I take account of what was said by the advocate-depute and I also take account of the consideration that it is, as it seems to me, impossible to lay down, as a matter of law, precisely when, in any case a caution should be administered. Leaving aside the making of a formal charge or its equivalent, that, in my view, must almost be a question of mixed fact and law which can only be determined by the jury acting under proper directions from the presiding judge and in the light of the whole evidence in the case including, it may be, any evidence of practice within the police force."

Thompson v. Crowe makes it plain that questions such as these are not "mixed questions of fact and law" to be determined in most cases by the jury, but questions of law for the judge alone.

(v) See also *Custerton v. Westwater*, 1987 S.C.C.R. 389; *Irving v. Tudhope*, 1987 S.C.C.R. 505.

(vi) However, contrast *McLory v. McInnes*, 1992 S.L.T. 501, in which the police found the accused asleep at the wheel of his car which was lying on the verge at a corner in the road. They awoke the accused and, without cautioning him, asked him what had happened, to which he replied that he had "lost it on the corner". It was held that this statement, if it amounted to a confession, was inadmissible, because of the likelihood that the accused was not fully aware of what he was doing or saying. The police ought to have waited until the accused was fully awake before inquiring into the circumstances.

The problem of statutory provisions which require an accused person to answer questions which may incriminate has long proved difficult—see for example *Foster v. Farrell*, 1963 S.L.T. 182; *H.M.A. v. Von*, 1979 S.L.T. (Notes) 62; and *Styr v. H.M.A.*, 1993 S.C.C.R. 278. The incorporation into Scots law of the European Convention on Human Rights has added a further dimension to the difficulty. In *Foster v. Farrell*, it was held that in cases brought under section 172 of the Road Traffic Act, no caution was necessary before requiring a person to give information as to the identity of the driver of a vehicle at a particular time. Lord Justice Clerk Grant said:

"I have no doubt that it is unnecessary to warn or caution a person before requiring him to give information under section 232. Such a warning or caution would be wholly inappropriate and out of place when the person concerned is bound by statute, and under penal sanction to give the information required."

In *Brown v. Stott*, the question was raised whether the lack of a caution in such circumstances amounted to a breach of the accused rights under Article 6 of the European Convention.

17.   Brown v. Stott
2001 S.L.T. 59

Section 172(3) of the Road Traffic Act 1988 provides that it is an offence for the keeper of a motor vehicle to fail to give information to the police, when required to do so under subsection (2), as to the identity of the driver of a motor vehicle when that driver is alleged to have committed an offence to which section 172 applies.

A woman was charged on complaint with driving after consuming excess alcohol, having admitted under police questioning in terms of section 172 of the 1988 Act that she had been the driver of her car at the relevant time. She raised as a devolution issue the question whether the Crown would be entitled to lead evidence of her reply, arguing that since she had been compelled to give an answer to the police, to do so would infringe her right to a fair trial under Article 6(1) of the Convention. The Crown admitted the intention to use the section 172 reply in evidence. The sheriff refused the devolution minute and the accused appealed. The High Court allowed the appeal and granted a declarator that, because of section 57 of the Scotland Act 1998, the Crown had no power to lead and rely on evidence of the admission which the accused had been compelled to make under section 172. The court held *inter alia* that the accused's admission under section 172 was self incriminating and that there was no justification for such infringement of the accused's Article 6 rights. The Crown and the Advocate General appealed to the Judicial Committee of the Privy Council. Much of the decision is concerned with the question whether a devolution issue arose at all. With respect to the merits, the court held that the requirements of section 172 did not amount to a breach of the accused's Convention rights.

LORD STEYN:
III. Article 6

"The present case is concerned with Article 6 of the Convention which guarantees to every individual a fair trial in civil and criminal cases. The centrality of this principle in the Convention system has repeatedly been emphasised by the European Court. But even in respect of this basic guarantee, there is a balance to be observed. First, it is well settled that the public interest may be taken into account in deciding what the right to a fair trial requires in a particular context. Thus in *Doorson v. The Netherlands* it was held that 'principles of fair trial also require that in appropriate cases the interests of the defence are balanced against those of witnesses or victims called upon to testify': at (1996) 22 E.H.R.R., p.358, para. 70. Only one specific illustration of this balanced approach is necessary. Provided they are kept 'within reasonable limits' rebuttable presumptions of fact are permitted in criminal legislation: *Salabiaku v. France*. Secondly, once it has been determined that the guarantee of a fair trial has been breached, it is never possible to justify such breach by reference to the public interest or on any other ground. This is to be contrasted with cases where a trial has been affected by irregularities not amounting to denial of a fair trial. In such cases it is fair that a court of appeal should have the power, even when faced by the fact of irregularities in the trial procedure, to dismiss the appeal if in the view of the court of appeal the defendant's guilt is plain and beyond any doubt. However, it is a grave conclusion that a defendant has not had the substance of a fair trial. It means that the administration of justice has entirely failed. Subject to the possible exercise of a power to order a retrial where appropriate, such a conviction can never be allowed to stand.

IV. The privilege against self incrimination

It is well settled, although not expressed in the Convention, that there is an implied privilege against self incrimination under Article 6. Moreover, section 172(2) undoubtedly makes an inroad on this privilege. On the other hand, it is also clear that the privilege against self incrimination is not an absolute right. While there is no decision of the European Court of Human Rights directly in point, it is noteworthy that closely related rights have been held not to be absolute. It is significant that the basic right of access to the courts has been held to be not absolute: *Golder v. United Kingdom*. The principle that everyone charged with a criminal offence shall be presumed innocent until proved guilty according to law is connected with the privilege against self incrimination. Yet the former has been held not to be absolute: *Salabiaku v. France*. The European Court has also had occasion to emphasise the close link between the right of silence and the privilege against self incrimination: *Murray v. United Kingdom*. In *Murray* the European Court held that the right of silence is not absolute.

In these circumstances it would be strange if a right not expressed in the Convention or any of its Protocols, but implied into Article 6 of the Convention, had an absolute character. In my view the right in question is plainly not absolute. From this premise it follows that an interference with the right may be justified if the particular legislative provision was enacted in pursuance of a legitimate aim and if the scope of the legislative provision is necessary and proportionate to the achievement of the aim.

V. Section 172(2)

In considering whether an inroad on the privilege against self incrimination can be justified, it is necessary to concentrate on the particular context. An intense focus on section 172(2) is required. It reads as follows: [his Lordship quoted its terms and continued]

The penalty for failing to comply with section 172(2) is a fine of not more than £1,000. In addition an individual may be disqualified from driving and endorsement of the driver's licence is mandatory. It is well established that an oral admission made by a driver under section 172(2) is admissible in evidence: *Foster v. Farrell*.

The subject of section 172(2) is the driving of vehicles. It is a notorious fact that vehicles are potentially instruments of death and injury. The statistics placed before the board show a high rate of fatal and other serious accidents involving vehicles in Great Britain. The relevant statistics are as follows: 1996, 40,601 fatal and serious accidents; 1997, 39,628; 1998, 37,770.

The effective prosecution of drivers causing serious offences is a matter of public interest. But such prosecutions are often hampered by the difficulty of identifying the drivers of the vehicles at the time of, say, an accident causing loss of life or serious injury or potential danger to others. The tackling of this social problem seems in principle a legitimate aim for a legislature to pursue.

The real question is whether the legislative remedy in fact adopted is necessary and proportionate to the aim sought to be achieved. There were legislative choices to be made. The legislature could have decided to do no more than to exhort the police and prosecuting authorities to redouble their efforts. It may, however, be that such a policy would have been regarded as inadequate. Secondly, the legislature could have introduced a reverse burden of proof clause which placed the burden on the registered owner to prove that he was not the driver of the vehicle at a given time when it is alleged that an offence was committed. Thirdly, and this was the course actually adopted, there was the possibility of requiring information about the identity of the driver to be revealed by the registered owner and others. As between the second and third techniques it may be said that the latter involves the securing of an admission of a constituent element of the offence. On the other hand, such an admission, if wrongly made, is not conclusive. And it must be measured against the alternative of a reverse burden clause which could without further investigation of the identity of the driver lead to a prosecution. In their impact on the citizen the two techniques are not widely different. And it is rightly conceded that a properly drafted reverse burden of proof provision would have been lawful.

It is also important to keep in mind the narrowness of the interference. Section 172(2) is directed at obtaining information in one category, namely the identity of the driver at the time when an offence was allegedly committed. The most important part of section 172(2) is para. (a), since the relevant information is usually peculiarly within the knowledge of the owner. But there may be scope for using (b) in a limited category of cases, e.g. when only the identity of a passenger in the car is known. Section 172(2) does not authorise general questioning by the police to secure a confession of an offence. On the other hand, section 172(2) does, depending on the circumstances, in effect authorise the police officer to invite the owner to make an admission of one element in a driving offence. It would, however, be an abuse of the power under section 172(2) for the police officer to employ improper or overbearing methods of obtaining the information. He may go no further than to ask who the driver was at the given time. If the police officer strays beyond his power under section 172(2) a judge will have ample power at trial to exclude the evidence. It is therefore a relatively narrow interference with the privilege in one area which poses widespread and serious law enforcement problems.

VIII. Conclusion on Article 6

That brings me back to the decision of the High Court of Justiciary. It treated the privilege against self incrimination as virtually absolute. That conclusion fits uneasily into the balanced Convention system, and cannot be reconciled with Article 6 in all its constituent parts and the spectrum of jurisprudence of the European Court on the various facets of Article 6.

I would hold that the decision of the High Court of Justiciary on the merits was wrong. The procurator fiscal is entitled to lead the evidence of Miss Brown's admission under section 172(2)."

LORD HOPE:

The scheme of Article 6(1)

"As the Lord Justice General (Rodger) observed (p.385J), the right of silence and the right against self incrimination are not lately minted. They have been recognised as general principles of the law of Scotland at least since the beginning of the nineteenth century. In neither case was the right regarded as absolute, but the judges saw it as their function to see that they were jealously safeguarded. It was appreciated from an early stage that the accused's right to silence at trial would be worthless if his right of silence and his right against self incrimination were not available to him from the outset of the criminal investigation. So rules were developed by the judges to ensure that these rights were respected by the court and the police.

In *Chalmers v. H.M.A.* at 1954 J.C., p.79; 1954 S.L.T., p.184 Lord Justice General Cooper said that the principles which regulate the duties of the police when questioning suspects had been stated and restated in over a score of decisions in the past 80 or 90 years. As the jurisprudence on this subject developed, the ultimate test was said to have been founded upon the principle of fairness. In *Brown v. H.M.A.* at 1966 S.L.T., p.107 Lord Justice General Clyde observed that the test applied in all such cases was a simple and intelligible test which had worked well in practice—has what has taken place been fair or not? Other dicta to the same effect were referred to in *Codona v. H.M.A.* at 1996 S.L.T., p.1105A–E, where it was emphasised that that simple test must never be permitted to become a formality. The statutory rules relating to the questioning of persons detained at a police station and to judicial examination as a part of petition procedure, which are now to be found in sections 13–15 and 35–38 of the Criminal Procedure (Scotland) Act 1995, have been framed in such a way as to provide appropriate checks and balances in the interests of fairness to the accused.

As these provisions show, and as the judges have repeatedly emphasised in the common law context, the common law principle of fairness has always to be reconciled with the interests of society in the detection and punishment of crime: *Lawrie v. Muir* at 1950 J.C., p.26; 1950 S.L.T., p.39, per Lord Justice General Cooper; *H.M.A. v. Hepper* at 1958 J.C., p.40; 1958 S.L.T., p.160, per Lord Guthrie. The rule of law requires that every person be protected from invasion by the authorities of his rights and liberties. But the preservation of law and order, on which the rule of law also depends, requires that those protections should not be framed in such a way as to make it impractical to bring those who are accused of crime to justice. The benefits of the rule of law must be extended to the public at large and to victims of crime also.

Now that the common law rights of the accused have been reinforced by the right under Article 6(1) of the Convention to a fair trial it is necessary to re-examine and revise these principles. The scheme of the article involves the application of different tests at each stage of the inquiry from those applied by the common law. It requires that a more structured approach be taken when the overriding test of fairness is applied to the facts. But it is important to recognise nevertheless that the rule of law lies at the heart of the Convention.

The final indent of the preamble to the Convention refers to the common heritage of the European countries whose governments were signatory thereto of "political traditions, ideals, freedom and the rule of law". In *Salabiaku v. France* at para. 28 the European Court of Human Rights said that Article 6, by protecting the right to a fair trial, was intended to enshrine "the fundamental principle of the rule of law". In *Golder v. United Kingdom* at para. 35 the court said that in civil matters one could scarcely conceive of the rule of law without there being a possibility of access to the courts. These statements assert the right of the individual to the protection of the rule of law against the state. But the other side of the balance, which respects the public interest in the rule of law and the general interest of the community, was also recognised by the court in *Salabiaku*. It said in para. 28 of its judgment in that case that the Convention did not prohibit presumptions of fact or of law in principle, and that they were not incompatible with Article 6(2) so long as they were confined within reasonable limits which take account of what is at stake and maintain the rights of the defence. In *Pullar v. United Kingdom* at para. 32, the court said that the principle that a tribunal is to be presumed to be free of personal prejudice or partiality unless there is evidence to the contrary reflects 'an important element of the rule of law', which is that verdicts of a tribunal should be final and binding unless set aside by a superior court on the basis of irregularity or unfairness. A similar approach to the function of the rule of law can be seen in the fact that the court has consistently recognised that, while the right to a fair trial is absolute in its terms and the public interest can never be invoked to deny that right to anybody under any circumstances, the rights which it has read into Article 6 are neither absolute nor inflexible.

It is important therefore to distinguish between those Convention rights which are to be regarded as absolute and those which are not. The scheme of Article 6, as Keir Starmer in European Human Rights Law (Legal Action Group, 1999), pp.118–119, para. 3.88, has explained, is that the rights listed in Articles 6(2) and 6(3) which are supplementary to Article 6(1) are not intended to be an exhaustive list of the requirements of fairness in criminal proceedings. Those which are listed in Article 6(3) are described as minimum rights. Once the meaning of those rights has been determined, there is no room in their case for any implied modifications or restrictions. But the European Court and the European Commission have interpreted the article broadly by reading into it a variety of other rights to which the accused person is entitled in the criminal context. Their purpose is to give effect, in a practical way, to the fundamental and absolute right to a fair trial. They include the right to silence and the right against self incrimination with which this case is concerned. As these other rights are not set out in absolute terms in the article they are open, in principle, to modification or restriction so long as this is not incompatible with the absolute right to a fair trial. As Keir Starmer, p.182, para. 4.75 has observed, where express restrictions are provided for by the Convention there is no room for implied restrictions. But where the European Court has read implied rights into the Convention, it has also read in implied restrictions on those rights.

The test of compatibility with Article 6(1) which is to be applied where it is contended that those rights which are not absolute should be restricted or modified, will not be satisfied if the modification or limitation "does not pursue a legitimate aim and if there is not a reasonable relationship of proportionality between the means employed and the aim sought to be achieved": *Ashingdane v. United Kingdom* at para. 57. In *Sporrong and Lönnroth v. Sweden* at para. 69 the court referred to the striking of a fair balance 'between the demands of the general interest of the community and the requirements of the protection of the individual's fundamental rights'. As that case and *Salabiaku v. France* both demonstrate, that approach has been used to support the view that, although the presumption of innocence in Article 6(2) is stated in absolute terms, it is not to be regarded as prohibiting the use of reverse onus clauses so long as they are confined within reasonable limits which strike a fair balance between these competing demands and requirements. The relevant principles described in *Ashingdane* were restated by the court in *Lithgow v. United Kingdom*, para. 194 and again in *Fayed v. United Kingdom*, para. 65.

I would hold therefore that the jurisprudence of the European Court tells us that the questions that should be addressed when issues are raised about an alleged incompatibility with a right under Article 6 of the Convention are the following: (1) is the right which is in question an absolute right, or is it a right which is open to modification or restriction because it is not absolute?; (2) if it is not absolute, does the modification or restriction which is contended for have a legitimate aim in the public interest?; (3) if so, is there a reasonable relationship of proportionality between the means employed and the aim sought to be realised? The answer to the question whether the right is or is not absolute is to be found by examining the terms of the article in the light of the judgments of the court. The question whether a legitimate aim is being pursued enables account to be taken of the public interest in the rule of law. The principle of proportionality directs attention to the question whether a fair balance has been struck between the general interest of the community in the realisation of that aim and the protection of the fundamental rights of the individual.

Saunders v. United Kingdom

It is plain from the opinion of the Lord Justice General, for reasons which I can well understand in view of the novelty of the question with which it was presented in this case, that the High Court found itself in some difficulty in obtaining clear guidance from the judgments of the European Court as to the scope of the right to silence and the right not to incriminate oneself: p.385C. They had been recognised by the European Court as rights which, although not specifically mentioned in Article 6, ought to be read in to that article to secure the right to a fair trial: *Funke v. France*, para. 44; see also *Murray v. United Kingdom* at para. 45. But the fullest description of those rights is to be found in *Saunders v. United Kingdom*, paras 68–69. So it was to be expected that the High Court would rely primarily on what was said in that case for guidance. Although this guidance was supplemented by the Lord Justice General, in his carefully researched opinion, by reference to generally recognised international standards such as those expressed in judgments of the Supreme Court of Canada and the Constitutional Court of South Africa, it was the approach of the European Court in *Saunders* which was his principal source. In the result it is not surprising that defects in the reasoning which are apparent on a close reading of *Saunders* are to be found in the judgment of the High Court also.

The main weakness in the reasoning of the court in *Saunders* lies in its failure to examine the issue, which is highlighted in the dissenting opinions of Judge Valticos and Judge Gölcüklü, as to whether the right to silence and the right not to incriminate oneself are or are not absolute rights the modification or restriction of which could in no circumstances ever be justified. The basis upon which the court proceeded, as it explained in the opening sentence of para. 68, was that these rights 'lie at the heart of the notion of a fair procedure under Article 6'. In the discussion which follows the rights are treated as if they were rights conferred by Article 6 which were not open to modification or restriction. The essence of the argument which the court accepted related to the use which was made of the evidence obtained under compulsion in the course of the criminal trial: para. 71. That was enough to persuade the court that the rights had been breached. It is true that in para. 74 of its judgment the court said that it did not find it necessary to examine the issue as to whether or not the rights were absolute in the light of its assessment of the use which was made at the trial of the interviews. But the reasoning upon which this observation seems to have been based appears to me, with respect, to be unconvincing. It was simply that the answers to questions put in the course of those interviews, whether directly self incriminating or not, were used in the course of the proceedings in a manner which sought to incriminate the applicant: para. 72. Questions as to whether the procedure which was followed was designed to pursue a legitimate aim and as to whether the means employed were proportionate were not addressed.

Although the European Court was careful to confine its observations in *Saunders* to the facts of that case only, the general approach which is revealed by the judgment appears to be out of keeping with the mainstream of the jurisprudence which the court itself has developed as to the nature and application of the rights which it has read into Article 6(1). Although it is possible as Lord Steyn has demonstrated to find indications in the judgment that the court did not regard the right of silence and the right against self incrimination as absolute, it is not easy to find any clear guidance to that effect. So when the Lord Justice General came, towards the end of his judgment at p.396G, to consider the circumstances of this case in accordance with the approach which in his view had been laid down by the court in *Saunders*, he appears to have regarded the right to silence and the right not to incriminate oneself as rights of a fundamental character which fell to be treated as if they were absolute rights. At p.396H he said that the respondent's right not to incriminate herself was a constituent element of the basic principles of fair procedure inherent in Article 6(1). He had already rejected arguments based on the recognition by the court in *Murray v. United Kingdom*, para. 47 that the right to silence was not absolute: see also *Condron v. United Kingdom* at para. 56. He said that he could find nothing in the circumstances of this case which would justify a restrictive interpretation or application of 'the right conferred by Article 6(1)'. Consequently he did not address the question as to the legitimacy of the aim pursued by the regulatory scheme of which section 172 of the Road Traffic Act 1988 forms part. Nor did he examine the question of proportionality. Lord Marnoch's opinion is open to the same criticism.

As the rights which are in question in this case are rights which are not specifically mentioned in Article 6 but are rights which have been read into that article by the court, they plainly do not have the status of rights which are expressed in the Convention as absolute rights. They are therefore open to modification or restriction so long as the relevant principles which apply to that exercise are satisfied. The crucial questions are the two questions which the decision of the High Court has left unanswered. It is to these two questions that I now turn.

Legitimate aim and proportionality

On the one hand there is the nature of the road traffic legislation of which section 172 of the Road Traffic Act 1988 forms part and the aims which it is designed to satisfy. Public safety is at the heart of the matter. Ever since use began to be made on our roads of fast moving motor vehicles it has been appreciated that the use of this means of transport has to be regulated. The risk of injury to the drivers of these vehicles, to passengers, to people in other vehicles on the same road and to members of the public generally led to the introduction of legislation to control the construction and use of motor vehicles and the manner in which they could be driven when they were on the highway and other places to which the public has access. This was combined with a system of registration which served a fiscal purpose but had the added benefit that it enabled both the vehicles and their keepers to be identified. Although there are differences in detail, all countries which are members of the Council of Europe employ similar systems to regulate the construction and use of motor vehicles in the interests of public safety.

I do not think that it can be doubted, against this background, that the system of regulation and the provisions which the legislation contains for the detection and prosecution of road traffic offences serve a legitimate aim. As for section 172 of the 1988 Act in particular, its purpose is to enable the driver of a vehicle alleged to be guilty of an offence to which that section applies to be identified. The offences to which the section applies are the result of a process of selection which has eliminated various minor offences and reserved its application to offences which can properly be regarded as serious. The system which the legislation has laid down for the prosecution of these offences requires the prosecution to prove that the accused was driving the vehicle at the time when the offence was committed. The purpose which these offences are designed to serve would be at risk of being defeated if no means were available to enable the police to trace the driver of a vehicle who, as so often happens, had departed from the place where the offence was committed before he or she could be identified. Here too, it seems to me that a legitimate aim is being pursued.

On the other hand there is the question whether the means which it employs are proportionate to that aim and are compatible with the right of the accused to a fair trial. Has a fair balance been achieved? In order to answer this question it is necessary to examine the provision in question more closely. It has several very important characteristics.

First, there are the qualifications which are written into section 172(2)(a) itself. The provision may be operated only when it is alleged that an offence has been committed of the kind to which the section applies: section 172(1). Then there is the fact that the requirement in section 172(2)(a) to give information as to the identity of the driver may be addressed only to the person keeping the vehicle. The expression 'keeping the vehicle' is not defined, but I take this to be a reference to the person in whose name the vehicle is registered under the Vehicle Excise and Registration Act 1994: see section 172(7) and (9) and the definition of the expression 'registered keeper' in section 172(10). A person who submits to registration as the keeper of a motor vehicle must be taken to have accepted responsibility for its use and the corresponding obligation to provide the information when required to do so. Furthermore the requirement for which provision is made is directed to one issue only, the identity of the driver of the vehicle. It is proper to recognise that the identity of the driver is likely to be an important and indeed crucial issue at any trial. But the provision does not permit open ended questioning of the person keeping the vehicle in order to secure an admission of guilt as to the offence. It seems to me that, bearing in mind the difficulties that may arise in tracing the driver of a vehicle after the event, this limited incursion into the right of silence and the right of the driver who is alleged to have committed an offence not to incriminate himself is proportionate.

Then there is the use which may be made of the response to the requirement in the event that the person keeping the vehicle admits that he or she was the driver of it. This is not the subject of any express provision in section 172 or of any other provision in the 1988 Act. But the approach which has been taken to provisions of this kind is that, unless the legislation provides otherwise, answers which a person is compelled to give in response to a statutory requirement can be used against that person in criminal proceedings. It was on that basis that Lord Justice Clerk Grant proceeded when he said in *Foster v. Farrell* at 1963 J.C., pp.53–54; 1963 S.L.T., p.185 that a statement obtained from the keeper as to the identity of the driver was admissible in evidence against him. The answer to the question whether the use of the driver's self incriminating statement at a trial for the offence with regard to which the requirement was made is proportionate to the legitimate aim is to be found partly in the characteristics of section 172(2)(a) which I have already identified and partly in the other respects in which the legislation preserves the accused's right to a fair trial. Under Scots law the driver's admission must be corroborated, and there must be other evidence to show beyond reasonable doubt that the driver committed the offence with which he is charged. All the usual protections against unreliable evidence and evidence obtained by oppression or other improper means remain in place.

I think therefore that it is reasonable to conclude that the limited modification which section 172(2)(a) makes, in pursuance of a legitimate aim in the public interest, to the right to silence and the right not to incriminate oneself is compatible with the right of the accused to a fair trial. I would hold that a fair balance has been achieved between these competing interests."

NOTES

It is arguable that the Scots approach—exemplified by cases such as *Lawrie v. Muir* and *Miln v. Cullen*—to evidence which is unfairly or illegally obtained is effectively the same as the European approach. What is required is a balancing of interests, in which no particular interest has absolute superiority or priority. In that context Lord Hope's review of the classic Scottish authorities on the "fairness test" is useful, linking this very modern authority on the applicable European jurisprudence, with the line of decisions reviewed by Lord Rodger in *Thompson v. Crowe*.

Chapter 9

COLLATERAL AND CHARACTER EVIDENCE

This branch of the law deals with the admissibility of evidence of events or actions which do not relate directly to the criminal charge or civil ground of action in a particular case, but to previous, similar incidents in which the accused or defender has been involved. It also regulates the extent to which evidence of a person's character may be led. The question, generally, is whether evidence of what has occurred on a previous occasion, is relevant to what has occurred on the particular occasion in question, and, even if it is considered relevant, whether it is also admissible. In general, the law answers this question in the negative, but there are exceptions. The leading case on collateral evidence is an English one.

(A) COLLATERAL EVIDENCE

1. Makin v. Attorney General for New South Wales
[1894] A.C. 57

Makin and his wife were charged with the murder of a baby whom it was alleged they had informally adopted. A sum of money had been paid to them by the child's mother, a sum which was admittedly inadequate to support the child. There was ample circumstantial evidence to convict the couple, but the prosecution sought in addition to adduce evidence of a number of other mothers who had placed their babies with the *Makins* in similar circumstances and of thirteen bodies found on premises which had been occupied by the *Makins* at various times. The prosecution argued that this evidence was relevant to rebut any possible defence of accident, and to show that the accused were engaged on a systematic course of conduct—sometimes known as "baby farming". The Privy Council held that the evidence relating to the other babies was admissible as supporting the other circumstantial evidence in the case.

OPINION OF THE BOARD: "In their Lordship's opinion the principles which must govern the decision of the case are clear, though the application of them is by no means free from difficulty. It is undoubtedly not competent for the prosecution to adduce evidence tending to shew that the accused has been guilty of criminal acts other than those covered by the indictment, for the purpose of leading to the conclusion that the accused is a person likely from his criminal conduct or character to have committed the offence for which he is being tried. On the other hand, the mere fact that the evidence adduced tends to shew the commission of other crimes does not render it inadmissible if it be relevant to an issue before the jury, and it may be so relevant if it bears upon the question whether the acts alleged to constitute the crime charged in the indictment were designed or accidental, or to rebut a defence which would otherwise be open to the accused. The statement of these general principles is easy, but it is obvious that it may often be very difficult to draw the line and to decide whether a particular piece of evidence is on the one side or the other."

NOTES

The law has been considerably developed in England, where this type of evidence is often referred to as "similar fact evidence"—and the courts there now require a "striking similarity" or "striking resemblance" between the subject matter of the charge and any evidence of additional similar acts, facts, or events—see *D.P.P. v. Boardman* [1975] A.C. 421. It is not, however, the striking similarity *per se* which allows the admission of such evidence, however. In *D.P.P. v. P.* [1991] 2 A.C. 447, in which *Boardman* was extensively considered, Lord Mackay of Clashfern explained that:

> "the essential feature of evidence which is to be admitted is that its probative force in support of the allegation that an accused person committed a crime is sufficiently great to make it just to admit the evidence, notwithstanding that it is prejudicial to the accused in tending to show that he was guilty of another crime. Such probative force may be derived from striking similarities in the evidence about the manner in which the crime was committed and the authorities provide illustrations of that . . . But restricting the circumstances in which there is sufficient probative force to overcome prejudice of evidence relating to another crime in which there is some striking similarity between them is to restrict the operation of the principle in a way which gives too much effect to a particular manner of stating it, and is not justified in principle. Hume on Crimes, 3rd ed., vol.11, p.384 said long ago: 'the aptitude and coherence of the several circumstances often as fully confirm the truth of the story as if all the witnesses were deponing to the same facts.'
>
> Once the principle is recognised, that what has to be assessed is the probative force of the evidence in question, the infinite variety of circumstances in which the question arises, demonstrates that there is no single answer in which this can be achieved. Whether the evidence has sufficient probative value to outweigh its prejudicial effect must in each case be a question of degree."

The law relating to collateral evidence in Scotland is relatively undeveloped, and the courts have sometimes appeared to treat the matter largely as one of expediency. However, it is thought that the question of relevance, or probative force, as Lord Mackay puts it, is also the governing feature of Scots law in this area. There are clearly cases in which evidence "tending to show that [the accused] was guilty of another crime" is admitted notwithstanding a lack of striking similarity—see, for example, the important, although rather different, case of *Nelson v. H.M.A.*, 1994 S.L.T. 389, below. Compare also the cases of *H.M.A. v. Joseph*, 1929 J.C. 55, the *Moorov* doctrine, considered in Chapter 5, above, and referred to by Lord Mackay in *D.P.P. v. P.*, above, and the New Zealand case of *R. v. Huijser* [1988] 1 N.Z.L.R. 577.

2. A. v. B.
(1895) 22 R. 402

In this case the pursuer in a civil case sued the defender for damages, averring that he had raped her. She averred and sought to lead evidence of other rapes carried out by the defender.

LORD PRESIDENT (ROBERTSON): "I agree with the Sheriff. I think the Sheriff rightly describes the averments, a proof of which he has disallowed, as irrelevant to the issues raised upon record.

The issues to be tried between the parties are whether, on two specified days of June 1894, the defender ravished the pursuer. What the pursuer wishes to prove under the articles in question is substantially whether, in July 1893, the defender attempted to ravish another woman, and whether, in April 1887, he attempted to ravish yet another woman. Article 2 is merely a general averment of system founded upon those two instances.

Now, it is quite plain that if these articles went to proof, the two collateral issues about the two other women would have to be tried out on the same scale as the main issues themselves, and this would be done, not because either of the other women claims it, but merely in order to lend some probability to this pursuer's case.

I cannot but feel that good sense is against such a proceeding, and I am satisfied that the law does not allow it.

In pronouncing any averment to be irrelevant to the issue, it is not implied that the matter averred has no bearing at all on the question in hand. For example, if the defender admitted at the trial that he had attempted to ravish those two other women, I think the jury might legitimately hold that this made it the more likely that he ravished the pursuer. But, then, Courts of law are not bound to admit the ascertainement of every disputed fact which may contribute, however slightly or indirectly, towards the solution of the issue to be tried. Regard must be had to the limitations which time and human liability to confusion impose upon the conduct of all trials. Experience shows that it is better to sacrifice the aid which might be got from the more or less uncertain solution of collateral issues, than to spend a great amount of time, and confuse the jury with what, in the end, even supposing it to be certain, has only an indirect bearing on the matter in hand.

I am for adhering to the interlocutor of the Sheriff. It may be right to add that, while the three articles are struck out of the record, this does not preclude the defender from being cross-examined about those two matters, for his credibility may be tested on matters going to character, although not relevant to the issues. Whatever his answer may be, however, it will not be competent for the pursuer to lead evidence on the subject."

NOTES

In spite of the emphasis in *A. v. B.* on considerations of expediency and, in particular, the avoidance of confusion and delay, the more principled view appears to be that the admissibility of collateral evidence is principally one of relevance—see Lord Justice-Clerk Thomson in *W. Alexander & Sons v. Dundee Corporation*, 1950 S.C. 123, above, Chapter 1 and below, where he says that.

"It was argued to us that the evidence ought to be excluded because this question of the behaviour of the vehicles is a 'collateral issue' in the sense in which that phrase is used in a number of cases which were cited to us. But if it is established that the skidding of these vehicles on these other occasions was truly due to the condition of the road, then it seems to me that that is not a collateral issue at all but something having a direct bearing on the decision of the present case. What we are searching for in a case like this is the cause of the accident. We have to carry out our search for the cause of the accident in a reasonably practical way, and the ultimate test of whether evidence is relevant or not is whether it has a reasonably direct bearing on the subject under investigation."

In this context, the recent case of *H.M.A. v. Beggs (No. 3)*, 2001 S.C.C.R. 891 is interesting. In that case the accused was charged with assault, sodomy and murder. Evidence was held to be admissible that the accused was in the habit of picking up young men and taking them back to his flat for the purpose of having sex with them. No authority on collateral evidence appears to have been before the court. An appeal has been marked at this time of writing, however.

3. W. Alexander & Sons v. Dundee Corporation
1950 S.C. 123

The facts of this case and part of Lord Justice-Clerk Thomson's opinion are set out in Chapter 1.

LORD MACKAY: "The case as against the Lord Ordinary's allowance of proof on the whole averments of both parties was opened almost entirely upon the authority of three cases, *A. v. B.* [(1895) 22 R. 402, above]; *H. v. P.* [(1905) 8 F. 232] and *Inglis v. The National Bank of Scotland Limited* [1909 S.C. 1038]. The Lord Ordinary distinguished these cases and, like your Lordship, I do not find anything wrong with the distinction which the Lord Ordinary made between them and the present case. All I would say is that perhaps the word 'collateral' has, both in the Lord Ordinary's opinion and in the arguments before us, appeared too largely in the character, as it were, of a decisive word—as if, that is to say, anything not collateral would eventually be allowed in, and anything 'collateral' ought everywhere and always to be excluded. For several reasons I think this exaltation of the word 'collateral' has been unfortunate in the history of our law on this class of matter. I do indeed find the word incidentally occurring in some three of the cited opinions. But the other and remaining points made against the various proposals of proof of prior instances are plainly more material, and are more helpful. Looking at the three cases as they stand, I think there is no doubt that a plain distinction falls to be taken between them and cases like the present, in which the real issue as to fault in the matter of causation of a slip of tyres is the alleged condition of a road—a road which has got to be, by admission, kept by the road authority (defenders) in a perpetual state of suitable repair for frequent access by wheel traffic; and which must (by the very hypothesis of the arguments) be examined and repaired from time to time.

What I thus affirm about the necessary upkeep of such a road is not only common sense but is the result of the defenders' own defences here, in which they put forward as a defence (and quite rightly so, if they prove it) that the time for overhaul and resurfacing of this road had only just arrived, and that they had even ordered such treatment by spraying, and that they did in fact proceed to do it within the next few weeks. What is the difference between a case like that and the three cited? The question in all the three cases was as to the probability of a delict (rape in one case, adultery in another, an alleged fraudulent misrepresentation by a bank in the third); and the only proposed link of causation—a link which was held to be insufficient to allow in as proof any previous incidents of other delicts, even though like in character—was that, in the constitution or habitual build-up of a particular man involved in both earlier and later instances, there was a tendency to do the sort of things which would throw light, or probability, on the real question as to whether he actually did the final delictual action. I find it enough, to establish the clear distinction, to cite the actual passage quoted to us from the third case (*Inglis*), that in which Lord McLaren says (at p.1040): 'Although that case in its merits and substance belongs to a very different region of law, yet in the only matter there considered, namely, the relevancy, it seems to me to be a good authority for the proposition that it is not evidence against a party of having committed *a delict* to show that he has committed delicts *of the like description* against other persons on other occasions.' It is obvious, firstly, on the statement of that proposition that it does not apply here, because here we have no case of delict. There is no case to be made that the Corporation was deliberately neglecting its duties, but simply that it delayed too long in taking the necessary remedial steps to keep the road in repair. It is not, therefore, a delict at all. Even '*quasi*-delict' is a pretty strong term. Just negligence or delay. Secondly, the statement of Lord McLaren assumes that the actual incident is to be another delict committed against a different person and a delict 'of the like description'. The three cases relied on were all of that sort. The only link was a human link consisting of a probability of a habitual class of delict.

It does not follow of course that, because the Lord Ordinary rightly distinguished these cases, an restricted proof of any earlier happenings or accidents is to be allowed in every case. The Court must do its best between rejecting proof which the ordinary man will think strong or convincing and, on the other hand, accumulating matters of proof to such an extent as to choke the course of justice.

I should like to add, more directly relative to the present case, that to ignore all proof of the sort suggested here would not be to do justice between the parties. The issue is not the commission even of a *quasi*-delict upon the particular occasion of August 21, 1948, and one directed against this particular omnibus. It is rather a gradual and progressive fault—a delay in the proper care required of road authorities to keep a viable road; but a road which, on the other hand, by their very own averments, is a road which requires vigilance to examine it against deterioration which in process of time is inevitable, from time to time and whenever seen to be nearing the margin of danger, and the duty, towards all the traffic on each and every day, is to take prompt steps to overcome the tendency to become slippery, oily or 'treacherous'. It seems to me that such a duty and such alleged failure are pre-eminently not comparable to an issue of a commission of a single delict against a particular person and at a particular time; it is the *quasi*-delict involved in being too slow in apprehension of the increasing danger, and too slow in applying a remedy. If there is any class of permissible evidence, apart from limiting all proof to some direct testimony that 'upon such and such a day' (that in question) I found the road oily and dangerous', it is surely evidence that many accidents occurred, near the same locus, and (if it be so) were ascribed to under capacity of the particular road surface at that point to hold tyres."

NOTES

In *Hart v. Royal London Mutual Insurance Co. Ltd*, 1956 S.L.T. (Notes) 55, Lord Guthrie approved the following passage from the opinion of the Lord Ordinary, Lord Strachan in *W. Alexander & Sons v. Dundee Corporation*, which presents a nicely composite view of the rationale behind the collateral evidence "rule":

"The principle of the cases is, I think, that, where the issues are truly collateral, evidence is excluded because it is irrelevant and because it is inexpedient to spend time and money on proving facts which have no direct bearing on the matter in hand and which could at the most only lend some probability to the case. Where, on the other hand, the facts are not collateral but have a direct bearing on the particular case under consideration, evidence in regard to them is not excluded."

See also the cases of *Knutsen v. Mauritzen* (1918) 1 S.L.T. 85 and *Morrison v. Maclean's Trustees* (1862) 24 D. 625.

4. Gallagher v. Paton
1909 S.C. (J.) 50

An advertising agent was charged with fraud. It was alleged that he had pretended to "a female shop assistant" that her employer paid yearly for an advertisement in a directory, and thus induced her to pay him the sum of 1s.6d. The prosecutor sought to lead evidence of similar attempts made on the same day as the one libelled in the complaint. This evidence was admitted by the Magistrate and the accused was convicted. On appeal to the High Court it was held that the evidence had been competently admitted.

LORD MCLAREN: "The second objection is that the Magistrate admitted incompetent evidence, *videlicet*, the evidence of persons to whom similar representation were made by the accused on the same day. Now, when the question is whether the accused person made false statements, knowing the statements to be false, and for the purpose of obtaining money to which he was not entitled, I do not know of any better way of establishing the criminal intention than by proof that he had made similar false statements on the same day to other people, and apparently with the same object. In a civil case such evidence would be admitted without doubt or difficulty, and in criminal practice there is a parallel case, where it has been adjudged that evidence of attempting to pass off base coin to other persons is proof of guilty knowledge in the case of the base coin which the accused person successfully passed off. A false statement made to one person may be explained away, but when a system of false statements is proved, the probability is very great that the statements were designedly made. Unless a decision to the contrary could be produced, I am unable to hold that the law will reject as inadmissible evidence on which every one would act in the ordinary affairs of life, and which is calculated to produce conviction to any fair-minded person who hears it. This view of the question, however, suggests a limitation, that the evidence of like representations must be confined to those that were made about the same time, because, if the prosecutor were allowed to prove statements made at an earlier period, this would only go to general character, and would not necessarily throw light on the particular act which is under consideration."

5. Dumoulin v. H.M.A.
1974 S.L.T. (Notes) 42

"Ernst Bernhard Heinrich Dumoulin was charged on an indictment which set forth that, having formed a criminal purpose of taking out a policy or policies of insurance on the life of another whose death he intended to bring about to enable him to claim the sum or sums assured under such policies, he did certain things. The first was that he obtained money by fraudulent transactions in Germany on . . . September 14 and 15, 1972 and lodged part of the proceeds to his credit in the Bank of Nova Scotia in Edinburgh. The second, which was the subject of charge 1, was that between . . . September 20 and 30, 1972 he attempted to obtain money from the bank by fraud. The third was that he induced the girl he later married to complete applications for insurance of her life for very large sums in the event of her accidental death and used the money at his credit at the bank to pay the initial premium. The fourth was that on October 13, 1972 he married the girl and fifth, which was the subject of charge 2, was that on the same date he murdered his wife by pushing her over a cliff on Salisbury Crags. The indictment ended thus: 'all this you did with the intent to obtain money by fraud in pursuance of said criminal purpose.'

Before the jury was empanelled objection was taken to the relevancy and competency of that part of the indictment which related to the fraudulent transactions in Germany and also to the relevancy of charge 1 to the criminal purposes libelled. The objections were repelled and in course of the trial evidence was led upon both these matters. At the end of the day the trial judge directed the jury that there was insufficient evidence in law to entitle them to hold that the applicant had formed the criminal purpose libelled before the transactions in Germany took place and that, accordingly, they must put completely out of their minds the evidence which they had heard about those transactions. Further, at the end of the day, the Crown intimated that a conviction was no longer sought on charge 1 and that the evidence led did not establish that the applicant's communings with the bank had reached the stage of an attempt to induce the making of a loan. The jury was accordingly directed to find the applicant not guilty of this charge.

In the result the jury, by majority, found the applicant guilty as libelled of charge 2 under deletion of the words 'in pursuance of said criminal purpose'. In effect, therefore, they found him guilty of the murder of his wife with intent to obtain money by fraud.

The accused sought leave to appeal against his conviction alleging error on the part of the presiding judge in repelling the objection which had been taken to the competency and relevancy.

In *refusing* the application the court (the Lord Justice-General (Emslie), Lords Cameron and Johnston) delivered an opinion from which the following excerpt is taken: 'The question for us, accordingly, is whether the presiding judge was right to repel the objection taken to that part of the indictment which narrated the fraudulent transactions in Germany. It is not in dispute that it is incompetent to charge, and to lead evidence about, a criminal offence committed in a foreign jurisdiction unless that criminal offence forms an integral part of the crime which is libelled as having taken place in Scotland or unless the nexus between the offence abroad and the crime in Scotland is sufficiently close, *ex facie* of the indictment, as to make it relevant to prove the offence abroad in course of proof of the crime in Scotland. In short, the competency of libelling and admitting evidence about the fraudulent transactions in Germany depends essentially on whether, considering the indictment as a whole, these transactions are prima facie relevant to proof of the crimes which, according to the indictment, were committed in Scotland. So viewing the problem, the presiding judge's decision upon this question was, in our opinion, plainly the right one. On the face of this indictment the Crown was setting out to prove a motive for the murder libelled in charge 2. In particularly [sic] the Crown was setting out to prove that the criminal purpose was conceived in Germany and that to enable the impecunious applicant to complete that purpose by the murder in Scotland he engaged in the fraudulent transactions in Germany as the first step in acquiring the funds necessary to the execution of the plan.' Indeed, as the indictment expressly states, all the acts alleged to have been done by the applicant, including his actings in Germany, were done in the pursuance of the antecedent criminal purpose formed in Germany. In these circumstances, *ex facie* of the indictment, the transactions in Germany were an integral part of the preparation for the commission of the crimes libelled in Scotland. It matters not where these transactions took place, for the nexus libelled between these transactions and the charge of murder in Scotland is clearly sufficiently close to make it impossible to sustain the objections to relevancy. It follows that the evidence as to the transactions in Germany was competently admitted."

6. H.M.A. v. Joseph
1929 J.C. 55

J was charged with a fraudulent scheme involving the forgery of bank documents and the uttering of them, in Scotland, as genuine. The indictment libelled that in pursuance of this scheme, he had uttered a forged document in an hotel in Brussels. It was objected that it was incompetent to charge a crime committed in Belgium, and that evidence of the Belgian uttering was inadmissible. The trial judge repelled the objection.

LORD MURRAY: "A second point was argued, which, however, relates rather to the competency and admissibility of evidence, and I may at this stage indicate my view upon it. It is said that, inasmuch as the incident in Belgium admittedly cannot proceed as a substantive charge, any evidence relating to this matter, which would otherwise be relevant and admissible as bearing on the first and second charges—see Macdonald's, *Criminal Law* (3rd ed.) pp.317, 318, and the case of Bell there cited. It is not disputed that our law does not allow proof of a crime other than that which is libelled merely to establish that it is probable or likely that the accused may have committed the crime charged. But I regard it as settled that evidence in regard to another incident of a similar character may be admitted in proof of a crime charge, notwithstanding that this evidence may incidentally show or tend to show the commission of another crime, provided there be some connection or 'nexus', which, in the opinion of the Court, is sufficiently intimate, between the two 'incidents'. There is ample authority for the view that, if the connection between the incident sought to be proved and the crime libelled is very close in point of time and character, so that they can hardly be dissociated, the evidence will be admitted. I need not resume the authorities. The only question in this case is whether I am satisfied that the nexus is prima facie sufficiently close to warrant the admission of evidence as to the foreign incident, if it be tendered by the Crown in support of the charges libelled. The mere fact that it is rather later in point of date is, in my opinion, not conclusive. No doubt, if the interval of time is of a considerable duration, this may affect the weight of the evidence, and it might then be the duty of the judge to point this out to the jury, but that is another matter. Accordingly, on the question of admissibility of evidence, I am of the opinion that it is the law in Scotland, as in England, that it is open to the prosecution to prove any facts relevant to the charge, notwithstanding that they may show or tend to show the commission of another crime, if they show or tend to show that the act charged was done of design and did not arise by accident, or if they tend to rebut a defence of innocence which might otherwise be open to the panel."

NOTES

There is a close connection here with the case of *Moorov v. H.M.A.*, 1930 J.C. 68. *Moorov*, of course, has very particular implications for the doctrine of corroboration—see Chapter 5 above—but like this case, and the others reproduced here, it is fundamentally a case about circumstantial evidence and its relevance. See *D.P.P. v. P.* [1991] 2 A.C. 447, discussed above, and *R. v. Kilbourne* [1973] A.C. 729, in which Lord Simon of Glaisdale said:

"In *Moorov v. H.M. Advocate* . . . the accused was convicted of a series of assaults and indecent assaults on various female employees. In respect of many of the charges the only direct evidence against the accused was that of the woman against whom the particular offence was alleged to have been committed. The evidence of each woman was, however, held to have been corroborative of that of the others, which involved that it was both admissible on and relevant to the other charges. Lord Clyde, Lord Justice-General, started his judgment at p.72: 'The question in the present case belongs to the department of circumstantial evidence. This consideration is vital to the whole matter. Circumstantial evidence is evidence of facts from which, taken with all the other evidence, a reasonable inference is a fact directly in issue. It works by cumulatively, in geometrical progression, eliminating other possibilities. Why should evidence of assault on the other women in *Moorov* be evidence from which it was a reasonable inference that the accused had committed the particular assault? The answer was [that] . . . there was such a striking similarity between the various offences as to show an underlying unity, to provide a connecting link between them, so that each confirmed another, rendering the other more probable. As it was put in *Rex v. Sims* [1946] K.B. 531, 540:
'The probative force of all the acts together is much greater than one alone; for, whereas the jury might think one man might be telling an untruth, three or four are hardly likely to tell the same untruth unless they were conspiring together. If there is nothing to suggest a conspiracy their evidence would seem to be overwhelming.' "

The admissibility of evidence relating to criminal offences not libelled on the indictment has now been authoritatively considered in the following case:

7. Nelson v. H.M.A.
1994 S.C.C.R. 192

The appellant was charged with being concerned in the supply of controlled drugs contrary to section 4(3)(b) of the Misuse of Drugs Act 1971. Evidence was led that when the police attempted to arrest the appellant, he went into a toilet and swallowed a small cellophane wrapped object. Objection was taken to this on the basis that it was evidence which disclosed an offence by the appellant which was not libelled, namely obstructing the police contrary to section 23 of the 1971 Act by attempting to conceal possession of controlled drugs. The objection was repelled by the trial judge and the appellant appealed to the High Court.

LORD PRESIDENT (HOPE): "The rule upon which the objection to the admissibility of the evidence was based is a familiar one which is well recognised. Renton and Brown, paragraph 18–89, sets out the rule in these terms.

> 'It is not competent to lead evidence of any crime not libelled in the indictment either as a specific charge, or as a specific averment, in which case it must be relevant evidence of the crime charged.'

In *Boyle,* Petitioner, at p.955E the Lord Justice-General said:

> 'The principle is that notice must be given in the indictment of the intention to lead evidence of anything done or omitted to be done by the accused which constitutes a crime. This is so even if the evidence is to be directed only to proof of the principal crime or crimes libelled against him.'

The point which requires to be examined is whether this rule has been expressed correctly or whether it requires to be qualified to prevent its being applied too widely or being pressed to lengths which are unreasonable. It would not be in the interests of justice if the rule were to be applied too generally in circumstances where there was no need for this. Indeed there are signs that this is tending to be the case. The rapid growth in the number of and range of statutory offences has created a situation which cannot have been envisaged in the early years when the rule was being evolved. The view has developed that it is necessary to libel every offence, whether statutory or otherwise, which the evidence shows the accused may have committed, even though the Crown has no intention of seeking a conviction for these offences. Yet it may be necessary for the Crown to lead the evidence of these facts as background to proving the principal charges in the indictment. This practice has tended to lead to the overloading of indictments with charges, many of which have no prospect of surviving a submission of no case to answer under section 140A of the Criminal Procedure (Scotland) Act 1975 and will almost certainly be withdrawn at the end of the Crown case. This in turn may lead to confusion in the minds of the jury as to why they were in the indictment in the first place and as to the effect on the remaining charges of these charges being withdrawn. In the result, the true issues in the case may be obscure, in circumstances where there was no real risk of prejudice to the accused if the charges had been omitted from the indictment.

The Lord Advocate accepted that, if some of the formulations of the rule which are to be found in the authorities were sound, the evidence which was objected to in this case would require to be held to have been inadmissible. He submitted, however, that when these authorities were properly understood, the rule could more appropriately be restated to this effect: that the Crown can lead any evidence relevant to the proof of a crime charged, even though it may show or tend to show the commission of another crime not charged, unless that other crime is so dissociated in time, place or character from the crime charged that the libel does not give fair notice to the accused that evidence relating to that other crime may be led. Applying that formulation of the rule to the circumstances of the present case, he said that, when the accused is served with an indictment which libels a crime committed by him on a particular date at a particular locus, he must expect the Crown to lead any evidence relating to the events which happened at that time and that place which are relevant to the crime charged. The appellant in this case was charged with being concerned in the supplying of controlled drugs to another or others in the public house on the date when he was seen there by the police and detained by them. So there could be no objection to evidence being led of his actions while he was there, including actions which tended to show that he was seeking to conceal that he had controlled drugs in his possession from the police.

Although the rule is, as we have said, a familiar one, there is little detailed discussion of it in the early cases by which it was established: *H.M.A. v. Pritchard* and *H.M.A. v. Monson*. The panel in both of these cases was charged with murder and in both cases the Crown sought to lead evidence that he had done things which showed or tended to show that he had committed another crime with which he had not been charged in the indictment. Dr Pritchard was charged with murdering his wife and her mother by poisoning. Evidence was led from a female servant in the house in which she said she had become pregnant by him and had had a miscarriage. Objection was taken when she was asked whether the panel had given her anything to cause the miscarriage, on the ground that there was no notice in the indictment of such a charge. The Lord Justice-Clerk, Lord Justice Inglis, sustained the objection after consulting with the other judges, holding that the proposed question was not competent. No reasons were given by him in that case. But in *Monson* at pp.7–8 Lord Justice-Clerk Macdonald gave this explanation for the decision.

> 'That was a case where the crime charged was poisoning a wife, and it was held competent to ask a witness whether the prisoner had been having relations of improper intimacy with his female servant, that not being a matter which could have been made the subject of a criminal charge, and being one which might be proved as an incidental fact tending to establish motive; but when it was further proposed to ask the question whether the prisoner in those circumstances had used means to procure premature delivery, that was not allowed. That was a suggestion of crime, and crime with which the prisoner might have been charged in the indictment, thus giving him notice that he had to meet that charge . . .
>
> In that particular case what was proposed to be asked could have had no connection with the question which was being tried. The question of the undue familiarity had to do with the question that was being tried. The question of the prisoner having tried to get rid of the consequences of that intimacy could have had nothing to do with it except to throw suspicion upon him as regards the charge upon which he was brought to the bar— suggesting that if he could do the one thing he might do the other—and the Court disallowed it.'

In *Monson's* case objection was taken to a question which the prosecutor proposed to ask of a witness about a document which was pertinent to the case as it related to the question of motive. It bore the name of the witness as a signature and the question was whether he had in fact signed the document. The suggestion was that the panel had forged the signature. Objection was taken on the ground that if the panel was to be charged with forgery, that crime should have been libelled against him and he was not prepared to meet the charge as he had no notice of it. Although the question might have been regarded as relevant, the objection was sustained on the ground of lack of notice for reasons which were explained by Lord Justice-Clerk in this passage at p.8.

> 'If the charge had been made, the prisoner, through his advisors, would have made all preparations to meet it, but his legal advisers have no notice of any such charge, and it is impossible for them at this stage competently to bring forward evidence to meet it. This document was produced by the Crown and laid before the prisoner, but it was not alleged in the indictment that the prosecutor proposed to prove that the document was a forged document. I am of opinion that it would not be safe to allow such a question, which would tend to prove a very serious crime—one of the most serious crimes known to the law—as part of the incidents of a charge of another kind. It appears to me that the only right and proper course is to make that serious crime also a matter of charge, if the public prosecutor considers it to be of such importance to his case, as regards the history of the other crime, that he wishes to have it proved.'

It seems to be clear from these passages that the foundation for the rule is to be found in the principles of relevancy and of fair notice. It is open to the Crown on the one hand to lead any evidence which is relevant to proof of the crime charged. And, as Lord Meadowbank said in

H.M.A. v. Ritchie and Morren at p.582, it is not necessary to set forth the evidence in the indictment. Similar views were expressed by Lord Justice-Clerk Hope at p.563 and Lord Mackenzie at p.582. To the same effect in Monson at p.7 the Lord Justice Clerk said:

> 'As regards all circumstances tending relatively to throw light on the particular offence charged in the indictment—all ordinary circumstances—which cannot be made matter of criminal charge, it is not necessary in the ordinary case for the public prosecutor to give any notice of them. A person charged with a crime is under the necessity along with his advisors of preparing for every ordinary matter which may be relevant to the charge, and I think that is well illustrated in the case of *Pritchard*.'

But the accused must be given fair notice if evidence is to be led which would tend to prove that he had committed another crime, as proof of this might prejudice him in his defence to the charge libelled against him in the indictment. The requirement for notice that such evidence is to be led is not removed simply because the evidence might be relevant to the proof of that crime.

The Lord Advocate drew our attention to an unreported case, the trial of *John Watson Laurie*, for what became known as the Arran Murder in November 1889. Details of the trial are given in the account of it in a volume of the Notable British Trials series published in 1932, which was edited by William Roughead. The indictment is set out at p.65 and it contains a single charge alleging that the panel assaulted the deceased near the head of Glen Sannox in the Isle of Arran 'and did throw him down, and did beat him, and did murder him'. Evidence was led, as recorded in the Lord Justice-Clerk's charge at pp.218–219, that on the morning after the two men walked together in Glen Sannox the panel disappeared from the house where they had been staying, taking with him his own bag and the bag of the deceased. When he was apprehended some days later by the police he said that he had robbed the deceased but did not murder him. This line was maintained for the defence at the trial, and the Lord Justice-Clerk said at p.220 that a great deal would depend on what the jury made of the suggestion in arriving at their decision in the case. Now, although there was plainly evidence in that case which tended to show that the panel had robbed the deceased of his bag, no charge to that effect was included in the indictment. There is no mention of any objection having been taken to the evidence on the ground of lack of notice. But is appears that no prejudice could have been alleged in that case, as the evidence was relevant to motive and the panel accepted all along that he had robbed the deceased and that he had his bag with him when he left the house.

The cases to which we have referred so far do not suggest that the mere fact that the evidence may show or tend to show that the accused committed a crime not charged in the indictment necessarily renders the evidence inadmissible. That the rule was not being pressed that far at this stage can be seen from *Gallagher v. Paton* and *H.M.A. v. Joseph*. In *Gallagher* the complainer was charged with making a pretence to a shop assistant and defrauding her of a sum of money by means of the false pretence. Evidence was led at his trial of similar false representations made by the complainer to other persons on the same day for the purpose of obtaining money from them to which he was not entitled. It was contended that this was incompetent evidence as it had no bearing on the charge in the complaint. The evidence was held to be admissible because it was relevant to establishing the appellant's criminal intention. Lord McLaren said at p.55:

> 'Now, when the question is whether the accused person made false statements, knowing the statements to be false, and for the purpose of obtaining money to which he was not entitled, I do not know of any better way of establishing the criminal intention than by proof that he had made similar false statements on the same day to other people, and apparently with the same object.'

Lord Pearson said at p.56 that this was one of a class of cases in which guilty knowledge might be proved by such evidence, so as to exclude the defence that the act complained of was a mere mistake. No point was taken in that case that the complainer did not have fair notice of the intention to lead the evidence.

In *Joseph* the accused was charged with fraud and among the actings libelled in the indictment was the allegation that, in pursuance of the scheme, in a hotel in Brussels, he pretended that a forged document was genuine. Objection was taken to the relevancy of this part of the indictment on the ground that the court had no jurisdiction to try the accused for a crime committed in Belgium and it was also said that the evidence as to the crime alleged to have been committed there was inadmissible. No point could be taken in that case about lack of notice, but it was conceded for the Crown that the accused could not be charged with the commission of a crime in Belgium and there was a question as to the relevancy of the evidence. Lord Murray dealt with this point at pp.56–57.

'It is not disputed that our law does not allow proof of a crime other than that which is libelled merely to establish that it is probable or likely that the accused may have committed the crime charged. But I regard it as settled that evidence in regard to another incident of similar character may be admitted in proof of a crime charged, notwithstanding that this evidence may incidentally show or tend to show the commission of another crime, provided there be some connection or "nexus" which, in the opinion of the Court, is sufficiently intimate, between the two "incidents".'

He concluded his opinion at p.57 with an observation which, insofar as it related to England, appears to have been based on what was said in *Makin v. Attorney-General for New South Wales* at p.65. What he said was:

'Accordingly, on the question of admissibility of evidence, I am of opinion that it is the law in Scotland, as in England, that it is open to the prosecution to prove any facts relevant to the charge, notwithstanding that they may show or tend to show the commission of another crime, if they show or tend to show that the act charged was done of design and did not arise by accident, or if they tend to rebut a defence of innocence which might otherwise be open to the panel.'

We note that neither *Pritchard* nor *Monson* were referred to in the argument or in the opinions in these cases, and the last sentence which we have quoted from Lord Murray's opinion in *Joseph* does not sit very easily with what Lord Justice-Clerk Macdonald said in Monson at p.8 giving his reasons for sustaining the objections in that case.

It appears, however, by now to have been accepted as a general rule that it was incompetent to lead evidence showing or tending to show that the accused was guilty of a crime with which he had not been charged. In *Cameron v. Waugh* the appellant was charged with theft. Evidence was led which tended to show that he had been guilty of the crime of forgery, although he had not been charged with that crime in the complaint. Objection was taken to that evidence but the objection was repelled by the sheriff-substitute. Lord Justice-General Normand observed at p.8 that it was not disputed that it would be incompetent to lead evidence tending to show that the accused was guilty of the crime of forgery when the only crime with which he was charged was theft and that it was held that, as that was the effect of the evidence, the sheriff-substitute had misdirected himself. In *Griffen v. H.M.A.* the appellant was charged with an attempt to defraud a building society and mention was made in the indictment that he had adhibited a false signature to a disposition as part of the actings incidental to the crime charged. There was no lack of notice in that case about the intention to lead that evidence, but an objection was taken to it on the ground that the appellant had not been charged with uttering. The objection was repelled by the trial judge on the ground that sufficient notice was given in the indictment of what the Crown was proposing to prove. An appeal was taken against this decision, based on what the Lord Justice-Clerk said in *Monson*, but it was held that the evidence was properly admitted by the trial judge as the Crown was not seeking to make a substantive case against the appellant that he had committed the crime of uttering and because fair notice of what it was proposed to prove had been given in the indictment.

All the judges in *Griffen* affirmed the soundness of the rule described by the Lord Justice-Clerk in *Monson*. Lord Justice-Clerk Aitchison said at p.5 that this was a most salutary rule and that it should be strictly observed. He restated the rule in these terms.

'If in order to prove the substantive crime libelled it is thought necessary by the Crown to prove the commission of some other crime that is relevant to the crime substantively charged, or to the motive for committing it, then I do not doubt for a moment that notice ought to be given in the indictment by setting forth the subsidiary crime in the form of a charge. I should be sorry if the rule laid down by the Lord Justice-Clerk in *Monson's* case were in any way weakened.'

Lord Mackay expressed the rule at p.7 in these terms.

'If the Crown thinks it necessary to prove guilt of a separate crime against a panel, indicted for other crime or crimes, it must charge or libel it.'

Lord Ward noted at p.8 that what was attempted to be done in *Pritchard* and *Monson* was to prove acts which by themselves might have been charged as criminal without any notice whatever in the indictment of the intention to prove any such acts. But he agreed with the other judges that the evidence was admissible because the appellant had full notice of it in the indictment and because the Crown were not seeking to maintain against him that he had committed the crime of uttering.

All the cases to which we have referred so far were concerned only with common law crimes. But in *Robertson v. Watson* the appellants were charged with an offence under section 2 of the Food and Drugs (Adulteration) Act 1928 and regulation 1 of the Sale of Milk Regulations 1901 by selling milk which was deficient in milk fat. Evidence was led about the method of conveying the milk from the farms to the purchasers' premises and this included evidence that the milk cans were not locked and sealed as required by the Milk and Dairies (Scotland) Order 1934. The appellants were not charged with a breach of the 1934 Regulations, but no objection was taken to this evidence and an appeal as to its admissibility failed on that ground. The application of the rule to the circumstances of that case was, however, affirmed by Lord Justice-General Cooper at p.87.

'The rule illustrated by the *Monson* and *Pritchard* trials and expounded with its limitations in *Griffen v. H.M.A.* was, in my view, contravened by the proof of infringements of the Order of 1934. Failure to seal or lock the cans cannot be regarded as a mere incident to the commission of the offence charged emerging accidentally in the course of evidence directed to the offence charged. It is a distinct offence, rendering the offender liable to substantial penalties, and its proof was evidently relied upon as an element in establishing the guilt of the appellants of the offence charged and as extending the area falling to be covered by them in their effort to overcome the statutory presumption of guilt. In all such cases, if the matter is to be proved, it should be made the subject of a separate charge.'

It is not easy to reconcile all these *dicta*, because there are various aspects to the rule and it is subject to limitations, as the Lord Justice-General observed in *Robertson*. Attempts have been made to state it in simple terms, as in *Griffen*, but they are liable to mislead, with the result that the rule is then applied in circumstances where this is unnecessary. But it is worth noting that in several versions of the rule emphasis is placed on the intention to prove guilt of the other crime, which requires notice to be given. In *Griffen* Lord Justice-Clerk Aitchison referred to proof of 'the commission of some other crime'. Lord Mackay refers to it being thought necessary 'to prove guilt of a separate crime'. In *Robertson* the Lord Justice-General referred to 'proof of the offence under the 1934 Order which required the matter to be separately charged in the complaint. As we said earlier, the foundation for the rule is to be found in the principles of fair notice and of relevancy. To take first the question of relevancy, the general rule is that the Crown can lead any evidence which is relevant to the crime charged. This may include evidence relating to motive as well as to things done to commit the crime. The fact that the evidence may show or tend to show that the accused committed a crime not charged is not in itself a reason for holding the evidence to be inadmissible, so long as to do so is relevant to the crime charged in the indictment. But evidence showing or tending to show that the accused committed another crime may be prejudicial to him. This will be so, especially in the case of serious common law crimes which would be obvious to a jury, where the evidence tends to show that the accused is of bad character. This was the point which Lord Justice-Clerk Macdonald observed in *Monson* at p.8. As he put it, such evidence may suggest that if the accused would do the one thing, he might do the other. He regarded it as unsafe to allow a question which tended to prove the commission of a very serious crime as part of the incidents of a charge of another kind.

In such cases the principle of fair notice requires that the other crime ought to be charged in the complaint or indictment or at least that it should be the subject of a distinct averment. There is less reason to be concerned on this point if the evidence tends merely to show incidentally that the accused may have committed an offence of a trivial or technical nature from which no inference could be drawn that he was of bad character. But if it is necessary for the Crown to go to the length of establishing that the accused was in fact guilty of another crime, as part of the evidence relating to the crime charged, fair notice requires that this should be distinctly libelled in the complaint or indictment. This was one of the points observed in *Griffen*, in which it was noted that the Crown were not seeking to establish that the accused was guilty of the crime of uttering but led the evidence merely in order to show the history of the fraudulent transaction. Conversely, in *Robertson* it appears that the Crown led evidence that the accused committed the statutory offence which had not been charged against them as part of the evidence directed to the offence charged in the complaint.

The suggestion by the Lord Advocate as to how the rule might be restated does not deal fully with all these points. But taking his wording as a basis for this, we consider that, in the light of the principles upon which the earlier decisions were based, the rule may more appropriately be restated in these terms. The Crown can lead any evidence relevant to the proof of a crime charged, even though it may show or tend to show the commission of another crime not charged, unless fair notice requires that that other crime should be charged or otherwise referred to expressly in the complaint or indictment. This will be so if the evidence sought to be led tends to show that the accused was of bad character and that that other crime is so different in time, place or character from the crime charged to establish that the accused was in fact guilty of that other crime.

In the present case, the evidence of what happened in the toilet was clearly related to the crimes charged against the appellant in this indictment. Fair notice was given, by reference to the date and the place, of the intention to lead evidence of what happened when the appellant was seen there by police officers. His actings in attempting to conceal from them his possession of controlled drugs were relevant to the question whether he was guilty of being concerned in the supplying of drugs. It was not necessary for the Crown to prove that he was guilty of the separate statutory offence of intentionally obstructing the police officers in the exercise of their powers under section 23 of the Act and the evidence did not seek to establish this as a fact. For these reasons it was not necessary on grounds of fair notice for the commission of an offence under section 23 to be libelled in order to render this evidence admissible.

It follows that the sheriff was right not to sustain the objection. There was no miscarriage of justice in this case and we must refuse the appeal."

NOTES

Nelson was distinguished in the case of *H.M.A. v. Cormack*, 1995 S.C.C.R. 477. Lord Marnoch found difficulty in understanding the following dictum of the court, (as did the learned commentator to the S.C.C.R. report):

"if it is necessary for the Crown to go to the length of establishing that the accused was in fact guilty of another crime, as part of the evidence relating to the crime charged, fair notice requires that this should be distinctly libelled in the complaint or indictment."

In *Cormack*, which concerned a charge of being concerned in the supply of drugs, the Crown sought unsuccessfully to lead evidence of actual supply of drugs to a witness on a particular occasion. Sheriff Gordon comments that the *dictum* quoted from *Nelson*, if applied literally, would provide a very restricted exception indeed. The preferable view is that only where it is absolutely necessary to prove the charge against an accused person that evidence of another offence can be led. Thus, in *Slack v.*

H.M.A., 1996 S.L.T. 1084 it was held that on a charge of driving while disqualified, evidence tending to show that the car in question had been removed unlawfully was not admissible. Compare also the strange case of *H.M.A. v. Carson,* 1997 S.L.T. 1119. The Crown may also require to give notice where it is intended to lead evidence of criminal offences committed by persons other than the accused. This will often arise in cases involving the supply of drugs, where evidence that the accused have been associating with particular people may be crucial to a conviction. This point was raised in the case of *Forsyth v. H.M.A.*, 1992 S.L.T. 189, where evidence was led from police officers that certain associates of the accused had drugs convictions. Quashing the convictions, the Lord Justice General said:

> "In our opinion the risk of unfairness by the leading of such evidence was such that the trial judge should have disallowed questions about the character of these persons. He should have done so on the ground that no notice had been given to the accused that evidence was to be led of their association with particular named individuals of bad character, or that evidence was to be given in their absence of their criminal record. This is not one of those cases where evidence about the character of the places named in the charge was in issue, nor was the charge one of associating with persons of bad character. There was no evidence that the appellants had referred to these persons in any statements given by them to the police or that they had in any other way put their character in issue in the case. We consider that the trial judge misdirected himself in repelling the objection which was taken to this evidence."

(B) CHARACTER EVIDENCE

8. H.M.A. v. Kay
1970 J.C. 68

"Mrs Marion Clark Wilson or Hirst or Kay was charged on an indictment which set forth that 'you did on May 3, 1970 in the common stair at 172, Dairy Road, Edinburgh, assault your husband David John Kay, residing there, and did stab him on the body with a knife and did murder him and you did previously evince malice and ill-will against him, brandish a knife in front of him and threaten to kill him.' She pled not guilty, and a special defence was lodged which set forth that 'the panel pleads not guilty, and specially and without prejudice to said plea, that on the occasion libelled she was acting in self-defence, she reasonably believing that there was imminent danger to her life due to an assault intended by the deceased David John Kay.'

The panel was tried before Lord Wheatley and a jury in the High Court of Justiciary at Edinburgh on July 20, 1970. In the course of the trial her counsel sought leave to lodge out of time certain hospital records relating to her which indicated that she had been assaulted by the deceased on five previous occasions. The Advocate-depute did not object to the late lodging of the records, but questioned the admissibility of evidence of previous specific assaults on the panel by the deceased. He referred to Macdonald, *Criminal Law of Scotland,* (5th ed.) p.309; *Irving* (1838) 2 Swin 109; and *Fletcher* (1846) Ark 171. Counsel for the panel submitted that evidence of such assaults would be admissible, and distinguished the case of *Fletcher* on the ground that in the present case the indictment libelled previous malice and the special defence averred the panel's reasonable belief that an assault was intended by the deceased, a belief the reasonableness of which could be proved only by showing that the same kind of thing had happened before.

Lord Wheatley allowed the records to be lodged and held that the evidence, if tendered, would be admissible."

LORD WHEATLEY: "While the law as set forth in Macdonald (5th ed.) at p.309, and in the case of *Fletcher*, which is cited in support of the proposition therein stated, is understandable in the normal case—since normally it would be undesirable to allow evidence on collateral matters in a criminal trial—in the circumstances of this case I am of the opinion that the evidence in relation to these five assaults, if it is tendered, should be allowed. The reason for my decision is that the indictment narrates that the accused evinced malice and ill-will against the deceased on previous occasions. The defence which has been lodged as a special defence is to the effect that there was imminent danger to her life due to an assault intended by the deceased. I consider that it would be unfair to allow detailed evidence by the Crown in support of that part of the indictment which alleges that the accused had previously evinced malice and ill-will towards the deceased, without allowing the accused the opportunity of proving in turn by detailed evidence that she had reason to apprehend danger from the deceased. It seems to me that in the circumstances of this case equity demands that such evidence should be allowed. In reaching this decision, I wish to make it clear that I am not seeking to establish any new rule of law. It may well be that normally the general rule referred to by Macdonald would have to be given effect to, but, if special circumstances be shown, and justice demands a departure from that rule, then of course such a departure requires to be made. Each case will depend on its circumstances. I am of the opinion that the circumstances of this case, as explained to me by both the learned Advocate-depute and by learned counsel for the accused, entitle me to regard this as an exception justifying a departure from the general rule."

NOTES

This case, and those following, deal with the issue of evidence relating to the character of a party. Again, the question appears to be one of relevance. In this case, evidence was admitted not only of the victim's character but also of specific acts of violence perpetrated by the victim on the accused. This, however, was an unusual case in which the collateral evidence was admitted as relevant to rebut very specific Crown allegations of malice and ill-will on the part of the accused, and to show that the accused had good reason to fear the deceased. The more usual rule is stated in the following case.

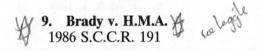

9. Brady v. H.M.A.
1986 S.C.C.R. 191

The appellant was charged with attempted murder and pleaded self-defence. Relying on *Kay v. H.M.A.*, above, he attempted to lead evidence of assaults by the complainer on third parties during a period between six months and four weeks before the incident libelled in the indictment. The trial judge ruled such evidence to be inadmissible and the appellant was convicted. On appeal, the High Court confirmed that the evidence was incompetent.

LORD JUSTICE-CLERK (ROSS): "The general rule is that it is not admissible to lead evidence on collateral matters in a criminal trial. Various justifications have been put forward for this rule. The existence of a collateral fact does not render more probable the existence of the fact in issue; at best a collateral matter can only have an indirect bearing on the matter in issue; a jury may become confused by having to consider collateral matters and may have their attention diverted from the true matter in issue. Whatever the justification for it, the general rule is clear. The general rule does, however, suffer certain exceptions. In accordance with this general rule and the recognised exceptions to it, in cases of murder or assault it has been decided that an accused may prove that the injured party was of a quarrelsome nature or violent disposition, but that he may not prove specific acts of violence committed previously by the injured party. The foundation of this particular rule is generally taken to be the case of *Margaret Shiells or Fletcher*. At p.174 the Lord Justice-Clerk said:

'The Court are of the opinion that they cannot allow a proof of these alleged prior assaults, but it is competent to lead evidence as to the general temper of the deceased, which may tend to throw some light upon the affray in question.'

Mr Hamilton sought to distinguish this case upon the view that in *Fletcher* the victim had died and so could not give evidence. I do not think that that detracts from the applicability of the rule. Indeed in *Fletcher* reference was made in the argument to the earlier case of *Irving* which was a case of assault and not murder. Thus it was a case where the victim was available as a witness. In that case the Lord Justice-Clerk observed that proof of individual acts of violence by the complainer was clearly incompetent, but that he would certainly allow it to be proved that the complainer was a passionate man. In the report in *Irving* reference is made to Alison's,

Practice of the Criminal Law, p.533. The learned author, writing in 1833, expressed the view that evidence of a fiery or quarrelsome disposition would probably be held competent. In Bell's notes to Hume on Crimes (1844) p.294, three cases are referred to, the most recent of which is *Irving*. *Irving* and *Fletcher* have been followed in a number of subsequent cases and have been referred to by a number of textbook writers. The decisions have stood for some 140 years and have been regarded, properly as I believe, as laying down a rule of general application. So far as textbooks are concerned reference may be made to Dickson on Evidence, Vol i, para.13, Macdonald (5th ed.) p.309, Renton and Brown (5th ed) para. 18–85 and Walkers on Evidence, p.15. Mr Hamilton drew attention to Alison's Practice at p.527 where it is stated:

'It is incompetent, in the general case, to put any questions to a witness as to his general character or conversation, but he may be asked as to particular offences or convictions.'

That statement was written in 1833 prior to the decisions in *Irving* and *Fletcher* and it must, in my opinion, be read along with what Allison says at pp.532–533 to which I have already referred. In *H.M.A. v. Kay* Lord Wheatley referred to *Fletcher* as setting forth the law in the normal case. However, in that case, exceptionally, evidence of specific assaults on the accused by the victim were held admissible because the indictment libelled previous malice and the accused was pleading self-defence. Lord Wheatley said:

'In reaching this decision, I wish to make it clear that I am not seeking to establish any new rule of law. It may well be that normally the general rule referred to by Macdonald would have to be given effect to, but, if special circumstances be shown, and justice demands a departure from that rule, then of course such a departure requires to be made. Each case will depend on its own circumstances.'

I regard *Kay* as a very special case and the general rule is in my opinion as laid down in *Fletcher* and referred to by, among others, Macdonald. In the present case Mr Hamilton reminded us that the appellant had lodged a special defence of self-defence. Under reference to the case of *Penning v. H.M.A.*, he submitted that in assessing the quality of the attack it was also necessary to consider the degree of force necessary to repel the attack; to use a hammer to repel an attack by a meek man might be excessive, but it would be different if the assailant was a man of known violence. I do not accept such a formulation. When self-defence is in issue one important consideration is that the retaliation must not be excessive; but what has to be measured is the violence used by the accused against the violence used or threatened by the victim at the time. What violence the victim may have used to third parties in the past is not properly in issue. It is clearly collateral and I see no justification for admitting evidence of violence used by the victim to the third parties in the past when considering the allegation that the appellant was acting in self-defence on the occasion libelled in the indictment. Mr Hamilton informed us that evidence of this kind would be admissible in England. Whether or not that is so I am not qualified to say. However, I am not persuaded that what occurs under another system of law is of any moment. What is in issue is the admissibility of evidence under the law of Scotland. In my opinion Mr Hamilton has failed to displace the rule laid down in *Fletcher* and *Irving* and followed since then. That rule is part of our law and can only be departed from in exceptional circumstances. Accordingly his first submission that the trial judge was bound to admit the evidence fails.

So far as his subsidiary arguments are concerned, the case of *Kay* was certainly an instance where the court departed from the strict application of the general rule. I am prepared to accept that in exceptional cases the court may depart from the strict application of the rule and that the matter lies within the discretion of the judge. However, I am quite satisfied that in the present case there were no exceptional circumstances which could have justified departure from the general rule. In all the circumstances I am of the opinion that the trial judge reached the correct conclusion on the question of admissibility and that the appellant has failed to make out ground 5."

NOTES

Of course, *Kay* is easily distinguishable from this case, since the previous acts of violence in the former case were directed not against third parties but against the accused herself. However, given that the overriding factor in relation to collateral evidence is relevance, it might be thought strange that a party may prove the victim's general character, but may not prove specific acts of violence. Why is general character any less collateral than specific acts of violence directed against third parties? Compare *H.M.A. v. Maan*, 2001 S.L.T. 408, and the American case of *Knapp v. The State*, 168 Indiana 153, 79 N.E. 1076 (1907), Chapter 1 above. Where an accused person does attack the character of the victim or complainer, or indeed any other Crown witness, he may then be subject to an investigation of his own character, either in cross-examination if he decides to give evidence, or through the leading of substantive evidence. The circumstances in which this may occur are governed by sections 266 and 270 of the Criminal Procedure (Scotland) Act 1995 and the case of *Leggate v. H.M.A.*, 1988 S.C.C.R. 391, below. Note, incidentally, Lord Ross's characterisation of the character of the victim as a "collateral" matter.

10. C. v. M.
1923 S.C. 1

This was an action for damages for slander in which a married woman averred that the defender had falsely stated that she had given birth to an illegitimate child some 10 years previously. The defender averred that the person herself had given him this information and in addition averred specific acts of adultery between the pursuer and a third party about a year before the date of the statement complained of. He also averred that the pursuer was well-known in the neighbourhood as a person of loose and immoral character.

LORD PRESIDENT (CLYDE): "In this case the pursuer asks for damages in respect of the harm done to her character by a slanderous statement alleged to have been made concerning her by the defender. It necessarily follows that she puts her character in issue; and therefore it is a relevant defence against her claim for damages to aver and prove that her character is such that it has not suffered any damage by the statement complained of. The point of such a defence is not that she is a bad character, but that she *has* a bad character. Accordingly, it appears to me that the amendment which the defender now proposes on answer 2, to the effect that 'the pursuer is well known in the neighbourhood in which she resides as a person of loose and immoral character, and she has suffered no damage as the result of the defender's statement,' is relevant and should be admitted. This amendment will provide a sufficient basis for evidence to the effect that the pursuer's reputation was a bad one, and has suffered either no damage, or, at any rate, not so much damage as might otherwise have been the case. There are still standing on record certain statements by which the pursuer is charged with specific acts of adultery said to have been committed at a date considerably later than the act alleged in the attack on her character which forms the subject of the present action. In the Outer House the Lord Ordinary found that those averments were irrelevant and ought not to be remitted to probation; but I think the proper course to be taken with regard to them is to order them to be deleted from the record. The reason for adopting this course is that which was given by Lord President Robertson in *A v. B*, and approved by Lord President Dunedin in *H v. P*, namely, that it is neither legitimate nor expedient that an inquiry into the particular slander complained of should open the door to a roving inquiry into collateral issues which have but an indirect bearing on the case in hand. I add, however, that in a question of this kind—as indeed in any question where character and credibility are concerned—it is competent, if notice has been fairly given, to put to the pursuer in cross-examination such specific instances of conduct as those made in the averments to which I have referred, notwithstanding that it is incompetent to present substantive evidence in support of their truth. It is a delicate matter of policy for the party concerned to consider whether he is either safe or wise in hazarding such cross-examination. But the cases to which I have already referred establish that such questions in cross-examination of the pursuer are legitimate, provided fair notice has been given of the subject-matter of the intended questions. With regard to the form in which fair notice should be given, it is enough to say that here sufficient notice has been given to the other side by the

statements now ordered to be deleted. I think it is fair that, as the expenses incurred in this reclaiming notice are entirely due to the course which the defender has pursued, those expenses should fall on him."
Lord Mackenzie, Lord Skerrington and Lord Cullen concurred.

NOTES

The general rule in civil cases is, therefore, similar to that in criminal cases—that evidence of general character of the pursuer or complainer is admissible, but evidence of specific similar acts is not. Compare the cases of *Whyte v. Whyte* (1884) 11 R. 712 and *Wilson v. Wilson,* 1955 S.L.T. (Notes) 81. In *Wilson* it was said that:

"It is, of course, well established that as a general principle of law, proof of collateral matters will not be permitted, *cf A v. B* (1885) 11R 402 . . . [above] and *H v. P* (1905) 8F. 232 . . . To this general rule there is a limited exception in consistorial causes in that evidence a defender's adultery or of indecent conduct with persons other than the named paramour or co-defender has been admitted in order to provide corroboration of the main case of adultery which the pursuer seeks to prove. That exception is one which has been recognised in practice for many years, both in England and Scotland, but the conduct must be either adulterous or at the very least indecent in character. That is made clear from the judgement of the court in *Whyte v. Whyte* (1884) 11R. 710 and is illustrated by the more recent case of *Nicol v. Nicol*, 1938 S.L.T. 98."

The exception made in adultery cases (*A. v. B.* was specifically a defamation case and not a consistorial one) will, it seems, be strictly limited to such cases—see Lord Stott in *Duff v. Duff*, 1969 S.L.T. (Notes) 53. As for the view expressed in *A v. B* that cross-examination, as opposed to the leading of evidence in chief, about specific acts of adultery would be permitted, see the doubts expressed by Lord Stott in *Duff v. Duff*, above, Lord Pearson in *H v. P* (1905) 8 F. 232 and, generally, by Macphail, *Evidence*, para. 16.05. In civil cases, such cross-examination would to some extent be useless, since, if the witness denies such acts, evidence cannot be led in rebuttal. In criminal cases, however, if a witness denies previous convictions, the Crown may produce a relevant extract conviction to demonstrate the falsity of the witness's denial—see *Dickie v. H.M.A.* (1897) 24 R. 82 and *H.M.A. v. Ashrif*, 1988 S.C.C.R. 197.

285-306 Tutorial 8

(C) THE CHARACTER AND PREVIOUS CONVICTIONS OF THE ACCUSED IN CRIMINAL CASES

11. Criminal Procedure (Scotland) Act 1995

"101.—(1) Previous convictions of the accused shall not be laid before the jury, nor shall reference be made to them in presence of the jury before the verdict is returned.
  (2) Nothing in subsection (1) above shall prevent the prosecutor—
  (a) asking the accused questions tending to show that he has been convicted of an offence other than that with which he has been charged, where he is entitled to do so under section 266 of this Act; or
  (b) leading evidence of previous convictions where it is competent to do so under section 270 of this Act . . .

266.—(1) Subject to subsections (2) to (8) below, the accused shall be a competent witness for the defence at every stage of the case, whether the accused is on trial alone or along with a co-accused.
  (2) The accused shall not be called as a witness in pursuance of this section except upon his own application or in accordance with subsection (9) or (10) below.
  (3) An accused who gives evidence on his own behalf in pursuance of this section may be asked any question in cross-examination notwithstanding that it would tend to incriminate him as to the offence charged.
  (4) An accused who gives evidence on his own behalf in pursuance of this section shall not be asked, and if asked shall not be required to answer, any question tending to show that he has

committed, or been convicted of, or been charged with, any offence other than that with which he is then charged, or is of bad character, unless—

(a) the proof that he has committed or been convicted of such other offence is admissible evidence to show that he is guilty of the offence with which he is then charged; or

(b) the accused or his counsel or solicitor has asked questions of the witnesses for the prosecution with a view to establishing the accused's good character or impugning the character of the complainer, or the accused has given evidence of his own good character, or the nature or conduct of the defence is such as to involve imputations on the character of the prosecutor or of the witnesses for the prosecution or of the complainer; or

(c) the accused has given evidence against any other person charged in the same proceedings.

(5) In a case to which Paragraph (b) of subsection (4) above applies, the prosecutor shall be entitled to ask the accused a question of a kind specified in that subsection only if the court, on the application of the prosecutor, permits him to do so.

(6) An application under subsection (5) above in proceedings in indictment shall be made in the course of the trial but in the absence of the jury.

(7) In subsection (4) above, references to the complainer include references to a victim who is deceased.

(8) Every person called as a witness in pursuance of this section shall, unless otherwise ordered by the court, give his evidence from the witness box or other place from which the other witnesses give their evidence.

(9) The accused may—

(a) With the consent of a co-accused, call that other accused as a witness on the accused's behalf or;

(b) ask a co-accused any question in cross-examination if that co-accused gives evidence, but he may not do both in relation to the same co-accused.

(10) The prosecutor or the accused may call as a witness a co-accused who has pleaded guilty to or been acquitted of all charges against him which remain before the court (whether or not, in a case where the co-accused has pleaded guilty to any charge, he has been sentenced) or in respect of whom the diet has been deserted; and the party calling such co-accused as a witness shall not require to give notice thereof, but the court may grant any other party such adjournment or postponement of the trial as may seem just.

(11) Where, in any trial, the accused is to be called as a witness he shall be so called as the first witness for the defence unless the court, on cause shown, otherwise directs.

270.—(1) This section applies where—

(a) evidence is led by the defence, or the defence asks questions of a witness for the prosecution, with a view to establishing the accused's good character or impugning the character of the Prosecutor, of any witness for the prosecution or of the complainer; or

(b) the nature or conduct of the defence is such as to tend to establish the accused's good character or to involve imputations on the character of the prosecutor, of any witness for the Prosecution or of the complainer.

(2) Where this section applies the court may, without prejudice to section 268 of this Act, on the application of the prosecutor, permit the prosecutor to lead evidence that the accused has committed, or has been convicted of, or has been charged with, offences other than that for which he is being tried, or is of bad character, notwithstanding that, in Proceedings on indictment, a Witness or production concerned is not included in any list lodged by the prosecutor and that the notice required by sections 67(5) and 78(4) of this Act has not been given.

(3) In proceedings on indictment, an application under subsection (2) above shall be made in the course of the trial but in the absence of the jury.

(4) In subsection (1) above, references to the complainer include references to a victim who is deceased."

NOTES

The general rule is that an accused person may not be cross-examined as to her character or previous convictions, and the prosecutor is not permitted to lead evidence on these matters. The provisions of section 266(4) have been interpreted to mean that, to fall foul of, the prohibition, the questioning must be calculated to reveal something not already known to the court—see *Dodds v. H.M.A.*, 1988 S.L.T. 194. It is the asking of the question which constitutes the contravention; it is not necessary that the question be answered. But if the accused fails to object at the time, she is taken to have waived the matter—see *Cordiner v. H.M.A.*, 1991 S.C.C.R. 652.

In certain circumstances, the accused may "throw away his shield" against character attacks— broadly speaking, where he puts his own character in issue, either by attacking the character of Crown witnesses or by trying to persuade the court that he is himself of good character.

Difficulties have arisen because certain attacks made by the accused on Crown witnesses may be inevitable in order to establish a defence. To accuse a witness of manufacturing evidence, for example, is an attack on character because it accuses the witness of dishonesty, perjury and an attempt to pervert the course of justice. The Criminal Justice (Scotland) Act 1995 introduced certain changes to section 141, now sections 266 and 270 of the Criminal Procedure (Scotland) Act 1995—see Sheldon, "Evidence in Criminal Trials" 1996 J.L.S.S. 25.

12. Leggate v. H.M.A.
1988 S.C.C.R. 391

The appellant was charged with assault and robbery. The evidence against him came from two police officers who spoke to an admission, and two other police officers who said that the appellant had taken them to where the weapon used in the crime had been hidden and had shown it to them. The appellant's counsel challenged the police evidence, putting questions which inferred that the police already knew the gun was there, and when the appellant came to give evidence he admitted in cross-examination that he was alleging that the police had known where the gun was and had conspired to 'fit him up'. The trial judge, applying section 141(1)(ii) and relying on *Templeton v. H.M.A.*, 1985 S.C.C.R. 357, but without considering whether he had any discretion to do otherwise, allowed the Crown to cross-examine the appellant as to character, and he admitted a number of previous analogous convictions. In his charge to the jury the judge directed them to disregard the appellant's previous convictions in assessing his credibility. The appellant was convicted and appealed to the High Court against the judge's decision to allow him to be cross-examined as to character. His appeal was heard by a bench of seven judges.

LORD JUSTICE-CLERK (ROSS): "The appellant went to trial in the High Court, Glasgow, along with a co-accused on an indictment libelling three charges. The first charge was a charge of theft, and on this charge the appellant was acquitted by the jury on the directions of the trial judge. The jury by a majority found the appellant guilty of each of charges (2) and (3) as libelled. Charge (2) was a charge of assault and robbery, and charge (3) was a contravention of sections l(l)(a) and 4(4) of the Firearms Act 1968. Against his conviction the appellant has now appealed. His note of appeal contained two grounds, but after the notes of certain evidence had been extended, together with the closing submissions of the advocate-depute, counsel for the appellant dropped the first ground of appeal. In presenting the appeal, counsel relied solely upon the second ground of appeal.

The second ground of appeal is in the following terms: *s. 346 Criminal Procedure (Sc) Act 1975*

'The trial judge erred in allowing the Crown to question the appellant regarding his previous convictions. The appellant was entitled, notwithstanding the terms of the recent decision in *Templeton v. McLeod* to the protection of section 346(1)(f) of the Criminal Procedure (Scotland) Act 1975. The attacks on the veracity of the Crown witnesses were made wholly and necessarily for the appellant fairly to establish his defence. The instant case is distinguishable from *Templeton* in that the Crown witnesses in Templeton spoke directly to the commission of the offence by the accused. There was no direct evidence of the commission of the crime in the instant case by any of the Crown witnesses whose evidence was attacked by the appellant. The trial judge ought not to have allowed the Crown to ask questions of the panel's previous record and a miscarriage of justice resulted.'

(It should be noted that in this ground of appeal the appellant has per incuriam referred to section 346(1)(f) of the Act of 1975 which applies to summary procedure instead of section 141(1)(f) which applies to solemn procedure.)

As counsel for the appellant pointed out, almost the entire evidence on charge (2) came from four police officers. Two of the police officers, Detective Inspector Logan and Police Constable Robertson, testified that after the appellant had been cautioned and charged he made a statement to them admitting his complicity in the offence. Their evidence was that he had said: 'Danny told me what the score is. I never meant to hit the old guy. It was his fault that I had to.'

He was then asked about the gun which had been used in the course of the robbery, and the appellant then said: 'It definitely wasn't loaded. Would it help me if I got it back?'

Evidence was also given by two other police officers, Detective Sergeant Sutherland and Police Constable Fletcher. Their evidence was that Detective Inspector Logan introduced them to the appellant and stated that he was to go with them to show them a shotgun. They took the appellant in a car and he gave them directions as to where to go. When they arrived at Huntersfield Drive, he told them to stop at a white fence and that they would then have to walk. He was handcuffed to *Fletcher*. He led them into fields and subsequently pointed to where there were hedges and grass at the side of the road and said, 'In there somewhere.' Detective Sergeant Sutherland said that he felt about in the grass at this point and came across a shotgun which was loaded with two cartridges.

Counsel explained that that was the totality of evidence against the appellant in relation to charges (2) and (3). He described the situation as a classic *'Manuel'* situation, except that prior to the shotgun being found the police had been aware that the men who had committed the robbery in charge (2) had been in this immediate vicinity after the robbery, and that the police had gone and searched the area to no avail. However, counsel recognised that if the evidence of Detective Sergeant Sutherland and Police Constable Fletcher was to be believed, then the appellant had not merely made an admission of his part in the crime charged, but had confirmed the contents of that admission by leading the police to the place where the shotgun had been left (*Manuel v. H.M.A.*).

The defence developed by the appellant during his trial was that he had had nothing to do with the robbery; he had made no reply to caution and charge, he had made no admission to Detective Inspector Logan and Police Constable Robertson, and he had not taken the other two officers to the field but had been taken there by them. The appellant also advanced an alibi, but this is not relevant to the ground of appeal.

In the course of the trial counsel for the appellant cross-examined the police witnesses. So far as Detective Inspector Logan and Police Constable Robertson were concerned the suggestion was that no interview with the appellant had taken place and that he had not made any offer to show the police where the gun was.

When Detective Sergeant Sutherland came to be cross-examined, however, it was put to him that the appellant had not directed them to the locus where the shotgun was but that the police had taken the appellant to the locus. Counsel for the appellant at the trial made it clear that his suggestion to the witness was that the two police officers had gone with the appellant to this locus and that Detective Sergeant Sutherland had picked up the gun. He agreed that the inference must be that the officer knew where the gun was. This was made absolutely clear in the cross-examination of Police Constable Fletcher, as the following passage shows:

'And that he was simply taken by you and your colleague from Rutherglen Police Office and was taken to the area you have pointed to in the photograph, that you walked along that pathway shown in the photograph, Photograph H, that you then turned right down the roadway we see in Photograph I, and to an area down there just about where you see the lamppost on the right, that Mr Sutherland searched in the hedgerow or in a ditch, in fact, and found a shotgun and said to Mr Leggate, "Right, Rodger, what is here?" and then said "Here, Rodger, this is yours"? I take it you disagree with all that?—Yes, sir.'

It was further put to Police Constable Fletcher in cross-examination that in response to these remarks by Mr Sutherland, the appellant had said, 'That is not my gun, and fine fucking well you know it.'

Mr Henderson for the appellant maintained that counsel for the appellant had done no more than to put his client's case to the police officers in clear and unequivocal terms; he had put the defence carefully, and had not suggested that there had been conspiracy between the police officers nor that the gun had been planted. That may well be so. At the start of the cross-examination, counsel confined himself to suggesting that the witnesses had been lying, and at no stage was it put to the police witnesses in cross-examination that they had formed a conspiracy to fabricate evidence. However, when the appellant came to give evidence, although he began by saying no more than that the police witnesses were not telling the truth, he made it clear in cross-examination that he agreed that what he was suggesting was the existence of a scheme to plant the gun or at least fix the gun on him as being something that he knew about and they did not. He agreed that his evidence was that five policemen (the four officers to whom we have referred plus the turnkey at Craigie Street Police Station) were not telling the truth, and he further agreed that it was a reasonable inference that he was suggesting that the police officers had conspired together. Indeed in re-examination, which admittedly took place after he had been cross-examined as to previous convictions, the following passage appears:

'Your position, however, in this case all along is that the police in fact have fitted you up?—Yes, that is correct.

And as has been put to you by the advocate-depute, quite a number of police officers in Rutherglen have in fact conspired to fit you up?—Yes, that is what I am saying.

Can you think of any reason why the police in fact would want to come in here and perjure themselves?—They reckon it is an easy conviction because of my previous convictions.

You are saying it is because of your record which explains the police behaviour in this case?—That is what I reckon, yes.'

However carefully the questions may have been put to the police witnesses in cross-examination, what was being put to them inevitably implied that there had been a conspiracy on the part of the police to fabricate evidence, and the appellant in his own evidence confirmed that that was true.

As already indicated, when the appellant was being cross-examined, the advocate-depute was permitted by the trial judge to cross-examine the appellant as to his previous criminal record. It is the trial judge's decision to allow this cross-examination which has led to this appeal being taken. The question raised in this appeal turns upon the provisions of section 141(1)(f)(ii) which provide as follows:

'(1) The accused shall be a competent witness for the defence at every stage of the case, whether the accused is on trial alone or along with a co-accused:
Provided that—
(i) the accused who gives evidence on his own behalf in pursuance of this section shall not be asked, and if asked shall not be required to answer, any question tending to show that he has committed, or been convicted of, or been charged with, any offence other than that with which he is then charged, or is of bad character, unless—
(ii) the accused or his counsel or solicitor has asked questions of the witnesses for the prosecution with a view to establish the accused's good character, or the accused has given evidence of his own good character, or the nature or conduct of the defence is such as to involve imputations on the character of the prosecutor or of the witnesses for the prosecution;'

In presenting his argument, Mr Henderson relied strongly upon the case of *O'Hara v. H.M.A.* [1948 J.C. 90]. He pointed out that an accused had become a competent witness by virtue of section 1 of the Criminal Evidence Act 1898, and that section 1(f) was the precursor of section 141(1)(f) of the Act of 1975. Although this alteration to the law had been made in 1898, Mr Henderson pointed out that *O'Hara v. H.M.A.* was the first reported case in Scotland dealing with the subject of the liability of an accused person to be cross-examined as to previous convictions. There had been a large number of judicial decisions in England upon the matter, but *O'Hara v. H.M.A.* had stood for 40 years and had been explained and applied in *Templeton v. McLeod* which was a decision of five judges.

In *O'Hara v. H.M.A.* the Lord Justice-Clerk (Thomson), after considering a number of English cases, concluded that the courts in Scotland were free to construe the subsection for themselves, and must do so in the background of the criminal law of Scotland. In determining what construction fell to be placed upon the subsection, the Lord Justice-Clerk concluded that in the subsection 'character' meant character generally and quite apart from the issue raised by the indictment. He also decided what construction was to be placed upon the words 'nature or conduct of the defence' and concluded that 'nature' was to be read not as meaning something which was inherent in the defence, but as referable to the mechanism of the defence; 'nature being the strategy of the defence and conduct the tactics'. His principal conclusion was stated as follows [at pp.98–99]:

⊕ O'Hara v HMA ⊗

> 'Accordingly, in my judgment, the statute warrants a distinction being drawn between two sets of cases, however difficult it may be to say on which side of the line any particular case falls, and perhaps for that reason it is undesirable to attempt too rigid a line of demarcation. Broadly, the two classes are (1) where the cross-examination is necessary to enable the accused fairly to establish his defence to the indictment albeit it involves an invitation to the jury to disbelieve the witnesses so cross-examined in so far as they testify in support of the indictment, and (2) where the cross-examination attacks the general character of the witnesses.'

The Lord Justice-Clerk also stressed that it was always within the discretion of the trial judge to refuse to allow cross-examination even where the nature or conduct of the defence involved imputation on character. He stated:

> 'I should add further that, even within the comparatively limited class of case where the nature or conduct of the defence involves imputations on character, it is still a question for the presiding Judge to decide whether cross-examination of the accused should be allowed. The fundamental consideration is a fair trial and there may be cases where the price which the accused may be called upon to pay if cross-examined will be out of all proportion to the extent and nature of the imputations cast on the witnesses who testify against him.'

Similar views were expressed by Lord Jamieson and Lord Stevenson. Both the Lord Justice-Clerk and Lord Jamieson appear to have cited with approval what was stated by Channel J. on the meaning of the words in the subsection in *R. v. Preston* at p.575:

> 'It appears to us to mean this: that if the defence is so conducted, or the nature of the defence is such, as to involve the proposition that the jury ought not to believe the prosecutor or one of the witnesses for the prosecution upon the ground that his conduct not his evidence in the case, but his conduct outside the evidence given by him makes him an unreliable witness, then the jury ought also to know the character of the prisoner who either gives that evidence or makes that charge, and it then becomes admissible to cross-examine the prisoner as to his antecedents and character with the view of showing that he has such a bad character that the jury ought not to rely upon his evidence. That is the general nature of the enactment and the general principle underlying it.'

Relying upon what was stated in *O'Hara v. H.M.A.*, Mr Henderson submitted that if what the accused does is for the proper conduct of his defence, and if this involves injurious reflections upon prosecution witnesses, provided that these injurious reflections relate to the facts of the case and not to extraneous matters, the protection afforded by the Act is unlimited, and the accused does not lose the protection of the subsection. He analysed the facts in *O'Hara v. H.M.A.* and submitted that although the appellant in that case was inferentially accusing two police witnesses of fabricating evidence and was accusing one police witness of being under the influence of drink, questions on these matters were clearly relevant to the defence. As the Lord

Justice-Clerk put it [at p.99]. 'Without these questions there was really no defence open to the accused at all.' Mr Henderson also referred to *Fielding v. H.M.A.* In that case, he submitted that the allegations made in cross-examination were unconnected with the charge, were unrelated to the charge and were not necessary to enable the accused to establish his defence. In these circumstances, he submitted that that was a clear case where the accused was not entitled to the protection of the Act.

Mr Henderson then proceeded to analyse the decision in *Templeton v. McLeod*. That was a case under summary procedure where the relevant statutory provision was section 346(1)(f)(ii). It was there held that there was no reason for rejecting the classification expressed by the Lord Justice-Clerk in *O'Hara* provided his formulation was properly interpreted and applied. In other words, although the Crown appear to have sought to challenge the correctness of the test laid down by the Lord Justice-Clerk in *O'Hara v. H.M.A.*, the court of five judges confined itself to explaining and applying that test in the case before it. In the course of delivering the opinion of the court, the Lord Justice-Clerk (Wheatley) said [at p.363]:

'In the contestation of a trial, credibility is normally a basic issue, and insofar as the evidence of a prosecution witness traverses the defence which is being proponed and supports the case for the prosecution, the credibility of such a witness is open to attack, even if it involves an accusation that the witness is not just mistaken but lying. Such a line of cross-examination can be said to be necessary for the accused fairly to establish his defence. This is the first type of case. Entirely different considerations attach to the second type of case. An attack on the general character of the witness is not restricted or qualified in any way, such as being necessary for the proper establishment of the defence. To accuse a witness of having committed a criminal offence is an attack on his general character, and falls within the second category whether or not the attack is considered to be necessary for the proper establishment of the defence. The distinction between the two classes is, in our opinion, to be seen as one between attacks upon the veracity of the witness for the prosecution which may be necessary for the accused fairly to establish his defence, and cross-examination of such a witness which goes further, and which can be seen to involve imputations upon his general character, as for example, by suggesting that he has been guilty of criminal conduct antecedent to his appearance in the witness box.'

Conner v. Lockhart was another case where *O'Hara v. H.M.A.* was followed. In that case an accused was tried summarily for attempted housebreaking with intent to steal by applying a chisel to a shop door. Part of the defence was an allegation that what appeared to be chisel marks on the door had in fact been placed there by one of the prosecution witnesses, namely a police officer. The allegation was put to the witness in cross-examination and was spoken to by two defence witnesses. The prosecutor obtained leave to cross-examine the accused as to character on the basis that the police officer had been accused of a criminal offence. On appeal the conviction was quashed. In the course of delivering his opinion in that case the Lord Justice-Clerk (Ross) stated [at p.363]:

'The crucial question is whether the cross-examination of P.C. Mullen, in which it was not merely suggested that his evidence was manufactured and indeed perjured, but in which it was put to him that after the appellant had been arrested, he (Mullen) had gone to the door and had produced a cutting tool and had caused the damage to the door spoken to by him and P.C. Nichol, involved an imputation on P.C. Mullen's character. In my opinion, the answer to that question is to be found in *O'Hara v. H.M.A.* and *Templeton v. McLeod*. It is clear from these cases that an accused does not lose the protection of the statute by attacking the credibility of a Crown witness, even if he goes the length of suggesting that the witness was not merely mistaken but was lying. That was the first type of case considered in *Templeton* and in relation to such a case, the court said: "Such a line of cross-examination can be said to be necessary for the accused fairly to establish his defence".'

The Lord Justice-Clerk proceeded to point out that in the case of *Conner v. Lockhart* the cross-examination had gone further, and that in effect the cross-examiner had accused the Crown witness of fabricating evidence. Subsequently he said [at p.365]:

> 'The present case is different on its facts from *Templeton* where the accused could have developed his defence without suggesting a conspiracy to commit perjury and the fabricating of evidence. Here, the allegation of fabricating evidence was an integral part of the defence so that the defence could not be established without making the allegation that P.C. Mullen had himself caused the damage after the appellant's arrest.'

In these circumstances he expressed the view that the cross-examination of P.C. Mullen was permissible, and that the appellant was entitled to embark upon that cross-examination without forfeiting his statutory protection. It would be fair to say that in *Conner v. Lockhart* all the judges followed *O'Hara v. H.M.A.* and distinguished *Templeton v. McLeod* on its facts. Mr Henderson also cited *R. v. Selvey*, although he submitted that it was not helpful in this context to consider English authorities. He submitted that we should follow *O'Hara v. H.M.A.*, and that in the circumstances of this case, any imputations were not made by the defence against the general character of the prosecution witnesses. The imputations that were made were necessary to enable the accused fairly to establish his defence. It had not been expressly suggested to the four Crown witnesses that they had got together to conspire or to fabricate their evidence, although Mr Henderson recognised that that might be inferred. Nevertheless, he submitted that the appellant should not have been cross-examined upon his previous convictions, and that he was entitled to the protection of the statute.

Mr Henderson also submitted that *O'Hara v. H.M.A.* and *Templeton v. McLeod* did not square with each other. He submitted that the statement in *Templeton v. McLeod* to the effect that accusing a Crown witness of having committed a criminal offence is always an attack on general character went too far. Accordingly he submitted that *Templeton v. McLeod* should be overruled. He submitted that the correct approach in cases of this kind is that the statutory protection afforded to an accused person is not lost if the proper conduct of the defence necessitates the making of injurious reflection upon a Crown witness provided that the injurious reflection is related to the facts in issue and does not introduce extraneous matters. Mr Henderson accordingly invited us to allow the appeal and to quash the conviction of the appellant. The advocate-depute stated that although criticism might be made of the language and expressions used in *Templeton v. McLeod*, nevertheless the law as laid down in that case was basically correct. He accepted, however, that the law might require to be restated. He agreed with Mr Henderson that *O'Hara v. H.M.A.* and *Templeton v. McLeod* did not square with each other. In the early stages of his argument he submitted that the court now had to choose between the reasoning in *O'Hara v. H.M.A.* and the approach which had been adopted in *Templeton v. McLeod*. His attitude towards *O'Hara v. H.M.A.* was that the actual decision might be correct but that the reasoning should not be followed. As his argument developed, however, the advocate-depute recognised that the court in *Templeton v. McLeod* had purported to explain and apply the decision in *O'Hara v. H.M.A.*, and at the end of the day his submission was that the approach of the courts in Scotland in *O'Hara v. H.M.A.* and all subsequent cases was erroneous, and that the approach adopted by the courts in England was the correct one and the one which should also be followed in Scotland. In presenting his very careful submissions, the advocate-depute submitted that part of the trouble had been that it had not been sufficiently appreciated that even where the nature or conduct of the defence was such as to fall within section 141(1)(f)(ii), none the less the court had a discretion as to whether or not to permit the Crown to cross-examine. One could readily conjure up situations where it would plainly be unfair to permit cross-examination of an accused upon his record, but the answer to that was that the court always had a discretion as to whether or not to permit such cross-examination even if an accused person was liable to be cross-examined under section 141(1)(f). At the forefront of the advocate-depute's submission lay the proposition that the words of the section fell to be interpreted according to their natural and ordinary meaning, and that it was illegitimate to seek to place a gloss upon the words used in the section. His submission was that where the nature or conduct of the defence [is] such as to involve imputations being made on the character of a Crown witness, then whatever the purpose of the imputations might be, the case falls within the terms of the subsection and so opens the door to the prosecutor, if so advised, to apply to the court to cross-examine the accused on character; but the court has a discretion to refuse to allow cross-examination, and in exercising its discretion, the court's aim is to ensure a fair trial. The advocate-depute then reminded us of how an accused person had come to be a competent witness, and he stressed that when an accused is giving evidence, he does so as a witness, although he is also an accused person. As a witness, an accused person would be open to cross-examination as to credibility, but Parliament has considered that an accused person should be given some protection in that regard when he is giving evidence. His right to give evidence is in effect qualified, and the advocate-depute submitted that what was enacted in section 141(1)(f)(ii) should not been seen as a penalty on an accused person or his advisers for bad behaviour in conducting the defence; rather it should be seen that Parliament was deciding that if an accused person adopted such a line of defence, fairness required that he should be subject to cross-examination as to his own character. The advocate-depute also stressed that the subsection refers to 'the character' and not 'general character'.

So far as accusing a Crown witness of perjury was concerned, the advocate-depute maintained that that might or might not involve an imputation on the character of the witness. In any event, at the end of the day, the advocate-depute accepted that merely to assert that a Crown witness was lying did not bring the case within section 141(1)(f)(ii); he maintained however, subject to that qualification, that in every case the crucial question was whether the cross-examination of the Crown witness involved an imputation on his character. If it did involve such an imputation, then the accused was liable to be questioned as to his own character although the court had a discretion as to whether or not such cross-examination should be permitted.

The approach for which the advocate-depute contended was clearly a different approach from that which commended itself to the judges in *O'Hara v. H.M.A.*, and from the approach which has been adopted in all subsequent cases in Scotland. Although any opinion of Lord Justice-Clerk Thomson is entitled to great respect, we have come to be of opinion that the approach described by the advocate-depute is the correct one, and that the approach in *O'Hara v. H.M.A.* can no longer be regarded as sound. In *O'Hara v. H.M.A.*, as already observed, the Lord Justice-Clerk held that the court was free to construe the subsection for itself. In our opinion, however, the construction favoured by the court in that case is seriously flawed. The fundamental error is that the court failed to give the words of the section their natural and ordinary meaning. Thus, in our opinion, in the subsection the word 'character' means 'character', and it is not proper to seek to draw a distinction between an attack on character and an attack on general character. The critical question must be whether the nature or conduct of the defence is such as to involve imputations on the 'character' of the prosecutor or of the witnesses for the prosecution, and it is not helpful or proper to confine the word 'character' to 'general character'. Having regard to the language used in the subsection, we are also of opinion that there was no warrant for drawing the distinction which the Lord Justice-Clerk drew between the two categories of cases identified by him. The words used in the subsection do not justify the conclusion that an accused will not be liable to cross-examination as to his previous convictions if the cross-examination on his behalf has been necessary to enable him fairly to establish his defence. In our opinion, the existence of the first of the two classes identified by the Lord Justice-Clerk involves reading into the subsection words which are not there. The subsection says nothing whatsoever about cross-examination on behalf of an accused which 'is necessary to enable the accused fairly to establish his defence'. We agree with the advocate-depute that where the nature or conduct of the defence is such as to involve imputations on the character of Crown witnesses, the case falls clearly within the terms of the subsection, and that it matters not whether it has been necessary for the accused to conduct his defence in this way to enable him fairly to establish his defence. Whether or not cross-examination on behalf of an accused person is necessary to enable the accused fairly to establish his defence is irrelevant to the question of whether or not he is liable to cross-examination upon his character in terms of the subsection. We agree, however, that even where a case is shown to fall within the terms of the subsection, it is still for the court to decide whether cross-examination of the accused about his character should be allowed, and that in exercising its discretion on this matter the fundamental consideration must be to ensure that there is a fair trial.

As already observed, the advocate-depute conceded that merely to assert that a Crown witness was lying would not bring a case within the terms of the subsection. The advocate-depute submitted that to accuse a Crown witness of perjury might or might not involve an imputation upon his character. In our opinion, however, to accuse any witness of perjury would necessarily involve some imputation upon his character. The qualification which the advocate-depute conceded, is, in our opinion, justified upon a different ground. Parliament cannot have intended that the subsection would come into play as soon as it was suggested on behalf of an accused person that a Crown witness was lying, because if that were so, it would be impossible in most cases for an accused person to conduct any real defence without losing the protection of the Act. Accordingly, in our opinion, it must be assumed that Parliament did not intend that the subsection should apply merely because it was asserted that a Crown witness was lying. The imputations on the character of a Crown witness which are referred to in the subsection must mean something more than mere assertions of perjury on the part of the Crown witness.

This approach to the construction of section 141(1)(f)(ii) appears to us to be fully justified when regard is had to the history of how an accused person came to be a competent witness. At common law an accused person was not a competent witness at his own trial. In terms of section 1 of the Criminal Evidence Act 1898 an accused person became a competent witness for the defence at every stage of the proceedings whether he was charged solely or jointly with any other person. Parliament, however, made that right a conditional one. The conditions relevant to the issues raised in the present appeal are to be found in section 1(f)(ii) of the Act of 1898. That subsection is the precursor of what is now section 141(1)(f)(ii). It follows that if an accused person wishes to take advantage of the statutory provision enabling him to be a competent witness for the defence, he must do so subject to the conditions imposed by Parliament. He is not, of course, obliged to give evidence, and he is entitled to remain silent. If he does give evidence, he can only do so as a witness. Since a witness is liable to cross-examination on his credibility, an accused person would similarly be subject to such cross-examination unless the statute provided for some restriction in that regard. That is just what has been done in section 141(1)(f)(ii); an accused person is given protection against cross-examination as to character and a restriction is placed upon the cross-examination of an accused who chooses to give evidence. In our opinion, the advocate-depute was well founded in contending that the subsection was not providing for a penalty against an accused person whose defence was such as to involve imputations on the character of Crown witnesses, but was merely spelling out the conditions which fell to be applied in the case of an accused person giving evidence.

It should be stressed that section 141(1)(f)(ii) does not provide that if the nature or conduct of the defence is such as to involve imputations on the character of Crown witnesses, the accused shall be open to cross-examination as to his own character or convictions; what it provides is that an accused who gives evidence on his own behalf shall not be questioned about his convictions or his character unless the conditions in *inter alia* section 141(1)(f)(ii) are satisfied. If they are satisfied, the result is that there is no statutory prohibition against the accused being cross-examined as to his convictions or character. In other words he then becomes liable to be questioned in this manner, but it is well established that the court is entitled to refuse to allow such cross-examination on the ground of fairness, as was recognised in *O'Hara v. H.M.A.* and in *Fielding v. H.M.A.*

Although the result arrived at in *O'Hara v. H.M.A., Fielding v. H.M.A., Templeton v. McLeod* and *Conner v. Lockhart* may have been correct, we are of opinion that the approach adopted in these cases was incorrect and that these four cases should be overruled. In future the approach laid down in the present case will require to be followed. This approach appears to be the same as that which is adopted in England. We were referred to *R. v. Selvey* [1970] A.C. 304. It is unnecessary to comment at any length upon the various dicta to which we were referred in this case. Although it is not easy to reconcile all the dicta in that case, it seems clear that the approach to this problem in the two jurisdictions is now substantially the same.

That the trial judge has a discretion as to whether to permit cross-examination of an accused person on his convictions or character where the defence has involved imputations on the character of the Crown witnesses is clear from *O'Hara v. H.M.A.* and *Fielding v. H.M.A.* An example of a trial judge exercising that discretion in favour of an accused may be seen in *H.M.A. v. Grudins.* It is also clear that such a discretion exists in England (*R. v. Selvey*).

There is, however, one important difference between England and Scotland when it comes to a trial judge exercising this discretion. In England judges appear to be provided with some at least of the previous convictions of an accused in the course of his trial, whereas in Scotland previous convictions must not be laid before the presiding judge until the prosecutor moves for sentence (section 161 of the Criminal Procedure (Scotland) Act 1975). This means that in Scotland the trial judge could not set about exercising his discretion in precisely the same manner as a judge in England. In *R. v. Selvey*, Lord Pearce observed at p.360H:

'But the courts have been right in thinking that the question is whether this attack on the prosecution ought to let in these convictions on the particular facts of the case, and on such a point rules are no substitute for a discretion in producing a fair trial.'

How then is a judge in Scotland to exercise this discretion during a trial? The first thing which is clear is that any discussion upon this matter ought to take place outwith the presence of the jury. Section 161 provides that previous convictions shall not be laid before the trial judge, whereas section 160 contains a prohibition against previous convictions both being laid before the jury or referred to in their presence before the verdict is returned. Having regard to the different language used in sections 160 and 161, we are of opinion that in the case of the trial judge, although previous convictions must not be laid before him, there is no reason why they should not be referred to in his presence in appropriate circumstances. The advocate-depute reminded us that the existence of previous convictions of an accused had not always been kept from the trial judge or the jury. Both in Hume on Crimes, vol. i, pp.94 to 95, and in Alison's Practice, p.305, para. 35, it is made clear that aggravations, such as that the accused was a habit and repute thief, were included in an indictment. As Alison points out [at p.306] this was usually done in these terms:

'And you the said A.B. are a habit and repute thief, and have been previously convicted of theft, conform to the convictions hereafter libelled on.'

Accordingly in former times the indictment might contain a reference to the previous convictions as part of the libel, and these were proved before the jury. This practice was altered by section 67 of the Criminal Procedure (Scotland) Act 1887 (the precursor of section 160 of the Act of 1975) which provided that previous convictions should not be laid before the jury nor should reference be made thereto in the presence of the jury although the prosecutor was entitled to lay before the jury evidence of such previous convictions where by the existing law it was competent to lead evidence of them as evidence in causa in support of the charge. In the case of the habit and repute thief, it was still the practice to libel previous convictions but they were no longer proved before the jury. This remained the position until the Criminal Justice (Scotland) Act 1949. Previous convictions continued to be libelled as aggravations, but in reading the charge to the jury no reference was made to the previous convictions so libelled (Renton and Brown (1st ed.), p.124). It is interesting to observe that *O'Hara v. H.M.A.* was before the passing of the Act of 1949 and that the indictment in that case libelled previous convictions as aggravation.

Section 39(1)(a) of the Criminal Justice (Scotland) Act 1949 provides that no mention shall be made in the indictment of previous convictions, and that extracts of previous convictions shall not be included in the list of productions annexed to the indictment. This provision now appears in section 68(1) of the Act of 1975. Section 39(1)(e) of the Act of 1949 provides that previous convictions shall not be laid before the presiding judge until the prosecutor moves for sentence, and that provision is now to be found in section 161(1) of the Act of 1975. The only other statutory provision which need be noted is section 30(1) of the Criminal Justice (Scotland) Act 1963 which provides that previous convictions shall not be libelled as an aggravation of an offence. That provision is now to be found in section 159(1) of the Act of 1975.

Having regard to the relevant statutory provisions, and in particular sections 160(1) and 161(1), we are of opinion that when the trial judge is determining whether to exercise his discretion to refuse to allow cross-examination on previous convictions or character, there is no reason why previous convictions should not be referred to before him. They must not be laid before him, but he can be given general information regarding previous convictions. For example, he can be told whether there are previous convictions, the date of these convictions and the general nature of them. Giving the trial judge information of that nature regarding the previous convictions would not, in our opinion, constitute laying the previous convictions before him. It is clearly essential that the trial judge should have some information regarding the accused's record of previous convictions before he can determine in the exercise of his discretion whether to allow cross-examination of the accused on his convictions and character.

In determining whether to allow cross-examination of an accused on his convictions or character, the trial judge requires to exercise a wide discretion. As Lord Justice-Clerk Thomson pointed out in *O'Hara v. H.M.A.*, the fundamental consideration is a fair trial. In England the view has been expressed that no firm rules can be laid down to govern the sort of circumstances which have to be considered by the trial judge in exercising his discretion, and, in our opinion, the same is true in Scotland. On the other hand, there are a number of factors which the trial judge will have to bear in mind when determining how to exercise his discretion. It is in this field that the two categories of case identified by Lord Justice-Clerk Thomson in *O'Hara v. H.M.A.* may become significant. If, for example, the trial judge was satisfied that the questions put to the Crown witnesses were truly an integral part of the defence, and were necessary to enable the appellant fairly to establish his defence, he might feel that the appellant should not be deprived of the protection of the Act. In other words, if the situation turned out to be similar to that described in *Conner v. Lockhart* that might be something which would lead the trial judge to exercise his discretion in favour of the accused. On the other hand, if the trial judge concluded that the cross-examination constituted a deliberate attack upon the character of the Crown witnesses, he might then be inclined to exercise his discretion in favour of the Crown. In *R. v. Selvey* at p.352D–E Lord Guest stated:

> 'the fact that the imputation was a necessary part of the accused's defence is a consideration which will no doubt be taken into account by the trial judge. If, however, the accused or his counsel goes beyond developing his defence in order to blacken the character of a prosecution witness, this no doubt will be another factor to be taken into account.'

The advocate-depute referred us to a number of English cases where views were expressed upon the way in which the trial judge should exercise his discretion in a situation of this kind. Each case turns on its own facts and in our opinion it is unnecessary to do more than refer to two further authorities. In *R. v. Cook* at pp.347–348, Devlin J. (as he then was) in delivering the judgment of the court said:

> 'In our opinion the difficulties created by this subsection are as a general rule best dealt with in accordance with the principle in *Rex v. Hudson* [[1912] 2 K.B. 464; 7 Cr. App. R. 256] as applied in *Rex v. Jenkins* [(1945) 31 Cr. App. R. 1]. The attempt to give the words a limited construction has led to decisions which it is difficult to reconcile; now that it is clearly established that the trial judge has a discretion and that he must exercise it so as to secure that the defence is not unfairly prejudiced, there is nothing to be gained by seeking to strain the words of the subsection in favour of the defence. We think, therefore, that the words should be given their natural and ordinary meaning and that the trial judge should, in his discretion, do what is necessary in the circumstances to protect the prisoner from an application of the subsection that would be too severe. It may be that, as indicated in *O'Hara v. H.M.A.*, cases of rape should be regarded as *sui generis*; certainly the peculiar questions to which they give rise have been settled by *Rex v. Turner* [[1944] K.B. 463] and that case has determined how the discretion should be exercised. No equally clear guidance can be given in cases where the subject-matter is not so specialised. In particular, no firm rule has been, or can be, laid down to govern the sort of

circumstances we have to consider here where the defence involves a suggestion of impropriety against a police officer. The cases on this subject-matter-in particular *Rex v. Preston; Rex v. Jones and Reg. v. Clark* [1955] 2 Q.B. 469; [1955] 3 W.L.R. 313; [1955] 3 All E.R. 29; 39 Cr. App. R. 120—indicate the factors to be borne in mind and the sort of question that a judge should ask himself. Is a deliberate attack being made upon the conduct of the police officer calculated to discredit him wholly as a witness? If there is, a judge might well feel that he must withdraw the protection which he would desire to extend as far as possible to an accused who was endeavouring only to develop a line of defence. If there is a real issue about the conduct of an important witness which the jury will inevitably have to settle in order to arrive at their verdict, then, as Singleton J. put it in *Rex v. Jenkins* and Lord Goddard C.J. repeated in *Rex v. Clark*, the jury is entitled to know the credit of the man on whose word the witness's character is being impugned.'

Similar views have been expressed in the High Court of Australia in *Phillips v. The Queen*. At p.56 the view was expressed that to impose a fetter on the exercise of the discretion in terms of exceptional circumstances was apt to mislead. However, [at p.57] the court referred with approval to a dictum of Gibbs J. in *R. v. Gramanatz* [1962] Q.W.N. at p.95.

'If the accused makes quite gratuitous imputations—accusations that are not necessarily involved in the proper conduct of his defence—the court will no doubt be more ready to exercise its discretion in favour of allowing cross-examination as to previous convictions or bad character than it would in a case where the accused in making imputations against prosecution witnesses is not doing anything more than presenting his defence.'

Only one further observation need be made on this topic. In cases where cross-examination of an accused on his previous convictions or character is permitted the reason is that these may have a bearing upon his credibility. Such evidence is not, however, relevant to his guilt of the offence charged on the indictment. It may therefore be necessary to consider whether allowing cross-examination of the accused might be unduly prejudicial to him so far as proof of the offence charged is concerned. As Lord Justice-Clerk Thomson pointed out in *O'Hara v. H.M.A.* in a passage cited above:

'. . . and there may be cases where the price which the accused may be called upon to pay if cross-examined will be out of all proportion to the extent and nature of the imputations cast on the witnesses who testify against him.'

We would, however, stress that a trial judge has a wide discretion as to whether to allow cross-examination of this kind. The fundamental consideration is fairness, and in applying the test of fairness one must have regard both to the position of an accused and the public interest in the detection of crime and the bringing of wrongdoers to justice. We would also add that we confidently expect that prosecutors will exercise a wise judgment as to whether it is really necessary in the particular circumstances to invite the court to exercise its discretion in favour of the Crown and thus to allow cross-examination of the accused about his character.

So far as this appeal is concerned, it is plain from the transcript of proceedings and the trial judge's report, that he was not invited to exercise any discretion when deciding whether or not to allow the appellant to be examined on his previous convictions and character. It is plain from the trial judge's report that he permitted the cross-examination upon the view that the attack which had been made upon the police witnesses fell clearly within the second classification in *O'Hara v. H.M.A.* which had been approved in *Templeton v. McLeod*. It does not appear that the trial judge appreciated that even if the case fell under the second of these two categories, it was still for him in the exercise of his discretion to determine whether the cross-examination of the accused should be allowed. In these circumstances we are satisfied that the approach which the trial judge made to this matter was fatally flawed. If the trial judge had been reminded, as he should have been, that he had a discretion in the matter, it is not possible now to say how he would have exercised that discretion. In his report the trial judge expresses the view that he has no doubts as to the correctness of his decision to allow the appellant to be questioned as to his previous convictions, but he has made that statement without apparently appreciating that he ought to have exercised his discretion having regard to the importance of securing that there was a fair trial.

Since the trial judge never applied his mind to the real question which was raised by the Crown's application to cross-examine the appellant upon his previous convictions and character, and since it is not now possible to say how he would have exercised his discretion, it follows that there was a miscarriage of justice in this case. The advocate-depute contended that any miscarriage of justice was avoided by the direction which the trial judge gave to the jury to the effect that they should disregard his record as far as his credibility was concerned. At p.21 of the charge the trial judge said:

> '*Leggate* didn't shrink from saying that having regard to the evidence which the police gave they had just fixed him up, was the words used, picked him up, "Because I had a record". That is a matter I would leave out of your consideration as far as his credibility is concerned, or lack of it. You have seen him: it is for you to decide whether you believe him or not. Never mind what sins he may have committed in the past. He asserted that the gun must have been planted in the hedge.'

Subsequently, at p.33 of the charge the trial judge said:

> 'I repeat in that connection, ladies and gentlemen, that while previous convictions, previous departures from the standard of honesty and so on expected of people were put to *Leggate*, I think you should forget about these when you are assessing his credibility and reliability.'

Having regard to the fact that the only justification for permitting cross-examination of an accused person on previous convictions or character is that questions of this kind have a bearing upon his credibility, it is somewhat surprising to discover that the trial judge here allowed the cross-examination and then directed the jury that they should disregard the appellant's admission of previous convictions when they came to assess his credibility. However that may be, we are not persuaded that these directions by the trial judge mean that there was no miscarriage of justice in this case. Although one must assume that a jury will normally comply with the directions which the trial judge gives them, since he failed in this case to exercise his discretion as to whether to allow the accused to be cross-examined on his previous convictions and character, the jury heard evidence about these matters which they would never have heard if the trial judge had exercised his discretion to refuse to allow the cross-examination, and his subsequent directions which we have quoted could not reasonably be expected to enable the jury to forget about that evidence in carrying out their task.

Our conclusion therefore is that in this case there was a miscarriage of justice which was not avoided by the directions given by the trial judge. It follows that the appellant's conviction on charges (2) and (3) must be quashed."

NOTES

For the opposite situation, in which the Crown attacks the character of the accused, see *Cordiner v. H.M.A.*, 1991 S.C.C.R. 652, and the commentary thereon at p.673. Compare *H.M.A. v. Beggs (No. 3)*, 2001 S.C.C.R. 891. The protection of section 266 is also lost where an accused gives evidence against any other person charged in the same proceedings. In the next case, the question arose whether one accused could "goad" another into giving hostile evidence, thereby allowing the first to lead evidence of the other's previous convictions.

13. Barnes v. H.M.A.
2001 S.L.T. 261

In this case two men were charged with murder. In cross examination counsel for the accused elicited evidence from the co-accused that he had seen the accused kicking the deceased, in order that counsel could then invoke section 266(4)(c) and question the co-accused on his record. Counsel for the co-accused objected. Counsel for the accused stated his intention to use the co-accused's record to attack his credibility and suggest that some witnesses had been in justified fear of him. The trial judge upheld the objection. The accused was convicted of murder and appealed, arguing that his counsel had been entitled as of right to cross examine the co-accused on his record in terms of section 266(4)(c).

OPINION OF THE COURT: —"[3] A relatively short account of the circumstances as revealed by the evidence is sufficient. The attack on the deceased was initiated by McGinley but the appellant soon joined in—they both claimed to have been acting in self defence. But the evidence generally indicated that the appellant continued the attack on the deceased after he was on the ground and that others joined in. It also indicated that the appellant and McGinley were still involved in attacking the deceased after the others had moved off. There was evidence that one of the attackers delivered blows with his feet after all the others had left. While the balance of the evidence suggested that the attacker in question was McGinley, one witness described the appellant's involvement in a way that could have been interpreted as indicating that he was last to break off the assault.

[4] McGinley, who was the first accused, gave evidence on his own behalf and, when his time came, so also did the appellant. The events giving rise to this appeal occurred, however, during McGinley's evidence. When his turn to cross examine McGinley came, Mr Hamilton, QC, the appellant's counsel at the trial, immediately made a motion to the trial judge for permission to cross examine McGinley on his previous convictions. Initially, Mr Hamilton argued that in his evidence in chief McGinley had 'given evidence against' the appellant, but he soon acknowledged that this was not so. Counsel who argued the appeal accepted that this was correct. It is therefore unnecessary to examine McGinley's evidence in chief. Despite the fact that McGinley had not given evidence against the appellant, Mr Hamilton proceeded to cross examine him, having given notice to the trial judge that he would renew his motion for leave to put questions to McGinley about his record. So, even before he began his cross examination, Mr Hamilton had indicated that he in effect intended to create a situation in which he could question McGinley about his record.

[5] In cross examination McGinley said that, after he had left the deceased on the ground, he saw Gary Richford kicking the deceased. Significantly enough, Richford had pled guilty to a lesser charge at the start of the trial and the Crown had accepted that plea. Mr Hamilton then asked McGinley about the appellant:

'Q. Now, did you see Barnes kicking him at all?—Yes.'

'Q. Where was he?—Standing in front of me.'

'Q. Standing in front of you. Was the man on the ground at the time?—Yes.'

'Q. And Barnes was kicking him?—Yes.'

'Q. You have a certain history, don't you, Mr McGinley?—What kind of history?'

At that point Mr Kerrigan, Q.C., counsel for McGinley objected and, after argument, the trial judge sustained the objection.

[6] In the course of the discussion, Mr Hamilton explained his position with admirable frankness: 'Quite simply put, the accused has given evidence against my client, however it was brought out, even if it was brought out by me and, indeed, my Lord, it was brought out by me for the deliberate and express purpose so that I could invoke this section. I say that so that there may be no equivocation or bones about it.'

More specifically, Mr Hamilton wished to use McGinley's record of crimes of violence in order to suggest that the evidence of certain witnesses had been affected by a justified fear of McGinley. He also wished to use it to attack McGinley's credibility and so to call into question his evidence that he was not the person involved in the closing stages of the assault. The trial judge plainly had doubts about the validity of both of these reasons for wishing to elicit

McGinley's evidence but we need not explore the matter further since they would be of relevance only if the trial judge would have had a discretion to decide whether to allow the cross examination. But Mr Hamilton's position at the trial—and the primary position of counsel at the appeal—was that, since McGinley had 'given evidence against' the appellant, by virtue of section 266(4)(c) his counsel was entitled as of right to cross examine McGinley on his record. They referred to the decision of this court in *McCourtney v. H.M.A.* [1977 J.C. 68]. Since a question about it was raised in the court below, we observe that the court in *McCourtney* gave its decision immediately but issued its reasons in writing later (1977 J.C. at p.69).

[7] At the trial the advocate depute argued somewhat tentatively that the passage of evidence which we have quoted might not be regarded as 'evidence against' the appellant. But, on the assumption that it was evidence against the appellant, the advocate depute concurred in Mr Hamilton's submission that counsel for the appellant had a right in terms of section 266(4)(c) to cross examine McGinley on his record. In formulating his initial objection Mr Kerrigan said in effect that what was proposed was not within the purpose of the section. His overall submission was that in the circumstances the court had a discretion which was to be exercised in such a way as to ensure a fair trial for all the accused. It was simply not a legitimate use of the provision for counsel for one accused to choose to engineer a means of bringing in purely prejudicial material against a co-accused in the form of his previous record.

[8] At the end of the argument the trial judge sustained the objection on the ground that, in his opinion, McGinley had not given evidence against the appellant in the sense meant by section 266(4)(c). In his report to this court the trial judge indicated that, since the trial, the more he had reflected on the point, the more he had come to think that the distinction which he made was mere semantics. Nevertheless he continued to feel unease at applying the approach in *McCourtney* in the circumstances of this case. Since he considered that it would have been unjust to permit the cross examination of McGinley on his previous convictions, he had grave doubts whether the opinion expressed in *McCourtney*, that the trial judge has no discretion to refuse to allow the co-accused to cross examine as to criminal record when section 266(4)(c) applies, was correct. Having analysed the authorities referred to in *McCourtney*, the trial judge expressed the view that the decision in *McCourtney* should be reconsidered and that the court should hold that a trial judge had a discretion which he or she could exercise in deciding whether to permit this type of cross examination.

[9] When the appeal first called before this court, the Crown had given an indication in writing that they favoured asking for a larger court to be convened to reconsider *McCourtney* and counsel would have consented to that. But by the time of that hearing, the Crown had modified their view and no longer wished that to be the first step. In any event the court indicated that we should wish to hear argument and then decide whether to convene a larger court or to deal with the case in some other way. In particular we wished counsel to address us on whether subsection (4)(c) applied at all in these circumstances. At the hearing where the appeal was eventually argued, therefore, counsel's primary position was essentially the same as Mr Hamilton's at the trial: McGinley had 'given evidence against' the appellant in terms of section 266(4)(c) and counsel for the appellant had therefore been entitled as a matter of right to cross examine McGinley on his record, even though counsel had deliberately engineered the situation, precisely with the aim of securing that right to cross examine. Only if the court were against him on this primary submission would counsel argue that *McCourtney* should be reconsidered. In that event, if it were held that the trial judge had had a discretion, counsel envisaged arguing that he should have exercised it in favour of allowing cross examination.

[10] For her part the advocate depute now argued that section 266(4)(c) did not apply either, first, because McGinley's answers were not truly 'evidence against' the appellant or, secondly, because the questioning had been deliberately engineered with the aim of eliciting the answers and so securing a right to cross examine McGinley on his record. It would be inconsistent with the aims of the legislation to hold that the subsection applied in that situation. On that basis the appeal should be refused. We note that the Crown did not present this argument at the trial. If the court did not accept this submission, then the appeal should be sent to a larger court to reconsider *McCourtney*: if the trial judge had a discretion, then he would properly have exercised it in favour of McGinley and so would have refused to permit the cross examination. On this second basis also the appeal should be refused.

[11] We are satisfied that the first limb of the advocate depute's argument is misconceived. As counsel pointed out, McGinley's evidence that the appellant kicked the deceased is evidence which would be included in any summary of the evidence supporting the Crown case against the appellant. It supported the Crown case in a material respect and tended to undermine the appellant's defence that he was not the person who had kicked the deceased at the end of the incident. We refer generally to *Murdoch v. Taylor* [[1965] A.C. 574], *McCourtney* at pp.72–73 (1978 S.L.T. at p.13) and *Burton v. H.M.A.* [1979 S.L.T. (Notes) 59]. In our view therefore it was indeed 'evidence against' the appellant.

[12] Counsel submitted that if that were so, then the subsection applied and, unless McCourtney were reconsidered, the appeal must succeed since the appellant's counsel had had a right to cross examine and the trial judge had had no discretion to exercise to prevent that cross examination.

[13] On an absolutely literal interpretation of subsection (4)(c), counsel's argument would, of course, succeed. But, in interpreting a statutory provision, the court must have regard to the overall legislative intention and interpret Parliament's words within that context. On that approach we have no hesitation in rejecting counsel's submission.

[14] Section 266 now embodies an amended version of a provision which first came into our law with the Criminal Evidence Act 1898. Until then, under both Scottish and English law, an accused person had not generally been allowed to give evidence in his own defence. The 1898 Act changed that and gave an accused the right, if he chose, to enter the witness box and give such evidence. While many of the usual rules were to apply to his evidence, in certain respects Parliament crafted a special set of rules which were, and are, designed to cater for his distinct position and to afford him a measure of protection not enjoyed by other witnesses. In particular, while he is to be subject to cross examination, limits are placed on the scope of that cross examination.

[15] So, under subsection (2) the accused's right not to incriminate himself is preserved by the rule that he cannot be called except on his own application. If, however, he chooses to give evidence, he loses the right not to incriminate himself in respect of the offence charged; in terms of subsection (3) he may therefore be asked any question about the offence even though the answer would tend to incriminate him in that regard. If an accused were treated as an ordinary witness, he would be liable to be cross examined about any previous conviction or about any criminal charge or indeed about his bad character, with a view to casting doubt on his credibility or reliability. But in subsection (4) Parliament has enacted a powerful protection of the accused against cross examination of that kind. He is not to be asked, and if asked is not to be required to answer, any question tending to show that he has committed or been convicted of, or been charged with, any offence other than that with which he is then charged. Similarly he is not to be questioned or required to answer questions tending to show that he is of bad character. The cumulative formulation ('shall not be asked, and if asked shall not be required to answer') makes for an emphatic declaration of the accused's right to this immunity.

[16] As Lord Justice Clerk Ross explained, giving the opinion of the court, in *Leggate v. H.M.A.* at 1988 J.C., pp.142–143; 1988 S.L.T., p.671, this right of the accused not to be cross examined on these matters is not absolute. It is conditional in the sense that it remains intact unless one of the conditions set out in paras (a)–(c) is fulfilled: if one of the conditions is fulfilled, then the right is lost and the accused may be cross examined on these matters—but, in the case of para. (b) at least, only if the court permits this in the exercise of its discretion.

[17] Since para. (a) deals with a distinct situation, we can ignore it for present purposes. While para. (b) has given rise to notorious difficulties of interpretation, its broad purpose at least can be discerned: the accused loses his right to immunity from this particular type of cross examination and is liable to be treated like any other witness, if his evidence or the conduct of his defence is of such a nature that it may be necessary, in order that the jury should be given a balanced picture of the evidence as a whole, for the Crown to be able to challenge the accused's credibility and reliability by bringing out these matters. Similarly, under para. (c), the accused loses his right to immunity and becomes like any other witness, open to the usual range of cross examination, if he gives evidence against a co-accused. If that were not so, the co-accused would be denied the possibility of defending himself fully.

[18] The structure of the provision is significant. The principal aim of subsection (4) is to confer on the accused a protection—albeit conditional—against a particular type of cross

examination. Any proper interpretation of the provision must, accordingly, be such as to promote rather than to frustrate that aim. If an accused gives evidence of a type falling within para. (b), he will lose that protection and the Crown may have the right to cross examine him on the forbidden topics. Similarly, if he gives evidence of a type falling within para. (c), he will lose that protection and, according to *McCourtney*, the co-accused will have the right to cross examine on those topics. But, in each case, the right of the Crown or of the co-accused is a subsidiary right which arises only in the event of the condition materialising. The subsidiary nature of these rights is seen from the very fact that the purpose of Parliament in conferring them was to guard against the risk of injustice arising out of something which the accused had said in evidence. In that sense they provide both the Crown and the co-accused with a measure of protection against certain kinds of harm done to their case by the accused. That is the nature of the 'benefit'—to use Lord Donovan's expression in *Murdoch v. Taylor* at [1965] A.C., p.590F—which is conferred upon them by paras (b) and (c).

[19] The construction which counsel invites us to put on the subsection turns the provision on its head and undermines the intention of Parliament to give an accused person the right, as a rule, to give evidence without the risk of finding his previous criminal actings or bad character being exposed, perhaps in considerable detail, to the jury, with all the possible repercussions for his case. On counsel's approach, counsel for the co-accused can use the subsection, not to provide the co-accused with a remedy for an injury which he has suffered, but to advance the co-accused's interests at the expense of the accused's by deliberately forcing the accused to injure the co-accused's case, with the express intention of thereby stripping away the accused's immunity and exposing him to this kind of cross examination. What was intended to be a remedial measure is transformed into a powerful weapon for deliberately inflicting on an accused the very type of harm from which Parliament intended to shield him. That cannot be right.

[20] In advancing his submission, counsel drew attention to the fact that in *Murdoch v. Taylor* Lord Pearce had specifically envisaged (at p.587D–F) the situation where one accused's counsel 'has deliberately led a co-defendant into the trap, or has, for the purpose of bringing in his bad record, put questions to him in cross-examination which will compel him, for the sake of his own innocence, to give answers that will clash with the story of the other defendant, or compel him to bring to the forefront implications which would otherwise have been unnoticed or immaterial'. In this passage Lord Pearce was describing one of the types of case where he, alone of their Lordships, envisaged that a trial judge might have a discretion to refuse to allow cross examination under the equivalent of subsection (4)(c). Nonetheless, the passage showed, said counsel, that the case of a deliberate stratagem had been before their Lordships and yet all the others had held that the provision applied and conferred an absolute right to cross examine. Even Lord Pearce, who considered that there was a discretion to refuse to allow such cross examination, did not question that the provision applied. Counsel went on to observe that in *McCourtney* 'the distinguished counsel' for the appellant, who referred to *Murdoch*, must equally have been aware of the possibility of counsel for one accused using this deliberate ploy in cross examining a co-accused. Despite this, senior counsel—and by implication his junior also—had not been able to suggest any situation where the trial judge might use his discretion to refuse to allow cross examination under the equivalent of subsection (4)(c) (see pp.73–74 (p.13)).

[21] Neither in *Murdoch* nor in *McCourtney* was the court concerned dealing with a case of this kind. Any observation or implication in their opinions must therefore be regarded as obiter. In particular, in the absence of any indication that their Lordships were ever asked to address the kinds of argument which we have just considered, we are not persuaded that we should treat their reasoning as being persuasive on this point.

[22] For similar reasons we reject counsel's argument based on a passage in Lord Donovan's opinion where he noted (at p.593B–D) that the wording of the equivalent provision in English law was sufficiently wide to suggest that, if one accused gave evidence against another, he would lose his immunity from the forbidden type of cross examination, even at the hands of the Crown. His Lordship said that, if the Crown sought to avail themselves of the provision, it should be construed as conferring on the trial judge a discretion to refuse that line of cross examination. Counsel argued that, even though he perceived difficulties to which the wording

of the provision could give rise, Lord Donovan did not for that reason deny the plain meaning of the words. Rather, while holding that the provision applied according to the full extent of its wording, he envisaged dealing with any resulting difficulties by implying a discretion in the judge. Similarly, said counsel, in this case the court should apply the plain meaning of the words and, if we thought that the provision so interpreted might give rise to injustice, send the appeal to a larger court to reconsider the decision in *McCourtney* denying the existence of a discretion. We simply observe, however, that in the passage in question Lord Donovan was dealing with a different point and in particular one where there was no suggestion of the Crown deliberately setting out to engineer the fulfilment of the condition now contained in para. (c).

[23] We are accordingly satisfied that the interpretation of subsection (4)(c) advanced on behalf of the appellant is unsound and that it was not intended to confer a right to cross examine on a co-accused whose counsel deliberately forced the accused to give evidence against the co-accused with the avowed purpose of putting himself in a position to exercise that right and thereby damage the credibility and reliability of the accused. We stress that our decision, and the reasoning upon which it is based, are confined to the situation where the questions are put with this one purpose in mind. Our reasoning would not apply, for instance, where the accused's answer resulted from a question put recklessly or carelessly. That being so, counsel failed to persuade us that there would be difficulty in knowing where to draw the line between cases falling within the provision and those cases, such as the present, where the court is asked to adopt an interpretation which frustrates the intention of Parliament in enacting it. We observe, finally, that our reasoning—which is, we suspect, much the same as that on which the trial judge rested his decision—is not based on mere semantics, but on what we regard as the real substance of the provision.

[24] The appellant's appeal against conviction is accordingly refused."

14. Graham v. H.M.A.
1983 S.C.C.R. 314

The appellant was tried on indictment on four charges. He offered to plead guilty to three of the four, but these pleas were not accepted. In the course of the Crown evidence the procurator fiscal depute asked a police officer what the appellant had replied when cautioned and charged with the second charge. The answer was, "That cow's got me the jail again." The sheriff held that this constituted a breach of section 160(1) of the Criminal Procedure (Scotland) Act 1975—now section 101 of the 1995 Act, above, and immediately directed the jury to disregard the answer. At the close of the Crown case the appellant again pleaded guilty to the second, third and fourth charges, and these pleas were accepted. The main issue on the remaining charge was credibility. In his charge to the jury the trial judge repeatedly told them to disregard the evidence led in respect of the charges to which the accused had pleaded guilty. The jury convicted on the first charge under deletion of part of the libel, and the appellant appealed against that conviction.

LORD JUSTICE-GENERAL (EMSLIE): "The appellant is Andrew Joseph Graham who was indicted on four charges. The first charge was that on various dates including November 16, 1982 in the house occupied by his wife Mrs Graham, he assaulted her, throwing her to the floor, punching and kicking her repeatedly about the head and body, tying a ligature round her neck, and so on, and threatening her with violence, all to her severe injury. Charges two, three and four represent the sequel to that event and consist of, in the shape of charge two, a charge of breach of the peace in the social security offices in Greenhill Road, Rutherglen. Charges three and four were charges arising out of that breach of the peace and in particular were charges of assault upon two employees of the Social Security Department. Before the trial began the appellant tendered pleas of guilty to charges two, three and four. The procurator fiscal declined to accept these pleas and the trial accordingly began with the indictment entire. The reason, one suspects, for the attitude taken by the procurator fiscal appears in what happened in the course of the trial. A police constable, McKean, was called to speak to the cautioning and charging of the appellant upon the breach of the peace libelled in charge two. The procurator fiscal then deliberately asked him: 'What was the reply?' At that stage the witness had begun to speak while the solicitor for the defence was attempting to object and in the result he completed his answer before the objection could be properly formulated. The sheriff, because of what was happening, did not hear the whole of the alleged reply spoken to by the police constable, nor did the shorthand writer. The reply, it is agreed, was, in its full form, this: 'That cow has got me the jail again', and that can only be a reference to the wife of the complainer mentioned in the libel to charge one. Now the jury may have heard the whole of that reply. We cannot assume that some of them did not hear it and the question at once arises whether in taking that answer deliberately from the witness, Police Constable McKean, there occurred a breach of the peremptory terms of section 160(1) of the Criminal Procedure (Scotland) Act 1975 as amended. That subsection enacts, repeating the language of earlier statutory provisions in all material respects, that previous convictions against an accused shall not be laid before the jury nor shall reference be made thereto in presence of the jury before the verdict is returned.

After the answer had been given there was a debate on the objection. The sheriff formed the opinion that what had happened was a breach of section 160(1) and that that breach was a material one but, in the event, what he decided to do was to say to the jury: 'If you have heard the reply allegedly given to caution and charge, on charge two, disregard it', and to allow the trial to proceed. At the conclusion of the Crown evidence one is not entirely surprised to notice that the procurator fiscal was then good enough to accept the pleas of guilty which had been tendered at the outset to charges two, three and four. The sheriff proceeded to charge the jury, accordingly, upon the only charge which was then before them for decision and that was charge one, and in his charge, without referring to the objectionable question and answer, as he thought, which has already been discussed in this opinion, he went out of his way to say to the jury from time to time in the course of his charge: 'Forget about charges two, three and four and put out of your minds all evidence led in relation to these charges.' He also said, as a reminder, that the jury was not there to try the appellant for his past or to inflict upon him a penalty as the result of his habits and behaviour.

This appeal is brought to challenge conviction on charge one upon the proposition, firstly, that there was a breach of section 160(1) in the circumstances which we have narrated, and secondly, upon the proposition that that breach was so material as to have resulted in miscarriage of justice. That these propositions bear to be answers to the correct questions can be discovered from the language of the new provisions governing appeals to this court in criminal matters, and from the cases of *McCuaig; McAvoy and Another* and *McLean v. Tudhope*, all reported in 1982 S.C.C.R. at pp.125, 263 and 555 respectively. Let us accordingly address ourselves to the first question and that is whether there was in the circumstances described a breach of section 160(1). In spite of a faint attempt by the learned advocate-depute to argue to the contrary we have not the slightest hesitation in holding that such a breach occurred and, indeed, in saying that that breach was deliberately engineered quite unnecessarily and without any justification by the procurator fiscal. The offending answer was deliberately taken in relation to caution on charge two and it is obvious, to us at least, that it was taken, not with a view to assisting in the prosecution of charge two but with a view to assisting in the prosecution of charge one. The second question accordingly arises at once and that is whether the breach was so material as to require us to quash the conviction as a miscarriage of justice. In spite of the sheriff's endeavours to undo the damage which was undoubtedly done by the soliciting of this answer from Police Constable McKean, both at the time when objection was taken and in the course of his charge, we are satisfied that in a case in which credibility was of the essence that the deliberate breach was so material as to have added a thoroughly damaging complication to the jury's task. In our judgment the reply of the appellant to charge two following upon caution indicated, and would indicate, to any Glasgow jury, that on the previous occasion the appellant had been convicted in relation to an offence involving his wife, the complainer in charge one. So grave was the breach, and so important was the issue of credibility that we are satisfied that the effect of the breach of the peremptory direction in section 160(1) upon the minds of the jurors could not reasonably be expected to have been obliterated by anything the sheriff tried to do and that the conviction must be quashed. The appeal will accordingly be allowed in so far as it relates to conviction on charge one in this indictment."

NOTES

The terms of section 160(1) of the Criminal Procedure (Scotland) Act 1975 are now contained in the consolidated Criminal Procedure (Scotland) Act 1995, s.101(1), which provides that "previous convictions against the accused shall not be laid before the jury, nor shall reference be made to them in presence of the jury before the verdict is returned." Why should the court be prevented from knowing about an accused person's previous convictions? Do you agree that their prejudicial effect outweighs their probative value? It should be noted that it is not every breach of section 101 that will lead to the quashing of a conviction on appeal. It must be shown that the breach led to a miscarriage of justice. See, for example, *McCuaig v. H.M.A.*, 1982 S.L.T. 383, in which a breach of section 160(1) was not fatal to the conviction. See also cases such as *Deeney v. H.M.A.*, 1986 S.C.C.R. 393, *Carmichael v. Monaghan*, 1986 S.C.C.R. 599, *Dudgeon v. H.M.A.*, 1988 S.L.T. 476, *Clampett v. Stott*, 2001 S.C.C.R. 860; *Penman v. Stott*, 2001 S.C.C.R. 911.

Under section 101, previous convictions may be laid before the court where they are necessary in order to prove a substantive charge. The obvious examples are charges of driving while disqualified and prison breaking, although even in such cases, if the previous convictions laid before the court go beyond what is strictly necessary to prove the charge, the section may again be breached—see, for example, *Mitchell v. Dean*, 1979 J.C. 62, in which the prosecution laid six previous convictions before the court in order to prove a charge of driving while disqualified. Less obvious situations are covered by this provision—in *Carberry v. H.M.A.*, 1975 J.C. 40, for example, the charge was one of conspiracy to rob a bank. The Crown were permitted to lead evidence disclosing that a car used in the robbery had been obtained by the accused from a man he had met a year earlier while they had both been in Barlinnie prison. In *Milne v. H.M.A.*, 1995 S.C.C.R. 751, it was held that a previous conviction was competently laid before the court in relation to a perjury charge.

In determining whether there has been any breach of the section, the conduct of the Crown is highly significant. In *Cordiner v. H.M.A.* 1978 J.C. 6 two men, *Cordiner* and Newby, were charged on an indictment containing three charges. The second charge alleged attempted extortion on two occasions in June 1976. However, during that month, *Cordiner* was serving a term of imprisonment. The Crown knew that, or could very easily have found it out. *Cordiner* lodged a special defence of alibi, narrating that at the time of the alleged offence, he had been an inmate in Saughton prison. That special defence was read to the jury at the commencement of the trial in accordance with the normal practice of the High Court. The Crown of course required to establish the month in which the offence alleged in the second charge had taken place, and the charge was withdrawn. *Cordiner*, giving evidence, stated, despite advice from the Court, that he had been "framed" by the police, and had been forced by the Crown to reveal his criminal record. Both accused were found guilty on the first and third charges. Both appealed against conviction. It was submitted for *Cordiner* that, by forcing him to reveal his criminal record, the Crown had been in breach of section 160(1); he had been prejudiced in the eyes of the jury; and there had been a miscarriage of justice. It was submitted on behalf of N that he was tainted by his association with C. The court accepted the argument on behalf of *Cordiner*, and rejected that on behalf of Newby. There had been no breach of the section in relation to Newby—merely to be associated with a co-accused who has a criminal record does not lead to a miscarriage of justice. In relation to *Cordiner*, the court said that:

> "It has to be noted that the Crown's original error in including the offensive date in the charge when his list of previous convictions prima facie disclosed that he could not have committed the offence on that date was compounded by the fact that after the special defence had been lodged at the pleading diet the Crown took no steps to seek to have the charge amended so as to exclude the date which occasioned the special defence in this respect to be lodged. This failure to take appropriate action in the face of their attention being specifically drawn to a fact which was almost instantly verifiable, in the knowledge that otherwise the disclosure that the appellant had been in prison would inevitably be drawn to the attention of the jury, was in our opinion quite unjustifiable. It may well be that the appellant deliberately exploited the situation which had arisen from the inexcusable conduct of the Crown which had led to disclosure of the previous conviction, but we cannot dissociate the appellant's admission and line of defence from the initial error made by the Crown and ignore the possible prejudicial effect on the jury. We cannot say that the jury would have convicted if the Crown has not erred at the outset in forcing the appellant to admit that he was in prison in June 1976."

This can be contrasted with *Andrew v. H.M.A.*, 2000 S.L.T. 402. In that case a witness unexpectedly revealed that the accused had previously been in prison in answer to an innocuous question about what the accused had said to the witness on a particular occasion. The court held that there had been no breach of section 101(1) of the 1995 Act where it was accepted that the advocate depute had had no idea that the witness was likely to answer the question in the way that he did. The court said:

"it is well recognised that the subsection and its predecessors are directed to the conduct of the prosecutor. In *Deighan v. MacLeod* the Lord Justice Clerk (Thomson) at 1959 J.C., p.29; 1960 S.L.T., p.4 said: 'The assumption of the provisions is that somebody who is exercising control over the trial is in a position to lay the prohibited information before the Court. There is an injunction clearly laid on the prosecutor, and if the prosecutor deliberately flouts it, then as the cases show, a conviction cannot stand. Where, on the other hand, in answer to a properly framed and competent question, a witness ultroneously includes in his answer something pointing to the accused's having been previously convicted, the injunction is not infringed because the contravention is not the act of the prosecutor and he cannot be regarded as having laid the information before the court . . . Intermediate cases may be difficult but it can safely be said that prosecutors must be very careful, and if by carelessness in framing a question or by pressing a witness too far despite the sort of warning signs one sometimes sees, the prohibited information is allowed to come out, then the prosecutor must pay the price, and rightly so, because as a rule the prosecutor knows quite a bit about the witnesses and their means of knowledge and ought to be on his guard'."

The court also noted that:

"Counsel did not persuade us that there was anything in the law relating to the interpretation and application of Article 6(1) or Article 6(2) [of the European Convention on Human Rights] which required that disclosure by a witness in answer to a question put by the prosecutor that the accused had a previous conviction automatically involved the infringement of the accused's right to a fair trial or his right to be presumed innocent until otherwise established."

It should be noted that where the Crown intends to lead evidence about the previous convictions of witnesses other than the accused, they may require to give notice of their intention to do so—see *Forsyth v. H.M.A.*, 1992 S.L.T. 189, above.

Finally, it seems that the Crown must take care not to lead evidence which is unduly prejudicial to the accused in comparison to its probative value. In *Cowan v. H.M.A.*, unreported, May 3, 2001 High Court of Justiciary, the Crown was allowed to lead evidence in relation to the practice of "grooming" children for the purposes of sexual abuse. The charge related to a single instance of lewd and libidinous practices allegedly directed against three young girls. The defence had cited a number of character witnesses who were to speak to the services and trustworthy character of the accused in his work with children, and it seems clear that the Crown evidence was designed to discredit those witnesses, or to inhibit the defence from leading them. The accused was convicted. The conviction was quashed on appeal. Delivering the Opinion of the Court, Lord Coulsfield said:

"In our view it is very plain that the evidence was wholly irrelevant and should never have been led. Further, we find it difficult to read what was said by the Procurator Fiscal Depute as anything other than an indication that the purpose of leading the evidence was to lay a foundation for cross-examination of witnesses to the accused's character in a way which would involve imputation that in his normal employment he might have been taking the opportunity to place himself in contact with children. Even without such cross-examination, the leading of the evidence was clearly intended to take away from any force which it otherwise might have. Having regard to all these factors, we cannot regard the evidence as other than significantly prejudicial to the accused's defence."

Compare the outcome in *H.M.A. v. Beggs (No. 3)*, 2001 S.C.C.R. 891. Where does the balance lie between probative value and prejudicial effect in that case?

15. Criminal Procedure (Scotland) Act 1995

"274.—(1) In any trial of a person on any charge to which this section applies, subject to section 275 of this Act, the court shall not admit, or allow questioning designed to elicit, evidence which shows or tends to show that the complainer—

    (a) is not of good character in relation to sexual matters;

    (b) is a prostitute or an associate of prostitutes; or

    (c) has at any time engaged with any person in sexual behaviour not forming part of the subject matter of the charge.

(2) This section applies to a charge of committing or attempting to commit any of the following offences, that is to say—

 (a) rape;
 (b) sodomy;
 (c) clandestine injury to women;
 (d) assault with intent to rape;
 (e) indecent assault;
 (f) indecent behaviour (including any lewd, indecent or libidinous practice or behaviour);
 (g) an offence under sections 106(1)(a) or 107 of the Mental Health (Scotland) Act 1984 (unlawful sexual intercourse with mentally handicapped female or with patient); or
 (h) an offence under any of the following provisions of the Criminal Law (Consolidation) (Scotland) Act 1995—
  (i) sections 1 to 3 (incest and related offences);
  (ii) section 5 (unlawful sexual intercourse with girl under 13 or 16);
  (iii) section 6 (indecent behaviour toward girl between 12 and 16);
  (iv) section 7(2) and (3) (procuring by threats etc);
  (v) section 8 (abduction and unlawful detention);
  (vi) section 13(5) (homosexual offences).

(3) In this section 'complainer' means the person against whom the offence referred to in subsection (2) above is alleged to have been committed.

(4) This section does not apply to questioning, or evidence being adduced, by the Crown.

275.—(1) Notwithstanding section 274 of this Act, in any trial of an accused on any charge to which that section applies, where the court is satisfied on an application by the accused—

 (a) that the questioning or evidence referred to in subsection (1) of that section is designed to explain or rebut evidence adduced, or to be adduced, otherwise than by or on behalf of the accused;
 (b) that the questioning or evidence referred to in paragraph (c) of that subsection—
  (i) is questioning or evidence as to sexual behaviour which took place on the same occasion as the sexual behaviour forming the subject matter of the charge; or
  (ii) is relevant to the defence of incrimination; or
 (c) that it would be contrary to the interests of justice to exclude the questioning or evidence referred to in that subsection,

the court shall allow the questioning or, as the case may be, admit the evidence.

(2) Where questioning or evidence is or has been allowed or admitted under this section, the court may at any time limit as it thinks fit the extent of that questioning or evidence.

(3) Any application under this section shall be made in the course of the trial but in the absence of the jury, the complainer, any person cited as a witness and the public."

NOTES

 Changes were introduced to the law in 1985 to limit the extent to which complainers in sexual offence cases could be questioned about their sexual character. A recent study indicates that these reforms have been only partially successful—see Brown, Burman and Jamieson, *Sex Crimes on Trial* (1993), an extract from which is reproduced in Chapter 1, above. See also the case of *Dickie v. H.M.A.* (1897) 2 Adam 331, also Chapter 1, above. The present law, which was extended by the Criminal Justice (Scotland) Act 1995 to cover the offences of clandestine injury to woman and incest, is now contained in sections 274 and 275 of the 1995 Act. There is very little reported case law on these provisions or their immediate predecessors. The findings of Brown *et al.* were, however, based on a survey of some 305 sexual offence cases, of which they actually observed more than 100.

16. Bremner v. H.M.A.

1992 S.C.C.R. 476

The appellant was charged with rape and advanced a defence of consent. Evidence was given that he and the complainer had had a relationship for a period of about six months which had ended some eight months before the date of the charge. An application was made under section 141B(1)(c) for leave to ask the complainer whether this relationship had involved regular sexual intercourse. The trial judge refused the application. In the course of his charge to the jury Lord Mayfield gave them, *inter alia*, the following direction:

> "Well, you heard an account of what happened this morning, the girl's account. It's clear I think that she was a previous girlfriend of the accused for about five or six months and that finished in January, this offence taking place in August, and they met together three, four, five times a week, as I remember, during that period, and spent some time together in both their parents' houses. There was, I think, some evidence that she wanted him back and there was some evidence that she visited his mother. One view is that it is said that she tried to persuade the mother to get the accused to resume the relationship. Well, you have to decide what happened in the factual matters and to decide what significance you attach to such attempts if they occurred."

The appellant was convicted and appealed to the High Court on the ground that the trial judge wrongly excluded evidence of the previous sexual relationship between the complainer and the accused. The appeal was first heard on December 20, 1991 by the Lord Justice-Clerk Ross, Lord Morison and Lord Weir, when it was continued for the shorthand notes of the debate on the section 141B application to be extended and for a supplementary report from the trial judge. In his supplementary report Lord Mayfield stated, *inter alia*:

> "In my view it is clear that section 141A is an absolute prohibition. Counsel for the defence did not satisfy me that it would be contrary to the interests of justice under section 141B(c) to exclude the proposed questioning. I had regard to the facts of the case. The motion by counsel for the defence was made at the conclusion of the evidence in chief of the complainer. It was clear on that evidence that a previous relationship between the parties had lasted for five or six months and had ended in January 1990. The offence did not occur until August 25, 1990. There had accordingly been a gap between the termination of the association and the offence. I took the view in such circumstances [that] the proposed line of questioning was not relevant to the issue before the court. The main issue was what happened on the occasion of the alleged offence. Another factor was that the accused, according to the complainer, struck her on a number of occasions. She stated that the rape occurred at the side of the road. Passing motorists saw the episode and stopped. The passengers asked the complainer, 'Are you being raped?' She said that she had been. In those circumstances I came to the conclusion that, as the relationship between the parties had ceased about eight months previously, that [sic] there had been violence by the accused against the complainer [and] the complainer maintained that she had been raped at the side of the road, the matter fell to be determined as the advocate depute maintained as to what had occurred that night. I was not persuaded in the particular circumstances that it was necessary in the interests of justice to allow the proposed line of evidence."

The appeal was heard again on March 19, 1992 by the Lord Justice-Clerk, Lord Morison and Lord Penrose.

LORD JUSTICE-CLERK (ROSS): "In his report to us the trial judge explains that at the conclusion of the examination in chief of the complainer counsel for the appellant made an application to the court under sections 141A and 141B of the Criminal Procedure (Scotland) Act 1975 to be allowed to ask the complainer about her previous association with the accused. He intimated that they had had a relationship which had been on a regular basis and that sexual intercourse between them had regularly taken place. He indicated that he wished to put to the complainer that that relationship had lasted for some five to six months. The situation apparently was that this relationship had come to an end in January 1990, that is, some eight months before the date of the alleged offence.

The relevant statutory provisions appear, as counsel submitted, in sections 141A and 141B. Reading these provisions shortly section 141A(1)(c) provides that in a trial for an offence such as rape, the court shall not admit or allow questioning designed to elicit evidence which shows or tends to show that the complainer has at any time engaged with any person in sexual behaviour not forming part of the subject-matter of the charge. Section 141B contains exceptions to that prohibition and provides *inter alia* that in any such trial where the court is satisfied that it would be contrary to the interests of justice to exclude the questioning or evidence referred to in section 141A(1) then the court shall allow such questioning or, as the case may be, admit such evidence. This was the motion which was made by counsel for the defence and, having heard counsel, the trial judge refused the motion to allow this question. That is what has given rise to the present appeal.

In presenting the appeal today Mr Watt has explained that the position of the appellant at the trial was that he accepted that sexual intercourse had taken place on the occasion libelled but maintained that that had been with the consent of the complainer and indeed at her instigation. There was nothing to prevent these allegations being put to the complainer and indeed it was put to her that intercourse had taken place at her instigation and with her consent. Mr Watt's complaint was that although the jury were also aware that there had been a relationship previously between the complainer and the appellant, because the trial judge did not permit the questioning which Mr Watt wished to address to the complainer, the jury were not aware that that previous relationship had been a sexual one. In some cases where the suggestion is that sexual intercourse between the complainer and an accused has taken place a short time before the alleged sexual attack, evidence as to the existence of the previous sexual intercourse may well have a bearing upon whether the complainer was disposed to consent to intercourse on the occasion in question. Mr Watt, however, recognised that there was this period of eight months between the end of the relationship and the alleged attack and he accordingly submitted that what he was hoping to do, if the questioning was permitted, was possibly to attack the credibility of the complainer. That of course would depend upon what answers she gave to the questions put.

The trial judge has explained in a supplementary report to us why he came to refuse the motion made to him by the defence. Mr Watt accepted that in dealing with a motion of this kind the trial judge had a discretion. He maintained that the trial judge had exercised his discretion wrongly. Recognising that this was a matter of discretion and that it is difficult for an appeal court to interfere in the exercise of discretion by a single judge, Mr Watt was driven to submit that the decision at which the trial judge had arrived was one at which no reasonable judge could have arrived. We are not persuaded that that is so. We recognise that another judge might well have allowed the questioning which the defence wished to address to the complainer, but it was a matter for the discretion of the trial judge and, particularly having regard to the period of time which had elapsed between the termination of the earlier relationship and the alleged offence, we are satisfied that the trial judge was entitled to reach the conclusion that it would not be contrary to the interests of justice to exclude the question. Where issues of that kind have to be determined, it is very much a matter for the impression of the trial judge and, having regard to the material before him, we are not persuaded that he exercised his discretion upon any wrong basis or that this court would be entitled to interfere with what he did. It follows that Mr Watt has been unable to persuade us that there was any miscarriage of justice upon this ground and the appeal against the conviction must therefore be refused."

NOTES

Note the passage in which the Lord Justice-Clerk says:

> "We recognise that another judge might well have allowed the questioning which the defence wished to address to the complainer, but it was a matter for the discretion of the trial judge and, particularly having regard to the period of time which had elapsed between the termination of the earlier relationship and the alleged offence, we are satisfied that the trial judge was entitled to reach the conclusion that it would not be contrary to the interests of justice to exclude the question."

The appeal court took the same approach in *Thomson v. H.M.A.*, 2001 S.C.C.R. 162. In that case the defence sought to lead evidence that the complainer had made false allegations of rape against two named individuals in 1991, and against medical staff at a hospital in 1995. The appeal court held that the trial judge had exercised his discretion correctly in excluding evidence in relation to both matters. He had applied the correct test, which was whether the admission of the evidence was in the interests of justice, and the appeal court would be justified in interfering with the exercise of his discretion only if they concluded that no judge acting reasonably would have excluded the evidence. Lord McEwan, delivering the opinion of the court said that "Other judges might have taken a different view, but there are no hard and fast rules". Is it satisfactory that so much should be left to the discretion of the trial judge? In particular, is section 275(1)(c) too widely stated, or even necessary? In what situations is questioning about sexual character or sexual history acceptable?

It is perhaps worthy of note, however, that in *Thomson*, the accused was not in a position to lead evidence about the 1991 allegations, and it was conceded that any cross-examination of the complainer about that matter would have been merely a "fishing" exercise. It may be that a different view would be taken of allegations about which the defence was in a position to lead evidence to contradict the complainer's account.

Chapter 10

OPINION EVIDENCE

In general, a witness should give evidence only as to fact, and should not be invited to express opinions. However, this rule is not applied strictly in practice, not least because it is often difficult to distinguish between matters of fact and matters of opinion. As Walker and Walker (2nd ed., 2000) (by Margaret Ross with James Chalmers) put it:

> "Testimony, which at first sight appears to be of fact, may prove to be actually of belief or opinion. Identification of a person is one instance (Dickson, *Evidence* 3rd ed., 392). This may range from 'That is my partner' to 'That is the stranger I saw in the close that night'. Each statement on analysis is one of belief founded on inferences, but, while the former would normally be accepted as equivalent to a statement of fact, the latter is obviously one of belief. Cross-examination on the former is unlikely to be effective, but may greatly reduce the weight of the latter."

Thus, there are many situations in which ordinary witnesses may, in effect, give evidence of their opinion on a certain matter. Identification of a person provides one example. Whether the identification relates to the witness's partner, or a total stranger, identification evidence from an eyewitness is clearly admissible in both cases. Indeed it is doubtful whether expert evidence on the matter would be admissible—see the Notes to *R. v. Turner*, below. Identification of handwriting and property provide other examples—see Walker and Walker para. 16.2.1.

Where the court requires assistance on a matter beyond the expertise or experience of ordinary witnesses, then evidence will be required from a "skilled witness"—see *Davie v. Magistrates of Edinburgh*, 1953 S.C. 34. In such cases, the expert may give evidence of matters of fact observed by her, and of her opinion on matters within her area of expertise. An ordinary witness will not usually be permitted to express an opinion on such matters, and the expertise of the witness must normally be established before she will be allowed to express an opinion. Formal qualifications are not required in every case, however, and in some cases, witnesses with particular experience—for example police officers—may give evidence of matters which might normally be regarded as being within the sphere of an expert. See for example *Main v. Russell*, 1999 G.W.D. 13–592, in which the High Court held that there was sufficient evidence to identify a substance as cannabis resin where the only evidence about the nature of the substance concerned came from lay witnesses who had seen and smoked cannabis before. It is here that the distinction between the ordinary and the skilled witness becomes blurred.

It does seem to be a firm principle that a witness, whether lay or skilled, should not be allowed to express an opinion as to the "ultimate issue"—that is, the very issue to be decided by the court. Thus, for example, an ordinary factual witness might give evidence in a criminal trial as to the speed at which a car was travelling shortly before a collision—evidence which is clearly the expression of an opinion—but would not be permitted to express an opinion as to whether the accused was driving carelessly or recklessly, that being the issue for the court to decide.

See generally Walker and Walker, *The Law of Evidence in Scotland* (2nd ed., 2000) (by Margaret Ross with James Chalmers); Stair Memorial Encyclopaedia, Vol. 10 paras. 647–656; Dickson, *Evidence*, paras. 391–392.

1. Hendry v. H.M.A.
1987 J.C. 63

The accused was charged with assaulting an elderly man, knocking him down and kicking him, whereby he suffered a heart attack and died. The assault caused only minor injuries, however, and the victim had been suffering from a severe degree of heart disease. A post-mortem examination indicated that he could have died at any time due to exertion, exercise or distress. Various stress factors were present in his case, as well as the obvious distress caused by the assault—he had, for example, recently eaten a heavy meal and had climbed a flight of stairs. It was argued that the assault did not cause the victim's death, and at the trial, one of the medical witnesses gave evidence that he could say that the assault had caused the heart attack only on a balance of probabilities, and that there was a reasonable doubt because of the presence of the other stress factors. The accused was convicted and he appealed on the ground that the medical evidence had not established causation to the required standard of proof. The appeal was heard by a Bench of five judges.

OPINION OF THE COURT: "Counsel drew attention to *H.M.A. v. McGinlay*, 1983 S.L.T. 562. In that case a similar question arose to the question which is raised in this appeal. The accused had been charged with the culpable homicide of one John Irvine. In delivering the opinion of the court, the Lord Justice-General said: 'All that is left is the important question of whether it was open to the jury to find beyond reasonable doubt that the death of Mr Irvine from the heart attack had been caused by the assault and the ensuing stress and fear.' The Lord Justice-General then proceeded to refer to the evidence which had been given by the two expert medical witnesses. The leading expert had not been prepared to go further than to say that there was a possible connection between the assault and the subsequent heart attack. The second expert witness was prepared, on a balance of probabilities, to conclude that a connection existed. He stated that he would plump for a connection. The Lord Justice-General added: 'Now this was a difficult field, a technical medical field. The jury would obviously require instruction in order to give proper attention to the important question of causation. The view we have come to is this. Where the medical experts were not prepared to express an opinion beyond reasonable doubt it cannot be maintained that there was material before the jury which would have justified them in reaching a conclusion beyond reasonable doubt.'

At the initial hearing in this appeal, junior counsel for the appellant based his argument almost entirely upon *McGinlay*. The Crown submitted that one *dictum* in *McGinlay* went too far, and it was for that reason that the appeal was sent for hearing by a full bench. In *McGinlay* the court decided that the jury were not entitled on the evidence before them to hold that either of the accused was guilty of the crime of culpable homicide. Although we are entirely satisfied with the correctness of the decision in that case, there is a passage in the opinion of the court which has given rise to difficulty. It must be kept in mind that the opinion of the court in *McGinlay* was delivered *ex tempore*, and was unrevised; it was reported in *The Scots Law Times* reports some six years after the case was decided. We are quite clear that the language used in one passage was language which would not have survived revision of the opinion. In the passage which we have quoted above, we are satisfied that the court did not intend to say: 'Where the medical experts were not prepared to express an opinion beyond reasonable doubt', but that what was intended to say was: 'Where the medical experts were not prepared to express a more confident opinion.' The opinion of the court in *McGinlay* should be read as if it contained a passage in the latter form.

We have little doubt that the form of question put to Dr Watson asking whether he could say beyond reasonable doubt that the occurrence of an assault had caused the heart attack was prompted by the passage in *McGinlay* to which I have referred. We were informed that since the decision in *McGinlay* was reported, counsel in a number of cases have addressed similar questions to medical witnesses. We agree with the Lord Advocate that it is improper to address such a question to a medical witness. Although a skilled witness may be asked to express an opinion, he should not be asked to express an opinion as to whether he is satisfied of some essential fact beyond reasonable doubt. Determining whether an essential fact has been established beyond reasonable doubt is within the province of the jury, and a witness should not be invited to usurp the function of the jury. It would have been in order for the medical witnesses in this case to have been asked how confident they were of the opinions which they expressed or whether they regarded the issue as difficult or doubtful. It was improper however to ask Dr Watson whether he could say beyond reasonable doubt that the occurrence of the assault had caused the heart attack. There is another reason why this form of question should not have been addressed to a medical witness. What is meant by 'beyond reasonable doubt' is a matter upon which a presiding judge will require to direct the jury, and it is not at all clear whether in expressing his opinion as a doctor, Dr Watson was using the words 'beyond reasonable doubt' in the legal sense.

As in *McGinlay*, the question in the present case was whether it was open to the jury to find beyond reasonable doubt that the death of the deceased from the heart attack had been caused by the earlier assault and the stress which it produced. We are quite satisfied that there was sufficient evidence before the jury to entitle them to reach a conclusion upon this matter. It is true that various other possible factors causing stress were referred to in evidence. These other factors were matters for the jury to determine on the evidence, thus there was evidence regarding the amount of alcohol which the deceased had apparently taken, and also evidence as to his familiarity with alcohol. On the evidence it was open to the jury to conclude that he had not consumed an amount of alcohol which was unusual for him to consume. The medical witnesses were unaware of his habits in relation to alcohol, but there were other witnesses who could speak to these habits. There was also evidence from witnesses who stated that he exhibited no signs of drunkenness before the alleged assault. The jury were entitled to accept that evidence. Likewise, the evidence of Mrs Love was such as to entitle the jury to conclude that climbing the stairs did not normally impose any undue stress upon the deceased, and that any difficulty which he may have had in ascending the stairs after the assault was therefore attributable to the assault. We would add that the statement of Dr Watson in cross examination to the effect that the deceased had had a 'very heavy meal' does not appear to be warranted on the evidence. In the post-mortem report, it is stated that his stomach was filled by a recently ingested meal, but there is nothing to indicate that that was a heavy meal far less a very heavy meal. The evidence of Mr Hodge was that he and the deceased had consumed pies and peas, and such evidence would not justify the inference that the appellant had consumed a heavy meal. All that evidence was before the jury, and in the light of it they would be entitled to conclude that a number of other factors which could produce stress were not in fact operative. This is important when one considers the passage in the evidence of Dr Watson to which we have already referred: 'There is reasonable doubt because of the alcohol, because of the climbing these stairs and because of a heavy meal. Those three factors must be taken into account as contributory factors towards his eventual demise so the assault was not the only factor.' In that passage Dr Watson appears to be accepting that the assault was one factor, but in the light of the evidence the jury would have been entitled to negative the other factors as being contributory at all.

In the light of the evidence of Dr Russell, to which we have referred, the jury were entitled to take his evidence as conveying his opinion that there was a definite connection between the assault and the subsequent heart attack. Likewise they were entitled to take the conclusion expressed in the report of the post-mortem examination as supporting the view that the assault had caused the subsequent heart attack. As already indicated, they were also entitled to regard Dr Watson's evidence as supporting that conclusion in view of the fact that the other factors referred to by Dr Watson could, as a matter of fact, be eliminated as contributory factors.

In our opinion, the trial judge correctly left it to the jury to determine whether they were satisfied beyond reasonable doubt that the assault had triggered off the heart attack and the ensuing death of the deceased, and there was ample evidence before the jury to entitle them to be so satisfied. For these reasons the appeal against conviction has been refused."

NOTES

The Court's willingness to put its own gloss on the report of *McGinley* is striking, and illustrates graphically the dangers of relying on *ex tempore* judgments, of which there are many in the criminal appeal court. *Hendry* was applied in *Paxton v. H.M.A.*, 2000 S.L.T. 771. See also *Nolan v. Macleod*, 1987 S.C.C.R. 558, in relation to identification evidence, and *Ingram v. Macari*, 1983 J.C. 1, below. In England and Wales, this rule, sometimes known as the "ultimate issue" rule, has been subject to criticism and reform.

2. Law Reform Committee Seventeenth Report
(Evidence of Opinion and Expert Evidence), Cmnd 4489

"2. In any civil litigation the first task of the judge is to ascertain, from the material put before him by the parties, what events have happened in the past and, it may be, what other events are likely to happen in the future. His second task is to form his own opinion as to whether those events are of such a character as would entitle the party complaining of them to a particular legal remedy against another party to the litigation. But this second task often involves his forming an opinion as to whether or not a person's conduct in relation to those events conformed to the standard of skill or care or candour to be expected of someone doing what that person did in the circumstances in which he did it. If in either of these tasks it will assist the judge to be informed of the opinion of some other person on any matter upon which he has to make up his own mind, evidence of that person's opinion should, in principle, be admissible. The test should be: has the witness who expresses his opinion some relevant knowledge not shared by the judge which makes the opinion of that witness more likely to be right than the opinion of someone who does not possess that knowledge?

Facts and opinions about what happened

3. The commonest kind of knowledge possessed by a witness and not shared by the judge is his knowledge of what he himself perceived with his physical senses of an event which happened in the past. We speak of him as a witness of fact; but it is seldom possible for him to communicate his knowledge of the event except in terms which include expressions of opinions which he himself formed by applying his previously acquired knowledge and experience to what he actually perceived with his physical senses at the time of the event. In one of the commonest kinds of civil action, for example, a motor accident case, speeds of vehicles and distances are highly relevant and are facts. But when a witness of a motor accident says: 'the car in which I was a passenger was travelling at thirty miles an hour when the child ran into the roadway ten yards in front of it', his statement as to the speed of the car (assuming that he was not looking at the speedometer) is an expression of an opinion which he has formed by comparing the physical sensations he experienced on other occasions when travelling in cars which he knew (perhaps from looking at the speedometer) to be travelling at thirty miles an hour. And his statement as to the distance of the child from the car is similarly an expression of an opinion based upon his previous experience and knowledge of what a distance of ten yards looks like to him. The witness's skill and experience in estimating speeds and distances may be shown by cross-examinations to be minimal; but this goes to the probative value of his opinion, not to its admissibility. For the witness has knowledge essential to the formation of an opinion on each of these matters which the judge can never possess—his recollection of what he himself perceived with his own physical senses at the time of the event he is attempting to describe. Unless opinions, estimates and inferences which men in their daily lives reach without conscious ratiocination as a result of what they have perceived with their physical senses were treated in the law of evidence as if they were mere statements of fact, witnesses would find themselves unable to communicate to the judge an accurate impression of the events they were seeking to describe.

4. But what if the witness says: 'there was nothing the driver could do to avoid the accident', or (which comes to the same thing) 'it was entirely the child's own fault'? The expression by a witness of the opinion which he formed as to the blameworthiness of the conduct of another person which he perceived with his physical senses may be the most vivid, as it is often the most natural, way of conveying to the judge an accurate impression of the event which the witness is describing. Yet where blameworthiness, in the sense of failure to exercise what an ordinary man would regard as reasonable care, is the very issue which the judge has to decide, as it is in many actions for negligence, an expression by a witness of his opinion as to the blameworthiness of a party to the accident is not admissible. In practice this rule can generally be circumvented and the opinion of the witness upon blameworthiness can be elicited circuitously by careful framing of the questions put to him. But this process, for which he cannot see the

reason, detracts from the spontaneity of the witness's description of the event and makes it more difficult for the judge to gain an accurate impression of what the witness actually perceived. Recognition of this by judges has led to considerable erosion of the rule in civil cases and a witness is often allowed to tell his story in his own way, notwithstanding that this may involve expressing his own opinion upon the very issue in the case. Nevertheless, the rule still forms part of the law of evidence. We do not think that today it forms any useful purpose. It makes it more difficult for the ordinary and honest witness of an event to give his evidence of what he perceived in the way it is most natural for him to do so—and so most helpful to the judge; and the methods which can legitimately be used to circumvent the rule tend to discredit the procedure of the courts in the eyes of ordinary men. We are not suggesting that it should be permissible to ask a non-expert witness a direct question as to his opinion of the blameworthiness of the conduct of another person where this is an issue in the action. To put such a question, even though the judge attaches no weight to the answer, suggests an encroachment on the decision-making function which is his alone. But we do recommend that the answer of a witness to a question put to him to elicit any fact which he has personally perceived should be admissible as evidence of the fact even though given in the form of an expression of his opinion upon a matter directly in issue in the action; we doubt whether this would entail any change in the existing law, but it would be convenient to have the point clearly stated in a statute. We also recommend that a similar rule should apply to statements admitted under the Civil Evidence Act 1968."

NOTES

The Law Reform Committee's recommendations were put into effect by the Civil Evidence Act 1972, s.3. Section 3(1) provides that:

". . . where a person is called as a witness in any civil proceedings, his opinion on any relevant matter on which he is qualified to give expert evidence shall be admissible in evidence."

However, no reform of the ultimate issue rule has yet been attempted in Scotland, perhaps because in practice it rarely poses any problems—although compare Macphail, *Evidence*, paras. 17.03–17.04. Opinion evidence is regularly elicited from ordinary witnesses, and, as the Law Reform Committee points out, the ultimate issue rule may in any event be circumvented by careful phrasing of questions. In the English context, Colin Tapper has said (*Cross on Evidence* (7th ed., 1990)), p.500:

"The better and simpler solution, largely implemented by English case-law, and in civil cases recognised in explicit statutory provision, is to abandon any pretence of applying any such rule, and merely to accept opinion whenever it is helpful to the court to do so, irrespective of the status or nature of the issue to which it relates."

The decision on both fact and law remains on any view a matter for the court, and depends on the evidence heard, and all the circumstances of the case—as Lord President Cooper puts it in *Davie v. Magistrates of Edinburgh*, below, "the parties have invoked the decision of a judicial tribunal and not an oracular pronouncement by an expert." For example, in both England and Scotland, expert psychological evidence about children, particularly their reaction to sexual and other forms of abuse is regularly admitted. However, the English courts have taken some care to limit use of such evidence. In such cases, the credibility of child witnesses is usually crucial and expert witnesses may be called to express views as to the likely accuracy of their evidence. However, in *Re FS (Child Abuse: Evidence)* [1996] 2 F.L.R. 158 it was emphasised that the role of the expert witness is to assist the court by a clinical assessment of the person interviewed and of his or her evidence. To tell the court that the evidence should or should not be believed is to usurp the function of the judge. Butler Sloss L.J. said: "I have to remind myself that the question is whether I believe the child, not whether I believe those who believe her"

In *K (Minors) (Alleged Sexual Abuse: Evidence)* [1996] 2 F.C.R. 425 it was again emphasised that the opinion of an expert as to whether or not a witness is telling the truth is not admissible; nor should the expert be asked to draw factual conclusions from the evidence of witnesses. The court said: "It is essential that greater care be exercised to ensure that in respect of accusations as damaging as these, inadmissible and prejudicial evidence is not put before the court."

In any event, a court is not bound to follow the views of an expert. See in the Scottish context *Stephen v. Scottish Boatowners Mutual Insurance Assocation*, 1989 S.L.T. 283; *Dingley v. Chief Constable of Strathclyde Police*, 1998 S.C. 548; 2000 S.C. (HL) 77; *Singh (Major) v. Secretary of State for the Home Department*, 2000 S.C.L.R. 610, and compare *Fyfe v. H.M.A.*, 1998 S.L.T. 195, and *Stewart v. H.M.A. (No. 1)*, 1997 S.C.C.R. 330. In the English case *M (A Minor)(Application for Care Order)* [1995] 3 F.C.R. 611 the court rejected psychological evidence about a child where the expert had reached sweeping conclusions based upon a number of unreliable "indications" that the child had been harmed. Finally, in *B (A Minor)(Rejection of Expert Evidence)* [1996] 1 FLR 667; [1996] 2 FCR 272 it was held that the court is entitled to reject the "unanimous opinion" of paediatricians, guardians *ad litem* and social workers, provided that they give proper reasons for doing so. This was an adoption case in which the trial judge found the expert witness to have taken a "scathing, dogmatic and merciless" stance against the mother, based on a mistaken impression that the mother was a abuser, or was deliberately covering up for a partner who was an abuser. The expert's evidence was contradicted by other evidence in the case, and in those circumstances did not require to be accepted.

3.   Davie v. Magistrates of Edinburgh
1953 S.C. 34

A number of dwelling houses were damaged during construction of a sewer. The owners of several of these houses attributed the damage to blasting operations which were carried out during the construction works, and sued in delict for reparation. The defenders led evidence from three expert witnesses, one of whom gave evidence that the blasting could not possibly have caused the damage. A second witness agreed with the first, but was cross-examined as to the adequacy of his qualifications, and the third witness materially contradicted the evidence of the first. In addition, the Lord Ordinary had regard to passages in a pamphlet which had not been spoken to by any of the witnesses, although the first witness had spoken to other passages in the pamphlet in cross-examination and re-examination.

LORD PRESIDENT (COOPER): "The only difficulty experienced by the Lord Ordinary and developed before us arose from the scientific evidence regarding explosives and their effect. This evidence was given by Mr Teichman, one of the technical staff of the ICI, with whom a fellow employee, Mr Sheddan, was taken as concurring. Mr Sheddan was cross-examined on his qualifications with considerable effect, and the point was taken that Mr Teichman was truly uncorroborated. I do not consider that in the case of expert opinion evidence formal corroboration is required in the same way as it is required for proof of an essential fact, however desirable it may be in some cases to be able to rely upon two or more experts rather than upon one. The value of such evidence depends upon the authority, experience and qualifications of the expert and above all upon the extent to which his evidence carries conviction, and not upon the possibility of producing a second person to echo the sentiments of the first, usually by a formal concurrence. In this instance it would have made no difference to me if Mr Sheddan had not been adduced. The true question is whether the Lord Ordinary was entitled to discard Mr Teichman's testimony and to base his judgement upon the other evidence in the case.

Founding upon the fact that no counter evidence on the science of explosives and their effects was adduced for the pursuer, the defenders went so far as to maintain that we were bound to accept the conclusions of Mr Teichman. This view I must firmly reject as contrary to the principles in accordance with which expert opinion evidence is admitted. Expert witnesses, however skilled or eminent, can give no more than evidence. They cannot usurp the functions of the jury or Judge sitting as a jury, any more than a technical assessor can substitute his advice for the judgement of the Court—*SS Bogota v. SS Alconda* (1923 S.C. 526). Their duty is to furnish the Judge or jury with the necessary scientific criteria for testing the accuracy of their conclusions, so as to enable the Judge or jury to form their own independent judgement by the application of these criteria to the facts proved in evidence. The scientific opinion evidence, if intelligible, convincing and tested, becomes a factor (and often an important factor) for consideration along with the whole other evidence in the case, but the decision is for the Judge or jury. In particular the bare *ipse dixit* of a scientist, however eminent, upon the issue in controversy, will normally carry little weight, for it cannot be tested by cross-examination nor independently appraised, and the parties have invoked the decision of a judicial tribunal and not an oracular pronouncement by an expert. I refer to Best on Evidence (9th ed.) p.400 ff.; Dickson on Evidence, (1st ed.) vol. ii, sec 1999; Wills on Circumstantial Evidence (7th ed.) p.176, and to the many authorities cited in these works.

That the Lord Ordinary was entitled to discard the evidence of Mr Teichman I do not doubt. It remains to consider whether he was right in doing so. [His Lordship considered Mr Teichman's evidence and, after expressing the opinion that the Lord Ordinary was justified in rejecting it, continued]—

Two further matters require mention. In addition to Mr Teichman and his assistant the defenders adduced another expert, Mr Sheddan, whose qualifications are impressive. This witness was asked, *inter alia*, with regard to the theory of the propagation of ground waves, and his answers are not only different from but in material respects contradictory of Mr Teichman's thesis—so much so that in opening this reclaiming motion counsel for the defenders did not read the evidence of Mr Sheddan at all. The Lord Ordinary treated Mr Sheddan's evidence as 'of no value,' but I cannot think that this is the end of the matter. If conflicting scientific expert evidence is adduced by a party, he cannot complain if on that account alone the whole of it is treated with more than suspicion.

The other matter is this. In the witness-box Mr Teichman produced as an item in the literature on the subject a pamphlet, No. 51 of process, by Dr Morris, entitled 'Vibrations due to Blasting and their Effects on Building Structures,' being a reprint of papers published towards the end of 1950. If the cross-examiner had had time to study that pamphlet he would have found material for pointed cross-examination, but he passed over it very lightly. In re-examination, however, Mr Teichman was taken back to the Morris pamphlet, and he assented to the view that Dr Morris was 'a recognised authority on the subject.' He was questioned in detail regarding matters on pp.12 and 13 of the pamphlet and utilised in support of his views the figures and graph there given. If we read pp.12 and 13, as we are surely entitled to do in order to understand the evidence, it becomes evident that Dr Morris's views are by no means identical with those of Mr Teichman. [His Lordship gave an example of this.]

The Lord Ordinary founded upon these and other passages on pages 12 and 13, but he went further by taking from other parts of the pamphlet passages materially inconsistent with Mr Teichman's evidence which had never been put to Mr Teichman. I do not think that he was entitled to do so. Passages from a published work may be adopted by a witness and made part of his evidence or they may be put to the witness in cross-examination for his comment. But, except in so far as this is done, the Court cannot in my view rely upon such works for the purpose of displacing or criticising the witness's testimony.

For myself I am prepared to discard the Morris pamphlet altogether, including pages 12 and 13, though a case can be made for examining these pages in order to test the evidence. Independently of this pamphlet there is in my view amply enough in the case before us to justify fully the rejection of the explosives evidence as insufficiently vouched, unconvincing, and insufficient to displace the inference arising from the remaining evidence in the case. I am accordingly for adhering to the interlocutor reclaimed against."

NOTES

The function of expert testimony is not in doubt—it is to help the court reach a conclusion on matters outwith its knowledge and expertise. Where the court is required to draw an inference of a technical nature, expert evidence must generally be led. Again, however, this rule is not applied strictly. In *Kenny v. Tudhope*, 1984 S.C.C.R. 290, for example, the charge against the accused was that he was unfit to drive through drink or drugs. Police evidence that his breath smelled of alcohol, his speech was slurred and his eyes glazed, was accepted as showing his unfitness. In most cases it will be obvious when expert evidence is required—for example, in medical negligence cases; complex company fraud trials; and litigation over defective aeroplane components, there would almost certainly be a need for expert assistance. There have been difficulties over the scope of expert testimony, however, and in particular, matters relating to "ordinary" human nature and behaviour—see the discussion of *Lowery v. R.* [1974] A.C. 85 and *R. v. Turner* [1975] 1 All E.R. 70, below.

Lord Cooper's dictum in *Davie* to the effect that corroboration of expert witnesses is not required should be read with caution. It is now partly true as a result of the general abolition by the Civil Evidence (Scotland) Act 1988, s.1, of the need for corroboration in civil causes—see the comments by Lord President Hope in *M. v. Kennedy*, 1993 S.C.L.R. 69, Chapter 14 below, (but compare Lord

Guthrie in *McKillen v. Barclay Curie & Co. Ltd*, 1967 S.L.T. 41 on the pre-1988 law). In criminal proceedings it remains the case that expert evidence in relation to any fact in issue must be corroborated—see Stair Memorial Encyclopaedia, Vol. 10, para. 651(5) and compare *Hendry v. H.M.A.*, 1987 J.C. 63, above.

Davie also makes clear that an expert is entitled to refer to books and unpublished works of others. In *Abadom* (1982) 76 Crim.App.R. 48, a crucial issue was whether shards of glass found on the accused's shoes corresponded to broken glass at the scene of a robbery. Expert evidence was given, based on Home Office statistics, as to the frequency of occurrence of glass with a given refractive index.

Provided that the qualifications of an expert are established, he or she may refer to works by experts in different but related fields. Thus, in *Main v. Andrew Wormald Ltd*, 1988 S.L.T. 141, a chest specialist was permitted to refer to a work by an epidemiologist. See also *Wilson v. H.M.A.*, 1988 S.C.C.R. 384, considered in the notes to *Hopes v. Lowery*, below.

In *Roberts v. British Railways Board*, 1998 S.C.L.R. (Notes) 577, it was held that published academic material may be put to an expert witness even although it has not previously been lodged as a production. Any prejudice to the other party may be cured by allowing recall of their own expert to deal with the matter, if necessary. However, a judge is not entitled to proceed on the basis of material to which she has not been referred at all.

4. Lowery v. R
[1974] A.C. 85

This was an Australian case which came before the Privy Council on appeal. Two men were accused of murdering a young girl in circumstances which suggested that one or other of them must have been the killer. Each blamed the other, and *Lowery* gave evidence to suggest that he was not the sort of person to have carried out what was a particularly brutal and sadistic killing. A clinical psychologist conducted intelligence and personality tests on both accused, and later gave evidence for *Lowery's* co-accused, King. This evidence was to the effect that *Lowery* displayed markedly aggressive tendencies, whereas King was easily led by more dominant personalities. On the basis of this evidence the jury were invited to draw the inference that *Lowery* was the more likely of the two to have committed the offence. In fact, both accused were convicted, and *Lowery* appealed on the basis that the psychologist's evidence ought not to have been admitted.

LORD MORRIS OF BORTH-Y-GEST: "Having referred fully to the nature of the evidence given by Professor Cox the question as to its admissibility may now be considered. There was no doubt that Rosalyn Mary Nolte was killed in the bush area some 10 miles out of Hamilton when *Lowery* and King were present and when no one else was present. As was pointed out in the Court of Criminal Appeal the very nature of the killing showed that it was 'a sadistic and otherwise motiveless killing.' Any prospect of the acquittal of either of the two accused could only have been on the basis that one alone was the killer and that the other took no part whatsoever. That was what *Lowery* alleged when he said that King alone was the killer and that he (*Lowery*) was powerless to save the girl. In *Rex v. Miller* [1952] 36 Cr.App.R. 169, Devlin J. referred to the duty of counsel for the defence to adduce any admissible evidence which is strictly relevant to his own case and assists his client whether or not it prejudices anyone else. The case for King was that *Lowery* had alone been the killer and that King had been heavily under the influence of drugs and had been powerless to stop *Lowery*. It was furthermore the evidence of each of them, in spite of what they said in their statements, that the idea or suggestion seeing 'what it would be like to kill a chick' emanated from the other. In these circumstances it was necessary on behalf of King to call all relevant and admissible evidence which would exonerate King and throw responsibility entirely on *Lowery*. If in imaginary circumstances similar to those of this case it was apparent that one of the accused was a man of great physical strength whereas the other was a weakling it could hardly be doubted that in forming an opinion as to the probabilities it would be relevant to have the disparity between the two in mind. Physical characteristics may often be of considerable relevance: see *Reg v. Toohey* [1965] A.C. 595. The evidence of Professor Cox was not related to crime or criminal tendencies: it was scientific evidence as to the respective personalities of the two accused as, and to the extent, revealed by certain well known tests. Whether it assisted the jury is not a matter that can be known. All that is known is that the jury convicted both the accused. But in so far as it might help in considering the probabilities as to what happened at the spot to which the girl was taken it was not only relevant to and indeed necessary for the case advanced by King but it was made relevant and admissible in view of the case advanced by *Lowery* and in view of *Lowery's* assertions against King.

The case being put forward by counsel on behalf of King involved posing to the jury the question 'which of these two men is the more likely to have killed this girl?' and inviting the jury to come to the conclusion that it was *Lowery*. If the crime was one which was committed apparently without any kind of motive unless it was for the sensation experienced in the killing then unless both men acted in concert the deed was that of one of them. It would be unjust to prevent either of them from calling any evidence of probative value which could point to the probability that the perpetrator was the one rather than the other.

Lowery put his character in issue. If an accused person puts his character in issue in the sense of asserting that he has never been convicted of any offence then provided that it is fair to do so it may be shown that he has had convictions. If an accused person puts his character in issue in the sense of adducing evidence that he is of good general reputation then it may be legitimate to call rebutting evidence of an equally general nature. When an accused person puts his character in issue he is in effect asking a jury to take the view that he is not one who would be disposed to have committed or would be likely to have committed the crime in question. An accused person of good character is permitted to advance such a consideration. But if an accused person is not of good character the law has been firm in the principle recognised by Lord Herschell L.C. in *Makin v. Attorney-General for New South Wales* [1894] A.C. 57, 65, when he said:

> 'It is undoubtedly not competent for the prosecution to adduce evidence tending to show that the accused has been guilty of criminal acts other than those covered in the indictment, for the purpose of leading to the conclusion that the accused is a person likely from his criminal conduct or character to have committed the offence for which he is being tried.'

Lord Herschell L.C. proceeded to refer to certain well known exceptions from the general rule.

It may be stated here that it was not suggested by the Solicitor-General that the contested evidence either could or would have been adduced by the prosecution.

In reference to this matter the Court of Criminal Appeal said, and in their Lordships' view rightly said:

> 'It is, however, established by the highest authorities that in criminal cases the Crown is precluded from leading evidence that does no more than show that the accused has a disposition or propensity or is the sort of person likely to commit the crime charged; . . .'

and further:

> 'It is, we think, one thing to say that such evidence is excluded when tendered by the Crown in proof of guilt, but quite another to say that it is excluded when tendered by the accused in disproof of his own guilt. We see no reason of policy or fairness which justifies or requires the exclusion of evidence relevant to prove the innocence of an accused person.'

The evidence of Professor Cox as will have been seen was not as such evidence in regard to the character of *Lowery* and King but rather was evidence as to their respective intelligences and personalities.

In this connection complaint was made of misdirection by the judge at the trial in that though he reminded the jury of the evidence of Professor Cox when dealing with King's defence he also referred to the evidence when dealing with the evidence of character adduced on behalf of *Lowery*. It was further said that the jury were given no guidance as to how they should consider or use the evidence. Though in the grounds of appeal advanced in the Court of Criminal Appeal there were complaints of misdirection they were not in that court pursued. In their Lordships' view if the evidence of Professor Cox was admissible the suggested misdirection was, in the setting of the case, of relatively minor significance and in their Lordships' view need not be further examined. *Lowery* and King were each asserting that the other was the completely dominating person at the time Rosalyn Nolte was killed: each claimed to have been in fear of the other. In these circumstances it was most relevant for King to be able to show, if he could, that *Lowery* had a personality marked by aggressiveness whereas he, King, had a personality which suggested that he would be led and dominated by someone who was dominant and aggressive. In support of King's case the evidence of Professor Cox was relevant if it tended to show that the version of the facts put forward by King was more probable than that put forward by *Lowery*. Not only however was the evidence which King called relevant to this case: its admissibility was placed beyond doubt by the whole substance of *Lowery's* case. Not only did *Lowery* assert that the killing was done by King and not only did he say that he had been in fear of King but, as previously mentioned, he set himself up as one who had no motive whatsoever in killing the girl and as one who would not have been likely to wreck his good prospects and furthermore as one who would not have been interested in the sort of behaviour manifested by the killer. While ascribing the sole responsibility to King he was also in effect saying that he himself was not the sort of man to have committed the offence. The only question now arising is whether in the special circumstances above referred to it was open to King in defending himself to call Professor Cox to give the evidence that he gave. The evidence was relevant to and necessary for his case which involved negativing what *Lowery* had said and put forward: in their Lordships' view in agreement with that of the Court of Criminal Appeal the evidence was admissible.

For these reasons their Lordships have humbly advised Her Majesty that the appeal should be dismissed."

5.   R. v. Turner
[1975] 1 All E.R. 70

The accused in *Turner* was charged with the murder of his girlfriend. His defence was that she had provoked him by revealing that she had been unfaithful to him, and he sought to lead evidence from a psychologist to bolster his contention that he was the sort of person likely to be provoked into violence by such a revelation. The evidence was excluded by the trial judge, *Turner* was convicted, and he appealed, arguing on the authority of *Lowery*, above, that the psychological evidence ought to have been admitted.

LORD JUSTICE LAWTON: "Before this court counsel for the appellant submitted that the psychiatrist's opinion as to the appellant's personality and mental make-up as set out in his report was relevant and admissible for three reasons: first, because it helped to establish lack of intent; secondly, because it helped to establish that the appellant was likely to be easily provoked; and thirdly, because it helped to show that the appellant's account of what had happened was likely to be true. We do not find it necessary to deal specifically with the first of these reasons. Intent was not a live issue in this case. The evidence was tendered on the issues of provocation and credibility. The judge gave his ruling in relation to those issues. In any event the decision which we have come to on counsel for the appellant's second and third submission would also apply to his first.

The first question on both these issues is whether the psychiatrist's opinion was relevant. A man's personality and mental make-up do have a bearing on his conduct. A quick-tempered man will react more aggressively to an unpleasing situation than a placid one. Anyone having a florid imagination or a tendency to exaggerate is less likely to be a reliable witness than one who is precise and careful. These are matters of ordinary human experience. Opinions from knowledgeable persons about a man's personality and mental make-up play a part in many human judgements. In our judgement the psychiatrist's opinion was relevant. Relevance, however, does not result in evidence being admissible: it is a condition precedent to admissibility. Our law excludes evidence of many matters which in life outside the courts sensible people taken into consideration when making decisions. Two broad heads of exclusion are hearsay and opinion. As we have already pointed out, the psychiatrist's report contained a lot of hearsay which was inadmissible. A ruling in this ground, however, would merely have trimmed the psychiatrist's evidence: it would not have excluded it altogether. Was it inadmissible because of the rules relating to opinion evidence?

The foundation of these rules was laid by Lord Mansfield C.J. in *Foulkes v. Chadd* and was well laid: 'The opinion of scientific men upon proven facts', he said, 'may be given by men of science within their own science.' An expert's opinion is admissible to furnish the court with scientific information which is likely to be outside the experience and knowledge of a judge or jury. If on the proven facts a judge or jury can form their own conclusions without help then the opinion of an expert is unnecessary. In such a case if it is given dressed up in scientific jargon it may make judgement more difficult. The fact that an expert witness has impressive scientific qualifications does not by that fact alone make his opinion on matters of human nature and behaviour within the limits of normality any more helpful than that of the jurors themselves; but there is a danger that they may think it does.

What, in plain English, was the psychiatrist in this case intending to say? First, that the appellant was not showing and never had shown, any evidence of mental illness as defined by the Mental Health Act 1959 and did not require any psychiatric treatment; secondly that he had had a deep emotional relationship with the girl which was likely to have caused an explosive release of blind rage when she confessed her wantonness to him; thirdly, that after he had killed her he behaved like someone suffering from profound grief. The first part of his opinion was within his expert province and outside the experience of the jury but was of no relevance in the circumstances of this case. The second and third points dealt with matters which are well within ordinary human experience. We all know that both men and women who are deeply in love can, and sometimes do, have outbursts of blind rage when discovering unexpected wantonness on the part of their loved ones; the wife taken in adultery is the classical example of the application of the defence of 'provocation'; and when death or serious injury results, profound grief usually follows. Jurors do not need psychiatrists to tell them how ordinary folk who are not suffering from any mental illness are likely to react to the stresses and strains of life. It follows that the proposed evidence was not admissible to establish that the appellant was likely to have been provoked. The same reasoning applies to its suggested admissibility on the issue of credibility. The jury had to decide what reliance they could put on the appellant's evidence. He had to be judged as someone who was not mentally disordered. This is what juries are empanelled to do. The law assumes they can perform their duties properly. The jury in this case did not need, and should not have been offered the evidence of a psychiatrist to help them decide whether the appellant's evidence was truthful.

Counsel for the appellant submitted that such help should not have been rejected by the judge because in *Lowery v. The Queen* the Privy Council had approved of the admission of the evidence of a psychologist on the issue of credibility. We had to consider that case carefully before we could decide whether it had in any way put a new interpretation on what have long been thought to be the rules relating to the calling of evidence on the issue of credibility, *i.e.* that in general evidence can be called to impugn the credibility to witnesses but not led in chief to bolster it up. In *Lowery v. The Queen* the issues were unusual; and the accused to whose disadvantage the psychologist's evidence went had in effect said before it was called that he was not the sort of man to have committed the offence. In giving judgement of the Board Lord Morris of Borth-y-Gest said:

> 'The only question now arising is whether in the special circumstances above referred to it was open to King in defending himself to call Professor Cox to give the evidence that he gave. The evidence was relevant to and necessary for his case which involved negativing what *Lowery* had said and put forward: in their Lordship's view in agreement with that of the Court of Criminal Appeal the evidence was admissible.'

We adjudge *Lowery v. The Queen* to have been decided on its special facts. We do not consider that it is an authority for the proposition that in all cases psychologists and psychiatrists can be called to prove the probability of the accused's veracity. If any such rule was applied in our courts trial by psychiatrists would be likely to take the place of trial by jury and magistrates. We do not find that prospect attractive and the law does not at present provide for it.

In coming to the conclusion we have in this case we must not be taken to be discouraging the calling of psychiatric evidence in cases where such evidence can be helpful within the present rules of evidence. These rules may be too restrictive of the admissibility of opinion evidence. The Criminal Law Revision Committee in its eleventh report thought they were and made recommendations for relaxing them. The recommendations have not yet been accepted by Parliament and until they are, or other changes in the law of evidence are made, this court must apply the existing rules (see *Myers v. Director of Public Prosecutions* per Lord Reid). We have not overlooked what Lord Parker C.J. said in *Director of Public Prosecutions A & BC Chewing Gum Ltd* about the advance of science making more and more inroads into the old common law principle applicable to opinion evidence; but we are firmly of the opinion that psychiatry has not yet become a satisfactory substitute for the common sense of juries or magistrates on matters within their experience of life. The appeal is dismissed."

NOTES

The rule laid down in *Turner* has been extensively criticised, both for its restrictive approach and for its vagueness. See *inter alia* Mackay and Colman, "Excluding Expert Evidence: A Tale of Ordinary Folk and Common Experience" [1991] Crim. L.R. 800; Sheldon and Macleod, "From Normative to Positive Data: Expert Psychological Evidence Re-examined" [1991] Crim. L.R. 811; D. H. Sheldon "The Admissibility of Psychological and Psychiatric Expert Testimony", 1992 S.L.T. (News) 301. For an alternative view, see Stone, *Proof of Fact in Criminal Trials* (1984), Chapter 1. In particular, the distinction which *Turner* purports to make between "normal" and "abnormal" mental states is difficult to apply in practice, and led to some arbitrary and, arguably, unfair results. In *R. v. Masih* [1986] Crim. L.R. 395, for example, it was argued that the defendant was unable, by reason of his very limited intellectual capacity to form the necessary *mens rea* for the offence involved. Expert evidence about the accused was excluded since, at 72, his IQ was within the limits of normality. It was agreed by the court however, that had the accused's IQ been 69 or below, expert evidence would have been admitted. *Masih* set a boundary between normality and abnormality which, although clear, has been variously described as "artificial" and "rather stringent" (see Beaumont, [1988] Crim. L.R. 290). In *Roberts* [1990] Crim. L.R. 122, the accused was an immature pre-lingually deaf person who had in the past been physically abused by his father. He was charged with murder and pleaded provocation. A psychiatrist was called to give evidence that irrational violence might be expected from persons such as the defendant when emotionally disturbed. This expert evidence was ruled inadmissible. In such cases the issue of provocation depends, in England, on the characteristics of a reasonable person sharing the characteristics of the defendant (*Camplin* (1978) 67 Cr.App.R. 14). The court held that the jury were aware of the defendant's special characteristics, and that the medical evidence would add nothing to that awareness. *Roberts'* conviction for murder was upheld. See also *R. v. Weightman* [1991] Crim. L.R. 204, in which expert evidence was excluded in spite of the undisputed fact that the accused suffered from a fairly serious personality disorder. More recent cases have taken a rather more flexible view.

6. R. v. Ward
[1993] 1 W.L.R. 619

Judith Ward was convicted in 1974 of certain terrorist offences. The Crown case at the time consisted largely of evidence of confessions and admissions made by her during police interviews, and partly on scientific evidence disclosing traces of nitroglycerine, an explosive, on her person and in the caravan in which she was living at the time of the alleged offences. The defence case was that she had lied to the police throughout and that no reliance could be placed on her admissions. She was convicted and did not immediately appeal. However, in 1991, the Home Secretary, concerned primarily about the reliability of the scientific evidence at the trial, referred the matter to the Court of Appeal. At the hearing of the appeal, fresh evidence was admitted from a psychologist and a psychiatrist as to Ward's hysterical personality disorder which made her particularly prone to making false claims about herself, and as to her abnormal suggestibility—that is, the extent to which a person can be led to agree with explicit or implicit suggestions made by another. There was no suggestion that she was suffering from any mental illness or disability. Quashing her conviction on a number of grounds, the Court of Appeal made the following comments on the admissibility of expert testimony on matters involving the personality of an accused.

LORDS JUSTICES: GLIDEWELL, NOLAN AND STEYN

Admissibility of evidence of psychiatrists and psychologists as to an accused's reliability

"At one time the authorities on this issue seemed fairly clear. In *Reg v. Toohey* [1965] A.C. 595 three men were charged with assault with intent to rob a boy aged 16. Their defence was, in essence, that they had neither assaulted nor robbed the boy, who was hysterical and had invented the whole matter. On behalf of the defence it was sought to call the evidence of a police surgeon who had expressed the view that from his examination of the boy he would consider him to be more prone to hysteria than a normal person, and that the hysteria might be exacerbated by alcohol. The judge at trial refused to allow these questions to be asked. The Court of Criminal Appeal dismissed an appeal following its own decision in *Rex v. Gunewardene* [1951] 2 K.B. 600. In a speech with which all the members of the House of Lords agreed in favour of allowing the appeal, Lord Pearce said, at p.608:

'Human evidence shares the frailties of those who give it. It is subject to many cross-currents such as partiality, prejudice, self-interest and, above all, imagination and inaccuracy. Those are matters with which the jury, helped by cross-examination and common sense, must do their best. But when a witness through physical (in which I include mental) disease or abnormality is not capable of giving a true or reliable account to the jury, it must surely be allowable for medical science or reveal this vital hidden fact to them.'

Lord Pearce drew an analogy and then added:

'So, too, must it be allowable to call medical evidence of mental illness which makes a witness incapable of giving reliable evidence whether through the existence of delusions or otherwise.'

His Lordship said at p.609:

'*Gunewardene's* case was, in my opinion, wrongly decided. Medical evidence is admissible to show that a witness suffers from some disease or defect or abnormality of mind that affects the reliability of his evidence. Such evidence is not confined to a general opinion to the unreliability of the witness, but may give all the matters necessary to show not only the foundation of and reasons for the diagnosis but also the extent to which the credibility of the witness is affected.'

Lowery v. The Queen [1974] A.C. 85 was a case in which the appellant and another young man were charged with the sadistic murder of a young girl. Each said it was the other who had killed the girl. Despite objection on the part of the appellant, the defence for the other man were allowed to call the evidence of a psychologist as to their respective personalities. On that evidence the jury were invited to conclude that the appellant was the more likely of the two to have killed the girl. They were both convicted, and the appellant appealed on the ground that the psychologist's evidence was inadmissible.

Giving the opinion of the Judicial Committee of the Privy Council dismissing the appeal, Lord Morris of Borth-y-Gest said, at p.103:

'it was most relevant for King to be able to show, if he could, that *Lowery* had a personality marked by aggressiveness whereas he, King, had a personality which suggested that he would be led and dominated by someone who was dominant and aggressive. In support of King's case the evidence of Professor Cox was relevant if it tended to show that the version of the facts put forward by King was more probable that that put forward by *Lowery*. Not only however was the evidence which King called relevant to this case, its admissibility was placed beyond doubt by the whole substance of *Lowery's* case. Not only did *Lowery* assert that the killing was done by King and not only did he say that he had been in fear of King but, as previously mentioned, he set himself up as one who had no motive whatsoever in killing the girl and as one who would not have been likely to wreck his good prospects and furthermore as one who would not have been interested in the sort of behaviour manifested by the killer. While ascribing the sole responsibility to King he was also in effect saying that he himself was not the sort of man to have committed the offence. The only question now arising is whether in the special circumstances above referred to it was open to King in defending himself to call Professor Cox to give the evidence he gave. The evidence was relevant to and necessary for his case which involved negativing what *Lowery* had said and put forward: in their Lordships' view in agreement with that of the Court of Criminal Appeal the evidence was admissible.'

So far the position seems reasonably clear, and the authorities would support the proposition that the evidence which we heard would be admissible in the present case and would have been admissible in 1974. However, a number of decisions thereafter showed a less clear picture. In *Reg v. Turner (Terence)* [1975] Q.B. 834, a decision of this court, a defendant on a charge of murder was not permitted to call a psychiatrist to prove the depth of his emotional state in order to support his defence of provocation. Giving the judgment of the court dismissing the appeal, Lawton L.J. said at p.842:

'We adjudge *Lowery v. The Queen* [1974] A.C. 85 to have been decided on its special facts. We do not consider that it is an authority for the proposition that in all cases psychologists and psychiatrists can be called to prove the probability of the accused's veracity. If any such rule was applied in our courts, trial by psychiatrists would be likely to take the place of trial by jury and magistrates. We do not find that prospect attractive and the law does not at present provide for it . . . we are firmly of the opinion that psychiatry has not yet become a satisfactory substitute for the common sense of juries or magistrates on matters within their experience of life.'

That decision was followed by another division of this court presided over by Lord Lane C.J. in *Reg v. Masih* [1986] Crim. L.R. 395.

However, *Reg v. Everett*, unreported, July 29, 1988, CA, was a decision to the opposite effect. The issue was whether the judge at trial should have ruled under section 76(2) of the Police and Criminal Evidence Act 1984 that a confession allegedly made by the appellant was inadmissible because, although the appellant was of very low mental age, he did not have a solicitor or other responsible person present when he was interviewed. The judge at trial had admitted the evidence. He had heard the evidence of a psychiatrist about the mental condition of the defendant, but had apparently given little or no weight to it. This court allowed the appeal. Giving the judgement of the court, Watkins L.J. said:

'Thus when the judge had to decide in making up his mind whether or not to admit these confessions, he had to take into account the evidence which he had listened to from experts as to that mental condition.'

Watkins L.J. then summarised the evidence and later said:

'What the judge in fact did was to rule in effect that he did not have to take account of the medical evidence of the mental condition of the appellant. On the contrary he listened to the tape recording and expressed himself, having done that, to be satisfied that the appellant understood the questions and made rational answers to them. That is not the function of a judge in such a situation as this. He cannot say to himself, "I am going to listen to a tape recording of the interviews and decide upon that alone whether it is proper to admit evidence of confessions." He must, as we have already said, regard the whole circumstances and take account of the medical evidence, which was here in no way contested. Having done so, he may decide, bearing in mind the terms of the provision I have referred to and the code, whether the prosecution has discharged the clear burden upon it. Here it most certainly had not.'

Most recently, in *Reg v. Raghip*, *The Times*, December 9, 1991, decided by this court, the court was directly concerned with the question whether the trial judge should have admitted the evidence of psychologists and a psychiatrist as to the appellant's lack of mental capacity. Giving the judgement of this court, Farquharson L.J. said of the decision in the *Masih* case:

> 'With respect to the Lord Chief Justice he is there endorsing the "judge for yourself" approach in respect of the jury which this court in *Everett's* case held was the wrong approach for the judge. The state of the psychological evidence before us as outlined earlier in this judgement—in contradistinction to that which was available to the defence at Raghip's trial and before this court on the renewed application—is such as to demonstrate that the jury would have been assisted in assessing the mental condition of Raghip and the consequent reliability of the alleged confessions . . . We emphasise that nothing we say in this judgement is intended to reflect upon the admissibility of psychiatric or psychological evidence going to the issue of the defendant's *mens rea*. But, in the context of assessment of reliability of a confessions pursuant to section 76(2)(b) we consider that the trial judge should ask himself the question posed earlier . . . [P]osing that question and applying those criteria in the instant case we consider that the psychological evidence as deployed before us was required to assist the jury and would have been admissible at Raghip's trial. We are therefore prepared to admit the evidence we heard *de bene esse* under section 23 of the Criminal Appeal Act 1968 as credible and admissible at Raghip's trial but not available at the time thereof. Having done so, it is apparent, for the reasons given earlier, that this fresh evidence renders Raghip's conviction unsafe and unsatisfactory and his appeal is allowed on this ground also.'

We appreciate that in *Reg v. Raghip* the fresh evidence was advanced in support of an argument that, if it had been available at the trial, it would have supported an application to the judge to rule that Raghip's confessions were inadmissible under section 76(2)(b) of the Police and Criminal Evidence Act 1984. The judgement in that case, however, applies equally to the admissibility of such evidence to prove that no reliance could be placed on the appellant's confessions and admissions.

We agree with what Lawton L.J. said in *Reg v. Turner* (Terence) [1975] Q.B. 834, that *Lowery v. The Queen* [1974] A.C. 85 is not an authority for the proposition that in all cases psychologists and psychiatrists can be called to prove the probability of the accused's veracity. Nor is the decision of this court in *Reg v. Raghip* authority for such a wide-ranging proposition. But we conclude on the authorities as they now stand that the expert evidence of a psychiatrist or a psychologist may properly be admitted if it is to the effect that a defendant is suffering from a condition not properly described as mental illness, but from a personality disorder so severe as properly to be categorised as mental disorder. Both Dr McKeith and Dr Bowden here so categorise the conditions from which, in their opinion, the appellant was suffering in 1974 and before. In our view such evidence is admissible on the issue whether what a defendant has said in a confession or admission was reliable and therefore likely to have been true.

We emphasise that the occasions on which such evidence will properly be admissible will probably be rare. This decision is not to be construed as an open invitation to every defendant who repents of having confessed and seeks to challenge the truth of his confession to seek the aid of a psychiatrist. But where evidence of the quality and force of that of Doctors McKeith and Bowden is tendered, it is in our view properly admissible. For that reason we admitted it and have taken account of it.

MR MACFARLAND'S OPINION: As to the admissibility of Mr MacFarland's opinion about the appellant, we have already quoted, and repeat, a passage from *Cross on Evidence*, at p.498. We add only that if the defence had had his statement in their possession, they could properly have used it in cross-examination of him, and no doubt without too much difficulty elicited his view.

CONCLUSIONS ON THIS ISSUE: The extent to which the appellant's confessions and admissions could be regarded as reliable and thus true was the major issue in the trial. We have already quoted the comment which the judge made, and on the evidence which had been called before him, was perfectly entitled to make, in his summing up. We believe that if Waller J. had had before him the evidence we have had, both the fresh evidence or evidence of that kind, and the evidence which was in existence at the time of the trial and was not disclosed, he would not have made the comment he did.

In the light of all this evidence, we cannot now be satisfied that reliance can be placed upon the truth of any of the appellant's confessions or admissions. Accordingly on this ground her conviction on all counts is unsafe and unsatisfactory."

NOTES

See also *R. v. King* [2000] Crim. L.R. 835. *Ward* moves away from the rather arbitrary distinction between normal and abnormal conditions and behaviour made in *Turner* and subsequent cases. It should be noted, however, that it is still rather a restrictive rule, being confined to evidence about the reliability of confessions, where a recognised personality disorder can be proved which shows a "substantial deviation from the norm"—*R. v. O'Brien* [2000] Crim. L.R. 676. Expert evidence as to *mens rea* is still apparently excluded, unless, once again, there is some suggestion of mental illness. Cases such as *Roberts* [1990] Crim. L.R. 122, above, would not, therefore, be affected by the more liberal view taken in *Ward* and *Raghip*, although *R. v. Weightman* [1991] Crim. L.R. 204, might well have been decided differently under the new approach. Certainly, the English courts appear to have held the *Turner* line in provocation cases—see *Home* [1994] Crim. L.R. 584 and *Cole* [1994] Crim. L.R. 820, criticised by Mackay and Colman in "Equivocal Rulings on Expert Psychological and Psychiatric Evidence: Turning Muddle into a Nonsense" [1996] Crim. L.R. 88.

Expert evidence on the issue of *credibility* is now admissible in some Commonwealth countries. See, for example, the Canadian case of *R. v. G.B.* [1990] 2 S.C.R. 30 and compare the New Zealand case *R. v. B.* [1987] 1 N.Z.L.R. 362. There are suggestions in some recent cases that evidence as to the *competency* of a witness is admissible in Scotland—see *M. v. Kennedy*, 1992 S.C.L.R. 69; *M. v. Ferguson*, 1994 S.C.L.R. 488; *K.P. v. H.M.A.*, 1991 S.C.C.R. 933—and the distinction between competency and credibility is a fine one. (Cases such as *M. v. Kennedy* must now be read in the light of *T. v. T.*, 2000 S.L.T. 1442, below, Chapter 13, but it is submitted that in those cases in which competency is an issue, the comments of Lord President Hope in this respect remain persuasive.) In *H.M.A. v. Grimmond*, 2001 S.C.C.R. 708, Lord Osborne excluded evidence from a child psychologist as to common patterns of disclosure in cases of child sexual abuse. Lord Osborne took the view that this was evidence of the complainers' credibility, and ruled it to be inadmissible, quoting with approval Lawton L.J.'s approach in *Turner*. Lord Osborne said:

"It respectfully appears to me that that approach is consistent with the approach which has hitherto been adopted in Scotland. It might be that, if it were established that a witness suffered from some form of mental illness which was relevant to a consideration of the quality of the evidence of that witness, psychiatric evidence concerning the implications of the illness might be admissible. However, in the present case, there is no suggestion that either of the children who are the complainers in this case is other than an ordinary and normal child. That being so it appears to me that the assessment of their credibility is exclusively a matter for the jury, taking into account their experience and knowledge of human nature and affairs."

This case may have implications for referrals brought under Chapter 3 of the Children (Scotland) Act 1995. In such proceedings, evidence from psychologists is regularly adduced for the purpose of setting up the credibility of child complainers. Lord Osborne distinguished *M. v. Kennedy* on the basis that the evidence led in that case was "directly relevant to the *de quo* of, the case, which was whether sexual abuse of the child in question had in fact taken place". It might be argued that that distinction is not a sustainable one, since in *Turner* expert evidence was excluded not merely in relation to credibility but also in relation to provocation, which was clearly a relevant issue in, if not the *de quo* of, the case. Even on the assumption that the distinction is sustainable, great care would be required in leading psychological evidence, and it might be argued that such evidence should be excluded altogether on the basis that:

"the fact that an expert witness has impressive scientific qualifications does not by that fact alone make his opinion on matters of human nature and behaviour within the limits of normality any more helpful than that of the jurors themselves; but there is a danger that they may think it does."

See also *Cowan v. H.M.A.*, unreported, High Court of Justiciary, May 3, 2001. It would appear that expert evidence as to the so-called "battered woman syndrome" may now be admissible in England

and Wales (*Aluwahlia* [1992] 4 All E.R. 889, *Emery* (1993) Cr. App. R. (S) 394), although arguably on the basis that it represents an "abnormal" mental state. See Sheldon, "Provocation and battered woman's syndrome" Criminal Law Bulletin, February 1993, p.4. In the Canadian case of *Lavallee v. R.* [1990] S.C.R. 852, Wilson J. held that "the mental state of abused women can hardly be appreciated without expert evidence". Expert evidence in relation to matters of identification has been excluded in Australia on the authority of *Turner*—see *R. v. Smith* [1987] V.R. 907, although there are a number of U.S. cases in which such evidence has been admitted—see, for example, *U.S. v. Stevens* 935F. 2d 1380 (3rd Circuit) (1991). In *R. v. Stockwell* (1993) 97 Cr. App. R. 260, in which *R. v. Turner* does not appear to have been before the court, evidence from a "facial mapping expert" was admitted.

There is comparatively little Scottish case law dealing explicitly with the admissibility of expert testimony. Macphail takes the view that the rule in *Turner* would also be applied in Scotland (Macphail, *Evidence*, para. 16.21) but apparently only insofar as the ratio of *Turner* prohibits expert evidence as to the *mens rea* of an accused person who is not said to be suffering from any mental illness or disability. That view is, on the whole, borne out by the cases.

In the Sheriff Court case of *Lockhart v. Stainbridge*, 1989 S.C.C.R. 220, a psychologist was permitted to testify as to the accused's fear of needles. While a phobia is can hardly be classified as a mental illness, it falls easily into the category of "abnormal" state of mind, if one was to apply the criteria set out in *Turner*.

In *Church v. H.M.A.*, 1995 S.L.T. 604, expert evidence was admitted, apparently without objection, of a sort very similar to that admitted in *R. v. Stockwell*, above. In *Ingram v. Macari*, 1983 J.C. 1, however, evidence from a psychologist as to the tendency of pornographic magazines to deprave and corrupt their readers was held to be inadmissible, that being a matter for the Sheriff alone to decide. This decision appears, however, to have been an application of the ultimate issue rule, referred to above.

In *Blagojevic v. H.M.A.*, 1995 S.C.C.R. 570, expert psychological evidence as to the accused's "suggestibility" was excluded, but only on the technical ground that since the accused had not himself given evidence, there was no proper evidential foundation for expert evidence regarding the stress or pressure to which the accused had been subjected in police interviews. The court declined on that basis to apply the case of *R. v. Ward* [1993] 1 W.L.R. 619, above. Compare the English case of *R. v. Robinson* [1994] All E.R. 346.

In *Martindale v. H.M.A.*, 1994 S.L.T. 1093, evidence of the accused's personality disorder was heard in support of a plea of diminished responsibility, but withdrawn from the jury in the absence of evidence of a recognised mental disorder, illness or disease.

7. Forrester v. H.M.A.
1952 J.C. 28

The accused was charged with "safe-blowing"—theft by opening lockfast places by means of explosives. The evidence against him was entirely circumstantial and based on three main points: (i) That when the accused was arrested he was in possession of some bank notes stolen from the safe in question; (ii) that a cut on one of his fingers matched that on a glove found near the scene; and (iii) that a small particle of material found in one of his pockets corresponded with the material of a cotton bedspread used in connection with the crime. The accused was convicted and appealed on the ground that the evidence had not established the source from which the material, spoken to by an expert witness, had been obtained.

LORD JUSTICE-GENERAL (COOPER): "The second ground of appeal and the third both relate to the particle of pink material which bulked largely in the evidence and also bulked to a considerable extent in the charge of the presiding Judge. The second ground I dismiss briefly, because it is admittedly a purely technical point and one which merely leads up to the third. The point is that, in making the comparison (which I shall meantime assume was otherwise adequately vouched) between the particle of material found in the pocket of the applicant and a thread or fibre taken from the bedspread discovered in the premises, no production was made of the particular fibre taken from the bedspread with which the comparison was made. Since, however, the whole bedspread was produced by the Crown, and as there is no suggestion that the defence could not have taken from that bedspread as many comparable fibres or threads as they wanted, I see no substance or merit in this second ground of appeal.

It is, however, the third ground of appeal that has given me much anxiety. It is stated as follows: 'The presiding Judge wrongly directed the jury that they were entitled to take into consideration the said evidence from Dr Fiddes relating to the comparison by him by means of microscopic examination of the respective fibres of thread aforementioned.' Now there is no doubt that the evidence of Dr Fiddes occupied considerable time during the trial, that it was founded upon by the advocate-depute in his address to the jury, and that it was the subject of detailed comment by the presiding Judge and was left by him to the jury as one of the elements in the case. The difficulty is that, on a narrow examination of the evidence, the position is left thus—that there is in my judgement no proper proof of the source of the slide 9A on which the Crown relied as being the specimen of pink material taken from the jacket of the applicant. The Lord Advocate strove, by a process of elimination and by reading to us much of the evidence of the police and of Dr Fiddes, to repair what is unquestionably a Crown omission in laying the foundation of this branch of the case. I have come to the conclusion, in the end without difficulty, that that chapter of the evidence has not been sufficiently vouched to justify its being laid before the jury at all. Where the mistake arose it is unnecessary to consider, but the matter unquestionably was left in a position of serious confusion. I am unable to find from repeated perusal of the evidence that the slide 9A was ever identified in the manner which alone would be appropriate in a criminal Court.

What, then, is to be the result? The case was presented to the jury as resting upon the cumulative effect of the various links in the chain of circumstantial evidence which I enumerated at the outset. I think it is just to say that the case was a narrow one, which might well have resulted in a verdict of 'not proven'; but when a thin case is put to a jury on the basis of three separate chapters of incriminating evidence, one of which is found to fail (as I think one of them has failed), it seems to me that it is difficult, if not impossible, for this Court, by considering what is left in the two links of the chain which will stand the strain, to determine whether the verdict (in this instance a majority verdict) can be supported or not; and so, though with reluctance and hesitation, I feel that in this case we have no option but to hold that the conviction cannot stand."

NOTES

Compare *Allan v. Ingram*, 1995 S.L.T. 1086. Before expert evidence can competently be led, the factual basis for it must be established. This may come from the expert herself, or from other witnesses. See, for example, *Blagojevic v. H.M.A.*, 1995 S.C.C.R. 570, above. In relation to the particular problem which arose in *Forrester* the Criminal Procedure (Scotland) Act 1995 provides:

"68.—(3) Where a person who has examined a production is adduced to give evidence with regard to it and the production has been lodged at least eight days before the trial diet, it shall not be necessary to prove—
(a) that the production was received by him in the condition in which it was taken possession of by the procurator fiscal or the police and returned to him after his examination of it to the procurator fiscal or the police; or
(b) that the production examined by him is that taken possession of by the procurator fiscal or the police,
unless the accused, at least four days before the trial diet, gives in accordance with subsection (4) below written notice that he does not admit that the production was received or returned as aforesaid or, as the case may be, that it is that taken possession of as aforesaid."

8.   Hopes v. Lavery
1960 J.C. 104

In this case, the police arranged, by means of a radio transmitter and a tape-recorder, for a recording to be made of a conversation between a blackmailer and his victim. Questions arose, first as to the admissibility of the tape; second as to the admissibility of evidence from a police officer who overheard the conversation by means of the transmitter—both matters considered in Chapter 8, above; and third, as to the admissibility of evidence from a court stenographer who made a transcript of the tape, parts of which were difficult to make out.

LORD JUSTICE-GENERAL (CLYDE): "Secondly, I turn to the objection to the competency of Miss McIntyre's evidence.

If it were possible to regard the wireless and tape recording equipment as having put the conversation in the Central Station into cold storage, as it were, so that, when the tape was played over to Miss McIntyre, she was hearing the actual conversation with the time factor eliminated, there is undoubtedly an argument for saying that her evidence is primary evidence. But I regard this as too fanciful an approach to the matter. Her shorthand notes and her transcript were the result of repeated replaying of the tape, and were really more in the nature of a reconstruction by her of what the conversation, in her view, must have been. The need for her evidence arose just because of the difficulty of comprehending from the tape what had in fact been said. In that situation her evidence was very doubtfully competent. For it was her reconstruction of what she interpreted of the conversation.

The difficulty with which the prosecution was faced was, however, a very real one. It was desirable that the jury should be afforded as accurate and intelligible a reproduction of the conversation as possible. It would never do for the trial to be prolonged by a long series of replayings of the tape, or of passages from it, either at the request of one of the parties, or of the jury, and it would be equally wrong for the jury to retire and replay the tape outwith the presence of the prosecutor or the accused, when they were considering their verdict. Practical considerations strongly point therefore in favour of leading evidence such as Miss McIntyre gave.

One way in which the problem could have been solved would have been to lead, in place of Miss McIntyre, a police witness skilled in reading tape recordings, where this type of difficulty occurs. He could have given skilled opinion evidence as an expert in the deciphering of the sounds emitted by the tape. This course was not adopted in the present case, for Miss McIntyre frankly admitted that she had no skill or experience in this type of work.

In the present case, however, I do not find it necessary to reach a definite conclusion as to the competency of Miss McIntyre's evidence. That matter would probably depend on the specialities of the present case which would have little value in the future. Even assuming that her evidence was incompetent, this is clearly a case where there has been no substantial miscarriage of justice. If the jury believed the victim's evidence, as they must have done, there was ample corroborative evidence in the tape itself, the evidence of Inspector George, the finding of the marked notes on Lavery when arrested, the evidence of the association of the victim with the two appellants, and the evidence of the deterioration in the victim's health. This is, therefore, a case to which the proviso to section 2(1) of the Criminal Appeal (Scotland) Act 1926 applies. On the whole matter, therefore, I would refuse the appeals."

LORD SORN: "The general rule is that it would be quite wrong, and inadmissible, to put a witness into the witness-box to tell the jury what the evidence they have been listening to ought to convey to them—and I subscribe to that general rule. But there are exceptions to that rule and the giving of evidence by qualified experts is the typical exception. But there is no rigid rule that only witnesses possessing some technical qualification can be allowed to expound their understanding of any particular item of evidence. Expositions of this kind are often given, subject to the control of the presiding Judge as to whether the person giving the exposition (without possessing some expert qualification) is equipped to do so, and as to whether it is fair to the accused that the exposition should be given. It is all a question of circumstances and, in the circumstances of the present case, I think Miss McIntyre's evidence was rightly admitted.

At the same time, I think that, on any future occasion of a similar kind, deliberate care should be taken by those preparing the Crown case in the selection of the individual who is to present the transcription. If there are persons with pre-existing qualifications for the task available, then the individual should be selected from such persons.

I shall only add that, even if I had thought Miss McIntyre's evidence to have been inadmissible, it would have made no difference to my view as to how the appeal should be dealt with. Even without her, there was ample evidence before the jury to justify the conviction of both accused."

NOTES

As well as establishing a factual basis for expert opinion, it is essential to establish that the expert is qualified to give an expert opinion. An expert need not have formal qualifications—although *Hopes v. Lavery* was clearly a marginal case—and it may be enough if she can demonstrate some experience, or has informally acquired expertise, in a particular area. In *White v. H.M.A.*, 1986 S.C.C.R. 224, for example, experienced police officers were permitted to give evidence as to the amount of a drug which a user might possess for his own consumption, and in *R. v. Murphy* [1980] Q.B. 434, as to the speed and displacement of vehicles involved in a road accident. See also *Wilson v. H.M.A.*, 1988 S.C.C.R. 384, in which police officers in the Drugs Squad were allowed to disclose "received wisdom of persons concerned in drugs enforcement" garnered at seminars and in discussions with customs officers.

Chapter 11

JUDICIAL KNOWLEDGE, AGREEMENT AND ADMISSIONS

(A) JUDICIAL KNOWLEDGE

1. Cross & Tapper on Evidence (9th ed., 1999) Butterworths, pp. 67–68

"When a court takes judicial notice of a fact, as it may, in civil and criminal cases alike, it declares that it will find that the fact exists, or directs the jury to do so, although the existence of the fact has not been established by evidence. If, for instance, the date of Christmas should be in issue, or relevant to the issue, it will not be necessary for the party who desires to establish that fact to call a witness to swear that the relevant date is December 25, because this is a matter of which judicial notice is taken. There are two classes of case in which the court will act in this way, for, to quote Lord Sumner:

> 'Judicial notice refers to facts which a judge can be called upon to receive and to act upon either from his own general knowledge of them, or from enquiries to be made by himself for his own information from sources to which it is proper for him to refer.'

From time to time statute has provided that judicial notice shall be taken of certain facts. It will therefore be convenient to illustrate the application of the doctrine by reference to facts which are judicially noticed without inquiry, facts judicially noticed after inquiry, and those of which notice must be taken under various statutory provisions . . .

It would be pointless to endeavour to make a list of cases in which the courts have taken judicial notice of facts without inquiry. The justification for their acting in this way is that the fact in question is too notorious to be the subject of serious dispute. Familiar examples are provided by the rulings that it is unnecessary to call evidence to show that a fortnight is too short a period for human gestation, that the advancement of learning is among the purposes for which the University of Oxford exists, that cats are kept for domestic purposes, that the streets of London are full of traffic and that a boy riding a bicycle in them runs a risk of injury, that young boys have playful habits, that criminals have unhappy lives, that the reception of television is a common feature of English domestic life enjoyed mainly for domestic purposes. The court may be taken to know the meaning of any ordinary expression in the English language, and that the value of money has declined since 1189. Judicial notice will also be taken of the fact that a post card is the kind of document which might be read by anyone, but not that husbands read their wives' letters. These conclusions have been reached without reference to any extraneous sources of information but there is a number of cases in which judicial notice has been taken only after such reference has been made . . .

Foremost among these are cases in which the court acts on information supplied by a Secretary of State with regard to what may loosely be described as political matters; but other illustrations are provided by cases concerning inquiries into historical facts, questions concerning the existence of various customs and matters of professional practice . . .

The sources consulted by the judge may include reports of previous cases, certificates from various officials, works of reference and oral statements of witnesses.

What was once a notorious fact to be noticed without further ado may become one of which notice will only be taken after the court's memory has been refreshed . . ."

NOTES

The Scottish position is very similar, if not identical. Walker and Walker, *Law of Evidence in Scotland*, put it thus:

> "It is unnecessary and sometimes incompetent, to lead evidence regarding matters which fall within judicial knowledge. The judge will himself take notice of these matters, either because he is bound by statute to do so, or because it is customary for judges to do so. In general they are matters which can be immediately ascertained from sources of indisputable accuracy, or which are so notorious as to be indisputable. If a matter is one which is judicially noticed, a judge may refresh his memory or supplement his knowledge regarding it by consulting recognised works of reference, such as dictionaries or text-books. While it is unnecessary to prove matters within judicial knowledge, evidence may sometimes be necessary regarding their applicability or inapplicability to the particular case. Apart from the matters which are recognised as being within judicial knowledge, it is improper for a judge to proceed upon his personal knowledge of the facts in issue, or upon his own examination of passages in text-books. Thus, he may not use his own observations of a locus or of documents, made after the conclusion of a proof, to contradict or supplement the evidence of the witnesses."

To the examples listed by Cross & Tapper, one might add that the basic facts of science and nature need not be proved; nor do well known historical or geographical facts, and certain aspects of business and social life. See, for example, *Williamson v. McClelland*, 1913 S.C. 678; *G's Trustees v. G's Curator Bonis*, 1936 S.C. 837; *The Fagernes* [1927] P. 311; *MacCormick v. The Lord Advocate*, 1953 S.C. 396; *Prentice v. Chalmers*, 1985 S.L.T. 168; *Lord Advocate's Reference (No. 1 of 1992)* 1992 S.C.C.R. 724. It has recently been held that the level of the National Minimum Wage is within judicial knowledge— *McKenzie v. H. D. Fraser & Sons*, 2001 S.L.T. 116, as is the fact that mortgage interest rates are variable—*Trotter v. Trotter*, 2001 S.L.T. (Sh. Ct.) 42.

2.   Oliver v. Hislop
1946 J.C. 20

The Tweed Fisheries Amendment Act, 1859, by sections 2 and 14, renders liable to a penalty a person who has in his possession within five miles of the river Tweed or its tributaries a rake hook or "similar engine of the description of those used for killing salmon."

An accused was charged with having contravened section 14 by being in possession on the right bank of the river Ettrick, a tributary of the river Tweed, of a "cleek attached to a stick, being an engine of the description of those used for killing salmon similar to a rake hook." The evidence for the prosecution established that the accused and another man were seen shortly before midnight on the bank of the river each holding what was described as a cleek bound to a stick with string. On the approach of water bailiffs, both men threw into the river the implements, which were not recovered. No evidence was adduced as to the nature and use of "cleeks" in general, or of the particular "cleek" which the accused was seen to be holding in his hand.

LORD JUSTICE-CLERK (COOPER): "By section 14 of the Tweed Fisheries Amendment Act, 1859, it is made an offence for any person to have in his possession within five miles from the river 'any pout net, rake hook or similar engine of the description of those used for killing salmon.' The respondent was charged with a contravention of that section in respect that on June 8, 1945 at the Selkirk Cauld he had in his possession a cleek attached to a stick, being an engine of the description of those used for killing salmon similar to a rake hook.

The evidence led in support of that complaint was very short, and it is embodied by the learned Sheriff-substitute in four findings in fact which I may briefly summarised as follows:— The time of the alleged offence was 11.45 p.m. and the place was the apron at the side of the Selkirk Cauld, where the accused was standing in company with another man unknown. Each man held in his hand what was described as a cleek tied to a stick with string, and I pause to emphasise that the implement to which our attention must be directed is an improvised device consisting of the stick plus the attached cleek. To return to the findings—when three water bailiffs approached the scene, the respondent and his companion threw their implements into the river and ran away across the Cauld to the opposite bank. The only further findings are negative in character, for they are to the effect that the two implements thrown into the river were not recovered, and that there was no evidence as to the nature and use of cleeks in general, or as to the nature and use of the cleek which the respondent was holding in particular.

On these findings the Sheriff-substitute found the respondent not guilty, and the question submitted for our opinion is 'On the facts stated was I entitled to acquit the respondent of the offence charged?'

I read that question as meaning, was I entitled to acquit the *respondent on the grounds stated by me*? And when I turn to the grounds stated by the Sheriff-substitute, as is his duty under the Act of 1908, I find that the reason for the acquittal was that the appellant had failed to prove that the cleek which the respondent had in his possession was an engine of the description of those used for killing salmon similar to a rake hook, and that this failure was fatal to the conviction which he sought. That I read as the sole basis of the acquittal. The Sheriff-substitute adds that he was fortified in this view by the observations of the Judges in *Gladstone and Another v. Stevenson* [4F. (J) 66], and by the fact that, in terms of section 16 of the Act, the use of a cleek in June is not necessarily illegal.

It appears to me from an examination of the Sheriff-substitute's grounds and the reasons which fortified him in these grounds that what he has in effect done has been to hold that it is indispensable for a conviction under this section that evidence should be led to satisfy the Court what a cleek is, and what a rake hook is, and to show that in outward semblance and characteristics as well as in potential use a cleek is similar to a rake hook. I am unable to approach the matter from that standpoint, and so far from finding fortification for the Sheriff-substitute's view in the case of *Gladstone v. Stevenson*, I am disposed to regard the opinions of the Judges in that case as pointing to an opposite conclusion.

The first thing to be said is this. When Parliament in 1857 and in 1859 enacted the Tweed Fisheries Acts, the operative provisions of these statutes were filled with technical terms of local significance, descriptive both of the implements and tackle used in taking fish lawfully and unlawfully, and of the fish themselves and I do not consider that a Border Sheriff, through whose territory the Tweed flows, requires, or ought to require, to be instructed by expert or other evidence as to the meaning of the terms which have been employed in the statutory regulation of the river for a period of close on ninety years. Indeed, if for his own enlightenment such a Sheriff required assistance as to the precise significance of such a technical term, I do not think that it is asking too much that he should have put the appropriate question to the water bailiffs when they were in the witness-box under examination.

A cleek is defined, according to the dictionary definitions given to us, in terms which conform to the ordinary popular understanding of the subject, as a large hook for catching hold of something. In section 16 of the Act it is used in a context which plainly shows that it is a synonym for a gaff. The implement in question here is a cleek attached to a stick with string. A rake hook is defined by dictionary definitions as a hook, or set of hooks fixed to a bar, dragged along the bottom of a river so as to catch fish. When one keeps in view these obvious definitions of the two articles, coupled with the fact that the statute refers to engines 'of the description of those used for killing salmon,' it becomes clear that the real issue before the Court, as Lord Stormonth Darling said in *Gladstone v. Stevenson* is whether the cleek in question—or rather, I should say in this case the improvised implement in question—was 'intended for the same kind of use as a rake hook'. The whole emphasis ought, in my view, to be placed not on the physical resemblance of the articles or engines, but upon their capacity for use in a similar way, namely for foul hooking the fish. I may add that the case of *Rodger v. Hislop and Others* [6R. (J) 16] which was cited to us, indicates that an ordinary salmon fly used with a rod and line can be used, and in that case was held to have been used, as a rake hook for the purpose of foul hooking and killing salmon.

Returning to the findings in this case, we have the fact to which I have already adverted, that the respondent was at a spot and at a time from which it is very difficult to draw any but one inference, and that the instrument in his hand was obviously capable of the use for which a rake hook is used. On the approach of the water bailiffs concerned to check operations of this kind, the respondent's conduct, both in relation to the implement and in relation to his own hurried departure, seems to confirm completely the inference as to what the true position of matters was, *viz.*, that the implement was being used, or was intended to be used, for foul hooking fish, just as a rake hook is used.

In that situation I read the case as meaning this, that but for the absence of the evidence which the Sheriff-substitute desiderated, but which, in my humble opinion, he had no right to ask, a conviction would have followed, and in my judgment, would necessarily have followed. Being of opinion that the further evidence was not required, and that the Sheriff-substitute's acquittal was therefore unjustified, I am of opinion that the question of law, should be answered in the negative.

I may add in conclusion that the Sheriff-substitute is not strictly accurate in saying that by the terms of section 16 of the 1859 Act the use of a cleek in June is not necessarily illegal. Even in June the use of a cleek to be legal must be used in fishing with rod and line and only for the purpose of landing fish, and not for killing fish."

Lords Mackay and Carmont agreed with the Lord Justice-Clerk.

NOTES

This case makes clear that what is "so notorious as to be indisputable" may vary from place to place. Thus, in *Henderson v. Henderson's Executor*, 2000 S.L.T. (Sh. Ct.) 6, it was held that in relation to an action raised in Wick Sheriff Court, it was within judicial knowledge that there were only two firms of solicitors in Wick. It may also vary according to particular circumstances. For example, whether a road is one which a local authority has a duty to maintain may be within judicial knowledge in some cases— a motorway would be an obvious example—but not in others. See *Russell v. Annan*, 1993 S.C.C.R. 234. As the passage from Cross & Tapper makes clear, it may also vary from time to time. One may wonder, for example, whether the matters taken to be within judicial knowledge in *Oliver v. Hislop*, would still be thought to be so today. On the other hand, it may be that in modern conditions, even quite technical matters may be deemed within judicial knowledge. *Doyle v. Ruxton*, 1999 S.L.T. 487 was an appeal from a prosecution under the Licensing (Scotland) Act 1976 for selling alcoholic drinks without a license. It was argued that the prosecution had failed to prove that certain brands of drink contained more than 0.5 per cent alcohol, thus falling within the definition of "alcoholic liquor" in the 1976 Act. The High Court disposed of the appeal on other grounds, and said that:

"it is accordingly unnecessary for us to pronounce a concluded opinion as to whether it is a matter of judicial knowledge that well known brand names such as McEwans Export, Guinness, Carlsberg Special Brew and the rest, are of such alcoholic strength that they can only be sold with an excise licence. Suffice it to say that we found the argument that judicial knowledge did not extend to these matters somewhat unattractive and unrealistic in the circumstances of this case. All the brands in question are well known and extensively advertised in the press, on television and in public places. They are widely known to consist of alcoholic liquor and to contain a sufficient percentage of alcohol to require them to be sold in licensed premises. In these circumstances we would be reluctant to hold that information of which the public is, in our opinion, so widely aware is not within judicial knowledge."

There are likely to be limits to this, however—compare *obiter* comments in *Beta Computers (Europe) Limited v. Adobe Systems (Europe) Limited*, 1996 S.L.T. 604.

3. The Commissioners of Inland Revenue v. Russell
1955 S.C. 237

The Finance Act 1936, enacts, by section 21(1), that "where, by virtue or in consequence of any settlement to which this section applies and during the life of the settlor, any income is paid to or for the benefit of a child of the settlor in any year of assessment, the income shall if at the commencement of that year the child was an infant and unmarried, be treated for all the purposes of the Income Tax Acts as the income of the settlor for that year and not as the income of any other person," and, by section 21(9)(a), that "the expression 'child' includes a stepchild, an adopted child and an illegitimate child." These provisions were repealed by the Income Tax Act 1952, and re-enacted by sections 397(1) and 403 thereof.

By a deed of trust a husband settled funds for the purpose, *inter alia*, of paying the income to or for behoof of his wife's daughter by a previous marriage. His wife's former husband was still alive. The truster having been assessed to surtax on income which included the income arising from the trust funds, the question arose whether the daughter was his stepchild within the meaning of section 21(9)(a) of the 1936 Act.

LORD PRESIDENT (CLYDE): "In this case the respondent granted a trust deed in May 1950 under which he settled certain funds in trust for the purpose, *inter alia*, of paying the income of the trust funds to or for behoof of Miss Susan Burnett. Miss Burnett was the infant daughter of the respondent's wife by a previous marriage. His wife had been divorced by her first husband in 1937, and he is still alive. In respect of the years 1950–1951 and 1951–1952 the respondent was assessed for surtax on the basis that the income from this trust fell to be treated as his income, and this course was taken in virtue of the provisions of section 21 of the Finance Act 1936. Under subsection (1) of that section, had Miss Burnett been the respondent's own child, the income from these settled funds would have fallen to be treated as his income for all the purposes of the Income Tax Acts. Subsection (9), it was maintained, extended this result to the case of Miss Burnett, since in that subsection 'child' is defined as including 'a stepchild, an adopted child, and an illegitimate child'.

The respondent appealed against these assessments and maintained that 'stepchild' did not include a child whose real father was alive, and this contention the Special Commissioners have sustained on the ground that it was not a natural use of the term 'stepchild' to include in it a child whose father was still living.

Authority upon this matter is sparse. Indeed Simon on Income Tax, vol. iii, p.103, leaves the matter open either way, and we were not referred to any decision in Scotland or England where the Courts have defined the precise meaning of the term 'stepchild.' It is true that in *Macdonald v. Macdonald*, where it was held that a stepmother was not liable to aliment a stepson, and where the real mother of the child was a party to the process, the Court did describe the former as a stepmother. But no argument on whether this designation was correct appears to have been presented, and the case cannot therefore be regarded as a decision favourable to the appellants in this case, for no point in the argument turned on the significance of the word 'stepmother.'

So far as the history of the definition in dictionaries of the word 'stepchild' is concerned, while originally it appears likely that the death of the real parent was an essential element in enabling a child to fall into the category of a 'stepchild', it is, in my view, clear that any such qualification on the definition is obsolete. In Murray's Oxford Dictionary 'stepchild' is defined as, first of all, an orphan—which is described as an obsolete definition—and then as a stepson or stepdaughter, and 'stepson' and 'stepdaughter' are defined in the dictionary as a son or a daughter by a former marriage of the husband or the wife. There is no indication of any requirement that the real parent must be dead before the child could become a stepchild. Similarly in the Shorter Oxford English Dictionary remarriage of the parent and not the death of one or other of the parents is the qualification for falling into the category of stepchild. None of the other dictionary definitions to which we were referred support any different conclusion as to the ambit of the term. On dictionary definitions, therefore, I am satisfied that the word is in modern parlance wide enough to cover the present case.

Apart from that aspect of the matter, however, it appears to me that the construction contended for by the respondent would lead to anomalous results. It seems to me surprising that the income from the settled funds should be treated as the income of the settlor only after a third party—the real father—happens to die, but that prior to such death the situation should be quite different. It appears to me much more reasonable to assume that no such accidental circumstance was intended to be treated as the criterion for ascertaining whether or not a child was a stepchild of the settlor. It was suggested that it would be anomalous that more than one settlor could be taxed in respect of income payable to or for behoof of the same child, as would happen if the contention for the Inland Revenue were correct. But in the case of an adopted child it is clear that there could be more than one settlor liable to tax in respect of funds settled on the same child, and, if that be so in the case of adoption, I see no reason why it should not also apply in the case of a stepchild.

On the whole matter accordingly, in my view, the conclusion arrived at by the Special Commissioners was wrong and the question which they put to us should be answered in the negative."

Lords Carmont, Russell and Sorn agreed with the Lord President.

NOTES

This case falls within the second of Cross's two categories—thus the court treated the definition of "stepchild" as being within judicial knowledge only after consulting two different dictionaries. Courts should be cautious when applying the concept of judicial knowledge, however. This is particularly so where inferences require to be drawn about a particular state of facts. In the following two cases, it was held that the court should not have proceeded without evidence.

4.   Kennedy v. Smith and Ansvar Insurance Company Limited
1976 S.L.T. 110

In 1961, a car owner completed a proposal for insurance by an insurance company in respect of the car which he owned. At the same time he signed a document called an "Abstinence and Membership Declaration". The abstinence declaration contained the following statement: "I am a total abstainer from alcoholic drinks and have been since birth. (A total abstainer never drinks a beverage the sale of which requires a licence or registration under the Clubs Act, including home-made wines and cider.)" According to the insurance company the form of policy governing the kind of insurance provided by the policy of 1961 was changed in 1967 insofar as it stated exceptions to the company's liability. These exceptions were expressed thus:—"5(a): Any claims arising while the insured or any other person otherwise indemnified under this policy is under the influence of intoxicating liquor. 5(b): Any claim arising while the insured vehicle is being driven by (i) the insured having consumed intoxicating liquor prior thereto in breach of the abstinence declaration." The car owner was a member of a bowling club. On July 3, 1971 he played in a county championship in which his club won. After the match he left with two friends in his car to drive home. At the suggestion of one of his friends they stopped at a public house where he had a pint, or perhaps a pint and a half of lager beer. He had eaten little food during the day. Shortly after 6 p.m. they left the public house intending to continue their journey home. About fifteen minutes later when the car, driven by the owner, was travelling on a dual carriageway it suddenly left the west-bound carriageway, crossed the central reservation, collided with an advance-warning sign, passing between two of its upright supporting pillars, and travelled a further thirty-five yards before coming to rest on the east-bound carriageway. The two passengers were killed and the driver was rendered unconscious. He was interviewed in hospital about 8.10 p.m. by a police constable who noticed a smell of alcohol. The families of the two passengers who were killed sued the car owner and driver for reparation. The defender called the insurance company as third party. The defender admitted liability and the amount of damages in each case was agreed. Decree for these sums was pronounced against the defender. The insurer refused to indemnify the defender, and proof before answer was allowed on the issue of the indemnity. The Lord Ordinary held that at the moment when the accident occurred the statement that the defender had been a total abstainer from birth was untrue, and that when the claim arose the defender was under the influence of intoxicating liquor. He found accordingly that the third party was not liable to indemnify the defender. The defender reclaimed.

THE LORD PRESIDENT (EMSLIE): "For the defender, the submission under reference to exception 5(a) is simple to state. There were no sufficient proved facts capable of supporting the inference that at the time of the accident the pursuer was 'under the influence of intoxicating liquor', as these words are properly to be understood. They mean, as the Lord Ordinary accepted 'under such influence of intoxicating liquor as disturbs the balance of a man's mind' this was the meaning given to them by Lord Coleridge. L.J., in *Mair v. Railway Passengers Assurance Co.* (1877) 37 L.T. 356 in which Denman, J. referred to the condition as 'disturbing the quiet, calm, intelligent exercise of the faculties', and was the meaning adopted by Lawton, J. in the later case of *Louden v. British Merchants Insurance Co.* [1961] 1 W.L.R. 798. The only proved facts are: (i) the admitted consumption by the defender of one pint of lager; and (ii) the happening of the accident. The Lord Ordinary was not entitled to rely as he did upon the facts that the defender drank the lager upon an empty stomach and was unaccustomed to alcohol, since there was no evidence whatever that either of these facts made it more probable that the amount of alcohol consumed would adversely affect the faculties of the defender. In so far as the Lord Ordinary refers to the erratic and unexplained behaviour of the defender's car this is only to be understood as a reference to the movement of the car at the time of the accident as the result, according to the defender, of the back wheels striking either the kerb or an object on the road surface. The happening of the accident is explicable as the result of momentary inattention or loss of concentration and it is sheer speculation to say that the defender's consumption of one or even one and a half pints of lager had placed him under such influence of alcohol as had disturbed the balance of his mind. The third party, who accepted the meaning of the critical expression adopted by the Lord Ordinary, argued that the exception was of a very wide character and would apply when, for example, a claim arose while the defender's wife, in a state of complete sobriety was driving the car in Scotland if it were proved that the defender was at the time under the influence of alcohol on holiday in Spain. I am happy to say that I need not comment upon this startling claim for the ambit of exception 5(a) for the question here relates to the state of the insured driver at the time of the accident. Upon this, the only relevant question, the third party contended that the Lord Ordinary was entitled, since it was within judicial knowledge, to rely on the defender's empty stomach and his being unaccustomed to alcohol as indicating a probability that the alcohol consumed would have greater and quicker effect upon the defender than would otherwise have been the case. They also argued that it was relevant to consider that this was a case of wholly unexplained and extraordinary movement of the motor car which the defender had driven accident-free for some years. It was further, they said, relevant in this connection to have regard to the plea tendered by the defender to the charge of contravening section 1(1) of the Road Traffic Act 1960.

In my opinion, the defender's submission in this matter is well founded. The Lord Ordinary was not, in my view, entitled to have regard to the fact that the lager drunk by the defender was consumed upon an empty stomach and that he was unaccustomed to alcohol. Whether or not a particular combination of circumstances is likely to exacerbate the effects of a particular consumption of alcohol is a matter of evidence (as was the case in *Louden*). In this case there was no evidence to show that the circumstances in question were other than neutral. In my opinion also, no weight can be given to the defender's plea of guilty. The Lord Ordinary gave no weight to this. Such a plea is explicable as soon as it is remembered that even a slight degree of carelessness may justify a conviction for driving in a manner dangerous to the public. In these circumstances, the 'inference' drawn by the Lord Ordinary rests only upon (i) proved consumption of one pint of lager and possibly—only possibly—another half pint, and (ii) the happening of the accident as it emerged in evidence. There was not one scintilla of evidence of any behaviour on the part of the defender, or of his car before the accident, which pointed to the alcohol he had consumed having to any material extent affected the balance of the defender's mind. For the exception to apply it is not enough to show that 1975 the defender had consumed a particular quantity of alcohol shortly before a claim arose. In my opinion mere proof that the defender had consumed at most a pint and a half of lager and that he had later been driving the car when it left the west-bound dual carriageway in the manner described, does not justify an inference that he was at the time of the accident under the influence of intoxicating liquor within the meaning of exception 5(a). The accident is consistent with momentary inattention and to say that he was under the influence of alcohol at the time can only on the facts proved in this case be speculation."

[The Lord President then proceeded to reject the pursuer's submission in relation to exception 5(b)(i), and allowed the reclaiming motion. Lords Johnston and Avonside concurred.]

5. McCann v. Adair
1951 J.C. 127

In an action of damages brought by a motor car dealer against a customer who had failed to take delivery of a car which he had purchased, the dealer and his book-keeper both gave evidence that the car had later been sold to another purchaser at a loss to the dealer of about £60. The dealer and book-keeper were subsequently charged with having so deponed in pursuance of a common design to pervert the course of justice, the truth, as they both well knew, being that the loss was £10. At the trial, the prosecution lodged as productions certain daybooks and extracts therefrom, which contained entries which were consistent with the evidence given by the two accused in the civil action. The day-books and extracts were formally proved but no further evidence was led regarding them. The Sheriff-substitute, having himself examined the relevant entries, held them to be false and convicted the accused.

LORD JUSTICE-GENERAL (COOPER): "A person named Rudin purchased from Norwood Motors, at a price of £710, a car of which he refused to take delivery. Norwood Motors raised an action of damages against him, in the course of which the present appellants deponed in evidence that this car, which had been sold to Rudin for £710, had subsequently been sold by Norwood Motors to a member of the trade for £650, which of course involved a loss of about £60. A prosecution was subsequently brought in Glasgow Sheriff Court against the appellants—the first of whom is the person who carries on the business of Norwood Motors and the second his salesman and book-keeper—the charge being that in pursuance of a common design to pervert the course of justice they had deponed in the sense which I have just indicated, the truth, as they both well knew, being that the car in question was sold on February 17, 1950 to a Mr Adam Cowan for £700. This means of course that the alleged damage of £60 would be reduced to about £10. The prosecution resulted in a conviction, and the imposition on the first appellant of a sentence of sixty days imprisonment, and on the second of a fine of £20 with the alternative of sixty days imprisonment.

The proceedings are now subjected to review by this stated case, and the whole difficulty arises, not in regard to the substance of the matter, with reference to which I am bound to say I do not entertain much doubt, but in regard to the very strange course which the proceedings took. The prosecution lodged as productions on their behalf the daybook and certain extracts from the day-book of Norwood Motors, and the day-book and certain extracts from the day-book of another firm called Sinclair Motors. The entries in these books at their face value showed that there had been an intermediate transaction between the abortive sale to Rudin and the final sale to Cowan, and that this transaction was one by which the car was sold for £650 to Sinclair Motors, and subsequently bought back from Sinclair Motors by Norwood Motors. I need not examine narrowly what the legal consequences of that intermediate transaction would be on the Norwood Motors' claim for damages against Rudin, because that is a civil question, and it is enough to say that, whatever arguments might be presented on that subject, if the substance of the matter was as appeared *ex facie* of the books it is very difficult to believe that any possible question of criminal prosecution could have arisen. The book entries supported the oral testimony which is now said to have been false. What happened at the prosecution was, as I say, that the books were produced, not by the defence, but by the Crown, and they were spoken to by a police witness who referred in evidence, we are told, to relevant entries. Evidently all the books of the two firms were not produced; anyhow all we are told about are the day-books. Taking these day-book entries, without the assistance of any evidence, the Sheriff-substitute, as he tells us, from an 'examination' of them and from deductions based upon the position of the relevant entries on the pages, drew the conclusion or 'inference' as he calls it that the entries in the books were false or, as he elsewhere puts it, 'fictitious'.

The first observation to be made is that the Crown had in their possession the books in question containing the entries which the Sheriff-substitute found on bare inspection to be suggestive of faking but no charge was preferred, either in this complaint or in any other complaint, of what would unquestionably have been just as much a criminal offence as the offence actually charged. Next it would appear that this additional charge, though never made, was held proved by the Sheriff-substitute as a result of his own private examination of the books, without any opportunity being afforded to the defence to cross-examine or otherwise explain the inferences or deductions adverse to them which the Sheriff-substitute drew. Finally it seems to me fairly obvious that, having formed by this method a conclusion that the appellants and this firm of Sinclair had apparently been guilty of deliberately faking their books, this conclusion must have had a powerful effect upon the mind of the Sheriff-substitute in dealing with the complaint actually before him. I do not think that it is legitimate in relation to any such crucial issue as this in a criminal trial that a conclusion so adverse to the accused should be drawn without evidence and without the opportunities afforded to the defence which are available to them when evidence is led.

The whole difficulty in this case arises from the method of procedure. If the books had been produced by the defence and if it had been possible, as I shall assume it would have been, for the prosecution in cross-examination to have satisfied the Sheriff-substitute that the entries, *ex hypothesi* relied upon by the defence as an answer to the charge of perjury, were faked, no question could have arisen. But because the method of procedure has been inverted, and has been inverted by the adoption of methods of which I do not think it is possible for this court to approve, I am of opinion that the conviction must be quashed."

Lord Russell and Keith agreed with the Lord Justice-General.

6.   Brims v. MacDonald
1993 S.C.C.R. 1061

The complainers were tried on summary complaint for dangerous driving. In the course of the evidence a witness described part of the locus as being a blind bend. Photographs of the bend were produced in cross-examination in order to challenge that evidence. The Sheriff examined the photographs and could not see that they contradicted the witness. He stated that he intended to visit the locus at lunchtime and invited the parties to accompany him if they wished to do so. The Sheriff visited the locus, but no one went with him. The complainers were convicted and appealed to the High Court by bills of suspension on the ground that the Sheriff's visit to the locus constituted an irregularity which vitiated the proceedings.

LORD JUSTICE-CLERK (ROSS): "These are bills of suspension at the instance of James Alexander Brims and John Mackay Munro. The respondent is the Procurator Fiscal, Wick. The complainers went to trial in the sheriff court at Wick on a complaint libelling a number of charges. It appears that the procurator fiscal did not ultimately seek conviction in respect of certain charges and the complainers were found not guilty of these charges but were found guilty of, respectively, charge (4) and charge (5), these each being charges of contravening the provisions of section 2 of the Road Traffic Act 1988.

They have presented these bills of suspension in which they seek to have their convictions and sentences suspended, and what has given rise to the presentation of these bills is the fact that during the trial the sheriff paid a visit to the locus. The Sheriff deals with this in his note and he explains how his visit to the locus came about. A Crown witness, Constable Duncan, gave evidence to the effect that two cars had come around a bend in Riverside Road which was a blind bend. It appears that the solicitor for one of the complainers sought to challenge the constable's evidence about the blindness of the bend by reference to a number of photographs. The photographs were handed to the sheriff and he states that he understood that the solicitor's purpose was to invite the sheriff to look at the photographs in order to assess the credibility and reliability of the constable's evidence in chief and in cross. The sheriff tells us that he looked at the photographs and so far as they were concerned could not see how they contradicted the evidence of the constable. However, he says that was his provisional view as he had not yet heard the whole evidence and he goes on to say this: 'It appeared to me that the matter might be of importance, but I could not know at that stage of the case.' The time had apparently come for the lunch-adjournment and the sheriff accordingly announced in open court that he would view the locus after lunch before the court resumed and that parties were welcome to accompany him if they wished, but that they did not need to do so if they did not. He tells us that no party objected to his proposal and that in the event no party accompanied him to the locus, which he viewed, having had it pointed out to him by his bar officer. The sheriff goes on to say that the reason why he viewed the locus was that he understood that the solicitor for one of the complainers was asking him to test the credibility and reliability of the constable's evidence by reference to the photographs. He felt that since the real thing was still readily available to be viewed in the flesh, it was appropriate that he should do so. He referred to Walkers on Evidence at p.48, where it is stated:

'Apart from the matters which are recognised as being within judicial knowledge, it is improper for a judge to proceed upon his personal knowledge of the facts in issue, or upon his own examination of passages in text-books. Thus he may not use his own observations of a locus or of documents, made after the conclusion of a proof, to contradict or supplement the evidence of the witnesses.'

Despite that statement in Walkers, the sheriff proceeded to view the locus after the evidence of the first Crown witness.

Mr Bell for the complainers maintained that in so acting the sheriff had acted improperly. The sheriff clearly thought that the matter of the evidence regarding the blindness of the bend was of importance and indeed, as we have observed, he says that in terms. Mr Bell referred first of all to Renton and Brown's Criminal Procedure (5th ed.), paras 14–68. That is a paragraph dealing with irregularities and it includes the statement: 'Nor should a judge examine a locus outwith the presence of the parties'.

The authority for that statement is given in a footnote as the case of *Sime v. Union* [(1897) 24R.(J) 70], although one is bound to say that it is not very clear that that case is indeed authority for the proposition which appears in that paragraph in Renton and Brown. There are, however, other authorities and although it is unnecessary to refer to all of these, reference was made during the hearing to *Hattie v. Leitch* [(1889) 16R. 1128]. That was a civil case and after the close of the proof in a sheriff court the sheriff-substitute, accompanied by the agents of the parties, examined the locus of the events which were the subject of the proof in order to see whether it was possible in the circumstances for certain witnesses to have seen the act which they deponed to have seen. With regard to that matter the Lord Justice-Clerk said at p.1130:

'Now, in this case the Sheriff-substitute has adopted a course which I think is most extraordinary and most reprehensible, because, after hearing the evidence of the witnesses, he goes to the spot without the witnesses to explain to him what they meant by their evidence, which he had taken without having seen the place. He goes without the witnesses to the place in order that, taking their evidence in his hand, he may form some Opinion of his own as to whether they could have seen or did see what they alleged. In so doing I think that the Sheriff is just turning himself into a witness in the case. He gives himself testimony by going there to look at the ground after the evidence had been led and in order to enable him to form his opinion, and what is the result of that?—that we, who cannot go and see the ground, are to rely upon evidence which he has given without cross-examination as to the possibility or impossibility of particular things being done and witnessed according to his view of the evidence which he had previously heard. That is not at all a satisfactory way of dealing with such a matter.'

That, as we say, was a civil case but the same principle can readily be applied to a criminal case and, indeed, in a criminal case there is the other feature that proceedings must take place in the presence of the accused. The advocate-depute very properly drew our attention to the case of *Aitken v. Wood* [1921 J.C. 84]. In that case, at a trial of an accused upon a charge of assaulting a woman by seizing and compressing her arm, the magistrates, one of whom was a medical doctor, at the conclusion of the evidence called the woman into their room so that her arm might be examined in private. The Lord Justice-General said this at p.86:

'This procedure, however well intended, and however harmless it may have been in this particular case, strikes at the principle—deeply rooted in the criminal law of Scotland— that no proceedings in a criminal trial, and particularly no proceedings connected with the taking of evidence, can go outwith the presence of the accused. The examination of the arm was just a means of taking evidence additional to that which was presented at the proof. The taking of such evidence, in the absence of the accused, is plainly an irregularity which vitiates the proceedings; and there is therefore nothing for it but to quash this conviction.'

The advocate-depute in the present case accepted that what the sheriff had done in this case was something which he ought not to have done. The advocate-depute, however, contended that even if one disregarded what the sheriff had said regarding the blindness of the bend, which is contained in finding four, there was still in the remaining findings, adequate findings to justify the sheriff in concluding that both of these complainers had been driving dangerously and in this connection he referred in particular to finding eight and findings 17 and 18. He also pointed out to us that in the sheriff's note he said:

'It will be noted that neither charge (4) nor charge (5) libels that the bend was blind. The fact that I have found that the bend was blind is merely a further circumstance making the driving of the appellants dangerous. I should stress that had I come to the view that the bend was not blind, I would still have found the appellants guilty as libelled.'

In these circumstances he suggested that this court, although disapproving of what the sheriff had done in relation to viewing the locus, should still uphold the conviction. It appears to us, however, that the situation is similar to that which obtained in *Aitken v. Wood* and that what was done in this case constituted an irregularity and that the only proper view is that it was an irregularity which vitiated the proceedings. As in that case, the sheriff, by going to the locus in order to determine whether the evidence of Constable Duncan regarding the blindness of the bend should be accepted, was in effect taking evidence, and that meant that part of the proceedings were being carried out outwith the presence of the complainers. That was a serious irregularity and as in the case of *Aitken v. Wood* we have come to the conclusion that it vitiated the proceedings. We shall accordingly pass the bills and suspend the convictions and sentence.

The advocate-depute submitted that if we were to follow that course, we should grant authority to the Crown to bring a fresh prosecution. Mr Bell suggested that it would not be appropriate to do so. He pointed out that the events which had given rise to this complaint had occurred in September 1992, that is over a year ago. We do not think that is a consideration which would tend to show that authority should not be granted to bring a new prosecution. In the present case we have passed these bills because of an irregularity which arose in the trial because of the action taken by the sheriff. In these circumstances it appears to us to be appropriate that, having set aside the convictions of the complainers in the bills, we should grant authority to the Crown to bring a new prosecution in accordance with section 452A(1)(d) and section 452B of the Criminal Procedure (Scotland) Act 1975."

NOTES

There appear to have been two problems in this case: first that the Sheriff proceeded upon his own investigation of the facts, when he should have proceeded solely on the evidence; and second that he effectively conducted part of the hearing outwith the presence of the parties. Thus, judges should be very wary of showing too much initiative in the context of an adversarial system, based on the idea that cases must be decided solely on evidence selected and placed before the court by the parties. The following case illustrates the converse of that proposition, however, which is that the adversarial system places a high onus on parties openly to assist and to advise the judge on the matters which she or he has to decide.

7. The Glebe Sugar Refining Company v. The Trustees of the Fort and Harbours of Greenock
1921 S.C. (H.L.) 72

LORD CHANCELLOR (BIRKENHEAD): "Their Lordships will give reasons in writing for the opinion which they have formed. But, as a point of very considerable general importance has arisen, I think it right to make this observation at once. It is not, of course, in cases of complication possible for their Lordships to be aware of all the authorities, statutory or otherwise, which may be relevant to the issues which in the particular case require decision. Their Lordships are therefore very much in the hands of counsel, and those who instruct counsel, in these matters, and this House expects, and indeed insists, that authorities which bear one way or the other upon matters under debate shall be brought to the attention of their Lordships by those who are aware of those authorities. This observation is quite irrespective of whether or not the particular authority assists the party which is so aware of it. It is an obligation of confidence between their Lordships and all those who assist in the debates in this House in the capacity of counsel. It has been made clear that Mr Sandeman, Sir John Simon, and Mr Macmillan were unaware of the existence of the section which appears to their Lordships to be highly relevant to, and in the event decisive upon, the matters under discussion here. Indeed the circumstances in which leading counsel are very often briefed at the last moment render such an absence of knowledge extremely intelligible. But I myself find it very difficult to believe that some of those instructing learned counsel were not well aware of the existence, and the possible importance and relevance, of the section in question. It was the duty of such persons, if they were so aware, to have directed the attention of leading counsel to the section and to its possible relevance, in order that they in turn might have brought it to the attention of their Lordships. A similar matter arose in this House some years ago, and it was pointed out by the then presiding Judge that the withholding from their Lordships of any authority which might throw light upon the matters under debate was really to obtain a decision from their Lordships in the absence of the material and the information which a properly informed decision requires; it was in effect to convert this House into a debating assembly upon legal matters, and to obtain a decision founded upon imperfect knowledge. The extreme impropriety of such a course cannot be made too plain. The learned counsel who has addressed their Lordships are acquitted of personal responsibility in this matter; but I very much hope that the observations I have thought it necessary to make will prevent a recurrence of that with which I have dealt. It is possible that the views their Lordships have formed upon this point will be reflected in the form of the order which their Lordships think it proper to make."

NOTES

The law of Scotland is, in general, within the judicial knowledge of the Scottish courts. The terms and authority of the recognised case reports and of statutes need not be proved, although the preceding case illustrates the extent of the duty incumbent on a pleader to refer the court to the relevant authorities. Statutory instruments are probably also within judicial knowledge, provided they are properly made under powers granted by statute, but the matter is not entirely settled—see Field and Raitt, *The Law of Evidence in Scotland*, (3rd ed., 2001) para. 4.06. Bye-laws and other Government orders require proof—see Stair Memorial Encyclopaedia, Vol. 10, para. 511; *Herkes v. Dickie*, 1958 J.C. 51; *Donnelly v. Carmichael*, 1996 S.L.T. 153. Compare *Valentine v. Macphail*, 1986 S.C.C.R. 321. However it appears that certain government orders contain matter which becomes so well-known that judicial notice can be taken of it. The judiciary must also take notice of EC law—European Communities Act 1972, ss.2–3, and the jurisprudence of the European Court of Human Rights, the Commission and the Committee of Ministers under the European Convention on Human Rights—Human Rights Act 1998, s.2. Customary International Law is also part of Scots law in relation to which expert evidence is neither required nor permitted—see *Lord Advocate's Reference (No. 1 of 2000)*, 2000 S.L.T. 507. Foreign law, by contrast, is regarded as a question of fact about which expert evidence must generally be submitted—see *Kolbin and Sons v. Kinnear*, 1930 S.C. (H.L.) 57 and compare *Baird v. Mitchell* (1854) 16 D. 1088. English law falls into the category of foreign law for most purposes, although the House of Lords takes judicial notice of the law of all the United Kingdom jurisdictions (*Elliot v. Joicey*, 1935 S.C. (H.L.) 57) and Scottish judges, anomalously, must apply the English law of charity in income tax cases—*I.R. v. Glasgow Police Athletic Association*, 1953 S.C. (H.L.) 57.

Matters of procedure associated with the legal process may also fall within judicial knowledge—for example in *Thorne v. Stott*, 2000 S.L.T. 113 the court noted that "it is within judicial knowledge that, where leave to appeal [in a criminal case where the appellant has been granted interim liberation] is refused, the court always grants warrant to all proper officers of law in possession of this warrant to apprehend and imprison or detain the appellant, said imprisonment or detention to continue during the period of the sentence detailed [overleaf] and to run from the date of the appellant's apprehension under this warrant, but always under deduction of any period of imprisonment or detention which the appellant is entitled to have reckoned as already undergone under that sentence, including any such period undergone during the currency of this appeal, the appellant to be conveyed by officers of law to the Prison of Saughton, Edinburgh or to any other lawful institution to be dealt with in due course of law."

In spite of all this, judges cannot realistically be expected to take judicial notice of the whole of the law, and accordingly it is the duty of solicitors or advocates to draw the attention of the court to all relevant authorities, whether favourable to their own case or not.

(B) ADMISSIONS AND AGREEMENT

8.   Lee v. The National Coal Board
1955 S.C. 151

A labourer brought an action against his employers for damages for injuries sustained by him when he was knocked down by a train of wagons on a colliery railway line belonging to and operated by them. He averred that the accident was caused by, *inter alia*, the defenders' breach of statutory duty in failing to comply with mining regulations and the failure of a shunter in his common law duties. At the trial the only evidence that the defenders or their servants were at fault was that of the pursuer; and the presiding Judge, on the defenders' motion, withdrew the case from the jury. In a motion for a new trial, the pursuer contended, *inter alia*, that, in so far as his case was based on the shunter's failure in his common law duties and the defenders' failure in their statutory duty, he was entitled to rely for corroboration on certain of the defenders' averments regarding the shunter's actings at the relevant time, as being equivalent to implied admissions of the facts which he was seeking to prove. These averments were made by way of explanations following a general denial of the pursuer's averments.

LORD RUSSELL: "In this action the pursuer seeks to recover from his employers damages for injuries sustained by him through being knocked down by a train of wagons on a colliery railway line belonging to and used by his employers. Proof in the action was led before a jury. At the conclusion of the evidence led for the pursuer the Lord Ordinary was moved by the defenders to withdraw the case from the jury on the ground of insufficient corroboration of the pursuer's evidence. The Lord Ordinary, after hearing counsel, granted the motion, and under his direction the jury found unanimously for the defenders. In this reclaiming motion the pursuer challenges that direction as being unwarranted and has moved that a new trial should be allowed.

Before noticing the averments of fault set out in the pursuer's pleadings I may observe that certain of the circumstances narrated therein are the subject of express and unqualified admission in the defenders' answers, *viz.*: [His Lordship gave the narrative quoted supra, and continued]—The averments of the pursuer are designed to support his plea that the accident was caused through the fault of the defenders at common law *et separatim* through the breach of statutory duty incumbent on the defenders in terms of the General Regulations under the Coal Mines Act 1911. The particular Regulations founded on are Regulation 161 and Regulation 167. These two Regulations occur in Part V. (of the General Regulations), which applies to lines of rails of not less than four feet eight inches and sidings, and the use of locomotives and wagons thereon. Regulation 161 provides that 'where a locomotive pushes more than one wagon and risk of injury may thereby be caused to persons employed, a man shall, wherever it is safe and reasonably practicable, accompany or precede the front wagon, or other efficient means shall be taken to obviate such risk.' It is not disputed that at the time of his accident the pursuer was a 'person employed' by the defenders; and that a jury might hold that the line on which he met with his accident was a place at which 'risk of injury . . . to persons employed' might be caused by the train of wagons being pushed by the locomotive. Three alternative duties were accordingly incumbent on the defenders in relation to the train in question, *viz.*, either (1) to cause a man to accompany the front wagon, or (2) to cause a man to precede the front wagon—one or other of those two duties being obligatory wherever it was safe and reasonably practicable so to act or (3) to take other efficient means (*i.e.*, other than a man accompanying or preceding the front wagon) to obviate the risk of injury. Regulation 167 relates to the giving of warning sound signals, the relevant words being 'the driver in charge of a locomotive or a man preceding it on foot shall give an efficient sound signal as a warning on approaching . . . any other point of danger to persons employed.'

The pursuer's averments of fact inferring that his accident was caused by the fault of the defenders are directed against the driver of the engine and the shunter respectively. In relation to the driver it is alleged that he did not keep a proper look-out, propelled the train carelessly and at an excessive speed, failed to halt the train short of the danger point at which the pursuer was knocked down, and proceeded without satisfying himself that no one was crossing or about to cross the line at that point; and that he gave no sufficient sound signal as a warning on the approach of the engine to the danger point. In relation to the shunter it is alleged that he signalled the train to proceed without taking care to satisfy himself that no one was crossing or about to cross the line; that he gave no warning of the train's approach; that instead of remaining close to the leading wagon he proceeded to a point 300 yards east of the leading wagon, from which point he was unable to see or warn any one crossing the line in front of the train; and that, although it was safe and reasonably practicable to do so, a man did not accompany or precede the front wagon and no other efficient means were taken to obviate risk of injury to persons employed. Those averments of fault are met in the defenders' answers by a general denial, followed by explanations giving notice of what the defenders offered to prove in order to rebut, if necessary, the alleged fault.

In the oral testimony adduced for the pursuer at the trial, evidence worthy of the jury's consideration was led as to some of the surrounding circumstances, for example, that the point on the line at which the pursuer was struck was about midway between the washery and the cone tower, and that on the morning of the accident the weather was wet and windy, smoke and steam were issuing from an adjacent bing, and a certain amount of noise was coming from the operations conducted inside the washery. But the only evidence directed to the establishing of the alleged negligent conduct of the driver and shunter was that given by the pursuer himself—the other employee (Durkan) who had been accompanying the pursuer at the time, and who was also knocked down, having been killed instantaneously. It is clear that, if on a survey of the evidence led before a jury the proof of fault depends on the uncorroborated testimony of one witness, that proof is not sufficient in point of law and it is the duty of the Court so to direct the jury. The substance of the testimony given by the pursuer himself in its most favourable aspect is briefly this: that on arriving at the railway line in question he was about 15 to 20 yards west of the washery; that he looked up and down the line to see if it was clear and did not see or hear anything approaching; that he walked on the line for 15 or 20 yards at an angle and had just reached the centre of the line when he was struck from behind; that there was no shunter there that morning; that he never saw a shunter standing at a signal fixed on the west end of the washery; and that he heard no sound or warning signal. It was maintained by the reclaimer that that testimony by itself was in law sufficient to establish a prima facie proof of one or other of the faults imputed to the driver and shunter, sufficient to impose on the defenders the duty of explanation and of proving that the accident happened without their negligence. In my opinion, that contention must be rejected. It was further maintained that, if corroboration of the pursuer's testimony is required, there exist facts and circumstances competent and sufficient to furnish such corroboration in respect of admissions in the defenders' answers on record. Those admissions are, it was argued, to be found in explanations made by the defenders, (first) in answer 3, to the effect that the front wagon of the train had been halted approximately 100 yards west of the washery building, and that the shunter went ahead to the south-east corner of the washery building and, having seen that there was nobody on the line between him and the train, waved the driver to come on; and (second) in answer 4, to the effect that it was not reasonably practicable for a man to accompany the front wagon of the train while it was passing between the washery and the cone tower, because the train owing to an incline had to be moved eastward at more than a walking pace, and that the shunter, after waving to the driver to come on, immediately walked eastwards and preceded the front wagon to some points further to the east. The reclaimer sought to deduce from those statements, divorced from their context, an implied admission by the defenders (corroborative of the pursuer's testimony) that the shunter had neither accompanied nor preceded the front wagon, and that in that situation the onus was upon them to prove (in terms of Regulation 161) that they took other efficient means to obviate risk to persons employed, at a place admittedly used by employees on their way to the silt pond. In my opinion, that argument cannot reasonably be accepted, and for these reasons—(a) the specific averments of fault set out on record by the pursuer are met by a general denial; (b) the particular statements founded on cannot be considered in isolation but must be conjoined with the whole explanations and qualifications embodied in the answers, and, so regarded, they are not admissions in the terms sought to be suggested and cannot competently or reasonably be assumed to be such by implication; (c) the written pleadings of parties are, in jury practice, not before the jury, and a presiding Judge would not be warranted in directing a jury in the present case that the defenders' answers contained implied admissions of facts corroborative of the pursuer's oral testimony. One further circumstance was sought in argument to be founded on by way of corroboration, *viz.*, that it is matter of reasonable implication from the evidence adduced for the pursuer that neither the driver nor the shunter was aware at the time that the train knocked down the pursuer and his fellow-worker; and that, if that be so, it affords prima facie evidence of negligence on their part. Having carefully scrutinised the evidence, I am of opinion that it does not reasonably support any such inference, and that the contrary suggestion is no more than conjecture.

On a survey of the situation in the light of the very full arguments addressed to us—and with time for deliberate consideration which the presiding Judge could not have at the trial have come to the conclusion, without hesitation but with some regret, that the reclaimer's challenge of the presiding Judge's direction cannot be sustained. It has been unfortunate that the pursuer himself was the only witness adduced on the topic of alleged fault in the attempt to prove his case, with the result that his claim was not supported by evidence which was in law sufficient to be considered by the jury.

I may add that, although we heard argument on the question where the onus lies in respect of the words in Regulation 161 'where safe and reasonably practicable,' I do not find it necessary to express any opinion on that question, which does not, in view of the conclusion to which I have come, arise for decision. I am for refusing the motion for a new trial, and it follows that the note of exceptions taken by the pursuer at the trial should also be refused."

LORD SORN: "In considering whether the trial Judge was right in deciding that there was insufficient evidence to go to the jury, it will be convenient to refer separately to the pursuer's case at common law and his case upon breach of statutory duty and to begin with the statutory case.

Once a person has established that his employers were in breach of a statutory Regulation he is in a strong position, but it is for him to prove the breach. It was argued by the defenders that under Regulation 161 the onus lay on the pursuer to prove not only that the specific precautions were omitted but also that it was 'safe and reasonably practicable' for the defenders to have taken them. On the other hand, it was argued for the pursuer that it was enough for him to prove omission of the precautions, the onus being on the defenders to prove that the taking of the precautions was not safe and reasonably practicable. In my opinion, it is not necessary to decide this point and I will assume (without by any means deciding) that the pursuer is right and that all he had to prove was omission of the specified precautions. The pursuer himself gave evidence to the effect that he saw no one with, or near, the leading wagon. This, of course, does not exclude the possibility that someone had preceded the wagons, but the word 'precede' in the Regulation is clearly used in a relative sense and the pursuer's evidence was perfectly good evidence to go before a jury on the question of breach. But was there any corroborative evidence to go to the jury? Breach of the Regulation was a major fact for the pursuer to prove, and our inflexible rule is that such facts cannot be proved by the evidence of one witness alone. Counsel for the pursuer could not suggest that the oral evidence of any other witness provided corroboration but argued that corroboration could be found in the defenders' averments in answer in the closed record—an argument which, it may be noted, was not advanced to the trial Judge when the motion for withdrawal was being debated. There is a passage in the defenders' answer 3 and another passage in answer 4 which, when read together, amount to an averment that the shunter had gone some distance ahead of the train and that, at the time of the accident, he was well to the east of the washery building. If this were the equivalent of evidence, it would, I consider, provide the necessary corroboration of the pursuer. But, in my opinion, the counter averments made by a defender in his defences cannot be used in this way. They are not evidence and they are not admissions. Admissions on record stand in quite a different position and are, no doubt, equivalent to proof; but averments have no factual significance unless and until they are proved. It would introduce the greatest confusion into our practice should we countenance the view that a pursuer, in order to supply deficiencies in his evidence, could select passages from his opponent's averments, construe them as a representation of certain facts, and then treat the result as if it was a judicial admission. In the present case it might have happened that the defenders' pleadings had been so drafted as to contain an admission of the very thing the pursuer had to prove, *i.e.*, that there was no one in the vicinity of the front wagon; but they were not so drafted and the proper course for the pursuer to have taken, seeing from the defenders' averments what the shunter's evidence was likely to be, and not being able to look elsewhere for corroboration, was to have cited the shunter as a witness.

Counsel for the pursuer submitted a further argument to the effect that corroboration of the pursuer might be found in inferences to be drawn from circumstances connected with the accident. It might be inferred that the train had not stopped until the rear part of it had passed the place where the men were knocked down; and it might also be inferred from the evidence of the witness Hunter that the shunter and driver were not at the scene of the accident when he arrived there. From these inferences, it was argued, the further inference might be drawn that the shunter and driver were not aware of the accident, leading to the ultimate inference that the shunter had not been near the leading wagon. I have considered this argument carefully, and not without sympathy, but I am afraid it amounts to mere speculation.

Having read the pleadings (which, it may be noted, do not go before the jury) one may have a shrewd idea that the shunter was not anywhere near the front wagon, but we cannot let that colour our minds to the effect of saying that the jury might legitimately have derived corroboration from the surrounding circumstances when, in fact, they would have been indulging in mere speculation had they done so. I accordingly conclude that the pursuer's evidence of a breach of Regulation 161 stood uncorroborated.

The pursuer also refers to Regulation 167 in his pleadings. The reference, rather curiously, occurs in the common law condescendence and it is doubtful whether it should be interpreted as an attempt to plead a breach of this Regulation, or merely as a reference to the Regulation in order to show that sound signals are thought to be proper under certain conditions. The point is not material, because, taking it as an averment of breach of the Regulation, the evidence of a breach, once again, rests upon the uncorroborated evidence of the pursuer.

As regards the common law case it seems clear that there was no evidence to go to the jury. The case on record, following the usual pattern, enumerates the duties alleged to be incumbent upon the shunter and the driver and states that they failed to carry out these duties. No evidence was led, however, to substantiate the existence of these duties and to show that they were duties which proper and usual practice imposed. The duties of shunters and pug-engine drivers cannot be treated as something that is common or judicial knowledge, and so the omission is a fatal one. I have not overlooked the evidence of one witness who said that, when he was a shunter, he used to ride on the buffer of the leading wagon. His evidence, however, is not in point, because he does not say that this was either a usual or proper practice and, indeed, he admitted that, in doing what he did, he not infrequently contravened the Regulations. In any event, even if it were to be assumed that the pursuer had established the existence of these duties, the evidence of failure to carry them out depends upon the uncorroborated evidence of the pursuer. I am, therefore, of the opinion that there was no legal evidence to go to the jury and that the trial Judge was right in withdrawing the case."

Lords Carmont and Strachan concurred.

NOTES

As this case makes clear, averments of fact made on Record by a party to a civil case have no evidential value until evidence is led in their support. An alternative view can be found in the opinion of Lord Sorn in *Dobson v. Colvilles Ltd*, 1958 S.L.T. (Notes) 30 (reported at 1959 S.C. 328) on which Sheriff Nigel Thomson based his decision in *Lord Advocate v. Gillespie*, 1969 S.L.T. (Sh. Ct.) 10. On this view "cases occur in which it is right to treat an averment in answer as equivalent to an admission. Whether this should be done must depend upon the particular case and the particular pleadings". However, the views expressed by Lord Sorn were *obiter*. It is submitted that Sheriff Thomson's view cannot stand with the decision of the First Division in *Lee* and with the following dictum of Lord Justice Clerk Thomson in *Wilson v. Clyde Rigging and Boiler Scaling Co. Ltd*, 1959 S.L.T. 59:

"There may be exceptional cases where one party in view of the way in which his opponent has coloured something in his pleadings may be entitled to a more benign interpretation of the evidence which he has led, but averment as such is not evidence and cannot be used as a substitute for evidence, or to eke out an otherwise defective proof."

Admissions made on record are generally conclusive against the party making them. Admissions which have been properly deleted from the record, however, cannot be founded upon—*Lennox v. N.C.B.*, 1955 S.C. 438. Mere averments, as Lord Sorn points out, require proof before any weight can be placed upon them, but if an averment is not specifically denied by a party, he may be taken to have admitted the point—see, generally, Black, *An Introduction to Written Pleading* (1982). In *Binnie v. Rederij Theodoro B.V.*, 1993 S.C. 71, it was held that the answer "believed to be true" in answer to an averment may be taken as an admission and no evidence need be led on that point. See also the procedure contained in the Sheriff Court Ordinary Cause Rules 1993, Rule 29.14, and its equivalent in the Rules of Court of Session whereby a party may serve notice on another party, calling on the latter to admit specified facts. Failure to respond to such a call has the effect that the latter party is deemed to admit the fact concerned.

Admissions may be contained in a minute of admissions prepared by the parties and such admissions are, once again, usually conclusive. In *London and Edinburgh Shipping Co. v. The Admiralty*, 1920 S.C. 309, Lord Dundas said:

> "In this case the parties elected to renounce probation upon an agreed joint minute of admissions in fact. This course has its advantages but also its risks. The adjustment of such a minute is, in my judgment, one of the most difficult and delicate tasks which fall to the lot of counsel. An unguarded admission, or an inadvertent omission, may be fatal. But, once adjusted, the minute forms the evidence in the case; it is the proof at large, in synthesis, and its statement of admitted facts must be accepted as final."

It seems, however, that in consistorial causes, any minute agreed by the parties may be re-opened by the court and evidence led as to the matters contained in it—*Robson v. Robson*, 1973 S.L.T. (Notes) 4. This is principally because of the overriding duty of the court to oversee the welfare of the child. Again, it seems that admissions made orally in court may not bind the party making the admission—see *Whyte v. Whyte* (1895) 23 R. 320.

9. Strathern v. Sloan
1937 J.C. 76

Thomas Graham and George Sloan were charged in the Sheriff Court at Glasgow on a complaint that while acting in concert, they stole a motor car. When the diet was called, Graham, against whom three other charges were libelled in the complaint, pleaded not guilty. *Sloan* tendered a plea of guilty. Before the latter plea was recorded, the procurator fiscal intimated that he declined to accept it, and he moved the Court to record a plea of not guilty, and to assign a diet for trial. After hearing argument upon the point, the Sheriff-substitute (Macdiarmid), on November 4, 1936, refused the motion of the procurator fiscal as incompetent, directed the plea of guilty to be recorded, and continued the cause for sentence at a later date. Thereafter the procurator fiscal presented a bill of advocation to the High Court, in which he craved the Court "to recall the interlocutor of judgment complained of; to remit to the Sheriff of the County of Lanark or his substitutes at Glasgow to proceed with the said complaint according to law; and to find the complainer entitled to expenses; or to do further or otherwise in the premises as to your Lordships shall seem proper."

LORD JUSTICE-CLERK (AITCHISON): "This is a bill of advocation brought by the Procurator-fiscal of Lanarkshire at Glasgow against a respondent, who is not represented. The question raised by the bill is whether the Procurator-fiscal was entitled to refuse to accept a plea of guilty tendered by the respondent in proceedings on summary complaint, and to require the Sheriff-substitute before whom the cause depended to assign a diet for trial. The complaint charged the respondent that he did, while acting in concert with another, steal a motor car. The other person named in the complaint was also charged in the complaint with three offences, all contrary to the Road Traffic Act, 1930. None of these offences concerns the respondent. On the diet being called on November 3, 1936, the respondent tendered a plea of guilty, whereupon the Procurator-fiscal intimated to the Sheriff-substitute, before the plea of guilty had been recorded, that he declined to accept the plea, and moved the Court to record a plea of not guilty and to assign a diet for trial. On the following day, after argument had been submitted by the Procurator-fiscal and by an agent on behalf of the respondent, the Sheriff-substitute refused the Procurator-fiscal's motion as being incompetent, directed the plea of guilty to be recorded, and continued the cause for sentence to be pronounced on a later date. Against the judgment of the Sheriff-substitute the Procurator-fiscal now appeals by bill of advocation.

It is well settled that, in criminal causes triable under solemn procedure, the Crown is not bound to accept a plea of guilty, but may insist upon the indictment proceeding to trial. This was affirmed in the case of *H.M. Advocate v. Peter and Smith* [2 Swinton 492]. In that case two persons were indicted in the High Court upon charges of robbery and the unlawful discharging of loaded firearms. One of the two tendered a plea of guilty, which was put on record. The Solicitor-General then claimed the right to lead evidence against both panels, and to read to the jury as evidence *in causa* the declaration of Smith, the panel who had pleaded guilty. The Court decided that this was within the right of the Crown. The leading opinion was given by Lord Medwyn, who said (at p.493): 'The panel has undoubtedly the privilege of making a judicial confession; but it is equally beyond doubt, that the public prosecutor is not bound to accept it unless he pleases, and may notwithstanding go into evidence. Baron Hume (ii, p.282) states the law both previous and subsequent to the statute 9 Geo. IV, cap. 29—prior to that statute the prosecutor had to proceed before a jury notwithstanding the confession of the prisoner—and I do not think that that Act militates in the least degree against the public prosecutor. The provision which it contains is not, that it shall not be competent, but merely that it shall no longer be necessary to go before a jury, in order to prove the case against a panel who has pleaded guilty. The prosecutor may still give the prisoner the chance of a trial. Alison (ii, p.368) says: "it need hardly be observed, that it is competent for a panel to plead guilty at any stage of his trial," but he shows that the Court may decline to accept the plea; and, in illustration, quotes the case of Stewart and Others [unreported], Glasgow, September 1826, where, a confession by one of the prisoners having been tendered when the jury were about to be enclosed, "the Lord Justice-Clerk declined to receive the confession at so late a stage, and the jury were charged with the case, and returned a verdict as to him of not proven." In the present case I am clearly of opinion that the public prosecutor has an alternative course, and may either accept the plea, or claim a verdict upon the other evidence which he is prepared to lead.' Lord Cockburn, who concurred, pointed out that, by the former law, a plea of guilty did not avoid a jury; there still required to be a verdict, and the plea of guilty was used merely as evidence; and, further, that the right of the public prosecutor to decline a plea still remained, and was applicable where there was one panel only just as much as where there were two or more panels; and he added that there were many cases where the panel had actually been acquitted after tendering his confession. Lord Meadowbank, who also concurred, spoke of 'the frequent practice of proceeding with the trial, notwithstanding a plea of guilty.' In *Pattison v. Stevenson* [5F. (J) 43] Lord Moncreiff similarly expressed the rule in these words: 'According to our law and practice, the prosecutor is not bound to accept a plea of guilty to the whole charge, and is entitled, notwithstanding the plea, to proceed to trial.' This opinion was concurred in by the Lord Justice-Clerk (Macdonald) and Lord Trayner.

It has never been doubted that the rule of *Peter's* case applies equally to criminal causes triable upon indictment in the Sheriff Court. The question now to be decided for the first time is whether the rule applies to causes that are triable upon summary complaint. The case in which the question was most nearly raised is *Kirkwood v. Coalburn District Co-operative Society* [1930 J.C. 38] which was a summary prosecution at the instance of H. M. Inspector of Factories in which alternative charges were libelled in the complaint. The panel tendered a plea of guilty to the minor of the alternative charges. The prosecutor objected to the plea being recorded, but the Sheriff recorded it. It was held on appeal that the prosecutor was entitled to proceed to trial with a view to proving the major charge, upon the ground that a prosecutor is never bound to accept a plea to the minor of two alternative charges so as to be compelled to give up the major alternative. In the course of his judgment the Lord Justice-General (Clyde) stated the wider proposition in these terms (at p.41): 'I do not think a prosecutor is ever bound to accept a plea, whether the charge be alternative or not, but is always entitled to insist on leading evidence before the jury and obtaining a verdict if he can—Macdonald on Criminal Law, (4th ed.), p.484, and authorities there collected.' I respectfully agree with this wider proposition, and, as the case Lord Clyde was dealing with arose upon a summary complaint, the observation must be taken as applying to summary complaints in the same way as to charges upon indictment.

This right of the public prosecutor may at first sight appear to be arbitrary, but consideration will point to many good grounds why the right should exist. In serious crime evidence may be necessary to bring out the full enormity of the crime, or perhaps to show mitigating circumstances; or again there may be concern as to whether the proper crime has been libelled, as, for example, where murder is charged, but where there is doubt whether the crime of the panel amounts to more than culpable homicide. Thus, the practice of our Courts in Scotland, and in England also, although not invariably in England, has been for the public prosecutor to refuse to accept a plea of guilty to a murder charge. Again, there may be a question, which can only be fully explored in evidence, as to the mental state of the panel. Or two or more persons may be charged, and the prosecutor may be unable, without inquiry, to assign the proper degree of guilt to each of the panels. There may be other reasons deemed sufficient by the public prosecutor for declining a plea of guilty. It is not necessary that he should assign any reason, the right being one which the law commits to his own judgment and discretion, and which he can exercise whether the proceedings are summary or on indictment. That being the general law, I desire to add one or two qualifications. (1) The right to refuse a plea of guilty is a right which is vested in the Lord Advocate, or his Deputes, or the Procurator-fiscal, who derives his authority from the Lord Advocate. How far the right extends to other prosecutors, public or private, is a more difficult question, and it may be difficult to differentiate, at any rate as between public prosecutors. (2) Where a plea of guilty is tendered by the panel, and is not accepted by the prosecutor, the formal entry on the record should not be an entry of not guilty, which is contrary to the fact, but should be to the effect that the panel has tendered a plea of guilty, and that the prosecutor has intimated that he declines to accept the plea. The practice of entering a plea of not guilty, contrary to an express and unqualified plea of guilty, is, in my opinion, wrong and should not be continued. In the case of summary complaints the entry of the plea on the record is expressly directed by section 41 of the Summary Jurisdiction Act, 1908. (3) Wherever a plea of guilty is tendered and not accepted by the prosecutor, the plea of guilty must under no circumstances be used against the panel, and, where the trial is on indictment, must not be disclosed to the jury. In all cases, therefore, under solemn procedure, where a plea of guilty is declined at the first diet, the panel should not be called upon to plead at the second diet, unless in the interval the prosecutor has made up his mind to accept the plea if again tendered. If the panel, notwithstanding his plea of guilty, chooses to enter the witness-box, he must have entire freedom to give his evidence, contrary to his plea of guilty which the prosecutor has declined to accept. This does not involve any encouragement of false testimony, as it is not unfamiliar that a panel may offer a plea of guilty, not because he is guilty of the offence charged, but because a public trial might disclose facts more hurtful to his own reputation, or the reputation of others, than the recording of a plea on his own confession. (4) If the prosecutor elects to proceed to trial, and in the course of the trial decides to accept a plea of guilty, he cannot do so unless the panel of new pleads guilty to the offence charged. Whether the panel is willing to do so can always be ascertained by communication with his counsel or agent, and until the panel's mind is known the question should not be put to him in open Court. There may be cases in which, the evidence having disclosed facts prejudicial to the panel, the panel may desire that the trial should proceed notwithstanding his recorded plea, either on the chance of his obtaining an acquittal, or for the purpose of bringing out circumstances that may go to alleviate the offence, if proved against him.

It is unnecessary to add that the right of the public prosecutor to decline a plea of guilty is a right which should be sparingly exercised, and, in my judgment, it should not be exercised where it may result in prejudice to another panel charged under the same indictment or complaint. The governing consideration in every case should be the public interest.

In the present case the learned Procurator-fiscal decided that the plea of guilty tendered by the respondent should not be accepted. The Sheriff-substitute, accordingly, should have assigned a diet for trial. The bill of advocation will, therefore, be passed. It will be enough if we recall the interlocutor of the Sheriff-substitute dated November 4, 1936, and the further interlocutor dated December 31, 1936, and remit to the Sheriff of the County of Lanark, or his Substitutes, at Glasgow, to proceed with the complaint according to law.

As the appeal has raised a question of general importance which it was necessary to have authoritatively ruled, and as the respondent has not in any way added to the expense by making appearance, this is a case in which no award of expenses should be made. I move your Lordships to pass the bill, and to remit to proceed as accords."

NOTES

A plea of guilty is the equivalent of an admission on record in civil cases and is generally conclusive against the accused. It may be possible to withdraw a plea of guilty—for example, if the accused pleaded guilty while unrepresented (compare *Tudhope v. Cullen*, 1982 S.C.C.R. 276) or where the court before which the plea is considerd is improperly constituted (see *Rimmer petitioner*, 2002 S.C.C.R. 1)—but is impossible once sentence has been recorded (*MacNeill v. McGregor*, 1975 J.C. 55). In this case, it was suggested that a person who wishes to withdraw a guilty plea might be able to petition the *nobile officium* of the High Court in the absence of a remedy under normal procedure). Compare also *Williamson v. H.M.A.*, 1978 S.L.T. 38 in which it was argued that a plea of self-defence which was later withdrawn was equivalent to a plea of guilty which the Crown had declined to accept. The effect of this was said to be that the accused should not have been cross-examined about his earlier plea and the reasons for its withdrawal. The court rejected this argument, saying—

"In a *Strathern v. Sloan* type of case one can see the force of the reasoning underlying the dictum of Lord Justice-Clerk Aitchison, namely, that it would be contrary to the concept of fairness that a prosecutor should reject an accused's plea of guilty and then cross-examine him on the basis that he had admitted his guilt by that plea. A special defence of self-defence, as previously noted, is merely notice to the Crown that it is proposed to take this line of defence. It is not an admission of guilt. On the contrary, a plea of not guilty is entered and the notice of the special defence is without prejudice to that plea and subject to the qualification contained in the notice. It is not in itself a plea. It is true that it indicates that the accused assaulted the complainer, albeit justifiably, and if it is withdrawn by the accused, as it was here, the plea of not guilty remains unqualified. This distinguishes the notice of such a special defence which is withdrawn by the accused from a plea of guilty which is rejected by the prosecutor. The unfairness which is attached to the latter situation does not attach to the former."

10. Walsh v. H.M.A.
1961 J.C. 51

A person charged on indictment with three charges of stealing motor cars originally pleaded not guilty to all charges, but at the trial diet pleaded guilty to the third charge, and otherwise adhered to his original pleas. A jury was empanelled to try the first and second charges, and thereupon the Sheriff Clerk read out to the jury all three charges in the indictment. Thereafter, in charging the jury, the presiding Sheriff directed them to bring in a verdict of guilty on the third charge, and, with reference to the first and second charges, he directed them that the doctrine of *Moorov v. H.M.A.*, 1930 J.C. 68, applied and, in effect, that they were entitled to take into account, along with the evidence, the third charge and the fact that the panel had pleaded guilty to it. The panel was convicted on all three charges.

LORD JUSTICE-CLERK (THOMSON): "This appeal brings out very clearly the difficulties into which a Court can get if it fails to adhere strictly to the well-tried rules of procedure.

The appellant was charged with three separate charges of theft of motor vehicles, in March 1960, June 1960 and July 1960. Originally he pleaded not guilty, but, at the second diet, when the case was called, he pleaded guilty to the third of these charges; the Procurator-fiscal accepted the plea, and the plea was signed and recorded in the ordinary way. What ought to have happened then was that, as far as the subsequent trial was concerned, the third charge should never have reappeared in the case until the Judge came to pronounce sentence. What did happen was that, immediately after the plea to the third charge had been recorded, a jury was empanelled, and the Sheriff Clerk proceeded to read to the jury all three charges. That was an error in procedure; only the two charges on which the trial was to proceed should have been read, as these were the only matters on which the jury could adjudicate. This initial error led to further trouble, and, in the end of the day, the Sheriff directed the jury as a matter of law to bring in a verdict of guilty on the third charge. No doubt the Sheriff felt he had to do something like this to try to rescue the situation. It was, of course, quite wrong. There had been a plea of guilty before the jury had been empanelled, and the jury had nothing to do with the third charge at all. Further trouble arose because the Sheriff made certain references to the third charge in the course of his charge to the jury. Some of these were innocuous enough, but one of them, as I shall point out in a moment, was anything but innocuous. In that state of circumstances, the appellant, having been found guilty of all three charges, the first two by the verdict on the facts, and the third by direction of the Judge, now appeals. The essence of the appeal is that the jury's mind must have been affected by the circumstances that they had this plea of guilty on the third charge before them in the course of their consideration of the first two charges. The attack was developed along two lines. The first was that to allow the plea of guilty on the third charge to be before the jury was really equivalent to laying a previous conviction before it. With regard to that matter it is not necessary for me to say anything further because as the case developed the point became academic, and I expressly reserve my opinion as to whether that is a sound argument or not. The other point, and the point on which the fate of the appeal has depended, was that the Sheriff misdirected the jury by referring to the third charge in a way which must have affected their minds to the appellant's prejudice. This arose out of what he said in purporting to apply the *Moorov* doctrine. It is agreed that this is not a case where the *Moorov* doctrine has application, and while it might not have mattered that he had brought in the *Moorov* doctrine, when he should not, had there been sufficient evidence otherwise, as to which I say nothing, the critical thing is that, after explaining about the *Moorov* doctrine to the jury, he said this: 'You have three alleged crimes, one of which has been admitted and you are quite entitled to use that doctrine in this particular case.' That seems to me to be clearly a misdirection because *Moorov* or no *Moorov* it was an invitation to the jury to found on something which was not properly before the jury at all. The Solicitor-General very properly agreed with that view, and, for reasons which he briefly developed, he conceded that he would not feel justified in appealing to the proviso in the particular circumstances of this particular case. He felt that, in view of the evidence, he could not say that the jury might not have been influenced by the fact that it had been brought to their notice that the appellant had pleaded guilty to the third charge, and he was affected also by the fact that on the second charge the verdict was a majority verdict only.

The Solicitor-General felt impelled to this view because of what was said by the Lord Justice-Clerk in *Tobin v. H.M.A.* [1934] J.C. 60. There, a direction was held to be a bad direction, and the question was whether or not the proviso ought to be applied. What the Lord Justice-Clerk said (at p.63) was this: 'In any case in which it appears that there has been either misdirection or non-direction amounting to misdirection, the greatest care must be taken in applying the proviso. It should only be applied if it can be affirmed that, with the proper direction, the jury would inevitably have reached the same conclusion.' Then his Lordship went on to say: 'In the present case I think the probabilities are very strong that, if the jury had been directed that the case of each accused must be considered separately, the same verdict would have been returned. On the other hand, I do not think that this can be affirmed with certainty, as it was a verdict by a majority only.' It is in that situation that the Solicitor-General felt that he could not on the particular facts of this particular case invite us to say that, had they been properly directed, the jury would inevitably have reached the same conclusion. In my view, the Solicitor-General took a very proper view in so approaching the case.

The result is that the appeal must succeed so far as the first two charges are concerned, but that leaves for our consideration the question of sentence on the third charge to which the appellant pleaded guilty in circumstances which are unexceptionable. The Sheriff-substitute when he was dealing with sentence proceeded immediately to sentence, and, in doing so, ignored the procedure laid down in section 18(2) of the Criminal Justice (Scotland) Act, 1949. He failed to observe that, in view of the appellant's age, it was necessary to obtain and consider information as to his circumstances before reaching a conclusion as to whether or not imprisonment was appropriate. Our proper course now is to obtain a probation report, and, when we have obtained it, we shall be in a position to proceed to impose the appropriate sentence."
Lords Macintosh and Strachan concurred.

NOTES

Compare *McColl v. Skeen*, 1980 S.L.T. (Notes) 53.

11. Criminal Procedure (Scotland) Act 1995

"256.—(1) In any trial it shall not be necessary for the accused or for the prosecutor—

    (a) to prove any fact which is admitted by the other; or

    (b) to prove any document, the terms and application of which are not in dispute between them,

        and, without prejudice to paragraph 1 of Schedule 8 to this Act, copies of any documents may, by agreement of the parties, be accepted as equivalent to the originals.

(2) For the purposes of subsection (1) above, any admission or agreement shall be made by lodging with the clerk of court a minute in that behalf signed—

    (a) in the case of an admission, by the party making the admission or, if that party is the accused and he is legally represented, by his counsel or solicitor; and

    (b) in the case of an agreement, by the prosecutor and the accused or, if he is legally represented, his counsel or solicitor.

(3) Where a minute has been signed and lodged as aforesaid, any facts and documents admitted or agreed thereby shall be deemed to have been duly proved.

257.—(1) Subject to subsection (2) below, the prosecutor and the accused (or each of the accused if more than one) shall each identify any facts which are facts—

    (a) which he would, apart from this section, be seeking to prove;

    (b) which he considers unlikely to be disputed by the other party (or by any of the other parties); and

    (c) in proof of which he does not wish to lead oral evidence,

        and shall, without prejudice to section 258 of this Act, take all reasonable steps to secure the agreement of the other party (or each of the other parties) to them; and the other party (or each of the other parties) shall take all reasonable steps to reach such agreement.

(2) Subsection (1) above shall not apply in relation to proceedings as respects which the accused (or any of the accused if more than one) is not legally represented.

    (3) The duty under subsection (1) above applies—

    (a) in relation to proceedings on indictment, from the date of service of the indictment until the swearing of the jury or, where intimation is given under section 76 of this Act, the date of that intimation; and

    (b) in relation to summary proceedings, from the date on which the accused pleads not guilty until the swearing of the first witness or, where the accused tenders a plea of guilty at any time before the first witness is sworn, the date when he does so."

NOTES

    Note that the duty imposed by section 257 exists only where the accused is represented. The onus is accordingly very much on his or her advisers to reach agreement with the Crown on matters considered to be uncontentious. No sanctions are provided in the Act for any failure to comply with the duty, although clearly it strengthens the hand of the Court in enquiring at an early stage in proceedings what steps have been taken by the parties to reach agreement. The purpose of the section is obviously to expedite proceedings by disposing of straightforward matters by agreement if possible.

"258.—(1) This section applies where, in any criminal proceedings, a party (in this section referred to as 'the first party') considers that facts which that party would otherwise be seeking to prove are unlikely to be disputed by the other parties to the proceedings.

    (2) Where this section applies, the first party may prepare and sign a statement—

    (a) specifying the facts concerned; or

    (b) referring to such facts as set out in a document annexed to the statement,
        and shall, not less than 14 days before the trial diet, serve a copy of the statement and
        any such document on every other party.

(3) Unless any other party serves on the first party, not more than seven days after the date of service of the copy on him under subsection (2) above or by such later time as the court may in special circumstances allow, a notice that he challenges any fact specified or referred to in the statement, the facts so specified or referred to shall be deemed to have been conclusively proved.

(4) Where a notice is served under subsection (3) above, the facts specified or referred to in the statement shall be deemed to have been conclusively proved only in so far as unchallenged in the notice.

(5) Subsections (3) and (4) above shall not preclude a party from leading evidence of circumstances relevant to, or other evidence in explanation of, any fact specified or referred to in the statement.

(6) Notwithstanding subsections (3) and (4) above, the court—
    (a) may, on the application of any party, where it is satisfied that there are special circumstances; and
    (b) shall, on the joint application of all the parties, direct that the presumptions in those subsections shall not apply in relation to such fact specified or referred to in the statement as is specified in the direction.

(7) An application under subsection (6) above may be made at any time after the commencement of the trial and before the commencement of the prosecutor's address to the court on the evidence.

(8) Where the court makes a direction under subsection (6) above it shall, unless all the parties otherwise agree, adjourn the trial and may, without prejudice to section 268 of this Act, permit any party to lead evidence as to any such fact as is specified in the direction, notwithstanding that a witness or production concerned is not included in any list lodged by the parties and that the notice required by sections 67(5) and 78(4) of this Act has not been given.

(9) A copy of a statement or a notice required, under this section, to be served on any party shall be served in such manner as may be prescribed by Act of Adjournal; and a written execution purporting to be signed by the person who served such copy or notice together with, where appropriate, the relevant post office receipt shall be sufficient evidence of such service."

NOTES

This section provides the procedural mechanism whereby the duty imposed in section 257 can be discharged.

    If the evidential provisions of the 1995 Act have a theme, it is the aspiration that agreement should be reached wherever possible on uncontroversial matters. Several of the provisions of the Act contain a procedure whereby uncontentious or technical matters will be taken to be proved unless objected to. For example, section 277 provides *inter alia* that:

    "(1) . . . for the purposes of any criminal proceedings, a document certified by the person who made it as an accurate transcript made for the prosecutor of the contents of a tape (identified by means of a label) purporting to be a recording of an interview between—
    (a) a police officer and an accused person; or
    (b) a person commissioned, appointed or authorised under section 6(3) of the Customs and Excise Management Act 1979 and an accused person,
shall be received in evidence and be sufficient evidence of the making of the transcript and of its accuracy.
    (2) Subsection (1) above shall not apply to a transcript—
    (a) unless a copy of it has been served on the accused not less than 14 days before his trial; or
    (b) if the accused, not less than six days before his trial, or by such later time before his trial as the court may in special circumstances allow, has served notice on the prosecutor that the accused challenges the making of the transcript or its accuracy."

Again, section 282 contains provisions to the effect that in criminal proceedings,

"(1) . . . evidence given by an authorised forensic scientist, either orally or in a report purporting to be signed by him, that a substance which satisfies either of the conditions specified in subsection (2) below is—

    (a) a particular controlled drug or medicinal product; or

    (b) a particular product which is listed in the British Pharmacopoeia as containing a particular controlled drug or medicinal product, shall, subject to subsection (3) below, be sufficient evidence of that fact notwithstanding that no analysis of the substance has been carried out.

(2) Those conditions are—

    (a) that the substance is in a sealed container bearing a label identifying the contents of the container; or

    (b) that the substance has a characteristic appearance having regard to its size, shape, colour and manufacturer's mark.

(3) A party proposing to rely on subsection (1) above ('the first party') shall, not less than 14 days before the trial diet, serve on the other party ('the second party')—

    (a) a notice to that effect; and

    (b) where the evidence is contained in a report, a copy of the report,

and if the second party serves on the first party, not more than seven days after the date of service of the notice on him, a notice that he does not accept the evidence as to the identity of the substance, subsection (1) above shall not apply in relation to that evidence."

The procedure of notice and counter-notice which the 1995 Act introduces in many of the evidential sections is clearly intended to reduce the need to lead evidence in relation to technical matters, saving the time of the court and that of the various technicians and agencies involved. It places the onus on an accused person to challenge the accuracy of such evidence. However, once the evidence is challenged, the onus is not placed on the accused to disprove the matters raised by the evidence; the Crown simply have to prove those matters by leading evidence about them in the conventional way.

Chapter 12

CONFIDENTIALITY, PRIVILEGE AND THE RECOVERY OF EVIDENCE

Once a legal action has been initiated (and occasionally before), a party is entitled to seek recovery of documents, papers, records of conversations and other communications from the other party, in order to assist in the preparation of her case. The party seeking to recover documents prepares a list of those documents—a "specification of documents"—and then enrols a motion asking the court to approve the specification and to grant a commission and diligence for the recovery of the documents listed. Recovery of the documents specified is overseen by a "commissioner"—usually an advocate or solicitor appointed by the court. The holder of the documents must usually produce the documents listed in the specification, but may object to their production on the ground that they are confidential or privileged. Confidentiality attaches to evidence, not to witnesses—see *H.M.A. v. Wilson*, High Court of Justiciary (Lord Reed), unreported, June 15, 2001, noted below. The categories of privileged communication are limited—although see Lord Sutherland's opinion in *W.P. v. Tayside Regional Council*, 1989 S.C.L.R. 165.

(A) LEGAL ADVISERS

1. McCowan v. Wright
(1852) 15 D. 229

This was an action of reduction by Robert McCowan, the trustee on the sequestrated estate of James Howie, of certain bonds and other deeds which had been granted by Howie to his brother-in-law John Wright. The action was founded on the Act of 1621, c.18, and also on fraud at common law. The Court granted a diligence for recovery of "all letters, and copies or drafts of letters, which passed between the defender and his agents about the time of, and in reference to the obtaining and preparation of the deeds and others under reduction, and in reference to the affairs of the bankrupt at and prior to the execution of the said deeds and others." A solicitor, Andrew Howden, W.S., having been examined as a haver, deponed that he had letters in his possession which had passed between the defender and his agents, Messrs Montgomerie and Fleming, but declined to produce them, on the ground of confidentiality.

The commissioner (under the diligence), having considered the objection and read the letters in question, sustained the objection to the haver producing the same, on the ground of confidentiality. The pursuer appealed this judgment to the Court.

LORD WOOD: "The rule by which the communications between clients and their legal advisers are protected from discovery, is one of great value and importance, and, within its legitimate limits, ought to be strictly observed.

According to the law of Scotland, such communications are privileged although they may not relate to any suit depending or contemplated, or apprehended; and so it was substantially decided in the case of *Lady Bath's executors* in 1811. It therefore required no authority from the law of England to support that proposition. But there are exceptions of a different kind which may exclude the privilege from being pleaded. And I think the objection to the production of the correspondence in question cannot be supported on any sound principle, and is not within the policy on which the rule is founded.

Looking to the pursuer's averments upon the record, as they relate to the issues upon which the case is to be tried, to these issues themselves, whether it be the issue on the statute 1621, or that on common law, and to the nature of the correspondence as described in the commissioner's report, so far as it could be explained without any improper disclosure of its contents, and which shows that it took place between the defender abroad and his agents in this country at the time the deeds under reduction were executed, and with reference to these deeds and their preparation, which deeds are said to have been granted to the defender, a conjunct or confident person, by the bankrupt after insolvency, without true, just, and necessary cause, and in order to defraud his prior creditors, and are represented as mere false and fraudulent devices to withdraw the funds of the bankrupt from his just and lawful creditors—a fraud which I must consider a moral fraud, whether it is taken on the statute or at common law—and during which correspondence it appears, that in relation to the matters to which it refers, the defender's agents had communication with the bankrupt;—I am clearly of opinion that the correspondence is not protected, and that, in ordering production of it, we shall adhere to the law as established in this country in regard to confidential communications between agent and client, and save the rule untouched in every case to which it properly applies.

To attempt to assimilate the present case to what has been called, a fraud upon an entail, or others of a like kind, seems to me altogether extravagant.

The grounds on which the objection to production ought to be repelled, have been already so fully stated by your Lordship, that I have nothing to add.

I at the same time agree with your Lordship, that there may be parts of the letters which fall within those communications between agent and client, and that advice asked and given, which ought not to be disclosed;—and, as your Lordship wishes, I shall be glad to look at the papers, with a view to make any selection that may appear to be necessary."

NOTES

The rule protecting communications between agent and client is clearly an important one—people should be free to discuss their legal problems and to seek advice without fear that their conversations or correspondence with their advisers will be used against them in court. The rule is not wholly inviolable, however, as the preceding case shows. In the following case, a dispute arose over the extent to which the general principle of confidentiality could be breached.

2. Micosta S.A. v. Shetland Islands Council
1983 S.L.T. 483

In an action of damages against a local authority in respect of alleged abuse of statutory powers, the pursuers were granted commission and diligence in respect of documents in the defenders' hands relating to the cause. The defenders produced letters between themselves and their law agents in a sealed envelope and opposed a motion for the envelope to be opened up, claiming confidentiality. The pursuers contended that where, as in this case, the subject-matter of the action was an alleged illegal act on the part of the defenders, such communications were recoverable as directly relevant to the intention or state of mind of the defenders at the relevant time.

THE LORD PRESIDENT (EMSLIE): "This is an action of damages by the owners of a Greek-registered bulk oil carrier, M.V. 'Mihalis'. It is directed against Shetland Islands Council as Sullom Voe harbour authority. From the pleadings it appears that the vessel was under charter to an oil company to load petroleum products at Sullom Voe for carriage to the United States. She arrived off Yell Sound, Shetland, on or about February 3, 1980 and was likely to be able to berth in Sullom Voe on February 7. While the vessel was some 13 miles from the coast after February 3, it was alleged that she had caused oil pollution. It is averred that a sequel to this allegation was that on February 11, 1980, the defenders' harbour master, acting upon the defenders' instructions, intimated to representatives of the pursuers a threat that if the vessel entered the harbour a special direction would be served under section 39 of the Zetland County Council Act 1974 prohibiting her from mooring at the oil jetty and inter alia from loading. When the charterers learned of this threat the charterparty was terminated. The basis of the pursuers' claim appears to be that the defenders deliberately abused their statutory powers relating to the management of the harbour for an ulterior and quite improper motive, namely, in order to punish the pursuers for having allegedly caused oil pollution outwith the waters within the defenders' jurisdiction. According to senior counsel for the pursuers there will arise in the action which goes to proof before answer on January 18, 1983, two important questions: (1) were the defenders behind the abuse of power?; and (2) if the defenders were responsible for the alleged threat being intimated by their harbour master what was their true motive?

In the foregoing circumstances the pursuers were granted commission and diligence for the recovery of documents in terms of a specific action of documents no. 15 of process. The particular terms of call 1 of that specification, so far as it is relevant for our consideration, were these:

> 'All letters, telegrams, telexes, reports, memoranda, minutes, records and other written documents dated prior to February 14, 1980 held by the defenders or Captain Flett, Harbour Master, Sullom Voe Terminal, Shetland, or anyone on the said parties behalf, referring to or relating to the matters mentioned on record in order that excerpts may be taken therefrom at the sight of the commissioner of all entries showing or tending to show . . . (b) that the defenders considered and subsequently instructed the issue of a threat to serve a special direction upon the vessel "Mihalis", should it enter the Sullom Voe harbour area; and (c) the reasons for such instruction.'

In response to that call the defenders produced documents falling under it. Included among these documents are, we are told, within a sealed envelope, certain communications and memoranda passing between the defenders and their solicitors. For the documents within the sealed envelope the defenders claim confidentiality.

The first matter with which we have to deal is a motion by the pursuers to allow the sealed envelope to be opened up so that the contents may be examined by the commissioner. In support of the motion senior counsel for the pursuers accepted the general rule that communications passing between a party and his law agent are confidential. His submission was, however, that there is an exception to that rule where the subject-matter of an action is an alleged illegal act on the part of a defender and where the communications are directly relevant to the intention or state of mind of the defender at the relevant time. That the law recognises an exception to the general rule in these circumstances is, it was said, to be deduced from the following cases: *McCowan v. Wright* (1852) 15D. 229; *Morrison v. Somerville* (1860) 23D. 232; and *Millar v. Small* (1856) 19D. 142. In this case the pursuers aver an illegal act—an abuse of power—by the defenders and a critical question is as to the intention behind the threat allegedly made by the defenders' harbour master on their instructions. In these circumstances the claim of confidentiality by the defenders cannot be maintained to prevent scrutiny of the communications in the sealed envelope in order that excerpts may be taken therefrom of all entries showing or tending to show the matters specified in heads (b) or (c) of call 1.

We are not persuaded that there is any warrant in authority for the recognition of an exception to the general rule in the terms contended for by senior counsel for the pursuers. The cases relied upon are cases of fraudulent transactions or collusive settlements by a defender in the carrying out of which his law agent was directly involved in his client's interest. The transactions themselves were the subject matter of investigation in the actions and in these circumstances it is not surprising that correspondence between the party and his law agent relating to these transactions was denied the privilege conferred by the general rule. 'A party is entitled to have advice, and to communicate with his law adviser confidentially, and such communication is not to be laid open except in particular circumstances and questions. Of course fraud supersedes all rules'. So said the Lord President (McNeill) in *Munro v. Fraser* (1858) 21D. 103 at p.107. So far as we can discover from the authorities the only circumstances in which the general rule will be superseded are where fraud or some other illegal act is alleged against a party and where his law agent has been directly concerned in the carrying out of the very transaction which is the subject-matter of inquiry. In this case it is not suggested that the defenders' solicitors were involved at all in the intimation of the alleged threat by the harbour master and any confidential correspondence as to the defenders' views at the relevant time—

for they were quite entitled to seek advice confidentially—clearly falls under the general rule (see *Executors of Lady Bath v. Johnston* November 12, 1811, F.C.). There is no trace in authority of any relaxation of the general rule, where the law agent of the party accused of an illegal act has played no part in the act itself, to permit examination of correspondence between that party and his law agent in order to discover that party's state of mind or intention at the relevant time. To admit of an exception of the kind contended for by the pursuers in this case would open the door so widely as largely to render worthless the general rule which our law has always regarded as of the highest importance. For these reasons the pursuers' motion will be refused."

NOTES

In *Kelly v. Vannet*, 2000 S.L.T. 75, it was made clear that the privilege flies off whether the legal adviser is knowingly involved in the commission of crime, or is merely an innocent agent. There appears to be some doubt over the confidentiality of communications between a potential client and a solicitor who declines to act—*H.M.A. v. Davie* (1881) 4 Coup. 450. Nor is it clear whether confidentiality applies to a lay representative, such as an advisor in a Citizens Advice Bureau, or to a solicitor who is acting in a non-professional capacity. See generally Black, "A Question of Confidence" (1982) 27 J.L.S.S. 299 and 389.

Confidentiality certainly does not apply to every professional relationship. It does not apply, for example, to Marriage Guidance Counsellors (although see the Civil Evidence (Family Mediation) (Scotland) Act 1995, s.1), nor to doctors, bankers, accountants and other professional groups. See Stair Memorial Encyclopaedia, Vol. 10, para. 686. Journalists are not usually bound to disclose their sources of information, but under the Contempt of Court Act 1981, s.10 there is a wide exception to this principle where it can be established that disclosure is necessary in the interests of justice, national security or the prevention of disorder or crime. In the unreported case of *Daniels* (1960), it was held by Lord Patrick that a priest is not bound to disclose matters revealed in the confessional (Beltrami, "The Defender" (1988), p.201). Compare Stair Memorial Encyclopaedia, Vol. 10, para. 685. Whatever degree of confidentiality attaches to the relationship between doctor and patient, a doctor cannot decline to give evidence which may incriminate her patient—see *H.M.A. v. Kelly*, unreported, February 20, 2001, High Court of Justiciary (Lord Mackay).

Neither does confidentiality apply to communications between family members—see *H.M.A. v. Parker*, 1944 J.C. 49. The only exception to this rule is in relation to communications between husband and wife—see Evidence (Scotland) Act 1853, s.3; Criminal Procedure (Scotland) Act 1995, s.264(2)(b) and *Hunter v. H.M.A*, 1984 J.C. 90, Chapter 14 below. The privilege appears to apply to communications made during the subsistence of the marriage, and is unaffected by the death or divorce of the spouses.

Parker emphasises that where information relates to the commission of a crime, the only situations in which information is privileged are where the information passes between solicitor and client, or husband and wife. However, subject to statutory exceptions (see Chapters 8 and 14), no witness can be compelled to answer questions the answers to which would be incriminating of that witness. See *e.g.* Dickson, *Evidence*, paras. 1786–1792. Similarly, questions which would implicate the witness in the commission of adultery need not be answered—see Stair Memorial Encyclopaedia, Vol. 10 para. 675. Do you consider that the latter example of privilege is justified in modern conditions? It would appear that there is no general rule that a witness may decline to answer questions which may expose her to a civil action.

(B) COMMUNICATIONS *POST LITEM MOTAM*

3. Hepburn v. Scottish Power plc
1997 S.L.T. 859

A fire broke out in a house causing considerable damage. A short circuit in the area of the electrical distribution board for the house was suspected as the cause. The electricity supply company instructed consulting scientists to investigate the cause of the fire. They visited the house and, with the consent of the householders, carried out an investigation which involved removing parts of the distribution board equipment. After they had completed their investigations, the company fitted a new distribution board and other equipment. The scientists then prepared a report for the company detailing the results of their investigations.

The householders sought to recover the scientists' report from the company by means of a summary application to the Sheriff brought under section 1(1) of the Administration of Justice (Scotland) Act 1972. The company opposed the application, arguing that the report was confidential to them as it had been prepared in contemplation of litigation. After a hearing at which evidence was led by the company as to the nature of the investigations which had been carried out, the sheriff ordered recovery of the report, but appointed a commissioner to excerpt from the report any professional advice or opinion given to the electricity supply company in contemplation of legal proceedings against them. The sheriff reached his decision on the basis that it was "in the interests of justice and fairness". Both parties appealed to the sheriff principal, who concluded that in the circumstances of a report being prepared a few days after the fire, with the consent of the householders, for a company in a monopoly position, and which had prevented the householders from having the distribution board examined themselves, the report was not one which had been prepared *post litem motam*, and ordered recovery of the whole report. The company appealed to the Court of Session which allowed the appeal and held:

(1) that the question of whether a report was one prepared *post litem motam* required the court to make a judgment as to whether or not the document had been prepared in anticipation of litigation, or in response to a development in litigation already raised;

(2) that it was not appropriate to take a broad brush approach to the issue of recovery, based upon issues of justice or fairness, and it was irrelevant to a consideration of whether a report was prepared *post litem motam* that the company was in a monopoly position or that the householders consented to the report being prepared;

(3) that having regard to the true character of the report it was prepared *post litem motam*;

(4) that there was, however, an exception to the rule that reports prepared *post litem motam* were not recoverable, namely that if the examination carried out was one which destroyed or materially altered the subject matter of the examination, with the result that the person in possession of the report of the examination was enabled to be in a position of knowledge as to the cause and circumstances of the incident involving the object and the other party was unable to acquire such knowledge, then the other party was entitled to know the results of that examination (*Black v. Bairds & Dalmellington*, 1939 S.C. 472, followed);

(5) that the correct course in relation to a report which had resulted in the destruction of the object was to appoint a commissioner to exclude from recovery material which was relevant only to matters of fault and liability.

OPINION OF THE COURT: "In presenting the appeal, senior counsel for the defenders drew attention to various matters which the sheriff and sheriff principal had had regard to and had taken into account in determining whether or not to grant the order. Only one of these factors was, in his submission, relevant to the issue. It was related to the circumstance that when Burgoynes carried out their inspection (with the consent of the householders), they removed parts of the distribution board equipment. A little later the defenders' workmen had done substantial work to restore a safe electricity supply. The defenders were now in the position that they were unable to explain what had happened to some of the electrical equipment after it had been removed by the defenders' workmen. That circumstance might be relevant to the issues raised by the application. But he submitted that in the court below, irrelevant considerations had been taken into account. A false and irrelevant distinction had been drawn between a report prepared to ascertain the true facts and a report prepared in contemplation of litigation. There was no necessary distinction of this kind. A report which was truly to be designated *post litem motam* would often and necessarily seek to ascertain and narrate the true facts. So this consideration was not relevant to determining whether or not the report fell to be treated as *post litem motam*. Equally it was an error to have regard to the fact that the defenders were said to be in a monopoly position as suppliers of electricity; for there was no rule of law that gave weight to such a consideration. The fact that the defenders were in the position similar to that of statutory undertakers was not relevant to the application of the rules about recovery of documents *post litem motam*. Nor was it relevant to have regard to the fact that the pursuers had given their consent to the carrying out of the examination which resulted in Burgoynes' report; nor did it make any difference that the investigation could not have been carried out without such consent. There was no implication to be drawn from the giving of consent that the report would be disclosed to the householders or that the defenders were obtaining it to help prepare their defences against some form of claim. Furthermore the inspection took place several days after the fire. Accordingly it did not fall within the recognised exception to the general rule, being an exception which allowed recovery of reports made at or about the time of the incident by persons actually present at the time of the incident. Although the defenders acknowledged that parts of the equipment had been removed for investigation these parts were still available. Nonetheless counsel acknowledged that the exact situation which could have been observed after the fire could not now be perfectly reconstructed and, at least in that sense, the effect of the inspection and the removal of some of the equipment was comparable to the destruction of part of the subject matter. Counsel particularly challenged the references in the court below to a broad general concept of 'the interests of justice' or fairness as being the test. Once the document was seen to be prepared *post litem motam* the general rule was clear. Reference was made to the opinion of the Lord Justice Clerk (Thomson) in *Young v. National Coal Board*, 1957 S.C. at p.105; 1957 S.L.T. at p.269:

> 'The Court will not, however, in the ordinary run of things, order production of documents which have been prepared in anticipation or in development of a party's case. Once the parties are at arm's length, or are obviously going to be at arm's length, the details of their preparation of weapons and ammunition are protected as confidential.'

That rule was reaffirmed in *Johnstone v. National Coal Board* and reference was made to the opinion of Lord President Clyde at 1968 S.L.T., pp.235–236: 'In our opinion the basic principle in Scots law regarding reports and records of accidents prepared by or on behalf of one side is that they are not recoverable under a specification of documents by the other side . . . To this general rule, however, all these judges recognise that there is one exception which relates to reports by employees present at the time of the accident and made to their employers at or about the time of the accident.'

The broad 'fairness' approach adopted by Sheriff Simpson in *Aitken v. Scottish Power plc* was not warranted in the light of the longstanding statements of the rule contained in *Young* and in *Johnstone*. Counsel drew our attention to similar statements to the same effect in *More v. Brown & Root Wimpey Highland Fabricators Ltd*. He distinguished the case of *Black v. Bairds & Dalmellington* in which recovery of a post mortem report had been allowed. That case had been explained in *Anderson v. St Andrews Ambulance Association*. He drew attention to the fact that in *Black* it was expressly stated in the opinion of Lord Mackay that when the parents of the deceased whose body was examined post mortem gave their consent to that examination, the giving of the consent was on a condition from which it might readily be inferred and implicitly understood that 'the results would be made commonly available'. Counsel acknowledged that *Black* could create a specific exception to the general rule but submitted that it did so only where it was appropriate to infer an understanding that the results would be made available to parties other than those who instructed the examination. The exception in relation to post mortem reports was further examined by Lord Cameron in *Waddington v. Buchan Poultry Products Ltd*, and counsel submitted that the conditions for the application of a *Black* exception as discussed by Lord Cameron in *Waddington* were not met in the present case. In *Young v. National Coal Board*, the Lord Ordinary, Lord Walker, had not ruled out a *Black* type of exception to the general rule, but the Inner House judges had reserved their opinion on that matter. It was submitted that this court should not follow the approach of Lord Hunter in *Marks & Spencer Ltd v. British Gas Corporation*. His observations as to the monopoly position and the statutory undertaker status of the defenders in that case were *obiter* and not relevant to the question as to whether or not the report was one prepared 'in anticipation or in development of a party's case'. It was not disputed that a report which would otherwise fall to be regarded as one prepared *post litem motam* might be recoverable if the subject matter of the examination had been destroyed by the examination or materially altered. It would be a question of circumstances as to whether or not the document should be recovered. No other issue was raised in the present application as to the applicability of the Administration of Justice (Scotland) Act 1972; the same considerations would apply even if the recovery had been sought after the closing of the record in an action of damages. The court was specifically invited to disapprove the general reasons given by the sheriff and the sheriff principal in support of their decisions and, in particular, to disapprove of references to broad and flexible concepts of fairness. The general principle enunciated in *Young* should be reaffirmed.

The solicitor advocate for the pursuers submitted that the decision of the sheriff principal was based on an exercise of judicial discretion which should not be disturbed unless he had exercised his discretion on a wrong principle or in a manner that was plainly wrong: he sought to illustrate this proposition by reference to *Britton v. Central Regional Council*. What lay at the root of the rule in *Young* was the concept of confidentiality. But, in his submission, confidentiality itself rested upon the notion of fairness; and, therefore, fairness was the guiding consideration in an application of this kind. It was his submission that the document could not be regarded as one prepared *post litem motam*. He drew attention to the Electricity Supply Regulations 1988 (S.I. 1988 No.1057), reg. 34(1)(a), which required the defenders to prepare a report after such an incident. However, he acknowledged that the report required by these regulations was not the report which the pursuers were seeking to recover. He submitted that the fact that the pursuers had consented to the making of the examination which resulted in the report was not irrelevant because, as in the case of *Black*, it was relevant to the question of fairness. He submitted that the most important factor, however, was that the investigation had—and this was hardly in dispute—changed the character of the material to be examined and that the pursuers had thus been permanently deprived of the opportunity to be in the position that the defenders had secured for themselves by having this investigation carried out. The question as to whether or not a document was truly to be regarded as *post litem motam* was to be decided on the basis of all the factors relevant to fairness. The solicitor advocate, however, had difficulty maintaining that position as he also submitted that the question as to whether or not a document fell to be regarded as having been prepared *post litem motam* was ultimately a question of fact, namely whether or not the document was one which a party to a litigation—whether already in court or simply in contemplation—had caused to be prepared 'in anticipation or in development of a party's case'. Even if the report in this case fell to be regarded as prepared *post litem motam*, however, he founded upon *Black* and upon the references in *Anderson* and *Waddington* to the destruction or material alteration of the subject matter of the examination. In essence, the report which the pursuers sought to recover contained the only available evidence of the condition of the equipment whose failure had caused the fire and it was now impossible to replicate that examination. A 'wrong' had been done by the defenders in removing relevant and significant material from the site and the defenders could not take advantage of that wrong.

In our opinion, the general rule is as stated very clearly in the cases of *Young, Johnstone* and *More*. We have not been asked to send this case to a larger court to allow consideration of these earlier authorities and, in any event, we would not have been persuaded that it was necessary to take such a step. The general rule requires the court to make a judgment as to whether or not the document which one party seeks to recover has been prepared in anticipation or in development of the case of the other party who has instructed preparation of the document. In the present case, the sheriff had the unusual advantage of hearing evidence from Mr Hay and his evidence does not appear to have been challenged. What is noteworthy is that he was employed at the relevant time not by the defenders nor by Burgoynes but by a firm of loss adjusters who had, as the sheriff put it, 'been employed by the defenders to protect their interests and carry out inquiries into the fire'. It is unfortunate that the sheriff did not approach the issue by expressly determining, as a matter of fact, in the light of the evidence, whether or not the report was, as the defenders averred, 'prepared in anticipation of litigation'. In our view it would have been difficult, in this case, to regard the report as not having been prepared in anticipation of litigation, given that it was instructed by loss adjusters in the circumstances narrated by Mr Hay. We have difficulty in seeing how the sheriff principal could come to a different view on the basis of considerations such as 'the fact that the defenders occupied a monopoly position' or the fact that the pursuers consented to the investigation. We do not consider that the authorities on this matter support a general proposition that it is appropriate just to take a broad brush approach to the issue of recovery, based upon regard to 'the interests of justice and fairness'. Without doubt, the interests of justice and fairness are relevant when the court is called upon to exercise a discretion; but the formulation of the rule in *Young, Johnstone* and *More* does not allow for the court to exercise a 'discretion' in order to determine whether or not the documents sought to be recovered fall to be classified as *post litem motam*. What the court has to do is to make a judgment as to the true character of the document. In our view, the report prepared by Burgoynes in this case falls to be regarded as one prepared *post litem motam* in the sense in which that expression has been used in the authoritative cases quoted.

That, however, does not end the matter at issue. We are of the view that *Black* created an exception to the general rule about non-recoverability of reports prepared by or on behalf of one side to a potential litigation. The question at issue in that case was the cause of death of a workman. On the day following his death, his employers, having obtained the deceased's parents' consent to a post mortem examination, had that examination carried out by a pathologist who conducted the examination in the presence of a medical representative of the family. In the Inner House the judges founded upon the fact that the result of the examination was the best evidence as to 'the state of the workman's body at death, the condition and appearances of its various organs, and the physical indications of injury or disease, which must be of the greatest value, and very probably conclusive, as to the cause of death' (per the Lord Justice Clerk (Aitchison) at 1939 S.C., p.476; 1939 S.L.T., p.418). Lord Mackay referred to the problem in the case as being able to be solved 'on grounds agreeable to the equities, without challenging, or infringing on, any of the well-settled and securely-buttressed principles according to which the documents of litigant A are made open to and are usable by litigant B, or are refused such a treatment'.

Lord Mackay regarded the fact that the examination was made post mortem would be enough, on its own, to justify an exception which would take the case out of the general rules of evidence and of confidentiality. He specifically referred to the circumstance that the nature of such an examination was that it destroyed the object of the examination so that no subsequent skilled examination on behalf of the other party could ever have the same effect. In our view, the opinions of the judges in *Black* support the existence of an exception to the general rule; the exception is that if the examination which is prepared in anticipation or development of a party's case is one which destroys or materially alters the subject matter of the examination with the result that the person in possession of the report of the examination is enabled to be in a position of knowledge as to the cause and circumstances of the incident involving the object and the other party is unable to acquire such knowledge because the object has been destroyed or materially altered, then the other party is entitled to know the results of that examination. We recognise, of course, that a report of an examination of the kind in question, whether it be an invasive examination of a corpse or of a piece of equipment which has to be dismantled for the purposes of the examination, may contain both observations of fact and expressions of opinion, whether they be expressions of technical expert opinion or of opinion in relation to fault and legal liability. Thus, although the exception may permit the recovery of the report it will not necessarily permit the recovery of the whole report, for that might deprive the party who instructed the preparation of the report of the privilege of confidentiality in relation to an expert opinion which he has instructed for the purposes of considering his legal liability. Such an opinion is, in principle, distinguishable from a factual record of things observed. We also recognise that there may be circumstances in which an opinion as to the cause of an incident which lies at the heart of a possible litigation may be difficult to disentangle and separate out from, on the one hand, observations of fact and, on the other, expressions of expert opinion. In our view, the correct course, to avoid any difficulty of this character, is to appoint a commissioner to take excerpts from the report so as to except from recovery material which is relevant only to matters of fault and liability. Ordinary cause rule 28.8 allows confidentiality to be claimed on the execution of commission and diligence for the recovery of the document in question and envisages that the matter of confidentiality will be resolved by the court on a motion to have the sealed packet opened up."

NOTES

Compare *Marks & Spencer Ltd v. British Gas Corporation*, 1983 S.L.T. 196 and *More v. Brown & Root Wimpey Highland Fabricators Ltd*, 1983 S.L.T. 669. Note the other important exception to this rule, mentioned in passing by the court in *Hepburn*:

"The exception relates to reports by employees present at the time of the accident and made to their employers at or about the time of the accident . . . all the judges who took part in the decision in *Young's* case recognised that this was an exception, incapable of being extended to cover any other reports. The justification for this exception, which is well settled in our practice, is that 'if such a report is made as part of a routine duty, and as a record of the reporter's immediate reaction before he has had the time, opportunity or temptation to indulge in too much reflection, it may well contain an unvarnished account of what happened and consequently be of value in the subsequent proceedings as a touchstone of truth' (Lord Justice-Clerk Thomson in *Young's* case), It is perfectly clear that this quotation from the Lord Justice-Clerk's opinion in *Young* is concerned with a report by someone present on the spot at the time of the accident."

(C) NEGOTIATIONS FOR SETTLEMENT OR CONCILIATION

In general, admissions or statements made during negotiations towards a settlement or in conciliation are inadmissible in any court proceedings. For example, section 1 of the Civil Evidence (Family Mediation) (Scotland) Act 1995, renders inadmissible any information as to what occurred during sessions conducted by accredited family mediators. A number of exceptions to this rule are provided by section 2 of the Act. Similarly, communications with a conciliation officer in an industrial dispute are not admissible in proceedings before an industrial tribunal—Industrial Tribunals Act 1996, s.18(7). Confidentiality also extends to communications made "without prejudice", a common method of preserving the position of parties to a negotiation. Again, there are exceptions to the rule.

4. Bell v. Lothiansure Ltd
1990 S.L.T. 58

Ian Bell and 57 other people sought, in conjoined actions, a remedy against Lothiansure Ltd, an insurance broker, in respect of moneys lost when the individuals had invested in bonds issued by an offshore company. The premiums paid had been paid to the offshore company and misappropriated. The case against the brokers and, after the liquidation of the brokers, against the professional indemnity insurer of the brokers, was that the brokers had not exercised reasonable care in advising the pursuers about the investment. At one stage an offer had been made by the solicitor acting on behalf of the professional indemnity insurer to provide a sum of money to settle the claims of the pursuer and of all others who had the same claim. The letter was marked "Without prejudice". The reason for referring to the letter was stated to be as an adminicle of evidence showing that the claims of the different pursuers were accepted as arising from "the same cause". The insurer sought to exclude averments about this offer from probation. In refusing probation of the averments, the Lord Ordinary (Lord McCluskey) said:

"I turn first to consider the submissions in relation to the first plea in law for the second defender, a plea to the effect that the pursuers averments relating to a letter from the second defender's solicitor should not be admitted to probation, on the ground of irrelevancy. The averments which appear in article 1 of the condescendence are: 'Solicitors for the insurers have offered to settle the pursuers' claims and all other claims arising from the same cause for the sum of £250,000. Reference is made to the letter from Messrs Reynold Porter Chamberlain to Messrs John C. Gray & Co. dated March 25, 1987 a copy of which is produced'. The letter is written 'Without prejudice'. Proceeding upon the narrative that the bondholders' claims are against the first defenders and do not concern the insurers, and expressing the view that any loss is not covered under the policies, the letter nevertheless contains an *ex gratia* offer in full and final settlement of all claims against the insurers.

Counsel for the insurer submitted several arguments in support of his first plea-in-law. In the first place, the contents of the letter could not be referred to and founded upon because it was written 'without prejudice'. He referred to *Walker v. Wilsher* (1889) 23 Q.B.D. 335, in which it was said that the general rule was that nothing written or said 'without prejudice' in such circumstances should be looked at, unless with the consent of both parties. That rule was applied there, in a case in which the question was whether in making an order as to the costs the court should have regard to a letter written 'without prejudice' and containing an offer which, if it had been accepted, could have resulted in the settlement of the action at a much earlier stage. It is plain, however, that the rule itself was seen as a much wider one. More recent examples of the application of the rule can be found in *Tomlin v. Standard Telephones and Cables Ltd.* [1969] 1 W.L.R. 1378, where it is said that the rule rests upon a view of the public interest, the view being that parties to a litigation should be encouraged to negotiate a settlement without prejudice in their positions if the negotiations should fail, and that, accordingly, such negotiations should be protected from later scrutiny by the court in event of their not leading to a negotiated settlement. The general rule was further affirmed in *Cutts v. Head & Another* [1984] Ch. 290.

In reply, the learned Dean of Faculty, appearing for the pursuers, argued that the letter was founded upon not because of the offer it contained but because, having regard to its terms, it could amount to an adminicle of evidence showing that the second defender's solicitors, as the insurers' agents, were not disputing that the various claims of the different pursuers arose from 'the same cause'. The point was therefore of some possible significance in relation to the application of insuring cll. nos. 3 and 4 in the relevant Lloyd's policy. I have to deal with this matter below.

For present purposes it is sufficient to note that whether or not the letter might be of any value in relation to that issue, it is plain that it can not be so used without looking at the contents of the letter. Accordingly, in my opinion the same general rule, referred to above, applies. The learned Dean of Faculty drew my attention to the observations by Lindley L.J. in *Walker v. Wilsher* (supra) at p.338 where his Lordship said: 'No doubt there are cases where letters written without prejudice may be taken into consideration, as was done the other day in a case in which a question of laches was raised. The fact that such letters have been written and the dates at which they were written may be regarded, and in so doing the rule to which I have adverted would not be infringed.' With respect that appears to me not to be a loophole in the general rule. The fact of writing a letter, or the date at which it was written, or the fact of its receipt might be relevant without regard to the contents which are protected by the 'without prejudice' rule. I do not think the pursuers in this case can escape from having to submit that what they are entitled to do is to refer to the contents of the letter with a view to founding upon a statement therein which was made in the context of an offer advanced during negotiations. In so doing they are seeking to avoid the rule which is general in both England and in Scotland. I also note, however, as counsel for the insurer pointed out, that the letter, whose terms are agreed in the joint minute, does not in fact say what the pursuers' averment suggests it says. Finally, if one tests the matter from the point of view of pure relevancy one has to ask what purpose these averments serve. If the averments were admitted to probation the pursuers would simply be allowed to prove that solicitors for the insurers made an *ex gratia* offer to the agent for the first defenders, but without admitting liability—albeit inferentially conceding, for the purposes of the proposed settlement only, a point that they might otherwise have argued. I do not see how this can be relevant in any way in any proof that takes place upon the pleadings in the present action. Accordingly I shall not admit to probation the two sentences in article I of the condescendence (being the 16th and 17th sentences) beginning, 'Solicitors for the insurers'. It follows that the final three sentences of ans. 1 for the second defender will not be admitted to probation. I sustain the first plea in law for the second defender."

5. Daks Simpson Group plc v. Kuiper
1994 S.L.T. 689

A company raised an action against a former executive director for count, reckoning and payment of secret commission paid to him by customers of the company and in respect of work done on the director's property and paid for by the company. In the course of negotiations the director's solicitors wrote to the company's solicitors in response to a draft agreement with an attached schedule of alleged secret commission payments. The letter concluded with the words "without prejudice" and commented on the accuracy of the figures shown in the schedule. The company sought summary decree for the amount accepted in the letter as accurate. The former director opposed the motion, arguing (i) that the motion was not "in terms of a conclusion" within rule 89B(3)(a), and (ii) that it was incompetent for the court to look at the letter since it had been written "without prejudice".

LORD SUTHERLAND: "The first defender was formerly employed as an executive director of the first pursuers until his resignation on December 9, 1992. The first pursuers aver that during the course of his employment with them the first defender obtained substantial sums of money by way of secret commission from customers of the pursuers. They also aver that a substantial amount of work was done on property owned by the first defender either by employees of the first pursuers during the time that they should have been working for the first pursuers or by independent contractors who were paid by way of invoices falsely submitted to the first pursuers. The conclusions of the summons are for count and reckoning for all undisclosed or secret profits made by the first defender and for payment to the pursuers by him of the balance found due to them, otherwise for payment by the first defender to the pursuers of £765,000 and for payment by the first and second defenders jointly and severally of the sum of £500,000. There is a further conclusion for payment by the first defender of £171,500 which is said to be the cost to the pursuers of investigating the first defender's wrongful activities. The second defender is the first defender's wife and she is sued on the basis that the property on which the work was done was conveyed to her gratuitously.

In cond. 5 it is averred that the secret commission paid to the first defender came to light following information supplied to the pursuers by the Inland Revenue. The pursuers estimate the amount of such secret commission at £850,000. They further aver that on December 9, 1992 a meeting was held in London attended by the first defender and his solicitor along with two representatives of the pursuers and the pursuers' accountant and solicitor. At that meeting it is said that the first defender admitted having received moneys by way of secret commission from a number of companies and admitted that the secret commission exceeded £600,000. By letter dated April 1, 1993 the pursuers' solicitors Messrs Allen & Overy wrote to the defender's solicitor enclosing a draft settlement agreement. Attached to the draft agreement there was a schedule showing a number of commission payments which in the view of the pursuers constituted secret commission paid to the first defender. By letter dated April 20, 1993 the defender's solicitor replied making certain comments on the draft settlement agreement. It was stated in that letter, *inter alia*: 'Mr Kuiper is prepared to accept that the first four commission payments stated by you are correct. However, he does not accept that the Bara figure is correct at £20,000. The true figure is in the region of £17,000 and he would accept a figure of £17,000. The estimated commission payments for the period prior to April 1, 1986 are not accepted. Mr Kuiper has spent some time endeavouring to rebuild the earlier payments which he would state as follows', and there followed a list of five payments totalling £108,056. This letter concluded with the words 'without prejudice'.

In the motion before me today the pursuers seek summary decree in the sum of £689,497. This sum is made up of the first four commission payments set out in the schedule to Allen & Overy's letter, £17,000 in respect of the Bara commission, and the amount stated in the defender's solicitor's letter of £108,056 as being the earlier payments received by him. Counsel for the pursuers argued that there was no defence stated in the defences and that accordingly a motion for summary decree was competent and appropriate. In ans. 5 it was said that the meeting on December 9, 1992 and subsequent correspondence were admitted under explanation that the parties met in order to negotiate a compromise of claims and that what was said by the first defender was said in that context. The letter of April 20, 1993 consistent with that context was marked 'without prejudice'. Apart from a blanket denial, there was no specific denial in that answer that these sums of secret commission had been paid to the defender. There was therefore no substantive defence stated; all that was being said was that the court could not look at what transpired at the meeting in December 1992 or the subsequent correspondence because it was all part of negotiations. Counsel for the pursuers accepted that if that was the true construction to be put on the words 'without prejudice', his present motion would have to fail, but he contended that those words did not mean that there was an absolute ban on looking at anything contained in the correspondence. He argued that if plain statements of fact were made in the course of a letter so marked, these could be looked at. What could not be looked at in a letter so marked was some hypothetical admission or concession or arrangement for the purpose of securing a settlement. Anything put forward as a bargaining counter in the course of the letter would be protected from further scrutiny, but a plain straightforward statement of fact or admission could be looked at because this was not something which was being used for the purposes of negotiation.

Counsel referred to the decision of Lord Wylie in *Watson Towers Ltd v. Macphail* [1986 S.L.T. 617]. In that case there was a letter from the defender which referred to 'plates of steel which were in stock at November 7, 1983 and which remain unpaid'. This statement came in a letter which offered a certain sum to the pursuers and it was said in the letter 'this offer is made without prejudice and would be in full and final settlement of your reservation of title claim'. It was held that the value of those plates of steel could be recovered by way of summary decree. In referring to the part of the letter which I have quoted, Lord Wylie said (at pp.618–619): 'These terms do not, in my view, infer a hypothetical admission or concession for the purpose of securing a settlement but are statements of fact. The use of the expression 'without prejudice' does not in my view protect the letter from subsequent use as an admission of fact.'

A very similar view was taken in the Canadian case of *Kirschbaum v. "Our Voices" Publishing Co.* [[1971] 1 OR 737], where it was said: 'Correspondence without prejudice is one of the exclusionary rules. Contrary to popular belief in some quarters, that the shibboleth 'without prejudice' written on a letter protects it from subsequent use as an admission is not accurate: see 4 Wigmore 2 Ed paras 1060–1062. That learned authority points out that the basis of the exclusion is a hypothetical admission or concession for the purpose of securing peace or settlement; and since it does not represent the parties' true belief it cannot be taken as a true admission. Therefore, the question to be considered is, what was the view and intention of the party in making the admission; whether it was to concede a fact hypothetically, in order to effect a settlement, or to declare a fact really to exist.'

Counsel contended that looking at the letter of April 20, 1993 in this light, it was clear that there was an admission of fact that the first four payments were correct, that the Bara payment was £17,000 and that the earlier payments were in the sum stated therein. This was not some form of hypothetical admission or concession for the purpose of securing a settlement but was a simple statement of fact. If these could be looked at as admissions, there was no conceivable defence to this part of the pursuers' claim and accordingly summary decree should be pronounced.

Counsel for the defender contended in the first place that the motion for summary decree was not in terms of a conclusion but was for a sum which constituted part of an alternative conclusion. Accordingly it did not fall within rule 89B(3)(a). In my opinion this argument is without substance. If I am entitled to look at the contents of the letter of April 20, 1993 and if I regard those contents as constituting an admission that certain sums are due, it does not appear that there is any need for a count and reckoning in respect of that amount. Furthermore, it is perfectly competent to seek a sum less than the whole of the sum sought in the conclusion and this can be done, if necessary, under sub para. (c) of the rule whereby the court can dispose of part of the subject matter. Counsel's main contention, however, was that because the letter of April 20, 1993 was written without prejudice, the contents of it could not be looked at and could not be held to constitute an admission. In that situation the defender was entitled to put the pursuers to their proof. He contended that Lord Wylie's approach in *Watson-Towers* was wrong and contrary to principle. He referred to *Cutts v. Head*. Although that case was concerned with the question special to English procedure as to whether or not a letter written without prejudice could be expressed to be subject to the reservation of a right to bring the letter to the notice of the judge on the issue of costs, certain observations were made as to the general nature of without prejudice letters. The general principle was stated by Oliver L.J. as follows: 'That the rule rests, at least in part, upon public policy is clear from many authorities, and the convenient starting point of the inquiry is the nature of the underlying policy. It is that parties should be encouraged so far as possible to settle their disputes without resort to litigation and should not be discouraged by the knowledge that anything that is said in the course of such negotiations (and that includes, of course, as much the failure to reply to an offer as an actual reply) may be used to their prejudice in the course of the proceedings. They should, as it was expressed by Clauson J. in *Scott Paper Co v. Drayton Paper Work Ltd* (1927)

44 RFC 151, 156, be encouraged fully and frankly to put their cards on the table. The public policy justification, in truth, essentially rests on the desirability of preventing statements or offers made in the course of negotiations for settlement being brought before the court of trial as admissions on the question of liability.

It was expressed thus by Romilly MR in *Jones v. Foxall* (1852) 15 Beav 388, 396: 'I find that the offers were in fact made without prejudice to the rights of the parties; and I shall, as far as I am able, in all cases, endeavour to repress a practice which, when I was first acquainted with the profession, was never ventured upon, but which, according to my experience in this place, has become common of late—namely, that of attempting to convert offers of compromise into admissions of acts prejudicial to the person making them. If this were permitted, the effect would be, that no attempt to compromise a dispute could ever be made.'

Reference was also made to *Bell v. Lothiansure Ltd* where Lord McCluskey held that the general rule applied that nothing written or said without prejudice should be looked at except with the consent of both parties. Lord McCluskey said (at p.59): 'I do not think the pursuers in this case can escape from having to submit that what they are entitled to do is to refer to the contents of the letter with a view to founding upon a statement therein which was made in the context of an offer advanced during negotiations. In so doing they are seeking to avoid the rule which is general in both England and Scotland.'

As the statements in the letter of April 20, 1993 were made in the context of a draft settlement agreement and were stated to be without prejudice, counsel argued that the general rule should apply and these statements should not be subject to scrutiny. If that is so there is no admission properly pled by the pursuers and accordingly the defender is entitled to put the pursuers to their proof. In any event even if the statements are to be looked at they do not constitute clear statements of admission. All that is said in relation to the first four payments is that the defender 'is prepared to accept' that they are correct. In relation to the Bara figure, the defender puts forward a suggestion. In relation to earlier matters again the defender is putting forward a proposal. Accordingly these are simply proposals put forward with a view to coming to a settlement by negotiation rather than any positive admission that the sums are actually due.

In my opinion the argument advanced by the pursuers is correct. The general principle underlying the rule is that if offers, suggestions, concessions or whatever are made for the purposes of negotiating a settlement, these cannot be converted into admissions of fact. I do not read Oliver L.J.'s statement as saying anything beyond that. The observations in *Bell* were made in the context of the averment being that solicitors for the insurers offered to settle the pursuers' claims and all other claims arising from the same cause for the sum of £250,000, but the letter proceeded on the narrative that the claims were against the first defenders and did not concern the insurers and expressing the view that any loss was not covered under the policies but nevertheless the insurers were prepared to make an *ex gratia* offer. Quite plainly, in my view, that could not be converted into some form of admission. 'Without prejudice' in my view means, without prejudice to the whole rights and pleas of the person making the statement. If, however, someone makes a clear and unequivocal admission or statement of fact, it is difficult to see what rights or pleas could be attached to such a statement or admission other perhaps than to deny the truth of the admission which was made. I see no objection in principle to a clear admission being used in subsequent proceedings, even though the communication in which it appears is stated to be without prejudice. I would adopt what is said by Lord Wylie in *Watson-Towers* and the Canadian view expressed in *Kirschbaum*.

As far as the statements themselves are concerned, three of the first four commission payments are stated in very precise figures to the nearest pound and accordingly the use of the words 'prepared to accept' appears to me to be quite reasonable as an admission that those payments are more or less accurate. In relation to the Bara figure, the letter reads 'he would accept a figure of £17,000', and that appears again to be a clear admission rather than a negotiating proposal. In relation to the other payments it is said that the defender 'has spent some time endeavouring to rebuild the earlier payments which he would state as follows'. Again therefore, this is not a negotiating figure but is a statement of what the defender himself has calculated as being the correct figure. In this context it must be borne in mind that the precise amounts received by the defender by way of unlawful payments are something which is particularly within his own knowledge. In my opinion therefore the defender has unequivocally admitted the fact that he has received improper payments to the extent of £689,497 and that being so there is no stated defence to this part of the pursuers' claim. I shall accordingly grant summary decree for that sum."

NOTES

See also *Assessor for Dundee v. Elder*, 1963 S.L.T. (Notes) 35; *Gordon v. East Kilbride Development Corporation*, 1995 S.L.T. 62.

(D) PUBLIC INTEREST IMMUNITY

6. The Corporation of the City of Glasgow v. The Central Land Board
1956 S.C. (H.L.) 1

Glasgow Corporation brought an action against the Central Land Board for declarator that certain determinations of the Board in respect of development charges were *ultra vires* and for their reduction. Proof having been allowed the Corporation moved for a commission and diligence to recover various documents in the possession of the defenders which related to the determination of the charges. This motion was met by the lodging in process of a certificate by the Secretary of State for Scotland that some of these documents "belonged to a class which it was necessary for the proper functioning of the public service to withhold from production".

LORD NORMAND: "In this appeal the Corporation of the City of Glasgow are the pursuers and appellants. They raised the action to have it declared that certain determinations made by the Central Land Board, the defenders and respondents, and purporting to determine certain development charges under the provisions of the Town and Country Planning (Scotland) Act 1947, were *ultra vires*. The respondents contested the relevancy of the case, and after debate the Lord Ordinary allowed a proof before answer. Thereafter the appellants moved the Lord Ordinary to grant a diligence for the recovery of certain documents in the possession of the respondents and of the Board of Inland Revenue. About some of these there was no dispute, but there were others which the respondents declined to produce, and before the appellants' specification was debated the Secretary of State for Scotland granted a certificate that he had examined the disputed documents and had formed the view that on grounds of public interest they ought not to be produced because they belonged to a class which it was necessary for the proper functioning of the public service to withhold from production. The Lord Ordinary, after hearing parties, allowed the recovery of the undisputed documents only. The appellants reclaimed and the First Division of the Court of Session adhered to the Lord Ordinary's interlocutor. The scheduled interlocutors are those of the Lord Ordinary and of the First Division dealing with the recovery of documents: the Lord Ordinary's interlocutor allowing a proof before answer was not reclaimed against and there is no question upon it before the House.

The first question that the House must consider is whether the Central Land Board is a body which can claim the benefit of the Crown's right to certify that a document or class of document should not be produced because its production would adversely affect the public interest, or, to put it shortly, whether the Board is the Crown for this purpose. On this question I agree with my noble and learned friend on the Woolsack, and have nothing to add.

The next question is whether there is a rule of law by which the Scottish Courts are bound to give effect to the certificate of the Secretary of State, or whether these Courts have an inherent jurisdiction not to review the certificate but to override it. It is conceded that the Courts do not know the exigencies and conditions of the public service and cannot be in a position to say that the Minister, to whom the exigencies and conditions are known, was wrong in certifying that the public interest would be injured by the publication of documents called for by a party to a litigation. One of the considerations which may move a Minister to grant a certificate like the present is that publication would or might be injurious to that freedom and candour of communication in writing between the officers of a department, which are of great importance to public administration: and the responsible Minister or the head of the public department must be the judge whether the disclosure of documents would have an adverse effect by inducing among public servants a cautious timidity in expressing their views. The judgments of Lord President Dunedin, Lord M'Laren, Lord Kinnear and Lord Pearson in *The Admiralty v. Aberdeen Steam Trawling and Fishing Co.* are conclusive on this point, but these judgments do not deal explicitly with the question whether the Courts in Scotland have the power to override the ministerial certificate. If such a power does exist, it must be based on the ground that the fair administration of justice between subject and subject and between the subject and the Crown is a public interest of a high order, and that its protection is the care of the Courts.

In the hundred years before the case of *Duncan v. Cammell, Laird & Co.* was decided, there can be no doubt that the Scottish Central Land Courts were satisfied that they possessed the inherent power I am now discussing. In the present case the Lord Ordinary and Lord Russell were of opinion that the Scottish Courts retain that power. Lord Carmont was, I think, disposed to agree with that opinion but he felt constrained to bow to the decision in *Duncan v. Cammell, Laird & Co.* Lord Sorn also held that the rule of law laid down in *Duncan v. Cammell, Laird & Co.* was binding on the Court of Session in any situation contemplated in the judgment of the Lord Chancellor in *Duncan v. Cammell, Laird & Co.*, but not in other cases.

It was argued for the respondents that the case of *Earl v. Vass* decided in principle that the Courts in Scotland were bound to give effect to a ministerial certificate that production of a document would be contrary to the public interest. In that case the pursuer [*Vass*], who had been seeking employment under the Board of Customs, raised an action of damages against the Earl of Home on the ground that he had falsely and maliciously made insinuations to the Board against the pursuer's character and so caused the pursuer to lose the opportunity of employment under the Board. The Lord Ordinary granted diligence for the recovery of letters written by the defender to the Board and to the Treasury. The Inner House affirmed. In the House of Lords the Lord Chancellor, Lord Eldon, reversed the judgments. He did so after consulting the Lord Chief Justice, who stated that 'he would not have permitted any such production as is here called for' for reasons of public interest. Lord Eldon heard no debate on the question which this House has now to decide and there was no appearance for the respondent. I can find in that case no authority for a general rule of law that the Scottish Courts have not the inherent power contended for. In Scotland the case has never been suffered to lay down any general rule. In *Henderson v. Robertson*, *Vass* was referred to but it was treated as a decision of narrow scope and Lord Eldon's opinion that the Crown cannot waive the right to withhold documents was rejected.

So, in *Donald v. Hart* Lord Justice-Clerk Hope, disallowing a call for a Crown precognition in an action for wrongous imprisonment directed against the Procurator-fiscal because malice did not appear in the issue, was free to say: 'I am not prepared to say that there is no case in which the Court would not, when it was necessary for the ends of justice, and when malice is averred as to the precognition, order production of a precognition.' From that time onwards for a hundred years there is a uniform tract of authority asserting the inherent power of the Court to disregard the Crown's objection to produce a document on grounds of public interest. It is necessary to refer to some only of the more important of these. In *Halcrow v. Shearer* the Court, consisting of Lord President Robertson, Lord Adam, Lord M'Laren and Lord Kinnear, granted diligence to recover a report on the character of a policeman made by the Procurator-fiscal to the Police Committee of the County Council although the Lord Advocate objected that its production would be prejudicial to the public service. It was ordered that the document should be transmitted to the Clerk of Court to lie in retentis and await the further order of the Court. This was done apparently in order to allow the Lord Advocate further time for consideration. The case, however, is not consistent with a rule of law that the Lord Advocate's objection, which had not been withdrawn was conclusive. *Arthur v. Lindsay* was an action for defamation against a Procurator-fiscal in which the pursuer had relevantly averred that the defender had inserted in precognitions statements which had not been made by the pursuer and had shown the precognitions to persons who had no concern with the preparation or the trial of the case. The pursuer moved for diligence to recover the precognitions and the Lord Advocate objected on the ground that it would be prejudicial to the public service. The First Division refused the diligence. Lord President Robertson said: 'They (the precognitions) are even of a high materiality, and it may be that the want of them will be prejudicial or even fatal to the pursuer's claim. But it is undoubted that private rights must sometimes yield to the requirements of general public policy, and it seems to me that the essential confidentiality of communications passing between a Procurator-fiscal and the head of the Criminal Department in Scotland is a paramount consideration.' The Lord President referred to an admission said to have been made by the Crown in *Donald v. Hart* that the general rule might yield to some great and overwhelming necessity but he found that the case did not fall within that description. Lord Adam and Lord M'Laren agreed with the Lord President, and Lord M'Laren added this: 'No doubt the Court has always maintained its power to make such an order in cases of emergency . . . but this is qualified by the fact that no authority has been found where the jurisdiction was in fact exercised, and it is most unlikely that, while the criminal administration remains as at present, the Court ever will exercise this supplemental power.' Lord Kinnear doubted whether the case was not one in which production of the precognition should have been ordered, but he was not prepared to override the Lord Advocate's objection. I think it is true that Lord President Robertson was disposed to hold that the recovery of a Crown precognition should never be ordered if it was opposed by the Lord Advocate, and it is also true that no case has been found where a Crown precognition was recovered when the Lord Advocate objected, but the Lord President did not deny the over-riding power of the court. In *Sheridan v. Peel* Lord President Dunedin, in granting an unopposed motion for diligence to produce, *inter alia*, a Crown precognition, said: 'It is quite clear that where documents sought to be recovered are in the custody of the Lord Advocate or of the Crown officials, the only proper course is to intimate to the Lord Advocate. He may then consent to produce the documents, or refuse to produce them on grounds of public interest. If he refuses to produce them, the Court can be asked to ordain him to do so. There are probably very few instances in which the Court would order the Lord Advocate to produce documents which he thought it inexpedient to produce, but the power to do so has always been recognised as inherent in the Court.' Lord M'Laren, Lord Kinnear and Lord Pearson concurred with the Lord President. In *Dowgray v. Gilmour* Lord President Dunedin referred to the steps which a party might have taken 'for seeing if he could not make the Lord Advocate produce' a document in his possession, and he referred to his remarks in *Sheridan v. Peel*.

The next case is *The Admiralty v. Aberdeen Steam Trawling and Fishing Co*. It arose out of a collision between a trawler and one of His Majesty's ships. The Admiralty objected to a motion for a diligence for the recovery of reports in its possession relating to the collision. The trawler owners argued that the Admiralty 'could not plead that it would be contrary to the public interest to produce the documents called for.' They did not argue that, if they were wrong on this point, the Admiralty's objection should nevertheless be overridden. The Court refused to order production, and the judgments of Lord President Dunedin and Lord Kinnear are important because they held that it is not for the Court to decide whether the production would be detrimental to the public interest and that that is a matter for the Board of Admiralty which alone had before it the necessary information. None of the learned Judges discussed the Court's inherent power to allow production in spite of the Lord Advocate's objection, but it cannot be inferred that they had changed the opinion they had all expressed so recently in *Sheridan v. Peel*. In *Henderson v. McGown* the First Division, reversing Lord Hunter, refused the defenders' crave for diligence to recover income tax returns. This was an action of damages in which the pursuer averred that his partners had falsely accused him of fraudulently understating the profits of the business managed by him. The defenders pleaded veritas. Many authorities, including *Earl v. Vass* and *The Admiralty v. Aberdeen Steam Trawling and Fishing Co*. were cited. The Court, before coming to a decision, consulted with the Judges of the Second Division. Lord President Strathclyde said: 'Undeniably, certain expressions to be found in some of the Opinions in the case of *The Admiralty v. Aberdeen Steam Trawling and Fishing Co* lend countenance to the Solicitor-General's contention, but, although the learned Judges in that case did not find it necessary to reassert the inherent power of this Court to order the recovery of a document, I cannot think that they intended to alter the law as it had previously been laid down and was generally understood, or to part with an inherent right in this Court which each of those Judges had on prior occasions expressly recognised. The true meaning and effect of the decision was that, when the objection is stated by the government department, this

Court will not consider whether the objection is well founded or not; this Court will not consider the merits of that question, but will grant or refuse the diligence at their discretion.' Having said that, he went on to consider whether the Court ought to exercise its inherent power in the case before it and decided that it should not. The same doctrine was reasserted by the Second Division in *Caffrey v. Lord Inverclyde* and by the First Division in *Rogers v. Orr*. It was, therefore, in 1939, a firmly established rule that in Scotland the Court has power to override the objection of a Minister or head of a government department that the production of a document would be contrary to public interest. The power has seldom been exercised and the Courts have emphatically said that it must be used with the greatest caution and only in very special circumstances. It was also a firmly established rule that the Court could not dispute the certificate and that the question whether production would be contrary to the public interest was for the Minister or the department concerned. The Courts have recognised that the refusal to exercise the jurisdiction to override the Crown's certificate may cause great injustice. It is, indeed, impossible to reconcile in all cases public interest and justice to individuals, yet the power is not a phantom power and in the last resort it is a real, though imperfect, safeguard of justice.

It was, however, contended by the Lord Advocate that *Duncan v. Cammell, Laird & Co.* has established that in England there is a rule of law by which the Courts are always bound to give effect to a valid certificate by the responsible Minister, or in some cases the head of a department, that production of a particular document either in itself or as forming an item of a class of documents would be contrary to the public interest, and that the same rule of law prevails in Scotland.

He also contended that the judgment of Lord President Cooper in *M'Kie v. Western Scottish Motor Traction Co.* shows that after *Duncan's* case the Scottish Courts were at least weakening in their assertion of their inherent power.

I will assume the Lord Advocate's contention, so far as the law of England is concerned, is well founded, but so far as the law of Scotland is concerned it cannot, in my opinion, be sustained. *Duncan's* case was an appeal from the English Court of Appeal and in it no question of Scots law fell to be decided. It is not binding on the Scottish Courts nor, of course, on this House sitting as a Court of ultimate appeal in a Scottish case. What was said in *Duncan's* case about the law of Scotland was said *obiter*, and, though it is not binding on the House must receive the most respectful consideration. It appears from the speech of the Lord Chancellor that after the hearing the case of *Earl v. Vass* was brought to his notice It was on that case and on *Admiralty v. Aberdeen Steam Trawling and Fishing Co.* that he formed the opinion that the Scots law was the same as that of England. The tract of authority which I have discussed was not brought to the notice of this House, and in particular the First Division judgment in *Henderson v. McGown*, delivered after consultation of the learned Judges of the Second Division, and its explanation of the Aberdeen case were never mentioned. In these circumstances I feel compelled to say that the Scots law did not receive sufficient consideration and that the observations upon it are of no weight. I cannot agree with Lord Carmont that the law of Scotland is to be altered by a side wind and that we are to have our long-established rules of law overturned by dicta pronounced without adequate citation of Scottish authorities and without debate. I do not find in Lord Cooper's judgment in *M'Kie* any acceptance of *Duncan's* case as determinative of Scots law. His judgment leaves that case over for future consideration and he does not commit himself. The result seems to lead to the conclusion that there is a difference between the law of England and the law of Scotland on an important constitutional question. That is no new thing, for until 1947 it was the law of England that the Crown could not be required to give discovery of any documents in a suit against it—*Thomas v. The Queen* and that was in my opinion, never the rule in Scotland.

It now becomes necessary to consider whether the interlocutor appealed from should be reversed in whole or in part, and the diligence granted in whole or in part. The case is narrow, and I would not have been disposed to interfere if the Courts below had granted the diligence craved. But not one of the learned Judges was in favour of granting the diligence, on the footing that the inherent power of the Court was unaffected by *Duncan's* case, and I do not find that there are sufficient reasons for interfering.

I am for dismissing the appeal."

NOTES

See also *P. Cannon (Garages) Ltd v. Lord Advocate*, 1983 S.L.T. (Sh. Ct.) 50.

The position in England is slightly different—see *Conway v. Rimmer* [1968] A.C. 910. There is a distinction between claims to privilege based on "class" and those based merely on "contents". Thus, in *Air Canada v. Secretary of State for Trade* [1983] 2 A.C. 396 the House of Lords refused to order disclosure of ministerial policy documents on the grounds of "class" based public interest privilege. In *Conway v. Rimmer*, Lord Reid said that:

> "I do not doubt that there are certain classes of documents which ought not to be disclosed whatever their content may be. Virtually everyone agrees that Cabinet minutes and the like ought not to be disclosed until such time as they are only of historical interest. But I do not think that many people would give as the reason that premature disclosure would prevent candour in the Cabinet. To my mind the most important reason is that such disclosure would create or fan ill-informed or captious public or political criticism. The business of government is difficult enough as it is, and no government could contemplate with equanimity the inner workings of the government machine being exposed to the gaze of those ready to criticise without adequate knowledge of the background and perhaps with some axe to grind. And that must, in my view, also apply to all documents concerned with policy making within departments including, it may be, minutes and the like by quite junior officials and correspondence with outside bodies. Further it may be that deliberations about a particular case require protection as much as deliberations about policy. I do not think that it is possible to limit such documents by any definition. But there seems to me to be a wide difference between such documents and routine reports. There may be special reasons for withholding some kinds of routine documents, but I think that the proper test to be applied is to ask, in the language of Lord Simon in *Duncan's* case, whether the withholding of a document because it belongs to a particular class is really 'necessary for the proper functioning of the public service.'"

7. Friel v. Chief Constable of Strathclyde
1981 S.C. 1

Police officers acting on information from an informer obtained a search warrant and searched the property of the petitioner in connection with the theft of a number of cases of whisky. They found nothing. The petitioner, who did not drink alcohol, was a respected local businessman. He believed that the information on which the police acted was given to them falsely and maliciously and without probable cause in order to damage his business standing and reputation. He wished to raise an action of damages against the informer, whose identity was unknown to him.

The petitioner therefore sought an order under section 1 of the Administration of Justice (Scotland) Act 1972 for the recovery of documents in the possession of the police force revealing the name of the informer. It was contended for the Chief Constable that there were insufficient averments to justify making an order. For the Lord Advocate it was contended that it would be injurious to the public interest to disclose the documents.

LORD MAXWELL: "This is a petition under section 1 of the Administration of Justice (Scotland) Act 1972 for an order, principally for recovery before the raising of an action of certain documents in the hands of the police. There is a reference in the petition to common law, as well as to the Act, but counsel for the petitioner accepted that he could not succeed unless he could bring himself within the Act. The petition is opposed by the Chief Constable of the force concerned and also by the Lord Advocate.

The petition narrates that on an evening in February 1979 officers of the Strathclyde Police called at the petitioner's home and stated that their visit was in connection with the theft of cases of whisky and that they had reason to believe that the cases were in the petitioner's house, garden, or garage. They produced a search warrant and carried out a search, which proved fruitless. It is stated in the petition *inter alia* that the petitioner does not drink alcohol and has had no dealing in whisky and that the petitioner is a respected local businessman. The petitioner further avers: [His Lordship quoted from paragraphs 3 and 4 of the petition, and continued]. I was also referred to two letters addressed to the petitioner's solicitors by the Strathclyde Police. The first of these is a letter of February 19, 1979 and reads:—'I refer to your letter of 14 instant regarding a search of your named client's premises by C.I.D. officers, I can only advise you that a consignment of whisky has been stolen and information came from a very reliable and respectable source that cases of what appeared to be whisky had been stored in your client's shed some time previously and were still therein. A search warrant was obtained and three cases of lemonade and some cans of lager were found in the shed. I am sure that your client as a law abiding citizen will recognise that the Police acted in good faith.' The second letter, which is dated March 9, reads as follows:—'I refer to your letter of February 21, 1979 and previous correspondence with Chief Superintendent McCallum of Greenock. No insinuation was intended nor is such apparent to me in the letter of reply dated February 19, 1979 with regard to the property found in the shed at your client's premises. The search warrant in question was obtained on the basis of information which, although subsequently found to be incorrect as occurs on occasions, appeared to be given in good faith. It may well be that you can justify your allegation against the informant, but the negative search of your client's premises while clarifying the issue for the Police does not of itself suggest that the information was maliciously given. You will appreciate that information which comes into the hands of the Police must be treated with confidentiality, irrespective of its source and only weighty considerations of public interest would warrant the Chief Constable in exercising his discretion to divulge it. I regret that your client is aggrieved, but in the circumstances I am unable to accede to your request to divulge the information you seek.' Without going into the details of the calls which are now sought to be enforced it was conceded that in substance what the petitioner seeks is an order to recover documents revealing the name of the person who gave the information on which the police proceeded. It is not suggested that the petitioner relies on any factual matter beyond that to which I have made reference.

Answers have been lodged on behalf of the police admitting that on information received they obtained a search warrant and made an unsuccessful search of the petitioner's premises for stolen whisky. They also state 'it is contrary to the public interest to divulge information given in confidence as to which matter the Police would follow the advice and instructions of the Lord Advocate.' The Lord Advocate also lodged Answers to which I shall refer in a moment.

Counsel for the Chief Constable, apart from certain criticisms of the details of the 'calls', confined his argument to the question of whether there is enough averred to justify an order under section 1 of the 1972 Act taking also into account the letters to which I was referred. Section 1 of the 1972 Act in subsection (1) is as follows:—'Without prejudice to the existing powers of the Court of Session and of the sheriff court those Courts shall have power, subject to the provisions of subsection (4) of this section, to order the inspection, photographing, preservation, custody and detention of documents and other property (including, where appropriate, land) which appear to the court to be property as to which any question may relevantly arise in any existing civil proceedings before that Court or in civil proceedings which are likely to be brought, and to order the production and recovery of any such property, the taking of samples thereof and the carrying out of any experiment thereon or therewith.' The question at issue relates to the words 'likely to be brought.' At one point counsel suggested that a Court can only say that proceedings 'are likely to be brought' if he can aver facts which would make an action relevant if averred on a Record. I think that this is probably going too far. I disagree with counsel for the petitioner that such a contention would render the section, as regards proceedings not already in Court, meaningless. The section is to a large extent, at least, concerned with the preservation of evidence and other corporeal property as opposed to the ascertainment of facts, but I do not think that a discretion to give an order in respect that proceedings are likely to be brought can be read as requiring full averments of fact which would make a relevant action. There is a real question, however, as to whether it can be said that proceedings are likely to be brought where, as here, it is clear that they cannot be brought unless the order is granted. That is to say, where the ascertainment of matters essential to the bringing of proceedings, such as the identity of the prospective defender, is itself the object of the application. I do not consider it necessary or desirable to determine that question in this case. I was referred to an English case *Dunning v. United Liverpool Hospital Board of Governors* [1973] 1 W.L.R. 586, dealing with a similarly, but not identically, worded English Act. This is a case which incidentally I have been informed has been over-ruled on other grounds. My impression from that case is that the judges would have given an affirmative answer to the question in certain circumstances. James L.J. however, said:—'In order to take advantage of the section the applicant for relief must disclose the nature of the claim he intends to make and show, not only the intention of making it, but also that there is a reasonable basis for making it. Ill-founded, irresponsible and speculative allegations or allegations based merely on hope would not provide a reasonable basis for an intended claim in subsequent proceedings.' I think that this would equally apply to an application for an order under section 1 of the 1972 Act on the ground that the proceedings 'are likely to be brought.' Assuming that the petitioner can use the section to discover his defender, as matter of degree I am of the opinion that he has not shown that proceedings are likely to be brought.

It is well settled that an informer is not liable for a false accusation, unless he is acting both from malice and without probable cause and that the presumption is that he has acted in good faith. (Glegg on Reparation (4th ed.) 195). I was referred to a number of authorities on this matter, but need not cite them as the principle is not disputed. Senior counsel for the petitioner frankly admitted that he did not know and would not know unless I granted the order sought whether he could eventually make a case of malice and want of probable cause. He submitted, however, that having regard to what is said in the petition, particularly about the respectable character of the petitioner and the fact that he does not drink, and having regard to the police admission in the letters that they proceeded on information from a respectable source, a probability of malice and want of probable cause could be sufficiently inferred for present purposes. I do not agree. The fact that the police proceeded on information to make an investigation which turned out to be without justification does not, in my opinion, make it probable that the information was given maliciously. It may, for example, have been given under wholly innocent error or it may have been misunderstood or misinterpreted by the police or it may have been correct information from which the police drew a prima facie inference which was not in fact warranted. For these reasons, apart altogether from the Lord Advocate's objection, I would have refused this motion.

In his Answers to the petition the Lord Advocate states *inter alia*—'The Lord Advocate objects to the disclosure of said documents on the grounds that to do so would be injurious to the public interest. In so doing the Lord Advocate exercises the discretion of withholding documents afforded by the common law relating to Crown privilege expressly preserved by the provisos to section 47 of the Crown Proceedings Act 1947 and section 1(4) of the Administration of Justice (Scotland) Act 1972, which are referred to for their terms. Explained that said documents fall into a class of documents which must be afforded protection from disclosure on the grounds of public policy in order to enable the detection and prosecution of crime in Scotland to function sufficiently and to allow citizens to offer assistance to the agencies of law subject to public disclosure at a later date. For these reasons the Lord Advocate objects to the recovery of the documents.'

Counsel for the petitioner asked me to override the Lord Advocate's objection. On this matter I was given a most interesting and elaborate citation of authority going back to the early nineteenth century. I trust counsel will excuse me for not reviewing the authorities, but I consider it unnecessary to do so, since there is really no dispute on the law as it now stands except perhaps in emphasis.

It is accepted that the appropriate Minister can take objection to the production of documents in the hands of a public body on grounds of public interest. It is accepted in particular that the Lord Advocate can take objection to the production of documents in the hands of the police (*Rogers v. Orr*, 1939 S.C. 492). It is accepted that the Court retains a discretionary power to order production of documents notwithstanding such an objection (*Glasgow Corporation v. Central Land Board*, 1956 S.C. (H.L.) 1). It is accepted that this power has, in practice, rarely, if ever, been exercised. It is accepted that the Lord Advocate's objection can, as here, competently be based on the public interest in non-disclosure of a class of documents as opposed to a particular document.

Counsel for the petitioner contended that, where the objection is taken in respect of a class of documents, the Court, in considering whether to override the objection, can take into account not only the interests of the particular petitioner, but the interests of the public as a whole in so far as other members of the public might find themselves in the same position as the petitioner. I agree with that submission.

It was suggested for the petitioner that the Court's function was to balance competing interests. That is, I think, correct only in a limited sense. The Court does not, in my opinion, balance competing interests in the same way, for example, as it seeks to balance convenience in relation to interdict, and the reason for that is that the Lord Advocate has access to information which may not be available to the Court and the Court is bound to accept his assertion that there is an aspect of public interest to be protected. The matter was put thus by Lord Radcliffe in *Glasgow Corporation v. Central Land Board*. I do not understand that the existence of the power involves that, in Scotland any more than in England, it is open to the Court to dispute with the Minister whether his view that production would be contrary to the public interest is well founded, or to arrive at a view contradictory of his, that production would not, in fact, be at all injurious to that interest. If weight is given to the argument that the Minister in forming his view may have before him a range of considerations that is not open to the Court and that he is not under any obligation to set out those considerations in public. I think that it must follow that the Minister's view must be accepted by the Court as incapable of being displaced by its own opinion. I understand the decision in *The Admiralty v. Aberdeen Steam Trawling & Fishing Co.*, 1909 S.C. 335 as a decision precisely to that effect and I do not think that there is anything in the later case of *Henderson v. McGown*, 1916 S.C. 821 which conflicts with the earlier case as so understood. The power reserved to the Court is therefore a power to order production, even though the public interest is to some extent affected prejudicially. This amounts to a recognition that more than one aspect of public interest may have to be surveyed in reviewing the question whether a document which would be available to a party in a civil suit between parties is not to be available to the party engaged in a suit with the Crown. The interests of Government, for which the minister should speak with full authority do not exhaust the public interest. Another aspect of that interest is seen in the need that impartial justice should be done in the Courts of law, not least between citizen and Crown and that a litigant who has a case to maintain should not be deprived of the means of its proper presentation by anything less than a weighty public reason. It does not seem to me unreasonable to expect that the Court would be better qualified than the Minister to measure the importance of such principles in application to the particular case that is before it.'

The argument was put thus for the petitioner. If the Lord Advocate's objection is sustained as regards this class of document it means that those members of the public who find themselves, or may find themselves, in the petitioner's position are in effect being deprived of access to the Courts and there is an overriding public interest that all persons should have access to the Court. I think that is a somewhat emotive and inaccurate way of stating the matter. The petitioner has access to the Courts. What he is being deprived of is the exercise of the Court's power to order others to produce confidential documents. It may follow from this that he is unable to raise an action which might otherwise be available to him, but that happens frequently and from many causes and is not equivalent to a deprivation of access to the Courts.

In my opinion it is plain that the risk to law enforcement on which the Lord Advocate relies could be a very serious risk indeed. It is not for me to measure the risk because I do not have the information to do it, but I could not override the Lord Advocate's objection unless I was satisfied that there is another public interest at stake so substantial that the risk to law enforcement must take second place. I am completely satisfied that the risk that perhaps in this case and perhaps occasionally in future cases a person, who has been the subject of malicious slander by an informer, will find it impossible to pursue a civil remedy against the informer does not represent a matter of public interest which outweighs the risk on which the Lord Advocate founds. I shall accordingly, for this reason also, refuse the motion.

I should add two points. First, counsel for the petitioner relied heavily on certain *dicta* in *Henderson v. Robertson* (1853) 15 D. 292. I do not think that the case assists him since it was the informer in that case, not the Lord Advocate, who sought to invoke the public interest. Second, one of the calls in the petition, in addition to calling for certain documents, proceeds as follows:—'and in any event an order ordaining the said Chief Constable to disclose the names and addresses of any informants referred to in the answers and the information relating to the petitioner upon which the said warrant was applied for and granted.' Even if I had been disposed to grant the other calls or any part of them I would not have granted this call. In my Opinion it is clear that there is nothing in section 1 of the 1972 Act which authorises the Court to order anybody to disclose anything. The section is concerned with the preservation or production of things, including documents, and in my opinion it has nothing to do with ordering persons to disclose information which is available to them. I do not agree with the submission of counsel for the petitioner that this is a mere technical distinction. It is accordingly unnecessary for me to decide in what circumstances, even without objection by the Lord Advocate, it might or might not be competent to order disclosure of names nor is it necessary for me to refer to certain authorities cited to me on that matter."

8. A.B. v. Glasgow and West of Scotland Blood Transfusion Service
1993 S.L.T. 36

LORD MORISON: "This is an application by a person who avers that he became infected with human immune deficiency virus as a result of blood transfusions administered to him in 1986 by the respondents, the Glasgow and West of Scotland Blood Transfusion Service. The petitioner proceeds upon provisions contained in section 1 of the Administration of Justice (Scotland) Act 1972, and in effect he seeks an order of the court for disclosure to him and his legal advisers of the name and address of the person who donated the blood which was transfused. The petitioner's only purpose in seeking such an order is to enable him to raise an action of damages against the donor, on the ground that he negligently failed to disclose to the respondents his high risk of HIV infection, negligently failed to complete accurately a health questionnaire which donors are asked to complete, and negligently donated blood for transfusion knowing that there was a high risk of it being infected. If the donor were voluntarily to disclose his identity to the petitioner, there would be no need to obtain an order from the court, but he has not done so yet, and the petitioner is accordingly unable to raise an action against him, although he is suing the respondents on the ground that their screening procedures were inadequate.

The case came before the court on December 13, 1989 when there was appearance both for the respondents and for the Lord Advocate, on whom the petition had also been served. It was continued for a week to enable the Lord Advocate to consider his position in relation to the public interest which it was submitted might be affected by the disclosure sought. At the continued hearing on December 20, the application was opposed both by the respondents and by the Secretary of State for Scotland as representing the public interest by virtue of his responsibility under the National Health Service (Scotland) Act 1978 to maintain and promote that service.

The Secretary of State opposes the disclosure sought, on the ground that it would be injurious to the public interest. That injury is particularised in answers to the petition lodged by him as follows: "These documents [i.e. those which disclose the donor's identity] . . . fall within the class of documents which ought to be afforded protection on the ground of public policy in order to ensure that there is and continues to be a sufficient supply of donor blood to the health service nationally. Such supply is required for necessary and often emergency medical procedures in the treatment of illness (including injury). The Secretary of State has duly considered the matter and has concluded that any infringement of donor anonymity would put such supply at risk. Prospective donors, he has concluded, would be discouraged from providing donations by reason of apprehension that they might be subjected to legal claims (whether justified or not) on the basis of some adverse effect resulting from the use of the blood for transfusion purposes.

It is to be noted that this conclusion relates to any infringement whatever of donor anonymity. The disclosure which the petitioner seeks is confined to himself and his legal advisers. It is not to be assumed, and it was not contended, that if the petitioner raised an action against the donor, the donor's name would necessarily be disclosed to the public. The attitude of prospective donors upon which the Secretary of State is relying is exclusively the apprehension that they might be sued, justifiably or not, in relation to their conduct, not that their names might thereby be publicised.

Such apprehension is one which anybody whose conduct affects other persons might experience. In the case of blood donors there seems to me to be every reason to suppose that they are actuated by the very highest motives of altruism and commitment to the public welfare. It is not immediately apparent to me why such persons would be deterred from pursuing these motives by an apprehension that they might be unjustifiably sued. If on the other hand there are any persons who give blood without due regard to their responsibilities, the public interest would plainly be served if they were discouraged from doing so. But it was conceded on behalf of the petitioner that I was not entitled to investigate the validity of the conclusion expressed by the Secretary of State unless it appeared that the conclusion was patently unreasonable or had been expressed on an erroneous basis, and this obviously cannot be said in the present case. In view of the observations contained in the speeches of Lord Normand and Lord Keith in the case of *Glasgow Corporation v. Central Land Board*, I consider that this concession was rightly made. Whilst in Scotland the court has the inherent power to override the objection of a responsible minister based on the public interest, that power is not to be exercised upon the basis of an assessment of the merits of the objection. Thus in the present case there may well be matters upon which the Secretary of State has been informed of which I am not aware and which are not contained in the information before me. For present purposes I must accept that 'any infringement of donor anonymity' would put at risk the sufficiency of the national supply of donor blood.

On this assumption, the scope for any reasoned argument as to whether or not the Secretary of State's objection should be overridden is limited. On behalf of the petitioner it was submitted that his private right to sue the donor was of such 'magnitude' (to use the word employed by Lord Moncrieff in *Rogers v. Orr*, 1939 S.L.T at p.406) as to prevail over the public interest advanced by the Secretary of State. But the only right which the petitioner seeks to assert in the proceedings which he proposes is the right to claim damages, and although his claim is a very large one, it seems to me to be impossible to hold that such a pecuniary interest should prevail over a material risk to the sufficiency of the national supply of blood for purposes of transfusion. It was submitted also that there were other persons apart from the petitioner whose right to claim damages would similarly be affected if disclosure were not made. I can conceive of cases in which such a consideration might be material, but I was not informed that there is a large number of persons likely to be prejudiced by nondisclosure to them of the names of donors, and I do not think that this matter substantially affects the issue. It was further submitted that it was a matter of public interest that the administration of justice should not be selective. This is undoubtedly true, but such an argument could be advanced in any case where disclosure of relevant information is subject to ministerial objection and counsel were unable to inform me of any case in which such an objection had been overridden by the court. However I entirely agree that it is offensive to any notion of justice that persons should be deprived of the ability to claim damages from those by whose negligence they have been injured. If public policy requires this, it seems to me that it would be reasonable for public policy to provide also some alternative means of compensation.

Counsel for the petitioner also pointed out that the extent of the alleged risk to the public blood supply was not indicated by the objection. Contrary to submissions made on behalf of the Secretary of State, I consider that this is indeed a relevant consideration in determination of the issue which is before me. It seems to me that it would be much easier for the court to override an objection based on a slight risk to the public interest than one based on a substantial probability of damage to that interest. But it is obvious that the consequences of a national deficiency in the supply of blood for transfusion would be appalling. If there is any material risk of such an occurrence resulting from disclosure of the donor's name in the present case—and this is what I have to assume—it seems to me to be clear that the objection to that disclosure must prevail over the interests advanced on the petitioner's behalf.

For these reasons I shall refuse to pronounce the order which the petitioner seeks. It was agreed that if this were my determination, I should refuse the motion, dismiss the petition and order the return to the respondents of the documents recovered from them. I shall issue an interlocutor in these terms.

I should add that the respondents advanced arguments similar to those of the Secretary of State, to support their submission that the donor's identity should not be revealed to the petitioner. The respondents are providing a public service and they have an obvious duty (subject only to an order of the court) to promote that valuable service and to maintain the confidentiality of persons upon whom they rely to provide it. Nevertheless I consider that the court's approach to their objection would be different from that which applies to a ministerial objection based on the public interest. In particular, it would in my opinion be legitimate for the court to consider and assess the merits of the respondents' objection in light of the nature of the work which they perform, so as to determine whether or not the petitioner's interest should prevail over that objection. This would involve consideration of the quality of the evidence upon which the respondents rely, and it might also involve a determination whether their own procedures are adequate to support the immunity which they say ought to be accorded to donors. However on the view which I have formed in respect of the Secretary of State's objection, it is unnecessary for me to reach any conclusion as to the respondents' contentions, and I refrain from doing so."

NOTES

Following *Conway v. Rimmer*, both Scots and English law recognise the power of the courts, at least in some circumstances, to overrule a Ministerial certificate claiming public interest immunity. In Scotland, the starting point must be that a ministerial certificate that the public interest will be damaged by recovery must be taken at face value. Thereafter the court must decide whether that certificate outweighs the fundamental public interest that justice be done. In *Hemming v. H.M.A.*, 1998 S.L.T. 213 production of police statements was ordered in the face of such a plea by the Lord Advocate. See also *H.M.A. v. Ward*, 1993 S.L.T. 1202, and below on the recovery of evidence in criminal cases.

The question remains whether public interest immunity, properly so-called, applies to bodies other than the Crown. In *D. v. National Society for the Prevention of Cruelty to Children* [1978] A.C. 171 the House of Lords granted immunity in respect of reports made to the Society on the ground that disclosure would deter informants from coming forward and would therefore hamper the important work of the society. However, in the Scottish case of *Higgins v. Burton*, 1968 S.L.T. (Notes) 52 it was held that records of a "Child Guidance Clinic" were not covered by public interest immunity and could be recovered. Lord Avonside said:

> "I would tend strongly to be of the opinion that there is no such thing as public interest in the sense in which that phrase is used in our Court unless the interest be a national one and put forward either by a Minister of the Crown or by the Lord Advocate. If the scope of such a claim was widened I can see no end to the repercussions which might arise and I would have thought that it should be strictly confined to the sources I have indicated. Even then, as is well-known, the courts in Scotland have always refused to be bound by a Minister's certificate, and its effect depends on the discretion of the Court."

In *W.P. v. Tayside Regional Council*, 1989 S.C.L.R. 165, a foster mother sued the Regional Council for damages having contracted Hepatitis B from a child whose natural mother was an intravenous drug user. She sought to recover records from the Council Social Work department in order to throw light upon the Council's state of knowledge as to the natural mother's health. Lord Sutherland granted the motion to recover the records holding that in this case the public interest in seeing justice done far outweighed the public interest in favour of confidentiality. He added the following comments about the nature of public interest privilege in Scotland:

> "Since 1968 there have been a number of decisions in England in which public interest privilege has been extended beyond national government to local authorities and to other bodies. In my view decisions of courts in England in this field have to be treated with some caution. In the first place, it is only comparatively recently that the English courts have been prepared to hold themselves not bound by a ministerial certificate. Furthermore, in certain types of proceedings in England, there appears always to have been a privilege attached to certain documents and I refer in particular to wardship proceedings. In the case of *D v. NSPCC* public interest privilege was extended to the situation where a litigant sought to recover from the NSPCC the name of an informer. It was held that because disclosure of the name of an informer would gravely damage the work of the NSPCC, public interest privilege should be extended to cover that situation . . . It is perhaps noteworthy that in the case of *Science Research Council* [1980] A.C. 1028, Lord Scarman regretted the passing of the term 'Crown Privilege' which in his view at least emphasised the very restricted area of public interest immunity. As he pointed out, the immunity

exists to protect information the secrecy of which is essential to the proper working of the government of the state. Whatever may be the position in England I would respectfully adopt what was said by Lord Avonside in *Higgins*, and had it been necessary for the purposes of my decision in this case I would also have been inclined to hold that public interest privilege in the strict sense is confined to the privilege of the Crown and the Lord Advocate. I do not, however, consider that it is really necessary to divide confidentiality into separate compartments, namely public interest privilege and private confidentiality. The interest of an individual in his own privacy is in itself a public interest. Any breach of confidentiality which infringes the individual's right to his own privacy is accordingly to some extent at least a breach of public interest. What has to be balanced in every case is the breach of public interest against the interest that is seen in the need that impartial justice should be done in the courts of law and that a litigant who has a case to maintain should not be deprived of the means of its proper presentation by anything less than a weighty public reason. It is therefore apparent that each case will depend upon its own particular facts. If there is only going to be a minimal breach of the privacy of an individual the public interest in maintaining that privacy may be overcome without too much difficulty by the public interest in maintaining the impartiality of justice between litigants. If, on the other hand, a Minister of the Crown certifies that disclosure of a particular piece of information would be gravely prejudicial to the national security, the court would be very slow to hold that this public interest should be outweighed by the private requirement of a litigant. It has always been accepted in Scotland that there is no such thing as absolute privilege and in any case the court may overrule an attempt to prevent the disclosure of information even though there are strong grounds put forward in the public interest for preventing that information being disclosed. That being so, there appears to me to be no valid reason for a rigid compartmentalisation between public interest privilege on the one hand and confidentiality on the other. The ultimate position taken up by counsel for the respondents was that the law of Scotland recognises a claim for confidentiality if it is strong enough to outweigh any interest to favour recovery. I would agree with this proposition and it does not seem to me to be necessary for the resolution of the problem in any particular case to decide whether or not there should be a division between public interest privilege and ordinary confidentiality which depends upon public interest for its existence. Thus if a case arose in Scotland in which a party sought to recover from the RSPCC the name of an informer, it would only be in very exceptional circumstances that such a motion would be granted. This would not be because public interest privilege is extended to the RSPCC, but because the nature of the work of that body is such that their claim to confidentiality would be awarded a high degree of protection."

In a sense, all forms of privilege or immunity are based on a public interest. The privilege attaching to communications between husband and wife appear to be based on the view that it would be destructive of the sanctity of the marriage bond to require spouses to disclose information which has passed between them. Similarly, the confidentiality which applies between solicitor and client appears to be based on the public interest in ensuring that everyone enjoys access to impartial legal advice without fear that disclosures to the agent may be admissible in court. Does Lord Sutherland's opinion in *W.P.*'s case imply that confidentiality may be claimed by anyone who can show a similar public interest in confidentiality?

In criminal cases, the public interest will almost always be in favour of disclosure (compare Sir Richard Scott in his Report of the Inquiry into the Export of Defence Equipment and Dual-use goods to Iraq and Related Prosecutions (HMSO, 1996). para. G18.83). However, the court will allow recovery only where the relevance of the documents to the defence case has been made abundantly plain.

9. McLeod, Petitioner
1998 S.L.T. 233

An accused person was charged on indictment with offences under the Misuse of Drugs Act 1971 and with selling alcohol to underage persons at a club occupied and managed by him. The club was raided by the police after a period of surveillance. The police detained and interviewed a large number of people, including the accused, during the raid and these persons' answers to police questioning were recorded on *pro forma* questionnaires. Only 30 of the persons who were interviewed were cited as Crown witnesses but the Crown had, at the accused's request, supplied a list of the other persons who had been interviewed. The Crown rejected the accused's request for disclosure of all of the questionnaires on the basis that they were privileged. The accused thereafter petitioned the High Court for commission and diligence to recover the 77 questionnaires on the ground that recovery was necessary for the proper preparation and presentation of the accused's defence. It was averred that difficulties had been experienced in precognoscing some of the detainees because they had no precise recollection of their answers to the questionnaires due to the lapse of time or because they had been drinking at the time. The petition was dismissed by a single judge and the accused appealed by way of petition to the *nobile officium*, arguing that in principle all statements and similar material generated in the course of an investigation leading to charges being brought should be made available, in absence of special reasons like the protection of an informer.

THE LORD JUSTICE GENERAL (RODGER): "In the Scottish system the accused's representatives have an opportunity to investigate the case against him. They can precognosce witnesses and, if need be, apply to the sheriff to precognosce them on oath. Another important aspect of our system derives from the role of the Crown, as it has been understood down the years. That role has been discussed in a number of cases. In *Slater v. H.M.A.* one of the grounds of appeal was that the Crown had not included the names of three individuals on the list of witnesses appended to the indictment. In dealing with that point Lord Justice General Clyde said (at 1928 J.C., p.103; 1928 S.L.T., pp.604–605): 'An accused person has no right to demand that the prosecution should—in addition to supplying him with the names and addresses of all the witnesses who may be called—communicate to him all the results, material or immaterial, of the investigations made by the Procurator-fiscal under direction of the Crown Office. No doubt a very different question would arise, if it could be shown that the prosecution had betrayed its duty by insisting in a charge in the knowledge of the existence of reliable evidence proving the innocence of the person accused which it concealed from him. Such a proceeding would constitute a violation of every tradition observed in the Scottish Crown Office. To assume, without evidence, that the responsible officers of the Crown concealed from an accused person anything known to them which it was material for him to know would be wholly unwarrantable; and nothing of that sort is suggested on behalf of the appellant.'

This passage positively affirms that an accused person has no right to demand that the Crown should communicate to him all the results of the investigation, irrespective of whether they are material or not. On the other hand the concluding sentence clearly recognises that it would be wrong for the Crown to conceal anything known to them which it was 'material' for the accused to know.

I have already quoted the passage from the opinion of Lord Cooper in *Downie* delivered in January 1952. Two months later in *Smith v. H.M.A.*, Lord Justice Clerk Thomson had occasion to comment on the role of the Crown. Having explained the duty of the police authorities in reporting to the procurator fiscal and the procurator fiscal's duty to investigate, the Lord Justice Clerk said (at 1952 J.C., p.72; 1952 S.L.T., p.289): 'If it is decided to prosecute, an indictment is prepared. The primary purpose of an indictment is to state the charge against the accused and to give the names of the witnesses and the productions on which the Crown rely to prove their case. A practice has grown up of including in the indictment the names of witnesses and productions which may have a bearing on the innocence of the accused. Just how far this practice goes has never been defined and indeed is hardly capable of definition. Obviously it is a question of circumstances and must turn on the nature of the case and the information available to the Crown.'

He then quoted part of the passage from *Slater* and continued:

> 'There can be little doubt, however, that the tendency in recent years has been for the defence to expect from the Crown, and indeed for the Crown to afford, a measure of assistance beyond what would have been in the contemplation of any previous generation of Scots lawyers. However that may be, the Crown does nowadays honour the practice of including witnesses and productions beyond what is strictly necessary for its own case.
>
> This practice springs from the Crown's recognition that it has opportunities for investigation which are not enjoyed by the defence. It is based also on the presumption of innocence and the consideration that an accused man is entitled to the benefit of the doubt. But the practice has not been pressed so far as to mean that the Crown is under any obligation to discover a line of defence. If, in a stabbing affray, the information

before the Crown showed that both assailant and victim had knives in their hands, it would be the duty of the Crown to include in the indictment the knife which was in the victim's hand and the witnesses who can speak to it. But, if there is nothing in the material before the Crown to suggest a possible defence of self-defence, it would appear unnecessary for the Crown to include something in the indictment just because it might have a possible bearing on such a defence if taken. It is a question of degree.'

This passage has been widely accepted as encapsulating the modern understanding of the duty of the Crown, not simply to put forward witnesses who support the Crown case but to include in the list other witnesses whose testimony may not be in line with the Crown case but which may have a bearing on the innocence of the accused and so may help the court to form a balanced view of the evidence relating to the incident in question. Indeed the representative of the Crown not infrequently leads the evidence of some at least of those witnesses. It was therefore all the more surprising that in *Higgins v. H.M.A.*, 1990 S.C.C.R. at p.269, when delivering the opinion of this court, Lord Cowie should have declared that 'there is no obligation on the Crown to disclose any information in their possession which would tend to exculpate the accused. Very often the Crown of their own free will are prepared to give that information'.

The Lord Advocate of the day repudiated this passage as an accurate depiction of the duty of the Crown and successive Lord Advocates have done too. Indeed in *H.M.A. v. Ward* the advocate depute expressly stated that the Crown did not wish to be associated with the statement in *Higgins* and in the present hearing also the Solicitor General rejected the statement. The written submissions for the Crown contain a succinct statement of the Crown's position on this point: 'The Crown accepts that it has an obligation to disclose any information which supports the defence case. This duty has long been set out in the Book of Regulations for the Procurator Fiscal Service and it extends to information which supports any known or stateable defence or which undermines the Crown case.'

In the circumstances I am satisfied that the passage in *Higgins* does not accurately reflect the duty of the Crown as it has long been understood both by the Crown and by the courts. Indeed the idea that the Crown could proceed with a trial without disclosing to the defence matters which would tend to exculpate the accused is wholly inconsistent with the basic premise of our law that the accused is entitled to a fair trial. In my view therefore this court should disapprove the passage in *Higgins*.

Counsel was ready to give the Crown credit for the generous way in which they interpreted their duty and he acknowledged the spirit of co-operation which they displayed. At the risk of sounding churlish, he nonetheless said that it was time for our system to stop relying on what he described as the 'paternalistic' attitude of the Crown and that the court should instead declare that accused persons have the right to have all the documents in a criminal investigation—and in particular any police statements—produced. There is, however, nothing paternalistic in the approach of the Crown. The Crown have no interest in securing the conviction of any but the guilty and must be astute to avoid asking for the conviction of the innocent. When the Crown provide the defence with information which supports the defence case, they are therefore not acting out of a sense of charity but out of an awareness of their duty in a system which is tenacious of the presumption of innocence and jealous of the right of accused persons to a fair trial. The relatively small role which applications for the production of documents have played in our system is indeed powerful testimony to the fact that as a rule the Crown have discharged this duty. I know of no reason to suppose that the Crown's attitude will change or that they will be less punctilious in fulfilling their duty in future.

Our system of criminal procedure therefore proceeds on the basis that the Crown have a duty at any time to disclose to the defence information in their possession which would tend to exculpate the accused. For his part counsel accepts that by and large the Crown perform that duty. Equally, as was seen in *Downie* and has been seen repeatedly over the years since then in cases such as *Ward*, the Crown will respond to specific requests from the defence for information or for the production of statements or other items where the defence can explain why they would be material to the defence. Counsel did not dispute that the Crown acted in this way or indeed that an offer to respond to any such request had been made in the present case. Again, when they respond in this way, the Crown are not merely acting out of kindness but are performing their duty to impart information which supports the defence case in the particular situation where they have been made aware of the possible significance of these items for the defence of the accused.

In a system which operates in this way there should for the most part be no need for an accused person to invoke the petition procedure to recover documents whose possible exculpatory effect can be appreciated by the Crown, whether spontaneously or when the defence ask for them. In such a system also it can be expected that the defence will have access to the documents which are material to the preparation and presentation of their case. If, however, it emerges at the trial that something has gone wrong and a material statement or other document comes to light at that stage, our procedure is well able to afford the necessary remedy, whether by adjournment, permission to lead additional evidence or, in an extreme case, by desertion of the diet. Indeed even supposing the statement or document came to light after conviction, the appeal court could allow an appeal on the ground of a miscarriage of justice if there were a reasonable explanation as to why evidence about it had not been heard at the trial (sections 106 and 175 of the Criminal Procedure (Scotland) Act 1995, as amended). Applications for the grant of a commission and diligence for the recovery of documents constitute only one part of this larger system for safeguarding the accused's right to a fair trial. This wider context has to be kept in mind in considering in what circumstances an application of this kind should be granted.

Like others in the past I am conscious of the difficulty of formulating the test which the court should apply when asked to order the production of documents in a criminal case where the charges are set out relatively succinctly and the only formal documents indicating a line of defence will be any transcript of the accused's judicial examination and any special defence or notice of incrimination. I consider, however, that an accused person who asks the court to take the significant step of granting a diligence for the recovery of documents, whether from the Crown or from a third party, does require to explain the basis upon which he asks the court to order the haver to produce the documents. The court does not grant such orders unless it is satisfied that they will serve a proper purpose and that it is in the interests of justice to grant them. This in turn means that the court must be satisfied that an order for the production of the particular documents would be likely to be of material assistance to the proper preparation or presentation of the accused's defence. The accused will need to show how the documents relate to the charge or charges and the proposed defence to them. Such a requirement imposes no great burden on an accused person or his advisers: the averments in the petition may be relatively brief and the court will take account of any relevant information supplied at the hearing. Moreover such a test is, I believe, consistent both with our native authority in cases such as *Slater*, *Smith* and *Hasson* and with the approach of the European Court [of Human Rights] in *Edwards* and *Benendoun*. How the test is to be applied in particular situations is best left to the court to work out as cases arise. I can record, however, that the Solicitor General accepted that the production of the police statements in *Hemming* would have been justified on this basis. He also accepted that it would probably be easier for an accused person to persuade the court that the test was satisfied in the case of police statements of Crown witnesses than in the case of police statements of other persons.

NOTES

The test laid down in *McLeod* is a strict one, and in practice full averments will be required in a petition seeking recovery of documents. The court will require to be satisfied that the documents sought will be of material assistance to the preparation of the defence case, and that they are required for a relevant legal purpose. See *e.g. Hoekstra v. H.M.A. (No. 6)*, 2001 S.L.T. 632. It should be noted that, while the defence does not have any positive duty of disclosure, they cannot suppress material obtained by instructing an expert report. In *H.M.A. v. Wilson*, unreported, June 15, 2001, High Court of Justiciary (Lord Reed), it was held that an expert witness cited by the defence may also be cited by another party, or by the Crown, if the defence decide not to lead the expert at trial. Confidentiality attaches to evidence, not to witnesses.

10. Maan v. H.M.A.
2001 S.L.T. 408

An order for production was made where an accused person charged with assault petitioned for commission and diligence for the recovery of certain parts of the criminal records of a number of Crown witnesses. The accused intended to plead self defence and to attack the credibility of the witnesses by questioning them in relation to previous acts of violence.

LORD MCFADYEN: "[23] The context in which the issues raised in this petition fall to be considered, in my view, is the undisputed right of the petitioner to a fair trial. Before the incorporation of the Convention into Scots law, albeit after consideration of Convention jurisprudence, it was recognised in *McLeod* (per Lord Justice General Rodger at p.98D (p.244F)) that Scottish criminal procedure proceeds on the basis that: 'the Crown have a duty at any time to disclose to the defence information in their possession which would tend to exculpate the accused'. Under the Convention, that is a requirement of article 6(1) (see for example *Rowe*, pp.29–30, para. 60). The duty extends, in my opinion, not only to information which bears directly on the guilt or innocence of the accused, but also to information which has a more indirect bearing, such as information which would tend to undermine the credibility of a Crown witness. That appears to have been recognised in *Jespers* (at para. 58).

[24] The accused's right to disclosure of relevant evidence is not absolute, and may have to yield to competing considerations. That was recognised in *McLeod* and also in *Rowe* (at p.31, para. 61). Where a competing consideration is put forward by the Crown as ground for refusal of disclosure, either absolutely or in the manner or at the time sought, the proper approach to the dispute is in my view the one outlined in *McLeod* at p.90D (p.239F–G). The court must consider on the one hand the public interest in securing for the accused a fair trial, and on the other hand the public interest put forward as justifying non-disclosure. In doing that, the court will attach the customary weight to any expression of view by the Lord Advocate as to public interest in maintaining the confidentiality of any document. It is, however, for the court to decide whether the former interest outweighs the latter.

[25] As I understood the advocate depute's submissions, she argued that in the present case the answer to the question which I require to ask myself as to the balance of competing interests is provided authoritatively by the case of *Ashrif* [*H.M.A. v. Ashrif*, 1998 S.L.T. 567]. Certainly that case, as an appellate decision of the High Court, is prima facie binding on me. It seems to me, however, that insofar as there is any inconsistency between the decision in *Ashrif* and the decision of the court of five judges in *McLeod*, *Ashrif* must yield. Moreover, *Ashrif* was decided long before the incorporation of the Convention into Scots law, and without reference to the Convention. If, therefore, *Ashrif* were in any respect inconsistent with a proper reflection of the petitioner's Convention rights, that too would afford ground for not following it.

[26] In my opinion, the court in *Ashrif* did not overtly follow the approach laid down in *McLeod*. It seems to me that there were three separate considerations which led to the conclusion that, aside from the question of the competency of making the application to the sheriff, commission and diligence should not be granted. One was that it was not in the public interest that the material sought, the schedule of previous convictions, should be disclosed. The second was that the schedule as such could not be used in evidence. The third was that the diligence sought was a fishing diligence. Dealing with these points in reverse order, the third is one that in my view requires to be considered individually in the circumstances of each case. The second, although of general application, is not one which in my view justifies refusal of the diligence. Although it is right that the schedule of previous convictions is not itself admissible in evidence, recovery of them is the only means by which the accused's advisers can ascertain the necessary information to enable them to obtain admissible evidence in the form of extracts of any convictions which they do wish to be in a position to prove should it become necessary to do so. The first point, however, the question whether commission and diligence should be refused for reasons of public policy, is the main point in issue. Although I do not doubt that the need to secure for the accused a fair trial was a consideration present in the minds of the members of the court, the reasons for the decision were not expressed in terms of balancing the public interest in securing a fair trial against the public interest in not disclosing the witnesses'

previous convictions. Moreover, the point was treated as one which is capable of decision in principle, without consideration of the relative strength of the competing interests in the particular case. In those respects, in my opinion, the approach adopted by the court was one which cannot now be regarded as consistent with that set out in *McLeod* or with proper consideration of the accused's Convention rights under article 6. I therefore conclude that I must approach the matter before me in the manner laid down in *McLeod* and with proper regard to the petitioner's rights under article 6. If, as a result of doing so, I come to the conclusion that the commission and diligence which the petitioner seeks should be granted, I do not consider that I am prevented from giving effect to that conclusion by *Ashrif*.

[27] The particular context in which the petitioner seeks commission and diligence is that in answer to a charge of aggravated assault he pleads that he acted in self defence and in defence of his father and brother, he and they having been attacked by the complainer, two other Crown witnesses and McIntosh. Over and above that, he has given notice of intention to attack the character of the complainer and the other two Crown witnesses. In my opinion, provided the witnesses' previous convictions are relevant to a legitimate attack on character or to their credibility, the material sought would plainly be relevant to his defence. It is therefore material which the petitioner is prima facie entitled to have disclosed to him. Moreover, in my view he is prima facie entitled to have it disclosed to him in advance of the trial. His right is to have disclosed to him material necessary for the proper preparation as well as the proper presentation of his defence. Possession of information about the witnesses' relevant criminal records would enable the petitioner's counsel or solicitor to make proper preparation for the cross examination of the witnesses in question. Lack of that information in advance would not wholly preclude the contemplated lines of cross examination, but would make embarking on them a much more uncertain course. Matters of credibility and character depend very much on the impressions made on the jury, and cross examination might well be less effective if embarked upon without knowledge of the detail of the witnesses' records. An impression unfairly unfavourable to the petitioner might be made on the jury if cross examination were embarked upon on his behalf, appeared to be unsuccessful, then was followed by re-examination which showed that the cross examiner had been ill informed.

[28] I note that the objection to disclosure of the witnesses' criminal records advanced by the advocate depute was put in general terms. No doubt there are some public interest points that are capable of being expressed in that way, but the approach is at variance with the changed approach to the disclosure of police statements adopted by the Crown in *McLeod*. The concern articulated by the Crown is that if disclosed before trial the witnesses' records may come into the hands of the accused himself. The apprehension is that the information in them may then be misused by the accused. That is not, however, said to be specifically apprehended in the circumstances of this particular case. The point is a general one. That formulation corresponds with the grounds relied upon by Lord Dunpark in *Ashrif* (at pp.207–208 (pp. 571–572)). The possibility of misuse would, in my view, be a telling consideration if there were ground for apprehension of such misuse in the particular case, but it is not in my view a weighty factor in the abstract. Lord Justice Clerk Ross's reasoning in *Ashrif* (at p.204 (p.569)) was slightly different. He apprehended that members of the public might be reluctant to come forward as witnesses if they knew that their criminal records might be disclosed to the accused and made public. It seems to me, however, that the disclosure of the witness's record in advance of the trial does not necessarily increase the likelihood of the convictions being disclosed in the course of the witness's evidence. The line of cross examination is available without disclosure, and disclosure ought to yield the result that no ill founded challenge to character or credibility is made. In some ways therefore it seems to me that disclosure in advance of trial will tend to the protection of the witness. Insofar as the public interest objection was seen in *Ashrif* as supported by a concern that more would be disclosed than could legitimately be used in an attack on character or on credibility, the answer seems to me to lie in properly narrow drafting of the calls in the specification (although I note that neither Lord Ross nor Lord Dunpark found the redrafting of the calls in more restricted form an adequate solution in that case: see p.205 (p.570) and p.208 (p.572)). There is, in my respectful view, no real force in Lord Ross's concern about ordering a search in SCRO records (p.204 (p.569)), when it is implicit in the Crown case that they will in any event arm themselves with the relevant schedule of previous convictions.

[29] Balancing these considerations as best I can, I have come to the conclusion that the petitioner's entitlement, as part of his right to disclosure of information in the hands of the Crown which would tend to exculpate him, to have sight of the relevant parts of the criminal records of the witnesses in question, is not outweighed by the public interest considerations put forward by the Crown as justifying non-disclosure.

[30] To obtain commission and diligence the petitioner must, in my opinion, satisfy the test formulated in *McLeod* at p.99A–D (p.244J–L), namely that making the order would serve a proper purpose and would be in the interests of justice. That involves, in my view, consideration of (i) whether the material sought can be put to legitimate use in support of the defence case or in attacking the prosecution case, (ii) whether the diligence is in the traditional sense a fishing diligence, and (iii) whether the calls in the specification are drafted so as to cover only material that can legitimately be covered. In my opinion, there are two aspects of the use to which the petitioner hopes to put the material he seeks to recover. The first is to enable an attack to be made on the character of the complainer and the others who, according to his special defence, attacked him, his brother and his father, by suggesting that they are men of a generally violent disposition. While there is in my view force in the advocate depute's submission that it would not be open to petitioner to prove specific previous instances of violence (*Brady*), and while I recognise that the petitioner has made no averments seeking to bring the case within the exceptional category of which *Kay* is an example, I am of opinion that it would be proper that the petitioner should have access to the witnesses' records of convictions for crimes of violence in support of a general assertion of a propensity to violence. The second aspect of the matter is the credibility of the witnesses. While I understand the basis for the suggestion that a record of crimes of dishonesty may cast doubt on the credibility of a witness, the relevance in that connection of convictions for crimes of violence is less obvious. Nevertheless, the authorities, although expressed in what may be thought to be somewhat old fashioned terms, support the proposition that a history of violence may affect the witness's credibility on the basis of general depravity. That must be a matter of degree. How far such an attack may be justified is a matter to be determined by the presiding sheriff at the trial. In my view, however, it would be wrong to refuse commission and diligence on the ground that the records, once disclosed, may not support an attack on credibility. In the context of the special defence, the notices to attack character and the averments in stat. 5 of the petition, I do not consider that the commission and diligence sought can be said to be a fishing diligence. The call as originally drafted would, in my opinion, have been too wide. As now adjusted in the form of calls 3, 4, 5 and 6, I am of opinion that it is adequately precise. On the whole matter, therefore, I conclude that the petitioner passes the 'proper purpose' test.

[31] There remains for consideration the advocate depute's submission that the proper time for disclosure will only arrive if and when a witness under cross examination gives false evidence about his criminal record. I do not consider that that submission is well founded. I have already said something in para. [27] above, in my assessment of the public interest in favour of disclosure, about why I consider that the petitioner's advisers should have the material in time to enable them properly to prepare as well as present the defence case. It is not in my view satisfactory for the defence to be conducted without access to relevant information, on the basis that if things go wrong the situation will be rescued by the prosecutor. It seems to me to be inappropriate for the defence to have to rely, in a matter which may be of some delicacy, on the Crown to intervene to correct false information provided by a witness. Moreover, in marginal cases there will be room for difference of opinion about what is relevant to the credibility of a witness or to whether he has a propensity to violence. The presentation of the defence case should not, in principle, depend on the judgment of the prosecutor on such matters. I do not rule out the possibility that in a different case, where for example there was specific ground for apprehension that an accused acting on his own behalf would misuse information about a witness's record, the balance of the competing public interests might be different, and the appropriate solution would be to defer disclosure of the record until false evidence had been given. In such a case, however, I would be inclined to think (but express no concluded view) that disclosure ought to be made as soon as the false evidence is given, so as to enable the matter to be dealt with in cross examination by the defence rather than in re-examination by the prosecutor. In the circumstances of the present case, however, I do not

consider that it is correct that the practice described in *Ashrif* and proposed to be followed by the Crown in the present case properly reflects the rights of the petitioner."

NOTES

Compare the rather restrictive approach taken in *Daly v. Vannet*, 1999 S.C.C.R. 346, a case in which no authority was cited. In *Daly* the High Court upheld a magistrates decision that a police notebook is confidential and could not be viewed by the defence. However, *Daly* was not a case involving a petition for recovery of documents, but one in which a defence agent sought to see the contents of a police officer's notebook in the course of a trial.

11.   Scottish Criminal Cases Review Commission v. H.M.A.
2001 S.L.T. 905

The Scottish Criminal Cases Review Commission was created in 1997 to examine cases in which a miscarriage of justice is alleged to have occurred, and if necessary to refer cases to the High Court for review. They are empowered to investigate cases, make inquiries, take statements and prepare reports on the matter in question, or to request the Lord Advocate or others to do so. Section 194I of the Criminal Procedure (Scotland) Act 1995 provides that where the Scottish Criminal Cases Review Commission "believe that a person or a public body has possession or control of a document or other material which may assist them in the exercise of any of their functions, they may apply to the High Court for an order requiring that person or body" to produce the document or provide them with access.

The commission sought an order in terms that section for production of documents and materials obtained and created by or on behalf of the Crown Office in certain linked criminal cases which were under investigation by the commission. Lengthy discussions with Crown Office had resulted in documents being made available but over time it appeared that more documents existed than the Crown had initially believed to be relevant to the charges. The Crown claimed confidentiality for certain papers and argued also that the petition was insufficiently specific as to why the documents were required.

LORD CLARKE: "[9] Without yet examining the provisions of section 194I, it is clear to me that . . . Parliament intended the petitioners to have the fullest investigative powers in reaching the decision whether or not a reference to the court should be made in any particular case and that in exercising these powers, in the performance of their investigative duties, they are to act independently and to be seen to act independently. There can be no question, in my judgment, of their powers of investigation being directed or circumscribed by any other person or body. Any circumscribing of their powers of investigation must arise, if at all, simply, in my opinion, as a matter of law. If it were to be otherwise, then public confidence in the body and its activities, and its independence, could be seriously compromised and the primary purpose in establishing the body would be defeated.

[10] The petitioners, shortly after they were established, began to investigate the cases of Thomas Campbell, Joseph Steele and Thomas Gray, who were convicted on indictment at Glasgow High Court on October 10, 1984. The petitioners aver that they are considering the whole background and history of that case which they refer to as 'the review case'. They also go on to aver that their investigation of the review case 'encompasses the connected case of Joseph Granger and Alexander Joseph Reynolds who were tried on indictment on charges of perjury committed in the course of the trial of Campbell, Steele and Gray'. These proceedings are referred to in the petition as 'the connected case'. At the time of the establishment of the petitioners, the cases of Campbell, Steele and Gray were before the Secretary of State, for the purpose of consideration by him as to whether, in the exercise of his powers, as they were prior to the passing of Pt XA of the 1995 Act, he should refer the case to the High Court. With the passing of the provisions of Pt XA of the 1995 Act, the Secretary of State's power to refer was abolished. The matter was, as I have just noted, then taken up by the petitioners. This involved the transfer of papers which had been before the Secretary of State. In a letter from the Crown Agent dated May 25, 1999 addressed to the petitioners' chief executive, a copy of which was produced, it was stated as follows:

'We confirmed at our meeting here on May 10, that we had asked the Scottish Office to withhold papers when they transferred this case to you in early April. The documents in question fell into two categories, the first being statements and precognitions, and the second being minutes or parts of minutes from Crown Office to Scottish Office relating to this case in response to requests from the Scottish Office. We explained at the meeting that the latter are in effect inter-departmental advice, analysis and comment, which we do not believe would be appropriate to provide to the commission. I understand that you would not in fact wish to seek material of that nature from the Crown Office.

There is, however, generally no problem so far as the provision of witness statements and precognitions is concerned, and I have asked Mr Miller to contact your case worker, Mr Johnstone, to make appropriate arrangements in that connection'.

In replying to that letter, the petitioners' chief executive by letter dated May 27, 1999 said:

'The position as indicated by you concerning the inter-departmental papers relating to the case is understood. I note what you say regarding the remaining papers and have advised Mr Johnstone to expect a call from Mr Miller'.

Thereafter there followed sundry correspondence between the petitioners and the Crown Office. The petitioners' investigations into the review case related to two charges on the indictment which were numbered 9 and 15 respectively. On June 22, 1999 the Crown Office provided the petitioners with seven documents consisting of police statements and precognitions. On November 23, 1999 the petitioners requested copies of all police statements held by the Crown Office relative to charge 15 which was a charge of murder. Under cover of a letter dated December 15, 1999 the Crown Office provided copies of certain material and said that it appeared that this was the extent of the documentation held by them that was relevant to the petitioners' inquiry in relation to charge 15. On December 17, 1999 the petitioners sought documents relevant to charge 9 which was a charge of attempted murder. On December 22, 1999 the Crown Office undertook to provide copies of statements relevant to charge 9. The petitioners aver that in that letter the Crown Office indicated that it would be helpful to them if the petitioners could specify any particular witnesses whose statements were of interest to the petitioners, otherwise the Crown Office could only provide the statements of those witnesses who appeared to the Crown Office to be relevant. The petitioners proceed to aver in the petition that: 'without unrestricted access to papers held by the Crown Office the petitioners cannot know the contents of the material held and therefore cannot give an exhaustive list of specific witnesses or specific documents that may be of assistance to them'.

Under cover of a letter dated February 9, 2000 the petitioners received from the Crown Office what they describe in the petition as 'a copy of another potentially relevant statement' in respect of charge 15, the production of which they say contradicted what the Crown Office had said in their letter of December 15, 1999. On February 14, 2000 the petitioners sought confirmation from the Crown Office that all statements relative to charges 9 and 15 had been produced. Under cover of a letter of March 23, 2000 the Crown Office sent to the petitioners copies of certain material. In their letter, the Crown Office indicated that it could suggest no further statements relative to charges 9 and 15 which might be relevant to the petitioners' inquiry.

[11] The petitioners, with the consent of the Crown Office, sought access to papers held by Strathclyde Police. Copy documentation was produced by the police, the original documents having apparently been destroyed. The petitioners aver that they understood that the copy documents were 'sourced by the police largely from the Crown Office and the Procurator Fiscal's Office in Glasgow'. The petitioners' averments continue as follows: 'On reviewing the documentation held by Strathclyde Police the petitioners found numerous witness statements, precognitions and other material not previously produced by the Crown Office which were valuable to the petitioners in furthering their investigation. These documents were relevant not only to existing lines of inquiry being pursued by the petitioners but also gave rise to new lines of inquiry which the petitioners have subsequently pursued. The fact that these additional papers were sourced by the police from the Crown Office and the Procurator Fiscal's Office in

Glasgow and that the Crown Office had not previously disclosed the material to the petitioners has led the petitioners to believe that the Crown Office may have in its possession or under its control further documents and material which may assist them in the discharge of their statutory functions'.

[12] In article 6 of the petition the petitioners explain that following a review of the documentation released from the police the petitioners wrote to the Crown Office, by letter dated March 23, 2000, seeking access to further papers held by the Crown Office. On May 31, 2000 the Crown Office produced to the petitioners a general inventory of documents held by the Crown Office relating to the cases. A copy of this inventory has been lodged in the present proceedings by the respondent. There are 22 categories of papers included in it. Among those categories are the following:

'14. Papers prepared by Crown in respect of appeal proceedings, divided into: collections of authorities; other documents assembled by the Crown in preparation for appeal proceedings, and indicated on the attached documents marked 'C'; and Crown analysis, comments and arguments relative to appeal proceedings.

15. Correspondence involving the Procurator Fiscal, police, Crown Office, Ministers, members of the public and defence solicitors including advice to Ministers between the time of the original inquiry and approximately December 1998, divided as follows: general correspondence between Procurator Fiscal, police, defence solicitors and Crown Office relating to original investigation, Love perjury investigation and appeal proceedings, including reports to law officers; folders specifically relating to ministerial correspondence; chronological files of correspondence relating to petitions to the Secretary of State including correspondence between Procurator Fiscal, police, defence solicitors, Crown Office and Scottish Office, including advice to Ministers and inter-departmental advice analysis and comment between 10/12/85 and 27/4/98. A list of the witness statements and precognitions contained within these files is given in Appendix H.'

The petitioners aver that, under cover of a letter from the Crown Office, dated June 1, 2000, there was sent to them a number of further statements and precognitions and statements which the Crown Office described in their letter as 'clearly relevant' to previous specific requests for information made by the petitioners. This material had apparently come to light during the compilation of the inventory just referred to. Then, on June 5, 2000, the Crown Office produced a further 16 documents being statements and precognitions which appeared to them to be potentially relevant to charges 9 and 15 but which had not been previously disclosed to the petitioners.

[13] None of the history of the correspondence passing between the parties, which I have just endeavoured to set out, was in any material respect disputed by the respondent in his answers to the petition, or indeed by the advocate depute on his behalf, in submission to me. I would simply observe, at this stage, that while both the petitioners and the Crown Office had clearly been acting in good faith throughout all of this correspondence, it is clear from the history of that correspondence, which I just set out, that the pace and extent of the petitioners' investigation has been, to date, in effect, to some extent at least, dictated by the Crown Office
. . .

[14] It is important for me to return to the correspondence to note the following. From the earliest point in that correspondence the Crown Office made it clear (in the Crown Agent's letter of May 25, 1999 referred to supra) that documents which fell to be considered as relating to inter-departmental advice, analysis and comment, would not be handed over to the petitioners and that position was accepted, as previously observed, by the petitioners, in their chief executive's letter of May 27, 1999. That appears to have remained the petitioners' attitude at least until March 23, 2000. On that date the petitioners' chairperson, Professor Sheila McLean wrote to the Crown Agent. In her letter she said *inter alia*: 'At present although the Commission has had sight of a substantial amount of that paperwork, in order to reach a thorough and informed conclusion on this case, it is necessary for the Commission to be apprised of as much information held on the cases as possible (obviously barring inter-departmental correspondence)' . . . It is clear also to me from a perusal of the correspondence

passing between the petitioners and the Crown Office that, at least until very recently, the petitioners' concentration, in their requests for material to be produced by the Crown Office, focused on precognitions, police statements and productions relative to the review case and that the requests did not extend to such documents in relation to the connected case. The order they now seek, if granted in its present terms, would entitle them to recover inter-departmental papers and, to be more specific, they would be entitled to documents embraced in categories 14 and 15 in the inventory referred to *supra*.

[15] The advocate depute explained to me that some of the material sought would be documents which the present law officers themselves had never seen, because of the established constitutional convention that ministers of a new administration did not have access to advice given to their predecessors by civil servants. I was somewhat surprised that this point was not fully elaborated upon, in submission before me. Be that as it may, it did appear to me that the respondent's position in respect of this application was to a some extent based on the view that such material should be irrecoverable though, as I have said, no legal argument was presented to me as to why that should be so. On the other hand, no explanation was given to me as to why the petitioners had, until at least March 23, 2000, apparently assumed and accepted that this type of material was not recoverable by them from the Crown Office.

[16] Against all of that background the question for me is one of relevancy and specification, namely have the petitioners averred a relevant and sufficiently specific case for an application for all the documents and material referred to in the schedule, in terms of section 194I, to be considered and to be granted by the court or do the provisions of that section, or some other principle or rule of law, require them to aver more than they have averred in this case before such an application can be considered and granted? The averments that support the need for the application in its present terms are as follows:

'7. The petitioners have a duty to have regard to all matters which appear to them to be relevant. Reference is made to section 194D(2)(c) of the Act. The petitioners believe the Crown Office to have in its possession documentation which may assist them in the exercise of their functions. Without an opportunity to study the papers held by the Crown Office the petitioners are unable to give an exhaustive list of the specific documentation that is relevant. Given the history of disclosure to date, hereinbefore condescended upon, the petitioners believe that they may be assisted in their investigation by having access to the whole papers held by the Crown Office relating to the review case and the connected case. The petitioners have concerns about (1) the time taken to date to secure production of documents from the Crown Office and (2) the fact that the Crown Office has discovered additional relevant documents on being pressed by the petitioners following assurances that all relevant documents had been produced. In the circumstances the petitioners have concluded that it is necessary for them to have access to all of the documents held by the Crown Office to identify for themselves those which do in fact assist them in their investigations.

8. The documents specified in the schedule are documents which the petitioners believe may assist them in the exercise of their function.

9. The Crown Office have been asked to give the petitioners unrestricted access to these papers but have refused to do so. Reasons given for refusing unrestricted access include confidentiality and possible contravention of the Data Protection Act 1998. Previously the Crown Office had raised a general concern about the possible human rights implications of release of documents to the petitioners, though it is not known if the Crown Office had any specific concerns on that ground in the present case. None of these considerations was an objection to production of the documents to the petitioners pursuant to an order of this court. Reference is made to section 194I(2) of the Act and section 35 of the Data Protection Act 1998.'

I should say that the learned advocate depute in his submissions to me did not rely on any points arising from the Data Protection Act 1998 or any human rights point in seeking to have the petition dismissed.

[17] I now turn to consider the provisions of section 194I. It is in the following terms: [his Lordship quoted its terms and continued:] It is clear that this section has been cast in very wide

terms, indeed. It will be seen, for example, that the provisions of the section do not seek to exclude from their ambit any particular classes of documents or any individual documents which may have any particular quality or character. It is noteworthy that section 194I(2) expressly provides that a duty to comply with an order under this section is not affected by any obligation of secrecy or other limitation on disclosure. That must mean, in my opinion, that an application to the court for an order is not to be considered as irrelevant, or otherwise inappropriate, if it seeks to recover documents which otherwise might be irrecoverable because of an obligation of secrecy or some other limitation on disclosure. The scope of the section, in this respect, is reinforced by the provisions of Sched. 9A, para. 6(5) to the Act which provides that: [his Lordship quoted its terms and continued:] It is apparent, accordingly, from those provisions the fact that a document may deal with questions of national security does not per se mean that a request for it by the petitioners is inept. That the documentation or material that may be recovered under section 194I goes beyond police statements, precognitions, productions and other material used in the preparation for, and in the course of, the original trial and any previous appeal, is, furthermore, established by the provisions of section 194I(3).

[18] Having regard to the provisions of section 194I as a whole, I have reached the conclusion that, in principle, there is nothing arising from those provisions, which makes it irrelevant or incompetent for the petitioners to seek the documents and the material to the extent which they do in the present petition. That that is the correct approach to be taken to the statutory provisions in Scotland, is supported, I think, by the approach of the legislation relating to the equivalent body to the petitioners which has been established for England and Wales. The Criminal Cases Review Commission was set up for England and Wales by the Criminal Appeal Act 1995 and its functions are similar to those of the petitioners. Section 17 of that Act provides: [his Lordship quoted the terms of section 17 and continued:] The language of section 17(3) and (4) is virtually identical to that which appears in section 194I(2) and (3) of the Scottish legislation, with regard to the documents or material that are recoverable by the commission. The provisions of section 18 differ materially, however, from those of section 194I in relation to the way in which documents and other material held on behalf of public bodies may be obtained. The provisions of the English legislation do not envisage an application to the court being required, but invest the commission with a statutory power to require the appropriate person to produce or give access to the material in question. The exercise of those powers is subject to two qualifications. They come into play when the commission believes that the document or material may assist them in the exercise of any of their functions and it is reasonable to request the production of or access to the documents or material in question. Section 18 of the English legislation deals expressly with one of the specific questions which arises in the present case. It provides as follows: [his Lordship quoted its terms and continued:] For present purposes, the significance, in my judgment, of those somewhat convoluted provisions, is that by section 18(3) it is recognised that documents or other material, which have been received by the Secretary of State in relation to a case which he has previously considered, or which he is in the process of considering with a view as to whether a reference to the court should be made or not, or that there should be a recommendation that the royal prerogative should be exercised, and where these documents or material were received by him from a person serving in a Government department, are not, in principle and by definition, to be excluded from recovery by the commission. The question as to whether they should be handed over or not is left to the discretion of the Secretary of State. Accordingly, it appears to me that in both jurisdictions the relevant legislation does not exclude, as a matter of law, the recovery of any class of documents or material, or any particular document or particular material, simply because of their nature or the circumstances in which they were created or received and, in particular, that both the English and Scottish legislation recognise the possibility of departmental papers and material being recovered, though this result is arrived at by different routes. Accordingly, in my opinion, insofar as the respondent's stance is based on any particular class of document or other material being irrecoverable by the petitioners, as a matter of law, standing the legislative provisions, such a stance would be misconceived. In that connection I should refer to a letter from the Solicitor General to the petitioners' chairperson dated June 14, 2000. In that letter the Solicitor General appears to adopt the approach that the only documents which the commission might recover are those which are 'evidential' in

character. He states: 'May I endeavour to make clear the Crown's position. The commission will be given access to all the evidential papers. You will be able to copy and take away any papers you wish subject only to us being able to identify and resolve any issues of confidentiality. In the very unlikely event that there is still an issue regarding any particular statement or precognition it will be quickly identified and you will still have the ability, as in any case, to make the appropriate application to the Court'. Quite apart from there being possibly some room for debate as to what is to be encompassed by the description 'evidential', I am of the opinion that if the Solicitor General was intending to circumscribe, by the use of that expression, the nature of documents and material which the petitioners might have, as a matter of law, because of the statutory provisions, then he was wrong to do so because, in my opinion, the relevant statutory provisions do not impose any such restrictions for the reasons I have already given.

[19] I should add this, that in reaching the view I have about the construction to be placed upon section 194I and its scope, I take some comfort from the following considerations. In the first place, it seems to me that it is unlikely that the intention was that the body set up to replace the Secretary of State in dealing with these matters should have more limited powers of investigation and more limited access to material than he did. Secondly, one must assume that the persons chosen to chair and to be the members of this very important body, are persons who were chosen for, among other things, their qualities of judgment and discretion, having regard to the material that would inevitably come into their possession in the exercise of their functions. Thirdly, section 194J creates statutory offences in relation to disclosure of information obtained by members of the commission or their staff, except when such disclosure is permitted by the Act.

[20] There does remain the important question, however, as to whether the present petition falls to be dismissed as being irrelevant, because of lack of specification, in relation to the precise reason or reasons why the order sought is cast in such universal terms. To put the matter another way, and perhaps more precisely, do the petitioners require, *ex limine* to set out more specific averments than they have as to why an order is required in respect of each and every document, and other pieces of material, they seek, or at least in respect of various classes of documents that might be encompassed in the order they seek. It was, as I understood the advocate depute's submissions, on this ground he took his principal stance, at this stage. Counsel for the petitioners accepted that the provisions of section 194I did not provide for a purely administrative procedure, whereby the court would simply rubber stamp any request made to it by the petitioners for recovery of any document or other material. He accepted that the court must have a discretion as to whether to grant or refuse any such application or part thereof. He contended, however, that the onus was on the haver of the documents, or other material, to specify a good reason why the documents or material should not be recovered or some 'fallacy in the commission's decision-making process' in bringing the petition in question. His submission was that, having regard to the provisions of section 194I(1), there was no obligation on the commission in making an application to the court to aver that the documents and material they sought were relevant to their investigation and why they were relevant. That was not the test. The commission simply had to believe that the documents or other material might assist them in the exercise of any of their functions. Their role was one of investigation. In exercising that role it would not be appropriate, or indeed possible, for them to say in advance what documents or other material would be relevant to their investigations. In an appropriate case they would require to have access to documents and materials simply to determine what was relevant and what was not relevant. It would be quite inappropriate for them to seek to prejudge the outcome or development of their investigations by restricting their request to documents and material which clearly appeared to be relevant at any particular point in their investigations. That was clearly so having regard to their duty to give reasons for making a reference to the court or refusing a reference once an application had been made to them. It was incumbent upon them, before setting out any such reasons, that they should be satisfied that they had had access to and had considered all the material that may have a bearing on their decision. The respondent's stance was flawed in that it failed adequately to recognise that the petitioners were not in the position of a litigant in a contested litigation, seeking recovery of documents or other material. In that connection, counsel for the petitioners

submitted that the position was to be contrasted with what was said by Lord Wilberforce in the case of *Air Canada v. Secretary of State for Trade* where his Lordship at [1983] 2 A.C., pp.438–439 said as follows: 'In a contest purely between one litigant and another, such as the present, the task of the court is to do, and be seen to be doing, justice between the parties—a duty reflected by the word 'fairly' in the rule. There is no higher or additional duty to ascertain some independent truth. It often happens, from the imperfection of evidence, or the withholding of it, sometimes by the party in whose favour it would tell if presented, that an adjudication has to be made which is not, and is known not to be, the whole truth of the matter: yet if a decision has been in accordance with the available evidence and with the law, justice will have been fairly done. It is in aid of justice in this sense that discovery may be ordered, and it is so ordered upon the application of one of the parties who must make out his case for it. If he is not able to do so, that is an end of the matter. There is no independent power in the court to say that, nevertheless, it would like to inspect the documents, with a view to possible production, for its own assistance'. Unlike the position in relation to a contested litigation, as set out in that passage from the speech of Lord Wilberforce, the position in the present case is that the petitioners have a statutory obligation to carry out a full, independent and impartial investigation into alleged miscarriages of justice and the legislation under which they act was clearly designed to give the widest powers to perform that duty.

[21] It seems to me that there is considerable force in those submissions. It is important also that I should note that counsel for the petitioners assured me that there was no question of such an application, like the present, being made in all cases which are being investigated by the petitioners. It was necessary to make such an application, in these terms, in the present case, because of the history of the case and because of the width of the inquiry that the petitioners felt obliged to conduct. That inquiry was not simply in relation to the original trial and appeal, but the sundry procedure that had occurred, over a very lengthy period of time, in relation to the review case and the connected case. The inquiry would cover allegations of police misconduct and alleged misconduct by the procurator fiscal service. I should note that the respondent does not, in his answers to the petition, it seems, demur from the petitioners being required to indulge in an inquiry of that scope in the present case.

[22] I am satisfied that the averments of the petitioners as to the history of the particular case to which the petition relates, and the attempts that have been made by them to recover documents and other materials from the Crown Office (by which I am not to be taken to imply any criticism of the Crown Office's conduct in relation thereto) are enough to satisfy, *prima facie*, the requirements of section 194I and that the petition, and the order sought, cannot be said to be irrelevant *in hoc statu*.

[23] I am of the opinion that, standing the repeated assertions in this case, by the Crown Office that they had handed over all the relevant material in their possession which, in the event, they have subsequently, by producing further material, accepted was not the case, and standing the apparent scope of the petitioners' investigations in this case and the history of the cases which are the subject of those investigations, the petitioners have a basis for averring a belief on their part that the documents and material they seek to receive may assist them in the exercise of their functions.

[24] The judgment as to whether the documents and material in question do, to any extent, assist them, and why they do, is one for the petitioners to arrive at, and is one which they cannot, by definition, reach until they have had access to the documents and material. This is what I take from the language of section 194I(1). To the extent, therefore, that the submission for the respondent was that the petitioners required to set out averments as to why the documents and material are relevant to their investigation, I consider that submission unsound, having regard to the wording of section 194I(1). Moreover, it seems to me that the position adopted by the Crown Office to date has, for the reasons I have endeavoured to give, been bedevilled by a wrong interpretation of the statutory provisions with regard to the nature of the documents and material that are recoverable by the petitioners. That has, in part, in my judgment, necessitated the petitioners bringing the petition and seeking the order they do."

NOTES

It is clear from this case that the SCCRC have very wide powers to recover material relevant to their investigations. Those powers arise from the breadth of the statutory provisions under which the

SCCRC operates. However, the question must arise whether it is right—or sensible—that a body which is in effect a tribunal of last resort, should have much wider power to recover evidence that of an accused person at first instance. It might be argued that it would be better if all relevant evidence was put before the court at first instance, thus perhaps increasing the chances of avoiding a miscarriage of justice in the first place. The difficulty for an accused person is that he has to establish under the *McLeod* test that material is likely to be of material assistance to the preparation of his case. But he has to do so before having sight of the material. The SCCRC is enabled simply to recover all material which may be relevant, and sift through it at its leisure—see para. [24] of Lord Clarke's opinion, above. Given the extent of the Crown's powers of investigation, it might be argued that the present law places accused persons at a disadvantage in comparison with the Crown. The Court has set its face against suggestions that the present law is unduly restrictive, or that it offends against article 6 of the Convention. Is it correct to do so?

In *Scottish Criminal Cases Review Commission, Petitioners*, 2001 S.L.T. 1198, the Court made detailed observations on the extent of the SCCRC's power to make inquiries of and take statements from members of a jury, where it is alleged that a miscarriage of justice has resulted from the conduct of jury members during a trial. In particular, the Court noted that the prohibition contained in section 8 of the Contempt of Court Act 1981 applies strictly to jury deliberations taking place after the jury have retired to consider their verdict, and neither the SCCRC nor the Crown have power to make inquiries of the jury as to events occurring after that time.

(E) COMMERCIAL CONFIDENTIALITY

11.   Iomega Corporation v. Myrica (UK) Ltd (No. 1)
1999 S.L.T. 793

A company obtained an order granting diligence for recovery of certain documents and property, and a number of items were produced and taken into the custody of the court. The petitioners enrolled a motion for authority to inspect the recoveries, including those contained in envelopes marked "confidential". The respondents objected, arguing that in view of their commercial confidentiality the documents should be disclosed only after commercially sensitive material had been blanked out, or where this could not be done satisfactorily, submitted to an independent expert appointed by the court who could call for other necessary material and report to the court.

LORD MCFADYEN: "The respondents' commercial confidentiality in the material recovered is not, in my view, *per se* a sound legal ground for refusing the petitioners access to it. I readily accept, however, that in ordering recovery of documents and making them available to an opposing party, the court will attach such conditions as are necessary to protect commercial confidentiality, so far as that can be achieved without frustrating the ends of justice (*Union Carbide*, at p.977).

In this case there seemed to me to be two possible ways of protecting the respondents' legitimate interests. One would be to blank out commercially sensitive material throughout the documents recovered. The other would be to restrict access to the documents to legal advisers and an independent expert, buttressing the protection with appropriate undertakings.

Initially the former approach was favoured, and accepted (indeed suggested) by the petitioners. Counsel for the respondents submitted that it was not possible now to change tack. I do not accept that. What was originally seen by the petitioners as expedient to accept in order to obtain prompt access to the recoveries did not achieve that result. Blanking out has been applied to only some of the documents, and to apply it comprehensively would involve material delay which would add to the delay which has already occurred. I therefore regard myself as free to make up my own mind as to how best to reconcile the petitioners' desire for access to the recoveries with the respondents' desire to protect their commercial confidentiality.

Counsel for the respondents submitted that the restricted access route was unreliable, because of the risk that confidential material might be 'blurted out' in the presence of the petitioners' personnel. I do not regard that risk as of such materiality as to preclude that approach.

The view which I have reached is that to occupy further time on blanking out allegedly confidential material would be inappropriate. I consider that the respondents will be adequately protected by allowing restricted and conditional access to the documents. While it might be possible, as counsel for the petitioners suggested, to release unconditionally the documents which have already been subjected to blanking out, I have decided not to do that, because of the additional blanking out which counsel for the respondents sought in respect of those documents. I therefore propose to authorise inspection of the recoveries, so far as documents 53–143 are concerned in blanked out form, but otherwise in unaltered form, by (a) the petitioners' counsel, (b) the petitioners' solicitors, provided they first sign an undertaking in a form which will be identified in the interlocutor by a number of process, and (c) an expert instructed by the petitioners' solicitors, provided that he (i) is not employed by the petitioners or any related company, and (ii) first signs an undertaking in the second form which will also be identified in the interlocutor by a number of process."

NOTES

Iomega (No. 1) emphasises that there is, strictly speaking, no such as thing as commercial confidentiality. Such considerations will not be allowed to hinder the public interest, that of litigating parties in recovering information which is relevant to the facts in issue. However, in so far as it is possible to do so, the courts will attempt to protect commercially sensitive information by attaching conditions to the recovery of documents, such as those imposed by Lord McFadyen in the preceding case. The sequel to this case is Iomega Corporation v. Myrica (UK) Ltd (No. 2), 1999 S.L.T. 796. In that case it was held that once information has been recovered, it is under the control of the court which can give authority for the information to be used in other proceedings, including proceedings abroad.

(F) CHILDREN

It has been held that a plea of confidentiality in a Referral under the Children (Scotland) Act 1995 will normally yield to the interests of the parties in a fair hearing where confidentiality is claimed by a local authority in social work records and the like—Reporter for Strathclyde v. B., 1997 Fam. L.R. 142. In M. v. British Railways Board, The Scotsman, September 13, 1995 it was held that production of confidential records held by an education authority about pupils' behavioural problems might be ordered if necessary in the interests of justice.

There is considerable controversy as to the question whether reports regarding the welfare of children, and in particular those referring to views expressed by children as to questions of parental rights and responsibilities, are confidential. The matter remains unsettled.

12. McGrath v. McGrath
1999 S.L.T. (Sh. Ct.) 90

After decree of divorce had been pronounced and access regulated, the father of a child lodged a minute seeking extensions of contact with her. At a child welfare hearing the sheriff was told that both parties were prepared to leave the decision as to the extent of increased contact to the child. The curator advised the sheriff of the child's views and also of the child's request that those views should not be repeated to her parents. The sheriff, taking that advice into account but not revealing what he had been told, declined to grant the orders sought. The defender appealed to the sheriff principal, submitting that the sheriff had acted contrary to the principles of natural justice:

SHERIFF PRINCIPAL E. F. BOWEN, Q.C.: "Counsel for the appellant submitted that in taking the views of the child into account in this fashion the sheriff had acted contrary to the principles of natural justice. It was a matter of principle that disclosure of information to a party was essential as part of the right to a fair hearing. In addition it was a basic requirement on a fact finder or decision maker to give reasons for a decision. That could not be complied with where there was a refusal to disclose the reasons for the decision. In support of these contentions counsel referred to MacDonald v. MacDonald, 1985 S.L.T. 244, in which the Second Division disapproved any practice of departing from the recognised procedure of determining disputed questions of access by proof in open court even with consent of parties. Counsel accepted that the situation was to some extent affected by the provisions of the

Children (Scotland) Act 1995, and in particular, sections 6 and 11(7) which underlined the obligation on the part of a court to take into account a child's views. The basic principles of natural justice were not however altered by that legislation. I was referred to the decision of the House of Lords in *Re D (Minors) (Adoption Reports: Confidentiality)* [1996] A.C. 593; [1995] 4 All E.R. 385. That was a case in which permission to view confidential documents in the context of adoption proceedings had been sought and refused in the lower courts. In remitting the matter to the court of first instance for reconsideration the House of Lords considered certain principles appropriate to situations where confidentiality of information was claimed which were set out in the concluding part of the speech of Lord Mustill at p.398. The fundamental principle was that a party was entitled to disclosure of all materials which may be taken into account by a court when reaching a decision adverse to that party. Before considering whether to depart from that fundamental principle the court had first to determine whether disclosure of the material would involve a real possibility of significant harm to the child. If it would involve such a risk the court was then required to consider whether the overall interests of the child would benefit from non-disclosure. Finally, if satisfied that the interests of the child pointed towards non-disclosure, the court then required to weigh that consideration against the interests of the parent or other party in having an opportunity to see and respond to the material, taking into account the importance of the material to the issues in the case. No attempt had been made to follow these principles in the present case. In viewing the matter purely from the point of view of the child the sheriff had erred in approach. The presumption, arising from the principles enunciated in *Re D*, was that when a child has something to say about the central issue in the case the parties should be told what that is. Counsel also referred to *McMichael v. United Kingdom* (1995) 20 E.H.R.R. 205, a decision of the European Court of Human Rights in which it was held that the withholding of the contents of reports in the context of proceedings under the Social Work (Scotland) Act 1968 contravened the right to a "fair hearing" granted by Article 6(1) of the European Convention on Human Rights. I was further referred to a decision of Sheriff Robertson in Edinburgh sheriff court on March 11, 1999 in the case of *Dosoo v. Dosoo*, 1999 S.L.T. (Sh. Ct.) 86. That decision was in relation to a motion to open up confidential envelopes which contained views expressed to a reporter by two children in relation to questions of contact. In refusing to allow the confidential information to be disclosed Sheriff Robertson expressed the view that the privacy of the views of children should be respected 'except in very compelling circumstances'. She considered that the case of *Re D* could be distinguished on the basis that it concerned adoption proceedings and that the law had developed from that expressed in *McMichael* because of the provisions of the Children (Scotland) Act 1995. Counsel argued that these views were wrong and the presumption that all information should be disclosed meant that there had to be compelling reasons to respect confidentiality. Counsel pointed out that ordinary cause rule 33.20 had been introduced to take account of the provisions of the 1995 Act. That rule required the sheriff to record the views of a child in writing and gave a discretion to place these in a sealed confidential envelope. That provision did not in itself impinge upon the common law requirement of openness and fairness. The effect of what had taken place in this case was that no proper reasons had been given for the refusal of the minute. The sheriff had 'taken into account' information provided to him but had not revealed any of it. He had proceeded to give reasons unrelated to the views of the child for refusing the minuter's request.

Counsel also indicated that the sheriff had erred in respect of the parties' position *quoad* para. 1(e) of the minute. He had recorded that 'this part was not opposed in principle but I did not think it was appropriate to pronounce an order in the detail there set out. That is quite unnecessary'. In fact there was an objection in principle and parties had indicated that they wished to be heard on this aspect separately. The sheriff had refused that aspect of the minute without any hearing at all.

In response the agent for the pursuer and respondent indicated that the provisions of the 1995 Act had made a difference to the approach to be adopted in issues of this nature. Sections 6 and 11 were significant, and OCR 33.20 acknowledged that an opportunity might have to be afforded to take the views of a child confidentially. That rule gave the sheriff an unfettered discretion in the matter. The need to provide children with an opportunity to express views freely, and consequently confidentially, had been recognised by the sheriff in *Dosoo*, and a distinction between contact cases and adoption cases was a legitimate one. His first submission was not that there was a presumption in favour of confidentiality, but that the sheriff had a wide discretion which he had exercised properly. He had acknowledged the problem of taking into account 'non-disclosed' information. The views of the child had played a part in his decision but were not the only basis for it. He had taken into account the interests of parties, but that was not the only factor. Furthermore he argued that the child welfare hearing had been fixed of consent to enable the views of the child to be ascertained. It was an implication that it was to bring matters to a conclusion. The parties had made submissions indicating that they were happy that the matter could be dealt with on the basis of the child's views. It was difficult to see what more the minuter could have said. The agent also acknowledged that the sheriff had misunderstood the position of the pursuer in relation to crave 1(e) which was to be dealt with by separate submissions.

In response counsel for the minuter maintained that it had never been agreed that the views of the child should be ascertained in the way that the sheriff had gone about it, and that because of the terms of the note he may not have acceded to the child's views. One simply could not tell.

I feel obliged to allow this appeal for two reasons. In the first place the decision is based not on what the child told the sheriff but on what was relayed to him by a third party. As a result the views of the child were not recorded as they would have been in accordance with OCR 33.20 had they been expressed directly to the sheriff or to a person appointed to obtain the views. The fact that a curator was involved rather than a reporter cannot be allowed to circumvent that requirement. The situation is that the views expressed by the child, and all the circumstances surrounding the expression of them, remain a secret shared only amongst the sheriff, the curator and the child. An appeal court is deprived of any opportunity of considering whether the discretion to withhold disclosure of the views was exercised properly.

Secondly, I do not consider that one can disregard the views of the House of Lords as set out in Re D, or for that matter the observations of the European Court of Human Rights in McMichael, by distinguishing this case from a case of adoption or by saying that the 1995 Act has altered the law. The forthcoming implementation of the Human Rights Act underlines the need to have regard to principles enshrined in the Convention. In Re D Lord Mustill, after referring to certain decisions of the European Commission and Court of Human Rights and of the Committee of Ministers including McMichael, said (at [1995] 4 All E.R., p.397h): 'in substance the principles to be derived from that jurisprudence are entirely consistent with those which I propose'. He also commented (p.388e) that 'it is a first principle of fairness that each party to a judicial process shall have an opportunity to answer by evidence and argument any adverse material which the tribunal may take into account when forming its opinion'. The ECHR made very similar observations when approaching the question of a contravention of Article 6. The approach of the House of Lords is thus in line with human rights law and should be seen as of general application, not simply of relevance to cases of adoption. There is of course as was pointed out in Dosoo a distinction between adoption cases and contact cases in that the former have a potential of finality which the latter do not necessarily possess. That in my view is simply one of the circumstances to be taken into account when applying the principles set out by Lord Mustill and is not a basis for distinction.

I agree with the submission by counsel for the minuter that the 1995 Act does not affect the basic principles involved in the right to a fair hearing and the open disclosure of information. The Act does not deal with confidential disclosure of views and does not purport to introduce any concept of a right to confidentiality. The requirement to regard the welfare of a child as its paramount consideration contained in section 11(7) relates to the making of orders under section 11(1), not to the question of whether a child's view should be kept confidential. I do not see how, in the absence of the specific creation of a right of confidentiality, the Act can be said to override the very clear principles mentioned by the House of Lords in Re D. Whilst section 11(7) requires a court to provide a child with an opportunity to express his views, it does not provide any clue as to how the courts are to encourage the expression of views 'freely' as provided in the UN Convention. The sheriff in Dosoo and the sheriff in the present case were in my view correct when they recognised that views can often be expressed 'freely' only where confidentiality can be assured. The practicalities involved in reconciling the right to a fair hearing and a child's right to express his views are thus of immense difficulty. They can best be resolved in my view by having regard to the principles set out by Lord Mustill, which involve taking the fundamental principle that a party is entitled to disclosure of all materials as the starting point and next considering whether disclosure of the material would involve a real possibility of significant harm to the child.

In these circumstances I consider that it is appropriate that the sheriff's interlocutor should be recalled and that matter remitted to be considered anew at a fresh child welfare hearing in the light of the principles which I have indicated above. The sheriff will have to decide, in the light of the submissions, how to obtain the views of the child and whether they should be treated as confidential. I do not propose that the matter should be heard again by the sheriff who dealt with it originally. He has in terms of his note stated fairly trenchant views regarding the conduct of the defender in relation to a number of matters. I shall not comment on these observations in detail. To my mind it is somewhat doubtful whether all these observations were necessary in the context of a minute and answers on the question of contact which on the face of the pleadings at least involved only issues of practicality. What is clear is that the sheriff has formed an adverse view of the defender and I doubt whether it would be fair to anyone, including the sheriff, to invite him to consider the matter again."

NOTES

In *Dosoo v. Dosoo*, 1999 S.L.T. (Sh. Ct.) 86, Sheriff Robertson went rather further than Sheriff Principal Bowen, noting that:

"the Children (Scotland) Act 1995 must be applied in issues relating to children, and section 6 thereof and OCR 33.21 have given effect to Article 12 of the UN Convention on the Rights of the Child. I agree that for a child to be able to express his views 'freely' he must be able to feel confident in privacy if he so wishes and the court should respect that privacy except in very compelling circumstances."

These two contrasting views take different starting points in attempting to resolve the question of confidentiality in this type of case, Sheriff Bowen starting from the—perhaps too broadly stated—premise that a party is entitled to the disclosure of all materials; Sheriff Robertson from the premise that a child has a "right" to express his or her views in confidence. The problem will no doubt prove to be a particularly thorny one to resolve. The matter has also been considered in the cases of *Grant v. Grant*, 2000 G.W.D. 5–177, and *Oyeneyin v. Oyeneyin*, 1999 G.W.D. 38–1836. In the latter case, Sheriff A. M. Bell followed the line taken in *McGrath* that the fundamental principle is that a party is entitled to know the basis upon which the court is dealing with an issue, and that the welfare of the child concerned must be subordinated to that. The difficulty with this approach is that it may involve the court in a breach of the rights of the child under the UN Convention of the Rights of the Child 1989, and conceivably also Article 8 of the European Convention on Human Rights. It seems that on either view, the court must undertake a balancing exercise, and it is submitted that the approach taken in *McGrath* is the correct one, focussing as it does on the general right of a party to recover material relevant to his or her case, and then considering whether that right ought to be cut down in the light of the consequences for the child involved. Whatever the correct approach, it seems clear that until the matter is resolved, those who prepare reports in such cases which include reference to the views of the child should take care to warn the children concerned that confidentiality may not at present be guaranteed.

Chapter 13

SOME SPECIALTIES OF CIVIL EVIDENCE

In Memorandum No. 46, *Law of Evidence* 1980, para. A.03(5), the Scottish Law Commission stated as a guiding principle that the law of evidence in civil and criminal proceedings ought to be identical unless good reason could be shown for divergence. In fact, there are significant differences, and in a more recent Report (on *Hearsay Evidence in Criminal Proceedings* Scot. Law Com. No. 149, 1995) the Commission accepted (para. 2.12) that there are good reasons for applying different, and perhaps more stringent rules in criminal cases. The Civil Evidence (Scotland) Act 1988 made far-reaching changes which take the law of civil evidence far from the law in criminal proceedings. For that reason it is appropriate to devote a separate section to the 1988 Act.

(A) THE ABOLITION OF CORROBORATION IN CIVIL CASES

1. Scottish Law Commission: (Scot. Law Com. No. 4, 1967)
Proposal for Reform of the Law of Evidence Relating to Corroboration

"I. Introduction

The Scottish Law Commission have received from individual members of the public, members of the legal profession and representatives of trade unions complaints relating to the rules requiring corroboration in civil actions, especially those arising from personal injury. When a man can prove, by his own testimony accepted as true by the Court that he has suffered injury through the fault of another, it is felt to be unjust that he cannot succeed in an action against that other unless he can produce corroborating evidence in support of his own. The number of persons whose rights have been affected by this rule of procedure can never be known, because it includes not only those whose cases have failed in Court, but also the presumably much larger number of those who have accepted legal advice, correct as the law now stands that they ought to abandon their claims because lack of corroboration makes them untenable.

2. Our First Programme includes the examination of the law of evidence with a view to reform and codification, and work is proceeding in that field, but it will necessarily be some time before this examination can be completed and comprehensive recommendations submitted. We are, however, satisfied (a) that the complaints we have been receiving with reference to the requirement of corroboration are well-founded, (b) that the amendment of the law is a matter of some urgency and (c) that this amendment need not await our presentation of a draft code of the whole law of evidence. For these reasons we now recommend that immediate effect be given to a proposal, which can properly be taken in isolation, substantially to curtail the doctrine of corroboration as it stands at present. From this recommendation we exclude criminal causes, consistorial causes, and actions of affiliations . . .

II. The Present Law and its History

The present law has been stated thus. 'By the law of Scotland, the testimony of one witness, however credible, is not full proof of any ground of action or defence, either in a civil or criminal cause. Accordingly, if the only evidence in support of a case is the uncorroborated testimony of one witness, it is the duty of the Court to direct the jury that the proof is not sufficient in point of law. But this rule does not require that two witnesses should swear to every fact in the case. The direct evidence of one witness supported by facts and circumstances, is sufficient.' Lord President Normand has said, 'There is sufficient corroboration if the facts and circumstances proved are not only consistent with the evidence of the single witness, but more consistent with it than with any competing account of the events spoken to by him. Accordingly, if the facts and circumstances proved by other witnesses fit in to his narrative so as to make it the most probable account of the events, the requirements of legal proof are satisfied.' Thus, a pursuer who has suffered injury by accident and is suing for damages must produce the evidence of at least a second witness to corroborate his own evidence either directly or by establishing facts and circumstances which corroborate it.

4. Historically, the rule was derived from the system of procedure in use in the ecclesiastical courts in medieval times, a system which was largely adopted by the Court of Session on its creation. Under that procedure the testimony of a single witness was not acceptable as proof: it was merely a 'half-proof' (*semiplena probatio*). A 'full proof' (*plena probatio*) required the evidence of two unexceptionable witnesses (*testes classici*) though the evidence of a single witness might be supplemented by other adminicles of evidence which together added up to another half-proof. There is ample evidence of the adoption of this theory of proof in the early practice of the Court of Session and it is analysed in the earliest treatise on its procedures, Skene's, *Ane Short forme of Proces* (see chapters XVI–XXX, especially chapter XXII). This theory of proof had the authority of various scriptural and Roman texts and was widely adopted throughout Europe. Nevertheless while its rigour was understandable at the time of its introduction when the alternatives were the ordeal or compurgation, it became increasingly obsolete with the passage of years. The safeguard which it provided against the decision of cases by the evidence of a single false witness was counterbalanced by the disadvantage that it excluded many legitimate claims. For this reason the rule was abolished in France after the Revolution and subsequently in many other European countries. The matter has been examined by Dr. H. A. Hammelmann who sums up the position as follows, 'The time is gone when in accordance with an artificial system of arithmetical proof, a verdict could only be secured if two or more witnesses were prepared to testify to the facts, so that in Napoleon's words one honest man could not, by his testimony, secure the conviction of a rogue while two rogues could secure the conviction of an honest man.'

5. The question of corroboration in civil cases was recently canvassed in the case of *Cleisham v. British Transport Commission* [1964 S.C. (HL) 8], per Lord Devlin (at page 24) stated the rule thus: 'it is unnecessary for the pursuer to do more than to establish that, in the light of the surrounding circumstances her account is more probable than any other account that is given in evidence or can reasonably be suggested so as not to leave it a case of one man's word against another's.' As the rule remains, however, it may still be necessary for a judge to say to an injured workman. 'I believe your evidence but I cannot hold your claim proved because the surrounding circumstances do not sufficiently corroborate it'. This is unsatisfactory: the Court should be entitled, when it is satisfied as to the truth of one version of the facts, to draw the legal conclusions which follow naturally from it. Corroborating evidence should not be a sine qua non as a matter of law. From enquiries which we have made, it is evident that there are many cases where pursuers having sustained injuries when working alone or in darkness, are unable to pursue a claim through absence of corroboration. Defenders lie under a similar disability in issues such as contributory negligence in which the burden of proof lies on them; they may be unable to discharge that onus through lack of corroboration.

III. Other Legal Systems

6. The law of England on this matter has been stated as follows. 'On the general rule that a single witness unconfirmed, is sufficient, the following exceptions have been engrafted either by statute or by rule of practice, there being this distinction that when corroboration is required by statute and is not forthcoming the case must be withdrawn from the jury, whereas when it is

merely required by the rule of practice, the case must be left to the jury.' There follow a number of exceptions of which all are in the criminal law except for breach of promise, bastardy, claims to property of deceased persons, and certain aspects of divorce proceedings. There thus seem to be three situations as to the requirement for corroboration: (a) in the general case it is not required, (b) in some matters it is required by statute, (c) in other circumstances it is the duty of the judge to warn a jury of the danger of convicting on uncorroborated evidence. Examples of the last situation are afforded by the evidence of accomplices, very young children, the prosecutrix on sexual charges, and disreputable people in general.

7. The following is a quotation from the Evidence Code of the State of California, 1965: 'Except where additional evidence is required by statute, the direct evidence of one witness who is entitled to full credit is sufficient for proof of any fact'. The similarity with the law of England is apparent.

8. The rule requiring corroboration, as already explained, has been abolished in most European countries. We are informed that in Sweden it was abolished by statute in 1948. Professor W. L. Haardt of The Hague has reported to us that new draft Rules of Evidence abolishing the corroboration rule in the Netherlands are expected to be enacted in 1967 or 1968. We understand that the rule remains only in Portugal. For the reasons given above, we consider that the law of Scotland in the matter of corroboration should be amended so as to bring it into harmony with most other systems.

IV. Recommendation

9. We therefore recommend legislation to the effect that in any civil cause not being a consistorial cause or an action of affiliation, the Court may treat the evidence of a single credible witness as sufficient proof of any averment which requires to be established by evidence given by a witness in person . . .

16. We have already indicated our view that the law of corroboration requires immediate reform. Any serious and unexpected difficulties or anomalies to which that reform may give rise can be dealt with as opportunities occur, and as the branches of law in which they arise become the subjects of examination. To wait for reform of any branch of the law until every possible anomaly could be dealt with would mean that the whole of the law would have to be examined before any proposal such as the present one could be put forward. This would be an example of the best being the enemy of the good . . .

V. Consultation

19. In accordance with a practice which we have found to be useful and convenient, an indication of our intention to submit recommendations on this topic was given to the Lord President of the Court of Session, the Faculty of Advocates, and the Law Society of Scotland, who were all asked for their informal comments. These were generally unfavourable to our proposals. At that stage it was our intention to confine the alteration of the law in relation to corroboration to actions of damages for personal injuries, on the view that this was the field in which reform was most urgently called for and at the same time one in which less controversy was likely to arise. The Faculty of Advocates submitted two informal memoranda, from both of which it was plain that the proposals as stated would probably not command the approval of the Faculty, and that the principal objection was to the difficulties and anomalies which would arise from the confining of any new rules to so narrow a class of action. Thus one of these memoranda states, 'It is of course accepted that some injustices occur. While that may be, it would appear that the Faculty would be strongly opposed to the present proposal, which is apparently confined to actions of damages for personal injuries.' We have come to the conclusion that the objection to the proposal as originally stated is sound. The shortcomings of the present rule are most obvious in actions of damages for personal injury, but there is no doubt that serious difficulties might arise in the application of different rules of evidence in

various classes of case. Obvious examples are actions of relief or for professional negligence which may require the proof of facts relating to personal injuries. Moreover, the criticism of the present rule is just as cogent in civil causes other than those arising from personal injury.

20. Both the Faculty of Advocates and the Law Society of Scotland expressed concern at the proposal to legislate piecemeal rather than by general review. This opinion is entitled to respect, but if the fact be that injustice is being done now, as we believe it is, and if it is possible to isolate this particular matter and to deal with it separately, then we submit that society ought not to be obliged to put up any longer with an unjust law which can easily be altered. An additional advantage of dealing with this matter separately is that some experience will have been gained of its working before the time comes to decide whether to incorporate it in our proposed Code of Evidence.

21. Another opinion expressed was that with a little diligence on the part of his advisers any party who has no eye-witness of his accident can secure the necessary corroboration from surrounding circumstances if his story is true. We were satisfied from our own experience that this suggestion had no foundation, but we made enquiries and were informed by a number of solicitors experienced in this branch of the law that such corroboration is not always available. A typical reply received in June, 1966 is as follows, 'In fact since January 1, 1966, I have opened up 116 files for such claims. In this number, I have had approximately ten repudiations of liability to date. In, I would say, half these repudiations my client was unable to press his or her claim because of inability to corroborate the circumstances of the accident even although it was quite apparent that if such evidence had been available, the claim was a sound one.' Another reply states, 'I find that, particularly in the textile industry with the ever increasing size of machinery coupled with the fact that one operator can now control many functions of a machine, people work in isolation. From this point of view it is becoming increasingly difficult to obtain corroborative evidence as to the circumstances surrounding an accident.'

VI. Conclusion

23. The rule requiring corroboration is a survival from the early history of Scots law. It is no longer justified in the class of case in which we recommend its abolition. It is unknown or has long been abandoned in most other systems of jurisprudence. We are not convinced by any of the reasons which have been advanced for its retention. It is causing real hardship to individuals in Scotland today."

Notes

Lord Devlin's dictum from *Cleisham v. B.T.C.*, quoted by the Commissioners, was criticised by Lord President Clyde in *Hughes v. Stewart*, 1964 S.C. 155 on the basis that it failed to state the full rigour of the rule requiring corroboration:

> "As a test for the credibility of a witness, it may well be justifiable, but it has never been regarded as satisfying the needs of corroborative evidence as understood in Scotland. A witness's account, however probable it may be, is not sufficient to constitute legal proof of a ground of action . . . In the present case it would not, in my opinion, have been enough in Scotland for the pursuer to have argued that in the light of an admitted collision between his vehicle and the defender's motor car his account of how that collision took place was sufficiently corroborated by the fact that his story was more probable than any other account. He can secure corroboration only if he leads other evidence than his own of facts more consistent with his account of how the collision occurred than any other account of it."

The "generally unfavourable" response to the Scottish Law Commission's proposals was maintained when draft legislation was placed before Parliament. Paradoxically, given the nature of the concerns which emerged during consultation, amendments made to the legislation as a result of Parliamentary opposition limited the reform to actions involving personal injury.

2.   Law Reform (Miscellaneous Provisions) (Scotland) Act
1968, s.9

Section 9, which came into operation on November 25, 1968, provided:

"(1) This section applies to any action of damages where the damages claimed consist of, or include, damages or solatium in respect of personal injuries (including any disease, and any impairment of physical or mental condition) sustained by the pursuer or any other person.

(2) Subject to subsection (4) of this section, any rule of law whereby in any proceedings evidence tending to establish any fact, unless it is corroborated by other evidence, is not to be taken as sufficient proof of that fact shall cease to have effect in relation to any action to which this section applies, and accordingly, subject as aforesaid, in any such action the court shall be entitled, if they are satisfied that any fact has been established by evidence which has been given in that action, to find that fact proved by that evidence, notwithstanding that the evidence is not corroborated.

(3) In relation to an action tried by jury, the reference in subsection (2) of this section to the court shall be construed as a reference to the jury.

(4) This section shall not—

(a) affect the operation of any enactment passed or made before the commencement of this Act, or

(b) apply for the purposes of any appeal or other proceedings arising out of any proceedings in which the proof or trial has taken place, or the evidence has otherwise been given, before such commencement.

(5) The references in this section to the giving of evidence are references to the giving of evidence in any manner, whether orally or by the production of documents or otherwise."

NOTES

In practice, this section met with a certain degree of judicial resistance—perhaps not surprising in view of the response of the Faculty of Advocates and the House of Lords to the reforms proposed by the SLC. This resistance was led by Lord President Clyde. In *Morrison v. J. Kelly and Sons Ltd*, 1970 S.C. 65 he said:

"Section 9(2) of the 1968 Act does not eliminate corroboration altogether. On the contrary, corroborative evidence still constitutes a valuable check on the accuracy of a witness's evidence. There may be cases where owing to the nature of the circumstances corroboration is unobtainable. Such a case may be an appropriate subject for the application of the subsection. But, where corroboration or contradiction of the pursuer's account of the matter is available, a court would obviously be very slow indeed to proceed upon the pursuer's evidence alone. The test under the subsection is a relatively high one. The Court must be 'satisfied that [the] fact has been established'. How could the Court be satisfied if corroborative evidence was available but without any explanation not produced? Or again, how could it be satisfied if a large body of directly contradictory evidence was led at the proof, the only criticism of which was that it differed from the pursuer's account?"

Morrison can be relatively easily distinguished, since in that case the pursuer was not only uncorroborated, he was actively contradicted by all of the other witnesses, including two witnesses for the pursuer. In those circumstances, the Lord Ordinary's decision to find for the pursuer would be open to criticism unless it adequately explained why an uncorroborated pursuer should be preferred to such a substantial body of evidence. In the event the Lord President makes clear in no uncertain terms that the Lord Ordinary's treatment of that question was very far from providing such an explanation.

Much of what Lord President Clyde says in *Morrison v. J. Kelly & Sons* is concerned with the right and duty of an Appellate court to review the Lord Ordinary's decision on the facts. Do you think that section 9 makes the trial judge's view of the witnesses' credibility and reliability more or less important? Compare Lord Stott's opinion in *McLaren v. Caldwell's Paper Mills Ltd*, 1973 S.L.T. 158, below, and see Chapter 15, below.

Lord President Clyde returned to the attack in the following case, *McGowan v. The Lord Advocate*.

3. McGowan v. Lord Advocate
1972 S.C. 68

LORD PRESIDENT (CLYDE): "This is a motion for a new trial in an action of damages brought by an injured workman against his employers. The defender is the Lord Advocate as representing the Ministry of Defence. The action is based on negligence on the part of the employers. After a trial before a jury the employers were found liable, and the pursuer was awarded a sum of £600 in name of damages. The defender has brought the present motion for a new trial before the Division.

The accident took place while the pursuer was assisting the unloading of certain boxes of ammunition from a trailer on to a platform, immediately behind which stood a railway wagon. The boxes were built up on to a pallet resting on the trailer. Two slings were placed round the pallet, and the ends of each sling were attached to the hook of an overhead crane, by means of which the loaded pallet was raised up from the trailer and swung over and then on to the platform. In addition to the pursuer who was engaged in this operation there was a craneman, who operated the crane, and two men who built up the boxes on the pallet and put on the two slings. The pursuer was assisting the lowering of the load on to the platform at the end of the operation.

The pursuer's case is that on the occasion in question one of the two slings slipped off one corner of the pallet as the load approached the platform. When it slipped, the load tilted and jammed and injured his hand against the railway wagon. The pursuer sought in evidence to explain why one of the two slings slipped off the edge of the pallet as it was being lowered on to the railway truck by stating that the sling was twisted when attached to the fall of the crane, and that, as the load descended, the twist came out with a jerk and caused the descending pallet to tilt over and swing out of its normal alignment.

The only witness on the merits called for the pursuer was one of the two slingers. He in no way corroborates the slipping of the load and positively contradicts the suggestion that a sling was twisted or that there was any tilt or jerk as the load was being lowered. It is fair to add that no attack of any kind was made on the accuracy or reliability of the evidence of this witness by the pursuer to the jury in support of his case.

The fault alleged is a defective system of slinging. The pursuer, without any experience of the work, expressed the opinion that it was unsafe. But it is established on the evidence that the method of slinging employed was the normal one, which had been in use for many years without trouble, and the slinger who gave evidence said that it was perfectly safe for the work being done. It may be that some safer method could have been devised, but this would not establish that the system in use was a negligent one. The jury had before them no evidence upon which they were entitled to hold that the system in operation was faulty.

The pursuer sought in argument before us to avoid the consequences of the lack of corroboration of the pursuer's evidence as to how the accident happened by founding upon section 9 of the Law Reform (Miscellaneous Provisions) (Scotland) Act, 1968. In our opinion that section, however, will not avail the pursuer in the present case. In the first place, this is not a case with which section 9 was primarily intended to deal, namely, one where the accident occurred in the absence of any eye-witness other than the pursuer himself: see *Morrison v. J. Kelly & Sons Ltd.*, at p.77. In the present case there were at least three other witnesses of the accident, whose evidence might have corroborated the pursuer. But in fact no material part of the pursuer's account of the accident was in any way corroborated. In the second place, the only one of the three other witnesses whose evidence the pursuer did lead, so far from corroborating his account of how the accident happened, directly contradicts the pursuer's account in every material respect. This other witness's evidence is not challenged as false or inaccurate. In such a situation section 9 will not assist the pursuer.

In this state of the evidence the jury were precluded from having before them in support of the essential elements in the pursuer's case any evidence upon which they could on any reasonable view find them to be proved: see *McGhee v. Glasgow Coal Co.* at p.298. It follows that there was no evidence upon which this jury could reasonably be satisfied within the meaning of section 9(2) that these essential elements were established. This is not a case in which the pursuer's evidence can be treated merely as if it stood alone and uncorroborated, and it seems clear that no reasonable jury would have been entitled to accept the unsupported evidence of the pursuer, which was contradicted by the evidence of the only other eye-witness to the accident led by the pursuer. In these circumstances, in our view, the verdict cannot stand."

NOTES

Lord President Clyde's view of section 9 appears to have been based upon what he perceived as the "mischief" with which that section was designed to deal—namely the problem of the pursuer injured while working alone, or at night, when no corroboration would be available. He was unhappy about the situation where there were witnesses to the accident who were not called to give their view of events. On one view his fear was perfectly justifiable. A decision not to call as a witness someone who may have relevant information about an event is often based on the view that his or her evidence is likely to be unhelpful or even hostile. On the other hand, it might be thought unreasonable that a pursuer should be required to do the defenders' work for them! This divergence of opinion about section 9 emerges very clearly from Lord Stott's opinion in the following case, *McLaren v. Caldwell's Paper Mill Company Ltd*.

4. McLaren v. Caldwell's Paper Mill Company Ltd
1973 S.L.T. 158

The pursuer was the driver of a crane which was being towed up a hill by a lorry belonging to the defenders. The pursuer averred that the tow rope broke while the crane was on the hill, and in order to hold the crane on the gradient, he had to apply such pressure to the clutch of the crane that he injured his knee. On the uncorroborated evidence of the pursuer the Lord Ordinary found the defenders to be at fault in failing to provide a tow rope of sufficient strength for use in towing up gradients. The defenders reclaimed on the ground that the Lord Ordinary was not entitled to make such a finding without corroboration of the pursuer's account.

LORD KISSEN: "In making his findings the Lord Ordinary relied for proof of essential facts on the evidence of the pursuer alone. Although there was some other evidence, which was far from satisfactory, that a towing rope was used to assist the said crane up gradients on the day of the said accident, the pursuer alone spoke to the breaking of the tow rope, the result of that breaking and its effect on his knee.

The major submission by defender's counsel was that, despite the terms of section 9(2) of the Law Reform (Miscellaneous Provisions) (Scotland) Act 1968, the Lord Ordinary was not entitled to make the crucial finding which he did on the pursuer's uncorroborated evidence. The Lord Ordinary said *inter alia* that, having regard 'to the pursuer's demeanour in the witness box', he formed the view that 'he was fully credible and reasonably reliable'. It was argued by junior counsel for the defenders that the Lord Ordinary was not entitled to make that finding on credibility and reliability and that even if he was, said section 9 could not be applied where there had been undue delay in raising the action or where a witness who might have been called to corroborate the pursuer had not been called. Senior counsel for the defenders was more moderate in regard to the alternative. He maintained that a court would have great difficulty in being satisfied that any essential fact had been proved by uncorroborated evidence, where there had been undue delay or failure to call a witness who might have corroborated the pursuer, but that a court could be so satisfied in appropriate circumstances. Both also founded on various other matters in their attack on the Lord Ordinary's finding in regard to the pursuer's credibility and reliability. I refer to these later but firstly, I state my own views on the effect of section 9(2) in a case like the present. The Lord Ordinary did not mention said section 9(2) in his opinion.

Reference was made to two cases where said section 9(2) had been considered. These cases were *Morrison v. Kelly*, 1970 S.L.T. 198 and *McGowan v. Lord Advocate*, 1972 S.L.T. 188. The facts in these two cases were very different from the facts of the present case in some important respects. The latter case was concerned with a motion for a new trial. In the former case, however, there were observations on the circumstances in which an appellate court could refuse to accept the views of a trial judge on the credibility and reliability of a witness and there were references to judicial dicta in the leading cases where this was considered. My opinion is that in a case where section 9(2) has to be applied, that is, in a case where the pursuer is not corroborated on crucial facts, the evaluation and assessment of a pursuer's evidence requires special care and attention because of the absence of corroborative evidence. A trial judge should, I think, be more hesitant in accepting such evidence as credible and reliable in the absence of supporting evidence from other sources. The difficulty of accepting such uncorroborated evidence will, in my opinion, be increased where there has been *mora* and therefore a heavier onus ... Likewise the difficulty of assessment and evaluation of uncorroborated evidence may be increased where the trial judge has to weigh and assess the importance of contrary evidence or the absence of other evidence which might have been led and which might have corroborated the uncorroborated evidence."

LORD STOTT: "A Lord Ordinary's view on the credibility of a witness is not sacrosanct. An appellate court, either because the reasons given by the trial judge are not satisfactory or because it is satisfied that he has not taken proper advantage of his having seen and heard the witnesses, is entitled to substitute its own view for his: *Thomas v. Thomas*, 1947 S.C. (HL) 45; 1948 S.L.T. 2, per Lord Thankerton at pp.5–6. But that jurisdiction has to be exercised within narrow limits. In the words of Lord Greene, M.R. in *Yuill v. Yuill* (approved by the House of Lords in *Thomas*): 'It can, of course, only be on the rarest occasions, and in circumstances where the appellate court is convinced by the plainest considerations, that it would be justified in finding that the trial judge had formed a wrong opinion'. In the present case counsel for the reclaimers has made certain criticisms of the pursuer's evidence some of which have been dealt with by the Lord Ordinary and some of which have not, but, in my opinion, anything that has been said in that regard falls far short of what has hitherto been required to enable an appellate court after making allowance for possible exaggeration to say that the Lord Ordinary's judgment of credibility was wrong.

But that, it was submitted, is not the proper approach when corroboration is no longer needed and the judge of first instance has decided an issue on the evidence of a single witness. In such a case, it was said, the appellate court must have a wider latitude to interfere. It is not clear why that should be so. It is plain from the terms of section 9 that 'the court' who have to be satisfied that a fact has been established by the evidence of a single witness must be, in the first instance at least, the judge who hears the proof, or if the action is tried by a jury, the jury. That being so one might perhaps be inclined to think that, since so much may turn on the evidence of one witness, the impression formed by the judge who saw and heard him in the witness box becomes more rather than less important. But that view of the effect of the section will not stand with the decision of the other division of this court in *Morrison v. J. Kelly & Sons*, 1970 S.L.T. 198, where it was held that section 9(2) did not alter or lessen the power of a court of appeal to review in appropriate cases the decision on an issue of fact of judge of first instance or the necessity for that judge to state adequate and sufficient reasons for his acceptance or rejection of evidence.

Morrison (supra) it is fair to say was a very different case from the present. It was a case in which the pursuer's evidence which was accepted by the Lord Ordinary was not only uncorroborated but was in direct conflict with the evidence of other witnesses whom the Lord Ordinary rejected for no other reason (so Lord President Clyde states at p.202) than that their evidence was inconsistent with the pursuer's. Here by contrast there was no competing version for the Lord Ordinary to assess. On that part of the case on which the Lord Ordinary has found for the pursuer the defenders relied on a simple *non probatum* and the credibility and reliability of the pursuer was necessarily the decisive factor.

Counsel for the reclaimer, however, has put forward three grounds on which it is submitted that the Lord Ordinary's assessment of credibility is vitiated. (1) The Lord Ordinary has made no comment on the failure of the pursuer to lead corroborative evidence which was not shown to be unavailable, *viz.* the evidence of the driver whose lorry according to the pursuer was at the other end of the tow rope when the rope broke. (2) He has said nothing about mora. (3) He has failed in weighing up the pursuer's credibility to have regard to contradictions between the pursuer's evidence and that of other witnesses on collateral matters.

(1) In the first of these submissions it seems to me that there is no substance whatever. It is to be observed that one of the grounds of action in the case as pled by the pursuer is fault on the part of the lorry driver. So far as I am aware it has never been normal practice for a party to a reparation action in Scotland to adduce as a witness a person whom he is blaming for his injuries. If the rule of law referred to in section 9 of the Act had still applied at the time of the proof, it might have been necessary for the pursuer to have adduced the lorry driver. But once that rule is gone I demur to the suggestion that it was incumbent upon the pursuer to adduce a witness who may or may not have been a hostile witness in order to see whether that witness's evidence corroborated or contradicted his own. The argument I think stems from some words of the Lord President in *Morrison* (at p.203 of the S.L.T. report) which counsel for the reclaimers tended to read as an indication that it is inappropriate to apply section 9 in a case where corroborative evidence might have been obtainable. I doubt if the words will bear the meaning that counsel sought to ascribe to them but if they do I respectfully disagree with them. The terms of the section do not suggest that it was intended to benefit only the man working alone. They are general and comprehensive and appear to have been chosen not with reference to any special set of circumstances but as a general remedy for the anomaly and injustice arising from a rule of law whereby the Court, convinced that an injured man had given a truthful account of his accident, were nevertheless bound to reject it from lack of corroboration. The Act now requires to be read subject to the ratio of the decision in *Morrison v. Kelly*. But it is one thing to say, as was said in *Morrison*, that the evidence of a single witness should not have been accepted when there was a weight of evidence the other way. It is quite another to say, as counsel for the reclaimers appears to say, that the evidence of the pursuer should have been rejected because there was an uncalled witness whose evidence might have been contradictory."

NOTES

The court in all of these cases was at pains to emphasise the need for care in the assessment of uncorroborated evidence and that any court should be slow to proceed on the basis of such evidence—see also *McCallum v. British Railways Board*, 1989 S.L.T. 296. However, *Morrison* and *McGowan* on the one hand, and *McLaren v. Caldwell's* on the other, suggest mutually exclusive views on the scope and effect of section 9(2). In spite of Lord Stott's efforts to distinguish *Morrison*, that case would appear to be authority for just the proposition that counsel for the reclaimers argued in *McLaren*. The weight of judicial opinion on section 9(2) favours the *Morrison* view. See further Field, "Going It Alone", 1989 S.L.T. (News) 216, *Sands v. George Waterston & Sons*, 1989 S.L.T. 174 and *McArthur v. Organon Laboratories*, 1982 S.L.T. 425. Lord Stott has made some pungent comments about Lord Clyde's decision in *Morrison v. Kelly & Sons*—see Stott, *Judge's Diary* (1995) pp.241–242. The full rigour of the *Morrison v. Kelly* "rule" appears in the following case: *Mason v. S L D Olding Ltd*.

5. Mason v. S.L.D. Olding Ltd
1982 S.L.T. 385

The pursuer in an action for reparation in respect of personal injuries sustained in an accident in the course of his employment with the defenders, blamed his employers *inter alia* for failure to institute a safe system of work and vicariously for the alleged negligence of their foreman, named Lundie. The pursuer averred that the accident happened when he was assisting Lundie in repairing a machine for laying asphalt on roads. Lundie, he averred, had instructed him to finish welding a lug on the bottom of a part of the machine called the hopper, the side of which was in accordance with usual practice propped up with a piece of wood. While he was so engaged, averred the pursuer, the prop slipped out of position and the side of the hopper fell upon and crushed his hand. The pursuer averred *inter alia* that the defenders should have required that such sides be supported by several independent means of support; that alternatively Lundie should have supported the hopper safely and securely by means *inter alia* of the nearby crane and that before instructing the pursuer to carry out the work, he should have inspected the prop to ensure that it was firmly wedged. At the proof the pursuer's evidence was wholly uncorroborated. He did not seek to lead Lundie as a witness nor did he give any explanation for his failure to do so. The pursuer submitted that provided he was accepted as a reliable witness, no corroboration of his account was required by virtue of section 9(2) of the 1968 Act. In rejecting this submission, Lord Robertson said:

"In order to succeed in the action as now pled, the pursuer must establish the facts as set out by him. In particular it is essential for him to establish that the job on which he was engaged was set up by Lundie, and that Lundie raised the side of the hopper, propped it, commenced to weld, was called away while welding, and instructed the pursuer to finish the welding. He must further establish that on Lundie's instructions he went in underneath the side, that when he was in there the side came down because the prop was disturbed, and that his hand was thereby jammed and injured.

Apart from the admissions on record by the defenders that on the day of the accident the pursuer was assisting Lundie, and that one of the sides of the hopper was being repaired, there is no evidence at all—apart from the pursuer's own evidence—that Lundie had anything to do with the accident or was there just before it. It was argued on behalf of the pursuer that, provided the pursuer was accepted as a credible and reliable witness, no corroboration of his account was required (Law Reform (Miscellaneous Provisions) (Scotland) Act 1968, section 9(2)). But I do not think that this argument is valid in the present case (see *Morrison v. J. Kelly & Sons Ltd.*, 1970 S.L.T 198, Lord President Clyde at p.203). Corroboration of the vital parts of the pursuer's account was obtainable from Lundie, and no explanation was produced as to why he was not led as a witness. Although the pursuer in his alternative case blamed Lundie, this was not his stronger case, and indeed, for reasons which I shall later mention, was of doubtful relevancy. Lundie was not present—according to the pursuer—at the time when the accident actually occurred, but his evidence would have accorded vital corroboration to the pursuer on the major branch of his case against the defenders. There is nothing unusual in a pursuer leading as a witness a fellow-workman, or superior, whom he blames for an accident. In the absence of the evidence of Lundie, without any explanation being offered to explain this absence, I am not satisfied that the pursuer has established, by the evidence he has led, the facts of the accident essential to his success (in terms of section 9(2) of the 1968 Act)."

NOTES

In *McDougall v. James Jones & Sons*, unreported, November 27, 1970, Lord Avonside said:

"I should add this, that even if I had at best been somewhat suspicious of the credibility of the pursuer that would have availed him nothing in the circumstances of this case. Section 9(2) of the Law Reform (Miscellaneous Provisions) (Scotland) Act, 1968, would allow me to accept uncorroborated evidence if I were satisfied that any fact had been established by evidence which had been given in the action. I could not possibly be so satisfied. It was said by [counsel for the pursuer] that the only other witness available was the foreman, Troup, and that since the foreman was, as it were, an agent of the defenders and himself blamed for the occurrence of the accident he could not be expected to call him. With this I disagree. If there is evidence available bearing on the proof of the matter it appears to me that that evidence *must* be led in any case in which the pursuer has spoken alone and where his testimony is of doubtful credit. Not only was there no suggestion that Mr Troup was not available, but in fact he was on the list of witnesses handed to me by agents for the pursuer as the pursuer's witness. It cannot be contemplated that the effect of the Act would be to allow a pursuer to succeed in these circumstances." [emphasis added]

McDougall and *Mason*, both Outer House cases, were decided before the opinions in *McLaren v. Caldwell's* were issued (*Mason* on June 14, 1972, in spite of the date of the report in Scots Law Times). Although both *Mason* and *McDougall* follow the *Morrison* line on the applicability of section 9, it seems that where a potential witness is being blamed for an accident, and can therefore be assumed to be likely to be a hostile witness, the *Morrison* rule does not apply and failure to call that witness will not be fatal to the pursuer's case. It appears further that a pursuer can succeed where he or she leads corroborative evidence which is subsequently rejected as unreliable—see *Thomson v. Tough Ropes*, 1978 S.L.T. (Notes) 5; *Comerford v. Strathclyde Regional Council*, 1987 S.C.L.R. 758 (Sh. Ct.).

6.   Civil Evidence (Scotland) Act 1988 (c.32), s.1

"1.—(1) In any civil proceedings the court or, as the case may be, the jury, if satisfied that any fact has been established by evidence in those proceedings, shall be entitled to find that fact proved by that evidence notwithstanding that the evidence is not corroborated.

(2) Any rule of law whereby any evidence may be taken to be corroborated by a false denial shall cease to have effect."

NOTES

In their Report on Evidence (Scot. Law Com. No. 100, 1986) the Scottish Law Commission made the following recommendations (p.43):

"1. The requirement of corroboration in civil proceedings in so far as it still applies should be abolished.
    2. The abolition of the requirement of corroboration in civil proceedings should extend to all civil proceedings, including consistorial proceedings."

The result of the 1986 Report was the Civil Evidence (Scotland) Act 1988, which gives legislative effect to the SLC's recommendation that the requirement of corroboration be abolished in all civil proceedings (and incidentally repeals section 9 of the 1968 Act). The question therefore arises as to whether the same approach—the *Morrison v. Kelly* approach—taken to section 9 also applies to the new provisions under the 1988 Act. There is little direct authority. In *McKay v. Yarrow Shipbuilders Ltd* (OH), unreported July 4, 1991. Lord Osborne said:

"In relation to section 9(2) of the Law Reform (Miscellaneous Provisions) (Scotland) Act 1968, the predecessor of section 1(1) of the Act of 1988, which applied only to actions of damages for personal injuries, it was said by Lord President Clyde in *Morrison v. J. Kelly and Sons Limited*, 1970 S.C. 65, at p.79, that corroborative evidence still constituted a valuable check on the accuracy of a witness' evidence. Where corroboration or contradiction of a pursuer's account of a matter was available, a Court would obviously be very slow indeed to proceed upon the pursuer's evidence alone. It appears to me that these expressions of opinion regarding the operation of section 9 of the Act of 1968 are equally applicable to the application of section 1(1) of the Act of 1988."

In *L v. L*, 1996 S.L.T. 767, Lord Hamilton said:

"In my view authorities on the application of section 9(2) of the Law Reform (Miscellaneous Provisions) (Scotland) Act 1968 are of assistance on the application of section 1(1) of the 1988 Act insofar as they indicate that, notwithstanding the abolition of the rule that corroboration is required for legal sufficiency, a failure to lead other evidence which might have supported the single witness speaking to the crucial fact may be material to the issue whether the court is satisfied that that fact has been proved by the evidence led. Failure to lead apparently available corroboration was a ground of judgment in *McGowan v. Lord Advocate*. Even where the single witness's evidence is or appears to be credible, corroborative evidence may still constitute a valuable check on the accuracy of the witness's evidence . . ."

Lord Hamilton also went on to hold that failure to lead a witness potentially supportive of credibility (by giving evidence of prior consistent statements) was also relevant to the *credibility* of the uncorroborated witness. That view was disapproved by the First Division in *L v. L*, 1998 S.L.T. 672; 1997 S.C.L.R. 866 per the Lord President at 871, discussed further below. Lord Coulsfield went further. He said (at p.875–876):

". . . I am uneasy about the so-called rule, derived from *McLaren v. Caldwell's Paper Mill Co. Ltd* and earlier cases, that failure to lead corroborative evidence which appears to have been available should lead a judge to regard evidence which has been led with special care and attention. Your Lordship has set out the arguments against the suggestion that any rule laid down in the *McLaren* case should be extended to the case of failure to lead evidence supportive of credibility and I entirely agree with those arguments. I would however, be inclined to go further and suggest that those same arguments cast doubt on the validity of any rule which may appear to have been laid down in *McLaren* and the earlier cases. The enactments which have rendered corroboration unnecessary in civil cases have provided that, in the appropriate circumstances, the evidence of a single witness is sufficient to establish any fact. I have never been clear what basis there could be for imposing some limitation upon the effect of those enactments by suggesting that there is some kind of rule that failure to lead corroborative evidence in some way qualifies the sufficiency of a single witness. In any event, none of the three decisions particularly referred to [*Morrison, McGowan, and McLaren*] is apt to provide the basis for a supposed rule . . . I would question whether the observations in the opinions in those cases, insofar as they do appear to suggest that there is some rule in the matter, were necessary for the decision. There was, however, no attempt to argue, in the present case, that the cases were wrongly decided or that the observations in them were not well founded. I content myself therefore with observing that the decisions, or at any rate the observations as to the proper treatment of the evidence of a single witness, may be open to reconsideration when a suitable opportunity offers."

See also comments by Lord President Hope in *M. v. Kennedy*, 1993 S.C.L.R. 69. Finally, in *Taylor v. Taylor*, 2000 S.L.T. 1419; 2001 S.C.L.R. 16, Lord Prosser, delivering the Opinion of the Court said that:

"It will always be a matter of circumstances, when corroboration is not required by law, whether the court will feel able to proceed upon uncorroborated evidence if potential witnesses can be identified who might have corroborated or contradicted the pursuer's account."

Two specialties should be mentioned. First, it is clear that Children's Hearing cases (under the Children (Scotland) Act 1995) are in a special position—see *W. v. Kennedy*, 1988 S.C.L.R. 236; 1988 S.L.T. 583, *K. v. Kennedy*, 1992 S.C.L.R. 386, *F. v. Kennedy (No. 2)*, 1992 S.C.L.R. 750. The *Morrison v. Kelly* "rule" has no application to them—see *K. v. Kennedy*, 1992 S.C.L.R. 386, above.

Second, section 8(3) of the 1988 Act provides that:

(1) In any action to which this subsection applies . . . no decree or judgment in favour of the pursuer shall be pronounced until the grounds of action have been established by evidence . . .
(3) Subject to subsection (4) below, in any action for divorce, separation or declarator of marriage or nullity of marriage, the evidence referred to in subsection (1) above shall consist of or include evidence other than that of a party to the marriage . . .

The court in *Taylor*, above, implied that section 8(3) does not impose a requirement for corroboration, and held that 8(3) certainly does not require "that all possible witnesses be brought to support the pursuer's account. It is enough that there is evidence other than that of the pursuer's which can be regarded as satisfying the requirements of section 8(3), even if that evidence comes from other member of the pursuer's family."

(B) The Abolition of the Rule Against Hearsay

7. Civil Evidence (Scotland) Act 1988 (c.32)

"2.—(1) In any civil proceedings
    (a) evidence shall not be excluded solely on the ground that it is hearsay;
    (b) a statement made by a person otherwise than in the course of the proof shall be admissible as evidence of any matter contained in the statement of which direct oral evidence by that person would be admissible; and
    (c) the court, or as the case may be the jury, if satisfied that any fact has been established by evidence in those proceedings, shall be entitled to find that fact proved by the evidence notwithstanding that the evidence is hearsay.

(2) Nothing in this section shall affect the admissibility of any statement as evidence of the fact that the statement was made.

(3) In paragraph (e) of section 5 of the Court of Session Act 1988 (power to make provision as regards the Court of Session for admission of written statements etc. in lieu of parole evidence), for the words 'the admission in lieu of parole evidence of written statements (including affidavits) and reports, on such conditions as may be prescribed' there shall be substituted the words 'written statements (including affidavits) and reports, admissible under section 2(1)(b) of the Civil Evidence (Scotland) Act 1988, to be received in evidence, on such conditions as may be prescribed, without being spoken to by a witness'.

(4) For paragraph (e) of section 32(1) of the Sheriff Courts (Scotland) Act 1971 corresponding power to make provision as regards the sheriff court) there shall be substituted the following paragraph:

'(e) providing in respect of any category of civil proceedings for written statements (including affidavits) and reports, admissible under section 2(1)(b) of the Civil Evidence (Scotland) Act 1988, to be received in evidence, on such conditions as may be prescribed, without being spoken to by a witness;'

3. In any civil proceedings a statement made otherwise than in the course of the proof by a person who at the proof is examined as to the statement shall be admissible as evidence in so far as it tends to reflect favourably or unfavourably on that person's credibility.

4.—(1) For the purposes of section 2 or 3 above, any person may at the proof, with leave of the court, at any time before the commencement of closing submissions—

(a) be recalled as a witness whether or not he has been present in court since giving evidence initially; or

(b) be called as an additional witness whether or not he has been present in court during the proof (or during any other part of the proceedings).

(2) Nothing in section 3 of the Evidence (Scotland) Act 1840 (presence in court not to disqualify witnesses in certain cases) shall apply as respects a witness called or recalled under subsection (1) above.

9. In this Act, unless the context otherwise requires—

'business' includes trade or profession;

'civil proceedings' includes, in addition to such proceedings in any of the ordinary courts of law—

(a) any hearing by the sheriff under section 42 of the Social Work (Scotland) Act 1968 of an application for a finding as to whether grounds for the referral of a child's case to a children's hearing are established, except in so far as the application relates to a ground mentioned in section 32(2)(g) of that Act (commission by the child of an offence);

(b) any arbitration, whether or not under an enactment, except in so far as, in relation to the conduct of the arbitration, specific provision has been made as regards the rules of evidence which are to apply;

(c) any proceedings before a tribunal or inquiry, except in so far as, in relation to the conduct of proceedings before the tribunal or inquiry, specific provision has been made as regards the rules of evidence which are to apply; and

(d) any other proceedings conducted wholly or mainly in accordance with rules of procedure agreed between the parties themselves (or as respects which it would have been open to them to agree such rules had they wished to do so) except in so far as any such agreement makes specific provision as regards the rules of evidence which are to apply;

'court' shall be construed in accordance with the definition of 'civil proceedings';

'document' includes, in addition to a document in writing,—

(a) any map, plan, graph or drawing;

(b) any photograph;

(c) any disc, tape, sound track or other device in which sounds or other data (not being visual images) are recorded so as to be capable (with or without the aid of some other equipment) of being reproduced therefrom; and

(d) any film, negative, tape or other device in which one or more visual images are recorded so as to be capable (as aforesaid) of being reproduced therefrom;

'film' includes a microfilm;

'hearsay' includes hearsay of whatever degree;

'made' includes 'allegedly made';

'proof' includes trial or other hearing of evidence, proof on commission and any continued proof;

'records' means records in whatever form;

'statement' includes any representation (however made or expressed) of fact or opinion but does not include a statement in a precognition; and 'undertaking' includes any public or statutory undertaking, any local authority and any government department."

NOTES

The commission concluded that the time had come for such a sweeping reform because of the uncertainty which had crept in to the operation of the rule, evidenced in part by the frequency with which it was being ignored in practice in matters which were non-contentious. The Commission was also aware that in those contexts in which the old hearsay rule was not applicable anyway (*e.g.* industrial tribunals) no major problem had been experienced, and that when the hearsay rule was enforced, the courts were occasionally being denied the best evidence available to them (*e.g.* an eyewitness statement made shortly after an incident; see *e.g. Waugh v. British Railways Board* [1980] A.C. 521). (See further Field, *Scottish Current Law Statutes*, annotations to 1988 Act.)

Section 2 thus sweeps away the hearsay rule in all "civil proceedings"—the latter term includes proceedings in any of the "ordinary courts of law"; hearings before a Sheriff under section 42 of the Social Work (Scotland) Act 1968 except where it is alleged that the child concerned has himself or herself committed an offence (*Harris v. F.*, 1991 S.L.T. 242); arbitrations; and proceedings for breach of interdict (*Byrne v. Ross*, 1993 S.L.T. 307). In contrast to recent reforms of the hearsay rule in criminal cases, the definition of hearsay includes "hearsay of whatever degree"—thus, hearsay of hearsay, etc., is admissible under the new provisions. Is it likely that the courts would be happy to proceed on the basis of such evidence?

8. K. v. F. J. Kennedy (Reporter to Children's Panel, Strathclyde Region) 1992 S.C.L.R. 386

The appellant was the father of a 14-year-old girl who was referred to the children's panel and subsequently to the sheriff for proof on three allegations. The third allegation was that the appellant had used lewd and libidinous practices towards the girl. The evidence before the sheriff included a statement made by the girl to a police officer shortly after the allegations came to light. During evidence before the sheriff the girl retracted the statement. The sheriff did not accept the girl's retraction and decided that the statement made to the police was sufficient and acceptable evidence to find the ground proved. The father appealed to the Inner House, which refused the appeal, finding that the sheriff was both entitled and justified in taking the hearsay evidence of the police officer as establishing the third ground.

LORD SUTHERLAND: "The appellant is the father of a girl now aged fourteen who was referred to a children's hearing on three grounds, namely lack of parental care likely to cause her unnecessary suffering; that an offence had been committed in respect of her involving assault, ill-treatment or exposure; and that an offence had been committed in respect of her, namely lewd and libidinous behaviour. The grounds of referral were not accepted and accordingly the matter was remitted to the sheriff to consider whether or not the grounds were established. The sheriff found that all three grounds were established. The present appeal is taken by the appellant only in respect of the third ground of referral, namely that an offence of lewd and libidinous behaviour had been committed by him in respect of the girl. In the stated case the sheriff has made eight findings of fact relating to lewd and libidinous behaviour on the part of the appellant. The peculiarity of this case is that the findings in fact were made largely on the basis of a statement made by the girl to a police officer. This statement was made on December 4, 1990 and at the children's hearing on December 7, it was retracted by the girl. Her retraction was repeated to the police on December 9, and before the sheriff the girl also maintained that although she had made this statement on December 4, it was not true. The sheriff, for reasons which he explains, did not accept the girl's retraction of the statement and has accepted that the statement admittedly made to the police on December 4, was in fact true. He founded on section 2 of the Civil Evidence (Scotland) Act 1988 to justify this course and in terms of section 1 of that Act it would not be necessary for there to be corroboration [sic]. The sheriff makes it clear that he did not take such a step lightly but only after weighing up all the sources of evidence. The sheriff sets out in his note what the sources of evidence were. In the first place, the police officer who took the statement on December 4, gave evidence and spoke not only to the terms of the statement but also to the fact that the girl was distressed while giving it. A friend of the family spoke to the girl telling her on December 2, 1990 about sexual interference from the appellant and it was this friend who arranged for the girl to see social workers and then the police. A cousin of the girl, who had been staying as a lodger for a few months in 1990, also gave evidence. She spoke to one occasion on which she went into the girl's bedroom and found the appellant sitting on the bed 'carrying on' with the girl. She said that on most nights the girl would bring bedclothes into her room and ask to sleep beside her but never said why. She also said that although she did not see any direct sexual interference, the appellant was always in the girl's bedroom with the door closed but she never really thought much about it. She denied that the girl ever complained to her about sexual interference although in the girl's statement to the police it was suggested that the girl had made such a complaint to her. The sheriff, however, found that this witness was not satisfactory in that she appeared more concerned to protect the appellant and, in particular, he did not accept her denial that the girl had complained to her. The girl herself in evidence admitted that she had made the statement to the police on December 4, but denied that the contents were true. The sheriff formed the view from her demeanour in the witness box that she appeared to be hiding something, was often silent and reluctant to speak, and gave the impression that there was far more behind what she was prepared to say. In these circumstances he rejected her retraction of the original statement. The appellant also gave evidence but the sheriff found that his demeanour was shifty, evasive and unreliable, and he accordingly rejected his evidence also.

Counsel for the appellant accepted that as a matter of law the sheriff would be entitled, in appropriate circumstances, to proceed upon the uncorroborated evidence of what was contained in a statement by the girl even though that statement was subsequently retracted. He argued, however, that in the circumstances of the present case no reasonable sheriff could be satisfied that the ground of referral had been made out. This was because the girl herself was admittedly found to be unreliable and there were a number of witnesses who were mentioned in the girl's statement who could have been called to give evidence but were not. Counsel argued that the test to be applied in a case of this nature was the same as was previously applied in cases under section 9 of the Law Reform (Miscellaneous Provisions) (Scotland) Act 1968. He referred in particular to *Morrison v. J. Kelly & Sons*, 1970 S.C. 65. In that case the Lord President set out the appropriate test to be applied in cases where it was sought to rely upon a pursuer's evidence alone even though corroborative evidence might have been available. In such circumstances a court would obviously be very slow to proceed upon the pursuer's evidence alone. The test under the subsection is a relatively high one and the court must be 'satisfied that the fact is established'. The Lord President then asks the rhetorical question, how could it be satisfied if corroborative evidence was available but without any explanation not produced? Counsel pointed to the fact that the sheriff in his note said that he did not know the reasons why this possible corroborative evidence was not produced. In these circumstances it was argued that the state of the evidence was so unsatisfactory that no reasonable sheriff could have been satisfied as to the truth of the original statement by the child.

Counsel for the respondent argued that the evidence led before the sheriff was sufficient to entitle him to come to the conclusion which he did. In addition to the original statement of the child there was positive evidence that the child had told the family friend about the alleged sexual interference before making the statement to the police and was distressed at the time. The girl did not dispute that she did make such a statement. The cousin, who was referred to in the girl's statement, might not have spoken to all the things that the girl suggested she could have spoken to but, nevertheless, she did give some evidence which would tend to show that the girl's statement was true. The possible witnesses who were not called could only have given similar evidence to that of the family friend rather than direct evidence of sexual interference. In these circumstances there was no need for any further evidence and this court should not interfere with the sheriff's findings, particularly as he had the very considerable advantage of seeing and hearing all the witnesses.

Counsel for the curator *ad litem* adopted the arguments advanced on behalf of the respondent. He also argued that section 9 of the Law Reform (Miscellaneous Provisions (Scotland)) Act had nothing whatever to do with the present case. That section was designed to do away with corroboration in personal injury actions where there were parties to a cause and where the process was adversarial. It is clear from *W v. Kennedy* (I.H.), 1988 S.C.L.R. 236; 1988

S.L.T. 583 that hearings before a sheriff under the Social Work (Scotland) Act are *sui generis* and that the purpose of the hearing is to consider what is in the best interests of the child. Strict rules of evidence and procedure which might be appropriate in adversarial cases are not necessarily appropriate in such hearings.

In our opinion the sheriff was entitled to come to the conclusion which he did and to make the findings of fact which he did on the basis of the child's original statement. Whatever may be the correct construction of section 9 of the Law Reform (Miscellaneous Provisions) (Scotland) Act we are of opinion that this does not assist in considering what is the appropriate approach to a referral under the Social Work Act. The sheriff has to proceed on the basis of the evidence that is before him and is not bound to refrain from relying upon it just because there might have been other evidence which could have been of assistance one way or the other. It is clear from his note that the sheriff considered the evidence very carefully in this case and it is also clear that he did not lightly take the step of proceeding on the basis of the original statement by the girl which was subsequently retracted. Support for the girl's original statement came from the evidence of the friend to whom the girl had made similar complaints two days beforehand and there was also some assistance, albeit slight, from the evidence of the cousin. From what appears in the girl's statement it is unlikely that the evidence from other witnesses mentioned in that statement would have added very much as they could only add indirect evidence which might at best be used to test the accuracy of the girl's statement on incidental matters. Such evidence had already come from the friend of the family and accordingly, in our view, the sheriff was entitled to be of the opinion that he could properly decide the issues of fact on the basis of the evidence which was adduced. While there is no doubt that the evidence in this case was thin, we are of opinion that it could not possibly be said that no sheriff was entitled to take the course which the sheriff did in this case.

The questions asked in the stated case are posed in terms of unnecessary detail and we shall substitute for these questions the one question, 'Was I entitled for the reasons stated in the above note to find the grounds of referral established?', and answer that question in the affirmative."

NOTES

The provisions of the 1988 Act allow for the theoretical possibility that a case could be established on the basis of an uncorroborated hearsay statement. It seemed unlikely that the courts would in practice proceed on the basis on such evidence, but in this case that is more or less what the court did. However, as the court noted, cases heard under the Social Work (Scotland) Act 1968 (now the Children (Scotland) Act 1995) may be in a rather special position, and it seems unlikely that such situations will regularly arise in ordinary civil actions. In any event while such evidence would constitute a bare sufficiency, the onus of proof remains on the Reporter (or pursuer). See the English case of *In re H. (Minors)* [1996] A.C. 563.

9. McVinnie v. McVinnie
1995 S.C.L.R. 480

Rule 72A of the Ordinary Cause Rules 1983 provides *inter alia*:

"(1) Any written statement (including an affidavit) or report, admissible under section 2(1)(6) of the Civil Evidence (Scotland) Act 1988 may be received in evidence in any ordinary cause without being spoken to by a witness subject to the provisions of this rule . . .

(3) Application to the sheriff to receive any such written statement or report in evidence without being spoken to by a witness shall be made by way of motion . . .

(6) On the hearing of such motion, the sheriff may grant the motion, with or without conditions, or may refuse it, or may continue the motion to enable such further information to be obtained as he may require for the purpose of determining the application."

Rule 29.3 of the Ordinary Cause Rules 1993 provides:

"(1) A party may apply by motion for the evidence of a witness to be received by way of affidavit; and the sheriff, after considering the affidavit, may make such order as he thinks fit.

(2) A party may apply by motion for a specified statement or document to be admitted as evidence without calling as a witness the maker of the statement or document; and the sheriff, after considering the statement or document, may make such order on such conditions, if any, as he thinks fit."

SHERIFF MACPHAIL: "This is a motion in an action of divorce which has been set down for proof on March 13 and 14, 1995. The pursuer is the wife. She seeks decree of divorce on the ground of non-cohabitation for more than five years, and payment of a capital sum of £20,000. The husband is defending the action only as regards the crave for a capital sum.

The pursuer's claim for a capital sum is founded on section 9(1)(b) of the Family Law (Scotland) Act 1985. That provision states the principle that fair account is to be taken of any economic advantage derived by either party from contributions by the other, and of any economic disadvantage suffered by either party in the interests of the other party or of the family. In their pleadings each party narrates a lengthy history of the marriage. The part of the pursuer's narrative which is material to the present motion consists of her averments that she made substantial financial contributions to the family. She avers that she had an interest in two properties in Australia, that these properties were sold, and that she contributed to the family her share of the net free proceeds of sale.

It appears that the two properties in Australia were jointly owned by the pursuer and her sister, Mrs Jill Chopping. The pursuer now tenders an affidavit which bears to have been sworn in Australia by Mrs Chopping, who lives in Brisbane. The affidavit runs to 19 paragraphs over nine pages and covers, among other things, the circumstances in which each property was sold and the amount of money the pursuer derived from each sale. It refers to a number of documents which have been lodged in process as productions. In the affidavit Mrs Chopping explains that she is a shop assistant and is unable, due to the distance and cost of travel to Scotland, to give evidence in person. I should add that both parties to this action are assisted persons.

The pursuer now moves that the affidavit should be received in evidence in terms of rule 72A of the First Schedule to the Sheriff Courts (Scotland) Act 1907. The defender opposes the motion. It is not disputed that the affidavit complies with the formal requirements of sub-paragraphs (4)(b) and (5) of rule 72A. The affidavits and the documents to which it refers were lodged in process on January 9, 1995. There was some dispute at the hearing of the motion as to for how long before January 9, the documents and the information in the affidavit had been available to the defender, but I did not understand that to be a live issue at the end of the day.

The fundamental difference between the parties was whether it was appropriate that the affidavit should be received in evidence. Each party's stance was determined by his or her view of the object of rule 72A. Counsel for the defender submitted that the purpose of the rule was to enable the court to have before it evidence which was largely of a non-controversial nature without the inconvenience of witnesses being brought to court. The more critical the evidence was, the less appropriate was the rule 72A procedure. Here the evidence in the affidavit was crucial to the pursuer's case for a capital sum. The defender, however, disputed the terms of a number of the paragraphs of the affidavit and the information in many other paragraphs was outwith his knowledge. Counsel for the defender maintained that the defender would be seriously prejudiced by the introduction of the information in the affidavit. Counsel stated that the defender disputed the contents of [certain] paragraphs . . . Further, the defender could not agree the contents of [certain other] paragraphs because they were outwith his knowledge . . .

Counsel for the Pursuer maintained that the scope of rule 72A was not restricted in the way submitted by counsel for the defender. The pursuer's counsel denied that the defender would suffer prejudice by the affidavit's being received in evidence: on the contrary, any prejudice would be suffered by the pursuer.

Both counsel made detailed submissions as to the contents of the affidavit. It will be appropriate, however, to consider first the dispute between the parties as to the purpose of rule 72A. If it is intended only for evidence which is largely uncontroversial, as the defender submitted, then the motion must be refused on the simple ground that the defender is not prepared to accept much of the information the affidavit contains.

The terms of rule 72A correspond substantially with those of rule 108A of the Rules of the Court of Session 1965. Rule 72A has been replaced by the much less elaborate rule 29.3 of the

Ordinary Cause Rules 1993. Rule 108A, on the other hand, has been replaced by the similarly worded rule 36.8 of the Rules of the Court of Session 1994. In any event, it is rule 72A which applies to this action. Both parties referred to two Outer House decisions under the equivalent rule 108A: *Ebrahem v. Ebrahem* and *Smith v. Alexander Baird Ltd.*

Ebrahem was an action for declarator of nullity of marriage in which the pursuer B moved for the reception in evidence of an affidavit sworn by her father. The pursuer maintained that, because of age and ill health, he could not travel from Egypt to Scotland. Lord Caplan observed that certain information in the affidavit, if accurately reported, would have a material bearing on the merits of the case. His Lordship said (at [p.541;] p.809I–L):

> 'I refused the motion. The motion was technically incompetent in that no reasons for allowing affidavit evidence had been set out, as the rules prescribe. However, more significantly, the situation is not one where evidence by affidavit would be appropriate. The 1988 Act allows the court to entertain affidavit evidence, but the power contained in the Act and in Rule of Court 108A is merely permissive. In certain situations, evidence by way of affidavit would obviously be a sensible option. The formal evidence of officials, speaking to transactions which are not seriously disputed, would be one clear example of a situation where evidence by affidavit alone could be considered appropriate. On the other hand, the affidavit procedure is not really suitable in cases where the witness is speaking to critical matters which are in dispute, and the fact that the witness cannot conveniently attend court does not render the procedure D any the more acceptable. In particular, procedure by way of affidavit evidence is not intended to supplant the taking of evidence by commission, where the latter procedure is available. Even if evidence is taken by way of interrogatories, the opponent has some opportunity to challenge the witness, if this is thought necessary. In the present case, the defender should have an opportunity to challenge the account of events which the witness is qualified to speak to, and if the witness cannot attend court, the pursuer should, at the appropriate stage, consider seeking to have his evidence taken by way of commission.'

Smith was concerned with a proof on quantum in an action of reparation. The pursuer moved for the reception in evidence of affidavits and other statements by witnesses who lived in the U.S.A. The defenders opposed the motion on the ground that, as the material contained in them was in issue and would be challenged by evidence led by the defenders, the defenders would be prejudiced by the absence of an opportunity to cross-examine the witnesses. Lord Cameron of Lochbroom granted the motion. His Lordship referred to *Ebrahem* and said (at p.564D–E):

> 'Without disagreeing with Lord Caplan's view expressed in the circumstances of that case, I observe that there is nothing in the provisions of section 2 of the Civil Evidence (Scotland) Act 1988 nor of Rule of Court 108A which is restrictive. There is nothing in their provisions to suggest that the evidence to which the procedure is to be related, has to be undisputed. The material in dispute may go to the heart of the case. Assessment of the witnesses' credibility may be crucial. But the court must in the end judge each case on its own circumstances against the general policy of the legislation to extend the modes in which evidence may be tendered at a proof.'

On the subject of prejudice his Lordship said (at p.565B–C):

> 'It is the pursuer who is accepting possible prejudice. The court will be bound, if contrary evidence is led which was subject to cross-examination, to take account of the fact that the evidence led for the pursuer in the matter was not subject to cross-examination.'

In my opinion an indication of the purpose of rule 72A may be obtained from a consideration of its origins. Both rule 72A and rule 108A were introduced after the enactment of the Civil Evidence (Scotland) Act 1988. The first paragraph of each rule is in essentially the same terms. Rule 72A(1) provides: [The sheriff quoted the rule as set out above and continued:]

It is therefore necessary to see what kind of written statement or report is admissible under section 2(1)(b) of the 1988 Act. Section 2(1) provides: [The sheriff quoted the section as set out above and continued:]

> 'Subsections (3) and (4) provide respectively for the amendment of section 5(e) of the Court of Session Act 1988 and the substitution of a new subsection (1)(e) in section 32 of the Sheriff Courts (Scotland) Act 1971. Each of these provisions is concerned with the power of the Court of Session to regulate procedure and practice and expressly confers on the court power to provide for written statements (including affidavits) and reports, admissible under section 2(1)(b) of the Civil Evidence (Scotland) Act 1988, to be received in evidence, on such conditions as may be prescribed, without being spoken to by a witness'.

The Acts of Sederunt introducing rules 108A and 72A (S.I.s 1989–435 and 436) bear to have been enacted under and by virtue of powers including those conferred respectively by section 5 of the Court of Session Act 1988 and by section 32 of the 1971 Act.

It appears to me that the following matters are clear from a consideration of the terms of section 2 of the Civil Evidence (Scotland) Act 1988. It is concerned with the admissibility of statements which are hearsay ('made by a person otherwise than in the course of the proof': section 2(1)(b)). Such a statement may be a written statement or 'documentary hearsay' ('statement' is very broadly defined in section 9). The essential point is that a statement which is hearsay 'shall be admissible' as evidence of any matter contained in the statement of which direct oral evidence by the maker of the statement would be admissible (section 2(1)(b)). It is not to be excluded solely on the ground that it is hearsay (section 2 (1)(a)). Thus it may be excluded on any other ground on which direct oral evidence by the maker of the statement would be inadmissible for example, on the ground that it is irrelevant, or that it contains an expression of Opinion on a matter on which only the evidence of a skilled witness would be admissible and the maker of the statement is not qualified as such a witness.

It is, I think, important to notice that the 1988 Act does not confer on the court any discretion to exclude hearsay evidence which is otherwise admissible in terms of section 2. Section 2(1)(b) expressly provides that if the statement contains any matter of which direct oral evidence by the maker of the statement would be admissible, then the statement 'shall be admissible as evidence of that matter'. This provision is neither permissive nor subject to qualification. If the court were to have a discretion to exclude a statement which was admissible in terms of section 2(1)(b), it would be necessary, in my view, for such a discretion to be expressly conferred by Parliament, because the judge or sheriff in a Scottish civil court has no discretion at common law to exclude evidence which is otherwise admissible. Such a discretion, if conferred, would be a novel and important power. It seems not unreasonable to suppose that it would be conferred not only in express terms, but with some specification of the factors which the court was required to consider in exercising its discretion to exclude the evidence. For a recent example of a statutory provision conferring a judicial discretion to exclude documentary hearsay which is otherwise admissible I refer to section 25 of the Criminal Justice Act 1988.

There are no comparable provisions in the Civil Evidence (Scotland) Act 1988. The Act does not provide that a hearsay statement shall be admissible subject to a discretion in the judge to exclude it, or shall be admissible provided that the subject-matter of the statement is formal or is not contentious. Rules 108A and 72A likewise, in my respectful opinion, do not impose any such restrictions. If they did so, they would adject to the admissibility of documentary hearsay important conditions which are not to be found in the primary legislation. The results would be strange. If the rules were to be understood to confer an exclusionary discretion, the judge or sheriff would have power to exclude documentary hearsay but not oral hearsay: a distinction which it might be difficult to justify. Further, since the power to exclude would be discretionary, it is quite possible that judges and sheriffs would make differing decisions in similar circumstances: *quot judices, tot sententiae*. If the rules were to be understood to restrict documentary hearsay to matters which were not in dispute, statements which were admitted under the rules would simply duplicate the function of joint minutes of admission. I respectfully agree with the view of Lord Cameron of Lochbroom in *Smith* that there is nothing in the provisions of section 2 or rule 108A which is restrictive, or which suggests that the evidence has to be undisputed.

I therefore consider that where a motion in terms of rule 72A is to be considered, the first issue to be resolved is whether the written statement or report is admissible under section 2(1)(b) of the Civil Evidence (Scotland) Act 1988. Here, the test prescribed by section 2(1)(b) is whether the matter contained in the statement is matter of which direct oral evidence by the maker of the statement would be admissible. If that test is satisfied, then, in terms of rule 72A(1), the written report or statement may be received in evidence in any ordinary cause without being spoken to by a witness subject to the provisions of this rule. For reasons I have already tried to explain, I do not regard the word 'may' in subparagraph (1) as qualifying the admissibility of a statement which has passed the test. Similarly, while rule 72A(6) provides that the sheriff 'may' grant the motion with or without conditions or 'may' refuse or continue it, he or she cannot, in my view, impose conditions or refuse' the motion on grounds based on his or her own views of the appropriateness of leading hearsay evidence on the matter dealt with in the statement.

I therefore consider that I am not entitled to refuse the motion on the ground that the defender disputes or is unable to agree a substantial part of the contents of the affidavit. The correct approach, in my view, is to begin by considering whether the affidavit satisfies the section 2(1)(b) test: does it contain matter of which direct oral evidence by Mrs Chopping would be admissible? The defender's counsel submitted that the pursuer had no record for some of the matters in the affidavit, and that other matters in the affidavit were inconsistent with the pursuer's averments. In other words, on all these matters direct oral evidence by Mrs Chopping would be inadmissible on the ground that it did not fall within the scope of the pursuer's averments on record.

I have had some difficulty in deciding how best to deal with this submission. Counsel for the pursuer accepted that some parts of the affidavit were at variance with her pleadings. She submitted that it would be open to me at this stage to exclude parts of the affidavit from being received in evidence. Counsel for the defender, on the other hand, submitted that such a course was not open to me.

The provisions in rule 72A(6) enabling the sheriff to grant the motion, with or without conditions did not empower the sheriff to delete *ex proprio motu* parts of the affidavit.

In my Opinion it would not necessarily be sensible to refuse a motion to receive an affidavit in evidence because some part of it was not admissible under section 2(1)(b). Refusal of the motion might be particularly unfortunate if the rest of the affidavit contained the best, or the only, available information on the matters with which it dealt. I do not consider that rule 72A(6) compels such a result. On the other hand, I do not consider that it would be appropriate for me in this case to accede to counsel for the pursuer's submission that I should, in effect, edit the affidavit. Both the affidavit and the pursuer's pleadings deal with matters at length and in detail. Where there are discrepancies, it is difficult at this stage to assess their significance and thus the extent to which it would be proper to adopt a charitable or benevolent approach or on the other hand to insist that the pursuer's evidence must fall strictly within her averments. It is also important to have in view that it is not impossible that at some stage before the conclusion of the proof the pursuer might move for leave to amend in order to cure any material discrepancy between her evidence and her pleadings. Whether such a motion might be granted cannot be predicted now.

In this situation I have decided to take the course of allowing the affidavit to be received in evidence under reservation of all questions as to the competency and relevancy of particular statements contained in the affidavit. It cannot be maintained, I think, that every statement in the affidavit is inadmissible. On the other hand the granting of the motion subject to the reservation I have mentioned neither implies any judgment that any part of the contents of the affidavit is admissible, nor excludes any argument at or after the proof that any part of its contents is inadmissible.

I now consider the submission for the defender that the defender would be prejudiced if the affidavit were to be received in evidence. The defender's counsel pointed out that the court would be deprived of the opportunity of seeing and hearing Mrs Chopping under cross-examination. In my opinion such issues are not relevant: a written statement is admissible if it meets the section 2(1)(b) test and cannot be excluded because the sheriff thinks it might prejudice the other party, or because the sheriff would prefer to see and hear the maker of the statement giving evidence in the witness box. It is only necessary to say that the granting of the motion does not imply any judgment that the information in the affidavit is credible and reliable, or that it must be accepted as true by the sheriff who hears the proof, or that it cannot be contradicted by other evidence at the proof. It should not be assumed that the court would not look critically at the contents of the affidavit. Indeed, I think it may be said that the pursuer, in electing to rely on hearsay evidence, is taking a course which may be fraught with peril. I respectfully agree with the observations of Lord Cameron of Lochbroom in *Smith* at p.565B–C, which I have quoted above. The defender's counsel will be entitled to remind the sheriff that he or she has not had the benefit of hearing Mrs Chopping's evidence tested in cross-examination and to submit that the sheriff should take that into consideration when considering how far he or she can safely rely on the evidence in the affidavit. Counsel may be able to develop this submission by pointing out particular features of the evidence in the affidavit which conflict with other evidence and which could have been explored in cross-examination. I have no doubt that the sheriff will be well aware of the need for caution in determining whether to accept any part of the evidence in the affidavit and how much weight, if any, to give to it.

Counsel for the defender also criticised the selection of the contents of the affidavit. He said that an earlier, longer version of it had been submitted to the defender's solicitors and that portions of that version had been excised from the present affidavit in order to give the false impression that Mrs Chopping's evidence was uncontroversial. It is not unusual, I think, for an affidavit to be carefully edited: that is a consideration which the sheriff at the proof might be expected to have in mind and it may diminish the weight to be attached to the affidavit. The defender's counsel also pointed to what he submitted were gaps in the information provided by the affidavit: again, these may go to its weight.

A further point taken by counsel for the defender was that there were in process three different accounts of the pursuer's movements between 1969 and 1984: in the B affidavit, in her pleadings and in No. 13 of Process, which bore to be an itinerary. In my view that might be a matter for exploration and comment at the proof, but it does not justify the refusal of the pursuer's motion."

NOTES

The presence in the Ordinary Cause rules (and the Court of Session Rules of Court—see Rule 36.8) of a procedure for enrolling affidavit evidence by way of motion tended to suggest a discretion on the part of the court to refuse to allow such evidence, a discretion exercised in *Ebrahem v. Ebrahem*, 1989 S.C.L.R. 540, one of the cases considered by Sheriff Macphail. Although a Sheriff Court decision, this case, and those of *Smith v. Alexander Baird*, 1993 S.C.L.R. 563, and *Glaser v. Glaser*, 1997 S.L.T. 456 held that the court has no discretion to exclude hearsay evidence, provided that the correct procedure is followed, and the statement satisfies the requirements of section 2 (see, *e.g. Lenaghan v. Ayrshire and Arran Health Board*, 1994 S.L.T. 765 and compare Sheldon, "Heard it on (sic.) the Grapevine", 1993 J.L.S.S. 294 at 295–296.) Rule 36.8 has now been amended, and there is no need to enrol a motion to have hearsay evidence admitted. The party seeking to adduce the evidence simply lodges the statement as a production and intimates it to the other parties to the case. See the Act of Sederunt (Rules of the Court of Session Amendment No. 4) (Miscellaneous) 2001 (S.S.I. 2001 No. 305). *McVinnie* also suggests that there is no rule equivalent to the *Morrison v. Kelly* rule in relation to hearsay. The fact that a witness is technically available is, it seems, no objection to the admission of hearsay evidence of that witness. This means (among other things) that, as in *Smith* and *McVinnie*, where a witness is abroad and it would be difficult or expensive or even simply inconvenient to bring the witness to court, hearsay evidence in the form of an affidavit may—indeed must—be admitted.

10. F. v. Kennedy (No. 2)
1992 S.C.L.R 750

The appellant was the father of two children, J and W who had been referred to a Children's Hearing on the ground that they had been subjected to sexual abuse by the appellant. The appellant did not accept the grounds for referral, but after a lengthy proof before the Sheriff, they were found to be established. The appellant appealed to the Court of Session arguing *inter alia* that (i) hearsay evidence of statements made by J was inadmissible since J himself had given evidence at the proof and had not been asked about the statements in question and (ii) hearsay evidence of statements made to social workers in the course of the investigation was not admissible in any event since they amounted to precognitions.

LORD JUSTICE-CLERK (ROSS): "Mr McGhie [Counsel for appellant] drew attention to the terms of section 2 of the Civil Evidence (Scotland) Act 1988 dealing with the admissibility of hearsay. He submitted, however, that the Act of 1988 did not in terms seek to alter the established rule of evidence relating to 'best evidence'. He recognised that proceedings of the kind with which we are concerned are proceedings *sui generis* but he contended that, since J had given evidence, what he had said on another occasion to a third party was not evidence. Under reference to question 5 he frankly stated that he did not attach great importance to (b), *i.e.*, the fact that J had not been questioned in his evidence as to the making of any previous statement of a different nature, but he submitted that it was important that J had not been asked in evidence about matters on which other witnesses subsequently gave hearsay evidence of what J had said on an earlier occasion.

In my opinion, these submissions are not soundly based. We are not concerned in the present case with the use of a statement made on another occasion to reflect favourably or unfavourably on the witness's credibility. That is provided for in section 3 of the Act of 1988. Any hearsay evidence of witnesses as to what J has previously said was not being led in order to challenge or support his credibility. There was accordingly no need at the proof before the sheriff to question J as to any statement made by him on another occasion. The purpose of leading hearsay evidence here was so that it could be treated as evidence of any matter contained in the statement (section 2(1)(b) of the Act of 1988). Of course, the fact that J was not asked in his evidence about the statements alleged to have been made by him earlier can no doubt be made a matter of comment, and to that extent it may reflect upon his credibility. In my opinion, however, the fact that J was not asked in evidence about statements made by him on an earlier occasion did not render incompetent hearsay evidence of witnesses as to what J had previously said.

Mr McGhie also submitted that in the present case it was not clear what were based on hearsay evidence and what facts on direct evidence; in that Mr McGhie contended that the whole evidence should be treated with suspicion and should be subjected to great scrutiny. In my opinion, it was for the sheriff to determine whether or not he accepted of the evidence adduced before him and I shall return to this matter later.

Mr McGhie's principal submission was that if a witness is available and has given evidence upon a particular matter, hearsay evidence of what he has said to others about that matter is not available. In my opinion, Mr Drummond Young was well founded in contending that that was not the effect of section 2(1)(b) of the Act of 1988. In my judgment section 2(1)(b) does not deal only with the situation where a witness has not given oral evidence. It is significant that 'statement' is defined in section 9 of the Act of 1988 as including 'any representation (however made or expressed) of fact or opinion'. There is no suggestion there that 'statement' is limited to a statement by a witness who has not given oral evidence. On the contrary, it is plain from section 9 that the only exception arises where the statement has been made in a precognition. Accordingly, reading section 2 and section 9 together, I am satisfied that the fact that the maker of the statement has given oral evidence does not prevent hearsay evidence being given of what he has said upon another occasion. In this connection the effect of these two sections is that the best evidence rule is overridden.

The provisions of the Act of 1988 apply to civil proceedings as defined in section 9. Included among such civil proceedings are hearings under section 42 of the Social Work (Scotland) Act 1968 of an application for a finding as to whether grounds for referral are established. It is plain that in many such applications the evidence of children will be critical, and there may well be occasions when it will be difficult to take the whole of a child's evidence in court. It may therefore be important for the sheriff to be able to rely to some extent at least on hearsay evidence of what the child has said on other occasions. Having regard to the interpretation which I would place on section 2 and section 9, I am satisfied that this is something which the sheriff can do. Except where an application to a sheriff relates to a ground mentioned in section 32(2)(g) of the Act of 1968, a sheriff is entitled to hold any fact to be established without there being corroboration, and he is entitled to rely on hearsay evidence (*Harris v. F*). I would stress, of course, that it is for the sheriff to determine what weight if any he is to place upon any of the evidence led before him, including the hearsay evidence.

For the foregoing reasons I would move your Lordships to answer both questions 3 and 5 in the affirmative."

Notes

See also *Ferguson v. S.*, 1993 S.C.L.R. 712. *F. v. Kennedy (No. 2)*, as the learned commentator in Scottish Civil Law Reports points out, has "potentially important implications for all civil cases". Perhaps even more strongly than *McVinnie v. McVinnie*, above, this case emphasises that admissibility is no longer an issue in relation to hearsay, at least where the objection to the evidence is confined to its status as hearsay. The question of the weight to be accorded such evidence is, of course, an entirely different one. *F. v. Kennedy (No. 2)* also called into question (at least the present writer questioned it—see "Heard it on (sic) the Grapevine", 1993 J.L.S.S. 294) the usefulness of section 3 of the Act. If hearsay is admissible in any circumstances, as *F. v. Kennedy (No. 2)* suggests, why insert a section into the Act to say that hearsay evidence may be adduced to attack or bolster a witness's credibility? One answer to this may be that it was desired to emphasise the change to the old rule that a witness's previous inconsistent statements could be used only to attack that witness's credibility, whereas previous consistent statements could not be used to shore it up. Under the new provisions, previous statements are admissible in so far as they reflect favourably or unfavourably on a witness's credibility. Another reason for the insertion of section 3 emerges from the following case, *Davies v. McGuire* 1995 S.L.T. 755. It is presumably the case, however, that the best evidence rule, insofar as there is anything of it left, is over-ridden only in respect of hearsay evidence and it will, in general, still be necessary to produce originals where certain types of real evidence are concerned (copy documents will now, in general, suffice to satisfy the court of the authenticity of the original, provided, the copy is properly authenticated—see section 6 of the 1988 Act). This view is borne out by the recent case of *Japan Leasing (Europe) plc v. Weir's Trustees (No. 2)* 1998 S.C. 543; 1998 S.L.T. 973, Chapter 6 above, which may be an attempt by the Court the limit the ambit of the decision in *F. v. Kennedy*. The proper view therefore seems to be that the best evidence rule is over-ridden only in relation to oral evidence.

See also *Stirling Aquatic Technology v. Farmocean AB (No. 2)*, 1996 S.L.T. 456 and *McIlveny v. Donald*, 1995 S.C.L.R. 802, above, Chapter 6.

11. Davies v. McGuire
1995 S.L.T. 755

Mr and Mrs Stephen Davies raised an action against Allan David McGuire for damages for the death of their 13-year-old son who had been run down and killed by a car driven by the defender. At a proof before the Lord Ordinary (Gill) the defender attempted to lead evidence from a police officer about statements made to him by witnesses to the accident during the officer's investigations. The police officer had been called by the pursuers to give evidence about the scene of the accident and the road layout in advance of any of the eyewitnesses. Some of the witnesses had been cited to give evidence at the proof while some had not. The Lord Ordinary sustained an objection to the evidence of the statements made to the police officer at that stage of the proof but allowed the officer to be recalled after the eyewitnesses had given evidence and then gave evidence of the content of the statements made to him. After the proof his Lordship held, without reference to the statements made to the police officer, that the accident had been solely the fault of the boy who had run in front of the car, leaving the driver with no opportunity to avoid the collision. His Lordship assoilzied the defender and, in relation to the questions raised under the 1988 Act, said:

"In these circumstances it is unnecessary for me to rely upon a further line of evidence which was pressed by senior counsel for the defender, namely the contents of a series of witness statements taken by D.C. Galbraith of Dalkeith CID shortly after the accident.

D.C. Galbraith was led as a witness for the pursuers before any eyewitness evidence had been heard. In his evidence in chief he described the scene at the locus on his arrival there shortly after the accident. He described the road and weather conditions and he spoke to the defender's statement under caution. In cross-examination, senior counsel for the defender sought to have this witness read from his notebooks certain statements which he had noted from a number of apparent eyewitnesses after the accident. Senior counsel's stated purposes were, first, to establish by hearsay the accounts given in the statements by those who would not in the event give evidence and, secondly, the credibility of those who would. He argued that sections 2 and 3 of the Civil Evidence (Scotland) Act 1988 expressly warranted such a course. He accepted that if he was right in this, it would be open to him to present his entire case in this way.

I sustained an objection to this line of evidence. In my opinion, sections 2 and 3 do not permit a cross-examiner in such circumstances to elicit hearsay evidence for either of these purposes.

Section 3 makes admissible as evidence any previous statement of a witness in so far as it tends to reflect favourably or unfavourably on the witness's credibility. This extends the previous law. Section 3 of the Evidence (Scotland) Act 1852, which the 1988 Act has repealed (section 10(1) and Sched.), made admissible as evidence any previous statement of a witness on any matter pertinent to the issue where that statement was different from the witness's evidence. Under section 3 of the 1852 Act it was not competent to discredit a witness in advance. It was only when the witness had given evidence that proof became admissible of his previous statement (*cf. Livingstone v. Strachan, Crerar & Jones*, 1923 S.C. 794; 1923 S.L.T. 525).

Section 3 of the 1988 Act is worded in a different form from section 3 of the 1852 Act, but in my opinion it implies the same precondition, namely that the witness must first give evidence before proof of his previous statement becomes admissible. If I am right, it follows that the objection to the proposed line of cross-examination is even stronger when it is already known that the maker of the statement will not be called as a witness.

As to senior counsel's reliance on section 2, I consider that that section, which provides for the general admissibility of hearsay, cannot of itself warrant the eliciting of hearsay in the manner proposed.

I am confirmed in these views by section 4 of the 1988 Act which, in the circumstances which arose in this case, permits a party to recall a witness to give evidence of hearsay statements for the purposes of sections 2 and 3. In the event, that is what senior counsel for the defender decided to do.

Senior counsel for the defender recalled D.C. Galbraith in the course of the defender's proof. He then asked him to read a number of witness statements from his notebooks. At this stage, senior counsel for the pursuers objected to this line evidence on the ground that such statements were precognitions. Having heard from the witness the circumstances in which these statements were noted by him, I held that these were typical police statements in the sense described in *Hall v. H.M.A.*, 1968 S.L.T. 275 and such distinguishable from precognitions (*cf. F. v. Kennedy (No. 2)*, 1993 S.L.T. 1284 at pp.1287–1288) which for this purpose sections 9 of the 1988 Act excludes.

The effect of the 1988 Act is to entitle the court not only to accept hearsay where the maker of the statement is not a witness (*Ferguson v. S*, 1993 S.C.L.R. 712) but to accept hearsay of a witness in preference to his evidence in court (*K. v. Kennedy*, 1993 S.L.T. 1281; *F. v. Kennedy (No. 2)*, supra). I consider that the court should proceed with extreme caution in applying the provisions of the 1988 Act in such circumstances."

NOTES

After the passage quoted, Lord Gill went on to consider the various witness statements read out by the police officer, D.C. Galbraith, and to explain the weight which he accorded to these statements. One statement in particular, from a witness who was named in the pursuer's list of witnesses but not in the defenders, and who without any explanation was not called to give evidence, he disregarded entirely.

Given the views expressed in *F. v. Kennedy (No. 2)* above and *McVinnie v. McVinnie*, above, was this something which, strictly speaking, he was entitled to do? In this area, questions of weight may be hard to distinguish from questions of admissibility.

This case attempts to give some meaning to section 3. How persuasive do you find Lord Gill's view of that section? Can it stand with Lord Justice-Clerk Ross's views in *F. v. Kennedy (No. 2)*? Note that in the latter case, although Lord Ross's comments about section 2 are very general, he carefully separates that section from section 3.

Precognitions form an exception to the general permission of hearsay evidence under the 1988 Act—see section 9 and the cases reproduced below.

12.   Highland Venison Mkt Ltd v. Allwild GmbH
1992 S.C.L.R. 415

The pursuers raised an action for payment for venison delivered to the defenders. The defenders averred that the pursuers had failed to sell and deliver venison in the quantity agreed and they counter-claimed for damages for the pursuers' alleged failure. The defenders, a German company, had used the services of an agent in the U.K., a Mr Epstein, to negotiate the terms of the contract with the pursuers. Mr Epstein died in May 1990 and the defenders sought to lead the evidence of a Miss Ryder, the solicitor acting for the defenders, as to what Mr Epstein had told her about the circumstances of the transaction. Objection was taken to the admissibility of Miss Ryder's evidence and it was heard under reservation. She produced a document which she said was a precognition prepared after the interview and which had been revised by Mr Epstein and signed by him. In argument at the conclusion of the evidence counsel for the pursuers submitted that the document was inadmissible in that it was a 'precognition'. Counsel for the defenders submitted that the document should be distinguished from a precognition in respect that the deceased had not only revised the document but had also signed it and he relied on section 2 of the Civil Evidence Scotland Act 1988. In the event the Lord Ordinary was able to decide the case without considering the evidence from Miss Ryder but he expressed certain views in relation to the admissibility of the document and her evidence.

LORD CULLEN: "Miss Ryder gave evidence that she interviewed Mr Epstein in London in December 1989 for a period of one and a half to two hours. She took notes with a view to preparing a precognition of his evidence. She sent a draft precognition to him later for his revisal. In due course he sent to her a retyped precognition which incorporated certain revisals which he had made and which was signed by him. She identified this document as No. 24–10 of Process. Counsel for the defenders objected to the line of evidence as to the contents of this document and to Miss Ryder's evidence as to the terms of her notes and the differences between this document and her copy of the draft precognition. I heard her evidence under reservation of this objection on which I heard full argument from counsel in their closing submissions. According to the notes of Miss Ryder, Mr Epstein told her that for over twenty years he had been engaged in business connected with Scottish venison. [His Lordship then dealt with the evidence given by the witness and continued:]

In his closing submissions counsel for the pursuers submitted that No. 24–10 of Process was inadmissible in respect that it was a precognition. In any event, it was inadmissible in respect that there was 'a reasonable suspicion, either that the statement was not in accordance with the truth, or that it was a coloured or one-sided version of the truth' (*Lauderdale Peerage Case* (1885) 10 App. Cas. 692, per Lord Watson at p.707). The latter objection also applied to Miss Ryder's notes. Mr Epstein had been an agent for a long time and hoped to remain one. He had told the defenders that he had made a contract for the sale of two containers and they had committed themselves at an early stage in reliance upon this. Any loss sustained by them would appear to be his fault. The objection applied with even greater strength in respect that Mr Epstein's statements were taken from him *post litem motam*. It was also unfair for the defenders to rely on these sources for Mr Epstein's account when they had failed to give the pursuers the opportunity to take his evidence on commission at an early stage in the case. Counsel for the defenders submitted that No. 24–10 of Process should be distinguished from a precognition in respect that the deceased had not only altered the statement but signed it, making it his own rather than a statement filtered through the mind of another person. Counsel also relied on the alteration in the law which was effected by section 2 of the Civil Evidence (Scotland) Act 1988. [The Lord Ordinary then quoted the term of s.2(1) as set out above and continued:]

Counsel submitted that this provision had the effect of rendering evidence as to Mr Epstein's statements admissible. An objection based on the line of authority of which the *Lauderdale*

Peerage Case is the best-known example fell to be regarded as an instance of evidence being objected to 'on the ground that it is hearsay'. On the basis that No. 24–10 of Process was not inadmissible the weight to be attached to it was for me to consider. It gave a general impression of being a truthful and not tendentious statement.

Counsel for the pursuers responded by arguing that paragraph (a) of section 2(1) of the 1988 Act qualified the scope of paragraph (b). If it did not do so, there would be no need for it. It was worded in such a way as to preserve an objection on a ground other than that the statement was hearsay. This kept open the objection of the type to which the *Lauderdale Peerage Case* related.

[After considering his decision on the matters at issue between the parties his Lordship continued:] I consider that the defenders have established on a balance of probabilities that he agreed to the sale of two containers.

In the circumstances I do not require to consider the evidence of Miss Ryder and the objection which was taken to it. However, since the matter was fully argued I will briefly give my views on these matters. I agree with counsel for the pursuers that paragraph (a) of section 2(1) of the 1988 Act falls to be regarded as qualifying the general proposition set out in paragraph (b). The subsection plainly should be read as a whole and, so read, its intention is clearly to deal with the hearsay objection and in that context to enlarge what is admissible as evidence. Paragraph (b) should not be read as if it ruled out objections other than an objection on the ground that the evidence is hearsay. One example of this may be given. If evidence is objected to on the ground of confidentiality, that objection would plainly be unaffected by paragraph (a). The same should apply to paragraph (b). Accordingly, in the present case the question is whether an objection of the type to which the *Lauderdale Peerage Case* relates is an instance of an objection on the ground of evidence being hearsay. In my view it is and the effect of paragraph (a) is that such evidence should not be excluded from consideration. Its weight is a matter for the court or, as the case may be, the jury. In the present case I consider that there is no sound reason why it should not be treated as credible and reliable evidence as to what happened. The evidence given by Miss Ryder as to her notes of the interview with Mr Epstein serves only to confirm the conclusion on fact to which I have already come. I should add that I consider that there is some force in the view that the statement contained in No. 24–10 of Process does not fall to be regarded as a precognition' for the purposes of the 1988 Act, for the reasons given by counsel for the defenders. However, this is not a matter on which I require to come to a conclusion."

13.   William Anderson v. Jas B. Fraser & Co. Ltd
1992 S.C.L.R. 417

The pursuer sued his employers for damages as a result of an accident at work. He gave evidence that he had damaged his back when he and a fellow employee (R) were moving certain parts of a house kit. The defenders *inter alia* denied that any such accident took place. R stated *inter alia* that he had witnessed the accident and gave an account not dissimilar to the pursuer's. He stated that he did not recall telling the defenders' production manager and a claims inspector from the insurance company that he had not witnessed the accident. He had been interviewed by a solicitor acting for the defenders and claimed that "We seemed to get mixed up". The production manager gave evidence that he had interviewed R, who had stated that he could recollect nothing about the accident. The claims inspector gave evidence that R had told him that he had no recollection of the accident. The solicitor for the defenders was called to give evidence but her evidence was objected to by the pursuer's counsel on the basis that she had been present in court during the pursuer's evidence and that she had been taking a precognition from R and thus the evidence was inadmissible. In deciding that the evidence was admissible and that the words 'statement in a precognition' in the Civil Evidence (Scotland) Act 1988 meant what was recorded in a document prepared by the precognoscer and not evidence of what the person said to the precognoscer in interview. The Lord Ordinary issued a note of which the following is an extract.

LORD MORTON OF SHUNA: "James Rehill in his evidence gave a broadly similar account to that which the pursuer gave in his evidence. He stated that he was to put his side down first and when he did so the panel collapsed. He could only think that this was because the panel was not put down square on to the blocks. In cross-examination he stated that the blocks on this side all couped over. He was not sure if they fell to the floor. He could not tell what had happened. He did not remember telling either Mr Roughhead, the defenders' production manager, or an insurance man that he had not witnessed the accident. When he was later interviewed by [a solicitor for the defenders], 'We seemed to get mixed up'. Mr Roughhead stated that the pursuer had been off work for some time before the defenders were aware that he claimed to have had an accident at work. Sometime in 1988 after the entry had been made in the accident book Mr Roughhead spoke to James Rehill who told him that he—Rehill— could recollect nothing about any accident to the pursuer. He spoke to Rehill because the pursuer and Rehill had worked together for years as a team. Mr McIlwham, a claims inspector with the defenders' insurers gave evidence that Rehill had told him he had no recollection of any accident to the pursuer. This was in response to a question whether he had witnessed any accident to the pursuer. A solicitor representing the defenders gave evidence of an interview with Rehill on December 11, 1991. This evidence was objected to by counsel for the pursuer and at [the solicitor's] suggestion was allowed under reservation of questions of competency and relevancy. The defenders' solicitor said that Rehill told her that he had seen the incident in which the section had jerked away from Rehill and towards the pursuer as they were landing it on the blocks. She said that Rehill did not appear at all confused, was willing to accept blame for the accident and stated, quite categorically, that the panel jerked away from him and towards the pursuer and not away from the pursuer and towards Rehill.

The objection to the defenders' solicitor's evidence was on the ground that she had been present in court when the pursuer gave evidence and also on the ground that she had been taking a precognition from Rehill and therefore the evidence about this was inadmissible. It does not appear to me that the fact that a solicitor acting for a party is present in court prevents the solicitor giving evidence. The question is whether what was said to the defenders' solicitor was inadmissible because it was a precognition is more complicated. [His Lordship then quoted the terms of sections 2 and 3 of the Civil Evidence (Scotland) Act 1988 and continued]:

Section 9, the interpretation section, provides that ' "Statement" includes any representation however made or expressed of fact or opinion but does not include a statement in a precognition'. The only case to which I was referred in which the effect of the Civil Evidence (Scotland) Act was considered was *Highland Venison Mkt Ltd v. Allwild GmbH* [reported at p.415. supra]. In that case a solicitor interviewed a Mr Epstein and took notes. She then drafted a precognition which she sent to Mr Epstein for his revisal. Mr Epstein revised the precognition and made alterations and signed the document which he had had retyped. Mr Epstein died prior to the proof. An objection was taken to the admission of the statement signed by him and to the evidence of the solicitor on the basis that the notes taken by the solicitor and the documents signed by Mr Epstein were a precognition and were inadmissible. Lord Cullen in the view he took of other evidence did not for his decision require to consider the evidence of the solicitor and the statement but expressed the view that the evidence was admissible and that the revised document was not a 'precognition' within the meaning of section 9 of the Act.

The objection to the admissibility of a precognition has been stated as that there was 'a reasonable suspicion, either that the statement was not in accordance with the truth, or that it was a coloured or one-sided version of the truth'. Lord Justice-Clerk Thomson was to much the same effect in *Kerr v. H.M.A.*, 1958 J.C. 14 at p.19, when he said:

> 'one reason why reference to precognition is frowned on is that in a precognition you cannot be sure that you are getting what the potential witness has to say in a pure and undefiled form. It is filtered through the mind of another, whose job is to put what he thinks the witness means into a form suitable for use injudicial proceedings. This process tends to colour the result. Precognoscers as a rule appear to be gifted with a measure of optimism which no amount of disillusionment can damp.'

It appears to me that in civil proceedings the only reason for the exclusion of Precognition is that what is stated in the precognition is or may be coloured by the mind of the precognoscer who produces in the precognition an edited version of what the witness has said. This would exclude the actual document prepared by the precognoscer but would not exclude evidence of what the witness actually said to the precognoscer prior to the preparation of the document. I am of opinion that the exception in the definition of 'statement' in the Civil Evidence (Scotland) Act excluding 'a statement in a precognition' means what is recorded in a document prepared by the precognoscer and does not exclude evidence of what the person said to the precognoscer in interview. On that basis the defenders' solicitor's evidence, for what it is worth, is admissible."

NOTES

Andersen was distinguished in *McAvoy v. City of Glasgow District Council*, 1993 S.C.L.R. 393; 1993 S.L.T. 859. In *Cavanagh v. B.P. Chemicals*, 1995 S.L.T. 1287 Lord Clyde suggests that where a precise record of questions asked and answers given in any interview is unavailable, hearsay evidence about that interview may be accorded little weight.

14. F. v. Kennedy (No. 2)
1992 S.C.L.R. 750

The facts of this case are set out on p.419.

LORD JUSTICE-CLERK (ROSS): "Mr McGhie dealt with questions 7 and 8 together. The issue raised in these questions is whether hearsay evidence of what J and W had said on previous occasions was in the nature of evidence taken on precognition. In section 9 of the Act of 1988 'statement' is defined as including 'any representation (however made or expressed) of fact or opinion but does not include a statement in a precognition'. Mr McGhie drew attention to the terms of finding 16 where a description was given of the interviewing of J and W. He emphasised that the children, and in particular J had been interviewed on numerous occasions, and virtually every day between June 7, and July 20 when the hearing began. No records had been kept by the social workers of the dates, times or duration of these interviews, and no notes were taken at the time of what the children said; the hearsay evidence of the social workers was based purely on their own recollections. Moreover, at the interviews anatomically correct dolls were regularly given to the children to demonstrate with, although none of the interviewers had had any special training in the use of anatomically correct dolls. No tape or video recordings were made of the interviews. Police officers were present at some of the interviews. During the interviews on occasion the children told the social workers fantasy stories. No psychiatrist or psychologist was consulted to examine the children although the children showed advanced signs of disturbance. In these circumstances Mr McGhie maintained that what each child had said amounted to a statement in a precognition. In this connection he drew attention to various tests which had been laid down in civil cases as to what amounted to a precognition. Section 2(1)(b) of the Act of 1988 provides for the admissibility of a statement made by a person otherwise than in the course of the proof, and section 9 makes it plain that 'statement' does not include a statement in a precognition. In my opinion Parliament must be taken to have used the word 'precognition' in the sense in which it has been used in previous case-law. As is made clear in Walker and Walker, *The Law of Evidence in Scotland*, the word 'precognition' is sometimes used as an abstract term to mean the act of taking a statement from a person for purpose of discovering what his evidence is to be in a cause which has commenced or at least been decided upon, and on other occasions the word 'precognition' is used in the concrete sense as referring to a written precognition where a witness's statements are put into consecutive narrative form. In *Traynor's Executrix v. Bairds & Scottish Steel Ltd* Lord Guthrie, in holding that a statement made by a deceased person to his solicitor was inadmissible, appears to have based his decision to some extent upon the view that the statement was tainted by self-interest. However, in *Young v. National Coal Board* Lord Guthrie held that the statement in question was of the nature of a precognition although the element of self-interest was absent. He appears to have been influenced by the fact that the statement in question had not been made in conversation in the ordinary course of the individual's daily life, but had been elicited from him by questions put to him by an investigator. In *Miller v. Jackson* the Lord Ordinary (Lord Emslie) excluded evidence of a statement made by a deceased upon the view that it was 'a statement akin to a precognition'. The statement in question had been deliberately solicited by a visit to the deceased after the raising of the action by an individual who had a clear interest in the outcome of the action and who was related to one of the parties.

Mr Drummond Young for the respondent drew attention to what the sheriff said about this matter in his note. The sheriff had been referred to *Kerr v. H.M.A.* which was a criminal case. The sheriff stated that he had no difficulty in deciding that the children's statements were not to be regarded as precognitions. He stated:

'The evidence related to remarks made by the children from time to time, often in casual conversation, and sometimes in a more "structured" interview, which I consider gives them considerable spontaneity, and they are very far removed from what is traditionally regarded as a precognition in the sense of a statement taken by the police or the procurator fiscal in a criminal investigation.'

Although Mr Drummond Young recognised that this case was not concerned with a precognition in the sense of a statement taken by the police or the procurator fiscal in a criminal investigation, he maintained that the sheriff's reasoning was sound and that the sheriff had reached the correct conclusion. He stressed that proceedings under section 42 of the Act of 1968 are not adversarial proceedings. They are proceedings which are undertaken in the interests of the children, and accordingly he submitted that the normal grounds of objection to a precognition were not present. He pointed out also that in the present case there was no suggestion that there ever had been any written precognition; it could not be said that the statement was in any way tainted by self-interest; and he submitted that it was not necessary in every case before a statement could be admitted that it could be regarded as a fair and spontaneous statement.

I have come to the conclusion that the sheriff arrived at the correct decision upon this matter. After the children's mother had alleged that her children had been the subject of abuse, it was plainly the duty of the social workers and the police to investigate the matter with a view to determining whether the children were in need of compulsory measures of care. The sheriff has described in finding 16 how the interviews were conducted. In my opinion, however, it is clear that the purpose of these interviews was not so much to take precognitions from the children for the purposes of a litigation, but rather to determine whether grounds existed for concluding that these children were in need of compulsory measures of care. There is no reason to think that any document was ever prepared by a precognoscer containing what the precognoscer thought that the child would say in evidence. The present case is therefore different from *Anderson v. Jas B. Fraser & Co. Ltd*, to which Mr McGhie drew attention at the continued hearing. Moreover there was no litigation in the normal sense in existence at the time. There was to be a hearing before the sheriff to determine whether the grounds of referral had been established, but these proceedings are recognised to be *sui generis* and they are not in any proper sense an adversarial litigation.

In the foregoing circumstances I am satisfied that the sheriff reached the correct conclusion in this case."

NOTES

Precognitions were always regarded as being inadmissible, whether or not they fell into any of the then recognised exceptions to the hearsay rule. See *inter alia Lauderdale Peerage case* (1885) 10 A.C. 692; *Traynor's Extr v. Baird's and Scottish Steel*, 1957 S.C. 311; *Young v. NCB*, 1960 S.C. 6; *Thomson v. Jamieson*, 1986 S.L.T. 72; *Miller v. Jackson*, 1972 S.L.T. (Notes) 31; *Wm Thyne v. Stenhouse*, 1979 S.L.T. (Notes) 93; *Hall v. Edinburgh Corporation*, 1974 S.L.T. (Notes) 14; *Cordiner v. British Railways Board*, 1986 S.L.T. 209. The 1988 Act preserves this rule. Is the justification for the exclusion of precognitions—set out in the passage quoted by Lord Morton of Shuna from *Kerr v. H.M.A.*, 1958 J.C. 14—a convincing one? Might it not be said that *all* evidence whether taken on precognition or not is, in a sense, "filtered through the mind of another", and that this objection is particularly potent in relation to all hearsay evidence?

15. T. v. T.
2000 S.L.T. 1442

The parents of a child (E) separated and later divorced. The father sought contact with E, who had remained in the care of her mother. When the father's action for contact came to proof the mother sought to adduce evidence from a police officer regarding answers given by E at an interview, shortly after her fourth birthday, which indicated that she had been sexually abused by her father during a contact visit supervised by his mother at his mother's home. A dispute arose as to the admissibility of that evidence. E's mother having accepted on the basis of previous authority—in particular the case of *L v. L*, 1996 S.L.T. 767—that the officer's evidence would only be admissible if E would be a competent witness at the proof, the sheriff examined E and found her to be a competent witness. Following proof the sheriff refused the father's application and made an order depriving him of all parental rights and responsibilities. The father appealed to the Court of Session and the case was remitted to a court of five judges in order that the whole question of the proper interpretation of section 2(1)(b) of the 1988 Act could be considered. The father argued that the relevant issue was whether E would have been a competent witness at the time of the police interview, and further that the sheriff had no proper basis for the order depriving him of parental rights and responsibilities.

THE LORD PRESIDENT (RODGER): "[9] In the course of the debate before the First Division it became apparent that counsel for both parties were, frankly, unhappy about the law as laid down in the authorities dealing with the interpretation of section 2(1)(b). In particular, counsel for both parties pointed out that the decisions of the Second Division in *F. v. Kennedy* [No. 1] and of the Lord Ordinary in *L. v. L.* meant that any prudent counsel, who wished to lead the hearsay evidence of a statement made by a child, felt constrained to bring the child to court and to proffer the child as a witness to be examined by the presiding sheriff. Not only could this examination be long and painful for all concerned, and especially for the child, but in addition the procedure could seem like a ritual and somewhat disconnected indeed from reality, since there was no actual intention to take the child's evidence, even if he or she proved to be competent. These authorities had also caused difficulties for reporters in social work proceedings where the grounds of referral were not accepted and the facts had to be proved. In some cases, where the relevant evidence was in the form of hearsay evidence of statements by young children, reporters had preferred not to take proceedings rather than to submit the children to the procedure for testing competence.

[10] The First Division were aware, of course, that it might have been possible to resolve this appeal without deciding how section 2(1)(b) actually fell to be interpreted. Indeed this has been done on a number of occasions in the past. I refer, for instance, to the decision of the First Division in *L. v. L.* at 1998 S.L.T, p.674J–L. But, in view of the representations made by counsel for both parties, the First Division decided that the question of the proper interpretation of section 2(1)(b) required to be addressed and that this could be done satisfactorily only by a court which was free to re-examine past decisions of the Inner House. In giving the opinion of the court, I suggested, under reference to part of an observation of Lord Hamilton in *L. v. L.*, at 1996 S.L.T., p.770F, that in addition to the two competing arguments advanced by counsel at the hearing before the First Division there was also room for another view. This would be to the effect that section 2(1)(b) was designed to ensure that a statement would not be admissible if it related to a particular matter on which evidence from the person concerned would not have been admissible, for example because it was confidential or sought to contradict the terms of a written contract. In other words, section 2(1)(b) might embody a test of the admissibility of the evidence rather than of the competence, as a witness, of the person whose statement was to be narrated by the witness giving the hearsay evidence.

[11] At the hearing before this court, there were therefore three rival interpretations in play. For their part, counsel for the pursuer adhered to the argument which junior counsel had advanced before the sheriff, that section 2(1)(b) involved a competence test which fell to be applied at the time when E made the statements in question. In their written submissions before this court, counsel for the defender still maintained, as their primary argument, that section 2(1)(b) embodied a competence test, to be applied at the date of any proof or jury trial. The sheriff had therefore applied the correct test. But, if they were wrong about that, they now argued that on a proper interpretation of section 2(1)(b) no competence test at all fell to be

applied and hearsay evidence was admissible unless direct evidence on the matter would be inadmissible if given by the person who had made the statement. In the course of the hearing, however, counsel for the defender modified their position to the extent of advancing the argument that there is no competence test as their primary contention and the other argument as their fallback argument.

[12] Counsel for the defender changed the emphasis of their submissions in this way in recognition of the very real and obvious difficulties in the argument that there is a competence test which falls to be applied at the time of the proof. Two opposing examples illustrate these difficulties, which arise independently of the exact wording of the provision.

[13] Suppose A overhears another adult, B, describing an event and B some months later, and quite independently, suffers a stroke which destroys his capacity to give evidence. If A's evidence is admissible under section 2(1)(b) only if B would be a competent witness as to the event at the time of the proof, then A's evidence is inadmissible. And yet, it is hard to see any sensible reason for excluding A's evidence on that basis since the trustworthiness of the account given by B would not be affected by his subsequent illness. The same must indeed apply if B dies, since in that case also he would not be a competent witness at any proof. For the reasons given in paras 40–42 below, when discussing the *res gestae* and *de recenti* rules, I am satisfied that this difficulty cannot be avoided by invoking the common law exception under which hearsay evidence was admitted if the maker of the statement had died.

[14] Now suppose that A overhears B, a child of two, make a statement about an event. Twenty years later A is called to give evidence as to B's statement about the event. By that time B will be 22 and plainly would be a competent witness. If the test of competence applies at the time of the proof, A's evidence will be admissible because at the proof B would be a competent witness as to the event. In this case it is hard to see any sensible reason for admitting A's evidence on that basis since the trustworthiness of B's statement at the age of two cannot be affected by her competence to give evidence at the age of 22.

[15] These are just two examples of the consequences of holding that a competence test falls to be applied to the maker of a statement at the time of the proof. They are at once so obvious and so absurd that I should find it impossible to adopt a construction of the provision which led to them, unless the words used by Parliament admitted of no other construction.

[16] While not overlooking these difficulties, counsel for the defender submitted that, nonetheless, this was precisely the construction which the Second Division had placed upon the paragraph in *F. v. Kennedy* and which had been followed by the Lord Ordinary in *L. v. L.* I turn accordingly to the first of these cases.

[17] *F. v. Kennedy* arose out of a referral by a reporter under the Social Work (Scotland) Act 1968 relating to allegations of lewd, indecent and libidinous practices in respect of three children. The grounds of referral were not accepted and a proof was accordingly held in front of the sheriff. Evidence was led of various statements which the children were said to have made in the course of interviews. One of the children, W, was three years old at the time of the proof and, when brought into court, he remained mute and did not give evidence. Nevertheless, the sheriff held that evidence of the statements allegedly made by W was admissible. Although the reports of the decision of the Second Division do not reproduce Sheriff Gow's note, it can be studied in the session papers. From that note it appears that the argument presented to him was somewhat convoluted. But it also appears that he decided that the evidence of W's statements was admissible even though W himself had been unable to give evidence when called in the proceedings. The sheriff then made use of that evidence in holding that the grounds of referral had been established.

[18] Against that background I am satisfied that the argument for the reporter in the appeal before the Second Division (1992 S.C. at p.31; 1993 S.L.T. at p.1280D–E) was to the effect that, even if a child did not know the difference between truth and falsehood, and so would fail the test of competence, hearsay evidence of statements made by that child would be admissible under section 2(1)(b). Contrary, therefore, to a suggestion by senior counsel for the pursuer in this case at one stage of his argument, the decision of the Second Division in *F. v. Kennedy* cannot be explained as having been given without the point having been argued.

[19] In delivering the opinion of the court, Lord Justice Clerk Ross began his decision by quoting the test for deciding when '[a] child is admissible' from Walker and Walker, *The Law*

of Evidence in Scotland, para. 349. He continued by referring to two criminal appeals where the procedure had been discussed and added (p.32 (p.1280F–H)): 'In the present case it was not possible for the sheriff to carry out any examination of the child to see whether he knew the difference between truth and falsehood nor was it possible for him to admonish the child to tell the truth because the child remained mute throughout. In these circumstances we are satisfied that the provisions of section 2(1)(b) of the Act of 1988 were not satisfied with regard to W. What he may have said to the social workers or others was not admissible as evidence of any matter contained in such statement because direct oral evidence by W of any such matter was not admissible since in the circumstances W himself was not an admissible witness. We recognise that W would have been an admissible witness if he had been examined by the sheriff as to his ability to distinguish between truth and falsehood and if, on being satisfied on that matter, the sheriff had cautioned him to tell the truth, but in our opinion, the terms of the subsection make it plain that hearsay is only admissible if it is hearsay of a person who was in fact an admissible witness.'

On that basis the court held that evidence as to statements made by W was not admissible under section 2(1)(b) and remitted the case to the sheriff so that he could inform them 'as to what the hearsay evidence of W. was', and also as to the extent to which he had relied on that evidence in making his findings in fact.

[20] In the passage which I have quoted the court can be seen to decide two points. First, they decide that evidence of statements made by W would have been admissible under section 2(1)(b) if, but only if, W had in fact been 'an admissible witness'. Secondly, they decide that W would have been 'an admissible witness' if the sheriff had successfully examined him as to his ability to distinguish between truth and falsehood and had cautioned him to tell the truth. Although the second of these points has led to the development of the unfortunate practice of children being brought to court simply to be subjected to an examination by the presiding sheriff, it is in fact the less fundamental of the two. And indeed in two later cases the First Division indicated to practitioners that, depending on the other evidence available, a sheriff might be able to decide whether a child was an admissible witness without the child actually having to be brought to court. See *M. v. Kennedy* at 1993 S.C., p.125A–E, per Lord President Hope giving the opinion of the court, and *M. v. Ferguson* at 1994 S.C.L.R., p.492C–E, *per* Lord President Hope, again giving the opinion of the court. In each case the court reached their decision for other reasons and these particular comments were obiter. Presumably because of this, practitioners have continued to be guided by *F. v. Kennedy* and have persisted in bringing children to court to be examined by the judge or sheriff. There may also have been difficulties in obtaining the kind of evidence envisaged by the First Division in the later cases.

[21] The second of the matters which I have identified arises only because of the Second Division's decision on the first matter. The correct starting point for any reconsideration of their decision is therefore with that first, and more fundamental, aspect.

[22] The use of language in the relevant passage in the opinion of the court is striking: the court repeatedly use the term 'admissible' to refer to witnesses. The use of 'admissible' in this way—which I shall call 'the first sense' of the word—is, of course, well established in our textbooks. When so used, the adjective refers to persons who are called to give evidence and who are competent to do so. For instance, the words quoted from Walker and Walker on Evidence, para 349: 'A child is admissible if he appears . . .', occur in a chapter which is introduced in the previous paragraph with the words 'witness is competent unless he is excluded by a rule of law'. The same usage is to be found in Dickson's, *Treatise on the Law of Evidence in Scotland*, para. 1542. Speaking of the former law, the author says: 'It was then more difficult to discover who were admissible, than who were incompetent witnesses.' As that comment suggests, at one time our law excluded many classes of persons from giving evidence but, largely as a result of the reforms of the nineteenth century, the only persons now regarded as incompetent are certain children and persons suffering from disease, whether physical or mental, affecting their ability to give evidence. If they are not competent to give evidence, they are not 'admissible' witnesses. Since they are not admissible witnesses, they do not give evidence.

[23] That usage of the term 'admissible' is to be distinguished from its use—in what I shall call 'the second sense'—to refer to particular kinds of evidence which an *ex hypothesi* admissible

witness may give. For instance, the common law protects the confidence of communings between a client and his lawyer and so, unless the client waives the lawyer's duty of confidentiality, evidence by the (admissible) solicitor as to those communings is inadmissible. Statute may also render certain evidence inadmissible. For instance, section 1(1) of the Civil Evidence (Family Mediation) (Scotland) Act 1995 provides: 'Subject to section 2 of this Act, no information as to what occurred during family mediation to which this Act applies shall be admissible as evidence in any civil proceedings.' Any evidence, which could otherwise be given by an (admissible) participant or mediator as to what occurred during family mediation, is not admissible in civil proceedings.

[24] With these two different uses of the adjective 'admissible' in mind, I turn to look at the language of section 2(1)(b) of the 1988 Act. It is immediately apparent that the legislature is using the term 'admissible' in the second sense, to refer to a 'statement' and to 'evidence' rather than to refer to a witness (first sense). A 'statement made by a person' is to be 'admissible as evidence' of any matter contained in the statement of which direct 'evidence' by that person would be 'admissible'. In one respect Parliament uses a kind of shorthand. When it speaks of a statement being admissible as evidence of the matter contained in the statement, it is really referring to evidence of the statement being admissible as evidence of the matter contained in the statement. Nevertheless, whether in shorthand form or when its meaning is teased out in this way, the paragraph is concerned exclusively with defining the classes of statement which are admissible as evidence. Since the provision uses the adjective 'admissible' in the second sense only, there is nothing in its language to suggest that Parliament was here concerned with the, distinct, issue of the admissibility of anyone to give evidence as a witness in proceedings. In other words, the paragraph presupposes that the maker of the statement would be a competent and admissible witness. If he were not, there would be no evidence, whether admissible or inadmissible. It is then concerned with the admissibility of any direct oral evidence which that person might give on particular matters. If such evidence would be inadmissible, then hearsay evidence of a statement by him to a similar effect is also inadmissible. Conversely, if such evidence would be admissible, hearsay evidence of a statement by him to a similar effect is also admissible.

[25] In *F. v. Kennedy*, the court's reasoning, that the provision does indeed deal with the admissibility of the child to give evidence, depends on running together the two distinct senses of 'admissible' in our law: the evidence of the social workers was regarded as inadmissible (second sense) because direct evidence of the matter by W was inadmissible (second sense) because he himself was not an admissible witness (first sense). In my view, having regard simply to the wording of the subsection, that reasoning is unsound. It might, perhaps, be justified if the words used by Parliament could not otherwise be given a sensible meaning. But that is very far from the case. If the adjective 'admissible' is given its second sense, to refer only to the admissibility of evidence relating to a particular matter, the provision not only makes sense but performs a vital role. If para. (b) did not exist, hearsay evidence could be led of a person making a statement about a matter as to which his direct oral evidence would not be admissible. I have already mentioned the solicitor who is asked to give evidence about communings with his client and a participant or mediator who is asked to give evidence about events at a mediation hearing. The policy of the law is that such evidence is not to be admissible. That policy would be undermined if it were open to a party either to give evidence himself or to lead the evidence of someone else as to what the solicitor or participant or mediator had said about these matters. Section 2(1)(b) exists to prevent this kind of potential misuse of hearsay evidence and to bolster the policy of the law, by virtue of which evidence of certain matters is to be inadmissible. This interpretation, it should be noted, gives full value to the words 'by that person' since, where evidence is inadmissible because of a duty of confidentiality on the witness or because, perhaps, the witness came by his knowledge in an unlawful manner, evidence as to the same matter may be admissible if given by someone else who obtained it in a different way.

[26] In *L. v. L.*, 1996 S.L.T. at p.770F–G, the Lord Ordinary recognises that the exclusion of evidence of this kind may have been the primary purpose behind the provision but adds, under reference to *F. v. Kennedy*, that it is 'also apt to include a situation of legal incapacity where no direct evidence by the maker of the statement would be admissible'. For the reasons which I

have given, I see nothing in its language which suggests that the provision should be given this extended meaning. Moreover, as Lord Hamilton goes on to demonstrate and as I explain in more detail below, if it is given that extended meaning, the conditional tense used in the words 'would be admissible' really compels the court to interpret the provision as requiring the court to decide the admissibility of the hearsay evidence by asking whether evidence by the maker of the statement would be admissible at the proof. As I have shown already and as counsel for the defender readily acknowledged, such an interpretation leads to absurd results. Those absurd results are themselves a powerful indication that the construction which gives rise to them is itself flawed.

[27] I find reinforcement of this view in the terms of section 259 of the Criminal Procedure (Scotland) Act 1995 which provides *inter alia*: [his Lordship quoted its terms set out supra and continued:]

[28] The provision is more elaborate than, and has a different scope from, section 2(1)(b) of the 1988 Act since it applies only where, for one of a number of specified reasons, the person who made the statement is not to be called to give evidence at the trial. What is significant for present purposes, however, is that in the 1995 Act Parliament has expressly dealt with both the admissibility of evidence as to the matter in question (in para. (b) of subs. (1)) and the competence of the maker of the statement (in para. (c) of subs. (1)). Even more significantly, the language of para. (b) is similar to the language of section 2(1)(b) of the 1988 Act. The similarity in the language suggests that the provision in the 1988 Act is intended to have the same restricted scope as para. (b) of section 259(1) of the 1995 Act. In both, 'admissible' is used in the second sense noted above.

[29] Another argument should be noticed. On behalf of the pursuer counsel attached some importance to the word 'solely' in section 2(1)(a) of the 1988 Act. This showed, they said, that Parliament had intended to do no more than abolish the hearsay rule; all the other rules remained intact and the provisions should be interpreted in such a way as to give effect to those rules. It followed that Parliament must have intended that the courts should exclude hearsay evidence of the statement of a child if the child herself would not be a competent witness, since otherwise the rules as to the admissibility of child witnesses would be undermined. This did not appear to be a separate argument, but simply a consideration which was said to support the pursuer's submission that subs. (1)(b) did indeed incorporate a competence test. The use of the word 'solely' does not, however, justify the approach which counsel sought to build on it. Paragraph (a) of subsection (1) is in fact the key provision which creates the general rule that hearsay evidence is admissible. If it said nothing more than that, however, it would mean that no hearsay evidence could ever be excluded, however irrelevant or incompetent it might be— for instance, because it related to a matter not falling within the scope of the pleadings or because it sought to contradict the terms of a written contract. By framing the paragraph in the way that it did, however, Parliament ensured that this new class of evidence would be treated like direct oral evidence of the same matter. In other words, even though hearsay evidence is in principle admissible, it can be excluded in the same way that certain direct oral evidence of a witness can be excluded. The general rules apply to this new form of evidence as they do to other types of evidence. The inclusion of the word 'solely' in subs. (1)(a) is not therefore a reason for saying that the subsection as a whole, or para. (b) in particular, embodies a test of competence of the maker of the statement.

[30] For the reasons which I have outlined so far, my provisional view is therefore that section 2(1)(b) should be given its straightforward meaning, according to which it deals only with the admissibility of evidence as to a statement about the matters in question and does not deal at all with the admissibility as a witness of the person making the statement.

[31] Counsel for the pursuer argued that such an approach would be mistaken and that the paragraph should be construed as importing a competence test, but that the test should be applied by reference to the time when the person made the statement. This interpretation enjoys support from certain *obiter* remarks by the Lord President in *M. v. Ferguson*, at 1994 S.C.L.R., p.492D–E and from Lord Hope's observations, again obiter, in *Sanderson v. McManus*, at 1997 S.C. (HL), p.60C; 1997 S.L.T., p.632K. It has the additional merit of making a certain kind of sense in policy terms: if the policy of the legislature was to exclude evidence of

statements by persons who could not have been competent witnesses on the matter, then the aim would be to exclude evidence of statements by people who were too young or too unfit to be able to give trustworthy evidence when they made the statement in question. That is simply the obverse of the argument as to the absurdity of applying a competence test at the date of the proof. The criticism of the pursuer's argument is not, therefore, that it leads to absurdity. Rather, as counsel for the defender made clear, the criticism is that the pursuer's interpretation finds no support in the language of section 2(1)(b) and is indeed inconsistent with it. It also tends to exclude evidence which might well be compelling.

[32] In the first place, the interpretation favoured by counsel for the pursuer is open to precisely the same basic objection as applies to the interpretation which imports a competence test at the time of the proof. It conflates the two senses of 'admissible' and ignores the language of the provision, which is concerned with the admissibility of evidence rather than with the admissibility of witnesses. I need not repeat what I have already said on that point. In addition, however, even on the assumption that this difficulty could be overcome, the pursuer's interpretation ignores the tenses of the verbs used by Parliament. An example makes this clear. The statement in question 'shall be admissible' if oral evidence by that person 'would be admissible'. Suppose that a child has made a statement about a particular matter at the age of three and is called to give evidence about it at a proof held when she is six. Having examined her in the usual way, the sheriff concludes that she is competent to give evidence. If she then gave oral evidence about the matter, it 'would be admissible'. That being so, even on the assumption that the provision embodied a competence test, in that situation, according to the words used in para. (b), the statement made about the same matter when the child was three would be admissible. The position becomes even clearer if the child has made, say, three statements relating to different incidents. When called to give evidence, she recalls two of them and gives admissible oral evidence about those two, but fails to remember the third. If she remembered the third incident, her direct oral evidence about it 'would be admissible'. I can therefore see no basis, standing the terms of para. (b), for holding that hearsay evidence of her earlier statement about that third incident would be inadmissible, simply because she would not have been a competent witness when she made the statement at the age of three.

[33] For the pursuer's approach to be acceptable, one would have to be able to read the paragraph as providing that, even though the direct oral evidence of the child would be admissible at the proof, hearsay evidence of the statement would be inadmissible if the child would not have been a competent witness at the time when she made the statement. I find it impossible to read the language of the paragraph in that way. Nor am I tempted to try, since we can see that, when Parliament later wished to introduce just such a twofold test in section 259 of the 1995 Act, it did so explicitly, using unambiguous language and creating a more complex scheme. As Lord Nimmo Smith pointed out during the hearing, under section 259 the child witness who refuses to accept the admonition to tell the truth or who refuses to give evidence, as envisaged in subsection (2), is *ex hypothesi* a competent witness at the date of the trial. But, nonetheless, in terms of subsection (1)(c), evidence of her statement is admissible only if the trial judge is satisfied that she would have been a competent witness at the time the statement was made. If Parliament had wished to make similar provision in the 1988 Act, it could have done so. Since it did not, I infer that Parliament did not intend to introduce a test of that kind. I therefore reject the construction of section 2(1)(b) of the 1988 Act advanced by counsel for the pursuer.

[34] In the result, simply on the basis of the language of the subsection, I conclude that it does not embody a competence test and that hearsay evidence of a statement is admissible unless it concerns a matter as to which direct oral evidence by the maker of the statement would not be admissible. I have preferred to base that conclusion on the language used by Parliament in section 2(1)(b), but in my view it is also consistent with a number of wider considerations which were urged upon us.

[35] As the long title suggests, the 1988 Act effected a revolution in our law of evidence. At times the courts have had difficulty in adjusting to all the implications of that revolution. As I had occasion to remark in *L. v. L.* at p.676G, our duty, however, is to give full effect to the changes which Parliament has made.

[36] Down the years before 1988, there was a more or less desultory debate about the advantages and disadvantages, on the one hand, of retaining the exclusionary rule and, on the other, of allowing in hearsay evidence. Some flavour of that debate is to be found in paras 19.01–19.21 of the published version of the research paper on the law of evidence which Sheriff Macphail wrote for the use of the Scottish Law Commission and which formed the basis of their Memorandum (no. 46) on the Law of Evidence published in 1980. The catalogue of issues reappears in much the same form in the commission's Report on "Corroboration, Hearsay and Related Matters in Civil Proceedings" (no. 100, 1986), paras 3.15–3.21. That debate is now of largely historical interest but it shows, of course, that the risk that hearsay evidence might be less reliable than direct oral evidence was among the arguments which could be, and were, deployed in support of retaining the pre-existing law. On the advice of ministers, who adopted a considerably more radical policy than the commission had proposed, Parliament nonetheless swept away the old exclusionary rule and replaced it with a rule which made hearsay evidence admissible in principle in all cases where primary evidence to the same effect would have been admissible. By passing the legislation Parliament resolved the antecedent debate, as far as Scottish courts at least are concerned, and replaced the old law with a new and completely different rule, to which we must give effect.

[37] On the interpretation of section 2(1)(b) which I prefer, this means that we must accept that hearsay evidence of a statement is admissible even though, perhaps, the maker of the statement would not have been an admissible witness. Senior counsel for the pursuer sought to dissuade us from adopting that interpretation on the simple ground that there was no hint of it in the previous authorities or in textbooks. As he himself recognised, that is not strictly speaking the case but, in any event, even if the interpretation had never been previously advanced, I should not find that a persuasive argument one way or the other. It is well known that, when once adopted, a particular approach will often tend to persist even if it is unsound, unless and until the whole question is thoroughly re-examined. In the case of section 2(1)(b) the basic approach to its interpretation adopted early on in *F. v. Kennedy* was really just accepted in all the subsequent cases, with attention being given to trying to manage the difficulties to which it gave rise in practice. This is the first opportunity which the court has had to look again at the fundamentals of the matter.

[38] More importantly, senior counsel for the pursuer urged upon us what they saw as the undesirable consequences of allowing in hearsay evidence without a competence test. It would mean that a judge or even a jury might have to hear evidence of a statement made by a child who was incapable of distinguishing truth from falsehood or of giving a trustworthy account. Those undesirable consequences were an indication that Parliament could never have intended the provision to have this effect. For my part, I find it helpful to keep in mind that hearsay evidence is, almost by definition, evidence by A of what B said when not on oath. Whoever B may be, it is evidence of what he said when he was not giving evidence in the proceedings in which the hearsay evidence is led. When he made the statement, B may have been drunk, affected by drugs, ill, distracted, engaged in a practical joke or impelled by sheer malice. These and a thousand other factors may mean that his statement is completely untrustworthy and the evidence of what he said equally valueless. Nonetheless the evidence of his statement is admissible under section 2 and the court or jury have to use their wisdom and common sense to assess what weight, if any, to give to that evidence. The statements of children and of persons suffering from mental disorder or disability raise not dissimilar issues. Even assuming that their statements can properly be regarded as inherently less trustworthy than statements by people affected in the ways which I have mentioned, it is a matter of degree only. If evidence of their statements is admitted, the judge or jury will again have to use their wisdom and common sense to decide whether the statements are trustworthy. The exercise is not au fond different. In carrying it out, in the case of young children in particular, the judge or jury will be able to draw not only on their own experience of listening to children in everyday life but also on any expert evidence which may be tendered in relation to the individual whose statement is in issue.

[39] To hold that evidence of the statements of a child is admissible only when the child could have given evidence on the same point is to equiparate the capacity to make a statement about something with the capacity to give evidence on the same point. They may, however, be entirely different. There must be many children who can state, perhaps casually but quite

accurately, what they happen to have seen but who, for a whole variety of reasons, could not give evidence on the same matter in court. The moves in Britain and elsewhere in recent years to change the ways in which children give evidence are eloquent of precisely that distinction. More particularly, we all know that even quite young children will try to explain what they have just seen happening and we do not simply reject all these explanations as fantasy or as wholly untrustworthy. It is not hard, for instance, to imagine a situation where a young child comes into a room, perhaps in distress, and says that she has just seen her father hit her mother or that her father has just hit the child herself. That child may be unable to pass the test of competence to give evidence, but what she said may still be extremely compelling and have the ring of truth. In real life you might well act on the strength of such a statement and, indeed, be open to criticism if you did not. On an application of the competence test as envisaged by the pursuer, however, evidence of what the child said would often be inadmissible as evidence of these matters.

[40] To avoid that uncomfortable conclusion, counsel for the pursuer argued that a statement of this kind would be admissible as part of the evidence of the *res gestae*. Perhaps to give this doctrine a more modern and shiny patina, senior counsel for the pursuer preferred to refer to such statements as 'excited utterances' and pointed out that in many other jurisdictions hearsay evidence of such spontaneous utterances is admissible. He also appeared to envisage that in a suitable case evidence of a *de recenti* statement by a young child might be admissible. The court was suddenly faced with the idea that, somewhere behind the terms of section 2 of the 1988 Act, the *res gestae* and *de recenti* doctrines survived to haunt the law. So far from making all things new, Parliament had impliedly preserved these troublesome rules.

[41] I reject that argument, as I would also reject any argument that hearsay evidence of statements by someone who had since died would be admissible by reason of the old common law, even though the person concerned could obviously not comply with a competence test applied at the time of the proof. The *res gestae*, *de recenti* and deceased persons rules were all exceptions to the former general rule that hearsay evidence was inadmissible. That general rule has passed away and, with it, any need for these former exceptions. Indeed, on counsel's analysis, these common law rules would not now be performing the role assigned to them by the common law. Rather, they would be common law exceptions to a supposed statutory exception to a statutory rule that hearsay statements are admissible. There is no warrant in the wording of the 1988 Act or in its long title for conjuring up common law exceptions or supplements of this kind to the rules laid down by Parliament. In this respect I agree with the court in *F. v. Kennedy* at p.32 (p.1280K) that the admissibility of statements depends on the provisions of the 1988 Act.

[42] The fact that counsel for the pursuer felt the need to resort to the desperate measure of calling up the spirits of the *res gestae* and *de recenti* rules is an indication that the interpretation of section 2(1)(b) which counsel favoured was not in itself satisfactory. It is therefore another reason for rejecting that interpretation. The same would apply to any invocation of the old exception for statements of deceased persons to avoid difficulties in applying any supposed competence test at the time of the proof. On the approach to section 2 which I favour, all these various classes of statement can be accommodated within the legislation enacted by Parliament without the need to disturb the repose of the old common law exceptions, whose work in our civil law is done.

[43] When looking at the position more generally, I am also struck by the way in which any competence test, whether applied at the time of the statement or at the time of the proof, tends to cut down what one might have thought would be potentially useful effects of the reform of the law of hearsay. Very often—though not invariably, of course—if a witness is available to give direct oral evidence on a matter, that will be the most compelling and effective evidence. If so, the party will tend to call the witness to give evidence, even if some other witness can speak to a statement which the person concerned has made on the point. It is precisely in those cases where, for whatever reason, that person cannot give evidence that hearsay evidence of the person's earlier statement may be most useful to the court. If that person is an adult, usually no difficulty arises and the evidence can be led. But if the person happens to be a child up to, say, 12 years of age, evidence of her earlier statement cannot be led, it is said, unless there is evidence available to demonstrate that she would be a competent witness. If available at all,

such evidence may be difficult and costly to obtain, involving the need to commission expert reports and, perhaps, to have the child interviewed. And, of course, if the evidence is to the effect that the child would not be or would not have been a competent witness, then on this approach the evidence of her statement will be inadmissible, however compelling it may appear to be.

[44] My uneasiness with such a conclusion increases when I contemplate the terms of section 23 of the (Irish) Children Act 1997 (no. 40) which counsel for the pursuer helpfully drew to our attention. The section provides *inter alia*: [his Lordship quoted its terms set out supra and continued:]

The provision is different in important respects from section 2 in our own legislation. For one thing, it deals only with the evidence of children and does not touch the general rules relating to hearsay evidence. Moreover, subsection (2) retains to the court a measure of control which is absent from the Scottish legislation. On the other hand I note in passing that the Irish provision distinguishes between the admissibility of evidence and the ability of a child to give evidence in language which tends to confirm the interpretation that I have placed on section 2(1)(b) of our own legislation.

[45] Despite the difference in approach, the Irish provision is of some assistance for present purposes, since it shows that the Irish legislature has made the evidence of statements by children admissible in the very kind of case where the competence test supposedly enshrined in our section 2 would make such evidence inadmissible. The rationale for the Irish provision must be that evidence of statements by children may be of value to the court, even though the child may not be capable of giving evidence or it would not be in the interests of the child for her to give oral evidence. That seems, with respect, a wholly justifiable balance for a legislature to strike and, though the balance is struck differently by section 2(1), I find no reason to recoil from the conclusion that Parliament intended to allow evidence to be led of statements made by children who are too young or are otherwise incapable of giving oral evidence. Indeed some confirmation that this was the intention of Parliament may be found in certain passages of the debates on the Civil Evidence (Scotland) Bill. Before turning to those passages, I should look further at the various documents which the Scottish Law Commission produced to pave the way for the 1988 Act.

[46] As already mentioned, the starting point is the research paper prepared by Sheriff Macphail. At para. 19.27 he observed that it did not seem logical to depart from the requirement that the maker of the statement must be a person who would have been a competent witness. He then quoted a passage from Walker and Walker on Evidence, para. 371, dealing with hearsay statements of deceased persons under the old law and suggesting that there were three possible dates for determining competence: the date when the statement was tendered in evidence, the day the maker of the statement died, and the day when the statement is alleged to have been made. Sheriff Macphail pointed out that Dickson on Evidence, paras 266–267, considered that the date should be the day when the statement was alleged to have been made, but that in *Deans' JF v. Deans*, at 1912 S.C., p.448; 1912 1 S.L.T., pp.200–201 Lord President Dunedin had reserved his opinion.

[47] In memorandum no. 46, which was prepared on the basis of Sheriff Macphail's paper, the commission observed (at para. T.08): 'The maker of the statement must be a person who would have been a competent witness. We propose that the date on which his competency should be tested is the time when the statement is tendered in evidence.'

In the published version of his research paper (Evidence, para. S19.27) Sheriff Macphail simply recorded this proposal. The striking thing about the proposal is that there is no indication whatever of the reasons for the commission's (prima facie strange) choice.

[48] When the commission eventually came to publish their report on the matter in 1986, they did not discuss this issue at all. In fact they made no mention of the need for a test of competence, far less of the date at which any such test should be applied. In para. 3.37 they concluded that the rule against the admission of hearsay evidence should be abolished, subject to certain safeguards. They then added: 'In making this recommendation we do not intend to render admissible evidence of statements made by another, if direct oral evidence of the matter contained in the statement would not have been admissible, if offered by the original maker of the statement. In other words we are concerned only with evidence which is presently

inadmissible because of the rule against hearsay, not with evidence which may be inadmissible for other reasons, for example, by reason of confidentiality. Therefore, subject to the safeguards outlined below, we recommend that: 8. The rule against hearsay should be abolished and any statement made by a person otherwise than as a witness in court should be admissible as evidence of any matter contained in the statement which could competently have been given by that person as direct oral evidence. We further recommend that this should apply to multiple as well as simple hearsay.'

This recommendation formed one of the bases for clause 2 in the draft Bill attached to the report. Paragraphs (a) and (b) of clause 2(1) are in all essential respects similar to the terms of section 2(1)(a) and (b) as eventually enacted by Parliament.

[49] Unfortunately, recommendation 8 is formulated somewhat loosely. In particular the relative clause at the end of the first sentence lacks any appropriate antecedent. In that situation I should not be inclined to attach weight to the particular words used by the commission in their recommendation. But, if the recommendation is read along with what the commission say immediately before, I infer that they intended to exclude the admission of hearsay evidence if direct oral evidence of the same matter would have been either incompetent or irrelevant. On the other hand, despite what they said in their memorandum in 1980, I find nothing at all to suggest that the commission intended to recommend that any legislation should contain a test of competence. The reason for this is hidden from our gaze: it may be that the commission changed their minds in the light of the responses to their memorandum, or else changes in the membership of the commission may have led to a change of view. Whatever the reason, it is sufficient that the commission did not recommend the inclusion of such a test and that on this matter Parliament enacted the provision in essentially the same terms as the commission had proposed. The appropriate inference from the Law Commission material seems therefore to be that the provision enacted by Parliament was not designed to incorporate a test of competence.

[50] Although I have indicated that I do not myself find section 2(1)(b) ambiguous, I readily acknowledge that a different interpretation has hitherto prevailed and has been regarded favourably, even in the House of Lords (*Sanderson v. McManus* at pp.59I–60D (p.632H–L). In those circumstances it would be wrong to exclude consideration of the passages in Hansard on any technical ground relating to perceptions of ambiguity or the lack of it.

[51] We were referred to the proceedings in the House of Commons. In the second reading debate on May 16, 1988 the only indication which appears to me to be of any possible assistance comes in the minister's reply to the debate in which he said that the member for Aberdeen, South (Mr Doran) had made an interesting comment on child abuse cases. The minister, Lord James Douglas-Hamilton, indicated that he believed that the Bill met his point (Hansard, HC, Sixth Series, Vol. 133, col. 774). The minister appears to be referring to Mr Doran's comment (col. 765) that many cases of child abuse are discovered outside the home, at school or nursery school, and that, under the pre-existing law, evidence from a teacher, a nursery nurse or a social worker would be inadmissible. The Bill would, he thought, provide a considerable improvement and the work of the social work departments and children's hearing system would be much more effective because courts would be able to deal with such cases. If Mr Doran's comments and the minister's reply are read together, it may be legitimate to infer that the minister was indicating that the Bill would indeed make it easier for hearsay evidence to be introduced even in the case of children of nursery school age. At the very least, this passage is important because it shows that Parliament was well aware of the possible implications of the new provision for evidence relating to statements by young children.

[52] This is confirmed by the debate in the standing committee in which several members, including the minister, were legally qualified and were well aware of the full implications of the legislation which they were discussing. On June 23, 1988 Mr Dewar was concerned about the possible adverse effects of the legislation on persons facing social work proceedings in relation to allegations of child abuse (First Scottish Standing Committee Debates, Session 1987–88, Vol. XI, cols 95–96). He put down an amendment designed to exclude such proceedings from the scope of the Bill. Mr Doran (cols 96–98), on the other hand, was worried that any such amendment would weaken the Bill's beneficent effect in giving more scope for the use of hearsay evidence of children's statements in such proceedings. He gave the example of the

difficulties which had occurred in a case involving a girl of four who made two graphic statements indicating that she had been abused by her father. The grounds of referral were not accepted and a hearing was held before the sheriff who was unable to find the grounds established because the statements were hearsay and there was no corroboration. The minister undertook to consider the matter and Mr Dewar withdrew the amendment.

[53] At third reading on July 4, 1988 Mr Dewar did not move his amendment again and, having considered the matter, the minister did not seek to amend the Bill in this way either. In replying to the short debate he said (Hansard, HC, Sixth Series, Vol. 136, col. 742), however, that Mr Doran had fairly and correctly pointed out that the ultimate aim should be the protection of the child. He added that Mr Doran had made it absolutely clear that he believed that the majority of reporters, social workers and police welcomed the fact that the Bill would do away with a major difficulty in the proof of child abuse. He had also stated his opposition to Mr Dewar's amendment and had expressed concern that the minister had agreed to reconsider the matter. Lord James concluded: 'Having considered the matter further, I should state that the weight of evidence is clearly in one direction, and I hope that the House will accept the position on that very important point.' The House then agreed that the Bill should be read a third time.

[54] While the passage in the minister's speech is not perhaps entirely clear on the matter, the fair interpretation seems to be that he recognised that, if passed, the Bill would indeed have an impact on social work proceedings by abolishing the need for corroboration and by permitting the introduction of hearsay evidence as to statements made by young children, who would not be called to give evidence themselves. If that is correct, then the passage from the minister's speech, when interpreted in the light of the debates, tends to support the view that Parliament envisaged that, by virtue of what is now section 2, parties would be able to introduce into civil proceedings evidence of statements of children who could not themselves give evidence. In this way proceedings would now be able to be brought where previously they could not be brought because the children were unable to give evidence. So construed, the minister's reply would give some support for the view, which I would reach in any event, that section 2(1)(b) does not import a competence test."

NOTES

(i) It is now necessary to conduct an examination into a child's competency only where it is proposed to lead that child as a witness. The admissibility of a hearsay statement made by the child is not dependent on the question of competency. The question remains whether a party would be permitted to lead evidence at proof as to the competency of a witness in order to cast doubt on his or her credibility.

(ii) In general, and apart from section 3 of the 1988 Act, it seems that evidence may *not* be led in so far as it bears only upon a witnesses credibility—see generally Macphail, *Evidence*, para. 16.19. Lord Hope's view in *M. v. Kennedy* that in certain cases evidence will have to be led about a child's "ability to give a trustworthy account" suggests that this rule is not to be strictly applied, or at least that the matter is one of competence and not credibility (compare Macphail, *Evidence*, para. 3.28). See in any event the old cases of *John Buchan* and *Malcolm Maclean* (1833) Bells Notes 293, 294, in which evidence as to the child's ability or tendency to speak the truth was admitted. These cases should be treated with some caution, however, and in particular should be read in the light of the English case of *Re F.S. (Child Abuse: Evidence)* [1996] 2 F.L.R. 158 and the other English cases reviewed in the Notes to Item 2 in Chapter 10. In *F.S.*, it was emphasised that the role of the expert witness is to assist the court by a clinical assessment of the person interviewed, and of his or her evidence. The expert is not there to to tell the court that the evidence should or should not be believed as that would be to usurp the function of the judge.

(iii) *M. v. Kennedy* makes clear, in spite of dicta to the contrary in Walker and Walker, *Evidence* and the Stair Memorial Encyclopaedia, Vol. 10, that spontaneity—in the sense of an ability to give an account of a particular event—is not a matter which necessarily affects the question of competency. It is enough that the child knows the difference between truth and falsehood. Of course, the weight to be accorded to evidence in circumstances where a witness has to be comprehensively led—as in *M. v. Kennedy*—might be thought to be negligible, but as we have seen, for example in relation to *K. v. Kennedy*, above, courts may be willing to proceed in Children's Hearing cases on the thinnest of evidence.

(iv) Note that if evidence of a hearsay statement *is* inadmissible for whatever reason, evidence that the statement was made may still be admissible *quantum valeat*—see *Sanderson v. McManus*, 1997 S.L.T. 629. Note, however, that comments by Lord Hope at p.632 to the effect that "it would have been sufficient that the child was competent at the time when the statements were made", were specifically *not* followed in *T. v. T.*

Chapter 14

WITNESSES—SOME SPECIALTIES

"The spirit of the old Scotch law was to exclude the evidence of every person whose character, whose connection with the parties, or whose interest in the cause, raised a doubt as to the trustworthiness of his evidence. It was then more difficult to discover who were admissible, than who were incompetent, witnesses. For a number of years, however, the prevailing spirit both in the courts and in the legislature has been to sweep away the grounds for excluding witnesses, leaving the old objections whatever effect they ought to have upon the credibility of witnesses who are open to them." (Dickson Vol. II, para. 1542). Even at the time Dickson was writing, however, there remained doubts as to the competency of deaf and mute people to give evidence, and atheists were absolutely prohibited. In modern practice, most people may be called as witnesses in any court proceedings and indeed may be compelled to attend and to answer questions. Some exceptions remain, the most notable being that of the accused in criminal proceedings. There are also complications relating to the spouses of accused persons and of parties in civil cases, those who are accused along with others in the same proceedings and those who give evidence as accomplices or *socii criminis*. Finally, this section considers some of the difficulties (and attempted solutions) in relation to child witnesses, again with the emphasis on child witnesses in criminal proceedings.

1.   Criminal Procedure (Scotland) Act 1995

"263.—(1) In any trial, it shall be competent for the party against whom a witness is produced and sworn *in causa* to examine such witness both in cross and *in causa*.

(2) The judge may, on the motion of either party, on cause shown order that the examination of a witness for that party ('the first witness') shall be interrupted to permit the examination of another witness for that party.

(3) Where the judge makes an order under subsection (2) above he shall, after the examination of the other witness, permit the recall of the first witness.

(4) In a trial, a witness may be examined as to whether he has on any specified occasion made a statement on any matter pertinent to the issue at the trial different from the evidence given by him in the trial; and evidence may be led in the trial to prove that the witness made the different statement on the occasion specified.

(5) In any trial, on the motion of either party, the presiding judge may permit a witness who has been examined to be recalled.

264.—(1) The spouse of an accused may be called as a witness—
   (a) by the accused;
   (b) by a co-accused or by the prosecutor without the consent of the accused.
(2) Nothing in this section shall—
   (a) make the spouse of an accused a compellable witness for a co-accused or for the prosecutor in a case where such spouse would not be so compellable at common law;
   (b) compel a spouse to disclose any communication made between the spouses during the marriage.
(3) The failure of the spouse of an accused to give evidence shall not be commented on by the defence or the prosecutor.
(4) The spouse of a person charged with bigamy may be called as a witness either for the prosecution or the defence and without the consent of the person charged.

265.—(1) Every person adduced as a witness who is not otherwise by law disqualified from giving evidence, shall be admissible as a witness, and no objection to the admissibility of a witness shall be competent on the ground of—

    (a) conviction of or punishment for an offence;

    (b) interest;

    (c) agency or partial counsel;

    (d) the absence of due citation to attend; or

    (e) his having been precognosced subsequently to the date of citation.

(2) Where any person who is or has been an agent of the accused is adduced and examined as a witness for the accused, it shall not be competent for the accused to object, on the ground of confidentiality, to any question proposed to be put to such witness on matters pertinent to the issue of the guilt of the accused.

(3) No objection to the admissibility of a witness shall be competent on the ground that he or she is the father, mother, son, daughter, brother or sister, by consanguinity or affinity, or uncle, aunt, nephew or niece, by consanguinity of any party adducing the witness in any trial.

(4) It shall not be competent for any witness to decline to be examined and give evidence on the ground of any relationship mentioned in subsection (3) above.

266.—(1) Subject to subsections (2) to (8) below, the accused shall be a competent witness for the defence at every stage of the case, whether the accused is on trial alone or along with a co-accused.

(2) The accused shall not be called as a witness in pursuance of this section except upon his own application or in accordance with subsection (9) or (10) below.

(3) An accused who gives evidence on his own behalf in pursuance of this section may be asked any question in cross-examination notwithstanding that it would tend to incriminate him as to the offence charged.

(4) An accused who gives evidence on his own behalf in pursuance of this Section shall not be asked, and if asked shall not be required to answer, any question tending to show that he has committed, or been convicted of, or been charged with, any offence other than that with which he is then charged, or is of bad character, unless—

    (a) the proof that he has committed or been convicted of such other offence is admissible evidence to show that he is guilty of the offence with which he is then charged; or

    (b) the accused or his counsel or solicitor has asked questions of the witnesses for the prosecution with a view to establishing the accused's good character or impugning the character of the complainer, or the accused has given evidence of his own good character, or the nature or conduct of the defence is such as to involve imputations on the character of the prosecutor or of the witnesses for the prosecution or of the complainer; or

    (c) the accused has given evidence against any other person charged in the same proceedings

(5) In a case to which paragraph (b) of subsection (4) above applies, the prosecutor shall be entitled to ask the accused a question of a kind specified in that subsection only if the court on the application of the prosecutor, permits him to do so.

(6) An application under subsection (5) above in proceedings in indictment shall be made in the course of the trial but in the absence of the jury.

(7) In subsection (4) above, references to the complainer include references to a victim who is deceased.

(8) Every person called as a witness in pursuance of this section shall, unless otherwise ordered by the court, give his evidence from the witness box or other place from which the other witnesses give their evidence.

(9) The accused may—

    (a) With the consent of a co-accused, call that other accused as a witness on the accused's behalf or;

    (b) ask a co-accused any question in cross-examination if that co-accused gives evidence, but he may not do both in relation to the same co-accused.

(10) The prosecutor or the accused may call as a witness a co-accused who has pleaded guilty to or been acquitted of all charges against him which remain before the court (whether or not, in a case where the co-accused has pleaded guilty to any charge, he has been sentenced) or in respect of whom the diet has been deserted; and the party calling such co-accused as a witness shall not require to give notice thereof, but the court may grant any other party such adjournment or postponement of the trial as may seem just.

(11) Where, in any trial, the accused is to be called as a witness he shall be so called as the first witness for the defence unless the court, on cause shown, otherwise directs.

267.—(1) The court may, on an application by any party to the proceedings, permit a witness to be in court during the proceedings or any part of the proceedings before he has given evidence if it appears to the court that the presence of the witness would not be contrary to the interests of justice.

(2) Without prejudice to subsection (1) above, where a witness has, without the permission of the court and without the consent of the parties to the proceedings, been present in court during the proceedings, the court may, in its discretion, admit the witness, where it appears to the court that the presence of the witness was not the result of culpable negligence or criminal intent, and that the witness has not been unduly instructed or influenced by what took place during his presence, or that injustice will not be done by his examination.

268.—(1) Subject to subsection (2) below, the judge may, on a motion of the prosecutor or the accused made—

    (a) in proceedings on indictment, at any time before the commencement of the speeches to the jury;

    (b) in summary proceedings, at any time before the prosecutor proceeds to address the judge on the evidence,

permit him to lead additional evidence.

(2) Permission shall only be granted under subsection (1) above where the judge—

    (a) considers that the additional evidence is prima facie material; and

    (b) accepts that at the commencement of the trial either—

        (i) the additional evidence was not available and could not reasonably have been made available; or

        (ii) the materiality of such additional evidence could not reasonably have been foreseen by the party.

(3) The judge may permit the additional evidence to be led notwithstanding that—

    (a) in proceedings on indictment, a witness or production concerned is not included in any list lodged by the parties and that the notice required by sections 67(5) and 78(4) of this Act has not been given; or

    (b) in any case, a witness must be recalled.

(4) The judge may, when granting a motion in terms of this section, adjourn or postpone the trial before permitting the additional evidence to be led.

(5) In this section "the commencement of the trial" means—

    (a) in proceedings on indictment, the time when the jury is sworn; and

    (b) in summary proceedings, the time when the first witness for the prosecution is sworn.

269.—(1) The judge may, on a motion of the prosecutor made at the relevant time, permit the prosecutor to lead additional evidence for the purpose of—

    (a) contradicting evidence given by any defence witness which could not reasonably have been anticipated by the prosecutor; or

    (b) providing such proof as is mentioned in section 263(4) of this Act.

(2) The judge may permit the additional evidence to be led notwithstanding that—

    (a) in proceedings on indictment, a witness or production concerned is not included in any list lodged by the parties and that the notice required by sections 67(5) and 78(4) of this Act has not been given; or

    (b) in any case, a witness must be recalled.

(3) The judge may when granting a motion in terms of this section, adjourn or postpone the trial before permitting the additional evidence to be led.

(4) In subsection (1) above, "the relevant time" means—

    (a) in proceedings on indictment, after the close of the defence evidence and before the commencement of the speeches to the jury; and

    (b) in summary proceedings after the close of the defence evidence and before the prosecutor proceeds to address the judge on the evidence.

270.—(1) This section applies where—

    (a) evidence is led by the defence, or the defence asks questions of a witness for the prosecution, with a view to establishing the accused's good character or impugning the character of the prosecutor, of any witness for the prosecution or of the complainer; or

    (b) the nature or conduct of the defence is such as to tend to establish the accused's good character or to involve imputations on the character of the prosecutor, of any witness for the prosecution or of the complainer.

(2) Where this section applies the court may, without prejudice to section 268 of this Act, on the application of the prosecutor, permit the prosecutor to lead evidence that the accused has committed, or has been convicted of, or has been charged with, offences other than that for which he is being tried, or is of bad character, notwithstanding that, in proceedings on indictment, a witness or production concerned is not included in any list lodged by the prosecutor and that the notice required by sections 67(5) and 78(4) of this Act has not been given.

(3) In proceedings on indictment, an application under subsection (2) above shall be made in the course of the trial but in the absence of the jury.

(4) In subsection (1) above, references to the complainer include references to a victim who is deceased."

NOTES

Most of the law relating to the competence and compellability of an accused person, spouses of such persons, and evidence of an accused's bad character or previous convictions is contained in these provisions of the consolidated Criminal Procedure (Scotland) Act 1995. Some of these matters have already been considered in Chapter 9 on collateral evidence. The main remaining issues are examined in the extracts reproduced below.

(A) THE ACCUSED

The accused is neither a competent nor a compellable witness for the prosecution (see Stair Memorial Encyclopaedia, Vol. 10, paras. 539–542). She may, of course, give evidence on her own behalf—see Criminal Procedure (Scotland) Act 1995, s.266, above—although cases such as *Todd v. H.M.A.*, 1984 J.C. 13, below, indicate that if the accused chooses to give evidence, she may be asked any question in cross-examination, notwithstanding that the answer may be incriminating. An accused may, however, be called as a witness for the prosecution where she has pleaded guilty to (1995 Act, s.266), or is acquitted of, all charges which remain before the court, or if the charges against her are dropped. Where an accused exercises her right to remain silent at her trial, the judge or prosecutor may comment upon that silence and invite the jury to draw adverse inferences from such silence. Such comment, however, may be made only in certain limited circumstances.

2. Scott v. H.M.A.
1946 J.C. 90

The accused was the driver of a motor car which had been involved in a collision. He was charged *inter alia* with an attempt to pervert the course of justice by inducing witnesses to give false evidence at his trial. Two witnesses gave evidence in support of this charge but their evidence was vague and inconsistent. The accused did not give evidence in his own defence and his silence was commented upon repeatedly by the trial judge, who told the jury erroneously that the evidence of the two witnesses was supported by a third witness and was all substantially to the same effect.

LORD MONCRIEFF: "[I share the reluctance of Lord Carmont] to entertain appeals in criminal cases upon a meticulous examination of the charge to the jury by the presiding Judge. I am even more reluctant to entertain such appeals where the objection to the charge is founded upon isolated passages in the charge and not on its general purport and tenor. In the present case, however, I agree with your Lordship that the presiding Judge failed to present to the jury for their consideration the very substance of the defence.

As regards the comment by the presiding Judge upon the failure of the accused to give evidence on his own behalf, I recognise that after the decision of the case of *Brown v. Macpherson* [1918 J.C. 3] such comment does not in itself afford a reason for appeal. In that case, however, the opinion of the Lord Justice-General, with which the Lord Justice-Clerk concurred, was only that such comment was permissible in exceptional cases. Lord Dundas, who was the third member of that Court, concurred with that opinion, though only with hesitation. I would, however, welcome a further consideration of that decision so far as it was directed towards this question. In my view, it is of the very substance of the remedy introduced by the Criminal Evidence Act 1898, that the evidence of the accused in criminal cases is to be made available to the Court only upon his own application. It is true that in a succeeding subsection it is for the prosecutor only that it is expressly made incompetent to comment upon the failure of the accused to avail himself of this privilege. I cannot, however, hold that this warrants an inference that comment by the Judge is to be competent. It rather appears to me to anticipate that a prohibition of judicial comment is not likely to be required. I do not think that the substance of the enactment, which secures that the privilege shall be available to the accused at his own option, will be preserved if the accused is also to realise that the exercise of the option according to his choice may result in a most gravely serious reaction against his defence . . . I entirely agree with your Lordship in holding that such comment, if made by the Judge, should, at most, be incidental comment and should in no case be reiterated and emphasised."

LORD JUSTICE-GENERAL (NORMAND): "I am also decidedly averse from favouring criticism of a Judge's charge based on isolated passages and not its general tenor. But here the criticism was directed against the tenor, although it was also supported and pointed by references to particular passages. After repeated study of the charge as a whole I am satisfied that the jury must have understood that all they had to decide was whether the two witnesses were telling the truth, and that, if they came to the conclusion that they were, their duty was to convict. The jury were thus led to ignore the substance of the defence that the two witnesses were vague and inconsistent in their evidence about the appellant's purpose in approaching them, and that one of them was even uncertain whether he had any serious purpose. The general effect of the inadequate presentation of the defence was certainly not diminished by the reiterated misstatement that there were three witnesses and not two who deponed against the appellant, or by the recurring comment that the appellant had not given evidence in contradiction of the three witnesses. Since the defence was not that the two witnesses were unveracious, but that their evidence was wholly inconclusive, the appellant had no occasion to give evidence contradicting them. The emphasis laid on his failure to go into the witness box therefore gave additional weight to the appellant's contention that the jury's minds were deflected from their duty to consider what was the true import of the evidence. Although comment of this kind is, in my view, competent, it should be made with restraint and only when there are special circumstances which require it; and, if it is made with reference to particular evidence which the panel might have explained or contradicted, care should be taken that the evidence is not distorted and that its true bearing is properly represented to the jury. I agree therefore with your Lordships that the appeal should be allowed."

NOTES

Lord Moncrieff's comments on the soundness of *Brown v. Macpherson*, 1918 J.C. 13 were disapproved in *Knowles v. H.M.A.*, 1975 J.C. 6. Lord Justice-General Normand's *dictum* on the question of comment by the trial judge on the accused's failure to give evidence is, however, frequently cited by the courts. In *Stewart v. H.M.A.*, 1980 S.L.T. 245, the court quoted that *dictum* and continued:

"This is a particularly delicate area in which comment has necessarily to [be] considered carefully lest a jury should receive the erroneous impression that they are entitled to treat the fact that the accused has not entered the witness box as a piece of evidence corroborative of the case for the prosecution, or worse, a piece of evidence which is to be added to a body of evidence which would be insufficient to satisfy them that guilt had been established beyond reasonable doubt."

In *Stewart*, the case for the defence was that an important Crown witness was lying, and the trial judge commented upon the accused's failure to give evidence contradicting that witness. The comment was held to be appropriate in the circumstances. See also *Dempsey v. H.M.A.*, 1996 S.L.T. 289, and *Paterson v. H.M.A.*, 2000 S.L.T. 833, which emphasises that comment by the trial judge will be appropriate only where "special circumstances" arising from the evidence demand it. Moreover, the trial judge must be careful to specify the particular parts of the evidence which may give rise to inferences of guilt and which call for an explanation from the accused—see *e.g. Mack v. H.M.A.*, 1999 S.L.T. 1163.

Comment by the prosecutor on the accused's failure to give evidence is now competent. The Criminal Justice (Scotland) Act 1995, s.32 abolished section 141(l)(b) and 346(l)(b) of the Criminal Procedure (Scotland) Act 1975. It remains to be seen how this permission to comment will be interpreted in practice but it is thought that comment by the prosecutor ought to be made with similar restraint to that exercised by judges. In the House of Lords debate on section 32 (see Hansard H.L. Vol. 560 col. 416), the then Lord Advocate, Lord Rodger of Earlsferry said:

"the prosecutor will only comment with restraint because of course he must have regard to the fact that as the law has been laid down it is only with restraint that this can be said to a jury, and it is only in special circumstances that it can be said. If he goes further than that, if he says something which goes beyond that, it will be the judge's duty to correct what the prosecutor has said and to give the proper direction to the jury. If he should fail to do so, or, in certain circumstances, if the appeal court thought that what was said by the prosecutor was so outrageous, then presumably the matter could be the basis for a ground of appeal. Where the law itself only allows comment with restraint, and only for inferences to be drawn in narrow circumstances, it would be a foolish prosecutor indeed who went further than that."

(B) THE CO-ACCUSED

A co-accused is, like any accused person, neither competent nor compellable at the instance of the prosecution, except in the circumstances outlined above. A co-accused may be called as a witness by another accused (see 1995 Act, s.266(9) above), but cannot be compelled to give evidence. It was at one time thought that evidence led for one accused could not be used as evidence against another accused. That suggestion was comprehensively rejected in the following case. However, an accused who gives evidence against a co-accused loses his protection against questioning on his character and previous convictions—see the 1995 Act, s.266(4)(c) and Chapter 9 above.

3. Todd v. H.M.A.
1984 J.C. 13

Three accused were charged on indictment with assault and robbery and maintained separate defences. The co-habitee of one of the accused, who had been on the list of witnesses for the prosecutor but was not called by him, gave evidence on behalf of her co-habitee. Her evidence in chief incriminated one of the co-accused and she was cross-examined on behalf of that co-accused. The witness was then cross-examined by the prosecutor who elicited further evidence incriminating the co-accused following an unsuccessful objection on behalf of the latter to the admissibility of such evidence. Counsel for the co-accused was, however, permitted to cross-examine the witness further. The trial judge also refused to direct the jury that the evidence by that witness which had been adduced on behalf of one accused could not be evidence against his co-accused. The co-accused was convicted and appealed on the ground that the trial judge had materially misdirected the jury in relation to that evidence. The appeal was heard by a bench of five judges.

LORD JUSTICE-CLERK (WHEATLEY): "This appeal relates to the question whether the evidence of a witness led by one accused in exculpation of that accused is competent evidence against a co-accused when separate defences are being maintained, or, put another way, whether such evidence can be extracted from such a witness. What happened was this. The appellant and two men were charged with assault and robbery. A Mrs Sandra Brodie, a co-habitee of one of the men, was a witness on the Crown list of witnesses. She was not called as a witness by the Crown, but her co-habitee, who was the first-named accused, called her as a witness in support of his defence of alibi. As the issue is a question of general law I find it unnecessary to go into details. It suffices to say that after this witness had given her evidence-in-chief and had been cross-examined by counsel for the appellant she was cross-examined by the advocate-depute on behalf of the Crown. In the course of that cross-examination, when the witness was being questioned on matters which could have had a bearing on the appellant's involvement in the offence, objection to the line of evidence was taken by the appellant's counsel on the ground that the advocate-depute was incompetently attempting to use a witness adduced by one accused to speak in his defence as a witness against another accused after the Crown case had been closed. The trial judge repelled the objection, but intimated to the appellant's counsel that he would allow counsel the opportunity of further cross-examination on this fresh evidence involving the appellant—an opportunity of which counsel duly availed himself. In the event, the trial judge allowed the evidence, to the line of which objection had been taken, to go to the jury together with the other evidence in the case quoad the appellant. In the course of his charge to the jury the trial judge warned them that 'statements made by one accused outwith the presence and hearing of another are not evidence against that person. On the other hand, whatever is said in the witness box under oath is evidence in the case and is evidence available in support rebuttal of any of the charges in respect of any of the accused'. It was the application of that general direction to the evidence objected to which forms the ground of appeal against the appellant's conviction.

When the appeal was first heard before a court of three judges it was represented that the dictum of Lord Justice-General Clyde in *Young v. H.M.A.*, 1932 J.C. 63 at p.74, insofar as it could have a bearing on the present issue, might have to be re-considered, and that accordingly a fuller court should be convened to hear the appeal. That representation was accepted and this fuller Court was convened.

The law of evidence in criminal trials has altered over the course of time and it is difficult to say what, if any, particular aspect of it is based on principle. It seems to me that it is more a question of practice than of principle, and the practice has progressively changed. So far as the evidence of an accused is concerned, there has been a progressive widening of the scope of an accused's evidence, or, put another way, a progressive loosening of the restrictions on an accused's evidence from the days when an accused was not allowed to give evidence at all to the position of an accused today. This has been effected by legislation, which reflects the general trend to loosen the restrictions on evidence which is relevant to the issue before the Court in the interest of the administration of justice. The extent of and limitation on the evidence which can be taken from a witness adduced by an accused have been conditioned, at least to some extent, by the position of the accused himself, and that, too, has been a broadening process. The vehicle for that has mainly been the common law, but the most recent extension of the broadening process has taken legislative form. Section 82A of the Criminal Procedure (Scotland) Act 1975, introduced into that statute by virtue of section 27 of the Criminal Justice (Scotland) Act 1980 provides: 'It shall be competent for the prosecutor to examine any witness or put in evidence any production included in any list or notice lodged by the accused, and it shall be competent for an accused to examine any witness or put in evidence any production included in any list or notice lodged by the prosecutor or by a co-accused'— Since by that section a right is given to 'examine', that right must also extend to 'cross-examine' at large such a witness who is adduced by another party. It seems to me that it would make a nonsense if the opposite view were taken. There is nothing in the section to indicate any restriction on the evidence of a witness so adduced. The positions of the prosecutor and the accused (whether one or more than one) are exactly the same. In a case where there are two accused, the witness could be named in the list of both accused. If the counter argument was correct it would mean that the first accused who called that witness could elicit evidence from the witness to support his defence, but the second accused would be debarred from cross-examining him to elicit support for his defence if that evidence was going to inculpate the first accused. This is obviously wrong. The position of a co-accused is affected by section 141(2) of the Criminal Procedure (Scotland) Act 1975 which enacts that an accused may, with the consent of a co-accused, call that co-accused as a witness on the accused's behalf, or ask a co-accused any question in cross-examination if that accused gives evidence, but he may not do both in relation to the same co-accused. And, of course, an accused who gives evidence may be asked any question in cross-examination of a relevant nature by any of the other parties—even a question which would tend to incriminate him on the offence charged.

I do not suggest that the position of a witness adduced by an accused is in exactly the same legal position as that of the accused himself, but it seems to me that it would be wholly illogical and an affront to common sense if a witness adduced by an accused to support his defence was placed by the law of Scotland in a more protected and a more limited position in the giving of evidence than the accused who adduced him. So much was admitted by counsel for the appellant, but a concession is not required to establish the obvious, and counsel argued that the established law left it in that position. If an accused can be asked any relevant question in cross-examination without reserve he can be asked a question by the prosecutor in relation to the offence charged even if the answer to that question implicates a co-accused. I can see no reason why a witness adduced by him should be in a more protected position. That, in my opinion, provides the answer to the question in issue, unless it can be established that there is a rule of the common law of Scotland still in operation of a nature and force which would debar a court of this composition from implementing that view.

From the various authorities cited to us I shall deal with only three, because these are the ones which seemed to me to carry the thrust of the appellant's argument so far as the law of Scotland is concerned. These authorities are the opinion expressed by Lord Justice-General Clyde in *Young v. H.M.A.*, 1932 J.C. 63, Alison's Criminal Law of Scotland, Vol. II, at pp.621–622, and *Hackston v. Millar*, 5 Adam 37.

I consider first the case of *Young*. The passage in the opinion of Lord Justice-General Clyde founded upon by the appellant is at p.74 and reads: 'In the ordinary case, therefore, once one of the accused goes into the box in support of his separate defence, the door opens for a general cross-examination by his co-accused for the purpose of vindicating their own separate defences. It does not follow that the Act opens any door for the cross-examination of ordinary witnesses called by one co-accused in support of his own separate defence'. It was submitted by counsel for the appellant that this was a positive and relevant statement of the law in the context of that case and was not an *obiter dictum*. I disagree with this. The issue under review related to whether anything said by any one of the accused could be held to be admissible against the others. That being so, an exposition of the law in relation to the admissibility of evidence from an ordinary witness adduced by one accused against a co-accused is clearly *obiter*. That being so, it is open to this Court of five judges to review that statement and, if need be, hold that, whether or not it was accurate at the time it was delivered, it represents the law of Scotland at the present time.

Lord Justice-General Clyde's statement of the law at p.74 stemmed from an earlier passage in his opinion at p.73, *viz*. 'The general principle of the law of Scotland—apart from the Act of 1898—is that evidence led for the defence of one co-accused is not admissible against another co-accused; and in *Hackston v. Millar* this general statement was stated by the Lord Justice-Clerk, and was made a matter of express reservation by Lord Stormonth Darling with regard to ordinary witnesses called by one co-accused in support of his separate defence—see Alison's Criminal Law, Vol. II, pp.621–622'.

I accordingly turn to these two authorities relied upon by Lord Justice-General Clyde. In *Hackston v. Millar* I find nothing in the judgment of Lord Justice-Clerk Macdonald to warrant the proposition. What the Court was dealing with there was the right of one accused to cross-examine another accused. Lord Stormonth Darling was non-committed [sic] and reserved his opinion on the position of ordinary witnesses. Alison *supra* at p.621, made reference to two cases when dealing with the situation when an accused might present evidence which incriminated a co-accused under the professed design of exculpating himself. In the first of these two cases the Court allowed writings which incriminated a co-accused to be produced. In the second case, Alison records that proof was offered by one accused which tended to fix the whole crime on a co-accused, and the Court allowed the evidence to be received, but with the observation that what was proved against one panel could not be evidence against the other, however powerfully it might operate in favour of the accused who presented the evidence. Alison goes on to consider the difficulty, which has presented itself to judges ever since of how the Court can effectively get it over to a jury that evidence which they have heard which is incriminatory of an accused should not influence their minds in their deliberations. The case quoted by Alison to vouch his proposition was *Malcolm Gillespie and J. Skene Edwards*, Aberdeen, Autumn 1827, which does not appear to have been reported.

With all due respect this seems to me to be rather a tenuous basis on which to found a general principle of the law of evidence. In any event, Alison was writing in 1833, when the law of evidence was quite different from what it is today. At that time an accused person was not allowed to give evidence, and he could only present his defence through the evidence of witnesses. In that situation, any stated rule of practice restricting the bounds of such evidence has to be looked at in that light. With the passage of 150 years and the steadily increasing removal of restrictions on evidence in the interval, I cannot regard the passages in Alison as representative of the current law.

I therefore do not consider that the authorities relied upon by Lord Justice-General Clyde warranted the opinion which he expressed *obiter* in *Young* in 1932. However that may be, I do not regard these authorities, or that *obiter* opinion of Lord Justice-General Clyde, as having the compelling weight to negative or stand in the way of the view I have formed on the law as it stands, and should stand, today.

In reaching that conclusion, and accordingly in affirming what I consider to be the very proper ruling of the trial judge on the subject, coupled with the proper direction in law which resulted, I feel that I am only endorsing the trend which seeks to remove artificial or illogical restrictions from the law of evidence. In my view, subject to appropriate safeguards, the objective should be to allow a person who has gone into the witness-box and taken the oath or affirmed to be examined on any evidence which is relevant to the basic subject matter of the trial, namely whether the Crown has proved beyond reasonable doubt that the offence libelled was committed and that the accused, or the respective accused if there are more than one, committed that offence. It seems to me that in the general public interest and for the proper administration of justice this should be so.

I would accordingly refuse the appeal."

LORD HUNTER: "So far as concerns conviction this note of appeal raises in two forms what is a single question, namely whether under the modern criminal law and practice of Scotland there is in existence a general principle that the evidence of witnesses called by one accused is not, in a case where separate defences are maintained, admissible for or against another co-accused. Counsel for the appellant submitted that the existence of such a principle in the common law was to be derived from a passage in Alison: Practice of the Criminal Law of Scotland, Vol. II, pp.621–622. In that passage the learned author referred to an observation by the Court in an unreported case in 1827, *Malcolm Gillespie and J. Skene Edwards*, Aberdeen, Autumn 1827, referred to in another connection in Alison: Principles of the Criminal Law of Scotland, Vol. I, pp.435–436. It appears that the observation was made when repelling an objection taken on behalf of one panel, who was charged with forgery and uttering, to proof offered by the other panel who was 'charged with the forgery only'. According to Alison, the Court when allowing the evidence objected to, observed 'that what was proved by one panel could not be evidence against the other, however, powerfully it may operate in his own favour'. This passage in Alison occurred in a commentary on a proposition that the objections of nonage, infamy, tutoring, interest and the like, were the same in proof in exculpation as in that adduced for the prosecution. This proposition and the commentary following it were contained in a chapter under the heading 'Of Proof in Exculpation'. It is apparent from earlier passages in Alison on the subject of parole proof, and also from passages in Hume to which we were referred, that relaxation of the very strict limits previously set to the competency and effect of evidence led in exculpation was a gradual process which was still continuing during the early part of the nineteenth century. Alison, Vol. II, p.547; Hume on Crimes, Vol. II, pp.296–297, 300 and 402 (including Note 1). In such circumstances I am of opinion that the passage in Alison is a very slender foundation on which to erect a supposed general principle, which is said still to survive a century and a half later, although in the meantime technical and artificial rules tending to prevent or restrict the taking into consideration of relevant evidence or to inhibit cross-examination on relevant matters have been largely discarded. Moreover, Alison himself, immediately after referring to the observation which I have quoted, remarks pointedly on the impracticability of persuading a jury by direction to apply such a rule. The comment is as apt today as it was when Alison wrote. I am not persuaded that any such general principle is now to be found in our common law. At best for the appellant there may at one time have been a technical rule of practice to the effect for which her counsel contended. Macdonald: Criminal Law of Scotland, 5th ed., p.337. If such a rule existed it must clearly, as was in effect conceded by counsel for the appellant, have been subject to exceptions, and modern writers on the law of evidence have observed that the Court has not been prepared to press the technical rules to the point of unfairness: Walkers on Evidence, p.387. I would go further and say, on the basis of my own experience, that if such a rule could be said to have survived into the second quarter of the twentieth century, it has in modern practice been as much honoured in the breach as in the observance. Moreover, as I have indicated, there has during the last century or more been a movement away from artificial and technical rules of practice in the law of evidence, so that courts and juries in criminal cases may be enabled to take into account all evidence relevant to the issues before them, unless fairness to an accused demands a modification, as it does, for example, in the case of statements made by one accused which tend to incriminate another accused who was not present when the statement was made.

The movement away from such artificial and technical rules of practice has in my opinion been assisted and signposted by legislation, of which the Criminal Evidence Act 1898 and, very recently, the provisions relating to evidence in the Criminal Justice (Scotland) Act 1980, including sections 27 and 28 thereof, are striking examples. The supposed rule of practice said to be based on a judicial observation in 1837 would, in my opinion, sit very awkwardly with the results of these statutory provisions. Of the authorities cited to us, only *Young v. H.M.A.*, 1932 J.C. 63 gives positive support to the survival into the twentieth century of a 'general principle' with the effect for which counsel for the appellant contended. I am satisfied that the observation at p.73 in the judgment of the Court delivered by the Lord Justice-General was *obiter*, since the actual decision was concerned with the admissibility of the evidence of a co-accused. I am, moreover, not convinced that authority is to be found in the somewhat unsatisfactory case of *Hackston v. Millar* 5 Adam 37; (1906 8 F. (J.)) 52 for the 'general principle' proposed in the *obiter* observation in *Young v. H.M.A.* to which I have referred. The opinion of the Lord Justice-Clerk in *Hackston v. Millar* does not appear to me to express any such general principle, nor, in my view, is any such principle expressed in the passage from the English case quoted by the Lord Justice-Clerk. Lord Stormonth Darling merely reserved his opinion as to the right of one accused person to cross-examine an ordinary witness called on behalf of another who is being tried along with him. Such a reservation of opinion does not suggest the survival in 1906 of a well-recognised general principle of the common law that evidence led for the defence of one co-accused was not admissible against another co-accused.

It would, in my opinion, require very convincing authority to establish that the supposed rule of practice is one which must be followed and applied at the present day. I consider that there is little to be said in support of a technical rule of practice, which rests on no statute, which was developed against a background of criminal law, evidence and procedure radically different from that which exists at the present day, which is based on no discernible modern principle, which consists ill with modern legislation, which is admittedly subject to exceptions, which is not uniformly enforced by the Court and, if enforced, would involve the giving of directions to juries in criminal cases which they are unlikely to comprehend, and which would artificially, and probably unsuccessfully, seek to prevent juries from considering and weighing evidence which may be highly relevant to the issue before them. At the trial in the present case during a discussion prior to the speeches of counsel the very experienced judge who presided at the trial described the rule, if it existed, as 'one of the most absurd rules of the common law'. I respectfully agree, and consider that the last vestige of such a supposed rule, namely an *obiter dictum* in *Young v. H.M.A.* more than half a century ago, should now be swept away.

For these reasons I agree with your Lordship in the chair that the appeal against conviction should be refused."

Lords Robertson, Dunpark and Ross agreed that the appeal should be refused.

NOTES

See also *Green v. O'Brien*, 1988 G.W.D. 10–401. The Criminal Procedure (Scotland) Act 1995, s.266(3) provides that: "An accused who gives evidence *on his own behalf* in pursuance of this section may be asked any question in cross-examination notwithstanding that it would tend to incriminate him *as to the offence charged*" [emphasis added]. Where an accused is called as a witness for a co-accused, is he bound to answer questions which would tend to incriminate him? See Macphail, *Evidence*, paras 5.41 and S5.36. In general, "It is a sacred and inviolable principle of the criminal jurisprudence of Scotland, that no man is bound to criminate himself"—Lord Gillies in *Livingston v. Murray* (1830) 9 S. 161. The position of the accused and that of accomplices, or *socii criminis*, represent exceptions to this fundamental principle. It seems doubtful whether the accused may be asked questions regarding criminal conduct not libelled in the indictment, although there is no doubt that the Crown can lead evidence of such conduct—see *Nelson v. H.M.A.*, 1994 S.C.C.R. 192, Chapter 9, above.

Where an accused does give evidence for or against a co-accused, he should not be treated as an accomplice—see *Slowey v. H.M.A.*, 1965 S.L.T. 309, and *Casey v. H.M.A.*, 1993 S.L.T. 33, below.

(C) ACCOMPLICES

4. Docherty v. H.M.A.
1987 J.C. 81

The appellant appeared for trial in the High Court of Justiciary on an indictment charging him with robbery whilst acting along with certain named individuals. Those individuals had earlier pled guilty to that crime on separate indictments and had been duly sentenced. They were called as witnesses on behalf of the Crown at the appellant's trial. There was independent evidence which inculpated the appellant in the commission of the crime. In these circumstances, the trial judge failed to give the jury a *cum nota* warning in respect of the evidence of the *socii criminis*. On being convicted, the appellant appealed to the High Court of Justiciary by way of note of appeal. The appeal was heard by a Bench of nine judges.

OPINION OF THE COURT: "The appellant was convicted after trial by the majority verdict of a jury of a charge in the following terms:

Walter Scott Ellis, William Leitch and James Neely Drysdale had earlier pled guilty on separate indictments to the crime libelled against *Docherty* and had been duly sentenced, and at *Docherty's* trial all three were called as witnesses for the Crown. Their evidence was to the effect that, while they had committed the crime libelled, they had set out from Craigneuk with a different intention. According to the evidence of Leitch, a group of youths, including one named Mooney, had raped his stepdaughter and he was determined to find and punish Mooney in particular. What he hoped to do was to assault Mooney severely with a baton, breaking his arms, and possibly his legs as well, and to tie him to a headstone in a graveyard as a public example. An expedition to find Mooney in particular was mounted by Leitch and Ellis and Drysdale agreed to join him in inflicting retribution upon Mooney. Leitch's understanding was that Mooney was to be found in a hostel in Broxburn and *Docherty*, who was told the purpose of this expedition, was persuaded to drive the three men to Broxburn and to drive them back to Craigneuk when they had achieved their purpose. Their evidence was that they took with them many balaclava helmets or masks, a short baton, some masking tape and probably a knife. All these items were in a plastic bag. Although Leitch did not think that *Docherty* knew what was in the bag, Ellis stated in evidence that *Docherty* had seen the various articles sticking out of the bag before the three men left him in Broxburn at a point some distance from the chapel house into which in the course of the night the three men forced entry. The evidence of all three proceeded to narrate that in an endeavour to find Mooney who, they thought, was living in the house, they tied up Father Tabone and Canon O'Connor and questioned them. When it became clear after a search of the house that Mooney was not to be found there, and that indeed they had probably come to the wrong village, they decided to rob the two priests, all as described in the libel. So far as Leitch, Ellis and Drysdale were concerned in the witness box at the trial of *Docherty*, far from attempting to inculpate *Docherty* in the robbery, they did their best to exculpate him of that crime by emphasising again and again that, so far as *Docherty* was concerned, he had agreed to be their driver on the understanding that the object of the expedition was merely the severe punishment of Mooney. As has been observed already, the robbery was, according to their evidence, an afterthought when they found out that they had come to the wrong house. All that remains to be said is the evidence of the three men about the appellant's part in the expedition except in so far as Ellis attributed to the appellant knowledge of the contents of the plastic bag, coincided with the evidence given by the appellant himself.

In charging the jury, the trial judge quite deliberately did not direct them that they should not accept the evidence of Leitch, Drysdale and Ellis unless they were fully satisfied that it was credible, and an appeal is taken against *Docherty's* conviction upon the following ground: 'The trial judge misdirected the jury by failing to direct them that the evidence of Leitch, Ellis and Drysdale could only be received *cum nota* they being *socii criminis*.'

When the appeal first called for hearing, it was appreciated that the position of the appellant was that there was a rule of law which requires the trial judge in every case in which a *socius criminis* is called as a witness by the Crown, and whether or not he gives crucial or indeed any evidence against the accused, to give to the jury a specific direction that the evidence of that *socius criminis* requires very narrow scrutiny and that they must not accept it unless they are fully satisfied that it is credible. Over the years since the first hint of the existence of such a rule of law was given, doubts have been entertained about the rule and its scope and, in the case of *Scott v. H.M.A.*, 1987 S.L.T. 389, the Lord Justice-Clerk (Ross), Lord Robertson and Lord McDonald indicated that when a suitable opportunity arose full consideration ought to be given to the soundness of the supposed rule. Since it was considered by the court that this appeal provided an opportunity for such consideration to be given, the appeal was continued for full hearing before this court—a bench of nine judges—and for extension of the notes of evidence given by Leitch and Scott Ellis.

In presenting the appeal, senior counsel submitted in the first place that Leitch, Drysdale and Ellis were *socii criminis* in that they had already been convicted of the crime which was charged against Docherty. In support of that proposition he drew our attention to the case of *Wallace v. H.M.A.*, 1952 J.C. 78, and, in particular, to the opinion of Lord Keith. His second submission was that in these circumstances the trial judge was bound as matter of law to give to the jury a special warning that they should scrutinise their evidence with special care and should not accept it unless they were fully satisfied that it was credible. In that connection senior counsel for the appellant recognised that, although their evidence was in the main exculpatory of *Docherty* so far as the charge of robbery was concerned, they did give some evidence which assisted the Crown case against *Docherty* in that they testified to *Docherty's* having been the driver during the expedition to Broxburn and, in the case of Scott Ellis at least, that *Docherty* was aware of the contents of the plastic bag. In support of the second submission, senior counsel traced the history of the development of the rule of law upon which he relied and took as his starting point certain *obiter dicta* in the case of *Dow v. MacKnight*, 1949 J.C. 38. Thereafter he examined a number of subsequent decisions of the High Court in which the *obiter dicta* in Dow were followed. The first of these cases was *Wallace v. H.M.A.* in which a convicted thief gave evidence for the Crown against an appellant who had been charged with reset of the stolen articles. In that case, the evidence of the convicted thief was crucial evidence and it appeared from his evidence that he harboured a grudge against the accused because he believed that he had not received from the accused a fair share of the proceeds of the crime.

In his opinion the Lord Justice-General (Cooper), at 1952 J.C. pp.81–82, said this: 'This situation seems to me a typical one for an application of the rule which was alluded to by several of the judges who gave the decision in the case of *Dow v. MacKnight*, 1949 J.C. 38. Some argument was directed against the observations made in that case with regard to what we then desiderated from presiding Judges in charging juries in cases where the evidence of a *socius criminis* is material, and I am prepared to say that where, as here, crucial evidence for a conviction is the evidence of a person who is in a reasonable sense an accomplice or associate in the crime with which the appellant is charged, such evidence ought always to be made the subject of a specific and particular warning to the jury that it is suspect evidence deserving of close scrutiny, and it will not suffice to rest content with the ordinary injunction as regards being satisfied as to credibility which falls to be given in most cases with regard to witnesses in any criminal trial. Now, in this case it is true that the learned Sheriff-Substitute when dealing with the evidence of Stewart referred to him as a prisoner who told the story of how he had committed a theft and of how he had been convicted of that theft and sent to prison, and, having said so, he then warned the jury that their first question must be: "Do I believe him? Do I believe that that man was telling a truthful story?" and to that note he reverts more than once. I have come to think that that was not in the circumstances of this case a sufficient compliance with the rule in *Dow v. MacKnight* particularly as laid down by Lord Jamieson in that case and as restated above, and I think that in every case of this kind it should be explicitly stated to the jury that our law regards with more or less suspicion the evidence of an accomplice or *socius criminis*, and that it is the duty of a jury to apply to such evidence a special scrutiny, over and above the general examination which a jury has to apply to all the material evidence in every case. As this conviction turned necessarily upon the evidence of Stewart and as Stewart's evidence was not adequately subjected to the cautionary note which I have indicated, I am inclined to think that that is sufficient for the disposal of this appeal in favour of the appellant.'

Lord Carmont and Lord Keith agreed with the Lord Justice-General and Lord Carmont in particular said this (at p.83): 'The statement made by Lord Jamieson that your Lordship has referred to seems to me to point strongly in the direction of requiring the Judge at a trial, when the evidence of a *socius criminis* [is] allowed before a jury, explicitly to bring to their notice the character and source of the evidence that is offered for their acceptance, and the Judge should be cautious to explain, and explain fully, the nature of the situation so that no rash or suspect evidence can form the basis of a jury's subsequent conviction.' The rule is mentioned again in the case of *H.M.A. v. Murdoch*, 1955 S.L.T. (Notes) 57 in which the leading opinion was given by Lord Sorn. The case involved a charge of theft and the entire evidence against the accused Gray was given by a Mr and Mrs Lawson to whose house the stolen goods were taken. The Lawsons had been charged by the police with the theft themselves but the charges were not proceeded with and they gave evidence for the Crown which of course conferred upon them immunity from prosecution. In the course of his opinion Lord Sorn said this at p.57: 'The only ground of appeal which remains for consideration is the argument that Mr and Mrs Lawson were *socii criminis* and that the presiding judge failed to give an express direction to the jury that, as such, their evidence was suspect and should be weighed with special care. The appellant founded on the case of *Wallace v. H.M.A.*, 1952 J.C. 78, and we were not asked to consider whether that case was rightly decided or whether the rule there laid down necessarily applied to every case where evidence is given by a *socius criminis*. The Crown did not dispute that the special warning should have been given if the Lawsons—or either of them—were *socii criminis* in the sense of *Wallace's* case and so the whole argument was directed to the question whether the presiding judge should have treated them as such.'

Senior counsel for the appellant also mentioned briefly the case of *Slowey v. H.M.A.*, 1965 S.L.T. 309 which decided merely that a co-accused was not a *socius criminis* of his fellow accused, and then cited two unreported decisions which appeared to decide that a special warning is to be given to the jury in every case, regardless of circumstances, in which a *socius criminis* gives evidence for the Crown. The first of these cases was *Dunstance v. H.M.A.*, unreported, in which opinions were delivered on July 13, 1951. In that case it appears that the most active participant in the crime libelled was a 15 year old boy named Wright who had acted as the decoy for the victim and had evidently done a good deal more. He gave evidence for the Crown in the trial of Dunstance, and in an application for leave to appeal the charge of the presiding sheriff was criticised because of his alleged failure adequately to direct the jury as to the value of the evidence of the boy Wright. In his opinion, the Lord Justice-General (Cooper) said this: 'The boy Wright was a *socius criminis* and, as has been observed in this Court on many occasions, it is right and proper that a jury should also be reminded of the suspicion which normally attaches to the evidence of a *socius criminis*, and therefore of the necessity for applying to that evidence a special scrutiny. In this instance the Sheriff-Substitute did give that warning, and described it in terms of a caution which applied to Wright; but then he went on to point out, in my judgment with justification, that in the case before the jury the circumstances which normally require such a caution to be given with regard to a *socius criminis* and his evidence were not present, or at least were not present to the extent normally encountered, because this boy Wright, so far from giving evidence for the Crown in order to exculpate himself and incriminate others, had gone a long way to taking the main responsibility for the assaults upon himself and said very little to incriminate the other three accused, apart from saying that they were standing by on both occasions and that they participated in the loot derived from these acts of violence. In my view the comment which the Sheriff-Substitute made was justified. The jury were sufficiently warned to scrutinise the evidence of Wright, while at the same time their attention was pointedly drawn to the unusual features which Wright's evidence presented, and to the fact that he was a *socius criminis* 'with a difference'.

The second of these cases was *McKenzie v. H.M.A.*, unreported, in which opinions were delivered on June 26, 1958. The charge against McKenzie was that while acting along with a man Cochrane he had stolen a quantity of confectionery and biscuits. The ground upon which his application for leave to appeal was supported was that the presiding Sheriff-Substitute misdirected the jury. It appears from the opinion of the Lord Justice-General (Clyde) that the alleged crime was perpetrated by a group of individuals who removed certain goods from the premises of a firm in Dundee. One of the group was Cochrane who pled guilty to his part in the theft and who had been sentenced prior to the trial of McKenzie. At McKenzie's trial, Cochrane was called as a witness for the Crown and, at the conclusion of the evidence, the learned Sheriff-Substitute dealt with the question of the extent to which a jury is entitled to rely upon the evidence of *socii criminis* in incriminating an accused person. He directed the jury quite properly to regard with circumspection the evidence of certain of the witnesses who had been involved in the alleged theft along with the appellant but in regard to Cochrane he directed them otherwise. He informed them, as was the fact, that Cochrane had pled guilty to the offence and had been sentenced for it, and he went on to say that, as far as he could see, Cochrane had no axe to grind in giving evidence in the appellant's trial. He informed them that they (the jury) could not reduce Cochrane's prison sentence and went on to say that: 'He would not be allowed out of prison any earlier by giving tainted evidence so I think you may accept it, if you are accepting it, you may accept that you can attach as much importance to him as to any of the other untainted witnesses.' The Lord Justice-General dealt with this direction tersely because he said this: 'This direction was fundamentally a bad one and is directly at variance with the decision in the case of *Dow v. MacKnight*, 1949 J.C. 38 and *Wallace v. H.M.A.*, 1952 J.C. 78 and in particular the opinion of the Lord Justice-General [1952] J.C. at the top of p.82.' Lord Sorn appeared to be less confident but he had this to say: 'I think the Sheriff-Substitute was quite justified in suggesting that there may be varying degrees of suspicion attached to the evidence given by a *socius criminis*. When a *socius* is purchasing immunity from prosecution by giving evidence there is plainly strong motive for him to do so and a high degree of suspicion may be thought to be attached to what he says. On the other hand when the *socius* has already pled guilty to the offence and is undergoing sentence he has a less obvious motive to give evidence and the degree of suspicion attached to that evidence may be less. But that is as far as it goes. Even in the latter case the witness still bears the character of a *socius criminis* and the presiding Judge must give a warning to the jury as to the reserve with which such evidence must always be accepted, as laid down in the case of *Dow* and in the case of *Wallace*.'

It is fair to say that senior counsel who presented his argument on behalf of the appellant recognised the problems which the existence of the rule for which he contended created in many cases, and he was very conscious too that many witnesses have a more obvious axe to grind than any *socius criminis*, and that it was very difficult to find any sound justification for the supposed rule of law, at least in the form in which it has emerged since *Dow v. MacKnight*.

There is no doubt that the decided cases, which proceeded upon acceptance of certain *obiter dicta* in *Dow v. MacKnight*, appear to declare that there is a rule of law in terms of which, whenever a witness is led by the Crown who is, as the Lord Justice-General (Cooper) put it in *Wallace*, 'in a reasonable sense' an accomplice or associate in the crime with which 'the accused is charged', the trial judge must give to the jury a specific and particular warning that the evidence of that witness is suspect evidence deserving of close or special scrutiny. It matters not whether the evidence which he gives inculpates or exculpates the accused or whether his evidence is or is not crucial or material to the success of the Crown case. It does not seem to matter either that there may not be a whisper of a suggestion at the trial that the witness has any axe to grind in giving the evidence which he does, or that he has the slightest interest to 'load and convict' his supposed accomplice. The primary question for us in this appeal is to discover whether there is any sound warrant for the existence of such a rule in the law of Scotland.

The case with which this appeal is concerned illustrates very well some, but by no means all, of the problems and absurdities which so frequently arise as the result of the authorities to which senior counsel for the appellant brought to our notice. A common problem in many cases is to know whether a particular Crown witness ought to be identified as being 'in a reasonable sense' an accomplice or associate in the crime libelled. Were Leitch, Drysdale and Ellis in this case to be regarded as associates or accomplices of the appellant in the robbery? They certainly did not suggest that *Docherty* was their accomplice in the crime of robbery at all. There was, in any event, no suggestion from any quarter, in particular from those acting for the appellant, that these three witnesses had any interest to 'load and convict' the appellant and the thrust of their evidence was to explain that *Docherty* knew nothing about the robbery and was entirely innocent of the charge. If, in this case, the trial judge had obeyed the so-called rule of law and had given to the jury the explicit direction which it appears to require it would not have surprised us if the giving of the direction had been challenged on the ground that Leitch, Drysdale and Ellis should not have been treated as accomplices of the appellant in the crime libelled against him, and in any event, that the giving of the direction had been prejudicial to the defence at the trial. It is, in our opinion, on the face of it, somewhat absurd that in a trial judge's charge to the jury which is intended to help the jury to make their decision in a fair trial, he should be obliged by law to give the special warning in relation to the evidence of a Crown witness who is or may be a *socius criminis*, where that witness has given evidence wholly favourable to the accused, or where there has been no suggestion that that witness has any motive to lie and to concoct testimony inculpating the accused, or where the adverse testimony of the supposed *socius* has not even been subject to cross examination. Further, the apparent absurdities engendered by the so-called rule of law do not end there. Since 1898 an accused has enjoyed a statutory right to give evidence. Since the Criminal Justice (Scotland) Act 1980 one of several accused who has pled guilty before the Crown case in evidence has concluded may be called as a witness by the Crown in the trial which proceeds against his co-accused. An accused person, too, may if he consents, be called as a witness for the defence of a co-accused and if he elects to give evidence he acquires no immunity. Again since 1980 the Crown and the defence may examine each other's witnesses on the respective lists. These statutory innovations can produce some very curious results. If a co-accused pleads guilty after the Crown has closed its case and is called as a witness for a co-accused, no special warning requires to be given by the trial judge. If, however, that same accused had pled guilty before the Crown closed its case and had given precisely the same evidence as a witness adduced by the Crown the so called rule of law would have demanded the giving of the special warning. For our part it is very difficult to see why if a stigma always attached to a *socius criminis* so that his evidence is always to be presumed to be tainted, it should be noticed where he is adduced as a Crown witness and ignored where he is called to give evidence for an accused person. His interest to load and convict that accused may be no less in the latter case. Again, where one co-accused gives evidence in his defence exculpating himself and implicating another the special warning will not be given because the co-accused is not a *socius criminis* in the crime charged.

In the light of all these considerations one is tempted to wonder whether there can really be any sound warrant for the existence of the rule of law upon which the appellant relies which, as has been seen, produces in its application problems which are difficult to solve and results which in so many cases seem to be absurd and prejudicial to the interests of the accused.

Our first task in this appeal must be to discover the source of the rule of law which was declared in the case of *Wallace* which, as senior counsel for the appellant put it, was the case 'which caused all the trouble'. Reference has already been made to the important passages in the opinions delivered in that case and we do not repeat them here. Suffice it to say it is perfectly clear that the rule of law declared in *Wallace* and affirmed in all the other cases to which we have referred was delivered from certain *obiter dicta* of certain judges in the case of *Dow v. MacKnight* which was decided by a bench of seven judges. Let us now see what the case of *Dow v. MacKnight* decided and what precisely was said by the judges whose observations were adopted by the court in *Wallace*.

In *Dow v. MacKnight* the appellant who had been charged with reset of a quantity of cigarettes was convicted upon the evidence of two persons who had stolen the cigarettes and who had already been convicted of the theft and sentenced. There was no other evidence which incriminated the accused. The only question for decision was whether the evidence of the two thieves (treated as *socii criminis*) uncorroborated by any other testimony, was sufficient, if believed, to support the conviction of the accused. That question (Lords Mackay and Carmont dissenting) was answered by the court in the affirmative.

The leading opinion was delivered by the Lord Justice-Clerk (Thomson) who with his usual lucidity began by giving an admirable summary of the development of the attitude of the modern law towards the *socius criminis*. His opinion begins as follows (1949 J.C. at pp.42–44): 'In our early criminal law there were a number of categories of persons who were disqualified from being witnesses. These categories were of the most varied character. At one time women were excluded. By Hume's time the main categories were unsoundness of mind, nonage, connection with the prosecutor, connection with the accused, infamy, enmity to the accused, and interest in the issue. When the prosecutor tendered a witness it was competent to the defence to move for his exclusion. This issue was tried as a separate issue, and the Court had to decide whether the witness "was admissible or not". The existence of such a system was the result of prevailing social conditions, and, as conditions improved and the administration of justice became more stable, the system of exclusion began to disintegrate. The disintegration operated by the refusal of the Court to apply the strict rules of exclusion in certain cases. The witness was admitted, but admitted *cum nota*. As time went on, the exceptional course tended to become the rule and the ground of exclusion disappeared altogether. Thus the general exclusion of women was modified in cases of occult or domestic crime. Hume (vol. ii, p.339) quotes an interlocutor of 1693, which illustrates the way in which the law was tending to develop, "The Lords allow the women to be received witness *cum nota* as to all things done without doors but admit them *simpliciter* as to all things done within doors." However, by Hume's time, this exclusion had gone. The same process operated in the other categories.'

His Lordship then proceeded to examine the position in Hume's time when the disqualification of persons in certain categories from being witnesses had disappeared, these persons thereafter being admitted *simpliciter*. The disqualification still however attached to a number of categories of persons but the tendency to admit them as witnesses *cum nota* was increasing. According to the Lord Justice-Clerk a witness who was admitted *cum nota* appeared before the jury as one whose credibility was suspect on a priori grounds and that this was so was put before the jury. But, he adds (at p.43), 'it was open to the jury to accept the witness as fully credible and I see no ground for thinking that a witness presented to the jury *cum nota* was unable to overcome the initial handicap and that his evidential value fell to be proportionately reduced. The "nota" was equivalent to a warning by the judge that the evidence of the witness was open to suspicion.' Thereafter the Lord Justice-Clerk made it clear that in Hume's time the objection that a witness was a *socius* was hardly maintainable and, quoting Hume, 'is now only moved in order to obtain, if the circumstances make it reasonable, a reservation of the credibility of the witness, as liable to be affected by his situation and the account he may give of his own misdeeds.' The important points which are emphasised are that the *nota* was only attached when the admission of a *socius* as a witness was objected to, that the *nota* was not necessarily attached even if moved for, and that *socii* were admitted in some cases without reservation, and that in any case the value to be put on his evidence was for the jury. We need only mention the final two paragraphs of this opinion. The second last paragraph (1949 J.C. at pp.44–45) is in these terms: 'It was, I think, consciousness of this which drove the Dean of Faculty to approach the matter from what at first sight seems rather a different angle. The evidence of *socii*, in his view, could not be enough, and there must be some evidence independent of the *socii* themselves. What he seemed to be seeking was some touchstone by which the reliability of the *socii* could be measured. I can see the force of that. The danger to be guarded against is concoction, and he sought some element contributed independently of the guilty parties which would point to the accused's guilt and so not leave the matter on their testimony alone. But the only reason for demanding such an independent element is that the *socii* are not fully credible in themselves, that they carry the *nota* with them, and that the jury must discount their evidence and find other evidence to restore the balance. Such a view, as I have already said, seems to me to be indefensible in principle.' From that paragraph it is clear that the Lord Justice-Clerk thought it indefensible in principle to argue that the *socii* are not fully credible in themselves and that they carry the *nota* with them. The last paragraph is in these terms: 'I should add that, in cases where the evidence against an accused person is entirely derived from *socii criminis*, it is the duty of the presiding judge to draw the jury's attention explicitly to the point.' This paragraph speaks for itself and we say at once, upon a consideration of the opinion of the Lord Justice-Clerk, that it contains no trace of any recognition of the existence of a rule of law of the kind declared in Wallace. Indeed there is much in the opinion to suggest that no such rule of law would be defensible, particularly where, in modern times, a *socius criminis* is just as admissible, *simpliciter*, as any other person tendered as a witness by the Crown.

Having given close attention to the opinion of the Lord Justice-Clerk in Dow we can now identify the observations of Lord Jamieson and the Lord Justice-General (Cooper) which inspired the decision in Wallace. Lord Jamieson (1949 J.C. at p.53) said this: 'The matter then resolves itself into a question of credibility, and if, after a proper direction, or the taking into consideration that the evidence of *socii* must be received *cum nota*, the evidence of two or more is believed by jury or judge, again on principle, there is no reason why a conviction should not follow.' He also at p.55 said this: 'I wish, however, to guard against being thought to imply that the evidence of *socii* is to be treated with just the same measure of scrutiny as that of witnesses unconnected with the crime. Whether they have already pled guilty or been convicted, or whether they have turned King's evidence, there is always a temptation to minimise their part in the crime and blacken the accused. Their evidence can only be received *cum nota*, and in every case this should be explained to the jury and they should be directed not to accept it unless fully satisfied that it is credible.' The Lord Justice-General, who adopted the reasoning of the Lord Justice-Clerk and Lord Jamieson, made the following observations at p.57: 'The appellant did not of course maintain that the evidence of *socii criminis* was inadmissible; but his contention that no conviction could stand on the evidence of *socii criminis* alone is in substance a revival of the old dogma that those with a presumed interest to lie are incapable of speaking the truth. That dogma I reject, in favour of the modern view that the appraisal of the value of evidence is a rational process. The evidence of *socii criminis* always requires very narrow scrutiny and juries must always be so warned. But the penitent thief is not a figment of the imagination, and the *socius criminis* is by no means the only type of witness likely to concoct false evidence.'

What we must now do is to test the soundness of the observations of Lord Jamieson and the Lord Justice-General by discovering if there is any trace in our law of the supposed necessity for a special direction to be given where a *socius criminis*, to whose admissibility objection had been taken, was admitted *cum nota* or without reservation. It will be recalled of course that the evidence of a *socius* in and after Hume's time was not necessarily received *cum nota*. It was only so received in some cases if objection to the admissibility of the *socius* as a witness had been taken, and where the defence wished to attack his credibility. Burnett in his Criminal Law (1811 ed.) discusses the grounds upon which a *socius* was held to be disqualified as a witness and at p.410 said this: 'After what has been said of legal infamy, few observations are necessary on the objection, which used formerly to be often discussed with regard to *socii criminis*. Whatever our law may have been antiently, in relation to this matter, where the *infamia facti* operated as a disqualification, and when the expediency, and even necessity of admitting the evidence of accomplices in many cases was not so much felt, no point is now more firmly established, than that *socii criminis* are admissible witnesses in every case. It is not, however, the *infamia facti* that is now the chief ground for excepting to the credibility of a *socius criminis*, but the *petium*, which (it is said), is held out or implied in the case of every accomplice brought forward to give evidence, namely, that of his being, *eo ipso*, relieved from any prosecution for that offence (of which afterwards), though, in truth, the objection of being a *socius*, unless cautiously qualified, implies an admission of the guilt of the person who pleads it.'. Later at p.417 he wrote as follows: 'It was nearly on the above principle, that some of our lawyers formerly held that the King's pardon, actually given to a witness previous to his deponing, whether as an accomplice with the party accused, or as having been guilty or convicted of other crimes, was alone a ground to disqualify him. But while an obvious distinction arises between a pardon actually tendered before the witness gives his evidence, and a promise to take effect afterwards, and in a particular event, that opinion does not appear ever to have been received in our Courts, and it is now completely exploded. In the case, indeed, of an accomplice, it is now held, that the very act of calling and examining him as a witness on the part of the Crown, goes far to operate as a discharge or acquittal to him from all prosecution for that crime; but as the witness is not bound to criminate his associates, or even to make a full disclosure of all he knows, so as to entitle him to this indemnity, the implied pardon, by his being brought forward as a witness for the prosecutor, ought to have no effect to disqualify him, or to impeach his testimony in any way.' Perhaps, however, the best indication of the attitude of the court to a *socius criminis* whose evidence was tendered by the Crown, can be found in charges to the jury delivered by the Lord Justice-Clerk (Boyle) and the Lord Justice-Clerk (Braxfield) respectively in the trials of Burke and Deacon Brodie.

In the *Burke* trial Hare and Mrs Hare gave evidence for the Crown. They were not admitted *cum nota*. Passages from the Lord Justice-Clerk's charge to the jury are to be found in Roughhead's Notable British Trials series at p.248. For our purposes the important passages are as follows. They are to be found in that chapter of his charge which begins thus: 'The remarks of the prisoners' counsel, on this part of the case, render it necessary for me shortly to explain to you the law with regard to the admissibility of *socii* in guilt, and the position in which persons in that predicament stand, in relation to their credibility.' In the course of giving the necessary explanation his Lordship gave the following directions to the jury at p.249: 'Most undoubtedly such persons are not to be received on the same footing as witnesses standing in a different situation; still, however, though their evidence may be liable to the greatest suspicion, and may be subjected to a more severe and strict examination than in the ordinary case, you must hear what they have to say.

It has been further argued, that Hare and his wife were placed in the situation of being themselves exposed to be tried for other charges of murder, and, indeed, for the other two charges contained in the present indictment; hence, that they have a clear interest to throw the blame of the actual perpetration of the crime on the prisoners, and represent themselves as comparatively or completely innocent. But here, gentlemen, I feel it necessary to state it to you, as the decided opinion both of myself and my brethren now present, that whatever may be the case with regard to other murders, or other crimes, the witnesses in question are as fully protected by the law, in relation to all those contained in the present indictment,—that is to say, against either trial or punishment for them,—as if they had been entirely free from any concern in their perpetration. These persons were called on to give evidence on the whole of the charges contained in the indictment. Eventually, and at a subsequent diet, they must still be examined in relation to the other two; and, therefore, so far as the plea of interest is rested on the alleged danger to which they are exposed, it is entirely and thoroughly without foundation. The public faith has been pledged to these persons, wicked and criminal as they may be, and certainly are; and it must, at all hazards, be kept sacred. As to their credibility however, that, as I have already stated, is a totally different matter. If their evidence be inconsistent, and at variance with itself, contradicted by other, and entirely unexceptionable, testimony, or standing alone, and unsupported by collateral corroborating circumstances,—it is for you to judge all this, and give such weight to the story told by them, as under the whole circumstances, appears to be rational and just. In estimating the degree of credibility due to persons of this description, you will keep in remembrance the manner in which they gave their evidence, and their whole demeanour and behaviour, while under examination. You will attend, likewise, in particular, to the story told by these two persons, and observe whether they differ from, or contradict each other, with regard to circumstances of importance, which they had the same or equal opportunities of observing. I do not see, however, that any other or different rules can, or ought to be applied, in comparing the evidence of the two witnesses in question, than is done in the ordinary case.'

In the trial of *Deacon Brodie*, an account of which also appears in the Notable British Trials series, a *socius criminis* Ainslie gave evidence. Objection had been taken to his admissibility as a witness. The objection was repelled and the court pronounced an interlocutor in these terms (at p.115): 'The Lord Justice-Clerk and Lords Commissioners of Justiciary having considered the foregoing objections with the answers thereto, they repel the objections stated, and allow the witness to be examined, reserving the credibility of his evidence to the jury.' In his charge to the jury the Lord Justice-Clerk (Braxfield) gave the following directions (at p.197): 'Now, to ascertain this point you have, in the first place, gentlemen, the evidence of Brown and Ainslie, and if they have sworn truth the prisoners must be guilty. To the admissibility of these witnesses there can be no objection. Were not evidence of this sort admissible, there would not be a possibility of detecting any crime of an occult nature. Had a corrupt bargain, indeed, been proved, by which they were induced to give their evidence, there might have been room for an objection to their admissibility. But no such bargain has even been alleged against the public prosecutor in the present case. And as to their being accomplices, this, gentlemen, is no objection at all. A proof by accomplices may display, it is true, a corruption of manners, which alone can render such proof necessary. But it is impossible to go into the idea that their testimony is therefore inadmissible.

Nor is there, in the present case, any reason to suppose that they were under improper temptations to give their evidence. Each of them was separately called upon by the Court, and it was explained to each of them that they ran no hazard unless from not speaking the truth, and that their being produced as witnesses secured them from all punishment, except what would follow upon their giving false evidence. Under such circumstances, you cannot suppose, gentlemen, that they would be guilty of perjury without any prospect of advantage to themselves, and merely to swear away the lives of these prisoners at the bar.

Their credibility, to be sure, rests with you, gentlemen; and if you find anything unnatural or contradictory in their evidence you will reject it.'

We can now say that the researches of counsel have disclosed no trace in the law of Scotland, before 1949, of any rule of law which required judges to warn juries that the evidence of a *socius* may only be received *cum nota* (whatever that may mean), and, in every case, to direct juries that they should not accept his evidence, after special scrutiny, unless fully satisfied that it is credible. On the contrary it is clear, under reference to Burnett, and to the charges of the two Lords Justice-Clerk which we have examined, that no such special warning or direction was considered to be appropriate. It is of importance also to notice what the expression *cum nota* was understood to mean in the days when it was attached to certain disqualified persons who were admitted as witnesses after objections had been taken by the defence. We take the meaning from Trayner's *Latin Maxims* (3rd ed.) and it is as follows: '*Cum nota.*—With a mark, or reservation. Formerly, when witnesses were disqualified by reason of agency, or partial counsel, etc., it was a frequent practice to admit persons as witnesses who were in some measure chargeable with the disqualification, and especially so where there happened to be a *penuria testium*. They were admitted, however, *cum nota*, that is, with a mark to call the attention of the Judge to the extent of agency, etc., which had been proved against them, and with a reservation to him to give such weight to their evidence as under the circumstances he should think proper. In effect, the evidence of a witness admitted *cum nota*, generally received as much weight as the evidence of those who were not so distinguished.'

In our opinion, in light of all that we have said so far in this opinion we are fully persuaded that Lord Jamieson and the Lord Justice-General fell into error in making the observations which we have quoted from their opinions in *Dow*. They appear to have proceeded upon the mistaken view (i) that all *socii criminis* are only admitted *cum nota* and (ii) that the evidence of *socii criminis* is always suspect and always requires very narrow scrutiny. This was not the view taken by the law in and since Hume's time. *Socii criminis* were frequently admitted without reservation and the meaning and significance of the *nota*, where it was attached, give no support for the proposition that the *socius*, admitted *cum nota*, carried a stigma with him which would lead to his credibility being examined by a jury in a way different from that in which they would assess the credibility of any other witness. The observations which we are considering are, in our opinion, clearly not supported by prior authority and, further, they are, in our judgment, indefensible in principle in a system of law which, long before 1949, had come to recognise that any *socius criminis* was just as admissible as any other witness, and that no person in that particular category was any longer admitted *cum nota*. Further, we cannot, with respect to Lord Jamieson and the Lord Justice-General in *Dow* and to judges in the decided cases from *Wallace* onwards, endorse the proposition that the evidence of any *socius criminis* is always suspect. There are no doubt cases in which the credibility of a *socius*, who gives important evidence for the Crown inculpating the accused, may be subject to attack by the defence on the ground of his alleged interest or motive to tell lies about the accused. But the same kind of attack must properly be made just as frequently in the case of witnesses who are not *socii criminis* and, as has been indicated earlier in this opinion, there are many cases in which the evidence of a *socius* led for the Crown is not challenged by the defence, many cases in which the evidence given by a *socius* called by the Crown is wholly exculpatory of the accused.

For all these reasons we have no hesitation in declaring that the decided cases which proceeded to erect the supposed rule of law upon the *obiter dicta* in *Dow* which we have held to be unsound, fall to be disapproved. In our opinion, it follows that in spite of the decided cases to which our attention was drawn in course of the hearing of this appeal, the trial judge was perfectly correct in declining to give the direction identified in the ground of appeal. His directions to the jury as to how they should approach their task of assessing the credibility of all the witnesses led before them were impeccable, as the Lord Advocate suggested, and we have only to add that, in future, trial judges need only give to juries in all cases, whether or not any *socius criminis* has been adduced as a witness for the Crown, the familiar directions designed to assist them in dealing with the credibility of witnesses and any additional assistance which the circumstances of any particular case may require. If, for example, the credibility of any Crown witness, including a *socius criminis*, is in any particular case attacked by the defence on the ground of alleged interest to load and convict the accused or, indeed, on any other ground, the trial judge will normally be well advised to remind the jury that, in assessing the credibility of the witness concerned, they should take into consideration the criticisms which have been made of the witness in the course of the presentation of the defence case.

Upon the whole matter, for all the reasons given in this opinion, the appeal against conviction will be refused."

NOTES

See also *Mason v. H.M.A.*, 2000 S.L.T. 1004. A *socius criminis*, broadly speaking is a person who gives evidence for the Crown on the basis that she admits having played a part in the offence. Lord Keith said in *Wallace v. H.M.A.*, 1952 J.C. 78:

"I am not satisfied that any witness can be treated as a *socius* unless he had already been convicted of the crime which is charged against an accused or is charged along with an accused or gives evidence in the witness-box confessedly as an accomplice in the crime charged. In all these three cases I think a witness is a *socius*. In the case of any other witness I should, as at present advised, hesitate to say that the court has any duty or right to arrogate to itself the task of saying that such a witness, who after all is not on trial, is a *socius* in the offence with which an accused is charged."

A co-accused is not generally to be regarded as a *socius criminis*—see *Slowey v. H.M.A.*, 1965 S.L.T. 309, and *Casey v. H.M.A.*, 1993 S.L.T. 33, below—but with that exception, Lord Keith's *dictum* seems consistent with the present law. A *socius* has no privilege in respect of self-incrimination and must answer all questions put by prosecution or defence. In return, the *socius* (provided he or she has not already pleaded guilty or been convicted) receives immunity from prosecution in relation to the offence about which she gives evidence. On all these points see the following case and *O'Neill v. Wilson*, 1983 J.C. 42, below.

5. McGinley and Dowds v. MacLeod
1963 J.C. 11

A, B and C were involved in a brawl which lasted a few minutes and began in one street in Penicuik and ended in a neighbouring street. A was charged with assaulting B in the first street with a bottle, and B and C were charged with assaulting A in both streets by kicking him. B and C were adduced as Crown witnesses at the trial of A, who was acquitted. Thereafter, on the same day, the trial of B and C took place conducted by a different depute procurator-fiscal and before a different Sheriff-substitute. B and C were convicted. They subsequently presented a bill of suspension on the ground that, having given evidence for the Crown in the trial of A, they were exempt from prosecution in regard to the matter concerned in the trial of A. It was held by the majority—Lord Guthrie dissenting—that, as the exemption from prosecution only applied to a *socius criminis* and only covered the libel in support of which he was called to give evidence, the bill should be refused.

LORD JUSTICE-GENERAL (CLYDE): "This bill of suspension arises out of convictions of each of the complainers of assaulting a Mr McBeth. The prosecution was brought in the Sheriff Court in Edinburgh on a complaint at the instance of the Procurator-fiscal.

It appears that cross allegations of different assaults had been made to the police by the complainers, on the one hand, and by Mr McBeth, on the other. The Procurator-fiscal therefore brought a complaint against Mr McBeth charging him with assaulting McGinley in Eastfield Farm Road, Penicuik, and striking him on the face with a bottle, and a further complaint was brought against McGinley and Dowds charging them with assaulting and kicking McBeth in Eastfield Farm Road, Penicuik, and on a footpath outside an inn in Edinburgh Road, Penicuik, on the same day.

All three pleaded not guilty and trials in both cases were fixed for June 20. The two present complainers were cited to give evidence for the prosecution against McBeth, and he was cited to give evidence for the prosecution against the present complainers. We were informed that no precognitions were taken from any of these parties on behalf of the prosecution.

The trial against McBeth proceeded in the morning before one of the Sheriff-substitutes in Edinburgh. Both the present complainers gave evidence for the prosecution. After the trial McBeth was found not guilty. In the afternoon of the same day the prosecution against the present complainers took place. It was heard by a different Sheriff-Substitute and a different depute fiscal conducted the prosecution. No evidence was led at this later prosecution of any statements made by the present complainers in the prosecution against McBeth. The present complainers were both found guilty.

The complainers now contend that it was incompetent for the prosecutor to have proceeded with the trial against them once they had given evidence for the Crown in the earlier trial, and that the convictions in the second trial should therefore be quashed. They put forward this contention, not upon the view that what ha[d] taken place had in any way prejudiced them, for no prejudice was involved. Moreover, we have an assurance from the Crown that no intimation was ever given to the complainers that the proceedings against them were to be dropped or that their trial would not proceed if they gave evidence in the prosecution against McBeth. Indeed, owing to the way in which the second trial was conducted—a different judge, a different prosecutor, and no reference in the second trial to any evidence which they gave in the first—it would be difficult to establish any basis for prejudice. The complainer's argument was based on what was described as an automatic rule of law under which, if A is called as a Crown witness in a charge against B, A *ipso facto* becomes exempt from any prosecution for any other offence connected with the incident in question. From this proposition it was contended that, because the complainers gave evidence in the case where McBeth was charged with assaulting one of them, they *ipso facto* became exempt from prosecution for a different assault by a different person which was connected with or followed upon the earlier assault.

I can find no warrant in principle or in authority for any such automatic exemption from prosecution. In principle it would go far to defeat the ends of justice which after all are designed to punish crime. So far as authority is concerned, none was quoted to us in support of this wide proposition.

It was sought to justify the contention by asking us to extend the rule of exemption from prosecution which is well settled in regard to evidence by a *socius criminis*. That rule took its origin in the doubts which existed in the minds of Scottish criminal jurists as to the competency of a prosecutor leading the evidence of one *socius criminis* in a prosecution against another. In an old statute [21 Geo. II, cap. 34, s.20] it was provided that, in trials for thefts of cattle, a *socius criminis* was a competent witness against an accused and that 'such witness should not be liable to prosecution on account of his accession to such offence.' This rule now extends to all offences, and as Hume [Vol. II, p.367] puts it: 'Thus the witness, when this has been explained to him, is absolutely free to tell what story he has a mind.' The basis of the rule would seem, therefore, to be the protection of a *socius* who has given evidence against his partner, which no doubt also implicates him, from being subsequently prosecuted for that offence. In all the earlier writers and the textbooks, and in the decided cases the rule is always dealt with in relation to *socius criminis*. The matter is summed up in the latest edition of Macdonald on Criminal Law thus: 'Where a witness is adduced by the Crown and gives evidence he cannot be charged later with the offence, even if it be plain that he was *particeps criminis*. By adducing him as a witness the prosecutor discharges him *ipso facto* from liability to prosecution, and a witness so adduced cannot refuse to give evidence on the ground that his evidence may implicate himself. The libel in support of which he is called is the measure of his indemnity although part of it may have been departed from.'

To apply this to the present case, the leading of evidence from the complainers in the prosecution against McBeth would preclude the prosecutor from charging either of them with being art and part in McBeth's assault with a bottle on McGinley. But that is as far as the automatic indemnity goes. It constitutes no indemnity against their being prosecuted for another offence libelled—*i.e.* their united attack on two occasions on him. This is not simply a case of a single brawl where there is a dispute as to who is the aggressor. The two offences are quite distinct. The offence alleged in the case against McBeth is an attack by McBeth with a bottle in Eastfield Farm Road, Penicuik, on one of the complainers. The offence alleged in the case of the complainers is two assaults on McBeth one in Eastfield Farm Road and another at a different locus in Penicuik.

In my opinion, in the first place, the rule invoked by the complainers only applies in the case of a *socius criminis*, and is designed to encourage him to tell the truth without fear of thereby incriminating himself and becoming liable to prosecution. The present case is not, therefore, within the ambit of the rule. The complainers and McBeth were not *socii criminis*, but antagonists mutually accusing each other. In the second place, the indemnity, in any event, only covers the libel in support of which the complainers were called to give evidence. It does not, therefore, cover a libel for a different offence against different people and including an offence at a different place.

The argument accordingly which was put forward in support of the complainers is, in my opinion, unsound in law, and the wide extension if the rule hitherto confined to a *socius criminis* which was urged by the complainers would be altogether unwarranted. In my opinion, the bill should be refused."

LORD GUTHRIE (DISSENTING): "The facts narrated in this bill of suspension and in the answers to it are novel, and consequently the question raised by them is not covered by any precedent.

An allegation was made to the police by Norman McBeth that he had been assaulted by the complainers, and they reported to the police that they had been assaulted by McBeth. The Procurator-fiscal then brought two complaints, one against McBeth charging him with assault upon the present complainers, and the other charging them with assault upon McBeth. On May 11, 1962 each pleaded not guilty to the charge against him. Diets of trial in the two cases were fixed for June 20, 1962. The present complainers were cited to give evidence in the prosecution against McBeth, and he was cited to give evidence for the prosecution against them. On June 20, the trial of McBeth took place first, and the complainers gave evidence for the prosecution. McBeth was found not guilty by the Sheriff-substitute. Later on the same day the trial of the complainers took place and they were both found guilty, and each was sentenced to 60 days' imprisonment. This trial was conducted by a different depute Procurator-fiscal before a different Sheriff-substitute. No evidence was led of statements by the complainers in their evidence at the previous trial. They now seek to have their convictions and sentences suspended, on the ground that, having given evidence for the Crown in the trial of McBeth, they became exempt from prosecution relating to the same matter as was concerned in the charge against and trial of McBeth.

The first matter for consideration is whether the second trial related the same matter as that with which the complaint against McBeth was concerned. McBeth was charged with assaulting the complainer McGinley on April 13, 1962 in Eastfield Farm Road, Penicuik, The charge against the complainers was that on the same date in Eastfield Farm Road, Penicuik, and on the footpath outside the Cuiken Inn Edinburgh Road, Penicuik, they assaulted McBeth by kicking him on the face, arms, legs and body to his injury. It is stated in the bill that both charges related to the same alleged incident which started in Eastfield Farm Road, Penicuik, shortly after 10 p.m. on April 13, 1962 and terminated a few minutes later at the Cuiken Inn nearby. This is borne out by the terms of the complaints, which disclose a coincidence in date and in place, Eastfield Farm Road. In these circumstances, it is clear that it is impossible to separate the subject matter of the two charges. Unfortunately the complainers were not represented at their trial by a solicitor, but it is obvious that any defence to the charge against them required reference to the alleged assault by McBeth which was the subject matter of the previous trial in which they had given evidence.

It is well settled that a *socius criminis* who has been adduced as a witness by the Crown cannot thereafter be prosecuted for his part in the matter libelled. But two questions require consideration, first, whether this protection is limited to *a socius criminis*, and, second, what is the scope of the indemnity of the party entitled to it. In order to answer these questions it is necessary to inquire into the justifications of the rule. Alison states that the immunity of the witness from prosecution is explained to him by the presiding judge as soon as he appears in Court, and adds: 'and consequently he gives his testimony under a feeling of absolute security as to the effect which it may have upon himself.' A second consideration is that it is a fundamental rule of our criminal law that an accused person is entitled to reserve his defence until he gives evidence at his trial, and cannot be compelled to disclose it in whole or in part by interrogation on the part of the Crown.

With these considerations in mind, I am of opinion that this plea in bar of trial, as it is rightly called in Macdonald is available to other persons than *socii criminis*. It would be inequitable if it were limited to *socii*. If A and B commit an assault on C, and A is charged with the crime and B gives evidence for the Crown, he is immune from subsequent prosecution although a *socius* of A. But if A engages in a fight with B and C, and is charged with assaulting C, and B is adduced as a witness by the Crown, surely B cannot be prosecuted thereafter for his part in the fight because he was not a *socius* of A, but was on the other side. The only logical and just rule is that stated by Macdonald (5th ed.) p.273—'Where a witness is adduced by the Crown and gives evidence, he cannot be charged later with the offence, even if it be plain that he was *particeps criminis*.' In *H.M.A. v. Weatherly* [4 Adam 353 at 355] Lord McLaren said: 'It is really a discharge by operation of law arising from the fact that the witness by the proper legal authority has been cited to give evidence.' It may be that there is an example of the application of the protection to a participant who was not a *socius* of the accused in the case of *William Dreghorn* referred to by Hume in a footnote in his work on Crimes, but the report is obscure. In my opinion, the *socius* is the obvious, but not the only, case for the benefit of the plea. Therefore, I think that the complainers are not excluded from the indemnity because they were not *socii* of McBeth.

It remains to be considered whether the protection of the rule is available to them in the circumstances. Hume says that by the very act of calling him as a witness, the prosecutor discharges all title to molest him for the future, with relation to the matter libelled. Now, according to the terms of the charge, the matter libelled against McBeth, on which they gave evidence, was the assault upon the first complainer, for which the present complainers could obviously not be prosecuted. But, in my opinion, the protection afforded by the rule does not depend upon the terms of the libel, but upon its subject matter. If A and B engage in a fight, and A is tried for assaulting B and B gives evidence for the prosecution, he would be immune from subsequent prosecution on a charge of assaulting A. In this case the subject matter of the complaint against McBeth was part of the subject matter of the charge against McGinley and Dowds, in the sense that the second charge could not be fairly and fully investigated without inquiry into the earlier part of the dispute. The two complaints dealt with two parts of the same incident. The course adopted by the Crown had the effect of compelling the complainers to give their version of the beginning of the affair before their case went to trial. McGinley was made to disclose the nature and extent of the provocation he had suffered. I think that the procedure adopted was irregular, and a violation of the two principles to which I have referred as the justification of the plea. In giving their testimony in the earlier trial, the complainers could not have absolute security as its effect upon their own trial. They were prevented from reserving completely their defence until their own trial.

If the prosecution of the complainers after giving their evidence in the first trial was not liable to cause injustice, why was it decided to have the second trial before a different Sheriff-substitute? Why was it decided to have the prosecution conducted by a different procurator-fiscal depute? Why should the respondent find it necessary to aver in his answers that at the trial of the complainers no evidence was led by the prosecution of statements made by them in their previous evidence?

I am, therefore, of opinion that the prayer of the bill should be granted, and the convictions and sentences quashed. As, however, your Lordships have reached a different conclusion, I must respectfully dissent."

The Court refused the bill.

NOTES

Does *McGinley and Dowds* define the concept of the *socius* too narrowly? What problems can you foresee in the application of the case? For example, would you have considered it appropriate, had *McGinley and Dowds* fallen to be regarded as *socii criminis*, to issue a *cum nota* warning about their evidence against McBeth. Should they have been warned that they need not answer incriminating questions? In the older case of *Macmillan v. Murray*, 1920 J.C. 13 it was held that a Crown witness in a criminal trial cannot refuse to give evidence implicating him as a *socius* since she is automatically discharged from liability to prosecution. *McGinley and Dowds* made clear that some Crown witnesses who admittedly took some part in an incident will not be granted immunity. The case is considered in an anonymous article "Socius or Hostis" in (1963) S.L.R. 21. Macphail suggests (Macphail, *Evidence* para. 5.03) that the ratio of *McGinley and Dowds* should be re-considered in any general legislative reform of the Scots law of evidence. No such reform has been adopted and indeed *M'Ginley and Dowds* was expressly approved in the following case, *O'Neill v. Wilson*.

6. O'Neill v. Wilson
1983 J.C. 42

O'Neill, a police officer, pursued a suspect, McLennan, to a house where there occurred a violent incident involving *O'Neill*, McLennan and another member of the McLennan family. Subsequently the McLennans were tried on a summary complaint which, *inter alia*, charged each with assaulting *O'Neill*. *O'Neill* was adduced as a witness by the Crown, and gave evidence against both McLennans who were acquitted. Thereafter, *O'Neill* was charged on a summary complaint with assaulting the McLennans. In the course of the trial, objection was taken to the competency of the proceedings against *O'Neill* on the ground that, having given evidence for the Crown in the trial of the McLennans, *O'Neill* was immune from prosecution for a crime alleged to have been committed in the course of the same incident. The Sheriff repelled the objection, adjourned the trial diet and granted leave to appeal to the High Court. The appeal was heard by a Bench of five judges.

LORD JUSTICE-GENERAL (EMSLIE): "The appellant, who is a police officer, was charged on summary complaint that he 'did on November 21, 1981 at the house at 28 Paton Street, Greenock occupied by Catherine McLennan assault Robert Stewart McLennan residing there and seize hold of him and strike him repeatedly on the head with a baton to his injury.' An objection was stated on his behalf to the competency of these criminal proceedings against him and the submission was that having been called, and having given evidence, at an earlier trial of the complainer who was charged, along with another, of assault upon the appellant in course of precisely the same incident in which the alleged assault by the appellant is said to have occurred, the appellant was immune from prosecution upon the charge libelled in the complaint against him. The Sheriff repelled the objection because he considered, correctly, that he was bound by the decision of this Court in *McGinley and Dowds v. MacLeod*, 1963 J.C. 11 in which it was held that the only Crown witness called to give evidence who is entitled to immunity from prosecution is a *socius criminis* and that the immunity extends only to the libel in support of which his evidence was given. In this appeal the primary submission for the appellant was that immunity from prosecution may in certain circumstances extend to witnesses other than *socii criminis*, that the majority decision in *McGinley and Dowds* was unsound, and that it should accordingly be overruled. In the circumstances of this case the immunity from prosecution which the law confers and should confer is available to the appellant. With this brief introduction I shall now attempt to summarise the circumstances in which it is contended that the appellant became immune from prosecution upon the charge of assaulting Robert Stewart McLennan.

On November 21, 1981 the appellant, who was on duty as a uniformed police officer in Bow Road, Greenock, became involved in an incident in which it appeared to him that Robert Stewart McLennan was committing a breach of the peace. While he was attempting to reason with McLennan, McLennan ran off. The appellant pursued him to the house of Catherine McLennan at 28 Paton Street and became involved in a violent incident with Robert Stewart McLennan and Alexander Stewart McLennan. The outcome was that with the assistance of other police officers, who had been summoned by the appellant using his personal radio, Robert Stewart McLennan and Alexander Stewart McLennan were arrested and were subsequently charged on a summary complaint, on which they went to trial, which contained two charges. The first charge was directed against Robert Stewart McLennan only and was a charge of breach of the peace in Bow Road on 21 November 1981. The second charge was that on the same date, at the house at 28 Paton Street, Robert Stewart McLennan and Alexander Stewart McLennan assaulted the appellant, a constable in uniform and in the execution of his duty, by punching and kicking him repeatedly on the head and body, attempting to strike him with a hammer and attempting to throw him over a wall to his injury; contrary to the Police (Scotland) Act 1967, section 41(1)(a).

At the trial the appellant was called as a witness for the Crown. In course of his evidence he was cross-examined at some length by counsel for the accused upon the line that he, and not either of the accused, had been the aggressor in the struggle which undoubtedly occurred, and that his evidence in support of the libel in charge 2 was untruthful. At no stage in the course of his evidence was the appellant warned that he need not answer any questions the answers to which might incriminate him. At the conclusion of the evidence for the prosecution Robert Stewart McLennan was acquitted by the Sheriff of the charge of breach of the peace in respect that there was not sufficient evidence to warrant his conviction upon that charge. Surprisingly, in view of the nature of the cross-examination of the appellant to which I have referred, neither of the accused elected to give evidence in relation to the remaining charge in the complaint, and at the conclusion of the trial what the Sheriff did was to find that charge Not Proven. Subsequently the complaint with which this appeal is concerned was served upon the appellant.

The particular submission for the appellant was that by virtue of the fact that the appellant gave evidence as a Crown witness in the trial of the complainer Robert Stewart McLennan on a charge of assault arising out of the encounter between the appellant and the complainer in the house at 28 Paton Street, the appellant is, according to the law of Scotland, immune from prosecution upon the charge of assaulting McLennan in course of precisely the same encounter. He was not a *socius criminis* of Robert Stewart McLennan in the crime libelled against McLennan and the charge in the complaint against the appellant libels a different crime. Accordingly, if the law of Scotland is as it was declared to be by the judges in the majority in *McGinley and Dowds* the appellant's claim to immunity from prosecution cannot be supported. However, as was recognised by Lord Guthrie, who delivered a dissenting opinion in *McGinley and Dowds*, the immunity which the law of Scotland confers upon certain witnesses who have given evidence for the Crown in a criminal trial is available to persons who are not, in the strict sense, *socius criminis*, and the scope of the immunity is not confined to a libel in terms essentially the same as that in support of which the witness was called to give evidence for the prosecution. The measure of immunity does not depend upon the terms of the libel but its subject matter, and a witness who has given evidence for the Crown in support of a particular libel is immune from prosecution upon any charge in which the subject matter of the libel is the same. Accordingly, where several persons are concerned in an encounter involving or resulting in violence, and one has given evidence for the Crown in support of a charge of assault, in course of or arising out of that encounter, by another, that witness is immune from prosecution upon a charge of assault by him, in course, or arising out of, the same encounter. There is no logical reason why the rule which affords protection to Crown witnesses should be restricted to *socius criminis*. The underlying reason for granting immunity to a *socius criminis* who has given evidence in support of a charge against his accomplices in the crime libelled, is that there will be a greater likelihood that the witness will tell the truth, and have no motive to load his evidence to convict the accused in order to minimise his own responsibility in the matter. The same considerations apply in the case of a Crown witness in a position such as that of the appellant at the trial of Robert Stewart McLennan.

In presenting this submission Counsel for the appellant sought to persuade us that authoritative support for it was to be found in the case of *H.M.A. v. William Dreghorn* in 1806 which is referred to in a footnote in Hume, *Commentaries on the Law of Scotland Respecting Crimes* (3rd ed.) Vol. ii p.367. This passage in Hume, and the footnote, were before the Court in *McGinley and Dowds* but the case of *Dreghorn* was not fully considered. It does not appear from the report that the record of the trial of *Dreghorn* in the Book of Adjournal November 4, 1806 to July 5, 1809 was drawn to the Court's attention, or that the fuller account of the facts which emerged at the trial, and the opinions of the judges to be found in Burnett, *Criminal Law* at p.82 and 83 and in Appendix lxvii, were referred to in the argument. Upon a proper appreciation of the case of *Dreghorn* the rule declared by the judges in *McGinley and Dowds* is too narrowly stated.

The circumstances in the case of *McGinley and Dowds* were these. A brawl involving these two men and McBeth began in a street in Penicuik and was continued, to end a few minutes later, outside the Cuiken Inn in a neighbouring street. The result was that McBeth was charged with assaulting McGinley in the street where the brawl began and McGinley and Dowds were charged in a separate complaint with, *inter alia,* an assault upon McBeth at the place where it ended. The trial of McBeth took place in the morning of June 20, 1962. The complainers gave evidence for the prosecution. McBeth was found not guilty. In the afternoon, the trial of the complainers took place before a different Sheriff. Both were found guilty and brought a Bill of Suspension complaining that it was incompetent for the prosecutor to have proceeded to trial against them once they had given evidence for the Crown in the trial of McBeth. Their contention was that they were immune from prosecution for any other offence connected with the incident in which the charge against McBeth arose. The Lord Justice-General (Clyde) observed correctly that no authority was cited in support of this extension of the rule of exemption from prosecution which is well settled in regard to evidence given for the Crown by a *socius criminis.* Having traced the origin of the rule to the Act 21 Geo. II, cap. 34, section 20 which provided that in trial for thefts of cattle a *socius criminis* was a competent witness against an accused and that 'such witness should not be liable to prosecution on account of his accession to such offence', he observed that the rule now extends to all offences, citing Hume on Crimes, Alison—Criminal Law and certain decided cases, and that it is always dealt with in relation to *socii criminis.* His conclusion was expressed in these terms: 'In my opinion, in the first place, the rule invoked by the complainers only applies in the case of a *socius criminis,* and is designed to encourage him to tell the truth without fear of thereby incriminating himself and becoming liable to prosecution. The present case is not, therefore, within the ambit of the rule. The complainers and McBeth were not *socii criminis,* but antagonists mutually accusing each other. In the second place, the indemnity in any event only covers the libel in support of which the complainers were called to give evidence. It does not, therefore, cover a libel for a different offence against different people and including an offence at a different place.'

> 'The argument accordingly which was put forward in support of the complainers is, in my opinion unsound in law, and the wide extension of the rule hitherto confined to a *socius criminis* which was urged by the complainers would be altogether unwarranted. In my opinion, the bill should be refused.'

Lord Carmont also found no good ground for extending the immunity to persons other than *socii criminis.* For the moment I shall say nothing of the dissenting opinion of Lord Guthrie for the first question to be answered is whether the case of *Dreghorn* provides reliable authoritative support for the view that *McGinley and Dowds* was wrongly decided, and that the immunity claimed by the appellant is afforded to him by the Law of Scotland.

Dreghorn, a corporal in the Stirlingshire Regiment of Militia, was indicted on a charge of murder or culpable homicide. From the record in the Book of Adjournal it can be seen that the charge libelled that in Penicuik, Dreghorn was ordered to carry a message to an officer at the House of Greenlaw, that accompanied by another corporal of his regiment he set out, that on the way they became involved in a quarrel or scuffle with Private Pinkerton and other soldiers of the Lanarkshire Regiment, and that, as a result, Dreghorn and his companion returned to Penicuik where they reported to their Commanding Officer what had occurred. The libel further states that Dreghorn, this time accompanied by a Sergeant, was ordered to set out once more for the House of Greenlaw, that on this occasion he carried a loaded musket, that once more on the way he encountered soldiers of the Lanarkshire Regiment, including Pinkerton and one Archibald Robertson, that an altercation took place, the outcome of which was that Dreghorn shot and mortally wounded a soldier of the Lanarkshire Regiment. At the trial Private Pinkerton was a Crown witness. Objection was taken by counsel for the accused (later Lord Justice-Clerk Boyle) to the admissibility of this witness who had a direct interest to incriminate the accused, upon the ground that he was in custody awaiting trial by court martial upon a military offence arising out of the affray, and that the Court could not protect him against the consequences of such proceedings. This witness was withdrawn by counsel for the prosecution before being sworn. Private Robertson was also a Crown witness and a similar objection was taken to his admissibility. He also was in military custody awaiting trial by court martial for a military offence arising out of the affray. Counsel for the prosecution did not withdraw this witness and the Court proceeded to repel the objection holding that Private Robertson was admissible as a witness, reserving his credibility to the jury.

Under reference to the substance of the opinions of the Court to be found in Burnett Appendix page lxvii it appears that Mr Gill is well founded in saying that although Private Robertson was not a *socius criminis* in the sense that he was an accomplice of Dreghorn in the shooting of the soldier who died, the objection to his admissibility as a witness for the Crown was repelled because, in the opinion of the majority of the judges, Robertson, in giving evidence, would be assured of protection from trial by court martial. As is evident from page lxix this opinion brought forth an immediate protest from Lord Cathcart the Commander of the Forces in Scotland.

The question I have to ask myself is whether the case of *Dreghorn* ought to be regarded as persuasive authority for the view that the immunity which our law affords to certain witnesses extends, in certain circumstances, to those who are not accomplices of the accused in the charge libelled against him. To that question the answer appears to me to be in the negative.

Dreghorn was an unusual case in which the Court does not appear to have addressed its mind to the limits of the rule first introduced by statute, which protected a *socius criminis* giving Crown evidence in support of a particular charge libelled, from subsequent prosecution upon that charge. In any event it cannot be left out of account that the libel in the indictment against Dreghorn included the two violent interruptions of Dreghorn's official journey by soldiers of the Lanarkshire Regiment including Robertson. For this reason the Court may have taken the view that Robertson was a *socius criminis* in the transactions which were the subject of the libel. This certainly seems to have been the view of the decision taken by counsel for Dreghorn [see the opinion of Lord Justice-Clerk Boyle in the trial of William Hare reported in the supplement to the trial of William Burke and Helen McDougal pp.134 and 135, in a passage in which he refers to *Dreghorn* in support of the proposition that a *socius criminis* who has given Crown evidence in support of a charge cannot be prosecuted on that charge]. The important and remarkable thing is, however, that the case of Dreghorn has not been treated by any subsequent text book writer or in any decided case, as having extended the rule first introduced by statute in 1747, for the protection of *socii criminis*. In the passage from Hume which was before the Court in McGinley and Dowds, in which Dreghorn is mentioned in a footnote, the immunity is said to be confined to *socii criminis* 'with relation to the matter libelled.' Alison, Criminal Law, Vol. ii, pp.452 to 456, is to the same effect, and at p.455, dealing with the immunity of a *socius criminis*, Alison refers to *Dreghorn* as a case concerned with a soldier 'adduced as a *socius criminis*.' In none of the editions of Macdonald on the Criminal Law of Scotland is there any suggestion that the rule is wider than it was held to be in *McGinley and Dowds* [see 5th ed., pp.273 & 298]. Although the learned author cites both Hume and Alison he does not mention *Dreghorn* at all. The same fate befell *Dreghorn* in the treatment of the immunity rule in Dickson on Evidence Vol. 2 section 1560. It will accordingly be seen that for at least 150 years it appears to have been regarded as clear that the rule, as it was declared in *McGinley and Dowds*, defines the only circumstance in which a Crown witness is afforded immunity from prosecution. That is that he is an accomplice in the crime charged and that his immunity covers only the libel in support of which he has given evidence. Consideration of the case of *Dreghorn* does not persuade me that there is any justification for extending that rule in 1983, even to the limited extent contended for by the appellant in this appeal. I am of opinion further that principle does not require extension of the rule. The justification for the rule is, in my opinion, a purely practical one, namely the public interest in the conviction and punishment of offenders. Reference to the language of section 20 of the Act of 1747 makes this abundantly clear. Unless the evidence of a *socius criminis* is available to the Crown in certain cases all the perpetrators would escape conviction. Without immunity the evidence of a *socius criminis* would not be available at all. Unlike any other witness the *socius criminis* is called by the Crown for the express purpose of testifying that he was an accomplice in the crime charged. If he did not have the protection of immunity he would not be bound to answer any questions, the answers to which would tend to incriminate him, and he would require to receive a warning to that effect. The position of all other witnesses including the appellant is quite different. For these the protection of immunity is not a necessity. The appellant was not led to confess that he participated in the crime libelled against the McLennans or, indeed, in any crime. Like any witness, except a *socius criminis*, he was entitled, at any stage of his evidence to decline to answer questions, the answers to which might in some way incriminate him. The immunity rule as it was stated *McGinley and Dowds* is clear, certain and easy to apply. If it were to be departed from, difficulty of application would at once arise and a wider immunity would carry a serious risk that the ends of justice might be defeated and thus conflict with public interest.

All that I now require to say is that I have considered with care the opinion of Lord Guthrie in *McGinley and Dowds* and that, with respect, I cannot approve of it. His Lordship appears to have been moved by what he regarded as equitable considerations but his reasoning is, I believe, seriously flawed in several respects. As can be seen in his opinion at p.20, he holds that the only logical and just rule is that stated by Macdonald: 'where a witness is adduced by the Crown and gives evidence, he cannot be charged later with the offence even if it be plain that he was *particeps criminis*.' That sentence taken by itself lends no support whatever for his dissenting opinion. In any event he has omitted to notice the context and the clear statement that the libel in support of which the witness is called is the measure of his indemnity [see pp.273 and 298]. Macdonald affords no support whatever for the view that anyone but a *socius criminis* is entitled to the immunity granted to a Crown witness by our law. His Lordship, further, in expressing his view of the scope of the immunity cites, in his opinion at p.21, Hume. In the quoted passage he professed to find support for his opinion, yet it is evident that he was only able to do so by substituting for Hume's words; 'the matter libelled' the words: 'the subject matter of the libel'. This is wholly unwarranted, especially when it is remembered that the quotation appears in a discussion of one subject only—the admissibility of a *socius criminis* as a witness and *his* immunity (the emphasis is mine). I have only to add that the case of *H.M.A. v. Weatherly* 4 Adam 353 cited by Lord Guthrie in his opinion at p.20 was clearly a case concerned with a *socius criminis*.

Upon the whole matter I am satisfied that the Sheriff rightly repelled the objection taken by the appellant, and that the appellant is afforded no immunity from prosecution upon the charge libelled in the complaint to which he has answered. The appeal should accordingly be refused."

All the other judges agreed with the opinion of the Lord Justice-General.

NOTES

For criticism of *O'Neill v. Wilson*, see the extensive comments by Sheriff Gordon in his commentary to *O'Neill v. Wilson* in 1983 S.C.C.R. at 272, and Stoddart, "The Immunity Rule" (1983) J.L.S.S. 453. This case appears to render the concept of the *socius criminis* synonymous with that of the accomplice. How does that view accord with Lord Keith's definition of *socii criminis* in *Wallace v. H.M.A.*, above? In *Jones v. H.M.A.*, 1992 S.L.T. 115 two men were convicted of murder art and part with a third man. The third man was tried separately, and they gave evidence for the Crown at his trial. In the circumstances, there was no question that they would have expected to receive immunity in respect of the murder charge. However, their convictions were set aside on appeal because of a misdirection by the trial judge on an unrelated point, and it was held that it would be inappropriate to authorise a fresh prosecution because of the general rule that a person cannot be prosecuted in relation to an offence about which he has given evidence. In other words, the immunity for *socii criminis* can apply retrospectively! Finally, note that even where a *socius* has been acquitted of a charge, the Crown may still bring similar charges against his or her associates—see *Howitt v. H.M.A.*, 2000 S.L.T. 449.

(D) SPOUSES/CO-HABITEES

7. Foster v. H.M.A.
1932 J.C. 75

A married woman was tried in the Sheriff Court on an indictment which charged her with uttering as genuine cheques on which her husband's signature had been forged by her. The indictment also contained a charge of assault upon her husband committed by her, but this charge was, at the trial, found not proven. The husband was adduced by the prosecutor as a witness at the trial, but his evidence with regard to the charge of forgery consisted merely of a repudiation of his signature, and the Sheriff, in charging the jury, directed them to disregard the evidence of the husband with regard to the forgery charge, and to consider, on that charge, only the evidence of other witnesses. The accused was convicted of the charge of forgery. In an appeal against the conviction the accused contended that her husband's evidence with regard to the forgery had been incompetently admitted, as that charge involved no injury to his person or deprivation of his liberty.

LORD ORMIDALE: "The applicant for leave to appeal in the present case is Mary Black Lee or Foster, who was convicted at the Sheriff Court of Ayr on June 15, last of forging the signature of her husband, John H. Foster, on three cheques, and uttering those cheques as genuine. She was tried by the Sheriff and a jury on an indictment which contained four charges in all. Three of them were the charges of forging and uttering on which she was found guilty by the unanimous verdict of jury. The fourth charge was one of assaulting her husband with intent to do him grievous bodily harm. On this fourth charge the jury returned a unanimous verdict of not proven.

Four reasons are stated for the application, but the substantive ground of the appeal is the first, namely, 'The admission of an incompetent witness and inadmissible evidence, in respect that the Sheriff (a) allowed the prosecutor, against the will of the appellant, to adduce the appellant's husband as a witness against her, and (b) himself asked questions and allowed the prosecutor to lead evidence of said witness tending to inculpate appellant of a crime not inferring personal violence, *viz.*, forgery.'

The combination of a charge of assault with charges of forgery is an unusual one, but it was explained that they were not indirectly related. The cheques were uttered by the panel to commission agents in satisfaction of losses incurred by the panel in connexion with gambling transactions betting on horse-races. They were three in number, (1) a cheque for £47, 17s., dated June 28, 1931; (2) a blank cheque, subsequently filled in for £826, 2s. 6d., dated July 1, 1931; and (3) a cheque for £20, dated March 7, 1932. All these the husband declined to pay. On the cheque for £826, 2s. 6d. coming to his knowledge, he remonstrated with his wife, and she promised to cease betting for large amounts, and promised to restrict her betting to a matter of shillings. This promise she did not keep, and the question of her betting heavily was again raised between the panel and her husband in the beginning of March. The alleged assault by the panel was committed on March 10. I understand that it was suggested by the prosecutor that in the heavy gambling and the husband's remonstrance was to be found the motive for the alleged assault. This charge, as I have said, was however found not proven.

Now, it cannot be disputed, and was not disputed, that, in connexion with the charge of assault, the infliction by violence of personal injuries, the husband was a competent witness and his evidence thereanent admissible. I regard this as of crucial importance, for, while it was obviously extremely difficult to put questions to the husband in the witness-box strictly relevant to the assault alone, the Fiscal was extremely careful and discreet in his examination.

But, apart from the special circumstances of the case, I shall deal with the general question raised by Mr Duffes's very interesting argument. The general rule at common law, he said, was that spouses cannot give evidence for or against each other, except where the spouse is the injured party—and 'injured,' in this connexion, means injured by personal violence—or, to express it more generally, injured in his or her safety. This last expression is taken from English law; but, in considering the question, I am not inclined to look for guidance in that quarter, and I do not therefore refer to the English authorities which were cited—Russell on Crimes and Taylor on Evidence. The Scots text-books which were cited were Hume, Alison and Macdonald. After stating the general rule, Hume says (vol. ii., p.349): 'One exception must, however, be allowed, in the case even of a wife—that of a prosecution at the instance of the Lord Advocate, for a crime committed by the husband against the woman herself, for she may here be a necessary witness'. I take it that the same observation applies to the crime of a wife against her husband. I cannot think that the statement of the exception confines it to crimes of violence, and the reason given for the exception is no less unlimited in its expression. Alison is definitely in favour of the view that the rule holds good except in the case of personal violence directed by the one spouse against the other, although he does express a reasoned doubt whether to apply the rule in cases of bigamy, as had been done in a Scots case to which he refers, is consistent either with justice or with principle. It is, of course, about a century since Alison wrote, and it would appear that, prior to that date, the cases cited as illustrative of the exception were concerned with violence done by one spouse to the other, the then state of society being such as to afford little opportunity of their committing other crimes inter se. In the other text book cited by Mr Duffes—Macdonald—both in its third and fourth editions, it is in these words affirmed: 'The injury need not be bodily. When a husband was charged with falsely accusing his wife of a crime, she was held admissible.' That was the case of *Elliot Millar* [Ark. 355]. The panel had falsely accused her of trying to poison him, and the charge against him was libelled falsehood, fraud, and wilful imposition. Macdonald goes on to say ((3rd ed.) p.449, (4th ed.) p.496): 'It has not been decided whether a spouse injured by forgery committed by the other is a competent witness.'—*Fegan* [Shaw 261]. That case I regard of importance, for, although the decision of the question was shelved, it shows at least that it was considered open and, further, that the case of *Armstrong* [2 Broun 251], on which Mr Duffes so strongly relied, was not—if within the knowledge of the two judges who dealt with *Fegan*, which I assume to have been the case—held to conclude the question. The case of *Muirhead* [13 R. (J) 52] cannot, in my opinion, be held to be in point, for the real ground of decision was that there had been a complete miscarriage of justice.

The question not being foreclosed by authorities, I can see no ground for holding that, in principle, the evidence of the panel's husband in the present case was not admissible. The crime of which she was said to be guilty, and was ultimately found to be guilty, was, in my opinion, a crime within the meaning of the word as used by Hume, that is, a crime against her husband. He was examined as a witness in a case where the wrong was primarily done to himself.

I have referred to the crime of assault being linked up with the charges of forgery as a special circumstance in this case, and as justifying the prosecution in calling the husband as a witness. In that connexion I would like to add that no question was put to the witness by the Fiscal which suggested that the panel was the person who had forged his name; and further that, in his charge to the jury, the Sheriff warned them not to proceed, in considering the question of guilty or not guilty of the forgery, on the evidence of the husband, but to confine their attention solely to the testimony of the bank officials and the expert in hand writing.

Very little was said in support of the other reasons stated for this application, and I am satisfied that no effect can be given to them. Treating this application for leave to appeal as having been granted, and treating it as an appeal, I advise your Lordships to dismiss it."

LORD ANDERSON: "The question for decision arises under the first ground of appeal proponed by the appellant. Some difficulty has been created by the inclusion in one indictment of the charges of assault and forgery. The husband of the accused was undoubtedly a competent witness in reference to the charge of assault, and the circumstances connected with the forgeries were probably explanatory of the motive which induced the assault. If the charges had been separately tried, or if the only charge had been forgery, the point for decision would have been purely raised—Can one spouse be competently put in the box by the prosecutor for the purpose of securing a conviction against the other on a charge of forgery? This question is open, and is of general importance.

The general rule of evidence in a Criminal Court is that one spouse cannot competently give evidence to incriminate the other. Under this general rule an accused spouse is entitled to have the other excluded from the prosecutor's list of witnesses and debarred from entering the witness-box to give any evidence for the prosecution. But exceptions to this general rule have been recognised. The appellant's counsel conceded that in cases of bodily injury or deprivation of personal liberty the injured spouse is a competent witness, but he maintained that the exceptions were limited to those two categories. The Lord Advocate maintained that the exceptions were not so limited, but extended, *inter alia*, to criminal offences against property.

The appellant founded on the cases of *Armstrong* and *Muirhead*. *Armstrong* was a case of bigamy, and judicial views were undoubtedly expressed to the effect that the only exception to the general rule was to be found in a case of bodily injury. *Muirhead* was a very special case where a wife was charged with stealing the property of her husband. The conviction in that case was regarded by the Court as a miscarriage of justice, on which ground it would appear that the conviction was quashed. On the other hand the general statements of the law to be found in Hume, II. 346, 349; Alison, II. 461 Dickson on Evidence, II, section 1572; and Macdonald, Criminal Law, (3rd ed.) 449, (4th ed.) 496, do not indicate that the exceptions are to be limited to the two categories suggested by the appellant. Macdonald states specifically in the 3rd edition, p.449, 'An injured spouse cannot decline to give evidence. The injury need not be bodily.' The same statement of the law is to be found in the 4th edition, p.496. Macdonald refers to the case of *Elliot Millar*, in which the evidence of a wife was admitted where the husband had been charged with falsely accusing her of the crime of attempted poisoning. The case of *Fegan* was also referred to, where the Court reserved decision of the question raised in the present case. The Lord Advocate referred to the rule of procedure which prevails in England. This is the creation of statute: to wit, the Married Women's Property Act, 1882, sections 12 and 16, and the Married Women's Property Act, 1884, section 1. These statutory provisions make it competent for one spouse to give evidence against the other where a criminal offence against property belonging to one spouse has been committed by the other spouse. The Lord Advocate maintained that the common law of Scotland effected the same result as the English statutes referred to.

If, in the absence of express decision, regard is had to considerations of principle, I am unable to hold that these warrant an exception to the rule in the case of bodily injury, but exclude all extension of the exception beyond that category. If the fundamental consideration, as the text writers seem to suggest, is necessity—the need for the evidence of the injured spouse to secure conviction—this would seem to operate as strongly in the case of offences against property as in the case of bodily injury. I am, therefore, prepared to affirm the general contention of the Crown that, in reference to a charge of forgery, the husband of the accused is a competent witness.

It seems to me that this is a necessary ground of decision, because I am unable to proceed on the alternative ground suggested by the Crown, which was based on the specialties of the case. It was pointed out that the Procurator-fiscal had refrained from putting questions to Foster directed to the charge of forgery, and that the Sheriff had charged the jury to disregard anything he had said in the witness-box relating to that charge. These considerations appear to me to be quite irrelevant and unavailing. If the appellant's view of the law is right, the evidence of Foster should have been rigidly confined to the charge of assault. If he gave any evidence bearing on the charge of forgery, whether in answer to questions by the prosecutor or ultroneously, the whole procedure was thereby, in my opinion, vitiated, and the conviction invalidated. I am therefore unable to decide the case on the alternative ground suggested by the Lord Advocate.

On the general question argued, however, I am in favour of the Crown and, for that reason, am of opinion that the appeal should be refused."
The Court dismissed the appeal.

NOTES

Whenever the spouse of an accused has been the victim, in a broad sense, of the accused's crime, he or she is a competent and compellable witness for the Crown (see 1995 Act, s.264). Lord Hunter puts the matter succinctly in *Foster* when he says:

"I am unable to justify in principle the admission of the evidence of a spouse in a case where there is injury to the person and the exclusion of such testimony where the injury has been to property."

It would appear that in order to apply this rule, the offence must have had a direct and adverse effect on the spouse as the victim of the offence. In *Hay v. McClory*, 1994 S.L.T. 520 it was held that the accused's spouse was not a compellable witness where the offence was one of vandalism directed against the house of which the spouse was the tenant. Lord Justice Clerk Ross, delivering the Opinion of the Court, suggested that the matter might have been different had there been evidence that the spouse would have had to pay the bill for the damage. In fact, it appeared that the local authority carried out repairs without charging the tenant.

What if the accused is charged on an indictment or complaint which libels one offence directed against his spouse and one not so directed? Is the spouse competent and compellable at the instance in relation to the second charge only, or not competent in the case at all? See the opinions of Lord Anderson and Lord Ormidale above, the case of *Bates v. H.M.A.*, 1989 S.C.C.R. 338, below and Sheriff Gordon's commentary to it at 1989 S.C.C.R. 348. The spouse is both competent and compellable at the instance of the accused spouse—see *Hunter v. H.M.A.*, 1984 J.C. 90, below, and the terms of the 1995 Act, s.264(2). For a summary see Stair Memorial Encyclopaedia, Vol. 10, para. 543.

8.   Hunter v. H.M.A.
1984 J.C. 90

An accused was charged on an indictment with assaulting his infant daughter and with murdering her. He lodged a notice in respect of the charge of assault incriminating his wife. At his trial evidence was led by the prosecutor that the accused was alone with the child when the injuries were sustained and that he had made statements to the police which incriminated himself. The accused's wife was called as a witness on his behalf. The trial judge first warned her that she need not answer any questions which might incriminate either herself or her husband. He later informed her that she did not require to answer any questions and the wife declined to give any evidence. After all the evidence was led the prosecutor withdrew the first charge and the accused was convicted of culpable homicide. He appealed against his conviction on the ground that the evidence of his wife was wrongly excluded by the trial judge. His appeal was heard by a bench of five judges.

LORD JUSTICE-CLERK (WHEATLEY): "The appellant was charged with the murder of his baby daughter Antonia, the libel being that on September 8, 1983 within his dwelling-house he assaulted her and struck and punched her repeatedly on the head, face, body and legs, whereby she sustained serious injuries from which she died later that day. In the event he was convicted of culpable homicide and sentenced to six years' imprisonment. He now appeals against that conviction on the ground that the trial judge erred in law as hereinafter explained, in consequence of which a miscarriage of justice resulted.

The circumstances were these. The appellant was also charged in the indictment with assaulting the baby to her severe injury on various occasions between her birth on June 15, 1983 and September 8, 1983. To that charge the appellant lodged a defence of incrimination, naming his wife as the person responsible for the assaults. At the end of all the evidence, including that of the appellant himself, the Crown withdrew that charge. No defence of incrimination was lodged in respect of the murder charge, and the wife was expressly excluded from involvement in it by the appellant. The appellant's wife was included in the Crown list of witnesses but was not called upon by the Crown to give evidence. The Crown closed its case and the appellant and other persons were adduced as witnesses by defence counsel. Counsel then called the appellant's wife to the witness-box to give evidence, as he was entitled to do. The trial judge thereupon warned her that she did not require to answer questions when the answers might incriminate her and that she did not require to answer questions when the answers might incriminate her husband. At that point the first charge was still before the jury and the defence of incrimination involving her was still live. After she had answered several questions of a general nature, the Court was adjourned for a short interval and on its resumption the trial judge gave her a further warning. He did so because, according to his report, he considered that the form of warnings which he had given earlier were less clear than was desired. He accordingly informed her that she did not require to answer questions but that it was a matter for her. He was thus treating her as a competent but not a compellable witness. On receiving this instruction the appellant's wife stated that she did not wish to give evidence and she was released from the witness-box.

The appellant now maintains that the said ruling was wrong in law and that it prejudiced him to the extent of causing him to suffer a miscarriage of justice, in that he was hoping to obtain from his wife evidence which would have been of assistance to his defence on the murder charge. He had been convicted of culpable homicide and sentenced to six years' imprisonment on that charge, something which might not have occurred if his wife had been compelled to give evidence. He had thus suffered substantial prejudice and loss as a result of the judge's error.

Counsel for the appellant took the Court through the development, both at common law and by statute, of the law regulating competency and confidentiality in the evidence of one spouse in the trial of another. It is but right to record that it had been suggested to him at a previous hearing, when the issue here was still a matter of contestation and the appeal was remitted to a fuller Court for determination, that such a course might be necessary. At this hearing the advocate-depute in due course intimated that the Crown was not disputing the submission that the trial judge's decision in law which is the subject-matter of the appeal was wrong. In these circumstances we feel that the proper approach is to consider the law on the subject as it stands today, and to examine the extent to which it is conditioned by earlier qualifications.

Section 143 of the Criminal Procedure (Scotland) Act 1975 (as substituted by section 29 of the Criminal Justice (Scotland) Act 1980) provides by subsection (1): 'The spouse of a person charged with an offence may be called as a witness; (a) by that person; (b) by a co-accused or by the prosecutor without the consent of that person.' A spouse is therefore a competent witness in the trial of the other spouse. A competent witness is obliged to answer any question relevant to the circumstances in a criminal trial, unless excused from doing so by some principle of the common law or by statute. Subsection (2) of section 143 aforesaid provides: 'Nothing in this section shall (a) make the spouse of an accused a compellable witness for a co-accused or for the prosecutor in a case where such spouse would not be so compellable at common law; (b) compel a spouse to disclose any communication made between the spouses during the marriage.' These are the only exemptions which the statute permits. The first of these is not applicable in the instant case, and the second is simply a restatement of what was enacted by section 1(d) of the Criminal Evidence Act 1898. The provisions of section 143 are symptomatic of the development of the principle that, subject to appropriate safeguards, all relevant evidence should be available to the Court at a criminal trial in the interests of justice. Subsection (2) of the section is an indication of that. It clearly follows from this that the general exemption given to the wife of the appellant by the trial judge was a misdirection in law. The only exemptions which might have had to be invoked here were (a) a direction under the common law that the witness need not answer any question where the answer might incriminate her in a criminal offence (charge 1 being still before the court at the time), and (b) a direction under section 143(2)(6) supra.

An error in law by the trial judge in regard to the evidence of a witness does not *eo facto* necessarily lead to a granting of an appeal. By the terms of section 228 of the said Act the appellant has to show that the error resulted in a miscarriage of justice. Counsel for the appellant submitted that the evidence which could hopefully have been obtained from his wife in view of her precognition 'was likely to be important in that it might have bolstered up the appellant's evidence in the witness-box or at least created a suspicion in the minds of the jurors about the Crown's case, so as to lead to an acquittal'. When asked to particularise on these vague generalities counsel gave an explanation which did more to support the Crown's case than to counter it. The Crown's case was virtually watertight. The appellant was in the house alone with the baby during the period when the non-accidental injuries were sustained according to any reasonable reading of the evidence. He made statements to the police under caution which were self-condemnatory. Even the challenge which he made in his evidence to these statements was only partial, and what he admitted both in relation to the statements and what he said in giving his evidence indicated that the non-accidental injuries which the child suffered and from which she died could only have been sustained at his hands. What was the hoped-for evidence which the appellant's wife could have given in that situation? Counsel said that it would be to the effect that the appellant was a kind and loving father and that it would be out of character for him to attack the child; that his behaviour on the previous night had been normal, as it was on her return to the house after an absence of several hours on the day of the tragedy; that it was only some time after her return to the house that it dawned upon both of them that the child was cold and a doctor was sent for; and that both of them had gone to the hospital with the child, at which time he was very concerned about the child. Even if such evidence had been given by the appellant's wife, no reasonable interpretation of it could have had any proper impact on the weighty case against the appellant or could even have created any reasonable doubt about its validity. That evidence, if it had any value, was in mitigation and not in exoneration.

In all the circumstances, therefore, while we are of the opinion that the trial judge erred in law in the manner complained of, we are also of the opinion that no miscarriage of justice resulted from it. We accordingly refuse the appeal."

9. Bates v. H.M.A.
1989 S.C.C.R. 338

The appellant and a man C were charged with possession of (i) heroin and (ii) di-substituted barbituric acid, with intent to supply to another, contrary to section 5(3) of the Misuse of Drugs Act 1971, an offence in relation to which the spouse of an accused is not a compellable Crown witness. The appellant lodged a notice of intention to lead evidence incriminating C. The Crown called C's wife as a witness and she was told by the trial judge that she was not obliged to answer questions the answers to which would incriminate her husband. She gave evidence against the appellant, but refused to answer any questions put to her in cross-examination. Later in the trial C pleaded guilty to charge (i) and (ii). There was evidence against the appellant on these charges other than that of Mrs C, and he was convicted of them. He appealed to the High Court by note of appeal against conviction on the ground that the trial judge's direction to Mrs C had been wrong, and that as a result the appellant had been restricted in the conduct of his defence.

LORD JUSTICE-CLERK (ROSS): "The appellant is William Bates, who went to trial along with several co-accused in the High Court at Glasgow on an indictment libelling a number of charges. The appellant faced a total of six charges, namely charges (1) to (6) on the indictment. Charges (3) and (4) were subsequently withdrawn by the Crown, and the jury found charges (5) and (6) not proven so far as the appellant was concerned. He was, however, found guilty of charges (1) and (2). Charges (1) and (2) libelled contraventions of section 5(3) of the Misuse of Drugs Act 1971. The appellant was sentenced to ten years' imprisonment on charge (1) and two years' imprisonment on charge (2). The appellant has now appealed against conviction and sentence.

In the note of appeal the appellant put forward two grounds of appeal against conviction, but Mr Morris intimated that he was not proposing to argue the second ground of appeal. Mr Morris submitted that the trial judge had erred in directing the wife of a co-accused (Campbell) that she need not answer any questions the answers to which might tend to incriminate her husband, but that she should answer all other questions. He submitted that this direction was erroneous and had led to a miscarriage of justice.

The first-named accused on the indictment was Malcolm Alexander Campbell, and he proceeded to trial along with the appellant. The wife of the said Malcolm Alexander Campbell was called to give evidence by the Crown. She was advised that she need not say anything which might tend to incriminate her husband. Mr Morris submitted that this resulted in unfairness to the appellant since he had lodged a notice of intention to incriminate Malcolm Alexander Campbell. He explained that Mrs Campbell gave evidence against the appellant but would not answer any questions in cross-examination on behalf of the appellant on the ground that her answers might incriminate her husband. He submitted that she should have been directed that although she was a competent witness, she was not compellable and that she did not have to give evidence, but that if she did, she would require to answer all questions put to her. Mr

Morris contended that the directions which the trial judge gave had restricted the conduct of the appellant's case; the witness indicated that she would not answer any questions which might incriminate her husband and yet, at the same time, she went on to give evidence upon which the Crown relied against the appellant although the appellant had no opportunity to cross-examine her fully on the appellant's allegation that the drugs concerned belonged to her husband. In support of his submissions Mr Morris founded upon *Hunter v. H.M.A.* He also drew attention to the terms of section 143 of the Criminal Procedure (Scotland) Act 1975.

Mr Morris submitted that the direction was erroneous and that there had been a miscarriage of justice. He stated that the result of the direction was to produce an unreal and artificial situation. He also stated that it was unfair that when he came to cross-examine Mrs Campbell she declined to answer questions which were designed to support the notice of incrimination of Campbell which had been lodged. He also submitted that there had been a paucity of evidence against the appellant. In these circumstances he contended that the alleged misdirection by the trial judge had caused a miscarriage of justice. Section 143 of the Act of 1975 provides as follows:

[His Lordship then quoted the terms of section 143, now re-enacted in substantially the same terms in section 264 of the Criminal Procedure (Scotland) Act 1995.]

The sharp question which arises in this appeal is whether the trial judge was correct in directing the wife of Campbell that she need not answer any questions the answers to which might tend to incriminate her husband but that she should answer all other questions, or whether he ought to have directed her that although she was a competent witness she was not compellable and did not require to give evidence, but that if she did elect to give evidence she would require to answer all questions put to her.

If Campbell had not been one of the accused on this indictment, there is no doubt that Mrs Campbell would have been a competent and compellable witness for the Crown. Likewise, if Campbell alone had been indicted, Mrs Campbell would have been a competent witness for the Crown but would not have been compellable. The difficulty arises because the appellant and Campbell have both been indicted on the one indictment. In his report, the trial judge makes it plain that he accepted the submission of the advocate-depute which involved drawing a distinction between Mrs Campbell as a compellable witness against the appellant but as a witness who was not compellable against her husband. In my opinion that approach is flawed. Mrs Campbell was a witness at the trial of those who were named on this indictment, and no distinction can properly be drawn between Mrs Campbell as a witness against her husband and Mrs Campbell as a witness against her husband's co-accused. She could not give evidence in more than one capacity. Mrs Campbell was undoubtedly a competent witness for the Crown but since she was the wife of one of the accused she was not a compellable witness in the trial. Accordingly, she should have been warned that she was entitled to give evidence but was not required to do so and she should also have been told that if she elected to give evidence, she would require to answer all questions put to her. It appears to be accepted that the trial judge directed Mrs Campbell that she need not answer any questions the answers to which might tend to incriminate her husband. In my opinion that was not a sound direction. Since Mrs Campbell was not compellable as a witness at this trial, she was entitled to refuse to give evidence, but she was not entitled to adopt the attitude that she was prepared to give evidence but only evidence which did not incriminate her husband. If after being warned Mrs Campbell elected to give evidence, then there was no reason why she should not be asked questions which might tend to incriminate her husband. There is no rule of law which says that a wife who is giving evidence cannot be asked questions which might tend to incriminate her husband.

I agree with Mr Morris that the direction which the trial judge gave to Mrs Campbell placed the appellant's counsel in an impossible situation. The result of the direction was that Mrs Campbell was free to give evidence against the appellant, and yet the appellant was unable to cross-examine her fully, and in particular was unable to put what was a substantial part of the appellant's defence, namely, the incrimination of Campbell.

Although it is no doubt tempting to seek to draw a distinction between Mrs Campbell as a witness against her husband and Mrs Campbell as a witness against the appellant, I am clearly of opinion that such an approach is unsound; moreover, there would be great practical difficulties consequent upon such an approach. The approach, particularly in this case where notice of incrimination had been given, meant that the appellant's counsel was unable properly to cross-examine Mrs Campbell. That must have resulted in unfairness to the appellant. The advocate-depute contended that the directions given by the trial judge were correct. He founded upon the case of *Deacon Brodie* in 1788 [see Trial of Deacon Brodie ed. Roughhead]. In that case objection on behalf of the co-accused Smith was taken to the calling of his wife as a witness. The Crown intimated that they did not intend to examine the witness in relation to the conduct of her husband but that she was an unexceptionable witness against the co-accused Brodie. At that date a wife was not a competent witness against her husband. The court, however, held that there was nothing to prevent the Crown from putting such questions to her as did not affect her husband but only the co-accused. The final ruling of the court given by the Lord Justice-Clerk was:

'The Court will take care not to allow the witness to give any answer against her husband. But, as she is a good witness against Brodie, the Court cannot help it if, by establishing his guilt, a presumption thereby arises against Smith. I am therefore for repelling the objection' . . .

In my opinion, however, it must be borne in mind that the case of *Deacon Brodie* arose long before there were statutory provisions dealing with evidence being given by the spouse of an accused. As I have already observed, in 1788 a spouse was not a competent witness against her husband. That is no longer the situation, and, accordingly, the situation in *Deacon Brodie* was different to the situation in the present case.

In the circumstances I am satisfied that the trial judge did give an erroneous direction in the present case and that he ought to have directed Mrs Campbell that, although she was entitled to give evidence, she could not be compelled to do so, but that, if she did give evidence, she would require to answer all questions put to her. An error of law by the trial judge on a matter of this kind does not necessarily mean that an appeal must succeed. Before an appeal can be allowed the court must be satisfied that there has been a miscarriage of justice. Accordingly, the next question is whether the error in law by the trial judge in this case resulted in a miscarriage of justice. In the present case I am satisfied that no miscarriage of justice resulted from the error in the direction which the trial judge gave. Mr Morris maintained that he had been inhibited from adducing evidence from Mrs Campbell which might have tended to incriminate Campbell. I accept that that is so, but we were reminded that ultimately Campbell pled guilty to charges (1) and (2). Accordingly, as the advocate-depute put it, at the end of the day the notice of incrimination bore fruit and the appellant cannot complain now that he was unable to ask questions tending to support the notice of incrimination. Mr Morris also maintained that there was a paucity of evidence in this case but, as the trial judge made plain in his charge in relation to the case against the appellant under charges (1) and (2), evidence came from four sources. There was fingerprint evidence, there was evidence of the relationship between the appellant and Campbell, the evidence of Mrs Campbell and the evidence of another co-accused, McKeen, who had incriminated the appellant quoad charges (1) and 2).

Accordingly, although the direction which the trial judge gave to Mrs Campbell was at the time unfair to the appellant, the lack of fairness to him was dissipated as soon as Campbell pled guilty to charges (1) and (2) and thus incriminated himself before the jury. It follows that in the special circumstances of this case the error in law of the trial judge did not result in any miscarriage of justice, and I would accordingly move your Lordships to refuse the appeal against conviction."

NOTES

See also *Hay v. McClory*, 1994 S.L.T. 520.

What reasons can be advanced in favour of the privilege afforded to spouses? Is it a rule suitable for a modern law of evidence? The privilege probably does not apply to a divorced spouse—see Clive, *Husband and Wife*, p.370; nor, it seems, does it apply to a co-habitee.

10. Casey v. H.M.A.
1993 S.L.T. 33

An accused person was tried in the High Court on a charge of *inter alia*, murder. A witness for the Crown was the accused's co-habitee with whom he had lived for six years and who called herself his common law wife. The trial judge did not warn her that she was not a compellable witness in terms of section 143(2) of the 1975 Act. A co-accused, in his own defence, spoke to an incrimination lodged against the accused. The trial judge, in his charge to the jury, failed to give them a *cum nota* warning in respect of the co-accused's evidence when they were considering the case against the accused. The Crown case rested partly on the evidence of the co-accused but the Crown invited the jury to convict both accused and accordingly to accept part and reject part of the co-accused's evidence. The accused was convicted and appealed, contending *inter alia* that: (i) the co-habitee should have been advised by the trial judge that she was not a compellable witness; and (ii) that the trial judge should have given a *cum nota* warning to the jury in respect of the evidence of the co-accused.

OPINION OF THE COURT: "(5) In this ground of appeal it is contended that the trial judge erred in law in failing to advise Mrs Isobel Casey that she was not a compellable witness. Apparently the situation is that this witness and the appellant were not married to one another although they had co-habited for six years. In his report, the trial judge states that they had cohabited for six years. In his report, the trial judge states that the view that the word 'spouse' in section 143 of the Criminal Procedure (Scotland) Act 1975 meant someone who had gone through a ceremony of marriage or been declared by law to be married to the person charged with the offence, and that it did not include what is often referred to as a common law wife.

In support of his submissions, the appellant sought to rely on *McKay v. H.M.A.*, 1992 S.L.T. 138. In that case it was held that sudden and overwhelming indignation on the discovery of infidelity, which the law recognised as constituting provocation, might be just as powerful in the case of cohabitees as it was in the case of people married to each other. In our opinion, however, that case does not assist the appellant. In *McKay v. H.M.A.*, the court was considering the application of a doctrine of the common law, whereas in the present case under section 143 of the Act of 1975, the question which arises is one as to the interpretation of a statute. In section 143, the word which is used is 'the spouse' and we are satisfied that it is only persons who are married to each other who are properly referred to in law as spouses. We see no justification for attaching the expression 'spouse' to persons who are cohabiting with one another but are not married. In the circumstances we are quite satisfied that the witness Mrs Isobel Casey was a compellable witness, and that the trial judge would have been in error if he had advised her that she was not compellable.

In any event, as the trial judge points out in his report, none of this witness's evidence incriminated the appellant directly in the murder of the victim, and there is accordingly no basis whatsoever for the assertion that a miscarriage of justice has occurred in this respect. [His Lordship dealt with other grounds of appeal with which this report is not concerned, and continued:]

The second additional issue which the appellant raised was related to his additional ground of appeal dated June 1, 1992. His complaint appeared to be that since his co-accused sought to incriminate him, the burden of proof had in some way been altered. At the same time the appellant returned to his first ground of appeal maintaining that the jury should have been directed to treat the evidence of his co-accused with particular care.

In our opinion this ground of appeal is misconceived. It is true that part of the Crown case against the appellant was based upon the evidence given by his co-accused, but the Crown were inviting the jury to find both the appellant and his co-accused guilty of the charge, and although they relied on some of the evidence given by the co-accused in support of their case against the appellant, they also invited the jury to reject parts of the evidence given by the co-accused. It was authoritatively laid down in *Docherty v. H.M.A.* that there was no rule that a trial judge must direct the jury that the evidence of a *socius criminis* should be scrutinised with special care. At the same time it was recognised that there might be cases where the trial judge would think it appropriate to give the jury directions which would assist them in dealing with the credibility of particular witnesses. We are quite clear however that there was no obligation upon the trial judge in this case to give the jury any warning to the effect that they required to scrutinise the evidence of the co-accused with care, and indeed that it would have been wrong for him to have done so. We agree with the Lord Advocate who appeared for the Crown in this appeal that for the trial judge to have given any such direction would have been contrary to the spirit of *McCourt v. H.M.A.* Throughout the trial the co-accused was entitled to the presumption of innocence, and accordingly the trial judge would not have been justified in directing the jury that they should treat the evidence of the co-accused with particular care.

[His Lordship then dealt with another ground of appeal with which this report is not concerned, and continued:]

Having duly considered all the grounds of appeal put forward by the appellant, and the submissions which he put forward, we have reached the clear conclusion that he has failed to demonstrate any miscarriage of justice in this case. There was sufficient evidence if the jury accepted it to entitle them to convict the appellant, and nothing which he has said would justify us in interfering with the jury's verdict. It follows that the appeal against conviction must be refused."

11.   Evidence (Scotland) Act 1853

"3. It shall be competent to adduce and examine as a witness in any action or proceeding in Scotland any party to such action or proceeding, or the husband or wife of any party, whether he or she shall be individually named in the record or proceedings or not; but nothing herein contained shall . . . render any person compellable to answer any question tending to criminate himself or herself, or shall in any proceeding render any husband competent or compellable to give against his wife evidence of any matter communicated by her to him during the marriage, or any wife competent or compellable to give against her husband evidence of any matter communicated by him to her during the marriage."

NOTES

It is generally accepted that this section renders the spouse of a party a compellable as well as a competent witness in civil proceedings in Scotland—see Macphail, *Evidence*, para. 4.03; Stair Memorial Encyclopaedia, Vol. 10, para. 538. There is some doubt, however, as to whether a party to a consistorial action is compellable—cases such as *Bird v. Bird*, 1931 S.C. 731 and *White v. White*, 1947 S.L.T. (Notes) 51, imply that the defender in such an action may refuse to give evidence, although the judges in those cases deplored defenders who did so. It should be noted, however, that these were cases involving allegations of cruelty, regarded as a marital offence. It is arguable that such a different view might be taken in these days of "no-fault" divorce. See also Macphail, *Evidence*, paras 4.16 and 4.17.

(E) CHILDREN AND OTHER VULNERABLE WITNESSES

In the old case of *Auld v. McBey* (1881) 18 S.L.R. 312, Lord President Inglis said:

"I have found that when the question is as to what happened on a particular occasion the best witnesses are boys and girls. Their eyes are generally open and they are not thinking of other things and they are not talking to their neighbours."

Although in England and certain other jurisdictions, children below a certain age are regarded as incompetent witnesses, it is accepted in Scotland that children of any age may be adduced as witnesses in criminal trials or civil proofs. Recent research suggests that children tend to be much more reliable witnesses than they have often (Lord President Inglis apart) been given credit for—see the survey in Spencer and Flin, *The Evidence of Children: the law and the psychology*, (2nd. Ed., 1993). The law takes the view that much depends on the ability of individual children to communicate and to communicate truthfully (although arguably, this is or ought to be the major consideration in relation to all types of witness). Accordingly, one of the main issues for the courts in dealing with child witnesses is ensuring that the child is capable of giving intelligible testimony which is reasonably reliable—this is a question considered in cases such as *Rees v. Lowe*, 1989 S.C.C.R. 664 and *Kelly v. Docherty*, 1991 S.C.C.R. 312, below. The other major difficulty which has exercised the law in recent years is the problem of the trauma caused to children when giving evidence, particularly in cases where the child witness has herself been the victim of the crime. A number of measures have been introduced recently to ameliorate such trauma—see the report on the "Evidence of Children and Other Potentially Vulnerable Witnesses" (1990) Scot. Law Com. No. 125, the Criminal Procedure (Scotland) Act 1995, s.271, as amended, below, and cases such as *Birkett v. H.M.A.*, 1992 S.C.C.R. 850 and *Brotherston v. H.M.A.*, 1995 S.C.C.R. 613.

12. Rees v. Lowe
1989 S.C.C.R. 664

The appellant was charged with using lewd and libidinous practices towards a three year old girl. The complainer—the girl—was the principal Crown witness and one of the crucial issues in the case was whether or not she was a competent witness. The Sheriff took the view that with a child as young as the complainer, a preliminary enquiry as to her ability to so recognise the truth would not be fruitful, and instead he simply instructed her to answer the questions of the solicitors as best she could, and to assess the reliability of the evidence as it came out. The appellant was convicted and appealed to the High Court.

LORD JUSTICE-CLERK (ROSS): "The appellant is Charles Cecil Rees who went to trial in the sheriff court at Edinburgh on a complaint charging him with using lewd, indecent and libidinous practices and behaviour towards a girl aged three years. He was found guilty of the charge and he has appealed against his conviction by way of stated case. The stated case contains some four questions of law. The advocate-depute at the outset intimated that the Crown were not seeking to support the conviction and he stated that he would consent to questions 1, 2 and 4 in the case being answered in the negative. Mr Bell for the appellant, of course, wished the questions to be answered in that sense.

Since the issue is an important one, however, it is right that we should explain now why the Crown adopted this course in this case. As is plain from the terms of the complaint, a critical matter was obviously whether the complainer, who was a child of three years, could give evidence. The sheriff allowed this child to give evidence and his findings are to some extent based upon what she said. On the issue of the competency of this three year old girl as a witness, the sheriff in his note said this:

'I took the view that for a child of those years there was little point in examining her as one would, say, a six or seven year old, to clarify that she knew what was meant by telling the truth and not telling lies, and contented myself with simply telling her that the two ladies sitting at the table would ask her things, and she was to answer as best she could, relying on a close watch to form my impression as to her intelligence and truthfulness.'

As the learned advocate-depute pointed out, it appears that the sheriff at no stage made any examination of the girl to ascertain whether she knew the difference between telling the truth and telling lies. He had no evidence regarding that and instead he applied to her evidence as it was given some continuous assessment so that he could form some judgment as the evidence went along as to whether the child knew the difference between the truth and telling lies. We entirely agree with the advocate-depute that this was not the proper approach for the sheriff to have taken. The proper approach to be followed is well recognised. In Dickson on the Law of Evidence, vol. ii, paragraph 1548, it is stated:

'The competency of a young witness has to be determined by the judge, after a preliminary examination of the child, and other evidence (if necessary) as to his intelligence.'

There is a further statement in paragraph 1549 to the following effect:

'Accordingly children under 12 years of age may not be sworn; they are examined on "declaration", *i.e.*, they are admonished to tell the truth.'

It is plain in this case that the sheriff was at fault in that he neither carried out any preliminary examination of the child to see whether she knew the difference between what was true and what was false, nor did he at any stage admonish her to tell the truth. On the contrary, all he said to her was that she should answer the questions as best she could. In our opinion that was an entirely inadequate admonition for the sheriff to have made. The same approach to evidence given by children is to be found in Walkers on Evidence at p.374 and also in Macdonald, *Criminal Law of Scotland* (5th ed.), pp.285–286. The way in which one should approach the question of whether a child of tender years can give evidence is, we would have thought, well recognised and is clearly laid down in the authorities to which we have referred. We take this opportunity of stressing that when witnesses of this age are tendered, it is important for a judge or sheriff to follow the rules which have been laid down and to examine whether the witness knows the difference between telling the truth and telling lies and further to admonish the witness as to the importance of telling the truth. As that was not done in the present case, we can well recognise why the advocate-depute has consented to questions 1, 2 and 4 being answered in the negative, and we shall answer them in that manner."

[The conviction was accordingly quashed.]

NOTES

Why should there be so much emphasis on the ability of a child to differentiate truth and falsehood when so many adults deliberately lie? See the critical comments in Spencer and Flin, *The Evidence of Children: the law and the psychology*, p.334. Is the continuous assessment approach taken by the Sheriff in *Rees v. Lowe* preferable? Would such an approach not be more consistent with the present ethos of the Scottish law of evidence? Is it not the case that a child may have difficulty in expressing or indeed in understanding the difference between truth and falsehood and yet still be able to give a perfectly truthful account? Note that in a number of cases the court has admitted or suggested that it would be prepared to admit extraneous evidence as to the truthfulness of child witnesses—see *K.P. v. H.M.A.*, 1991 S.C.C.R. 933, below, and older cases such as *John Buchan* and *Malcolm Maclean* (1833) Bells Notes 293, 294. There is a very fine line, however, between evidence about the ability of a child to speak the truth, and the question whether in relation to the particular occasion concerned, the child *was* speaking the truth. Compare the Butler Sloss L.J.'s comments in Re F.S. "Child Abuse: Evidence" [1996] 2 F.L.R. 158, quoted above, chapter 10.

13. Kelly v. Docherty
1991 S.C.C.R. 312

The appellant was charged with breach of the peace and assault, allegedly committed in May 1990. One of the principal witnesses for the Crown was a seven year old boy. The sheriff did not carry out an examination of the boy to determine whether he knew the difference between truth and falsehood, but asked him to tell the truth, which the boy said he would. The appellant was convicted and appealed to the High Court on the ground that, as the sheriff had not carried out the proper procedure in relation to the child, the latter was not a competent witness.

LORD JUSTICE-GENERAL (HOPE): "The appellant is Charles Kelly who was charged in the sheriff court at Greenock with three charges on summary complaint. The first was a charge of breach of the peace, the second was a charge of assault on his wife to her injury and the third was a related breach of a condition of bail, bail having been granted to the appellant the day previous to these two offences. He pled not guilty and went to trial on July 10, 1990 when evidence was led. At the end of the trial he was found guilty as libelled on the first charge, he was found guilty on the second charge under deletion of part of the narrative of the assault, and he was also found guilty on the breach of the condition of bail. He was sentenced to three months on each of these charges, these sentences to run concurrently.

He has now appealed against his conviction on two grounds, but the only one which is of relevance to what we have to say in this case is the first, which is whether it was competent for the sheriff simply to ask the witness [A], aged seven, to promise to tell the truth without first having carried out a preliminary examination as to whether the witness knew the difference between telling the truth and telling lies. The background to this question is to be found in the narrative of the evidence which the sheriff has provided in the stated case. He describes how the appellant came to see his wife in the house at which they had been living, how he refused to leave the house and there was an argument on the landing of the house and a further argument later in the street when his wife went to collect their child [A], who was aged seven years of age, at a phone box in the street. That was the basis for the charge of breach of the peace in the first charge in the complaint. The narrative then describes how the appellant assaulted his wife at the phone box in the manner described in the amended charge of assault by hitting her on the head and trying to kick her. Corroboration was sought to be obtained from the child . . . who gave evidence which was not in all respects consistent with that of his mother. He did, however, provide the essential elements to prove the breach of the peace and also the assault on his mother in the vicinity of the telephone box. The only other evidence in the case came from a police officer who arrived shortly afterwards and was able to speak to the complainer's condition after the assault.

The question which we are asked to consider is whether it was competent for the sheriff to ask the witness [A] to promise to tell the truth, without interrogating him as to whether he knew the difference between telling the truth and telling lies, and whether, in these circumstances, the sheriff was entitled to proceed on his accepting his answer to his question that he would tell the truth. The sheriff has described at some length in the stated case the approach which he took when the child entered the witness box. We understand that what he did was simply ask the child to promise to tell the truth, and that he did not carry out a preliminary examination to discover whether he knew the difference between telling the truth and telling lies. On the other hand the sheriff assures us that he did not simply ask the witness to tell the truth. He told him that the child was going to be asked questions by the procurator fiscal and the solicitor for the appellant, and he asked him if in answering these questions he would tell him the truth. It was on the basis of his answer to that question that the sheriff says that he was satisfied that the child understood his question and that it was appropriate that the evidence should proceed.

> 'Children, however young, may be examined if they have sufficient intelligence to understand the obligation to speak the truth, and of this it is the duty of the Judge to satisfy himself by examination and also, if he sees fit, by the evidence of others.'

In *Rees v. Lowe* the opportunity was taken to examine the procedure in a case where the sheriff had not examined a three year old girl who was called to give evidence in order to discover whether or not she knew the difference between what was true and what was false. Indeed in that case the sheriff did not even admonish the child to tell the truth, but told her to answer the questions as best she could and then relied on a close watch to form his impression as to her intelligence and truthfulness. In his opinion at p.667[E] the Lord Justice-Clerk said this:

> 'It is plain in this case that the sheriff was at fault in that he neither carried out any preliminary examination of the child to see whether she knew the difference between what was true and what was false, nor did he at any stage admonish her to tell the truth.'

It can be seen from this passage that there are in fact two stages in the procedure which should be followed in these cases. The first is the preliminary examination, and the second is the admonition to tell the truth. The Lord Justice-Clerk went on to say this:

> 'The way in which one should approach the question of whether a child of tender years can give evidence is, we would have thought, well recognised and is clearly laid down in the authorities to which we have referred. We take this opportunity of stressing that when witnesses of this age are tendered, it is important for a judge or sheriff to follow the rules which have been laid down and to examine whether the witness knows the difference between telling the truth and telling lies and further to admonish the witness as to the importance of telling the truth.'

It can be seen again from this passage that the procedure which should be followed is in two stages, and that it is only if stage one is satisfied and the sheriff has satisfied himself by examination of the witness, and if necessary by other evidence, that the child does indeed know the difference between telling the truth and telling lies, that he can proceed to the second stage, which is the stage of admonishing the child to tell the truth.

It appears from what the sheriff has told us in this case that he overlooked what was said in *Rees v. Lowe*. He maintains that he was satisfied, the longer the child's evidence went on, that he was telling the truth, but for the reasons given in that case a process of continuous assessment of this kind is no substitute for the proper procedure. We are satisfied that the learned advocate-depute was correct when he said that it was not open to the sheriff to proceed as he did straightaway to tell the child to tell the truth and then listen to his evidence without having carried out the preliminary examination which is so important in all these cases where young children are called upon to give evidence.

It follows from what we have said so far that the conviction which was returned in this case cannot stand. The advocate-depute suggested that what we should do by way of disposal of this appeal is to exercise the power mentioned in section 453C(1) of the Criminal Procedure (Scotland) Act 1975 which would permit the Crown to bring a fresh prosecution against the appellant. This submission was made upon the basis that it appears from what the sheriff says in the stated case that there was a sufficiency of evidence and, furthermore, that the circumstance which has led to our quashing the conviction was not attributable in any way to the fault of the Crown. On the other hand, Mr Douglas for the appellant submitted that that course would not be appropriate in this particular case, because of the lapse of time which has occurred and the fact that the critical evidence came from a child whose evidence was already at variance from that of his mother in some respects and might be adversely affected by a further passage of time.

We have decided, very much for the reasons advanced by Mr Douglas, that it would not be appropriate to give authority to the Crown to bring a further prosecution in this case. We also have in mind that it might distress the child, and thus be contrary to his best interests, were he to be required to give evidence again about the circumstances which he was asked to describe. For these reasons what we shall do is answer the first question in the stated case in the negative, and that means that we shall simply allow the appeal and quash the conviction."

14. Quinn v. Lees
1994 S.C.C.R. 159

LORD JUSTICE-GENERAL (HOPE): "The appellant is Keith Christopher Quinn, who went to trial in the sheriff court at Edinburgh charged with assaulting three boys by setting a dog on them whereby one of the boys was knocked to the ground and bitten by the dog, to his injury.

In the course of the trial two questions arose which were the subject of a submission at the end of the Crown case that there was no case to answer. The first related to the procedure that was followed before two of the three boys gave their evidence. The three boys, who were the complainers, were aged 13, 13 and 16 respectively. As two of the three boys were under the age of 14, the question arose whether it was appropriate for them to take the oath before they gave their evidence. The submission to the sheriff was that he had failed to follow the proper procedure. It was said that he had administered the oath to these younger boys without determining whether they knew the difference between truth and falsehood and accordingly that their evidence was incompetent. If that submission was well founded, then the only remaining witness was the 16 year old boy and his evidence would be uncorroborated. The second submission related to the facts of the case and it was to the effect that the whole incident was really no more than a joke and that the appellant did not have the *mens rea* necessary for a conviction of assault. The sheriff repelled the submission on both of these grounds. The appellant then gave evidence, but he was found guilty of the charge and the sheriff decided to defer sentence for six months for good behaviour. An application has now been made for the conviction to be reviewed on grounds which raise again the two points which were the basis for the submission that there was no case to answer.

The incident occurred during the evening when the three boys, named [C.A.D.], [R.M.] and [D.D.] were walking home at about 9.30 p.m. along Easter Drylaw Drive, Edinburgh. They saw the appellant and a companion with an Alsatian dog on the other side of the road. Both [C.D.] and [D.D.] were wearing woollen hats which they had pulled down to their eyes and covered their ears. The appellant asked the witnesses, 'Are youz robbers?' The reply came from one of them that they were not, whereupon the appellant instructed his dog, while pointing to the three boys, 'King, fetch,' The dog then went across the road towards the boys and attacked [C.A.D.] knocking him to the ground and biting him on the leg. That was the incident as described in the evidence of all three witnesses and it is the background against which the two questions which were raised by way of a motion for no case to answer fell to be considered.

We shall take first the question relating to the competency of the evidence of the two younger boys. As we have said, [D.D.] was aged 16 years and no question arises about the competency of his evidence. In the case of [C.D.] and [R.M.] the sheriff decided that, although they were under the age of 14, he should administer the oath to them and he duly did so. The question which is raised is whether he went through the proper procedure before he took that course. The rules of practice in this matter are not in doubt. A child who is under the age of 12 is not normally put on oath at all. He is admonished to tell the truth, after the procedure which is described in *Kelly v. Docherty* has been carried out. On the other hand, a child who is aged 14 years or more is normally put on oath, and no question arises as to any preliminary procedure. Where a child is between the ages of 12 and 14 the judge must satisfy himself that the child understands the nature of the oath. Unless he is so satisfied, it is not appropriate for him to put a child who is under the age of fourteen on oath.

In the present case the appellant maintains that, at least in the case of one of these two witnesses, the sheriff did not follow the proper procedure. The propositions on which this argument depends are set out conveniently in paragraph 11 of the note of proposed adjustments. The account given here is that when the witness [C.A.D.] came to the witness box the sheriff asked him whether he knew what taking an oath meant, whereupon he replied 'No'. The sheriff then said, 'I am going to put you on oath', and then administered the oath to him. When the witness [R.M.] came to the witness box the sheriff put the same question to him, to which he received the reply 'Yes' and the sheriff then put him on oath. The sheriff for his part tells us in his note that he followed the following procedure in the case of both boys. He says that before the oath was administered he asked them whether they were aware of the truth and what the administration of the oath meant. Both boys answered in the affirmative, and he was fully satisfied in both cases that the witnesses knew what the administration of the oath entailed.

On the face of the sheriff's account there can be no question as to the competency of the evidence of either of these two witnesses. On the account given in paragraph 11 of the note of adjustments, the way he dealt with only one of the two boys appears to fall outside the proper procedure. This is because [R.M.], when asked the appropriate question, replied in the affirmative. On this version of what occurred the argument does not appear to advance the appellant's position at all on competency because, if [R.M.'s] evidence was available, then there was corroboration for the evidence of [D.D.] and there was therefore sufficient evidence for the Crown case to succeed. However that may be, the proposition which is made in regard to [C.A.D.] is contradicted by what the sheriff himself has told us in his note. Miss Gilchrist informed us that her instructions contradicted the sheriff, and there was a suggestion that the sheriff had not had his notes available to him at the time when he came to prepare the stated case. We must, however, take the case as it has been presented to us by the sheriff and on his account, and having regard also to what is said in paragraph 11 of the note of adjustments, it appears to us that there is no point of substance in this ground of appeal."

[The Lord Justice-General then went on to consider the other ground of appeal, with which this extract is not concerned]

NOTES

In civil cases, examination of a child for competence to give evidence is no longer necessary where it is proposed simply to lead hearsay evidence of what the child has said on a previous occasion—*T. v. T.*, 2000 S.L.T. 1442. This can be contrasted with the position in criminal cases, in which, where it is proposed to lead hearsay evidence, it is explicitly required that the maker of the hearsay statement would have been a competent witness at the time the statement was made—see s.259(1)(c).

If it is proposed to lead a child as a witness at a hearing—in civil or criminal matters—then steps must be taken to ensure that the child has a sufficient degree of understanding to qualify as a competent witness. The nature and extent of the steps required remains controversial. As the extract from *Quinn v. Lees*, above, demonstrates, the requirements for examination are fairly basic. There are limits, however. In the case of *A.R. v. Walker*, 1999 S.L.T. 1233 the Sheriff merely asked the child, who was five, whether she knew the difference between truth and falsehood, to which she responded by nodding. It was held that this was not enough to constitute a sufficient examination of competency. Lord Prosser, delivering the Opinion of the Court said:

> "we are satisfied that an examination for this purpose might be very brief: we would respectfully concur with the observation made by the Lord Justice Clerk in *S. v. Kennedy* at p.22 of his opinion, where he says: 'How to carry out a preliminary examination of a child witness is very much up to the judge or sheriff faced with that task. Different judges or sheriffs will no doubt approach this task in different ways. Much will also depend upon the way in which the child responds to initial questioning.
>
> Nonetheless, it does not appear to us that this single question, met with only a simple affirmative, can constitute a sufficient examination for this purpose. The question of whether the child knows the difference between truth and falsehood is a question for the court, and not simply a question to be put to the child. A child who on fuller examination is held to understand the crucial difference between truth and falsehood may initially, if faced with a bald question on the matter, give a negative answer—as occurred in *S. v. Kennedy*. Equally, it seems to us that a child who does not know the difference between what is true and what is false might well give an affirmative answer. While much may turn on impression and demeanour, we do not think that such a simple affirmative by the child can provide a sufficient basis for an affirmative answer by the court."

The Sheriff also took into account reports prepared prior to the proof by the safeguarder and a social worker to the effect that the child was "articulate and outgoing". The court disregarded these reports on the basis that they contained insufficient material to indicate that the child knew the difference between truth and falsehood. Nevertheless, the court emphasised that a Sheriff is entitled to take other matters into account in assessing the question of competence. It seems, however, that there must be at least some element of personal interaction between Sheriff and child:

> "In addition to what actually passes between the court and the child, before the child is admitted as a witness, it was accepted by counsel for the appellant that the court may have recourse to other evidence and material, in judging whether the child knows the difference between truth and falsehood. Reference was made to *P. v. H.M.A.*, where it was held that it was for the trial judge himself to decide, in all the circumstances, whether or not it was necessary to have evidence from another source before determining the issue. We were referred also to *L. v. L.* at 1996 SLT, p.772, where Lord Hamilton says: 'This preliminary exercise may at times be lengthy and difficult; at other times it may be relatively brief. It involves however the judge not only questioning the child but directly observing him or her in the course of such questioning. He is thus enabled to form an impression from direct observation of the child. That impression may be reinforced or negatived by evidence from others who have directly addressed themselves to the question of the child's capacity to give evidence; but I find nothing in the authorities to justify the proposition that this judicial examination may be altogether dispensed with and a child's capacity to give evidence determined solely on other evidence.
>
> Counsel for the appellant acknowledged that the evidence of others envisaged in these cases might not merely be expert or opinion evidence from persons 'who have directly addressed themselves to the question of the child's capacity to give evidence', but might be evidence of past conversations with the child which from their content might be of considerable assistance to the judge or sheriff, as demonstrating that the child did or did not understand the difference between truth and falsehood. And while such past conversations might be on wholly extraneous subjects, nothing to do with the case in hand, it was accepted that in principle one might have regard, for this initial and preliminary purpose, to evidence of what the child had said on a prior occasion in relation to precisely those issues which would be in point if and when the child came to give evidence, or indeed if others gave admissible hearsay evidence of what the child had said during those same prior conversations. That appears to us to be correct in principle; and while it may at first sight seem paradoxical to use for this preliminary purpose the very material which will be relied upon as evidence if the preliminary hurdle is surmounted, we are satisfied that there is no inherent problem—although it will of course be important to bear in mind the

fundamental distinction between looking at the material at this stage, to judge the child's capacity to give evidence, and looking at it subsequently as evidence, to be evaluated in terms of credibility and reliability."

The matter is also considered in *M. v. Kennedy*, 1993 S.C.L.R. 69. In that case Lord President Hope said, *obiter*, that:

". . . it is well recognised in the authorities that a decision as to whether a child's evidence is or is not to be admissible does not require to be based only on a preliminary examination of the child himself. Dickson says in paragraph 1548 that the competency of a young witness has to be determined after a preliminary examination of the child and other evidence (if necessary). Macdonald at p.286, under reference to Dickson, says that the judge must satisfy himself by examination 'and also, if he sees fit, by the evidence of others'. Walkers make the same point about hearing, if necessary, other evidence at p.374. This point was not discussed in *F. v. Kennedy* [(No. 1)], but it is a course which might have been followed in that case had it appreciated that the decision about admissibility was crucial not only to the question whether to hear the child but also as to the admissibility of the child's statements to the social workers. The sheriff would have been entitled to rely on the evidence of other witnesses whom he accepted as reliable and had addressed their minds to the point, if there was an explanation as to why the child would not speak to him. That also is a course which would have been open in the present case, if an opinion about the child's ability to tell the difference between truth and falsehood had been obtained from the psychiatrists and a sufficient explanation given as why the child could not communicate with the sheriff in such a way as to satisfy him on this point."

Lord Hope comes close to suggesting in this passage that, at least in certain circumstances—and *M. v. Kennedy* was a rather unusual case in which the child was an elective mute who would communicate only by nodding or shaking his head—a determination of competency may be made on the basis *purely* of evidence from others who have had contact with the child. The court in *T. v. T.* did not appear to criticise that view, albeit that the matter was not focused before the court in that case.

15. K.P. v. H.M.A.
1991 S.C.C.R. 933

LORD JUSTICE-CLERK (ROSS): "The appellant is [K.P.] who went to trial in the High Court at Kilmarnock on an indictment containing four charges. Charges (1) and (3) were both charges of indecent assault and rape, and charges (2) and (4) were both charges of indecent assault and sodomy. The jury by a majority found charges (1) and (2) not proven, and by a majority found the appellant guilty of charges (3) and (4). Against this conviction he has now appealed.

The complainer in charge (3) was the appellant's daughter who was born on June 4, 1983. The charge libelled that the offence had been committed on various occasions between February 1, 1987 and June 15, 1987 and June 29, 1987 and April 5, 1988, at which times the child was aged between three and four. The complainer in charge (4) was the appellant's son who was born on April 18, 1985. The offences libelled in this charge were said to have been committed on various occasions between the same dates as those libelled in charge (3), at which times this complainer must have been aged between twenty-two months and nearly three years of age.

The mother of the two children had given evidence relevant to charges (1) and (2) but had given no evidence relevant to charges (3) and (4). Incriminating evidence in relation to those charges came from the two children only. As regards charges (3) and (4) the Crown relied upon *Moorov v. H.M.A.* Accordingly, the evidence of both children was essential for convictions on charges (3) and (4).

The ground of appeal put forward on the appellant's behalf was that the trial judge had erred in allowing evidence to be led from the appellant's son in view of the child's age at the date of the trial, his age at the date of the alleged offence, the lengthy time gap between the date of the alleged offence and the date of the trial, the inability of the child to understand properly what was meant by the truth, the absence of any independent evidence to demonstrate any such ability, and the failure of the trial judge to make full enquiry as to the child's ability to understand what was meant by the truth. When the case was first heard before this court, the appeal was continued and the court authorised extension of the notes of evidence given by the complainer in charge (4). The notes of evidence are now available. At the time of the trial when the said child gave evidence he was aged five years and nine months. When the child was tendered as a witness, the following exchange took place between the presiding judge and the child: [His Lordship narrated the examination of the witness by the trial judge as set out above, and continued:]

At that stage counsel for the accused submitted that although the presiding judge had asked a number of questions there still remained a problem of being satisfied as to the child's proper understanding of what the truth was. Counsel maintained that the court required to be satisfied that a witness of this age properly understood what was meant by the truth, and that in the present case there was still a difficulty in being sure that the child understood what someone meant by truth. Counsel stated that he would not presume to suggest to the presiding judge how things might be done, but he contended that it was not clear at that stage what the child's understanding was. Counsel further submitted that there was a very real risk that a child of this age had really no understanding of the idea of truth. He contended that a young child with no understanding of truth would still be able to tell factual things.

In reply to these observations, the presiding judge indicated that all that he could do was to ascertain if the child was to be of the sort of intelligence which one might expect of a child of his age, and to understand simple questions and accept at least that there is a distinction between the truth and telling lies. Subsequently he indicated that from the replies which he had received it appeared to him that there was sufficient understanding in the child of the difference between the truth and lies. Subsequently he added:

'But I am not satisfied that his understanding of the truth is so limited that he could not properly be tendered as a witness.'

The child accordingly gave evidence.

In presenting the appeal, Mr Bell for the appellant pointed out that although charges (1) and (2) had been found not proven, it was important to observe that charge (2) related to offences said to have been committed against the said child over a period when his age varied from six days old to barely four months. Although the Crown relied upon the rule of *Moorov*, it was not a pure *Moorov* case, and there had been evidence about opportunity from the child's grandmother pointing to the earlier part of the period as the time when any such offences might have taken place. As the trial judge correctly observed in his report, the evidence indicated that the offences were more likely to have taken place in the earlier part of the period running from April 1, 1987 to April 5, 1988. Mr Bell also explained that a special feature of the case had been that the female complainer had not been a stranger to abuse, because she had been the victim of sexual abuse at the hands of her grandfather who had been convicted on December 19, 1988 in the sheriff court. An extract conviction had been produced before the jury, and the conduct giving rise to the charges had occurred almost contemporaneously with the conduct referred to in charge (3). There was, however, no suggestion that the younger child had been abused by his grandfather. Nonetheless the suggestion had been that the older child or his mother might have influenced the younger child.

Mr Bell accepted that it was for the trial judge to decide as a matter of competency whether the younger child could give evidence. The evidence showed that the children had been removed from the family home for quite some time before they gave evidence, and that they were living with foster parents whom they referred to as 'uncle' and 'aunt'. Mr Bell recognised that in determining whether a child should be examined as a witness, the normal procedure was for the trial judge to carry out a preliminary interrogation of the child, but he submitted that in the present case it was not sufficient merely to do that, but that the trial judge should also have investigated the child's ability to give evidence by hearing evidence from third parties. He stated that it was only by carrying out the latter exercise that the trial judge could satisfy himself that the child knew what it meant to tell the truth. He submitted that the present case was a special one because of the previous history of sexual abuse in the family, because of the age of the child when the offences had been committed, and because of the considerable lapse of time between the commission of the alleged offences and the child's giving evidence.

As counsel pointed out, the admissibility of a child as a witness is dealt with in Dickson on Evidence (3rd ed.), paragraphs 1543, 1548; Alison, *Practice of the Criminal Law of Scotland*, pp.432–435; Macdonald on the Criminal Law of Scotland (5th ed.), pp.295–296, and Walker and Walker, *The Law of Evidence in Scotland*, p.374. Counsel also referred to *Rees v. Lowe* and *Kelly v. Docherty*. It is clear from these authorities that, as the matter is put in Walker and Walker:

> 'It is for the judge to determine whether a child should be examined, after a preliminary interrogation of the child and, if necessary, after hearing other evidence.'

The critical question in the present case is whether it was sufficient for the trial judge to question the child as he did, or whether it was necessary for him to hear other evidence as to whether the child was able to understand and appreciate the duty of speaking the truth. Mr Bell maintained that the trial judge ought to have made further enquiries from third parties such as the foster parents, and he submitted at the end of the day that no reasonable judge could have been satisfied without hearing evidence from some other source regarding this matter.

The advocate-depute, on the other hand, stressed that it was clearly established that it was for the judge to determine whether he was satisfied that the child could understand the difference between truth and falsehood. In *Kelly v. Docherty* the procedure was described by the Lord Justice-General under reference to what had been said in *Rees v. Lowe*. After quoting from that case the Lord Justice-General said [at p.315E]:

> 'It can be seen again from this passage that the procedure which should be followed is in two stages, and that it is only if stage one is satisfied and the sheriff has satisfied himself by examination of the witness, and if necessary by other evidence, that the child does indeed know the difference between telling the truth and telling lies, that he can proceed to the second stage, which is the stage of admonishing the child to tell the truth.'

The advocate-depute maintained that it was plain from the transcript of the evidence that the presiding judge had followed the proper procedure, and that in the circumstances he was entitled to conclude that the child was able to understand the difference between telling the truth and telling lies. The advocate-depute recognised that the trial judge had put the matter in the wrong way when he said:

> 'But I am not satisfied that his understanding of the truth is so limited that he could not properly be tendered as a witness.'

The real issue was whether the trial judge was satisfied that the witness understood the difference between telling the truth and telling lies. Before stating the matter thus, however, the trial judge had said this:

> '[F]rom the replies which have been received it appears to me that there is sufficient understanding in this witness of the difference between truth and lies.'

Having studied the interrogation of the witness which the trial judge carried out, we are of opinion that he followed the correct procedure, and that he was entitled to be satisfied that the child did understand the difference between telling the truth and telling lies. It must be kept in mind that the trial judge had an advantage which this court does not have of having seen and heard the child answering his questions; in determining an issue of this kind the demeanour of the child may be of considerable importance. In his report the trial judge says:

'Before he gave evidence I asked him such questions as I thought necessary to try to ascertain as far as one can whether he understood the difference between telling the truth and telling lies and that he knew that it was wrong to tell lies. The answers which I received gave me no reason to suppose that he did not understand the distinction between truth and untruth.'

Whether or not it was necessary for the trial judge to have evidence from another source before he could determine this issue was for the trial judge himself to decide in all the circumstances. It may be that, faced with this particular case, another judge would have required evidence from another source, but we are not persuaded that after carrying out the interrogation which was carried out here, no reasonable judge could have been satisfied that the child knew the difference between telling the truth and telling lies. In our opinion, after he had questioned the child, the trial judge was entitled to be satisfied that the child did indeed know the difference between telling the truth and telling lies.

Since the only ground of appeal put forward is that the trial judge should not have allowed evidence to be led from the younger child, and as that ground of appeal has not been established, it follows that the appellant has failed to demonstrate that there was any miscarriage of justice in this case. The appeal against conviction must therefore be refused."

NOTES

It certainly seems to have been accepted in this case that extrinsic evidence as to the child's competency in a criminal case is admissible—whether it should be sought in any particular case is a matter for the judge's discretion. However, in *H.M.A. v. Grimmond*, 2001 S.C.C.R. 708, Lord Osborne took the view that evidence of a child's credibility will not be admitted unless it can be shown that the child was suffering from some form of mental illness. As noted above, the distinction between competency and credibility is a very fine one, particularly where young children are concerned, and particularly given the test of competency which is applied to the testimony of such children. The children in *Grimmond* were aged six (almost seven) and eight. There is no basis in Lord Osborne's reasoning to say that any different rule should be applied in civil cases—for example, referrals to the Sheriff for proof in cases brought under Chapter of the Children (Scotland) Act 1995. Where it is sought to lead hearsay of a child witness under section 259 of the Criminal Procedure (Scotland) Act 1995 the child's competency will have to be established, because of the specific provisions of s.259(1)(c). Finally, hearsay evidence of a child witness cannot be led simply because a child is becomes distressed and is unwilling to speak up in court. A specific direction must be given to the child that he or she must answer a particular question, and the child must have refused to answer before the provisions of s.259 can be invoked—see *MacDonald (Robert Grant) v. H.M.A.*, 1999 S.L.T. 533.

16. Criminal Procedure (Scotland) Act 1995, s.271

Evidence of vulnerable persons: special provisions

"271.—(1) Subject to subsections (7) and (8) below, where a vulnerable person has been or could be cited to give evidence in a trial the court may appoint a commissioner to take the evidence of that person if—

(a) in solemn proceedings, at any time before the oath is administered to the jury;

(b) in summary proceedings, at any time before the first witness is sworn;

(c) in exceptional circumstances in either solemn or summary proceedings, during the course of the trial,

application is made in that regard; but to be so appointed a person must be, and for a period of five years have been, a member of the Faculty of Advocates or a solicitor.

(2) Proceedings before a commissioner appointed under subsection (1) above shall be recorded by video recorder.

(3) An accused shall not, except by leave of the commissioner, be present in the room where such proceedings are taking place but shall be entitled by such means as seem suitable to the commissioner to watch and hear the proceedings.

(4) Subsections (2) to (6), (8) and (9) of section 272 of this Act shall apply to an application under subsection (1) above and evidence taken by a commissioner appointed under that subsection as those subsections apply to an application under subsection (1) of that section and evidence taken by a commissioner appointed on such an application.

(5) Subject to subsections (7) and (8) below, where a vulnerable person has been or is likely to be cited to give evidence in a trial, the court may, on an application being made to it, authorise the giving of evidence by that person by means of a live television link.

(6) Subject to subsections (7) and (8) below, where a vulnerable person has been or is likely to be cited to give evidence in a trial, the court may, on application being made to it, authorise the use of a screen to conceal the accused from the sight of that person while that person is present to give evidence; but arrangements shall be made to ensure that the accused is able to watch and hear as the evidence is given by the vulnerable person.

(7) The court may grant an application under subsection (1), (5) or (6) above only on cause shown having regard in particular to—

    (a) the possible effect on the vulnerable person if required to give evidence, no such application having been granted;

    (b) whether it is likely that the vulnerable person would be better able to give evidence if such an application were granted; and

    (c) the views of the vulnerable person.

(8) In considering whether to grant an application under subsection (1), (5) or (6) above the court may take into account, where appropriate, any of the following—

    (a) the nature of the alleged offence;

    (b) the nature of the evidence which the vulnerable person is likely to be called upon to give;

    (c) the relationship, if any, between the person and the accused; and

    (d) where the person is a child, his age and maturity.

(9) Where a sheriff to whom an application has been made under subsection (1), (5) or (6) above would have granted the application but for the lack of accommodation or equipment necessary to achieve the purpose of the application, he may by order transfer the case to any sheriff court which has such accommodation and equipment available, being a sheriff court in the same sheriffdom.

(10) The sheriff court to which a case has been transferred under subsection (9) above shall be deemed to have granted an application under, as the case may be, subsection (1), (5) or (6) above in relation to the case.

(11) Where a court has or is deemed to have granted an application under subsection (1), (5) or (6) above in relation to a vulnerable person, and the vulnerable person gives evidence that he recalls having identified, prior to the trial, a person alleged to have committed an offence, the evidence of a third party as to the identification of that person by the vulnerable person prior to the trial shall be admissible as evidence as to such identification.

(12) In this section—

"child" means a person under the age of 16 years;

"court" means the High Court or the sheriff court;

"trial" means a trial under solemn or under summary procedure; and

"vulnerable person" means—

    (a) any child; and

    (b) any person of or over the age of 16 years

        (i) who is subject to an order made in consequence of a finding of a court in any part of the United Kingdom that he is suffering from mental disorder within the meaning of section 1(2) of the Mental Health (Scotland) Act 1984, section 1(2) of the Mental Health Act 1983, or Article 3(1) of the Mental Health (Northern Ireland) Order 1986 (application of enactment); or

        (ii) who is subject to a transfer direction under section 71(1) of the 1984 Act, section 47 of the 1983 Act, or Article 53 of the 1986 Order (transfer directions); or

        (iii) who otherwise appears to the court to suffer from significant impairment of intelligence and social functioning."

NOTES

In its Report "The Evidence of Children and other Vulnerable Witnesses" (Scot. Law Com. No.125, 1990), the Scottish Law Commission recommended the introduction of a number of measures designed to reduce the trauma caused to children by the prospect and experience of giving evidence in court. Their proposals were partially implemented by the Law Reform (Miscellaneous Provisions) (Scotland) Act 1990, ss.56–59 which introduced the possibility of giving evidence by live television link and specifically adopted the ratio of *Muldoon v. Herron*, 1970 J.C. 30, above, Chapter 7, to allow identification of the accused to be made by child witnesses in less stressful conditions than those obtaining during a trial. The Prisoners and Criminal Proceedings (Scotland) Act 1993, ss.33–35, introduced further measures including the idea of giving video-taped evidence on commission and the use of screens to "shelter" the witness in court. These measures were consolidated by the Criminal Procedure (Scotland) Act 1995 and are all now contained in section 271 of that Act. The present section 271 was recast by the Crime and Punishment (Scotland) Act 1997, s.29. The original s.271 applied only to children—*i.e.* persons under the age of 16. The new provisions have been extended to other vulnerable witnesses as defined in s.271(12), above. The measures apply specifically to criminal proceedings, but there is nothing to prevent a party in a civil case adducing as evidence statements made by vulnerable persons in documents or on video-tape, since hearsay is admissible in such cases thanks to the Civil Evidence (Scotland) Act 1988, s.2. A number of other measures, however, are competent without recourse to these statutory provisions:

17. Lord Justice General's Memorandum on Child Witnesses, July 26, 1990

Renton and Brown Appendix F

"1. The following memorandum of guidance has been prepared at the suggestion of the Scottish Law Commission: see Report on the Evidence of Children and Other Potentially Vulnerable Witnesses (Scot. Law Com. No. 125). Its purpose is to provide guidance to judges in the exercise of their discretionary powers, where a child is to give evidence by conventional means in open court, to put the child at ease while giving evidence and to clear the court of persons not having a direct involvement in the proceedings.

2. The general objective is to ensure, so far as is reasonably practicable, that the experience of giving evidence by all children under the age of 16 causes as little anxiety and distress to the child as possible in the circumstances.

3. The following are examples of the measures which may be taken, at the discretion of the presiding judge, with a view to achieving that objective—

    (a) The removal of wigs and gowns by the judge, counsel and solicitors;

    (b) The positioning of the child at a table in the well of the court along with the judge, counsel and solicitors, rather than requiring the child to give evidence from the witness box;

    (c) Permitting a relative or other supporting person to sit alongside the child while he or she is giving evidence;

    (d) The clearing from the court-room of all persons not having a direct involvement in the proceedings.

4. In deciding whether or not to take these or similar measures, or any of them, the presiding judge should have regard to the following factors—

    (a) The age and maturity of the child.

        In general the younger the child the more desirable it is that steps should be taken to reduce formality and to put the child at ease while giving evidence.

    (b) The nature of the charge or charges, and the nature of the evidence which the child is likely to be called upon to give.

        Particular care should be taken in cases with a sexual element or involving allegation of child abuse especially where the child is the complainer or an eye-witness. Children directly involved in such cases are likely to be especially vulnerable to trauma when called upon to give evidence in the presence of the accused. The giving of evidence of a relatively formal nature, especially in the case of an older child, is unlikely to cause anxiety or distress and in such cases it will rarely be necessary to take special measures in the interests of the child.

(c) The relationship, if any, between the child and the accused.

A child who is giving evidence at the trial of a close relative may be especially exposed to apprehension or embarrassment, irrespective of the nature of the charge. The positioning of the child and the support of a person sitting alongside the child while giving evidence are likely to be of particular importance in these cases.

(d) Whether the trial is summary or on indictment.

While informality may be easier to achieve in summary cases, the presence of a jury in cases taken on indictment is likely to present an anxious or distressed child with an additional cause for anxiety or distress. This makes it all the more necessary under solemn procedure that steps should be taken to put the child at ease.

(e) Any special factors placed before the court concerning the disposition, health or physique of the child.

All children are different, and judges should take each child's particular circumstances into account before deciding what steps, if any, should be taken to minimise anxiety or distress.

(f) The practicability of departing from normal procedure, including the size and layout of the court and the availability of amplification equipment.

Whatever steps are taken, a child witness who gives evidence by conventional means must remain visible and audible to all those who have to hear and assess the evidence, including the jury and the accused.

5. In all cases before a witness under 16 years of age is led in evidence an opportunity should be given to those representing the Crown and the defence to address the judge as to what special arrangements, if any, are appropriate. Under solemn procedure such representations should be made outwith the presence of the jury and preferably before the jury is empanelled or at least before the commencement of the evidence.

6. If a relative or other supporting person is to sit alongside the child, that person should not be a witness in the case and he or she should be warned by the judge at the outset not to prompt or seek to influence the child in any way in the course of the evidence.

7. The clearing of the court while a child is giving evidence will normally be appropriate in all cases which involve an offence against, or conduct contrary to, decency or morality: see section 166 and section 362 of the Criminal Procedure (Scotland) Act 1975. In other cases this should only be done if the judge is satisfied that this is necessary in order to avoid undue anxiety or distress to the child. The statutory provisions that bona fide representatives of newspaper or news agency should not be excluded should be applied in all cases.

8. When taking any of the measures described above the judge should have regard to the court's general duty to ensure that the accused receives a fair trial and is given a proper opportunity to present his defence."

NOTES

As these guidelines have been interpreted, it is not only children who may now be regarded as vulnerable, a view that seems entirely justifiable in the light of the changes made to s.271. *McGinley v. H.M.A.*, 2001 S.L.T. 198 was a case involving charges of lewd and libidinous practices said to have taken place when the complainer was aged between 12 and 14. By the time of the trial the complainer was 28. Nevertheless, she was allowed to have her boyfriend sit close to her in court as a "comforting presence". The trial judge's decision to allow this was upheld on appeal. The appeal court noted that if, as in *McGinley*, there is any suggestion of improper communication between the witness and the supporter, then that matter should be specifically raised with the trial judge, not just the witness, and if necessary, a motion made to desert the trial.

18. H.M.A. v. Birkett
1992 S.C.C.R. 850

The accused was charged with the attempted murder of a three year old child, A.G.B., and with assaulting the child's mother. The prosecutor petitioned the court to be allowed to take the evidence of A.G.B., two of his siblings, aged six and eight, and two other children, aged four and six, by live television link. In the case of A.G.B. it was averred that he was frightened of the accused, but in the cases of the other children, it was averred only that they were quiet and hesitant witnesses and that their evidence would be of a traumatic nature which they would be better able to give outwith the presence of the accused. The accused objected to the petition and a hearing was held before the Lord Justice-Clerk (Ross) on July 10, 1992.

LORD JUSTICE-CLERK (ROSS): "This is a petition at the instance of the Lord Advocate seeking an order under section 56 of the Law Reform (Miscellaneous Provisions) (Scotland) Act 1990 authorising the giving of evidence by five children by means of a live television link. The children are [A.G.B.], [L.J.B.], [C.J.B.], [W.S.G.] and [A.D.G.].

[A.G.B.] is the complainer in charge (1) and I was informed that he is aged three. He has been precognosced by the procurator fiscal himself, and I was informed that he is frightened of the accused, and that the view of the procurator fiscal is that he would be better able to give evidence outwith the presence of the accused. Miss Scott for the accused did not oppose the application in respect of [A.G.B.], and accordingly I agreed to grant the application so far as he was concerned.

As regards the children [L.J.B.] (aged six) and [C.J.B.] (aged eight), who are the sister and brother respectively of [A.G.B.], it was said that they are both quiet and hesitant witnesses and that they will be required to give evidence of a traumatic nature. It was said that [L] might be inhibited in the presence of the accused. It was also said that [A.S.P.], who is the complainer in charge (2), might be ready to protect the accused. As regards [C.J.B.], I was informed that he felt loyalty both to his mother [A.S.P.] and the accused with whom he had had a close relationship. It was felt that there was divided loyalty in his case. It was suggested that they would be better able to give evidence outwith the accused's presence.

As regards [W.S.G.] (aged four) and [A.D.G.] (aged six), it was said that they were to give evidence regarding charge (1) and in particular evidence regarding the use of a knife. It was said that the evidence they could give was of a frightening nature, and again that they would be better able to give evidence outwith the accused's presence.

In terms of section 56(2) of the Act of 1990, cause has to be shown before the court may grant an application such as this. In determining whether cause has been shown regard must be had in particular to the possible effect on the child required to give evidence, no such application having been granted, and whether it is likely that the child would be better able to give evidence if the application were granted.

Section 56(3) specifies the criteria to be taken into account when considering whether to grant an application such as this. Miss Scott for the accused maintained that the application should be refused in relation to the four children other than [A.G.B.]. She stressed that it was not suggested in their case that they were frightened, and she emphasised that age was not in itself a sufficient ground for granting the application. She stated that [L.J.B.] and [C.J.B.] had had a close relationship with the accused, and that [C] had had a particularly good relationship with him. They only spoke to part of the matters libelled. As regards the other two children, they were not related to the accused or the complainers and they had not lived in the same household as them. She recognised that the children would be speaking to a somewhat frightening event, but she emphasised that that would be so whether they gave evidence in open court or by means of live television link. This was not a case involving sexual abuse.

On the information placed before me I was not satisfied that cause had been shown at this stage for the granting of the application. On the other hand I was conscious that difficulties might be encountered when the evidence of the children was sought to be taken in open court, and I was anxious that at that stage the trial judge, if he thought fit, could order that the evidence of these children should be taken by means of a television link. A question then arose in my mind as to whether it would be competent to continue the matter for consideration by the trial judge. The Act of Adjournal (Consolidation Amendment No. 2) (Evidence of Children) 1991 sets out the form of applications under section 56 of the Act of 1990, and prescribes the procedure to be followed. Rule 61A [of the Act of Adjournal (Consolidation) 1988, as inserted by paragraph 2 of the 1991 Amendment] provides for an application for this purpose being made by petition not later than 14 clear days before the trial diet (except on special cause shown). In my opinion, the purpose of providing that applications should be made fourteen days before the trial diet is to ensure that the trial takes place within a building where facilities exist for taking evidence by means of a live television link. If an application is granted then arrangements will be made for the trial to take place in such a building. On the other hand, if an application is refused, there will be no need for any such arrangements to be made. The advocate-depute agreed that it would not be incompetent to continue an application of this kind for consideration by the trial judge, but he stressed that it would be undesirable to do so. He explained that where child witnesses are concerned, steps have to be taken before a trial to put them at their ease. They are given guidance by procurators fiscal, and other agencies may also be involved in this respect. They are visited before the trial and it is explained to them what is going to happen. In order to reduce any uncertainties that the children may have it will be explained to them where they will have to stand when giving their evidence, and they may be taken and shown a courtroom for that purpose. He accordingly submitted that if the application were to be continued and it was uncertain whether a particular child's evidence was to be given in open court or by means of a live television link, the result would be most unsatisfactory. I fully appreciate the force of these observations which the advocate-depute made. On the other hand I was concerned that if I refused the application out of hand, and it subsequently transpired that any of the witnesses was having difficulty in giving evidence in court, it might be desirable if the trial judge could arrange to have the evidence of the child taken by means of a live television link. Since the application was being granted in relation to the complainer in charge (1), the trial would be taking place within a building where that facility existed. I appreciate that the Act of Adjournal does not envisage successive applications being made in relation to the evidence of particular children, nor does it envisage the application being dealt with by a trial judge at the trial. None the less, if a trial is taking place in a building where facilities for taking evidence by a live television link exist, I see no reason why the trial judge should not be able to order that the evidence of a child should be taken in that way. I recognise, however, that if in relation to that child an application had previously been refused, the trial judge might be reluctant to order the child's evidence to be taken by means of a live television link in the event of that facility being available. Since I was not satisfied in relation to the four children to whom I have referred that cause had been shown at this stage for the granting of the application, I was not prepared to grant the application. I have, however, refused to grant the application in *hoc statu* in order to emphasise that if circumstances have changed by the time of the trial, and if it appears appropriate to the trial judge to order that the evidence of all or any of these children should be taken by means of a live television link, he will be able to do so by making an order in terms of the petition which is presently before me.

For the sake of completeness, it should be noted that the advocate-depute contended that even if an application had been refused by one judge before the trial had commenced, it would be open to the Crown or the accused to lodge a further petition before the trial judge seeking an order for the taking of the evidence of the child by means of a live television link. Special cause might be shown as to why that petition had not been lodged 14 clear days before the trial diet, and the advocate-depute contended that in the event of a change of circumstances there was no reason why a subsequent petition should not be granted. It is unnecessary for me to determine whether successive petitions under this procedure would be competent, since by refusing the present application in *hoc statu* I have kept the existing petition in existence and left it open to the trial judge, if so advised, to grant the application which has at present been refused in *hoc statu*. However, since the application has at present been refused, the Crown should proceed upon the basis that the evidence of these children is to be taken in open court, and the guidance which is given to the children pre-trial should proceed upon that basis."

NOTES

This decision indicates that live television link evidence will not be permitted in every case where a vulnerable person has to give evidence. It seems that there must be specific averments about the trauma likely to be suffered by the witness in giving evidence and about the reasons for it. It suggests that it is not enough merely to narrate that the evidence is of a traumatic or frightening nature; the witness must have some reason to fear giving evidence in open court, such as a well-founded fear of the accused, as in the case of the child "A.G.B." in *Birkett*. Section 271(8)(b) of the 1995 Act does specifically refer, however, to the nature of the evidence which the child is likely to be called upon to give as a factor which may be taken into account by the court in deciding whether or not to grant an application. Does *Birkett* suggest therefore that what is required is evidence which is traumatic for some reason specifically related to the witness, rather than merely frightening *per se*? See *inter alia* John Fotheringham, "Trials of the Small Screen" (1996) 41 J.L.S.S. 60; Kathleen Murray, "CCTV in Scottish Courts" (1995) 40 J.L.S.S. 314; K. Murray, "Live Television Link: an Evaluation of its Use by Child Witnesses in Criminal Proceedings" (Scottish Office: Central Research Unit 1995).

19.   Brotherston v. H.M.A.
1995 S.C.C.R. 613

The appellant was convicted of murder. Prior to the trial, authority had been obtained to take the evidence of three child witnesses by live TV link. At the trial, defence counsel asked the trial judge to reconsider the matter because of the importance of identification in the trial. The trial judge refused to do so. One of the child witnesses who gave evidence by live TV link named a number of people, including the accused, as having been involved in the incident, although she had not attended an identity parade prior to the trial. The advocate-depute then asked the trial judge to allow her to come to court to determine whether she could identify the persons she had named. Again, the trial judge refused to do so. However, the judge granted the advocate-depute's motion to allow an identification by means of the TV camera. The camera then showed the witness a general view of the court and then panned across the court. The witness was then asked whom she had seen and she named several people, including the appellant. She then separately identified in the dock all the people she had named, including the appellant. The appellant appealed against his conviction, arguing that the identification evidence was incompetent.

LORD JUSTICE-GENERAL (HOPE): "The appellant went to trial at the High Court in Glasgow with five others charged with the murder of William Barclay by striking and stabbing him repeatedly on the head and body with knives and various other instruments. There were a number of other charges on the indictment with which we are not concerned in this appeal. At the end of the trial the appellant and his co-accused Edward Lyon were found guilty of the murder. Two other co-accused were found guilty on reduced charges of assault and the other two, were acquitted.

The appellant has appealed against his conviction on four grounds. The fourth ground in his note of appeal was not argued. The third ground is that the trial judge misdirected the jury on the need for care with regard to identification evidence. The first and second grounds relate to the fact that a number of child witnesses gave evidence by means of a live television link under section 56 of the Law Reform (Miscellaneous Provisions) (Scotland) Act 1990. The second ground is that the trial judge misdirected the jury insofar as he suggested to them that evidence by means of the live television link was obviously of less value than direct evidence. The first ground is that the trial judge erred insofar as he allowed a child named [P.D.] to make a dock identification by means of a television camera. We have stated these grounds of appeal in reverse order—because that was how Mr Taylor presented his argument, and it is convenient to follow that order in this opinion.

The murder took place after dark in the course of a running battle between two groups of youths in Drysdale Street, Blawarthill Street and Dumbarton Road, Glasgow. The deceased and his brothers Mark and Stephen Barclay were returning home from a public house where they had been drinking when they became involved in a confrontation with Lyon and a number of other youths including the appellant. In the ensuing scuffle Stephen Barclay was beaten up in a close by a number of youths and took little further part in the incident. Mark Barclay, who was in the street outside, engaged in a fight with a number of youths who were armed with various weapons. The deceased William Barclay emerged from a crowd, having been hit by an axe. He was dragged away by his brother Mark Barclay and they both ran away in the direction of Dumbarton Road. They were followed into that street by a number of youths carrying various weapons. In the course of the chase in Dumbarton Road William Barclay sustained a single stab wound to the right side of his neck, as a result of which he collapsed and died behind Mark Barclay near a bus shelter.

It was accepted at the trial that the appellant was among the group of youths who were running about in the course of this incident. It was also accepted that the group as a whole, although engaged in a violent disturbance, could not be held responsible for the murder. The jury were told by the trial judge that there was insufficient evidence for them to infer that there was a concerted attack with murderous intent on the deceased by persons armed with weapons other than knives. Mark Barclay was not an eyewitness of his brother's stabbing, as he did not see the fatal blow being delivered. But he was just in front of him, heard a thud and turned round to see his brother collapse on the ground. He saw two youths running away from the place where his brother was lying. Both had knives and both were heading back towards the street from where they had come. He positively identified the appellant and Lyon as the two youths with knives whom he saw leaving the vicinity of the deceased's body. The Crown case against the appellant and Lyon thus depended upon Mark's evidence, corroborated by other witnesses who spoke to what they saw before William Barclay collapsed in Dumbarton Road, by circumstantial evidence including bloodstains on the road and by forensic evidence.

Lyon had lodged a special defence of alibi, but the appellant did not plead alibi. He accepted that he was in Blawarthill Street during the incident, but he denied following the deceased into Dumbarton Road to the place where he was stabbed. This aspect of the case provides the background to the third ground of appeal which relates to the trial judge's directions on the identification evidence. As he pointed out at p.7E . . . identification was right at the centre of the disputed issues of fact in the case.

Mr Taylor submitted that the trial judge failed to give sufficient directions to the jury on the need for care to be taken in their examination of this evidence, which he said was particularly important in the appellant's case. The incident took place at night and it involved a considerable disturbance. Much of the evidence of identification came from children and young persons. We were referred to the Lord Justice-Clerk's observation in *McAvoy v. H.M.A.* [1991 S.C.C.R. 123] at p.131A–B that the trial judge may feel it desirable to remind the jury that errors can arise in identification and that, as there have been cases of mistaken identity, the jury must consider the evidence of identification with some care. Mr Taylor accepted that it was in the discretion of the trial judge what precisely he should say to the jury on this matter and that no fixed formula need be used: *Blair v. H.M.A.* [1993 S.C.C.R. 483] at p.486F; *Chalmers v. H.M.A.* [1994 S.C.C.R. 651] at p.655D–E. But he maintained that what the trial judge said at pp.7–9 of the charge [. . .] was inadequate and that he then gave the jury a misdirection at p.22C when he said, when dealing with the special defence of alibi:

> 'By its very nature alibi puts in issue, even more than it might otherwise be, the identification of an accused at a locus. So you would want to give special consideration to identification for this reason, as well as for the reasons that I have already given to you.'

In our opinion the directions which the trial judge gave on this matter cannot be faulted on the ground that they were inadequate. At pp.7F–8A [. . .] he told the jury that, because of its obvious scope for error, evidence of identification of a person which proceeds not so much on knowing a person as on a witness's impression of that person's appearance requires to be scrutinised with care. He went on to explain the need for that evidence to be corroborated and to explain the approach which the jury should take to identification evidence. This direction was not repeated, but it appears in the context of important directions of a general nature about the approach to be taken to evidence. We consider that enough was said here to alert the jury to the need for care when they came to examine the evidence of identification.

The trial judge returned to the point . . . in the passage which we have quoted when dealing with the special defence of alibi [. . .]. This passage was criticised on the ground that the judge was suggesting here by implication that the need for care in the scrutiny of the identification evidence was of importance where, as in the appellant's case, there was no special defence alibi. It was suggested that there was lack of balance here, which might suggest to the jury that an accused who pled alibi was in a different position and that his special defence of alibi had some special significance in regard to the question of identification. We do not read the passage in this way. The trial judge made it clear that he was dealing here with the particular matters which arise in the special defence of alibi. He was drawing their attention to the points which have to be considered where an accused person claims that at the material time he was at a different place from that where the crime was committed. The emphasis was on the need for proof that he was at the locus, where this put in issue by this special defence. We do not find here, however, any suggestion that the jury's scrutiny of the identification in regard to the accused required to be carried out with less care. For these reasons we do not think that this passage constituted a misdirection.

The second ground of appeal relates to a passage in the charge where the trial judge was dealing with the approach which the jury should take to the evidence which the child witnesses had given by the live television link. Authority had been given for the evidence of [P.D., N.McD. and T.H.] to be given by this means. In the event all three witnesses gave their evidence in this way and it was to the evidence of [T.H.] that Mr Taylor made reference in support of this ground of appeal. This witness spoke to seeing a person putting a knife down a stank in Blawarthill Street in the course of the incident. This knife was recovered by the police and it was found to have bloodstaining on it which could have come from the deceased but not from anyone else who was involved. It was a large, stainless steel Wiltshire Staysharp kitchen knife, similar to two kitchen knives which were found in the appellant's grandparents' house on top of a dresser in a Staysharp container. The container was designed to hold three knives of different sizes and one of the set was missing. There was evidence that, although the knife in the stank was not in all respects identical to the other knives, it could be fitted into this container. [T.H.'s] evidence, however, that the person he saw putting the knife into the stank was not the appellant whom he had previously identified at an identification parade. Mr Taylor said that the evidence of this witness on this point was crucial to the appellant that, although it was given by means of a live television link, it was evidence which the jury were entitled to accept as having the same weight as if it had been given from the witness box.

It was for this reason that Mr Taylor submitted that the trial misdirected the jury when he said at pp.9E–10E:

'Clearly, evidence on a live television link may not be as good—that is for you to decide, you hear it, you see it—may not be as good as evidence given by a witness directly in court before you. Mention has been made about matters such as the demeanour of a witness. It may be quite obvious to you that seeing somebody, a witness, on a television link, that witness equally not being present in court with the rest of us, does diminish the value of any evidence led by that witness and you will take due note of that. The extent of the diminution of value and weight of that evidence is entirely for you to assess . . . So, you having seen it in action with all its faults, and there are many, obviously, and you have to decide—obviously it is of less value than direct evidence—you have to decide whether it is of any value and, if it is of value, what value you can give it. Various detailed criticisms were made in the process of speeches by the various advocates and I won't rehearse them, I will simply leave that general observation with you and you will make of it what you can.'

Mr Taylor said that the will of Parliament as expressed in section 56 of the 1990 Act was to enable a child to give evidence by means of the live television link which was of the same value as if that evidence had been given in the witness box. The jury were entitled to attach the same importance to it as they would have done if the child had been in court when giving the evidence and it was wrong for the judge to suggest otherwise. There was a misdirection here which was prejudicial to the appellant in view of the importance to him of [T.H.'s] evidence.

The trial judge has explained in his report that the quality of the television link evidence in this case was the subject of considerable and continuing criticism by counsel for the appellant and other defence representatives. He says that the problems of the television link communication in this case must have been all too evident to the jury as they were to everyone else involved in the case. His intention in this passage was to draw attention to these problems in relation generally to the witnesses who had been led by means of the television link for the Crown and to the one Crown witness who had been led on the television link for the defence.

In view of the detailed criticisms which had been made of this evidence, it is hard to see how the trial judge can reasonably be criticised for dealing with the matter in this way in his charge. It would no doubt have been better if he had said in terms that the jury were entitled, if they thought fit, to attach the same value to the evidence given by this means as to evidence given in court by the other witnesses. But the effect of his direction was to leave this whole matter to the jury to decide. His comment that this evidence was obviously of less value than direct evidence has to be seen in the context of the direction as a whole and the atmosphere of the trial, bearing in mind the considerable and continuing criticism of the quality of the television link evidence in which the appellant's counsel, among others, participated.

Any risk of prejudice to the appellant in this passage was removed when the trial judge came to deal . . . with the evidence against the appellant. He dealt in particular with the significance which might be attached to [T.H.'s] evidence at pp.44D–45A:

'Again, so far as Brotherston is concerned, there is a knife similar in make to two of a set of three in his grandmother's kitchen. A set of Staysharp knives seems to have been on top of a dresser not hidden. Ladies and gentlemen, there was a knife similar to that found in a stank near to where the murderous chase began. It may be that there is circumstantial evidence pointing to the accused Carry Brotherston. There may be nothing at all, because after all when you got the evidence of [T.H.] about seeing somebody putting, a boy putting something in a stank, or a knife in a stank, he seemed to exclude any of the accused from being present when that happened. So, that may not matter at all, it may have no significance in the case.'

There is no hint here that [T.H.'s] evidence was obviously of less value than the other evidence. We do not think that the jury would be likely to have been misled into thinking that they should be influenced in their approach to this evidence simply because it was given by means of the live television link. For these reasons the appellant's contention that there was a miscarriage of justice on the grounds set out in the second and third grounds of appeal must be rejected.

We turn now to the first ground of appeal, which is that the trial judge erred in allowing [P.D.] to make a dock identification by means of a television camera. The background to this argument is to be found partly in the provisions of the statute and partly in the events at the trial which preceded the giving of this evidence. It is important to note before we examine this background that Mr Taylor's submission was of a general nature directed to the principle of the matter, not to any particular difficulty which had arisen in this case. He submitted that the trial judge had no power to permit the witness to give evidence of identification by this means and that what he did here was not only unfair to the appellant but was also incompetent.

Section 56 of the 1990 Act is in these terms.

'(1) Subject to subsections (2) and (3) below, where a child has been cited to give evidence in a trial, the court may, on an application being made to it, authorise the giving of evidence by the child by means of a live television link.
(2) The court may grant an application under subsection (1) above only on cause shown having regard in particular to—
    (a) the possible effect on the child if required to give evidence, no such application having been granted; and
    (b) whether it is likely that the child would be better able to give evidence if such application were granted.
(3) In considering whether to grant an application under subsection (1) above, the court may take into account, where appropriate, any of the following—
    (a) the age and maturity of the child;
    (b) the nature of the alleged offence;
    (c) the nature of the evidence which the child is likely to be called on to give; and
    (d) the relationship, if any, between the child and the accused.'

There are a number of features in the provisions of this section which may be noted at this stage. First, the court has a discretion as to whether or not to grant the application, in regard to which it may take account of the matters referred to in subsection (3). Second, what the court may authorise the child to do by means of the live television link is to give evidence. What this may involve is not further defined, although one of the factors which the court may take into account under subsection (3) is the nature of the evidence which the child is likely to be called upon to give. Third, what the court is empowered to do is to 'authorise' the giving of evidence by this means. It does not order this to be done, so the fact that authorisation has been given does not make it incompetent for the party who wishes to lead the evidence to dispense with the use of a live television link altogether and bring the child into court to give the evidence. Fourth, the section says nothing about dock identification. It neither prohibits identification by this method if the child is to give evidence by means of a live television link, nor does it make provision as to how this may be done.

The only provision in the group of sections dealing with the giving of evidence by this means which deals with evidence of identification is section 58, which is in these terms.

'Where a court has, or is deemed to have, granted an application made under section 56 of this Act in relation to a child cited to give evidence in a trial, and the child gives evidence that he recalls having identified, prior to the trial, a person alleged to have committed an offence, the evidence of a third party as to the identification of that person by the child prior to the trial shall be admissible as evidence as to such identification.'

This section, which is based upon the principle in *Muldoon v. Herron* [1970 J.C. 30], provides one solution to the problem about identification evidence which arises where a child may find it distressing to give evidence in court and an application under section 56 has been granted. But it does not say that this is the only means by which a child who has been authorised to give evidence by means of a live television link may give evidence of identification. It provides an alternative to dock identification but, like section 56, it does not prohibit identification by this method if the child is to give evidence by this means.

When the advocate-depute reached the stage in the trial when he wished evidence to be given by means of a live television link, he moved the court to adjourn the trial to the sheriff court in Glasgow where this equipment was available. Mr Taylor objected to the adjournment and submitted that the trial judge should reconsider the question whether the child witnesses should give their evidence by this means. He said that it had become clear that identification of the appellant was an issue which would be put to these witnesses and that they should give their evidence in court. The trial judge refused to reconsider the matter and repelled the objection. It has not been suggested that he was wrong to do this and in our opinion it would not have been competent for him to recall the order by which the giving of evidence by this means had been authorised.

[P.O.] was then called upon to give evidence. Unlike [T.H.] she had not viewed an identification parade. She gave evidence that various people whom she named, including Carry Brotherston, were present at the incidents which she described and that Carry Brotherston had had a knife with him which had blood on it. The advocate-depute, in the absence of the jury, then moved the court to allow her to come into court to see whether she could identify the persons whom she had named. When the trial judge expressed the opinion that this would not be competent, as the Crown had elected to take this witness's evidence by means of the television link and not in open court, the advocate-depute suggested that the witness should be shown pictures of the people who were in the courtroom by means of a television camera to enable her to make her identification by this means. These proposals were objected to by Mr Taylor on the appellant's behalf and by counsel for all but one of the appellant's co-accused. After hearing submissions on this matter, the trial judge ruled against bringing the witness into court. The advocate-depute then renewed his motion for the television equipment to be used so that he could ask the witness whether she could identify the people whom she had named by this means. The trial judge reserved his opinion on this matter to allow investigations to be made as to whether this proposal was technically feasible. Having been satisfied on this point when the trial resumed the next day, he allowed the witness to be asked whether she could identify the people she had named by means of the television camera.

The advocate-depute began this chapter of the evidence by reminding the witness that she had named various people the previous day as doing various things. He asked her whether she knew the people that she had named. When she answered this question in the affirmative, he showed her a general view of the court and asked her to tell him if she saw any of the people she had named in the courtroom. As the camera panned across the court, she identified by name all the people she had named in the earlier part of her evidence including the appellant. Mr Taylor gave the following description of what had been done to identify the appellant [in] the transcript of this witness's evidence . . .

'For the purposes of the notes, what happened there was the camera panned from left to right and then stopped so that the third accused was clearly in the sight of the camera. Counsel with his hand to his face then bent his head forward to enable this witness to see the person who was behind the head.'

[P.D.'s] identification of the appellant as being the person whom she had named as Carry Brotherston and as having a knife in his hand with blood on it was not challenged by Mr Taylor in cross-examination. As the trial judge says in his report, and is clear also from a reading of the transcript, the witness appeared to have no difficulty in identifying the appellant and the other persons whom she had named by means of the television camera. There was no indication that she was distressed by giving her identification evidence by this means or that she was affected in any other way by what was done. Mr Taylor did not suggest that the equipment which was used for this purpose was unsatisfactory, nor did he suggest that the way in which it was used was objectionable on any grounds other than that its use was incompetent. He did not suggest that it was used in a way which amounted to leading the witness. We are satisfied that what was done here was as close to an identification given by the witness from the witness box as was practicable. The only difference was that the witness was in another room. She was being shown by means of the live television link the same view of those who were in court as she would have seen if she had been standing in the witness box.

Mr Taylor submitted that, if authority was sought for a child to give evidence by means of a live television link and identification was in issue, the party wishing to lead evidence of the identification must take the step referred to in section 58. He said that it would be open to that person to seek a warrant from the sheriff for the accused to be put on an identification parade to enable this step to be taken, if the child had not previously identified the accused. What sections 56 and 58 did not do was to authorise the child to see a television broadcast of what was in the courtroom. Statutory authority for that would be required and he maintained that section 56 did not enable the court to give that authority. In any event, a camera on a tripod in the witness box was not to be equiparated with the eye of the witness in the witness box and to allow evidence of identification to be given by this means was unfair.

The advocate-depute submitted that the giving of evidence of identification by this means was competent and that there was no unfairness in this case. She pointed out that the witness said that she knew Carry Brotherston and she submitted that it was not unfair for the witness to be asked whether she saw him in court. Nor was it unfair for her to be shown views of the courtroom by means of the television camera. A dock identification by this witness from the witness box would clearly not have been unfair in these circumstances and since there was no technical difficulty in allowing her to view the courtroom by means of the television camera, it was not unfair for her to be asked to give that identification by this means. As for the question of competency she submitted that there was nothing in section 56 or 58 which rendered what was done in this case incompetent. These sections were permissive and enabling in character. They did not prohibit what had been done here and the test as to what should be done was one of fairness in each case according to its own circumstances. She submitted that the same test should be applied in deciding whether or not a child who had given part of the evidence by means of the television link could come into court to provide an identification from the witness box.

In our opinion the procedure which was adopted in this case was competent. As we said earlier in our analysis of the section, section 56 does not define what may be involved in the giving of evidence. What it does is to enable the court to authorise the giving of evidence by a method which allows the child to remain outside the courtroom. That method is described as a live television link. The section assumes that the child will be able to communicate with those in the courtroom by means of television. It assumes that visual images will be transmitted from the courtroom to the child and from the room where the child is to the courtroom. It assumes that the equipment will link both places to each other so that the child can both see and hear the people in the courtroom with whom she is being asked to communicate.

For these reasons it cannot be said that the authority which was given by section 56 does not extend to enabling the child to see a television picture of what is in the courtroom. Mr Taylor submitted that there was no authority for a picture of what was in the courtroom to be broadcast to the child. Broadcasting could of course be inappropriate, but the television link is on the closed-circuit system so that there can be no broadcast. So long as a closed circuit system is being used, the showing of pictures of what is in the courtroom to the child by this means to enable her to give evidence cannot be said to be incompetent, if the giving of evidence by means of a live television link has been authorised. Various situations can be imagined where the child may require to look at objects as well as people when giving evidence. Counsel may require to demonstrate things to the child by reference to productions which they will need to have with them in the courtroom if they are to do this effectively or there may be productions which cannot conveniently be moved from the courtroom to the place where the child is. The giving of evidence by means of the live television link would be greatly inhibited if this were not to be competent and we do not find anything in the section which has this effect. Once the position is accepted that it is competent for the child by means of the television link to be shown things which are in the courtroom, it is a short and inevitable step to accept that the child may be shown views of the courtroom to enable identification evidence to be given by this means. The fact that section 58 provides for one method of giving evidence of identification does not imply that other methods are incompetent.

We were referred to paragraphs 3.7–3.20 of the report of the Scottish Law Commission on the Evidence of Children and Other Potentially Vulnerable Witnesses (Scot. Law Com. No. 125) and to passages in Hansard where the clause to permit the evidence of child witnesses to be given through the live television link was being debated in the House of Commons and in the House of Lords. But we have not found anything there which is of direct assistance to us on this issue. All that can be said is that no mention was made either in the report of the Scottish Law Commission or when the clause was being debated in Parliament of the possibility that a child might be required to provide evidence of identification by means of the live television link. It was, however, appreciated that the expected benefits from the use of the live television link would be reduced if the child witness still had to identify the accused in court in a face-to-face identification. This led to the introduction of what is now section 58 of the 1990 Act. But the purpose of this section was to render admissible another method of identification, not to lay down the only way in which identification evidence could be given by the child witness.

We agree with the advocate-depute that the use of this method for the giving of identification evidence raises questions of fairness, the answer to which will depend on the circumstances. The first consideration must of course be for the child, if the possible effect on the child of giving evidence in court is to justify making an application under section 56. The purpose of the legislation is to minimise distress to the child and a child who is likely to be distressed by being shown pictures of the accused by means of the television link should not be asked to give evidence of identification by this means. Fortunately, that problem did not arise in this case, but if the child had been distressed this would have raised questions about the fairness of the procedure to the accused. One of the purposes of allowing a child who is likely to be distressed by giving evidence in court to give evidence by means of the television link is to assist the child to give evidence. But fairness to the accused requires that this procedure be used fairly and in a way which minimises distress to the child throughout the giving of the evidence. It would be unfair if the cross-examiner were to be at a disadvantage in putting questions to the witness because the child had become distressed by having to identify the accused by means of the live television link while giving evidence. A child whose evidence has been authorised to be given by this means should not be asked to identify by using the television link unless it is clear that this will not cause the child to become distressed. We should add that the granting of authority under section 56 does not make it incompetent for the child to be asked to give evidence in court from the witness box. But once the child has started to give evidence by means of television link, fairness requires that the whole of that evidence should be given by this means. It would not be fair for the child to be asked to give a dock identification from the witness box without being available for examination in court upon that evidence. For the child then to be cross-examined in the courtroom would defeat the purpose for which authority had been given under section 56. In our opinion the trial judge was right not to permit the child to be brought into court to identify the appellant, advocate-depute had decided to use the live television link as the means by which he was to take evidence from the child.

We do not need to consider the advocate-depute's alternative submission in regard to this matter, which was that there was no miscarriage of justice because there was ample evidence from other witnesses to support the appellant's conviction on this charge. In our opinion this ground of appeal fails, because it was not incompetent for the trial judge to allow [P.D.] to make a dock identification by means of a television camera and the procedure which was adopted in this case did not result in any unfairness.

On the whole matter we are satisfied that there was no miscarriage of justice in this case and the appeal against conviction must be refused."

NOTES

On what basis do you think the application for live TV link in this case could have been granted? On the question of identification evidence see the cases in Chapter 5, above.

20.   F. v. Kennedy (No. 2)
1992 S.C.L.R. 750

The facts of this case are set out in Chapter 13, above. A further point on which the appellant attacked the Sheriff's decision was by arguing that the hearsay evidence of the children used at the proof had been obtained by interviewing methods which were in breach of guidelines laid down in the Report on the Cleveland Inquiry [Into Allegations of Child Abuse] by Lord Justice Butler-Sloss (DHSS, 1988).

LORD JUSTICE-CLERK (ROSS): "In addressing this court on question 12, Mr McGhie maintained that the facts spoken to in evidence included no evidence independent of the children. He stressed that these children had been exposed to a long series of interviews designed to lead to disclosures by them. Under reference to the Cleveland Report he maintained that children are susceptible to suggestions made by adults, that they readily respond to cues and that they say what is expected of them. He further submitted that any statements made by children are reinforced by acceptance and repetition, and that it is difficult for children to know what is truth and what is not. At the end of the day his submission was that the sheriff had not been entitled to proceed upon the basis of what the children had said. He reminded the court that the solicitor for the appellant had drawn the attention of the sheriff to these criticisms. He had stressed that the social workers had had little or no experience in the use of anatomically correct dolls, that they had not approached the interviews with an open mind, that they had carried out too many interviews, that there had been no proper recording of interviews, no video recordings had been made of the interviews of J. and W. and any notes of interviews had not been produced. He also drew the sheriff's attention to certain of the criticisms made by Dr Furnell, the child psychologist.

Mr McGhie maintained that the sheriff had missed the point in holding that the children were truthful and reliable. He accepted that the sheriff was entitled to hold that the children were telling the truth as they saw it, but he maintained that they were not reliable. Mr McGhie referred to a number of English cases and under reference to these he submitted that because of the way in which the children had been interviewed in this case, serious doubt must necessarily be thrown upon their reliability, and the sheriff was not entitled to treat them as reliable witnesses.

In my opinion Mr McGhie's submission is not a sound one. His approach appears to me to be misconceived. He seeks to elevate the status of the Cleveland Report to something approaching gospel. The Cleveland Report is an important document and the recommendations which were made in the report no doubt show what good practice is in interviewing children and in the light of present-day views and, unless and until other guidelines for Scotland are devised, the recommendations of the Cleveland Report should in general be followed. In any case, however, it is for the judge who hears the evidence to determine what evidence is truthful and reliable. Where criticisms are made of the way in which children have been interviewed, that is something which the sheriff requires to take into account. But the mere fact that the guidelines in the Cleveland Report have not been followed does not mean that the sheriff is not entitled to accept the evidence of children as reliable. It is significant that in one of the cases to which Mr McGhie referred, namely *Re C and L (Child Abuse: Evidence)* [[1991] F.C.R 361], Hollings J. appears to have held that care orders should be made in respect of five children although there had been many breaches of the guidelines laid down in the Cleveland Report. In that case it was held that there had been serious faults in the way the children had been interviewed, and that in almost every respect the guidelines of the Cleveland Report had not been followed. There had been a failure to approach the interviews with an open mind, leading questions had been asked, there were too many interviews of the children, and there were inadequate video recordings. Despite that, Hollings J. did hold that care orders should be made in respect of some of children.

In the present case it is clear that many of the guidelines laid down in the Cleveland Report had not been followed. This is regrettable but the sheriff was well aware that there had been a failure to observe all these guidelines. The sheriff had the assistance of Dr Furnell, who spent a day in the witness box. He criticised the methods used by the social workers, but the sheriff tells us that his evidence did not vitiate the hearsay evidence obtained at the interviews. Dr Furnell made it clear that he made no personal criticism of the social workers themselves; the most he could say was that they were perhaps rather over-zealous in their anxieties to protect the interests of the children and their lack of experience in the rapidly expanding field of research in child sex abuse had left them somewhat out of their depth. The sheriff tells us that although minor criticisms could be made of the interviewing techniques used in this case and that methods could no doubt be improved and refined in the light of experience, none the less he did not consider such criticism sufficient to invalidate any of the hearsay evidence obtained at the various interviews. It may be that the criticisms made were more than 'minor' but none the less, in my opinion, the sheriff was fully entitled to arrive at the conclusion which he reached. Credibility and reliability were matters for the sheriff. It was for him to consider the weight of the evidence and to ask himself whether the grounds for referral had been established. It appears to me that the sheriff decided that issue in the light of the evidence before him and taking into account all the criticism which had been made on behalf of the appellant. The evidence is not before this court and this court cannot substitute its views on evidence for those of the sheriff.

In all these circumstances I am satisfied that the challenge which Mr McGhie sought to mount against the sheriff's assessment of the witnesses must fail. Having regard to the evidence which was before the sheriff, he was plainly entitled to conclude that the grounds for referral had been established . . . I would move your Lordships to answer question 12, as amended, in the affirmative."

Chapter 15

APPEALS

1. Thomas v. Thomas
1947 S.C. (H.L.) 45

This was an action for divorce brought by a husband on the grounds of his wife's cruelty. The evidence was equivocal, and there were clearly faults on both sides. At all events, the Lord Ordinary assoilzied the defender. The Second Division, differing from the Lord Ordinary on the effect of the evidence and in particular on the credibility of certain witnesses, recalled the Lord Ordinary's interlocutor and granted decree of divorce. The House of Lords restored the interlocutor of the Lord Ordinary, holding that the evidence disclosed no grounds for interfering with his decision.

VISCOUNT SIMON: "Before entering upon an examination of the testimony at the trial, I desire to make some observations as to the circumstances in which an appellate Court may be justified in taking a different view on facts from that of a trial Judge. For convenience, I use English terms, but the same principles apply to appeals in Scotland. Apart from the classes of case in which the powers of the Court of Appeal are limited to deciding a question of law (for example, on a case stated or on an appeal under the County Courts Act) an appellate Court has, of course, jurisdiction to review the record of the evidence in order to determine whether the conclusion originally reached upon that evidence should stand; but this jurisdiction has to be exercised with caution. If there is no evidence to support a particular conclusion (and this is really a question of law), the appellate Court will not hesitate so to decide. But if the evidence as a whole can reasonably be regarded as justifying the conclusion arrived at, at the trial, and especially if that conclusion has been arrived at on conflicting testimony by a tribunal which saw and heard the witnesses, the appellate Court will bear in mind that it has not enjoyed this opportunity and that the view of the trial Judge as to where credibility lies is entitled to great weight. This is not to say that the Judge of the first instance can be treated as infallible in determining which side is telling the truth, or is refraining from exaggeration. Like other tribunals, he may go wrong on a question of fact, but it is a cogent circumstance that a Judge of first instance, when estimating the value of verbal testimony, has the advantage (which is denied to Courts of appeal) of having the witnesses before him and observing the manner in which their evidence is given. What I have just said reproduces in effect the view previously expressed in this House—for example, by Viscount Sankey in *Powell and Wife v. Streatham Manor Nursing Home* (1935 A.C. 243 at p.50), and in earlier cases there quoted. Lord Greene, MR, admirably states the limitations to be observed in the course of his judgement in *Yuill v. Yuill* (1945 P. 15 at p.19). Lord President Clyde, in *Dunn v. Dunn's Trustees* (1930 S.C. 131), summarised the scope of the appellate correction, with copious citation of earlier authority, and I agree with him that the true role is that expounded by Lord President Inglis in *Kinnell v. Peebles* (1890 17 R. 416), that a Court of Appeal should 'attach the greatest weight to the opinion of the Judge who saw the witnesses and heard their evidence and consequently should not disturb a judgement of fact unless they are satisfied that it is unsound.

It not infrequently happens that a preference for A's evidence over the contrasted evidence of B is due to inferences from other conclusions reached in the Judge's mind, rather than from an unfavourable view of B's veracity as such; in such cases it is legitimate for an appellate tribunal to examine the grounds of these other conclusions and the inferences drawn from them, if the materials admit of this; and if the appellate tribunal is convinced that these inferences are erroneous, and that the rejection of B's evidence was due to the error, it will be justified in taking a different view of the value of B's evidence. I would only add that the decision of an appellate Court whether or not to reverse conclusions of fact reached by the Judge at the trial must naturally be affected by the nature and circumstances of the case under consideration. What I have said applies to appeals from a Judge sitting alone. Conclusions of fact embodied in the verdict of a jury cannot be subjected to the same degree of re-examination—for the course of reasoning by which the verdict has been reached is not disclosed—and consequently the verdict of a jury on fact must stand if there was any evidence to support it and if the conclusion is one at which a reasonable jury when properly directed might reasonably arrive."

LORD THANKERTON: "(1) Where a question of fact has been tried by a Judge without a jury, and there is no question of misdirection of himself by the Judge, an appellate Court which is disposed to come to a different conclusion on the printed evidence should not do so unless it is satisfied that any advantage enjoyed by the trial Judge by reason of having seen and heard the witnesses could not be sufficient to explain or justify the trial Judge's conclusion. (2) The appellate Court may take the view that, without having seen or heard the witnesses, it is not in a position to come to any satisfactory conclusion on the printed evidence. (3) The appellate Court, either because the reasons given by the trial Judge are not satisfactory, or because it unmistakably so appears from the evidence, may be satisfied that he has not taken proper advantage of his having seen and heard the witnesses, and the matter will then become at large for the appellate Court. It is obvious that the value and importance of having seen and heard the witnesses will vary according to the class of case, and, it may be, the individual case in question."

NOTES

See also *Clarke v. Edinburgh and District Tramways Co.*, 1919 S.C. (HL), pp.36–37; 1919 1 S.L.T., p.248. This case is accepted as providing an authoritative statement of the law relating to appeals. In *Macintosh v. N.C.B.*, 1988 S.L.T. 348, Lord Justice-Clerk Ross said, under reference to *Dunn v. Dunn's Trustees*, 1930 S.C. 131 and *Thomas v. Thomas*, above, that:

"It is well settled that a court of appeal may reverse a decision on fact by a judge of first instance if the judge has misapprehended the meaning of the evidence or if it is clear that the evidence of a witness who has been accepted is clearly unreliable because it is inconsistent with itself or with other evidence."

See also *Zenel v. Haddow*, 1993 S.L.T. 975. The abolition of the requirement for corroboration in civil cases (Civil Evidence (Scotland) Act 1988, s.1) does not affect the right and duty of an appellate court to examine, and if necessary to reverse, a trial judge's view of the facts—*Morrison v. J. Kelly and Sons*, 1970 S.C. 65. Compare Lord Stott's view in *McLaren v. Caldwell's Paper Mill*, 1973 S.L.T. 158, above, Chapter 13. In the latter case Lord Stott said:

"An appellate court, either because the reasons given by the trial judge are not satisfactory or because it is satisfied that he has not taken proper advantage of his having seen and heard the witnesses, is entitled to substitute its own view for his: *Thomas v. Thomas*, 1947 S.C. (H.L.) 45; 1948 S.L.T. 2, per Lord Thankerton at pp.5–6. But that jurisdiction has to be exercised within narrow limits. In the words of Lord Greene, M.R. in *Yuill v. Yuill* (approved by the House of Lords in Thomas): 'It can, of course, only be on the rarest occasions, and in circumstances where the appellate court is convinced by the plainest considerations, that it would be justified in finding that the trial judge had formed a wrong opinion'. In the present case counsel for the reclaimers has made certain criticisms of the pursuer's evidence some of which have been dealt with by the Lord Ordinary and some of which have not, but, in my opinion, anything that has been said in that regard falls far short of what has hitherto been required to enable an appellate court after making allowance for possible exaggeration to say that the Lord Ordinary's judgment of credibility was wrong.

But that, it was submitted, is not the proper approach when corroboration is no longer needed and the judge of first instance has decided an issue on the evidence of a single witness. In such a case, it was said, the appellate court must have a wider latitude to interfere. It is not clear why that should be so. It is plain from the terms of section 9 that 'the court' who have to be satisfied that a fact has been established by the evidence of a single witness must be, in the first instance at least, the judge who hears the proof, or if the action is tried by a jury, the jury. That being so one might perhaps be inclined to think that, since so much may turn on the evidence of one witness, the impression formed by the judge who saw and heard him in the witness box becomes more rather than less important. But that view of the effect of the section will not stand with the decision of the other division of this court in *Morrison v. J. Kelly & Sons*, 1970 S.L.T. 198, where it was held that section 9(2) did not alter or lessen the power of a court of appeal to review in appropriate cases the decision on an issue of fact of judge of first instance or the necessity for that judge to state adequate and sufficient reasons for his acceptance or rejection of evidence."

Before an appellate court can review the decision of the court of first instance on the facts, there must have been a patent error in the assessment of the evidence. The task of the appellate court is easier where the dispute concerns the proper inferences to be drawn from the facts found, rather than about the particular facts which were found. The latter question may depend heavily on the impression made by the witnesses, whom, of course, the appellate court do not hear or see. In *Montgomerie & Co v. Wallace-James*, (1903) 6 F. (H.L.) 10, Lord Halsbury, L.C. said that:

"Where no question arises as to truthfulness, and where the question is as to the proper inferences to be drawn from truthful evidence, then the original tribunal is in no better position to decide than the judges of an appellate court."

2. Edwards v. Bairstow
[1956] A.C. 14

The two respondents bought a spinning plant and, without using it themselves, sold it on for profit. The Inspector of Taxes wished to tax the respondents on this transaction under Schedule D of the Incomes Taxes legislation then in force as an adventure in nature of trade. The General Commissioners, however, would not so classify it and the Inspector appealed. It was argued for the respondents that the finding of the Commissioners was one of fact and one which could not therefore be disturbed on appeal. A number of Scottish cases were cited in support of this argument.

VISCOUNT SIMONDS: "I must turn now to the question of the apparent divergence between the English and Scottish Courts and venture to approach it by a brief consideration of the nature of a problem which has many aspects, *e.g.* the finding of a jury, the award of an arbitrator, or the determination of a tribunal which is by statute made the judge of fact. And the present case affords an exact illustration of the considerations which I would place before your Lordships.

When the commissioners, having found the so-called primary facts which are stated in paragraph 3 of their case, proceed to their finding in the supplemental case that 'the transaction, the subject matter of this case, was not an adventure in the nature of trade', this is a finding which is in truth no more than an inference from the facts previously found. It could aptly be preceded by the word 'therefore'. Is it, then, an inference of fact? My Lords, it appears to me that the authority is overwhelming for saying that it is. Such cases as *Cooper v. Stubbs* (1925 2 K.B. 753), *Jones v. Leeming* (1930 A.C. 415) and *Inland Revenue Commissioners v. Lysaght* (1928 A.C. 234; 44 T.L.R. 374) (a case of residence) amongst many others are decisive. Yet it must be clear that to say that such an inference is one of fact postulates that the character of that which is inferred is a matter of fact. To say that a transaction is or is not an adventure in the nature of trade is to say that it has or has not the characteristics which distinguish such an adventure. But it is a question of law, not of fact, what are those characteristics, or, in other words, what the statutory language means. It follows that the inference can only be regarded as an inference of fact if it is assumed that the tribunal which makes it is rightly directed in law what the characteristics are and that, I think, is the assumption that is made. It is a question of law what is murder: a jury finding as a fact that murder has been committed has been directed on the law and acts under that direction. The commissioners making an inference of fact that a transaction is or is not an adventure in the nature of trade are assumed to be similarly directed, and their finding thus becomes an inference of fact.

If that is, as I hope it is, a just analysis of the position, the somewhat different approach to the question in some, but by no means all, of the Scottish cases is easily explicable. For as the Lord President (Lord Normand) put it in *Inland Revenue Commissioners v. Fraser* (1942 S.C. 493, 501; 24 TC 498, 504): " . . . the commissioners here have either misunderstood the statutory language (which I think is the probable explanation of their error) or, having understood it, have made a perverse finding without evidence to support it.' He might equally well have said that the assumption that they were rightly directed in law was displaced by a finding which was upon that assumption inexplicable. The misdirection may appear upon the face of the determination. It did so here, I think, in the case as originally stated: for in effect that determination was that the transaction was not an adventure in the nature of trade because it was an isolated transaction, which was clearly wrong in law. But sometimes, as in the case as it now comes before the court, where all the admitted or found facts point one way and the inference is the other way, it can only be a matter of conjecture why that inference has been made. In such a case it is easy either to say that the commissioners have made a wrong inference of fact because they have misdirected themselves in law or to take a short cut and [say] that they have made a wrong inference of law, and I venture to doubt whether there is more than this in the divergence between the two jurisdictions which has so much agitated the revenue authorities.

But, my Lords, having said so much, I think it right to add that in my opinion, if and so far as there is any divergence between the English and Scottish approach, it is the former which is supported by the previous authority of this House to which reference has been made. It is true that the decision of the commissioners is only impeachable if it is erroneous in law, and it may appear paradoxical to say that it may be erroneous in law where no question of law appears on the face of the case stated. But it cannot be, and has not been, questioned, that an inference, though regarded as a mere inference of fact, yet can be challenged as a matter of law on the grounds that I have already mentioned, and this is I think the safest way to leave it."

NOTES

The distinction between questions of fact and questions of law is of importance because of the number of statutory provisions which render an appeal competent only where the appeal is on a point of law. Appeals from Sheriff Court summary cause and small claims cases are in this category, for example— see Sheriff Courts (Scotland) Act 1971, s.38; as are prosecution appeals in summary criminal proceedings—Criminal Procedure (Scotland) Act 1995, s.175(3), and appeals from a determination of an Industrial Tribunal—Employment Protection (Consolidation) Act 1978, s.136. As *Edwards v. Bairstow* makes clear, however, the distinction is not so sharp as it might at first appear. In certain circumstances, a mistaken inference of fact may amount to an error of law.

3. Melon v. Hector Powe Ltd
1980 S.C. 188

In this case, a manufacturing company assigned the lease of its factory to another firm, and dismissed its entire workforce. On the same day as the dismissal, however, the employees were all re-employed by the successor company on terms no less favourable than before. Certain employees applied for a redundancy payment on the grounds that they had been dismissed by reason of redundancy, and an Industrial Tribunal found in their favour. The company appealed against this decision.

LORD PRESIDENT (EMSLIE): "It hardly requires to be mentioned that an appeal lies from a decision of the industrial tribunal to the Employment Appeal Tribunal, and from a decision of that Tribunal, to this Court, only upon a question of law. This being so I am happy to say that the parties are not in dispute as to the extent to which the appellate tribunal, or this Court, is entitled to interfere with a decision of first instance, and to substitute their own decision for that arrived at by the industrial tribunal. The law is clear that where it cannot be shown that the tribunal of original jurisdiction has either misdirected itself in law, entertained the wrong issue, or proceeded upon a misapprehension or misconstruction of the evidence, or taken into account matters which were irrelevant to its decision, or has reached a decision so extravagant that no reasonable tribunal properly directing itself on the law could have arrived at, then its decision is not open to successful attack. It is of no consequence that the appellate tribunal or court would itself have reached a different conclusion on the evidence. If there is evidence to support the decision of the tribunal of first instance then in the absence of misdirection in law—which includes the tribunal's selection of the wrong question to answer—that is an end of the matter."

NOTES

See also *Saltire Press Ltd v. Boyd*, 1999 S.L.T. 438, another employment case, in which it was said that:

> "... there was no dispute that the approach which an appeal court must apply was to be found conveniently set out in the opinion of Stephenson L.J. in *Nethermere (St Neots) Ltd v. Gardiner* [1984] ICR at p 621G: 'This court has therefore to do what the appeal tribunal should have done: apply *Edwards v. Bairstow* as this court applied it, for instance, in *Coates v. Modern Methods & Materials Ltd* [1982] I.C.R. 763 and the House of Lords applied it in *Melon v. Hector Powe Ltd* [1981] I.C.R. 43, and to decide whether the industrial tribunal misdirected itself in law or reached a decision which was unreasonable to the point of perversity. We must not ourselves decide what is the right inference to draw from the facts as found so as to determine the true nature of the arrangement because we may be in that 'grey area', as Fox L.J. called it in *O'Kelly v. Trusthouse Forte Plc.* [1983] I.C.R. 728, 758H, where it may be a contract of service or a contract for services and either the majority opinion or the minority opinion of it may come 'within the band of possible reasonable decisions' which excludes a court from judging whether they are right or mistaken: see the observations of Lord Hailsham of St. Marylebone L.C. in *In re W. (An Infant)* [1971] A.C. 682, 700D.' "

The distinction between questions of law and those of fact is not an easy one to draw. Many questions which have to be resolved by the courts involve a mixture of law and fact. Such questions have sometimes been called questions of degree, and are regarded essentially as questions of fact for the tribunal of first instance to decide in all the circumstances of the case. See Wilson, "A Note on Fact and Law" (1963) 26 M.L.R. 609, and "Questions of Degree" (1969) 32 M.L.R. 361.

4. O'Kelly v. Trust House Forte
[1984] Q.B. 90

This case concerned the dismissal of a number of people who worked for Trust House Forte (T.H.F.) as "regulars". They were people who worked regularly—in some cases to the exclusion of all other work—for the company at banquets and other functions, but who had no formal contract of employment with T.H.F. They applied to an Industrial Tribunal for a ruling that they had been unfairly dismissed. A preliminary question arose as to whether the applicants were employees or independent contractors for the purposes of the Employment Protection (Consolidation) Act 1978.

LORD-JUSTICE FOX: "The preliminary issue with which we are concerned is whether the applicants were 'employees' under a 'contract of employment' within section 153(1) of the Employment Protection (Consolidation) Act 1978 or whether they were independent contractors working under a contract for service.

Under section 136(1) of the Act an appeal lies to the appeal tribunal 'on a question of law' arising from a decision of the industrial tribunal. The first question which we have to determine is the extent of the jurisdiction of the appeal tribunal to interfere with the decision of the industrial tribunal. It is said, by the applicants, that the question whether a contract is a contract of service or a contract for services is a question of law; that section 136(1) permits an appeal on a question of law; and that accordingly the appeal tribunal were free to make up their own minds on that question of law upon the basis of the facts found by the industrial tribunal.

I accept that the question whether a contract is a contract of service can, in a general sense, be called one of law. But I doubt if that is useful in relation to the present problem. It gives too general an answer to a more complex matter. Thus it is evident from the authorities that a question can, in a general sense, be characterised as one of law without excluding the possibility that, in the end, it resolves itself into a question of fact in individual cases. In *Currie v. Inland Revenue Commissioners* [1921 2 K.B. 332], the question was whether a person was carrying on a 'profession' within the meaning of exception (c) of section 39 of the Finance (No. 2) Act 1915. Lord Sterndale MR said, at pp.335–336:

> 'Is the question whether a man is carrying on a profession or not a matter of law or a matter of fact? I do not know that it is possible to give a positive answer to that question; it must depend upon the circumstances with which the court is dealing. There may be circumstances in which nobody could arrive at any other conclusion than that what the man was doing was carrying on a profession; and therefore, looking at the matter from the point of view of a judge directing a jury, the judge would be bound to direct them that on the facts they could only find that he was carrying on a profession.
>
> That reduces it to a question of law. On the other hand, there may be facts on which the direction would have to be given the other way. But between those two extremes there is a very large tract of country in which the matter becomes a question of degree; and where that is the case the question is undoubtedly, in my opinion, one of fact; . . .'

In *Edwards v. Bairstow* [1956] A.C. 14 the question was whether a transaction was 'an adventure or concern in the nature of trade' and so taxable under Case 1 of Schedule D of the Income Tax Act 1918. Lord Radcliffe said that was a question of law (at p.33). But he also said that the law provided no precise definition of the word 'trade' and that there were many combinations of circumstances in which it could not be said to be wrong to arrive at a conclusion one way or the other. All such cases could be described 'as questions of degree and, therefore, as questions of fact.'

Simmons v. Heath Laundry Co [1910] 1 K.B. 543 is a much earlier example of the principle stated in *Currie v. Inland Revenue Commissioners* [1921] 2 K.B. 332 and *Edwards v. Bairstow* [1956] A.C. 14. The case turned on the meaning of the term 'contract of service' in the Workmen's Compensation Act 1906; the problem related to part-time earnings of the applicant from giving piano lessons and giving accompaniments on the piano. The arbitrator decided that the earnings did not arise under contracts of service. That was held to be a question of fact for the arbitrator, and accordingly the Court of Appeal refused to interfere. Fletcher Moulton L.J. said, at p.549:

> 'Some cases present no difficulty. For example, where the proprietor of a private boarding school engages ushers to teach the boys and to maintain discipline, it does not, in my opinion, admit of reasonable doubt that the contracts into which those ushers enter are "contracts of service" within the Act. On the other hand it is in my mind equally clear that where a person goes to a music or singing master to take lessons it would be absurd to hold that the person giving the lessons is the servant of the person taking them in any sense of the word. The contract between them is a contract for services, but it is not a contract of service. Between these two extreme cases lie an infinite number of intermediate cases where the special circumstances point with greater or less force towards the one conclusion or the other, and in my opinion it is impossible to lay down any rule of law distinguishing the one from the other. It is a question of fact to be decided by all the circumstances of the case.'

Woods v. W. M. Car Services (Peterborough) Ltd [1982] I.C.R. 693, which was concerned with the question whether the employer had repudiated the contract of service, seems to me to follow the same principles as those stated by Lord Sterndale, M.R., Fletcher Moulton L.J. and Lord Radcliffe.

Lord Denning, M.R. said in *Woods v. W. M. Car Services (Peterborough) Ltd* [1982] I.C.R. 693, 698:

'In each case, it depends on whether the misconduct amounted to a repudiatory breach
. . . The circumstances are so infinitely various there can be, and is, no rule of law saying
what circumstances justify and what do not. It is a question of fact for the tribunal of
fact—in this case the industrial tribunal.'

Now what is said on behalf of the applicants in the present case is this. It is accepted that in
Woods v. W. M. Car Services (Peterborough) Ltd, for example, the nature of the issue before the
court was such that there was a grey area, or a band of uncertainty, where one could not say
that it would be wrong for the tribunal to decide the case one way or the other. The confines of
the law were imprecise and, within the grey area, it was a matter of degree in individual cases
whether the case was within the statutory provision or not. That, however, is not, so it is said,
the position here. There can only be one correct answer to the question whether a contract of
service exists. Reliance is placed upon the decision of this court in *Young & Woods Ltd v. West*
[1980] I.R.L.R. 201 and, in particular, the observations of Stephenson L.J. at p.205.

I do not feel able to accept that argument. The issue seems to me to be no more susceptible
of the analysis that there is a right and a wrong answer to be determined as a matter of pure
law than was the issue in the *Heath Laundry* case [1910] 1 K.B. 543 or *Currie v. Inland Revenue
Commissioners* [1921] 2 K.B. 332 or *Woods v. W M Car Services (Peterborough) Ltd* [1982]
I.C.R. 693. The precise quality to be attributed to various individual facts is so much a matter
of degree that it is unrealistic to regard the issue as attracting a clear 'legal' answer.

I do not think that the *Heath Laundry* case [1910] 1 K.B. 543 was wrongly decided. It seems
to me to be consistent with the principles applied by the Court of Appeal in *Currie v. Inland
Revenue Commissioners* [1921] 2 K.B. 332 and in the House of Lords in *Edwards v. Bairstow*
[1956] A.C. 14, and if there be any conflict between it and *Young & Woods v. West* [1980]
I.R.L.R. 201 (in which, in fact, the Court of Appeal was of the opinion that the decision of the
industrial tribunal was right and did not have to interfere with it), I would follow the *Heath
Laundry* case.

I should add that I do not detect in the more recent authorities any tendency to depart from
the *Edwards v. Bairstow* [1956] A.C. 14 principles. In *Melon v. Hector Powe Ltd* [1981] I.C.R. 43
they were applied by the House of Lords in an appeal from an industrial tribunal under the
Redundancy Payments Act 1965: see the speech of Lord Fraser of Tullybelton at p.48. And in
Pioneer Shipping Ltd v. BTP Tioxide Ltd [1982] A.C. 724, 752, Lord Roskill said that in
Edwards v. Bairstow the House of Lords made it clear that the court should only interfere with
the conclusion of special commissioners if it were shown either that they had erred in law or
had reached a conclusion which no reasonable tribunal, properly instructed, could have
reached. And he went on to deprecate the suggestion that since the question whether a
contract was frustrated was one of law the court was free to decide the matter itself and
contrary to the decision of the arbitrators.

In the present case the industrial tribunal in their full and careful reasons list nine
circumstances which are consistent with the existence of a contract of employment, four which
are not inconsistent with it and five of which are inconsistent with it. It seems to me that the
case was indeed one where the answer, in the end, was a matter of degree and, therefore, of
fact. For example, there may, I think, be a narrow line between the conclusion that the
company were undertaking to offer work to the regular casuals in return for the regular casuals
undertaking to accept the work which was offered (*i.e.* a contract of employment) and the
conclusion that there was no contract to employ and that the arrangement was simply the
consequence of market forces (in effect, the dominant economic position of the company). It
was essentially a matter of fact for the individual tribunal to decide which was correct after
considering the evidence."

5. Criminal Procedure (Scotland) Act 1995

"106.—(1) Any person convicted on indictment may, with leave granted in accordance with
section 107 of this Act, appeal in accordance with this Part of this Act, to the High Court—

(a) against such conviction;

(b) subject to subsection (2) below against the sentence passed on such conviction;

(c) against his absolute discharge or admonition;

(d) against any probation order or any community service order;

(e) against any order deferring sentence;

(f) against both such conviction and, subject to subsection (2) below, such sentence or disposal or order.

(2) There shall be no appeal against any sentence fixed by law.

(3) By an appeal under subsection (1) above a person may bring under review of the High Court any alleged miscarriage of justice, which may include such a miscarriage based on—

(a) subject to subsections (3A) to (3D) below, the existence and significance of evidence which was not heard at the original proceedings; and

(b) the jury's having returned a verdict which no reasonable jury, properly directed, could have returned.

(3A) Evidence such as is mentioned in subsection (3)(a) above may found an appeal only where there is a reasonable explanation of why it was not so heard.

(3B) Where the explanation referred to in subsection (3A) above or, as the case may be, (3C) below is that the evidence was not admissible at the time of the original proceedings, but is admissible at the time of the appeal, the court may admit that evidence if it appears to the court that it would be in the interests of justice to do so.

(3C) Without prejudice to subsection (3A) above, where evidence such as is mentioned in paragraph (a) of subsection (3) above is evidence—

(a) which is—

(i) from a person; or

(ii) of a statement (within the meaning of section 259(1) of this Act) by a person, who gave evidence at the original proceedings; and

(b) which is different from, or additional to, the evidence so given,

it may not found an appeal unless there is a reasonable explanation as to why the evidence now sought to be adduced was not given by that person at those proceedings, which explanation is itself supported by independent evidence.

(3D) For the purposes of subsection (3C) above, "independent evidence" means evidence which—

(a) was not heard at the original proceedings;

(b) is from a source independent of the person referred to in subsection (3C) above; and

(c) is accepted by the court as being credible and reliable."

NOTES

The present section 106 was revised and substituted by section 26 of the Crime and Punishment (Scotland) Act 1997. Its provisions relating to appeals based on fresh evidence closely follow the test laid down by Lord Justice General Hope in *Church v. H.M.A.*, 1995 S.L.T. 604. That test was controversial, and departed significantly from the previous understanding of the law. *Church* was consequently overruled by a bench of five judges presided over by Lord Justice Clerk Ross a week later in *Elliot v. H.M.A.*, 1995 S.L.T. 612. Section 26 overrules *Elliot* and restores the *Church* test, albeit considerably hedged with qualifications and safeguards.

For comment on this odd episode, see Ferguson, "Fresh Evidence Appeals" (1995) 40 J.L.S.S. 264; Scott, *Criminal Appeals and Additional Evidence—A Missed Opportunity;* Sheldon, "Additional Evidence and the Ancient Regime", 1995 S.L.T. (News) 189; 1995 J.R. 539. Under the old test, additional evidence could be considered only where it was "not available and could not reasonably have been made available at the trial". The new test, contained in section 106(3A) above, is on one view less stringent than the old. However, where an appeal is based upon the evidence of a person who gave evidence at the original trial—as is frequently the case—and that person comes forward with a different version of events, then the test is heavily qualified. There must be a reasonable explanation for the failure to give the new version at the trial, and the new version must itself be supported by independent evidence. One of the first cases to come before the court under these new provisions was *Campbell v. H.M.A.*, 1998 S.L.T. 923. This was one of several appeals brought by Messrs Campbell and Steele in the infamous "ice-cream wars" case.

6. Campbell v. H.M.A.
1998 S.L.T. 923

Two accused persons, C and S, were found guilty in 1984 of the murder of six people by setting fire to their flat. The Crown relied partly on the evidence of an accomplice, L, who gave evidence that he had heard a conversation among various people including C and S in which C spoke with another man about setting fire to the deceased's flat door. S was listening to the conversation and agreeing with what was said. C was also convicted of assault by shooting at an ice cream van. The Crown case was that he had instigated the attack but had not been present when it was carried out. The Crown relied on evidence from L that he had driven C's car to the locus of the shooting and afterwards had been thanked by C for his involvement in the attack, as corroboration of C's admission to the police that he had been involved in the crime. Appeals on the ground of insufficiency of evidence were refused in 1985. In 1996 the Secretary of State, under section 124(3), referred C and S's case to the High Court and they lodged grounds of appeal, arguing *inter alia* that (1) there was new evidence from L that showed that he had lied at the trial as a result of police pressure and inducements, (2) there was new evidence from L's sister, who had been cited at the original trial by S and two other accused but never called, to the effect that L had been guilty of committing the shooting himself but had been released by the police and never prosecuted for the shooting, and (3) there was insufficient evidence for conviction. The Crown argued that the third ground was incompetent as it had been determined by the High Court in the appeal in 1985.

THE LORD JUSTICE CLERK (CULLEN): "Both appellants seek to adduce evidence for the purposes of their appeals which was not heard at the original trial. Before turning to the proposed evidence it is necessary for me to consider the statutory provisions in the light of which it requires to be considered. Section 17(1) of the Crime and Punishment (Scotland) Act 1997 provides that in section 106 of the 1995 Act, which deals with the right of appeal in solemn proceedings, the following should be substituted for subs. (3): [his Lordship quoted the terms of section 106 set out *supra* and continued:]

The main features of the substitution effected by section 17 can be summarised as follows.

First, subs. (3) retains 'any alleged miscarriage of justice' as a general ground on which an appellant may exercise his right of appeal. This was introduced originally by the Criminal Justice (Scotland) Act 1980 in substitution for section 228(2) of the Criminal Procedure (Scotland) Act 1975. Prior to that the legislation had taken the form of setting out a number of grounds on which the verdict of the jury could be set aside, one of which was that 'on any ground there was a miscarriage of justice'. However, unlike the subsection which it supersedes, the new subs. (3) does not include the words 'in the proceedings in which he was convicted' which had formed part of the language introduced by the 1980 Act. It may be noted that these words were commented on by Lord McCluskey in *Elliott v. H.M.A.* at 1995 J.C., pp.113–114; 1995 S.L.T., p.623. The Sutherland committee, "Report of the Committee on Appeals Criteria and Alleged Miscarriages of Justice", Cm 3245 (1996) recommended removal of these words on the ground that they were unduly restrictive and unrealistic (para. 2.30).

Secondly, the new para. (a) of subs. (3) replaces the single specific instance of an alleged miscarriage of justice which had been attached by the 1980 Act to the general ground of appeal, namely 'including any alleged miscarriage of justice on the basis of the existence and significance of additional evidence which was not heard at the trial and which was not available and could not reasonably have been made available at the trial'.

These words were regarded by the Sutherland committee as unduly restrictive in the light of a number of decisions relating to the meaning of 'additional evidence' (*McCormack v. H.M.A.*; *Mitchell v. H.M.A.* and *Maitland v. H.M.A.*, and the interpretation of 'not available and could not reasonably have been made available at the trial' (*Salusbury-Hughes v. H.M.A.* and *Elliott v. H.M.A.*) (see paras 2.35–2.53).

The terms of the new subs. (3)(a) are expressly subject to subs. (3A)–(3D) which set out a number of entirely new conditions which are intended to regulate what new evidence may or may not found an appeal.

From the time when appeal against conviction in solemn proceedings was introduced by the 1926 Act provision was made for the hearing of new evidence in connection with such appeals. Section 6 of the 1926 Act enabled the court to exercise various powers 'if they think it necessary or expedient in the interest of justice'. These included, under para. (b) of that section, the power to order the taking of evidence of witnesses, whether or not they had been called at the trial. This power was considered by the court in a number of cases including *Gallacher v. H.M.A.*, to which I will refer later in this opinion. Similar provision was made by section 252(b) of the 1975 Act. The 1980 Act replaced this with a power to hear or order the hearing of 'any additional evidence relevant to any alleged miscarriage of justice', which plainly referred to the specific ground in section 228(2) of the 1975 Act, as amended, on which an appellant could exercise his right of appeal. Similar provision was made by section 104(1)(b) of the 1995 Act, from which the 1997 Act has now removed the word 'additional'.

Thirdly, subs. (3)(b) introduces a second specific instance of a miscarriage of justice, in accordance with the recommendation made by the Sutherland committee (paras 2.59–2.71). It may be noted that one of the grounds on which the verdict of the jury could be set aside under section 2(1) of the 1926 Act was that 'the verdict was unreasonable'. It was also an express ground of appeal under the 1975 Act, but it was removed by the 1980 Act, when the general right of appeal in respect of an alleged miscarriage of justice was introduced.

During the course of his submissions counsel for *Campbell* submitted that subs. (3)(b) was of assistance when considering the effect of evidence which was not heard at the trial but is now sought to be adduced. It is plain that this ground of appeal is concerned with the evidence which the jury heard at the trial. In *Gallacher* the Lord Justice Clerk (Thomson) said at 1951 J.C., p.46; 1951 S.L.T., p.161, when referring to the ground that 'the verdict was unreasonable': 'We can likewise leave out of consideration the question whether the verdict of the jury should be set aside on the ground that it is unreasonable. The only way in which we can in any practical or effective way approach that problem is on the basis of the evidence actually before the jury. A verdict is reasonable or unreasonable only on the basis of the evidence on which the verdict was reached.' Counsel went on to suggest that, while subs. (3)(b) did not directly apply, it was nonetheless of assistance in determining whether a miscarriage of justice had occurred. However, this cannot mean that it is possible for an appellant whose appeal relies upon evidence which was not heard at the trial to avoid the necessity of satisfying the various conditions laid down under subs. (3A)—(3D), and base his case on the simple proposition that on the hypothesis that had this evidence been heard by the jury, their verdict would have been unreasonable. I find no warrant for that approach, and accordingly I do not consider that the ground set out in subs. (3)(b) is of relevance in the present case.

The Evidence of Mrs Agnes Carlton:

Both appellants seek to rely on the evidence of Mrs Carlton, who is a sister of William McDonald Love and who did not give evidence at the trial.

Where an appellant relies for the purposes of his appeal upon the existence and significance of evidence which was not heard at the trial, subs. (3A) provides that such evidence 'may found an appeal only where there is a reasonable explanation of why it was not so heard'. Subsection (3B) makes special provision in regard to the question of admissibility, but this is of no relevance to the present case and accordingly I do not require to give it further consideration.

In approaching the meaning of 'a reasonable explanation' it is of some assistance to examine the background to the introduction of this expression.

This test was introduced on the recommendation of the Sutherland committee, who noted that it reflected the views of the Thomson committee in their first report (Criminal Appeals in Scotland, Cmnd 5038 (1972)) and the terminology used in England in section 23 of the Criminal Appeal Act 1968, as amended by section 4 of the Criminal Appeal Act 1995 (para. 2.44).

The Sutherland committee stated that they believed that this test would bring about a significant change in the way in which the appeal court would have to consider appeals on the basis of fresh evidence. It appeared to be less stringent than the current wording but still provide the necessary degree of control by the court to avoid allowing too many unmeritorious appeals to be brought forward (para. 2.50). They observed: 'In relation to any appeal brought forward on the basis of fresh evidence the dominating consideration for the appeal court, if our recommendations are adopted, would be that there should be a reasonable explanation for the failure to adduce the evidence and we would not wish to try to circumscribe what might be a reasonable explanation in any particular circumstances. We believe that is a matter for the court to decide' (para. 2.52).

In that connection I note that they considered that the words of the Lord Justice Clerk (Thomson) in *Gallacher* at p.45 (pp. 160–161) would continue to be of relevance (para. 2.51). The words to which they referred were as follows: 'We might observe, however, that the first question which the Court is bound to ask of any appellant who tenders fresh evidence is why it was not tendered at the trial. We do not propose to canvass the issue of what might or might not be an adequate explanation. No general rule can possibly be laid down and the explanation in any particular case must be viewed, not in the light of any technicality or rule of practice or of procedure, but solely in the light of the dominating consideration that we may order new evidence if we think it necessary or expedient in the interests of justice.'

It is clear that in using the words 'necessary or expedient in the interests of justice' the Lord Justice Clerk was referring directly to the terms of section 6 of the 1926 Act. Similar wording does not appear in subs. (3A), but I consider that in determining whether its terms have been satisfied the court should have regard to the interests of justice according to the circumstances of the particular case.

Subsection (3A) applies whether or not the evidence which was not heard at the trial is from a person who gave evidence at that time. In the case of a witness who did not give evidence at the trial the question is, in effect, whether there is a reasonable explanation of why that witness was not adduced at that time. It is also plain from the language, and in particular the words 'may found an appeal only where there is a reasonable explanation', that it is for the appellant to show that the test is satisfied.

The parties to the appeal appear to be at one in agreeing that the expression 'a reasonable explanation' fell to be interpreted in an objective way. It has two aspects. If what is put forward by the appellant is rejected as not genuine it cannot be an explanation. The advocate depute submitted that the appellant required to show that the explanation was true. If this entails that full legal proof is called for, I consider that this is over-exacting. It is enough in my view if the court is persuaded to treat the explanation as genuine. However, an explanation cannot be 'a reasonable explanation' if it is not adequate to account for the fact that the witness's evidence was not heard. Thus, in a case where the defence take a deliberate decision not to lead a witness at the trial for technical reasons, it is difficult to see how this could provide 'a reasonable explanation' when it was sought at the stage of appeal to lead the evidence which could have been led at the trial. It would not be enough to say that at the trial the appellants' advisers were of a different mind.

In that connection the advocate depute referred the court to the decision in England in *R. v. Shields and Patrick* which related to section 23(2) of the Criminal Appeal Act 1968. That subsection required the court to receive evidence if a number of conditions were satisfied, one of which was that the evidence was not adduced at the trial 'but there is a reasonable explanation for the failure to adduce it'. In that case the court observed that it would seldom, if ever, be a reasonable explanation for not calling a witness that the risk of calling him was at the time considered too great and counsel advised that he should not be called. Accordingly, in my view, it would be difficult, if not impossible, for evidence to be admitted at the stage of an appeal if a tactical decision was taken not to adduce it at the trial. Likewise, if the explanation were merely that the appellant was not aware of the existence of the witness; or, where he was aware of the existence of the witness, he was not aware that he was able or willing to give evidence of any significance, this would hardly provide 'a reasonable explanation'. But it might be different if the appellant also could show that at the time of the trial he had no good reason for thinking that the witness existed, or, as the case might be, that he would give the evidence in question. Thus much might depend on the steps which the appellant could reasonably be expected to have taken in the light of what was known at the time. The underlying intention of the new legislation is that the court should take a broad and flexible approach in taking account of the circumstances of the particular case.

The requirement of subs. (3A) appears to me to precede consideration of the significance of the evidence in question as fresh evidence in the case. Thus, if there is not 'a reasonable explanation' of why it was not heard at the trial, access to it is denied; and questions as to the effect which it might have had at the trial do not arise for consideration. Accordingly it is appropriate to consider in the first place whether the conditions for the admission of that evidence can be satisfied. Where the appellant proposes to lead evidence as to that explanation, the initial question for the court is whether, on the information which it has been given about the proposed evidence, it could provide 'a reasonable explanation' which would satisfy the terms of subs. (3A).

I turn then to consider the evidence which is sought to be adduced from Mrs Carlton. The letter of the Secretary of State dated August 1, 1996 refers to statements made by her without further specification.

The most recent statement given by her was an affidavit dated July 12, 1997. In that affidavit she states that, on the night of the shooting to which charge 9 relates, Love, who was living with her at the time, left the house with a sawn off shotgun which he had previously shown to her. She was curious about what he was going to do, and she stood at her window which overlooked Balveny Street, from which she saw the incident. She saw her brother climb out of a car, fire the shotgun into the ice cream van and then climb back into the car with the shotgun. About two and half hours later he came back to the house with the gun . . .

Counsel for *Campbell*, whose submissions were adopted by the solicitor advocate for Steele, submitted that if the jury had been aware of Mrs Carlton's evidence that her brother had shot at the van, his credibility and reliability would have been seen in a very different light. That evidence showed that he was a major actor in the incident and had a motive for minimising his involvement. She clearly denied any possibility that the shooting was done by the co-accused Gray.

There was a very clear issue between the appellants and the Crown as to whether the evidence which Mrs Carlton could give is significant in regard to the case against *Campbell* on charge 9 and against each of the appellants on charge 15. The advocate depute submitted that her evidence had no bearing on these matters, and moreover was not convincing or trustworthy.

However, the initial question is whether the information which is provided by her affidavit and statements could satisfy the requirement for 'a reasonable explanation' of why her evidence was not heard at the trial. She was not on the Crown list of witnesses but she was on the lists of witnesses for Steele and the co-accused Lafferty and John Campbell. When Love gave evidence he was cross examined by counsel for the co-accused Gray, who shared a common solicitor with *Campbell*. In the course of that cross examination counsel put to him that he had been staying at Mrs Carlton's house, left it carrying a sawn off shotgun, went along the street and fired the shots at the van, returning to the house 10 minutes later. The cross examination of Love by counsel for John Campbell was to the same effect. In addition he put to him that before the shooting he had appeared to her to be edgy and upset. When she asked him what was wrong he told her that he was going to shoot up an ice cream van. Further, when he returned to the house he told her that he had done so and that he had been surprised at the amount of kick he felt when he had fired the gun.

The advocate depute pointed out that Love had given evidence on September 11 and 12. If it was true that Mrs Carlton last attended court on one of these days, that was almost a fortnight before the defence case opened on September 25. No application was made to the court for a warrant to secure her attendance or for the trial to be adjourned to enable her evidence to be led. There was nothing in her account of her meeting with the man in a black robe to explain why she was not called as a defence witness. She did not say that he put pressure on her either to avoid giving evidence or at least not to attend court. She was on her own account mystified as to why she was not called as a defence witness. It appeared that if she had been adduced as a witness she would have given evidence as to Love's actions.

Counsel frankly accepted that he was unable to offer any explanation as to why she was not called to give evidence as a witness for *Campbell*. He did not doubt that the lists of defence witnesses were known to his representatives. He accepted that she should have been led on his behalf. He suggested that *Campbell's* representatives might have assumed that she would be led as a witness for Steele, although the fact that Steele was not accused on charge 9 might indicate that this was not likely. Counsel also suggested that an explanation could have been that the full import of her evidence was not known to them at the time.

On behalf of Steele the solicitor advocate drew attention to a statement by the solicitor who had represented him at the time of the trial. He stated that the reason why Mrs Carlton was not called as a witness for Steele was that he had been informed that she was to change her evidence. He thought that his first source of his information was senior counsel for Steele. He did not know counsel's source of information. When she asked him after the trial why she had not been called, he gave her this explanation, which she said was incorrect. He also stated that he could categorically deny that he had been informed that anyone had sought to persuade Mrs Carlton to change her evidence. The solicitor advocate said that it was relevant that at the trial a police officer, Detective Constable Lewis, denied a suggestion that he had put pressure on a Crown witness, Lynn Chalmers, to give evidence that her boyfriend, Joseph Grainger, had gone out in the later part of the evening on which the fire took place at the Doyles' house. When he was asked at the later trial of Grainger for perjury whether he had said to her that it was in Grainger's best interests that she changed her statement, because if she did not do so he would be charged with conspiracy to murder and could get 30 years' imprisonment, he said: 'I may have said that. I don't recollect'. The solicitor advocate said that this tended to support the statement by Steele's solicitor that at the trial allegations abounded regarding intimidation by the police and manipulation of evidence. The solicitor advocate suggested that this might have put the defence off calling Mrs Carlton as a witness. The solicitor advocate added that it was a legitimate consideration that much had been done at the trial to discredit Love. He pointed out that evidence had been given by Douglas Thomson and John McCaffrey as to statements made to them by Love when they were fellow prisoners in Barlinnie prison during Love's remand there in 1984. In particular, Thomson gave evidence that Love told him that he hated the Doyles and had fired two shots with a shotgun at the windscreen of an ice cream van. He also told him he was making a deal with the police, trying to give false information about someone else for his own benefit.

In my view neither appellant is in a position to show that there was 'a reasonable explanation' for Mrs Carlton not being called to give evidence in their defence. So far as *Campbell* is concerned no explanation has been put forward. It is plainly right to infer that if Mrs Carlton had been precognosced she would have given information on the lines of her police statement dated July 7, 1984, which indicated that Love had fired the shots. If, as is submitted on behalf of *Campbell*, she is in a position to give significant evidence affecting the issue as to Love's credibility, substantially the same applied at the time leading up to and during the trial. There is nothing to indicate that, so far as *Campbell* is concerned, the position had changed. As I have already pointed out, counsel for Gray, who shared a common solicitor with counsel for *Campbell*, put a number of allegations to Love which were apparently based on information which she had supplied. There is nothing to indicate that any inquiry was made of Mrs Carlton to check whether her position had changed in any respect since she had supplied that information. As regards Steele it is clear from the statement given by his then solicitor that she would have been called as a witness but for the information to the effect that she was to change her evidence. However, there is nothing to explain why this information, so far as it went, was taken at face value. No attempt appears to have been made to check with her whether this information had any substance to it. I am unable to attach any significance to the attitude which Detective Constable Lewis adopted towards another witness.

In these circumstances I am satisfied that the appellants have not demonstrated that the evidence of Mrs Carlton should be admitted for the purposes of their appeals. Accordingly it is unnecessary for me to go on to discuss the significance of that evidence, including the questions as to the credibility and reliability of her evidence which were raised by the advocate depute.

The New Evidence of William McDonald Love

Where an appellant relies for the purposes of his appeal upon the existence and significance of evidence which was not given by a witness who gave evidence at the trial, it is also necessary for subs. (3C) and (3D) to be satisfied. In the present case the appellants seek to adduce evidence from Love which falls within para. (a)(i) of subs. (3C).

Prior to the alteration in the law effected by section 17 of the 1997 Act the appeal court would not have entertained different or additional evidence from a witness who gave evidence at the trial. The Lord Justice General (Emslie) in *Mitchell v. H.M.A.* at 1989 S.C.C.R., p.511 said: 'Putting the matter shortly we shall say that the court will never entertain an appeal upon the proposition that a witness who has given evidence at a trial merely wishes to change his story' (*cf. Brodie v. H.M.A.* per Lord Justice General Hope at 1993 J.C., p.100).

The Sutherland committee recommended that an appeal based on fresh evidence in the form of a change of witness testimony should be possible. They recognised that a relaxation of the previous legislation relating to such evidence might encourage the intimidation of witnesses and that there was a real risk of abuse. In order to avoid what they saw as the very obvious pitfalls of opening the door to this kind of appeal they made the further recommendation that the reasons given for the change of testimony should be supported by some additional credible and reliable evidence. If the reasons for the change of testimony were so supported, it should be considered. If they were not so supported, it should not be considered (paras 2.57–2.58).

The provisions of subs. (3C) and (3D) broadly reflect the recommendations of the Sutherland committee. However, they are in certain respects more stringent. During the course of the discussion the advocate depute pointed out that fears of intimidation of witnesses had caused the initial rejection by the Government of the committee's recommendations. Further safeguards were incorporated in order to define the limited circumstances in which a change of witness evidence could be the basis of an appeal. In that connection the advocate depute drew our attention to the speech of the Lord Advocate at the committee stage of consideration of the Crime and Punishment (Scotland) Bill (Hansard, March 10, 1997). Differing from the recommendation of the Sutherland committee, subs. (3D) provides that the 'independent evidence' is to be evidence which was not heard at the original trial. Further, subs. (3C) states that, without prejudice to subs. (3A), the witness's different or additional evidence 'may not found an appeal unless there is a reasonable explanation as to why the evidence now sought to be adduced was not given' by the witness at the trial. Accordingly subs. (3C) imposes a requirement for 'a reasonable explanation' which is separate from that imposed under subs. (3A).

The terms in which subs. (3C) are expressed indicate that what is required is an explanation relating to the witness, which would normally, if not invariably, come from him or her. Subsection (3A) would still require a reasonable explanation from the appellant but in a case which was concerned with a change in the witness's evidence it might well be that there was little which the appellant required to explain. However, in some cases in which it was sought to adduce the witness to give additional evidence the appellant might seek to account for the fact that the witness did not give that evidence at the trial by explaining that at the time he had no reason to think that the witness could give that evidence.

I require to consider the interpretation and application of the expression 'a reasonable explanation' in the context of subs. (3C), but I will leave that discussion until I have set out the evidence sought to be adduced from Love and the arguments which were submitted in regard to it. Whatever is treated as 'a reasonable explanation' must be 'supported' by 'independent evidence', which itself has to satisfy the three requirements of subs. (3D). It is important to note that it is one thing for independent evidence to provide support for the content of the different or additional evidence; it is another thing for it to provide support for the explanation itself. At the stage where the 'independent' evidence has not yet been heard the question is whether, on the information provided to the court, that evidence could support the explanation. Likewise, at that stage the question is whether it is capable of being regarded as credible and reliable.

Before turning to the evidence which is proposed to be adduced from Love, it is necessary for me to deal with certain statements which were made on his behalf in connection with his prosecution in the armed robbery case in 1984. Counsel for *Campbell* founded on the fact that, following his arrest on March 25, at his judicial examination on April 2, he stated that from about 9.00 p.m. on March 23, he had been at 961 Gartloch Road, in the company of others, including Mrs Carlton. This was repeated in the terms of a special defence which was lodged in that case on his behalf, although it was withdrawn before the trial commenced. It was replaced with a different version in which it was stated that he was at that address from midnight on that date. The armed robbery took place in the early hours of March 24. Counsel submitted that this threw doubt on his evidence that he had been at the Netherfield bar on March 23 or 24.

The advocate depute submitted that this argument sought to attribute to Love's evidence a degree of precision which it had not borne. Love was uncertain as to the date of the meeting, as the appeal court had emphasised in 1985. In any event it did not follow from his alibi that he could not have heard the conversation in the bar. The advocate depute also pointed out that at the trial with which the present appeal is concerned, Love was cross examined about his alibi in the armed robbery case by counsel for the co-accused Gray, who, as I have already said, shared a common solicitor with *Campbell*. In the result the jury were aware that he had put forward an alibi for March 23 and 24. In any event if this had been new evidence, there was no reasonable explanation for its not having been heard at the trial, particularly when several of those who were most closely involved in the armed robbery case were also involved in this trial. It was an obvious step to investigate the alibi at least when the significance of the particular weekend became clear during the examination in chief of Love about one month before the trial ended. It was accepted that no such investigation had taken place until after the trial had finished, although it was said that the defence had been refused a request for a copy of the transcript of Love's judicial examination.

In my view the submissions made by the advocate depute on this point were well founded. Insofar as any aspect of the alibi put forward by Love in connection with the armed robbery case was not brought out before the jury in the trial with which the present appeals are concerned, there is no reasonable explanation as to why evidence relating to it was not heard at the trial.

I turn next to the evidence proposed to be adduced from Love. In his letter dated August 1, 1996 the Secretary of State referred to an affidavit sworn by Love on February 22, 1992. In that affidavit Love stated that when he was first seen by the police at Barlinnie after the fire, he did not ask to see a senior police officer. This was suggested to him by a CID officer who said to him that he knew all about the shooting and the fire. On the following morning he was seen by Detective Supt Walker and Detective Insp McKillop. He denied all knowledge of the ice cream wars. They told him 'how various things were supposed to have happened' and offered him bail. They said to him that there had been a meeting at the Netherfield bar and they talked about a discussion that was supposed to have taken place there. They wanted him to go along and say that. When they came to see him three to four days later they said that he would not be charged in regard to the shooting; he was to do what they wanted him to do, and they would look after him. They offered to relocate him and his family, give him money and make sure he was all right and did not want for anything. He had not so far admitted any involvement in the shooting. He was able to give them information about it. He had met the co-accused Lafferty while he was walking his dog, but Lafferty never mentioned Campbell's name. He spoke to him about a 'message', which he understood to be about a shooting. Lafferty never paid him £30 and told him that Campbell would see him and square him up later. That was something which was put into his head by the police. It was also untrue that Campbell thanked him for the 'message' or said that he would square up with him later. After the shooting Campbell merely indicated to him that it was because of him (Campbell) that it had happened. He said nothing to admit responsibility for it. He merely said: 'Thanks very much for doing that van for us'.

The police officers wanted him to say various things about the fire although he had no knowledge of them. There were a number of meetings to clarify what the Crown had agreed to do, and the police officers told him the questions they wanted him to answer and what they wanted him to say. He was never present at a meeting at the Netherfield bar or any other bar between the appellants and the co-accused Gray, at which starting a fire at Fat Boy's was discussed. He said that in evidence because he was told to do so.

Detective Supt Walker raised the subject of a precognition on oath and told him about, or made, promises about what he was going to do for him. He also discussed what might happen if he fulfilled his promises and he did not go through with his part of the bargain. They wanted it on oath and that was what the Crown was wanting as well. In exchange for helping him he was to be relocated and get a new house out of the country and be given a job.

He himself did not bring up the matter of bail, but Detective Supt Walker did so, saying that he would be out of prison as soon as the precognition on oath was signed. He (Love) wanted bail after he signed as he did not want to go back to Barlinnie since Campbell and others would be coming in. When the officers came to collect him for the precognition on oath he said that he was not going through with it, because he did not trust them. The procurator fiscal depute, Mr Spiers, told him that if he refused to give the precognition he would be charged with offences on the basis of the statements which he had made to the police officers. However, once he had given the precognition and signed it, he would be given bail.

Between getting bail and giving evidence he lived at various addresses but the police gave him no assistance in moving. Detective Supt Walker wanted him to obtain more information about what was going on in Garthamlock. He did not have a job and got no money apart from state benefits. He said to police officers that he wanted to tell the truth about the Doyle case if they did not give him special treatment, such as bail on other alleged offences or getting the charges dropped. He wanted them to fulfil their promises to get a house for his wife and children and money to live on, but they did not want to provide that. He now wanted to come forward to tell the truth.

The terms of this affidavit follow the terms of the transcript of an interview of Love by solicitors for the appellants on January 19, 1989. According to that transcript Love also said that when the two police officers first visited him they stated that in addition to offering bail they 'said they would get the armed robbery and that dropped against us if I did them a favour. I just went along with what they were saying'. In a separate affidavit dated February 22, 1992 Love adopted the transcript of the interview as accurate and truthful. Also before this court was a letter from Love, using the alias 'W McDonald', to Campbell's solicitor, dated January 19, 1989, in which he retracted everything that he had said at the meeting and reaffirmed that the evidence which he gave at the trial was the whole truth.

The court was also referred to the transcript of an interview of Love by officers of Strathclyde Police on February 27, 1994 as part of an investigation into his alleged perjury at the trial. In that interview Love repeated that he had been threatened by Mr Spiers, as also by the two police officers, that he would be charged with offences if he did not proceed with the precognition on oath. He also alleged that when he was brought before the sheriff to be precognosced he told him that he was giving his statement under duress. The sheriff responded that duress was a matter to be put before the court when the case came to trial. His position in regard to his evidence at the trial was that it was mostly untrue, but that he had not committed perjury since 'duress was a defence'. I should also add that in the course of the interview Love also stated that he was put under duress when the police officers threatened that his sister, Mrs Carlton, and others might be charged for 'perjury' if he did not give them what they wanted. So far as Mrs Carlton is concerned, this appears to have been a reference to statements which she had made in his defence in connection with the armed robbery case in which he was acquitted in August 1984.

Finally, I note that in the precognition on oath Love made statements to the same general effect as he did during the course of giving evidence at the trial. It is true, as the solicitor advocate pointed out, that he merely said that Steele was present, rather than saying that he was positively agreeing what was being said during the course of the meeting at the Netherfield bar. However, it is plain from his statement to the police dated May 2, 1984, which was produced during the course of the hearing, that his position was the same as when he gave evidence in court. He said that 'everybody was involved in the discussion'.

Counsel for *Campbell*, whose submissions were adopted by the solicitor advocate for Steele in regard to charge 15, submitted that the evidence which Love gave at the trial was of crucial importance to the Crown case against *Campbell* on charges 9 and 15. The new evidence which he was able to provide showed that he had not been as truthful or reliable as he had been made out at the trial. The jury would have been bound to acquit if they accepted that he had lied. In any event this would have been bound to have had a material bearing on his credibility which was a critical issue at the trial. Counsel made it plain that *Campbell's* position was that while Love was now telling the truth, the object of adducing his different evidence was to show that his evidence at the trial was in fact unreliable.

Once more there was a dispute between the appellants and the Crown as to the significance of the evidence sought to be adduced from Love, including in particular the credibility and reliability of his 'different' evidence. However, as before, it is necessary in the first instance to consider the issues which arise in regard to the conditions for admission of this evidence.

Counsel submitted that the appellant was in a position to show for the purpose of subs. (3A) that there was a reasonable explanation as to why the 'different evidence of Love was not heard at the trial'. He said that 'a reasonable explanation' must be one based on reason which the court had discretion to accept or reject. Those who represented Campbell at the trial did not have the means of demonstrating that Love was a liar which his post-trial statements had provided. The mere fact that his credibility was challenged at the trial on the ground that he was attempting to gain advantage for himself did not mean that the same point could not found an appeal based on the 'different' evidence.

As regards the explanation which Love gave for not giving evidence at the trial to the same effect as his post-trial statements, counsel submitted that his explanation should be viewed objectively in considering whether it was 'a reasonable explanation' for the purpose of subs. (3C). His statements showed that he had been offered and received advantages which he would not otherwise have had. First, as soon as he gave the statements which the Crown were looking for, he was released on bail. Although counsel did not go so far as to say that his previous record was so bad he would never have obtained bail, he was a repeated offender and was being prosecuted for serious offences. Secondly, he avoided prosecution for attempted murder. If he had been convicted of carrying out the shooting himself, he could have received a sentence of 14 years, as did the co-accused Gray. He clearly had a strong motive to minimise his involvement in regard to charge 9. He was offered preferment in return for which he involved *Campbell* in both charges. Having given statements he was liable to be charged with perjury if he denied in the witness box that he had made them. Counsel pointed out that this is what happened in regard to the Crown witness Joseph Grainger, who denied making a statement as to what happened when he was present at a meeting in the Netherfield bar.

The advocate depute disputed what counsel had submitted. He adopted two alternative approaches. First, he directed his remarks towards the conduct of those who represented Campbell at the trial. They could reasonably have been expected to precognosce Love with some care. If he disclosed, as he now maintained, that he had been pressurised into giving false evidence, they could reasonably have been expected to advise him that he must tell the truth at the trial, and that, if he failed to do so, he would be committing perjury; that he could not be prosecuted in respect of any of the matters on the indictment in which he was involved as he had been precognosced on oath by the Crown as a *socius*; and that he would in any event be immune from prosecution as soon as he was adduced by the Crown as a witness. Furthermore he could not be prosecuted for perjury in respect of his precognition on oath if he had given false testimony only under duress; and in any event he was unlikely to be prosecuted if he had been pressurised. They would have been expected in any event to report the matter to the authorities for investigation. On any view when he came to give evidence the obvious thing for him to do was to say that he had been pressurised into making false statements.

Secondly, the advocate depute directed his remarks to the conduct of Love himself. In his post-trial statements he claimed that the fact that he had not given true evidence at the trial was due to a combination of his being offered inducements and being threatened and pressurised. However, so far as the alleged inducements were concerned, they had not materialised by the time when he gave his evidence at the trial. He had been acquitted in the armed robbery case, the charges for which had not been dropped. He was being held on remand on an unrelated charge. The police had, according to him, reneged on their promises to assist him. Furthermore, if it was true that he had been threatened and pressurised, he had ample opportunity to report this to his solicitor, who acted for him in the armed robbery case and whom he had seen on a number of occasions during the trial with which the present appeals are concerned, both before and after the stage at which he gave evidence. It was to be expected that he would have been given advice on the lines already mentioned. In any event he had the opportunity to discuss the matter with the procurator fiscal depute, the sheriff, the defence solicitors, the prison authorities and ultimately to disclose it to the court at the trial. If he had reported this conduct, it was highly unlikely that he would have given the perjured evidence. The advocate depute underlined his submissions by referring to two previous decisions which, while they were concerned with the application of the previous legislation relating to 'additional evidence which was not heard at the trial and which was not available and could not reasonably have been made available at the trial', were, in his submission, still of relevance. In *Brodie v. H.M.A.* a number of Crown witnesses who had given statements to the police which were favourable to the Crown case wished to change their evidence at the stage of appeal, alleging that they had been subjected to police pressure. At 1993 J.C., p.99 the Lord Justice General observed that precognition of those witnesses by the defence would have revealed the nature of those statements. However, if what those witnesses now said was to be believed, namely that what they said in their statements was not true, it was highly unlikely that this information would not have been revealed to the appellant's solicitors if the matter had been properly investigated before the case went to trial. In *MacKenzie v. H.M.A.*, where the appeal was based on additional evidence from the appellant which he did not give at the trial because, as he claimed, he had been threatened by a co-accused and his family, the court held that it would not be enough for the appellant to show that he had been threatened and that because of this he had simply chosen not to give evidence. At 1995 S.C.C.R., p.151; 1995 S.L.T., p.747 the Lord Justice General (Hope) said that if a case of inability due to threats was to be made out, that inability must include the inability to report these threats to those who could give advice and take action to deal with them at the trial. In the present case there was no question of Love being subject to a very serious threat; nor, on the other hand, was it a case of his being subjected to a threat in regard to a very minor piece of evidence. The court should not entertain the view that it was reasonable *prima facie* for Love to commit perjury in these circumstances.

Are the appellants able to provide "a reasonable explanation" as to why Love did not give at the trial the evidence which is now sought to be adduced?

It is in my view of some importance that it was considered necessary to provide that there should be "a reasonable explanation" as to why a witness failed to give the different or additional evidence at the trial. As in the case of subs. (3A), it is for the appellant to show that this test is satisfied. The expression should have essentially the same meaning as it does in subs. (3A), although the contexts are different. Thus it would not be an "explanation" unless the court is persuaded to treat what is said as genuine.

What else is required for "a reasonable explanation" for the purposes of subs. (3C)? It is difficult to see why the mere fact that the witness has changed his evidence—which would in most cases imply perjury at the trial—would satisfy this test as it would deprive "reasonable" of most of its meaning. It is possible to envisage a case in which a witness gives perjured evidence because of a serious threat made to himself or his family. In such a case the test could be met. But between these examples are a variety of circumstances in which, if meaning is to be given to the expression "a reasonable explanation", the court is apparently expected to make the difficult judgment as to whether the test is met or not. I would observe that throughout it has to be borne in mind that if the explanation does not meet the test, it is the appellant who suffers the loss of being unable to adduce the evidence which the witness says is the truth. However, that appears to be the possible result, in the light of the requirement of "a reasonable explanation" in subs. (3C).

In the present case I reject the advocate depute's submission which was directed towards the conduct of those who represented Campbell at the trial. There is nothing to indicate that Love would have disclosed that the account which he had given to the police or in his precognition on oath was untrue or that he had been pressurised into giving false evidence.

As regards Love's own explanation, the information before the court is that he would give evidence that his evidence at the trial was false in certain respects, namely that he was at a meeting when the starting of a fire at Fat Boy's door was discussed by Campbell in the presence of Steele, that Lafferty mentioned Campbell's name in connection with the shooting, and that Campbell thanked him for the "message" after the shooting. Love would state that in return for being offered certain inducements by the police he agreed to make these false statements which they concocted with his co-operation. One of these inducements was that he would not be charged with the shooting. The granting of bail and the support of Love and his family would, if carried out, be consequential on his co-operation in giving a precognition on oath in line with what had been suggested to him by the police. His explanation is unrelated to the extent of his involvement in the shooting. He does not admit or suggest that he was the person who shot at the van, or that he lied about his part in the shooting.

Thus far it appears that, on his own account, Love was a willing participant in the arrangements which the police officers had suggested. However, matters advanced to the stage at which, he claims, he was the subject of duress. This appears to have taken two forms. First, at some stage which is not easy to determine, he was told that unless he went ahead with the false evidence, his sister and others would be prosecuted for "perjury" in connection with the information which they had given in his defence in the armed robbery case. Secondly, he was threatened with being charged with offences if he did not proceed with the precognition on oath. The latter appears to mean that the statements which he had already given to the police, on the strength of their assurance that he would not be prosecuted for the shooting, would be used after all as evidence against him. In these circumstances his perjury was the alternative to being charged with offences on the basis of those statements.

In the circumstances I consider that, assuming Love's explanation is genuine, it is arguable that it provides "a reasonable explanation" for his having failed to give a true account at the trial. This is in two respects. First, if his explanation is genuine, police officers who could have charged him with participation in the shooting, initiated discussion with him by offering various inducements in return for his co-operation in giving evidence which they knew would be false. In these circumstances it would not be surprising that someone in Love's position considered that it was more prudent to co-operate in this way than not to do so. Secondly, and again assuming that his explanation is genuine, he was subjected to some pressure to repeat the false statements on precognition; and, so far as his own involvement on charge 9 is concerned, unfair advantage was taken of his having incriminated himself after he had been assured that he would not be prosecuted in respect of that charge. I am not persuaded that the approach of the advocate depute in maintaining that Love's explanation could not be "a reasonable explanation" unless he was unable to complain to his solicitor or others is well founded. Underlying what was said in *Brodie* and *MacKenzie* was the approach adopted by the court to the previous test, and in particular the question whether evidence was not "reasonably available". In the present case we have to deal with a different test.

However, before an appeal on this basis can make any further headway, the question is whether there is "independent evidence" within the meaning of subs. (3D) which could support the explanation.

Counsel for Campbell submitted that for the purposes of these provisions he relied on the evidence which would be given by the police officers who conducted the interview with Love on April 24, 1994; and on the evidence of Mrs Carlton. For this purpose her evidence has to be considered again. However, in this case there does not require to be "a reasonable explanation" of why she did not give evidence at the trial, since that is not one of the conditions which "independent evidence" requires to satisfy.

I can deal briefly with the evidence of the police officers since it is plain that on no view could their evidence qualify as "independent evidence" having regard to the terms of para. (b) of subs. (3D). All that those officers could do would be to provide evidence as to statements coming from the same source, namely Love himself.

As regards Mrs Carlton, counsel pointed out that she satisfied paras (a) and (b) of subs. (3D). It was, he said, self evident that her evidence would be both credible and reliable. In any event at this stage it was at least capable of being regarded as credible and reliable, and the court could reach the conclusion that it satisfied para. (c) after hearing it.

On the question of whether the explanation "is itself supported by" her evidence, counsel submitted that, although she did not explain how Love came to be released, she provided a check on his evidence that he was released, despite the serious charges which were pending against him, and that he went to other addresses. Although she could not explain why he was not charged with charge 9, she also showed, through her evidence as an eyewitness, that Love had a reason for minimising his involvement. She supported the conclusion that he had a reason for giving the statements which the prosecution authorities sought from him, and refraining from saying what he stated after the trial.

The advocate depute submitted that Mrs Carlton did not support the explanation. She could not provide that support, as distinct from contradicting the substance of the evidence which Love had given in regard to charge 9, a charge in which he was on any view a *socius*. The fact that Love was granted bail and was not prosecuted in respect of the shooting could not support his explanation as to how that came about. His application for bail was based on the danger from those on whom he had informed. There was nothing unusual about using an accomplice as a witness, with the result that he could not be prosecuted. This was a matter for the prosecutor's decision as to what was in the public interest. These facts did not support the proposition that he was offered bail in return for a statement or was threatened with prosecution unless he co-operated. It was noteworthy that in the police statement dated April 26, 1994 Mrs Carlton stated that she had no idea why Love did what he did and said what he did in court. Furthermore, evidence of Love's being granted bail and not being prosecuted on charge 9 was brought out in the evidence of a number of witnesses at the trial, namely Detective Supt Walker, Detective Inspector McKillop and Mr Spiers. In itself, this was not evidence "which was not heard at the original proceedings". So far as Love's involvement on charge 9 was concerned, he was on his own evidence at the trial a *socius*, and not to a minor extent. The jury heard evidence that he had admitted to two fellow prisoners that he had been the gunman. Accordingly, evidence of his involvement was before the jury in a number of respects.

In my view, the arguments presented by the advocate depute are compelling. The question is whether the evidence of Mrs Carlton is capable of supporting the explanation given by Love that he did not give true evidence at the trial because he had been offered inducements by the police and put under pressure by them and the procurator fiscal depute to give false evidence. Evidence that he had obtained immunity from prosecution in regard to charge 9 and had obtained bail in the armed robbery case is not evidence which was not heard at the trial. It was brought out in evidence, and moreover the circumstances in which this happened formed a significant part of Love's cross examination. In any event that evidence cannot support Love's account as to inducements and pressure. There was nothing unusual about an accomplice being used as a Crown witness so that he could not be prosecuted in respect of the crime to which he testified. This was a matter for the prosecutor to decide in considering what was in the public interest. On any view Love had exposed himself to danger in making statements which incriminated others who would be likely to be remanded in custody as a consequence. Mrs Carlton is unable to give evidence which can provide independent support for the proposition that Love gave false evidence as a result of the alleged inducements and pressure. She is able to give evidence which, if it is true, indicates that Love would have wished to minimise his own involvement in the shooting. That could support the proposition that he gave false evidence as to his own involvement, but that does not tend to show that he was induced or pressured by others to give false evidence on other matters relating to charge 9, let alone charge 15. In any event it does not provide independent support for an explanation given by Love, since he does not say that he lied as to the extent of his own involvement in the shooting. In these circumstances I am not satisfied that evidence which Mrs Carlton would give could support Love's explanation that he was induced and put under pressure to give false evidence against the appellants in regard to the charges with which I am concerned.

In these circumstances, it is not necessary for me to go on to consider whether the evidence which Mrs Carlton would give is capable of being regarded at this stage as credible and reliable, as counsel submitted.

Assuming that the necessary preconditions for the admission of Love's evidence had been fulfilled, it would have been necessary for me to go on to consider the significance of his evidence.

In that connection, the advocate depute submitted two arguments. The first was that since, as he maintained, a retrial was not possible, the court should not quash the conviction *simpliciter* unless it was satisfied that if the jury had heard the new evidence, it would have come to a different result. Secondly, he submitted that the well known test set out in the opinion of the Lord Justice General (Emslie) in *Cameron v. H.M.A.*, 1987 S.C.C.R., pp 618–619; 1988 S.L.T., p.170 was to be preferred to the re-formulation adopted by the Lord Justice General (Hope) in *Church No (2) v. H.M.A.*, 1996 S.C.C.R. (No 2), p.33; 1996 SLT, p.385. However, these are issues with which, in my view, I do not require to deal in order to resolve the present appeals; and accordingly I reserve my opinion in regard to them."

LORD SUTHERLAND: "Subsection (3A) provides that such evidence may found an appeal only where there is a reasonable explanation of why it was not so heard. The first question is therefore what can constitute a reasonable explanation. It was a matter of agreement that it is for the appellant to establish this explanation. Clearly the explanation advanced would have to be accepted by the court as apparently genuine before it could begin to be established. An explanation which is held to be untrue is not an explanation at all. What, however, is the significance of 'reasonable'? Plainly the word must have some significance as a qualification of the explanation. I do not consider that 'reasonable' in this context can be equiparated with 'rational'. An explanation that it was decided not to lead evidence, the existence of which was known to the appellants' advisers, for tactical reasons, would undoubtedly be perfectly rational but it would be contrary to the interests of justice to permit the defence to keep some evidence up its sleeve only to be produced to the appeal court in the event of the verdict of the jury being unfavourable. I agree with the comments of the Court of Appeal (Criminal Division) in *R. v. Shields and Patrick*. Similarly, the fact that the defence solicitors failed to precognosce a witness on the Crown list and were thus unaware of the existence of favourable evidence could not be regarded in general as a reasonable explanation, although again perfectly rational. In my opinion what is required is an explanation which, in the circumstances of the particular case, is one which the court is persuaded to regard as some justification for the failure to lead the evidence, bearing in mind the context that what is being inquired into is an alleged miscarriage of justice which in turn involves the concept of the interests of justice as a whole.

Subsection (3B) is not relevant to this case, being concerned with evidence which at the time of the trial was inadmissible but is admissible at the time of the appeal, but it is perhaps of interest to note that such evidence may only be admitted if 'it would be in the interests of justice to do so'.

Moving on to subs. (3C), the first thing to note is that it is specifically stated to be without prejudice to subs. (3A), which plainly implies that an appellant must first satisfy the subs. (3A) qualification. Evidence from a person or of a statement by a person which is different from or additional to evidence given at the original proceedings may not found an appeal unless there is a reasonable explanation as to why the evidence was not given by that person at those proceedings and that explanation requires to be supported by independent evidence. From whom does that explanation require to come? It cannot be encompassed in the explanation which is to be given by the appellant under subs. (3A), as if that were so it would be unnecessary to include in subs. (3C) the additional requirement for a reasonable explanation. In my view there is only one person who can give that explanation, namely the witness who wishes to alter or add to his evidence. If, for example, the witness wishes to add to his evidence he might explain that he did not give the additional evidence because he was never asked about it at the trial. From the witness's point of view that would appear to be a reasonable explanation, although it may cause difficulties to the appellant in providing his reasonable explanation under subs. (3A). If the witness purported, albeit with some doubt, to identify the appellant at the trial he may explain that he has subsequently seen the perpetrator whom he could positively identify and therefore wishes to retract his original identification of the appellant. This, if true, is something to which only the witness could speak. The position is even clearer if the witness now wishes to say that the whole of his original evidence was false and perjured as only he can provide the explanation as to why he gave that false evidence. Obviously the explanation will be advanced by or on behalf of the appellant, but so far as examination of the explanation is concerned it is the witness's explanation which must be examined to see if it satisfies the requirements of subs. (3C). As far as 'reasonable' is concerned I am of the view that the same considerations apply in subs. (3C) as apply in subs. (3A), namely that in the circumstances of the particular case the explanation is one which the court is persuaded to regard as some justification for the failure to lead the evidence at the original trial. It is unlikely that Parliament intended the word 'reasonable' to have a different meaning in the two subsections. Can there ever be justification for committing perjury? In my view there may be exceptional circumstances to provide at least some justification for a witness to take that exceptional course. The example given during the course of the hearing was that of the witness whose wife was being held hostage. This would be a fairly clear case and in my view the principle could legitimately be extended to situations where serious threats of personal injury were made to the witness himself. At the other end of the scale I do not consider that it could ever be regarded as reasonable for a witness to give wholly false evidence just because it suited his convenience at the time to do so. The fact that he perceived some advantage to himself in giving perjured evidence equally, in my view, could not be regarded as reasonable. The more difficult cases are the ones which fall between these two extremes. If the witness says that he was persuaded by police officers to give evidence along the lines of words put into his mouth by the police this may be a reasonable explanation. The important feature in such a case would be the complete impropriety of the actings of the police. If officers who are supposed to maintain law and order act in such a way as to suborn, the witness may with some justification feel that he also can act in a wholly improper way by acceding to the police suggestions. Each case will obviously depend on its own facts but there must, in my view, be some element of justification rather than pure self interest before an explanation can be regarded as reasonable.

The final qualification is that the explanation must be supported by independent evidence, which is defined in subs. (3D). It requires to be credible and reliable evidence not heard at the original trial from a source independent of the witness who is altering or adding to his evidence given at the original trial. It is clear from subs. (3D)(c) that it is the appeal court that has to decide on the credibility and reliability of this source. The source requires to be independent. The concept of an independent source is well understood in the context of corroboration. For example, in a rape case, the corroboration of the complainer's evidence cannot come from another witness speaking to what he or she was told by the complainer, the source in both instances being the same. It would follow that a person giving evidence that he had been told by the witness who is changing his evidence why he had initially committed perjury would not be a source independent of the witness. I appreciate that the obtaining of independent evidence of what may be a state of mind of the witness may be difficult but it is in my opinion clear that Parliament intended that there should be a truly independent check. Quite apart from what I regard as the clear wording of subs. (3D) to that effect, it is in accordance with what the Sutherland committee recommended and with the observations of the Lord Advocate when introducing in the House of Lords the amendments which became the new section 106."

NOTES

Lord McCluskey dissented on the question whether the reasonable explanation required under subs. (3A) imposes a separate requirement from that imposed under subs. (3C). He said:

> "I consider that in a section 106(3C) case we are not necessarily required to look for two reasonable explanations, one from the appellant, under subs. (3A), and a separate one from the witness, under subs. (3C). One should be sufficient, whatever its source, if the court can properly accept that it is a reasonable explanation as to why the trial jury were deprived of it. This reading of subs. (3C) does not, in any sense, prejudice subs. (3A)."

A number of other points were decided in *Campbell*, notably:
  (a) That the appeal court is entitled to re-consider a ground of appeal which has already been heard and decided at a previous appeal, as happened in *Campbell*.
  (b) It will be difficult if not impossible to offer as a reasonable explanation for not calling a witness at the trial that a tactical decision had been taken not to lead the evidence at trial—see also *Mills v. H.M.A.*, 1999 S.L.T. 680, and compare *Hynd v. P.F. (Kilmarnock)*, 2000 S.C.C.R. 231.

A major difficulty in additional evidence appeals is in deciding what effect, if any, the additional evidence would have had on the outcome of the case. In the final passage reproduced from *Campbell*, above, the Lord Justice Clerk decided that he did not require to consider the argument as to the appropriate formulation of the test to be applied. In *Kidd v. H.M.A.*, 2000 S.L.T. 1068 the matter arose again. Delivering the Opinion of the Court Lord Justice Clerk Cullen said:

> "In approaching this question, it is important, in our view, that a number of matters should be borne in mind. First, the governing question in any appeal based on additional evidence is whether the fact that it was not heard at the trial represents a miscarriage of justice. It is not a matter of whether the additional evidence is significant—as if that represented some absolute quality—but whether it is of such significance as to lead to the conclusion that a verdict returned in ignorance of it must be regarded as a miscarriage of justice. Secondly, while it is convenient to describe the judicial approach to determining whether evidence is of that significance as a 'test', it should not be forgotten that the sole test which is laid down by section 106(3)(a) is that of miscarriage of justice. It is clear, as a matter of common sense, that the 'significance' of evidence includes considerations as to its relevance, materiality and importance. It also is plain, as was pointed out by Lord Justice General Emslie [in *Cameron v. H.M.A.*, 1987 S.C.C.R. 618; 1988

S.L.T. 170] that it includes its quality in point of credibility and reliability. None of these factors is determinative. What matters is the overall impression which is created. Thirdly, we are in full agreement with the distinction which Lord Justice General Hope [in *Church (No. 2) v. H.M.A.*, at 1996 S.C.C.R. 33; 1996 S.L.T. 385] drew between the trial court and the appeal court. The latter is not only different in function from the former but it does not enjoy the advantages which the former has of hearing and seeing the original witnesses. Further there are inherent limitations in an appeal court determining what the former would have made of the additional evidence when considered in the context of the original evidence.

[24] For these reasons we consider that, for the purposes of this aspect of the significance of additional evidence, it is sufficient that the appeal court is satisfied that it is capable of being regarded by a reasonable jury as both credible and reliable. However, in saying that, we must emphasise the importance of the quality of the additional evidence. As we have pointed out above, the cogency of the additional evidence is of critical importance. It requires to be of such significance, in the words of Lord Justice General Emslie, 'that it will be reasonable to conclude that the verdict of the jury, reached in ignorance of its existence, must be regarded as a miscarriage of justice'.

[25] A distinction can be drawn between the language used by the court in *Cameron* and that used in *Church*. However, in *Cameron*, as the court pointed out at p.619, there was no reason to doubt that the additional witness honestly believed in the truth of her evidence, and accordingly it was not necessary for the court to give close consideration to what a jury might have concluded as to her credibility. If the court intended that there should be a difference between the approach to credibility and that to reliability, one would have expected that the reasons for observing such a difference would have been spelled out. For these reasons, and in the light of the considerations which we have discussed earlier in this opinion, we do not consider that there was any essential difference of approach between that in *Cameron* and that more fully spelled out in *Church*."

See also *Maclay v. H.M.A. (No. 2),* 2000 S.L.T. 1076, in which the court applied the test set out in *Church (No. 2)*, and in which it was *provisionally* held that s.106(3C) applies only to a person who has given evidence at the original trial. Thus, where a co-accused did not give evidence at the original trial, but provides additional evidence for an appeal by the accused, it may be that his additional evidence does not require to satisfy the test laid down in s.106(3C).

It might be argued that any attempt by an appellate court to second-guess what the jury would have made of particular evidence is futile, and that any decision should be taken purely on the basis that all that is required is that the appeal court be satisfied that the absence of the particular evidence from the original trial amounted to a miscarriage of justice. The test to be applied under the 1995 Act should be contrasted with the recent English case of *R. v. Pendleton* [2001] UKHL 66, December 13, 2001. In that case the House of Lords disapproved of the "reasonable jury" test, emphasising that the question was really one for the Court of Appeal to decide on the basis of its own evaluation of the evidence (although it should be noted that this was a matter of construction of the particular English legislative provisions). Lord Hobhouse of Woodborough said:

" . . . in my judgment it is not right to attempt to look into the minds of the members of the jury. Their deliberations are secret and their precise and detailed reasoning is not known. For an appellate court to speculate, whether hypothetically or actually, is not appropriate. It is for the Court of Appeal to answer the direct and simply stated question: Do we think that the conviction was unsafe?"

In *Smith v. H.M.A.*, 2001 S.L.T. 438 the court was faced with an even more difficult question. The accused had been convicted of murder. The appeal court heard that highly significant medical evidence given at the original trial in 1977 was "entirely without foundation and misconceived". That evidence was to the effect that the deceased had been kicked in the head. In fact, his injuries had been received when he fell over backwards and struck his head. The court required to decide whether to quash his conviction *simpliciter*, or to substitute a verdict of guilty of culpable homicide. Delivering the Opinion of the Court, Lord Justice General Rodger said that "[we] should substitute an amended verdict of guilty of culpable homicide only if we are satisfied that, on the basis of all the relevant evidence, a reasonable jury, properly instructed, would have found the appellant guilty of culpable homicide." In the event, the test could not be satisfied, and the conviction was quashed.

Craig v. H.M.A., unreported, May 18, 2001, High Court of Justiciary, provides an example of a case in which the court accepted that the significance of the additional evidence was such that it was willing to quash a murder conviction and substitute one of culpable homicide. Craig was a case in which five out of six psychiatrists who gave evidence at the appeal took the view that the accused had been suffering from diminished responsibility at the time of the killing. See also the contrasting case of *Chant v. H.M.A.*, unreported, April 26, 2001, High Court of Justiciary.

7. Criminal Procedure (Scotland) Act 1995

The Scottish Criminal Cases Review Commission

"194A.—(1) There shall be established a body corporate to be known as the Scottish Criminal Cases Review Commission (in this Act referred to as 'the Commission').

(2) The Commission shall not be regarded as the servant or agent of the Crown or as enjoying any status, immunity or privilege of the Crown; and the Commission's property shall not be regarded as property of, or held on behalf of, the Crown.

(3) The Commission shall consist of not fewer than three members.

(4) The members of the Commission shall be appointed by Her Majesty on the recommendation of the Secretary of State.

(5) At least one third of the members of the Commission shall be persons who are legally qualified; and for this purpose a person is legally qualified if he is an advocate or solicitor of at least ten years' standing.

(6) At least two thirds of the members of the Commission shall be persons who appear to the Secretary of State to have knowledge or experience of any aspect of the criminal justice system; and for the purposes of this subsection the criminal justice system includes, in particular, the investigation of offences and the treatment of offenders.

(7) Schedule 9A to this Act, which makes further provision as to the Commission, shall have effect."

References to the High Court

"194B.—(1) The Commission on the consideration of any conviction of a person or of the sentence (other than sentence of death) passed on a person who has been convicted on indictment may, if they think fit, at any time, and whether or not an appeal against such conviction or sentence has previously been heard and determined by the High Court, refer the whole case to the High Court and the case shall be heard and determined, subject to any directions the High Court may make, as if it were an appeal under Part VIII of this Act.

(2) The power of the Commission under this section to refer to the High Court the case of a person convicted shall be exercisable whether or not that person has petitioned for the exercise of Her Majesty's prerogative of mercy.

(3) This section shall apply in relation to a finding under section 55(2) and an order under section 57(2) of this Act as it applies, respectively, in relation to a conviction and a sentence.

(4) For the purposes of this section 'person' includes a person who is deceased.

194C. The grounds upon which the Commission may refer a case to the High Court are that they believe—
    (a) that a miscarriage of justice may have occurred; and
    (b) that at it is in the interests of justice that a reference should be made.

194D.—(1) A reference of a conviction, sentence or finding may be made under section 194B of this Act whether or not an application has been made by or on behalf of the person to whom it relates.

(2) In considering whether to make a reference the Commission shall have regard to—
    (a) any application or representations made to the Commission by or on behalf of the person to whom it relates;
    (b) any other representations made to the Commission in relation to it; and
    (c) any other matters which appear to the Commission to be relevant.

(3) In considering whether to make a reference the Commission may at any time refer to the High Court for the Court's opinion any point on which they desire the Court's assistance; and

on a reference under this subsection the High Court shall consider the point referred and furnish the Commission with their opinion on the point.

(4) Where the Commission make a reference to the High Court under section 194B of this Act they shall—

    (a) give to the Court a statement of their reasons for making the reference; and

    (b) send a copy of the statement to every person who appears to them to be likely to be a party to any proceedings on the appeal arising from the reference.

(5) In every case in which—

    (a) an application has been made to the Commission by or on behalf of any person for the reference by them of any conviction, sentence or finding; but

    (b) the Commission decide not to make a reference of the conviction, sentence or finding, they shall give a statement of the reasons for their decision to the person who made the application.

194E.—(1) The Secretary of State may by order provide for this Part of this Act to apply in relation to convictions, sentences and findings made in summary proceedings as they apply in relation to convictions, sentences and findings made in solemn proceedings, and may for that purpose make in such an order such amendments to the provisions of this Part as appear to him to be necessary or expedient.

(2) An order under this section shall be made by statutory instrument, and shall not have effect unless a draft of it has been laid before and approved by a resolution of each House of Parliament.

194F. The Commission may take any steps which they consider appropriate for assisting them in the exercise of any of their functions and may, in particular—

    (a) themselves undertake inquiries and obtain statements, opinions or reports; or

    (b) request the Lord Advocate or any other person to undertake such inquiries or obtain such statements, opinions and reports.

194G.—(1) The Secretary of State may by order make such incidental, consequential, transitional or supplementary provisions as may appear to him to be necessary or expedient for the purpose of bringing this Part of this Act into operation, and, without prejudice to the generality of the foregoing, of dealing with any cases being considered by him under section 124 of this Act at the time when this Part comes into force, and an order under this section may make different provision in relation to different cases or classes of case.

(2) An order under this section shall be made by statutory instrument subject to annulment in pursuance of a resolution of either House of Parliament."

Powers of investigation of Commission

"194H.—(1) Where it appears to the Commission that a person may have information which they require for the purposes of carrying out their functions, and the person refuses to make any statement to them, they may apply to the sheriff under this section.

(2) On an application made by the Commission under this section, the sheriff may, if he is satisfied that it is reasonable in the circumstances, grant warrant to cite the person concerned to appear before the sheriff in chambers at such time or place as shall be specified in the citation, for precognition on oath by a member of the Commission or a person appointed by them to act in that regard.

(3) Any person who, having been duly cited to attend for precognition under subsection (2) above and having been given at least 48 hours notice, fails without reasonable excuse to attend shall be guilty of an offence and liable on summary conviction to a fine not exceeding level 3 on the standard scale or to imprisonment for a period not exceeding 21 days; and the court may issue a warrant for the apprehension of the person concerned ordering him to be brought before a sheriff for precognition on oath.

(4) Any person who, having been duly cited to attend for precognition under subsection (2) above, attends but—

    (a) refuses to give information within his knowledge or to produce evidence in his
        possession; or

    (b) prevaricates in his evidence, shall be guilty of an offence and shall be liable to be
        summarily subjected to a fine not exceeding level 3 on the standard scale or to
        imprisonment for a period not exceeding 21 days.

194I.—(1) Where the Commission believe that a person or a public body has possession or
control of a document or other material which may assist them in the exercise of any of their
functions, they may apply to the High Court for an order requiring that person or body—

    (a) to produce the document or other material to the Commission or to give the
        Commission access to it; and

    (b) to allow the Commission to take away the document or other material or to make
        and take away a copy of it in such form as they think appropriate, and such an order
        may direct that the document or other material must not be destroyed, damaged or
        altered before the direction is withdrawn by the Court.

(2) The duty to comply with an order under this section is not affected by any obligation
of secrecy or other limitation on disclosure (including any such obligation or limitation
imposed by or by virtue of any enactment) which would otherwise prevent the production of
the document or other material to the Commission or the giving of access to it to the
Commission.

(3) The documents and other material covered by this section include, in particular, any
document or other material obtained or created during any investigation or proceedings
relating to

    (a) the case in relation to which the Commission's function is being or may be exercised;
        or

    (b) any other case which may be in any way connected with that case (whether or not any
        function of the Commission could be exercised in relation to that other case).

(4) In this section—

    'Minister' means a Minister of the Crown as defined by section 8 of the Ministers of the
Crown Act 1975;

    'police force' means any police force maintained for a local government area under
section 1(1) of the Police (Scotland) Act 1967 and references to a chief constable are
references to the chief constable of such a force within the meaning of that Act; and

    'public body' means

    (a) any police force;

    (b) any government department, local authority or other body constituted for the
        purposes of the public service, local government or the administration of justice;
        or

    (c) any other body whose members are appointed by Her Majesty, any Minister or any
        government department or whose revenues consist wholly or mainly of money
        provided by Parliament."

Disclosure of Information

"194J.—(1) A person who is or has been a member or employee of the Commission shall not
disclose any information obtained by the Commission in the exercise of any of their functions
unless the disclosure of the information is excepted from this section by section 194K of this
Act.

    (2) A member of the Commission shall not authorise the disclosure by an employee of the
Commission of any information obtained by the Commission in the exercise of any of their
functions unless the authorisation of the disclosure of the information is excepted from this
section by section 194K of this Act.

    (3) A person who contravenes this section is guilty of an offence and liable on summary
conviction to a fine of an amount not exceeding level 5 on the standard scale.

194K.—(1) The disclosure of information, or the authorisation of the disclosure of information, is excepted from section 194J of this Act by this section if the information is disclosed, or is authorised to be disclosed—

    (a) for the purposes of any criminal, disciplinary or civil proceedings;

    (b) in order to assist in dealing with an application made to the Secretary of State for compensation for a miscarriage of justice;

    (c) by a person who is a member or an employee of the Commission to another person who is a member or an employee of the Commission;

    (d) in any statement or report required by this Act;

    (e) in or in connection with the exercise of any function under this Act; or

    (f) in any circumstances in which the disclosure of information is permitted by an order made by the Secretary of State.

(2) The disclosure of information is also excepted from section 194J of this Act by this section if the information is disclosed by an employee of the Commission who is authorised to disclose the information by a member of the Commission.

(3) The disclosure of information, or the authorisation of the disclosure of information, is also excepted from section 194J of this Act by this section if the information is disclosed, or is authorised to be disclosed, for the purposes of—

    (a) the investigation of an offence; or

    (b) deciding whether to prosecute a person for an offence, unless the disclosure is or would be prevented by an obligation or other limitation on disclosure (including any such obligation or limitation imposed by, under or by virtue of any enactment) arising otherwise than under that section.

(4) Where the disclosure of information is excepted from section 194J of this Act by subsection (1) or (2) above, the disclosure of the information is not prevented by any obligation of secrecy or other limitation on disclosure (including any such obligation or limitation imposed by, under or by virtue of any enactment) arising otherwise than under that section.

(5) The power to make an order under subsection (1)(f) above is exercisable by statutory instrument which shall be subject to annulment in pursuance of a resolution of either House of Parliament.

194L.—(1) Where a person or body is required by an order under section 194I of this Act to produce or allow access to a document or other material to the Commission and notifies them that any information contained in the document or other material to which the order relates is not to be disclosed by the Commission without his or its prior consent, the Commission shall not disclose the information without such consent.

(2) Such consent may not be withheld unless—

    (a) (apart from section 194I of this Act) the person would have been prevented by any obligation of secrecy or other limitation on disclosure from disclosing the information without such consent; and

    (b) it is reasonable for the person to withhold his consent to disclosure of the information by the Commission.

(3) An obligation of secrecy or other limitation on disclosure which applies to a person only where disclosure is not authorised by another person shall not be taken for the purposes of subsection (2)(a) above to prevent the disclosure by the person of information to the Commission unless—

    (a) reasonable steps have been taken to obtain the authorisation of the other person; or

    (b) such authorisation could not reasonably be expected to be obtained."

NOTES

In *Scottish Criminal Cases Review Commission v. H.M.A.*, 2001 S.L.T. 905 Lord Clarke gave the following exposition of the background to the creation of the Commission:

> "The genesis of the petitioners is to be found in the recommendations of the committee chaired by Professor Stewart Sutherland on Criminal Appeals and Miscarriages of Justice Procedures in their report of June 1996. One of that committee's important recommendations was that a new

body should be established with power to consider alleged miscarriages of justice cases and to refer deserving cases to the court of appeal for determination. The recommendation was that this new body should replace the existing system whereby the Secretary of State had powers to refer cases to the appeal court, which powers were formerly to be found in section 263 of the Criminal Procedure (Scotland) Act 1975, as subsequently amended. Having considered various options in relation to procedures for having the cases of convicted persons referred back to the appeal court, on the basis of alleged miscarriages of justice, the committee reached the conclusion that the one which was most likely to command public confidence was the removal of the Secretary of State from the process altogether and the establishment of a new body, completely independent of the executive, with powers to consider alleged miscarriages of justice cases and to refer deserving cases to the appeal court. This was the only option which the committee considered would properly address the issue of the separation of powers between the executive and the judiciary, which they regarded as the fundamental weakness of the current system and the remedying of which was the single most important consideration—see paras 5.50 and 5.52 of the report. Such a body had already been established for England and Wales under the Criminal Appeals Act 1995, following the recommendation of the Royal Commission on Criminal Justice. In discussing the composition of the proposed body the committee stated that: 'the most important consideration in appointing chairman and members will be that they have the personal authority, impartiality and integrity to command public confidence in the body's operations'—see para. 5.54 of the report. The committee recommended that the new body should be able to refer cases to the appeal court: 'where the normal appeals procedures have been exhausted; where it believes a miscarriage of justice may have occurred and it is in the interests of justice that the case should be referred'—see recommendation 7.19.

In discussing the powers which the body should have, the committee said that: 'the review body will also need to be able to acquire, or have access to, any necessary and relevant information, for example, documents, reports, witness statements and special advice . . . when the new body is carrying out its own investigations it may require the power to obtain appropriate court orders for the precognition of witnesses or the production of documents. We recommend that the body should be empowered to petition the Court to obtain such orders'—see para. 5.68 of the report.

[6] In an earlier part of the report, which dealt with the scope of criminal appeals, the committee recommended that the general basis for an appeal should remain that a miscarriage of justice had occurred and that this ground should not be qualified or limited in any way (see para. 2.30 of the report). The committee went on to say: 'Put simply, the Court should be empowered to review any and all relevant considerations relating to the case—whenever they may have arisen—in determining whether a miscarriage of justice has, in fact, occurred'. There is no suggestion in the report that in using the phrase 'miscarriage of justice' in relation to the remit of the proposed new body, the committee were envisaging any narrower meaning to be placed upon it in that context.

[7] The committee's recommendations were, in the event, enacted in Pt XA of the Criminal Procedure (Scotland) Act 1995. There was apparently very little parliamentary discussion of the provisions relating to the setting up of the new body and its powers. The Government of the day had initially rejected the committee's recommendations that such a body was necessary in Scotland but, ultimately, however, the Lord Advocate announced in the House of Lords that he was moving certain amendments which became Part XA of the Act. In doing so the Lord Advocate said: 'Ultimately we came down on one side on this issue whilst the Committee came down on the other. After further consideration and taking account of the views expressed in your Lordships' House at Committee stage, we are prepared to accept that an independent body to review alleged miscarriages of justice should be set up, replacing the current statutory involvement of the Secretary of State. This group of amendments and in particular amendment no. 26 provide for that. In general they are based on the recommendations put forward by the Sutherland Committee, but some of the detail and mechanics of what it has proposed correspond to some of the provisions of the Criminal Appeal Act 1995, which established the Criminal Cases Review Commission in England and Wales. These have required to be adjusted, where appropriate, for the Scottish context. I am not sure that it is necessary to go through these in detail'—see Hansard, HL, March 19, 1997, col. 944.

[8] The petitioners were established by section 194A as a body corporate. Section 194A(2) provides that they shall not be regarded as the servant or agent of the Crown or as enjoying any status, immunity or privilege of the Crown; and the commission's property shall not be regarded as property of, or held on behalf of, the Crown. Section 194B(1) provides: [his Lordship quoted section 194B(1) set out *supra* and continued] Section 194C echoes the words of the committee's recommendation by providing that: [his Lordship quoted section 194C(a) and (b) and continued]

The width of the petitioners' power is demonstrated by the provisions of section 194D(1) and (2) which are in the following terms: [his Lordship quoted its terms and continued] The petitioners are obliged to give reasons for making a reference to the court and also must give reasons for refusing to make a reference to the person or persons who have applied to them for such a reference to be made—see section 194D(4) and (5). Once again the width of the petitioners' powers can be seen in the provisions of section 194F which states: [his Lordship quoted section 194F (a) and (b) and continued]. Section 194H confers powers on the petitioners to apply to the sheriff for precognition of persons to be taken on oath.

[9] Without yet examining the provisions of section 194I, it is clear to me that, from all the foregoing, Parliament intended the petitioners to have the fullest investigative powers in reaching the decision whether or not a reference to the court should be made in any particular case and that in exercising these powers, in the performance of their investigative duties, they are to act independently and to be seen to act independently. There can be no question, in my judgment, of their powers of investigation being directed or circumscribed by any other person or body. Any circumscribing of their powers of investigation must arise, if at all, simply, in my opinion, as a matter of law. If it were to be otherwise, then public confidence in the body and its activities, and its independence, could be seriously compromised and the primary purpose in establishing the body would be defeated."

In *Scottish Criminal Cases Review Commission, Petitioners*, 2001 S.L.T. 1198, the Commission sought advice from the High Court as to the limits of their powers of investigation, as they are entitled to do under s.194D(3). The advice sought related to the investigation of jury deliberations. The High Court's advice regarding section 8 of the Contempt of Court Act 1981 provides an example of the sort of limitations on the Commission's powers which may arise 'as a matter of law'.

In examining a case which is referred to it, the High Court must review case on the basis of the law and standards applicable at the present day, not at the time the case was originally heard. In *Boncza-Tomaszewski v. H.M.A.*, 2001 S.L.T. 336, Lord Justice General Rodger, delivering the Opinion of the Court said that:

"In *R. v. Bentley* [[1999] Crim.L.R. 330], the Court of Appeal held that they required to deal with the matter on the basis of the standards applied by the courts in 1998 rather than by reference to the standards of 1952 or 1953. Similarly, they required to apply their current understanding of the common law. We respectfully adopt their Lordships' reasoning and deal with the issues in this case on the basis of our current understanding of the common law and on the basis of present day standards. This approach may involve the risk that we seem to criticise our predecessors by reference to criteria which are different from those which they were applying. But that risk is inherent in section 194B which is specifically designed to allow this court to reconsider the soundness of a conviction even though it was subject to appeal. The operation of that section would be both artificial and ineffective if the court were forced to consider the issues by reference to the practice and legal approach of a bygone age. The purpose of the section must be to permit the court to re-examine cases to see whether, by the common law and standards of the time when the reference is considered, there has been a miscarriage of justice, even if, due to their understanding of the common law or by the standards applied at the time of the original proceedings and appeal, the appeal court would then have reached a different conclusion."

The mere fact that a case is referred by the Commission is no guarantee of success. The Appeal Court is not bound by the Commission's reasoning. Moreover, by s.194B, where a reference is made it requires to proceed as a normal appeal, with all that that entails by way of procedure. Thus in *Crombie v. Clark*, 2001 S.L.T. 635, the appeal failed because the Bill of Suspension lodged by the appellant contained insufficient averments to disclose a miscarriage of justice, and the court did not proceed to any factual investigation of the circumstances.

INDEX

References are to page numbers

Accomplices, 449–467
  immunity, 462
  socius criminis, 449–458, 458–462
  warning as to evidence of, 462
  witnesses, as, 449–467
Accused, 442–444
  admission against interest, 171–174
  incriminating statements by, 225–231
  previous convictions, 285–310
  statements by
    exceptions to hearsay rule, 188
  witness, as, 442–444
Admissibility of evidence, 194–267. *See also* **Hearsay**
  adultery, 223
  blood samples, 205–206
  caution, need for, 255–260
  civil causes, 223–225
  collateral evidence, 2–3
  consent to search, 211–212, 217–220
  criteria in Scots law, 241
  deception by police officer as to identity, 196–204
  diary found during search, 220–223
  documents, 210–211
  entrapment, 203–204
  extrajudicial confessions, 231–251
  fairness, 196, 224–225, 254
  hearsay, 164
  human rights, 249, 260–267
  improperly obtained, 194–267
  incriminating statements by accused, 225–231
  knowledge and intention of police, 212
  licensing investigation cases, 196–204
  obscene videos, 212–216
  procedure, 235–236
  "public interest in the rule of law", 196
  recorded statements, 251–254
  reply to police questioning, 255–260
  respective roles of judge and jury, 236
  search, consent to, 207–208
  searches without warrants, 194–196, 208–211, 216–217
  self–incrimination, 198–199
  test of, 237–243
  trial within trial, 231–251
  warrant, 203–205
Admissions, 343–354. *See also* **Agreement**
  effect, 343–347
  guilty, plea of, 347–350
  procedural mechanism, 350–354
Agency for foreign principal,
  presumption, 50–51
Agreement, 343–354. *See also* **Admissions**
  procedural mechanism, 350–354
Alibi,
  burden of proof, 33–34

Appeals, 501–529
  fresh evidence, 507–524
    reasonable explanation, 522
    "reasonable jury" test, 523
    significance, 523–524
  industrial tribunal, findings of, 506–507
  question of law and fact distinguished, 501–503, 503–504, 504–505
  reversal of finding of fact, 501–503
  Scottish Criminal Cases Review Commission, 524
Averment,
  evidential value, 343–347

Balance of probabilities,
  accused, on, 76
  burden of proof, and, 25–28
  standard of proof, 64–62, 70–72
Best evidence, 124–145
  biological material, 126–129
  company records, 135–142
  convenience of production, 133–135
  expert evidence, 135
  financial records, 135–142
  fish, possession of, 126–129
  hearsay. *See* **Hearsay**
  material prejudice, and, 126–129, 130–131
  objection to inadmissible evidence, 125
  practicality of production, 133–135
  real evidence, 145
  rule, 124–125
  secondary evidence of documents, 142–145
  "statement", 144–145
  tyres, condition of, 131–133
Biological material,
  evidence of, 126–129
Blood sample, 214–206
Blood test, 48–50
Burden of proof, 16–38. *See also* **Presumptions**
  alibi, 33–34
  balance of probabilities, and, 25–28
  causation, 17–18
  claimant, 16–17
  frustration, 18–20
  incidence, 16–38
  "knowing or suspecting", 36–38
  legal, 30–32, 39
  provisional, 30–32, 39–44
  reasonable steps, 20–25
  safe workplace, 20–25
  shifting, 45–46
  shifts, 28–30
  special defence of incrimination, 32–36
  special defences, 32–36
  statutory defence, 20–25
  ultimate, 44–45

Causation,
burden of proof, 17–18
Caution,
admissibility of evidence, and, 255–260
Character evidence, 281–310
collateral matters, 281–284
criminal cases, 285–310
cross–examination, 285–303
general evidence, 285
previous convictions of accused, 285–310
prejudicial effect, 304–306
proof of substantive charge, 305–306
rape, 307–310
relevance, 6–7, 282
sexual offences, 306–310
slander, 284–285
violent disposition of accused, 282–284
Chastity,
relevance, 7–8
Children, 394–397
confidentiality, and, 394–397
liability, 48
views of, 394–397
witnesses, as, 476–500
avoiding anxiety and distress, 488–489
corroboration, 480–483
differentiation between truth and falsehood, 478–480
extrinsic evidence of competency, 483–486
hearsay, 481–483
interviewing methods, 499–500
preliminary examination, 483
television link evidence, 489–491, 492–499
Circumstantial evidence,
corroboration, and, 91–88, 93–103
relevance, 9–12, 12–14
Civil proceedings,
meaning, 409
Claimant,
burden of proof, 16–17
Co–accused, 444–449
compellability, 444–449
competence, 444–449
Cohabitees, 467–476
compellability, 467–476
competence, 467–476
Collateral evidence, 268–281. *See also* **Character evidence**
corroboration, 273–274
evidence of other offences, 274–281
intention, of, 272–273
rationale behind rule, 270–272
relevance, 269–270
Commercial confidentiality, 393–394
Communications *post litem motam*,
privilege, 358–363
Company records,
best evidence, 135–142
Conciliation negotiations,
privilege, 363–367
Confessions, 225–231
corroboration, and, 106–108, 110–111, 111–114
"self–corroborating", 113–114
Confidentiality, 355–397. *See also* **Privilege**
children. *See* **Children**
commercial. *See* **Commercial confidentiality**
fairness test, 231
protection for accused, 231

Corroboration,
basis for rule, 79–80
circumstantial evidence, and, 91–88, 93–103
civil cases, abolition in, 398–407
consultation, 400–401
credibility, and, 407–408
credibility of pursuer, and, 405–406
effect, 404–405
history, 398–399
"mischief", 403–404
other legal systems, 399–400
recommendation, 400
statutory provision, 402
clandestine injury, 93–103
collateral evidence, and, 273–274
conduct, by, 82
confession, and, 106–108, 110–111, 111–114
"course of criminal conduct", 116–117
distressed state of complainer, 82–79, 84–91
evidence in relation to separate charges, 114–116
expert witness, of, 317–318
false denial, 121–123
hearsay, 180–182
identification, 121–123
identification evidence, 108–110
identity of property stolen, 119
inconsistent evidence, 93–103
insider dealing, 96–97
instigation to murder, 103–106
jury, and, 102
meaning, 116
mutual, 114–116
relevance, and, 14–15
relevance of other offences, 116–117
risk of human fallibility, and, 83–84
self–incrimination, 80–82
sequence of events, 99
special knowledge, 82
standard of, 106
traditional view, 83–84
Course of criminal conduct,
corroboration, and, 116–117
Credibility,
expert evidence, 326–327
Cross–examination,
character, as to, 285–303
Crown office,
public interest immunity, and, 386–393
Crown privilege. *See* **Public interest immunity**

Direct evidence,
relevance, 9–12
Distressed state of complainer,
corroboration, and, 82–79, 84–91
Divorce,
standard of proof, 63–64
Document,
admissibility, 210–211
meaning, 188
post litem motam, 358–363
secondary evidence, 142–145

Entrapment,
human rights, and, 203–204
Exculpatory statement,
hearsay, 164–171

Expert evidence, 311–330. *See also* **Opinion evidence**
admissibility, 320–322
best evidence, and, 135
corroboration, 317–318
credibility, 326–327
factual basis for, 327–328
function, 317
"indications", 316
personality of accused, as to, 322–328
psychologist, 318–320, 320–322
qualifications of expert, 328–330
reliability of accused, as to, 322–328
scientific criteria, 316–317

Feminist issues,
relevance, 8–9
Financial records,
best evidence, 135–142
Fingerprints,
relevance, 12
Frustration,
burden of proof, 18–20

Guilty, plea of
effect, 347–350

Hearsay, 146–193
abolition of rule against, 408–438
admissibility, 417–419
affidavit evidence by way of motion, 412–417
child, competency of, 425–438
competency, and, 438
credibility of witness, and, 425–438
'precognition', 420–423, 422–424, 424–425
weight, questions of, 419–420
admissibility, 164
admission by accused against interest, 171–174
child witness, 481–483
corroboration, 180–186
credibility of witness, 183–184
evidence about prior statement, 155
exceptions, 184–188
qualifications, 186–187
exculpatory statement,164–171
fundamental nature of rule against, 158–159
history of rule, 146–147
human rights, 189–193
identification evidence, 174–178, 178–179, 180–182
implied assertions, 162–164
incriminating statements, 225–231
maker of statement not available to give evidence in person, 186
meaning, 146
"mixed statement", 171–174
police evidence of telephone calls, 155–162
prior statements of witnesses, 187–188
probative effect of evidence, and, 158–159, 160
rationale, 147–148
res gestae, 150–151, 151–155
self–exonerating statement, 164–171
statements by accused, 188
statements made after time for deliberation, 153–155
uncorroborated statement, 410–412
victim, statement by, 152–153
words spoken, 151–155
Homosexuality,
relevance, 6–7

Human rights,
admissibility of evidence, 249
Article 6(1), European Convention, 260–267
entrapment, and, 203–204
fair trial, 189–193
hearsay, 189–193
privacy, 219–220
procedural safeguards, 189–193
section 172(2) Road Traffic Act 1988, 260–267
legitimate aim, 265–266
proportionality, 265–266
self–incrimination, 260–267

Identification,
corroboration, 121–123
hearsay, 174–178, 178–179, 180–182
Identification evidence,
corroboration, 108–110
Improperly obtained evidence. *See* **Admissibility of evidence**
Inadmissible evidence,
objection to, 125
Incrimination,
special defence
burden of proof, 32–36
Insanity,
standard of proof, 76–77
Insider dealing,
corroboration, and, 96–97

Judicial knowledge, 331–342
alcohol, effects of, 336–337
cleek, meaning of, 332–334
examples, 331–332
false accounts, 337–339
investigation of facts, 339–341
law of Scotland, 341–342
limits, 334
meaning, 331
stepchild, 334–336
Jury,
corroborative evidence, and, 102

Knowing or suspecting,
burden of proof, 36–38

Legal advisers,
privilege, 355–358
Legitimacy,
presumption, 48–50

Material prejudice,
best evidence, and, 126–129, 130–131
Murder, instigation to
corroboration, 103–106

"No case" submission, 78–79

Opinion evidence, 311–330. *See also* **Expert evidence**
reasonable doubt, as to, 312–313
relevant knowledge, 314
"ultimate issue", 311–313

Paternity,
standard of proof, 62–63

Police,
deception as to identity, 196–204
knowledge and intention, 212
misinterpretation of warrant, 219–220
Possession,
movable property, 51–53
recently stolen goods, 47–48
Precognition,
hearsay, and, 420–423, 422–424, 424–425
Presumptions, 39–56. *See also* **Burden of proof**
agency for foreign principal, 50–51
blood test, 48–50
children, liability of, 48
compelling, 44
conclusive, 45
conflicting, 46
fact, of, 45
law, of, 45
legitimacy, 48–50
meaning, 39
possession of movable property, 51–53
possession of recently stolen goods, 47–48
provisional 39–44
res ipsa loquitur, 53–56
trigger facts, 46
Previous convictions,
accused, of, 285–310
Primary evidence. *See* **Best evidence**
Prior statements of witnesses,
hearsay, 187–188
Privilege, 355–397. *See also* **Public interest immunity**
communications post litem motam, 358–363
conciliation negotiations, 363–367
legal advisers, 355–358
public interest immunity. *See* **Public interest immunity**
settlement negotiations, 363–367
"without prejudice", 363–367
Public interest immunity, 368–393
blood donor, identity of, 376–379
"class", 371–372
criminal records of Crown witnesses, 382–385
Crown Office, 386–393
development charges, 368–371
documents of material assistance to defence case, 379–382
informer, identity of, 372–375
police questionnaires, 379–382
power of courts to overrule certificate, 378–379
scope of application, 378–379
Scottish Criminal Cases Review Commission, 386–393

Quasi–criminal proceedings,
standard of proof, 72–75

Rape,
character evidence, 307–310
Reasonable doubt,
opinion evidence, 312–313
standard of proof, 59–58, 63–64
Reasonable steps,
burden of proof, 20–25
Reasoning,
use in evidence, 4–6
Recorded statements,
admissibility, 251–254

Relevance, 1–15
character, 6–7
chastity, 7–8
circumstantial evidence, 9–12, 12–14
collateral evidence, 2–3
corroboration, 14–15
definition, 1–2
direct evidence, 9–12
disputed evidence, 3–4
feminist issues, 8–9
fingerprint evidence, 12
homosexuality, 6–7
reasoning, use of, 4–6
remoteness, 2–3
sexual promiscuity, 7–8
Res gestae,
meaning, 150–151, 151–155
Res ipsa loquitur, 53–56
effect of doctrine, 54–55
reasonable care, and, 55–56

Scottish criminal cases review commission, 524
background to creation of, 527–528
basis for review of cases, 529
disclosure of information, 526–527
limits of powers, 529
powers of investigation, 525–526
public interest immunity, and, 386–393
references to High Court, 524–525
Search,
consent to, 207–208, 211–212, 217–220
urgency, matter of, 216–217
without warrant, 194–196, 208–211, 216–217
Secondary evidence. *See* **Best evidence**
Self–exonerating statement,
hearsay, 164–171
Self–incriminating,
corroborating, and, 80–82
human rights, and, 260–267
Settlement negotiations,
privilege, 363–367
Sexual offences,
character evidence, 306–310
Sexual promiscuity,
relevance, 7–8
Similar fact evidence, 268–270, 272
Slander,
character evidence, 284–285
Social Work (Scotland) Act 1968,
standard of proof, 69–70
Socius criminis, 449–458, 458–462
Special defences,
burden of proof, 32–36
Special knowledge,
corroboration, and, 82
Spouses, 467–476
compellability, 467–476
competence, 467–476
Standard of proof, 57–77
balance of probabilities, 64–62, 70–72
burden of proof on accused, where, 76
civil cases, 58–59
credibility, 57–58
criminal cases, 59
different standards, 58
divorce, 63–64
evasion of VAT, 72–75
final direction, 60–62

Standard of proof—*cont.*
  gravity of issue, and, 66–67
  higher than normal, 68–70
  highly sensitive or emotive allegations, 67–68
  insanity, 76–77
  paternity, 60–63
  probability, 57–58
  quasi–criminal proceedings, 72–75
  reasonable doubt, 59–58, 63–64
  seriousness of allegations, and, 70–72
  Social Work (Scotland) Act 1968, 69–70
  variable civil standard, 68–70
Statement,
  meaning, 144–145
Sufficiency of evidence, 78–123
  no case submission, 78–79

Telephone calls,
  hearsay, 155–162
Television link,
  vulnerable witnesses, 489–491, 492–499

Trial within trial, 231–251

Value added tax,
  evasion
    standard of proof, 72–75
Videotapes,
  obscene, 212–216
Vulnerable witnesses, 476–500
  television link, 489–491, 492–499

Warrant,
  incompetent, 203–205
  misinterpretation by police, 219–220
  search, for. *See* **Search**
Without prejudice, 363–367
Witnesses, 439–500
  accused. *See* **Accused**
  compellability, 439–442
  competence, 439–442
  vulnerable, 476–500